THE OXFORD HANDBOOK OF

THE HISTORY
OF ANALYTIC
PHILOSOPHY

During the course of the twentieth century, analytic philosophy developed into the dominant philosophical tradition in the English-speaking world. In the last two decades, it has become increasingly influential in the rest of the world, from continental Europe to Latin America and Asia. At the same time there has been deepening interest in the origins and history of analytic philosophy, as analytic philosophers examine the foundations of their tradition and question many of the assumptions of their predecessors. This has led to greater historical self-consciousness among analytic philosophers and more scholarly work on the historical contexts in which analytic philosophy developed. This historical turn in analytic philosophy has been gathering pace since the 1990s, and the present volume is the most comprehensive collection of essays to date on the history of analytic philosophy. It contains state-of-the-art contributions from many of the leading scholars in the field, all of the contributions specially commissioned. The introductory essays discuss the nature and historiography of analytic philosophy, accompanied by a detailed chronology and bibliography. Part One elucidates the origins of analytic philosophy, with special emphasis on the work of Frege, Russell, Moore, and Wittgenstein. Part Two explains the development of analytic philosophy, from Oxford realism and logical positivism to the most recent work in analytic philosophy, and includes essays on ethics, aesthetics, and political philosophy as well as on the areas usually seen as central to analytic philosophy, such as philosophy of language and mind. Part Three explores certain key themes in the history of analytic philosophy.

THE OXFORD HANDBOOK OF

THE HISTORY
OF ANALYTIC
PHILOSOPHY

Edited by
MICHAEL BEANEY

OXFORD
UNIVERSITY PRESS

Great Clarendon Street, Oxford, OX2 6DP,
United Kingdom

Oxford University Press is a department of the University of Oxford.
It furthers the University's objective of excellence in research, scholarship,
and education by publishing worldwide. Oxford is a registered trade mark of
Oxford University Press in the UK and in certain other countries

Published in the United States of America by Oxford University Press
198 Madison Avenue, New York, NY 10016, United States of America

British Library Cataloguing in Publication Data
Data available

Library of Congress Cataloging in Publication Data
Data available

ISBN 978–0–19–923884–2 (Hbk.)
ISBN 978–0–19–874799–4 (Pbk.)

PREFACE

In the preface to his pioneering book on Frege, published in 1973, Michael Dummett remarked that a book without a preface is like arriving at someone's house for dinner and being shown straight to the table. There is a huge feast on offer in the present volume, and even though the starters may be more than enough to whet the appetite, an *amuse bouche* should be offered first in the reception lounge. Given that one of the aims of this volume is to elucidate the historical origins of analytic philosophy, which is now the dominant tradition in the philosophical world, it is only right that I say something here about the origins of this book and the form it came to take. Menus, too, have a history.

The publication of this book is the clearest sign yet that history of analytic philosophy is now recognized as a subfield of philosophy in its own right. As Peter Momtchiloff emailed me back in September 2006, in inviting me to edit this volume in the Oxford Handbook series, 'I believe that now is an ideal time for this, a collective study of a subject that is really taking off.' Over the weeks that followed I had extensive discussion with Peter and several colleagues and friends, some of whom have contributed to this Handbook, about the form the Handbook should take and the possible chapters and authors. The proposal drawn up went to four advisers, and valuable comments and suggestions were received. I then began the process of inviting contributors, and the negotiations and correspondence we engaged in helped shape other chapters and fed back into the discussions that continued throughout the editorial project. Several contributors kept in touch with others writing on related topics, and drafts were circulated and comments passed. It was an exciting period, as I became more aware myself of just what interesting stories there were to tell and of what issues became important in the analytic tradition.

Right from the beginning, the Handbook was intended as more than a mere survey of developments in analytic philosophy, and I encouraged contributors to take their own line through the material they covered and to reflect on what doing history of analytic philosophy involved. This is not a history of analytic philosophy by many hands, in other words, though much light has certainly been shed on key chapters in that history. Rather, it is a genuine *handbook*, representing and bringing together the best work in the area over recent years, making room for a variety of voices, and opening up new perspectives and lines of investigation, with the aim of enthusing, informing, and orienting all those with an interest in the history of analytic philosophy.

Inevitably, some chapters turned out to be rather different than I had anticipated, and the organization of the volume altered accordingly. Some people who had originally agreed to contribute found that they could not, after all, deliver, whether because of illness, other commitments, or the realization (so they said) that they had nothing new to say, and two people disappeared into a black hole of electronic silence. This was when the most difficult decisions had to be taken: whether to recommission, to find ways in which the resultant gaps might be filled in other chapters, or simply to drop the topic. As more and more chapters came in, the options for recommissioning reduced, as the obligations to those who had already sent in their chapters built up. I am especially grateful to several authors for agreeing to contribute at a later stage in the project and to a much tighter schedule. In the end, with much regret, I did have to call it a day on a few of the originally planned contributions. Perhaps I should have cracked the whip earlier, but I hope I achieved the right balance between inclusion and delay.

I was often conscious of the paradox of editing—or more precisely, of the paradox that arises from setting deadlines to contributors. Contributors would want to know when the final (or final final) deadline was, understanding by that the date when all the contributions bar their own would have been sent in. No one actually said 'Let me know when you've received the last chapter but mine, and I promise to send you mine within two weeks from then', though an editor of another Oxford Handbook told me that this had indeed been said to them, and I am sure that something like this thought crossed the minds of one or two of the present contributors (and it does not help when they are in contact with one another!). Although I will never edit something as large as this ever again (I say to myself with some determination), I may yet do some further editing, so I had best not own up in public to the strategy I adopted for resolving the paradox, or the more ruthless strategy that I sometimes wondered whether I should have followed.

All these facts are salutary reminders of the contingencies that affect the publication of all books, which the historian of analytic philosophy should bear in mind just like every other historian. Looking back at the original proposal submitted to Oxford University Press, I am aware of how much has changed. Excellent papers have been added that were not envisaged, but equally, some chapters originally planned have had to be dropped, for one reason or another. I am extremely happy with the resultant set of contributions, although I would have recommissioned chapters on one or two topics had time not been running out (and the constraints of space allowed). The Handbook will be made available online, however, and I have been told that further chapters can be added for the online edition. I also look forward to updating the chronology and bibliography as a continual resource for future work in history of analytic philosophy. I would be delighted to receive suggestions for additions to the online edition.

This book has taken up far more of my life than I anticipated when I agreed to edit it: thousands of emails have been exchanged since that first email from Peter Momtchiloff, and I have often read and commented on more than one draft of a chapter, most chapters ending up rather longer than originally intended. When I look at the size of my mailbox folder for this Handbook, I realize just how impossible it would have been to edit it without email. (The effect of all our new technology on both the practice of philosophy and the study of its history has scarcely begun to be appreciated, and strikes me as both facilitating and terrifying, in equal measure, for future historians of philosophy.)

There have been the usual highs and lows involved in any editorial project, but I regard it as an enormous privilege to have been given the opportunity to work with so many of the leading scholars in the field. What has been most satisfying is the sense of having contributed to a genuinely cooperative enterprise that I am certain will be valued for a long time to come.

I am grateful to many people both for help and support with this project and for inspiration and advice over the years in my own work on the history of analytic philosophy. I would like to thank, first, each and every contributor to this volume: I have learnt much from their chapters and from our discussions, which have helped shape both the volume as a whole and my own editorial material. Many of the contributors have encouraged and influenced me in all sorts of other ways over the years, especially Tom Baldwin, Stewart Candlish, Sean Crawford, Jonathan Dancy, Cora Diamond, Juliet Floyd, Gottfried Gabriel, Hanjo Glock, Nick Griffin, Peter Hacker, Gary Hatfield, Peter Hylton, Michael Kremer, Bernard Linsky, Robert May, Erich Reck, Sanford Shieh, Peter Simons, John Skorupski, Charles Travis, and Thomas Uebel.

Second, I would like to thank all those others who have helped me, in various ways, in my work on the history of analytic philosophy, whether in email correspondence or in discussion at conferences and seminars. Here the list is extensive, and I can only mention a few: Andy Arana, Ken Blackwell, Rosalind Carey, Chen Bo, James Connelly, Josie D'Oro, Philip Ebert, Sébastien Gandon, Warren Goldfarb, Dirk Greimann, Han Linhe, Chris Hookway, Jiang Yi, Wolfgang Künne, Dermot Moran, Koji Nakatogawa, John Ongley, Marco Panza, Carlo Penco, Eva Picardi, Michael Potter, Aaron Preston, Tom Ricketts, Marcus Rossberg, Eric Schliesser, Peter Sullivan, Amie Thomasson, Maria van der Schaar, Pierre Wagner, Crispin Wright, and Yu Junwei.

Third, I have been fortunate to have had many colleagues and students over the years, in a number of institutions, with whom I have had fruitful discussions of analytic philosophy, its history, and methodological and historiographical issues. Again, I can only list a few here (not already mentioned): David Bell, Hanno Birken-Bertsch, Dan Brigham, Cristina Chimisso, Wonbae Choi, Bob Clark, James Clarke, Martin Davies, Mauro Engelmann, Jeremy Gray, Wolfgang Kienzler, Peter Lamarque, Sandra Lapointe, Marie McGinn, Peter Millican, Volker Peckhaus, Barry Smith, Tom Stoneham, Christian Thiel, Roger White, David Wiggins, Adrian Wilson, and Rachael Wiseman.

Fourth, I am grateful to all those who have been involved in the production of this volume for Oxford University Press. Peter Momtchiloff has been the perfect editor, initiating the project with enthusiasm, guiding it with encouragement and sound advice, and responding at every stage promptly and adeptly. In the final stages, Jo North has done a superb job in copy-editing such a huge text, and Ellie Collins has been equally efficient in handling the cover design and publicity, and Sree Viswananthan in coordinating the production process. I am also indebted to Jim Driscoll for his help in proof-reading the entire volume, and to James Bridge for compiling the index.

Last, but not by any means least, I thank my family for living through this project with me: my wife Sharon and our children Tara, Thomas, and Harriet. Tara's work on German literature and philosophy and Thomas's medical training and research in the history of

medicine have informed our family discussions of historical and historiographical topics. Taking Harriet through her AS-level course in philosophy was more valuable to me
than I think she realizes. I would especially like to thank Harriet for suggesting the work
of Paul Nash for the front cover, the design of which was also a matter of family discussion. Born in the same year as Wittgenstein, Collingwood, and Heidegger, Nash was
one of the pioneers and promoters of modernism in Britain, founding the Unit One art
movement with Henry Moore, Barbara Hepworth, Ben Nicholson, and others in 1933.
He painted 'Kinetic Feature', one of the few examples of his own abstract art, in 1931, and
it was first exhibited in 1933. As made clear in Chapter 2 of this Handbook, this was just
the time that the phrases 'analytic philosopher' and 'analytic philosophy' began to be
used, suggesting that a new philosophical tradition was emerging.

My greatest debt, as ever, is to Sharon Macdonald, whose own work as an anthro-
pologist and her wide-ranging intellectual interests have inspired and informed my own
writing and thinking in ways that no historian, and least of all myself, could possibly do
justice to. The final stages of completing the editing of this book have coincided with the
finishing of Sharon's own book on memorylands; and we have shared both the excite-
ments and frustrations of trying to complete major projects. I dedicate my own contribution to this volume to her. The volume as a whole is dedicated to all those who work
on the history of analytic philosophy.

Michael Beaney
3 March 2013

Note to Paperback Edition
The opportunity has been taken to make some minor corrections and revisions.
May 2015

Contents

PART II THE DEVELOPMENT OF ANALYTIC PHILOSOPHY

PART III THEMES IN THE HISTORY OF ANALYTIC PHILOSOPHY

Notes on Contributors

Maria Baghramian is Professor of Philosophy at University College Dublin, Ireland. She received her Ph.D. from Trinity College Dublin under Tim Williamson's supervision. Her books include *Modern Philosophy of Language* (1999), *Pluralism* (edited with Attracta Ingram, 2001), *Relativism* (2004), *Reading Putnam* (ed. 2012), *Donald Davidson: Life and Words* (ed. 2012) and *Hilary Putnam* (forthcoming). She was the chief editor of the *International Journal of Philosophical Studies* from 2003 to 2013. She is a founding member of Aporo: The Irish Network of Research in Philosophy and the Society of Women in Philosophy–Ireland. She was elected a Member of the Royal Irish Academy in 2010.

Thomas Baldwin is Emeritus Professor of Philosophy at the University of York. He is the author of *G. E. Moore* (1990) and *Contemporary Philosophy: Philosophy in English since 1945* (Oxford University Press, 2001). He has edited several of Moore's writings, including a revised edition of *Principia Ethica* (1993), Moore's *Selected Writings* (1993), and (together with Consuelo Preti) an edition of Moore's *Early Philosophical Writings* (2011). He also edited *The Cambridge History of Philosophy 1870–1945* (2003). He was editor of *Mind* from 2005 to 2015.

Michael Beaney is Professor of History of Analytic Philosophy at the Humboldt University in Berlin and Professor of Philosophy at King's College London. He is the author of *Frege: Making Sense* (1996) and *Imagination and Creativity* (2005), and editor of *The Frege Reader* (1997), *Gottlob Frege: Critical Assessments of Leading Philosophers* (with Erich Reck; 4 vols., 2005), and *The Analytic Turn* (2007). He is also editor of the *British Journal for the History of Philosophy*, and general editor of a series on the history of analytic philosophy published by Palgrave Macmillan.

Tyler Burge is Distinguished Professor of Philosophy at UCLA. He has authored many articles in philosophy of mind, philosophy of psychology, epistemology, philosophy of language, philosophy of logic, and history of philosophy. Two books of essays on his work with replies are *Reflections and Replies: Essays on the Philosophy of Tyler Burge* (2003) and *Meaning, Basic Self-Knowledge, and Mind* (2003). The first three of several projected volumes of his essays are *Truth, Thought, Reason: Essays on Frege* (2005), *Foundations of Mind* (2007), and *Cognition Through Understanding* (2013) (all Oxford University Press). In 2010 he published *Origins of Objectivity* (Oxford University Press). He is past president of the American Philosophical Association, Pacific Division, and a current member of the American Academy of Arts and Sciences, British Academy, Institut International de Philosophie, and American Philosophical Society.

Stewart Candlish is Senior Honorary Research Fellow at The University of Western Australia, former Editor of the *Australasian Journal of Philosophy* (2007–2013), and Fellow of the Australian Academy of the Humanities. He is the author of *The Russell/ Bradley Dispute and Its Significance for Twentieth-Century Philosophy* (2007) and wrote the chapters 'British Idealism: Theoretical Philosophy' in the *Routledge Companion to Nineteenth-Century Philosophy* (2010) and 'Philosophy and the Tide of History: Bertrand Russell's Role in the Rise of Analytic Philosophy' in *The Historical Turn in Analytic Philosophy* (ed. Erich Reck, 2013). With Nic Damnjanovic, he has also contributed the chapters 'The *Tractatus* and the Unity of the Proposition' to *Wittgenstein's Early Philosophy* (ed. José L. Zalabardo, Oxford University Press, 2012), and 'The Identity Theory of Truth' to *The Oxford Handbook of Truth* (ed. Michael Glanzberg, Oxford University Press, forthcoming).

Annalisa Coliva is Associate Professor of Philosophy at the University of Modena and Reggio Emilia, Italy. She is the author of *Moore and Wittgenstein: Scepticism, Certainty and Common Sense* (2010), as well as of several other books in Italian, such as *Scetticismo. Dubbio, paradosso e conoscenza* (2012) and *I modi del relativismo* (2009). She is the editor of *Mind, Meaning and Knowledge: Themes from the Philosophy of Crispin Wright* (Oxford University Press, 2012) and of *The Self and Self-Knowledge* (Oxford University Press, 2012). She is the Associate Director of COGITO Research Centre in Philosophy.

Sean Crawford is Lecturer in Philosophy at the University of Manchester. He has written articles on a variety of topics in the philosophy of mind and language and is the author of *Aspects of Mind* (2005) and the editor of *Philosophy of Mind: Critical Concepts in Philosophy* (2010).

Nic Damnjanovic is Honorary Research Fellow at The University of Western Australia (where he was formerly a tenured Assistant Professor) and a practising lawyer. He has previously held a visiting position at the University of Colorado, Boulder. His publications include articles and reviews on psychopathology and responsibility, truth, essentialism, and consciousness, in a range of collections and philosophy and law journals including *Philosophical Quarterly* and *Erkenntnis*. With Stewart Candlish, he has contributed the chapters 'A Brief History of Truth' to *Handbook of the Philosophy of Science, vol. 5: Philosophy of Logic* (ed. Dale Jacquette, 2007), and 'The Myth of the Coherence Theory of Truth' to *Judgement and Truth in Early Analytic Philosophy and Phenomenology* (ed. Mark Textor, 2013).

Jonathan Dancy is Professor of Philosophy at the University of Texas at Austin. Previously he taught in Britain, first at the University of Keele and then at the University of Reading.

He has worked mainly in epistemology, moral philosophy, and the philosophy of action, and has a special interest in George Berkeley and in the history of twentieth-century ethics. His books include *Moral Reasons* (1993), *Practical Reality* (Oxford University Press, 2000), and *Ethics Without Principles* (Oxford University Press, 2004). He has published over 75 articles in academic journals and elsewhere.

Cora Diamond is University Professor and Kenan Professor of Philosophy Emerita at the University of Virginia. She is the author of *The Realistic Spirit: Wittgenstein, Philosophy, and the Mind* (1991) and the editor of *Wittgenstein's Lectures on the Foundations of Mathematics, Cambridge, 1939* (1976).

Julia Driver is Professor of Philosophy at Washington University in St. Louis. She received her Ph.D. at the Johns Hopkins University. Her main areas of research interest are normative ethics, moral psychology, moral agency, and the moral philosophy of David Hume. She has published three books, *Uneasy Virtue* (2001), *Ethics: The Fundamentals* (2006), and *Consequentialism* (2012), as well as articles in a variety of journals.

Juliet Floyd is Professor of Philosophy at Boston University. She has written articles on Kant, Frege, Russell, Wittgenstein, Quine, Rawls, Turing, and Gödel. She edited (with Sanford Shieh) *Future Pasts: The Analytic Tradition in Twentieth-Century Philosophy* (Oxford University Press, 2001; Oxford Scholarship Online, 2004). She is currently an editor in Twentieth-Century Philosophy for *The Stanford Encyclopedia of Philosophy*, an associate editor of the *Journal for the History of Analytical Philosophy*, and on the Editorial Board of the series on the history of analytic philosophy published by Palgrave Macmillan.

Gottfried Gabriel is Professor of Philosophy at the University of Jena (Germany), since 2009 Professor Emeritus. He works in the areas of epistemology, logic, aesthetics, political iconography, and philosophy of language. His publications include the monographs: *Definitionen und Interessen* (1972), *Fiktion und Wahrheit* (1975), *Zwischen Logik und Literatur. Erkenntnisformen von Dichtung, Philosophie und Wissenschaft* (1991), *Grundprobleme der Erkenntnistheorie* (1993, 3rd edn. 2008), *Logik und Rhetorik der Erkenntnis. Zum Verhältnis von wissenschaftlicher und ästhetischer Weltauffassung* (1997), *Ästhetik und Rhetorik des Geldes* (2002), *Einführung in die Logik* (2005, 3rd edn. 2007). He is co-editor of Frege's *Correspondence* and *Lectures on Logic*. He is also editor of *Historisches Wörterbuch der Philosophie*, vols. 11–13 (2001–7).

Richard Gaskin is Professor of Philosophy at the University of Liverpool. He is author of *Experience and the World's Own Language: A Critique of John McDowell's Empiricism* (Oxford University Press, 2006), *The Unity of the Proposition* (Oxford University Press, 2008), and *Language, Truth, and Literature: A Defence of Literary Humanism* (Oxford University Press, 2013).

Hans-Johann Glock is Professor of Philosophy at the University of Zurich (Switzerland), and Visiting Professor at the University of Reading (UK). He is the author of *A Wittgenstein Dictionary* (1996), *Quine and Davidson on Language, Thought and Reality* (2003), *La mente de los animals* (2009), and *What is Analytic Philosophy?* (2008). He has published numerous articles on the philosophy of mind, the philosophy of language, the history of analytic philosophy, and Wittgenstein. At present he is working on a book on animal minds and co-editing *The Blackwell Companion to Wittgenstein*.

Nicholas Griffin is Director of the Bertrand Russell Centre at McMaster University, Hamilton, Ontario, where he holds a Canada Research Chair in Philosophy. He has written widely on Russell, is the author of *Russell's Idealist Apprenticeship* (Clarendon Press, 1991), and the general editor of *The Collected Papers of Bertrand Russell*.

P. M. S. Hacker is Emeritus Research Fellow at St John's College, Oxford. He is author of *Insight and Illusion* (Clarendon Press, 1972, 2nd revised edn. 1986), of the four-volume *Analytical Commentary on the* Philosophical Investigations, the first two volumes co-authored with G. P. Baker, of *Wittgenstein's Place in Twentieth-Century Analytic Philosophy* (1996), and of *Wittgenstein: Connections and Controversies* (Oxford University Press, 2001). He has written extensively on philosophy and the neurosciences, most recently *Philosophical Foundations of Neuroscience* (2003) and *History of Cognitive Neuroscience* (2008) co-authored with M. R. Bennett. He is currently writing a three-volume work on human nature, the first volume of which, *Human Nature: The Categorial Framework*, was published in 2007. The sequel, *The Intellectual Powers: A Study of Human Nature*, was published in 2013. A further volume of his essays, *Wittgenstein: Comparisons and Context,* was also published in 2013 (Oxford University Press).

Gary Hatfield is Professor of Philosophy at the University of Pennsylvania. He is the author of *The Natural and the Normative: Theories of Spatial Perception from Kant to Helmholtz* (1990), *Descartes and the Meditations* (2003), and *Perception and Cognition: Essays in the Philosophy of Psychology* (Clarendon Press, 2009); co-editor (with Sarah Allred) of *Visual Experience: Sensation, Cognition, and Constancy* (Oxford University Press, 2012), and translator of Kant's *Prolegomena to Any Future Metaphysics* (2004).

Richard G. Heck Jr. is Romeo Elton Professor of Natural Theology at Brown University. He is the author of two books: *Frege's Theorem* (Oxford University Press, 2011) and *Reading Frege's* Grundgesetze (Oxford University Press, 2012). He is also Associate Editor for Philosophy of Mathematics for *Thought*, a member of the Editorial Board of the *Journal of Philosophical Logic*, *Philosopher's Imprint*, and *Philosophia Mathematica*, and of the Advisory Board of the *Journal for the History of Analytical Philosophy*.

David Hyder studied philosophy and computer science at Yale, after which he worked for several years as a software developer on Wall Street. He took his Ph.D. from the University of Toronto in 1997 with Ian Hacking and Alasdair Urquhart. From 1997–2000 he was Lorenz Krüger Fellow at the Max Planck Institute for the History of Science, 2000–2004 Assistant Professor of Philosophy at the Universität Konstanz, 2004–present Assistant, then Associate Professor at the University of Ottawa. He is the author of *The Mechanics of Meaning* (2002) and *The Determinate World* (2009), and co-editor with Hans-Jörg Rheinberger of *Science and the Life-World* (2010). He is now writing a book on Kant's theory of time.

Peter Hylton was educated at King's College, Cambridge, and at Harvard University. He is Professor of Philosophy and Distinguished Professor at the University of Illinois, Chicago. He is the author of *Russell, Idealism, and the Emergence of Analytic Philosophy* (Oxford University Press, 1990), of *Quine* (2007), and of numerous essays, chiefly on the history of analytic philosophy, some of which are collected in *Propositions, Functions, and Analysis* (Oxford University Press, 2005).

Andrew Jorgensen was educated at the University of Waikato and Temple University. He works on the history of analytic philosophy, especially the work of Alexius Meinong, and the philosophy of language, including Robert Brandom's inferentialist approach to meaning and arguments for scepticism about meaning. He was an Irish Research Council Postdoctoral Fellow and an Aporo Research Fellow in the School of Philosophy, University College Dublin.

Mark Eli Kalderon is Professor of Philosophy at University College London. He is the author of *Moral Fictionalism* (Oxford University Press, 2005) and editor of *Fictionalism in Metaphysics* (Oxford University Press, 2005). He is former editor of the *Proceedings of the Aristotelian Society* and has served on the Editorial Board for *Mind*.

Michael Kremer is Mary R. Morton Professor of Philosophy and in the College at the University of Chicago. His articles include 'Kripke and the Logic of Truth' (1988), 'The Argument of "On Denoting"' (1994), 'Contextualism and Holism in the Early Wittgenstein' (1997), 'The Purpose of Tractarian Nonsense' (2001), and 'Sense and Reference: The Origins and Development of the Distinction' (2010). He serves on the Editorial Boards of the *Notre Dame Journal of Formal Logic* and *Notre Dame Philosophical Reviews*.

Peter Lamarque is Professor of Philosophy at the University of York. His books include *Truth, Fiction, and Literature*, with Stein Haugom Olsen (Clarendon Press, 1994), *Fictional Points of View* (1996), *The Philosophy of Literature* (2009), and *Work and Object:*

Explorations in the Metaphysics of Art (Oxford University Press, 2010). He was editor of the *British Journal of Aesthetics* from 1995–2008.

Bernard Linsky is a Professor of Philosophy at the University of Alberta, Canada. He is the author of *Russell's Metaphysical Logic* (1999) and *The Evolution of* Principia Mathematica: *Russell's Manuscripts and Notes for the Second Edition* (2011), and editor with Guido Imaguire of *On Denoting 1905–2005* (2005). He is a member of the Editorial Board of *Russell: The Journal of Bertrand Russell Studies*.

Robert May is Distinguished Professor of Philosophy and Linguistics at the University of California, Davis. He is the author of *Logical Form: Its Structure and Derivation,* and with Robert Fiengo of *Anaphora and Identity* and *De Lingua Belief.* He is well known for his work in the syntax and semantics of natural language, especially on natural language quantification, and has written extensively on Frege, along with other topics in philosophy of language and philosophy of logic.

Alex Miller is Professor of Philosophy at the University of Otago. He is author of *Philosophy of Language* (2nd edn., 2007) and *Contemporary Metaethics: An Introduction* (2nd edn., 2013). He is co-editor (with Crispin Wright) of *Rule Following and Meaning* (2002) and editor of *Logic, Language and Mathematics: Essays for Crispin Wright* (Oxford University Press, forthcoming).

Cheryl Misak is Professor of Philosophy and former Vice-President and Provost at the University of Toronto. She is the author of *The American Pragmatists* (Oxford University Press, 2013), *Truth, Politics, Morality* (2000), and *Truth and the End of Inquiry* (Oxford University Press, 1991). She is currently working on a book titled *Cambridge Pragmatism* on the influence of Peirce and James on Ramsey and Wittgenstein.

Jaroslav Peregrin is Research Professor of Logic at the Academy of Sciences of the Czech Republic and Professor of Philosophy at the University of Hradec Králové, Czech Republic. Aside from books in Czech he is the author of *Doing Worlds with Words* (1995), *Meaning and Structure* (2001), and a number of articles in books and journals, including *Journal of Philosophical Logic*, *Erkenntnis*, *Studia Logica*, and *Synthèse*.

Erich H. Reck is Professor of Philosophy at the University of California at Riverside, USA. He is the author of a number of articles on early analytic philosophy, the history and philosophy of logic, and the philosophy of mathematics. He is also the editor, or co-editor, of *From Frege to Wittgenstein: Perspectives on Early Analytic Philosophy* (Oxford University Press, 2002), *Frege's Lectures on Logic: Carnap's Student Notes, 1910–1914* (with Steve Awodey, 2004), *Gottlob Frege: Critical Assessments of Leading Philosophers* (with Michael Beaney, 4 vols., 2005), and *The Historical Turn in Analytic Philosophy* (2013).

Sanford Shieh is Associate Professor of Philosophy at Wesleyan University. He specializes in philosophy of logic, metaphysics, and the history of analytic philosophy. He has written on the anti-realist critiques of classical logic, Frege on definitions, and is co-editor, with Juliet Floyd, of *Future Pasts: The Analytic Tradition in Twentieth-Century Philosophy* (Oxford University Press, 2001).

Peter Simons FBA holds the Chair of Moral Philosophy (1837) at Trinity College Dublin. Prior to that he held posts at Bolton, Salzburg, and Leeds. His main research areas in philosophy are metaphysics and ontology, the philosophy of logic; and in its history, the philosophy and logic of Austria and Poland as well as early analytic philosophy. He is the author of *Parts* (1987, 2000), *Philosophy and Logic in Central Europe from Bolzano to Tarski* (1992), and over 200 articles.

John Skorupski is Professor Emeritus of Moral Philosophy at the University of St Andrews. His main interests are in moral and political philosophy, metaethics, epistemology, and the history of nineteenth- and twentieth-century philosophy. He is the author of *English-Language Philosophy 1750–1945* (Oxford University Press, 1993); his most recent book is *The Domain of Reasons* (Oxford University Press, 2010).

David Woodruff Smith is Professor of Philosophy at the University of California, Irvine. He has written on various theories and historical figures in phenomenology, philosophy of mind, and philosophy of language. He is the author of *Husserl* (2007, 2nd edn., 2013) and *Mind World* (2004), and co-editor (with Amie L. Thomasson) of *Phenomenology and Philosophy of Mind* (2005).

Jamie Tappenden is Associate Professor of Philosophy at the University of Michigan. He has written on the logic of vagueness and the liar paradox, negation, and most recently on historical and philosophical issues arising out of research practices in mathematics. In his writings on the history of analytic philosophy he has worked to illuminate the ways that some of the characteristic dimensions of early analytic philosophy arose from problems arising in concurrent mathematical and scientific research.

Mark Textor is Professor of Philosophy at King's College London. He is the author of *Bolzanos Propositionalismus* (1996), *Über Sinn und Bedeutung von Eigennamen* (2005), and *Frege on Sense and Reference* (2010). He has edited several collections, among them *Bolzano and Analytic Philosophy* (together with W. Künne and M. Siebel, *Grazer Philosophische Studien* 53 (1997)), *The Austrian Contribution to Analytic Philosophy* (2006), and *Judgement and Truth in Early Analytic Philosophy and Phenomenology* (2013). He edited the *Journal for the History of Analytical Philosophy* from 2010 to 2013.

Charles Travis received his doctorate from UCLA in 1967. Since then he has taught at various universities in the USA, Canada, The Netherlands, and the UK. The last three of these are the University of Stirling, Northwestern University, and King's College London. His first efforts were in philosophy of language. He has gone on to work on problems of thought, perception, and knowledge, and on the interpretation of Frege and of Wittgenstein. He is currently working on a book on Frege. He now lives in Portugal.

Thomas Uebel is Professor of Philosophy at the University of Manchester, England. He is the author of *Overcoming Logical Positivism from Within* (1992), *Vernunftkritik und Wissenschaft* (2000), and *Empiricism at the Crossroads* (2007); co-author (with N. Cartwright, J. Cat, and K. Fleck) of *Otto Neurath: Philosophy Between Science and Politics* (1996); editor of *Rediscovering the Forgotten Vienna Circle* (1991); co-editor of, amongst others, *Otto Neurath: Economic Writings 1904–1945* (with R. S. Cohen, 2004), *Wiener Kreis: Texte zur wissenschaftlichen Weltauffassung* (with M. Stoeltzner, 2005) and *The Cambridge Companion to Logical Empiricism* (with A. Richardson, 2007).

Jonathan Wolff is Professor of Philosophy and Dean of Arts and Humanities at University College London. His recent books include *Disadvantage* (with Avner de-Shalit, Oxford University Press 2007), *Ethics and Public Policy* (2011), and *The Human Right to Health* (2012). He is the editor of G. A. Cohen, *Lectures in the History of Moral and Political Philosophy* (2013).

INTRODUCTION

ANALYTIC PHILOSOPHY AND ITS HISTORIOGRAPHY

CHAPTER 1

···

WHAT IS ANALYTIC
PHILOSOPHY?

···

MICHAEL BEANEY

All concepts in which a whole process is semiotically summarized elude definition; only that which has no history is definable. (Nietzsche, 'On the Genealogy of Morals', 1887, Second Essay, § 13)

I am an analytic philosopher. I think for myself. (Searle, as reported by Mulligan 2003, p. 267; cf. Glock 2008a, p. 211)

Analytic philosophy is characterized above all by the goal of clarity, the insistence on explicit argumentation in philosophy, and the demand that any view expressed be exposed to the rigours of critical evaluation and discussion by peers. (European Society for Analytic Philosophy, homepage of website <http://www.dif.unige.it/esap>; accessed 18 October 2011)

ANALYTIC philosophy is now generally seen as the dominant philosophical tradition in the English-speaking world,[1] and has been so from at least the middle of the last century. Over the last two decades its influence has also been steadily growing in the non-English-speaking world. One sign of this is the proliferation of societies for

---

[1] Even with my best Austinian hat on, I have been unable to detect any significant differences (whether semantic or pragmatic) between uses of 'analytic' and uses of 'analytical'. Some talk of 'analytical' philosophy, others of 'analytic' philosophy, but the latter are in the clear majority, and I will follow the majority use here. One suggestion might be that the former have a methodologically based conception in mind, while the latter are referring more to a tradition or movement. I discuss this distinction in section 1.4 of this chapter; but I have no found no grounds for it in uses of 'analytic' and 'analytical'. For all philosophical (and present) purposes, they can be treated as synonymous. In the German philosophical literature, as well as 'analytisch' there is 'sprachanalytisch', which tends to be used, more specifically, for linguistic philosophy or analytic philosophy of language (see e.g. Tugendhat 1976).

analytic philosophy around the world.[2] The growing dominance of the analytic tradition, however, does not mean that there has been any convergence of aims, methods, or views. If anything, the reverse is true: analytic philosophy now encompasses a far wider range of approaches, ideas, and positions than it ever did in its early days. From its original concern with epistemological and metaphysical questions in the philosophy of logic and mathematics (in the case of Frege and Russell) and in ethics and the theory of judgement (in the case of Moore), it has ramified—via the linguistic turn (taken first by Wittgenstein)—into all spheres of philosophy. As well as mainstream analytic philosophy in the areas of philosophy of language, logic, mathematics, mind and science, and analytic ethics, there are also fields as diverse as analytic aesthetics, analytic Marxism,

[2] In Europe there are societies for analytic philosophy in Austria (WFAP, founded 2009, with around 20 members), Croatia (CSAP, founded 2001), France (SoPhA, founded 1993), Germany (GAP, founded 1990, with around 900 members, claiming to be one of the biggest philosophical societies in Europe), Italy (SIFA, founded 1992, with over 400 members), the Netherlands (and Flemish-speaking Belgium; VAF, founded 2006), Portugal (SPFA, founded 2004), Romania (SRFA, founded 2007), Slovenia (DAF, founded 1991), and Spain (SEFA, founded 1995, with some 100 members). Most of these are constituent members of the European Society for Analytic Philosophy (ESAP, founded 1991), whose website <http://www.dif.unige.it/esap> contains links to its member societies. Analytic philosophy has been strong in the Nordic countries since the early twentieth century, from the work of Hägerström, Kaila, and Naess onwards. On Scandanavian and Nordic philosophy, see Olson and Paul 1972; Manninen and Stadler 2010; and on Finnish analytic philosophy, in particular, see Pihlström 2001; Haaparanta and Niiniluouto 2003. Poland and Austria, too, boast a proud history of analytic philosophy, through the work of the Lvov–Warsaw school and the Austrian realists, in particular. For references, see n. 20 below.

In Latin America, there are societies in Argentina (SADAF, founded 1972, with over 200 members), Brazil (SBFA, founded 2008, with over 50 members), Chile (SCFA, founded 2007, with some 20 members), and Peru (CESFIA, founded 2006), with Mexico hosting the Asociación Latinoamericana de Filosofía Analítica (ALFAn, founded 2006, with over 120 members). On analytic philosophy in Latin America, see Gracia *et al.* 1984; Martí 1998.

In Japan, analytic philosophy is promoted through such societies as the Association for Philosophy of Science and the Association for the Study of American Philosophy (cf. Piovesana 1962 [1997], pp. 219–21). In China, there is a Center for Analytical Philosophy (founded 2003) in the Institute of Foreign Philosophy at Peking University, as well as a Society for Analytic Philosophy (founded 2005).

There are also related societies such as the Institut Wiener Kreis (founded 1991), devoted to the study and further development of the work of the original Vienna Circle, the History of Early Analytic Philosophy Society (HEAPS, founded 2003, with over 60 members), and the Society for the Study of the History of Analytical Philosophy (SSHAP, founded 2009). Mention, too, should be made of the various societies and networks devoted to the work of individual analytic philosophers, such as the extremely active and long-established Bertrand Russell Society (BRS, founded 1974, with some 100 members) and Austrian Ludwig Wittgenstein Society (ALWS, founded 1974, with around 120 members), and the newer British Ludwig Wittgenstein Society (BWS, founded 2007, with over 300 members), Internationale Ludwig Wittgenstein Gesellschaft (formerly the Deutsche Ludwig Wittgenstein Gesellschaft, founded 1994, becoming the ILWG in 2006), Nordic Network for Wittgenstein Research (NNWR, founded 2006, with over 110 members), and North American Wittgenstein Society (NAWS, founded 2000). All this adds up, then, to tremendous and burgeoning interest in analytic philosophy, its past and its future, across the world.

analytical feminism, analytic theism, and analytical Thomism, for example.[3] There have also been complete reversals of views as well as diversification. One central strand in early analytic philosophy was logical positivism, in which the repudiation of metaphysics was fundamental. In the second half of the twentieth century, however, metaphysics has undergone a revival, and while earlier analytic philosophers would have regarded 'analytic metaphysics' as an oxymoron, the term now designates a respectable subdiscipline.[4] Analytic philosophy supposedly originated in reaction to Kantian and Hegelian forms of idealism, yet analytic Kantianism has been alive and flourishing for many years and there is now talk of analytic philosophy being ushered from its Kantian to its Hegelian stage.[5] Phenomenology has generally been seen as the main rival to the analytic tradition in the first half of the twentieth century, yet analytic phenomenology, especially analytic phenomenology of mind, is both reputable and thriving in the twenty-first century.[6]

Faced with these developments, one might wonder whether it makes sense to talk of 'analytic philosophy' any longer; as Frege once remarked, the wider the extension of a

---

[3] On analytic aesthetics, see Lamarque's chapter in this Handbook; on analytic Marxism, see Cohen 1978 and Wolff's chapter (which discusses analytic political philosophy, more generally); on analytic feminism, see Garry 2004, and the website of the Society for Analytical Feminism (founded in 1991; <https://sites.google.com/site/analyticalfeminism>; accessed 9 January 2012); on analytic theism (associated with the work of Plantinga, in particular), see Sennett 1998; on analytical Thomism, see Haldane 1995, 1997, 2006, and Paterson and Pugh 2006. Today, 'analytic' (or 'analytical') can qualify most philosophical approaches or areas. This practice of 'analytic' qualification was firmly established in the late 1960s and early 1970s when Danto published a trilogy of books on analytical philosophy of history (1965), analytical philosophy of knowledge (1968), and analytical philosophy of action (1973).

[4] On analytic metaphysics, see Simons' chapter in this Handbook; cf. Tooley 1999; Loux and Zimmerman 2003; Lowe 2008a; Chalmers *et al.* 2009. Lowe (1998, p. vi) treats it as the fundamental subdiscipline of analytic philosophy, although he also has reservations about the use of the term 'analytic metaphysics' and its close relative 'analytic ontology' (2008b, 2011). On metaphysics in early analytic philosophy, see Bradford 1981; Beaney 2012b; Shieh 2012. The latter two are contained in Haaparanta and Koskinen 2012, which traces the development of the relationship between logic and metaphysics from Aristotle to recent analytic metaphysics.

[5] The work of Strawson, especially Strawson 1959 and 1966, was the main source of the Kantian turn in analytic philosophy. For discussion of Kant and analytic philosophy, see Hanna 2001, 2008; Glock 2003b (Glock's own contribution, 2003c, talks explicitly of 'analytic Kantianism'); O'Shea 2006. On the move to a Hegelian stage in analytic philosophy, see Rorty's introduction to Sellars 1997, pp. 8–9; cf. Redding 2007, p. 1. Redding discusses the work of McDowell and Brandom, in particular. Brandom's inferentialism is explained in Peregrin's chapter in this Handbook, and McDowell's views on perception are considered in the context of the Oxford realist tradition in Travis and Kalderon's chapter.

[6] 'Analytic phenomenology' was used in the title of a book as far back as 1970 (Erickson 1970). A more recent use is in the subtitle of Huemer 2005. For discussion of analytic phenomenology, see Smith's chapter in the present volume. Other examples of prima facie oxymoronic 'analytic' qualification include 'analytic idealism' (which has been used to describe e.g. Ewing's work), 'analytic hermeneutics' (used e.g. as the title of ch. 1 of Howard 1982), and 'analytic existentialism' (used as the title of a conference held in Cape Town in 2001).

term, the less content it has (1884, § 29). Wanting to restrict the label to the early phase of the tradition, some have argued that analytic philosophy had exhausted itself by the 1970s (at the latest), and that we are now in a 'post-analytic' age.[7] These views, however, do not reflect the widespread use of 'analytic philosophy' to refer to much contemporary philosophy, and the term 'early analytic philosophy' has been introduced to refer to the early period.[8] It seems best, then, to respect the current use of the term as much as possible and treat analytic philosophy as a tradition that is healthier and stronger today, albeit more diverse, than it has ever been in the past. Certainly, a concern with the *history* of analytic philosophy should err on the side of inclusiveness. Even if there are some philosophers, schools of thought, or periods that some would wish to exclude from the tradition, their relationship to analytic philosophy, on whatever narrower conception is favoured, will still be relevant in understanding the nature and development of analytic philosophy, so conceived.

As a first approximation, then, in its most inclusive sense, analytic philosophy can be characterized as the tradition that originated in the work of Gottlob Frege (1848–1925), Bertrand Russell (1872–1970), G. E. Moore (1873–1958), and Ludwig Wittgenstein (1889–1951) and developed and ramified into the complex movement (or set of interconnected subtraditions) that we know today. I say more about the origins of analytic philosophy in the first section of this chapter, and more about its development in the second section. In the third section I discuss the question of what themes have been particularly important in the history of analytic philosophy and hence might reveal something about the character of the analytic tradition. These first three sections correspond (more or less) to the three main parts of this Handbook. In the fourth and final section I draw on these sections—and the Handbook as a whole— in directly addressing the question that forms the title of this chapter. I shall leave until the next chapter consideration of the historical turn that has taken place in analytic philosophy over the last two decades, the histories that have been written of the analytic tradition, and the questions that these raise as to the relationship between

---

[7] Quine's attack on the analytic/synthetic distinction and Wittgenstein's later critique of his own earlier philosophy have been seen as inaugurating the 'post-analytic' age. 'Post-analytic philosophy' is the title of a book published in 1985 (Rajchman and West), though only American philosophy is here discussed. Wang published a book in the same year called *Beyond Analytic Philosophy*. Quine describes himself as 'post-analytic' in Borradori 1994. The University of Southampton established a Centre for Post-Analytic Philosophy in 1997 (inaugurated with a lecture by Bernard Williams, later published as ch. 17 of Williams 2006a), but it soon became a Post-Centre. A collection entitled *Post-Analytic 'Tractatus'* appeared in 2004 (Stocker 2004). For further discussion of 'post-analytic' philosophy, see e.g. Mulhall 2002; Reynolds *et al.* 2010.

[8] The first book to have 'Early Analytic Philosophy' in its title was Cocchiarella 1987. Later books include Clarke 1997; Tait 1997; Reck 2002a; Beaney 2007a; and Textor 2013. As noted above (n. 2), the History of Early Analytic Philosophy Society was founded in 2003. An analogy can be drawn with the way that 'early modern philosophy' came to be used to refer to the first phase of 'modern philosophy', the phase that is generally taken to run from Descartes (or just before) to Kant, whose work marks the end of early modern philosophy, whether or not Kant's work itself is counted as part of it.

analytic philosophy and history of philosophy.[9] This Handbook is itself both an historical product of that historical turn and philosophically conceived to consolidate and deepen that historical turn.

1.1 THE ORIGINS OF ANALYTIC PHILOSOPHY

Russell's and Moore's rebellion against British idealism has often been taken as signalling the birth of analytic philosophy.[10] Certainly, it is one of the key events in the emergence of analytic philosophy, and the nature of the rebellion is explained by Griffin in chapter 11 of this Handbook. For Russell, what was crucial was his concern with the foundations of mathematics. After his initial flirtation with neo-Hegelianism, he came to the conclusion that it was only by rejecting the neo-Hegelian doctrine of internal relations that an adequate account of mathematics could be provided. Relational propositions are fundamental in mathematics, and according to Russell, relations had to be treated as 'real' (i.e. independent and irreducible) constituents of propositions in order for mathematics to consist of truths. For Moore, what was crucial was his dissatisfaction with the idealist's denial of mind-independent objects. Moore came to believe that the world is quite literally composed of concepts, propositions being nothing other than complex concepts. In understanding propositions, according to Moore, we grasp the constituent concepts that the propositions are actually *about*. Both Russell and Moore, then, came to adopt a crude form of direct realism, and this was at the heart of their rebellion against British idealism.

In his own description of their rebellion in *My Philosophical Development*, Russell just talked of their 'new philosophy',[11] and nowhere in their early work does either Russell or Moore speak of 'analytic' or 'analytical' philosophy. (I trace the development of talk of 'analytic philosophy', and the corresponding construction of analytic philosophy as a tradition, in the next chapter.) What we do find, however, is emphasis on the role of analysis. Russell's first endorsement is in his book on Leibniz, where he asserts as an 'evident' truth that 'all sound philosophy should begin with an analysis of propositions' (1900, p. 8). For Moore, such analysis consists in decomposing propositions into their constituent concepts, and this decompositional conception is also in play in the first chapter of *Principia Ethica*, where he argues that 'good'

---

[9] In what follows I use 'history of philosophy' to denote the discipline or practice of history of philosophy and 'the history of analytic philosophy' to denote the actual history of analytic philosophy. The title of this Handbook should be understood in both senses, however. It is both a handbook of the history of analytic philosophy and a handbook of history of analytic philosophy.

[10] See e.g. Hylton 1990; Griffin 1991; Hacker 1996.

[11] Russell 1959, ch. 5, pp. 42, 48–9. I say more about Russell's own talk of the 'new philosophy' in §§ 2 and 3 of the following chapter.

is indefinable, that is, that what 'good' denotes has no parts into which it can be decomposed.[12]

As Griffin notes, we have a clear sense in which Russell's and Moore's 'new philosophy' is 'analytic': at the core of their method is the decompositional analysis of propositions. For Moore, this is *conceptual* analysis; Russell's position, however, is more complex. While Moore and Russell agreed that the aim of philosophical analysis is to uncover the fundamental constituents of propositions,[13] Russell understood this within a broader programme of *logical* analysis. This involved the identification, first, of the logical constituents of propositions, that is, the logical constants,[14] but second, more importantly, of the logical propositions themselves, and in particular, of the fundamental propositions or logical principles from which all other logical propositions can be derived. It is this idea that lay at the core of his work on the foundations of mathematics from 1901, when his logicist project was first announced—the project of showing how the propositions of mathematics can be derived from purely logical propositions.[15]

What made logicism feasible was the creation of modern logic, the system of propositional and predicate logic whose use has been a major force in the development of analytic philosophy. It is here that Frege comes into the story and obliges us to acknowledge him as one of the co-founders of analytic philosophy. For it was Frege who created quantificational logic, and although Russell learnt of this logic through Giuseppe Peano (1858–1932), and adapted Peano's notation rather than Frege's, there is no doubt that once Russell properly studied Frege's writings, after completing *The Principles of Mathematics* in May 1902, he both learnt from them and developed his own position in critique of some of Frege's key ideas.[16] Frege was also an influence on Wittgenstein, whose early thinking was prompted by the problems he found in Frege's and Russell's work, taking over some of their ideas and assumptions but criticizing others. So on

---

[12] Cf. Beaney 2009, § 6.4. Moore also endorses analysis in his preface to *Principia Ethica*, although here what he means is the disentangling of questions so that we can be clear about what exactly the question is that we are asking before we try to answer it. Moore writes that 'the work of analysis and distinction is often very difficult', but if we can do it, then we can resolve the philosophical problems that face us (1903, p. vii). A decompositional conception of analysis is still at work here, and we might bring his various descriptions of analysis together by suggesting that the aim of philosophy, on Moore's view, is to get clear about the constituent concepts of propositions that give rise to philosophical problems.

[13] For the early Moore, the fundamental constituents are all concepts. For Russell in the *Principles*, they are all *terms*, of which there are two kinds, things and concepts, concepts in turn being divided into predicates and relations (1903, p. 44). So there are differences between Moore's and Russell's views here (cf. Russell 1903, p. 44, n.*).

[14] See e.g. Russell, 1903, p. 9: 'the method of discovering the logical constants is the analysis of symbolic logic'; cf. p. xx.

[15] See Russell 1901. Two years later he writes: 'The fact that all Mathematics is Symbolic Logic is one of the greatest discoveries of our age; and when this fact has been established, the remainder of the principles of mathematics consists in the analysis of Symbolic Logic itself' (1903, p. 5).

[16] For details of the relationship between Frege and Russell, with particular reference to their logic and philosophy of mathematics, see Beaney 2005a.

this score, too, Frege must be counted as one of the co-founders of analytic philosophy. Moore's and Russell's rebellion against British idealism occurred independently of Frege, but both Russell's subsequent work and Wittgenstein's thinking were inextricably linked to Frege's ideas.[17]

Quantificational logic was first presented in Frege's *Begriffsschrift* of 1879, where he announces that his ultimate aim is to give a logical analysis of number (1879, p. viii). Over twenty years before Russell, then, Frege set out to demonstrate that arithmetic is reducible to logic. (Unlike Russell, Frege was never a logicist about geometry.) He gave his first, informal account in *Die Grundlagen der Arithmetik* of 1884, and the formal proof was his aim in *Grundgesetze der Arithmetik*, of which Volume I appeared in 1893 and Volume II in 1903. It was while the second volume was in press that Russell informed him, in June 1902, of the contradiction that undermined his system, and Frege was soon led to abandon his logicist project. The task of demonstrating logicism was passed on to Russell, who found it necessary to construct a complex theory of types to avoid the contradiction (and related ones). In pursuing his logicist project, however, Frege had been led to develop many of the ideas that became influential in subsequent analytic philosophy. Many courses in the philosophy of language today, for example, begin with Frege's key distinctions between concept and object, and *Sinn* and *Bedeutung*; and the internalism/externalism debate in current philosophy of mind goes back to Frege's theory of thought and his views about indexicality. An account of Frege's influence is provided by Tyler Burge in chapter 10 of this Handbook (see also Burge 1992).

Frege's creation of quantificational logic and the rebellion by Russell and Moore against British idealism are the two most significant events in the emergence of analytic philosophy, events that lie at the root of many of the ideas and achievements that we associate with early analytic philosophy, such as Frege's logical analysis of existential and number statements, Moore's critique of naturalism, Russell's theory of descriptions and theory of types, and Wittgenstein's conception of logical propositions as tautologies. A deeper understanding of the origins of analytic philosophy, then, requires appreciation of the background to these events—in particular, the German philosophical and scientific background to Frege's and Wittgenstein's work, the British philosophical background to Russell's and Moore's rebellion, and the mathematical and logical background to Frege's and Russell's logicist projects. The chapters by David Hyder, Gottfried Gabriel, John Skorupski, and Jamie Tappenden offer an account of these backgrounds. I also say more about this in the first section of the next chapter, and further details are provided in the chronology that forms chapter 3. Here I simply note that to place a philosopher's work in historical context is not necessarily to dissolve away its originality or significance: it may help, instead, to identify just what was new and important.

---

[17] On the influence of Frege and Russell on Wittgenstein, the relative strengths of which is a matter of controversy, see Anscombe 1959; Diamond 1981, 1984, 2010, chapter 30 below; Dummett 1981b; Baker 1988; Hacker 1996, ch. 2, 1999; Ricketts 1996, 2002, 2010; Reck 1997, 2002b; Green 1999; Conant 2000, 2002; Goldfarb 2002; Travis 2006a; Carey 2007; Landini 2007; Floyd 2009; Potter 2009; Kienzler 2011; Beaney 2012b.

Originality and significance, however, are often only appreciated with hindsight. Frege's work was recognized by very few at the time. Russell claimed that it was he who first drew attention to Frege. The claim is false, but he is right that he wrote the first exposition of Frege's philosophy in English, and it was through this exposition that Wittgenstein learnt of Frege's work.[18] Frege's influence on Russell and (to a much greater extent) Wittgenstein, however, was not appreciated until after the Second World War, and Frege's work was overlooked in the early histories of analytic philosophy (see the next chapter). Even today, he is still sometimes omitted,[19] but the general consensus firmly locates him at the heart of analytic philosophy.

In recent years there has been growing interest in the work of Bernard Bolzano (1781–1848). Bolzano was critical of Kant's account of mathematics, just as Frege and Russell were, and his conceptions of analyticity, apriority, logical consequence, and propositionality, as well as his use of the method of variation, anticipate the ideas of later analytic philosophers. Bolzano did not directly influence the four acknowledged main founders of analytic philosophy, but he did influence Kazimierz Twardowski (1866–1938), the founder of the Lvov–Warsaw School, whose work fed into the later analytic tradition through Alexius Meinong (1853–1920) and Alfred Tarski (1902–83), among others. Recognizing the Polish and Austrian influences on analytic philosophy—or better, the Polish and Austrian *branches* of analytic philosophy, then, brings Bolzano into its family tree, as a granduncle of the analytic tradition.[20] Whether or not we agree to count Bolzano himself as an analytic philosopher, however, consideration of his work certainly has a place in understanding the history of analytic philosophy. Mark Textor explains Bolzano's critique of Kant in chapter 5 of this Handbook.

If there is anything that might provide a defining characteristic of 'analytic' philosophy, then the obvious candidate—as the very name suggests—is the role played by *analysis*. As indicated above, Russell's and Moore's early philosophy was indeed 'analytic' in the sense that the decompositional analysis of propositions was central to their methodology. As Russell himself announced in 1900, 'That all sound philosophy should begin with an analysis of propositions, is a truth too evident, perhaps, to demand a proof' (1900, p. 8). This remark is made in his book on Leibniz, and he immediately went on to note: 'That Leibniz's philosophy began with such an analysis, is less evident, but seems

---

[18] Russell makes the claim in his *History of Western Philosophy* (1945, p. 784), for example, and his exposition is offered in Appendix A of *The Principles of Mathematics* (1903), which Wittgenstein read in 1909. It was Peano who drew Russell's own attention to Frege, though, and Frege's work was also familiar to many German and Polish logicians and mathematicians at the time.

[19] Hacker (rather surprisingly, given his work on Wittgenstein) tends to play down Frege's role in the history of analytic philosophy (see e.g. Hacker 1996, 2007, and his chapter in the present volume); but the most egregious recent omission occurs in Soames' two-volume history (2003). Soames claims that it was his hope to write a companion volume on the 'highly technical parts' of the analytic tradition (2003, I, pp. xvii f.), but Frege's ideas about concept and object, sense and reference, thought, compositionality, indexicality, analyticity, analysis, and the context principle, among others, hardly count as 'highly technical' (cf. Beaney 2006b, §3).

[20] On the Polish and Austrian branches of analytic philosophy, see Woleński 1989, 1999; Simons 1992; Nyíri 1996; Textor 2006; Lapointe *et al.* 2009; Mulligan *et al.* 2013; and for discussion of Bolzano in relation to analytic philosophy, see Künne, Siebel, and Textor 1997; Lapointe 2011.

to be no less true' (ibid.). Russell's first remark is frequently cited; the implication of the second is less often recognized: that Leibniz might count as an analytic philosopher just like Russell. But if Leibniz so counts, then how far back can we go? To Descartes? To Ockham, Buridan, and other medieval logicians? To Aristotle or even Plato? As Richard Gaskin shows in chapter 29, there are logical atomist themes in Plato's *Theaetetus*, as Ryle and others have explored.

In fact, the decompositional conception of analysis that Moore and Russell adopted was neither new nor definitively characteristic of later analytic philosophy, even in the case of Russell's and Moore's own later philosophy. Arguably, Moore inherited his early conception from Brentano via Stout and Ward,[21] and Moore in turn influenced Russell, reinforced by Russell's own work on Leibniz in 1899.[22] Moore's and Russell's early conception of analysis was extremely crude, reflecting as it did their initial naïve realism, but richer and more interesting conceptions soon developed. By far the most significant and influential conception was that embodied in Russell's theory of descriptions, first put forward in 1905 and famously described by Ramsey as a 'paradigm of philosophy' (1931b, p. 263). Much has been written about this;[23] what is important for present purposes is the role played by what I have called 'interpretive' or 'transformative' analysis.[24] The first step in the analysis of a sentence of the (grammatical) form 'The F is G' consists in interpreting it as, or transforming it into, a sentence of a different (quantificational) form, namely, 'There is one and only one F, and whatever is F is G', taken to represent the real logical form of the proposition expressed by the sentence—or at least, as a step nearer the goal of complete representation. (For discussion of the idea of a logically perfect language involved in this, see Hylton's chapter.)

Russell's theory of descriptions opened up the prospect of a whole new philosophical programme: making clear the 'real' logical form of propositions to both reveal the fundamental structure and composition of the world and resolve philosophical perplexity that arises from misunderstanding the logic of our language and thought. Developing the associated ideas of 'incomplete symbols' and 'logical fictions', Russell applied the theory in attempting to solve the paradoxes that threatened his logicist project, and then turned to what he later called 'logical constructions' in other areas of philosophy, as Bernard Linsky explains in chapter 12.[25]

There was development in Moore's views on analysis, too, as Thomas Baldwin shows in chapter 13. Moore's early (crude) decompositional conception of analysis underlies both his attack in *Principia Ethica* (1903a) on the supposed naturalistic fallacy and his idea that philosophical disagreements arise from failing to disentangle questions that get fused together (1903a, p. vii). After that, Moore's views become more complex. Moore

[21] See Bell 1999; Beaney 2002/2007c; Schaar 1996, 2013.
[22] I say more about the significance of Russell's work on Leibniz in section 2.2 of the next chapter. Cf. Beaney 2013a, §5.1.
[23] See especially Hylton 1990, ch. 6; 2003; Linsky and Imaguire 2005; Neale 2005; Stevens 2011.
[24] See especially Beaney 2007b, 2007c, 2009a; cf. n. 62 below.
[25] For further discussion of logical constructions, in the broader context of the debates that were then going on in Britain at the time, see Nasim 2008.

(1944) endorsed Ramsey's praise of Russell's theory of descriptions, for example, but he did not advocate any systematic project of analysis such as Russell did. Influenced, too, by Wittgenstein's *Tractatus* (1921), Moore insisted that one could understand the meaning of an expression without being able to give a correct analysis of its meaning. This enabled him to claim, in 'A Defence of Common Sense' (1925), that one could know that certain deliverances of common sense are true even if one has no analysis of the relevant statements to hand. The idea also underlies Moore's 'Proof of an External World' (1939), as Annalisa Coliva makes clear in section 34.1 of chapter 34 (and see also section 35.3 of Juliet Floyd's chapter).

Russell's, Moore's, and Wittgenstein's ideas all helped form what became known as the Cambridge School of Analysis, which reached the peak of its influence in the 1930s, as Baldwin describes in the second half of his chapter. As well as Russell, Moore, and Wittgenstein, key figures in Cambridge were C. D. Broad (1887–1971), Frank Ramsey (1903–30), and John Wisdom (1904–93), and in London (though Cambridge educated) Susan Stebbing (1885–1943). The journal *Analysis* was founded in 1933, and in the pages of both it and the *Proceedings of the Aristotelian Society* there was both lively discussion of the nature of analysis and examples of its use that also generated debate. It was with respect to the Cambridge School that the term 'analytic philosophy' was first used, and I say much more about this and the construction of the analytic tradition in the following chapter.

Wittgenstein's *Tractatus* was the single most important influence on the Cambridge School, and it is generally regarded as *the* key text of early analytic philosophy, influencing every subsequent generation of analytic philosophers. In the final chapter of Part I of this Handbook, Michael Kremer offers an account of its main ideas by focusing on the summary of the whole sense of the book that Wittgenstein himself offered in his preface: 'what can be said at all can be said clearly; and whereof one cannot speak thereof one must be silent' (1922, p. 27). At the end of his book, Wittgenstein notoriously claimed that the propositions of the *Tractatus* were nonsensical, to be kicked away once one has used them as a ladder to climb up to the correct view. Traditionally, commentators have interpreted Wittgenstein as holding that the nonsense is nevertheless 'illuminating', intended to express ineffable truths about language, logic, and the world.[26] In recent years, however, a new 'therapeutic' or 'resolute' reading has been developed that challenges this traditional view; and this has stirred a great deal of debate. According to the new reading, we should take Wittgenstein at his word and not 'chicken out' by talking of illuminating nonsense and ineffable truths.[27] Kremer sides more with the new than the old reading, and uses his discussion to elucidate Wittgenstein's famous remark (in a letter to Ficker in 1919) that the point of his book was in fact ethical.

[26] The term 'illuminating' is Hacker's (1986, p. 18). Hacker is the most prominent current advocate of the traditional reading. For his criticisms of the new reading, see Hacker 2000, 2003.

[27] See especially Diamond 1988, where the phrase 'chickening out' is used ([1991a], p. 181), 1991b; Ricketts 1996a; Goldfarb 1997b, where the term 'resolute' is used (p. 64); Conant 2002, 2007; Conant and Diamond 2004. For an 'elucidatory' reading that attempts to steer between the traditional and new readings, see McGinn 1999, 2006; and for further discussion of the debate, see Kremer 2001, 2007; Proops 2001; Sullivan 2002, 2003.

1.2 THE DEVELOPMENT OF ANALYTIC PHILOSOPHY

Wittgenstein's *Tractatus* can be regarded as marking the culmination of the early period of analytic philosophy. Wittgenstein's own statement in his preface that he is 'indebted to Frege's great works and to the writings of my friend Mr Bertrand Russell' (1922, p. 3) reinforces the case for regarding Frege as one of the founders of the analytic tradition, and for classifying Frege's invention of quantificational logic alongside Moore's and Russell's rebellion against British idealism as the two most significant events in the emergence of analytic philosophy. Its further development is characterized by its gradual broadening and ramifying, as the ideas of Frege, Russell, Moore, and Wittgenstein in its early period were applied, criticized, extended, and transformed. Russell, Moore, and Wittgenstein themselves played major roles in this development. An account of Russell's project in *The Analysis of Matter* of 1927 is included in Linsky's chapter, and Moore's 'Proof of an External World' of 1939 is examined by Annalisa Coliva in chapter 34. Both Russell's and Moore's views on perception and sense-data are also discussed by Gary Hatfield in chapter 33. Hans-Johann Glock provides a survey of Wittgenstein's later philosophy in chapter 18, concluding by addressing the disputed questions of his legacy and of whether the later Wittgenstein is an 'analytic' philosopher.

In the development of analytic philosophy in its second phase, Russell, Moore, and Wittgenstein were joined by a broad range of philosophers of the next generation, who, with different backgrounds and interests, introduced new approaches and ideas in responding not only to earlier philosophical views but also to subsequent advances in logic, mathematics, science, and other disciplines. The work of the Cambridge School of Analysis in the 1920s and 1930s has already been mentioned. Standard stories of analytic philosophy in Britain simply then switch, after the Second World War, to Oxford and so-called ordinary language philosophy, with Gilbert Ryle (1900–76), J. L. Austin (1911–60), and P. F. Strawson (1919–2006) taking over as the dominant figures.[28] In fact, however, there was an earlier movement in Oxford that in some ways parallels developments in Cambridge. Indeed, in its own rejection of British idealism, it begins several years before Moore's and Russell's rebellion, and defends anti-psychologistic and realist views of knowledge and perception that are interestingly related to Moore's and Russell's. Certainly, they were all part of the vigorous epistemological debate that took place in Britain in the first half of the twentieth century—and continues to the present day. The key figures were John Cook Wilson (1848–1915) and H. A. Prichard (1871–1947), and

---

[28] The standard story can be found in its crudest form in Milkov 2003, but it is also reflected, for example, in Warnock 1958/1969, Stroll 2000, and Soames 2003, very different as all these are. The centre of gravity of British analytic philosophy did indeed shift from Cambridge to Oxford after the Second World War (cf. Beaney 2006c, 2006f), but as I have come to appreciate much more now, Oxford ordinary language philosophy has deep roots in earlier Oxford realism, and Cook Wilson's work, in particular (Beaney 2012a).

Part II of this Handbook opens with an account of Oxford realism by Charles Travis and Mark Kalderon. As they argue, the work of later Oxford philosophers, especially Austin and, more recently, John McDowell (1942–), must be seen in the broader historical context of the Oxford tradition. I say more about Oxford realism in section 2.3 of the next chapter, and there is further discussion in Hatfield's chapter.

The most important event in the development of analytic philosophy in its second phase, though, was the establishment of the Vienna Circle, following on from the founding of the Verein Ernst Mach in 1928 and with its collaborative name-bestowing manifesto launched in 1929 (Carnap, Hahn, and Neurath 1929). The movement of logical positivism—or logical empiricism (the two terms are often used synonymously)—proved to be far more influential than the Cambridge School of Analysis. Indeed, while both were seen as forms of analytic philosophy in the 1930s (see the next chapter), analytic philosophy came to be identified more in the public mind as logical positivism, especially when A. J. Ayer (1910–89) popularized it in the English-speaking world in *Language, Truth and Logic* (1936) and Wittgenstein's influence on the Vienna Circle and his own verificationist phase in the early 1930s suggested (mistakenly) that he, too, counted as a logical positivist.[29] In chapter 16 of this Handbook, Thomas Uebel stresses the heterogeneity of logical empiricism, which in fact included not only the work of members of the Vienna Circle, from Moritz Schlick (1882–1936) and Friedrich Waismann (1896–1959), who had the closest connection to Wittgenstein, to Otto Neurath (1882–1945) and Rudolf Carnap (1891–1970), but also the work of the Berlin Society for Empirical Philosophy, led by Hans Reichenbach (1891–1953).[30]

Vienna in the late 1920s and early 1930s was not only a centre for logical empiricism. It was also at the forefront of developments in logic, as Erich Reck explains in chapter 17.[31] Carnap made contributions to logic as well as to philosophy, and one of the younger members of the Vienna Circle was Kurt Gödel (1906–78), who published his famous incompleteness theorems in 1931. Alfred Tarski (1901–83), one of the leading figures in the Lvov–Warsaw School of Logic, maintained close links with Carnap and Gödel, and his seminal paper on truth appeared in Polish in 1933 and in German in 1935. This influenced not only Carnap's philosophy, as his 'syntactic turn' gave way to a 'semantic turn',[32]

---

[29] On the controversial relationship between Wittgenstein and the Vienna Circle, see Baker 1988, 2003; McGuinness 1991; Carus 2007, ch. 7; Stern 2007. For Wittgenstein's conversations with members of the Vienna Circle, see Waismann 1979.

[30] On the Berlin Society, see Hoffmann 2007. For fuller discussion of logical empiricism, see Hanfling 1981a; Uebel 1992, 2007; Giere and Richardson 1996; Stadler 1997/2001, 2003; Friedman 1999; Richardson and Uebel 2007. On Carnap and Reichenbach, see Spohn 1992; and on Carnap, in particular, see Richardson 1998; Awodey and Klein 2004; Carus 2007; Friedman and Creath 2007. The classic collection of readings is Ayer 1959; a later collection is Hanfling 1981b.

[31] See also Mancosu, Zach, and Badesa 2009, and other chapters in Haaparanta 2009 for a fuller account of the development of modern logic.

[32] Carnap's conception of philosophy as the logic of science, understood as formalizing the logical syntax of the language of science, is articulated in Carnap 1934/1937; his 'semantic turn' is represented in Carnap 1942, 1943, 1947. On the former, see Friedman 1999, Part 3; Wagner 2009. On the development of Carnap's views, see Coffa 1991, chs. 15–17; Ricketts 1996b; Creath 1999; Awodey 2007.

but also many subsequent philosophers, most notably, Donald Davidson (1917–2003) in his work on theories of meaning thirty years later. Alexander Miller explains Davidson's use of Tarski's theory of truth in chapter 21.

The 1930s, however, also saw the rise of Nazism in Germany, and this led to the exodus of many of the logical positivists and logicians in continental Europe by the beginning of the Second World War, most of them ending up in the United States. Carnap emigrated at the end of 1935, for example, Tarski had to stay when he was stranded there at the outbreak of war, after a trip to a congress, and Gödel went to Princeton in 1940. Reichenbach went to UCLA in 1938 after five years in Istanbul. Together with the visits from British philosophers, including both Russell and Moore, that increasingly took place, these events transformed philosophy in the States.[33] American philosophers had visited Europe to learn about and report back on developments in philosophy there,[34] but it was only when European philosophers went to the States, and started taking up jobs there, that analytic philosophy began to grow. Seen by some in the States as a healthy import, by others as a threat to existing American philosophical traditions, especially pragmatism, it soon took firm root in American soil and began to develop its own character in critical interaction with those other traditions and with earlier and continuing European analytic philosophy. An account of the relationship between American pragmatism and analytic philosophy is provided by Cheryl Misak in chapter 38.[35]

The most famous American visitor to the Vienna Circle had been W. V. O. Quine (1908–2000), who spent a year in Europe in 1932–3. The dispute that he subsequently had with Carnap over the analytic/synthetic distinction is perhaps the most well-known of all in the history of analytic philosophy, taken by some to mark the beginning of the end of analytic philosophy but by most as heralding a new phase in analytic philosophy. Much has been written about this dispute,[36] and aspects of it are discussed by Maria Baghramian and Andrew Jorgensen in chapter 19 and by Sanford Shieh in chapter 36. Quine's work has had enormous influence on both American philosophy and analytic philosophy in general. Davidson, Hilary Putnam (1926–) and Saul Kripke (1940–) are three of the most prominent American analytic philosophers who have critically engaged at the deepest level with Quine's ideas. Baghramian and Jorgensen explain Putnam's and Kripke's critique of Quine's views on meaning and reference, and Shieh

---

[33] Further details of all these events are provided in the chronology that forms chapter 3 of this Handbook. Russell was a regular—if controversial—visitor to the States (see his *Autobiography*, 1967–9/1975, especially ch. 13). After his retirement from Cambridge, Moore went to the States in October 1940 and taught at various institutions during the war (Moore 1942a, pp. 38–9). For one testament to his influence, see White 1999, ch. 5.

[34] A notable example is Ernest Nagel, who first reported on 'analytic philosophy' for an American audience in 1936; see section 2.4 of the following chapter.

[35] For further accounts of the complex development of analytic philosophy in America, see Kuklick 2001, Part III; Isaac 2005; Reisch 2005, 2007; and especially Misak 2008, chs. 14ff.

[36] See, for example, Ebbs 1997, Part II; Hylton 2001a; 2007a, chs. 2–3; Creath 2007. For Quine's and Carnap's own correspondence, see Quine and Carnap 1990. Morton White's role in the story is frequently overlooked; see especially White 1950; 1956, ch. 8; cf. 1999, Appendix.

discusses some of the responses to Quine's views on modality, in particular, from Kripke and Ruth Barcan Marcus (1921–2012).

On a widespread view of analytic philosophy, the focus of interest in its early period was on questions of meaning in the areas of (philosophical) logic and philosophy of mathematics, with philosophy of language coming to be seen as fundamental to other areas of philosophy, not least metaphysics, which increasingly became the target of attack. Certainly, the development of philosophy of language has been a central thread— arguably even *the* central thread—in the history of analytic philosophy. The construction of theories of meaning has played a key role in this development, as Alexander Miller explains in chapter 21. In fact, however, traditional epistemological and metaphysical concerns were present right from the beginning of analytic philosophy. Frege and Russell were both concerned with the epistemology of mathematics, and made metaphysical assumptions or came to meta-physical conclusions in support of their logical and logicist views.[37] Moore's objection to idealism was primarily epistemological and he, too, advocated a metaphysics of concepts to support his critique.[38] Of course, it is true that logical positivism urged the repudiation of metaphysics, but this was relatively short-lived, and logical positivism came under attack for its own metaphysical assumptions. By the time we come to the work of Quine and Strawson, metaphysics, whether qualified as 'analytic' or 'descriptive', is firmly back on the agenda. The story of metaphysics in analytic philosophy is charted by Peter Simons in chapter 23.[39]

If philosophy of language has often been seen as central in early analytic philosophy, then philosophy of mind is sometimes taken to have usurped its place in later analytic philosophy. There is no doubt that there has been an explosion of interest in a wide range of issues in philosophy of mind over the last 50 years.[40] One fundamental debate concerns the mind/body problem, and in chapter 20 Sean Crawford explains the origins of the identity theory. On the standard story, this emerged in critique of the various forms of so-called logical behaviourism proposed by the logical positivists and Ryle. As Crawford shows, however, the 'logical behaviourism' that was attacked was to some extent constructed by its critics into a 'shadow position'; and the actual history is both more interesting and philosophical revealing.

A similar strategy is adopted by Stewart Candlish and Nic Damnjanovic in chapter 22, in discussing a second—and related—debate that is fundamental to both philosophy of mind and philosophy of action. This concerns the distinction—or lack of it—between reasons and causes. Here the standard picture has been of an anti-causalist consensus in earlier analytic philosophy, in which the distinction was stressed, being demolished by Davidson's paper of 1963 on 'Actions, Reasons and Causes'. Candlish

---

[37] See Beaney 2012b.

[38] See Baldwin 1990, chs. 1–2.

[39] For further discussion, see Loux and Zimmerman 2003b, and the other chapters of Loux and Zimmerman 2003a; Lowe 2008a; Moore 2012, Part 2.

[40] For a good sense of the breadth of this explosion, see the 4 vols. of Crawford 2011. For a survey of developments in both philosophy of language and philosophy of mind between 1950 and 1990, see Burge 1992. Cf. Crane and Patterson 2000; Kim 2004.

and Damnjanovic argue, though, that the supposed neo-Wittgensteinian 'behaviourist' position attacked by Davidson is a caricature of the views actually held by Wittgenstein, Ryle, and G. E. M. Anscombe (1919–2001), and that the current causalist consensus is not as well-grounded as many people think.[41]

There have been major developments in analytic philosophy in other areas as well. From Moore's earliest work, analytic philosophers have concerned themselves with ethics, and emotivism and prescriptivism, in particular, were closely related to logical positivism and ordinary language philosophy, respectively. In later analytic ethics, there has been a 'naturalistic turn' that parallels developments in philosophy of mind, although this, too, has generated much debate and Kantian theories (among others) have been revived in response. In chapter 24 Jonathan Dancy provides an account of meta-ethics in twentieth-century analytic philosophy, and in chapter 25 Julia Driver discusses normative ethical theory.[42] As mentioned at the beginning of this chapter, there are now 'analytic' traditions in virtually all areas of philosophy. In chapter 26, Peter Lamarque identifies the beginnings of analytic aesthetics in a collection on *Aesthetics and Language* published in 1954 (Elton 1954) and outlines its growth and concerns. In 1956 there appeared the first in a series of edited volumes on *Philosophy, Politics and Society* (Laslett 1956), and in chapter 27, Jonathan Wolff considers this series in charting the development of analytic political philosophy. These dates are significant; as I suggest in section 2.5 of the next chapter, it is only in the 1950s that analytic philosophy properly becomes recognized as a tradition. That this should have happened as it ramified into all areas of philosophy is not a coincidence.

1.3 THEMES IN THE HISTORY OF ANALYTIC PHILOSOPHY

In the previous two sections, in introducing the chapters in Parts I and II of this Handbook, a sketch has been provided of some of the main developments in the history of analytic philosophy. Those chapters fill out the sketch by focusing on particular figures, movements, periods, or areas of philosophy. But this is not the only way to contribute to history of analytic philosophy. The chapters in Part III also shed light on the history of analytic philosophy by exploring certain themes that are characteristic of, or have been particularly associated with, analytic philosophy.[43]

---

[41] For more on this debate, see D'Oro and Sandis 2013.

[42] For more on the history of analytic ethics, see Darwall, Gibbard, and Railton 1992; Railton 1998; Hurka 2004, 2011; Irwin 2009; Deigh 2013.

[43] This is not to say that there is a hard and fast division between the three parts. Chapters 21 and 22 might have been allocated to Part III, for example, and chapter 38 might have been placed in Part I. But the Handbook was planned with the division in mind, allowing for some flexibility in deciding its final shape.

At the foundation of Frege's creation of quantificational logic in his *Begriffsschrift* of 1879 was his use of function–argument analysis, which replaced the subject–predicate analysis of traditional logic. Frege came to characterize functions as 'unsaturated' (reflecting the gap in functional expressions, such as '( ) is mortal', that indicates where the argument term goes), distinguishing them thereby from objects, seen as 'saturated'. The distinction provided Frege with a way to solve what has become known as the problem of the unity of the proposition, concerning the compositionality of propositions. In chapter 28 Robert May and Richard Heck argue that the origins of Frege's conception of unsaturatedness lay in his confrontation with George Boole, which occurred *after* the *Begriffsschrift* was published. Frege was led to take propositions of the form '*Fa*' as logically primary, and this entailed maintaining that the composition of such atomic propositions is essentially and irreducibly predicative.

Compositionality is also the theme of chapter 29, but here there is a contrasting conclusion, with the focus shifting to a later figure in the analytic tradition, Gilbert Ryle, and to a confrontation with a much earlier philosopher, Plato. Richard Gaskin argues that Ryle read Plato's *Theaetetus* through the spectacles of Russell's and Wittgenstein's logical atomism, and offered a 'propositional' interpretation of Socrates' dream theory. On Gaskin's account, Ryle overplays the distinction between naming and saying, which is not required to solve the problem of the unity of the proposition. Gaskin's discussion shows how the concerns and ideas of analytic philosophy affect the interpretation of past philosophers, and how diagnosis of the distortions that may be involved in such interpretations can be aided by appreciation of their own historical context.

The development of interpretations of Wittgenstein's *Tractatus*, one of the seminal works of analytic philosophy, is itself the theme of chapter 30. Cora Diamond argues that Anscombe effected a transformation in our understanding of the history of analytic philosophy that reflects the transformation of philosophy that Wittgenstein himself had hoped his work would achieve. What is central here is recognition of the influence that Frege had on Wittgenstein, and the significance of Frege's 'judgement-based' approach to meaning as opposed to Russell's 'object-based' approach. Seeing the *Tractatus* through a Russellian lens, Diamond argues, yields a realist 'metaphysical' reading that fails to do justice to Wittgenstein's conception of philosophy as an elucidatory activity. Thinking through the deep implications of Frege's influence and of judgement-based approaches, however, yields an interpretation of Wittgenstein's work that places its methodological revolution at its heart. Here we find history of analytic philosophy employed in philosophical elucidation itself. I consider some of the methodological issues raised by Gaskin's and Diamond's chapters in the final section of the next chapter.

In his introduction to the *Tractatus*, Russell remarked that Wittgenstein 'is concerned with the conditions for a logically perfect language' (1922, p. 8). Russell misunderstood Wittgenstein's aims, but the concern with a logically perfect language was indeed part of Russell's own project in his logical atomist period. In chapter 31 Peter Hylton explains the role that the idea of a logically perfect language plays in this project and traces the development of the idea in the works of Carnap, Quine, and David Lewis (1941–2001). The idea, he argues, lingers on in analytic philosophy, in conceptions of regimented theory that supposedly present metaphysical conclusions drawn from philosophical analysis, even though the reasons that originally motivated the idea have long since ceased to convince.

The misunderstanding of Wittgenstein's *Tractatus* that Russell showed in his introduction has often been taken to reflect two different traditions in analytic philosophy, 'ordinary language philosophy' and 'ideal language philosophy'. Both are seen as resulting from 'the linguistic turn' that philosophy took in giving rise to analytic philosophy. This term was introduced in 1960 by Gustav Bergmann (1906–87), and later formed the title of an influential collection that was published in 1967, edited by Richard Rorty (1931–2007). In chapter 32 Peter Hacker critically examines Bergmann's and Rorty's conception of the linguistic turn, and argues that its origin lies in the *Tractatus*, and that it should be distinguished from an earlier 'logicist turn' that was taken in the mid-nineteenth century. He outlines its development in the work of the Vienna Circle, Wittgenstein's later thought, and Oxford philosophy, and defends it against some criticisms.[44]

Turning now to epistemology, there are two interconnected debates that might be seen as especially characteristic of analytic philosophy. One concerns the idea of sense-data and their supposed role in perception, and the other concerns scepticism about the external world. The debate about sense-data figured prominently in epistemological discussions in the first half of the twentieth century. Russell and Moore made important contributions to this debate, but their own positions were by no means the only ones, as Gary Hatfield explains in chapter 33. Hatfield charts the development of this debate from the end of the nineteenth century to the middle of the twentieth century, discussing the Oxford realists as well as the American 'new realists' and 'critical realists', the attack on the 'myth of the given' by Wilfrid Sellars (1912–89), and Austin's critique of appeals to sense-data.

The problem of the external world is perhaps the most notorious philosophical problem of all, a source of continual fascination and frustration. In 1939 Moore offered a famous 'proof' of an external world that has been controversial ever since. In chapter 34 Annalisa Coliva discusses this proof and some of the different interpretations of it, from its initial reception right up to the most recent debate. Drawing on both Wittgenstein's ideas in *On Certainty*, which was inspired by Moore's work and written in the last 18 months of Wittgenstein's life, and contemporary arguments for epistemic externalism, Coliva offers a 'new Wittgensteinian' analysis of Moore's proof and response to the problem of the external world.

Moore's 'proof' is one of the examples that Juliet Floyd gives in chapter 35 of the concern with 'rigour' that is also often taken to be characteristic of analytic philosophy. She uses it to illustrate the varieties of 'rigorous experience' to which analytic philosophers aspire, a goal which is not unique to those working in the tradition of ideal language philosophy, but which is also involved, in ordinary language philosophy, in attempts to

---

[44] It has recently been argued that the linguistic turn has now been displaced by a 'representational turn' in analytic philosophy; see e.g. Williamson 2003; 2007, ch. 1. For his reply, see Hacker 2007.

remind us of the familiar. Every analysis or rigorization, she writes in section 35.1, 'leaves an interpretive need behind, the trail where the human serpent brings philosophy and knowledge into the garden'. This 'residue', as she calls it, must always be explained; and once this is pointed out, we can see it recognized, in some form or other, by analytic philosophers from Frege onwards. Frege spoke of the importance of pre-theoretical 'elucidation' of basic logical concepts,[45] for example, and Floyd suggests that Alan Turing (1912–54) was especially sensitive to the need for a 'common sense basis' for logic.

One area where rigorization has a played a crucial role in the development of analytic philosophy is modality. Kant located the analytic/synthetic, a priori/a posteriori, and necessary/contingent distinctions at the conceptual core of his philosophy, and critique of Kant's understanding of these distinctions has driven much analytic philosophy. The story here is highly complex, but one theme stands out: the gradual waning of distrust in modal notions. In chapter 26 Sanford Shieh provides an account of this waning, identifying two major phases. The first begins with Frege's, Moore's, and Russell's views and consists of the critique of Russell's conception of logic, in particular, by C. I. Lewis (1883–1964) and Wittgenstein in the *Tractatus*. The second phase begins with Carnap's *Logical Syntax* (1934/1937) and Quine's modal scepticism and consists of the rejection of Quine's scepticism by Ruth Barcan Marcus (1921–2012) and Saul Kripke, among others.

Issues of modality are intimately connected with questions of inference and normativity. Various accounts have been given of the notions here and different paths have been taken through their history, paths chosen to support the accounts given.[46] In recent years, one particular account has been powerfully articulated through a new reading of the history of analytic philosophy that has sought to construct an 'inferentialist' tradition, to use the term introduced by its main architect, Robert Brandom (1950–). In chapter 37 Jaroslav Peregrin explains inferentialism, outlining its main ideas and distinguishing it from the representationalism that has been the more dominant paradigm in analytic philosophy. He traces its history through the work of Frege, Wittgenstein, Carnap, and Sellars, and draws also on Gentzen's development of the natural deduction system of logic.

Brandom's inferentialism is rooted not only in the analytic tradition but also in the related tradition of pragmatism. The two traditions have had a close but complicated relationship throughout their history, especially in the States. In chapter 38 Cheryl Misak provides an account of this relationship, discussing the work of Chauncey Wright (1830–75), Charles Sanders Peirce (1839–1914), William James (1842–1910), John Dewey (1859–1952), Quine, and Rorty. Although there are differences between pragmatism and analytic philosophy, Misak argues, they share a basic emphasis on argumentative rigour, logic, and scientific methodology.

The final chapter, by David Woodruff Smith, concerns the relationship between analytic philosophy and what is generally seen as its main rival, especially in the first half of

---

[45] See especially Frege 1914 [1997], pp. 313–18. On the importance of 'elucidation', see Weiner 1990, ch. 6; 2005; Conant 2002; Beaney 2006a.

[46] One prominent—and controversial—recent account is that provided by Soames (2003), who takes the gradual advance in our understanding of modal notions, culminating in Kripke's work, as *the* central story of analytic philosophy.

the twentieth century, phenomenology. As Smith points out, however, in their origins in the work of Frege and Husserl, respectively, it is hard to find any clear differences of concern or methodology. Both were occupied with the analysis of meaning or content, and both argued against psychologism, for example. After its emergence, phenomenology may have placed more emphasis on conceptual rather than linguistic structures, but as the focus in analytic philosophy shifted from philosophy of language to philosophy of mind, there was greater engagement with phenomenology. Concern with intentionality and consciousness has brought phenomenology and analytic phenomenology closer together, and the existence now of 'analytic phenomenology' is only one sign of the rapprochement that has taken place, at least in some quarters. At any rate, there is now much more dialogue between analytic philosophy and phenomenology,[47] as indeed between analytic philosophy and other traditions, which bodes well for the future of philosophy.

1.4 Can 'Analytic Philosophy' be Defined?

At least in outline, a certain view of the nature of analytic philosophy should now have emerged in introducing the chapters in the three main parts of this Handbook. Of course, it might be objected that this view was presupposed in the outline provided—or indeed, further back, in the commissioning of the chapters themselves. So can more be said in justifying this view? I provide an account of how the analytic tradition came to be constructed, historically, in the next chapter. Here I focus on the question of whether 'analytic philosophy' can be defined. In their chapters, the contributors to this Handbook either say something explicit about what they take analytic philosophy to be or else show what they take it to be through their discussions. It may be misguided to seek necessary and sufficient conditions for philosophy to be 'analytic', but can some kind of consensus as to its general characterization be extracted from their discussions? And if so, then does this reflect a consensus in the wider philosophical community?[48]

---

[47] See e.g. Mays and Brown 1972; Durfee 1976; Dreyfus and Hall 1982; Petitot *et al.* 1999; Horgan *et al.* 2002; Smith and Thomasson 2005; Tieszen 2005; Beaney 2007a; Textor 2013.

[48] There is no shortage of reflections on the nature of analytic philosophy. By far the most helpful and comprehensive discussion is provided by Glock (2008). I agree with a lot of what Glock says, although (as will become clear in what follows), I do not think he does justice either to the role of analysis in analytic philosophy (which can provide the basis for a satisfying account of analytic philosophy) or to the importance of history of philosophy for philosophy; cf. Beaney 2011b. Here is an alphabetically ordered list of other works that offer a characterization or account of analytic philosophy, which have helped inform the view sketched in the present section: Akehurst 2010; Ammerman 1965b; Baldwin 1998; Beaney 1998, 2006c, 2006f, 2007b; Boundas 2007b; Bouveresse 1983; Charlton 1991, ch. 1; Cohen 1996; Cozzo 1999; Danto 1980; Engel 1988, 1999; Floyd and Shieh 2001, introd.; Føllesdal 1997; Hacker 1996, 1998, 2007, 2011; Martin 2002; Martinich 2001a; Monk 1996b, 1997; E. Nagel 1936; Preston 2006, 2007; Quinton 1995a; Rorty 1981, 2007b; J. Ross 1998; Schwartz 2012, introd.; Soames 2003, 2005, 2008; Stroll 2000, ch. 1; Urmson 1956; van Inwagen 2006; von Wright 1993b; Weitz 1966, introd., 1967; White 1955, editorial material; Williams 1996. For discussion of the relationship between analytic and 'continental' philosophy, see the references given in n. 60 of chapter 2 below.

We have already noted one particular disagreement as to who counts as a founder of the analytic tradition. Everyone agrees that Russell and Moore, through their rebellion against British idealism, and Wittgenstein, through his *Tractatus*, are founders, but some, even today, exclude Frege. Hacker, for example, quite explicitly does so, and Frege was left out in Soames' story of analytic philosophy.[49] Frege's exclusion might be seen as implicit in some discussions of Russell and Moore, although most authors would say that this is just because it was not in their brief to include Frege.[50] Others clearly take Frege to be the main inspiration behind the analytic tradition. This is explicit in Burge's chapter in this Handbook and in his other work, for example, and rampantly explicit throughout Dummett's writings.[51] As Diamond shows in her chapter, there is also increasing recognition of the crucial influence that Frege had on Wittgenstein. In any case, given the importance of logic in the analytic tradition, Frege's creation of quantificational theory alone entitles him to a secure place in the analytic pantheon.

Agreement on the key founders already gives some shape to the analytic tradition—as a first approximation, we can characterize it as what is inspired by their work. With this in mind, we can then identify two subsequent strands in analytic philosophy that develop the ideas of its four founders. The first is the Cambridge School of Analysis, building on the work of Russell, Moore, and Wittgenstein, and the second is logical empiricism, influenced by Frege, Russell, and Wittgenstein. Of course, there were other influences on both of these, most notably, by the German-speaking philosophers of science, neo-Kantians, and Polish logicians on logical empiricism. This brings further philosophers into the frame, strengthening and broadening analytic philosophy: Stebbing, Broad, Ramsey, Wisdom, Black (on the Cambridge side); Schlick, Neurath, Carnap, Waismann, Tarski, Popper, Feigl, Hempel, Gödel, Bergmann, Hung, Ayer (on the logical empiricist side). As has often been remarked, the establishment of a tradition proceeds not only by developing new ideas but also by securing suitable predecessors. In this way, retrospectively, the analytic tradition can then be backdated to include such figures as Stout, Twardowski and Leśniewski, and even Bolzano.[52]

[49] See e.g. Hacker 1996b, 2007, 2011, as well as his chapter in the present volume; Soames 2003. For criticism of both, see Floyd 2009; cf. Beaney 2006b. Frege is also omitted in Schwartz's recent history of analytic philosophy on the ground that he 'published in mathematics journals' (2012, p. 197). Not a single one of Frege's three books (1879, 1884, 1893/1903), three seminal essays of 1891–2, and three articles of his 'Logical Investigations' (1918–23) was published in a mathematics journal. Five of the latter six were published in philosophy journals, the other (1891) appeared as a booklet.

[50] The titles of Hylton 1990 and Stevens 2005, for example, suggest that Russell is taken as the key founder of analytic philosophy. But neither would wish to exclude Frege.

[51] See especially Burge 2005a; Dummett 1973, 1981a, 1991a, 1991b, 1993a. In the latter, on the origins of analytic philosophy, Dummett focuses solely on Frege, though there is a lot of comparison with Husserl. Russell and Moore are excluded 'because this ground has been fairly well worked over' (1993a, p. 1).

[52] Logical empiricism provides an excellent example of backdating. In the manifesto of the Vienna Circle (Carnap, Hahn, and Neurath 1929), the following predecessors were all co-opted: Avenarius, Bentham, Boltzmann, Brentano, Comte, Duhem, Einstein, Enriques, Epicurus, Feuerbach, Frege, Helmholtz, Hilbert, Hume, Leibniz, Mach, Marx, Menger, Mill, Müller-Lyer, Pasch, Peano, Pieri, Poincaré, Popper-Lynkeus, Riemann, Russell, Schröder, Spencer, Vailati, Whitehead, Wittgenstein. Cf. Ayer 1959, p. 4. On the need to find predecessors in constructing a (self-justificatory) grand narrative for a tradition, cf. Moran 2008, pp. 23–4.

The process of consolidation and ramification continued after the Second World War, with logical empiricism emigrating to the States, where its growth was nourished by interaction with native pragmatism, and with British analytic philosophy moving house to Oxford to nurture ordinary language philosophy. A whole host of new names enter the pantheon: most prominently, Goodman, Quine, Stevenson, Sellars, Chisholm, Davidson, Putnam, and Kripke in the States, and Ryle, Austin, Grice, Hare, and Strawson in Oxford. This suggests a further way to characterize analytic philosophy: by simply listing those in the pantheon. This is essentially what Martinich and Sosa do in their *Companion to Analytic Philosophy* (2001a): 39 chapters deal with 42 philosophers in turn.[53] In the introduction, Martinich makes some brief remarks on the history of analytic philosophy, but having found nothing to define or characterize analytic philosophy, concludes: 'The multiplicity of analytical styles is one reason for organizing the volume by individual philosopher and not by theme' (2001a, p. 5).

Turning to theme, then, is there anything here by means of which to characterize analytic philosophy? There are obvious candidates, most notably, the focus on questions of language. That analytic philosophy arose when the linguistic turn was taken is one of its most popular creation myths.[54] In chapter 32, however, Hacker argues that the linguistic turn was only properly taken by Wittgenstein in the *Tractatus*, which would mean that the early Russell and Moore would be excluded from the analytic tradition. Dummett, on the other hand, has claimed that it was first taken in section 62 of Frege's *Foundations*.[55] This may restore Frege to the pantheon, but would still exclude early Russell and Moore. If we also add that linguistic turns have occurred in both twentieth-century hermeneutics and in earlier German philosophy,[56] then it cannot be taken to provide either necessary or sufficient conditions for philosophy to be 'analytic'.

---

[53] Tarski, Church, and Gödel are all covered in one chapter. For the record, the full list is given in the chronology in chapter 3 below, in the entry for 2001. Martinich reports that there are others who were considered but in the end excluded: Black, Bergmann, Feigl, Feyerabend, Evans, C. I. Lewis, Mackie, E. Nagel, Price, Prichard, Prior, Reichenbach, Schlick, Vlastos, Waismann, Wisdom. Yet others were excluded 'because they do not fit squarely within the tradition of analytic philosophy as ordinarily understood': Dewey, James, Peirce, Cook Wilson, Whitehead (2001a, p. 5). All of these have been included in the chronology below. For the different selection made in their anthology (Martinich and Sosa 2001b), see the entry for 2001 in the chronology below.

[54] The term 'creation myth' is used by Gerrard (1997, p. 40), referring to Moore's and Russell's rebellion against British idealism. Gerrard argues that Moore and Russell took over much more from Bradley's idealism than they admitted, most notably, his anti-psychologism.

[55] Dummett 1991a, p. 111. Dummett writes that '§ 62 is arguably the most pregnant philosophical paragraph ever written'—arguably the most hyperbolical claim ever made in history of philosophy.

[56] On the linguistic turn in hermeneutics (especially in the work of Heidegger and Gadamer), see Gadamer 1960, Part 3; 1962; 1972; Habermas 1999; Lafont 1999; Davey 2008. On Husserl and the linguistic turn, see Parsons 2001. On earlier linguistic turns, see Losonsky 2006. Preston (2007) takes the linguistic turn to provide the basis for characterizing analytic philosophy as a school, and then, having shown (rightly) that this does not give us necessary and sufficient conditions, argues that the history of analytic philosophy is the history of an illusion. The illusion is Preston's assumption that analytic philosophy has to be seen as a school at all, defined by a set of doctrines. See Beaney 2007e; cf. n. 46 in chapter 2 below.

We find ourselves in a similar predicament whatever other themes or doctrines we consider. Hostility to metaphysics is often suggested as another candidate. As Simons shows in chapter 23, however, while this was characteristic of logical positivism and Wittgenstein's thinking, it was not true of either Frege's philosophy or Russell's and Moore's early realism, and analytic metaphysics is very much alive today. Other candidates include anti-psychologism, endorsement of the analytic/synthetic distinction, naturalism, and ahistoricism. In each case, however, counterexamples can readily be found, showing that any suggested characterization either excludes some philosophers who would definitely be counted as analytic or includes some who would definitely be counted as not analytic—or indeed both. Husserl, for example, was also a critic of psychologism (from his *Logical Investigations* onwards), as were the neo-Kantians and the British idealists. Many philosophers today follow Quine in rejecting the (absoluteness of the) analytic/synthetic distinction while still regarding themselves as working in the analytic tradition. While there might have been a 'naturalistic turn' in later analytic philosophy partly inspired by this Quinean rejection, naturalism is far from universally accepted today, and was in any case explicitly repudiated by the early analytic philosophers.[57] As to ahistoricism, I shall say more about this in the next chapter. Here we need only note that the very existence of this Handbook is a counterexample.[58]

Far greater potential for characterization of analytic philosophy lies in considerations of method and style. As far as style is concerned, analytic philosophy is widely regarded as placing emphasis on argumentation, clarity, and rigour.[59] In the preface to his *Begriffsschrift*, Frege wrote that his concept-script was 'intended to serve primarily to test in the most reliable way the validity of a chain of inference and to reveal every presupposition that tends to slip in unnoticed, so that its origin can be investigated' (1879/1997, pp. 48–9). The quantificational logic Frege developed has been seen ever since as a means to sharpen and evaluate argumentation. But the use of logic is hardly itself new; logic was invented by Aristotle, systematized and deployed by the medieval logicians, and further extended and exploited by Leibniz and Bolzano, among others. Of course, the logic Frege developed was far more powerful than anything hitherto available, but emphasis on argumentation has always been central—and self-consciously so—in philosophy.[60]

As far as clarity is concerned, it is easy to find passages in, say, Bradley, Heidegger, or Derrida and place them alongside passages in, say, Frege, Russell, or Putnam, to show some major difference of style. But Collingwood, for example, writes at least as clearly as Russell, and while Wittgenstein is certainly an anomaly, his aphoristic remarks make

---

[57] For recent defence of analytic non-naturalist approaches to philosophy, see Corradini, Galvan, and Lowe 2006, and in particular, van Inwagen 2006.

[58] For further discussion of the difficulties involved in defining analytic philosophy thematically or doctrinally, see Glock 2008, chs. 4–5.

[59] See e.g. the website of the European Society for Analytic Philosophy, quoted at the beginning of this chapter; Soames 2003, I, p. xiii. Cf. Føllesdal 1997; Ross 1998.

[60] On the development of logic, see Kneale and Kneale 1962, and its recent update, Haaparanta 2009.

more interpretive demands than Nietzsche's. In much analytic philosophy today there is also a keenness for jargon and technical sophistication to more than match the fondness for neologism and allusion to profundity characteristic of some non-analytic philosophy. I share the view that clarity is one of the most important virtues of philosophical thinking and writing, but it is by no means exhibited only in the best analytic philosophy. The virtue was expressed with poetic clarity by Pope long before Frege and Russell: 'True wit is nature to advantage dressed, / What oft was thought, but ne'er so well expressed; / Something whose truth convinced at sight we find, / That gives us back the image of our mind.'[61] If an idea is worth thinking, then it is worth saying clearly; and if it is said clearly, then it will crystallize thinking in others.

As far as rigour is concerned, there is far more involved here than is often assumed, as Floyd shows in chapter 35. However 'rigorous' one might be, there is always a 'residue' requiring elucidation, where one can only appeal, in some informal way, to 'common sense', 'intuitions', or a 'meeting of minds'.[62] In any case, once again, it is not only analytic philosophy that values rigour. In his critique of Dilthey's historical hermeneutics, Husserl also argued that philosophy is a rigorous science (1911); phenomenology involved a different conception of rigour, but the difference between this conception and, say, Frege's or Russell's, is no greater than the difference between Moore's and Frege's or Russell's.

While it would be wrong to deny that analytic philosophy places emphasis on argumentation, clarity, and rigour, then, the most that could really be claimed is that analytic philosophy, on the whole, places more emphasis on these virtues than other traditions of philosophy. If we want to characterize analytic philosophy more substantially, then it is to method that we should turn, and more specifically, to the method of analysis. For the obvious suggestion is that analytic philosophy is 'analytic' because of the central role played by analysis. Here the immediate objection is that analysis, too, has been central to philosophy from its very birth in ancient Greek thought and hardly distinguishes analytic philosophy. As I have argued elsewhere, however, there were new methods and kinds of analysis that were indeed introduced into analytic philosophy, beginning with Frege's logical and logicist analyses, his use of contextual definition, and Russell's theory of descriptions.[63] These were developed further in Russell's method of logical construction (see Linsky's chapter), by Wittgenstein in the *Tractatus* (see Kremer's

---

[61] Pope, *An Essay on Criticism*, Part 2, ll. 297–300. On clarity, see also Price 1945; Lewis 1963; Hart 1990; Glock 2008, pp. 168–73.

[62] For discussion of the role of 'intuitions' in philosophy, see chapter 19 by Baghramian and Jorgensen. On the need to appeal to a 'meeting of minds', see Frege 1892b/1997, p. 192; 1914/1997, p. 313. I discuss the importance of this in Beaney 2006a.

[63] See especially Beaney 2009a (first pub. 2003); cf. 2002, 2007b, 2007c. I argue that 'interpretive' forms of analysis, drawing on the new logic to transform or paraphrase sentences to exhibit their 'real' logical form and content, come to the fore in early analytic philosophy, reflection on their nature and justification then inspiring the linguistic turn that is consolidated in the second phase of analytic philosophy. I also argue that analytic philosophy, in its Fregean and Russellian manifestations, should be seen as 'analytic' much more in the sense that analytic geometry is 'analytic' than in the crude decompositional sense exhibited in Moore's and Russell's early naïve realism.

chapter), by other members of the Cambridge School of Analysis (see Baldwin's chapter), and by Carnap in *The Logical Construction of the World* (1928a) and in his work on logic and semantics (see Reck's chapter).[64] The ideas were introduced to Oxford by Ryle in his 'Systematically Misleading Expressions' of 1932 and by Ayer in his *Language, Truth and Logic* of 1936 (see Uebel's chapter), and Quine gave them a powerful presence in America through his own logical and philosophical work (see Baghramian and Jorgensen's and Hylton's chapters), with others such as C. I. Lewis, Marcus, and Kripke contributing to the analysis of modal notions (see Shieh's chapter).

This Fregean strand in analytic philosophy is complemented by a Moorean strand, the creative tension between these two main strands forming the central core of the internal dynamic of the analytic tradition.[65] The Moorean strand begins with Moore's early emphasis on carefully distinguishing and clarifying the philosophical questions we ask and his decompositional conception of the analysis of propositions (see Griffin's chapter), and proceeds (also) through the elucidatory project of Wittgenstein's *Tractatus* (see Diamond's chapter), his later philosophy (see Glock's chapter), and Moore's later appeal to common sense in responding to scepticism (see Coliva's chapter). After the Second World War, conceptual analysis is developed further in Oxford ordinary language philosophy, exhibited by Austin's philosophically motivated linguistic analyses (see Travis and Kalderon's chapter) and the connective analyses of Ryle, Strawson, and others (see Hacker's chapter).

All these different conceptions and techniques of analysis, and the variations and modifications introduced by many other analytic philosophers, have become part of the methodological toolbox of analytic philosophy. The analytic philosopher might then be characterized as someone who knows how to use these tools, through training in modern logic and study of the work of their predecessors. Each analytic philosopher may have different aims, ambitions, backgrounds, concerns, motivations, presuppositions, and projects, and they may use these tools in different ways to make different constructions, criticisms, evaluations, and syntheses; but there is a common repertoire of analytic techniques and a rich fund of instructive examples to draw upon; and it is these that form the methodological basis of analytic philosophy. As analytic philosophy has developed and ramified, so has its toolbox been enlarged and the examples of practice (both good and bad) expanded.

This methodologically based conception makes sense of a number of other features of analytic philosophy and disputes that often arise regarding it. First of all, it explains why analytic philosophy is sometimes said to adopt (and to be criticized for adopting) a piecemeal approach, encouraging small-scale investigations rather than grand

---

[64] In George's 1967 translation of *Der logische Aufbau der Welt*, the title is rendered as 'The Logical Structure of the World', but this misses the sense of 'Aufbau'. On Carnap's *Aufbau* project, see especially Richardson 1998. I discuss Carnap's key conception of analysis in this work—what he calls 'quasi-analysis'—in Beaney 2004b.

[65] I tell this story in a little more detail in Beaney 2006c, 2006f, 2009, §6, 2012a (on the Moorean strand).

system-building.[66] 'Divide and conquer' is the maxim of success, Russell remarked in advocating the scientific method in philosophy (1914d, p. 86). Analytic techniques clearly lend themselves to piecemeal approaches and to collaborative work of the kind familiar in science. Concepts can be analysed one by one, and in very specific contexts of use; intermediate steps can be inserted in chains of argument and further assumptions added; Gettier-style counterexamples to purported definitions can be presented in brief articles; and so on. No doubt those techniques can be employed in idle cog-spinning or epicycling, or Gettier games played for their own sake, or massive logical hammers used to crack tiny philosophical nuts, all of which provide grounds for criticism; but analytic philosophy is not intrinsically piecemeal, and grand narratives can indeed be pursued, bringing together the results of many different kinds of analysis.

Secondly, we have an explanation of the success of analytic philosophy—of why analytic philosophy, despite occasional talk of 'post-analytic' philosophy and the objections and fears of 'continental' philosophers, has established itself so firmly and widely over the last hundred years. The toolbox is full of useful instruments, with concepts clarified, distinctions drawn, doctrines refined, and logical theories enriched. The big philosophical questions may seem as fascinating and frustrating as ever, but there is a range of responses available to entice and enrage further. A major reason for its global success, however, is its relatively democratic and meritocratic nature. There is no ideological baggage to acquire in the way that there is in Marxism, no creed to avow as there is in Thomism, no doctrines or attitudes to adopt as there is in Kantianism or Hegelianism or phenomenology. One doesn't need an 'ism' to be an analytic philosopher,[67] although if one wants to be an 'ist', one can be an analytic 'ist'. It is no surprise that analytic philosophy has taken off in those countries that have shed or are shedding their Marxism-Leninism. The turn to analytic philosophy in Eastern Europe, for example, happened almost immediately after the communist regimes crumbled in 1989.[68] And analytic philosophy is gradually growing in China. With widening educational opportunities and the proliferation of online resources, journals, and textbooks, access to philosophy is open

[66] See e.g. Soames 2003, I, p. xv; Glock 2008, pp. 164–8. For criticism of this feature, see e.g. Ryle 1957/1971b, p. 385; Boundas 2007c, pp. 33–4.

[67] In 'Taking Sides in Philosophy', Ryle wrote: 'The gist of my position is this. There is no place for "isms" in philosophy' (1937b/1971b, p. 161). In concluding his article, he conceded that the 'ism' labels are 'applicable and handy, as terms of abuse, commiseration, or apologia', but urged that they be reserved 'for our intervals of gossip and confession' (1937b/1971b, p. 175). Consistently with this, Ryle avoided talk of 'analytic philosophy', too, though here there was the additional reason that he regarded the word 'analysis' as misleading in its suggestion that philosophical problems could be tackled piecemeal (cf. the previous footnote)—despite the fact that it 'contrasts well with such expressions as "speculation", "hypothesis", "system-building" and even "preaching" and "writing poetry"' (1957/1971b, p. 385). Ayer also claimed that 'there is nothing in the nature of philosophy to warrant the existence of conflicting philosophical parties or "schools"' (1936, p. 176). More recently, van Inwagen has written: 'being an analytical philosopher does not involve commitment to any philosophical doctrine.... A philosopher may take any position on any philosophical question and still be an analytical philosopher in good standing' (2006, p. 88).

[68] Societies for analytic philosophy began to be formed as early as 1991; see n. 2 above.

as never before, and at its best, analytic philosophy, in particular, lends itself to ready engagement, its piecemeal character encouraging participation.[69] Everyone can in principle contribute, even if it is only to find a counterexample to a definition of knowledge; and on any topic, there is some position available that may accord with one's 'intuitions', however shaky or robust they may be. And even if—or when—someone comes up with a confused or mistaken view, it can be misguided in a revealing way, and analysis of it can spur further debate. For someone with individualistic leanings in an oppressive or repressive environment, analytic philosophy can be intellectually liberating. As Searle is reported as having once said (quoted at the beginning of this chapter), 'I am an analytic philosopher. I think for myself.'[70]

Thirdly, and following on from this, we can see what is mistaken about talk of 'post-analytic' philosophy, and why 'analytic' can qualify just about any philosophical position or tradition. Talk of 'post' anything is to suggest having gone beyond something, its errors or limitations recognized, the problems solved or shown to be insoluble, its possibilities exhausted. Such critical distancing is always overdone. But if analytic philosophy is seen as methodologically based, and the toolbox is still in use, even if some tools have been added and some have dropped to the bottom, then talk of 'post-analytic' makes little sense. No one is a post-carpenter or post-plumber, though they can be an ex-carpenter or ex-plumber. As noted at the beginning of this chapter, far from being replaced by 'post-analytic', 'analytic' is being used as a qualifier with ever greater frequency. But this, too, is unsurprising, if to talk of something being 'analytic' is just to say that it can be done in an analytic *way*, that is, by using the analytic toolbox.

While the methodologically based conception makes sense of many of the uses of 'analytic', however, it does not do justice to all those uses, and in particular, to when we talk of analytic philosophy as a tradition or movement. Perhaps we should simply distinguish two meanings of 'analytic philosophy', depending on whether we have in mind the activity ('analytic philosophizing') or the tradition ('the analytic tradition'). But the two are clearly related, both historically and conceptually. As I show in the next chapter, talk of the analytic (or logico-analytic) method came before talk of analytic philosophy, which only began in the 1930s and only became widespread in the 1950s, which is when an analytic *tradition* was finally recognized. The methods provided the basis for the tradition, their application in specific projects, from Frege's and Russell's logicism onwards, providing the analyses, approaches, arguments, concepts, doctrines, moves, positions, texts, themes, and theories that gradually accumulated in all their interconnections to form that tradition.

None of these analyses, approaches, and so on can be singled out as somehow definitive of the analytic tradition. But there is an underlying interconnectedness, grounded

---

[69] This is no doubt helped by the fact that analytic philosophy is pursued almost entirely through the medium of English, which has now established itself as the international language of communication.

[70] Searle is reported as having said this on being introduced to a phenomenologist (Mulligan 2003, p. 26; Glock 2008, p. 211). It may be an example of the speech act of tongue-in-cheeky goading, but it captures the sentiment at issue here.

in methodological, conceptual, and causal relations, that a philosophically perceptive, historically sensitive account can bring out. There are many, mutually supporting ways of doing this—comparing the analyses, contextualizing the approaches, reconstructing the arguments, clarifying the concepts, identifying anticipations of the doctrines in earlier philosophy, explaining the moves in the debates in which they occurred, refining the positions in considering their reception by critics and interpreters, exploring the intertextual references, drawing out underlying themes, synthesizing the theories, and so on. There is no royal road through the history of analytic philosophy, and certainly no single track that a single chapter can take to do that history justice; but in a multi-authored Handbook such as this, enough different paths can be taken, and enough different aspects of the philosophical debates can be elucidated, to show something of the richness and complexity of that history. In the end, the only way to answer the question 'What is analytic philosophy?' is to provide a history of the analytic tradition. I consider some examples of such histories in the next chapter, in saying more about the historical construction of the analytic tradition and some of the historiographical issues they raise. The chapters that then follow make contributions both to providing such a history and to elucidating the philosophical debates and themes that have been central in the history of analytic philosophy.

CHAPTER 2

....

THE HISTORIOGRAPHY OF ANALYTIC PHILOSOPHY

....

MICHAEL BEANEY

If you are to venture to interpret the past you can do so only out of the fullest exertion of the vigour of the present. (Nietzsche, 'On the Uses and Disadvantages of History for Life', 1874, p. 94)

The past alone is truly real: the present is but a painful, struggling birth into the immutable being of what is no longer. Only the dead exist fully. (Russell, 'On History', 1904c, p. 61)

History begins only when memory's dust has settled. (Ryle, 'Introduction' to *The Revolution in Philosophy*, 1956, p. 1)

NIETZSCHE opens his brilliant early essay 'On the Uses and Disadvantages of History for Life' with a quote from Goethe: 'In any case, I hate everything that merely instructs me without augmenting or directly invigorating my activity.' He goes on to argue that we need history 'for the sake of life and action', and this forms a central theme throughout his subsequent work. We find it expressed again, for example, in *On the Genealogy of Morals*, where he attacks modern historiography for aspiring merely to mirror and hence resisting any kind of judgement (1887, 'Third Essay', § 26). In his early essay, Nietzsche distinguishes three species of history, which he calls 'monumental', 'antiquarian', and 'critical', corresponding to three ways in which history relates to the living person: 'as a being who acts and strives, as a being who preserves and reveres, as a being who suffers and seeks deliverance' (1874, p. 67). Monumental history provides a supply of the greatest moments in history for emulation and inspiration; antiquarian history gives a sense of the local coherence and rootedness of previous life and thought to satisfy our nostalgia for their imagined certainties; while critical history submits the events of the past to the tribunal of reason for examination and critique. Nietzsche argues that all three types of history are needed, each correcting the excesses of the other. Antiquarian history reminds monumental history of the terrain that makes possible the mountain peaks, for example, while monumental history rectifies the myopia of antiquarian history. Critical history encourages us to tackle the mountain peaks for ourselves, while foiling the epistemological escapism of antiquarian history.

The historiography of analytic philosophy provides excellent illustrations of Nietzsche's three species of history. Standard textbooks tend to represent analytic philosophy as a progression from one mountain peak to another, from Frege's *Begriffsschrift* through Russell's theory of descriptions to Wittgenstein's *Tractatus*, to name but three familiar summits. There are detailed works of scholarship that offer antiquarian powder to explode monumental mythology, such as Griffin's book on Russell's break with idealism (1991) and Uebel's account of the Vienna Circle debate about protocol sentences (1992, 2007). As to critical history, this has been alive and kicking from the very dawn of analytic philosophy, from Frege's criticisms of the views of his predecessors in the first half of *The Foundations of Arithmetic* (1884), Russell's reconstruction of Leibniz's philosophy (1900), and Moore's simplification of idealist arguments (1899a, 1903b), onwards.[1] Kripke's use of Frege and Russell as the stalking-horses for his own theory of reference (1980) and his interpretation of Wittgenstein's discussion of rule-following to motivate his idea of a 'sceptical solution' to a 'sceptical paradox' (1982) are just two more recent examples to illustrate the power and prevalence of the genre.

However, it would be misleading to suggest that any of these examples involve only one of Nietzsche's three species of history. Rather, each combines different aspects of those species in varying degrees. Dummett's first book on Frege's philosophy of language (1973), for example, might be seen as combining the monumentalizing of Frege with critical reconstruction to further his own concern with developing a theory of meaning. Candlish's recent book on the dispute between Russell and Bradley (2007) does not just provide a much-needed corrective to received views of this dispute but has its own underlying agenda—to argue for a view of philosophy that does justice to its historical dimension. Nietzsche's tripartite distinction, though, offers a useful initial typology to indicate the range of accounts of the history of analytic philosophy and of analytic approaches to history, and a fruitful framework to explore some of the historiographical issues that arise from these accounts and approaches.

2.1 CONTEXT AND CONNECTION

Nietzsche's essay was written in 1874, which was a significant year in the development of modern philosophy.[2] Lotze's so-called 'greater' *Logic* was published, an expanded version of his 1843 'lesser' *Logic*. Whether or not Lotze counts as a neo-Kantian

---

[1] I discuss the role of what I call 'historical elucidation' in Frege's *Foundations* in Beaney 2006a, and the significance of Russell's 'rational reconstruction' of Leibniz in Beaney 2013a. For an account of Moore's 'refutation' of idealism, see Baldwin 1990, ch. 1.

[2] See the chronology of analytic philosophy and its historiography that follows this chapter.

himself, he undoubtedly had a major influence on both neo-Kantianism and analytic philosophy as it originated in its two main—German and British—branches.[3] This was especially true of his anti-psychologism and the Kantian distinction he drew between psychological genesis and logical justification.[4] A new edition of Hume's *Treatise* was also published, to which the British idealist Green wrote long introductions attacking what he called 'the popular philosophy', a form of empiricism with roots in Locke's *Essay* and confusions that became clear in Hume's *Treatise*, according to Green. Green's Cambridge contemporary and sparring partner, Sidgwick, also published his main work, *The Methods of Ethics*, in 1874. While Sidgwick may be far less well known today than Mill, he developed a more sophisticated form of utilitarianism which had a major influence on Moore and many subsequent ethical theorists such as Hare, Parfit, and Singer.[5]

Lotze was the dominant philosopher in Germany at the time, and both Green and Sidgwick were leading figures in British philosophy. Green became White's Professor of Moral Philosophy at Oxford in 1878 (although unfortunately he died just four years later), and Sidgwick became Knightbridge Professor of Moral Philosophy at Cambridge in 1883. In 1874, though, there were two further significant publications by philosophers who, like, Nietzsche, were at the beginning of their careers: Brentano and Bradley. Brentano was the oldest of the three, and in 1874 he published his first major work, *Psychology from an Empirical Standpoint*, in which he sought to establish a new science of mental phenomena, thereby sowing the seed of the phenomenological tradition that came to fruition in the work of Husserl. Bradley had been taught by Green, and he was to succeed Green as the main representative of British idealism. Bradley's first publication appeared in 1874, too, offering an interesting comparison with Nietzsche's essay. Entitled 'The Presuppositions of Critical History', it discusses a conception of 'critical

---

[3] Defining 'neo-Kantianism' has proved controversial. In its narrowest sense, it covers the philosophy of the so-called Marburg and Southwest Schools, originating in the work of Hermann Cohen and Wilhelm Windelband, respectively, dating from the early 1870s. More broadly, it also covers earlier philosophers writing after Kant, who in some way concerned themselves with Kant's philosophy, such as Kuno Fischer, Hermann Lotze, and Otto Liebmann (who originated the 'Back to Kant' slogan in 1865), as well as other philosophers not directly associated with the two main schools such as Hans Vaihinger and, more controversially, Wilhelm Dilthey. Gabriel (2002) suggests that Lotze is the founder of neo-Kantianism; while Anderson (2005) distinguishes between 'orthodox' and 'non-orthodox' neo-Kantianism, the former corresponding to the narrower sense just identified. In his helpful account of the relationship between neo-Kantianism and anti-psychologism, Anderson defines orthodox neo-Kantianism precisely by its commitment to anti-psychologism, in emphasizing both the objectivity and the normativity of logical and philosophical principles. The concern with normativity is an important feature, according to Anderson, and rules out as orthodox neo-Kantians others such as Frege and Husserl who also stressed the objectivity of logic (2005, pp. 291, 305–6). On the nature of neo-Kantianism, cf. also Köhnke 1986; Adair-Toteff 2003; Makkreel and Luft 2010.

[4] On Lotze's influence on Frege, see Gabriel's chapter in this Handbook. On the importance of the distinction between psychological genesis and logical justification in analytic philosophy, see Beaney 2013a.

[5] See Schultz 2011.

history' close to Nietzsche's. History, for Bradley, involves a 'union' of 'the past in fact' with 'the present in record' (1874, p. 8), and he rejects empiricist accounts that assume that past facts can simply be read off from present records. Instead, those records need to be subjected to interpretation and critical judgement. This idea was to influence Collingwood's later insistence on the need to interrogate sources.[6] Whereas Nietzsche offers, essentially, a pragmatic rationale for critical history, namely, that it invigorates our current thinking, Bradley digs deeper and argues that history inevitably involves interpretation and criticism. The main themes of his idealist metaphysics are already visible in this early work.[7]

1874 also saw two important publications by mathematicians. Both give little indication in their title of their revolutionary implications. One is called 'On a Property of the Set of Real Algebraic Numbers'. In this paper Cantor first showed that the class of real numbers is not countable, thereby inaugurating his theory of transfinite numbers, which led—via the development of set theory—to the emergence of the paradoxes that are central to the story of early analytic philosophy.[8] The second is called 'Methods of Calculation based on an Extension of the Concept of Magnitude', and was Frege's *Habilitationsschrift*, written to qualify him to teach back at Jena, where he had first gone to university and where he was to stay for the rest of his career. Still five years before his *Begriffsschrift* of 1879, which is what truly revolutionized logic, this earlier work nevertheless anticipates the main idea of his logicist project. The seed from which the whole of arithmetic grows, he argues, is addition, which he associates with the iteration of an operation, represented by an appropriate function. So the concept of a function holds the key to connecting the different areas of arithmetic (1874, pp. 57–8).

The other significant publication of 1874, which—together with Lotze's *Logic*—marks the emergence of a debate that is central to the story of analytic philosophy right from the beginning, is Wilhelm Wundt's *Principles of Physiological Psychology*. Described as 'the most important book in the history of modern psychology' (Boring 1950, p. 322), Wundt here lays the foundations of empirical psychology by arguing that 'consciousness', or 'inner experience' as he defines it, can be investigated scientifically by direct self-observation. Wundt rejected Kantian criticisms of the scientific status of psychology, and five years later, he established Germany's—and Europe's—first psychology laboratory. (The very first in the world was founded just a year after Wundt's *Principles*, in 1875, by William James at Harvard.) With Lotze leading the Kantian opposition, the battle-lines were thus drawn up in the debate about psychologism that raged well into the twentieth century, as both analytic philosophy and phenomenology sought to establish themselves in opposition to psychologizing tendencies in

---

[6] See especially Collingwood 1946/1993. On the development of Collingwood's views on historiography, see Wilson 2001.

[7] For further discussion of this work, see Walsh 1984.

[8] See Tappenden's chapter in this Handbook.

philosophy and, on the other hand, empirical psychology broke away from philosophy to launch itself as a separate discipline. Indeed, although the debate has sometimes gone quiet, as in the 1920s and 1930s, it has never really left the philosophical agenda, and arguments about the relationship between philosophy and psychology were reinvigorated by the naturalistic forms of analytic philosophy that developed after the Second World War.[9]

In one year, 1874, then, we have works published which either represent or herald most of the great traditions of late nineteenth- and twentieth-century Western philosophy: neo-Kantianism, idealism, utilitarianism, phenomenology, scientific philosophy, as well as analytic philosophy—or at any rate, that branch of analytic philosophy that had its roots in work on the foundations of mathematics. Perhaps all we are missing are works representing positivism and pragmatism. Mach's *Analysis of Sensations* was not to be published until 1886, although positivism counts as a form of scientific philosophy and Mach was both influenced by and made contributions to empirical (or physiological) psychology. The term 'pragmatism' did not make its public appearance until 1898, although Peirce's essays of 1877–8 are often taken to mark the emergence of pragmatism and we might, in any case, see pragmatist ideas in Nietzsche's philosophy.[10] As far as the history of analytic philosophy is concerned, this reminds us that the analytic tradition did not emerge in an intellectual vacuum, or in a space informed only by certain mathematical developments and local hostility to British idealism.[11] On the contrary, in the latter half of the nineteenth century, there was both intense debate about existing philosophical positions, such as empiricism, idealism, Kantianism, and psychologism, and germination of the seeds of the new traditions of the twentieth century, including phenomenology and pragmatism as well as analytic philosophy itself. Any proper understanding of the development of analytic philosophy, then, has to take account of its place in the broader intellectual context and its changing and contested interconnections with other traditions and disciplines.[12]

---

[9] For an account of the debates about psychologism, especially around the turn of the twentieth century, see Kusch 1995, 2011; cf. Travis 2006b. On the relationship between philosophy and psychology, see also Reed 1994; Hatfield 2002, 2012. On the development of naturalistic forms of analytic philosophy of mind, see Crawford's chapter in this Handbook.

[10] Hookway (2008) and Bernstein (2010) do not mention Nietzsche at all in their accounts of pragmatism. But Rorty (1998) does count Nietzsche as a fellow pragmatist, citing Berthelot 1911 as the first work in which Nietzsche is classified with James and Dewey and where Nietzsche is first called a 'German pragmatist'. Cf. also Rorty 1991, p. 2.

[11] One of the aims of the detailed chronology that follows this chapter is to provide further reminders of the richness not only of the analytic tradition itself but also of the broader scientific and philosophical context in which analytic philosophy developed.

[12] On aspects of the background to analytic philosophy, see the chapters by Gabriel, Skorupski, Tappenden, and Hyder in this Handbook, and on the relationship of analytic philosophy to British idealism, pragmatism, and phenomenology, see the chapters by Griffin, Misak, and Smith, respectively. For substantial accounts of British idealism, American pragmatism, and phenomenology, see Mander 2011, Misak 2013, and Moran 2000, respectively.

2.2 ANALYTIC PHILOSOPHY AND AHISTORICISM

As the two essays by Nietzsche and Bradley indicate, there was much discussion about the nature and role of historical understanding in the second half of the nineteenth century—in the period in which analytic philosophy itself has its origins. As is well known, however, analytic philosophy emerged with an entirely ahistorical self-image. Indeed, it might be said that its official ideology was strongly anti-historical. In one of his great purple passages, Frege has this to say about historical investigations in the introduction to *The Foundations of Arithmetic*:

> The historical mode of investigation, which seeks to trace the development of things from which to understand their nature, is certainly legitimate; but it also has its limitations. If everything were in continual flux and nothing remained fixed and eternal, then knowledge of the world would cease to be possible and every-thing would be thrown into confusion. We imagine, it seems, that concepts originate in the individual mind like leaves on a tree, and we suppose that their nature can be understood by investigating their origin and seeking to explain them psychologically through the working of the human mind. But this conception makes everything subjective, and taken to its logical conclusion, abolishes truth. What is called the history of concepts is really either a history of our knowledge of concepts or of the meanings of words. Often it is only through enormous intellectual work, which can last for hundreds of years, that knowledge of a concept in its purity is achieved, by peeling off the alien clothing that conceals it from the mind's eye. (1884, p. VII/1997, p. 88)

Frege took himself to have revealed the 'pure' concept of a natural number, by defining the natural numbers as extensions of logical concepts. To show that this was indeed the right account, however, he had to explain what was wrong with previous conceptions of number, and he does this in the first half of the *Foundations*, discussing the views of Locke, Leibniz, Berkeley, Hume, Kant, and Mill, among others. To a certain extent, then, Frege himself does history of philosophy. It may only be 'critical history' of a fairly simple kind, but it is important nevertheless in motivating his own views. I have called this 'historical elucidation', alluding to Frege's use of 'elucidation' ('*Erläuterung*') to refer to that pre-theoretical work that must be undertaken to get the basic (indefinable) concepts understood.[13] Although Frege does not talk of elucidation having an historical

---

[13] See Beaney 2006a. For Frege's use, see Frege 1899 [1980], pp. 36–7 (where Frege talks of 'Erläuterungssätze'—'elucidatory propositions'); 1906 [1967], pp. 288–9 (in Frege 1984, pp. 300–1, 'Erläuterung' is mistranslated as 'explication'); 1914 [1997], pp. 313–14 (in Frege 1979, pp. 207–8, 'Erläuterung' is mistranslated as 'illustrative example'). For further discussion of elucidation, see e.g. Weiner 1990, ch. 6, 2001, 2005; Conant 2002; Reck 2005, 2007.

dimension, his work shows that it does. New views always need to be positioned in the historical space of past conceptions, as Frege realized after it was clear from the reviews of *Begriffsschrift* that no one had appreciated his achievement or project.[14] He recognized that an informal account of the kind offered in the *Foundations* was a necessary preliminary to the formal demonstration of his logicism that he later sought to carry out in the *Basic Laws*.[15]

Russell's and Moore's contribution to the founding of analytic philosophy proceeded quite explicitly by critical engagement with the views of previous thinkers. Their rebellion against British idealism is the most familiar part of the story.[16] Less well known is the significance of the book Russell published in 1900: *A Critical Exposition of the Philosophy of Leibniz*.[17] This can justifiably be regarded as the first work of 'analytic' history of philosophy, heralding what later came to be known as 'rational reconstruction'.[18] What is interesting about this book is that it was written *before* Russell's conversion to the new quantificational logic of Frege and Peano.[19] This is not to say that it was composed while Russell was still under the influence of British idealism, however. It was written in the short transitional period in which Russell was rebelling against British idealism—and indeed, played a key role in that rebellion. As Russell himself later remarked (1959a, p. 48), what he realized in working on Leibniz was the importance of the question of relations, and he was led to reject what he called 'the doctrine of internal relations'—that 'Every relation is grounded in the natures of the related terms', as he put it (1959a, p. 43). He saw this doctrine as characteristic of both British idealism (and Bradley's monism, in particular) and Leibniz's monadism. His rejection of British idealism was thus partly effected through his critique of Leibniz.[20]

What a commentator must do, Russell writes, 'is to attempt a reconstruction of the system which Leibniz should have written—to discover what is the beginning, and what the end, of his chains of reasoning, to exhibit the interconnections of his various opinions' (1900, p. 2). In reconstructing Leibniz's philosophy, Russell identifies five main

---

[14] Frege was prompted, in particular, to read and criticize Boole's work; see May and Heck's chapter in this Handbook.

[15] His three seminal papers of 1891–2 can also be seen as essentially elucidatory papers, though here there is less historical positioning.

[16] See Griffin's chapter in this Handbook.

[17] One of the few commentators to recognize its significance is Hunter (1993).

[18] For a fuller account of this, see Beaney 2013a.

[19] Russell first met Peano in August 1900, an event that Russell described as 'a turning point in my intellectual life' (1975, p. 147). His book on Leibniz was published in October, but he had finished writing it in March and had received the proofs in June. Only the preface was written after this turning point, in the same month—September 1900—as he first started extending Peano's calculus to the logic of relations. (Cf. the chronology in Russell 1993, pp. liii–liv.) Russell called this month 'the highest point of my life' (1975, p. 148): a month that included both his recognition of the revolutionary power of the new logic and his presentation to the world of the first rational reconstruction in analytic history of philosophy.

[20] Russell's concern with Leibniz, however, was accidental. He was asked to give a course of lectures on Leibniz in Cambridge in Lent Term 1899, in place of McTaggart, who was away at the time. Cf. Russell 1975, p. 136, 1993, p. 511.

premises that he argues generate not only Leibniz's characteristic doctrines but also the inconsistencies that affect his philosophy. Exposition thus goes hand-in-hand with criticism, according to Russell. Indeed, the two are virtually inseparable, since the views need to be set out as clearly as possible to make judgements about them, and being alert to inconsistencies means respecting all the passages where claims are asserted or denied (cf. 1900, p. 3).

Russell's conception of history of philosophy is further clarified in the preface to the book, where he distinguishes a 'mainly historical' from a 'mainly philosophical' approach. The first is concerned with influences, causes, context, and comparisons, while the second aims to discover 'the great types of possible philosophies', the understanding of which enables us to 'acquire knowledge of important philosophic truths' (1900, pp. xv–xvi). On this second approach, Russell writes, 'the philosopher is no longer explained psychologically: he is examined as the advocate of what he holds to be a body of philosophic truth. By what process of development he came to this opinion, though in itself an important and interesting question, is logically irrelevant to the inquiry how far the opinion itself is correct' (1900, p. xvi). Like Frege and the neo-Kantians, then, Russell draws a sharp distinction between psychological genesis and logical justification, which underlies his distinction between the two approaches to history of philosophy and his own obvious preference for the 'mainly philosophical' approach.

Both Russell's distinction and preference have been characteristic of analytic historiography throughout the history of analytic philosophy, at any rate until fairly recently. Indeed, as the cases of Frege and Russell suggest, this analytic conception of history of philosophy is both historically and logically prior to the systematic projects pursued by analytic philosophers. Following Frege and Russell, analytic philosophers have offered (or borrowed) rational reconstructions in criticizing previous philosophical doctrines to motivate their own philosophical views, and presupposed the validity of the distinction between psychological genesis and logical justification in their methodology.

On Frege's and Russell's view, then, the history of philosophy is just a repository of different philosophical positions, understood as eternally given and towards which different philosophers take different attitudes.[21] The adoption of these attitudes may be explained either psychologically or logically, and the task of the 'philosopher' (as opposed to 'historian') is to sift out the logical reasons from the psychological causes in arguing for the correctness of their own philosophical position and incorrectness of all other positions. That this view itself emerges out of a particular intellectual context (late nineteenth-century anti-psychologism) is obscured by the very anti-psychologism it presupposes. It might also account for why Frege and (early) Russell did not see themselves as offering a 'new philosophy'. The forms of realism they adopted (Platonism in the case of Frege, naïve realism in the case of Russell in his initial rebellion against British idealism) were hardly new positions—but more

[21] On this conception, cf. Rée 1978.

importantly, could not be seen as new by the approach to history of philosophy they adopted. What was new was their methodology, based on logical analysis and contextual definition.[22]

Alternative conceptions of history of philosophy were available to Frege and Russell at the time they were writing. One such alternative was presented to Russell by Cassirer in his review of Russell's book on Leibniz.[23] Cassirer appreciates the value of Russell's 'systematic interest', which enables questions to be asked that are rarely raised in traditional accounts (1902, p. 533). But he criticizes Russell for his obsession with identifying contradictions. Conflicting views might well be found in Leibniz's writings when taken as a whole, but the conflict may simply be the result of intellectual development or of different dialectical contexts, where different pressures or concerns are involved. Cassirer's main example is Leibniz's conception of substance, which in reworking the traditional Aristotelian conception by giving it a dynamic character, looked both backwards and forwards. Cassirer writes that 'It would be entirely one-sided and unhistorical to judge this opposition, on which, as it were, the whole inner tension of the system rests, as simply a contradiction' (1902, p. 539). According to Cassirer, there may be 'tensions' in philosophical systems, but this is what drives philosophical thinking, the proper understanding of which requires a synthesis of 'historical' and 'philosophical' approaches. We will come back to this in due course.

2.3   RUSSELL'S ROLE IN THE CONSTRUCTION OF ANALYTIC PHILOSOPHY

As the cases of Frege and (early) Russell suggest, then, a philosopher's general position shapes, and in turn is shaped by, their view of history of philosophy. Analytic philosophers ever since have tended to endorse critical history: past philosophical work is selected and rationally reconstructed for present purposes, providing both alternative views by means of which to situate one's own view as well as ideas and arguments, judged to be good, upon which to build. In this second case, but even to an extent in the first case, this leads to a certain degree of monumentalizing, whereby key figures or doctrines are singled out for approval. Despite criticizing Kant's conception of arithmetic, for example, Frege still referred to him as 'a genius to whom we can only look up with grateful admiration', and suggested that he was merely refining Kant's notion of analyticity in pursuing his logicist project (cf. 1884, §§ 88–9/1997, pp. 122–3).

---

[22]   See the previous chapter in this Handbook.

[23]   The review occurs in an appendix to Cassirer's own book on Leibniz (1902, pp. 532–41). Another review was by the Leibniz scholar and translator Robert Latta (1901). Both reviews are briefly discussed in Hunter 1993, pp. 407–9.

Russell engaged in a great deal of critical history throughout his life. As well as writing on past philosophers such as Leibniz and Kant, he also discussed the work of many of his contemporaries, including James, Bradley, Frege, Meinong, Poincaré, Bergson, Dewey, Broad, Ryle, and Strawson, to name just some of the most prominent.[24] All this engagement can be seen as culminating in his *History of Western Philosophy*, published in 1945. Its subtitle reveals that there is an element of antiquarianism here, too, though: 'and its Connection with Political and Social Circumstances from the Earliest Times to the Present Day'. The book is an unreliable guide to either the philosophers or the circumstances covered, but the brief final chapter makes clear Russell's own position and also the critical function that his antiquarianism performs. Entitled 'The Philosophy of Logical Analysis', Russell argues that one of the main attractions of the philosophy he endorses is that it does not allow itself to be influenced by 'mistaken moral considerations' or 'religious dogmas'. 'In the welter of conflicting fanaticisms', Russell writes, 'one of the few unifying forces is scientific truthfulness, by which I mean the habit of basing our beliefs upon observations and inferences as impersonal, and as much divested of local and temperamental bias, as is possible for human beings' (1945/1961, p. 789). The antiquarianism thus turns out to be employed in criticizing the philosophies Russell rejects.

The scientific truthfulness of which Russell here speaks is a further reflection of that distinction between logical justification and psychological (or social or political) explanation that lies at the heart of both his and Frege's methodology. It was also central to the methodology of logical positivism, especially in the work of Carnap and Reichenbach, for whom 'scientific philosophy' was seen as the way forward.[25] Indeed, the term 'rational reconstruction' was first brought to prominence in the book Carnap published in 1928, *The Logical Construction of the World*, and Reichenbach develops the idea further in his *Experience and Prediction* of 1938, in which he draws his famous distinction between the context of discovery and the context of justification.[26] Of course, these ideas themselves had a 'context of discovery' that we should not pass over without comment: they would certainly have had a special resonance in the 1930s and 1940s, as 'conflicting fanaticisms' were indeed raging across the world.[27]

Through his critical histories and rational reconstructions, and his methodological discussions of logical analysis and justification, Russell did more than any other philosopher to establish analytic philosophy as the tradition that it is now generally recognized as being. But this did not happen overnight or in ways that it might seem natural to assume

[24] For the range of Russell's writings on other philosophers, see the various volumes of his *Collected Papers*.

[25] See especially Reichenbach 1951.

[26] For an account of the development of the idea of rational reconstruction, see Beaney 2013a. Cf. Schickore and Steinle 2006.

[27] As Nagel described one of the functions of analytic philosophy in 1936, 'it requires quiet green pastures for intellectual analysis, wherein its practitioners can find refuge from a troubled world and cultivate their intellectual games with chess-like indifference to its course' (1936, p. 9).

now, and the history of its establishment is instructive. Russell's and Moore's rebellion against British idealism took place during a relatively short period of time, between 1898 and 1903, but the naïve realism they initially adopted was hardly distinctive in itself. Indeed, realism had already been taking over from idealism in Oxford at the time of their rebellion. Thomas Case, who was Waynflete Professor of Moral and Metaphysical Philosophy from 1889 to 1910, had published his *Physical Realism* in 1888, a book that even had 'analytical philosophy' in its subtitle, a term that is not used in any of Russell's or Moore's early writings. John Cook Wilson, who was Wykeham Professor of Logic from 1889 to 1915, was by then consolidating his position as the leading figure in Oxford realism and on the Oxford scene generally, although he published little in his lifetime and his *Statement and Inference* only appeared posthumously, edited from his lecture notes by one of his former students.[28] In the United States, there was also a realist movement, instigated by the so-called 'new realists' and continued by the 'critical realists'. The former, comprising Holt, Marvin, Montague, Perry, Pitkin, and Spaulding, published their manifesto in 1910 and their book, *New Realism*, in 1912.[29] The latter, including Lovejoy, Santayana, and Roy Wood Sellars, published their *Essays in Critical Realism* in 1920.[30] There were realist movements elsewhere, such as in Berlin, where Trendelenburg's work inspired an Aristotelian realism with similarities to Oxford realism, and in Austria, led by Meinong, influenced by Bolzano and Brentano.[31]

What was distinctive of Moore's and Russell's realism was the emphasis placed on analysis, even if this, too, was initially conceived rather naïvely, as simply involving decomposition. With the emergence of the theory of descriptions in 1905, however, Russell's analytic methodology (and to a lesser extent Moore's) became more sophisticated.[32] There was still no talk of 'analytic philosophy', but in 1911 Russell gave a lecture to the Société Française de Philosophie entitled 'Analytic Realism'. He described his philosophy as realist 'because it claims that there are non-mental entities and that cognitive relations are external relations, which establish a direct link between the subject and a possibly non-mental object', and as analytic 'because it claims that the existence of the complex depends on the existence of the simple, and not vice versa, and that the

---

[28] Wilson 1926. For discussion of the Oxford realists, and in particular, Case and Cook Wilson, see Marion 2000, 2006a, 2006b, 2009. On Case's and Cook Wilson's perceptual realism, see Hatfield's chapter in this Handbook; and on Cook Wilson's influence on later Oxford philosophers, see Beaney 2012a, and Travis and Kalderon's chapter.

[29] Spaulding's contribution was called 'A Defense of Analysis', certainly suggesting that Russell and the new realists were kindred spirits.

[30] Drake *et al.* 1920. See also Sellars 1916. For a brief account of early twentieth-century American realism, see Kuklick 2001, ch. 11. The movement is often forgotten: it receives virtually no discussion in *The Oxford Handbook of American Philosophy* (Misak 2008), for example.

[31] On the Austrian tradition in analytic philosophy, see Nyíri 1981, 1986; Simons 1992, 1999; Smith 1994; Textor 2006. Australian realism can be taken to begin in 1927, when Anderson (who had been influenced by Alexander, in particular) went to Sydney as Challis Professor of Philosophy and published 'Empiricism'; see Baker 1986; Armstrong 2001.

[32] See §1.1 of the previous chapter; and for more on Russell's and Moore's conceptions of analysis, and the range of conceptions that we find in the history of philosophy, see Beaney 2007c, 2009a.

constituent of a complex, taken as a constituent, is absolutely identical with itself as it is when we do not consider its relations' (1911c/1992, p. 133). He went on to characterize his philosophy as an 'atomic philosophy', and by the late 1910s, he was describing his position as 'logical atomism', a term that also came to be used, though not by Wittgenstein himself, for some of the central ideas of the *Tractatus*.[33]

In 1924 Russell wrote an article entitled 'Philosophy of the Twentieth Century',[34] in which he divides academic philosophy into three groups: adherents of classical German philosophy, including Kantians and Hegelians; pragmatists and Bergson; and 'realists', understood as those who are scientifically minded (1924b/1943, p. 228). He admits that the division is not exclusive, suggesting that William James can be regarded as a founder of both pragmatism and realism. Russell quickly dismisses Hegelianism, taken as represented by Bradley, and goes on to consider the views of James and Bergson. In the final ten pages, he discusses the 'new philosophy' of realism, 'characterized by analysis as a method and pluralism as a metaphysics' (1924b/1943, p. 240). He claims that it had three main sources, in theory of knowledge, logic, and the principles of mathematics. In logic, he notes that the 'organic' view of the idealists is replaced by atomism, and as far as the principles of mathematics are concerned, he remarks that only the new philosophy has managed to accommodate the results of the work of Cantor, Frege, and others. In theory of knowledge, Russell claims that the new philosophy, as against Kant, maintains that 'knowledge, as a rule, makes no difference to what is known'. This was one of the slogans of the Oxford realists, which Collingwood later notoriously thought he could refute in three sentences.[35] So although Cook Wilson and the other Oxford realists of the period failed to appreciate the significance of the development of mathematical logic,[36] there is an extent to which they might be seen as enlisted by Russell in his group of twentieth-century philosophers. Whether or not one counts the Oxford realists as 'analytic philosophers' alongside Russell, Moore, and

[33] See Russell 1918, 1924a; repr. together in Russell 1972. Russell's and Wittgenstein's logical atomism are discussed together in, for example, Urmson 1956, Part I. The first monograph on Wittgenstein's logical atomism is Griffin 1964. On Russell's logical atomism, see also Klement 2009, and on Wittgenstein's logical atomism, see Proops 2007.

[34] The article was later reprinted in *Twentieth Century Philosophy: Living Schools of Thought*, edited by Runes (1943). It opens Part II, which also includes chapters on Kantianism, Hegelianism, Thomist humanism, transcendental absolutism (by Santayana), personalism, phenomenology, logical empiricism (by Feigl), American realism, pragmatism (by Dewey), dialectical materialism, naturalism, and philosophies of China. The crudity of Russell's typology is thus shown up by the rest of the book. The book also shows that 'analytic philosophy' is still far from being recognized as a distinct, let alone dominant, tradition.

[35] Collingwood 1939, p. 44, in the chapter entitled 'The Decay of Realism'. For an account of his critique of the Oxford realists, see Beaney 2013b.

[36] In commenting on Russell's paradox, in correspondence with Bosanquet in 1903, Cook Wilson had written: 'I am afraid I am obliged to think that a man is conceited as well as silly to think such puerilities are worthy to be put in print: and it's simply exasperating to think that he finds a publisher (where was the publisher's reader?), and that in this way such contemptible stuff can even find its way into examinations' (1926, II, p. 739). As Ayer later put it, Cook Wilson 'had sat like Canute rebuking the advancing tide of mathematical logic' (1977, p. 77).

Wittgenstein, their views are clearly important in the bigger story of the history of analytic philosophy.[37]

2.4 THE EARLY HISTORICAL CONSTRUCTION OF ANALYTIC PHILOSOPHY

The first use of the term 'analytic philosopher' to refer to at least some of those whom we would now count as analytic philosophers does not occur until 1931, when we find it in Wisdom's *Interpretation and Analysis in Relation to Bentham's Theory of Definition*. Wisdom recognizes an anticipation of Russell's theory of descriptions, in its use of contextual definition to do eliminativist work, by Bentham in his theory of fictions. Key here is what Bentham calls 'paraphrasis': 'that sort of exposition which may be afforded by transmuting into a proposition, having for its subject some real entity, a proposition which has not for its subject any other than a fictitious entity'.[38] Wisdom talks first of 'logico-analytic philosophers' and then just 'analytic philosophers', understanding analysis as the analysis of facts we already know (1931, pp. 13–15). A year later, the idea of paraphrasis, though not the term, is picked up by Ryle in 'Systematically Misleading Expressions' (1932), in which he argues that the philosophical problems that are generated by certain kinds of expression (such as ones that appear to denote non-existent objects) can be resolved by rephrasing the relevant sentences. Neither Wisdom nor Ryle talk of 'analytic philosophy' (Wisdom just talks of 'analytic philosophers'), but the explicit articulation of the idea of paraphrasis in the work of both Wisdom in Cambridge and Ryle in Oxford represents a definite stage in the construction of analytic philosophy as a tradition.[39]

The first use of the term 'analytic philosophy' to refer to at least part of what we would now regard as the analytic tradition occurs in Collingwood's *Essay on Philosophical Method* of 1933. He uses it to refer to one of two 'sceptical positions' that he attacks in chapter 7. What he has in mind, in particular, is the view according to which philosophy aims solely to analyse knowledge we already possess. He does not refer to Wisdom, but

---

[37] In *A Hundred Years of British Philosophy* (1935 [1938]), Metz has a chapter on 'The Older Realism' (52 pages), discussing Case and Cook Wilson, among others, and a chapter on 'The New Realism' (175 pages), discussing Moore, Russell, and Whitehead, among others.

[38] Bentham 1843, p. 246; quoted by Wisdom 1931, p. 92. On the significance of the idea of paraphrasis, see Beaney 2009a, §6. Cf. also Quine 1981b, pp. 68–9.

[39] Three years later, in *Problems of Mind and Matter*, Wisdom does indeed talk of 'analytic philosophy': he writes that his book is intended as an introduction to it, though he stresses that analytic philosophy 'has no special subject matter' (1934, p. 2). Ryle, by contrast, never uses the term. In fact, his attack on 'isms' in philosophy (1937b) and his qualms about the notion of analysis (see e.g. 1957, pp. 263–4) suggests outright opposition to its use, even though he would agree with Wisdom that philosophy is an activity rather than a science. Cf. § 1.4 of the previous chapter.

does mention Moore and Stebbing as advocates of this view. It is a 'sceptical position', he argues, because it denies that 'constructive philosophical reasoning' is possible (1933, p. 137), and he criticizes it for neglecting to examine its own presuppositions. Stebbing had herself drawn attention to this neglect in 'The Method of Analysis in Metaphysics' (1932), to which Collingwood refers, and she had attempted to identify these presuppositions, while admitting, however, that she could not see how they were justified. It is worth noting that what seems to have been the first use of 'analytic philosophy' occurs in a critique: it is often the case that positions are first clearly identified in attacking them.[40]

Stebbing's role in the story of analytic philosophy is frequently overlooked. In 1930, she had published *A Modern Introduction to Logic*, which might be regarded as the first textbook of analytic philosophy. Her preface to the first edition opens with the remark that 'The science of logic does not stand still', and she notes that all the textbooks then in use in British universities make no reference to the developments in logic that had taken place in the previous 50 years. In setting out to correct this, she covers a wide range of topics, from the logical ideas of *Principia Mathematica* and Russell's theory of descriptions, to various issues in scientific methodology and the theory of definition. In 1933, together with Duncan-Jones, Mace, and Ryle, she founded the journal *Analysis*, initially conceived as the mouthpiece of the Cambridge School of Analysis. In the 'Statement of Policy' that introduces the first issue, we read: 'the contributions to be published will be concerned, as a rule, with the elucidation or explanation of facts, or groups of facts, the general nature of which is, by common consent, already known; rather than with attempts to establish new kinds of fact about the world, of very wide scope, or on a very large scale'. Although it has long since allowed a broader range of contributions, *Analysis* continues to be one of the flagships of analytic philosophy. In the first five volumes of the journal, there was a lot of discussion of the nature of analysis, a debate in which Stebbing's work was influential.[41]

One of Stebbing's key papers in this debate was the lecture she gave to the British Academy in 1933, in which she compared the conceptions of analysis of the Cambridge School and logical positivism.[42] This was one of the first attempts to bring together the two kinds of philosophy. It was also Stebbing who invited Carnap to London in 1934 to talk on philosophy and logical syntax, which introduced logical positivism to Britain, and where Carnap first met both Russell and Ayer. Stebbing thus played a crucial role in creating the dialogue between the Cambridge School of Analysis and logical positivism that was to provide a central theme in analytic philosophy as it developed in the 1930s.

[40] For an account of Collingwood's critique of analytic philosophy, see Beaney 2001; cf. 2005c.

[41] On analysis, see also the supplementary volumes of the *Proceedings of the Aristotelian Society* published in 1934, where the question 'Is analysis a useful method in philosophy?' is debated by Black, Wisdom, and Cornforth, and 1937, where the question 'Does philosophy analyse common sense?' is debated by Duncan-Jones and Ayer.

[42] Stebbing 1933a. Cf. Black 1938. For an account of Stebbing's work on analysis, see Beaney 2003b. On the debate about analysis in the Cambridge School of Analysis, see Baldwin's chapter in this Handbook.

Although 'analytic philosophy' was first used to refer to the Cambridge School of Analysis, it was soon extended to include logical positivism as well. Here, too, though, the term was not initially used by the positivists themselves. There had been no mention of it in the manifesto of the Vienna Circle, published in 1929, where the key phrase was 'scientific world-conception'. Frege, Russell, and Wittgenstein were mentioned as precursors, but as just three in a long list of other philosophers and scientists. In 1930 Carnap and Reichenbach founded *Erkenntnis* as the journal of logical positivism, and the first issue opens with an article by Schlick entitled 'The Turning Point in Philosophy'. This turning point was made possible by the development of the new logic, Schlick argues, but what was crucial was the insights it fostered: into the nature of logic as purely formal and the nature of philosophy as an activity clarifying meaning rather than a science establishing truth. Schlick talks here of 'the profound inner rules of logical syntax discovered by the new analysis' (1930/1959, p. 56), though not of 'analytic philosophy'. There is similar talk in Carnap's famous contribution to the second volume of *Erkenntnis*, 'The Elimination of Metaphysics through Logical Analysis of Language' (1932a).

Talk of 'logical analysis', and the obvious influence of Wittgenstein's *Tractatus* on the ideas of the logical positivists, clearly connected logical positivism to the Cambridge School of Analysis, and this connection was obvious to those who visited Europe from elsewhere. One such visitor was Ernest Nagel from Columbia University, who spent the academic year 1934–5 in Europe, and reported on his experiences for *The Journal of Philosophy* in 'Impressions and Appraisals of Analytic Philosophy in Europe', published in January 1936. This is the first article with 'analytic philosophy' in its title, and the first article that refers to both Cambridge philosophy and the work of the Vienna Circle (and indeed the Lvov–Warsaw School) as analytic philosophy. Nagel reports on 'the philosophy professed at Cambridge, Vienna, Prague, Warsaw, and Lwów' (1936, p. 6), but singles out the work of Moore, Wittgenstein, and Carnap for detailed discussion.

Carnap never took to the term 'analytic philosophy'. In July 1935 he wrote to Quine about the titles of the courses that he had agreed to give in the States, to where he emigrated in December that year. He notes that Nagel had suggested 'analytic philosophy' for the elementary course he had proposed on 'wissenschaftliche Philosophie', given that translating it as 'scientific philosophy' might suggest that his subject was philosophy of natural science, which would be too narrow. But, he goes on, 'I should not like this title very much' (Quine and Carnap 1990, p. 181). In describing his work many years later in his intellectual autobiography (1963), he does not use the term.

The term 'analytic philosophy' did not really catch on until after the Second World War.[43] By then many of the logical positivists who had emigrated to the States after the Nazis had come to power in Germany had established themselves in key philosophy

---

[43] As mentioned in n. 34 above, the collection on *Twentieth Century Philosophy* published in 1943, for example, makes no reference to 'analytic philosophy' as a distinct tradition.

departments, most notably, at Chicago, UCLA, Harvard, Princeton, Berkeley, Iowa, and Minnesota. There was also increasing contact between British and American philosophers. Many philosophers from the States, either as students or as faculty, spent at least a year at either Oxford or Cambridge, and many British philosophers visited the States to give lectures.[44] The dialogue and cross-fertilization that this fostered made it natural to see a much broader movement developing, for which the umbrella term 'analytic philosophy' seemed eminently suitable. The first book to have this term in its title was Pap's *Elements of Analytic Philosophy*, published in 1949. Pap distinguishes four main factions: Carnapians, Mooreans, Wittgensteinians or 'therapeutic positivists', and philosophers concerned to clarify the foundations of science and knowledge. That same year saw the publication of Feigl and Sellars' classic collection, *Readings in Philosophical Analysis*. The title suggests that the emphasis is on the method of philosophical analysis rather than on a school or tradition of philosophical thought, but although the term 'analytic philosophy' is not used, the book made a major contribution to laying down the canon of analytic philosophy,[45] and the new methodology was taken as marking 'a decisive turn in the history of philosophy' (1949, p. vi). A further collection on *Philosophical Analysis* was published the following year, edited by Black (1950a). Black does talk here of 'analytical philosophy' (though only once, in the preface), but he cautions against treating 'Philosophical Analysis' as forming 'a "School" having well defined articles of association' (1950b, p. 2). Rather, 'analysis' is used merely 'to identify philosophers who share a common intellectual heritage and are committed to the clarification of basic philosophical concepts' (1950a, p. v).[46]

Further events strengthened this growing sense that a distinctive style or methodologically rooted tradition of philosophy had established itself. In 1950 Feigl and Sellars followed up their collection by founding the journal *Philosophical Studies*, which they edited until 1971. Reichenbach wrote a Whiggish history of the rise of scientific philosophy (1951). 1952 saw Austin and Hart become Professors at Oxford and Wisdom become Professor at Cambridge, and both Quine and Strawson published textbooks on logic. Wittgenstein's *Philosophical Investigations* finally appeared

---

[44] For details of some of the most significant visits, see the chronology that follows this chapter.

[45] For the record, the philosophers whose work is canonized are (in order of appearance): Feigl, Kneale, Quine, Tarski, Frege, Russell, Carnap, Lewis, Schlick, Aldrich, Ajdukiewicz, Nagel, Waismann, Hempel, Reichenbach, Moore, Stace, Sellars, Broad, Chisholm, Mace, Ducasse, Stevenson. Davidson (1980, p. 261) reports that he got through graduate school by reading Feigl and Sellars.

[46] The same caution had been urged by Black twelve years earlier (1938, p. 24). Black's caution provides a straightforward counterexample to Preston's claim that, from its earliest uses until at least the 1960s, '"analytic philosophy" in the nominative sense was employed clearly and consistently to refer to…a school of philosophy', understood as defined doctrinally (2007, p. 79). Preston does not mention Black's work. As I hope this chapter shows, the history of the construction of the analytic tradition is much more complex—and explicable—than Preston makes out in his claim that it is just the history of an illusion (on the grounds that there are no defining doctrines); cf. n. 56 in chapter 1 above. For criticism of Preston's claim, see Beaney 2007e.

in 1953, and both Quine and Wisdom published collections of their papers. 1953 also saw the first edition of Hospers' *Introduction to Philosophical Analysis*. It was to go through three further editions over the next four decades and remains in print today, having introduced tens of thousands of students to analytic philosophy across the world.[47]

In 1955 White edited the sixth volume, on twentieth-century philosophers, in a series on 'The Great Ages of Western Philosophy'. Although the work of Croce, Santayana, Bergson, Husserl, and Sartre was represented, it was clear from the title—'The Age of Analysis'—where the main action was now seen as taking place, in the analytic and pragmatist traditions. As White wrote in his preface, 'the twentieth century has witnessed a great preoccupation with analysis as opposed to the large, synthetic, system-building of some other periods in the history of philosophy' (1955, p. 9). The other philosophers covered were Moore, Whitehead, Peirce, James, Dewey, Russell, Carnap, and Wittgenstein. Even if there was still reluctance to use the name itself, analytic philosophy did indeed appear to have come of age.

2.5 ANALYTIC PHILOSOPHY AND THE EARLY CONSTRUCTION OF ITS OWN HISTORY

In retrospect, it might seem remarkable that even in the 1950s, the term 'analytic philosophy' was far from being widely used for the tradition that is now generally regarded as having originated more than half a century before then. However, traditions do not, of course, spring up overnight. Methodologies must be sufficiently developed and examples of their application (whether successful or instructively controversial) must be readily available. Their place in methodological space must be secured and recognizably defined, with appropriate contrasts drawn in opposition to rival traditions. They also need to have constructed enough of their history to boast a pedigree. 1956 heralded something of a watershed in all these respects.

Four influential articles were published in 1956: Austin's 'A Plea for Excuses', which offers the fullest statement of his methodology and illustrates its use; Grice and Strawson's reply to Quine's attack on the analytic/synthetic distinction, which

---

[47] The first edition was published in the United States in 1953, but not in Britain until 1956, however. The first and second editions open with a chapter on philosophy and language, aimed at showing how philosophical problems can be clarified and some of them solved or dissolved by attention to the language in which they are formulated. The chapter was deleted in the third edition of 1990, but—after complaints—restored in a shorter form in the fourth edition of 1997, a history that is itself revealing of the development of analytic philosophy. The first chapter of the first edition is entitled 'Words and the World' and of the second edition (1967) 'Meaning and Definition', for example. The original title was restored in the fourth edition. On the changes here, see Hospers' preface to the fourth edition.

highlighted a debate that has been central to the history of analytic philosophy;[48] Sellars' 'Empiricism and the Philosophy of Mind', where his famous critique of the 'myth of the given' was first articulated; and Place's 'Is Consciousness a Brain Process?', which helped inaugurate a new phase in the development of philosophy of mind by arguing for the mind/brain identity thesis.[49] The first edition of Wittgenstein's *Remarks on the Foundations of Mathematics* was also published that year, as well as two collections of the most important of their papers by Russell and Tarski—*Logic and Knowledge* and *Logic, Semantics, Metamathematics*, respectively. These three books made clear just how deeply interconnected the concern with the foundations of mathematics is with issues in semantics and the philosophy of language, interconnections that have also been at the heart of analytic philosophy.[50]

Two monographs helped consolidate the place of analytic philosophy in the history of philosophy, though in different ways. Urmson's *Philosophical Analysis: Its Development between the Two World Wars* (1956) was the first history of analytic philosophy, discussing the rise and fall of both logical atomism and logical positivism, partly with the aim of clearing the ground for the new philosophy that was then emerging. ('Philosophical Analysis' is the title of the book, but Urmson also talks of 'analysts', 'analytic theories', 'analytic philosophers', and the like.) What was conceived as the 'analytic movement' was, in fact, something whose obituary was being written (cf. 1956, pp. 186–7). Historiography is always rich in irony, but it is certainly ironic that at the very point at which its obituary was being written, analytic philosophy was about to blossom into the dominant tradition in twentieth-century philosophy that it is now recognized as being. (It gives a twist to Russell's remark, quoted at the beginning of this chapter, that 'only the dead exist fully'.) Of course, it did so by greatly broadening the meaning of 'analysis', as a limited number of reductive forms of analysis gave way to various forms of connective analysis, and in turn to the whole range of forms combining reductive and connective analysis in different ways that characterizes the contemporary scene.[51]

One account that brought together some of these different forms of analysis was offered in White's *Toward Reunion in Philosophy* (1956), which sought to show how the various strands of the analytic tradition merge with pragmatism once we recognize that describing, performing, and evaluating are all part of philosophizing. The book was based on a course on 'Problems of Analytic Philosophy' that White had begun teaching in the early 1950s at Harvard, which may have been the first course with 'analytic

---

[48] For discussion of this debate, see the chapters by Baghramian and Jorgensen and by Shieh in this Handbook.

[49] See Crawford's chapter in this Handbook. For some other articles published in 1956, see the chronology that follows this chapter. Mention might also be made, for example, of the article by Chisholm in which he defends Brentano's thesis that intentionality is the mark of the psychological. A translation of Tarski's seminal paper on truth (1933) was also published that year.

[50] On the importance of recognizing this, see Floyd 2009, especially p. 164; and for more on this theme, see Floyd's chapter in this Handbook.

[51] For an account of the range of different conceptions of analysis, see Beaney 2009a. On the distinction between reductive and connective analysis, see Strawson 1992, ch. 2.

philosophy' in its title, although White remarks that it might just as well have been called 'the Philosophy of Russell, Moore, Wittgenstein, Carnap, and a Few Others with Whom They Have Succeeded in Communicating' (1999, p. 129). White's teaching at Harvard influenced a generation of analytic philosophers, including Cavell and Dreben, who were assistants on his course (1956, p. xi).

Two other books published in 1956 deserve mention here, which illustrate the growing dominance of analytic philosophy in all areas of philosophy and in perceptions of philosophy outside the academy. The first is Laslett's collection of essays, *Philosophy, Politics and Society*, which might be taken to mark the beginning of analytic political philosophy. The collection was the first in a series of volumes edited by Laslett and others over the next 50 years, which show how analytic political philosophy developed. This first volume was published just two years after Elton's collection on *Aesthetics and Language* (1954), which marks the beginning of analytic aesthetics.[52]

The second book, *The Revolution in Philosophy*, consists of essays that originated in a series of talks given on the Third Programme of the BBC. In introducing the book, Ryle remarks that 'History begins only when memory's dust has settled' (Ayer *et al.* 1956, p. 1), and suggests that twentieth-century philosophy is largely the story of the notion of 'meaning' (Ayer *et al.* 1956, p. 8), implying, though not explicitly asserting, that concern with meaning is the 'revolution' to which the title of the book refers. Chapters on Bradley (by Wollheim), Frege (by Kneale), logical atomism (by Pears), Moore (by Paul), the Vienna Circle (by Ayer), the later Wittgenstein (also by Paul), and two chapters on analysis (by Strawson and Warnock) follow. The chapter on Frege is worth noting: it marks the entry of Frege into the pantheon of analytic philosophers. We will return to this in the next section.

In the decade that followed, many more classics of analytic philosophy appeared, from Anscombe's *Intention* (1957) and Chisholm's *Perceiving* (1957), through Strawson's *Individuals* (1959) and Quine's *Word and Object* (1960), to Rorty's collection on *The Linguistic Turn*, to mention just some of the highlights.[53] After positivist savaging, Strawson's book restored metaphysics to analytic respectability, albeit in a 'descriptive' rather than 'revisionary' form. Rorty's collection gave wide currency not only to talk of 'the linguistic turn' but also to the idea of there being two conflicting strands within linguistic philosophy—ideal language philosophy and ordinary language philosophy.[54] During the same period, further books on the history of philosophy appeared, including two editions of Passmore's *A Hundred Years of Philosophy* (1957, 1966), G. J. Warnock's *English Philosophy since 1900* (1958, 1969), and Mary Warnock's *Ethics since 1900* (1960, 1966). G. J. Warnock's book is highly parochial, giving the false impression that English

---

[52] On the development of analytic political philosophy and analytic aesthetics, respectively, see Wolff's and Lamarque's chapters in this Handbook.

[53] For many more see the chronology that follows this chapter.

[54] Rorty notes in his introduction (1967, p. 9) that the term 'the linguistic turn' was introduced by Bergmann. Bergmann uses it in his review of Strawson's *Individuals* (Bergmann 1960). On Bergmann and the significance of the linguistic turn, see Hacker's chapter in this Handbook.

philosophy is simply analytic philosophy: he discusses Moore, Russell, logical positivism, and Wittgenstein before passing on to his Oxford colleagues.[55] Passmore's book, by contrast, is admirably comprehensive, even from the English perspective he admits he has. Beginning with Mill, he covers various forms of idealism, naturalism, realism, and pragmatism, as well as developments in logic, logical positivism, ordinary language philosophy, existentialism, and phenomenology. Cook Wilson, Collingwood, and Heidegger are discussed, for example, as well as Russell, Moore, and Wittgenstein.[56] Mary Warnock's book is also written from an English perspective, spiced by token exotic flavours from America and France, with chapters on Bradley, Moore, Prichard's and Ross' intuitionism, Ayer's and Stevenson's emotivism, Hare, and Sartre's existentialism.[57]

One other event from this period deserves mention here: the Royaumont colloquium of 1958.[58] Entitled 'La Philosophie Analytique', this was intended to facilitate dialogue between analytic philosophers and philosophers from continental Europe. Participants included Ryle, Austin, Strawson, Quine, Williams, Urmson, Hare, Merleau-Ponty, Wahl, and van Breda (the founder of the Husserl archives at Leuven). Various myths have grown up about this conference, and it is often seen as having only further cemented the idea of a rift between analytic and 'continental' philosophy. Many of the myths have now been exploded,[59] and the term 'continental philosophy' is highly problematic and unfortunate, not least because it both includes and excludes far too much.[60]

---

[55] The first edition contains a (weak) chapter on logic, removed in the second edition on the (mistaken) grounds that it was no longer characteristic of English philosophy. However, he does add (justifiably) some paragraphs on Cook Wilson. (Cf. his preface to the second edition.)

[56] As well as incorporating revisions, the second edition also contains an additional final chapter entitled 'Description, Explanation or Revision?', responding to the issues raised by Strawson's *Individuals* (1959).

[57] Only six years separate the first and second editions, but a third edition was published in 1978. Here Warnock adds a postscript on, among other works, Rawls' *Theory of Justice*, noting in her preface that it no longer seems possible to distinguish moral from political philosophy. On developments in ethics and political philosophy in the analytic tradition, see the chapters by Dancy, Driver, and Wolff in this Handbook.

[58] The proceedings were published in *Cahiers de Royaumont*, 1962.

[59] See especially Overgaard 2010; Vrahimis 2013.

[60] Despite making this point, Leiter and Rosen persist in using the term 'continental philosophy' for what they call '(primarily) philosophy after Kant in Germany and France in the nineteenth and twentieth centuries', on the grounds of there being no better alternative term, though they only consider 'post-Kantian' and 'post-Hegelian' (2007b, p. 2). Of course, they can hardly avoid so persisting in a *Handbook of Continental Philosophy*, but that the 'Continent' should be identified (even 'primarily') with Germany and France is only the most immediately obvious objection. For much fuller discussion of the question 'What is continental philosophy?', and attempts to (re)construct a tradition out of all the disparate 'non-analytic' traditions of nineteenth- and twentieth-century Western philosophy, see Critchley 1997, 2001; Glendinning 1999b, 2006; Boundas 2007c; cf. Mulligan 1991b. A far more monumental construction is provided by Schrift 2010–. On the controversial relationship between analytic and 'continental' philosophy, see Agostini 1997; Akehurst 2008; Buckle 2004; Campbell 2001; Carman 2007; Chase and Reynolds 2011; Cooper 1994; Dascal 2001; Egginton and Sandbothe 2004; Glendinning 2002; Glock 2008, ch. 3; Himanka 2000; Levy 2003; Mandelbaum 1962; May 2002; Prado 2003; Reynolds *et al.* 2010; Richmond 1996; Rosen 2001; Simons 2001; Staten 1984; Williams 1996 (where the analytic/continental distinction is compared to dividing cars into front-wheel drive and Japanese; p. 25).

In fact, just as in the case of 'analytic philosophy', the term 'continental philosophy' only gained currency well over 50 years after the relevant supposed origins. In his own paper at the conference, Ryle uses the term in talking of 'the wide gulf that has existed for three-quarters of a century between Anglo-Saxon and Continental philosophy', meaning by 'Continental philosophy' primarily phenomenology.[61] The term was also used, in a similar sense, by Mandelbaum in his Presidential Address to the American Philosophical Association in December 1962. Mandelbaum talks here of 'two movements which, together, may be said to dominate philosophy', namely, 'that species of analytic philosophy which stems from Moore and the later Wittgenstein' and 'the phenomenological–existentialist movement which is characteristic of philosophy on the Continent', which he immediately goes on to call 'Continental philosophy' (1962, p. 7). That there is a 'phenomenological–existentialist' tradition is uncontroversial, though some may prefer to talk of two—albeit connected—traditions here; but it is misleading to use a geographical term to designate this. Nevertheless, its misleading character aside, many of the arguments that inevitably go on in philosophy departments when new appointments are made and public profiles are produced gradually came to be construed as battles between 'analytic' and 'continental' philosophers, especially in the United States and Britain. These battles further illustrate just how the analytic tradition was partly constructed and consolidated in opposition to rival (constructed) traditions.

2.6   The Canonization of Frege

With the exception of selections from the *Basic Laws of Arithmetic* published in *The Monist* in 1915–17, there were no English translations of Frege's work until 1948, when Black published his translation of 'Über Sinn und Bedeutung' in the *Philosophical Review*. A second translation was published by Feigl the following year in Feigl and Sellars' *Readings in Philosophical Analysis*. In 1950 Austin's translation of *The Foundations of Arithmetic* appeared, and in 1952 Geach and Black published their *Translations from the Philosophical Writings of Gottlob Frege*. Russell, Wittgenstein, and Carnap, in particular, had all acknowledged the importance and influence upon them of Frege's work; but it was only once Frege's writings were readily available in translation that English-speaking analytic philosophers began to pay attention to Frege.[62] Articles on Frege started to appear in

---

[61]   Ryle 1962 [1971a], p. 189. Ryle's paper was called 'Phenomenology versus "The Concept of Mind"', and he provocatively suggests that his own book 'could be described as a sustained essay in phenomenology, if you are at home with that label' (p. 196). A few years earlier, Austin had suggested that he was doing 'linguistic phenomenology' (1956 [1979], p. 182).

[62]   The exception, of course, was Russell, who had provided the first account in English of Frege's philosophy in Appendix A of *The Principles of Mathematics* in 1903. Carnap's *Meaning and Necessity* of 1947 also contains significant discussion of Frege's ideas.

the main philosophical journals in the 1950s,[63] and as mentioned above, Kneale contributed a chapter on Frege to *The Revolution in Philosophy*, published in 1956.

Two books stand out as crucial in the subsequent canonization of Frege as an analytic philosopher. The first is Anscombe's *Introduction to Wittgenstein's Tractatus*, published in 1959, in which she argued that failure to appreciate Frege's work was the main cause of the 'irrelevance' of much of what had hitherto been published on Wittgenstein.[64] The early Wittgenstein ceased to be either bracketed with (middle) Russell as a logical atomist or regarded as a proto-positivist, but instead was seen as responding, at a deep level, to problems in Frege's philosophy. The second book is Dummett's monumental work, *Frege: Philosophy of Language*, published in 1973, in which Frege finally emerged from the shadows of other philosophers and came to be seen as a significant philosopher in his own right, with a semantic theory, so Dummett argued, that could be developed and employed in reformulating and solving many of the traditional problems of philosophy.[65]

Dummett was not the only philosopher who held that the development of semantic theory was the key to dealing with a whole host of problems in the philosophy of language and mind. In a series of papers from the late 1960s, Davidson had advocated a similar programme.[66] In seeing a theory of truth as providing the basis for a theory of meaning, Davidson drew on Tarski's work as well as Frege's, further widening the sphere of analytic philosophy and reconnecting with earlier philosophers and logicians.[67] The so-called Davidsonic boom hit Oxford in the 1970s, combining with Dummett's work to gradually loosen the hold that 'ordinary language philosophy' had had in Britain after the Second World War. This decline of ordinary language philosophy may also have increased willingness to use 'analytic philosophy' rather than 'linguistic philosophy' as the generic term for the various strands of the analytic tradition, including both ordinary language philosophy and 'ideal language philosophy'.[68]

In the States, the work of Quine, Kripke, and Putnam, criticizing many of the assumptions and doctrines of earlier analytic philosophy concerning meaning and the analytic/synthetic, a priori/a posteriori, and necessary/contingent distinctions, led to further distancing from that period.[69] For some, this was seen as inaugurating an era

---

[63] Many of these were reprinted in Klemke 1968, the first collection of papers on Frege.

[64] Cf. Anscombe 1959, p. 12. On the importance of Anscombe's book for our understanding of Wittgenstein, see Diamond's chapter in this Handbook. For further discussion of the influence of Frege on Wittgenstein, see the works cited in n. 17 of the previous chapter.

[65] For more on the importance of Frege in the development of history of analytic philosophy, see Floyd 2009, § 4.

[66] See the papers collected in Davidson 1984.

[67] On the development of theories of meaning, see Miller's chapter in this Handbook.

[68] On linguistic philosophy as comprised of these two strands, see especially Rorty 1967 (as mentioned above). The rise and fall (and historical construction) of linguistic philosophy deserves its own separate treatment. For accounts, see Hacking 1975; Hanfling 2000; Hallett 2008; Beaney 2012a. For classic critiques of linguistic philosophy, see Gellner 1959; Mundle 1970.

[69] For an account of the work of Quine, Kripke, and Putnam, see Baghramian and Jorgensen's chapter in this Handbook.

of 'post-analytic philosophy',[70] but most simply saw it as initiating a new phase of analytic philosophy, with a deepening and broadening of its various concerns in a revised form. With metaphysics firmly back on the agenda, 'analytic metaphysics' developed, bringing with it a whole range of issues, from the ontology of possible worlds to the metaphysics of mind.[71] This reinforced reconnection with the earliest phase of analytic philosophy, when metaphysics had not been repudiated,[72] and even pushed back the boundaries of what counts as this earliest phase, to include such remoter ancestors as Bolzano, who had criticized Kantian modal conceptions long before Quine, Kripke, and others.[73]

2.7   THE HISTORICAL TURN IN ANALYTIC PHILOSOPHY

In his introduction to *Frege: Philosophy of Language*, Dummett notoriously claimed that Frege's *Begriffsschrift* 'is astonishing because it has no predecessors: it appears to have been born from Frege's brain unfertilized by external influences' (1973, p. xxxv). He repeats the claim in his second book on Frege, alleging further that the philosophical system Frege constructed on the basis of his logic 'owed, I believe, not very much more to previous philosophical work than did his formal logic to previous work in that field' (1981a, p. xvii). In creating quantificational logic, Frege's *Begriffsschrift* was indeed revolutionary, and his philosophy was undoubtedly driven by concern to articulate a corresponding epistemology and metaphysics;[74] but all this was far from unfertilized by external influences. Sluga was the first to show how mistaken Dummett's historiography was, and since then much light has been shed on both the philosophical and the mathematical context of Frege's work.[75] To take just one example: we now know that the

---

[70]   For references, see n. 7 of the previous chapter.

[71]   For an account of metaphysics in the analytic tradition, see Simons' chapter in this Handbook.

[72]   On the metaphysics of early analytic philosophy, see Beaney 2012b.

[73]   On Bolzano's critique of Kant, see Lapointe 2011, and Textor's chapter in this Handbook.

[74]   I talk neutrally here of 'corresponding', since the question of the relative priority of Frege's logic, epistemology, and metaphysics is controversial. I am convinced, however, that Frege's philosophy essentially arose from thinking through the implications of his use of function–argument analysis, extended from mathematics to logic. For elaboration of this, see e.g. Beaney 2007d, 2011a, 2012b.

[75]   See especially Sluga 1980, and for subsequent accounts of Frege that are more historically informed, see e.g. Baker and Hacker 1984a; Weiner 1990; Carl 1994; Beaney 1996; Burge 2005 (which collects together his papers on Frege from 1979 onwards); Kienzler 2009; Künne 2010. On the historical context of Frege's work, see especially Gabriel and Kienzler 1997; Gabriel and Dathe 2000; the papers in vol. 1 of Beaney and Reck 2005; and Gabriel's chapter in this Handbook. On the mathematical background, see the papers in vol. 3 of Beaney and Reck 2005; Tappenden 2005, 2006; Wilson 2010; Hallett 2010; and Tappenden's chapter in this Handbook. On Frege's influence on subsequent philosophy, see Burge's chapter.

very name 'Begriffsschrift' shows the influence of Trendelenburg and, through him, of Wilhelm von Humboldt.[76]

The controversy over the interpretation of Frege brought to a head the growing sense, even within the analytic tradition, of the impoverished understanding that analytic philosophers had of their own history and of historiographical issues.[77] Historiographical debates had already been going on in history and philosophy of science, inspired, in particular, by Kuhn's paradigm-shifting work of 1962, *The Structure of Scientific Revolutions*. This had encouraged more detailed investigation of the historical development of science, and deeper reflection about methodology, led, most notably, by Lakatos, whose work was published in the 1970s. In history of ideas, and especially history of political thought, too, there was increasing discussion of historiography, Skinner's 'Meaning and Understanding in the History of Ideas' of 1969 being particularly influential. In 1979 Rorty's *Philosophy and the Mirror of Nature* appeared, which put grand narratives back on the table at the same time as questioning the continued existence of analytic philosophy (see e.g. p. 172), thereby raising the stakes for the historiographical self-consciousness of analytic philosophers.

In 1984, Rorty, Schneewind, and Skinner edited a landmark collection of papers entitled 'Philosophy in History'. Part I contains historiographical essays and Part II case-studies, including three in history of analytic philosophy: on Frege (by Sluga), Moore (by Baldwin), and Russell (by Hylton). In his own contribution to Part I Rorty distinguishes and discusses four genres in the historiography of philosophy: rational reconstruction, historical reconstruction, *Geistesgeschichte*, and doxography. The first three correspond, more or less, to Nietzsche's three species of history: critical, antiquarian, and monumental, respectively. Rational reconstruction we have already noted is illustrated by Russell's early book on Leibniz and is the most characteristic genre in analytic philosophy. Dummett's first book on Frege provides another example, though here there are also aspects of *Geistesgeschichte*—monumentalizing Frege in the history of philosophy as the first person (rightly, on Dummett's view) to make the theory of meaning the foundation of all philosophy.[78] Rorty characterizes *Geistesgeschichte* as 'big sweeping' stories that aim at 'self-justification in the same way as does rational reconstruction, but on a different scale' (1984, pp. 56–7). His own *Philosophy and the Mirror of Nature* clearly falls into this category. *Geistesgeschichte* play a central role in canon-formation, unlike doxography, which takes a canon for granted. Doxography, as Rorty conceives it, is based on the assumption that philosophical positions are eternally given, implying

[76] See Thiel 1995/2005; Gabriel's chapter in this Handbook.

[77] Other controversies that might be mentioned here include the debate about Kripke's interpretation of Wittgenstein's remarks on rule-following and private language, and the question of the influences on Carnap and other members of the Vienna Circle. Early criticisms of Kripke's interpretation include Baker and Hacker 1984b and McGinn 1984. Investigation of the influences on Carnap was spearheaded by Coffa and Friedman in the early 1980s. Coffa's work was eventually published in 1991, and a collection of Friedman's papers appeared in 1999.

[78] See especially 1973, ch. 19; 1981a, ch. 3.

that history of philosophy is simply a matter of working out which positions a philosopher holds. As we have also already noted, doxography is illustrated in Frege's and Russell's writings on the history of philosophy.

Rational reconstructions and *Geistesgeschichte* inevitably prompt historical reconstruction, where antiquarian impulses seek to correct the distortions that the former involve. Sometimes this results in very detailed studies where antiquarianism rules; but it usually inspires accounts that combine rational and historical reconstruction in more satisfying ways. This is exactly what happened in the history of analytic philosophy—or the history of the historiography of analytic philosophy. At the beginning of the 1990s a wealth of works appeared that marked the beginning of history of analytic philosophy as a recognized subfield of philosophy. Two books on Russell, by Hylton (1990) and Griffin (1991), offered careful reconstructions of the development of Russell's early views, setting new standards of scholarship. This was reinforced by Baldwin's book on Moore (1990), which provided the first substantial account of the full range of Moore's philosophy. Weiner's book on Frege sought to show how Frege's philosophical thinking emerged out of his mathematical concerns, rejecting the assumption that Frege could be treated as 'truly one of us' (1990, p. 2). A collection of Diamond's papers appeared (1991), which included her influential readings of Frege and Wittgenstein that were to inspire the 'New Wittgenstein' debate a decade later (see especially Crary and Read 2000). Monk's biography of Wittgenstein was published (1990), which, alongside McGuinness' earlier biography of the young Wittgenstein (1988), provided much-needed context to Wittgenstein's often enigmatic remarks. A new collection on the analytic tradition reflected the historical turn that was taking place (Bell and Cooper 1990), and Coffa's long-awaited book on logical positivism appeared, reconstructing a 'semantic tradition', as he called it (1991). Uebel also published a monograph on logical positivism (1992), elucidating the internal debates within the Vienna Circle. Simons brought out a collection of essays on the Central European tradition in analytic philosophy (1992). Dummett made two further important contributions: *Frege: Philosophy of Mathematics* (1991a), the sequel to his first book on Frege, was far more sensitive to the development of Frege's thinking; and *Frege and Other Philosophers* (1991b), a collection of his papers, contained responses to some of his critics. Two years later he also published *Origins of Analytical Philosophy* (1993a), goaded by the Zeitgeist, but bizarrely, discussing only Frege and Husserl. Bell's book on Husserl (1990), written from an analytic perspective, also helped encourage dialogue between analytic philosophers and phenomenologists, even if controversy is never far away in such dialogue.

These books transformed the landscape of analytic philosophy.[79] In the new constituent field of history of analytic philosophy, articles, monographs, collections, biographies, and autobiographies have been appearing with ever increasing frequency.[80] Coupled with a stream of new editions and translations of the work of analytic

---

[79] For further discussion of the historical turn in analytic philosophy, see the papers in Reck 2013.
[80] For some of the highlights, see the chronology and bibliography that follow this chapter.

philosophers (both well-known and lesser-known) and the burgeoning textbook industry that seeks to introduce that work to new generations of students right across the world, history of analytic philosophy now rivals more established areas of history of philosophy, such as history of ancient Greek philosophy and history of early modern philosophy, in terms of the number of academics that record it as one of their research and teaching interests.[81]

In general, however, standards of historical scholarship in history of analytic philosophy have not yet reached the level that they are in history of ancient Greek philosophy and early modern philosophy. Rational reconstructions are still offered that have not learnt from the historical studies that are now available. Impressive as it may be as a series of rational reconstructions of canonical texts in the history of analytic philosophy, Soames' *Philosophical Analysis in the Twentieth Century* (2003), for example, still presents Russell's theory of descriptions without mentioning Russell's earlier theory of denoting; thinking through the problems faced by the latter is what actually led Russell to the former.[82] Doxography, too, will always be a temptation that serious history of philosophy must avoid. It is all too easy to take a canon for granted and ignore broader questions of context and connection, questions that are essential to address in developing awareness of the contingency and negotiability of canons.

In his discussion of historiography, Rorty criticizes doxography for its complacency about canon-formation. But he stresses how the other three genres complement one another. He notes that there is a 'hermeneutic circle' of rational and historical reconstruction, around which one must go many times before doing either sort of reconstruction, and talks of the tension between rational and historical reconstruction that generates the need for the self-justification that *Geistegeschichte* provides.[83] Ideally, balance between the genres should be struck in all work in history of philosophy; but this would be unrealistic. A more tolerant attitude is to recognize the diversity of approaches and encourage that diversity in the hope that the balance will be achieved over time in the ongoing and self-correcting work of the academic community as a whole.[84]

---

[81] Ten years ago, only a handful of philosophers recorded history of analytic philosophy as an area of research specialism or teaching competence. Today most medium or large English-speaking departments have at least one person who gives this as one of their areas. In Leiter's 'Philosophical Gourmet Report' <http://www.philosophicalgourmet.com>, history of analytic philosophy (including Wittgenstein) is one of the specialities evaluated, one of nine history of philosophy specialities.

[82] Soames' work has been especially controversial. For reviews, see e.g. Kremer 2005; Rorty 2005; Beaney 2006b; Hacker 2006; Wilson 2006b. For his replies to critics, see Soames 2006a, 2006b. Cf. also Floyd 2009. For deeper understanding of Russell's theory of descriptions, see Hylton 1990, 2003; Linsky and Imaguire 2005; Stevens 2011.

[83] 1984, p. 53, fn. 1; p. 68. I discuss rational and historical reconstruction further, and offer my own resolution of the tension in what I call 'dialectical reconstruction', in Beaney 1996, ch. 1; 2013a.

[84] This has been the editorial policy in the present Handbook, within the obvious constraints of seeking representative coverage of the main philosophers, views, and themes.

In 2007 a new book series on the history of analytic philosophy was established, the first series of its kind, and the first volume was published in 2008.[85] In 2010, following the founding of the Society for the Study of the History of Analytical Philosophy, an online *Journal for the History of Analytical Philosophy* was launched, again the first of its kind, and its first issue appeared in 2011.[86] In the case of both the series and the journal, 'history of analytic philosophy' is understood broadly, to include interconnections with other traditions and the work of philosophers who might be regarded as outside the analytic tradition. In both cases, too, the interaction between history of analytic philosophy and contemporary analytic philosophy is stressed, an interaction that is seen as mutually beneficial. The present Oxford Handbook draws on and deepens the historical turn that has taken place in analytic philosophy, and the range of contributions from leading scholars that it contains testifies to the richness and significance of the work that is now being done in the field.

2.8 Analytic Philosophy and History of Analytic Philosophy

The historical turn in analytic philosophy has given fresh impetus and added relevance to the debates about the relationship between philosophy and history of philosophy that have taken place since the emergence of analytic philosophy. Analytic philosophers are now more aware that their rational reconstructions are contested, that interpretations of the views even of their own immediate predecessors cannot be taken for granted, that their own concepts, doctrines, positions, and problems have a history, that their assumptions have a context that may need to be explained, that there have been changes and fashions in their own tradition, and so on. I conclude this chapter by saying something in defence of the historical turn that has taken place.

As we have seen, from its origins in the work of Frege and Russell, analytic philosophy has had ahistorical tendencies. Analytic philosophers have engaged in history of philosophy, but often only to the extent of offering—or sometimes simply borrowing—rational

---

[85] The series was inspired by Candlish's monograph on the Russell/Bradley dispute (2007), which was reissued in paperback as the third volume of the series (see Beaney 2009b). The first volume was Nasim 2008, and there are now over 20 volumes published, with many more in the pipeline. For the record, the volumes are, in order: Nasim 2008, Wagner 2009, Candlish 2009 [2007], Venturinha 2010, Coliva 2010, Lapointe 2011, Stevens 2011, Patterson 2012, Landini 2012, Duke 2012, Wagner 2012, Gandon 2012, Pardey 2012, Textor 2013, Korhonen 2013, Chapman 2013, Engelmann 2013, Reck 2013, D'Oro and Sandis 2013, Mulligan, Kijania-Placek and Placek 2013, Schaar 2013, Griffin and Linsky 2013. For details, see the website for the series: <http://www.palgrave.com/products/series.aspx?s=hap>. See also the chronology that follows this chapter.

[86] Information on the Society and Journal can be found at: <http://www.humanities.mcmaster. ca/~philos/sshap> and <http://jhaponline.org>, respectively.

reconstructions to further their own projects. They have tended to be uninterested in doing justice to the philosophers whose work they reconstruct, or in getting the historical facts right.[87] Given that the early analytic philosophers were all realists, this might seem ironic. Their mathematical and scientific realism, or epistemological and metaphysical realism, seems not to have been matched by any respect for historical realism. Such analytic philosophers need not repudiate historical realism; they may complain as loudly as anyone else when their own views are misinterpreted. Rather, they simply deny its relevance: while there are historical facts of the matter about philosophers' actual views, this is for the historian to establish, not the philosopher. On their view, philosophical concepts, doctrines, positions, and problems are independent of their articulation by any particular person, and hence their attribution or misattribution to anyone is of no ultimate significance.

This is not the place for a full critique of ahistoricism.[88] I will make just four points here, drawing on what has been said in both this and the previous chapter. First of all, philosophical terminology is created and shaped by the uses of the past, and is essentially and inevitably contested, even if there are periods of consensus or local contexts where there is relative agreement. In the historical longer run, clarification is always needed, which requires serious engagement with past philosophical views. This is most obviously so when terms like 'Kantian', 'Fregean', or 'Russellian' are in play. To use such terms is to accept a commitment to justify that use by reference to some view that Kant, Frege, or Russell, respectively, actually held at some point. But there are similar commitments in the case of terms such as 'analytic' or 'necessary'. In defining 'analytic' in the way he did in the *Foundations*, for example, Frege transformed Kant's notion, even if he himself wrote that he did not intend to introduce a new sense, 'but only to capture what earlier writers, in particular *Kant*, have meant' (1884, § 3). To what extent this is actually so requires investigation of what Kant meant and any assessment of a claim about the 'analyticity' of a proposition requires explanation of the intended sense.

Of course, one might respond that as long as one defines what one means by a term, one can use it (Humpty-Dumpty-like) in whatever way one wants. However, any such definition will itself use further terms, and as Frege recognized, not everything can be defined, and at some point, at the most basic level, we have to rely on a 'meeting of minds'. So elucidation, as he called it, is always required; and this, too, as I suggested in section 2.2, has an historical dimension, since new views need to be positioned within the historical space of previous views if they are to be properly understood.[89]

[87]   As Kripke notoriously put it in introducing his 'sceptical interpretation' of Wittgenstein's remarks on rule-following, 'my method is to present the argument as it struck me, as it presented a problem for me' (1982, p. viii). Light was eventually shed on those remarks, but only by recognizing the differences between Kripkenstein, as Kripke's Wittgenstein came to be called, and Wittgenstein himself.

[88]   For fuller discussion, see especially the essays in Rorty, Schneewind, and Skinner 1984; Hare 1988; Sorell and Rogers 2005; Reck 2013. See also Glock 2008, ch. 4, and some of the replies in the special issue (no. 1) of *Teorema*, 30 (2011). For an account of the German historicist tradition, see Beiser 2011.

[89]   Cf. Floyd's discussion in her chapter in this Handbook of the 'interpretive need' that is left behind by every analysis or rigorization. Satisfying this interpretive need will also have an historical dimension.

This leads on to a second criticism of ahistoricism. Philosophical concepts, doctrines, positions, and problems can indeed be regarded as independent of their articulation by any particular person—but only up to a point, or within local contexts, contexts that embed shared presuppositions or where a 'meeting of minds' can be relied upon. Debates involving those concepts, doctrines, positions, and problems depend on these shared presuppositions, which may not be explicitly articulated by the protagonists, but some of which may well need to be recognized for the debates to progress—whether to deepen the arguments, resolve the disagreements, overcome any stalemates, or diagnose any mistaken assumptions. As mentioned in section 2.4 above, Stebbing admitted that the Cambridge School of Analysis involved presuppositions that she was unable to justify, and this prompted Collingwood to criticize analytic philosophy for this failing, and later, more constructively, to articulate a view of philosophy in which the identification of presuppositions was its primary goal. Arguably, Collingwood went too far in the other direction, in advocating too strong a form of historicism, but I think he was right to see the identification of presuppositions as an important aim of philosophy, and one which requires history of philosophy in its pursuit.

Logicism provides a good example. In denying that mathematics is reducible to logic, Kant presupposed that logic was Aristotelian logic (and was right in his denial). In arguing that arithmetic can be reduced to logic, Frege had to expand the domain of logic, and today it is often presupposed that logic means Fregean logic (or some extension of it). Resolving debates about logicism, then, cannot proceed without clarification of what is meant by 'logic', in other words, without identification of the relevant presuppositions.[90] Another example is the distinction between psychological genesis and logical justification, which might be seen as one of the most fundamental presuppositions of analytic philosophy, from which its ahistoricism follows. Once we recognize this presupposition and understand its historical source, however, we see that it is shared with neo-Kantianism and British idealism, and hence that ahistoricism is not an inevitable consequence. It may have been questioned only relatively recently in the analytic tradition; but history of philosophy reveals alternative views of the relationship between philosophy and history of philosophy that are much healthier.

Ahistoricism is undermined, thirdly, when we appreciate how much of actual philosophical discourse involves engagement with the ideas of past philosophers. Philosophy is essentially 'talking with a tradition', to use Brandom's words.[91] This can be obscured by the scientism that inhabits some regions of analytic philosophy. This is reflected, for example, in views of philosophical research based on scientific models: to work at the 'cutting-edge' of the discipline involves reading the very latest articles published in, say,

[90] For discussion of the issues here, see MacFarlane 2002.
[91] The phrase forms the title of Part One of Brandom 2002. On Brandom's inferentialist reworking of Gadamerian hermeneutics, grasp of conceptual content itself is understood as 'the ability to *navigate* and *negotiate* between the different perspectives from which such a content can be interpreted (implicitly) or specified (explicitly)' (2002, p. 109). Conversing with tradition is thus *constitutive* of understanding meaning. Brandom's view is also influenced by Sellars' conception of history of philosophy as the *lingua franca* of philosophy; Sellars 1973; cf. Floyd 2009, p. 167.

Mind or *Analysis*, and coming up with criticisms, counterexamples, further arguments, or alternative theories in response. To read only the very latest articles, however, is not to philosophize in some purified atmosphere: one cannot breathe in an ahistorical vacuum. The past is simply telescoped into a shorter time-frame; and once debate develops, the time-frame inevitably expands to reveal its historical roots and engagement with tradition becomes more and more explicit.[92]

Finally, bringing these last two points together, philosophizing always reflects, invokes, or presupposes some kind of underlying narrative, whether grand or modest, which reveals the location in the historical space of philosophical traditions. This narrative may be explicitly articulated in the main text of publications, but more often than not is implicitly exhibited in what Derrida (1972) called the 'margins' of philosophy—in prefaces, footnotes, correspondence, off-the-cuff remarks, gossip, and so on. It is imbibed in learning to philosophize in a certain way, and is in turn transmitted through teaching and discussion. It may be publicly defended, but will typically be taken for granted in the culture or context in which the philosophizing occurs, and may function at subconscious levels. We are thrown into a particular philosophical life-world, in other words, and history of philosophy is required to appreciate our philosophical *Dasein* and hence to transcend our historical embodiment.

The narratives that form our philosophical self-identity may well involve distorted views of the past, myths, misinterpretations, and so on. These 'shadow histories', as Watson (1993) called them, may be even more important than real histories.[93] Dummett saw Frege as rebelling against German idealism, for example,[94] while Russell is all too readily assumed to have slain Bradley.[95] Carnap's infamous attack on Heidegger's supposed 'pseudo-statement' that 'The Nothing itself nothings' ('*Das Nichts selbst nichtet*') has become a classic of uncharitable interpretation,[96] and the literature on Wittgenstein is full of exotic characters, from Russellstein to Kripkenstein and now New Wittgenstein (or various New Wittgensteins).[97] Myths are contagious, however, and sooner or later

---

[92] In discussing the relationship between analytic philosophy and history of philosophy in correspondence with Isaiah Berlin, Morton White remarks: 'Curiously enough, if one treats a *contemporary* writer one is thought to be original, whereas if one treats a far greater figure of the past, one is thought to be derivative or parasitical, or what have you. Nonsense, I say.' He goes on to suggest how an historical work can be transformed into a 'pure', 'original' one: 'One writes the first, with references to other people, pages, chapters, verses, expounding them and criticizing them; then one goes over the manuscript, carefully eliminating all the inverted commas and references, and starts talking about the theory of the ghost-in-the-machine or category mistakes or traditional dualism, etc., etc. Immediately one ceases to be Byzantine and becomes Greek, thereby becoming original and unparasitical. Nonsense, I say' (1999, p. 248).

[93] For discussion and critique of one such shadow history, see Crawford's chapter in this Handbook.

[94] See e.g. Dummett 1973, pp. 197–8, 541, 683–4.

[95] For critique of this assumption, see Candlish 2007.

[96] Carnap 1932a, § 5. Carnap's attack is discussed by Friedman in *A Parting of the Ways* (2000); cf. Friedman 1996; Inwood 1999; Gabriel 2003; Witherspoon 2003.

[97] See Russell 1922; Kripke 1982; Crary and Read 2000; Read and Lavery 2011. On readings of Wittgenstein, see the chapters by Kremer, Glock, and Diamond in this Handbook.

these shadow histories require correction. If analytic philosophers prize truth, clarity, and rigour, and wish to divest themselves of the 'local and temperamental bias' of which Russell spoke (see section 2.3 above), then they should extend their analytic methods to investigating and correcting their own narratives and self-identities.

All four points suggest ways in which philosophy has an intrinsically historical dimension and in which history of philosophy is essential to philosophy. History of philosophy plays a crucial role in clarifying concepts, doctrines, positions, and problems; it identifies presuppositions and opens up alternative views; it makes us appreciate the tradition in which our conversations take place; and it develops self-consciousness and corrects shadow histories. Analytic philosophy has become the tradition in which much philosophizing is now pursued, so that talking with the analytic tradition may form one's first conversations. In this context, it is inevitable that history of analytic philosophy should have emerged. History of analytic philosophy is analytic philosophy come to self-consciousness; it provides the forum for richer dialogues with the past, combining in multifarious ways monumental, antiquarian, and critical history, rational and historical reconstruction. This has also expanded the repertoire of methods of analysis on which philosophers can draw, through various forms of historical and textual analysis— genealogical analysis, presuppositional analysis, hermeneutics, deconstructional analysis, among others. Analysis itself has been deepened and broadened, synthesizing, we might say, logical/conceptual and historical/textual modes of analysis.

The spread of analytic philosophy across the world, and its ramification into all subfields of philosophy and into interdisciplinary projects, is also cultivating new dialogues with other traditions and disciplines, which will in turn transform them all, reconfiguring their conceptual and historical interconnections. This will require new analyses, interrogations, and narratives that renegotiate the positioning and oppositioning involved in those traditions and disciplines, in the ways we have seen exemplified in the account given here of the construction of the analytic tradition. The future for history of analytic philosophy—and for augmented and invigorated analytic philosophy—promises new enlightenment. *Explicare aude!* Have courage to offer your own (historically informed) analyses!

CHAPTER 3

....

CHRONOLOGY OF ANALYTIC PHILOSOPHY AND ITS HISTORIOGRAPHY

....

MICHAEL BEANEY

THIS chronology condenses as much information as possible in as succinct a form as possible in 25,000 words about the key thinkers, publications, and events in the history of analytic philosophy and its historiography. Under each year, the entries are ordered as follows: publications; events; births and deaths. The aim is to show something not only of the 'internal' history of analytic philosophy but also of the wider philosophical context in which analytic philosophy developed. So selected publications and events of related philosophical traditions, such as neo-Kantianism, pragmatism, and phenomenology, as well as relevant scientific texts, are also included (indicated in shaded lines). The entries are by no means limited to just this, but 150 philosophers and other thinkers have been selected for particular coverage—with dates of births, deaths, and key events and publications. Of these 150, 100 are either generally recognized as analytic philosophers or closely connected with the analytic tradition, such as certain mathematicians and pragmatists, and the other 50 are generally recognized as not analytic philosophers (indicated in shaded lines). For the record, these 150 are noted in the following table, together with works of reference where further information about their life and work can be found:

Thinker	Dates	Accounts of life and work, biographies, chronologies
Ajdukiewicz, Kazimierz	1890–1963	Sinisi & Woleński 1995
Alexander, Samuel	1859–1938	Stout 1940a, 1940b; Slater 2006
Anderson, John	1893–1962	Baker 1986; Weblin 2006
Anscombe, G. E. M.	1919–2001	Müller 2001; Teichman 2001; Diamond 2006; Driver 2009
Armstrong, David	1926–2014	Jackson 2001

(Continued)

Thinker	Dates	Accounts of life and work, biographies, chronologies
Austin, J. L.	1911–60	Fann 1969; Warnock 1969, 1989; Berlin *et al.* 1973; Searle 2001; Cave 2006a
Ayer, A. J.	1910–89	Ayer 1977, 1985, 1992; Foster 1985; Ayer & Honderich 1991; Hahn 1992; Rogers 1999; Sprigge 2001; Hunter 2006a; Macdonald 2010
Bergmann, Gustav	1906–87	Gram & Klemke 1974; Addis 2005; Anellis 2005a
Bergson, Henri	1859–1941	Lawlor & Moulard 2011
Berlin, Isaiah	1909–97	Ignatieff 1998; Cherniss 2006; Cherniss & Hardy 2010
Black, Max	1909–88	Schrader 2005
Boltzmann, Ludwig	1844–1906	Blackmore 1995
Bolzano, Bernard	1781–1848	Morscher 2007
Boole, George	1815–64	MacHale 1985; Gasser 2006; Burris 2010
Bradley, F. H.	1846–1924	Ferreira 2006; Candlish & Basile 2009
Braithwaite, R. B.	1900–90	Cave 2006
Brandom, Robert B.	1950–	Weiss & Wanderer 2010
Brentano, Franz	1838–1917	Jacquette 2004; Huemer 2010
Broad, C. D.	1887–1971	Broad 1959; Schilpp 1959; Britton 1978; van Cleve 2001; Seager 2006; Gustavsson 2010
Brouwer, L. E. J.	1881–1966	van Atten 2011
Burge, Tyler	1946–	Hahn & Ramberg 2003
Cantor, Georg	1845–1918	Dauben 1979; Hallett 1984
Carnap, Rudolf	1891–1970	Carnap 1963; Schilpp 1963; Hintikka 1975; Sarkar 2001; Carus 2005, 2007; Friedman & Creath 2007
Case, Thomas	1844–1925	Marion 2006a
Cassirer, Ernst	1874–1945	Gawronsky 1949; Schilpp 1949a; T. Cassirer 2003; Friedman 2011
Cavell, Stanley	1926–	Eldridge 2003; Brino-Dean 2005; Cavell 2010
Chisholm, Roderick	1916–99	Chisholm 1997; Hahn 1997b; Foyer & Zimmerman 2001; Feldman 2005; Feldman & Feldman 2008
Chomsky, Noam	1928–	Barsky 1997; Ludlow 2001; McGilvray 2005; Szabó 2005
Church, Alonzo	1903–95	Manzano 1997; Anderson 2001; Drucker 2005; Enderton forthcoming
Collingwood, R. G.	1889–1943	Collingwood 1939; Boucher 2006; Inglis 2009; D'Oro & Connelly 2010; Boucher & Smith 2013
Darwin, Charles	1809–82	Browne 1995, 2000
Davidson, Donald	1917–2003	Davidson 1999; Hahn 1999; Lepore 2001, 2005a; Malpas 2009
Dedekind, Richard	1831–1916	Reck 2008
Deleuze, Gilles	1925–95	Smith & Protevi 2008
Dennett, Daniel	1942–	Ross *et al.* 2000; Viger 2005a
Derrida, Jacques	1930–2004	Peeters 2010; Lawlor 2011

Thinker	Dates	Accounts of life and work, biographies, chronologies
Dewey, John	1859–1952	Dewey 1939; Hook 1939; Schilpp 1939; Dykhuizen 1973; Eldridge 2005
Dilthey, Wilhelm	1833–1911	Makkreel 2008
Dreben, Burton	1927–99	Gibson 2005
Duhem, Pierre	1861–1916	Martin 1991
Dummett, Michael	1925–2011	Green 2001; Miller 2001; Weiss 2002; Auxier & Hahn 2007; Dummett 2007
Einstein, Albert	1879–1955	Einstein 1949; Schilpp 1949b; Clark 1971
Engels, Friedrich	1820–95	Carver 1989
Evans, Gareth	1946–80	Mandik 2006
Feigl, Herbert	1902–88	Feyerabend 1966; Aune 1998; Reisch 2005b
Feyerabend, Paul	1924–93	Feyerabend 1995; Oberheim 2005; Preston 2009
Fodor, Jerry	1935–	Rey 2001; Viger 2005b
Foot, Philippa	1920–2010	Lawrence 2001; Hoy 2005; Kirchin 2006
Foucault, Michel	1926–84	Gutting 2008
Frege, Gottlob	1848–1925	Dummett 2001; Kreiser 2001; Thiel & Beaney 2005
Freud, Sigmund	1856–1939	Gay 1988
Gadamer, Hans-Georg	1900–2002	Gadamer 1997; Hahn 1997a; Grondin 2003; Malpas 2009b
Geach, Peter T.	1916–2013	Lewis 1991, 2006
Gödel, Kurt	1906–78	Dawson 1997; Anderson 2001; Parsons 2005; Kennedy 2011
Goodman, Nelson	1906–98	Scheffler 2001
Green, T. H.	1836–82	Tyler 2006, 2011
Grice, H. Paul	1913–88	Neale 2001; Stainton 2005; Grandy & Warner 2006; Hogan 2006
Habermas, Jürgen	1929–	Wiggershaus 2004; Bohman & Rehg 2011
Hägerström, Axel	1868–1939	Mindus 2009
Hare, R. M.	1919–2002	Sinnott-Armstrong 2001; Pybus 2006
Hart, H. L. A.	1907–92	Shapiro 2001; Lacey 2004; Brooks 2006
Hegel, G. W. F.	1770–1831	Pinkard 2000; Redding 2010
Heidegger, Martin	1889–1976	Guignon 1993; Wheeler 2011
Helmholtz, Hermann von	1821–94	Königsberger 1902–3; Patton 2010
Hempel, Carl G.	1905–97	Kitcher 2001; Reisch 2005c
Herbart, Johann	1776–1841	Asmus 1968/1970
Hertz, Heinrich	1857–94	Fölsing 1997; Baird et al. 1998; Lützen 2005
Hilbert, David	1862–1943	Reid 1970
Hintikka, Jaakko	1929–	Niiniluoto 2005; Hintikka 2006; Auxier & Hahn 2006
Hung, Tscha	1909–92	Cohen 1992; Dainian 1992
Husserl, Edmund	1859–1938	Smith & Smith 1995; Smith 2007; Beyer 2011
James, William	1842–1910	Myers 1986; Suckiel 2005; Goodman 2009
Joachim, Harold H.	1868–1938	Mander 2006b

(Continued)

Thinker	Dates	Accounts of life and work, biographies, chronologies
Kant, Immanuel	1724–1804	Kuehn 2001
Kim, Jaegwon	1934–	Greco 2005
Kneale, William	1906–90	Smiley 1995, 2006
Kotarbiński, Tadeusz	1886–1981	Woleński 1990
Kripke, Saul	1940–	Sosa 2001; Green 2005
Kuhn, Thomas S.	1922–96	Grandy 2001; Fuller 2005
Lakatos, Imre	1922–74	Wright 2006
Leśniewski, Stanisław	1886–1939	Simons 2011
Lewis, C. I.	1883–1964	Lewis 1968; Schilpp 1968; Murphey 2005; Colella 2005; Hunter 2007
Lewis, David	1941–2001	Stalnaker 2001; Hawthorne 2005; Weatherson 2009
Lotze, Hermann	1817–81	Sullivan 2010
Łukasiewicz, Jan	1878–1956	Woleński 1989
Mach, Ernst	1838–1916	Blackmore 1972; Wolters 2000; Pojman 2009
Mackie, John L.	1917–81	McDowell 1990; Sherratt 2006
Malcolm, Norman	1911–90	Ginet 2001; Blair 2005
Marcus, Ruth Barcan	1921–2012	Cresswell 2001, Garrett 2005; Marcus 2010
Marx, Karl	1818–83	Berlin 1939; McLellan 1973; Wolff 2010
McDowell, John	1942–	Thornton 2006
McTaggart, J. M. E.	1866–1925	Armour 2006
Meinong, Alexius	1853–1920	Marek 2008
Merleau-Ponty, Maurice	1908–61	Flynn 2004
Mill, John Stuart	1806–73	Skorupski 1989; Capaldi 2004; Wilson 2007
Moore, G. E.	1873–1958	Moore 1942; Schilpp 1942; Baldwin 1990, 2004; Sosa 2001
Nagel, Ernest	1901–85	Suppes 1994; Anellis 2005b
Neurath, Otto	1882–1945	Nemmeth & Stadler 1996; Cat 2010
Nietzsche, Friedrich	1844–1900	Wicks 2011b
Peano, Giuseppe	1858–1932	Kennedy 1980
Peirce, Charles S.	1839–1914	Hookway 1985; Brent 1998; Misak 2004; de Waal 2005; Burch 2010
Perry, Ralph Barton	1876–1957	Papas 2005
Plantinga, Alvin	1932–	Plantinga 1985; Tomberlin & van Inwagen 1985; Sennett 2005
Poincaré, Henri	1854–1912	Gray 2012
Popper, Karl	1902–1994	Popper 1974, 1976; Schilpp 1974; Hacohen 2000; Newton-Smith 2001
Price, Henry H.	1899–1984	Hunter 2006b
Prichard, Harold A.	1871–1947	Stratton-Lake 2006a; Dancy 2010
Prior, Arthur N.	1914–69	Copeland 2006, 2007
Putnam, Hilary	1926–	Heil 2001; Pihlström 2005; Auxier & Hahn 2013

Thinker	Dates	Accounts of life and work, biographies, chronologies
Quine, W. V.	1908–2000	Quine 1985, 1986; Schilpp & Hahn 1986/1998; Føllesdal 2001; Hylton 2001b, 2007a, 2010; Lepore 2005b
Ramsey, Frank P.	1903–30	Sahlin 1990; Armendt 2001; Cave 2006c
Rawls, John	1921–2002	Daniels 2001; Boettcher 2005; Pogge 2007
Reichenbach, Hans	1891–1953	Traiger 2005; Hoffmann 2007
Rickert, Heinrich	1863–1936	Faust 1927; Ollig 1998
Rorty, Richard	1931–2007	Williams 2001; Rumana 2005; Ramberg 2007; Gross 2008; Auxier & Hahn 2010; Rorty 2010
Ross, W. D.	1877–1971	Stratton-Lake 2006b
Russell, Bertrand	1872–1970	Russell 1944, 1959a, 1975; Schilpp 1944; Schoenman 1967; Clark 1975; Tait 1975; Moorehead 1992; Monk 1996a, 2000; Baldwin 2001b
Ryle, Gilbert	1900–76	Stroll 2001; Sprague 2006
Santayana, George	1863–1952	Santayana 1940, 1944; Schilpp 1940; Holzberger 2005; Saatkamp 2010
Sartre, Jean-Paul	1905–80	Sartre 1981; Schilpp 1981; Flynn 2011
Schiller, F. C. S.	1864–1937	Shook 2006
Schlick, Moritz	1882–1936	Haller 1982
Schopenhauer, Arthur	1788–1860	Wicks 2011a
Searle, John R.	1932–	Martinich 2001b; Elugardo 2005
Sellars, Wilfrid	1912–89	Rosenberg 2001, 2009; Delaney 2005; deVries 2011
Sidgwick, Henry	1838–1900	Schultz 2004; Skelton 2006
Skinner, B. F.	1904–90	Bjork 1997; Rutherford 2005
Stebbing, L. Susan	1885–1943	Beaney 2006e; Chapman 2013
Stegmüller, Wolfgang	1923–91	Kleinknecht 1993
Stevenson, Charles	1908–79	Dreier 2001; Stroh 2005
Stout, George F.	1860–1944	Keene 2006b; Schaar 2013
Strawson, Peter F.	1919–2006	Strawson 1998; Hahn 1998; Snowdon 2001; Shieber 2006
Tarski, Alfred	1901–83	Anderson 2001; Feferman & Feferman 2004; Anellis 2005c; Patterson 2012
Trendelenburg, Friedrich	1802–72	Morris 1874
Turing, Alan	1912–54	Hodges 1983, 2007
Twardowski, Kazimierz	1866–1938	Woleński 1989, 2011; Lapointe *et al.* 2009
Vlastos, Gregory	1907–91	Graham 2005
von Wright, Georg Henrik	1916–2003	Schilpp & Hahn 1989; von Wright 1989; Stoutland 2001
Waismann, Friedrich	1896–1959	Ellis 2006a
Watson, John B.	1879–1958	Cohen 1979; Buckley 1989
White, Morton	1917–	White 1999; Føllesdal 2005
Whitehead, A. N.	1861–1947	Whitehead 1941; Schilpp 1941; Lowe 1985–90; Lucas 2005; Weber 2006

(Continued)

Thinker	Dates	Accounts of life and work, biographies, chronologies
Wiggins, David	1933–	S. Williams 2006
Williams, Bernard	1929–2003	Cullity 2005
Wilson, John Cook	1849–1915	Marion 2006b, 2010
Windelband, Wilhelm	1848–1915	Rickert 1915; Ollig 1998
Wisdom, John	1904–93	Bambrough 1974; Ellis 2006b
Wittgenstein, Ludwig	1889–1951	Malcolm 1958/1984; Rhees 1981; McGuinness 1988; Monk 1990; Flowers 1999; Hacker 2001c
Wright, Crispin	1942–	Byrne 2006
Wundt, Wilhelm	1832–1920	Kim 2006

Information about the founding of the following 40 philosophy journals is also included: *Analysis* (1933), *Analytic Philosophy* (1960, as *Philosophical Books*; name changed 2011), *Archiv für Geschichte der Philosophie* (1888), *Australasian Journal of Philosophy* (1923), *British Journal of Aesthetics* (1960), *British Journal for the History of Philosophy* (1993), *British Journal for the Philosophy of Science* (1950), *Canadian Journal of Philosophy* (1971), *Dialectica* (1947), *Erkenntnis* (1930/1975), *Ethics* (1890, as *International Journal of Ethics*; name changed 1938), *European Journal of Philosophy* (1993), *Grazer Philosophische Studien* (1975), *History and Philosophy of Logic* (1980), *History of Philosophy Quarterly* (1984), *Inquiry* (1958), *Journal of the British Society for Phenomenology* (1970), *Journal for the History of Analytical Philosophy* (2010), *Journal of the History of Ideas* (1940), *Journal of the History of Philosophy* (1963), *Journal of Philosophical Logic* (1972), *Journal of Philosophy* (1904), *Journal of Symbolic Logic* (1936), *Mind* (1876/1892), *Mind and Language* (1986), *The Monist* (1888), *Noûs* (1967), *Pacific Philosophical Quarterly* (1920, as *The Personalist*; name changed 1980), *Philosophers' Imprint* (2001), *Philosophical Perspectives* (1987), *Philosophical Quarterly* (1950), *Philosophical Review* (1891), *Philosophical Studies* (1950), *Philosophy and Phenomenological Research* (1940), *Philosophy of Science* (1934), *Proceedings of the Aristotelian Society* (1888/1900), *Ratio* (1957/1988), *Russell* (1971/1981), *Synthese* (1936), *Theoria* (1935). (This is not to be taken as reflecting a judgement on the 'top 40' journals; they have been selected for their significance in the history of analytic philosophy.)

In compiling this chronology, I have drawn especially on *The Continuum Encyclopedia of British Philosophy* (Grayling, Pyle, and Goulder 2006), *The Dictionary of Modern American Philosophers* (Shook 2005), and the online *Stanford Encyclopedia of Philosophy*. I have also made use of the various Cambridge Companions, the volumes in 'The Library of Living Philosophers' series, the biobibliographical appendix to *The Cambridge History of Philosophy 1870–1945* (Baldwin 2003), and the *Routledge Encyclopedia of Philosophy* (Craig 1998). For the Frege entries, I drew on the more detailed chronology in Thiel and Beaney 2005, and for the Russell entries, the chronologies in each volume of Russell's *Collected Papers* (1983–).

I have made no attempt to do justice to work in analytic philosophy after (roughly) 1980. This is not only because the sheer amount of work being published is unsurveyable except in specific subfields, but also because it takes at least 30 years for the dust to settle to allow significance to be recognized. What I have focused on instead is selecting key works in the emerging subfield of analytic philosophy that is history of analytic philosophy. In selecting the entries I have been guided by the contributions to the present Handbook and by further recommendations sent to me by several of the contributors.[1] While I have tried to avoid factual mistakes by minimizing reliance on any single source, there will inevitably be embarrassing errors, egregious omissions, controversial inclusions, and idiosyncratic comments, and I can only hope that these will be outweighed by the usefulness of the chronology (which helped me in writing the first two chapters). Analytic philosophy has become increasingly complex in its ramifications, and historians of analytic philosophy have become increasingly aware of the broader context, so there is value in simply juxtaposing key events and publications in such a condensed way to provide a sense of the bigger picture, and to indicate some of the gaps in existing accounts, including in the present Handbook. (That said, I should note that I have not sought to include anything about the extra-philosophical context other than a few developments in mathematics and science; so there is nothing on artistic, literary, or political events, for example. That would have taken up even more months of my life.) Whatever its deficiencies may be, I hope that this chronology can at least provide a basis for adapted and revised versions to assist future work in history of analytic philosophy.

Year	Event	Further details and/or significance
1781	Kant, *Critique of Pure Reason*	• the work to which much subsequent philosophy responds • 2nd edn. 1787
	Birth of Bernard Bolzano	• 5 October, Prague
1784	Kant, 'An Answer to the Question: "What is Enlightenment?"'	• '*Sapere aude!* Have courage to use your *own* understanding!' (1784 [1991], p. 54)
1788	**Birth of Arthur Schopenhauer**	• 22 February, Danzig, Prussia (now Gdansk, Poland)
1802	**Birth of Friedrich Trendelenburg**	• 30 November, Eutin, near Lübeck
1804	**Death of Kant**	• 12 February, Königsberg, Prussia (now Kaliningrad)
1806	**Birth of John Stuart Mill**	• 20 May, Pentonville, London
1807	Hegel, *Phenomenology of Spirit*	• his first main work
1808	Herbart, *Main Points of Logic*	• criticizes Kant's table of judgements
1809	**Birth of Charles Darwin**	• 12 February, Shrewsbury, Shropshire
1810	Bolzano, *Contributions...*	• criticizes Kant's a priori/a posteriori distinction in offering a better grounded account of mathematics
1813	Herbart, *Textbook Introducing Philosophy*	• rejects psychologism
1815	**Birth of George Boole**	• 2 November, Lincoln

[1] I would especially like to thank Annalisa Coliva, Sean Crawford, Julia Driver, Gottfried Gabriel, and Sanford Shieh.

(Continued)

Year	Event	Further details and/or significance
1817	**Birth of Hermann Lotze**	• 21 May, Bautzen, Saxony
1818	**Birth of Karl Marx**	• 5 May, Trier
1819	Schopenhauer, *The World as Will and Representation*	• 2nd edn. 1844; 3rd edn. 1859 • first tr. 1883
1820	**Birth of Friedrich Engels**	• 28 November, Barmen, Rhineland
1821	**Birth of Hermann von Helmholtz**	• 31 August, Potsdam
1831	**Birth of Richard Dedekind**	• 6 October, Braunschweig
	Death of Hegel	• 14 November, Berlin
1832	**Birth of Wilhelm Wundt**	• 16 August, Neckarau, Mannheim
1833	**Birth of Wilhelm Dilthey**	• 19 November, Biebrich, Wiesbaden
1836	**Birth of Thomas H. Green**	• 7 April, Birkin, Yorkshire
1837	Bolzano, *Theory of Science*	• his main work, 4 vols.
1838	Bentham, *Works*	• 11 vols. 1838–43
	Birth of Ernst Mach	• 18 February, Chrlice, near Brno, Moravia
	Birth of Henry Sidgwick	• 31 May, Skipton, Yorkshire
	Birth of Franz Brentano	• 16 June, Marienberg am Rhein, Germany
1839	**Birth of Charles S. Peirce**	• 10 September, Cambridge, Massachusetts
1840	Trendelenburg, *Logical Investigations*	• offers an 'organic' view of logic • 2nd edn. 1862; 3rd edn. 1870
1841	**Death of Herbart**	• 14 August, Göttingen, Germany
1842	**Birth of William James**	• 11 January, New York
1843	Mill, *System of Logic*	• his main work; 2nd edn. 1846; 3rd edn. 1851; 4th edn. 1856; 5th edn. 1862; 6th edn. 1865; 7th edn. 1868; 8th edn. 1872
	Lotze, *Logic*	• his 'lesser' *Logic*; expanded version 1874 • distinguishes logical validity from psychological genesis
1844	Lotze succeeds Herbart	• Professor, Göttingen 1844–80
	Birth of Ludwig Boltzmann	• 20 February, Vienna
	Birth of Thomas Case	• 14 July, Liverpool
	Birth of Friedrich Nietzsche	• 15 October, Röcken, Saxony
1845	**Birth of Georg Cantor**	• 3 March, St Petersburg, Russia
1846	**Birth of F. H. Bradley**	• 30 January, Clapham, London
1847	Boole, *The Mathematical Analysis of Logic*	• treats Aristotelian logic algebraically
	Helmholtz, *On the Conservation of Force*	• formulates law of conservation of energy
1848	Marx and Engels, *Communist Manifesto*	• opens with claim that the history of all society is the history of class struggles
	Birth of Wilhelm Windelband	• 11 May, Potsdam
	Birth of Gottlob Frege	• 8 November, Wismar, Germany
	Death of Bolzano	• 18 December, Prague
1849	**Birth of John Cook Wilson**	• 6 June, Nottingham

Year	Event	Further details and/or significance
1850	Přihonský, *New Anti-Kant*	• expounds Bolzano's critique of Kant
1851	Bolzano, *Paradoxes of the Infinite*	• anticipates some ideas of later set theory
1853	**Birth of Alexius Meinong**	• 17 July, Lemberg (later Lvov, now Lviv, Ukraine)
1854	Boole, *The Laws of Thought*	• develops his algebra of logic further
	Dedekind, 'On the Introduction of New Functions in Mathematics'	• announces programme of explaining generation of numbers • lecture for his *Habilitation*
	Birth of Henri Poincaré	• 29 April, Nancy
1856	Trendelenburg, *On Leibniz's Design for a Universal Characteristic*	• uses term 'Begriffsschrift'
	Birth of Sigmund Freud	• 6 May, Freiberg in Mähren, Moravia
1857	**Birth of Heinrich Hertz**	• 22 February, Hamburg
1858	**Birth of Giuseppe Peano**	• 27 August, Spinetta, Piedmont, Italy
1859	Darwin, *The Origin of Species*	• theory of evolution
	Mill, 'On Liberty'	• argues for freedom of speech • formulates harm principle
	Birth of Samuel Alexander	• 6 January, Sydney, Australia
	Birth of Edmund Husserl	• 8 April, Prossnitz, Moravia
	Birth of Henri Bergson	• 18 October, Paris
	Birth of John Dewey	• 20 October, Burlington, Vermont
1860	**Birth of George F. Stout**	• 6 January, South Shields, Durham
	Death of Schopenhauer	• 21 September, Frankfurt
1861	Mill, 'Utilitarianism'	• based on 'greatest happiness principle'
	Birth of A. N. Whitehead	• 15 February, Ramsgate, Kent
	Birth of Pierre Duhem	• 10 June, Paris
1862	**Birth of David Hilbert**	• 23 January, Königsberg, Prussia (now Kaliningrad)
1863	**Birth of Heinrich Rickert**	• 25 May, Danzig, Prussia (now Gdansk, Poland)
	Birth of George Santayana	• 16 December, Madrid
1864	**Birth of F. C. S. Schiller**	• 16 August, Schleswig-Holstein, Denmark
	Death of Boole	• 8 December, Ballintemple, Cork, Ireland
1865	Carroll, *Alice's Adventures in Wonderland*	• *Through the Looking-Glass and what Alice found there* 1872
	Stirling, *The Secret of Hegel*	• beginning of Hegelian turn in Britain
1866	Green at Oxford	• Fellow, Balliol College 1866–78
	Birth of J. M. E. McTaggart	• 3 September, London
	Birth of Kazimierz Twardowski	• 20 October, Vienna
1867	Marx, *Capital*, vol. 1	• his main work; vol. 2 1885; vol. 3 1894
	Mach to Prague	• Professor of Experimental Physics 1867–95
1868	**Birth of Harold H. Joachim**	• 28 May, London
	Birth of Axel Hägerström	• 6 September, Vireda, near Jönköping, Sweden
1869	Frege to Jena	• studies mathematics, physics, chemistry, philosophy, 4 semesters

Year	Event	Further details and/or significance
1870	Peirce, 'Description of a Notation for the Logic of Relatives'	• invention of quantifier notation
	Helmholtz, 'On the Origin and Significance of the Axioms of Geometry'	• discusses implications of non-Euclidean geometries • influences logical positivists
	Bradley at Oxford	• Fellow, Merton College; stays there for the rest of his life
1871	Cohen, *Kant's Theory of Experience*	• neo-Kantian interpretation from the Marburg School
	Frege to Göttingen	• studies mathematics, physics, philosophy of religion (with Lotze), 5 semesters
	Birth of Harold A. Prichard	• 31 October, London
1872	Dedekind, *Continuity and Irrational Numbers*	• defines real numbers in terms of 'cuts' in the series of rational numbers
	Boltzmann, 'Further Studies…'	• formulates Boltzmann equation and H-theorem (as now known), offering 'analytical proof' of second law of thermodynamics
	Death of Trendelenburg	• 24 January, Berlin
	Birth of Bertrand Russell	• 18 May, Ravenscroft, Monmouthshire, Wales
1873	Frege's doctorate	• 'On a Geometrical Representation of Imaginary Forms in the Plane', Göttingen
	Sigwart, *Logic*	• 2nd edn. 1878; 3rd edn. 1904
	Death of Mill	• 8 May, Avignon, France
	Birth of G. E. Moore	• 4 November, London
1874	Lotze, *Logic*	• vol. 1, in 3 books, of his *System of Philosophy* • his 'greater' *Logic*: expanded version of 1843 *Logic*
	Brentano, *Psychology from an Empirical Standpoint*	• seeks to establish a science of mental phenomena • vol. 2 repr. 1911
	Sidgwick, *The Methods of Ethics*	• discusses rational egoism, dogmatic intuitionism, and utilitarianism, and offers a qualified defence of latter
	Wundt, *Principles of Physiological Psychology*	• seeks to investigate the inner experiences of consciousness through direct self-observation • described as 'the most important book in the history of modern psychology' (Boring 1950, p. 322)
	Cantor, 'On a Property of the Set of Real Algebraic Numbers'	• first proof that the class of real numbers is not countable • beginning of theory of the transfinite
	Green, 'Introductions'	• introds. to his edition (with Grose) of Hume's *Treatise* • attacks 'the popular philosophy' of empiricism
	Frege's *Habilitation*	• 'Methods of Calculation based on an Extension of the Concept of Magnitude'
	Nietzsche, 'On the Uses and Disadvantages of History for Life'	• distinguishes monumental, antiquarian, and critical history • argues that history should serve life and action
	Bradley, 'The Presuppositions of Critical History'	• argues that historical facts are constructs • influences Collingwood

Year	Event	Further details and/or significance
	Frege to Jena	• returns to teach analytic geometry, theory of functions, and later, analytic mechanics; stays for rest of his career
	Brentano to Vienna	• Professor 1874–80; Privatdozent 1880–95
	Birth of Ernst Cassirer	• 28 July, Breslau, now in Poland
1875	America's first psychology laboratory	• founded by W. James at Harvard
1876	Bradley, *Ethical Studies*	• includes 'My Station and its Duties'
	Founding of *Mind*	• subtitled 'A Quarterly Review of Psychology and Philosophy' (ref. to psychology dropped in 1974) • founded and funded by Alexander Bain (cf. Sorley 1926) • first editor George Croom Robertson 1876–91 • first philosophy journal in Britain and longest-running English-language philosophy journal in the world
	Birth of Ralph Barton Perry	• 3 July, Poultney, Vermont
1877	Peirce, 'Illustrations of the Logic of Science'	• 6 essays pub. in *Popular Science Monthly* 1877–8 • 1st: 'The Fixation of Belief' • 2nd: 'How to Make Our Ideas Clear'
	Birth of W. D. Ross	• 15 April, Thurso, Scotland
1878	Meinong's *Habilitation*	• on Hume, supervised by Brentano
	Green at Oxford	• White's Professor of Moral Philosophy 1878–82
	Birth of Jan Łukasiewicz	• 21 December, Lwów, Galicia (now Lviv, Ukraine)
1879	Frege, *Begriffsschrift*	• inaugurates modern logic by applying function-argument analysis from mathematics, developing his 'Begriffsschrift' ('concept-script') • axiomatizes propositional logic; constructs first system of predicate logic by introducing quantifier notation (independently of Peirce) • lectures on his new logical system, a course he then offers most years until he retires in 1918
	Germany's first psychology laboratory	• Institute for Experimental Psychology founded by Wundt at Leipzig
	Johannes Thomae to Jena	• Professor of Mathematics • maintains good relations with Frege until mid-1900s, when they dispute over formalist theories of arithmetic
	Birth of John B. Watson	• 9 January, Travelers Rest, South Carolina
	Birth of Albert Einstein	• 14 March, Ulm, Germany
1880	Founding of the Aristotelian Society	• first meeting 3 May, Bloomsbury (see Carr 1929) • President Shadworth H. Hodgson 1880–94
	Lotze to Berlin	• Professor 1880–1
1881	**Birth of L. E. J. Brouwer**	• 27 February, Overshie, Rotterdam
	Death of Lotze	• 1 July, Berlin
1882	Windelband, 'What is Philosophy?'	• argues that philosophy should be critical philosophy (in Kantian sense)

(Continued)

Year	Event	Further details and/or significance
	Meinong to Graz	• Professor; remains until his death in 1920
	Death of Green	• 15 March, Oxford
	Birth of Moritz Schlick	• 14 April, Berlin
	Death of Darwin	• 19 April, Downe, Kent
	Birth of Otto Neurath	• 10 December, Vienna
1883	Bradley, *The Principles of Logic*	• rejects empiricist view of judgement
	Cantor, *Foundations of a General Theory of Manifolds*	• fullest account of the underlying ideas of his theory of the transfinite
	Green, *Prolegomena to Ethics*	• argues that knowledge of nature presupposes an a priori or spiritual principle
	Seth & Haldane, eds., *Essays in Philosophical Criticism*	• provides manifesto of neo-Hegelianism • dedicated to Green
	Dilthey, *Introduction to the Human Sciences*	• introduces idea of the *Geisteswissenschaften*
	Windelband, 'Critical or Genetic Method?'	• distinguishes critical method of philosophy from genetic method of psychology and history
	Mach, *Mechanics*	• a critical and historical account of its development
	Sidgwick at Cambridge	• Knightbridge Professor of Moral Philosophy 1883–1900, when he resigns due to ill health
	Death of Marx	• 14 March, London
	Birth of C. I. Lewis	• 12 April, Stoneham, Massachusetts
1884	Frege, *The Foundations of Arithmetic*	• criticizes previous views of arithmetic and outlines his own logicist view—that arithmetic is reducible to logic • not pub. in English until 1950
	Keynes, *Studies and Exercises in Formal Logic*	• exposition of Aristotelian logic • revised and enlarged 1887, 1894, 1906
	Stout at Cambridge	• Fellow, St John's College 1884–96
	Whitehead at Cambridge	• Fellow in Mathematics, Trinity College 1884–1910
1885	Kerry, series of articles	• 8 parts 1885–91; discusses Bolzano and Frege
	Birth of L. Susan Stebbing	• 2 December, London
1886	Mach, *The Analysis of Sensations*	• naturalist account of the dynamic relationship between experience and (a priori) cognitive structures
	Nietzsche, *Beyond Good and Evil*	• first section 'On the Prejudices of Philosophers'
	Ward, 'Psychology'	• influential Encyclopedia article
	Birth of Stanisław Leśniewski	• 30 March, Serphukhov, near Moscow
	Birth of Tadeusz Kotarbiński	• 31 March, Warsaw
1887	Nietzsche, *On the Genealogy of Morals*	• develops critique of Christianity • §12 of third essay: statement of his perspectivism
	Brentano, 'Descriptive Psychology'	• lectures, Vienna 1887–91; first pub. 1982 • distinguishes descriptive from genetic psychology
	Birth of C. D. Broad	• 30 December, Harlesden, London

Year	Event	Further details and/or significance
1888	Dedekind, *What are the numbers and what are they for?*	• seeks to reduce arithmetic to 'logic', i.e., set theory • defines both natural numbers and a notion of infinity • formulates (Dedekind-)Peano axioms, as now called
	Case, *Physical Realism*	• early statement of Oxford realism • subtitled 'An analytical philosophy from the physical objects of science to the physical data of sense'
	Founding of *Proceedings of the Aristotelian Society*	• first symposium of Aristotelian Society on 'Is Mind Synonymous with Consciousness?'
	Founding of *The Monist*	• founding editor Edward C. Hegeler • first issue 1890
	Founding of *Archiv für Geschichte der Philosophie*	• founding editor Ludwig Stein • first article by Zeller (1888), Berlin
1889	Peano, 'The principles of arithmetic…'	• formulation of (Dedekind-)Peano axioms
	Cook Wilson succeeds Thomas Fowler	• Wykeham Professor of Logic, Oxford 1889–1915
	Thomas Case at Oxford	• Waynflete Professor of Moral and Metaphysical Philosophy 1889–1910
	Santayana at Harvard	• Professor 1889–1912, when he retires early to live and write in Europe
	Birth of R. G. Collingwood	• 22 February, Cartmel Fell, Lancashire
	Birth of Ludwig Wittgenstein	• 26 April, Vienna
	Birth of Martin Heidegger	• 26 September, Meßkirch, Germany
1890	James, *The Principles of Psychology*	• his main work
	Founding of *International Journal of Ethics*	• founding editor S. Burns Weston 1890–1914 (Tufts 1923) • became *Ethics: An International Journal of Social, Political, and Legal Philosophy* in 1938
	Russell to Cambridge	• Trinity College; BA in Mathematics 1893; Moral Sciences Part II 1894
	Birth of Kazimierz Ajdukiewicz	• 12 December, Ternopil, Galicia (now in Ukraine)
1891	Frege, 'Function und Concept'	• lecture given 9 January • explains his conception of concepts as functions • first draws distinction between sense and reference
	Husserl, *Philosophy of Arithmetic*	• criticizes Frege's *Foundations* • sends Frege a copy in April/May, prompting an exchange of letters; they correspond again 1906–7
	Cantor, 'On an Elementary Question in the Theory of Manifolds'	• first appearance of 'diagonal argument' for the existence of non-denumerable sets • cardinality of power set $\wp(X)$ > cardinality of set X
	Mind changes hands	• Sidgwick takes over financial support • Stout becomes editor, 1891–1920 • new series begun, 1892 onwards

(Continued)

Year	Event	Further details and/or significance
	Founding of *Philosophical Review*	• part of endowment of Sage School of Philosophy, Cornell • founding editor Jacob Gould Schurman; first issue 1892
	Founding of *Rivista di matematica*	• founding editor Peano
	Birth of Rudolf Carnap	• 18 May, Ronsdorf, Germany
	Birth of Hans Reichenbach	• 26 September, Hamburg
1892	Frege, 'On Sense and Reference'	• classic account of distinction
	Frege, 'On Concept and Object'	• defends absolute distinction between concept and object • last of his three seminal papers of 1891–2
	Rickert, *The Object of Knowledge*	• sees acknowledgement of truth value as expression of a 'will to truth'
	Moore to Cambridge	• studies classics and then philosophy; meets Russell
	Cassirer at Berlin	• studies 1892–6
1893	Frege, *Basic Laws of Arithmetic*, vol. 1	• his main work, seeking to formally demonstrate logicism; vol. 2 1903 • selections first tr. into English 1915–17; further trs. 1952, 1964; no complete tr. until 2013
	Bradley, *Appearance and Reality*	• fullest development of his absolute idealism • argues for the unreality of relations
	McTaggart, *A Further Determination of the Absolute*	• his first (short) work, outlining neo-Hegelian programme
	Alexander to Manchester	• Samuel Hall Professor of Philosophy 1893–1924, when he retires
	Boltzmann to Vienna	• Professor of Theoretical Physics 1893–1906
	Hägerström at Uppsala	• teaches; Professor 1911–33 • founds Uppsala School of Philosophy and Scandinavian legal realist tradition
	Birth of John Anderson	• 1 November, Stonehouse, near Glasgow
1894	Twardowski, *On the Content and Object of Presentations*	• *Habilitationsschrift*, Vienna; most influential work • reworks Bolzano's content/object distinction in a Brentanian framework • reviewed by Stout (1894)
	Frege, review of Husserl	• criticizes Husserl's *Philosophy of Arithmetic* • helps convert Husserl to anti-psychologism
	Poincaré, 'On the Nature of Mathematical Reasoning'	• rejects (logicist) view that mathematical induction can be analysed purely logically
	Dilthey, 'Ideas for a Descriptive and Analytic Psychology'	• distinguishes natural sciences from human sciences (*Geisteswissenschaften*) • psychology included in latter
	Hertz, *The Principles of Mechanics*	• geometrizes mechanics to eliminate forces
	Death of Hertz	• 1 January, Bonn
	Death of Helmholtz	• 8 September, Charlottenburg, Germany

Year	Event	Further details and/or significance
1895	Russell, 'The Foundations of Geometry'	• Cambridge Fellowship dissertation, awarded 10 October • refashions a Kantian view in light of non-Euclidean geometry • rev. and pub. 1897; reviewed by Moore (1899b)
	Peano, *Formulaire de Mathématiques*, vol. 1	• vol. 2 1897–9; vol. 3 1901; vol. 4 1903
	Lewis Carroll, 'What the Tortoise said to Achilles'	• presents paradox of inference • distinguishes between assumption and rule of inference
	Frege meets Hilbert in Lübeck	• talks on Peano's notation at a convention in September • writes to Hilbert 1 October, prompting a dispute over the foundations of geometry
	Hilbert to Göttingen	• Professor of Mathematics 1895–1930, when he retires
	Mach to Vienna	• Professor of the History and Philosophy of the Inductive Sciences 1895–1901, when he retires
	Twardowski to Lvov	• Professor 1895–1930, when he retires • founds Lvov School, later known (after First World War) as Lvov–Warsaw School
	Death of Engels	• 5 August, London
1896	Stout, *Analytic Psychology*	• analytic distinguished from genetic psychology • theory of thought reference
	Bergson, *Matter and Memory*	• tr. 1911; discussed by Russell (1912c)
	McTaggart, *Studies in the Hegelian Dialectic*	• first of his books on Hegel
	Santayana, *The Sense of Beauty*	• offers naturalistic account
	Hobhouse, *Theory of Knowledge*	• develops perceptual realism
	Rickert, *The Limits of Concept Formation in Natural Science*	• subtitled 'A Logical Introduction to the Historical Sciences' • 1st vol.; 2nd vol. 1902
	Founding of chair at Cambridge	• Professorship of Mental Philosophy and Logic • first holder: James Ward 1897
	Stout to Aberdeen	• Anderson Lecturer in Comparative Psychology 1896–9
	Cassirer to Marburg	• Ph.D. with Cohen 1896–9; pub. as introduction to book on Leibniz (1902)
	Birth of Friedrich Waismann	• 21 March, Vienna
1897	Moore, 'The Metaphysical Basis of Ethics'	• Cambridge Fellowship dissertation, unsuccessful in 1897 • revised 1898, successful; Fellow 1898–1904
	McTaggart at Cambridge	• Lecturer in Moral Sciences, Trinity College 1897–1923
	Łukasiewicz at Lwów	• begins university, studying with Twardowski • Lecturer 1906, Professor 1911–15

(Continued)

Year	Event	Further details and/or significance
1898	Stout, *A Manual of Psychology*	• genetic approach (unlike Stout 1896) • theory of embodied self • becomes standard textbook; 5th edn. 1938
	Whitehead, *A Treatise on Universal Algebra*	• comparative study of algebras
	Russell, 'An Analysis of Mathematical Reasoning'	• formulates a 'contradiction of relativity' which depends on doctrine of internal relations
	Moore, 'The Elements of Ethics'	• lectures given in London; form basis of first 3 chapters of *Principia Ethica*
1899	Moore, 'The Nature of Judgment'	• first published rejection of Bradley's idealism • naïve realism asserted instead • discussed by Ryle (1970b)
	Russell, draft of *Principles of Mathematics*	• rejects doctrine of internal relations to avoid contradictions in mathematics (see 1899/1900, p. 93)
	Meinong, 'On Objects of Higher Order...'	• distinguishes between object and mental content • discussed by Russell (1904a)
	Hilbert, *Foundations of Geometry*	• develops axiomatic approach • approach discussed further in Hilbert 1918
	Freud, *The Interpretation of Dreams*	• presents his theory of dreams as unconscious wish-fulfilments
	Stout to Oxford	• first Wilde Reader in Mental Philosophy 1899–1903
	Birth of Henry H. Price	• 17 May, Neath, Wales
1900	Russell, *A Critical Exposition of the Philosophy of Leibniz*	• first work of 'analytic' history of philosophy • seeks to show that Leibniz's philosophy follows from just five premises, which also generate inconsistencies • distinguishes two conceptions of history of philosophy, one 'mainly historical', the other 'mainly philosophical' • reviewed by Cassirer (1902)
	Husserl, *Logical Investigations*	• vol. 1 (*Prolegomena*) long critique of psychologism • vol. 2 1901
	Moore, 'Necessity'	• reduces necessity to relative logical priority
	Hilbert, 'On the Concept of Number'	• applies axiomatic method to number theory • distinguishes axiomatic from genetic method
	Hilbert, 'Mathematical Problems'	• address to International Congress of Mathematicians, Paris, where he presents his 23 unsolved problems, incl. continuum hypothesis and consistency of arithmetic
	Bergson, *Laughter*	• brings up the rire?
	Russell meets Peano	• International Congress of Philosophy, Paris, August • 'a turning point in my intellectual life' (1975, p. 147) • learns new logic and begins to develop logic of relations • September 'the highest point of my life' (1975, p. 148)
	William Ritchie Sorley succeeds Sidgwick	• Knightbridge Professor of Moral Philosophy, Cambridge • Sorley, an idealist, retires 1933

Year	Event	Further details and/or significance
	New series of *Proceedings of the Aristotelian Society*	• now pub. annually
	Mind Association founded	• formed on Sidgwick's death to manage *Mind*
	Birth of R. B. Braithwaite	• 15 January, Banbury
	Birth of Hans-Georg Gadamer	• 11 February, Marburg
	Birth of Gilbert Ryle	• 19 August, Brighton
	Death of Nietzsche	• 25 August, Weimar
	Death of Sidgwick	• 28 August, Terling, Essex
1901	Russell, 'The Logic of Relations'	• first fruit of work on new logic (1901a)
	Baldwin, ed., *Dictionary of Philosophy and Psychology*	• highly influential dictionary • 3 vols. 1901–2
	Couturat, *The Logic of Leibniz*	• reviewed by Russell (1903b)
	Mauthner, *Contributions to a Critique of Language*	• 3 vols. on 'Language and Psychology' (1901), 'On Linguistics' (1901), 'On Grammar and Logic' (1902)
	Russell discovers paradox	• first formulation of eponymous paradox (1901b, p. 195)
	Founding of American Philosophical Association	• breakaway from American Psychological Association, founded 1891 (cf. Gardiner 1926; Campbell 2006)
	Birth of Alfred Tarski	• 14 January, Warsaw (born Alfred Tajtelbaum)
	Birth of Ernest Nagel	• 16 November, Vágújhely (now Nové Mesto nad Váhom, Slovakia)
1902	James, *The Varieties of Religious Experience*	• Gifford lectures, Edinburgh 1901–2
	Meinong, *On Assumptions*	• theory of assumptions; 2nd edn. 1910 • discussed by Russell (1904a)
	Brentano, *The Origin of the Knowledge of Right and Wrong*	• first work tr. into English • reviewed by Moore (1903c)
	Cassirer, *Leibniz's System*	• contains review of Russell's book on Leibniz
	Schiller, 'Axioms as Postulates'	• first statement of British pragmatism
	Russell writes to Frege	• having started to read Frege properly, informs Frege on 16 June of the contradiction in his logical system • prompts correspondence over the next two years, with occasional letters later • paradox devastates Frege, eventually leading him to abandon his logicism and concentrate on explaining his logical ideas • Russell develops first theory of types in August
	Perry to Harvard	• teaches; Professor 1913–46, when he retires
	Birth of Karl Popper	• 28 July, Vienna
	Birth of Herbert Feigl	• 14 December, Reichenberg, Bohemia
1903	Frege, *Basic Laws of Arithmetic*, vol. 2	• in press when he received Russell's letter • hastily written appendix responding to Russell's paradox—unsuccessfully, Frege soon realized

(Continued)

Year	Event	Further details and/or significance
	Russell, *The Principles of Mathematics*	• first attempt at a comprehensive account of mathematics • early theory of denoting • app. A: first exposition of Frege's philosophy
	Moore, *Principia Ethica*	• critique of ethical naturalism, focused on the supposed 'naturalistic fallacy'
	Moore, 'The Refutation of Idealism'	• fullest early critique of idealism
	Frege, 'On the Foundations of Geometry: First Series'	• first of Frege's essays on Hilbert's work
	Bergson, 'Introduction to Metaphysics'	• criticizes analysis and valorizes 'intuition' • tr. 1912
	Schiller, *Humanism: Philosophical Essays*	• first collection elaborating his pragmatism • second collection 1907
	Weininger, *Sex and Character*	• distinguishes masculinity and femininity as ideal types • Weininger kills himself a few months after publication
	Stout to St Andrews	• Professor of Logic and Metaphysics 1903–36, when he retires
	Cassirer to Berlin	• *Habilitation* 1903–6; published as Cassirer 1906 • Privatdozent 1906–19
	Birth of Frank P. Ramsey	• 22 February, Cambridge
	Birth of Alonzo Church	• 14 June, Washington, DC
1904	Russell, 'Meinong's Theory of Complexes and Assumptions'	• critique of Meinong 1899 and 1902 • Stout had recommended the former to Russell and Meinong had sent him the latter
	Meinong, 'On the Theory of Objects'	• reviewed by Russell (1905b)
	Stout, 'Primary and Secondary Qualities'	• defends form of representative realism
	Founding of *The Journal of Philosophy*	• original title 'The Journal of Philosophy, Psychology, and Scientific Methods'; changed 1923 • founding editors Frederick J. E. Woodbridge and J. McKeen Cattell; pub. Columbia University
	Birth of B. F. Skinner	• 20 March, Susquehanna, Pennsylvania
	Birth of John Wisdom	• 12 September, London
1905	Russell, 'On Denoting'	• first formulation of theory of descriptions • a 'paradigm of philosophy', as Ramsey later called it
	Einstein, *annus mirabilis* papers	• on photoelectric effect, Brownian motion, special theory of relativity, and $E = mc^2$
	Santayana, *The Life of Reason*	• offers naturalistic account of reason in common sense, society, religion, art, science; 5 vols. 1905–6 • 'Those who cannot remember the past are condemned to repeat it' (I, p. 284)
	Mach, *Knowledge and Error*	• subtitled 'Sketches on the Psychology of Enquiry'
	Birth of Carl Hempel	• 8 January, Oranienburg, near Berlin
	Birth of Jean-Paul Sartre	• 21 June, Paris

Year	Event	Further details and/or significance
1906	Frege, 'On the Foundations of Geometry: Second Series'	• second and much longer of Frege's essays on Hilbert's work
	Joachim, *The Nature of Truth*	• criticizes correspondence theory, and offers qualified defence of coherence theory (in idealist tradition) • criticizes Russell's early view in ch. 2
	Joseph, *An Introduction to Logic*	• exposition of traditional Aristotelian logic
	MacColl, *Symbolic Logic*	• summary of his logic, including systems of modal logic • reviewed by Russell (1906)
	Duhem, *The Aim and Structure of Physical Theory*	• formulates Duhem thesis, as now known, that theory is underdetermined by empirical fact • criticizes idea of crucial experiments • 2nd edn. 1914; tr. 1954
	Correspondence between Frege and Husserl	• second exchange of letters October 1906–January 1907
	Wittgenstein to Berlin	• studies mechanical engineering at the Technische Hochschule, 3 semesters
	Birth of Kurt Gödel	• 28 April, Brünn (now Brno), Moravia
	Birth of Gustav Bergmann	• 4 May, Vienna
	Birth of William Kneale	• 22 June, Liverpool
	Birth of Nelson Goodman	• 7 August, Somerville, Massachusetts
	Death of Boltzmann	• 5 September, Duino, near Trieste, Italy
1907	James, *Pragmatism*	• subtitled 'A New Name for Some Old Ways of Thinking' • discussed by Moore (1907), Russell (1908b, 1909)
	Russell, 'The Regressive Method…'	• paper given at Cambridge Mathematical Club, 9 March
	Birth of H. L. A. Hart	• 18 July, Harrogate, Yorkshire
	Birth of Gregory Vlastos	• 27 July, Istanbul
1908	Russell, 'Mathematical Logic as Based on the Theory of Types'	• develops theory of types to solve the logical and semantic paradoxes • formulates the Vicious Circle Principle
	Poincaré, *Science and Method*	• part 2: 'Mathematical Reasoning' • criticizes Cantor, Couturat, Russell, Hilbert
	Brouwer, 'The unreliability of the logical principles'	• first publication of argument against law of excluded middle
	McTaggart, 'The Unreality of Time'	• argues for the unreality of time by distinguishing A-series and B-series
	Birth of Maurice Merleau-Ponty	• 14 March, Rochefort-sur-Mer
	Birth of W. V. O. Quine	• 25 June, Akron, Ohio
	Birth of C. L. Stevenson	• 27 June, Cincinnati, Ohio
1909	Prichard, *Kant's Theory of Knowledge*	• argues that knowledge is *sui generis* and that there can be no 'theory' of knowledge
	Wittgenstein to Manchester	• studies aeronautical engineering • becomes interested in foundations of mathematics • reads Russell 1903, Frege 1893/1903; tries to solve Russell's paradox

(Continued)

Year	Event	Further details and/or significance
	Brouwer at Amsterdam	• teaches; Professor 1912–51, when he retires
	Birth of Max Black	• 24 February, Baku, then in Russia
	Birth of Isaiah Berlin	• 6 June, Riga, Latvia
	Birth of Tscha Hung	• 21 October, Anhui, China
1910	Whitehead & Russell, *Principia Mathematica*	• their main work, attempting to demonstrate logicism • vol. 1 December 1910, vol. 2 April 1912, vol. 3 April 1913
	Russell, *Philosophical Essays*	• collection of papers mainly on pragmatism and truth
	Moore, 'Some Main Problems of Philosophy'	• lectures 1910–11; not published until 1953 • talks of 'sense-data'
	Perry, 'The Ego-Centric Predicament'	• criticizes idealism
	Manifesto of American realism	• 'The Program and First Platform of Six Realists': Holt, Marvin, Montague, Perry, Pitkin, and Spaulding
	Cassirer, *Substance und Function*	• critique of empiricist abstractionism, drawing on mathematical logic, especially the notion of function
	Russell at Cambridge	• Lecturer in Logic and the Principles of Mathematics 1910–15
	Carnap studies at Jena	• philosophy, mathematics, physics 1910–14 • attends Frege's course on 'Begriffsschrift', winter semester 1910/11
	Whitehead to London	• UCL 1910–14; Professor of Applied Mathematics, Imperial College, 1914–24
	J. A. Smith succeeds Thomas Case	• Waynflete Professor of Moral and Metaphysical Philosophy, Oxford 1910–35
	Death of James	• 26 August, Chocorua, New Hampshire
	Birth of A. J. Ayer	• 29 October, London
1911	Russell, 'The Basis of Realism'	• clarifies his realism in relation to the manifesto of American realism (Holt *et al.* 1910)
	Russell, 'Knowledge by Acquaintance and Knowledge by Description'	• first formulation of distinction • read to Aris. Soc. 6 March
	Russell, 'Analytic Realism'	• lecture to Société française de philosophie 23 March • analytic realism described as an 'atomic philosophy'
	Russell, 'On the Relation of Universals and Particulars'	• Presidential Address to Aris. Soc., 30 October; attended by Bergson • argues that the division of objects into particulars and universals is fundamental
	Hägerström, 'On the Truth of Moral Propositions'	• defends axiological nihilism, a form of emotivism • inaugural lecture; key event in founding of Uppsala School of Philosophy
	Wittgenstein visits Frege for the first time	• Wittgenstein writes first letter to Frege, outlining his philosophical ideas and asking to visit him • beginning of a correspondence that lasts until 1920 • Frege recommends that Wittgenstein study with Russell

Year	Event	Further details and/or significance
	Moore to Cambridge	• Lecturer 1911–25
	Wittgenstein meets Russell	• 18 October, Cambridge; attends Russell's lectures and has discussions with him
	Broad to St Andrews	• assistant to Stout, then lecturer in Dundee • also holds Cambridge Prize Fellowship, but non-resident
	Bruno Bauch succeeds Otto Liebmann	• Professor of Philosophy, Jena • Bauch interested in Frege's work and later encourages his 'Logical Investigations', pub. in journal Bauch founded: *Beiträge zur Philosophie des deutschen Idealismus*
	C. I. Lewis to Berkeley	• teaches 1911–20
	Birth of J. L. Austin	• 26 March, Lancaster
	Birth of Norman Malcolm	• 11 June, Selden, Kansas
	Death of Dilthey	• 1 October, Seis am Schlern, Italy
1912	Russell, *The Problems of Philosophy*	• Russell's 'shilling shocker', pub. January (completed August 1911) • discusses matter, idealism, knowledge, universals, truth
	Russell, 'On the Notion of Cause'	• Presidential Address to Aris. Soc., 4 November (re-elected for a second year) • argues that the notion of causation is confused
	Lewis, 'Implication and the Algebra of Logic'	• critique of Russell, outlining paradoxes of material implication
	Brouwer, 'Intuitionism and Formalism'	• inaugural lecture 14 October; tr. 1913 • first presentation of intuitionism
	Holt *et al.*, *New Realism*	• cooperative work of the six American realists
	Perry, *Present Philosophical Tendencies*	• subtitled 'a Critical Survey of Naturalism, Idealism, Pragmatism and Realism Together with a Synopsis of the Philosophy of William James'
	Moore, *Ethics*	• shorter restatement of *Principia Ethica*, with a chapter on free will
	Prichard, 'Does Moral Philosophy Rest on a Mistake?'	• argues that the mistake lies in seeking a unifying moral principle • defends a pluralist intuitionism
	Jourdain, 'Gottlob Frege'	• survey of Frege's ideas
	Schiller, *Formal Logic*	• criticizes emphasis on deductive logic
	Russell, 'The Philosophy of Bergson'	• critique of Bergson, whom he had met for the first time on 28 October 1911
	Wittgenstein to Cambridge	• Trinity College, February; works with Russell
	5th International Congress of Mathematicians	• Cambridge, 22–28 August • Russell presides over section on philosophical questions; he had invited Frege, who declined, but Peano attends

(Continued)

Year	Event	Further details and/or significance
	Wittgenstein visits Frege for the second time	• Brunshaupten, on the Mecklenburg coast • discusses the 'complex problem', as he writes to Russell afterwards (2008, p. 36)
	Birth of Wilfrid Sellars	• 20 May, Ann Arbor, Michigan
	Birth of Alan Turing	• 23 June, Paddington, London
	Death of Poincaré	• 17 July, Paris
1913	Wittgenstein, 'Notes on Logic'	• compiled for Russell, October (*Notebooks*, App. 1)
	Russell, 'The Nature of Sense-Data'	• reply (written October 1912) to Dawes Hicks' (1912) critique of Russell 1912b
	Husserl, *Ideas* I	• full title 'Ideas Pertaining to a Pure Phenomenology and to a Phenomenological Philosophy'; first tr. 1931
	Watson, 'Psychology as a Behaviorist Views It'	• behaviourist manifesto
	Wittgenstein criticizes Russell	• Wittgenstein attacks Russell's theory of judgement, May • Russell abandons work on his *Theory of Knowledge*
	Carnap attends Frege's lectures	• 'Begriffsschrift II', summer semester
	Wittgenstein to Norway	• arrives 14 October and stays until June 1914, with a break at Christmas
	Wittgenstein visits Frege for the third time	• has discussions over several days in December
	Birth of H. Paul Grice	• 13 March, Birmingham
1914	Frege, 'Logic in Mathematics'	• lectures which Carnap attends, summer semester • pub. 1969
	Russell, 'On the Nature of Acquaintance'	• pub. in 3 parts in *Monist* • analyses experience as relation of acquaintance between a subject and an object, and criticizes neutral monism
	Russell, 'The Relation of Sense-Data to Physics'	• written January, introducing talk of 'sensibilia' • formulates his 'supreme maxim' that 'logical constructions are to be substituted for inferred entities'
	Russell, *Our Knowledge of the External World*	• Lowell lectures, Harvard, March–April; invited by Perry; meets James and Sheffer; pub. August • argues that all philosophy is logic and extends the method of logical construction
	Moore and Stout debate sense-data	• at Joint Session
	Russell, 'On Scientific Method in Philosophy'	• Herbert Spencer Lecture, Oxford, 18 November • argues that the essence of philosophy is logical analysis
	Wittgenstein, 'Notes dictated to G. E. Moore'	• dictated in Norway, April • pub. as App. 2 of *Notebooks 1914–1916*
	Broad, *Perception, Physics, and Reality*	• based on 1911 Cambridge Prize Fellowship dissertation

Year	Event	Further details and/or significance
	Alexander, 'The Basis of Realism'	• argues for his form of direct realism
	Bradley, *Essays on Truth and Reality*	• collection of his papers, including several on truth
	Watson, *Behavior*	• classic behaviourist work; rev. edn. 1930
	Wittgenstein to Vienna	• returns July and enlists in Austrian army • serves on the Eastern Front, and later on the Italian Front
	Einstein to Berlin	• Professor and Director of the Kaiser Wilhelm Physical Institute 1914–33
	Death of Peirce	• 19 April, Milford, Pennsylvania
	Birth of Arthur N. Prior	• 4 December, Masterton, New Zealand
1915	Russell, 'The Ultimate Constituents of Matter'	• address to Phil. Soc. of Manchester, February • articulates a realism 'not remote' from Alexander 1914
	Selections from Frege's *Basic Laws* translated	• first translation of any of Frege's work • tr. Jourdain and Stachelroth, pub. *Monist* 1915–17
	Stebbing at London	• Bedford College: Lecturer (part-time) 1915; Lecturer 1920; Reader 1927; Professor 1933
	Łukasiewicz to Warsaw	• Professor 1915–44
	Death of Cook Wilson	• 11 August, Oxford
	Death of Windelband	• 22 October, Heidelberg, Germany
1916	Einstein, 'The Foundation of the General Theory of Relativity'	• first full exposition of the theory
	Russell loses lectureship at Cambridge	• dismissed by Trinity College because of opposition to war
	Death of Dedekind	• 12 February, Braunschweig, Germany
	Death of Mach	• 19 February, Vaterstetten, Germany
	Birth of Peter T. Geach	• 29 March, Chelsea, London
	Birth of G. H. von Wright	• 14 June, Helsinki
	Death of Duhem	• 14 September, Cabesprine, near Carcassonne, France
	Birth of Roderick Chisholm	• 27 November, North Attleboro, Massachusetts
1917	Hägerström, *On the Question of the Notion of Law*	• develops theory of valuation combining emotivism and an error theory
	Stebbing meets Moore	• Stebbing reads paper at the Aris. Soc. and is persuaded by Moore that she is wrong • converted to a more Moorean philosophy
	Birth of Donald Davidson	• 6 March, Springfield, Massachusetts
	Death of Brentano	• 17 March, Zurich
	Birth of Morton White	• 29 April, New York
	Birth of John L. Mackie	• 25 August, Sydney, Australia
1918	Frege, 'Thought' and 'Negation'	• first two essays of his 'Logical Investigations'

(Continued)

Year	Event	Further details and/or significance
	Russell, 'The Philosophy of Logical Atomism'	• course of 8 lectures given in London 22 January–12 March • claims to explain ideas learnt from Wittgenstein • introduces talk of 'logical construction'
	Russell, *Mysticism and Logic*	• collection of key papers 1911–15, plus 3 earlier ones
	Schlick, *General Theory of Knowledge*	• defends scientific realism and a form/content distinction in rejecting the synthetic a priori • first mind/brain identity theory • 2nd edn. 1925
	C. I. Lewis, *A Survey of Symbolic Logic*	• surveys existing logical systems and introduces his modal system of strict implication (chs. 5–6) • repr. 1960 without chs. 5–6
	Brouwer, 'Founding Set Theory…'	• begins intuitionist reconstruction of set theory
	Frege retires from Jena	• moves to Bad Kleinen, near Wismar • gift of money from Wittgenstein helps buy a house
	Russell in Brixton prison	• jailed for an anti-war article, May–September • writes *Introduction to Mathematical Philosophy*
	Wittgenstein back in Austria	• during leave from the war in the summer, completes more or less final version of *Tractatus*
	Wittgenstein in prisoner-of-war camp	• Cassino, Italy, October 1918–August 1919
	Death of Cantor	• 6 January, Halle, Germany
1919	Russell, *Introduction to Mathematical Philosophy*	• his clearest, non-technical exposition of his logical and logicist views
	Russell, 'On Propositions'	• comes to agree with James in rejecting the subject • contains discussion of Watson's *Behavior* (1914)
	Moore, 'External and Internal Relations'	• critique of the claim (attributed to Bradley) that all relations are internal
	Correspondence between Wittgenstein and Frege	• Frege receives a copy of the *Tractatus* in early 1919, but writes on 28 June that he finds it hard to understand
	Wittgenstein in Vienna	• trains to be a school teacher October 1919–July 1920
	Russell meets Wittgenstein	• The Hague, 12 December • they spend a week discussing the *Tractatus*
	Stout gives Gifford lectures	• Edinburgh 1919, 1921; later pub. as Stout 1931, 1952 • introduces idea of philosophical zombie, as now known
	Leśniewski to Warsaw	• Professor of the Foundations of Mathematics 1919–39
	Kotarbiński at Warsaw	• teaches; Professor from 1929
	Joachim succeeds Cook Wilson	• Wykeham Professor of Logic, Oxford • retires 1935
	Cassirer to Hamburg	• Professor 1919–33, when he emigrates • Rector 1929–30

Year	Event	Further details and/or significance
	Birth of Elizabeth Anscombe	• 18 March, Limerick, Ireland
	Birth of Richard M. Hare	• 21 March, Backwell, Somerset
	Birth of Peter F. Strawson	• 23 November, Ealing, London
1920	Alexander, *Space, Time, and Deity*	• his main work, developing a speculative metaphysics based on a form of direct realism • sees metaphysics as just more comprehensive than the special sciences
	Reichenbach, *The Theory of Relativity and A Priori Knowledge*	• *Habilitationsschrift*; tr. 1965
	Brouwer, 'Does Every Real Number Have a Decimal Expansion?'	• inaugurates foundational debate between intuitionists and formalists in the 1920s (cf. Mancosu 1998)
	Ajdukiewicz, *From the Methodology of the Deductive Sciences*	• 3 essays on logical concept of proof, proofs of consistency of axioms, notion of existence • orig. in Polish; tr. 1966
	Łukasiewicz, 'On Three-Valued Logic'	• presents three-valued logic, discovered in 1918 • invents Polish notation around same time
	Sorley, *A History of English Philosophy*	• offers a critical history, using the criticisms of philosophers made by their successors
	Founding of *The Personalist*	• founding editor Ralph Tyler Flewelling • becomes *Pacific Philosophical Quarterly* in 1980
	C. I. Lewis to Harvard	• Professor 1920–53, when he retires; Edgar Peirce Professor 1948–53
	Broad to Bristol	• Professor 1920–3
	Reichenbach to Stuttgart	• instructor in physics, then Professor, 1920–6
	Russell visits Russia	• May–June, accompanied by Dora Black
	Wittgenstein teaches	• Trattenbach September 1920–June 1922; Hassbach September–October 1923; Puchberg November 1923–July 1924; Otterthal September 1924–April 1926 (when he resigned after hitting a child)
	Russell and Black visit China	• October–July, though Russell spends his last 3 months recovering from a near-fatal illness • meets Dewey, October • gives 5 series of lectures in Beijing
	Death of Wundt	• 31 August, Grossbothen, Leipzig
	Birth of Philippa Foot	• 3 October, Owston Ferry, Lincolnshire
	Death of Meinong	• 27 November, Graz
1921	Wittgenstein, *Logisch-Philosophische Abhandlung*	• original German publication of *Tractatus* • tr. Ogden and Ramsey, introd. by Russell, 1922
	Russell, *The Analysis of Mind*	• rejecting both the subject and sense-data, hence no longer treating sensation as relational, adopts neutral monism
	McTaggart, *The Nature of Existence*, vol. 1	• his main work, in idealist tradition; vol. 2 1927 • argues that ultimate reality consists of loving spirits

(Continued)

Year	Event	Further details and/or significance
	Stout, 'The Nature of Universals and Propositions'	• British Academy lecture • argues for the existence of tropes, as now called
	Carnap, *Der Raum*	• doctoral dissertation, Jena
	Johnson, *Logic*, vol. 1	• vol. 2 1922; vol. 3 1924 • distinguishes sentences, assertions, and propositions
	Helmholtz, *Epistemological Writings*	• ed. Hertz and Schlick
	Moore succeeds Stout	• Editor of *Mind* 1921–47
	Birth of John Rawls	• 21 February, Baltimore, Maryland
	Birth of Ruth Barcan Marcus	• 2 August, New York (born Ruth Barcan)
1922	Wittgenstein, *Tractatus Logico-Philosophicus*	• …? (7)
	Russell, 'Introduction' to *Tractatus*	• not well-received by Wittgenstein himself
	Moore, *Philosophical Studies*	• first collection of papers
	Hilbert, 'The New Grounding of Mathematics'	• develops his formalism • identifies a finitary core of 'contentual' number theory, based on the operation of signs
	Husserl, lectures	• 4 lectures on 'Phenomenological Method and Phenomenological Philosophy', London, June
	Russell visits Wittgenstein	• Austria, August
	Schlick at Vienna	• Professor of the History and Philosophy of the Inductive Sciences 1922–36
	Birth of Thomas Kuhn	• 18 July, Cincinnati, Ohio
	Birth of Imre Lakatos	• 9 November, Debrecen, Hungary (born Imre Lipschitz)
1923	Frege, 'Compound Thoughts'	• third essay of 'Logical Investigations' • fourth essay, on 'Logical Generality', never completed
	Ramsey, review of *Tractatus*	• after its publication, visits Wittgenstein in Puchberg for 2 weeks in September, discussing the *Tractatus*
	C. I. Lewis, 'A Pragmatic Conception of the *A Priori*'	• introduces his 'conceptual pragmatism'
	Broad, *Scientific Thought*	• develops sense-datum theory of perception
	Ogden & Richard, *The Meaning of Meaning*	• subtitled 'A Study of The Influence of Language upon Thought and of The Science of Symbolism' • many subsequent edns., up to 10th edn. 1949
	Cassirer, *The Philosophy of Symbolic Forms*, vol. 1	• his main work • vol. 2 1925; vol. 3 1929
	Santayana, *Scepticism and Animal Faith*	• naturalistic critique of epistemological foundationalism
	Founding of *Australasian Journal of Philosophy*	• founded as *The Australasian Journal of Psychology and Philosophy* by Australasian Association of Philosophy • founding editor Francis Anderson, Sydney

Year	Event	Further details and/or significance
	Carnap meets Reichenbach	• Erlangen conference on logic and scientific philosophy
	Broad succeeds McTaggart	• Lecturer, Cambridge
	Birth of Wolfgang Stegmüller	• 3 June, Natters, near Innsbruck, Austria
1924	Russell, 'Logical Atomism'	• Russell's contribution to Muirhead 1924
	Russell, 'Philosophy of the Twentieth Century'	• distinguishes three (not exclusive) groups: adherents of German idealism; pragmatists, incl. James and Bergson; realists, also incl. James • repr. as first chapter of Part II of Runes 1943
	Bradley, 'Relations'	• his final account of relations, replying to Russell
	Muirhead, ed., *Contemporary British Philosophy (First Series)*	• contributors: Baillie, Bosanquet, Broad, Carr, Haldane, Hobhouse, Inge, Laird, Mackenzie, McTaggart, Morgan, Muirhead, Read, Russell (1924a), Schiller, Temple
	Whitehead to Harvard	• Professor of Philosophy 1924–37, when he retires
	Carnap attends Husserl's lectures	• summer semesters 1924 and 1925, Freiburg
	Founding of the British Institute of Philosophy	• inaugural meeting 10 November; attended by Russell • now the Royal Institute of Philosophy
	Birth of Paul Feyerabend	• 13 January, Vienna
	Death of Bradley	• 18 September, Oxford
1925	Moore, 'A Defence of Common Sense'	• lists truisms he claims to know with certainty • distinguishes between understanding the meaning of an expression and being able to give its correct analysis
	Ramsey, 'The Foundations of Mathematics'	• defends logicism by amending *Principia Mathematica* • distinguishes between logical and semantic paradoxes
	Russell & Whitehead, 2nd edn. *Principia Mathematica*	• contains long new introduction (see Linsky 2011)
	Broad, *The Mind and its Place in Nature*	• emergence of emergentism
	Whitehead, *Science and the Modern World*	• challenges scientific materialism
	Dewey, *Experience and Nature*	• develops an event ontology
	Muirhead, ed., *Contemporary British Philosophy (Second Series)*	• contributors: Ward, Bax, Fawcett, Dawes Hicks, Hoernlé, Joad, Moore (1925), Smith, Sorley, Taylor, Thomson, Webb
	Moore succeeds Ward	• Professor, Cambridge 1925–39, when he retires
	Wittgenstein visits England	• August, meets Keynes, Johnson; argues with Ramsey
	Carnap visits Vienna	• meets Schlick
	Hempel to Berlin	• Ph.D. 1934; studies with Reichenbach
	Passing away of McTaggart	• 18 January, London

(Continued)

Year	Event	Further details and/or significance
	Differentiation of Gilles Deleuze	• 18 January, Paris
	Birth of Michael Dummett	• 27 June, London
	Death of Frege	• 26 July, Bad Kleinen, Germany
	Death of Case	• 31 October, Falmouth
1926	Cook Wilson, *Statement and Inference*	• main work of Oxford realism • edited from his lecture courses by Farquharson; 2 vols.
	Durant, *The Story of Philosophy*	• final two chs. on contemporary European philosophy (Bergson, Croce, Russell) and American philosophy (Santayana, James, Dewey)
	Carnap to Vienna	• teaches philosophy 1926–31
	Reichenbach to Berlin	• Professor 'for epistemological issues in physics' 1926–33
	Wittgenstein in Vienna	• joins Engelmann in designing and supervising the building of a house for his sister Gretl, 1926–8
	Birth of David Armstrong	• 8 July, Melbourne, Australia
	Birth of Hilary Putnam	• 31 July, Chicago
	Birth of Stanley Cavell	• 1 September, Atlanta
	Birth of Michel Foucault	• 15 October, Poitiers, France
1927	Russell, *The Analysis of Matter*	• three parts on the logical analysis of physics, physics and perception, and the structure of the physical world
	Ramsey, 'Facts and Propositions'	• introduces redundancy theory of truth
	Anderson, 'Empiricism'	• founding statement of Australian realism • paper read at annual congress of AAPP
	Heidegger, *Being and Time*	• reviewed by Ryle (1929), who calls it an 'advance' but 'towards disaster' • not tr. until 1962
	Santayana, *The Realms of Being*	• vol. 1 on essence, 1927; vol. 2 on matter, 1930; vol. 3 on truth, 1937; vol. 4 on spirit 1940
	Hägerström, *The Roman Concept of Obligation…*	• key text in founding of Scandinavian legal realist tradition; vol. 2 1941
	Schlick meets Wittgenstein	• February, Vienna; begins discussions and persuades him to meet other members of Vienna Circle
	Correspondence between Wittgenstein and Ramsey	• over Ramsey 1925 (cf. Wittgenstein 2008, pp. 158–61)
	Founding of Berlin Society for Empirical Philosophy	• 27 February; changes name to Society for Scientific Philosophy 1930; members include Reichenbach, Lewin, Grelling, von Mises, Hempel (see Hoffmann 2007)
	Brouwer lectures in Berlin	• Reichenbach attends; eventually pub. as Brouwer 1992

Year	Event	Further details and/or significance
	Anderson to Sydney	• Challis Professor of Philosophy 1927–58, when he retires
	Birth of Burton Dreben	• 27 September, Boston
1928	Carnap, *The Logical Construction of the World*	• attempts to 'rationally reconstruct' our concepts through a 'constitution system'
	Carnap, *Pseudoproblems in Philosophy*	• argues that theses of realism and idealism are scientifically meaningless
	Ramsey, 'On a Problem of Formal Logic'	• proves Ramsey's theorem, instigating Ramsey theory, as both now called
	Founding of Verein Ernst Mach	• November, with Schlick elected President
	Prichard at Oxford	• White's Professor of Moral Philosophy 1928–37, when he retires
	Brouwer lectures in Vienna	• 10 March (Brouwer 1929), 14 March (Brouwer 1930) • attended by Wittgenstein, Gödel, Waismann, Feigl
	Bergmann at Vienna	• Ph.D. in mathematics; joins Vienna Circle; law degree 1935
	Birth of Chomsky	• 7 December, Philadelphia, Pennsylvania
1929	Vienna Circle manifesto	• Carnap, Hahn, & Neurath 1929
	Wittgenstein, 'Some Remarks on Logical Form'	• written for Joint Session, but Wittgenstein talked about infinity instead
	C. I. Lewis, *Mind and the World-Order*	• develops his 'conceptual pragmatism'
	Ramsey, 'Theories'	• introduces idea of a 'Ramsey sentence', as now called
	Whitehead, *Process and Reality*	• argues that process rather than substance is metaphysically fundamental • founding text of process philosophy
	Russell, *Marriage and Morals*	• argues for a new sexual ethics based on respect for the personality and freedom of others
	Kotarbiński, *Gnosiology*	• subtitled 'The Scientific Approach to the Theory of Knowledge'; orig. pub. in Polish; tr. 1966 • introduces his 'reism', later called 'concretism'
	Husserl, *Formal and Transcendental Logic*	• tr. D. Cairns 1969
	Köhler, *Gestalt Psychology*	• classic account
	Wittgenstein to Cambridge	• returns January; awarded Ph.D. for the *Tractatus*, viva 18 June, examined by Moore and Russell • receives grant from Trinity College to pursue research
	Davos encounter	• 'International University Course' held at Davos, Switzerland, 17 March–6 April • debate between Cassirer and Heidegger, attended by Carnap (see Friedman 2000, Gordon 2010)
	Ryle meets Wittgenstein	• Joint Session, Nottingham • become friends, and go on walking holidays together

(Continued)

Year	Event	Further details and/or significance
	Wittgenstein in Vienna	• holds discussions with Schlick and Waismann, Christmas vacation; recorded in Waismann 1979
	Hempel to Vienna	• studies with members of the Vienna Circle, one semester
	Church to Princeton	• Professor 1947; stays until 1967
	Birth of Jaakko Hintikka	• 12 January, Vantaa, Finland
	Birth of Jürgen Habermas	• 18 June, Düsseldorf
	Birth of Bernard Williams	• 21 September, Westcliff, Essex
1930	Wittgenstein, *Philosophical Remarks*	• written between February 1929 and April 1930 • pub. in German 1964; tr. 1979 • read by Russell and Littlewood in recommending him for a Fellowship at Trinity
	Stebbing, *A Modern Introduction to Logic*	• first textbook of analytic philosophy • covers both traditional and modern logic, scientific method, and definition and the nature of logic • 2nd edn. 1933, with 4 apps. added, one on 'Logical Constructions', one on 'Postulational Systems' • 3rd edn. 1942; four further edns. after her death in 1943, the last in 1950; repr. into the 1960s
	Schlick, 'The Turning Point in Philosophy'	• argues that philosophy is not a system of cognitions but an activity of clarifying meaning
	Kaila, 'Logical Positivism'	• introduces logical positivism to Finland
	Broad, *Five Types of Ethical Theory*	• discusses Spinoza, Butler, Hume, Kant, Sidgwick • endorses a form of intuitionism
	Ross, *The Right and the Good*	• presents his ethical intuitionism
	Russell, *The Conquest of Happiness*	• Part I: causes of unhappiness; Part II: causes of happiness • written 'as a hedonist'
	Wittgenstein in Cambridge	• begins teaching in January • elected to a 5-year Fellowship at Trinity, 5 December
	Founding of *Erkenntnis*	• founding editors Carnap and Reichenbach • takes over *Annalen der Philosophie* (1919–29)
	Wittgenstein in Vienna	• holds discussions with Schlick and Waismann, Christmas vacation; recorded in Waismann 1979
	Quine to Harvard	• Ph.D. 1932, on *Principia Mathematica*, supervised by Whitehead
	Stevenson to Cambridge	• BA 1933; influenced by Moore and Wittgenstein
	Tarski visits Vienna	• lectures on metamathematics, February
	Death of Ramsey	• 19 January, Guy's Hospital, London
	Birth of Jacques Derrida	• 15 July, El-Biar, Algiers
1931	Gödel's incompleteness theorems	• 'On Formally Undecidable Propositions of *Principia Mathematica* and Related Systems I'

Year	Event	Further details and/or significance
	Wisdom, *Interpretation and Analysis in Relation to Bentham's Theory of Definition*	• explores connection between Russell's theory of descriptions and Bentham's use of 'paraphrasis' • talks of the 'logico-analytic philosophers' (p. 13) and 'analytic philosophers' (p. 15)
	Wisdom, 'Logical Constructions'	• 5-part series of papers, 1931–3 • first talk of 'paradox of analysis' in Part V (1933)
	Ramsey, *The Foundations of Mathematics*	• posthumous collection of papers
	Blumberg & Feigl, 'Logical positivism'	• subtitled 'A new movement in European philosophy' • introduces the term 'logical positivism'
	Neurath, two papers on physicalism	• one subtitled 'The Philosophy of the Vienna Circle' • term 'physicalism' first introduced
	Ajdukiewicz, 'On the Meaning of Expressions'	• presents his theory of meaning, developed further in Ajdukiewicz 1934a
	Carnap to Prague	• Professor of Natural Philosophy 1931–5
	Feigl to Iowa	• Lecturer 1931–40
	Stebbing to Columbia	• Visiting Professor 1931–2
	Nagel at Columbia	• joins faculty; University Professor 1967–70, when he retires
	Birth of Richard Rorty	• 4 October, New York
1932	Ryle, 'Systematically Misleading Expressions'	• argues that misleading statements have to be reformulated to clear up confusions
	Stebbing, 'The Method of Analysis in Metaphysics'	• read to Aris. Soc., December • attempts to articulate the methodological assumptions of Moorean philosophy • influences Collingwood
	Carnap, 'The Elimination of Metaphysics…'	• argues that metaphysical statements are revealed to be pseudo-statements through logical analysis of language • nothings Heidegger over nothing (§5)
	Carnap, 'The Physical Language as Universal Language of Science'	• claims that all scientific knowledge is expressible in the language of physics • tr. as 'The Unity of Science' 1934
	Carnap & Neurath debate protocol sentences	• Carnap 1932c and Neurath 1932 • Neurath anti-foundationalist: science like a ship on the open sea
	Lewis & Langford, *Symbolic Logic*	• first full account of systems of strict implication
	Price, *Perception*	• takes sense-data as the given, and offers a synthesis of phenomenalism and realism
	Quine and Ayer to Vienna	• become members of the Vienna Circle, Quine for a year, Ayer for 4 months
	Death of Peano	• 20 April, Turin, Italy
	Birth of John Searle	• 31 July, Denver, Colorado
	Birth of Alvin Plantinga	• 15 November, Ann Arbor, Michigan

(Continued)

Year	Event	Further details and/or significance
1933	Wittgenstein, *Philosophical Grammar*	• written 1930–3 • tr. and pub. 1975
	Wittgenstein, *Blue Book*	• dictated 1933–4; pub. 1958
	Wittgenstein, *The Big Typescript*	• 1st version 1933; rev. 1933–7 • tr. and pub. 2005
	Tarski, 'The Concept of Truth in Formalized Languages'	• seminal paper • orig. pub. in Polish; German 1935; English 1956
	Collingwood, *An Essay on Philosophical Method*	• ch. 7: criticizes 'analytical philosophy', as he calls the kind of philosophy practised by Moore and Stebbing
	Stebbing, 'Logical Positivism and Analysis'	• lecture given to British Academy, March • compares the different conceptions of analysis of the Cambridge (Moorean) School and logical positivism
	Stebbing, 'Constructions'	• Presidential Address to Aris. Soc.
	Broad, *Examination of McTaggart's Philosophy*	• vol. 1; vol. 2 1938
	Founding of *Analysis*	• ed. Duncan-Jones, helped by Stebbing, Mace, and Ryle • first issue November; stops 1940 but restarts 1947 • M. Macdonald editor 1948–54
	Broad succeeds Sorley	• Knightbridge Professor of Moral Philosophy, Cambridge • retires 1953
	Quine at Harvard	• Junior Fellow 1933–6; Instructor 1936; Associate Professor 1941; Professor 1948; Edgar Pierce Professor of Philosophy 1956; retires 1978
	Stevenson to Harvard	• Ph.D. 1935, working with Perry; Instructor 1935–8
	Malcolm to Harvard	• Ph.D. 1940 (Cambridge 1938–9)
	Cassirer to Oxford	• 1933–5
	Reichenbach to Istanbul	• 1933–8
	Einstein to Princeton	• Professor of Theoretical Physics 1933–45, when he retires
	Birth of David Wiggins	• 8 March, London
1934	Carnap, *The Logical Syntax of Language*	• argues for philosophy to be replaced by logic of science • distinguishes 'material' and 'formal' modes of speech • introduces his principle of tolerance in logic • tr. 1937
	Popper, *Logik der Forschung*	• seeks to replace verificationism by falsificationism • tr. as *The Logic of Scientific Discovery* 1959
	Wittgenstein, *Brown Book*	• dictated 1934–5; pub. 1958
	Wisdom, *Problems of Mind and Matter*	• in his introduction, states that 'Analytic philosophy has no special subject-matter' (p. 2)

Year	Event	Further details and/or significance
	Black, Wisdom and Cornforth debate analysis	• symposium on 'Is Analysis a Useful Method in Philosophy?', Joint Session, July
	Gentzen, 'Investigations into Logical Deduction I'	• introduces natural deduction system of logic • provides basis for inferentialism about logical constants • part II 1936
	Ajdukiewicz, 'The World-Picture and the Conceptual Apparatus'	• presents his radical conventionalism, later revised
	Dewey, *Art as Experience*	• his main work on aesthetics • William James Lectures, Harvard 1931
	Founding of *Philosophy of Science*	• journal of Philosophy of Science Association • founding editor William Malisoff 1934–47 • editorial board includes: Carnap, Feigl, Stebbing
	Stebbing invites Carnap to London	• Carnap gives three lectures, published as *Philosophy and Logical Syntax* (1935), reviewed by Stebbing (1935) • Carnap meets Russell and Ayer for the first time
	Hempel to Belgium	• works with Paul Oppenheim
	Sellars to Oxford	• BA in PPE 1936
	Birth of Jaegwon Kim	• 12 September, Taegu, Korea
1935	Hempel, 'The Logical Analysis of Psychology'	• introduces term 'logical behaviorism'
	Ryle criticizes Collingwood	• 'Mr Collingwood and the Ontological Argument' • occasions correspondence (Collingwood 2005b)
	Frege's *Nachlaß* given to Heinrich Scholz	• Frege's adopted son Alfred hands over papers to Scholz at Münster, who plans an edition of Frege's works • copies made of most of the important pieces
	Founding of Association for Symbolic Logic	• publishes *Journal of Symbolic Logic* (*JSL*) • first issue 1936, ed. Church and Langford • Church edits reviews until 1979
	Founding of *Theoria*	• subtitled 'A Swedish journal of philosophy and psychology'; reference to psychology dropped 1966 • first Swedish journal of philosophy (see Hansson 2009) • founding editor Åke Petzäll 1935–57 • first 2 vols. in Swedish, thereafter in English, French, and German
	Carnap to the US	• arrives in December to teach from 1936 • becomes American citizen 1941
	Collingwood succeeds Smith	• Waynflete Professor of Metaphysical Philosophy, Oxford 1935–43
	Price succeeds Joachim	• Wykeham Professor of Logic, Oxford • retires 1959
	Cassirer to Sweden	• Göteborg 1935–41

(Continued)

Year	Event	Further details and/or significance
	Birth of Jerry Fodor	• 22 April, New York
1936	Ayer, *Language, Truth and Logic*	• Ayer's 'young man's' version of logical positivism • ch. 1: 'The Elimination of Metaphysics' • repr. with new introd. 1946
	Waismann, *Introduction to Mathematical Thinking*	• concerned with mathematical concept formation • tr. 1951
	Tarski, 'On the Concept of Logical Consequence'	• pub. in both Polish and German; English 1956
	Carnap, 'Testability and Meaning'	• revises verifiability principle • defines analyticity semantically, not syntactically
	Quine, 'Truth by Convention'	• questions idea that mathematical and logical truths are true by convention
	Nagel, 'Impressions and Appraisals of Analytic Philosophy in Europe'	• first paper published with 'analytic philosophy' in its title • reports on 'the philosophy professed at Cambridge, Vienna, Prague, Warsaw, and Lwów' (p. 6)
	Weinberg, *An Examination of Logical Positivism*	• first book-length critique
	Church–Turing thesis	• Church, 'An Unsolvable Problem of Elementary Number Theory': emergence of the lambda-calculus • Turing, 'On Computable Numbers, with an Application to the Entscheidungsproblem': term 'Turing machine' introduced in Church's review of paper
	Church's theorem	• Church, 'A Note on the Entscheidungsproblem'
	Naess, *Knowledge and Scientific Behaviour*	• doctoral dissertation, introducing logical positivism to Norway
	Lovejoy, *The Great Chain of Being*	• develops concept of 'unit-idea', here tracing those of plenitude, continuity, and gradation
	Founding of *Synthese*	• founded as a Dutch journal • Hintikka editor 1966–2002 • subtitled 'An International Journal for Epistemology, Methodology and Philosophy of Science'
	Founding of Association for Symbolic Logic	• *Journal of Symbolic Logic* founded at same time • *Bulletin of Symbolic Logic* founded 1995 • *Review of Symbolic Logic* founded 2008, to include more historical work
	Carnap at Chicago	• Professor 1936–52
	Turing visits Princeton	• stays to complete Ph.D. with Church • awarded 1938, when he returns to Cambridge
	Death of Schlick	• 22 June (murdered), Vienna
	Death of Rickert	• 25 July, Heidelberg, Germany
1937	Wittgenstein, *Remarks on the Foundations of Mathematics*	• written 1937–44; tr. and pub. 1956 • 3rd edn. 1978, incl. new material (Part VI) on rule-following

Year	Event	Further details and/or significance
	Wisdom, 'Philosophical Perplexity'	• argues that philosophical statements are verbal recommendations
	Russell, 'On Verification'	• Presidential Address to Aris. Soc., 8 November
	Stevenson, 'The Emotive Meaning of Ethical Terms'	• his first paper on emotivism
	Quine, 'New Foundations for Mathematical Logic'	• introduces NF set theory
	Duncan-Jones and Ayer debate common sense	• symposium on 'Does Philosophy Analyse Common Sense?', Joint Session, July
	Black, 'Vagueness: An Exercise in Logical Analysis'	• first analysis of 'vague sets'
	Hempel to Chicago	• works as Carnap's assistant for a year
	Popper to New Zealand	• Canterbury 1937–46
	Waismann to Cambridge	• teaches 1937–9
	Death of Schiller	• 9 August, Los Angeles
1938	Reichenbach, *Experience and Prediction*	• advocates realism but anti-foundationalist and probabilistic
	Prichard, 'The Sense-Datum Fallacy'	• Presidential Address to Aris. Soc.
	Stevenson, 'Persuasive Definitions'	• definitions that seek to change attitudes
	Skinner, *The Behavior of Organisms*	• develops first account of operant behaviour
	Metz, *A Hundred Years of British Philosophy*	• Part II on 'Recent Schools of Thought': chs. on neo-idealism (208 pages), pragmatism, older realism, new realism (175 pages), mathematical logic, philosophy of natural science, psychology, theism • orig. pub. in German, 1935
	Russell to Chicago	• Visiting Professor 1938–9 • seminars, on what becomes Russell 1940a, attended by Carnap and Morris
	Grice at Oxford	• begins teaching at St John's College; stays until 1967
	Reichenbach to UCLA	• 1938–53
	Bergmann to the US	• emigrates
	Sellars to Iowa	• Assistant Professor; stays until 1946
	Malcolm to Cambridge	• 1938–9; influenced by Moore and Wittgenstein
	Death of Twardowski	• 11 February, Lvov
	Death of Husserl	• 26 April, Freiburg, Germany
	Death of Joachim	• 30 July, Croyde, Devon
	Death of Alexander	• 13 September, Manchester
1939	Moore, 'Proof of an External World'	• 🖐 🖐
	Wittgenstein, early version of *Philosophical Investigations*	• CUP agree to publish it, but Wittgenstein abandons plan
	Wittgenstein, lectures	• lectures on the foundations of mathematics; pub. 1975

(Continued)

Year	Event	Further details and/or significance
	Ross, *The Foundations of Ethics*	• further development of his ethical intuitionism
	Stebbing, *Thinking to some Purpose*	• popular book on critical thinking
	Collingwood, *An Autobiography*	• attack on his Oxford Realist colleagues
	Schilpp, ed., *The Philosophy of John Dewey*	• 1st vol. in 'The Library of Living Philosophers', a series in which the philosophers chosen write an autobiographical essay and reply to the papers included • contributors include Russell
	Wittgenstein succeeds Moore	• Professor of Philosophy 1939–47, when he resigns
	Russell to UCLA	• Professor 1939–40, when he resigns • again teaches on what becomes Russell 1940a
	von Wright to Cambridge	• works with Broad 1939, meets Moore and Wittgenstein
	Stevenson to Yale	• Assistant Professor 1939–46
	Hempel to New York	• Hempel takes up post at City College of New York • moves to Queen's College, where he stays until 1948
	Tarski to US	• attends a 'Unity of Science' congress in August • has to stay after war breaks out
	Death of Leśniewski	• 13 May, Warsaw
	Death of Hägerström	• 7 July, Uppsala, Sweden
	Death of Freud	• 23 September, London
1940	Russell, *An Inquiry into Meaning and Truth*	• William James Lectures, Harvard, autumn
	Quine, *Mathematical Logic*	• rev. edn. 1951, expounding ML set theory
	Ayer, *The Foundations of Empirical Knowledge*	• refinement of his logical positivism
	Collingwood, *An Essay on Metaphysics*	• critique of Ayer's logical positivism • metaphysics seen as articulating absolute presuppositions
	Schilpp, ed., *The Philosophy of George Santayna*	• 2nd vol. in 'The Library of Living Philosophers' • contributors include Russell
	Founding of *Philosophy and Phenomenological Research*	• founding editor Marvin Farber 1940–80 • later editors: Chisholm 1980–6; Ernest Sosa 1986–
	Founding of *Journal of the History of Ideas*	• founding editor Arthur Lovejoy
	Moore to US	• visits for first time in October; lectures at Smith College
	Carnap at Harvard	• Visiting Professor 1940–1 • Tarski also there that year; Russell there autumn 1940
	Waismann to Oxford	• Lecturer in phil. of science and maths 1945; Reader in phil. of maths 1950; Reader in phil. of science 1955
	Gödel to Princeton	• Institute of Advanced Study; tenure 1946; Professor 1953 • stays for rest of his career

Year	Event	Further details and/or significance
	Bergmann to Iowa	• research associate in psychology; lecturer in philosophy; Assistant Professor 1944; Professor of Philosophy and Psychology 1950–74, when he retires
	Black to the US	• University of Illinois 1940–6
	Birth of Saul Kripke	• 13 November, Bay Shore, New York
1941	Moore, 'Certainty'	• Howison lecture, Berkeley; pub. 1959
	Church, *The Calculi of Lambda-Conversion*	• exposition of the lambda-calculus
	von Wright, *The Logical Problem of Induction*	• Ph.D. thesis, Helsinki
	Schilpp, ed., *The Philosophy of Alfred North Whitehead*	• 3rd vol. in 'The Library of Living Philosophers'
	Russell in Philadelphia	• lectures at Barnes Foundation January 1941–December 1942, on what becomes Russell 1945
	Moore in US	• lectures at Princeton, then Mills College, California
	Feigl to Minnesota	• Professor 1941–71, when he retires, but remains Director of the Minnesota Center for the Philosophy of Science
	Cassirer to Yale	• 1941–4; influences Pap; meets Langer
	Anscombe and Geach marry	• Oxford
	Death of Bergson	• 3 January, Paris
	Birth of David Lewis	• 28 September, Oberlin, Ohio
1942	Carnap, *Introduction to Semantics*	• 1st vol. of his *Studies in Semantics* • 2nd vol. 1943: *Formalization of Logic*
	Langer, *Philosophy in a New Key*	• subtitled 'A Study in the Symbolism of Reason, Rite and Art'; influenced by Cassirer
	Hempel, 'The Function of General Laws in History'	• sets out covering law (later called 'deductive-nomological') model of explanation
	Schilpp, ed., *The Philosophy of G. E. Moore*	• 4th vol. in 'The Library of Living Philosophers' • first collection on Moore • contributors include Broad, Stevenson, Bouwsma, Ducasse, Langford, Malcolm, Lazerowitz, Ambrose, Wisdom, Stebbing
	Moore in New York	• lectures at Columbia
	Tarski to Berkeley	• Department of Mathematics; tenure 1945; Professor 1948 • stays for rest of his life
	Anscombe to Cambridge	• studies with Wittgenstein 1942–6
	Birth of John McDowell	• 7 March, Boksburg, South Africa
	Birth of Daniel Dennett	• 28 March, Boston, Massachusetts
	Birth of Crispin Wright	• 21 December, Bagshot, Surrey

(Continued)

Year	Event	Further details and/or significance
1943	Stebbing, *A Modern Elementary Logic*	• intended as textbook for first-year students • widely used for a decade, until superseded by Quine 1950 and Strawson 1952
	Quine, 'Notes on Existence and Necessity'	• first assault on modality; reply by Church (1943), appealing to Frege's sense/reference distinction
	Runes, ed., *Twentieth Century Philosophy*	• Part I on areas of philosophy (ethics, etc.) • Part II: after general survey by Russell (1924b), chs. on Kantianism, Hegelianism, Thomism, absolutism, personalism, phenomenology, logical empiricism, American realism, pragmatism, dialectical materialism, naturalism, Chinese philosophies
	Sartre, *Being and Nothingness*	• subtitled 'Essay on Phenomenological Ontology' • tr. 1956
	Death of Collingwood	• 9 January, Coniston, Lancashire
	Death of Hilbert	• 14 February, Göttingen
	Death of Stebbing	• 11 September, London
1944	Stevenson, *Ethics and Language*	• fullest account of his emotivism • denied tenure at Yale as a result
	Popper, *The Poverty of Historicism*	• pub. in book form 1957
	Tarski, 'The Semantic Conception of Truth…'	• defends a 'realist' conception of truth
	Gödel, 'Russell's mathematical logic'	• his first philosophical paper
	Adorno & Horkheimer, *Dialectic of Enlightenment*	• orig. title 'Philosophical Fragments'; pub. as book 1947 • key text of the Frankfurt School
	Cassirer, *An Essay on Man*	• English introduction to his philosophy of symbolic forms
	Schilpp, ed., *The Philosophy of Bertrand Russell*	• 5th vol. in 'The Library of Living Philosophers' • contributors include Reichenbach, Weitz, Gödel, Moore, Black, Einstein, E. Nagel, Chisholm, Hook
	Russell back to England	• 5-year Lectureship at Trinity College, Cambridge
	Cassirer to Columbia	• 1944–5
	Death of Stout	• 18 August, Sydney
1945	Russell, *History of Western Philosophy*	• subtitled 'and its Connection with Political and Social Circumstances from the Earliest Times to the Present Day' • last 4 chs. on Bergson, James, Dewey, and the Philosophy of Logical Analysis
	Hung, *The Philosophy of Vienna Circle*	• introduces logical positivism to China
	Merleau-Ponty, *Phenomenology of Perception*	• develops concept of the body-subject to avoid dualisms such as that between empiricism and intellectualism • tr. 1962

Year	Event	Further details and/or significance
	Popper, *The Open Society and its Enemies*	• defends democratic liberalism against totalitarianism
	Destruction of Frege's *Nachlaß*	• Frege's *Nachlaß* purportedly destroyed in a bombing raid on Münster on 25 March • only the copies made earlier remain
	Ryle succeeds Collingwood	• Waynflete Professor of Metaphysical Philosophy, Oxford 1945–67 • inaugural lecture: 'Philosophical Arguments'
	Tarski to Berkeley	• takes up permanent post; Professor of Mathematics 1948; remains until his death in 1983
	Death of Cassirer	• 13 April, New York
	Death of Neurath	• 22 December, Oxford
1946	Wittgenstein, final version of *Philosophical Investigations*	• pub. as Part I in 1953 • taken as main text in 4th edn. of 2009
	C. I. Lewis, *An Analysis of Knowledge and Valuation*	• mature exposition of his views
	Collingwood, *The Idea of History*	• criticizes 'scissor-and-paste' historiography • sees history as re-enactment of past experience
	Wisdom & Austin debate	• Joint Session, symposium on 'Other Minds'
	Barcan (Marcus), 'A Functional Calculus…'	• first axiomatic system of modal predicate logic • introduces 'Barcan formula'
	Carnap, 'Modalities and Quantification'	• first 'semantical' system of modal predicate logic
	Wimsatt & Beardsley, 'The Intentional Fallacy'	• argues for anti-intentionalism
	Hospers, *Meaning and Truth in the Arts*	• discusses truth in art
	Ayer to London (UCL)	• Grote Professor of the Philosophy of Mind and Logic
	Popper to London	• Reader 1946–9, Professor of Logic and Scientific Method 1949–69, LSE
	Anscombe to Oxford	• Research Fellow; Lecturer 1951; Fellow 1964–70; Somerville College
	von Wright takes up Chair	• Professor, Helsinki, 1946–61, but in Cambridge 1947–51
	Brouwer lectures in Cambridge	• gives annual lecture 1946–51; eventually pub. as Brouwer 1981
	Malcolm to Cambridge	• 1946–7; second visit
	Goodman to Pennsylvania	• Associate Professor 1946–51; Professor 1951–64
	Stevenson to Michigan	• Associate Professor; stays until 1978
	Sellars to Minnesota	• Assistant Professor; Professor 1951–8
	Black to Cornell	• Professor of Philosophy; Susan Linn Sage Professor 1954–77, when he retires

(Continued)

Year	Event	Further details and/or significance
	Łukasiewicz to Dublin	• Professor of Mathematical Logic, Royal Irish Academy, 1946–56
	Wittgenstein brandishes poker	• Moral Sciences Club 25 October, when Popper speaks on 'Are there philosophical problems?' (see Edmonds & Eidinow 2001)
	Birth of Gareth Evans	• 12 May, London
1947	Carnap, *Meaning and Necessity*	• subtitled 'A Study in Semantics and Modal Logic' • repr. 1956 with additional essays (incl. Carnap 1950b)
	Barcan (Marcus), 'The Identity of Individuals…'	• first axiomatic system of modal predicate logic with identity • offers proof of necessity of identity
	Ewing, *The Definition of Good*	• offers non-naturalistic definition of 'good' in terms of 'ought'; a work of 'analytic idealism'
	Macdonald, 'Natural Rights'	• sees statements of natural rights as akin to reason-based decisions
	Bocheński, *Contemporary European Philosophy*	• part II on 'Philosophy of Matter': ch. 5 on Russell, ch. 6 on neo-positivism, ch. 7 on dialectical materialism • last section of ch. 6 on 'analytical philosophy', taken as evolved from Moore and neo-positivism
	Founding of *Dialectica*	• founding editors Gaston Bachelard, Paul Bernays and Ferdinand Gonseth • became official journal of the European Society for Analytic Philosophy 1996
	Ryle succeeds Moore	• Editor of *Mind* 1947–71
	Malcolm to Cornell	• 1947–78
	Death of Prichard	• 29 December, Oxford
	Death of Whitehead	• 30 December, Cambridge, Massuchusetts
1948	Russell, *Human Knowledge*	• subtitled 'Its Scope and Limits'
	Quine, 'On what there is'	• seen as making analytic ontology respectable
	Hempel & Oppenheim, 'Studies in the Logic of Explanation'	• expounds D-N (deductive-nomological) model of explanation
	Frege, 'On Sense and Reference' translated	• first tr. by Black • also tr. as 'On Sense and Nominatum' by Feigl, 1949
	Wiener, *Cybernetics*	• founding text
	Shannon, 'A Mathematical Theory of Communication'	• founding work of information theory
	von Wright succeeds Wittgenstein	• Professor, Cambridge; resigns 1951 to return to Helsinki
	Strawson to Oxford	• Fellow, University College 1948–68
	Turing to Manchester	• develops University computer • meets Polanyi, who encourages philosophical interests

Year	Event	Further details and/or significance
	Hempel to Yale	• 1948–55
	Vlastos to Cornell	• Sage Professor 1948–55
	White to Harvard	• Assistant Professor 1948–50; Associate Professor 1950–3; Professor 1953–70
	Skinner to Harvard	• Professor of Psychology 1948–74, when he retires; Edgar Pierce Professor of Psychology 1958–74
1949	Ryle, *The Concept of Mind*	• attacks Cartesian dogma of the 'Ghost in the Machine' as a 'category-mistake' • concern with 'logical geography' of our concepts
	Pap, *Elements of Analytic Philosophy*	• first book to have 'analytic philosophy' in its title • distinguishes four major factions: Carnapians, followers of Moore, Wittgensteinians or 'therapeutic positivists', and philosophers concerned to clarify the foundations of science and knowledge • ch. 17: 'The Nature of Logical Analysis'
	Feigl & Sellars, eds., *Readings in Philosophical Analysis*	• first reader in 'modern philosophical analysis', described as originating in logical empiricism and the Cambridge movement deriving from Moore and Russell • contributors include W. Kneale, Quine, Tarski, Frege, Russell, Carnap, C. I. Lewis, Schlick, Aldrich, Adjukiewicz, E. Nagel, Waismann, Hempel, Reichenbach, Moore, Stace, Broad, Chisholm, Mace, Ducasse, Stevenson • 2nd edn. 1972
	Prichard, *Moral Obligation*	• posthumous collection of his papers; 2nd edn. 1968
	Malcolm, 'Defending common sense'	• Wittgensteinian critique of Moore's use of 'I know' in stating truisms
	Schilpp, ed., *Albert Einstein: Philosopher-Scientist*	• 7th vol. in 'The Library of Living Philosophers'
	Wittgenstein to Ithaca	• visits Malcolm, August and September • meets Bouwsma (cf. Bouwsma 1986)
1950	Strawson, 'On Referring'	• reply to Russell's 'On Denoting' (1905a)
	Frege, *Foundations* translated	• first English tr. by Austin
	Austin & Strawson debate truth	• Joint Session, symposium on 'Truth'
	Turing, 'Computing machinery and intelligence'	• introduces idea of the Turing Test, as now called
	Carnap, 'Empiricism, Semantics, and Ontology'	• distinguishes 'internal' and 'external' questions
	Carnap, *Logical Foundations of Probability*	• ch. 1 on explication
	White, 'The Analytic and the Synthetic'	• subtitled 'An Untenable Dualism'
	Prichard, *Knowledge and Perception*	• posthumous collection of his papers

(Continued)

Year	Event	Further details and/or significance
	Black, ed., *Philosophical Analysis*	• authors asked to provide 'specimens' of phil. analysis • contributors: Ambrose, Anscombe, Ayer, Bouwsma, Chisholm, Feigl, Frankena, Lazerowitz, Lewy, Macdonald, Mace, Malcolm, Marhenke, Ryle, Stevenson, Will, Wisdom
	Founding of *Philosophical Studies*	• edited by Feigl and Sellars until 1971, and then just Sellars until 1974
	Founding of *The Philosophical Quarterly*	• ed. T. M. Knox, pub. at St Andrews for the Scots Philosophical Club
	Founding of *British Journal for Philosophy of Science*	• following formation (in 1948) of Philosophy of Science Group of the British Society for the History of Science • founding editor A. C. Crombie
	Russell wins Nobel Prize in Literature	• in recognition of his writings 'in which he champions humanitarian ideals and freedom of thought'
	Dreben to Oxford	• studies with Austin for a year
	Birth of Robert Brandom	• 13 March, Buffalo, New York
1951	Quine, 'Two Dogmas of Empiricism'	• classic attack on analytic/synthetic distinction
	Reichenbach, *The Rise of Scientific Philosophy*	• sees history of philosophy as having proceeded from speculation to science, culminating in logical empiricism, where new methods of logical analysis provide key to the resolution of philosophical problems
	Goodman, *The Structure of Appearance*	• critique of Carnap's *Aufbau*
	von Wright, 'Deontic Logic'	• creation of deontic logic • *An Essay in Modal Logic* pub. same year
	Łukasiewicz, *Aristotle's Syllogistic…*	• expounded 'from the Standpoint of Modern Formal Logic', as rest of title says
	Arrow, *Social Choice and Individual Values*	• inaugurated social choice theory • formulates Arrow's impossibility theorem, as now known
	Davidson to Stanford	• Professor 1951–67
	Death of Wittgenstein	• 29 April, Cambridge
1952	Frege, *Translations…*	• first English edn. of a selection of his published writings, tr. Geach and Black • Wittgenstein advised on selection
	Quine, *Methods of Logic*	• textbook on logic
	Strawson, *Introduction to Logical Theory*	• argues that ordinary language lacks an exact logic • distinguishes presupposition from entailment
	Carnap, 'Meaning Postulates'	• first response to Quine 1951, defining analytic statements as those derived from 'meaning postulates'

Year	Event	Further details and/or significance
	Hare, *The Language of Morals*	• ethics 'the logical study of the language of morals' (p. iii) • argues for what he calls 'universal prescriptivism'
	Stegmüller, *Main Currents in Contemporary Philosophy*	• introduces post-war analytic philosophy to German-speaking world • 2nd edn. 1960, tr. 1969
	Austin at Oxford	• White's Professor of Moral Philosophy 1952–60
	Wisdom succeeds von Wright	• Professor of Philosophy, Cambridge • retires 1968
	Carnap at Princeton	• Institute of Advanced Study 1952–4
	Hart to Oxford	• Professor of Jurisprudence 1952–69
	Dreben at Harvard	• Junior Fellow 1952–5; Assistant Professor 1956; Associate Professor 1961; Professor 1965; Edgar Pierce Professor 1981–90
	Searle to Oxford	• Rhodes Scholar 1952–9 • studies with Austin, Strawson, and Geach
	Rawls to Oxford	• studies with Hart, Berlin, and Hamphire 1952–3
	Death of Dewey	• 1 June, New York
	Death of Santayana	• 26 September, Rome
1953	Wittgenstein, *Philosophical Investigations*	• tr. Anscombe • 4th edn. 2009, with rev. tr. Hacker and Schulte
	Quine, *From a Logical Point of View*	• collection of his papers, incl. 'Two Dogmas' • rev. edn. 1961
	Wisdom, *Philosophy and Psycho-Analysis*	• collection, incl. papers on methodology, Moore, Russell
	Braithwaite, *Scientific Explanation*	• his main work
	Price, *Thinking and Experience*	• offers empiricist account of thinking
	Naess, *Interpretation and Preciseness*	• subtitled 'A Contribution to the Theory of Communication' • key text of Norwegian analytic philosophy
	D. Williams, 'On the Elements of Being'	• introduces term 'trope'
	Weldon, *The Vocabulary of Politics*	• positivist approach to political philosophy
	Skinner, *Science and Human Behavior*	• uncompromising behaviourist account of human activity
	Hospers, *An Introduction to Philosophical Analysis*	• best-selling introduction to philosophy in analytic style • 2nd edn. 1967, 3rd edn. 1990, 4th edn. 1997 • first two edns. begin with a long ch. on philosophy and language, cut in the 3rd edn., but restored in a shortened form in the 4th edn. after complaints
	Founding of Minnesota Center for Philosophy of Science	• directed by Feigl 1953–71 • first vol. of *Minnesota Studies in Philosophy of Science* pub. 1956

(Continued)

Year	Event	Further details and/or significance
	R. B. Braithwaite succeeds Broad	• Knightbridge Professor of Moral Philosophy, Cambridge • retires 1967
	Brouwer lectures in US	• MIT, Princeton, Chicago, Berkeley, among others
	Cavell at Harvard	• Junior Fellow 1953–6
	Death of Reichenbach	• 9 April, Los Angeles
1954	Reviews of *Philosophical Investigations*	• Malcolm in *Phil. Review* • Strawson in *Mind* • Feyerabend in *Phil. Review* (1955)
	Turing, 'Solvable and Unsolvable Problems'	• argues that incompleteness theorems show need to appeal to 'common sense'
	Bergmann, *The Metaphysics of Logical Positivism*	• collection of his papers
	Macdonald, ed., *Philosophy and Analysis*	• selection of articles from *Analysis* 1933–40, 1947–53 • introduction by Macdonald on history of *Analysis* and development of analytic philosophy
	Elton, ed., *Aesthetics and Language*	• marks effective beginning of analytic aesthetics
	Vlastos, 'The Third Man Argument in the *Parmenides*'	• pioneering work in analytic history of ancient Greek thought
	Carnap to UCLA	• succeeds Reichenbach as Professor
	Death of Turing	• 7 June (suicide), Wilmslow, Cheshire
1955	Goodman, *Fact, Fiction and Forecast*	• elaborates new riddle of induction
	Braithwaite, *Theory of Games*	• offered 'as a tool for the moral philosopher'
	Hart, 'Are There Any Natural Rights?'	• interprets debates about the 'ontological status' of rights not as denying their existence
	Kotarbiński, *Praxiology*	• subtitled 'An Introduction to the Science of Efficient Action'; orig. pub. in Polish; tr. 1965 • sets up Laboratory of Praxiology in 1958
	White, ed., *The Age of Analysis: Twentieth Century Philosophers*	• vol. 6 of 'The Great Ages of Western Philosophy' • contains work by Moore, Croce, Santayana, Bergson, Whitehead, Husserl, Sartre, Peirce, James, Dewey, Russell, Carnap, Wittgenstein
	Hempel to Princeton	• 1955–73
	Vlastos to Princeton	• Stuart Professor of Philosophy 1955–76, when he retires
	Death of Einstein	• 18 April, Princeton
1956	Wittgenstein, *Remarks on the Foundations of Mathematics*	• written 1937–44 • 2nd edn. 1967; 3rd edn. 1978, incl. new material on rule-following
	Austin, 'A Plea for Excuses'	• clearest statement of his methodology, which he suggests calling 'linguistic phenomenology' (p. 182)

Year	Event	Further details and/or significance
	Sellars 'Empiricism and the Philosophy of Mind'	• critique of 'myth of the given' • lectures given in London • reissued 1997 with a study guide by Brandom
	Grice & Strawson, 'In Defense of a Dogma'	• reply to Quine's attack on analytic/synthetic distinction
	Place, 'Is Consciousness a Brain Process?'	• mind/brain identity thesis
	Chisholm, 'Sentences about Believing'	• defends Brentano's thesis that intentionality is the mark of the psychological
	Quine, 'Quantifiers and Propositional Attitudes'	• suggests sententialist account of propositional attitudes
	Gallie, 'Essentially Contested Concepts'	• offers 7 criteria of 'contestedness'
	Ayer, *The Problem of Knowledge*	• context-based account of knowledge
	Church, *Introduction to Mathematical Logic*	• early version pub. 1944
	Russell, *Logic and Knowledge*	• collection of essays 1901–50, incl. Russell 1905a, 1918–19 • obsequiously edited by R. C. Marsh
	Tarski, *Logic, Semantics, Metamathematics*	• papers 1923–38, tr. Woodger
	Urmson, *Philosophical Analysis: Its Development between the Two World Wars*	• first history of analytic philosophy, covering logical atomism, logical positivism, and 'the beginnings of contemporary philosophy' • reviewed by Russell (1956c)
	White, *Toward Reunion in Philosophy*	• seeks to synthesize analytic and pragmatist traditions • based on Harvard course on 'Problems of Analytic Philosophy' taught from early 1950s
	Ayer et al., *The Revolution in Philosophy*	• essays by Wollheim on Bradley, Kneale on Frege, Pears on logical atomism, Paul on Moore and on later Wittgenstein, Ayer on Vienna Circle, and both Strawson and Warnock on analysis • introduced by Ryle, who describes twentieth-century philosophy as the story of 'meaning' • originated as talks given on the BBC Third Programme
	Flew, ed., *Essays in Conceptual Analysis*	• collection of papers published in early 1950s, incl. Strawson 1950a
	Laslett, ed., *Philosophy, Politics and Society*	• marks emergence of analytic political philosophy • subsequent vols. 1962, 1967, 1972, 1979, 1992, 2003, 2010 (Fishkin & Goodin)
	Nagel, *Logic Without Metaphysics*	• collection of essays
	Russell, *Portraits from Memory*	• collection of occasional pieces, incl. portraits of Santayana, Whitehead, Mill, among others

(Continued)

Year	Event	Further details and/or significance
	Kuhn to Berkeley	• teaches history of science; Professor 1961
	Cavell to Berkeley	• teaches 1956–62
	Death of Łukasiewicz	• 13 February, Dublin
1957	Anscombe, *Intention*	• critique of idea that intentions are interior acts or events
	Geach, *Mental Acts*	• criticizes abstractionism, Russell's theory of judgement
	Chisholm, *Perceiving: A Philosophical Study*	• his first book
	Chomsky, *Syntactic Structures*	• introduces his theory of transformational grammar • argues for an innate 'universal grammar'
	Prior, *Time and Modality*	• seminal presentation of tense logic • John Locke lectures 1956
	Grice, 'Meaning'	• distinguishes natural and non-natural meaning
	Passmore, *A Hundred Years of Philosophy*	• a history of philosophy from Mill to Wittgenstein and Sartre • 2nd edn. 1966, revising later chapters and adding a final chapter on 'Description, Explanation or Revision?'
	Wood, *Bertrand Russell: The Passionate Sceptic*	• first biography of Russell
	Skinner, *Verbal Behavior*	• offers behaviourist account of language learning • reviewed by Chomsky (1959)
	Founding of *Ratio*	• new series 1988
	Berlin at Oxford	• Chichele Professor of Social and Political Theory, Oxford 1957–67, when he becomes founding President of Wolfson College, retiring 1975
	Kotarbiński at Warsaw	• President of Polish Academy of Sciences 1957–62
	Death of Perry	• 22 January, Cambridge, Massachusetts
1958	Wittgenstein, *Blue and Brown Books*	• dictated 1933–4 and 1934–5
	Winch, *The Idea of a Social Science*	• applies Wittgensteinian ideas in critique of empirical science
	Pap, *Semantics and Necessary Truth*	• subtitled 'An Inquiry into the Foundations of Analytic Philosophy'
	Feigl, 'The "Mental" and the "Physical"'	• proposes version of the identity theory of mind
	Sellars & Chisholm debate intentionality	• 'Intentionality and the Mental'; Chisholm gives priority to intentional thought, Sellars to language
	Foot, 'Moral Beliefs'	• rejects radical subjectivism
	Anscombe, 'Modern Moral Philosophy'	• renewed interest in moral psychology, especially concerning virtues
	Berlin, 'Two Concepts of Liberty'	• inaugural lecture • distinguishes negative and positive liberty

Year	Event	Further details and/or significance
	Rawls, 'Justice as Fairness'	• first development of his theory of justice
	Geach, 'Imperative and Deontic Logic'	• first formulation of Frege–Geach problem, as now known (cf. Geach 1960, 1965; Searle 1962; anticipated by Ross 1939, pp. 33–4)
	Warnock, *English Philosophy Since 1900*	• discusses Moore, Russell, logical positivism, Wittgenstein, Ryle, and Austin • 2nd edn. 1969, removing chapter on logic and adding more on Austin
	White, *G. E. Moore: A Critical Exposition*	• first monograph on Moore's philosophy
	Malcolm, *Ludwig Wittgenstein: A Memoir*	• with biographical sketch by von Wright • 2nd edn. 1984 with Wittgenstein's letters to Malcolm
	Føllesdal, *Husserl und Frege*	• first (short) monograph on Husserl and Frege
	Royaumont colloquium	• conference on 'La Philosophie Analytique', aimed to facilitate dialogue between analytic and non-analytic philosophers, but often seen to have failed • participants include Ryle, Austin, Strawson, Quine, Williams, Urmson, Hare, Merleau-Ponty, Wahl, Van Breda • Ryle distinguishes 'Anglo-Saxon' from 'Continental' philosophy (1962, p. 189) • proceedings pub. 1962 (*Cahiers de Royaumont*)
	Founding of *Inquiry*	• founding editor Arne Naess
	Sellars to Yale	• visitor, then Professor until 1963
	Stegmüller to Munich	• Professor 1958–90, when he retires
	Death of Watson	• 25 September, New York
	Death of Moore	• 24 October, Cambridge
1959	Strawson, *Individuals*	• engages in 'descriptive'—rather than 'revisionary'—metaphysics
	Anscombe, *An Introduction to Wittgenstein's Tractatus*	• argues for the importance of Frege to Wittgenstein
	Hampshire, *Thought and Action*	• sees freedom as based on capacity for reasoning and (self-)knowledge
	Smart, 'Sensations and Brain Processes'	• proposes identity theory of mind
	Kripke, 'A Completeness Theorem in Modal Logic'	• his first paper
	Malcolm, *Dreaming*	• claims that dreams are not occurrences during sleep
	Brandt, *Ethical Theory*	• introduces distinction between act and rule utilitarianism
	Sibley, 'Aesthetic Concepts'	• seeks to distinguish aesthetic from non-aesthetic concepts
	Russell, *My Philosophical Development*	• contains replies to Urmson (1956), Warnock (1956), Strawson (1950a), and Ryle (1949)

(Continued)

Year	Event	Further details and/or significance
	Moore, *Philosophical Papers*	• second collection of his papers, prepared shortly before his death
	Ayer, ed., *Logical Positivism*	• 2nd vol. in 'The Library of Philosophical Movements' series (ed. P. Edwards), the only one dealing with any form of analytic philosophy; extensive bib. • contributors: Russell, Schlick, Carnap, Hempel, Hahn, Neurath, Ayer, Stevenson, Ramsey, Ryle, Waismann (the last three in a section on 'Analytical Philosophy')
	Gellner, *Words and Things*	• famous polemic, subtitled 'An Examination of, and an Attack on, Linguistic Philosophy'; foreword by Russell • Ryle controversially refuses to review it in *Mind*
	Schilpp, ed., *The Philosophy of C. D. Broad*	• 10th vol. in 'The Library of Living Philosophers'
	Charlesworth, *Philosophy and Linguistic Analysis*	• discusses Moore, Russell, Wittgenstein, Ayer, the Cambridge School, the Oxford School
	Snow, *The Two Cultures*	• Rede lecture, Cambridge, 7 May; 2nd edn. 1963 • argues that there is a sciences/humanities cultural divide
	Ayer succeeds Price	• Wykeham Professor of Logic, Oxford; retires 1978
	Searle to Berkeley	• Assistant Professor 1959–64; Associate Professor 1964–7; Professor 1967–
	Prior to Manchester	• Professor (newly established second chair) 1959–66
	Death of Waismann	• 4 November, Oxford
1960	Quine, *Word and Object*	• introduces idea of indeterminacy of translation • offers def. of ordered pair as philosophical paradigm
	Gadamer, *Truth and Method*	• key text of hermeneutics • part 1 on art, part 2 on history, part 3 on language • first tr. 1975
	Ayer, 'Philosophy and Language'	• inaugural lecture • critique of linguistic philosophy
	Bergmann, 'Strawson's Ontology'	• review of Strawson's *Individuals* • introduction of term 'the linguistic turn'
	Putnam, 'Minds and Machines'	• introduces Turing machines into philosophy of mind
	Prior, 'The Runabout Inference-ticket'	• gets us into contonktions
	Hook, *Dimensions of Mind*	• collection from interdisciplinary conference • contributors include Ducasse, Feigl, Köhler, E. Nagel, Putnam, Skinner, Wiener
	Popkin, *The History of Scepticism from Erasmus to Descartes*	• argues that modern philosophy developed out of a sceptical crisis in the sixteenth century • expanded editions 1979, 2003
	M. Warnock, *Ethics since 1900*	• discusses Bradley, Moore, intuitionism, emotivism, moral psychology, existentialism • 3rd edn. 1978, omitting chapter on Bradley

Year	Event	Further details and/or significance
	Founding of the *British Journal of Aesthetics*	• journal of the British Society of Aesthetics, founded 1960 • editor H. Osborne 1960–77
	Lakatos to London	• LSE, where he remains until his death in 1974
	Kneale succeeds Austin	• White's Professor of Moral Philosophy 1960–6, when he retires due to ill health
	Death of Austin	• 8 February, Oxford
1961	Wittgenstein, *Notebooks 1914–1916*	• 2nd edn. 1979, with different version of 'Notes on Logic'
	Wittgenstein, *Tractatus* retranslated	• tr. Pears and McGuinness
	Austin, *Philosophical Papers*	• 2nd edn. 1970; 3rd edn. 1979
	Russell, *Basic Writings*	• first selection from the full range of Russell's writings (1903–59)
	Grice, 'The Causal Theory of Perception'	• introduces idea of implication, later called 'implicature' (e.g. 1975a, 1981)
	Marcus, 'Modalities and Intensional Languages'	• defends quantified modal logic against Quine's criticisms
	Robinson, 'Non-standard Analysis'	• introduces infinitesimals
	Nagel, *The Structure of Science*	• subtitled 'Problems in the Logic of Scientific Explanation' • classic account of reductionism
	Hart, *The Concept of Law*	• develops legal positivism, described as an exercise in 'analytic jurisprudence' • 2nd edn. 1994 with reply to critics
	von Wright in Finland	• Research Professor, Academy of Finland 1961–86
	Putnam to MIT	• Professor of Philosophy of Science 1961–65
	Fodor at MIT	• Assistant Professor; Associate Professor 1963; Professor 1969–86
	Death of Merleau-Ponty	• 4 May, Paris
1962	Kuhn, *The Structure of Scientific Revolutions*	• rejects cumulative view of scientific progress and emphasizes role played by 'paradigm shifts'
	Austin, lectures published	• *How to Do Things with Words* • *Sense and Sensibilia*
	Geach, *Reference and Generality*	• subtitled 'An Examination of Some Medieval and Modern Theories'
	Kneale & Kneale, *The Development of Logic*	• monumental account from the ancient Greeks to the theory of deductive systems (Gödel, Tarski)
	Putnam, 'The Analytic and the Synthetic'	• argues that analytic statements are true by 'implicit convention'
	Sellars, 'Philosophy and the Scientific Image of Man'	• distinguishes 'scientific image' and 'manifest image'
	Strawson, 'Freedom and Resentment'	• argues for a form of compatibilism by appeal to our 'participant reactive attitudes'

(Continued)

Year	Event	Further details and/or significance
	Mandelbaum, 'Philosophy, Science, and Sense Perception'	• Presidential Address to APA, December • distinguishes analytic from 'continental' philosophy (understood as phenomenological–existential tradition)
	Blanshard, *Reason and Analysis*	• critical study of analytic philosophy over the previous 40 years • discusses logical positivism, logical atomism, linguistic philosophy
	Hintikka, *Knowledge and Belief*	• first main work, exploring logic of the two notions, developing possible-worlds semantics
	Moore, *Commonplace Book 1919–1953*	• selection from his notebooks
	Anderson, *Studies in Empirical Philosophy*	• collection of his writings from 1926
	Rawls to Harvard	• Professor 1962–91; University Professor 1979–2002
	Death of Anderson	• 6 July, Sydney
1963	Davidson, 'Actions, Reasons, and Causes'	• argues that reasons are causes
	Gettier, 'Is Justified True Belief Knowledge?'	• generated the genre of Gettier counterexamples
	Putnam, 'Brains and Behaviour'	• critique of logical behaviourism
	Kenny, *Action, Emotion and Will*	• offers Wittgensteinian, anti-causalist account
	Hare, *Freedom and Reason*	• argues that one can be both free and rational in thinking morally
	Popper, *Conjectures and Refutations*	• subtitled 'The Growth of Scientific Knowledge' • essays elaborating his falsificationism
	Sellars, *Science, Perception and Reality*	• first collection of his papers
	Malcolm, *Knowledge and Certainty*	• collection of his papers
	Stevenson, *Facts and Values*	• collection of his papers
	von Wright, *The Varieties of Goodness*	• his own favourite book
	von Wright, *Norm and Action*	• develops his logic of norms
	Schilpp, ed., *The Philosophy of Rudolf Carnap*	• 11th vol. in 'The Library of Living Philosophers' • 80-page 'Intellectual Autobiography' • contributors include Frank, Popper, Feigl, Ayer, Davidson, Quine, Sellars, Beth, Strawson, Bar-Hillel, Goodman, Pap, Hempel, Putnam, E. Nagel
	Caton, ed., *Philosophy and Ordinary Language*	• first anthology of ordinary language philosophy • contributors: Austin, Cartwright, Hall, Linsky, Rhees, Ryle, Searle, Strawson, Toulmin & Baier, Urmson
	H. D. Lewis, ed., *Clarity Is Not Enough*	• subtitled 'Essays in Criticism of Linguistic Philosophy' • contributors include: Price (1945), Blanshard (1952), Quine (1951), Ayer (1960)

Year	Event	Further details and/or significance
	Mehta, *The Fly and the Fly-bottle*	• interviews Gellner, Russell, Hare, Murdoch, G. Warnock, Strawson, Ayer, Hampshire
	Alston & Nakhnikian, eds., *Readings in Twentieth-Century Philosophy*	• parts on James, Bergson, Maritain, Whitehead, Dewey, Moore, Russell, logical positivism, ordinary language philosophy, Husserl, Heidegger, Tillich, Sartre
	Founding of the *Journal of the History of Philosophy*	• first journal for the history of philosophy established in the English-speaking world
	Sellars to Pittsburgh	• Professor 1963–89
	Cavell to Harvard	• Walter M. Cabot Professor of Aesthetics and the General Theory of Value 1963–97, when he retires
	Dennett to Oxford	• studies with Ryle; Ph.D. awarded 1965
	Plantinga to Calvin College	• Professor 1963–82
	Death of Ajdukiewicz	• 12 April, Warsaw
1964	Wittgenstein, *Philosophical Remarks*	• written 1929–30 • pub. in German; tr. 1975
	Frege, *Basic Laws* translated in part	• introduction and §§ 1–52 of vol. 1; appendix to vol. 2 • tr. M. Furth
	Benacerraf & Putnam, eds., *Philosophy of Mathematics*	• classic collection of readings • 2nd edn. 1983
	Black, *A Companion to Wittgenstein's Tractatus*	• first detailed commentary
	Taylor, *The Explanation of Behaviour*	• argues that teleological explanations are indispensable and non-causal
	Chappell, ed., *Ordinary Language*	• contains Malcolm 1942, Ryle 1953, Austin 1956, Mates 1958, Cavell 1958
	Simpson, *Logical Forms, Reality and Significance*	• pioneering work of Latin American analytic philosophy
	Goodman to Brandeis	• Professor 1964–7
	Habermas to Frankfurt	• Professor of Philosophy and Sociology 1964–71; 1984–93, when he retires
	Death of C. I. Lewis	• 2 February, Menlo Park, California
1965	Waismann, *The Principles of Linguistic Philosophy*	• Waismann's account of Wittgenstein's ideas as he understood them in the early 1930s
	Hempel, *Aspects of Scientific Explanation*	• collection of his papers
	Benacerraf, 'What Numbers Could Not Be'	• argues that arithmetic is concerned with progressions, not objects
	Rorty, 'Mind-Body Identity…'	• argues for eliminative materialism, as now known
	Ammerman, ed., *Classics of Analytic Philosophy*	• work by Austin, Ayer, Broad, Carnap, Grice, Hempel, Moore, Quine, Russell, Ryle, Strawson, Wisdom • contains 'A Short History of Analytic Philosophy' by ed.

(Continued)

Year	Event	Further details and/or significance
	Thiel, *Sense and Reference in Frege's Logic*	• first monograph in German on Frege's philosophy • pub. in English 1968
	Jeremy Walker, *A Study of Frege*	• first monograph in English on Frege's philosophy
	Danto, *Analytical Philosophy of History*	• distinguishes substantival and analytical philosophy of history; repr. in Danto 1985
	Barry, *Political Argument*	• adopts 'analytical' rather than 'causal' approach
	Putnam to Harvard	• Professor of Philosophy; Walter Beverley Pearson Professor of Modern Mathematics and Mathematical Logic 1976–2000, when he retires
	Kuhn to Princeton	• Professor of Philosophy and History of Science 1964–79
	von Wright visits Cornell	• Professor-at-large, Cornell, 1965–77
	Dennett to Irvine	• Assistant Professor 1965–70; Associate Professor 1970–1
1966	Chisholm, *Theory of Knowledge*	• offers definitions of epistemic terms and principles • 2nd edn. 1977; 3rd edn. 1989
	Quine, *The Ways of Paradox*	• second collection of his essays
	Donnellan, 'Reference and Definite Descriptions'	• distinguishes referential and attributive uses, in response to Russell (1905a) and Strawson (1950a)
	D. Lewis, 'An Argument for the Identity Theory'	• first statement of his analytic functionalism, as now known
	Strawson, *The Bounds of Sense*	• reconstructs Kant, playing down his transcendental idealism
	Bennett, *Kant's Analytic*	• 'fighting Kant tooth and nail' to learn from him (p. viii) • sequel 1974
	Weitz, ed., *Twentieth-Century Philosophy: The Analytic Tradition*	• parts on realism and common sense (Moore, Russell, Lovejoy); logical analysis (Russell, Ryle); logical positivism (Carnap, Hahn, Stevenson, Hempel, Urmson); conceptual elucidation (Wisdom, Ryle, Wittgenstein, Austin, Hart & Honoré, Baier)
	Williams & Montefiore, eds., *British Analytical Philosophy*	• contributors: Pears, Searle, Quinton, Lemmon, Harré, Kenny, Ishiguro, Montefiore, MacIntyre, Taylor, Wollheim, Gardiner, Hepburn, Mészáros
	Copi & Beard, *Essays on Wittgenstein's Tractatus*	• collection incl. Wittgenstein 1929
	Pitcher, *Wittgenstein*	• collection on the *Philosophical Investigations*
	Copleston, *A History of Philosophy*, vol. 8	• entitled 'Bentham to Russell' • Part V on 'The Revolt against Idealism': ch. 17 on realism in Britain and America; ch. 18 on Moore; chs. 19–21 on Russell
	Foucault, *The Order of Things*	• contains critique of representation in modern philosophy • tr. 1973

Year	Event	Further details and/or significance
	Hare at Oxford	• White's Professor of Moral Philosophy, Oxford 1966–83
	Prior to Oxford	• Fellow, Balliol College 1966–9, when he dies
	Death of Brouwer	• 2 December, Blaricum, near Amsterdam
1967	Frege, *Kleine Schriften*	• first complete edition of published papers • tr. as *Collected Papers* 1984
	Russell, *Autobiography*	• 3 vols. 1967–9; repub. together in 1975
	Wittgenstein, *Zettel*	• fragments mainly written 1945–8
	Rorty, ed., *The Linguistic Turn*	• classic collection on linguistic philosophy, covering both 'ordinary language' and 'ideal language' philosophy • contains papers by Schlick, Carnap, Bergmann, Ryle, Wisdom, Malcolm, Copi, Black, Ambrose, Chisholm, Cornman, Quine, Passmore, Maxwell & Feigl, Thompson, Hare, Henle, Geach, Urmson, Hampshire, Warnock, Cavell, Shapere, Strawson, Katz, Bar-Hillel • 39-page introd. and 33-page bib. covering 1930–65
	Edwards, ed., *The Encyclopedia of Philosophy*, 8 vols.	• entry on 'Analysis, Philosophical' (Weitz 1967), covering Russell, Moore, Wittgenstein, Wisdom, Ryle, Carnap, Ayer • 2nd edn. 2005, ed. Borchert; includes new entry on 'Analysis, Philosophical' (Soames 2005)
	Grice, 'Logic and Conversation'	• William James Lectures, Harvard • parts published later, but only fully in 1989
	Davidson, 'Truth and Meaning'	• argues that a theory of meaning must be built on a Tarskian theory of truth
	Davidson, 'The Logical Form of Action Sentences'	• repr. 1980 with replies to criticism
	Goldman, 'A Causal Theory of Knowing'	• inspires reliabilism
	Putnam, 'The Nature of Mental States'	• defends machine state functionalism
	Wiggins, *Identity and Spatio-Temporal Continuity*	• argues against idea that identity is continuity • reworked as Wiggins 1980 and again as Wiggins 2001
	Foot, 'The Problem of Abortion ...'	• discusses the doctrine of double effect • introduces the trolley problem, as now known
	Fann, ed., *Ludwig Wittgenstein*	• first collection with many memoirs and recollections
	van Heijenoort, ed., *From Frege to Gödel*	• subtitled 'A Source Book in Mathematical Logic, 1879–1931', with first complete tr. of Frege's *Begriffsschrift*, and many other subsequent works in the history of logic
	McCall, ed., *Polish Logic 1920–1939*	• first collection of work by Polish logicians in translation

(Continued)

Year	Event	Further details and/or significance
	Skolimowski, *Polish Analytical Philosophy*	• subtitled 'A Survey and a Comparison with British Analytical Philosophy'
	Derrida, triple event announcing his presence	• *Speech and Phenomena*: critique of Husserl • *Of Grammatology*: critique of logocentrism • *Writing and Difference*: collection of essays • introduces deconstruction
	Founding of *Noûs*	• founding editor Hector-Neri Casteñeda
	Founding of British Society for Phenomenology	• founded by Wolfe Mays • *Journal of the British Society for Phenomenology* founded 1970
	Williams succeeds Braithwaite	• Knightbridge Professor of Philosophy, Cambridge (the 'Moral' in the title now dropped) • resigns 1979, when he becomes Provost of King's
	Grice to Berkeley	• Professor 1967–88
	Church to UCLA	• Professor 1967–90
1968	Goodman, *Languages of Art*	• develops theory of symbols, theory of notation
	Sellars, *Science and Metaphysics*	• subtitled 'Variations on Kantian Themes' • John Locke Lectures, Oxford 1965–6
	Armstrong, *A Materialist Theory of the Mind*	• fullest account of his identity theory: central state materialism
	Fodor, *Psychological Explanation*	• develops functionalism as a position between behaviourism and dualism
	Wollheim, *Art and its Objects*	• distinguishes artworks as individuals and as types • 2nd edn. 1980
	Danto, *Analytical Philosophy of Knowledge*	• bases account on distinction between descriptive and semantic concepts
	Quine, 'Epistemology Naturalized'	• criticizes Carnapian rational reconstruction • urges that epistemology be seen as part of psychology
	Grice, 'Utterer's Meaning, Sentence Meaning, and Word-Meaning'	• followed by 'Utterer's Meaning and Intentions' (1969)
	Kaplan, 'Quantifying In'	• discusses quantification into epistemological contexts
	Cornman, 'On the elimination of "sensations" and sensations'	• 'eliminative materialism' coined, distinguished from 'reductive materialism'
	Habermas, *Knowledge and Human Interests*	• first articulation of his critical social theory
	Deleuze, *Difference and Repetition*	• presents a metaphysics of difference
	Derrida, 'Différance'	• deconstructs meaning into differing and deferring
	Ayer, *The Origins of Pragmatism*	• subtitled 'Studies in the Philosophy of Charles Sanders Peirce and William James'
	Klemke, ed., *Essays on Frege*	• first collection of papers on Frege • dedicated to Bergmann

Year	Event	Further details and/or significance
	Schilpp, ed., *The Philosophy of C. I. Lewis*	• 13th vol. in 'The Library of Living Philosophers'
	Strawson succeeds Ryle	• Waynflete Professor of Metaphysical Philosophy, Oxford • retires 1987
	Goodman to Harvard	• Professor 1968–77
	Kripke to Rockefeller	• Associate Professor; Professor 1972–7
1969	Frege, *Nachgelassene Schriften*	• *Nachlaß* finally published, based on surviving material • tr. as *Posthumous Writings* 1979
	Wittgenstein, *On Certainty*	• remarks written 1949–51, on Moore 1925 and 1939
	Bolzano, collected works	• first of c.150 vols. appears
	Searle, *Speech Acts*	• classic account of his speech act theory
	Cavell, *Must We Mean What We Say?*	• collection, incl. his essay with that title • includes 'Austin at Criticism' (1965)
	Dretske, *Seeing and Knowing*	• defends epistemological direct realism
	Dennett, *Content and Consciousness*	• first book, dividing philosophy of mind into theory of content and theory of consciousness
	Strawson, 'Meaning and Truth'	• Inaugural Lecture, Oxford • talks of 'Homeric struggle' between communication-intention theorists and theorists of formal semantics
	Skinner, 'Meaning and understanding...'	• argues for contextualist history
	Klemke, ed., *Studies in the Philosophy of G. E. Moore*	• 3 parts: ethics; ontology; methodology and epistemology
	Fann, ed., *Symposium on J. L. Austin*	• papers on his life and work
	Ishiguro, 'Use and Reference of Names'	• rejects realist readings of *Tractatus*
	Stegmüller, *Problems and Results...*	• vol. 1 of *Problems and Results of Philosophy of Science and Analytic Philosophy* (1969–74); 2nd edn. 1983
	Foucault, *The Archaeology of Knowledge*	• sees 'epistemes' (systems of thought) as governed by unconscious rules requiring excavation • tr. 1972
	Deleuze, *The Logic of Sense*	• explores structure and genesis of sense
	Death of Prior	• 6 October, Norway
1970	Davidson, 'Mental Events'	• argues for anomalous monism
	Dretske, 'Epistemic operators'	• offers relevant-alternatives account of knowledge • gives first counterexamples to Principle of Closure
	Sen, *Collective Choice and Social Welfare*	• builds on Arrow 1951 in developing social choice theory by considering informational broadening

(Continued)

Year	Event	Further details and/or significance
	Mundle, *A Critique of Linguistic Philosophy*	• criticizes Ayer, Ryle, Austin, Warnock, and Strawson in Part One, and Wittgenstein in Part Two
	Klemke, ed., *Essays on Bertrand Russell*	• contributors include Quine, Bergmann, Hochberg, Strawson, Sellars, Geach, Linsky, Carnap, Ramsey • 3 parts on ontology, theory of reference and descriptions, philosophy of logic and mathematics
	Ambrose & Lazerowitz, eds., *G. E. Moore: Essays in Retrospect*	• contributors include Braithwaite, Malcolm, Lazerowitz, Findlay, Ambrose, Ryle, Bouwsma, Ewing, Broad, Ayer, W. & M. Kneale, Lewy, Duncan-Jones, Urmson
	Wood & Pitcher, ed., *Ryle*	• first collection on Ryle
	Lakatos & Musgrave, eds., *Criticism and the Growth of Knowledge*	• collection on Kuhn's work • includes Lakatos 1970
	Łukasiewicz, *Selected Works*	• first collection of his logical and philosophical writings in translation
	Fain, *Between Philosophy and History*	• subtitled 'The Resurrection of Speculative Philosophy of History Within the Analytic Tradition'
	Gross, *Analytic Philosophy: An Historical Introduction*	• two main themes: sense-data; meaning and reference • discusses Moore, Russell, Wittgenstein, logical positivism, Ryle, Austin, Quine, Strawson
	Anscombe succeeds Wisdom	• Professor of Philosophy, Cambridge; retires 1986
	White to Princeton	• Professor, Institute for Advanced Study, 1970–87, when he retires
	Death of Russell	• 2 February, Penrhyndeudraeth, Wales
	Death of Carnap	• 14 September, Santa Monica, California
1971	Rawls, *A Theory of Justice*	• uses idea of the 'original position' to argue for a view of 'justice as fairness'
	von Wright, *Explanation and Understanding*	• rejects reduction of reasons to causes
	Cornman, *Materialism and Sensations*	• advocates adverbial materialism, steering between eliminative and reductive materialism
	Ayer, *Russell and Moore: The Analytical Heritage*	• William James Lectures, Harvard 1970 • 5 chapters on Russell, 4 chapters on Moore
	Ryle, *Collected Papers*	• vol. 1: *Critical Essays* • vol. 2: *Collected Essays 1929–1968*
	Strawson, *Logico-Linguistic Papers*	• his classic papers, beginning with 'On Referring' (1950a)
	Kripke, 'Identity and Necessity'	• distinguishes rigid and non-rigid designators
	Dennett, 'Intentional Systems'	• defines 'intentional system' and distinguishes design stance, physical stance, and intentional stance
	Thomson, 'A Defence of Abortion'	• uses violinist thought experiment • in first issue of *Philosophy and Public Affairs*

Year	Event	Further details and/or significance
	Derrida, 'Signature Event Context'	• discusses Austin, prompting debate with Searle (Derrida 1977/1988; Searle 1977)
	Founding of *Canadian Journal of Philosophy*	• founded by John King-Farlow, Kai Nielsen, T. M. Penelhum, and W. W. Rozeboom, Alberta
	Founding of *Russell: the Journal of the Bertrand Russell Archives*	• founding editor Kenneth Blackwell, McMaster • new series 1981, subtitle changed to 'the Journal of Bertrand Russell Studies'
	Dennett to Tufts	• Associate Professor; Professor 1975; Director of Center for Cognitive Studies 1985
	Kim to Michigan	• Professor 1971–87
	Death of Broad	• 11 March, Cambridge
	Death of Ross	• 5 May, Oxford
1972	Kripke, 'Naming and Necessity'	• criticizes descriptivist theories of names and develops a causal theory of reference • pub. in book form 1980
	Popper, *Objective Knowledge*	• rejects 'commonsense theory of knowledge' • dedicated to Tarski
	Frege, *Conceptual Notation*	• tr. by Bynum of *Begriffsschrift* and related material • contains first substantial biography of Frege
	Foot, 'Morality as a System of Hypothetical Imperatives'	• compares ethics with etiquette
	Clarke, 'The legacy of skepticism'	• first account of epistemic contextualism
	Ayer, *Bertrand Russell*	• draws on Ayer 1971
	Hacker, *Insight and Illusion*	• 2nd edn. 1986, with many revisions to his interpretation of Wittgenstein
	Feigl & Sellars, eds., *New Readings in Philosophical Analysis*	• rev. edn. of Feigl & Sellars 1949
	Derrida, *Margins of Philosophy*	• essays on Hegel, Husserl, Heideger, Saussure, and Austin, among others
	Deleuze & Guattari, *Anti-Oedipus*	• sees 'desiring-production' as the 'universal primary process'
	Founding of *Journal of Philosophical Logic*	• founding editor B. C. van Fraassen
	Hamlyn succeeds Ryle	• Editor of *Mind* 1972–84
1973	Dummett, *Frege: Philosophy of Language*	• groundbreaking work, establishing Frege's status as a founder of analytic philosophy • in emphasizing his philosophy of language, provoked critical reaction from those who saw Frege as primarily having other interests, rooted in his logicism • 2nd edn. 1981 (with refs. added)
	Davidson, 'Radical Interpretation'	• concerned with the conditions that make interpretation possible

(Continued)

Year	Event	Further details and/or significance
	Benacerraf, 'Mathematical Truth'	• poses dilemma for mathematical realism
	Evans, 'The Causal Theory of Names'	• critique of Kripke 1972
	Kim, 'Causation, Nomic Subsumption and the Concept of Event'	• presents his view of events as property exemplifications
	Williams, *Problems of the Self*	• first collection of his papers, incl. on personal identity
	Lewis, *Counterfactuals*	• applies possible world semantics to conditionals
	Hinton, *Experience*	• source of talk of 'disjunctivism'
	Danto, *Analytical Philosophy of Action*	• develops notion of a 'basic action'
	Ayer, *The Central Questions of Philosophy*	• ch. 3 on 'Philosophical Analysis'
	Berlin *et al.*, *Essays on J. L. Austin*	• first collection on Austin • Berlin describes 'Oxford philosophy' in introd.
1974	Wittgenstein, *Philosophical Grammar*	• written 1930–3
	Davidson, 'On the Very Idea of a Conceptual Scheme'	• attacks dualism of scheme and content—the 'third dogma of empiricism'
	Nagel, 'What is it like to be a bat?'	• started the bat-wagon about phenomenal consciousness
	Kirk, 'Sentience and Behaviour'	• coins term 'zombie'
	Plantinga, *The Nature of Necessity*	• develops actualist possible worlds semantics • applies modal metaphysics to ontological argument and to free will response to problem of evil
	Montague, *Formal Philosophy*	• selected papers
	Nozick, *Anarchy, State and Utopia*	• adopts 'flashy' analytic style (cf. p. x)
	Brandt, *A Theory of the Good and the Right*	• John Locke Lectures, Oxford • pub. 1979
	Schilpp, ed., *The Philosophy of Karl Popper*	• 14th vol. in 'The Library of Living Philosophers' • first collection on Popper
	Death of Lakatos	• 2 February, London
1975	Putnam, *Philosophical Papers*	• vols. 1–2; vol. 3 1983
	Putnam, 'The meaning of "meaning"'	• uses Twin Earth thought experiment to argue that '"meanings" just ain't in the *head*!' • advocates causal theory of reference
	Grice, 'Logic and Conversation'	• develops idea of conversational implicatures
	Grice, 'Method in Philosophical Psychology'	• Presidential address to APA, San Diego, 28 March
	Shoemaker, 'Functionalism and Qualia'	• argues that functionalism can account for qualia
	Fodor, *The Language of Thought*	• develops his representational theory of mind • argues for the innateness of concepts
	Sellars, *Essays in Philosophy and its History*	• 'variations on Sellarsian themes' (p. vii)

Year	Event	Further details and/or significance
	Feyerabend, *Against Method*	• subtitled 'Outline of an anarchistic theory of knowledge' • originally planned as *For and Against Method*, co-authored with Lakatos
	Hacking, *Why Does Language Matter to Philosophy?*	• discusses heydays of ideas, meanings, sentences • answer: because sentences interface between knower and known, and perhaps even constitute knowledge
	Corrado, *The Analytic Tradition in Philosophy*	• Part 1: 'The Background'; 2 chs. on logic and metaphysics; knowledge and meaning • Part II: 'The Problems'; 4 chs. on theory of knowledge; philosophy of mind; ethics; logic and analytic philosophy
	Clark, *The Life of Bertrand Russell*	• second biography
	Relaunch of *Erkenntnis*	• editors Essler, Hempel and Stegmüller • vol. 9 (see Hempel 1975, Hegselmann & Siegwart 1991)
	Founding of *Grazer Philosophische Studien*	• subtitled 'International Journal for Analytic Philosophy' • founding editor Rudolf Haller
1976	Frege, *Wissenschaftlicher Briefwechsel*	• first edn. of Frege's correspondence (as known then) • tr. as *Philosophical and Mathematical Correspondence* 1980
	Lakatos, *Proofs and Refutations*	• subtitled 'The Logic of Mathematical Discovery'
	Chisholm, *Person and Object*	• argues that a satisfactory metaphysics of persons must accord with certain pre-analytic data
	Dummett, *The Logical Basis of Metaphysics*	• William James Lectures, Harvard • pub. 1991, revised
	Wiggins, 'Truth, Invention, and the Meaning of Life'	• applies Wittgenstein's ideas about objectivity in mathematics to ethics
	Thomson, 'Killing, Letting Die,...'	• discusses trolley problem
	Geach, 'Saying and Showing in Frege and Wittgenstein'	• inspires later debate about the 'new Wittgenstein'
	Evans & McDowell, eds., *Truth and Meaning*	• collection marking the 'Davidsonic boom' hitting Oxford in 1970s
	Popper, *Unended Quest*	• intellectual autobiography
	Lewis, ed., *Contemporary British Philosophy (Fourth Series)*	• contributors: Anscombe, Bambrough, Dummett, Flew, Geach, Hamlyn, Hare, Harrison, Hepburn, Körner, Strawson, Swinburne, Urmson, Vesey, Walsh, Warnock, Williams, Winch
	Schirn, ed., *Studien zu Frege*, 3 vols.	• first multi-volume collection of papers on Frege
	Fogelin, *Wittgenstein*	• 'Arguments of the Philosophers' series; 2nd edn. 1987
	Ackermann, *The Philosophy of Karl Popper*	• first monograph on Popper

(Continued)

Year	Event	Further details and/or significance
	Tugendhat, *Lectures...*	• introduces analytic philosophy of language in German-speaking world; tr. 1982
	Death of Heidegger	• 26 May, Freiburg, Germany
	Death of Ryle	• 6 October, Whitby, Yorkshire
1977	Wittgenstein, *Remarks on Colour*	• written 1950–1
	Mackie, *Ethics: Inventing Right and Wrong*	• argues against objective values, using 'argument from relativity' and 'argument from queerness'
	Dworkin, *Taking Rights Seriously*	• criticizes legal positivism and utilitarianism
	Kuhn, *The Essential Tension*	• subtitled 'Selected Studies in Scientific Tradition and Change'
	McDowell, 'On the Sense and Reference of a Proper Name'	• reconstructs Frege's notion of sense in a Davidsonian framework, arguing for 'object-dependent' thoughts
	Kaplan, 'Demonstratives'	• first presentation of his theory of demonstratives • pub. 1989, though widely circulated before
	Perry, 'Frege on Demonstratives'	• argues that demonstratives pose a problem for Frege • response by Evans (1981)
	Ayer, *Part of my Life*	• autobiography up to 1946; sequel 1984 (*More of my Life*)
	Hempel to Pittsburgh	• Professor 1977–85
	Kripke to Princeton	• McCosh Professor of Philosophy 1977–97
1978	Lakatos, *Philosophical Papers*, 2 vols.	• vol. 1: 'The methodology of scientific research programmes' • vol. 2: 'Mathematics, science and epistemology' • published four years after his death
	Goodman, *Ways of Worldmaking*	• pluralism about right yet conflicting world-versions
	Dummett, *Truth and Other Enigmas*	• first collection of his papers
	Dennett, *Brainstorms*	• essays on mind and psychology
	Armstrong, *Universals and Scientific Realism*	• argues for the existence of universals, as required for there to be laws of nature
	Block, 'Troubles with Functionalism'	• presents absent qualia argument
	Foot, *Virtues and Vices*	• first collection of her papers
	Cohen, *Karl Marx's Theory of History*	• founding text of analytic Marxism • 2nd edn. 2000
	Rée, Ayers & Westoby, *Philosophy and its Past*	• criticizes analytic philosophers' approach to history of philosophy
	Malcolm to London	• Visiting Professor, King's College
	Wright to St Andrews	• Professor of Logic and Metaphysics 1978–2009
	Death of Gödel	• 14 January, Princeton
	Death of Stevenson	• 14 March, Bennington, Vermont
1979	Rorty, *Philosophy and the Mirror of Nature*	• attacks epistemological foundationalism, seen as characteristic of philosophy since Descartes
	Kripke, 'A Puzzle about Belief'	• raises his puzzle about Pierre

Year	Event	Further details and/or significance
	Burge, 'Individualism and the Mental'	• argues for social externalism, using thought experiment concerning 'arthritis', among others
	Perry, 'The Problem of the Essential Indexical'	• he makes a mess
	Goldfarb, 'Logic in the Twenties'	• discusses development of understanding of quantification
	Wittgenstein, *Ludwig Wittgenstein and the Vienna Circle*	• conversations recorded by Waismann 1929–32
	Cavell, *The Claim of Reason*	• subtitled 'Wittgenstein, Skepticism, Morality, and Tragedy'
	Churchland, *Scientific Realism and the Plasticity of Mind*	• his first book, arguing for eliminative materialism, rejecting folk psychology
	Sainsbury, *Russell*	• 'Arguments of the Philosophers' series
	Platts, *Ways of Meaning*	• first book defending Davidsonian theory of meaning
	Diamond, 'Frege and Nonsense'	• her first paper exploring issue of nonsense in connection with Frege and Wittgenstein; followed by Diamond 1981
	Brandt, *A Theory of the Good and the Right*	• develops his utilitarianism
	Levy, *Moore: G. E. Moore and the Cambridge Apostles*	• first biography of Moore—but only covering his life up to First World War • remains, to date, the only biography
	Dummett succeeds Ayer	• Wykeham Professor of Logic, Oxford; retires 1992
	Kuhn to MIT	• Professor of Philosophy 1979–89
1980	Wittgenstein, *Remarks on the Philosophy of Psychology*, 2 vols.	• remarks in vol. 1 written 1946–7 (TS 229) • remarks in vol. 2 written 1947–8 (TS 232)
	Davidson, *Essays on Actions and Events*	• first collection of his papers
	Searle, 'Minds, Brains and Programs'	• introduces Chinese Room argument
	Fodor, 'Methodological Solipsism...'	• defends a form of rational, as opposed to naturalistic, psychology, based on methodological solipsism
	van Fraassen, *The Scientific Image*	• develops his constructive empiricism
	Field, *Science Without Numbers*	• defends nominalism
	Block, ed., *Readings in the Philosophy of Psychology*	• vol. 1 on mental representation, imagery, innate ideas • vol. 2 on behaviourism, physicalism, functionalism
	Sluga, *Gottlob Frege*	• written in reaction to Dummett 1973 • sought to position Frege more accurately in the history of philosophy, as influenced by a host of German thinkers • 'Arguments of the Philosophers' series (but more historical than most in the series)

(Continued)

Year	Event	Further details and/or significance
	Resnik, *Frege and the Philosophy of Mathematics*	• first monograph devoted to Frege's philosophy of mathematics
	Baker and Hacker, *Wittgenstein: Understanding and Meaning*	• vol. 1 of their analytical commentary on *Philosophical Investigations* (§§ 1–184); rev. Hacker 2005 • vol. 2 1985 (§§ 185–242); rev. Hacker 2009 • vol. 3 1990 (§§ 243–427), by Hacker alone • vol. 4 1996 (§§ 428–693), by Hacker alone
	Wright, *Wittgenstein on the Foundations of Mathematics*	• pioneering work on the topic
	Lyons, *Gilbert Ryle*	• first monograph on Ryle
	O'Hear, *Karl Popper*	• 'Arguments of the Philosophers' series
	Founding of *History and Philosophy of Logic*	• founding editor Ivor Grattan-Guinness
	Timothy Smiley succeeds Williams	• Knightbridge Professor of Philosophy, Cambridge • retires 1998
	Death of Sartre	• 15 April, Paris
	Death of Evans	• 10 August, London
1981	Dummett, *The Interpretation of Frege's Philosophy*	• Dummett's substantial reply to his critics, written as he was preparing the 2nd edn. of Dummett 1973
	Putnam, *Reason, Truth and History*	• ch. 1: 'Brains in a vat'
	Chisholm, *The First Person*	• subtitled 'An Essay on Reference and Intentionality'
	Dretske, *Knowledge and the Flow of Information*	• bases theory of knowledge and belief on theory of information
	Fodor, *RePresentations*	• essays on functionalism and propositional attitudes
	Nozick, *Philosophical Explanations*	• offers truth-tracking account of knowledge
	Hare, *Moral Thinking*	• argues that universal prescriptivism entails preference utilitarianism
	MacIntyre, *After Virtue*	• critique of modern (post-Enlightenment) moral theory and defence of an Aristotelian virtue ethics
	Habermas, *Theory of Communicative Action*	• critique of theories of rationality and development of his universal pragmatics and discourse theory • 2 vols. tr. 1984. 1987
	Dworkin, 'What is Equality?'	• part 1: equality of welfare; part 2: equality of resources
	Holtzman & Leich, eds., *Wittgenstein: To Follow a Rule*	• contributors include Baker, Peacocke, Wright, Evans, McDowell, Blackburn
	Block, ed., *Perspectives on the Philosophy of Wittgenstein*	• includes Kripke on rules and private language
	French *et al.*, eds., *The Foundations of Analytic Philosophy*	• 32 papers, from Chisholm on Brentano and Benacerraf on Frege to Devitt on Donnellan
	Munitz, *Contemporary Analytic Philosophy*	• chs. on Peirce, Frege, Russell, early Wittgenstein, verificationism, later Wittgenstein, Quine

Year	Event	Further details and/or significance
	Death of Kotarbiński	• 3 October, Warsaw
	Death of Mackie	• 12 December, Oxford
1982	Wittgenstein, *Last Writings on the Philosophy of Psychology*, vol. 1	• remarks written 1948–9: preliminary studies for Part II of *Philosophical Investigations* • vol. 2 1992: 'The Inner and the Outer 1949–1951'
	Kripke, *Wittgenstein on Rules and Private Language*	• interprets Wittgenstein as offering a 'sceptical solution' to a sceptical paradox • provokes much controversy among Wittgenstein scholars
	Evans, *The Varieties of Reference*	• begins with Frege, Russell, and Kripke
	McDowell, 'Criteria, Defeasibility and Knowledge'	• criticizes 'highest common factor' (hybridist or conjunctivist) conception of experience
	Jackson, 'Epiphenomenal Qualia'	• birth of Mary the colour scientist and formulation of the knowledge argument
	Wolf, 'Moral Saints'	• finds the idea unattractive, criticizing Kantianism and utilitarianism
	Ayer, *Philosophy in the Twentieth Century*	• intended as a sequel to Russell's *History of Western Philosophy* • concentrates on the 'two main schools for which I have a personal predilection, the American pragmatists…and what is loosely called the analytic movement' (p. vii) • six chapters on philosophers of these schools, one on Collingwood, one on phenomenology and existentialism (to 'diminish what might appear to be a bias in favour of Anglo-Saxon thought'; p. viii)—Husserl receives one page and Heidegger five pages
	von Wright, *Wittgenstein*	• collection of his papers, some on composition of texts
	Mohanty, *Husserl and Frege*	• second monograph on Husserl and Frege (after Føllesdal 1958)
	Plantinga to Notre Dame	• John A. O'Brien Professor of Philosophy • director of Center for Philosophy of Religion 1984–2002
1983	Russell, *Collected Papers*, vol. 1	• 'Cambridge Essays 1888–99' • 1st vol. published, with 28 vols. planned
	Wright, *Frege's Conception of Numbers as Objects*	• reinvigorated work on Frege's logicism
	Fodor, *The Modularity of Mind*	• argues that the mind contains 'modules'
	Searle, *Intentionality*	• theory of intentionality seen as central to philosophy of mind
	Stich, *From Folk Psychology to Cognitive Science*	• argues for eliminative materialism
	Barwise & Perry, *Situations and Attitudes*	• develop situation semantics

(Continued)

Year	Event	Further details and/or significance
	Levine, 'Materialism and Qualia'	• formulates explanatory gap argument
	Parsons, *Mathematics in Philosophy*	• selected essays
	Grice, 'The Conception of Value'	• Carus lectures, pub. 1991
	Death of Tarski	• 27 October, San Francisco
1984	Russell, *Collected Papers*, vol. 7	• 'Theory of Knowledge: The 1913 Manuscript' • 2nd vol. published
	Davidson, *Inquiries into Truth and Interpretation*	• second collection of his papers
	Parfit, *Reasons and Persons*	• parts on self-defeating theories, rationality and time, personal identity, and future generations
	Stroud, *The Significance of Philosophical Skepticism*	• discusses Austin, Carnap, Moore, and Quine • explores internal/external distinction
	Stalnaker, *Inquiry*	• applies possible worlds semantics to theory of belief
	Millikan, *Language, Thought and Other Biological Categories*	• naturalistic account of intentionality • teleological theory of mental content
	Shoemaker, *Identity, Cause, and Mind*	• collection of his essays
	Baker & Hacker, *Frege: Logical Excavations*	• sought to correct some of the perceived deficiencies of Dummett's view of Frege—like Sluga (1980), but from a different (Wittgensteinian) perspective • critically reviewed by Dummett (1984), prompting further heated exchange in *Phil. Quar.* (Baker and Hacker 1987, 1989; Dummett 1988b)
	Rorty, Schneewind, & Skinner, eds., *Philosophy in History*	• collection of essays addressing both methodological questions and specific developments in the history of analytic philosophy • reacting to the ahistorical approach to history of philosophy of many analytic philosophers • contributors: C. Taylor, MacIntyre, Rorty (identifying four genres of historiography), Krüger, Hacking, Kuklick, Lepenies, Schneewind, Skinner, Burnyeat, M. Frede, Dunn, Ayers, Sluga (on Frege), Baldwin (on Moore), Hylton (on Russell)
	Gracia *et al.*, eds., *Philosophical Analysis in Latin America*	• collection of work by Latin American analytic philosophers (cf. Gracia 1984)
	Kim, 'Concepts of Supervenience'	• distinguishes 'weak', 'strong', and 'global' supervenience
	Mulligan, Simons & Smith, 'Truth-makers'	• first full discussion of idea of truth-makers • first published use of term Simons 1982
	Railton, 'Alienation…'	• argues for 'objective consequentialism'
	Founding of the British Society for the History of Philosophy	• 'to promote and foster all aspects of the study and teaching of the history of philosophy' • its journal, the *BJHP*, founded in 1993
	Founding of *History of Philosophy Quarterly*	• founding editor Nicholas Rescher

Year	Event	Further details and/or significance
	Blackburn succeeds Hamlyn	• Editor of *Mind* 1984–90
	Death of Foucault	• 25 June, Paris
	Death of Price	• 20 November, Oxford
1985	Quine, *The Time of My Life*	• autobiography
	Rosen, *The Limits of Analysis*	• criticizes analytic philosophy for failing to do justice to its limits and context
	Williams, *Ethics and the Limits of Philosophy*	• describes his approach as 'analytical' (p. vi)
	Foster, *A. J. Ayer*	• first monograph on Ayer • 'Arguments of the Philosophers' series
	Hookway, *Peirce*	• 'Arguments of the Philosophers' series
	Wright, 'Facts and certainty'	• sees failure of transmission of warrant in Moore's proof of an external world
	Herman, 'The Practice of Moral Judgment'	• offers normative reconstruction of Kantian ethics
	Tomberlin & van Inwagen, eds., *Alvin Plantinga*	• collection of essays, incl. Plantinga's 'Self-Profile'
	Passmore, *Recent Philosophers*	• supplement to Passmore 1957/1966 • discusses theories of meaning; realism and relativism
	Rajchman & West, eds., *Post-Analytic Philosophy*	• contributors include: Rorty, Putnam, Nagel, Danto, Cavell, Davidson, Hacking, Kuhn, Rawls, Scanlon • restricted to American philosophy
	Death of E. Nagel	• 20 September, New York
1986	Lewis, *On the Plurality of Worlds*	• fullest defence of his modal realism and counterpart theory
	Burge, 'Individualism and Psychology'	• argues for anti-individualism about perceptual states • discusses Marr's theory of vision
	Salmon, *Frege's Puzzle*	• defends naïve theory of information content
	Patricia Churchland, *Neurophilosophy*	• subtitled 'Toward a Unified Science of the Mind/Brain'
	Cohen, *The Dialogue of Reason*	• subtitled 'An Analysis of Analytical Philosophy' • chs. on language, reasoning, rationality, computation
	Nagel, *The View from Nowhere*	• explores tension between subjective and objective standpoints
	Railton, 'Moral Realism'	• defends 'stark, raving moral realism'
	Ayer, *Ludwig Wittgenstein*	• short, critical account of all main works
	Malcolm, *Nothing is Hidden*	• subtitled 'Wittgenstein's Criticism of his Early Thought'
	Haaparanta & Hintikka, eds., *Frege Synthesized*	• contributors: Weiner, van Heijenoort, Sluga, Ricketts, Burge, Haaparanta. Resnik, Cocchiarella, Brandom, Kitcher, Currie, A. Moore & Rein
	Schilpp & Hahn, eds., *The Philosophy of W. V. Quine*	• 18th vol. in 'The Library of Living Philosophers'

(Continued)

Year	Event	Further details and/or significance
	Proust, *Questions of Form*	• subtitled 'Logic and the Analytic Proposition from Kant to Carnap', discussing Bolzano and Frege as well
	Canfield, ed., *The Philosophy of Wittgenstein*	• 15-vol. collection on Wittgenstein
	Shanker, ed., *Ludwig Wittgenstein: Critical Assessments*	• 4-vol. collection on Wittgenstein • second series 2002 (Shanker & Kilfoyle)
	Founding of *Mind and Language*	• founding editors M. K. Davies and S. D. Guttenplan
	McDowell to Pittsburgh	• Professor 1986–
	Fodor to New York	• Distinguished Professor, CUNY 1986–8
1987	Dennett, *The Intentional Stance*	• full exposition of his view that mental states are ascribed from the intentional stance
	Fodor, *Psychosemantics*	• defends folk psychology
	Schiffer, *Remnants of Meaning*	• criticizes theories of meaning and content, advocating 'no-theory theory'
	Davidson, 'Knowing One's Own Mind'	• creates Swampman
	Cocchiarella, *Logical Studies in Early Analytic Philosophy*	• collection of his essays on Frege, Russell, Meinong, and Wittgenstein, reconstructing logicism and logical atomism; first use of 'early analytic philosophy' in a title
	Founding of *Philosophical Perspectives*	• founding editor James E. Tomberlin 1987–2002 • supplement to *Noûs* from 1996
	Kim to Brown	• Professor
	Death of Bergmann	• 21 April, Iowa City
1988	Putnam, *Representation and Reality*	• criticizes his earlier functionalism
	Dretske, *Explaining Behavior*	• subtitled 'Reasons in a World of Causes' • representational theory of belief, desire, and action
	Baker, *Wittgenstein, Frege and the Vienna Circle*	• first monograph exploring connections between Frege, Wittgenstein, and logical positivism
	McGuinness, *Wittgenstein: A Life: Young Ludwig 1889–1921*	• first book-length biography of Wittgenstein, though covering only first half of his life • 2nd vol. has never appeared
	Haller, *Questions on Wittgenstein*	• considers Wittgenstein in the context of Austrian philosophy
	New series of *Ratio*	• subtitled 'An International Journal of Analytic Philosophy'
	Fodor to Rutgers	• Professor
	Death of Feigl	• 1 June, Minneapolis
	Death of Black	• 27 August, Ithaca, New York
	Death of Grice	• 28 August, Berkeley, California
1989	Publication of Frege's letters to Wittgenstein	• tr. Dreben and Floyd, pub. 2011

Year	Event	Further details and/or significance
	Taylor, *Sources of the Self*	• subtitled 'The Making of the Modern Identity'
	O'Neill, *Constructions of Reason*	• subtitled 'Explorations of Kant's Practical Philosophy'
	Brink, *Moral Realism and the Foundations of Ethics*	• criticizes non-cognitivism and defends moral realism
	Kim, 'The Myth of Nonreductive Materialism'	• Presidential Address to Central Division of APA, April • critique of nonreductive materialism
	Quinn, two papers on 'Actions, Intentions, and Consequences'	• discusses 'doctrine of doing and allowing' and doctrine of double effect
	Warnock, *J. L. Austin*	• first monograph; 'Arguments of the Philosophers' series
	Schilpp & Hahn, eds., *The Philosophy of Georg Henrik von Wright*	• 19th vol. in 'The Library of Living Philosophers'
	Death of Ayer	• 27 June, London
	Death of Sellars	• 2 July, Pittsburgh
1990	Russell, *Collected Papers*, vol. 2	• 'Philosophical Papers 1896–99' • 7th vol. published
	Quine & Carnap, *Dear Carnap, Dear Van*	• Quine–Carnap correspondence, ed. Creath
	Hylton, *Russell, Idealism, and the Emergence of Analytic Philosophy*	• first substantial scholarly account of the development of Russell's philosophy (up to 1913) • introduction: argues for the importance of studying the history of analytic philosophy
	Baldwin, *G. E. Moore*	• examines full range of Moore's work • remains the most substantial account to date
	Weiner, *Frege in Perspective*	• first monograph on Frege from the Harvard school
	Monk, *Ludwig Wittgenstein: The Duty of Genius*	• first (and to date only) full-length complete biography of Wittgenstein (McGuinness 1988 only covered first half of his life)
	Sahlin, *The Philosophy of F. P. Ramsey*	• first monograph on Ramsey
	Bell & Cooper, eds., *The Analytic Tradition*	• contributors: Bell, Skorupski, Burge, Hookway, Dummett, Künne, Baldwin, Hylton, Sacks, Hart
	Neale, *Descriptions*	• defends and develops Russell's theory
	Etchemendy, *The Concept of Logical Consequence*	• criticizes Tarksi's conception
	van Inwagen, *Material Beings*	• explores problem of material composition
	Gibbard, *Wise Choices, Apt Feelings*	• offers naturalistic theory of normative judgement
	Nussbaum, *Love's Knowledge*	• subtitled 'Essays on Philosophy and Literature'
	Walton, *Mimesis as Make-Believe*	• offers eliminativist account of fiction
	Bell, *Husserl*	• offers an analytic philosopher's account • 'Arguments of the Philosophers' series
	Sainsbury succeeds Blackburn	• Editor of *Mind* 1990–2000
	Williams at Oxford	• White's Professor of Moral Philosophy 1990–6

(Continued)

Year	Event	Further details and/or significance
	Death of Braithwaite	• 21 April, Cambridge
	Death of Kneale	• 24 June, Grassington
	Death of Malcolm	• 4 August, London
	Death of Skinner	• 18 August, Cambridge, Massachusetts
1991	Dummett, *Frege: Philosophy of Mathematics*	• long-awaited sequel to his book on Frege's philosophy of language, finally correcting imbalance in view fostered • adopts an approach more sensitive to the development of Frege's philosophy
	Dummett, *Frege and Other Philosophers*	• collection of Dummett's papers on Frege, incl. replies to some of his critics
	Coffa, *The Semantic Tradition from Kant to Carnap*	• a history of the development of views on the a priori • Part I: 'The semantic tradition' • Part II: 'Vienna, 1925–1935'
	Griffin, *Russell's Idealist Apprenticeship*	• offers detailed account of the development of Russell's thought up to his final break with idealism • draws on the extensive archives at McMaster
	Diamond, *The Realistic Spirit*	• collection, incl. papers on Frege and Wittgenstein
	Dennett, *Consciousness Explained*	• proposes 'multiple drafts' view of consciousness • rejects qualia, and hence 'hard problem'
	Hill, *Autonomy and Self-Respect*	• collection of essays
	Jackson, 'Decision-Theoretic Consequentialism…'	• argues that consequentialism can accommodate concern with nearest and dearest
	Vlastos, *Socrates: Ironist and Moral Philosopher*	• presents Socrates as not merely a critical thinker but as having positive views
	Deleuze & Guattari, *What is Philosophy?*	• argues that philosophy is the creation of concepts
	Köhnke, *The Rise of Neo-Kantianism*	• subtitled 'German Academic Philosophy between Idealism and Positivism'
	Dreben to Boston	• Professor 1991–99
	Death of Stegmüller	• 1 June, Munich
	Death of Vlastos	• 12 October, Berkeley
1992	Strawson, *Analysis and Metaphysics*	• seeks to replace 'reductive' by 'connective' analysis
	Russell, *Selected Letters*	• Vol. 1: 'The Private Years, 1884–1914' • Vol. 2: 'The Public Years, 1914–1970'; pub. 2001
	Searle, *The Rediscovery of the Mind*	• develops his theory of consciousness, based on Chinese Room argument (1980)
	Williams, *Unnatural Doubts*	• subtitled 'Epistemological Realism and the Basis of Skepticism' • defends epistemological contextualism
	Campbell, *Truth and Historicity*	• first history of development of conceptions of truth
	Hahn, ed., *The Philosophy of A. J. Ayer*	• 21st vol. in 'The Library of Living Philosophers'

Year	Event	Further details and/or significance
	Simons, *Philosophy and Logic…*	• essays on Central European analytic tradition
	DeRose, 'Contextualism and knowledge attributions'	• first semantic contextualist account of knowledge attributions
	Death of Hung	• 27 February, Beijing
	Death of Hart	• 19 December, Oxford
1993	Rawls, *Political Liberalism*	• moves from his earlier Kantian constructivism to 'political constructivism'
	Dummett, *Origins of Analytical Philosophy*	• offered not as a history but 'a series of philosophical reflections on the roots of the analytical tradition' (p. viii) • argues that analytic philosophy and phenomenology have the same roots, focusing on Frege and Husserl, with no discussion of Russell, Moore, or the Vienna Circle • claims that analytic philosophy was born when the 'linguistic turn' was taken—in Frege's *Foundations* • orig. pub. in German 1988
	Dummett, *The Seas of Language*	• collection, incl. papers on theory of meaning
	Blackburn, *Essays in Quasi-Realism*	• develops expressivism
	Dancy, *Moral Reasons*	• defends moral particularism; elaborated in Dancy 2004
	Kim, *Supervenience and Mind*	• selected essays
	Plantinga, two books on warrant	• argues that knowledge requires warrant rather than justification (1993a) • develops theory of warrant as proper function (1993b)
	von Wright, 'Analytical Philosophy'	• subtitled 'A Historico-Critical Survey'
	Russell, *Collected Papers*, vol. 3	• 'Toward the 'Principles of Mathematics' 1900–02' • 9th vol. published
	Irvine & Wedeking, eds., *Russell and Analytic Philosophy*	• contributors include Sainsbury, Blackburn & Code, Neale, Griffin, B. Linsky, Shanker, Detlefsen, Hylton, Landini, Hunter
	Sluga, ed., *The Philosophy of Frege*, 4 vols.	• the second multi-volume collection on Frege, containing many of the classic papers published up to 1988 • vol. 1: general assessments and historical accounts • vol. 2: logic and foundations of mathematics • vol. 3: meaning and ontology • vol. 4: sense and reference
	Moore, *Selected Writings*	• the first Moore reader, ed. Baldwin
	(Barcan) Marcus, *Modalities*	• collection of her papers
	Founding of *British Journal for the History of Philosophy*	• journal of the BSHP • founding editor G. A. J. Rogers 1993–2011
	Founding of *European Journal of Philosophy*	• founding editor Mark Sacks

(Continued)

Year	Event	Further details and/or significance
	Wiggins succeeds Dummett	• Wykeham Professor of Logic, Oxford; retires 2000
	Death of Feyerabend	• 11 February, Genolier, Vaud, Switzerland
	Death of Wisdom	• 9 September, Cambridge
1994	Brandom, *Making It Explicit*	• main work presenting his inferentialism • introd. to main ideas later provided in Brandom 2000
	McDowell, *Mind and World*	• aims to show that there is no gulf between mind and world to be bridged
	Skorupski, *English-Language Philosophy 1750–1945*	• vol. 6 in OUP 'History of Western Philosophy' series • first half of the twentieth century discussed as 'modernism', with one chapter on Frege and Cambridge, one on Vienna
	Carl, *Frege's Theory of Sense and Reference*	• places Frege in Kantian epistemological tradition • pub. in CUP 'Modern European Philosophy' series
	Smith, *Austrian Philosophy: The Legacy of Franz Brentano*	• defends the 'Neurath–Haller thesis', that there is a distinctive Austrian tradition of analytic philosophy (cf. Haller 1991)
	Steiner, *An Essay on Rights*	• analytic Marxist account
	Death of Popper	• 17 September, Croydon
1995	Dretske, *Naturalizing the Mind*	• defends representational theory of consciousness
	Demopoulos, ed., *Frege's Philosophy of Mathematics*	• first collection bringing together work inspired by the rediscovery of Frege's theorem
	Hintikka & Puhl, eds., *The British Tradition in 20th Century Philosophy*	• proceedings of 17th International Wittgenstein Symposium
	Malcolm, *Wittgensteinian Themes*	• essays 1978–89
	Kusch, *Psychologism*	• offers account of debates about psychologism in late nineteenth- and early twentieth-century Germany • subtitled 'A case study in the sociology of philosophical knowledge'
	Smith & Smith, eds., *The Cambridge Companion to Husserl*	• contributors: B. Smith, D. Smith, Mohanty, Hintikka, Simons, Willard, Mulligan, Philipse, Tieszen, Fine
	Founding of *Stanford Encyclopedia of Philosophy*	• founding editor Edward N. Zalta • initial funding from Center for the Study of Language and Information, Stanford, directed by John Perry
	Death of Church	• 11 August, Hudson, Ohio
	Death of Deleuze	• 4 November (suicide), Paris
1996	Chalmers, *The Conscious Mind*	• raises the 'hard' problem of consciousness • argues against reductive materialist accounts
	Korsgaard, *Creating the Kingdom of Ends*	• develops and defends Kant's ethics
	Korsgaard, *The Sources of Normativity*	• defends Kantian appeal to autonomy, synthesizing voluntarism, realism and reflective endorsement
	Publication of Carnap's notes on Frege's lectures	• tr. as *Frege's Lectures on Logic* 2004

Year	Event	Further details and/or significance
	Hacker, *Wittgenstein's Place in Twentieth-Century Analytic Philosophy*	• an account of analytic philosophy with Wittgenstein's philosophy (both early and late) firmly at the centre • Frege and Russell are discussed as part of the background and Quine in a later chapter on 'post-positivism' • final chapter on 'The Decline of Analytic Philosophy'
	Beaney, *Frege: Making Sense*	• focuses on development of Frege's conception of sense
	Dejnozka, *The Ontology of the Analytic Tradition and Its Origins*	• subtitled 'Realism and Identity in Frege, Russell, Wittgenstein, and Quine'
	Monk, *Bertrand Russell: The Spirit of Solitude*	• vol. 1 of biography • vol. 2 2000, subtitled 'The Ghost of Madness'
	Monk & Palmer, eds., *Bertrand Russell and the Origins of Analytical Philosophy*	• contributors: Monk, Griffin, Noonan, Candlish, Sainsbury, Palmer, Hylton, Rodríguez-Consuegra, Grayling, Kilmister, Landini, Pigden, Greenspan
	Sluga and Stern, eds., *The Cambridge Companion to Wittgenstein*	• contributors: Sluga, Fogelin, Ricketts, Summerfield, Garver, Gerrard, Glock, Diamond, Cavell, Stroud, Bloor, Scheman, Kober, Stern
	Giere & Richardson, eds., *Origins of Logical Empiricism*	• described as 'an effort on the part of the Minnesota Center for Philosophy of Science to recover its own historical origins' (p.vii)
	Sarkar, ed., *Science and Philosophy in the Twentieth Century*	• collection of works on logical empiricism, 6 vols.
	Baillie, ed., *Contemporary Analytic Philosophy: Core Readings*	• readings divided into six sections: (1) Frege, Russell, Moore; (2) Wittgenstein; (3) Logical Empiricism (Schlick, Carnap); (4) Ordinary Language Philosophy (Ryle, Austin, Strawson, Grice); (5) Quine; (6) Truth, Meaning and Interpretation (Tarski, Davidson) • 2nd edn. 2002, with 7th section added on 'Reference and Essence' (Kripke, Putnam, Burge)
	Ewald, ed., *From Kant to Hilbert*	• source book on foundations of mathematics
	Sokal, 'Transgressing the Boundaries...'	• hoax article submitted to *Social Text*, provoking debate about postmodernism as part of the 'Science Wars'
	Death of Kuhn	• 17 June, Cambridge, Massachusetts
1997	Frege, *The Frege Reader*	• first single-volume edition to include all Frege's seminal papers as well as substantial selections from his three major works; ed. Beaney
	Gabriel & Kienzler, eds., *Frege in Jena*	• first collection devoted to Frege's Jena context
	Tait, ed., *Early Analytic Philosophy: Frege, Russell, Wittgenstein*	• contributors: Burge, Friedman, Gerrard, Goldfarb, Hylton, B. Linsky, Reck, Ricketts, Tait, Weiner
	Glock, ed., *The Rise of Analytic Philosophy*	• contributors: Føllesdal on analytic philosophy, Sluga on Frege, Monk on Russell, Hacker on the rise of analytic philosophy, and Skorupski on why language mattered

(Continued)

Year	Event	Further details and/or significance
	Künne, Siebel, & Textor, eds., *Bolzano and Analytic Philosophy*	• first book on Bolzano's relation to analytic philosophy • signals recognition not so much of his direct influence but of his anticipation of ideas of analytic philosophy
	Clarke, *Philosophy's Second Revolution*	• subtitled 'Early and Recent Analytic Philosophy' • argues against the naturalistic—and more specifically, materialistic—turn that took place in the 1960s
	Hahn, ed., *The Philosophy of Hans-Georg Gadamer*	• 24th vol. in 'The Library of the Living Philosophers'
	Hahn, ed., *The Philosophy of Roderick M. Chisholm*	• 25th vol. in 'The Library of the Living Philosophers'
	Haldane, ed., *Analytical Thomism*	• special issue of *Monist* • first use of term in title of book; earlier use Haldane 1995
	Death of Berlin	• 5 November, Oxford
	Death of Hempel	• 9 November, Princeton
1998	Scanlon, *What We Owe to Each Other*	• development of his contractualism
	Blackburn, *Ruling Passions*	• develops expressivist theory of practical reasoning
	Jackson, *From Metaphysics to Ethics*	• subtitled 'A Defence of Conceptual Analysis'
	McDowell, collected papers	• vol. 1: *Mind, Value, and Reality* • vol. 2: *Meaning, Knowledge, and Reality*
	Lowe, *The Possibility of Metaphysics*	• argues for the foundational nature of metaphysics in analytic philosophy
	Richardson, *Carnap's Construction of the World*	• stresses neo-Kantian roots of Carnap's philosophy
	Kamm, *Morality, Mortality*	• vol. 1 entitled 'Death and Whom to Save from It'
	Biletzki & Matar, eds., *The Story of Analytic Philosophy*	• subtitled 'Plot and Heroes' • contributors include Hacker, Hylton, Sacks, Skorupski, Floyd, Friedlander, Putnam, Hintikka
	Mancosu, ed., 1998, *From Brouwer to Hilbert*	• subtitled 'The Debate on the Foundations of Mathematics in the 1920s'
	Hahn, ed., *The Philosophy of P. F. Strawson*	• 26th vol. in 'The Library of the Living Philosophers'
	Craig, ed., *Routledge Encyclopedia of Philosophy*	• 10 vols. • online from 2000: <http://www.rep.routledge.com>
	Death of Goodman	• 25 November, Needham, Massachusetts
1999	Friedman, *Reconsidering Logical Positivism*	• collection of papers, mainly on Carnap
	Hursthouse, *On Virtue Ethics*	• fullest presentation of her virtue ethics

Year	Event	Further details and/or significance
	Irvine, ed., *Bertrand Russell: Critical Assessments*, 4 vols.	• vol. 1: life, work and influence • vol. 2: logic and mathematics • vol. 3: language, knowledge, and the world • vol. 4: history of philosophy, ethics, education, religion, and politics
	Hahn, ed., *The Philosophy of Donald Davidson*	• 27th vol. in 'The Library of the Living Philosophers'
	Tooley, ed., *Analytical Metaphysics*	• 5 vol. collection of essays
	O'Hear, ed., *German Philosophy Since Kant*	• includes: Simons on Austrian realism, Glock on German analytic tradition, Bell on Brentano's influence on Moore and Russell, Hacker on Frege and Wittgenstein, Uebel on the Vienna Circle, Inwood on nothing
	White, *A Philosopher's Story*	• autobiography
	Rogers, *A. J. Ayer: A Life*	• first biography
	Death of Chisholm	• 19 January, Providence, Rhode Island
	Death of Dreben	• 11 July, Boston
2000	Wittgenstein, *Nachlass*	• Bergen electronic edition
	Williamson, *Knowledge and Its Limits*	• defends knowledge-first approach to epistemology
	Stroll, *Twentieth-Century Analytic Philosophy*	• main chapters on Frege's and Russell's philosophical logic, logical positivism and the *Tractatus*, Moore, later Wittgenstein, Ryle and Austin, Quine, and direct reference theories
	Friedman, *A Parting of the Ways*	• account of the meeting at Davos in 1929 between Cassirer, Heidegger, and Carnap
	Crary and Read, eds., *The New Wittgenstein*	• contributors include Diamond, Conant, Floyd, Hacker
	Timothy Williamson succeeds Wiggins	• Wykeham Professor of Logic at Oxford
	M. Martin succeeds Sainsbury	• Editor of *Mind* 2000–5
	Death of Quine	• 25 December, Boston
2001	Baldwin, *Contemporary Philosophy*	• subtitled 'Philosophy in English since 1945' • final vol. in OUP 'History of Western Philosophy' series
	Floyd & Shieh, eds., *Future Pasts: The Analytic Tradition in Twentieth-Century Philosophy*	• dedicated to Dreben, most contributors having Harvard connection • organized around key events in the history of analytic philosophy from Frege's *Begriffsschrift* • contributors: Goldfarb, Weiner, Føllesdal, Hintikka, Ricketts, Parsons, Floyd, Minar, Quine, Friedman, Hylton, Putnam, Neiman, Scheman, Parikh, Cavell, Hart, Shieh, Hatfield, Sacks, Rawls
	Hale and Wright, *Reason's Nearest Kin*	• essays on neo-Fregean philosophy of mathematics

(Continued)

Year	Event	Further details and/or significance
	Crane, *Elements of Mind*	• defends Brentano's thesis, that intentionality is the mark of the mental
	Martinich & Sosa, eds., *A Companion to Analytic Philosophy*	• 39 chapters summarizing the work of the 41 greatest analytic philosophers, according to the editors: Frege, Russell, Moore, Broad, Wittgenstein, Carnap, Popper, Ryle, Tarski, Church, Gödel (the last three treated together), Ramsey, Hempel, Goodman, Hart, Stevenson, Quine, Ayer, Austin, Malcolm, Sellars, Grice, von Wright, Chisholm, Davidson, Anscombe, Hare, Strawson, Foot, Marcus, Rawls, Kuhn, Dummett, Putnam, Armstrong, Chomsky, Rorty, Searle, Fodor, Kripke, David Lewis
	Martinich & Sosa, eds., *Analytic Philosophy: An Anthology*	• 7 sections: philosophy of language, metaphysics, epistemology, philosophy of mind, freedom and personal identity, ethics, methodology • selections from the work of those in the editors' *Companion*, except Broad, Popper, Ryle, Tarski, Church, Gödel, Ramsey, Hart, von Wright, Hare, Marcus, Kuhn, Dummett, Chomsky, Rorty, Fodor • includes work, instead, by Black, Gettier, Nagel, Williams, Langford, hence offering a different perspective on the canon
	Hanna, *Kant and the Foundations of Analytic Philosophy*	• an account of the relationship between the views of Kant and analytic philosophers on the notions of the analytic and synthetic, a priori and a posteriori
	Kreiser, *Gottlob Frege: Leben—Werk—Zeit*	• first (and to date only) full-length biography of Frege
	Kuklick, *A History of Philosophy in America 1720–2000*	• Part II: 'The Age of Pragmatism, 1859–1934' • Part III: 'Professional Philosophy, 1912–2000', with chapters on 'Professional Realism', 'Europe's Impact on the United States', 'Harvard and Oxford', and 'The Tribulations of Professional Philosophy'
	Founding of *Philosophers' Imprint*	• pub. online by University of Michigan
	Death of Anscombe	• 5 January, Cambridge
	Death of D. Lewis	• 14 October, Princeton
2002	Brandom, *Tales of the Mighty Dead*	• inferentialist reading of certain texts in the history of philosophy; two essays on Frege
	Williams, *Truth and Truthfulness*	• subtitled 'An Essay in Genealogy'
	Reck, ed., *From Frege to Wittgenstein: Perspectives on Early Analytic Philosophy*	• explores work of Frege and early Wittgenstein • contributors: Reck, Gabriel, Gerrard, Sluga, Shieh, Ruffino, Weiner, Goldfarb, Macbeth, Ricketts, Diamond, Proops, Floyd, Ostrow, Conant (89-page essay on 'The Method of the *Tractatus*')
	Horgan *et al.*, eds., *Origins*	• collection on the common sources of the analytic and phenomenological traditions
	Death of Hare	• 29 January, Ewelme, Oxfordshire

Year	Event	Further details and/or significance
	Death of Gadamer	• 13 March, Heidelberg
	Death of Rawls	• 24 November, Lexington, Massachusetts
2003	Soames, *Philosophical Analysis in the Twentieth Century*, 2 vols.	• vol. 1: 'The Dawn of Analysis'; 5 parts: Moore; Russell; early Wittgenstein; logical positivism; early Quine • vol. 2: 'The Age of Meaning'; 7 parts: later Wittgenstein; Ryle, Strawson and Hare; Malcolm and Austin; Grice; later Quine; Davidson; Kripke • series of rational reconstructions of some canonical texts • no discussion of Frege or Carnap • narrative: the Whiggish story of gradual clarifications of modal notions culminating in Kripke's work
	Baldwin, ed., *The Cambridge History of Philosophy 1870–1945*	• Part I 1870–1914, Part II 1914–45, each Part divided into sections covering different areas of philosophy • first section of Part I on positivism, idealism, and pragmatism • first section of Part II on 'the analytic programme', with chapters on logical atomism (Simons), logical positivism (Richardson), Polish logic (Woleński), and logic and philosophical analysis (Baldwin)
	Griffin, ed., *The Cambridge Companion to Bertrand Russell*	• contributors: Griffin, Grattan-Guinness, Cartwright, Beaney, Godwyn and Irvine, Hylton, Landini, Urquhart, Hager, Tully, Linsky, Demopoulos, Baldwin, Grayling, Pigden
	Stalnaker, *Ways a World Might Be*	• collection of his papers on metaphysics
	Gibbard, *Thinking How To Live*	• develops expressivism
	Beaney, 'Analysis'	• *Stanford Encyclopedia* entry, outlining the history of conceptions of analysis, with extensive bibliography • § 6 on analytic philosophy
	Lamarque and Olsen, eds., *Aesthetics and the Philosophy of Art*	• subtitled 'The Analytic Tradition: An Anthology'
	Shields, ed., *Process and Analysis*	• first book exploring connection between Whitehead, Hartshorne, and the analytic tradition
	Haaparanta & Niiniluuoto, eds., *Analytic Philosophy in Finland*	• first survey of Finnish analytic philosophy
	Founding of British Philosophical Association	• established out of the National Committee for Philosophy, set up in early 1980s
	Kripke to New York	• Professor CUNY
	Death of Williams	• 10 June, Rome
	Death of von Wright	• 16 June, Helsinki
	Death of Davidson	• 30 August, Berkeley, California
2004	Wittgenstein, complete correspondence	• Innsbruck electronic edition
	Armstrong, *Truth and Truthmakers*	• defends truth-maker principle

(Continued)

Year	Event	Further details and/or significance
	Pryor, 'What's wrong with Moore's argument'	• defends Moore's proof of an external world
	Baker, *Wittgenstein's Method*	• collection of his last papers, seeing Wittgenstein more as a psychotherapist than a policeman (cf. p. 1)
	Awodey & Klein, eds., *Carnap Brought Home: The View from Jena*	• exemplifies growing interest in the history of analytic philosophy in Germany, as scholars there seek to reclaim the work of those philosophers—such as Carnap—who were forced to leave Germany as a result of Nazism
	Feferman & Feferman, *Alfred Tarski*	• first biography
	Gibson, ed., *The Cambridge Companion to Quine*	• contributors: Gibson, Fogelin, Creath, de Rosa and Lepore, Bergström, Hylton, Kirk, Føllesdal, Isaacson, Ullian, Dreben
	Complete translation of Frege's *Basic Laws* underway	• work begins on a complete translation, directed by Crispin Wright at St Andrews • eventually published 2013
2005	Wittgenstein, *The Big Typescript*	• composed 1933–7
	Davidson, *Truth and Predication*	• discusses problem of the unity of the proposition
	Burge, *Truth, Thought, Reason*	• collection of his papers on Frege • substantial introduction
	Hylton, *Propositions, Functions, Analysis*	• collection of his essays on Russell
	Neale, ed., *100 Years of 'On Denoting'*	• special issue of *Mind* marking centenary
	Stevens, *The Russellian Origins of Analytic Philosophy*	• offers account of development of Russell's philosophy focusing on problem of the unity of the proposition
	Beaney & Reck, eds., *Gottlob Frege: Critical Assessments*, 4 vols.	• third multi-volume collection on Frege • contains key papers pub. 1986–2005 • vol. 1: Frege's philosophy in context • vol. 2: Frege's philosophy of logic • vol. 3: Frege's philosophy of mathematics, • vol. 4: Frege's philosophy of thought and language • comparison with Sluga 1993 shows increasing concern with philosophy of mathematics
	Sorell & Rogers, eds., *Analytic Philosophy and History of Philosophy*	• essays by historians of early modern philosophy reflecting on the relationship between analytic philosophy and history of philosophy • but no essays on the history of analytic philosophy itself
	Jackson & Smith, eds., *The Oxford Handbook of Contemporary Philosophy*	• 'contemporary philosophy' understood as contemporary analytic philosophy
	Baldwin succeeds Martin	• Editor of *Mind* 2005–

Year	Event	Further details and/or significance
2006	McGinn, *Elucidating the Tractatus*	• seeks a way between 'metaphysical' and 'resolute' readings
	Travis, *Thought's Footing*	• reads Wittgenstein as responding to Frege
	Wilson, *Wandering Significance*	• subtitled 'An Essay on Conceptual Behavior'
	Textor, ed., *The Austrian Contribution to Analytic Philosophy*	• collection exploring roots of analytic philosophy in work of Bolzano, Brentano, Meinong, and others
	Auxier & Hahn, eds., *The Philosophy of Jaakko Hintikka*	• 30th vol. in 'The Library of the Living Philosophers'
	Horgan & Timmons, eds., *Metaethics after Moore*	• marking centenary of Moore 1903
	Corradini, Galvan, & Lowe, eds., *Analytic Philosophy Without Naturalism*	• defends analytic non-naturalism in epistemology, ontology, philosophy of religion, philosophy of mind, practical philosophy
	Death of Strawson	• 13 February, Oxford
2007	Williamson, *The Philosophy of Philosophy*	• ch. 1: 'The Linguistic Turn and the Conceptual Turn' • ch. 6: 'Thought Experiments', discussing Gettier
	Sosa, *A Virtue Epistemology*	• manifesto of virtue epistemology
	Burge, *Foundations of Mind*	• collection of papers defending his anti-individualism • substantial introd.
	Candlish, *The Russell/Bradley Dispute and its Significance for Twentieth-Century Philosophy*	• first monograph devoted to the dispute • argues against received view that Russell 'won' • repr. 2009 as 3rd vol. in 'History of Analytic Philosophy' series
	Hylton, *Quine*	• views Quine's philosophy as rooted in his naturalism • 'Argument of the Philosophers' series
	Carus, *Carnap and Twentieth-Century Thought*	• subtitled 'Explication as Enlightenment'
	Friedman & Creath, eds., *The Cambridge Companion to Carnap*	• contributors: Creath, Friedman, Carus, Mormann, Gabriel, Ryckman, Pincock, Uebel, Reck, Ricketts, Awodey, Demopoulos, Zabell, Richardson
	Richardson & Uebel, eds., *The Cambridge Companion to Logical Empiricism*	• contributors: Richardson, Uebel, Stadler, Hoffmann, Reisch, Friedman, Galavotti, Mormann, Awodey and Carus, Ryckman, Hardcastle, Nemeth, Stern, Creath • 47-page bib.
	Auxier & Hahn, eds., *The Philosophy of Michael Dummett*	• 31st vol. in 'The Library of Living Philosophers'
	Beaney, ed., *The Analytic Turn*	• subtitled 'Analysis in Early Analytic Philosophy and Phenomenology'
	Green & Williams, eds., *Moore's Paradox*	• first collection of essays on the paradox
	Nuccetelli & Seay, eds., *Themes from G. E. Moore*	• subtitled 'New Essays in Epistemology and Ethics'

(Continued)

Year	Event	Further details and/or significance
	Preston, *Analytic Philosophy: The History of an Illusion*	• attempts to show that the idea of analytic philosophy is a myth • mistakenly assumes that analytic philosophy can only be a 'school' with a defining set of doctrines
	Founding of new book series on history of analytic philosophy	• series editor Beaney, published by Palgrave Macmillan • first series of its kind, inspired by Candlish 2007
	Death of Rorty	• 8 June, Palo Alto, California
2008	Glock, *What is Analytic Philosophy?*	• characterizes analytic philosophy as a tradition held together by ties of influence and family resemblances • ch. 2: historical survey
	Wittgenstein, *Wittgenstein in Cambridge*	• subtitled 'Letters and Documents 1911–1951'
	Brandom, *Between Saying and Doing*	• subtitled 'Towards an Analytic Pragmatism' • John Locke Lectures, Oxford 2006 • first ch.: 'Extending the Project of Analysis'
	Moran, ed., *The Routledge Companion to Twentieth Century Philosophy*	• part I on 'Major themes and movements': early and later analytic philosophy, Hegelianism, Kant, American philosophy, naturalism, feminism
	Gaskin, *The Unity of the Proposition*	• discusses Frege, Russell, and Bradley's regress
	Nasim, *Bertrand Russell and the Edwardian Philosophers*	• explores debate over the problem of the external world in Britain 1900–16 • 1st vol. in 'History of Analytic Philosophy' series
	Misak, ed., *The Oxford Handbook of American Philosophy*	• includes chapters on analytic philosophy by Hookway, Ahmed, Richardson, Glock, Lance, Ramberg, Soames, Macbeth
	Hallett, *Linguistic Philosophy: The Central Story*	• discusses Plato, Aquinas, Wittgenstein, Carnap, Tarski, Flew, Russell, Malcolm, Austin, Kripke, Putnam, Quine, Rorty, Stich, Habermas
2009	Wittgenstein, *Philosophical Investigations*	• 4th edn., rev. tr. by Hacker & Schulte • Part I taken as the main text • Part II retitled 'Philosophy of Psychology—A Fragment'
	Irwin, *The Development of Ethics*, vol. 3	• entitled 'From Kant to Rawls' • first two vols. pub. 2007, 2008
	Floyd, 'Recent Themes in the History of Early Analytic Philosophy'	• state-of-the-art review article for *Journal of the History of Philosophy*
	Wagner, ed., *Carnap's 'Logical Syntax of Language'*	• first collection devoted to *Logical Syntax* • 2nd vol. in 'History of Analytic Philosophy' series
	Braddon-Mitchell and Nola, eds., *Conceptual Analysis and Philosophical Naturalism*	• explores the 'Canberra Plan', building on Ramsey 1929 and Lewis 1970
2010	Burge, *Origins of Objectivity*	• develops theory of perception • critique of Strawson, Evans, Quine, Davidson

Year	Event	Further details and/or significance
	Künne, *Gottlob Frege's Philosophical Logic*	• detailed commentary on Frege 1918a, 1918b, 1923 • pub. in German
	Cavell, *Little Did I Know*	• philosophical autobiography
	Auxier & Hahn, eds., *The Philosophy of Richard Rorty*	• 32nd vol. in 'The Library of Living Philosophers'
	Venturinha, ed. *Wittgenstein after his Nachlass*	• explores implications of *Nachlass* now being available • 4th vol. in 'History of Analytic Philosophy' series
	Coliva, *Moore and Wittgenstein*	• subtitled 'Scepticism, Certainty, and Common Sense' • 5th vol. in 'History of Analytic Philosophy' series
	Founding of *Journal for the History of Analytical Philosophy*	• journal of the Society for the Study of the History of Analytical Philosophy • editor Mark Textor • first issue 2011
	Death of Foot	• 3 October, Oxford
2011	Moore, *Early Philosophical Writings*	• contains Moore's 1897 and 1898 dissertations • ed. Baldwin & Preti
	Kripke, *Philosophical Troubles*	• vol. 1 of collected papers
	Parfit, *On What Matters*	• discusses reasons and rationality; offers synthesis of Kantianism, consequentialism and contractualism; responds to critics; defends a 'non-metaphysical' meta-ethics
	Kuusela & McGinn, eds., *The Oxford Handbook of Wittgenstein*	• covers full range of Wittgenstein's philosophy
	Heck, *Frege's Theorem*	• collection of his essays
	Lapointe, *Bolzano's Theoretical Philosophy*	• 6th vol. in 'History of Analytic Philosophy' series
	Stevens, *The Theory of Descriptions*	• offers account of development and reception of Russell's theory of descriptions, and a systematic defence • 7th vol. in 'History of Analytic Philosophy' series
	Linsky, *The Evolution of Principia Mathematica*	• subtitled 'Bertrand Russell's Manuscripts and Notes for the Second Edition'
	Mander, *British Idealism*	• comprehensive history
	Gustafsson and Sørli, eds., *The Philosophy of J. L. Austin*	• first collection on Austin since Berlin *et al.* 1973
	Special issue of *Teorema*	• symposium on Glock's *What is Analytical Philosophy?* • contributors: Glock (précis of book, and replies), Dummett, Marconi, Monk, García-Carpintero, Preston, Acero, Hacker, Beaney, Alvarez, Mulligan
	Philosophical Books changes name	• becomes *Analytic Philosophy* • first issue 1960
	Death of Dummett	• 27 December, Oxford

(Continued)

Year	Event	Further details and/or significance
2012	Schwartz, *A Brief History of Analytic Philosophy*	• chapters on Russell and Moore; Wittgenstein and logical positivism; responses to logical positivism; ordinary language philosophy; responses to ordinary language philosophy; metaphysics; naming and necessity; ethics • excludes Frege
	Patterson, *Alfred Tarski*	• first monograph on his philosophy of language and logic • 8th vol. in 'History of Analytic Philosophy' series
	Death of Marcus	• 19 February, New Haven, Connecticut
2013	Reck, ed., *The Historical Turn in Analytic Philosophy*	• contributors: Reck, Baldwin, Beaney, Candlish, Carus, Glock, Hatfield, Heis, Hylton, Kremer, Richardson, Tanney • 15th vol. in 'History of Analytic Philosophy' series
	Frege, *Basic Laws of Arithmetic*	• first complete English translation, tr. Ebert & Rossberg
	Beaney, ed., *The Oxford Handbook of the History of Analytic Philosophy*	

CHAPTER 4

BIBLIOGRAPHY OF ANALYTIC PHILOSOPHY AND ITS HISTORIOGRAPHY

MICHAEL BEANEY

THIS bibliography includes all works referred to in the first three chapters of this Handbook and the key works referred to in the other chapters. A selection of other works has also been made to round out the picture of analytic philosophy and its historiography that this Handbook provides, at the start of the second decade of the twenty-first century. In what follows, the entries starred (*) indicate that the author is one of the 150 philosophers and other thinkers listed in the table that precedes the chronology in Chapter 3.

Of the four main founders of analytic philosophy, bibliographies of their writings can be found in Thiel and Beaney 2005 (on Frege); Schilpp 1944, Blackwell, and Ruja 1994 (on Russell); Schilpp 1942 (on Moore); and Wittgenstein 2000 (the Bergen electronic edition, on Wittgenstein). Bibliographies of secondary literature on Frege can be found in Bynum and Bynum 1972, Beaney and Reck 2005, vol. 1; on Russell in Irvine 1999, vol. 1; on Moore in Baldwin 2004; and on Wittgenstein in Shanker and Shanker 1986, Frongia and McGuinness 1990. Of the other figures in the history of analytic philosophy (and twentieth-century philosophy, more generally), where they have a volume in 'The Library of Living Philosophers' series devoted to their work, full bibliographies of their writings are included. Bibliographies can also be found in the relevant encyclopaedia entries and companions cited in the table that precedes the chronology in Chapter 3.

Ackermann, Robert (1976). *The Philosophy of Karl Popper*. Amherst: University of MA Press.

Addis, Laird (2005). 'Gustav Bergmann 1906–1987', online at: <http://www.uiowa.edu/~phil/gustavbergmann.shtml> [accessed 28 May 2012].

Adorno, Theodore and Max Horkheimer (1944). *Dialectic of Enlightenment: Philosophical Fragments*; pub. in book form 1947; ed. G. S. Noerr, tr. E. Jephcott. Stanford: Stanford University Press, 2002.

Agostini, F. D. (1997). *Analitici e Continentali*. Milan: Raffaello Cortina.

Ahmed, Arif (2008). 'W. V. Quine', in Misak 2008, pp. 290–338.

*Ajdukiewicz, Kazimierz (1920). *From the Methodology of the Deductive Sciences*. Lwów, 1921 (post-dated), orig. in Polish; tr. J. Giedymin in *Studia Logica* 19 (1966), 9–45.

—— (1931). 'On the Meaning of Expressions', tr. in Ajdukiewicz 1978, pp. 1–34; orig. pub. in Polish.

—— (1934a). 'Language and Meaning', tr. in Ajdukiewicz 1978, pp. 35–66; orig. pub. in Polish.

—— (1934b). 'The World-Picture and the Conceptual Apparatus', tr. in Ajdukiewicz 1978, pp. 67–89; orig. pub. in Polish.

—— (1949). *Problems and Theories of Philosophy*, tr. Henryk Skolimowski and Anthony Quinton. Cambridge: Cambridge University Press, 1973.

—— (1974). *Pragmatic Logic*. Dordrecht: D. Reidel.

—— (1978). *The Scientific World-Perspective and Other Essays, 1931–1963*, ed. J. Giedymin. Dordrecht: D. Reidel.

Akehurst, Thomas L. (2008). 'The Nazi Tradition: The Analytic Critique of Continental Philosophy in Mid-century Britain', *History of European Ideas* 34: 548–57.

—— (2009). 'British Analytic Philosophy: The Politics of an Apolitical Culture', *History of Political Thought* 30: 678–92.

—— (2010). *The Cultural Politics of Analytic Philosophy: Britishness and the Spectre of Europe*. London: Continuum.

*Alexander, Samuel (1914). 'The Basis of Realism', *Proceedings of the British Academy* 6: 279–314.

—— (1920). *Space, Time, and Deity*, 2 vols. London: Macmillan.

Almog, Joseph, John Perry, and Howard Wettstein (eds.) (1989). *Themes from Kaplan*. Oxford: Oxford University Press.

Alston, William P. and George Nakhnikian (eds.) (1963). *Readings in Twentieth-Century Philosophy*. London: Macmillan/Free Press of Glencoe.

Ambrose, Alice (1966). *Essays in Analysis*. London: George Allen & Unwin.

Ambrose, Alice and Morris Lazerowitz (eds.) (1970). *G. E. Moore: Essays in Retrospect*. London: George Allen & Unwin.

Ammerman, Robert R. (ed.) (1965a). *Classics of Analytic Philosophy*. New York: McGraw-Hill.

—— (1965b). 'A Short History of Analytic Philosophy', in Ammerman 1965a, pp. 1–12.

Anderson, C. Anthony (2001). 'Alfred Tarski, Alonzo Church, and Kurt Gödel', in Martinich and Sosa 2001a, pp. 124–38.

*Anderson, John (1927). 'Empiricism', in Anderson 1962, pp. 3–14.

—— (1962). *Studies in Empirical Philosophy*. Sydney: Angus and Robertson.

Anderson, R. Lanier (2005). 'Neo-Kantianism and the Roots of Anti-psychologism', *British Journal for the History of Philosophy* 13: 287–323.

Anellis, Irving H. (2005a). 'Bergmann, Gustav (1906–87)', in Shook 2005, I, pp. 209–12.

—— (2005b). 'Nagel, Ernest (1901–85)', in Shook 2005, III, pp. 1787–90.

—— (2005c). 'Tarski, Alfred (1901–83)', in Shook 2005, IV, pp. 2380–4.

Angelelli, Ignacio (1967). *Studies on Gottlob Frege and Traditional Philosophy*. Dordrecht: D. Reidel.

Annas, Julia (2004). 'Ancient Philosophy for the Twenty-First Century', in Leiter 2004, pp. 25–43.

*Anscombe, G. E. M. (1957). *Intention*. Oxford: Blackwell; 2nd edn. 1963.

—— (1958). 'Modern Moral Philosophy', *Philosophy* 33: 1–19.

—— (1959). *An Introduction to Wittgenstein's Tractatus*. London: Hutchinson; 2nd edn. 1963; 3rd edn. 1967; 4th edn. 1971.

—— (1981). *Collected Philosophical Papers*, 3 vols. Minneapolis: University of Minnesota Press.

Anscombe, G. E. M. and P. T. Geach (1961). *Three Philosophers*. Oxford: Blackwell.

Arana, Andrew and Carlos Alvarez (eds.) (forthcoming). *Analytic Philosophy and the Foundations of Mathematics*. Basingstoke: Palgrave Macmillan.

Armendt, Brad (2001). 'Frank P. Ramsey', in Martinich and Sosa 2001a, pp. 139–47.

Armour, Leslie (2006). 'McTaggart, John McTaggart Ellis (1866–1925)', in Grayling, Pyle, and Goulder 2006, III, pp. 2047–51.

*Armstrong, D. M. (1968). *A Materialist Theory of the Mind*. London: Routledge & Kegan Paul; rev. edn. 1993.

—— (1978). *Universals and Scientific Realism*. Cambridge: Cambridge University Press.

—— (1997). *A World of States of Affairs*. Cambridge: Cambridge University Press.

—— (2001). 'Black Swans: The Formative Influences in Australian Philosophy', in Brogaard and Smith 2001, pp. 11–17.

—— (2004). *Truth and Truthmakers*. Cambridge: Cambridge University Press.

Armstrong, D. M. and Norman Malcolm (1984). *Consciousness and Causality: A Debate on the Nature of Mind*. Oxford: Blackwell.

Arrington, R. and H.-J. Glock (eds.) (1991). *Wittgenstein's Philosophical Investigations*. London: Routledge.

Arrow, Kenneth J. (1951). *Social Choice and Individual Values*. New York: Wiley; 2nd edn. 1963.

Asmus, Walter (1968/1970). *Johann Friedrich Herbart. Eine pädagogische Biographie*, 2 vols. Heidelberg: Quelle & Meyer.

Aspray, William and Philip Kitcher (eds.) (1988). *History and Philosophy of Modern Mathematics*. Minneapolis: University of Minnesota Press.

Aune, Bruce (1998). 'Feigl and the Development of Analytic Philosophy at the University of Minnesota', online at: <http://www.umass.edu/philosophy/PDF/Aune/feigl.pdf> [accessed 28 May 2012].

*Austin, J. L. (1946). 'Other Minds', *Proceedings of the Aristotelian Society*, Supplementary Vol. 20; repr. in Austin 1979, pp. 76–116.

—— (1950). 'Truth', *Proceedings of the Aristotelian Society*, Supplementary Vol. 24; repr. in Austin 1979, pp. 117–33.

—— (1954). 'Unfair to Facts', in Austin 1979, pp. 154–74; orig. written 1954.

—— (1956). 'A Plea for Excuses', *Proceedings of the Aristotelian Society* 56; repr. in Chappell 1964, pp. 41–63; also repr. in Austin 1979, pp. 175–204.

—— (1962a). *How to Do Things with Words*, ed. J. O. Urmson and M. Sbisà. Oxford: Oxford University Press.

—— (1962b). *Sense and Sensibilia*, ed. G. J. Warnock. Oxford: Oxford University Press.

—— (1979). *Philosophical Papers*, 3rd edn., ed. J. O. Urmson and G. J. Warnock. Oxford: Clarendon Press; 1st edn. 1961.

Auxier, Randall E. and Lewis Edwin Hahn (eds.) (2006). *The Philosophy of Jaakko Hintikka*. Chicago: Open Court.

—— (eds.) (2007). *The Philosophy of Michael Dummett*. Chicago: Open Court.

—— (eds.) (2010). *The Philosophy of Richard Rorty*. Chicago: Open Court.

—— (eds.) (2013). *The Philosophy of Hilary Putnam*. Chicago: Open Court.

Awodey, Steve (2007). 'Carnap's Quest for Analyticity: The *Studies in Semantics*', in Friedman and Creath 2007, pp. 226–47.

Awodey, Steve and Carsten Klein (eds.) (2004). *Carnap Brought Home: The View from Jena*. Chicago: Open Court.

*Ayer, A. J. (1936). *Language, Truth and Logic*. London: Victor Gollancz; 2nd edn. 1946; repr. London: Penguin.

—— (1937). 'Does Philosophy Analyse Common Sense?', *Proceedings of the Aristotelian Society*, Supplementary Vol. 16: 162–76.

—— (1940). *The Foundations of Empirical Knowledge*. London: Macmillan.

—— (1956). *The Problem of Knowledge*. Harmondsworth: Pelican.

—— *et al.* (1956). *The Revolution in Philosophy*. London: Macmillan.

—— (ed.) (1959). *Logical Positivism*. Glencoe, IL: The Free Press.

—— (1960). 'Philosophy and Language' [inaugural lecture]; repr. in Lewis 1963, pp. 401–28.

—— (1968). *The Origins of Pragmatism: Studies in the Philosophy of Charles Sanders Peirce and William James*. London: Macmillan.

—— (1971). *Russell and Moore: The Analytical Heritage*. London: Macmillan.

—— (1972). *Bertrand Russell*. London: Fontana.

—— (1973). *The Central Questions of Philosophy*. London: Weidenfeld & Nicolson.

—— (1977). *Part of my Life*. Oxford: Oxford University Press.

—— (1982). *Philosophy in the Twentieth Century*. London: Weidenfeld & Nicolson.

—— (1984). *More of my Life*. Oxford: Oxford University Press.

—— (1986). *Ludwig Wittgenstein*. London: Penguin.

—— (1992). 'Intellectual Autobiography', in Hahn 1992, pp. 1–53.

Ayer, A. J. and Ted Honderich (1991). 'An Interview with A. J. Ayer', in Griffiths 1991, pp. 209–26.

Ayers, Michael (1978). 'Analytical Philosophy and the History of Philosophy', in Rée, Ayers, and Westoby 1978, pp. 42–66.

Baggini, Julian and Jeremy Stangroom (eds.) (2002). *New British Philosophy: The Interviews*. London: Routledge.

Baillie, James (ed.) (1996). *Contemporary Analytic Philosophy: Core Readings*. Englewood Cliffs, NJ: Prentice Hall.

Baird, Davis, R. I. G. Hughes, and Alfred Nordmann (eds.) (1998). *Heinrich Hertz: Classical Physicist, Modern Philosopher*. Dordrecht: Kluwer.

Baker, A. J. (1986). *Australian Realism: The Systematic Philosophy of John Anderson*. Cambridge: Cambridge University Press.

Baker, Gordon P. (1988). *Wittgenstein, Frege and the Vienna Circle*. Oxford: Blackwell.

—— (ed.) (2003). *The Voices of Wittgenstein: Ludwig Wittgenstein and Friedrich Waismann*. London: Routledge.

—— (2004). *Wittgenstein's Method: Neglected Aspects*, ed. and introd. Katherine J. Morris. Oxford: Blackwell.

Baker, G. P. and P. M. S. Hacker (1980). *Wittgenstein: Understanding and Meaning*. Oxford: Blackwell; repub. in 2 vols. in paperback as Baker and Hacker 1983a and 1983b.

—— (1983a). *An Analytical Commentary on Wittgenstein's Philosophical Investigations*. Oxford: Blackwell

—— (1983b). *Wittgenstein: Meaning and Understanding*. Oxford: Blackwell.

—— (1983c). 'Dummett's Frege or Through a Looking-Glass Darkly', *Mind* 92: 239–46.

—— (1984a). *Frege: Logical Excavations*. Oxford: Blackwell.

—— (1984b). *Scepticism, Rules and Language*. Oxford: Blackwell.

—— (1985). *Wittgenstein: Rules, Grammar and Necessity*. Oxford: Blackwell; 2nd edn. rev. P. M. S. Hacker, 2009.

—— (1987). 'Dummett's Dig: Looking-Glass Archaeology', *Philosophical Quarterly* 37: 86–99.

—— (1989). 'The Last Ditch', *Philosophical Quarterly* 39: 471–7.

—— (2005a). *Wittgenstein: Understanding and Meaning, Part I: Essays*, 2nd edn. of Baker and Hacker 1983b, rev. P. M. S. Hacker. Oxford: Blackwell.

—— (2005b). *Wittgenstein: Understanding and Meaning, Part II: Exegesis §§ 1–184*, 2nd edn. of Baker and Hacker 1983a, rev. P. M. S. Hacker. Oxford: Blackwell.

Baldwin, James Mark (ed.) (1901–2). *Dictionary of Philosophy and Psychology*, 3 vols. London: Macmillan.

Baldwin, Thomas (1990). *G. E. Moore*. London: Routledge.

—— (1998). 'Analytical Philosophy', in Craig 1998, I, pp. 223–9.

—— (2001a). *Contemporary Philosophy*. Oxford: Oxford University Press.

—— (2001b). 'Bertrand Russell', in Martinich and Sosa 2001a, pp. 21–44.

—— (ed.) (2003). *The Cambridge History of Philosophy 1870–1945*. Cambridge: Cambridge University Press.

—— (2004). 'George Edward Moore', *The Stanford Encyclopedia of Philosophy*, online at: <http://plato.stanford.edu/entries/moore> [accessed 28 May 2012].

—— (2006). 'Philosophy of Language in the Twentieth Century', in Lepore and Smith 2006, pp. 60–99.

Bambrough, Renford (ed.) (1974). *Wisdom: Twelve Essays*. Totowa, NJ: Rowman & Littlefield.

*Barcan, Ruth C. (1946). 'A Functional Calculus of First Order Based on Strict Implication', *Journal of Symbolic Logic* 11: 1–16.

—— (1947). 'The Identity of Individuals in a Strict Functional Calculus of Second Order', *Journal of Symbolic Logic* 12: 12–15.

Barry, Brian (1965). *Political Argument*. London: Routledge.

Barsky, Robert F. (1997). *Noam Chomsky: A Life of Dissent*. Cambridge, MA: MIT Press.

Barwise, Jon and John Perry (1983). *Situations and Attitudes*. Cambridge, MA: MIT Press.

Beaney, Michael (1996). *Frege: Making Sense*. London: Duckworth.

—— (1998). 'What is Analytic Philosophy? Recent Work on the History of Analytic Philosophy', *British Journal for the History of Philosophy* 6: 463–72.

—— (2001). 'Collingwood's Critique of Analytic Philosophy', *Collingwood and British Idealism Studies* 8: 99–122.

—— (2002). 'Decompositions and Transformations: Conceptions of Analysis in the Early Analytic and Phenomenological Traditions', *Southern Journal of Philosophy*, Supplementary Vol. 40 (Horgan *et al.* 2002): 53–99.

—— (2003a). 'Russell and Frege', in Griffin 2003, pp. 128–70.

—— (2003b). 'Susan Stebbing on Cambridge and Vienna Analysis', in Stadler 2003, pp. 339–50.

—— (2004a). 'Gottlob Frege: The Light and Dark Sides of Genius' (Essay Review of Lothar Kreiser, *Gottlob Frege: Leben—Werk—Zeit*). *British Journal for the History of Philosophy* 12: 159–68.

—— (2004b). 'Carnap's Conception of Explication: From Frege to Husserl?', in Awodey and Klein 2004, pp. 117–50.

—— (2005a). 'Frege, Russell and Logicism' [shortened and revised version of Beaney 2003a], in Beaney and Reck 2005, I, pp. 213–40.

—— (2005b). 'Sinn, *Bedeutung* and the Paradox of Analysis', in Beaney and Reck 2005, IV, pp. 288–310.

—— (2005c). 'Collingwood's Conception of Presuppositional Analysis', *Collingwood and British Idealism Studies* 11(2): 41–114.

—— (2006a). 'Frege and the Role of Historical Elucidation: Methodology and the Foundations of Mathematics', in Ferreirós and Gray 2006, pp. 49–71.

——(2006b). 'Soames on Philosophical Analysis' (Critical Notice of Scott Soames, *Philosophical Analysis in the Twentieth Century*), *Philosophical Books* 7: 255–71.

——(2006c). 'Analytic Philosophy', in Grayling, Pyle, and Goulder 2006, I, pp. 85–92.

——(2006d). 'Duncan-Jones, Austin Ernest (1908–67)', in Grayling, Pyle, and Goulder 2006, II, pp. 916–17.

——(2006e). 'Stebbing, Lizzie Susan (1885–1943)', in Grayling, Pyle, and Goulder 2006, IV, pp. 3023–8.

——(2006f). 'Analytic Philosophy', in Brown 2006, I, pp. 203–6.

——(ed.) (2007a). *The Analytic Turn: Analysis in Early Analytic Philosophy and Phenomenology*. London: Routledge.

—— (2007b). 'The Analytic Turn in Twentieth-Century Philosophy', introduction to Beaney 2007a, pp. 1–30.

——(2007c). 'Conceptions of Analysis in the Early Analytic and Phenomenological Traditions: Some Comparisons and Relationships', in Beaney 2007a, pp. 196–216 [abridged and revised version of Beaney 2002].

——(2007d). 'Frege's Use of Function-Argument Analysis and his Introduction of Truth-Values as Objects', *Grazer Philosophische Studien* 75 (Greimann 2007): 93–123.

—— (2007e). 'Is Analytic Philosophy an Illusion? A Reply to Preston', *The Bertrand Russell Society Quarterly* 132–5 (Quadruple Issue, November 2006–August 2007): 27–34.

—— (2009a). 'Analysis', *The Stanford Encyclopedia of Philosophy*, online at: <http://plato.stanford.edu/entries/analysis> [accessed 28 January 2013].

——(2009b). 'Foreword' to Candlish 2009 [2007], pp. ix–xi.

——(2011a). 'Frege', in Lee 2011, ch. 1.

——(2011b). 'Putting Analysis Rightfully Back into Analytic Philosophy', *Teorema* 30: 87–94.

——(2012a). 'Ordinary Language Philosophy', in Russell and Fara 2012, pp. 873–84.

——(2012b). 'Logic and Metaphysics in Early Analytic Philosophy', in Haaparanta and Koskinen 2012, pp. 257–92.

——(2013a). 'Analytic Philosophy and History of Philosophy: The Development of the Idea of Rational Reconstruction', in Reck 2013.

——(2013b). 'Collingwood's Critique of Oxbridge Realism', in Boucher and Smith 2013.

—— (forthcoming). 'Frege's Logicism and the Significance of Interpretive Analysis', in Arana and Alvarez 2013.

Beaney, Michael and Erich H. Reck (eds.) (2005). *Gottlob Frege: Critical Assessments of Leading Philosophers*, 4 vols. London: Routledge.

Beiser, Frederick C. (2011). *The German Historicist Tradition*. Oxford: Oxford University Press.

Bell, David (1979). *Frege's Theory of Judgement*. Oxford: Oxford University Press.

——(1990). *Husserl*. London: Routledge.

——(1999). 'The Revolution of Moore and Russell: A Very British Coup?', in O'Hear 1999, pp. 193–208.

Bell, David and Neil Cooper (eds.) (1990). *The Analytic Tradition*. Oxford: Blackwell.

Benacerraf, Paul (1965). 'What Numbers Could Not Be', *Philosophical Review* 74: 47–73; repr. in Benacerraf and Putnam 1983, pp. 272–94.

——(1973). 'Mathematical Truth', *Journal of Philosophy* 70: 661–79.

——(1981). 'Frege: The Last Logicist', in French *et al.* 1981, pp. 17–36.

Benacerraf, Paul and Hilary Putnam (eds.) (1964). *Philosophy of Mathematics: Selected Readings*. Englewood Cliffs, NJ: Prentice-Hall; 2nd edn. Cambridge: Cambridge University Press, 1983.

Bennett, Jonathan (1966). *Kant's Analytic*. Cambridge: Cambridge University Press.

—— (1971). *Locke, Berkeley, Hume: Central Themes*. Oxford: Oxford University Press.

—— (1974). *Kant's Dialectic*. Cambridge: Cambridge University Press.

Bentham, Jeremy (1838–43). *The Works of Jeremy Bentham*, 11 vols. Edinburgh.

—— (1843). 'Essay on Logic', in Bentham 1838–43, Vol. 8, pp. 213–93.

*Bergmann, Gustav (1954). *The Metaphysics of Logical Positivism*. New York: Longmans, Green, and Co.; 2nd edn. Madison: University of Wisconsin Press, 1967; 3rd edn. Westport, CT: Greenwood Press, 1978.

—— (1960). 'Strawson's Ontology', *Journal of Philosophy* 57: 601–22; repr. in Bergmann 1964.

—— (1964). *Logic and Reality*. Madison: University of Wisconsin Press.

*Bergson, Henri (1896). *Matière et mémoire*. Paris: Alcan; tr. N. M. Paul and W. S. Palmer as *Matter and Memory*. New York: Swan Sonnenschein, 1911.

—— (1900). *Le Rire: essai sur la signification du comique*. Paris: Alcan; tr. C. Brereton and F. Rothwell as *Laughter: An Essay on the Meaning of the Comic*. London: Macmillan, 1911.

—— (1903). 'Introduction à la métaphysique', *Revue de métaphysique et de morale* 29: 1–36; repr. in Bergson 1934; tr. T. E. Hulme as *Introduction to Metaphysics*. New York: Putnam, 1912.

—— (1907). *L'Evolution créatrice*. Paris: Alcan; tr. Arthur Mitchell as *Creative Evolution*. London: Macmillan, 1911.

—— (1934). *La Pensée et le mouvant*. Paris: Alcan; tr. M. L. Andison as *The Creative Mind: An Introduction to Metaphysics*. New York: Philosophical Library, 1946.

*Berlin, Isaiah (1939). *Karl Marx: His Life and Environment*. London: Home University Library; 2nd edn. 1948; 3rd edn. 1963; 4th edn. 1978. Oxford: Oxford University Press.

—— (1958). 'Two Concepts of Liberty' [inaugural lecture], in Berlin 1969, pp. 118–72.

—— (1969). *Four Essays on Liberty*. Oxford: Oxford University Press.

—— (1973). 'Austin and the Early Beginnings of Oxford Philosophy', in Berlin *et al.* 1973, pp. 1–16.

—— *et al.* (1973). *Essays on J. L. Austin*. Oxford: Clarendon Press.

—— (1978). *Concepts and Categories: Philosophical Essays*. London: Hogarth; repr. Oxford: Oxford University Press, 1980.

—— (1997). *The Proper Study of Mankind: An Anthology of Essays*. London: Chatto & Windus.

Bernstein, Richard (2010). *The Pragmatic Turn*. Cambridge: Polity Press.

Bertholet, René (1911). *Un Romantisme Utilitaire: Étude sur le Mouvement Pragmatiste*. Paris: F. Alcan.

Betti, Arianna (2010). 'Kazimierz Twardowski', *The Stanford Encyclopedia of Philosophy*, online at: <http://plato.stanford.edu/entries/twardowski> [accessed 28 May 2012].

Beyer, Christian (2011). 'Edmund Husserl', *The Stanford Encyclopedia of Philosophy*, online at: <http://plato.stanford.edu/entries/Husserl> [accessed 28 May 2012].

Biletzki, Anat (2003). *(Over)Interpreting Wittgenstein*. Dordrecht: Kluwer.

Biletzki, Anat and Anat Matar (eds.) (1998). *The Story of Analytic Philosophy*. London: Routledge.

Bird, Alexander (2004). 'Thomas Kuhn', *The Stanford Encyclopedia of Philosophy*, online at: <http://plato.stanford.edu/entries/thomas-kuhn> [accessed 28 May 2012].

Bird, Graham (ed.) (2006). *A Companion to Kant*. Oxford: Blackwell.

Birjukov, B. V. (1964). *Two Soviet Studies on Frege*, tr. and ed. I. Angelelli. Dordrecht: D. Reidel.

Bjork, Daniel W. (1997). *B. F. Skinner: A Life*. Washington, DC: American Psychological Association.

*Black, Max (1934). 'Is Analysis a Useful Method in Philosophy?', *Proceedings of the Aristotelian Society*, Supplementary Vol. 13: 53–64.

—— (1937). 'Vagueness: An Exercise in Logical Analysis', *Philosophy of Science* 4: 427–55.

—— (1938). 'Relations between Logical Positivism and the Cambridge School of Analysis', *Erkenntnis* 8: 24–35.

——(ed.) (1950a). *Philosophical Analysis: A Collection of Essays*. Englewood Cliffs, NJ: Prentice-Hall.

——(1950b). 'Introduction', in Black 1950a, pp. 1–13.

——(1954). *Problems of Analysis: Philosophical Essays*. Ithaca, NY: Cornell University Press.

—— (1964). *A Companion to Wittgenstein's Tractatus*. Cambridge: Cambridge University Press.

——(ed.) (1965). *Philosophy in America*. London: George & Unwin.

——(1968). *The Labyrinth of Language*. Harmondsworth: Penguin.

Blackburn, Simon (1993). *Essays in Quasi-Realism*. Oxford: Oxford University Press.

——(1998). *Ruling Passions: A Theory of Practical Reasoning*. Oxford: Oxford University Press.

Blackmore, J. (1972). *Ernst Mach: His Work, Life, and Influence*. Berkeley: University of California Press.

——(1995). *Ludwig Boltzmann: His Later Life and Philosophy, 1900–1906*. Dordrecht: Kluwer.

Blackwell, Kenneth and Harry Ruja (1994). *A Bibliography of Bertrand Russell*, 3 vols. London: Routledge.

Blair, Daniel (2005). 'Malcolm, Norman Adrian (1911–90)', in Shook 2005, III, pp. 1589–93.

Blanchette, Patricia (2012). *Frege's Conception of Logic*. Oxford: Oxford University Press.

Blanshard, Brand (1952). 'The Philosophy of Analysis', *Proceedings of the British Academy* 38; repr. in Lewis 1963, pp. 76–109.

——(1962). *Reason and Analysis*. London: George Allen & Unwin.

——(1980). 'Reply to Mr. Fogelin', in Schilpp 1980, pp. 725–41 [reply to Fogelin 1980].

Block, Irving (ed.) (1981). *Perspectives on the Philosophy of Wittgenstein*. Oxford: Blackwell.

Block, Ned (1978). 'Troubles with Functionalism', *Minnesota Studies in the Philosophy of Science* 9: 261–325; repr. in Block 1980, I, pp. 268–306.

—— (ed.) (1980). *Readings in the Philosophy of Psychology*, 2 vols. London: Routledge.

Bloor, David (1976). *Knowledge and Social Imagery*. London: Routledge; 2nd edn. Chicago: University of Chicago Press, 1991.

Blumberg, Albert E. and Herbert Feigl (1931). 'Logical Positivism: A New Movement in European Philosophy', *Journal of Philosophy* 28: 281–96.

Bocheński, I. M. (1956). *Contemporary European Philosophy*, tr. D. Nicholl and K. Aschenbrenner. Berkeley: University of California Press; orig. pub. in German, 1947.

Boettcher, James W. (2005). 'Rawls, John Bordley (1921–2002)', in Shook 2005, IV, pp. 2014–21.

Bohman, James and William Rehg (2011). 'Jürgen Habermas', *The Stanford Encyclopedia of Philosophy*, online at: <http://plato.stanford.edu/entries/habermas> [accessed 28 May 2012].

Boisvert, Daniel R. (2011). 'Charles Leslie Stevenson', *The Stanford Encyclopedia of Philosophy*, online at: <http://plato.stanford.edu/entries/Stevenson> [accessed 28 May 2012].

*Boltzmann, Ludwig (1872). 'Weitere Studien über das Wärmegleichgewicht unter Gasmolekülen', *Wiener Berichte* 66: 275–370; repr. in Boltzmann 1909, I, ch. 23.

——(1909). *Wissenschaftliche Abhandlungen*, 3 vols., ed. F. Hasenöhrl. Leipzig: Barth; repr. New York: Chelsea, 1969.

*Bolzano, Bernard (1810). *Beyträge zu einer begründeteren Darstellung der Mathematik*. Prague: Caspar Widtmann; tr. S. Russ as *A Better Grounded Presentation of Mathematics* in Bolzano 2004, pp. 83–139.

—— (1837). *Wissenschaftslehre*, 4 vols. Sulzbach: Seidel; repr. in Bolzano 1969–, Series I, Vols. 11–14; selections tr. Rolf George as *Theory of Science*. Oxford: Oxford University Press, 1972; and by Jan Berg as *Theory of Science*. Dordrecht: D. Reidel, 1973.

—— (1851). *Paradoxien des Unendlichen*, ed. Franz Přihonský. Leipzig: Reclam; selections tr. Donald A. Steele as *Paradoxes of the Infinite*. London: Routledge & Kegan Paul, 1950; also tr. S. Russ in Bolzano 2004, pp. 591–678.

—— (1969–). *Bernard Bolzano Gesamtausgabe*, *c.*150 vols. Stuttgart-Bad Cannstatt: Frommann–Holzboog.

——(2004). *The Mathematical Works of Bernard Bolzano*, ed. S. Russ. Oxford: Oxford University Press.

Bonk, Thomas (ed.) (2003). *Language, Truth and Knowledge: Contributions to the Philosophy of Rudolf Carnap*. Dordrecht: Kluwer.

*Boole, George (1847). *The Mathematical Analysis of Logic, Being an Essay Towards a Calculus of Deductive Reasoning*. Cambridge: Macmillan; repr. in *Collected Logical Works*, vol. 1, ed. R. Rhees. La Salle, IL: Open Court, pp. 45–124.

—— (1854). *An Investigation of The Laws of Thought on Which are Founded the Mathematical Theories of Logic and Probabilities*. London: Macmillan; repr. in *Collected Logical Works*, vol. 2, ed. Philip E. B. Jourdain. La Salle, IL: Open Court.

Boolos, George (1998). *Logic, Logic, and Logic*. Cambridge, MA: Harvard University Press.

Borchert, Donald M. (ed.) (2005). *Encyclopedia of Philosophy*, 2nd edn. Detroit: Thomson Gale.

Boring, E. G. (1929). *A History of Experimental Psychology*. New York: Appleton-Century-Crofts; 2nd edn. 1950.

—— (1942). *Sensation and Perception in the History of Experimental Psychology*. New York: Appleton-Century-Crofts; 2nd edn. 1950.

Borradori, Giovanna (1994). *The American Philosopher: Conversations with Quine, Davidson, Putnam, Nozick, Danto, Rorty, Cavell, Macintyre, and Kuhn*. Chicago: University of Chicago Press.

Borst, C. V. (ed.) (1970). *The Mind/Brain Identity Theory*. London: Macmillan.

Boucher, David (2006). 'Collingwood, Robin George (1889–1943)', in Grayling, Pyle, and Goulder 2006, I, pp. 677–80.

Boucher, David and Teresa Smith (eds.) (2013). *R. G. Collingwood's An Autobiography*, rev. edn. Oxford: Oxford University Press.

Boundas, Constantin V. (ed.) (2007a). *The Edinburgh Companion to Twentieth-Century Philosophies*. Edinburgh: Edinburgh University Press.

—— (2007b). 'How to Recognize Analytic Philosophy', in Boundas 2007a, pp. 29–35.

—— (2007c). 'How to Recognize Continental European Philosophy', in Boundas 2007a, pp. 367–74.

Bouveresse, Jacques (1983). 'Why I am so very unFrench', in Montefiore 1983, pp. 9–33.

Bouwsma, O. K. (1986). *Wittgenstein: Conversations 1949–1951*, ed. J. L. Craft and R. E. Hustwit. Indianapolis: Hackett.

Braddon-Mitchell, David and Robert Nola (eds.) (2009). *Conceptual Analysis and Philosophical Naturalism*. Cambridge, MA: MIT Press.

Bradford, Dennis E. (1981). 'Moore, Russell, and the Foundations of Analytic Metaphysics', *Philosophy Research Archives* 7: 553–81.

*Bradley, F. H. (1874). 'The Presuppositions of Critical History'. Oxford: James Parker; repr. in Bradley 1935, pp. 1–70.

—— (1876). *Ethical Studies*, 2nd edn. Oxford: Clarendon Press, 1927.

—— (1883). *The Principles of Logic*, 2nd edn. Oxford: Clarendon Press, 1922.

—— (1893). *Appearance and Reality*. London: Swan Sonnenschein; 2nd edn. 1897; 9th impression, Oxford: Clarendon Press, 1930.

—— (1914). *Essays on Truth and Reality*. Oxford: Oxford University Press.

—— (1924). 'Relations', in Bradley 1935, pp. 629–76.

—— (1935). *Collected Essays*. Oxford: Clarendon Press.

—— (1999). *The Collected Works of F. H. Bradley*, 12 vols., ed. Carol A. Keene and W. J. Mander. Bristol: Thoemmes.

*Braithwaite, R. B. (1953). *Scientific Explanation: A Study of the Function of Theory, Probability and Law in Science*. Cambridge: Cambridge University Press.

—— (1955). *Theory of Games as a Tool for the Moral Philosopher*. Cambridge: Cambridge University Press.

Brandl, Johannes L. (2002). 'Gilbert Ryle: A Mediator between Analytic Philosophy and Phenomenology', *Southern Journal of Philosophy*, Supplementary Vol. 40 (Horgan *et al.* 2002): 143–51.

*Brandom, Robert B. (1994). *Making It Explicit*. Cambridge, MA: Harvard University Press.

—— (2000). *Articulating Reasons: An Introduction to Inferentialism*. Cambridge, MA: Harvard University Press.

—— (2002). *Tales of the Mighty Dead*. Cambridge, MA: Harvard University Press.

—— (2008). *Between Saying and Doing: Towards an Analytic Pragmatism*. Oxford: Oxford University Press.

—— (2009). *Reason in Philosophy: Animating Ideas*. Cambridge, MA: Harvard University Press.

Brandt, Richard B. (1959). *Ethical Theory: The Problems of Normative and Critical Ethics*. Englewood Cliffs, NJ: Prentice-Hall.

—— (1979). *A Theory of the Good and the Right*. Oxford: Oxford University Press.

Brent, Joseph (1998). *Charles Sanders Peirce: A Life*, 2nd edn. Bloomington, IN: Indiana University Press; 1st edn. 1993.

*Brentano, Franz (1874). *Psychologie vom empirischen Standpunkt*. Leipzig: Duncker & Humblot; 2nd edn. Leipzig: Felix Meiner, 1924; tr. A. C. Rancurello, D. B. Terrell, and L. McAlister as *Psychology from an Empirical Standpoint*. London: Routledge, 1973; 2nd edn. 1995, introd. Peter Simons.

—— (1902). *The Origin of the Knowledge of Right and Wrong*, tr. Cecil Hague. Westminster: Archibald Constable; also tr. Roderick Chisholm and Elizabeth Schneewind. London: Routledge, 1969.

—— (1911). *Von der Klassifikation der psychischen Phänomene* [repr. of Brentano 1874, Vol. 2, with additional material]. Leipzig: Duncker und Humblot, 1911.

—— (1982). *Deskriptive Psychologie*, ed. R. Chisholm and W. Baumgartner. Hamburg: Meiner; tr. Benito Müller. London: Routledge, 1995.

Brink, David O. (1989). *Moral Realism and the Foundations of Ethics*. Cambridge: Cambridge University Press.

Brino-Dean, Terry (2005). 'Cavell, Stanley Louis (1926–)', in Shook 2005, I, pp. 459–63.

Britton, K. (1978). 'Charlie Dunbar Broad, 1887–1971', *Proceedings of the British Academy* 64: 289–310.

*Broad, C. D. (1914). *Perception, Physics, and Reality*. Cambridge: Cambridge University Press.

—— (1923). *Scientific Thought*. London: Kegan Paul.

—— (1924). 'Critical and Speculative Philosophy', in Muirhead 1924, pp. 77–100.

—— (1925). *The Mind and Its Place in Nature*. London: Kegan Paul.

—— (1930). *Five Types of Ethical Theory*. London: Kegan Paul.

—— (1933). *Examination of McTaggart's Philosophy*, Vol. I. Cambridge: Cambridge University Press.

—— (1938). *Examination of McTaggart's Philosophy*, Vol. II. Cambridge: Cambridge University Press.

—— (1957). 'The Local Historical Background of Contemporary Cambridge Philosophy', in Mace 1957, pp. 13–61.

—— (1959). 'Autobiography', in Schilpp 1959, pp. 3–68.

Brogaard, Berit and Barry Smith (eds.) (2001). *Rationality and Irrationality/Rationalität und Irrationalität: Proceedings of the 23rd International Wittgenstein Symposium*. Vienna: öbv & hpt.

Brooks, Thom (2006). 'Hart, Herbert Lionel Adolphus (1907–92)', in Grayling, Pyle, and Goulder 2006, II, pp. 1387–9.

*Brouwer, L. E. J. (1908). 'De onbetrouwbaarheid der logische principes', *Tijdschrift voor Wijsbegeerte* 2: 152–8; tr. as 'The Unreliability of the Logical Principles' in Brouwer 1975, pp. 107–11.

—— (1912). 'Intuitionisme en Formalisme', Amsterdam: Clausen; inaugural lecture; tr. A. Dresden as 'Intuitionism and Formalism', *Bulletin of the American Mathematical Society* 20 (November 1913): 81–96; repr. in Benacerraf and Putnam 1964 [1983], pp. 77–89; also in Brouwer 1976, pp. 123–38.

—— (1918). 'Begründung der Mengenlehre unabhängig vom logischen Satz vom ausgeschlossenen Dritten. Erster Teil, Allgemeine Mengenlehre', *KNAW Verhandelingen* 5: 1–43; tr. in Brouwer 1975, pp. 151–90.

—— (1921). 'Besitzt jede reelle Zahl eine Dezimalbruchentwicklung?', *Mathematische Annalen* 83: 201–10; tr. as 'Does Every Real Number Have a Decimal Expansion?', in Mancosu 1998, pp. 28–35.

—— (1929). 'Mathematik, Wissenschaft und Sprache', *Monatshefte für Mathematik und Physik* 36: 153–64; tr. as 'Mathematics, Science, and Language' in Mancosu 1998, pp. 45–53; also in Brouwer 1975, pp. 417–28.

—— (1930). 'Die Struktur des Kontinuums', Vienna; tr. as 'The Structure of the Continuum' in Mancosu 1998, pp. 54–63; also in Brouwer 1976, pp. 429–40.

—— (1975). *Collected Works, Vol. 1: Philosophy and Foundations of Mathematics*, ed. A. Heyting. Amsterdam: North-Holland.

—— (1976). *Collected Works, Vol. 2: Geometry, Analysis, Topology and Mechanics*, ed. H. Freudenthal. Amsterdam: North-Holland.

—— (1981). *Brouwer's Cambridge Lectures on Intuitionism*, ed. D. van Dalen. Cambridge: Cambridge University Press; lectures given 1946–51.

—— (1992). *Intuitionismus*, ed. D. van Dalen, Mannheim: BI-Wissenschaftsverlag

Brown, Keith (ed.) (2006). *Encyclopedia of Language and Linguistics*, 2nd edn. Oxford: Elsevier.

Browne, E. J. (1995). *Charles Darwin: A Biography, Vol. 1: Voyaging*. Princeton, NJ: Princeton University Press.

—— (2000). *Charles Darwin: A Biography, Vol. 2: The Power of Place*. Princeton, NJ: Princeton University Press.

Buckle, Stephen (2004). 'Analytic Philosophy and Continental Philosophy: The Campbell Thesis Revised', *British Journal for the History of Philosophy* 12: 111–50.

Buckley, Kerry W. (1989). *Mechanical Man: John Broadus Watson and the Beginnings of Behaviorism*. New York: Guilford Press.

Bunnin, Nicholas and Eric P. Tsui-James (eds.) (1996). *The Blackwell Companion to Philosophy*. Oxford: Blackwell.

Burch, Robert (2010). 'Charles Sanders Peirce', *The Stanford Encyclopedia of Philosophy*, online at: <http://plato.stanford.edu/entries/peirce> [accessed 28 May 2012].

*Burge, Tyler (1979). 'Individualism and the Mental', *Midwest Studies in Philosophy* 4: 73–121; repr. in Burge 2007, pp. 100–50.

—— (1986). 'Individualism and Psychology', *Philosophical Review* 95: 3–45; repr. in Burge 2007, pp. 221–53.

—— (1992). 'Philosophy of Language and Mind: 1950–1990', *Philosophical Review* 101: 3–51; second half repr. in rev. form in Burge 2007, pp. 440–64.

—— (2003). 'Perceptual Entitlement', *Philosophy and Phenomenological Research* 67(3): 503–48.

—— (2005a). *Truth, Thought, Reason: Essays on Frege*. Oxford: Oxford University Press.

—— (2005b). 'Introduction', in Burge 2005a, pp. 1–68.

—— (2007). *Foundations of Mind*. Oxford: Oxford University Press.

—— (2010). *Origins of Objectivity*. Oxford: Oxford University Press.

Burgess, John P. (2005). *Fixing Frege*. Princeton, NJ: Princeton University Press.

Burnham, James and Philip Wheelwright (1932). *Introduction to Philosophical Analysis*. New York: Henry Holt.

Burris, Stanley (2010). 'George Boole', *The Stanford Encyclopedia of Philosophy*, online at: <http://plato.stanford.edu/entries/boole> [accessed 28 May 2012].

Butler, R. J. (ed.) (1962). *Analytical Philosophy*. Oxford: Blackwell.

—— (ed.) (1965). *Analytical Philosophy: Second Series*. Oxford: Blackwell.

Bynum, Terrell Ward (1972). 'On the Life and Work of Gottlob Frege', in Frege 1972, pp. 1–54.

Bynum, T. W. and A.W. Bynum (1972). 'A Frege Bibliography, 1873–1966', in Frege 1972, pp. 239–87.

Byrne, Darragh (2006). 'Wright, Crispin (1942–)', in Grayling, Pyle, and Goulder 2006, IV, pp. 3528–31.

Cahiers de Royaumont, [no ed.] (1962). *Philosophie No. IV: La Philosophie Analytique*. Paris: Les Éditions de Minuit.

Campbell, James (2006). *A Thoughtful Profession: The Early Years of The American Philosophical Association*. Chicago: Open Court.

Campbell, Richard (1992). *Truth and Historicity*. Oxford: Oxford University Press.

—— (2001). 'The Covert Metaphysics of the Clash between "Analytic" and "Continental" Philosophy', *British Journal for the History of Philosophy* 9: 341–59.

Candlish, Stewart (2007). *The Russell/Bradley Dispute and its Significance for Twentieth-Century Philosophy*. Basingstoke: Palgrave Macmillan; paperback edn. 2009.

Candlish, Stewart and Pierfrancesco Basile (2009). 'Francis Herbert Bradley', *The Stanford Encyclopedia of Philosophy*, online at:<http://plato.stanford.edu/entries/Bradley> [accessed 28 May 2012].

Canfield, John V. (ed.), (1986). *The Philosophy of Wittgenstein*, 15 vols. New York: Garland.

—— (ed.) (1997). *Philosophy of Meaning, Knowledge and Value in the Twentieth Century*. Routledge History of Philosophy, vol. X. London: Routledge.

*Cantor, Georg (1874). 'Über eine Eigenschaft des Inbegriffs aller reelen algebraischen Zahlen', *Journal für die reine und angewandte Mathematik* 77: 258–62; repr. in Cantor 1932, pp. 115–18; tr. in Ewald 1996, II, pp. 839–43.

—— (1883). *Grundlagen einer allgemeinen Mannigfaltigkeitslehre*. Leipzig: Teubner; repr. in Cantor 1932, pp. 165–209; tr. in Ewald 1996, II, pp. 878–920.

——(1891). 'Über eine elementare Frage der Mannigfaltigkeitslehre', *Jahresbericht der Deutschen Mathematiker-Vereinigung* 1: 75–8; repr. in Cantor 1932, pp. 278–80; tr. in Ewald 1996, II, pp. 920–2.

——(1932). *Gesammelte Abhandlungen mathematischen und philosophischen Inhalts*, ed. Ernst Zermelo. Berlin: Springer.

Capaldi, Nicholas (2000). *The Enlightenment Project in the Analytic Conversation*. Dordrecht: Kluwer.

——(2004). *John Stuart Mill: A Biography*. Cambridge: Cambridge University Press.

Capitan, W. H. and D. D. Merrill (eds.) (1967). *Art, Mind and Religion*. Pittsburgh: University of Pittsburgh Press.

Carey, Rosalind (2007). *Russell and Wittgenstein on the Nature of Judgement*. London: Continuum.

——(forthcoming). *Russell on Meaning: The Emergence of Scientific Philosophy from the 1920s to the 1940s*. Basingstoke: Palgrave Macmillan.

Carl, Wolfgang (1994). *Frege's Theory of Sense and Reference: Its Origins and Scope*. Cambridge: Cambridge University Press.

Carman, Taylor (2007). 'Continental Themes in Analytic Philosophy', in Boundas 2007a, pp. 351–63.

*Carnap, Rudolf (1921). *Der Raum. Ein Beitrag zur Wissenschaftslehre* [doctoral dissertation], Jena: University of Jena; repr. in *Kant-Studien*, Ergänzungshefte, 56 (1922).

——(1928a). *Der logische Aufbau der Welt*. Berlin-Schlachtensee: Weltkreis-Verlag; 2nd edn. Hamburg: Felix Meiner, 1961; tr. (together with Carnap 1928b) as Carnap 1967.

——(1928b). *Scheinprobleme in der Philosophie: Das Fremdpsychische und der Realismusstreit*. Berlin-Schlachtensee: Weltkreis-Verlag; tr. R. A. George as *Pseudoproblems in Philosophy: The Heteropsychological and the Realism Controversy* and inc. in Carnap 1967.

——(1932a). 'Überwindung der Metaphysik durch logische Analyse der Sprache', *Erkenntnis* 2: 219–41; tr. Arthur Pap as 'The Elimination of Metaphysics through Logical Analysis of Language', in Ayer 1959, pp. 60–81.

——(1932b). 'Die physikalische Sprache als Universalsprache der Wissenschaft', *Erkenntnis* 2: 432–65; tr. Max Black as *The Unity of Science*. London: Kegan, Paul, 1934.

——(1932c). 'Über Protokollsätze', *Erkenntnis* 3: 215–28; tr. R. Creath and R. Nollan as 'On Protocol Sentences', *Noûs* 21: 457–70.

——(1934). *Logische Syntax der Sprache*. Wien: Julius Springer; rev. and tr. as Carnap 1937.

——(1935). *Philosophy and Logical Syntax*. London: Kegan Paul.

——(1936). 'Testability and Meaning', *Philosophy of Science* 3: 419–71; 4: 1–40.

——(1937). *The Logical Syntax of Language*, tr. A. Smeaton. London: Kegan, Paul.

——(1942). *Introduction to Semantics, Studies in Semantics*, Vol. 1. Cambridge, MA: Harvard University Press.

——(1943). *Formalization of Logic, Studies in Semantics*, Vol. 2. Cambridge, MA: Harvard University Press.

——(1946). 'Modalities and Quantification', *Journal of Symbolic Logic* 11: 33–64.

——(1947). *Meaning and Necessity: A Study in Semantics and Modal Logic*. Chicago: University of Chicago Press, 2nd edn. 1956.

——(1950a). *Logical Foundations of Probability*. Chicago: University of Chicago Press.

——(1950b). 'Empiricism, Semantics, and Ontology', *Revue internationale de philosophie* 4: 20–40; repr. in Carnap 1956, pp. 205–21.

——(1952). 'Meaning Postulates', *Philosophical Studies* 3: 65–73; repr. in Carnap 1956, pp. 222–9.

—— (1956). *Meaning and Necessity: A Study in Semantics and Modal Logic*, 2nd edn. expanded. Chicago: University of Chicago Press.

—— (1963). 'Intellectual Autobiography', in Schilpp 1963, pp. 1–84.

—— (1967). *The Logical Structure of the World*, tr. Rolf A. George. Berkeley: University of California Press; repr. Chicago: Open Court, 2003.

—— (forthcoming). *Collected Works*, 13 vols. Chicago: Open Court.

Carnap, Rudolf, Hans Hahn, and Otto Neurath (1929). 'Wissenschaftliche Weltauffassung: Der Wiener Kreis', Vienna: Artur Wolf/Ernst Mach Society; tr. as 'The Scientific Conception of the World: The Vienna Circle', in Neurath 1973, pp. 299–318.

Carr, H. Wildon (1929). 'The Fiftieth Session: A Retrospect', *Proceedings of the Aristotelian Society* 29: 359–86.

Carroll, Lewis (Dodgson, Charles Lutwidge) (1865). *Alice's Adventures in Wonderland*. London: Macmillan, 1866.

—— (1872). *Through the Looking-Glass and what Alice found there*. London: Macmillan.

—— (1895). 'What the Tortoise said to Achilles', *Mind* 4: 278–80.

Cartwright, Nancy, Jordi Cat, Lola Fleck, and Thomas Uebel (1996). *Otto Neurath: Philosophy Between Science and Politics*. Cambridge: Cambridge University Press.

Carus, A. W. (2005). 'Carnap, Rudolf (1891–1970)', in Shook 2005, I, pp. 429–36.

—— (2007). *Carnap and Twentieth-Century Thought: Explication as Enlightenment*. Cambridge: Cambridge University Press.

Carver, Terrell (1989). *Friedrich Engels: His Life and Thought*. Basingstoke: Macmillan.

*Case, Thomas (1888). *Physical Realism, Being an Analytical Philosophy from the Physical Objects of Science to the Physical Data of Sense*. London: Longmans, Green, and Co.

*Cassirer, Ernst (1902). *Leibniz' System in seinen wissenschaftlichen Grundlagen*. Marburg: Elwert.

—— (1906). *Das Erkenntnisproblem in der Philosophie und Wissenschaft der neueren Zeit. Erster Band*. Berlin: Bruno Cassirer.

—— (1907). *Das Erkenntnisproblem in der Philosophie und Wissenschaft der neueren Zeit. Zweiter Band*. Berlin: Bruno Cassirer.

—— (1910). *Substanzbegriff und Funktionsbegriff: Untersuchungen über die Grundfragen der Erkenntniskritik*. Berlin: Bruno Cassirer; tr. as *Substance and Function*. Chicago: Open Court, 1923.

—— (1923). *Philosophie der symbolischen Formen. Erster Teil: Die Sprache*. Berlin: Bruno Cassirer; tr. as *The Philosophy of Symbolic Forms. Volume One: Language*. New Haven, CT: Yale University Press, 1955.

—— (1925). *Philosophie der symbolischen Formen. Zweiter Teil: Das mythische Denken*. Berlin: Bruno Cassirer; tr. as *The Philosophy of Symbolic Forms. Volume Two: Mythical Thought*. New Haven, CT: Yale University Press, 1955.

—— (1929). *Philosophie der symbolischen Formen. Dritter Teil: Phänomenologie der Erkenntnis*. Berlin: Bruno Cassirer; tr. as *The Philosophy of Symbolic Forms. Volume Three: The Phenomenology of Knowledge*. New Haven, CT: Yale University Press, 1957.

—— (1944). *An Essay on Man*. New Haven, CT: Yale University Press.

Cassirer, Toni (2003). *Mein Leben mit Ernst Cassirer*. Hamburg: Meiner.

Castañeda, Hector-Neri (ed.) (1975). *Action, Knowledge and Reality: Critical Studies in Honor of Wilfrid Sellars*. Indianapolis: Bobbs-Merrill.

Cat, Jordi (2010). 'Otto Neurath', *The Stanford Encyclopedia of Philosophy*, online at: <http://plato.stanford.edu/entries/neurath> [accessed 28 May 2012].

Caton, Charles E. (ed.) (1963). *Philosophy and Ordinary Language*. Urbana: University of Illinois Press.

Cave, Peter (2006a). 'Austin, John Langshaw (1911–60)', in Grayling, Pyle, and Goulder 2006, I, pp. 167–71,

—— (2006b). 'Braithwaite, Richard Bevan (1900–90)', in Grayling, Pyle, and Goulder 2006, I, pp. 412–15,

—— (2006c). 'Ramsey, Frank Plumpton (1903–30)', in Grayling, Pyle, and Goulder 2006, IV, pp. 2649–54,

*Cavell, Stanley (1958). 'Must We Mean What We Say?', *Inquiry* 1: 172–212; repr. in Chappell 1964, pp. 75–112; also repr. in Cavell 1969, pp. 1–43.

—— (1965). 'Austin at Criticism', *Philosophical Review* 74: 204–19; repr. in Rorty 1967, pp. 250–60; also in Cavell 1969, pp. 97–114.

—— (1969). *Must We Mean What We Say?* New York: Charles Scribner's Sons; 2nd edn. Cambridge: Cambridge University Press, 1976; updated edn. 2002.

—— (1979). *The Claim of Reason: Wittgenstein, Skepticism, Morality, and Tragedy*. New York: Oxford University Press.

—— (1996). *The Cavell Reader*, ed. Stephen Mulhall. Oxford: Blackwell.

—— (2010). *Little Did I Know: Excerpts from Memory*. Palo Alto: Stanford University Press.

Chalmers, David (1996). *The Conscious Mind*. New York: Oxford University Press.

Chalmers, David, David Manley, and Ryan Wasserman (eds.) (2009). *Metametaphysics: New Essays on the Foundations of Ontology*. Oxford: Oxford University Press.

Chapman, Siobhan (2005). *Paul Grice: Philosopher and Linguist*. Basingstoke: Palgrave Macmillan.

—— (2013). *Susan Stebbing and the Language of Common Sense*. Basingstoke: Palgrave Macmillan.

Chappell, V. C. (ed.) (1964). *Ordinary Language: Essays in Philosophical Method*. Englewood Cliffs, NJ: Prentice-Hall.

Charlesworth, Maxwell John (1959). *Philosophy and Linguistic Analysis*. Pittsburgh: Duquesne University Press.

Charlton, William (1991). *The Analytic Ambition: An Introduction to Philosophy*. Oxford: Blackwell.

Chase, James and Jack Reynolds (2011). *Analytic versus Continental: Arguments on the Methods and Value of Philosophy*. Durham: Acumen.

Cheney, David R. (ed.) (1971). *Broad's Critical Essays in Moral Philosophy*. London: George Allen & Unwin.

Cherniss, Joshua L. (2006). 'Berlin, Isaiah (1909–97)', in Grayling, Pyle, and Goulder 2006, I, pp. 312–16.

Cherniss, Joshua and Henry Hardy (2010). 'Isaiah Berlin', *The Stanford Encyclopedia of Philosophy*, online at: <http://plato.stanford.edu/entries/berlin> [accessed 28 May 2012].

Child, William (2011). *Wittgenstein*. London: Routledge.

Chimisso, Cristina (2008). *Writing the History of the Mind: Philosophy of Science in France, 1900 to 1960s*. Aldershot: Ashgate.

*Chisholm, Roderick M. (1951). 'Philosophers and Ordinary Language', *Philosophical Review* 60: 317–28; repr. in Rorty 1967, pp. 175–82.

—— (1956). 'Sentences about Believing', *Proceedings of the Aristotelian Society* 56: 125–48.

—— (1957). *Perceiving: A Philosophical Study*. Ithaca, NY: Cornell University Press.

—— (ed.) (1960). *Realism and the Background of Phenomenology*. Glencoe, IL: Free Press.

—— (1966). *Theory of Knowledge*. Englewood Cliffs, NJ: Prentice-Hall; 2nd edn. 1977; 3rd edn. 1989.

—— (1976). *Person and Object: A Metaphysical Study*. La Salle, IL: Open Court.

—— (1981a). *The First Person: An Essay on Reference and Intentionality*. Minneapolis: University of Minnesota Press.

—— (1981b). 'Brentano's Analysis of the Consciousness of Time', in French *et al.* 1981, pp. 3–16.

—— (1997). 'Intellectual Autobiography', in Hahn 1997, pp. 1–41.

*Chomsky, Noam (1957). *Syntactic Structures*. The Hague: Mouton.

—— (1959). 'Review of [Skinner's] *Verbal Behavior*', *Language* 35: 26–58.

—— (1966). *Cartesian Linguistics*. New York: Harper & Row.

*Church, Alonzo (1936a). 'An Unsolvable Problem of Elementary Number Theory', *American Journal of Mathematics* 58: 345–63.

—— (1936b). 'A Note on the Entscheidungsproblem', *Journal of Symbolic Logic* 1: 40–1.

—— (1937). 'Review of [Turing 1936]', *Journal of Symbolic Logic* 2: 42–3.

—— (1941). *The Calculi of Lambda-Conversion*. Princeton, NJ: Princeton University Press.

—— (1943). 'Review of Quine, "Notes on Existence and Necessity"', *Journal of Symbolic Logic* 8: 45–7.

—— (1956). *Introduction to Mathematical Logic*. Princeton, NJ: Princeton University Press; early version pub. in *Annals of Mathematics Studies*, 1944.

—— (forthcoming). *Collected Works*, ed. H. B. Enderton. Cambridge, MA: MIT Press.

Churchland, Patricia Smith (1986). *Neurophilosophy: Toward a Unified Science of the Mind/ Brain*. Cambridge, MA: MIT Press.

Churchland, Paul (1979). *Scientific Realism and the Plasticity of Mind*. Cambridge: Cambridge University Press.

—— (1981). 'Eliminative Materialism and Propositional Attitudes', *Journal of Philosophy* 78: 67–90.

Clark, Ronald William (1971). *Einstein: The Life and Times*. New York: HarperCollins.

—— (1975). *The Life of Bertrand Russell*. London: J. Cape.

—— (1981). *Bertrand Russell and His World*. London: Thames and Hudson.

Clarke, David S. (1997). *Philosophy's Second Revolution: Early and Recent Analytic Philosophy*. Chicago and La Salle, IL: Open Court.

Clarke, Thomson (1972). 'The Legacy of Skepticism', *Journal of Philosophy* 69(20): 754–69.

Cocchiarella, Nino B. (1987). *Logical Studies in Early Analytic Philosophy*. Columbus, OH: Ohio State University Press.

Coffa, J. Alberto (1991). *The Semantic Tradition from Kant to Carnap*. Cambridge: Cambridge University Press.

Cohen, David (1979). *J. B. Watson, The Founder of Behaviourism: A Biography*. London: Routledge & Kegan Paul.

Cohen, G. A. (1978). *Karl Marx's Theory of History: A Defence*. Oxford: Oxford University Press; 2nd edn. 2000.

Cohen, Hermann (1871). *Kants Theorie der Erfahrung*. Berlin: Dümmler.

Cohen, L. Jonathan (1986). *The Dialogue of Reason: An Analysis of Analytical Philosophy*. Oxford: Clarendon Press.

Cohen, Robert S. (1992). 'Recollections of Tscha Hung', in Cohen, Hilpinen, and Qiu 1992, pp. xiii–xvi.

Cohen, Robert S., Risto Hilpinen, and Qiu Renzong (eds.) (1992). *Realism and Anti-Realism in the Philosophy of Science*. Dordrecht: Kluwer.

Cole, Peter (ed.) (1981). *Radical Pragmatics*. New York: Academic Press.

Cole, Peter and Jerry L. Morgan (eds.) (1975). *Syntax and Semantics, Vol. 3: Speech Acts*. New York: Academic Press.

Colella, E. Paul (2005). 'Lewis, Clarence Irving (1883–1964)', in Shook 2005, III, pp. 1455–61.

Coliva, Annalisa (2010). *Moore and Wittgenstein: Scepticism, Certainty, and Common Sense*. Basingstoke: Palgrave Macmillan.

*Collingwood, R. G. (1933). *An Essay on Philosophical Method*. Oxford: Oxford University Press.

—— (1939). *An Autobiography*. Oxford: Oxford University Press; repr. in Boucher and Smith 2012.

—— (1940). *An Essay on Metaphysics*. Oxford: Oxford University Press.

—— (1946). *The Idea of History*, ed. T. M. Knox. Oxford: Oxford University Press; 2nd rev. edn. 1993, ed. J. van der Dussen.

—— (1993). *The Idea of History*, rev. edn., ed. J. van der Dussen. Oxford: Oxford University Press.

—— (1998). *An Essay on Metaphysics*, rev. edn., ed. R. Martin. Oxford: Clarendon Press.

—— (2005a). *An Essay on Philosophical Method*, rev. edn., ed. J. Connelly and G. D'Oro. Oxford: Oxford University Press.

—— (2005b). 'The Correspondence between R. G. Collingwood and Gilbert Ryle', in Collingwood 2005a, pp. 253–326.

Colodny, Robert (ed.) (1962). *Frontiers of Science and Philosophy*. Pittsburgh: University of Pittsburgh Press.

Conant, James (2000). 'Elucidation and Nonsense in Frege and Early Wittgenstein', in Crary and Read 2000, pp. 174–217 [excerpted from Conant 2002].

—— (2002). 'The Method of the *Tractatus*', in Reck 2002, pp. 374–462.

—— (2007). 'Mild Mono-Wittgensteinianism', in Crary 2007, pp. 31–142.

Conant, James and Cora Diamond (2004). 'On Reading the *Tractatus* Resolutely: Reply to Meredith Williams and Peter Sullivan', in Kölbel and Weiss 2004, pp. 46–99.

Cooper, David E. (1994). 'Analytic and Continental Philosophy', *Proceedings of the Aristotelian Society* 94: 1–18.

Copeland, B. Jack (2006). 'Prior, Arthur Norman (1914–69)', in Grayling, Pyle, and Goulder 2006, III, pp. 2599–602.

—— (2007). 'Arthur Prior', *The Stanford Encyclopedia of Philosophy*, online at: <http://plato.stanford.edu/entries/prior> [accessed 28 May 2012].

Copi, Irving M. and Robert W. Beard (eds.) (1966). *Essays on Wittgenstein's Tractatus*. London: Routledge & Kegan Paul.

Copleston, Frederick (1966). *A History of Philosophy*, Vol. 8: *Bentham to Russell*. Tunbridge Wells: Burns and Oates, 1999.

Cornforth, Maurice (1934). 'Is Analysis a Useful Method in Philosophy?', *Proceedings of the Aristotelian Society*, Supplementary Vol. 13: 90–118.

Cornman, James W. (1966). *Metaphysics, Reference, and Language*. New Haven, CT: Yale University Press.

—— (1968). 'On the Elimination of "Sensations" and Sensations', *Review of Metaphysics* 22: 15–35.

—— (1971). *Materialism and Sensations*. New Haven, CT: Yale University Press.

—— (1975). *Perception, Common Sense, and Science*. New Haven, CT: Yale University Press.

—— (1980). *Skepticism, Justification and Explanation*. Dordrecht: D. Reidel.

Corradini, A., S. Galvan, and E. J. Lowe (eds.) (2006). *Analytic Philosophy Without Naturalism*. London and New York: Routledge.

Corrado, Michael (1975). *The Analytic Tradition in Philosophy*. Chicago: American Library Association.

Couturat, Louis (1901). *La Logique de Leibniz*. Paris: Alcan.

Cozzo, Cesare (1999). 'What is Analytical Philosophy?', in Egidi 1999, pp. 55–63.

Craig, Edward (ed.) (1998). *Routledge Encyclopedia of Philosophy*. London: Routledge; online at: <http://www.rep.routledge.com> [accessed 28 May 2012].

Crane, Tim (2001). *Elements of Mind*. Oxford: Oxford University Press.

Crane, Tim and Sarah Patterson (eds.) (2000). *The History of the Mind–Body Problem*. London: Routledge.

Crary, Alice (ed.) (2007). *Wittgenstein and the Moral Life: Essays in Honor of Cora Diamond*. Cambridge, MA: MIT Press.

Crary, Alice and Rupert Read (eds.) (2000). *The New Wittgenstein*. London: Routledge.

Crawford, Sean (ed.) (2011). *Philosophy of Mind: Critical Concepts in Philosophy*, 4 vols. London: Routledge.

Creath, Richard (1999). 'Carnap's Move to Semantics: Gains and Losses', in Woleński and Köhler 1999, pp. 65–76.

—— (2007). 'Quine's Challenge to Carnap', in Friedman and Creath 2007, pp. 316–35.

Cresswell, Max (2001). 'Ruth Barcan Marcus (1921–)', in Martinich and Sosa 2001a, pp. 357–60.

Crisp, Roger (ed.) (2013). *The Oxford Handbook of the History of Ethics*. Oxford: Oxford University Press.

Critchley, Simon (1997). 'What is Continental Philosophy?', *International Journal of Philosophical Studies* 5: 347–65.

—— (2001). *Continental Philosophy: A Very Short Introduction*. Oxford: Oxford University Press.

Cullity, Garrett (2005). 'Williams, Bernard Arthur Owen (1929–2003)', in Shook 2005, IV, pp. 2602–8; also in Grayling, Pyle, and Goulder 2006, IV, pp. 3450–4.

Dainian, Fan (1992). 'Hong Qian (Tscha Hung) and the Vienna Circle', in Cohen, Hilpinen, and Qiu 1992, pp. xvii–xxii.

Dancy, Jonathan (1993). *Moral Reasons*. Oxford: Blackwell.

—— (2004). *Ethics Without Principles*. Oxford: Oxford University Press.

—— (2010). 'Harold Arthur Prichard', *The Stanford Encyclopedia of Philosophy*, online at: <http://plato.stanford.edu/entries/Prichard> [accessed 28 May 2012].

Daniels, Norman (2001). 'John Rawls (1921–2002)', in Martinich and Sosa 2001a, pp. 361–70.

Danto, Arthur C. (1965). *Analytical Philosophy of History*. Cambridge: Cambridge University Press; repr. in Danto 1985.

—— (1968). *Analytical Philosophy of Knowledge*. Cambridge: Cambridge University Press.

—— (1973). *Analytical Philosophy of Action*. Cambridge: Cambridge University Press.

—— (1980). 'Analytical Philosophy', *Social Research* 47: 612–34.

—— (1985). *Narration and Knowledge*. New York: Columbia University Press.

Darwall, Stephen, Allan Gibbard, and Peter Railton (1992). 'Toward Fin de Siècle Ethics: Some Trends', *Philosophical Review* 101: 115–89.

*Darwin, Charles (1859). *On the Origin of Species*. London: John Murray.

—— (1871). *The Descent of Man, and Selection in Relation to Sex*. London: John Murray.

Dascal, Marcelo (2001). 'How Rational can a Polemic across the Analytic–Continental "Divide" be?', *International Journal of Philosophical Studies* 9: 313–39.

Dauben, Joseph Warren (1979). *Georg Cantor: His Mathematics and Philosophy of the Infinite.* Cambridge, MA: Harvard University Press.

Davey, Nicholas (2008). 'Twentieth-Century Hermeneutics', in Moran 2008a, pp. 693–735.

*Davidson, Donald (1963). 'Actions, Reasons, and Causes', *Journal of Philosophy* 60: 685–700; repr. in Davidson 1980, pp. 3–19.

—— (1967a). 'Truth and Meaning', *Synthese* 17: 304–23; repr. in Davidson 1984, pp. 17–36.

—— (1967b). 'The Logical Form of Action Sentences', in Rescher 1967; repr. in Davidson 1980, pp. 105–22, with 'Criticism, Comment, and Defence', pp. 122–48.

—— (1970). 'Mental Events', in Foster and Swanson 1970; repr. in Davidson 1980, pp. 207–25.

—— (1973). 'Radical Interpretation', *Dialectica* 27: 314–28; repr. in Davidson 1984, pp. 125–39.

—— (1974). 'On the Very Idea of a Conceptual Scheme', *Proceedings and Addresses of the American Philosophical Association* 47: 5–20; reprinted in Davidson 1984, pp. 183–98.

—— (1980). *Essays on Actions and Events.* Oxford: Oxford University Press; 2nd edn. 2001.

—— (1984). *Inquiries into Truth and Interpretation.* Oxford: Oxford University Press; 2nd edn. 2001.

—— (1987). 'Knowing One's Own Mind', *Proceedings and Addresses of the American Philosophical Association* 60: 441–58; repr. in Davidson 2001, pp. 15–38.

—— (1999). 'Intellectual Autobiography', in Hahn 1999, pp. 1–70.

—— (2001). *Subjective, Intersubjective, Objective.* Oxford: Oxford University Press.

—— (2004). *Problems of Rationality.* Oxford: Oxford University Press.

—— (2005a). *Truth, Language, and History.* Oxford: Oxford University Press.

—— (2005b). *Truth and Predication.* Cambridge, MA: Harvard University Press.

Davidson, Donald and Gilbert Harman (eds.) (1972). *Semantics of Natural Language.* Dordrecht: D. Reidel.

Davidson, Donald and Jaakko Hintikka (eds.) (1969). *Words and Objections: Essays on the Work of W. V. Quine.* Dordrecht: D. Reidel.

Dawes Hicks, George (1912). 'The Nature of Sense-Data', *Mind* 21: 399–409; repr. in Russell 1992, pp. 433–43.

Dawson, John W. (1997). *Logical Dilemmas: The Life and Work of Kurt Gödel.* Wellesley, MA: A. K. Peters.

De Pellegrin, E. (ed.) (2011). *Interactive Wittgenstein: Essays in Memory of Georg Henrik von Wright.* Dordrecht: Springer.

De Waal, Cornelis (2005). 'Peirce, Charles Sanders (1839–1914)', in Shook 2005, III, pp. 1895–902.

*Dedekind, Richard (1854). 'Über die Einführung neuer Funktionen in der Mathematik', *Habilitationsvorlesung*; tr. as 'On the Introduction of New Functions in Mathematics' in Ewald 1996, II, pp. 754–62.

—— (1872). 'Stetigkeit und irrationale Zahlen', tr. as 'Continuity and Irrational Numbers' in Ewald 1996, II, pp. 765–79.

—— (1888). *Was sind und was sollen die Zahlen?*, tr. in Ewald 1996, II, pp. 787–833.

Deigh, John (2013). 'Ethics in the Analytic Tradition', in Crisp 2013.

Dejnozka, Jan (1996). *The Ontology of the Analytic Tradition and Its Origins.* Lanham, MD: Littlefield Adams; paperback edn. repr. with corrections 2002, 2003.

Delaney, C. F. (2005). 'Sellars, Wilfrid Stalker (1912–83)', in Shook 2005, IV, pp. 2192–6.

*Deleuze, Gilles (1968). *Différence et repetition.* Paris: PUF; tr. Paul Patton as *Difference and Repetition.* New York: Columbia University Press, 1994.

—— (1969). *Logique du sens.* Paris: Minuit; tr. Mark Lester and Charles Stivale as *The Logic of Sense.* New York: Columbia University Press, 1990.

Deleuze, Gilles and Félix Guattari (1972). *L'Anti-Oedipe*. Paris: Minuit; tr. Robert Hurley, Mark Seem, and Helen R. Lane as *Anti-Oedipus*. New York: Viking, 1977.

——(1991). *Qu'est-ce que la philosophie?* Paris: Minuit; tr. Hugh Tomlinson and Graham Burchell as *What is Philosophy?* London: Verso, 1994.

Demopoulos, William (ed.) (1995). *Frege's Philosophy of Mathematics*. Cambridge, MA: Harvard University Press.

*Dennett, Daniel (1969). *Content and Consciousness*. London: Routledge.

——(1971). 'Intentional Systems', *Journal of Philosophy* 68: 87–106.

——(1978). *Brainstorms: Philosophical Essays on Mind and Psychology*. Cambridge, MA: MIT Press.

——(1984). *Elbow Room: The Varieties of Free Will Worth Wanting*. Cambridge, MA: MIT Press.

——(1987). *The Intentional Stance*. Cambridge, MA: MIT Press.

——(1991). *Consciousness Explained*. Boston: Little, Brown & Co.

DeRose, Keith (1992). 'Contextualism and Knowledge Attributions', *Philosophy and Phenomenological Research* 52(4): 913–29.

——(2009). *The Case for Contextualism*. Oxford: Oxford University Press.

*Derrida, Jacques (1962). *Introduction à 'L'Origine de la géométrie' de Husserl*. Paris: Presses Universitaires de France; 2nd edn. 1974; tr. John P. Leavey as *Edmund Husserl's Origin of Geometry: An Introduction*. Lincoln: University of Nebraska Press, 1989.

——(1967a). *La Voix et le phénomène*. Paris: Presses Universitaires de France; tr. David B. Allison as *Speech and Phenomena*. Evanston, IL: Northwestern University Press, 1973.

——(1967b). *De la grammatologie*. Paris: Minuit; tr. Gayatri Spivak as *Of Grammatology*. Baltimore, MD: Johns Hopkins University Press, 1974.

——(1967c). *L'Ecriture et la différence*. Paris: Seuil; tr. Alan Bass as *Writing and Difference*. London: Routledge, 1978.

——(1968). 'Différance', *Bulletin de la société française de philosophie*, 1968; in Derrida 1972 [1982], pp. 1–27.

——(1971). 'Signature Event Context', in Derrida 1972 [1982], pp. 307–30; tr. in *Glyph* 1 (1977): 172–97; also in Derrida 1988, pp. 1–23; talk orig. given in French 1971.

——(1972). *Marges de la philosophie*. Paris: Les Editions de Minuit; tr. Alan Bass as *Margins of Philosophy*. Hemel Hempstead: Harvester, 1982.

——(1977). 'Limited Inc a b c…', *Glyph* 2: 162–254; also in Derrida 1988, pp. 29–110.

——(1988). *Limited Inc*. Evanston, IL: Northwestern University Press.

Devitt, Michael (1981). 'Donnellan's Distinction', in French *et al.* 1981, pp. 511–26.

deVries, Willem (2011). 'Wilfrid Sellars', *The Stanford Encyclopedia of Philosophy*, online at: <http://plato.stanford.edu/entries/sellars> [accessed 28 May 2012].

*Dewey, John (1925). *Experience and Nature*; repr. New York: Dover, 1958.

——(1934). *Art as Experience*; repr. in *The Later Works, 1925–1953*, Vol. 10, ed. J. Boydston. Carbondale: Southern Illinois University Press.

——(1939). 'Biography of John Dewey', ed. Jane M. Dewey, in Schilpp 1939, pp. 3–45.

Diamond, Cora (1979). 'Frege and Nonsense', in Diamond and Teichman 1979, pp. 195–218; repr. in Diamond 1991a, pp. 73–93.

——(1981). 'What Nonsense Might Be', *Philosophy* 56: 5–22; repr. in Diamond 1991a, pp. 95–114.

——(1984). 'What Does a Concept-Script Do?', *Philosophical Quarterly* 34: 343–68; repr. in Diamond 1991a, pp. 115–44.

——(1988). 'Throwing Away the Ladder: How to Read the *Tractatus*', *Philosophy* 63: 5–27; repr. in Diamond 1991a, pp. 179–204.

—— (1991a). *The Realistic Spirit*. Cambridge, MA: MIT Press.

—— (1991b). 'Ethics, Imagination and the Method of Wittgenstein's *Tractatus*', in Heinrich and Vetter 1991, pp. 55–90; repr. in Crary and Read 2000, pp. 149–73.

—— (2006). 'Anscombe, Gertrude Elizabeth Margaret (1919–2001)', in Grayling, Pyle, and Goulder 2006, I, pp. 114–19.

—— (2010). 'Inheriting from Frege: The Work of Reception, as Wittgenstein did it', in Potter and Ricketts 2010, pp. 550–601.

Diamond, Cora and Jenny Teichman (eds.) (1979). *Intention and Intentionality: Essays in Honour of G. E. M. Anscombe*. Brighton: Harvester Press.

Dicker, Georges (1980). *Perceptual Knowledge: An Analytical Historical Study*. Dordrecht: D. Reidel.

Dickstein, Morris (ed.) (1998). *The Revival of Pragmatism*. Durham, NC: Duke University Press.

*Dilthey, Wilhelm (1883). *Introduction to the Human Sciences*, tr. in Dilthey 1985–2002, vol. 1.

—— (1894). 'Ideas for a Descriptive and Analytic Psychology', in Dilthey 1914–2006, vol. 5.

—— (1914–2006). *Gesammelte Schriften*, 26 vols. Göttingen: Vandenhoeck & Ruprecht.

—— (1985–2002). *Selected Works*, 5 vols., ed. R. A. Makkreel and F. Rodi. Princeton, NJ: Princeton University Press.

Domski, Mary and Michael Dickson (eds.) (2010). *Discourse on a New Method: Reinvigorating the Marriage of History and Philosophy of Science*. Chicago: Open Court.

Donnellan, Keith (1966). 'Reference and Definite Descriptions', *Philosophical Review* 75: 281–304.

D'Oro, Giuseppina and James Connelly (2010). 'Robin George Collingwood', *The Stanford Encyclopedia of Philosophy*, online at: <http://plato.stanford.edu/entries/Collingwood> [accessed 28 May 2012].

D'Oro, Giuseppina and Constantine Sandis (eds.) (2013). *Reasons and Causes: Causalism and Non-Causalism in the Philosophy of Action*. Basingstoke: Palgrave Macmillan.

Drake, Durant *et al.* (1920). *Essays in Critical Realism: A Co-operative Study of the Problem of Knowledge*. London: Macmillan.

Dray, William H. (ed.) (1966). *Philosophical Analysis and History*. New York: Harper & Row.

Dreier, James (2001). 'Charles Stevenson (1908–1979)', in Martinich and Sosa 2001a, pp. 175–80.

Dretske, Fred I. (1969). *Seeing and Knowing*. Chicago: University of Chicago Press.

—— (1970). 'Epistemic Operators', *Journal of Philosophy* 67: 1007–23.

—— (1981). *Knowledge and the Flow of Information*. Cambridge, MA: MIT Press.

—— (1988). *Explaining Behavior: Reasons in a World of Causes*. Cambridge, MA: MIT Press.

—— (1995). *Naturalizing the Mind*. Cambridge, MA: MIT Press.

Dreyfus, Hubert L. and Harrison Hall (eds.) (1982). *Husserl, Intentionality and Cognitive Science*. Cambridge, MA: MIT Press.

Driver, Julia (2009). 'Gertrude Elizabeth Margaret Anscombe', *The Stanford Encyclopedia of Philosophy*, online at: <http://plato.stanford.edu/entries/anscombe> [accessed 28 May 2012].

Drucker, Thomas (2005). 'Church, Alonzo (1903–95)', in Shook 2005, I, pp. 487–91.

Ducasse, Curt (1941). *Philosophy as a Science: Its Matter and its Method*. New York: Oskar-Piest.

*Duhem, Pierre (1906). *La théorie physique, son objet et sa structure*. Paris: Chevalier et Rivière; 2nd edn. 1914; tr. P. Wiener as *The Aim and Structure of Physical Theory*. Princeton, NJ: Princeton University Press, 1954.

—— (1996). *Essays in History and Philosophy of Science*, ed. and tr. Roger Ariew and Peter Barker. Indianapolis: Hackett.

Duke, George (2012). *Dummett on Abstract Objects*. Basingstoke: Palgrave Macmillan.

*Dummett, Michael (1973). *Frege: Philosophy of Language*. London: Duckworth; 2nd edn. 1981.

—— (1978). *Truth and Other Enigmas*. London: Duckworth.

—— (1981a). *The Interpretation of Frege's Philosophy*. London: Duckworth.

—— (1981b). 'Frege and Wittgenstein', in Block 1981, pp. 31–42; repr. in Dummett 1991b, pp. 237–48.

—— (1984). 'An Unsuccessful Dig' [review of Baker and Hacker 1984], *Philosophical Quarterly* 34: 379–401; repr. with revisions in Dummett 1991b, pp. 158–98.

—— (1988a). *Ursprünge der analytischen Philosophie*. Frankfurt: Suhrkamp; rev. and pub. in English as Dummett 1993a.

—— (1988b). 'Second Thoughts', *Philosophical Quarterly* 38: 87–103; repr. with revisions in Dummett 1991b, pp. 199–216.

—— (1991a). *Frege: Philosophy of Mathematics*. London: Duckworth.

—— (1991b). *Frege and Other Philosophers*. Oxford: Oxford University Press.

—— (1991c). *The Logical Basis of Metaphysics*. Cambridge, MA: Harvard University Press.

—— (1993a). *Origins of Analytical Philosophy*. London: Duckworth; rev. English edn. of Dummett 1988a.

—— (1993b). *The Seas of Language*. Oxford: Clarendon Press.

—— (2001). 'Gottlob Frege', in Martinich and Sosa 2001a, pp. 6–20.

—— (2007). 'Intellectual Autobiography', in Auxier and Hahn 2007, pp. 3–32.

—— (2010). *The Nature and Future of Philosophy*. New York: Columbia University Press.

Duncan-Jones, A. E. (1933). 'A Statement of Policy', *Analysis* 1: 1–2.

—— (1937). 'Does Philosophy Analyse Common Sense?', *Proceedings of the Aristotelian Society*, Supplementary Vol. 16: 139–61.

Durant, Will (1926). *The Story of Philosophy*. New York: Simon & Schuster; 2nd edn. 1933.

Durfee, Harold A. (ed.) (1976). *Analytic Philosophy and Phenomenology*. The Hague: Martinus Nijhoff.

Dworkin, Ronald (1977). *Taking Rights Seriously*. Cambridge, MA: Harvard University Press.

—— (1981). 'What is Equality?', *Philosophy and Public Affairs* 10: 228–40 (Part I: 'Equality of Welfare'), pp. 283–345 (Part 2: 'Equality of Resources').

Dykhuizen, George (1973). *The Life and Mind of John Dewey*. Carbondale: Southern Illinois University Press.

Ebbs, Gary (1997). *Rule-Following and Realism*. Cambridge, MA: Harvard University Press.

Edmonds, David and John Eidinow (2001). *Wittgenstein's Poker: The Story of a Ten-Minute Argument Between Two Great Philosophers*. New York: Harper & Collins.

Edwards, Paul (ed.) (1967). *The Encyclopedia of Philosophy*. New York: Macmillan.

Egginton, William and Mike Sandbothe (2004). *The Pragmatic Turn in Philosophy: Contemporary Engagements between Analytic and Continental Thought*. Albany. NY: State University of New York Press.

Egidi, Rosaria (1963). *Ontologia e Conoscenza Matematica: un saggio su Gottlob Frege*. Firenze: Sansoni.

—— (ed.) (1999). *In Search of a New Humanism: The Philosophy of Georg Henrik von Wright*. Dordrecht: Kluwer.

*Einstein, Albert (1916). 'Die Grundlage der allgemeinen Relativitätstheorie', *Annalen der Physik* 49: 769–822.

——(1918). 'Prinzipielles zur allgemeinen Relativitätstheorie', *Annalen der Physik* 55: 240–4.

——(1949). 'Autobiographical Notes', in Schilpp 1949b, pp. 1–95.

Eldridge, Michael (2005). 'Dewey, John (1859–1952)', in Shook 2005, II, pp. 629–36.

Eldridge, Richard (ed.) (2003). *Stanley Cavell*. Cambridge: Cambridge University Press.

Ellis, Anthony (2006a). 'Waismann, Friedrich (1896–1959)', in Grayling, Pyle, and Goulder 2006, IV, pp. 3279–80.

——(2006b). 'Wisdom, Arthur John Terence (1904–93)', in Grayling, Pyle, and Goulder 2006, IV, pp. 3482–5.

Elton, William (ed.), (1954). *Aesthetics and Language*. Oxford: Blackwell.

Elugardo, Reinaldo (2005). 'Searle, John Rogers (1932–)', in Shook 2005, IV, pp. 2175–81.

Enderton, Herbert B. (forthcoming). 'Alonzo Church: Life and Work', introduction to Church forthcoming.

Engel, Pascal (1988). 'Continental Insularity: Contemporary French Analytical Philosophy', in Griffiths 1988, pp. 1–19.

——(1997). *La Dispute: une Introduction à la Philosophie Analytique*. Paris: Minuit.

——(1999). 'Analytic Philosophy and Cognitive Norms', *The Monist* 82: 218–34.

Engelmann, Mauro (2013). *Wittgenstein's Philosophical Development: Phenomenology, Grammar, Method, and the Anthropological View*. Basingstoke: Palgrave Macmillan.

Engelmann, Paul (1967). *Letters from Ludwig Wittgenstein with a Memoir*. Oxford: Blackwell.

Erickson, Stephen (1970). *Language and Being: An Analytic Phenomenology*. New Haven: Yale University Press.

Etchemendy, John (1990). *The Concept of Logical Consequence*. Cambridge, MA: Harvard University Press.

*Evans, Gareth (1973). 'The Causal Theory of Names', *Proceedings of the Aristotelian Society*, Supplementary Vol. 47: 187–208; repr. in Evans 1985, pp. 1–24.

—— (1981). 'Understanding Demonstratives', in Parret and Bouveresse 1981; rev. and repr. in Evans 1985, pp. 291–321.

——(1982). *The Varieties of Reference*. Oxford: Oxford University Press.

——(1985). *Collected Papers*. Oxford: Oxford University Press.

Evans, Gareth and John McDowell (eds.) (1976). *Truth and Meaning: Essays in Semantics*. Oxford: Clarendon Press.

Ewald, William (ed.) (1996). *From Kant to Hilbert: A Source Book in the Foundations of Mathematics*, 2 vols. Oxford: Oxford University Press.

Ewing, A. C. (1947). *The Definition of Good*. London: Routledge & Kegan Paul.

——(1950). 'Philosophical Analysis in Ethics', *Philosophical Studies* 1: 74–80.

Fain, Haskell (1970). *Between Philosophy and History: The Resurrection of Speculative Philosophy of History Within the Analytic Tradition*. Princeton, NJ: Princeton University Press.

Fann, K. T. (ed.) (1967). *Ludwig Wittgenstein: The Man and His Philosophy*; repr. Sussex: Harvester Press, 1978.

——(ed.) (1969). *Symposium on J. L. Austin*. London: Routledge & Kegan Paul.

Faust, A. (1927). *Heinrich Rickert und seine Stellung innerhalb der deutschen Philosophie der Gegenwart*. Tübingen: Mohr.

Feferman, Anita and Solomon Feferman (2004). *Alfred Tarski: Life and Logic*. Cambridge: Cambridge University Press.

Feferman, Solomon, Charles Parsons, and Stephen G. Simpson (eds.) (2010). *Kurt Gödel: Essays for his Centennial*. Cambridge: Cambridge University Press.

*Feigl, Herbert (1943). 'Logical Empiricism', in Runes 1943, pp. 371–416; repr. in Feigl and Sellars 1949, pp. 3–26.

—— (1958). 'The "Mental" and the "Physical"', in Feigl, Scriven, and Maxwell 1958; repub. as a book with additional material. Minneapolis: University of Minnesota Press, 1967.

—— (1981). *Inquiries and Provocations: Selected Writings 1929–1974*. Dordrecht: D. Reidel.

Feigl, Herbert and Michael Scriven (eds.) (1956). *The Foundations of Science and the Concepts of Psychology and Psychoanalysis, Minnesota Studies in the Philosophy of Science*, 1. Minneapolis: University of Minnesota Press.

Feigl, Herbert, Michael Scriven, and Grover Maxwell (eds.) (1958). *Concepts, Theories, and the Mind/Body Problem, Minnesota Studies in the Philosophy of Science*, 2. Minneapolis: University of Minnesota Press.

Feigl, Herbert and Wilfrid Sellars (eds.) (1949). *Readings in Philosophical Analysis*. New York: Appleton-Century.

Feigl, Herbert, Wilfrid Sellars, and Keith Lehrer (eds.) (1972). *New Readings in Philosophical Analysis*. New York: Appleton-Century-Crofts.

Feldman, Richard (2005). 'Chisholm, Roderick Milton (1916–99)', in Shook 2005, I, pp. 475–9.

Feldman, Richard and Fred Feldman (2008). 'Roderick Chisholm', *The Stanford Encyclopedia of Philosophy*, online at: <http://plato.stanford.edu/entries/Chisholm> [accessed 28 May 2012].

Ferreira, Phillip (2006). 'Bradley, Francis Herbert (1846–1924)', in Grayling, Pyle, and Goulder 2006, I, pp. 403–7.

Ferreirós, José (2007). *Labyrinth of Thought: A History of Set Theory and Its Role in Modern Mathematics*. Basel: Birkhaüser.

Ferreirós, José and Jeremy Gray (eds.) (2006). *The Architecture of Modern Mathematics: Essays in History and Philosophy*. Oxford: Oxford University Press.

Fetzer, James H. (ed.) (2001). *The Philosophy of Carl G. Hempel: Studies in Science, Explanation, and Rationality*. Oxford: Oxford Univesity Press.

—— (2010). 'Carl Hempel', *The Stanford Encyclopedia of Philosophy*, online at: <http://plato.stanford.edu/entries/hempel> [accessed 28 May 2012].

*Feyerabend, Paul (1955). 'Wittgenstein's *Philosophical Investigations*', *Philosophical Review* 64: 449–83; repr. in Pitcher 1966, pp. 104–50; Feyerabend 1981b, pp. 99–130.

—— (1966). 'Herbert Feigl: A Biographical Sketch', in Feyerabend and Maxwell 1966, pp. 3–14.

—— (1975). *Against Method*. London: Verso; rev. edn. 1988.

—— (1981a). *Realism, Rationalism and Scientific Method, Philosophical Papers*, vol. 1. Cambridge: Cambridge University Press.

—— (1981b). *Problems of Empiricism, Philosophical Papers*, vol. 2. Cambridge: Cambridge University Press.

—— (1995). *Killing Time: The Autobiography of Paul Feyerabend*. Chicago: University of Chicago Press.

Feyerabend, Paul K. and Grover Maxwell (eds.) (1966). *Matter, Mind, and Method: Essays in Philosophy and Science in Honor of Herbert Feigl*. Minneapolis: University of Minnesota Press.

Field, Hartry (1980). *Science Without Numbers: A Defence of Nominalism*. Oxford: Blackwell.

Fishkin, James and Robert Goodin (eds.) (2010). *Population and Political Theory: Philosophy, Politics and Society, Eighth Series*. Oxford: Blackwell.

Flew, Antony (ed.) (1951). *Essays in Logic and Language*. Oxford: Blackwell.

—— (ed.) (1953). *Logic and Language (Second Series)*. Oxford: Blackwell.

—— (ed.) (1956). *Essays in Conceptual Analysis*. London: Macmillan.

—— (1979). 'The Cultural Roots of Analytical Philosophy', *Journal of Chinese Philosophy* 6: 1–14.

Flowers, F. A. (ed.) (1999). *Portraits of Wittgenstein*, 4 vols. Bristol: Thoemmes Press.

Floyd, Juliet (2009). 'Recent Themes in the History of Early Analytic Philosophy', *Journal of the History of Philosophy* 47: 157–200.

—— (2011a). 'Prefatory Note to the Translation [of the Frege–Wittgenstein correspondence]', in de Pellegrin 2011, pp. 1–14.

—— (2011b). 'The Frege–Wittgenstein Correspondence: Interpretive Themes', in de Pellegrin 2011, pp. 75–107.

Floyd, Juliet and Sanford Shieh (eds.) (2001). *Future Pasts: The Analytic Tradition in Twentieth-Century Philosophy*. New York: Oxford University Press.

Flynn, Bernard (2004). 'Maurice Merleau-Ponty', *The Stanford Encyclopedia of Philosophy*, online at: <http://plato.stanford.edu/entries/merleau-ponty> [accessed 28 May 2012].

Flynn, Thomas (2011). 'Jean-Paul Sartre', *The Stanford Encyclopedia of Philosophy*, online at: <http://plato.stanford.edu/entries/sartre> [accessed 28 May 2012].

*Fodor, Jerry (1968). *Psychological Explanation*. New York: Random House.

—— (1975). *The Language of Thought*. New York: Thomas Y. Crowell.

—— (1980). 'Methodological Solipsism Considered as a Research Strategy in Cognitive Psychology', *The Behavioral and Brain Sciences* 3: 63–109.

—— (1981). *RePresentations: Philosophical Essays on the Foundations of Cognitive Science*. Cambridge, MA: MIT Press.

—— (1983). *The Modularity of Mind: An Essay on Faculty Psychology*. Cambridge, MA: MIT Press.

—— (1987). *Psychosemantics: The Problem of Meaning in the Philosophy of Mind*. Cambridge, MA: MIT Press.

Fogelin, Robert J. (1976). *Wittgenstein*. London: Routledge & Kegan Paul; 2nd edn. 1987.

—— (1980). 'Blanshard's Critique of the Analytic Movement', in Schilpp 1980, pp. 696–724.

—— (2009). *Taking Wittgenstein at His Word: A Textual Study*. Princeton, NJ: Princeton University Press.

Foley, Richard and Dean Zimmerman (2001). 'Roderick Chisholm (1916–1999)', in Martinich and Sosa 2001a, pp. 281–95.

Føllesdal, Dagfinn (1958). *Husserl und Frege*. Oslo: Aschehoug.

—— (1997). 'Analytic Philosophy: What is it and why should one engage in it?', in Glock 1997, pp. 1–16.

—— (ed.) (2001). *Philosophy of Quine*, 5 vols. New York: Garland.

—— (2005). 'White, Morton Gabriel (1917–)', in Shook 2005, IV, pp. 2568–73.

Fölsing, Albrecht (1997). *Heinrich Hertz: Eine Biographie*. Hamburg: Hoffmann und Campe.

*Foot, Philippa (1958). 'Moral Beliefs', *Proceedings of the Aristotelian Society* 59: 83–104; repr. in Foot 1978, pp. 110–31.

—— (1967). 'The Problem of Abortion and the Doctrine of the Double Effect', *Oxford Review* 5: 5–15; repr. in Foot 1978, pp. 19–32.

—— (1972). 'Morality as a System of Hypothetical Imperatives', *Philosophical Review* 81: 305–16; repr. in Foot 1978, pp. 157–73.

—— (1978). *Virtues and Vices and Other Essays in Moral Philosophy*. Oxford: Blackwell.

Forguson, L. (2001a). 'Oxford and the "Epidemic" of Ordinary Language Philosophy', *Monist* 84: 325–46.

—— (2001b). 'Oxford Philosophy: A Case Study in Cognitive Epidemiology', in Brogaard and Smith 2001, pp. 101–9.

Foster, John (1985). *A. J. Ayer*. London: Routledge.

Foster, L. and J. W. Swanson (eds.) (1970). *Experience and Theory*. London: Duckworth.

*Foucault, Michel (1966). *Les mots et les choses*. Paris: Gallimard; tr. as *The Order of Things*. New York: Vintage, 1973.

—— (1969). *L'archéologie du savoir*. Paris: Gallimard; tr. A. Sheridan Smith as *The Archaeology of Knowledge*. New York: Harper & Row, 1972.

Frank, Philipp (1957). *Philosophy of Science: The Link Between Science and Philosophy*. Englewood Cliffs, NJ: Prentice-Hall; repr. New York: Dover, 2004.

*Frege, Gottlob (1873). 'On a Geometrical Representation of Imaginary Forms in the Plane', in Frege 1967, pp. 1–49; tr. H. Kaal in Frege 1984, pp. 1–55.

—— (1874). 'Methods of Calculation based on an Extension of the Concept of Quantity [Magnitude]', in Frege 1967, pp. 51–84; tr. H. Kaal in Frege 1984, pp. 56–92.

—— (1879). *Begriffsschrift, eine der arithmetischen nachgebildete Formelsprache des reinen Denkens*. Halle: L. Nebert; repr. in Frege 1964a, pp. VII–XVI, 1–88; tr. T. W. Bynum as 'Conceptual Notation' in Frege 1972, pp. 101–203; tr. S. Bauer-Mengelberg in van Heijenoort 1967, pp. 5–82; most of Part I (§§ 1–12) tr. P. T. Geach in Frege 1952, pp. 1–20; Preface and most of Part I tr. M. Beaney in Frege 1997, pp. 47–78.

—— (1880/81). 'Boole's Logical Calculus and the Concept-script', in Frege 1969/1983, pp. 9–52; tr. in Frege 1979, pp. 9–46.

—— (1882). 'Boole's Logical Formula-language and my Concept-script', in Frege 1969/1983, pp. 53–9; tr. in Frege 1979, pp. 47–52.

—— (1884). *Die Grundlagen der Arithmetik*. Breslau: W. Koebner; repr. in Frege 1986; tr. as Frege 1950; Introd., §§ 1–4, 45–69, 87–91, 104–9 tr. M. Beaney in Frege 1997, pp. 84–129.

—— (1891). 'Function and Concept'. Jena: Hermann Pohle; repr. in Frege 1962, pp. 17–39; Frege 1967, pp. 125–42; Frege 1999, pp. [I–IV], 1–31 (original pagination); tr. P. T. Geach in Frege 1952, pp. 21–41; Frege 1984, pp. 137–56; Frege 1997, pp. 130–48.

—— (1892a). 'On *Sinn* and *Bedeutung*', *Zeitschrift für Philosophie und philosophische Kritik* 100: 25–50; repr. in Frege 1962, pp. 40–65; Frege 1967, pp. 143–62; tr. M. Black as 'On Sense and Reference', *Philosophical Review*, 1948; repr. in Frege 1952, pp. 56–78; Frege 1984, pp. 157–77; Frege 1997, pp. 151–71; also tr. H. Feigl as 'On Sense and Nominatum', in Feigl and Sellars 1949, pp. 85–102.

—— (1892b). 'On Concept and Object', *Vierteljahrsschrift für wissenschaftliche Philosophie* 16: 192–205; repr. in Frege 1962, pp. 66–80; Frege 1967, pp. 167–78; Frege 1969/1983, pp. 96–127; tr. P. T. Geach in Frege 1952, pp. 42–55; Frege 1979, pp. 87–117; Frege 1984, pp. 182–94; Frege 1997, pp. 181–93.

—— (1893). *Grundgesetze der Arithmetik, begriffsschriftlich abgeleitet*. Jena: H. Pohle, Vol. I; repr. with Vol. II (Frege 1903a). Hildesheim: Georg Olms, 1962; repr. 1998 with corrigenda by C. Thiel; Preface, Introd., and §§ 1–7 of Vol. I tr. P. E. B. Jourdain and J. Stachelroth in Frege 1915–17, selections repr. in Frege 1952, pp. 137–58; Preface, Introd., and §§ 1–52 of Vol. I tr. M. Furth in Frege 1964b; most of Preface, Introd., and §§ 1–7, 26–9, 32–3 of Vol. I tr. M. Beaney in Frege 1997, pp. 194–223.

—— (1894). 'Review of E. G. Husserl, *Philosophie der Arithmetik I*', *Zeitschrift für Philosophie und philosophische Kritik* 103: 313–32; repr. in Frege 1967, pp. 179–92; tr. H. Kaal in Frege 1984, pp. 195–209; illustrative extracts tr. P. T. Geach in Frege 1952, pp. 79–85; extract tr. H. Kaal in Frege 1997, pp. 224–6.

—— (1903a). *Grundgesetze der Arithmetik, begriffsschriftlich abgeleitet.* Jena: H. Pohle, Vol. II; repr. with Vol. I (Frege 1893). Hildesheim: Georg Olms, 1962; repr. 1998 with corrigenda by C. Thiel; §§ 56–67, 86–137, 139–44, 146–7, and 'Nachwort' of Vol. II tr. P. T. Geach and M. Black in Frege 1952, pp. 159–244; 'Nachwort' of Vol. II tr. M. Furth in Frege 1964b; §§ 55–67, 138–47, and 'Nachwort' of Vol. II tr. P. T. Geach (with additions by M. Beaney) in Frege 1997, pp. 258–89.

—— (1903b). 'On the Foundations of Geometry: First Series', *Jahresbericht der Deutschen Mathematiker-Vereinigung* 12: 319–24, 368–75; repr. in Frege 1967, pp. 262–72; tr. E.-H. W. Kluge in Frege 1971, pp. 22–37; Frege 1984, pp. 273–84.

—— (1904). 'What is a Function?', in *Festschrift Ludwig Boltzmann gewidmet zum sechzigsten Geburtstage 20. Februar 1904*. Leipzig: Ambrosius Barth, pp. 656–66; repr. in Frege 1962, pp. 81–90; Frege 1967, pp. 273–80; tr. P. T. Geach in Frege 1952, pp. 107–16; Frege 1984, pp. 285–92.

—— (1906). 'On the Foundations of Geometry: Second Series', *Jahresbericht der Deutschen Mathematiker-Vereinigung* 15: 293–309, 377–403, 423–30; repr. in Frege 1967, pp. 281–323; tr. E.-H. W. Kluge in Frege 1971, pp. 49–112; Frege 1984, pp. 293–340.

—— (1912). 'Notes to Philip E. B. Jourdain, "The Development of the Theories of Mathematical Logic and the Principles of Mathematics"', *The Quarterly Journal of Pure and Applied Mathematics* 43: 237–69; repr. in Frege 1967, pp. 334–41; 1980, pp. 179–206.

—— (1914). 'Logic in Mathematics', in Frege 1969/1983, pp. 219–70; tr. in Frege 1979, pp. 203–50; extract in Frege 1997, pp. 308–18.

—— (1915–17). 'The Fundamental Laws of Arithmetic', *The Monist* 25: 481–94; 26, pp. 182–99; 27, pp. 114–27, tr. of Preface, Introd., and §§ 1–7 of Frege 1893, tr. P. E. B. Jourdain and J. Stachelroth; selections repr. in Frege 1952, pp. 137–58.

—— (1918a). 'Der Gedanke. Eine logische Untersuchung', *Beiträge zur Philosophie des deutschen Idealismus* 2: 58–77; repr. in Frege 1966, pp. 30–53; Frege 1967, pp. 342–61; tr. A. M. and Marcelle Quinton as 'The Thought: A Logical Inquiry' in *Mind* 65 (1956): 289–311; tr. P. T. Geach as 'Thoughts' in Frege 1977; Frege 1984, pp. 351–72; tr. as 'Thought' in Frege 1997, pp. 325–45.

—— (1918b). 'Der Verneinung. Eine logische Untersuchung', *Beiträge zur Philosophie des deutschen Idealismus* 1: 143–57; repr. in Frege 1966, pp. 54–71; Frege 1967, pp. 362–77; tr. P. T. Geach as 'Negation' in Frege 1952, pp. 117–36; Frege 1977; Frege 1984, pp. 373–89; Frege 1997, pp. 345–61.

—— (1923). 'Logische Untersuchungen. Dritter Teil: Gedankengefüge', *Beiträge zur Philosophie des deutschen Idealismus* 3: 36–51; repr. in Frege 1966, pp. 72–91; Frege 1967, pp. 378–94; tr. R. H. Stoothoff as 'Compound Thoughts' in *Mind* 72 (1963): 1–17; Frege 1977; Frege 1984, pp. 390–406.

—— (1950). *The Foundations of Arithmetic*, tr. of Frege 1884, tr. J. L. Austin, with German text. Oxford: Blackwell; 2nd edn. 1953.

—— (1952). *Translations from the Philosophical Writings of Gottlob Frege*, tr. and ed. Peter T. Geach and Max Black. Oxford: Blackwell; 2nd edn. 1960; 3rd edn. 1980 [without Frege 1918b].

—— (1962). *Funktion, Begriff, Bedeutung: Fünf logische Studien*, ed. G. Patzig. Göttingen: Vandenhoeck and Ruprecht.

—— (1964a). *Begriffsschrift und andere Aufsätze*, ed. I. Angelelli. Hildesheim: Georg Olms.

—— (1964b). *The Basic Laws of Arithmetic: Exposition of the System*, tr. of Frege 1893, Introd. and §§ 1–52, and of Frege 1903a, 'Nachwort', ed. with an introd. by Montgomery Furth. Los Angeles: University of California Press.

—— (1966). *Logische Untersuchungen*, ed. G. Patzig. Göttingen: Vandenhoeck and Ruprecht.

—— (1967). *Kleine Schriften*, ed. I. Angelelli. Hildesheim: Georg Olms; tr. as Frege 1984.

—— (1969). *Nachgelassene Schriften*, ed. H. Hermes, F. Kambartel. and F. Kaulbach. Hamburg: Felix Meiner; tr. as Frege 1979; 2nd edn. 1983 (see below).

—— (1971). *On the Foundations of Geometry and Formal Theories of Arithmetic*, tr. with an introd. by E.-H. Kluge. New Haven, CT: Yale University Press.

—— (1972). *Conceptual Notation and Related Articles*, ed. and tr. with a biog. and introd. by T. W. Bynum. Oxford: Clarendon Press.

—— (1976). *Wissenschaftlicher Briefwechsel*, ed. G. Gabriel, H. Hermes, F. Kambartel, C. Thiel, and A. Veraart. Hamburg: Felix Meiner; selection in Frege 1980a; abr. and tr. as Frege 1980b.

—— (1977). *Logical Investigations*, tr. of Frege 1918a, 1918b, 1923, ed. P. T. Geach, tr. P. T. Geach and R. H. Stoothoff. Oxford: Blackwell; now contained in Frege 1984.

—— (1979). *Posthumous Writings*, tr. of Frege 1969, tr. P. Long and R. White. Oxford: Blackwell.

—— (1980a). *Gottlob Freges Briefwechsel*, selection from Frege 1976, ed. G. Gabriel, F. Kambartel, and C. Thiel. Hamburg: Felix Meiner.

—— (1980b). *Philosophical and Mathematical Correspondence*, tr. of Frege 1976, ed. B. McGuinness, tr. H. Kaal. Oxford: Blackwell.

—— (1983). *Nachgelassene Schriften*, ed. H. Hermes, F. Kambartel, and F. Kaulbach. Hamburg: Felix Meiner, 2nd edn. of Frege 1969, revised and enlarged.

—— (1984). *Collected Papers on Mathematics, Logic, and Philosophy*, tr. of Frege 1967, ed. B. McGuinness, tr. M. Black *et al.* Oxford: Blackwell.

—— (1986). *Die Grundlagen der Arithmetik*, ed. C. Thiel, German centenary critical edition. Hamburg: Felix Meiner.

—— (1989). 'Briefe an Ludwig Wittgenstein', ed. A. Janik, in McGuinness and Haller 1989, pp. 5–33; tr. Burton Dreben and Juliet Floyd as 'Frege–Wittgenstein Correspondence' in de Pellegrin 2011, pp. 15–73.

—— (1994). 'Gottlob Freges politisches Tagebuch', ed. with an introd. by G. Gabriel and W. Kienzler, *Deutsche Zeitschrift für Philosophie* 42: 1057–98.

—— (1996). 'Vorlesungen über Begriffsschrift', ed. G. Gabriel, *History and Philosophy of Logic* 17: 1–48; tr. in Frege 2004.

—— (1997). *The Frege Reader*, ed. with an introd. by M. Beaney. Oxford: Blackwell.

—— (1999). *Zwei Schriften zur Arithmetik*, ed. W. Kienzler. Hildesheim: Georg Olms.

—— (2000). 'Vorschläge für ein Wahlgesetz', ed. U. Dathe and W. Kienzler, in Gabriel and Dathe 2000, pp. 297–313.

—— (2004). *Frege's Lectures on Logic: Carnap's Student Notes, 1910–1914*, with an introd. by G. Gabriel, tr. and ed. with an introd. by E. H. Reck and S. Awodey. Chicago: Open Court.

—— (2013). *Grundgesetze der Arithmetik, begriffsschriftlich abgeleitet*, tr. Philip Ebert and Marcus Rossberg. Oxford: Oxford University Press.

French, P. A., T. E. Uehling, and H. K. Wettstein (eds.) (1981). *The Foundations of Analytic Philosophy, Midwest Studies in Philosophy VI*. Minneapolis: University of Minnesota Press.

*Freud, Sigmund (1899). *Die Traumdeutung*. Leipzig and Vienna: Franz Deuticke.

Friedman, Michael (1996). 'Overcoming Metaphysics: Carnap and Heidegger', in Giere and Richardson 1996, pp. 45–79.

—— (1999). *Reconsidering Logical Positivism*. Cambridge: Cambridge University Press.

—— (2000). *A Parting of the Ways: Carnap, Cassirer, and Heidegger*. Chicago: Open Court.

—— (2011). 'Ernst Cassirer', *The Stanford Encyclopedia of Philosophy*, online at: <http://plato.stanford.edu/entries/Cassirer> [accessed 28 May 2012].

Friedman, Michael and Richard Creath (eds.) (2007). *The Cambridge Companion to Carnap.* Cambridge: Cambridge University Press.

Frongia, G. and B. McGuinness (1990). *Wittgenstein: A Bibliographical Guide.* Oxford: Blackwell.

Fuller, Steve (2005). 'Kuhn, Thomas Samuel (1922–96)', in Shook 2005, III, pp. 1372–9.

Gabbay, Dov M. and John Woods (eds.) (2004). *Handbook of the History of Logic, Volume 3— The Rise of Modern Logic: From Leibniz to Frege.* Amsterdam: Elsevier.

—— —— (eds.) (2009). *Handbook of the History of Logic: Volume 5—Logic from Russell to Church.* Amsterdam: Elsevier.

Gabriel, Gottfried (2002). 'Frege, Lotze, and the Continental Roots of Early Analytic Philosophy', in Reck 2002, pp. 39–51; repr. in Beaney and Reck 2005, I, pp. 161–75.

——(2003). 'Carnap's "Elimination of Metaphysics Through the Logical Analysis of Language": A Retrospective Consideration of the Relationship between Continental and Analytic Philosophy', in Parrini *et al.* 2003, pp. 30–42.

Gabriel, Gottfried and Uwe Dathe (eds.) (2000). *Gottlob Frege—Werk und Wirkung.* Paderborn: Mentis.

Gabriel, Gottfried and Wolfgang Kienzler (eds.) (1997). *Frege in Jena: Beiträge zur Spurensicherung.* Würzburg: Königshausen & Neumann.

*Gadamer, Hans-Georg (1960). *Wahrheit und Methode.* Tübingen: J. C. B. Mohr; 2nd edn. 1965; 5th edn. 1986; 6th edn. 1990, repr. as Gadamer 1985–95, vol. 1; tr. W. Glen-Doepel as *Truth and Method.* London: Sheed & Ward, 1975; tr. rev. by J. Weinsheimer and D. Marshall, 1989.

—— (1962). 'The Philosophical Foundations of the Twentieth Century', in Gadamer 1976, pp. 107–29.

——(1972). 'Semantics and Hermeneutics', in Gadamer 1976, pp. 82–94.

——(1976). *Philosophical Hermeneutics*, tr. and ed. David E. Linge. Berkeley: University of California Press.

——(1985–95). *Gesammelte Werke*, 10 vols. Tübingen: J. C. B. Mohr.

——(1997). 'Reflections on My Philosophical Journey', tr. Richard E. Palmer, in Hahn 1997a, pp. 3–63.

Gallie, W. B. (1956). 'Essentially Contested Concepts', *Proceedings of the Aristotelian Society* 56: 167–98; repr. in a rev. form in Gallie 1964, pp. 157–91.

——(1964). *Philosophy and the Historical Understanding.* London: Chatto & Windus.

Gandon, Sébastien (2012). *Russell's Unknown Logicism: A Study in the History and Philosophy of Mathematics.* Basingstoke: Palgrave Macmillan.

Gardiner, H. N. (1926). 'The First Twenty-Five Years of the American Philosophical Association', *Philosophical Review* 35: 145–58.

Garrett, Don (2004). 'Philosophy and History in the History of Modern Philosophy', in Leiter 2004a, pp. 44–73.

——(2005). 'Marcus, Ruth Charlotte Barcan (1921–[2012])', in Shook 2005, III, pp. 1599–604.

Garry, Ann (2004). 'Analytic Feminism', *The Stanford Encyclopedia of Philosophy*, online at: <http://plato.stanford.edu/entries/femapproach-analytic> [accessed 28 May 2012].

Gaskin, Richard (ed.) (2001). *Grammar in Early Twentieth-Century Philosophy.* London: Routledge.

——(2008). *The Unity of the Proposition.* Oxford: Oxford University Press.

Gasking, D. T. A. (1954). 'The Philosophy of John Wisdom', *Australasian Journal of Philosophy* 32: 136–56, 185–212.

Gasser, James (2006). 'Boole, George (1815–64)', in Grayling, Pyle, and Goulder 2006, I, pp. 377–80.

Gawronsky, Dimitry (1949). 'Ernst Cassirer: His Life and His Work', in Schilpp 1949a, pp. 1–38.

Gay, Peter (1988). *Freud: A Life for Our Time*. London: J. M. Dent & Sons.

*Geach, Peter T. (1957). *Mental Acts*. London: Routledge & Kegan Paul.

—— (1958). 'Imperative and Deontic Logic', *Analysis* 18: 49–56; repr. in Geach 1972, pp. 270–8.

—— (1960). 'Ascriptivism', *Philosophical Review* 69: 221–5; repr. in Geach 1972, pp. 250–4.

—— (1961). 'Frege', in Anscombe and Geach 1961, pp. 129–62.

—— (1962). *Reference and Generality: An Examination of Some Medieval and Modern Theories*. Ithaca. NY: Cornell University Press.

—— (1965). 'Assertion', *Philosophical Review* 74: 449–65; repr. in Geach 1972, pp. 254–69.

—— (1972). *Logic Matters*. Oxford: Blackwell.

—— (1976). 'Saying and Showing in Frege and Wittgenstein', in Hintikka 1976, pp. 54–70.

—— (ed.) (1988). *Wittgenstein's Lectures on Philosophical Psychology, 1946–47*. Chicago: University of Chicago Press.

Gellner, Ernest (1959). *Words and Things: An Examination of, and an Attack on, Linguistic Philosophy*. London: Routledge & Kegan Paul; rev. edn. 1979.

Gentzen, Gerhard (1934). 'Untersuchungen über das logische Schliessen I', *Mathematische Zeitschrift* 39: 176–210.

—— (1936). 'Untersuchungen über das logische Schliessen II', *Mathematische Zeitschrift* 41: 405–31.

Geraets, T. S. (ed.) (1979). *Rationality Today*. Ottawa: University of Ottawa Press.

Gerrard, Steve (1997). 'Desire and Desirability: Bradley, Russell and Moore versus Mill', in Tait 1997, pp. 37–74.

Gettier, E. L. (1963). 'Is Justified True Belief Knowledge?', *Analysis* 23: 121–3.

Giaquinto, Marcus (2002). *The Search for Certainty: A Philosophical Account of Foundations of Mathematics*. Oxford: Clarendon Press.

Gibbard, Allan (1990). *Wise Choices, Apt Feelings: A Theory of Normative Judgment*. Oxford: Oxford University Press.

—— (2003). *Thinking How To Live*. Cambridge, MA: Harvard University Press.

Gibson, Roger F. (ed.) (2004). *The Cambridge Companion to Quine*. Cambridge: Cambridge University Press.

—— (2005). 'Dreben, Burton Spencer (1927–99)', in Shook 2005, II, pp. 659–60.

Giere, Ronald N. and Alan W. Richardson (eds.) (1996). *Origins of Logical Empiricism*. Minneapolis: University of Minnesota Press.

Gillies, Donald (ed.) (1992a). *Revolutions in Mathematics*. Oxford: Clarendon Press.

—— (1992b). 'The Fregean Revolution in Logic', in Gillies 1992a, pp. 265–305.

Ginet, Carl (2001). 'Norman Malcolm (1911–1990)', in Martinich and Sosa 2001a, pp. 231–8.

Glendinning, Simon (ed.) (1999a). *The Edinburgh Encyclopedia of Continental Philosophy*. Edinburgh: Edinburgh University Press.

—— (1999b). 'What is Continental Philosophy?', in Glendinning 1999a, pp. 3–20.

—— (2002). 'The Analytic and the Continental', in Baggini and Stangroom 2002, pp. 201–18.

—— (2006). *The Idea of Continental Philosophy: A Philosophical Chronicle*. Edinburgh: Edinburgh University Press.

Glock, Hans-Johann (1996). *A Wittgenstein Dictionary*. Oxford: Blackwell.

—— (ed.) (1997). *The Rise of Analytic Philosophy*. Oxford: Blackwell.

—— (1999). 'Vorsprung durch Logik: The German Analytic Tradition', in O'Hear 1999, pp. 137–66.

—— (ed.) (2001). *Wittgenstein: A Critical Reader*. Oxford: Blackwell.

—— (2003a). *Quine and Davidson on Language, Thought and Reality*. Cambridge: Cambridge University Press.

—— (ed.) (2003b). *Strawson and Kant*. Oxford: Oxford University Press.

—— (2003c). 'Strawson and Analytic Kantianism', in Glock 2003b, pp. 15–42.

—— (2004). 'Was Wittgenstein an Analytic Philosopher?', *Metaphilosophy* 35: 419–44.

—— (2008a). *What is Analytic Philosophy?*. Cambridge: Cambridge University Press.

—— (2008b). 'Analytic Philosophy and History: A Mismatch?', *Mind* 117: 867–97.

—— (2008c). 'The Development of Analytic Philosophy: Wittgenstein and After', in Moran 2008a, pp. 76–117.

—— (2008d). 'The Influence of Wittgenstein on American Philosophy', in Misak 2008, pp. 375–402.

Glock, Hans-Johann and John Hyman (eds.) (2009). *Wittgenstein and Analytic Philosophy*. Oxford: Oxford University Press.

Glymour, Clark and Frederick Eberhardt (2008). 'Hans Reichenbach', *The Stanford Encyclopedia of Philosophy*, online at: <http://plato.stanford.edu/entries/reichenbach> [accessed 28 May 2012].

*Gödel, Kurt (1931). 'Über formal unentscheidbare Sätze der *Principia Mathematica* und verwandter Systeme I', *Monatshefte für Mathematik und Physik* 38: 173–98; tr. as 'On Formally Undecidable Propositions of *Principia Mathematica* and Related Systems I', in Gödel 1986–2005, I, pp. 144–95.

—— (1944). 'Russell's Mathematical Logic', in Schilpp 1944, pp. 123–53; repr. in Gödel 1986–2005, II, pp. 119–41.

—— (1986–2005). *Collected Works*, 4 vols., ed. S. Feferman *et al*. Oxford: Oxford University Press.

Goldfarb, Warren (1979). 'Logic in the Twenties: The Nature of the Quantifier', *Journal of Symbolic Logic* 44: 351–68.

—— (1997a). 'Wittgenstein on Fixity of Meaning', in Tait 1997, pp. 75–89.

—— (1997b). 'Metaphysics and Nonsense: on Cora Diamond's *The Realistic Spirit*', *Journal of Philosophical Research* 22: 57–73.

—— (2002). 'Wittgenstein's Understanding of Frege: The Pre-Tractarian Evidence', in Reck 2002, pp. 185–200.

—— (2011). 'Das Überwinden: Anti-metaphysical Readings of the *Tractatus*', in Read and Lavery 2011, pp. 6–21.

Goldman, Alvin (1967). 'A Causal Theory of Knowing', *Journal of Philosophy* 64: 357–72.

Gómez-Torrente, Mario (2011). 'Alfred Tarski', *The Stanford Encyclopedia of Philosophy*, online at: <http://plato.stanford.edu/entries/tarski> [accessed 28 May 2012].

*Goodman, Nelson (1951). *The Structure of Appearance*. Cambridge, MA: Harvard University Press.

—— (1955). *Fact, Fiction and Forecast*. Cambridge, MA: Harvard University Press; 3rd edn. 1979.

—— (1968). *Languages of Art*. Indianapolis: Bobbs-Merrill; 2nd edn. 1976.

—— (1978). *Ways of Worldmaking*. Indianapolis: Hackett.

Goodman, Russell (2009). 'William James', *The Stanford Encyclopedia of Philosophy*, online at: <http://plato.stanford.edu/entries/james> [accessed 28 May 2012].

Gordon, Peter E. (2010). *Continental Divide: Heidegger, Cassirer, Davos*. Cambridge, MA: Harvard University Press.

Gracia, Jorge J. E. (1984). 'Philosophical Analysis in Latin America', *History of Philosophy Quarterly* 1: 111–12.

—— (1992). *Philosophy and Its History: Issues in Philosophical Historiography*. Albany: State University of New York Press.

Gracia, J. J. E., E. Rabossi, E. Villanueva, and M. Dascal (eds.) (1984). *Philosophical Analysis in Latin America*. Dordrecht: D. Reidel.

Graham, Daniel W. (2005). 'Vlastos, Gregory (1907–91)', in Shook 2005, IV, pp. 2488–9.

Gram, M. S. and E. D. Klemke (eds.) (1974). *The Ontological Turn: Studies in the Philosophy of Gustav Bergmann*. Iowa City: University of Iowa Press.

Grandy, Richard (2001). 'Thomas S. Kuhn (1922–1996)', in Martinich and Sosa 2001a, pp. 371–7.

Grandy, Richard E. and Richard Warner (2006). 'Paul Grice', *The Stanford Encyclopedia of Philosophy*, online at: <http://plato.stanford.edu/entries/grice> [accessed 28 May 2012].

Grattan-Guinness, Ivor (1977). *Dear Russell, Dear Jourdain: A Commentary on Russell's Logic, Based on His Correspondence with Philip Jourdain*. New York: Columbia University Press.

—— (ed.) (1994). *Companion Encyclopedia of the History and Philosophy of the Mathematical Sciences*, 2 vols. London: Routledge.

—— (2000). *The Search for Mathematical Roots, 1870–1940: Logics, Set Theories and the Foundations of Mathematics from Cantor through Russell to Gödel*. Princeton, NJ: Princeton University Press.

Gray, Jeremy (2008). *Plato's Ghost: The Modernist Transformation of Mathematics*. Princeton, NJ: Princeton University Press.

—— (2012). *Henri Poincaré: A Scientific Biography*. Princeton, NJ: Princeton University Press.

Grayling, Anthony, Andrew Pyle, and Naomi Goulder (eds.) (2006). *The Continuum Encyclopedia of British Philosophy*, 4 vols. London: Thoemmes Continuum.

Greco, John (2005). 'Kim, Jaegwon (1934–)', in Shook 2005, III, pp. 1302–7.

Green, Karen (1999). 'Was Wittgenstein Frege's Heir?', *Philosophical Quarterly* 49: 289–308.

—— (2001). *Dummett: Philosophy of Language*. Cambridge: Cambridge University Press.

Green, Mitchell S. (2005). 'Kripke, Saul (1940–)', in Shook 2005, III, pp. 1360–7.

Green, Mitchell and John N. Williams (eds.) (2007). *Moore's Paradox: New Essays on Belief, Rationality, and the First Person*. Oxford: Clarendon Press.

*Green, T. H. (1874). 'General Introduction to Vol. I' and 'Introduction to Moral Part of the Treatise', in David Hume, *Treatise of Human Nature*, ed. T. H. Green and T. H. Grose, London; repr. in Green 1885–9, I, pp. 1–371.

—— (1883). *Prolegomena to Ethics*. Oxford: Clarendon Press; 5th edn. 1907.

—— (1885–9). *Works of Thomas Hill Green*, 3 vols., ed. R. Nettleship. London: Longmans, Green, and Co.

Greimann, Dirk (ed.) (2007). *Essays on Frege's Conception of Truth*, Grazer Philosophische Studien 75.

*Grice, H. P. (1957). 'Meaning', *Philosophical Review* 66: 377–88; repr. in Grice 1989, pp. 213–23.

—— (1961). 'The Causal Theory of Perception', *Proceedings of the Aristotelian Society*, Supplementary Vol. 35: 121–52; repr. abridged in Grice 1989, pp. 224–47.

—— (1968). 'Utterer's Meaning, Sentence Meaning, and Word-Meaning', *Foundations of Language* 4: 225–42; repr. in Grice 1989, pp. 117–37.

—— (1969). 'Utterer's Meaning and Intentions', *Philosophical Review* 68: 147–77; repr. in Grice 1989, pp. 86–116.

—— (1975a). 'Logic and Conversation', in Cole and Morgan 1975, pp. 41–58; repr. in Grice 1989, pp. 22–40.

—— (1975b). 'Method in Philosophical Psychology (From the Banal to the Bizarre)', *Proceedings and Addresses of the American Philosophical Association* 48: 23–53; repr. in Grice 1991, pp. 121–61.

—— (1981). 'Presupposition and Conversational Implicature', in Cole 1981, pp. 183–97; repr. in Grice 1989, pp. 269–82.

—— (1989). *Studies in the Way of Words*. Cambridge, MA: Harvard University Press.

—— (1991). *The Conception of Value*. Oxford: Clarendon Press.

Grice, H. P. and P. F. Strawson (1956). 'In Defense of a Dogma', *Philosophical Review* 65: 141–58; repr. in Grice 1989, pp. 196–212.

Griffin, James P. (1964). *Wittgenstein's Logical Atomism*. Oxford: Clarendon Press.

Griffin, Nicholas (1991). *Russell's Idealist Apprenticeship*. Oxford: Clarendon Press.

—— (ed.) (2003). *The Cambridge Companion to Bertrand Russell*. Cambridge: Cambridge University Press.

Griffin, Nicholas and Dale Jacquette (eds.) (2009). *Russell vs. Meinong: The Legacy of 'On Denoting'*. London: Routledge.

Griffiths, A. P. (ed.) (1988). *Contemporary French Philosophy*. Cambridge: Cambridge University Press.

—— (ed.) (1991). *A. J. Ayer: Memorial Essays*. Cambridge: Cambridge University Press.

Grondin, Jean (2003). *Hans-Georg Gadamer: A Biography*, tr. Joel Weinsheimer. New Haven, CT: Yale University Press.

Gross, Barry R. (1970). *Analytic Philosophy: An Historical Introduction*. New York: Pegasus.

Gross, Neil (2008). *Richard Rorty: The Making of an American Philosopher*. Chicago: University of Chicago Press.

Guignon, Charles (ed.) (1993). *The Cambridge Companion to Heidegger*. Cambridge: Cambridge University Press.

Gustafsson, Martin and Richard Sørli (eds.) (2011). *The Philosophy of J. L. Austin*. Oxford: Oxford University Press.

Gustavsson, Kent (2010). 'Charlie Dunbar Broad', *The Stanford Encyclopedia of Philosophy*, online at: <http://plato.stanford.edu/entries/broad> [accessed 28 May 2012].

Gutting, Gary (2008). 'Michel Foucault', *The Stanford Encyclopedia of Philosophy*, online at: <http://plato.stanford.edu/entries/foucault> [accessed 28 May 2012].

—— (2009). *What Philosophers Know: Case Studies in Recent Analytic Philosophy*. Cambridge: Cambridge University Press.

Haaparanta, Leila (ed.) (1994). *Mind, Meaning and Mathematics: Essays on the Philosophy of Husserl and Frege*. Dordrecht: Kluwer.

—— (ed.) (2009). *The Development of Modern Logic*. Oxford: Oxford University Press.

Haaparanta, Leila and Jaakko Hintikka (eds.) (1986). *Frege Synthesized*. Dordrecht: D. Reidel.

Haaparanta, Leila and Heikki Koskinen (eds.) (2012). *Categories of Being: Essays on Metaphysics and Logic*. Oxford: Oxford University Press.

Haaparanta, Leila and Ilkka Niiniluoto (eds.) (2003). *Analytic Philosophy in Finland*. Amsterdam: Rodopi.

*Habermas, Jürgen (1968). *Erkenntnis und Interesse*. Frankfurt am Main: Suhrkamp; tr. J. J. Shapiro as *Knowledge and Human Interests*. Boston: Beacon, 1971.

—— (1981). *Theorie des kommunikativen Handelns*, vol. 1: *Handlungsrationalität und gesellschaftliche Rationalisierung*; vol. 2: *Zur Kritik der funktionalistischen Vernunft*. Frankfurt am

Main: Suhrkamp; tr. T. McCarthy as *The Theory of Communicative Action*. Boston: Beacon, vol. 1 1984, vol. 2 1987.

—— (1999). 'Hermeneutic and Analytic Philosophy: Two Complementary Versions of the Linguistic Turn?', in O'Hear 1999, pp. 413–42.

Hacker, P. M. S. (1972). *Insight and Illusion: Wittgenstein on Philosophy and the Metaphysics of Experience*. Oxford: Clarendon Press.

—— (1986). *Insight and Illusion: Themes in the Philosophy of Wittgenstein*, rev. edn. of Hacker 1972. Oxford: Clarendon Press.

—— (1990). *Wittgenstein: Meaning and Mind*. Oxford: Blackwell.

—— (1996a). *Wittgenstein: Mind and Will*. Oxford: Blackwell.

—— (1996b). *Wittgenstein's Place in Twentieth-Century Analytic Philosophy*. Oxford: Blackwell.

—— (1997). 'The Rise of Twentieth Century Analytic Philosophy', in Glock 1997, pp. 51–76.

—— (1998). 'Analytic Philosophy: What, Whence, and Whither?', in Biletzki and Matar 1998, pp. 3–34.

—— (1999). 'Frege and the Later Wittgenstein', in O'Hear 1999, pp. 223–47; repr. in Hacker 2001a, pp. 219–41.

—— (2000). 'Was he trying to whistle it?', in Crary and Read 2000, pp. 353–88; repr. in Hacker 2001a, pp. 98–140.

—— (2001a). *Wittgenstein: Connections and Controversies*. Oxford: Clarendon Press.

—— (2001b). 'Frege and the Early Wittgenstein', in Hacker 2001a, pp. 191–218.

—— (2001c). 'Ludwig Wittgenstein', in Martinich and Sosa 2001a, pp. 68–93.

—— (2003). 'Wittgenstein, Carnap and the New American Wittgensteinians', *Philosophical Quarterly* 53: 1–23.

—— (2006). 'Soames' History of Analytic Philosophy', *Philosophical Quarterly* 56: 121–31.

—— (2007). 'Analytic Philosophy: Beyond the Linguistic Turn and Back Again', in Beaney 2007a, pp. 125–41.

—— (2011). 'Analytic Philosophy: The Heritage', *Teorema* 30: 77–85.

Hacking, Ian (1975). *Why Does Language Matter to Philosophy?* Cambridge: Cambridge University Press.

Hacohen, Malachi Haim (2000). *Karl Popper: The Formative Years, 1902–1945*. Cambridge: Cambridge University Press.

Haddock, Guillermo E. Rosado (2008). *The Young Carnap's Unknown Master: Husserl's Influence on* Der Raum *and* Der logische Aufbau der Welt. Aldershot: Ashgate.

Hager, Paul J. (1994). *Continuity and Change in the Development of Russell's Philosophy*. Dordrecht: Kluwer.

—— (2003). 'Russell's Method of Analysis', in Griffin 2003, pp. 310–31.

*Hägerström, Axel (1911). 'Om moraliska föreställningars sanning'; tr. R. T. Sandin as 'On the Truth of Moral Propositions' in Hägerström 1964; inaugural lecture.

—— (1917). *Till frågan om den objektiva rättens begrepp*. Uppsala: KHVU; tr. C. D. Broad as 'On the Question of the Notion of Law' in Hägerström 1953.

—— (1927/1941). *Der römische Obligationsbegriff im Lichte der allgemeinen römischen Rechtsanschauung*, vol. 1 1927, vol. 2 1941. Uppsala: Almqvist & Wiksell.

—— (1953). *Inquiries into the Nature of Law and Morals*, ed. Karl Olivecrona, tr. C. D. Broad. Stockholm: Almqvist & Wiksell.

—— (1964). *Philosophy and Religion*, tr. Robert T. Sandin. London: George Allen & Unwin.

Hahn, Hans (1980). *Empiricism, Logic, Mathematics*, ed. B. McGuinness. Dordrecht: D. Reidel.

Hahn, Lewis Edwin (ed.) (1992). *The Philosophy of A. J. Ayer*. Chicago: Open Court.

—— (ed.) (1997a). *The Philosophy of Hans-Georg Gadamer*. Chicago: Open Court.

—— (ed.) (1997b). *The Philosophy of Roderick M. Chisholm*. Chicago: Open Court.

—— (ed.) (1998). *The Philosophy of P. F. Strawson*. Chicago: Open Court.

—— (ed.) (1999). *The Philosophy of Donald Davidson*. Chicago: Open Court.

Hahn, Martin and Bjørn Ramberg (eds.) (2003). *Reflections and Replies: Essays on the Philosophy of Tyler Burge*. Cambridge, MA: MIT Press.

Haldane, John (1995). 'Analytical Thomism', in Honderich 1995.

—— (ed.) (1997). *Analytical Thomism*, special issue of *The Monist* 80(4).

—— (2006). 'Analytical Thomism: How We Got Here, Why It Is Worth Remaining and Where We May Go To Next', in Paterson and Pugh 2006, pp. 303–10.

Hale, Bob and Crispin Wright (1997). *A Companion to the Philosophy of Language*. Oxford: Blackwell.

—— (2001). *The Reason's Proper Study: Essays towards a Neo-Fregean Philosophy of Mathematics*. Oxford: Clarendon Press.

Hales, Stephen D. (ed.) (2002). *Analytic Philosophy: Classic Readings*. Belmont, CA: Wadsworth.

Haller, Rudolf (ed.) (1982). *Schlick und Neurath—ein Symposion, Grazer Philosophische Studien*, special issue, Vols. 16–17.

—— (1988). *Questions on Wittgenstein*. London: Routledge.

—— (1991). 'On the Historiography of Austrian Philosophy', in Uebel 1991, pp. 41–50.

—— (1993). *Neopositivismus: Eine historische Einführung in die Philosophie des Wiener Kreises*. Darmstadt: Wissenschaftliche Buchgesellschaft.

Hallett, Garth L. (2008). *Linguistic Philosophy: The Central Story*. Albany, NY: State University of New York Press.

Hallett, Michael (1984). *Cantorian Set Theory and Limitation of Size*. Oxford: Clarendon Press.

—— (2010). 'Frege and Hilbert', in Potter and Ricketts 2010, pp. 413–64.

Hampshire, Stuart (1959a). *Thought and Action: A New Approach to Moral Philosophy and to the Problem of Freedom of the Will*. London: Chatto & Windus.

—— (1959b). 'J. L. Austin', *Proceedings of the Aristotelian Society* 60: 2–14; repr. in Rorty 1967, pp. 239–47.

Hanfling, Oswald (1981a). *Logical Positivism*. Oxford: Blackwell.

—— (ed.) (1981b). *Essential Readings in Logical Positivism*. Oxford: Blackwell.

—— (1989). *Wittgenstein's Later Philosophy*. London: Macmillan.

—— (2000). *Philosophy and Ordinary Language*. London: Routledge.

Hanna, Robert (2001). *Kant and the Foundations of Analytic Philosophy*. Oxford: Oxford University Press.

—— (2008). 'Kant in the Twentieth Century', in Moran 2008a, pp. 149–203.

Hansson, Sven Ove (2009). 'A History of *Theoria*', *Theoria* 75: 2–27.

Hardcastle, Gary L. and Alan W. Richardson (eds.) (2003). *Logical Empiricism in North America*. Minneapolis: University of Minnesota Press.

Hare, Peter H. (ed.) (1988). *Doing Philosophy Historically*. Buffalo, NY: Prometheus Books.

*Hare, R. M. (1952). *The Language of Morals*. Oxford: Oxford University Press.

—— (1963). *Freedom and Reason*. Oxford: Oxford University Press.

—— (1971). *Essays on Philosophical Method*. London: Macmillan.

—— (1981). *Moral Thinking: Its Levels, Method, and Point*. Oxford: Oxford University Press.

*Hart, H. L. A. (1955). 'Are There Any Natural Rights?', *Philosophical Review* 64: 175–91.

—— (1961). *The Concept of Law*. Oxford: Clarendon Press; 2nd edn. 1994.

—— (1982). *Essays on Bentham*. Oxford: Clarendon Press.

Hart, H. L. A. and A. M. Honoré (1959). *Causation in the Law*. Oxford: Clarendon Press.

Hart, W. D. (1990). 'Clarity', in Bell and Cooper 1990, pp. 197–222.

—— (2010). *The Evolution of Logic*. Cambridge: Cambridge University Press.

Hatfield, Gary (2002). 'Psychology, Philosophy, and Cognitive Science: Reflections on the History and Philosophy of Experimental Psychology', *Mind and Language* 17: 207–32.

—— (2005). 'The History of Philosophy as Philosophy', in Sorell and Rogers 2005, pp. 83–128.

—— (2006). 'Psychology and Philosophy', in Grayling, Pyle, and Goulder 2006, III, pp. 2613–21.

—— (2013). 'Psychology, Epistemology, and the Problem of the External World: Russell and Before', in Reck 2013.

Hawthorne, John (2005). 'Lewis, David Kellogg (1941–2001)', in Shook 2005, III, pp. 1461–6.

Heck, Richard G. (2011). *Frege's Theorem*. Oxford: Oxford University Press.

—— (2012). *Reading Frege's Grundgesetze*. Oxford: Oxford University Press.

*Hegel, Georg W. F. (1807). *Phänomenologie des Geistes*; tr. as *Phenomenology of Spirit* by A. V. Miller. Oxford: Oxford University Press, 1977.

Hegselmann, Rainer and Geo Siegwart (1991). 'Zur Geschichte der "Erkenntnis"', *Erkenntnis* 35: 461–71.

*Heidegger, Martin (1927). *Sein und Zeit, Jahrbuch für Philosophie und phänomenologische Forschung*, VIII; tr. John Macquarrie and Edward Robinson. Oxford: Blackwell, 1962.

Heil, John (2001). 'Hilary Putnam (1926–)', in Martinich and Sosa 2001a, pp. 393–412.

Heinrich, R. and H. Vetter (eds.) (1991). *Bilder der Philosophie*. Vienna: Oldenbourg.

Heis, Jeremy (2013). 'Frege, Lotze, and Boole', in Reck 2013.

*Helmholtz, Hermann von (1847). *Über die Erhaltung der Kraft*. Berlin: Reimer.

—— (1870). 'Über den Ursprung und Bedeutung der geometrischen Axiome', in *Vorträge und Reden*, vol. 2. Leipzig: Johann Ambrosius Barth.

—— (1921). *Schriften zur Erkenntnistheorie*, ed. P. Hertz and M. Schlick. Berlin: Springer; tr. Malcolm Lowe as *Epistemological Writings. The Paul Hertz/Moritz Schlick Centenary Edition of 1921*, ed. Robert S. Cohen and Yehuda Elkana. Dordrecht: D. Reidel, 1977.

*Hempel, Carl G. (1935). 'The Logical Analysis of Psychology', *Revue de Synthèse*; tr. from the French original by W. Sellars in Feigl and Sellars 1949, pp. 373–84.

—— (1942). 'The Function of General Laws in History', *Journal of Philosophy* 39: 35–48.

—— (1952). *Fundamentals of Concept Formation in Empirical Science*. Chicago: University of Chicago Press.

—— (1965). *Aspects of Scientific Explanation*. New York: Free Press.

—— (1975). 'The Old and the New "Erkenntnis"', *Erkenntnis* 9: 1–4.

—— (1979). 'Scientific Rationality: Analytic vs. Pragmatic Perspectives', in Geraets 1979, pp. 46–58.

Hempel, Carl and Paul Oppenheim (1948). 'Studies in the Logic of Explanation', *Philosophy of Science* 15: 135–75; repr. in Hempel 1965, ch. 10.

*Herbart, J. F. (1808). *Hauptpuncte der Logik*, in *Sämtliche Werke*, II, ed. K. Kehrbach and O. Flügel. Langensalza: Beyer, 1887; repr. Aalen: Scientia, 1989.

—— (1813). *Lehrbuch zur Einleitung in die Philosophie*; repr. 1912, ed. K. Häntsch. Leipzig: Meiner.

Herman, Barbara (1985). 'The Practice of Moral Judgment', *Journal of Philosophy* 82: 414–36.

*Hertz, Heinrich (1894). *Die Prinzipien der Mechanik in neuem Zusammenhange dargestellt*, Leipzig; tr. as *The Principles of Mechanics Presented in a New Form*. London: Macmillan, 1899.

*Hilbert, David (1899). *Grundlagen der Geometrie*, in *Festschrift zur Feier der Enthullung des Gauss-Weber Denkmals in Göttingen*. Leipzig: Teubner; tr. E. J. Townsend. Chicago: Open Court, 1902.

—— (1900a). 'On the Concept of Number', tr. in Ewald 1996, II, pp. 1089–95.

—— (1900b). 'Mathematische Probleme', *Nachrichten von der Königlichen Gesellschaft der Wissenschaften zu Göttingen, Math.-Phys. Klasse*, pp. 253–97; partly tr. in Ewald 1996, II, pp. 1096–1105.

—— (1918). 'Axiomatic Thought', tr. in Ewald 1996, II, pp. 1105–15.

—— (1922). 'The New Grounding of Mathematics. First Report', tr. in Ewald 1996, II, pp. 1115–34; also in Mancosu 1998, pp. 198–214.

Hill, Christopher (ed.) (1988). *Analytic Philosophy, Philosophical Topics*, 25, no. 2. Fayetteville: University of Arkansas Press.

Hill, Claire Ortiz (1991). *Word and Object in Husserl, Frege and Russell: The Roots of Twentieth-Century Philosophy*. Athens, OH: Ohio University Press.

—— (1997). *Rethinking Identity and Metaphysics: On the Foundations of Analytic Philosophy*. New Haven, CT: Yale University Press.

Hill, Claire Ortiz and Guillermo E. Rosado Haddock (2003). *Husserl or Frege? Meaning, Objectivity, and Mathematics*. La Salle, IL: Open Court.

Hill, Thomas E. (1991). *Autonomy and Self-Respect*. Cambridge: Cambridge University Press.

Himanka, Juha (2000). 'Does The Earth Move? A Search for a Dialogue Between Two Traditions of Contemporary Philosophy', *The Philosophical Forum* 31: 57–83.

Hinich, Melvin J. and Michael C. Munger (1997). *Analytical Politics*. Cambridge: Cambridge University Press.

*Hintikka, Jaakko (1962). *Knowledge and Belief*. Ithaca, NY: Cornell University Press.

—— (ed.) (1975). *Rudolf Carnap, Logical Empiricist: Materials and Perspectives*. Dordrecht: D. Reidel.

—— (ed.) (1976). *Essays on Wittgenstein in Honour of G. H. von Wright, Acta Philosophica Fennica*, 28. Amsterdam: North-Holland.

—— (1996). *Ludwig Wittgenstein: Half-Truths and One-and-a-Half Truths*. Dordrecht: Kluwer.

—— (1998). 'Who is About to Kill Analytic Philosophy?', in Biletzki and Matar 1998, pp. 253–69.

—— (2006). 'Intellectual Autobiography', in Auxier and Hahn 2006, pp. 1–84.

Hintikka, Jaakko and Klaus Puhl (eds.) (1995). *The British Tradition in 20th Century Philosophy: Proceedings of the 17th International Wittgenstein Symposium*. Vienna: Hölder-Pichler-Tempsky.

Hinton, J. M. (1973). *Experience: An Inquiry into Some Ambiguities*. Oxford: Clarendon Press.

Hobhouse, L. T. (1896). *Theory of Knowledge*. London: Methuen.

Hochberg, Herbert (1978). *Thought, Fact, and Reference: The Origins and Ontology of Logical Atomism*. Minneapolis: University of Minnesota Press.

—— (2001). *Russell, Moore, and Wittgenstein: The Revival of Realism*. Egelsbach, Germany: Ontos Verlag.

—— (2003). *Introducing Analytic Philosophy: Its Sense and Its Nonsense, 1879–2002*. Frankfurt am Main: Ontos Verlag.

Hoche, Hans-Ulrich and Werner Strube (1985). *Analytische Philosophie*. Freiburg/München: Karl Alber.

Hodges, Andrew (1983). *Alan Turing: The Enigma*. New York: Simon & Schuster.

—— (2007). 'Alan Turing', *The Stanford Encyclopedia of Philosophy*, online at: <http://plato.stanford.edu/entries/turing> [accessed 28 May 2012].

Hoffmann, Dieter (2007). 'The Society for Empirical/Scientific Philosophy', in Richardson and Uebel 2007, pp. 41–57.

Hogan, Melinda (2006). 'Grice, Herbert Paul (1913–88)', in Grayling, Pyle, and Goulder 2006, II, pp. 1293–6.

Holt, Edwin B., Walter T. Marvin, William Pepperell Montague, Ralph Barton Perry, Walter B. Pitkin, and Edward Gleason Spaulding (1910). 'The Program and First Platform of Six Realists', *Journal of Philosophy, Psychology and Scientific Methods* 7: 393–401; repr. in Holt 1912, pp. 471–80.

—— et al. (1912). *New Realism: Cooperative Studies in Philosophy*. New York: Macmillan.

Holtzman, Steven and Christopher Leich (eds.) (1981). *Wittgenstein: To Follow a Rule*. London: Routledge.

Holzberger, William G. (2005). 'Santayana, George (1863–1952)', in Shook 2005, IV, pp. 2119–26.

Honderich, Ted (ed.) (1995). *The Oxford Companion to Philosophy*. Oxford: Oxford University Press.

Hook, Sidney (1930). 'A Personal Impression of Contemporary German Philosophy', *Journal of Philosophy* 27: 141–60.

—— (1939). *John Dewey: An Intellectual Portrait*; repr. New York: Prometheus, 1995.

—— (ed.) (1950). *John Dewey: Philosopher of Science and Freedom*. New York: Dial Press.

—— (ed.) (1960). *Dimensions of Mind*. New York: New York University Press.

Hookway, Christopher (1985). *Peirce*. London: Routledge.

—— (1988). *Quine*. Cambridge: Polity Press.

—— (2008a). 'Pragmatism', *The Stanford Encyclopedia of Philosophy*, online at: <http://plato.stanford.edu/entries/pragmatism> [accessed 28 May 2012].

—— (2008b). 'Pragmatism and the Given: C. I. Lewis, Quine, and Peirce', in Misak 2008, pp. 269–89.

Horgan, Terry, John Tienson, and Matjaz Potrc (eds.) (2002). *Origins: The Common Sources of the Analytic and Phenomenological Traditions, Southern Journal of Philosophy*, Supplementary Vol. 40.

Horgan, Terry and Mark Timmons (eds.) (2006). *Metaethics after Moore*. Oxford: Clarendon Press.

Hospers, John (1946). *Meaning and Truth in the Arts*. Chapel Hill: University of North Carolina Press.

—— (1953). *An Introduction to Philosophical Analysis*. Englewood Cliffs, NJ: Prentice Hall; repr. London: Routledge & Kegan Paul, 1956; 2nd edn. 1967, 3rd edn. 1990, 4th edn. 1997.

Howard, Roy J. (1982). *Three Faces of Hermeneutics*. Berkeley: University of California Press.

Hoy, Jocelyn (2005). 'Foot, Philippa Ruth (1920–[2010])', in Shook 2005, II, pp. 836–41.

Huemer, Wolfgang (2005). *The Constitution of Consciousness: A Study in Analytic Phenomenology*. London and New York: Routledge.

—— (2010). 'Franz Brentano', *The Stanford Encyclopedia of Philosophy*, online at: <http://plato.stanford.edu/entries/brentano> [accessed 28 May 2012].

*Hung, Tscha (1945). *The Philosophy of Vienna Circle*. Shanghai: Commercial Press; repr. 1989.

—— (1949). 'Moritz Schlick and Modern Empiricism', *Philosophy and Phenomenological Research* 9: 690–708.

—— (1985). 'Remarks on Affirmations [*Konstatierungen*]', *Synthese* 64: 297–306.

—— (1992). 'Ayer and the Vienna Circle', in Hahn 1992, pp. 279–300.

Hunter, Bruce (2006a). 'Ayer, Alfred Jules (1910–89)', in Grayling, Pyle, and Goulder 2006, I, pp. 174–8.

—— (2006b). 'Price, Henry Habberley (1899–1984)', in Grayling, Pyle, and Goulder 2006, III, pp. 2571–4.

—— (2007). 'Clarence Irving Lewis', *The Stanford Encyclopedia of Philosophy*, online at: <http://plato.stanford.edu/entries/lewis-ci> [accessed 28 May 2012].

Hunter, Graeme (1993). 'Russell Making History: The Leibniz Book', in Irvine and Wedeking 1993, pp. 397–414.

Hurka, Thomas (2004). 'Normative Ethics: Back to the Future', in Leiter 2004a, pp. 246–64.

—— (ed.) (2011). *Underivative Duty: British Moral Philosophers from Sidgwick to Ewing*. Oxford: Oxford University Press.

Hursthouse, Rosalind (1999). *On Virtue Ethics*. Oxford: Oxford University Press.

*Husserl, Edmund (1891). *Philosophie der Arithmetik*. Halle: Pfeffer.

—— (1900/1). *Logische Untersuchungen*. Halle: Max Niemeyer; 2nd edn. 1913; tr. N. Findlay as *Logical Investigations*. London: Routledge, 1970; repr. 2001 with a new introduction by Dermot Moran.

—— (1911). *Philosophy as a Rigorous Science*, tr. in Husserl 1965.

—— (1913). *Ideas Pertaining to a Pure Phenomenology and to a Phenomenological Philosophy*, tr. W. R. Boyce Gibson. London: George Allen & Unwin, 1931; also tr. F. Kersten. The Hague: Nijhoff, 1982.

—— (1929). *Formal and Transcendental Logic*, tr. Dorion Cairns. The Hague: Martinus Nijhoff, 1969.

—— (1939a). 'The Origin of Geometry', tr. J. P. Leavey in Derrida 1962 [1989], pp. 157–80.

—— (1939b). *Experience and Judgment*, ed. L. Landgrebe, tr. J. S. Churchill and K. Ameriks. London: Routledge, 1973.

—— (1965). *Phenomenology and the Crisis of Philosophy*, tr. Quentin Lauer. New York: Harper & Row.

Hyder, David (2002). *The Mechanics of Meaning: Propositional Content and the Logical Space of Wittgenstein's Tractatus*. Berlin and New York: Walter de Gruyter.

Hyder, David, and Hans-Jörg Rheinberger (eds.) (2009). *Science and the Life-World: Essays on Husserl's Crisis of the European Sciences*. Stanford: Stanford University Press.

Hylton, Peter (1990). *Russell, Idealism, and the Emergence of Analytic Philosophy*. Oxford: Clarendon Press.

—— (1993). 'Functions and Propositional Functions in *Principia Mathematica*', in Irvine and Wedeking 1993, pp. 342–60; repr. in Hylton 2005a, pp. 122–37.

—— (1998). 'Analysis in Analytic Philosophy', in Biletzki and Matar 1998, pp. 37–55.

—— (2001a). '"The Defensible Province of Philosophy": Quine's 1934 Lectures on Carnap', in Floyd and Shieh 2001, pp. 257–75.

—— (2001b). 'W. V. Quine (1908–2000)', in Martinich and Sosa 2001a, pp. 181–204.

—— (2003). 'The Theory of Descriptions', in Griffin 2003, pp. 202–40; repr. in Hylton 2005a, pp. 185–215.

—— (2005a). *Propositions, Functions, Analysis: Selected Essays on Russell's Philosophy*. Oxford: Oxford University Press.

—— (2005b). 'Frege and Russell', in Hylton 2005a, pp. 153–84; also in Potter and Ricketts 2010, pp. 509–49.

—— (2007a). *Quine*. London: Routledge.

—— (2007b). '"On Denoting" and the Idea of a Logically Perfect Language', in Beaney 2007, pp. 91–106.

—— (2010). 'Willard van Orman Quine', *The Stanford Encyclopedia of Philosophy*, online at: <http://plato.stanford.edu/entries/quine> [accessed 28 May 2012].

Ignatieff, Michael (1998). *Isaiah Berlin: A Life*. London: Chatto & Windus.

Inglis, Fred (2009). *History Man: The Life of R. G. Collingwood*. Princeton, NJ: Princeton University Press.

Inwood, Michael (1999). 'Does the Nothing Noth?', in O'Hear 1999, pp. 271–90.

Irvine, A. D. (ed.) (1999). *Bertrand Russell: Critical Assessments*, 4 vols. London: Routledge.

Irvine, A. D. and G. A. Wedeking (eds.) (1993). *Russell and Analytic Philosophy*. Toronto: University of Toronto Press.

Irwin, Terence (2007–9). *The Development of Ethics: A Historical and Critical Study*, 3 vols., vol. 1 2007, vol. 2 2008, vol. 3 2009. Oxford: Oxford University Press.

Isaac, Joel (2005). 'W. V. Quine and the Origins of Analytic Philosophy in the United States', *Modern Intellectual History* 2: 205–34.

Ishiguro, Hidé (1969). 'Use and Reference of Names', in Winch 1969, pp. 20–50.

Jackson, Frank (1982). 'Epiphenomenal Qualia', *Philosophical Quarterly* 32: 127–36.

—— (1991). 'Decision-Theoretic Consequentialism and the Nearest and Dearest Objection', *Ethics* 101: 461–82.

—— (1998). *From Metaphysics to Ethics: A Defence of Conceptual Analysis*. Oxford: Oxford University Press.

—— (2001). 'David M. Armstrong (1926–)', in Martinich and Sosa 2001a, pp. 413–18.

Jackson, Frank and Michael Smith (eds.) (2005). *The Oxford Handbook of Contemporary Philosophy*. Oxford: Oxford University Press.

Jacquette, Dale (ed.) (2002). *A Companion to Philosophical Logic*. Oxford: Blackwell.

—— (ed.) (2004). *The Cambridge Companion to Brentano*. Cambridge: Cambridge University Press.

*James, William (1890). *The Principles of Psychology*, 2 vols. New York: Henry Holt.

—— (1902). *The Varieties of Religious Experience*. New York: Longmans, Green, and Co.

—— (1907). *Pragmatism: A New Name for Some Old Ways of Thinking*. New York: Longmans, Green, and Co.

—— (1995). *Selected Writings*, ed. G. H. Bird. London: J. M. Dent.

Jarvie, Ian, Karl Milford, and David Miller (eds.) (2006). *Karl Popper: A Centenary Assessment*, 3 vols. Aldershot: Ashgate.

*Joachim, Harold H. (1906). *The Nature of Truth*. Oxford: Oxford University Press; 2nd edn. 1939.

Johnson, W. E. (1921–4). *Logic*, 3 vols., 1921, 1922, 1924. Cambridge: Cambridge University Press.

Joseph, H. W. B. (1906). *An Introduction to Logic*. Oxford: Clarendon Press; 2nd edn. 1916.

—— (1926). 'Universals and the "Method of Analysis"', *Proceedings of the Aristotelian Society*, Supplementary Vol. 6: 1–16.

—— (1932–3). 'A Defence of Free-Thinking in Logistics', Part I, *Mind* 41: 424–40; Part II, *Mind* 42: 417–42.

Jourdain, Philip E. B. (1912). 'The Development of the Theories of Mathematical Logic and the Principles of Mathematics', *The Quarterly Journal of Pure and Applied Mathematics*, 43; chapter on 'Gottlob Frege' repr. in Frege 1980b, pp. 179–206.

Juhl, Cory and Eric Loomis (2010). *Analyticity*. London: Routledge.

Kahane, Guy, Edward Kanterian, and Oskari Kuusela (eds.) (2007). *Wittgenstein and His Interpreters*. Oxford: Blackwell.

Kaila, Eino (1930). *Der logische Neupositivismus: Eine kritische Studie*. Turku: Annales Universitatis Aboensis; tr. as 'Logical Positivism' in Kaila 1979, pp. 1–58.

——(1979). *Logic and Experience*, ed. R. S. Cohen. Dordrecht: D. Reidel.

Kamm, Frances (1998). *Morality, Mortality, Volume I: Death and Whom to Save from It*. Oxford: Oxford University Press.

Kampis, George, Ladislav Kvasz, and Michael Stöltzner (eds.) (2002). *Appraising Lakatos: Mathematics, Methodology and the Man*. Dordrecht: Kluwer.

*Kant, Immanuel (1781/1787). *Critique of Pure Reason*, tr. and ed. P. Guyer and A. Wood. Cambridge: Cambridge University Press, 1997.

——(1784). 'An Answer to the Question: "What is Enlightenment?"', *Berlinische Monatsschrift* 4: 481–94; tr. in Kant 1991, pp. 54–60.

——(1991). *Political Writings*, ed. Hans Reiss, tr. H. B. Nisbet, 2nd edn. Cambridge: Cambridge University Press; 1st edn. 1970.

Kanterian, Edward (2005). *Analytische Philosophie*. Frankfurt: Campus.

Kaplan, David (1968). 'Quantifying In', *Synthese* 19: 178–214.

——(1977). 'Demonstratives', in Almog, Perry, and Wettstein 1989, pp. 481–563; orig. written 1977.

——(1989). 'Afterthoughts', in Almog, Perry, and Wettstein 1989, pp. 565–614.

Keene, Carol A. (2006a). 'Histories of British Philosophy', in Grayling, Pyle, and Goulder 2006, II, pp. 1480–9.

——(2006b). 'Stout, George Frederick (1860–1944)', in Grayling, Pyle, and Goulder 2006, IV, pp. 3066–9.

Kennedy, Hubert C. (1980). *Peano: Life and Works of Giuseppe Peano*. Dordrecht: D. Reidel.

Kennedy, Juliette (2011). 'Kurt Gödel', *The Stanford Encyclopedia of Philosophy*, online at: <http://plato.stanford.edu/entries/goedel> [accessed 28 May 2012].

Kenny, Anthony (1963). *Action, Emotion and Will*. London: Routledge & Kegan Paul; repr. with new preface, 2003.

——(1973). *Wittgenstein*. London: Penguin.

——(ed.) (1986). *Rationalism, Empiricism, and Idealism*. Oxford: Oxford University Press.

——(2007). *Philosophy in the Modern World, A New History of Western Philosophy*, vol. 4. Oxford: Clarendon Press.

Kerry, Benno (1885–91). 'Über Anschauungen und ihre psychische Verarbeitung', Parts I–VIII, *Vierteljahrezeitschrift für wissenschaftliche Philosophie*, Part I, 9 (1885). pp. 433–93; Part II, 10 (1886). pp. 419–67; Part III, 11 (1887). pp. 53–116; Part IV, 11 (1887). pp. 249–307; Part V, 13 (1889). pp. 71–124; Part VI, 13 (1889). pp. 392–414; Part VII, 14 (1890). pp. 317–53; Part VIII, 15 (1891). pp. 126–67.

Keynes, J. N. (1884). *Studies and Exercises in Formal Logic*; 2nd edn. 1887; 3rd edn. 1894; 4th edn. 1906.

Kienzler, Wolfgang (1997). *Wittgensteins Wende zu seiner Spätphilosophie 1930–1932*. Frankfurt am Main: Suhrkamp.

——(2009). *Begriff und Gegenstand: Eine historische und systematische Studie zur Entwicklung von Gottlob Freges Denken*. Frankfurt: Klostermann.

——(2011). 'Wittgenstein and Frege', in Kuusela and McGinn 2011, pp. 79–104.

Kim, Alan (2006). 'Wilhelm Maximilian Wundt', *The Stanford Encyclopedia of Philosophy*, online at: <http://plato.stanford.edu/entries/wilhelm-wundt> [accessed 28 May 2012].

*Kim, Jaegwon (1973). 'Causation, Nomic Subsumption and the Concept of Event', *Journal of Philosophy* 70: 217–36; repr. in Kim 1993, pp. 3–21.

—— (1984). 'Concepts of Supervenience', *Philosophy and Phenomenological Research* 45: 153–76; repr. in Kim 1993, pp. 53–78.

—— (1989). 'The Myth of Nonreductive Materialism', *Proceedings and Addresses of the American Philosophical Association* 63: 31–47; repr. in Kim 1993, pp. 265–84.

—— (1993). *Supervenience and Mind: Selected Philosophical Essays*. Cambridge: Cambridge University Press.

—— (2004). 'The Mind–Body Problem at Century's Turn', in Leiter 2004a, pp. 129–52.

Kirchin, Simon (2006). 'Foot, Philippa Ruth (1920–)', in Grayling, Pyle, and Goulder 2006, II, pp. 1120–4.

Kirk, Robert (1974). 'Sentience and Behaviour', *Mind* 83: 43–60.

Kitcher, Philip (1984). *The Nature of Mathematical Knowledge*. Oxford: Oxford University Press.

—— (2001). 'Carl G. Hempel', in Martinich and Sosa 2001a, pp. 148–59.

Klagge, James C. (ed.) (2001). *Wittgenstein: Biography and Philosophy*. Cambridge: Cambridge University Press.

—— (2010). *Wittgenstein in Exile*. Cambridge, MA: MIT Press.

Kleinknecht, Reinhard (1993). 'Nachruf auf Wolfgang Stegmüller', *Journal for General Philosophy of Science* 24: 1–16.

Klement, Kevin C. (2009). 'Russell's Logical Atomism', *The Stanford Encyclopedia of Philosophy*, online at: <http://plato.stanford.edu/entries/logical-atomism> [accessed 28 May 2012].

Klemke, E. D. (ed.) (1968). *Essays on Frege*. Chicago: University of Illinois Press.

—— (1969a). *The Epistemology of G. E. Moore*. Evanston, IL: Northwestern University Press.

—— (ed.) (1969b). *Studies in the Philosophy of G. E. Moore*. Chicago: Quadrangle.

—— (ed.) (1970). *Essays on Bertrand Russell*. Urbana: University of Illinois Press.

—— (ed.) (1983). *Contemporary Analytic and Linguistic Philosophies*. New York: Prometheus Books.

*Kneale, William (1956). 'Gottlob Frege and Mathematical Logic', in Ayer *et al.* 1956, pp. 26–40.

Kneale, William and Martha Kneale (1962). *The Development of Logic*. Oxford: Clarendon Press.

Köhler, Wolfgang (1929). *Gestalt Psychology*. New York: Liveright.

Köhnke, Klaus Christian (1991). *The Rise of Neo-Kantianism: German Academic Philosophy between Idealism and Positivism*, tr. R. J. Hollingdale. Cambridge: Cambridge University Press.

Kölbel, Max and Bernhard Weiss (eds.) (2004). *Wittgenstein's Lasting Significance*. London: Routledge.

Königsberger, Leo (1902–3). *Hermann von Helmholtz*, 3 vols. Braunschweig: Georg Olms; abr. and tr. Frances A. Welby. Oxford: Clarendon Press, 1906.

Korhonen, Anssi (2013). *Logic as Universal Science: Russell's Early Logicism and its Philosophical Context*. Basingstoke: Palgrave Macmillan.

Korsgaard, Christine (1996a). *Creating the Kingdom of Ends*. Cambridge: Cambridge University Press.

—— (1996b). *The Sources of Normativity*. Cambridge: Cambridge University Press.

*Kotarbiński, Tadeusz (1929). *Elementy teorii poznania, logiki formalnej i metodologii nauk*. Lvov: Ossolineum; 2nd edn. 1961; tr. as Kotarbiński 1966.

——(1955). *Traktat o dobrej roboci*. Warsaw: PWN; tr. as Kotarbiński 1965.

——(1965). *Praxiology: An Introduction to the Science of Efficient Action*. Oxford: Pergamon Press.

——(1966). *Gnosiology: The Scientific Approach to the Theory of Knowledge*. Oxford: Pergamon Press.

Kraft, Victor (1953). *The Vienna Circle: The Origin of Neo-Positivism*. New York: Philosophical Library.

Kreiser, Lothar (2001). *Gottlob Frege: Leben—Werk—Zeit*. Hamburg: Felix Meiner.

Kremer, Michael (1994). 'The Argument of "On Denoting"', *Philosophical Review* 103: 249–97.

——(2001). 'The Purpose of Tractarian Nonsense', *Noûs* 35: 39–73.

——(2005). 'Review of Scott Soames, *Philosophical Analysis in the Twentieth Century*', *Notre Dame Philosophical Reviews*, online at: <http://ndpr.nd.edu/review.cfm?id=4061> [accessed 28 May 2012].

——(2007). 'The Cardinal Problem of Philosophy', in Crary 2007, pp. 143–76.

——(2013). 'What is the Good of Philosophical History?', in Reck 2013.

*Kripke, Saul A. (1959). 'A Completeness Theorem in Modal Logic', *Journal of Symbolic Logic* 24: 1–14.

——(1971). 'Identity and Necessity', in Munitz 1971, pp. 135–64.

——(1972). 'Naming and Necessity', in Davidson and Harman 1972, pp. 253–355, 763–9; pub. in book form as Kripke 1980.

——(1979). 'A Puzzle about Belief', in Margalit 1979, pp. 239–83; repr. in Salmon and Soames 1988, pp. 102–48.

——(1980). *Naming and Necessity*. Oxford: Blackwell.

——(1982). *Wittgenstein on Rules and Private Language*. Oxford: Blackwell; earlier version in Block 1981, pp. 238–312.

——(2011). *Philosophical Troubles, Collected Papers*, vol. 1. Oxford: Oxford University Press.

Kuehn, Manfred (2001). *Kant: A Biography*. Cambridge: Cambridge University Press.

*Kuhn, Thomas S. (1962). *The Structure of Scientific Revolutions*. Chicago: University of Chicago Press, 2nd edn., enlarged, 1970.

——(1977). *The Essential Tension: Selected Studies in Scientific Tradition and Change*. Chicago: University of Chicago Press.

Kuklick, Bruce (2001). *A History of Philosophy in America 1720-2000*. Oxford: Clarendon Press.

——(2006). 'United States, Relationship with', in Grayling, Pyle, and Goulder 2006, IV, pp. 3233–9.

Künne, Wolfgang (2010). *Die Philosophische Logik Gottlob Freges*. Frankfurt: Klostermann.

Künne, Wolfgang, Mark Siebel, and Mark Textor (eds.) (1997). *Bolzano and Analytic Philosophy*. Amsterdam: Rodopi.

Kusch, Martin (1995). *Psychologism*. London: Routledge.

——(2011). 'Psychologism', *The Stanford Encyclopedia of Philosophy*, online at: <http://plato.stanford.edu/entries/psychologism> [accessed 28 May 2012].

Kuusela, Oskari (2008). *The Struggle against Dogmatism: Wittgenstein and the Concept of Philosophy*. Cambridge, MA: Harvard University Press.

Kuusela, Oskari and Marie McGinn (eds.) (2011). *The Oxford Handbook of Wittgenstein*. Oxford: Oxford University Press.

Lacey, Nicola (2004). *A Life of H. L. A. Hart: The Nightmare and the Noble Dream*. Oxford: Oxford University Press.

Lafont, Cristina (1999). *The Linguistic Turn in Hermeneutic Philosophy*. Cambridge, MA: MIT Press.

*Lakatos, Imre (1970). 'Falsification and the Methodology of Scientific Research Programmes', in Lakatos and Musgrave 1970, pp. 91–196; repr. in Lakatos 1978a, pp. 8–101.

—— (1971). 'History of Science and its Rational Reconstructions', in Lakatos 1978a, pp. 102–38; orig. pub. 1971.

——(1976). *Proofs and Refutations: The Logic of Mathematical Discovery*. Cambridge: Cambridge University Press.

—— (1978a). *The Methodology of Scientific Research Programmes, Philosophical Papers Volume 1*, ed. John Worrall and Gregory Currie. Cambridge: Cambridge University Press.

—— (1978b). *Mathematics, Science and Epistemology, Philosophical Papers Volume 2*, ed. John Worrall and Gregory Currie. Cambridge: Cambridge University Press.

Lakatos, Imre and Alan Musgrave (eds.) (1970). *Criticism and the Growth of Knowledge*. Cambridge: Cambridge University Press.

Lamarque, Peter and Stein Haugom Olsen (eds.) (2003). *Aesthetics and the Philosophy of Art: The Analytic Tradition: An Anthology*. Oxford: Blackwell.

Lance, Mark (2008). 'Placing in a Space of Norms: Neo-Sellarsian Philosophy in the Twenty-first Century', in Misak 2008, pp. 403–29.

Landini, Gregory (1998). *Russell's Hidden Substitutional Theory*. Oxford: Oxford University Press.

—— (2007). *Wittgenstein's Apprenticeship with Russell*. Cambridge: Cambridge University Press.

—— (2011). *Russell*. London: Routledge.

—— (2012). *Frege's Notations: What They Are and How They Mean*. Basingstoke: Palgrave Macmillan.

Langer, Susanne (1942). *Philosophy in a New Key: A Study in the Symbolism of Reason, Rite and Art*. Cambridge, MA: Harvard University Press.

Lapointe, Sandra (2011). *Bolzano's Theoretical Philosophy*. Basingstoke: Palgrave Macmillan.

Lapointe, Sandra, Mathieu Marion, Wioletta Miskiewicz, and Jan Woleński (eds.) (2009). *The Golden Age of Polish Philosophy: Kazimierz Twardowski's Philosophical Legacy*. New York: Springer.

Laslett, Peter (ed.) (1956). *Philosophy, Politics and Society*. Oxford: Blackwell.

Laslett, Peter and James Fishkin (eds.) (1979). *Philosophy, Politics and Society, Fifth Series*. Oxford: Blackwell.

—— —— (eds.), (1992). *Philosophy, Politics and Society, Sixth Series: Justice Between Age Groups and Generations*. Oxford: Blackwell.

—— —— (eds.) (2003). *Philosophy, Politics and Society, Seventh Series: Debating Deliberative Democracy*. Oxford: Blackwell.

Laslett, Peter and W. G. Runciman (eds.) (1962). *Philosophy, Politics and Society, Second Series*. Oxford: Blackwell.

—— —— (eds.) (1967). *Philosophy, Politics and Society, Third Series*. Oxford: Blackwell.

Laslett, Peter, W. G. Runciman, and Quentin Skinner (eds.) (1972). *Philosophy, Politics and Society, Fourth Series*. Oxford: Blackwell.

Latta, Robert (1901). 'Critical Notice of B. Russell: *A Critical Exposition of the Philosophy of Leibniz*', *Mind* 10: 525–33.

Laudan, Larry (1981). *Science and Hypothesis*. Dordrecht: D. Reidel.

Lawlor, Leonard (2011). 'Jacques Derrida', *The Stanford Encyclopedia of Philosophy*, online at: <http://plato.stanford.edu/entries/derrida> [accessed 28 May 2012].

Lawlor, Leonard and Valentine Moulard (2011). 'Henri Bergson', *The Stanford Encyclopedia of Philosophy*, online at: <http://plato.stanford.edu/entries/bergson> [accessed 28 May 2012].

Lawrence, Gavin (2001). 'Philippa Foot (1920–)', in Martinich and Sosa 2001a, pp. 350–6.

Lazerowitz, Morris (1968). *Philosophy and Illusion*. London: George Allen & Unwin.

Lee, Barry (ed.) (2011). *Key Thinkers: Philosophy of Language*. London: Continuum.

Lee, O. H. (ed.) (1936). *Philosophical Essays for A. N. Whitehead*. New York: Longmans.

Lehrer, Keith (ed.) (1975). *Analysis and Metaphysics: Essays in Honor of R. M. Chisholm*. Dordrecht: D. Reidel.

Leinfellner, W. and J. C. Schank (eds.) (1982). *Language and Ontology* (Proceedings of the 6th Wittgenstein Symposium, 1981). Vienna: Hölder-Pichler-Tempsky.

Leiter, Brian (ed.) (2004a). *The Future for Philosophy*. Oxford: Oxford University Press.

—— (2004b). 'Introduction' to Leiter 2004a, pp. 1–23.

Leiter, Brian and Michael Rosen (eds.) (2007a). *The Oxford Handbook of Continental Philosophy*. Oxford: Oxford University Press.

—— —— (2007b). 'Introduction' to Leiter and Rosen 2007a, pp. 1–5.

Lepore, Ernest (2001). 'Donald Davidson (1917–2003)', in Martinich and Sosa 2001a, pp. 296–314.

—— (2005a). 'Davidson, Donald Herbert (1917–2003)', in Shook 2005, II, pp. 583–92.

—— (2005b). 'Quine, Willard Van Orman (1908–2000)', in Shook 2005, II, pp. 1983–8.

Lepore, Ernest and Barry C. Smith (eds.) (2006). *The Oxford Handbook of Philosophy of Language*. Oxford: Oxford University Press.

Levine, James (2002). 'Analysis and Decomposition in Frege and Russell', *Philosophical Quarterly* 52: 195–216; repr. in Beaney and Reck 2005, IV, pp. 392–414.

Levine, Joseph (1983). 'Materialism and Qualia: The Explanatory Gap', *Pacific Philosophical Quarterly* 64: 354–61.

Levy, Neil (2003). 'Analytic and Continental Philosophy: Explaining the Differences', *Metaphilosophy* 34: 284–304.

Levy, Paul (1979). *Moore: G. E. Moore and the Cambridge Apostles*. London: Weidenfeld & Nicolson; paperback edn. Oxford: Oxford University Press, 1981.

*Lewis, C. I. (1912). 'Implication and the Algebra of Logic', *Mind* 21: 522–31.

—— (1917). 'The Issues Concerning Material Implication', *Journal of Philosophy* 14: 350–6.

—— (1918). *A Survey of Symbolic Logic*. Berkeley: University of California Press; repr. New York: Dover, 1960, excluding chs. 5–6.

—— (1923). 'A Pragmatic Conception of the *A Priori*', *Journal of Philosophy* 20: 169–77; repr. in Lewis 1970, pp. 231–9.

—— (1929). *Mind and the World-Order: Outline of a Theory of Knowledge*. New York: Charles Scribner's.

—— (1941). 'Logical Positivism and Pragmatism', in Lewis 1970, pp. 92–112.

—— (1944). 'The Modes of Meaning', *Philosophy and Phenomenological Research* 4; repr. in Linsky 1952, pp. 50–63; Lewis 1970, pp. 303–16.

—— (1946). *An Analysis of Knowledge and Valuation*. La Salle, IL: Open Court.

—— (1968). 'Autobiography', in Schilpp 1968, pp. 1–21.

—— (1970). *Collected Papers of Clarence Irving Lewis*, ed. John D. Goheen and John L. Mothershead. Stanford: Stanford University Press.

Lewis, C. I. and C. H. Langford (1932). *Symbolic Logic*. New York: Century Company.

*Lewis, David (1966). 'An Argument for the Identity Theory', *Journal of Philosophy* 63: 17–25; repr. in Lewis 1983, pp. 99–107.

—— (1969). *Convention*. Cambridge, MA: Harvard University Press.

—— (1970). 'How to Define Theoretical Terms', *Journal of Philosophy* 67: 427–46; repr. in Lewis 1983, pp. 78–95.

—— (1973). *Counterfactuals*. Oxford: Blackwell.

—— (1983). *Philosophical Papers*, vol. 1. Oxford: Oxford University Press.

—— (1986a). *Philosophical Papers*, vol. 2. Oxford: Oxford University Press.

—— (1986b). *On the Plurality of Worlds*. Oxford: Blackwell.

Lewis, Harry A. (ed.) (1991). *Peter Geach: Philosophical Encounters*. Dordrecht: Kluwer.

—— (2006). 'Geach, Peter Thomas (1916–)', in Grayling, Pyle, and Goulder 2006, II, pp. 1190–4.

Lewis, Hywel D. (ed.) (1956). *Contemporary British Philosophy: Personal Statements* (Third Series). London: George Allen & Unwin.

—— (ed.) (1963). *Clarity Is Not Enough: Essays in Criticism of Linguistic Philosophy*. London: George Allen & Unwin.

—— (ed.) (1976). *Contemporary British Philosophy: Personal Statements* (Fourth Series). London: George Allen & Unwin.

Linsky, Bernard (1999). *Russell's Metaphysical Logic*. Stanford: CSLI Publications.

—— (2007). 'Logical Analysis and Logical Construction', in Beaney 2007a, pp. 107–22.

—— (2011). *The Evolution of Principia Mathematica: Bertrand Russell's Manuscripts and Notes for the Second Edition*. Cambridge: Cambridge University Press.

Linsky, Bernard and Guido Imaguire (eds.) (2005). *On Denoting: 1905–2005*. München: Philosophia Verlag.

Linsky, Leonard (ed.) (1952). *Semantics and the Philosophy of Language*. Chicago: University of Illinois Press.

—— (1977). *Names and Descriptions*. Chicago: University of Chicago Press.

Livingston, Paul M. (2004). *Philosophical History and the Problem of Consciousness*. Cambridge: Cambridge University Press.

—— (2005). 'Rationalist Elements of Twentieth-Century Analytic Philosophy', in Nelson 2005, pp. 379–98.

Losonsky, Michael (2006). *Linguistic Turns in Modern Philosophy*. Cambridge: Cambridge University Press.

*Lotze, Hermann (1843). *Logik*. Leipzig: Weidmann.

—— (1874). *System der Philosophie, I: Drei Bücher der Logik*. Leipzig: Hirzel; 2nd edn. 1880.

Loux, Michael J. and Dean W. Zimmerman (eds.) (2003a). *The Oxford Handbook of Metaphysics*. Oxford: Oxford University Press.

—— (2003b). 'Introduction' to Loux and Zimmerman 2003a, pp. 1–8.

Lovejoy, Arthur O. (1936). *The Great Chain of Being: A Study of the History of an Idea*. Cambridge, MA: Harvard University Press.

Lowe, E. J. (1998). *The Possibility of Metaphysics*. Oxford: Oxford University Press.

—— (2002). *A Survey of Metaphysics*. Oxford: Oxford University Press.

—— (2008a). 'Metaphysics', in Moran 2008a, pp. 438–68.

—— (2008b). 'New Directions in Metaphysics and Ontology', *Axiomathes* 18: 273–88.

—— (2011). 'The Rationality of Metaphysics', *Synthese* 178: 99–109.

Lowe, Victor (1985–90). *Alfred North Whitehead: The Man and His Work*, 2 vols. Baltimore, MD: Johns Hopkins University Press.

Lucas, George R. (2005). 'Whitehead, Alfred North (1861–1947)', in Shook 2005, IV, pp. 2573–80.

Ludlow, Peter (2001). 'Noam Chomsky (1928–)', in Martinich and Sosa 2001a, pp. 419–27.

*Łukasiewicz, Jan (1920). 'On Three-Valued Logic', tr. in McCall 1967; also tr. in Łukasiewicz 1970; orig. pub. in Polish.

—— (1951). *Aristotle's Syllogistic from the Standpoint of Modern Formal Logic*. Oxford: Clarendon Press; 2nd edn. 1957.

—— (1970). *Selected Works*, ed. L. Borkowski. Amsterdam: North-Holland.

Lund, Matthew D. (2010). *N. R. Hanson: Observation, Discovery, and Scientific Change*. New York: Prometheus.

Lützen, Jesper (2005). *Mechanistic Images in Geometric Form: Heinrich Hertz's Principles of Mechanics*. Oxford: Oxford University Press.

Lyons, William E. (1980). *Gilbert Ryle: An Introduction to his Philosophy*. Brighton: Harvester.

—— (2008). 'Logic and the Foundations of Mathematics', in Misak 2008, pp. 482–514.

Macbeth, Danielle (2005). *Frege's Logic*. Cambridge, MA: Harvard University Press.

McCall, Stuart (ed.) (1967). *Polish Logic 1920–1939*. Oxford: Clarendon Press.

McCarthy, Timothy G. and Sean C. Stidd (eds.) (2001). *Wittgenstein in America*. New York: Oxford University Press.

MacColl, Hugh (1906). *Symbolic Logic and its Applications*. London: Longmans, Green & Co.

Macdonald, Graham and Crispin Wright (eds.) (1986). *Fact, Science and Morality: Essays on A. J. Ayer's Language, Truth and Logic*. Oxford: Blackwell.

Macdonald, Graham (2010). 'Alfred Jules Ayer', *The Stanford Encyclopedia of Philosophy*, online at: <http://plato.stanford.edu/entries/ayer> [accessed 28 May 2012].

Macdonald, Margaret (1947). 'Natural Rights', *Proceedings of the Aristotelian Society* 47: 225–50; repr. in Laslett 1956, pp. 35–55.

—— (ed.) (1954a). *Philosophy and Analysis: A Selection of Articles Published in Analysis between 1933–40 and 1947–53*. Oxford: Blackwell.

—— (1954b). 'Introduction', in Macdonald 1954a, pp. 1–14.

*McDowell, John (1977). 'On the Sense and Reference of a Proper Name', *Mind* 86: 159–85; repr. in McDowell 1998b, pp. 171–98.

—— (1982). 'Criteria, Defeasibility and Knowledge', *Proceedings of the British Academy* 68: 455–79; repr. in McDowell 1998b, pp. 369–94.

—— (1990). 'John Leslie Mackie', *Proceedings of the British Academy* 76: 487–98.

—— (1994). *Mind and World*. Cambridge, MA: Harvard University Press; paperback edn. 1996.

—— (1998a). *Mind, Value, and Reality*. Cambridge, MA: Harvard University Press.

—— (1998b). *Meaning, Knowledge, and Reality*. Cambridge, MA: Harvard University Press.

—— (2009). *Having the World in View: Essays on Kant, Hegel, and Sellars*. Cambridge, MA: Harvard University Press.

Mace, C. A. (ed.) (1957). *British Philosophy in the Mid-Century: A Cambridge Symposium*. London: George Allen & Unwin; 2nd edn. 1966.

MacFarlane, John (2002). 'Frege, Kant, and the Logic in Logicism', *Philosophical Review* 111: 25–65; repr. in Beaney and Reck 2005, I, pp. 71–108.

McGilvray, James (ed.) (2005). *The Cambridge Companion to Chomsky*. Cambridge: Cambridge University Press.

McGinn, Colin (1984). *Wittgenstein on Meaning*. Oxford: Blackwell.

McGinn, Marie (1989). *Sense and Certainty: A Dissolution of Scepticism*. Oxford: Blackwell.

—— (1999). 'Between Metaphysics and Nonsense: The Role of Elucidation in Wittgenstein's *Tractatus*', *Philosophical Quarterly* 49: 491–513.

—— (2006). *Elucidating the Tractatus*. Oxford: Clarendon Press.

McGuinness, Brian (1988). *Wittgenstein: A Life: Young Ludwig 1889–1921*. London: Duckworth.

—— (1991). 'Relation with and within the Vienna Circle', in McGuinness 2002, pp. 184–200; orig. pub. in German.

—— (2002). *Approaches to Wittgenstein: Collected Papers*. London: Routledge.

—— (ed.) (2008). *Wittgenstein in Cambridge: Letters and Documents 1911–1951*. Oxford: Blackwell.

McGuinness, Brian and Rudolf Haller (eds.) (1989). *Wittgenstein in Focus—Im Brennpunkt: Wittgenstein*. Amsterdam: Rodopi.

*Mach, Ernst (1883). *Die Mechanik in ihrer Entwickelung historisch-kritisch dargestellt*. Leipzig: Brockhaus, 4th edn. 1901; tr. T. J. McCormack as *The Science of Mechanics: A Critical and Historical Account of its Development*. La Salle, IL: Open Court, 1960.

—— (1886). *Die Analyse der Empfindungen und des Verhältnis des Physischen zum Psychischen*, tr. C. M. Williams and S. Waterlow as *The Analysis of Sensations and the Relation of the Physical to the Psychical*. New York: Dover, 1959.

—— (1905). *Erkenntnis und Irrtum: Skizzen zur Psychologie der Forschung*; tr. T. J. McCormack and P. Foulkes as *Knowledge and Error: Sketches on the Psychology of Enquiry*. Dordrecht: D. Reidel, 1976.

MacHale, Desmond (1985). *George Boole: His Life and Work*. Dublin: Boole Press.

MacIntyre, Alasdair (1958). *The Unconscious: A Conceptual Analysis*. London: Routledge & Kegan Paul.

—— (1966). *A Short History of Ethics*. London: Routledge & Kegan Paul; 2nd edn. 1998.

—— (1981). *After Virtue*. London: Duckworth; 2nd edn. 1984; 3rd edn. 2007.

*Mackie, J. L. (1973). *Truth, Probability and Paradox*. Oxford: Clarendon Press.

—— (1977). *Ethics: Inventing Right and Wrong*. Harmondsworth: Penguin.

McLaughlin, Brian P., Ansgar Beckermann, and Sven Walter (eds.) (2009). *The Oxford Handbook of Philosophy of Mind*. Oxford: Oxford University Press.

McLellan, David (1973). *Karl Marx: His Life and Thought*. London: Macmillan.

McManus, Denis (ed.) (2004). *Wittgenstein and Scepticism*. London: Routledge.

—— (2006). *The Enchantment of Words: Wittgenstein's Tractatus Logico-Philosophicus*. Oxford: Oxford University Press.

*McTaggart, J. M. E. (1893). *A Further Determination of the Absolute*; repr. in McTaggart 1934, pp. 210–72.

—— (1896). *Studies in the Hegelian Dialectic*. Cambridge: Cambridge University Press.

—— (1901). *Studies in Hegelian Cosmology*. Cambridge: Cambridge University Press.

—— (1908). 'The Unreality of Time', *Mind* 17: 457–74.

—— (1910). *A Commentary on Hegel's Logic*. Cambridge: Cambridge University Press.

—— (1921). *The Nature of Existence*, Vol. 1. Cambridge: Cambridge University Press.

—— (1927). *The Nature of Existence*, Vol. 2. Cambridge: Cambridge University Press.

—— (1934). *Philosophical Studies*, ed. S. V. Keeling. London: E. Arnold.

Makin, Gideon (2000). *The Metaphysicians of Meaning: Russell and Frege on Sense and Denotation*. London: Routledge.

Makkreel, Rudolf (2008). 'Wilhelm Dilthey', *The Stanford Encyclopedia of Philosophy*, online at: <http://plato.stanford.edu/entries/dilthey> [accessed 28 May 2012].

Makkreel, Rudolf A. and Sebastian Luft (eds.) (2009). *Neo-Kantianism in Contemporary Philosophy*. Bloomington: Indiana University Press.

*Malcolm, Norman (1942). 'Moore and Ordinary Language', in Schilpp 1942, pp. 343–68; repr. in Chappell 1964, pp. 5–23; Rorty 1967, pp. 111–24.

—— (1949). 'Defending Common Sense', *Philosophical Review* 58: 201–20; repr. in Klemke 1969b, pp. 200–19.

—— (1954). 'Wittgenstein's *Philosophical Investigations*', *Philosophical Review* 63: 530–59; repr. in Malcolm 1963, pp. 96–129; Pitcher 1966, pp. 65–103.

—— (1958). *Ludwig Wittgenstein: A Memoir*. Oxford: Oxford University Press; 2nd edn. 1984 with Wittgenstein's letters to Malcolm.

—— (1959). *Dreaming*. London: Routledge & Kegan Paul.

—— (1963). *Knowledge and Certainty*. Ithaca: Cornell University Press.

—— (1986). *Nothing is Hidden: Wittgenstein's Criticism of his Early Thought*. Oxford: Blackwell.

—— (1995). *Wittgensteinian Themes: Essays 1978–1989*, ed. G. H. von Wright. Ithaca: Cornell University Press.

Malpas, Jeff (2009a). 'Donald Davidson', *The Stanford Encyclopedia of Philosophy*, online at: <http://plato.stanford.edu/entries/davidson> [accessed 28 May 2012].

—— (2009b). 'Hans-Georg Gadamer', *The Stanford Encyclopedia of Philosophy*, online at: <http://plato.stanford.edu/entries/gadamer> [accessed 28 May 2012].

Mancosu, Paolo (ed.) (1998). *From Brouwer to Hilbert: The Debate on the Foundations of Mathematics in the 1920s*. Oxford: Oxford University Press.

—— (ed.) (2008). *The Philosophy of Mathematical Practice*. Oxford: Oxford University Press.

Mancosu, Paolo, Richard Zach, and Calixto Badesa (2009). 'The Development of Mathematical Logic from Russell to Tarski, 1900–1935', in Haaparanta 2009, pp. 318–470.

Mandelbaum, Maurice (1938). *The Problem of Historical Knowledge*. New York: Liveright.

—— (1962). 'Philosophy, Science, and Sense Perception', *Proceedings and Addresses of the American Philosophical Association* 36: 5–20.

—— (1977). *The Anatomy of Historical Knowledge*. Baltimore, MD: Johns Hopkins University Press.

Mander, W. J. (2006a). 'Idealism, British', in Grayling, Pyle, and Goulder 2006, II, pp. 1605–10.

—— (2006b). 'Joachim, Harold Henry (1868–1938)', in Grayling, Pyle, and Goulder 2006, II, pp. 1027–8.

—— (2011). *British Idealism: A History*. Oxford: Oxford University Press.

Mandik, Pete (2006). 'Evans, Michael Gareth Justin (1946–80)', in Grayling, Pyle, and Goulder 2006, II, pp. 1027–8.

Manninen, Juha and Friedrich Stadler (eds.) (2010). *The Vienna Circle in the Nordic Countries: Networks and Transformations of Logical Empiricism*. Dordrecht: Springer.

Manser, Anthony and Guy Stock (eds.) (1984). *The Philosophy of F. H. Bradley*. Oxford: Oxford University Press.

Manzano, Maria (1997). 'Alonzo Church: His Life, His Work, and Some of His Miracles', *History and Philosophy of Logic* 18: 211–32.

*Marcus, Ruth Barcan (1961). 'Modalities and Intensional Languages', *Synthese*, 13: 303–22.

—— (1993). *Modalities*. New York: Oxford University Press.

—— (2010). 'A Philosopher's Calling', *Proceedings and Addresses of the American Philosophical Association*, November.

Marek, Johann (2008). 'Alexius Meinong', *The Stanford Encyclopedia of Philosophy*, online at: <http:// plato.stanford.edu/entries/meinong> [accessed 28 May 2012].

Margalit, Avishai (ed.) (1979). *Meaning and Use*. Dordrecht: D. Reidel.

Marion, Mathieu (2000). 'Oxford Realism: Knowledge and Perception', Parts I and II, *British Journal for the History of Philosophy* 8: 299–338 (Part I), 485–519 (Part II).

—— (2006a). 'Case, Thomas (1844–1925)', in Grayling, Pyle, and Goulder 2006, I, pp. 577–80.

—— (2006b). 'Cook Wilson, John (1849–1915)', in Grayling, Pyle, and Goulder 2006, I, pp. 710–13.

—— (2009). 'John Cook Wilson', *The Stanford Encyclopedia of Philosophy*, online at: <http://plato.stanford.edu/entries/wilson> [accessed 28 May 2012].

Martí, Oscar R. (1998). 'Analytical Philosophy in Latin America', in Craig 1998, I, pp. 229–34.

Martin, Michael (2002). 'The Concerns of Analytic Philosophy', in Baggini and Stangroom 2002, pp. 129–46.

Martin, R. N. D. (1991). *Pierre Duhem: Philosophy and History in the Work of a Believing Physicist*. La Salle, IL: Open Court.

Martin, Wayne M. (2006). *Theories of Judgment: Psychology, Logic, Phenomenology*. Cambridge: Cambridge University Press.

Martinich, A. P. (2001a). 'Introduction' to Martinich and Sosa 2001a, pp. 1–5.

—— (2001b). 'John R. Searle (1932–)', in Martinich and Sosa 2001a, pp. 434–50.

Martinich, A. P. and David Sosa (eds.) (2001a). *A Companion to Analytic Philosophy*. Oxford: Blackwell; paperback edn. 2005.

—— —— (eds.) (2001b). *Analytic Philosophy: An Anthology*. Oxford: Blackwell.

*Marx, Karl (1867). *Capital*, vol. 1, in Marx and Engels 1975–, vol. 35.

Marx, Karl and Friedrich Engels (1848). *The Communist Manifesto*, tr. Samuel Moore (1888), introd. A. J. P. Taylor. London: Penguin, 1967; also in Marx and Engels 1975–, vol. 6, pp. 477–519.

—— —— (1975–). *Collected Works*. New York and London: International Publishers.

Mates, Benson (1958). 'On the Verification of Statements about Ordinary Language', *Inquiry* 1; repr. in Chappell 1964, pp. 64–74.

Mauthner, Fritz (1901–2). *Beiträge zu einer Kritik der Sprache*, 3 vols. Stuttgart: J. G. Cotta.

Max, Ingolf and Werner Stelzner (eds) (1995). *Logik und Mathematik. Frege-Kolloquium Jena 1993*. Berlin and New York: Walter de Gruyter.

Maxwell, Grover and Herbert Feigl (1961). 'Why Ordinary Language Needs Reforming', *Journal of Philosophy* 58: 488–98; repr. in Rorty 1967, pp. 193–200.

May, Todd (2002). 'On the Very Idea of Continental (or for that Matter Anglo-American) Philosophy', *Metaphilosophy* 33: 401–25.

Mays, Wolfe and S. C. Brown (eds.) (1972). *Linguistic Analysis and Phenomenology*. London: Macmillan.

Mehta, Ved, (1963). *The Fly and the Fly-bottle: Encounters with British Intellectuals*. London: Weidenfeld & Nicolson.

*Meinong, Alexius (1899). 'Ueber Gegenstände höhere Ordnung und deren Verhältniss zur inneren Wahrnehmung', *Zeitschrift für Psychologie und Physiologie der Sinnesorgane* 21: 162–272.

—— (1902). *Ueber Annahmen*. Leipzig: Barth; 2nd edn. 1910; tr. James Heanue as *On Assumptions*. Berkeley: University of California Press, 1983.

—— (1904a). *Untersuchungen zur Gegenstandstheorie und Psychologie*. Leipzig: Barth.

—— (1904b). 'Über Gegenstandstheorie', in Meinong 1904a, pp. 1–51; tr. as 'The Theory of Objects' in Chisholm 1960, pp. 76–117.

Menand, Louis (2001). *The Metaphysical Club: A Story of Ideas in America*. New York: Farrar, Straus and Giroux.

*Merleau-Ponty, Maurice (1945). *Phénoménologie de la Perception.* Paris: Gallimard; tr. Colin Smith as *The Phenomenology of Perception.* New York: Humanities Press, 1962.

Metz, Rudolf (1938). *A Hundred Years of British Philosophy,* tr. J. W. Harvey, T. E. Jessop, and H. Sturt, ed. J. H. Muirhead. London: Allen & Unwin; orig. pub. in German. Leipzig: Felix Meiner, 1935, 2 vols.

Milkov, Nikolay (2003). *A Hundred Years of English Philosophy.* Dordrecht: Kluwer.

—— (2004). 'G. E. Moore and the Greifswald Objectivists on the Given and the Beginning of Analytic Philosophy', *Axiomathes* 14: 361–79.

*Mill, John Stuart (1843). *System of Logic, Ratiocinative and Inductive,* in *Collected Works,* vols. 7–8.

—— (1859). 'On Liberty', in *Collected Works,* vol. 18, pp. 213–310.

—— (1861). 'Utilitarianism', in *Collected Works,* vol. 10, pp. 203–59.

—— (1963–81). *Collected Works of John Stuart Mill,* 33 vols., ed. J. M. Robson. Toronto: University of Toronto Press.

Miller, Alexander (2001). 'Michael Dummett (1925–)', in Martinich and Sosa 2001a, pp. 378–92.

Miller, Alexander and Crispin Wright (eds.) (2002). *Rule-Following and Meaning.* Chesham: Acumen.

Millikan, Ruth Garrett (1984). *Language, Thought and Other Biological Categories.* Cambridge, MA: MIT Press.

Mindus, Patricia (2009). *A Real Mind: The Life and Work of Axel Hägerström.* Dordrecht: Springer.

Misak, Cheryl (ed.) (2004). *The Cambridge Companion to Peirce.* Cambridge: Cambridge University Press.

—— (ed.) (2007). *New Pragmatists.* Oxford: Oxford University Press.

—— (ed.) (2008). *The Oxford Handbook of American Philosophy.* Oxford: Oxford University Press.

Mittelstraß, Jürgen (ed.). *Enzyklopädie Philosophie und Wissenschaftstheorie,* 2 vols. Mannheim: Bibliographisches Institut.

Mohanty, J. N. (1982a). *Husserl and Frege.* Bloomington: Indiana University Press.

—— (1982b). 'Husserl and Frege: A New Look at Their Relationship', with response by D. Føllesdal, in Dreyfus and Hall 1982, pp. 43–56.

Monk, Ray (1990). *Ludwig Wittgenstein: The Duty of Genius.* London: Jonathan Cape.

—— (1996a). *Bertrand Russell: The Spirit of Solitude.* London: Jonathan Cape.

—— (1996b). 'What is Analytical Philosophy?', in Monk and Palmer 1996, pp. 1–22.

—— (1997). 'Was Russell an Analytical Philosopher?', in Glock 1997, pp. 35–50.

—— (2000). *Bertrand Russell: The Ghost of Madness.* London: Jonathan Cape.

Monk, Ray and Anthony Palmer (eds.) (1996). *Bertrand Russell and the Origins of Analytical Philosophy.* Bristol: Thoemmes.

Montague, Richard (1974). *Formal Philosophy: Selected Papers of Richard Montague,* ed. R. Thomason. New Haven, CT: Yale University Press.

Montefiore, Alan (ed.) (1983). *Philosophy in France Today.* Cambridge: Cambridge University Press.

Moore, Adrian (2012). *The Evolution of Modern Metaphysics: Making Sense of Things.* Cambridge: Cambridge University Press.

*Moore, G. E. (1899a). 'The Nature of Judgment', *Mind* 8: 176–93; repr. in Moore 1993, pp. 1–19.

—— (1899b). 'Review of Russell's *Essay on the Foundations of Geometry', Mind* 8: 397–405.

—— (1900). 'Necessity', *Mind* 9: 289–304.

—— (1903a). *Principia Ethica*. Cambridge: Cambridge University Press; 2nd edn. 1993, ed. T. Baldwin.

—— (1903b). 'The Refutation of Idealism', *Mind* 12: 433–53; repr. in Moore, 1922; Moore 1993, pp. 23–44.

—— (1903c). 'Review of [Brentano 1902]', *International Journal of Ethics* 14: 115–23.

—— (1907). 'Professor James's "Pragmatism"', *Proceedings of the Aristotelian Society* 8: 33–77.

—— (1912). *Ethics*. London: Home University Library.

—— (1914). 'Symposium: The Status of Sense-Data', *Proceedings of the Aristotelian Society* 14: 355–80.

—— (1919). 'External and Internal Relations', *Proceedings of the Aristotelian Society* 20: 40–62; rev. and repr. in Moore 1922, pp. 276–309; Moore 1993, pp. 79–105.

—— (1922). *Philosophical Studies*. London: Kegan Paul.

—— (1925). 'A Defence of Common Sense', in Muirhead 1925, pp. 193–223; repr. in Moore 1959, pp. 32–59; Moore 1993, pp. 106–33.

—— (1936). 'Is Existence a Predicate?', *Proceedings of the Aristotelian Society* Supplementary Vol. 15: 154–88; repr. in Moore 1959, pp. 115–26; Moore 1993, pp. 134–46.

—— (1939). 'Proof of an External World', *Proceedings of the British Academy* 25: 273–300; repr. in Moore 1959; Moore 1993, pp. 147–70.

—— (1941). 'Certainty', in Moore 1959, pp. 226–51; Moore 1993, pp. 171–96; lecture orig. given in 1941.

—— (1942). 'An Autobiography', in Schilpp 1942, pp. 3–39.

—— (1944). 'Russell's "Theory of Descriptions"', in Schilpp 1944, pp. 175–225; repr. in Moore 1959, pp. 151–95.

—— (1953). *Some Main Problems of Philosophy*. London: George Allen & Unwin.

—— (1954–55). 'Wittgenstein's Lectures in 1930–33', *Mind* 63: 289–316; 64: 1–27; repr. in Moore 1959, pp. 252–324.

—— (1959). *Philosophical Papers*. London: George Allen & Unwin.

—— (1962). *Commonplace Book 1919–1953*, ed. Casimir Lewy. London: George Allen & Unwin.

—— (1986). *The Early Essays*, ed. Tom Regan. Philadelphia: Temple University Press.

—— (1991). *The Elements of Ethics*, ed. T. Regan. Philadelphia: Temple University Press.

—— (1993). *Selected Writings*, ed. Thomas Baldwin. London: Routledge

—— (2011). *G. E. Moore: Early Philosophical Writings*, ed. Thomas Baldwin and Consuelo Preti. Cambridge: Cambridge University Press.

Moorehead, Caroline (1992). *Bertrand Russell*. New York: Viking.

Moran, Dermot (2000). *Introduction to Phenomenology*. London: Routledge.

—— (ed.) (2008a). *The Routledge Companion to Twentieth Century Philosophy*. London: Routledge.

—— (2008b). 'Introduction: Towards an Assessment of Twentieth-Century Philosophy', in Moran 2008a, pp. 1–40.

Mormann, Thomas (2000). *Rudolf Carnap*. München: Beck.

Morris, George Sylvester (1874). *Friedrich Adolf Trendelenburg*. Ann Arbor, MI: University of Michigan Press.

Morscher, Edgar (2007). 'Bernard Bolzano', *The Stanford Encyclopedia of Philosophy*, online at: <http://plato.stanford.edu/entries/bolzano> [accessed 28 May 2012].

Moyal-Sharrock, Danièle (ed.) (2004). *The Third Wittgenstein: the Post-Investigations Works*. Aldershot: Ashgate.

Moyal-Sharrock, Danièle and William H. Brenner (eds.) (2005). *Readings of Wittgenstein's 'On Certainty'*. Basingstoke: Palgrave Macmillan.

Muirhead, J. H. (ed.) (1924). *Contemporary British Philosophy: Personal Statements* (First Series). London: George Allen & Unwin.

—— (ed.) (1925). *Contemporary British Philosophy: Personal Statements* (Second Series). London: George Allen & Unwin.

Mulhall, Stephen (1994). *Stanley Cavell: Philosophy's Recounting of the Ordinary*. Oxford: Oxford University Press.

—— (2001). *Inheritance and Originality: Wittgenstein, Heidegger, Kierkegaard*. Oxford: Oxford University Press.

—— (2002). 'Post-Analytic Philosophy', in Baggini and Stangroom 2002, pp. 237–52.

Müller, Anselm (2001). 'G. E. M. Anscombe (1919–2001)', in Martinich and Sosa 2001a, pp. 315–25.

Mulligan, Kevin (ed.) (1991a). *Continental Philosophy Analysed*, special issue of *Topoi* 10(2).

—— (1991b). 'Introduction: On the History of Continental Philosophy', in Mulligan 1991a, pp. 115–20.

—— (1997). 'Sur l'histoire de l'approche analytique de l'histoire de la philosophie: de Bolzano et Brentano à Bennett et Barnes', in Vienne 1997, pp. 61–103.

—— (2003). 'Searle, Derrida, and the Ends of Phenomenology', in Smith 2003, pp. 261–86.

Mulligan, Kevin, Katarzyna Kijania-Placek, and Tomasz Placek (eds.) (2013). *Studies in the History and Philosophy of Polish Logic: Essays in Honour of Jan Woleński*. Basingstoke: Palgrave Macmillan.

Mulligan, Kevin, Peter Simons, and Barry Smith (1984). 'Truth-makers', *Philosophy and Phenomenological Research* 44: 287–321.

Mundle, C. W. K. (1970). *A Critique of Linguistic Philosophy*. Oxford: Clarendon Press.

Munitz, Milton K. (ed.) (1971). *Identity and Individuation*. New York: New York University Press.

—— (1981). *Contemporary Analytic Philosophy*. New York: Macmillan.

Munz, Peter (2004). *Beyond Wittgenstein's Poker: New Light on Popper and Wittgenstein*. Aldershot: Ashgate.

Murphey, Murray G. (2005). *C. I. Lewis: The Last Great Pragmatist*. Albany: State University of New York Press.

Myers, Gerald (1986). *William James: His Life and Thought*. New Haven, CT: Yale University Press.

Naess, Arne (1936). *Erkenntnis und wissenschaftliches Verhalten*. Oslo: Jacob Dybwad.

—— (1953). *Interpretation and Preciseness: A Contribution to the Theory of Communication*. Oslo: Jacob Dybwad; repr. in *The Selected Works of Arne Naess*, vol. 5. Dordrecht: Springer, 2005.

*Nagel, Ernest (1936). 'Impressions and Appraisals of Analytic Philosophy in Europe', *Journal of Philosophy* 33(1): 5–24; 33(2): 29–53; repr. in Nagel 1956, ch. 9.

—— (1956). *Logic Without Metaphysics*. Glencoe, IL: Free Press.

—— (1961). *The Structure of Science: Problems in the Logic of Scientific Explanation*. New York: Harcourt, Brace and World.

Nagel, Thomas (1974). 'What is it Like to be a Bat?', *Philosophical Review* 83; repr. in Nagel 1979, pp. 165–80.

—— (1979). *Mortal Questions*. Cambridge: Cambridge University Press.

—— (1986). *The View from Nowhere*. Oxford: Oxford University Press.

Nasim, Omar W. (2008). *Bertrand Russell and the Edwardian Philosophers: Constructing the World.* Basingstoke: Palgrave Macmillan.

Neale, Stephen (1990). *Descriptions.* Cambridge MA: MIT Press.

——(2001). 'H. P. Grice (1913–1988)', in Martinich and Sosa 2001a, pp. 254–73.

——(ed.) (2005). *100 Years of 'On Denoting'*, Mind 114(456), special issue (October).

Neiman, Susan (2001). 'Sure Path of a Science: Kant in the Analytic Tradition', in Floyd and Shieh 2001, pp. 291–313.

Nelson, Alan (ed.) (2005). *A Companion to Rationalism.* Oxford: Blackwell.

Nemeth, Elisabeth and Friedrich Stadler (eds.),(1996). *Encyclopedia and Utopia: The Life and Work of Otto Neurath (1882–1945).* Dordrecht: Kluwer.

*Neurath, Otto (1931a). 'Physicalism: The Philosophy of the Vienna Circle', *The Monist* 41: 618–23; repr. in Neurath 1983, pp. 48–51.

—— (1931b). 'Physikalismus', *Scientia* 50: 297–303; tr. as 'Physicalism' in Neurath 1983, pp. 52–7.

—— (1932). 'Protokollsätze', *Erkenntnis* 3: 204–14; tr. as 'Protocol Statements' in Neurath 1983, pp. 91–9.

——(1973). *Empiricism and Sociology*, ed. R. S. Cohen and M. Neurath. Dordrecht: D. Reidel.

—— (1983). *Philosophical Papers 1913–1946*, ed. R. S. Cohen and M. Neurath. Dordrecht: D. Reidel.

Newton-Smith, W. H. (ed.) (2000). *A Companion to the Philosophy of Science.* Oxford: Blackwell.

——(2001). 'Karl Popper', in Martinich and Sosa 2001a, pp. 110–16.

Nickles, Thomas (ed.) (2003). *Thomas Kuhn.* Cambridge: Cambridge University Press.

Nidditch, P. H. (1962). *The Development of Mathematical Logic.* London: Routledge & Kegan Paul.

*Nietzsche, Friedrich (1874). 'Vom Nutzen und Nachtheil der Historie für das Leben', tr. R. J. Hollingdale as 'On the Uses and Disadvantages of History for Life' in *Untimely Meditations.* Cambridge: Cambridge University Press, 1983, pp. 57–123.

——(1886). *Jenseits von Gut und Böse*; tr. Marion Faber as *Beyond Good and Evil.* Oxford: Oxford University Press, 1998.

—— (1887). *Zur Genealogie der Moral: Eine Streitschrift*; tr. Carol Diethe as *On the Genealogy of Morality: A Polemic*, ed. Keith Ansell-Pearson. Cambridge: Cambridge University Press, 1994; also tr. Douglas Smith. Oxford: Oxford University Press, 1996.

Niiniluoto, Ilkka (2005). 'Hintikka, Kaarlo Jaakko Juhani (1929–)', in Shook 2005, II, pp. 1119–23.

Nozick, Robert (1974). *Anarchy, State and Utopia.* New York: Basic Books.

——(1981). *Philosophical Explanations.* Cambridge, MA: Harvard University Press.

Nuccetelli, S. and G. Seay (eds.) (2007). *Themes from G. E. Moore: New Essays in Epistemology and Ethics.* Oxford: Oxford University Press.

Nussbaum, Martha (1990). *Love's Knowledge: Essays on Philosophy and Literature.* Oxford: Oxford University Press.

Nyirí, J. C. (ed.) (1981). *Austrian Philosophy: Studies and Texts.* Munich: Philosophia.

——(ed.) (1986). *From Bolzano to Wittgenstein: The Tradition of Austrian Philosophy.* Vienna: Hölder-Pichler-Tempsky.

Oberheim, Eric (2005). 'Feyerabend, Paul Karl (1924–94)', in Shook 2005, II, pp. 772–8.

O'Connor, David (ed.) (1964). *A Critical History of Western Philosophy.* London: Macmillan.

——(1982). *The Metaphysics of G. E. Moore.* Dordrecht: D. Reidel.

Ogden, C. K. and I. A. Richards (1923). *The Meaning of Meaning: A Study of The Influence of Language upon Thought and of The Science of Symbolism*. London: Routledge & Kegan Paul; 2nd edn. 1926; 3rd edn. 1930; 4th edn. 1936; 10th edn. 1949.

O'Hear, Anthony (1980). *Karl Popper*. London: Routledge.

—— (ed.) (1999). *German Philosophy Since Kant*. Cambridge: Cambridge University Press.

—— (ed.) (2003). *Karl Popper: Critical Assessments of Leading Philosophers*, 4 vols. London: Routledge.

Ollig, Hans-Ludwig (1998). 'Neo-Kantianism', in Craig 1998, VI, pp. 776–92.

Olson, Raymond E. and Anthony M. Paul (eds.) (1972). *Contemporary Philosophy in Scandanavia*. Baltimore, MD: Johns Hopkins University Press.

O'Neill, Onora (1989). *Constructions of Reason: Explorations of Kant's Practical Philosophy*. Cambridge: Cambridge University Press.

Orenstein, Alex (2002). *W. V. Quine*. London: Acumen.

O'Shea, James (2006). 'Conceptual Connections: Kant and the Twentieth-Century Analytic Tradition', in Bird 2006, pp. 513–26.

Overgaard, Søren (2010). 'Royaumont Revisited', *British Journal for the History of Philosophy* 18: 899–924.

Palmer, Anthony (1988). *Concept and Object: The Unity of the Proposition in Logic and Psychology*. London: Routledge.

Pap, Arthur (1949). *Elements of Analytic Philosophy*. New York: Macmillan.

—— (1958). *Semantics and Necessary Truth: An Inquiry into the Foundations of Analytic Philosophy*. New Haven, CT: Yale University Press.

Papas, Dean (2005). 'Perry, Ralph Barton (1876–1957)', in Shook 2005, III, pp. 1914–19.

Pardey, Ulrich (2012). *Frege on Absolute and Relative Truth*. Basingstoke: Palgrave Macmillan.

Parfit, Derek (1984). *Reasons and Persons*. Oxford: Oxford University Press.

—— (2011). *On What Matters*, 2 vols. Oxford: Oxford University Press.

Parret, H. and J. Bouveresse (eds.) (1981). *Meaning and Understanding*. Berlin: Walter de Gruyter.

Parrini, Paolo, Wesley C. Salmon, and Merrilee H. Salmon (eds.) (2003). *Logical Empiricism: Historical and Contemporary Perspectives*, Pittsburgh: University of Pittsburgh Press.

Parsons, Charles (1983). *Mathematics in Philosophy: Selected Essays*. Ithaca, NY: Cornell University Press.

—— (2001). 'Husserl and the Linguistic Turn', in Floyd and Shieh 2001, pp. 123–41.

—— (2005). 'Gödel, Kurt Friedrich (1906–78)', in Shook 2005, II, pp. 940–6.

—— (2012). *From Kant to Husserl: Selected Essays*. Cambridge, MA: Harvard University Press.

Passmore, John (1957). *A Hundred Years of Philosophy*. London: Duckworth; 2nd edn. London: Penguin, 1966.

—— (1967). 'Historiography of Philosophy', in Edwards 1967.

—— (1985). *Recent Philosophers*. London: Duckworth.

Pataut, Fabrice (1996). 'An Anti-Realist Perspective on Language, Thought, Logic and the History of Analytic Philosophy: An Interview with Michael Dummett', *Philosophical Investigations* 19: 1–33.

Paterson, Craig and Matthew S. Pugh (eds.) (2006). *Analytical Thomism: Traditions in Dialogue*. Aldershot: Ashgate.

Patterson, Douglas (ed.) (2008). *New Essays on Tarski and Philosophy*. Oxford: Oxford University Press.

—— (2012). *Alfred Tarski: Philosophy of Language and Logic*. Basingstoke: Palgrave Macmillan.

Pattison, Mark (1876). 'Philosophy at Oxford', *Mind* 1: 82–97.

Patton, Lydia (2010). 'Hermann von Helmholtz', *The Stanford Encyclopedia of Philosophy*, online at: <http://plato.stanford.edu/entries/hermann-helmholtz> [accessed 28 May 2012].

Paul, G. A. (1936). 'Is There a Problem about Sense-Data?', *Proceedings of the Aristotelian Society*, Supplementary Vol. 15: 61–77.

*Peano, Giuseppe (1889). 'The Principles of Arithmetic, presented by a New Method', tr. in van Heijenoort 1967, pp. 83–97.

——(1895–1903). *Formulaire de Mathématiques*, 4 vols. Turin: Bocca.

Pears, David (1967). *Bertrand Russell and the British Tradition in Philosophy*. London: Collins.

——(1971). *Wittgenstein*. Glasgow: Fontana.

——(ed.) (1972). *Bertrand Russell: A Collection of Critical Essays*. New York: Doubleday.

——(1987/88). *The False Prison: A Study of the Development of Wittgenstein's Philosophy*, 2 vols. Oxford: Oxford University Press.

Peckhaus, Volker (1997). *Logik, Mathesis universalis und allgeneine Wissenschaft*. Berlin: Akademie Verlag.

Peeters, Benoît (2010). *Derrida*. Paris: Flammarion.

*Peirce, Charles Sanders (1870). 'Description of a Notation for the Logic of Relatives, Resulting from an Amplification of the Conceptions of Boole's Calculus of Logic', *Memoirs of the American Academy of Arts and Sciences* 9: 317–78; repr. in Peirce 1931–58,vol. 3, pp. 45–149.

——(1877). 'The Fixation of Belief', *Popular Science Monthly* 12: 1–15 (November); repr. in Peirce 1931–58, vol. 5, pp. 358–87.

——(1878). 'How to Make Our Ideas Clear', *Popular Science Monthly* 12: 286–302(January); repr. in Peirce 1931–58, vol. 5, pp. 388–410.

—— (ed.) (1883). *Studies in Logic by Members of the Johns Hopkins University*. Boston, MA: Little, Brown, and Company.

——(1931–58). *The Collected Papers of Charles Sanders Peirce*, 8 vols., vols. 1–6 ed. C. Hartshorne and P. Weiss, vols. 7–8 ed. A. Burks. Cambridge, MA: Harvard University Press.

—— (2010). *Philosophy of Mathematics: Selected Writings*. Bloomington, Indiana: Indiana University Press.

Perry, John (1977). 'Frege on Demonstratives', *Philosophical Review* 86: 474–97; repr. in Yourgrau 1990, pp. 50–70.

——(1979). 'The Problem of the Essential Indexical', *Noûs* 13: 3–21; repr. in Salmon and Soames 1988, pp. 83–101.

*Perry, Ralph Barton (1910). 'The Ego-Centric Predicament', *Journal of Philosophy, Psychology and Scientific Methods* 7: 5–14.

—— (1912). *Present Philosophical Tendencies: A Critical Survey of Naturalism, Idealism, Pragmatism and Realism Together with a Synopsis of the Philosophy of William James*. New York: Longmans, Green, and Co.

——(1926). *Philosophy of the Recent Past*. New York: Charles Scribner's Sons.

Petitot, Jean, Francisco J. Varela, Bernard Pachoud, and Jean-Michel Roy (eds.) (1999). *Naturalizing Phenomenology: Issues in Contemporary Phenomenology and Cognitive Science*. Stanford: Stanford University Press.

Pettit, Philip (1973). 'The Early Philosophy of G. E. Moore', *Philosophical Forum* 4: 260–98.

Philipp, P. (1996). *Bibliographie zur Wittgenstein-Literatur*. Bergen: Wittgenstein Archives.

Piercey, Robert (2009). *The Uses of the Past from Heidegger to Rorty: Doing Philosophy Historically*. Cambridge: Cambridge University Press.

Pihlström, Sami (2001). 'Philosophy in Finland—Analytic and Post-Analytic', in Brogaard and Smith 2001, pp. 273–83.

——(2005). 'Putnam, Hilary Whitehall (1926–)', in Shook 2005, III, pp. 1971–8.

Pinkard, Terry (2000). *Hegel: A Biography*. Cambridge: Cambridge University Press.

Piovesana, Gino K. (1997). *Recent Japanese Philosophical Thought 1862–1996: A Survey*. Richmond, Surrey: Japan Library; 1st edn. 1963 [Survey 1862–1962].

Pitcher, George (ed.) (1966). *Wittgenstein: The Philosophical Investigations*. London: Macmillan.

Place, U. T. (1956). 'Is Consciousness a Brain Process?', *British Journal of Psychology* 47: 44–50; repr. in Borst 1970, pp. 42–51.

*Plantinga, Alvin (1974). *The Nature of Necessity*. Oxford: Oxford University Press.

——(1985). 'Self-Profile', in Tomberlin and van Inwagen 1985, pp. 3–97.

——(1993a). *Warrant: The Current Debate*. Oxford: Oxford University Press.

——(1993b). *Warrant and Proper Function*. Oxford: Oxford University Press.

——(2000). *Warranted Christian Belief*. Oxford: Oxford University Press.

Platts, Mark (1979). *Ways of Meaning*. London: Routledge; 2nd edn. 1997.

Pogge, Thomas (2007). *John Rawls: His Life and Theory of Justice*. Oxford: Oxford University Press.

*Poincaré, Henri (1894). 'Sur la Nature du Raisonnement mathématique', *Revue de métaphysique et de morale* 2: 371–84; repr. in Poincaré 1902; also tr. in Ewald 1996, II, pp. 972–82.

——(1902). *La Science et l'Hypothèse*. Paris: Flammarion; tr. W. J. Greenstreet as *Science and Hypothesis*. London: Walter Scott, 1905.

——(1908). *Science et Méthode*. Paris: Flammarion; tr. F. Maitland as *Science and Method*, with preface by B. Russell. London: Routledge, 1914.

Pojman, Paul (2009). 'Ernst Mach', *The Stanford Encyclopedia of Philosophy*, online at: <http://plato.stanford.edu/entries/ernst-mach> [accessed 28 May 2012].

Popkin, Richard H. (1960). *The History of Scepticism from Erasmus to Descartes*. Assen, Netherlands: Van Gorcum.

——(1979). *The History of Scepticism from Erasmus to Spinoza*. Berkeley: University of California Press.

——(2003). *The History of Scepticism: From Savonarola to Bayle*. Oxford: Oxford University Press.

*Popper, Karl (1934). *Logik der Forschung*. Vienna: Julius Springer; tr. as Popper 1959.

——(1945). *The Open Society and its Enemies*, 2 vols. London: Routledge.

——(1957). *The Poverty of Historicism*. London: Routledge; 2nd edn. 1960; orig. pub. in three parts in *Economica* 11 and 12 (1944–5).

——(1959). *The Logic of Scientific Discovery*. London: Hutchinson; repr. London: Routledge, 1992.

——(1963). *Conjectures and Refutations: The Growth of Scientific Knowledge*. London: Routledge.

——(1972). *Objective Knowledge: An Evolutionary Approach*. Oxford: Clarendon Press; 2nd edn. 1979.

——(1974). 'Intellectual Autobiography', in Schlipp 1974, pp. 3–181; repr. as Popper 1976.

——(1976). *Unended Quest: An Intellectual Autobiography*. London: Collins.

Poser, Hans and Ulrich Dirks (eds.) (1998). *Hans Reichenbach: Philosophie im Umkreis der Physik*, Berlin: Akademie Verlag.

Potter, Michael (2000). *Reason's Nearest Kin: Philosophies of Arithmetic from Kant to Carnap*. Oxford: Oxford University Press.

——(2008). 'The Birth of Analytic Philosophy', in Moran 2008a, pp. 43–75.

——(2009). *Wittgenstein's Notes on Logic*. Oxford: Oxford University Press.

Potter, Michael and Thomas Ricketts (eds.) (2010). *The Cambridge Companion to Frege*. Cambridge: Cambridge University Press.

Prado, C. G. (ed.) (2003). *A House Divided: Comparing Analytic and Continental Philosophy*. Amherst, NY: Humanity Books.

Preston, Aaron (2006). 'Analytic Philosophy', *Internet Encyclopedia of Philosophy*, online at: <http://www.iep.utm.edu/analytic> [accessed 28 May 2012].

——(2007). *Analytic Philosophy: The History of an Illusion*. London: Continuum.

Preston, John (2009). 'Paul Feyerabend', *The Stanford Encyclopedia of Philosophy*, online at: <http://plato.stanford.edu/entries/feyerabend> [accessed 28 May 2012].

Preti, Consuelo (2008). 'On the Origins of the Contemporary Notion of Propositional Content: Anti-Psychologism in Nineteenth-Century Psychology and G. E. Moore's Early Theory of Judgment', *Studies in the History and Philosophy of Science* 39: 176–85.

——(forthcoming). *The Metaphysical Basis of Ethics: The Early Philosophical Development of G. E. Moore*. Basingstoke: Palgrave Macmillan.

*Price, H. H. (1932). *Perception*. Oxford: Oxford University Press; 2nd edn. 1950.

——(1945). 'Clarity is Not Enough', *Proceedings of the Aristotelian Society*, Supplementary Vol. 19: 1–31; repr. in Lewis 1963, pp. 15–41.

——(1953). *Thinking and Experience*. Oxford: Oxford University Press; 2nd edn. 1969.

*Prichard, H. A. (1906). 'Appearances and Reality', *Mind* 15: 223–9.

——(1909). *Kant's Theory of Knowledge*. Oxford: Clarendon Press.

——(1912). 'Does Moral Philosophy Rest on a Mistake?', *Mind* 21: 21–37; repr. in Prichard 2002, pp. 7–20.

——(1915). 'Mr. Bertrand Russell on our Knowledge of the External World', *Mind* 24: 145–85.

——(1938). 'The Sense-Datum Fallacy', *Proceedings of the Aristotelian Society* 17: 1–18.

——(1949). *Moral Obligation: Essays and Lectures*, ed. W. D. Ross. Oxford: Oxford University Press; 2nd edn. 1968.

——(1950). *Knowledge and Perception: Essays and Lectures*, ed. W. D. Ross. Oxford: Clarendon Press.

——(2002). *Moral Writing*, ed. Jim MacAdam. Oxford: Clarendon Press.

Priest, Graham (2002). *Beyond the Limits of Thought*, 2nd edn. Oxford: Oxford University Press; 1st edn. Cambridge: Cambridge University Press, 1995.

Příhonský, F. (1850). *Neuer Anti-Kant oder Prüfung der Kritik der reinen Vernunft nach den in Bolzano's Wissenschaftslehre niedergelegten Begriffen*. Bautzen: A. Weller.

*Prior, Arthur N. (1957). *Time and Modality*. Oxford: Oxford University Press.

——(1960). 'The Runabout Inference-ticket', *Analysis* 21: 38–9; repr. in Prior 1976, pp. 85–7.

——(1976). *Papers in Logic and Ethics*, ed. P. T. Geach and A. J. P. Kenny. London: Duckworth.

Proops, Ian (2001). 'The New Wittgenstein: A Critique', *European Journal of Philosophy* 9: 375–404.

——(2002). *Logic and Language in Wittgenstein's Tractatus*. New York: Garland Publishing.

——(2007). 'Wittgenstein's Logical Atomism', *The Stanford Encyclopedia of Philosophy*, online at: <http://plato.stanford.edu/entries/wittgenstein-atomism> [accessed 28 May 2012].

Proust, Joelle (1986). *Questions de forme*. Paris: Fayard, tr. A. A. Brenner as *Questions of Form: Logic and the Analytic Proposition from Kant to Carnap*. Minneapolis: University of Minnesota Press, 1989.

Pryor, James (2004). 'What's Wrong with Moore's Argument', *Philosophical Issues* 14: 349–78.

Pulkkinen, Jarmo (2005). *Thought and Logic: The Debates between German-Speaking Philosophers and Symbolic Logicians at the Turn of the 20th Century*. Frankfurt: Peter Lang.

*Putnam, Hilary (1960). 'Minds and Machines', in Hook 1960; repr. in Putnam 1975b, pp. 362–85.

—— (1962). 'The Analytic and the Synthetic', in *Minnesota Studies in the Philosophy of Science* 3; repr. in Putnam 1975b, pp. 33–69.

—— (1963). 'Brains and Behaviour', in Butler 1963; repr. in Putnam 1975b, pp. 325–41.

—— (1967). 'The Nature of Mental States', in Putnam 1975b, pp. 429–40; orig. pub. as 'Psychological Predicates' in Capitan and Merrill 1967.

—— (1975a). *Mathematics, Matter and Method, Philosophical Papers*, vol. 1. Cambridge: Cambridge University Press, 2nd edn. 1979.

—— (1975b). *Mind, Language and Reality, Philosophical Papers*, vol. 2. Cambridge: Cambridge University Press.

—— (1975c). 'The Meaning of "Meaning"', in Putnam 1975b, pp. 215–71.

—— (1981). *Reason, Truth and History*. Cambridge: Cambridge University Press.

—— (1983a). *Realism and Reason, Philosophical Papers*, vol. 3. Cambridge: Cambridge University Press.

—— (1983b). 'Beyond Historicism', in Putnam 1983a, pp. 287–303.

—— (1988). *Representation and Reality*. Cambridge, MA: MIT Press.

—— (1995). *Pragmatism*. Oxford: Blackwell.

—— (1997). 'A Half Century of Philosophy, Viewed from Within', *Daedalus* 126: 175–208.

Pybus, Elizabeth (2006). 'Hare, Richard Mervyn (1919–2002)', in Grayling, Pyle, and Goulder 2006, II, pp. 1364–7.

*Quine, W. V. (1936). 'Truth by Convention', in Lee 1936; repr. in Feigl and Sellars 1949, pp. 250–73; Benacerraf and Putnam 1964 [1983], pp. 329–54; Quine 1966a [1976], pp. 77–106.

—— (1937). 'New Foundations for Mathematical Logic', *American Mathematical Monthly* 44: 70–80.

—— (1940). *Mathematical Logic*. New York: Harper & Row; rev. edn. Cambridge, MA: Harvard University Press, 1951.

—— (1943). 'Notes on Existence and Necessity', *Journal of Philosophy* 40: 113–26; repr. in Linsky 1952, pp. 77–91; fused with Quine 1947 into Quine 1953b.

—— (1947). 'The Problem of Interpreting Modal Logic', *Journal of Symbolic Logic* 12: 43–8; fused with Quine 1943 into Quine 1953b.

—— (1948). 'On What There Is', *Review of Metaphysics* 48: 21–38; repr. in Quine 1953a, pp. 1–19.

—— (1950). *Methods of Logic*. New York: Holt; 2nd edn. 1959; 3rd edn. 1972; 4th edn. Cambridge, MA: Harvard University Press, 1982.

—— (1951). 'Two Dogmas of Empiricism', *Philosophical Review* 60: 20–43; repr. in Quine 1953a, pp. 20–46; Lewis 1963, pp. 110–32.

—— (1953a). *From a Logical Point of View*. Cambridge, MA: Harvard University Press; 2nd edn. 1961.

—— (1953b). 'Reference and Modality', in Quine 1953a, pp. 139–59.

—— (1954). 'Carnap and Logical Truth', in Schilpp 1963, pp. 385–406; repr. in Benacerraf and Putnam 1964 [1983], pp. 355–76; Quine 1966a [1976], pp. 107–32.

—— (1956). 'Quantifiers and Propositional Attitudes', *Journal of Philosophy* 53; repr. in Quine 1966a, pp. 185–96.

—— (1960). *Word and Object*. Cambridge, MA: MIT Press.

——(1966a). *The Ways of Paradox and Other Essays*. New York: Random House; 2nd enlarged edn. Cambridge, MA: Harvard University Press, 1976.

——(1966b). 'Existence and Quantification', in Quine 1969, pp. 91–113.

——(1968). 'Epistemology Naturalized', in Quine 1969, pp. 69–90.

——(1969). *Ontological Relativity and Other Essays*. New York: Columbia University Press.

——(1981a). *Theories and Things*. Cambridge, MA: Harvard University Press.

——(1981b). 'Five Milestones of Empiricism', in Quine 1981a, pp. 67–72.

——(1985). *The Time of My Life: An Autobiography*. Cambridge, MA: MIT Press.

——(1986). 'Autobiography of W. V. Quine', in Schilpp and Hahn 1986, pp. 1–46.

Quine, W. V. and Rudolf Carnap (1990). *Dear Carnap, Dear Van: The Quine–Carnap Correspondence and Related Work*, ed. Richard Creath. Berkeley: University of California Press.

Quinn, Warren (1989a). 'Actions, Intentions, and Consequences: The Doctrine of Doing and Allowing', *Philosophical Review* 98: 287–312.

——(1989b). 'Actions, Intentions, and Consequences: The Doctrine of Double Effect', *Philosophy and Public Affairs* 18: 334–51.

Quinton, Anthony (1964). 'Contemporary British Philosophy', in O'Connor 1964, pp. 530–56.

——(1971). 'Absolute Idealism', *Proceedings of the British Academy* 57: 303–29; repr. in Kenny 1986, pp. 124–50.

——(1995a). 'Analytic Philosophy', in Honderich 1995, pp. 28–30.

——(1995b). 'Continental Philosophy', in Honderich 1995, pp. 161–3.

Railton, Peter (1984). 'Alienation, Consequentialism, and the Demands of Morality', *Philosophy and Public Affairs* 13: 134–71; repr. in Railton 2003, pp. 151–86.

——(1986). 'Moral Realism', *Philosophical Review* 95: 163–207; repr. in Railton 2003, pp. 3–42.

——(1998). 'Analytic Ethics', in Craig 1998, I, pp. 220–3.

——(2003). *Facts, Values, and Norms: Essays toward a Morality of Consequence*. Cambridge: Cambridge University Press.

Rajchman, John and Cornel West (eds.) (1985). *Post-Analytic Philosophy*. New York: Columbia University Press.

Ramberg, Bjørn (2007). 'Richard Rorty', *The Stanford Encyclopedia of Philosophy*, online at: <http://plato.stanford.edu/entries/rorty> [accessed 28 May 2012].

——(2008). 'Rorty, Davidson, and the Future of Metaphysics in America', in Misak 2008, pp. 430–48.

*Ramsey, F. P. (1923). 'Critical Notice of L. Wittgenstein's *Tractatus Logico-Philosophicus*', *Mind* 32: 465–78; repr. in Copi and Beard 1966, pp. 9–23.

——(1925). 'The Foundations of Mathematics', *Proceedings of the London Mathematical Society*, Series 2, 25(5): 338–84; repr. in Ramsey 1978, pp. 152–212.

——(1927). 'Facts and Propositions', *Proceedings of the Aristotelian Society*, Supplementary Vol. 7: 153–70; repr. in Ramsey 1978, pp. 40–57.

——(1928). 'On a Problem of Formal Logic', *Proceedings of the London Mathematical Society*, Series 2, 30(4): 338–84.

——(1929). 'Theories', in Ramsey 1978, pp. 101–25.

——(1931a). *The Foundations of Mathematics and Other Logical Essays*, ed. R. B. Braithwaite. London: Routledge & Kegan Paul.

——(1931b). 'Philosophy', in Ramsey 1931a, pp. 263–9.

——(1978). *Foundations: Essays in Philosophy, Logic, Mathematics and Economics*, ed. D. H. Mellor. London: Routledge & Kegan Paul; rev. version of Ramsey 1931.

*Rawls, John (1958). 'Justice as Fairness', *Philosophical Review* 67: 164–94; repr. in Laslett and Runciman 1962, pp. 132–57.

—— (1971). *A Theory of Justice*. Cambridge, MA: Harvard University Press; rev. edn. 1999.

—— (1993). *Political Liberalism*. New York: Columbia University Press; 2nd edn. 2005.

Read, Rupert and Matthew A. Lavery (eds.) (2011). *Beyond the Tractatus Wars: The New Wittgenstein Debate*. London: Routledge.

Reck, Erich H. (1997). 'Frege's Influence on Wittgenstein: Reversing Metaphysics via the Context Principle', in Tait 1997, pp. 123–85; repr. in a shorter form in Beaney and Reck 2005, I, pp. 241–89.

—— (ed.) (2002a). *From Frege to Wittgenstein: Perspectives on Early Analytic Philosophy*. New York: Oxford University Press.

—— (2002b). 'Wittgenstein's "Great Debt" to Frege: Biographical Traces and Philosophical Themes', in Reck 2002a, pp. 3–38.

—— (2007). 'Frege–Russell Numbers: Analysis or Explication?', in Beaney 2007a, pp. 33–50.

—— (2008). 'Dedekind's Contributions to the Foundations of Mathematics', *The Stanford Encyclopedia of Philosophy*, online at: <http://plato.stanford.edu/entries/dedekind-foundations> [accessed 28 May 2012].

—— (ed.) (2013). *The Historical Turn in Analytic Philosophy*. Basingstoke: Palgrave Macmillan.

Redding, Paul (2007). *Analytic Philosophy and the Return of Hegelian Thought*. Cambridge: Cambridge University Press.

—— (2010). 'Georg Wilhelm Friedrich Hegel', *The Stanford Encyclopedia of Philosophy*, online at: <http://plato.stanford.edu/entries/hegel> [accessed 28 May 2012].

Rée, Jonathan (1978). 'Philosophy and the History of Philosophy', in Rée, Ayers, and Westoby 1978, pp. 1–39.

Rée, Jonathan, Michael Ayers, and Adam Westoby (eds.) (1978). *Philosophy and its Past*. Brighton: Harvester Press.

Reed, Delbert (2007). *The Origins of Analytic Philosophy: Kant and Frege*. London: Continuum.

Reed, Edward S. (1994). 'The Separation of Psychology from Philosophy: Studies in the Sciences of Mind 1815–1879', in Ten 1994, pp. 297–356.

Regan, Tom (1986). *Bloomsbury's Prophet: G. E. Moore and the Development of his Moral Philosophy*. Philadelphia: Temple University Press.

*Reichenbach, Hans (1920). *Relativitätstheorie und Erkenntnis apriori*. Berlin: Springer, tr. M. Reichenbach as *The Theory of Relativity and A Priori Knowledge*. Los Angeles: University of California Press, 1965.

—— (1935a). 'Logical Empiricism in Germany and the Present State of its Problems', *Journal of Philosophy* 33: 141–60.

—— (1938). *Experience and Prediction: An Analysis of the Foundations and the Structure of Knowledge*. Chicago: University of Chicago Press.

—— (1951). *The Rise of Scientific Philosophy*. Berkeley: University of California Press.

Reid, Constance (1970). *Hilbert*. New York: Springer.

Reisch, George A. (2005a). *How the Cold War Transformed Philosophy of Science: To the Icy Slopes of Logic*. Cambridge: Cambridge University Press.

—— (2005b). 'Feigl, Herbert (1902–88)', in Shook 2005, II, pp. 757–60.

—— (2005c). 'Hempel, Carl Gustav (1905–97)', in Shook 2005, II, pp. 1085–8.

—— (2007). 'From the "Life of the Present" to the "Icy Slopes of Logic"', in Richardson and Uebel 2007, pp. 58–87.

Rescher, Nicholas (ed.) (1967). *The Logic of Decision and Action.* Pittsburgh: University of Pittsburgh Press.

——(1969). *Essays in Philosophical Analysis.* Pittsburgh: University of Pittsburgh Press.

Resnik, Michael (1980). *Frege and the Philosophy of Mathematics.* Ithaca, NY: Cornell University Press.

—— (1981). 'Frege and Analytic Philosophy: Facts and Speculations', in French *et al.* 1981, pp. 83–103.

Rey, Georges (2001). 'Jerry Fodor (1935–)', in Martinich and Sosa 2001a, pp. 451–65.

Reynolds, Jack, James Chase, James Williams, and Edwin Mares (eds.) (2010). *Postanalytic and Metacontinental: Crossing Philosophical Divides.* London: Continuum.

Rhees, Rush (ed.) (1981). *Ludwig Wittgenstein: Personal Recollections.* Oxford: Blackwell.

Rheinberger, Hans-Jörg (2010). *On Historicizing Epistemology: An Essay,* tr. David Fernbach. Stanford: Stanford University Press.

Richardson, Alan (1998). *Carnap's Construction of the World.* Cambridge: Cambridge University Press.

——(2008). 'Philosophy of Science in America', in Misak 2008, pp. 339–74.

Richardson, Alan and Thomas Uebel (eds.) (2007). *The Cambridge Companion to Logical Empiricism.* Cambridge: Cambridge University Press.

Richardson, Joan (2007). *A Natural History of Pragmatism.* Cambridge: Cambridge University Press.

Richmond, Sarah (1996). 'Derrida and Analytical Philosophy: Speech Acts and their Force', *European Journal of Philosophy* 4: 38–62.

Rickert, Heinrich (1892). *Der Gegenstand der Erkenntnis.* Freiburg: J. C. B. Mohr.

—— (1896–1902). *Die Grenzen der naturwissenschaftlichen Begriffsbildung. Eine logische Einleitung in die historischen Wissenschaften,* 2 vols. Freiburg and Leipzig: J. C. B. Mohr; 2nd edn. 1913; abridged and tr. Guy Oakes as *The Limits of Concept Formation in Natural Science: A Logical Introduction to the Historical Sciences.* Cambridge: Cambridge University Press, 1986.

——(1915). *Wilhelm Windelband.* Tübingen: J. C. B. Mohr.

Ricketts, Thomas (1996a). 'Pictures, Logic, and the Limits of Sense in Wittgenstein's *Tractatus*', in Sluga and Stern 1996, pp. 59–99.

—— (1996b). 'Carnap: From Logical Syntax to Semantics', in Giere and Richardson 1996, pp. 231–50.

—— (2002). 'Wittgenstein against Frege and Russell', in Reck 2002a, pp. 227–51.

—— (2010). 'Concepts, Objects and the Context Principle', in Potter and Ricketts 2010, pp. 149–219.

Roberts, G. W. (ed.) (1979). *Bertrand Russell Memorial Volume.* London: George Allen & Unwin.

Robinson, Abraham (1961). 'Non-standard Analysis', *Proceedings of the Royal Academy of Sciences, Amsterdam,* series A, 64: 432–40.

——(1966). *Non-standard Analysis.* Amsterdam: North-Holland; 2nd edn. 1974; repr. Princeton, NJ: Princeton University Press, 1996.

Robinson, Richard, (1954). *Definition.* Oxford: Oxford University Press.

Rockmore, Tom (2005). *Hegel, Idealism, and Analytic Philosophy,* New Haven, CT: Yale University Press.

Rodriguez-Consuegra, Francisco A. (1991). *The Mathematical Philosophy of Bertrand Russell: Origins and Development,* Basel: Birkhäuser.

Rogers, Ben (1999). *A. J. Ayer: A Life*. London: Chatto & Windus.

Rollinger, Robin D. (2010). *Philosophy of Language and Other Matters in the Work of Anton Marty: Analysis and Translations*. Amsterdam and New York: Rodopi.

Romanos, George D. (1983). *Quine and Analytic Philosophy*. Cambridge, MA: MIT Press.

*Rorty, Richard (1965). 'Mind–Body Identity, Privacy, and Categories', *Review of Metaphysics* 19: 24–54.

—— (ed.) (1967). *The Linguistic Turn*. Chicago: University of Chicago Press; 2nd edn. 1992 with two retrospective essays.

—— (1979). *Philosophy and the Mirror of Nature*. Princeton, NJ: Princeton University Press; repr. Oxford: Blackwell, 1980.

—— (1981). 'Philosophy in America Today', in Rorty 1982, pp. 211–30; orig. pub. 1981.

—— (1982). *Consequences of Pragmatism*. Minneapolis: University of Minnesota Press.

—— (1984). 'The Historiography of Philosophy: Four Genres', in Rorty, Schneewind, and Skinner 1984, pp. 49–75.

—— (1991a). *Objectivity, Relativism, and Truth, Philosophical Papers*, vol. 1. Cambridge: Cambridge University Press.

—— (1991b). *Essays on Heidegger and others, Philosophical Papers*, vol. 2. Cambridge: Cambridge University Press.

—— (1998). 'Pragmatism as Romantic Polytheism', in Dickstein 1998, ch. 1.

—— (2005). 'How many grains make a heap?' [review of Soames 2003], *London Review of Books* 27(2) (20 January).

—— (2007a). *Philosophy as Cultural Politics, Philosophical Papers*, vol. 4. Cambridge: Cambridge University Press.

—— (2007b). 'Analytic and Conversational Philosophy', in Rorty 2007a, pp. 120–30.

—— (2010). 'Intellectual Autobiography', in Auxier and Hahn 2010.

Rorty, Richard, J. B. Schneewind, and Quentin Skinner (eds.) (1984). *Philosophy in History*. Cambridge: Cambridge University Press.

Rosen, Stanley (1985). *The Limits of Analysis*. New Haven: Yale University Press; 1st edn. New York: Basic Books, 1980.

—— (2001). 'The Identity of, and the Difference between, Analytic and Continental Philosophy', *International Journal of Philosophical Studies* 9: 341–8.

Rosenberg, Jay F. (2001). 'Wilfrid Sellars (1912–1989)', in Martinich and Sosa 2001a, pp. 239–53.

—— (2009). 'Wilfrid Sellars', *The Stanford Encyclopedia of Philosophy*, online at: <http://plato.stanford.edu/archives/fall2009/entries/sellars> [accessed 28 May 2012].

Ross, Don, Andrew Brook, and David Thompson (eds.) (2000). *Dennett's Philosophy: A Comprehensive Assessment*. Cambridge, MA: MIT Press.

Ross, J. J. (1998). 'Analytic Philosophy as a Matter of Style', in Biletzki and Matar 1998, pp. 56–70.

*Ross, W. D. (1930). *The Right and the Good*. Oxford: Oxford University Press.

—— (1939). *The Foundations of Ethics*. Oxford: Oxford University Press.

Roy, Jean-Michel (2004). 'Carnap's Husserlian Reading of the *Aufbau*', in Awodey and Klein 2004, pp. 41–62.

Rumana, Richard (2005). 'Rorty, Richard McKay (1931–[2007])', in Shook 2005, IV, pp. 2072–7.

Runes, Dagobert D. (ed.) (1942). *Who's Who in Philosophy*. New York: Greenwood Press.

—— (ed.) (1943). *Twentieth Century Philosophy: Living Schools of Thought*. New York: Philosophical Library.

*Russell, Bertrand (1897). *An Essay on the Foundations of Geometry*. Cambridge: Cambridge University Press.

—— (1898). 'An Analysis of Mathematical Reasoning', in Russell 1990, pp. 155–242.

—— (1899). 'The Fundamental Ideas and Axioms of Mathematics', in Russell 1990, pp. 261–306.

—— (1899/1900). 'The Principles of Mathematics, Draft of 1899–1900', in Russell 1993, pp. 9–180.

—— (1900). A Critical Exposition of the Philosophy of Leibniz, 2nd edn. 1937; repr. London: Routledge, 1992.

—— (1901a). 'The Logic of Relations with Some Applications to the Theory of Series', Revue de mathématiques 7: 115–48; repr. in Russell 1956a, pp. 1–38; 1993, pp. 310–49.

—— (1901b). 'Part I of the Principles, Draft of 1901', in Russell 1993, pp. 181–208.

—— (1903a). The Principles of Mathematics. Cambridge: Cambridge University Press; 2nd edn. 1937; repr. London: Routledge, 1992.

—— (1903b). 'Recent Works on the Philosophy of Leibniz' [review of Couturat 1901 and Cassirer 1902], Mind 12: 177–201.

—— (1903c). 'On Meaning and Denotation', in Russell 1994, pp. 314–58.

—— (1904a). 'Meinong's Theory of Complexes and Assumptions', Mind 13: 204–19, 336–54, 509–24; repr. in Russell 1994, pp. 431–74.

—— (1904b). 'Fundamental Notions', in Russell 1994, pp. 111–269.

—— (1904c). 'On History', The Independent Review 3: 207–15; repr. in Russell 1966, ch. 2; also in Russell 1985, pp. 73–82.

—— (1905a). 'On Denoting', Mind 14: 479–93; repr. in Russell 1956a, pp. 39–56; Russell 1973, pp. 103–19.

—— (1905b). 'Review of Meinong and Others, Untersuchungen zur Gegenstandstheorie und Psychologie', Mind 14: 530–8.

—— (1906). 'Review of H. MacColl's Symbolic Logic and Its Applications', Mind 15: 255–60.

—— (1907). 'The Regressive Method of Discovering the Premises of Mathematics', in Russell 1973, pp. 272–83.

—— (1908a). 'Mathematical Logic as Based on the Theory of Types', American Journal of Mathematics 30: 222–62; repr. in Russell 1956a, pp. 57–102.

—— (1908b). 'Transatlantic "Truth"', Albany Review 2: 393–410; repr. as 'William James's Conception of Truth' in Russell 1910, ch. 5.

—— (1909). 'Pragmatism', Edinburgh Review 209: 363–88; repr. in Russell 1910, ch. 4.

—— (1910). Philosophical Essays. London: Longmans, Green and Co.; repr. as Russell 1966 with two chapters replaced.

—— (1911a). 'The Basis of Realism', Journal of Philosophy, Psychology and Scientific Methods 8: 158–61; repr. in Russell 1992a, pp. 125–31.

—— (1911b). 'Knowledge by Acquaintance and Knowledge by Description', Proceedings of the Aristotelian Society 11: 108–28; repr. in Russell 1918, ch. 10; Russell 1992a, pp. 147–61.

—— (1911c). 'Le Réalisme analytique', Bulletin de la société française de philosophie 11: 282–91; repr. in Russell 1992, pp. 409–32; tr. as 'Analytic Realism' in Russell 1992a, pp. 132–46.

—— (1912a). 'On the Relation of Universals and Particulars', Proceedings of the Aristotelian Society 12: 1–24; repr. in Russell 1956a, pp. 103–24; Russell 1992a, pp. 162–82.

—— (1912b). The Problems of Philosophy. London: Home University Library; repr. Oxford: Oxford University Press, 1967.

—— (1912c). 'The Philosophy of Bergson', The Monist 22: 321–47; repr. in Russell 1992a, pp. 313–37.

—— (1913a). 'On the Notion of Cause', Proceedings of the Aristotelian Society 13: 1–26; repr. in Russell 1918, ch. 9; Russell 1992a, pp. 190–210.

—— (1913b). 'The Nature of Sense-Data: A Reply to Dr. Dawes Hicks', *Mind* 22: 76–81; repr. in Russell 1992a, pp. 183–9.

—— (1913c). *Theory of Knowledge: The 1913 Manuscript*, ed. E. R. Eames, in Russell 1984, pp. 1–178.

—— (1914a). 'On the Nature of Acquaintance', *The Monist* 24: 1–16, 161–87, 435–53; repr. in Russell 1956a, pp. 125–74.

—— (1914b). 'The Relation of Sense-Data to Physics', *Scientia* 4; repr. in Russell 1918, ch. 8.

—— (1914c). *Our Knowledge of the External World*. London: George Allen & Unwin; repr. London: Routledge, 1993.

—— (1914d). 'On Scientific Method in Philosophy', Herbert Spencer Lecture, Oxford; repr. in Russell 1918, ch. 6.

—— (1914e). 'Definitions and Methodological Principles in Theory of Knowledge', *The Monist* 24: 582–93.

—— (1915). 'The Ultimate Constituents of Matter', *The Monist* 25: 399–417; repr. in Russell 1918, ch. 7.

—— (1918). *Mysticism and Logic*. London: George Allen & Unwin.

—— (1918–19). 'The Philosophy of Logical Atomism', *The Monist* 28: 495–527; 29: 32–63, 190–222, 345–80; repr. in Russell 1956a, pp. 175–281; Russell 1972, pp. 31–142.

—— (1919a). *Introduction to Mathematical Philosophy*. London: George Allen & Unwin; repr. London: Routledge, 1993.

—— (1919b). 'On Propositions: What They Are and How They Mean', *Proceedings of the Aristotelian Society*, Supplementary Vol. 2: 1–43; repr. in Russell 1956a, pp. 283–320.

—— (1921). *The Analysis of Mind*. London: George Allen & Unwin.

—— (1922). 'Introduction [to Wittgenstein's *Tractatus*]', in Wittgenstein 1922 [1921], pp. 7–23; 1961 [1921], pp. ix–xxii.

—— (1924a). 'Logical Atomism', in Muirhead 1924, pp. 356–83; repr. in Russell 1956a, pp. 321–43; Russell 1972, pp. 143–65.

—— (1924b). 'Philosophy of the Twentieth Century', *Dial* 77: 271–90; repr. in Russell 1928, ch. 5; Runes 1943, pp. 227–49.

—— (1927). *The Analysis of Matter*. London: Kegan Paul; repr. London: Routledge, 1992.

—— (1928). *Sceptical Essays*. London: George Allen & Unwin.

—— (1929). *Marriage and Morals*. London: George Allen & Unwin.

—— (1930). *The Conquest of Happiness*. London: George Allen & Unwin.

—— (1937). 'On Verification', *Proceedings of the Aristotelian Society* 38: 1–20.

—— (1939). 'Dewey's New Logic', in Schilpp 1939, pp. 135–56.

—— (1940a). *An Inquiry into Meaning and Truth*. London: George Allen & Unwin.

—— (1940b). 'The Philosophy of Santayana', in Schilpp 1940, pp. 451–74.

—— (1943). *How to Read and Understand History: The Past as the Key to the Future*. Girard, KS: Haldeman-Julius.

—— (1944). 'My Mental Development', in Schilpp 1944, pp. 1–20.

—— (1945). *History of Western Philosophy*. London: George Allen & Unwin; 2nd edn. 1961.

—— (1948). *Human Knowledge: Its Scope and Limits*. London: George Allen & Unwin.

—— (1950). 'Logical Positivism', *Revue Internationale de Philosophie* 4: 3–19; repr. in Russell 1956a, pp. 365–82.

—— (1953). 'Cult of "Common Usage"', *British Journal for the Philosophy of Science* 3: 303–7.

—— (1956a). *Logic and Knowledge: Essays 1901–1950*, ed. R. C. Marsh. London: George Allen & Unwin.

—— (1956b). *Portraits from Memory and Other Essays*. London: George Allen & Unwin.

—— (1956c). 'Review of Urmson's *Philosophical Analysis*', *The Hibbert Journal*; repr. in Russell 1959, ch. 18, pp. 215–30.

—— (1959a). *My Philosophical Development*. London: George Allen & Unwin; repr. Unwin Paperbacks, 1985.

—— (1959b). 'Foreword' to Gellner 1959, pp. xiii–xv.

—— (1961). *The Basic Writings of Bertrand Russell: 1903–1959*, ed. Robert E. Egner and Lester E. Denonn. London: George Allen & Unwin.

—— (1966). *Philosophical Essays*. London: George Allen & Unwin; repr. of Russell 1910 with two chapters replaced.

—— (1972). *Russell's Logical Atomism*, ed. David Pears. London: Fontana/Collins.

—— (1973). *Essays in Analysis*, ed. D. Lackey. London: George Allen & Unwin.

—— (1975). *Autobiography*. London: George Allen & Unwin; orig. pub. in 3 vols., 1967–9.

—— (1983). *Cambridge Essays, 1888–99*, *Collected Papers*, Vol. 1, ed. Kenneth Blackwell *et al.* London: George Allen & Unwin.

—— (1984). *Theory of Knowledge: The 1913 Manuscript*, *Collected Papers*, Vol. 7, ed. E. R. Eames. London: George Allen & Unwin.

—— (1985). *Contemplation and Action 1902–14*, *Collected Papers*, Vol. 12, ed. Richard A. Rempel, Andrew Brink, and Margaret Moran. London: George Allen & Unwin.

—— (1986). *The Philosophy of Logical Atomism and Other Essays, 1914–19*, *Collected Papers*, Vol. 8, ed. John G. Slater. London: George Allen & Unwin.

—— (1988). *Essays on Language, Mind and Matter, 1919–26*, *Collected Papers*, Vol. 9. London: Unwin Hyman.

—— (1990). *Philosophical Papers 1896–99*, *Collected Papers*, Vol. 2, ed. N. Griffin and A. C. Lewis. London: Unwin Hyman.

—— (1992a). *Logical and Philosophical Papers, 1909–13*, *Collected Papers*, Vol. 6. London and New York: Routledge.

—— (1992b). *The Selected Letters of Bertrand Russell: The Private Years, 1884–1914*, ed. Nicholas Griffin. London: Penguin Group; repr. London: Routledge, 2002.

—— (1993). *Towards the 'Principles of Mathematics' 1900–02*, *Collected Papers*, Vol. 3, ed. Gregory H. Moore. London: Routledge.

—— (1994). *Foundations of Logic 1903–05*, *Collected Papers*, Vol. 4, ed. A. Urquhart. London: Routledge.

—— (1996). *A Fresh Look at Empiricism, 1927–42*, *Collected Papers*, Vol. 10. London and New York: Routledge.

—— (1997). *Last Philosophical Testament, 1943–68*, *Collected Papers*, Vol. 11. London and New York: Routledge.

—— (2001). *The Selected Letters of Bertrand Russell: The Public Years, 1914–1970*, ed. Nicholas Griffin. London: Routledge.

Russell, Gillian and Delia Graff Fara (eds.) (2012). *The Routledge Companion to Philosophy of Language*. London: Routledge.

Rutherford, Alexandra (2005). 'Skinner, Burrhus Frederic (1904–90)', in Shook 2005, IV, pp. 2228–34.

Ryckman, Thomas (2005). *The Reign of Relativity: Philosophy in Physics 1915–1925*. Oxford and New York: Oxford University Press.

—— (2007). 'Carnap and Husserl', in Friedman and Creath 2007, pp. 81–105.

*Ryle, Gilbert (1929). 'Heidegger's *Sein und Zeit*', *Mind* 38: 355–70; repr. in Ryle 1971a, pp. 205–22.

—— (1932). 'Systematically Misleading Expressions', *Proceedings of the Aristotelian Society* 32: 139–70; repr. in Rorty 1967, pp. 85–100; Ryle 1971b, pp. 41–65.

—— (1935). 'Mr Collingwood and the Ontological Argument', *Mind* 44: 137–51; repr. in Ryle 1971b, pp. 105–19.

—— (1937a). 'Back to the Ontological Argument', *Mind* 46: 53–7; repr. in Ryle 1971b, pp. 120–5.

—— (1937b). 'Taking Sides in Philosophy', *Philosophy* 12: 317–32; repr. in Ryle 1971b, pp. 160–77.

—— (1945). 'Philosophical Arguments', Inaugural Lecture; repr. in Ryle 1971b, pp. 203–21.

—— (1949). *The Concept of Mind*. London: Penguin.

—— (1953). 'Ordinary Language', *Philosophical Review* 62: 167–86; repr. in Chappell 1964, pp. 24–40; Ryle 1971b, pp. 314–31.

—— (1956). 'Introduction' to Ayer *et al.* 1956, pp. 1–11.

—— (1957). 'The Theory of Meaning', in Mace 1957, pp. 237–64; repr. in Ryle 1971b, pp. 363–85.

—— (1962). 'Phenomenology versus "The Concept of Mind"', pub. in French in *Cahiers de Royaumont* 1962; repr. in Ryle 1971a, pp. 186–204.

—— (1966). *Plato's Progress*. Cambridge: Cambridge University Press.

—— (1968). 'The Genesis of "Oxford" Philosophy', *The Linacre Journal* 3 (November 1999), *The Gilbert Ryle Issue*, pp. 109–14.

—— (1970a). 'Autobiographical', in Wood and Pitcher 1970, pp. 1–15.

—— (1970b). 'G. E. Moore's "The Nature of Judgment"', in Ambrose and Lazerowitz 1970, pp. 89–101.

—— (1971a). *Critical Essays, Collected Papers*, Volume 1. London: Hutchinson; repr. Abingdon: Routledge, 2009.

—— (1971b). *Collected Essays 1929–1968, Collected Papers*, Volume 2. London: Hutchinson; repr. Abingdon: Routledge, 2009.

—— (1990). 'Logical Atomism in Plato's *Theaetetus*', *Phronesis* 35: 21–46.

Saatkamp, Herman (2010). 'George Santayana', *The Stanford Encyclopedia of Philosophy*, online at: <http://plato.stanford.edu/entries/Santayana> [accessed 28 May 2012].

Sahlin, Nils-Eric (1990). *The Philosophy of F. P. Ramsey*. Cambridge: Cambridge University Press.

Sainsbury, R. M. (1979). *Russell*. London: Routledge & Kegan Paul.

Salmon, Nathan (1981). *Reference and Essence*. Princeton, NJ: Princeton University Press; 2nd edn. Amherst, NY: Prometheus Books, 2005.

—— (1986). *Frege's Puzzle*. Cambridge, MA: MIT Press; 2nd edn. Atascadero, CA: Ridgeview, 1991.

Salmon, Nathan and Scott Soames (eds.) (1988). *Propositions and Attitudes*. Oxford: Oxford University Press.

*Santayana, George (1896). *The Sense of Beauty: Being the Outlines of Aesthetic Theory*. New York: Scribner's Sons.

—— (1905–6). *The Life of Reason: or the Phases of Human Progress*, 5 vols. New York: Scribner's Sons.

—— (1923). *Scepticism and Animal Faith: Introduction to a System of Philosophy*. New York: Scribner's Sons.

—— (1927–40). *The Realms of Being*, 4 vols. New York: Scribner's Sons; pub. in one volume 1942.

—— (1940). 'A General Confession', in Schilpp 1940, pp. 3–30.

—— (1944). *Persons and Places: The Background of My Life*. New York: Scribner's Sons.

Sarkar, Sahotra (ed.) (1996). *Science and Philosophy in the Twentieth Century: Basic Works of Logical Empiricism*, 6 vols. New York: Garland.

—— (2001). 'Rudolf Carnap (1891–1970)', in Martinich and Sosa 2001a, pp. 94–109.

*Sartre, Jean-Paul (1943). *L'Être et le Néant: Essai d'ontologie phénoménologique*. Paris: Gallimard; tr. Hazel E. Barnes as *Being and Nothingness*. New York: Philosophical Library, 1956.

—— (1981). 'An Interview with Jean-Paul Sartre', in Schilpp 1981, pp. 1–52.

Sayre-McCord, Geoffrey (ed.) (1988). *Essays on Moral Realism*. Ithaca, NY: Cornell University Press.

Scanlon, T. M. (1998). *What We Owe to Each Other*. Cambridge, MA: Harvard University Press.

Schaar, Maria van der (1991). 'G. F. Stout's Theory of Judgment and Proposition', Doctoral Dissertation, Leiden.

—— (1996). 'From Analytic Psychology to Analytic Philosophy: The Reception of Twardowski's Ideas in Cambridge', *Axiomathes* 7: 295–324.

—— (2013). *G. F. Stout's Theory of Judgement: From Psychology to Philosophy*. Basingstoke: Palgrave Macmillan.

Scheffler, Israel (2001). 'Nelson Goodman (1906–1998)', in Martinich and Sosa 2001a, pp. 160–8.

Schickore, Jutta and Friedrich Steinle (eds.) (2006). *Revisiting Discovery and Justification: Historical and Philosophical Perspectives on the Context Distinction*. Dordrecht: Springer.

Schiffer, Stephen (1987). *Remnants of Meaning*. Cambridge, MA: MIT Press.

*Schiller, F. C. S. (1902). 'Axioms as Postulates', in Sturt 1902, pp. 47–133.

—— (1903). *Humanism: Philosophical Essays*. London and New York: Macmillan; 2nd edn. 1912.

—— (1907). *Studies in Humanism*. London and New York: Macmillan; 2nd edn. 1912.

—— (1912). *Formal Logic: A Scientific and Social Problem*. London and New York: Macmillan; 2nd edn. 1931.

—— (1920). 'The Meaning of "Meaning"', *Mind* 29: 385–414.

Schilpp, Paul A. (ed.) (1939). *The Philosophy of John Dewey*. La Salle, IL: Open Court; 2nd edn. 1971; 3rd edn. 1989.

—— (ed.) (1940). *The Philosophy of George Santayana*. La Salle, IL: Open Court; 2nd edn. 1951.

—— (ed.) (1941). *The Philosophy of Alfred North Whitehead*, La Salle, IL: Open Court; 2nd edn. 1951.

—— (ed.) (1942). *The Philosophy of G. E. Moore*. La Salle, IL: Open Court; 2nd edn. 1952; 3rd ed. 1968.

—— (ed.) (1944). *The Philosophy of Bertrand Russell*. La Salle, IL: Open Court; 2nd edn. 1971.

—— (ed.),(1949a). *The Philosophy of Ernst Cassirer*. La Salle, IL: Open Court.

—— (ed.) (1949b). *Albert Einstein: Philosopher-Scientist*. La Salle, IL: Open Court; 2nd edn. 1970.

—— (ed.) (1959). *The Philosophy of C. D. Broad*. La Salle, IL: Open Court.

—— (ed.) (1963). *The Philosophy of Rudolf Carnap*. La Salle, IL: Open Court.

—— (ed.) (1968). *The Philosophy of C. I. Lewis*. La Salle, IL: Open Court.

—— (ed.) (1974). *The Philosophy of Karl Popper*. La Salle, IL: Open Court.

—— (ed.) (1980). *The Philosophy of Brand Blanshard*. La Salle, IL: Open Court.

—— (ed.) (1981). *The Philosophy of Jean-Paul Sartre*. La Salle, IL: Open Court.

Schilpp, Paul A. and Lewis E. Hahn (eds.) (1986). *The Philosophy of W. V. Quine*. La Salle, IL: Open Court; 2nd expanded edn. 1998.

—— —— (eds.) (1989). *The Philosophy of Georg Henrik von Wright*. La Salle, IL: Open Court.

Schirn, Matthias (ed.) (1976). *Studien zu Frege*, 3 vols. Stuttgart-Bad Cannstatt: Frommann.

—— (ed.) (1996). *Frege: Importance and Legacy*. Berlin: de Gruyter.

*Schlick, Moritz (1918). *Allgemeine Erkenntnislehre*. Berlin: Springer; 2nd edn. 1925; tr. A. Blumberg as *General Theory of Knowledge*. La Salle, IL: Open Court, 1985.

—— (1930). 'Die Wende der Philosophie', *Erkenntnis* 1: 4–11; tr. P. Heath as 'The Turning Point in Philosophy' in Schlick 1979, vol. 2, pp. 154–60; also tr. D. Rynin in Ayer 1959, pp. 53–9.

—— (1979). *Philosophical Papers*, 2 vols., ed. H. L. Mulder and B. van de Velde-Schlick. Dordrecht: D. Reidel.

—— (2008-12). *Kritische Gesamtausgabe*, ed. Friedrich Stadler and Hans Jürgen Wendel, 5 vols. Vienna: Springer.

Schneider, Herbert W. (1951). 'Philosophic Thought in France and the United States', *Philosophy and Phenomenological Research* 11: 376–85.

Schnieder, Benjamin and Moritz Schulz (eds.) (2011). *Themes from Early Analytic Philosophy: Essays in Honour of Wolfgang Künne, Grazer Philosophische Studien*, 82. Amsterdam: Rodopi.

Schoenman, Ralph (ed.) (1967). *Bertrand Russell: Philosopher of the Century*. London: George Allen & Unwin.

*Schopenhauer, Arthur (1819). *Die Welt als Wille und Vorstellung*; 2nd edn. in 2 vols., 1844; tr. R. B. Haldane and J. Kemp as *The World as Will and Idea*, 3 vols. London: Routledge & Kegan Paul, 1883; also tr. E. F. J. Payne as *The World as Will and Representation*, 2 vols. New York: Dover, 1958.

Schrader, David E. (2005). 'Black, Max (1909–88)', in Shook 2005, I, pp. 234–8; repr. in Grayling, Pyle, and Goulder 2006, I, pp. 336–9.

Schrift, Alan D (ed.) (2010–). *The History of Continental Philosophy*, 8 vols. Chicago: University of Chicago Press.

Schultz, Bart (2004). *Henry Sidgwick: Eye of the Universe—An Intellectual Biography*. Cambridge: Cambridge University Press.

Schwartz, Stephen P. (ed.) (1977). *Naming, Necessity, and Natural Kinds*. Ithaca: Cornell University Press.

—— (2012). *A Brief History of Analytic Philosophy: From Russell to Rawls*. Chichester: Wiley-Blackwell.

Seager, William (2006). 'Broad, Charlie Dunbar (1887–1971)', in Grayling, Pyle, and Goulder 2006, I, pp. 428–32.

*Searle, John (1962). 'Meaning and Speech Acts', *Philosophical Review* 71: 423–32.

—— (1969). *Speech Acts: An Essay in the Philosophy of Language*. Cambridge: Cambridge University Press.

—— (1977). 'Reiterating the Differences: A Reply to Derrida', *Glyph* 1: 198–208.

—— (1980). 'Minds, Brains and Programs', *Behavioral and Brain Sciences* 3: 417–57.

—— (1983). *Intentionality: An Essay in the Philosophy of Mind*. Cambridge: Cambridge University Press.

—— (1992). *The Rediscovery of the Mind*. Cambridge, MA: MIT Press.

—— (1995). *The Construction of Social Reality*. New York: The Free Press.

—— (2001). 'J. L. Austin (1911–1960)', in Martinich and Sosa 2001a, pp. 218–30.

Sellars, Roy Wood (1916). *Critical Realism: A Study of the Nature and Conditions of Knowledge*. New York: Rand, McNally and Co.

*Sellars, Wilfrid (1949). 'Realism and the New Way of Words', in Feigl and Sellars 1949, pp. 424–56.

—— (1953). 'Inference and Meaning', *Mind* 62: 313–38; repr. in Sellars 2007, pp. 3–27.

—— (1956). 'Empiricism and the Philosophy of Mind', in Feigl and Scriven 1956, pp. 253–329; repr. in Sellars 1963, pp. 127–96; Sellars 1997.

—— (1962). 'Philosophy and the Scientific Image of Man', in Colodny 1962; repr. in Sellars 1963, pp. 1–40; Sellars 2007, pp. 369–408.

—— (1963). *Science, Perception and Reality*. London: Routledge & Kegan Paul.

—— (1968). *Science and Metaphysics: Variations on Kantian Themes*. London: Routledge & Kegan Paul.

—— (1973). 'Autobiographical Reflections: (February, 1973)', in Castañeda 1975, pp. 277–93.

—— (1975). *Essays in Philosophy and its History*. Dordrecht: D. Reidel.

—— (1997). *Empiricism and the Philosophy of Mind*, ed. R. Brandom. Cambridge, MA: Harvard University Press.

—— (2007). *In the Space of Reasons: Selected Essays of Wilfrid Sellars*, ed. Kevin Scharp and Robert B. Brandom. Cambridge, MA: Harvard University Press.

Sellars, Wilfrid and Roderick M. Chisholm (1958). 'Intentionality and the Mental: A Correspondence', in Feigl, Scriven, and Maxwell 1958 (*Minnesota Studies in the Philosophy of Science*, 2), pp. 507–39.

Sen, A. K. (1970). *Collective Choice and Social Welfare*. San Francisco: Holden Day.

Sennett, James F. (ed.) (1998). *The Analytic Theist: An Alvin Plantinga Reader*. Grand Rapids, MI: William B. Eerdmans.

—— (2005). 'Plantinga, Alvin Carl (1932–)', in Shook 2005, III, pp. 1927–32.

Seth, Andrew and R. B. Haldane (eds.) (1883). *Essays in Philosophical Criticism*. London: Longmans, Green, and Co.; repr. New York: Franklin, 1971.

Shanker, Stuart (ed.) (1986). *Ludwig Wittgenstein: Critical Assessments*, 4 vols. Kent: Croom Helm.

—— (ed.) (1996). *Philosophy of Science, Logic and Mathematics in the Twentieth Century*, Routledge History of Philosophy, vol. 9. London: Routledge.

Shanker, Stuart and David Kilfoyle (eds.) (2002). *Ludwig Wittgenstein: Critical Assessments of Leading Philosophers*, Second Series, 4 vols. London: Routledge.

Shanker, V. A. and S. G. Shanker (1986). *A Wittgenstein Bibliography*. Kent: Croom Helm.

Shannon, Claude E. (1948). 'A Mathematical Theory of Communication', *Bell System Technical Journal* 27: 379–423 (July), 623–56 (October).

Shapiro, Scott (2001). 'H. L. A. Hart (1907–1992)', in Martinich and Sosa 2001a, pp. 169–74.

Shapiro, Stewart (ed.) (2005). *The Oxford Handbook of Philosophy of Mathematics and Logic*. Oxford: Oxford University Press.

Sherratt, Anna (2006). 'Mackie, John Leslie (1917–81)', in Grayling, Pyle, and Goulder 2006, III, pp. 2021–3.

Shieber, Joseph H. (2006). 'Strawson, Peter Frederick (1919–2006)', in Grayling, Pyle, and Goulder 2006, IV, pp. 3070–5.

Shieh, Sanford (2012). 'Logic, Modality, and Metaphysics in Early Analytic Philosophy: C. I. Lewis Against Russell', in Haaparanta and Koskinen 2012, pp. 293–318.

Shields, George W. (ed.) (2003a). *Process and Analysis: Whitehead, Hartshorne, and the Analytic Tradition*. Albany: State University of New York Press.

—— (2003b). 'Introduction: On the Interface of Analytic and Process Philosophy', in Shields 2003a, pp. 3–47.

Shoemaker, Sydney (1975). 'Functionalism and Qualia', *Philosophical Studies* 27: 291–315; repr. in Block 1980, II, pp. 251–67; Shoemaker 1984, pp. 184–205.

—— (1984). *Identity, Cause, and Mind*. Cambridge: Cambridge University Press.

Shook, John R. (ed.) (2005). *The Dictionary of Modern American Philosophers*, 4 vols. Bristol: Thoemmes Continuum.

Shope, Robert (1983). *The Analysis of Knowing: A Decade of Research*. Princeton, NJ: Princeton University Press.

Sibley, Frank (1959). 'Aesthetic Concepts', *Philosophical Review* 68: 421–50.

*Sidgwick, Henry (1874). *The Methods of Ethics*. London: Macmillan; further editions 1877, 1884, 1890, 1893, 1901, 1907.

—— (1876). 'Philosophy at Cambridge', *Mind* 1: 235–46.

—— (1883). 'A Criticism of the Critical Philosophy', *Mind* 8: 313–37.

Sigwart, Christoph von (1873). *Logik*, 2 vols.; 2nd edn. 1878; 3rd edn. 1904. Tübingen: J. C. B. Mohr.

Simons, Peter (1982). 'Moments as Truth-Makers', in Leinfellner and Schank 1982, pp. 159–61.

—— (1986). 'The Anglo-Austrian Analytic Axis', in Nyírí 1986, pp. 98–107.

—— (1992). *Philosophy and Logic in Central Europe from Bolzano to Tarski: Selected Essays*. Dordrecht: Kluwer.

—— (1999). 'Bolzano, Brentano and Meinong: Three Austrian Realists', in O'Hear 1999, pp. 109–36.

—— (2001). 'Whose Fault? The Origins and Evitability of the Analytic–Continental Rift', *International Journal of Philosophical Studies* 9: 295–311.

—— (2011). 'Stanisław Leśniewski', *The Stanford Encyclopedia of Philosophy*, online at: <http://plato.stanford.edu/entries/lesniewski> [accessed 28 May 2012].

Simpson, T. M. (1964). *Formas lógicas, realidad y significado*. Buenos Aires: Editorial Universitaria de Buenos Aires.

Sinisi, Vito and Jan Woleński (1995). *The Heritage of Kazimierz Ajdukiewicx*. Amsterdam: Rodopi.

Sinnott-Armstrong, Walter (2001). 'R. M. Hare (1919–2002)', in Martinich and Sosa 2001a, pp. 326–33.

Skelton, Anthony (2006). 'Sidgwick, Henry (1838–1900)', in Grayling, Pyle, and Goulder 2006, IV, pp. 2922–8.

*Skinner, B. F. (1938). *The Behavior of Organisms: An Experimental Analysis*. New York: Appleton-Century-Crofts.

—— (1953). *Science and Human Behavior*. New York: Macmillan.

—— (1957). *Verbal Behavior*. New York: Appleton-Century-Crofts.

Skinner, Quentin (1969). 'Meaning and Understanding in the History of Ideas', *History and Theory* 8: 3–53.

Skolimowski, Henryk (1967). *Polish Analytical Philosophy: A Survey and a Comparison with British Analytical Philosophy*. London: Routledge.

Skorupski, John (1989). *John Stuart Mill*. London: Routledge.

—— (1994). *English-Language Philosophy 1750–1945*. Oxford: Oxford University Press.

—— (1997). 'Why did Language Matter to Analytic Philosophy?', in Glock 1997, pp. 77–91.

Slater, John G. (2006). 'Alexander, Samuel (1859–1938)', in Grayling, Pyle, and Goulder 2006, I, pp. 61–6.

Sluga, Hans (1980). *Gottlob Frege*. London: Routledge.

—— (ed.) (1993). *The Philosophy of Frege*, 4 vols. New York: Garland Publishing.

—— (1998). 'What has History to do With Me? Wittgenstein and Analytic Philosophy', *Inquiry* 41: 99–121.

Sluga, Hans and David Stern (eds.) (1996). *The Cambridge Companion to Wittgenstein*. Cambridge: Cambridge University Press.

Smart, J. J. C. (1959). 'Sensations and Brain Processes', *Philosophical Review* 68: 141–56; repr. in Borst 1970, pp. 52–66.

——(1963). 'Materialism', *Journal of Philosophy* 60: 651–62.

Smiley, Timothy (1995). 'William Calvert Kneale', *Proceedings of the British Academy* 87: 385–97.

——(2006). 'Kneale, William Calvert (1906–90)', in Grayling, Pyle, and Goulder 2006, III, pp. 1775–7.

Smith, Barry (1994). *Austrian Philosophy: The Legacy of Franz Brentano*. Chicago and La Salle, IL: Open Court.

——(ed.) (2003). *John Searle*. Cambridge: Cambridge University Press.

Smith, Barry and David Smith (eds.) (1995). *The Cambridge Companion to Husserl*. Cambridge: Cambridge University Press.

Smith, Daniel and John Protevi (2008). 'Gilles Deleuze', *The Stanford Encyclopedia of Philosophy*, online at: <http://plato.stanford.edu/entries/deleuze> [accessed 28 May 2012].

Smith, David Woodruff (2007). *Husserl*. London: Routledge.

Smith, David Woodruff and Amie L. Thomasson (eds.) (2005). *Phenomenology and Philosophy of Mind*. Oxford and New York: Clarendon Press.

Smullyan, Arthur (1947). 'Review of Quine, "The Problem of Interpreting Modal Logic"', *Journal of Symbolic Logic* 12: 139–41.

Snow, C. P. (1959). *The Two Cultures*. Cambridge: Cambridge University Press.

——(1963). *The Two Cultures: And a Second Look*. Cambridge: Cambridge University Press; 2nd expanded edn. of Snow 1959.

Snowdon, Paul (2001). 'P. F. Strawson (1919–)', in Martinich and Sosa 2001a, pp. 334–49.

—— (2009). 'Peter Frederick Strawson', in the *Stanford Encyclopedia of Philosophy*, online at <http://plato.stanford.edu/entries/strawson> [accessed 28 May 2012].

Soames, Scott (2003). *Philosophical Analysis in the Twentieth Century*, Volume 1: *The Dawn of Analysis*, Volume 2: *The Age of Meaning*. Princeton, NJ: Princeton University Press.

—— (2005). 'Analysis, Philosophical', in Borchert 2005, I, pp. 144–57.

—— (2006a). 'What is History for? Reply to Critics of *The Dawn of Analysis*', *Philosophical Studies* 129: 645–65.

—— (2006b). 'Hacker's Complaint', *Philosophical Quarterly* 56: 426–35.

—— (2008). 'Analytic Philosophy in America', in Misak 2008, pp. 449–81.

Sokal, Alan (1996). 'Transgressing the Boundaries: Towards a Transformative Hermeneutics of Quantum Mechanics', *Social Text* 46/47: 217–52; repr. in Sokal and Bricmont 1998, pp. 199–240.

Sokal, Alan and Jean Bricmont (1998). *Intellectual Impostures*. London: Profile.

Sorell, Tom and G. A. J. Rogers (eds.) (2005). *Analytic Philosophy and History of Philosophy*. Oxford: Oxford University Press.

Sorley, W. R. (1920). *A History of English Philosophy*. Cambridge: Cambridge University Press.

——(1926). 'Fifty Years of "Mind"', *Mind* 35: 409–18.

Sosa, David (2001). 'Saul Kripke (1940–)', in Martinich and Sosa 2001a, pp. 466–77.

Sosa, Ernest (2001). 'G. E. Moore', in Martinich and Sosa 2001a, pp. 45–56.

——(2007). *A Virtue Epistemology*. Oxford: Oxford University Press.

Spaulding, Edward Gleason (1912). 'A Defense of Analysis', in Holt *et al.* 1912, pp. 153–247.

Spengler, Oswald (1918–23). *Der Untergang des Abendlandes*, vol. 1 1918, rev. 1922, vol. 2 1923. München: C. H. Beck; tr. C. F. Atkinson as *The Decline of the West*. Oxford: Oxford University Press, 1991.

Spohn, Wolfgang (ed.) (1991). *Hans Reichenbach, Rudolf Carnap: A Centenary*, Erkenntnis 35, special issue.

Sprague, Elmer (2006). 'Ryle, Gilbert (1900–1976)', in Grayling, Pyle, and Goulder 2006, IV, pp. 2799–803.

Sprigge, T. L. S. (2001). 'A. J. Ayer (1910–1989)', in Martinich and Sosa 2001a, pp. 205–17.

Stadler, Friedrich (1997). *Studien zum Wiener Kreis. Ursprung, Entwicklung und Wirkung des Logischen Empirismus im Kontext*. Frankfurt am Main: Suhrkamp; tr. as *The Vienna Circle: Studies in the Origins, Development and Influence of Logical Empiricism*. Vienna and New York: Springer, 2001.

——(ed.) (2003). *The Vienna Circle and Logical Positivism*. Vienna Circle Institute Yearbook, 10 [2002]. Dordrecht: Kluwer.

——(2007). 'The Vienna Circle: Context, Profile, and Development', in Richardson and Uebel 2007, pp. 13–40.

Stadler, Friedrich and Hans Jürgen Wendel (eds.) (2009). *Stationen. Dem Philosophen und Physiker Moritz Schlick zum 125. Geburtstag*, Schlick-Studien, Vol. 1. Vienna: Springer.

Stainton, Robert J. (2005). 'Grice, Herbert Paul (1913–88)', in Shook, II, pp. 983–8.

Stalnaker, Robert (1984). *Inquiry*. Cambridge, MA: MIT Press.

——(2001). 'David Lewis (1941–2001)', in Martinich and Sosa 2001a, pp. 478–88.

——(2003). *Ways a World Might Be*. Oxford: Oxford University Press.

Staten, Henry (1984). *Wittgenstein and Derrida*. Lincoln: University of Nebraska Press.

*Stebbing, L. Susan (1930). *A Modern Introduction to Logic*. London: Methuen; 2nd edn., revised and enlarged, 1933.

——(1932). 'The Method of Analysis in Metaphysics', *Proceedings of the Aristotelian Society* 33: 65–94.

——(1933a). 'Logical Positivism and Analysis', *Proceedings of the British Academy* 1933: 53–87.

——(1933b). 'Constructions', *Proceedings of the Aristotelian Society* 34: 1–30.

——(1935). 'Critical Notice of Carnap, *Logische Syntax der Sprache, Die Aufgabe der Wissenschaftslogik, Philosophy and Logical Syntax, The Unity of Science*', *Mind* 44: 499–511.

——(1939). *Thinking to some Purpose*. London: Penguin.

——(1942). 'Moore's Influence', in Schilpp 1942, pp. 515–32.

——(1943). *A Modern Elementary Logic*. London: Methuen; 5th edn., rev. C. W. K. Mundle, 1952.

*Stegmüller, Wolfgang (1952). *Hauptströmungen der Gegenwartsphilosophie*. Vienna: Humboldt-Verlag; 2nd edn. Stuttgart: Kröner, 1960; tr. Albert E. Blumberg as *Main Currents in Contemporary German, British, and American Philosophy*. Dordrecht: D. Reidel, 1969.

——(1969–74). *Probleme und Resultate der Wissenschaftstheorie und Analytischen Philosophie*, 4 vols. Berlin: Springer; 2nd rev. edn. 1983.

Steiner, Hillel (1994). *An Essay on Rights*. Oxford: Blackwell.

Stelzner, Werner (1996). *Gottlob Frege: Jena und die Geburt der modernen Logik*. Jena: Richter.

Stenius, Erik (1960). *Wittgenstein's Tractatus: A Critical Exposition of its Main Lines of Thought*. Oxford: Blackwell.

Stern, David (2007). 'Wittgenstein, the Vienna Circle, and Physicalism: A Reassessment', in Richardson and Uebel 2007, pp. 305–31.

Sternfeld, Robert (1966). *Frege's Logical Theory*. Carbondale and Edwardsville, IL: Southern Illinois University Press.

Stevens, Graham (2005). *The Russellian Origins of Analytic Philosophy*. London: Routledge.

——(2011). *The Theory of Descriptions*. Basingstoke: Palgrave Macmillan.

*Stevenson, C. L. (1937). 'The Emotive Meaning of Ethical Terms', *Mind* 46: 14–31; repr. in Ayer 1959, pp. 264–81; Stevenson 1963, pp. 10–31.

—— (1938). 'Persuasive Definitions', *Mind* 47: 331–50; repr. in Stevenson 1963, pp. 32–54.

—— (1944). *Ethics and Language*. New Haven, CT: Yale University Press.

—— (1963). *Facts and Values: Studies in Ethical Analysis*. New Haven, CT: Yale University Press.

Stewart, J. A. (1876). 'Psychology—A Science or a Method?', *Mind* 1: 445–51.

Stich, Stephen (1983). *From Folk Psychology to Cognitive Science: The Case Against Belief.* Cambridge, MA: MIT Press.

Stirling, J. H. (1865). *The Secret of Hegel.* Edinburgh: Oliver and Boyd, 1898.

Stocker, Barry (ed.) (2004). *Post-Analytic Tractatus*. Aldershot: Ashgate.

*Stout, G. F. (1894). 'Review of [Twardowski 1894]', *Mind* 3: 274–5.

—— (1896). *Analytic Psychology*, 2 vols. London: Swan Sonnenschein.

—— (1898/9). *A Manual of Psychology*, 2 vols. London: Swan Sonnenschein; 2nd edn. 1901; 3rd edn. 1913; 4th edn. 1929; 5th edn. 1938, with C. A. Mace.

—— (1904). 'Primary and Secondary Qualities', *Proceedings of the Aristotelian Society* 4: 141–60.

—— (1914). 'Symposium: The Status of Sense-Data', *Proceedings of the Aristotelian Society* 14: 381–406.

—— (1921). 'The Nature of Universals and Propositions', *Proceedings of the British Academy* 10: 157–72; repr. in Stout 1930.

—— (1930). *Studies in Philosophy and Psychology.* London: Swan Sonnenschein.

—— (1931). *Mind and Matter.* Cambridge: Cambridge University Press.

—— (1940a). 'The Philosophy of Samuel Alexander', *Mind* 49: 1–18, 137–49.

—— (1940b). 'S. Alexander (1859–1938): Personal Reminiscences', *Mind* 49: 126–9.

—— (1952). *God and Nature*, ed. A. K. Stout. Cambridge: Cambridge University Press.

Stoutland, Frederick (2001). 'G. H. von Wright (1916–2003)', in Martinich and Sosa 2001a, pp. 274–80.

Stratton-Lake, Philip (2006a). 'Prichard, Harold Arthur (1871–1947)', in Grayling, Pyle, and Goulder 2006, III, pp. 2580–4.

—— (2006b). 'Ross, William David (1877–1971)', in Grayling, Pyle, and Goulder 2006, IV, pp. 2764–8.

*Strawson, P. F. (1950a). 'On Referring', *Mind* 59: 320–44; repr. in Strawson 1971, pp. 1–27.

—— (1950b). 'Truth', *Proceedings of the Aristotelian Society*, Supplementary Vol. 24; repr. in Strawson 1971, pp. 190–213.

—— (1952). *Introduction to Logical Theory.* London: Methuen.

—— (1954). 'Review of Wittgenstein's *Philosophical Investigations*', *Mind* 63: 70–99; repr. in Pitcher 1966, pp. 22–64; Strawson 1974b, pp. 147–85.

—— (1956). 'Construction and Analysis', in Ayer *et al.* 1956, pp. 97–110.

—— (1959). *Individuals.* London: Methuen.

—— (1962a). 'Freedom and Resentment', *Proceedings of the British Academy* 48: 1–25; repr. in Strawson 1974b, pp. 1–28.

—— (1962b). 'Analysis, Science, and Metaphysics', together with discussion of the paper, in Rorty 1967, pp. 312–30.

—— (1963). 'Carnap's Views on Constructed Systems versus Natural Languages in Analytic Philosophy', in Schilpp 1963, pp. 503–18.

—— (1964a). 'Identifying Reference and Truth-Values', *Theoria* 30; repr. in Strawson 1971, pp. 75–95.

—— (1965). 'Truth: A Reconsideration of Austin's Views', *Philosophical Quarterly* 15: 289–301; repr. in Strawson 1971, pp. 234–49.

—— (1966). *The Bounds of Sense*. London: Methuen.

—— (1969). 'Meaning and Truth', Inaugural Lecture, Oxford; in Strawson 1971, pp. 170–89.

—— (1971). *Logico-Linguistic Papers*. London: Methuen.

—— (1974a). *Subject and Predicate in Logic and Grammar*. London: Methuen; 2nd edn. Aldershot: Ashgate, 2004.

—— (1974b). *Freedom and Resentment and Other Essays*. London: Methuen; 2nd edn. London: Routledge, 2008.

—— (1992). *Analysis and Metaphysics: An Introduction to Philosophy*. Oxford: Oxford University Press.

—— (1998). 'Intellectual Autobiography', in Hahn 1998, pp. 1–22; repr. in Strawson 2008 [1974b], pp. xvi–xxxix.

Stroh, Guy W. (2005). 'Stevenson, Charles Leslie (1908–79)', in Shook 2005, IV, pp. 2328–32.

Stroll, Avrum (1994). *Moore and Wittgenstein on Certainty*. New York: Oxford University Press.

—— (2000). *Twentieth-Century Analytic Philosophy*. New York: Columbia University Press.

—— (2001). 'Gilbert Ryle', in Martinich and Sosa 2001a, pp. 117–23.

Stroud, Barry (1984). *The Significance of Philosophical Skepticism*. Oxford: Oxford University Press.

Sturt, Henry (ed.) (1902). *Personal Idealism: Philosophical Essays by Eight Members of the University of Oxford*. London: Macmillan.

Suckiel, Ellen Kappy (2005). 'James, William (1842–1910)', in Shook 2005, II, pp. 1225–32.

Sullivan, Arthur (ed.) (2003). *Logicism and the Philosophy of Language: Selections from Frege and Russell*. Calgary, ON: Broadview Press.

Sullivan, David (2010). 'Hermann Lotze', *The Stanford Encyclopedia of Philosophy*, online at: <http://plato.stanford.edu/entries/hermann-lotze> [accessed 28 May 2012].

Sullivan, Peter (2002). 'On Trying to be Resolute: A Response to Kremer on the *Tractatus*', *European Journal of Philosophy* 10: 43–78.

—— (2003). 'Ineffability and Nonsense', *Proceedings of the Aristotelian Society*, Supplementary Vol. 77: 195–223.

Suppes, Patrick (1994). 'Ernest Nagel: 1901–1985', *Biographical Memoirs*. Washington, DC: National Academy of Sciences, pp. 256–72.

Szabó, Zoltán Gendler (2005). 'Chomsky, Noam Avram (1928–)', in Shook 2005, I, pp. 480–6.

Tait, Katharine (1975). *My Father Bertrand Russell*. New York: Harcourt Brace Jovanovich.

Tait, William W. (ed.) (1997). *Early Analytic Philosophy: Frege, Russell, Wittgenstein*. Chicago: Open Court.

—— (2005). *The Provenance of Pure Reason: Essays in the Philosophy of Mathematics and its History*. Oxford: Oxford University Press.

Tanney, Julia (2009). 'Gilbert Ryle', *The Stanford Encyclopedia of Philosophy*, online at: <http://plato.stanford.edu/entries/ryle> [accessed 28 May 2012].

Tappenden, Jamie (2005). 'The Caesar Problem in its Historical Context: Mathematical Background', *Dialectica* 59: 237–64.

—— (2006). 'The Riemannian Background to Frege's Philosophy', in Ferreirós and Gray 2006, pp. 97–132.

*Tarski, Alfred, (1933). 'The Concept of Truth in Formalized Languages', tr. in Tarski 1956, pp. 152–278; orig. pub. in Polish.

—— (1935). 'On the Concept of Logical Consequence', tr. in Tarski 1956, pp. 409–20; orig. pub. in Polish and German.

—— (1944). 'The Semantic Conception of Truth and the Foundations of Semantics', *Philosophy and Phenomenological Research* 4: 341–76.

—— (1956). *Logic, Semantics, Metamathematics: Papers from 1923 to 1938*, ed. and tr. J. H. Woodger. Oxford: Clarendon Press.

—— (1986). *Collected Papers*, 4 vols., ed. S. Givant and R. McKenzie. Basel: Birkhäuser.

Taylor, Charles (1964a). *The Explanation of Behaviour*. New York: The Humanities Press.

—— (1964b). 'Review of *Cahiers de Royaumont, La Philosophie Analytique*', *Philosophical Review* 73: 132–5.

—— (1989). *Sources of the Self: The Making of the Modern Identity*. Cambridge, MA: Harvard University Press.

Teichman, Jenny (2001). 'Gertrude Elizabeth Margaret Anscombe, 1919–2001', *Proceedings of the British Academy* 115: 31–50.

Teichmann, Roger (2008). *The Philosophy of Elizabeth Anscombe*. Oxford: Oxford University Press.

Ten, C. L. (ed.) (1994). *The Nineteenth Century, Routledge History of Philosophy*, vol. 8. London: Routledge.

Textor, Mark (ed.) (2006). *The Austrian Contribution to Analytic Philosophy*. London: Routledge.

—— (2011). *Frege on Sense and Reference*. London: Routledge.

—— (ed.) (2013). *Judgement and Truth in Early Analytic Philosophy and Phenomenology*. Basingstoke: Palgrave Macmillan.

Thiel, Christian (1968). *Sense and Reference in Frege's Logic*, tr. T. J. Blakeley. Dordrecht: D. Reidel; first pub. 1965.

—— (1995). '"Nicht aufs Gerathewohl und aus Neuerungssucht": Die Begriffsschrift 1879 und 1893', in Max and Stelzner 1995, pp. 20–37; tr. M. Beaney as 'Not Arbitrarily and Out of a Craze for Novelty: The Begriffsschrift 1879 and 1893', in Beaney and Reck 2005, II, pp. 13–28.

Thiel, Christian and Michael Beaney (2005). 'Frege's Life and Work: Chronology and Bibliography', in Beaney and Reck 2005, I, pp. 23–39.

Thomasson, Amie L. (2002). 'Phenomenology and the Development of Analytic Philosophy', *Southern Journal of Philosophy*, Supplementary Vol. 40 (Horgan *et al.* 2002): 115–42.

Thomson, Judith Jarvis (1971). 'A Defence of Abortion', *Philosophy and Public Affairs* 1: 47–66.

—— (1976). 'Killing, Letting Die, and the Trolley Problem', *The Monist* 59: 204–17.

Thornton, Stephen (2009). 'Karl Popper', *The Stanford Encyclopedia of Philosophy*, online at: <http://plato.stanford.edu/entries/popper> [accessed 28 May 2012].

Thornton, Tim (2006). 'McDowell, John Henry (1942–)', in Grayling, Pyle, and Goulder 2006, III, pp. 2001–2.

Tieszen, Richard (2005). *Phenomenology, Logic, and the Philosophy of Mathematics*. Cambridge and New York: Cambridge University Press.

—— (2011). *After Gödel: Platonism and Rationalism in Mathematics and Logic*. Oxford: Oxford University Press.

Tomberlin, James E. and Peter van Inwagen (eds.) (1985). *Alvin Plantinga*. Dordrecht: D. Reidel.

Tooley, Michael (ed.) (1999). *Analytical Metaphysics: A Collection of Essays*, 5 vols. New York: Garland.

Traiger, Saul (2005). 'Reichenbach, Hans (1891–1953)', in Shook 2005, IV, pp. 2029–35.

Travis, Charles (1989). *The Uses of Sense*. Oxford: Oxford University Press.

—— (2006a). *Thought's Footing: A Theme in Wittgenstein's Philosophical Investigations*. Oxford: Oxford University Press.

—— (2006b). 'Psychologism', in Lepore and Smith 2006, pp. 103–26.

—— (2011). *Objectivity and the Parochial*. Oxford: Oxford University Press.

*Trendelenburg, Friedrich Adolf (1840). *Logische Untersuchungen*, 2 vols. Leipzig: Hirzel; 2nd edn. 1862; 3rd edn. 1870.

—— (1842). *Erläuterungen zu den Elementen der aristotelischen Logik*. Berlin: G. Bethge; 3rd edn. 1876.

—— (1856). *Über Leibnizens Entwurf einer allgemeinen Charakteristik, Abhandlungen der Königl. Akademie der Wissenchaften zu Berlin, In Commission bei F. Dümmler*, Berlin; repr. in Trendelenburg 1867, pp. 1–47.

—— (1867). *Historische Beiträge zur Philosophie, III, Vermischte Abhandlungen*. Berlin: G. Bethge.

Tufts, James H. (1923). 'The Future of the Journal', *International Journal of Ethics* 34: 1–5.

Tugendhat, Ernst (1976). *Vorlesungen zur Einführung in die sprachanalytische Philosophie*. Frankfurt am Main: Suhrkamp; tr. P. A. Gorner as *Traditional and Analytical Philosophy: Lectures on the Philosophy of Language*. Cambridge: Cambridge University Press, 1982.

—— (1979). *Selbstbewusstsein und Selbstbestimmung*. Frankfurt: Suhrkamp; tr. Paul Stern as *Self-consciousness and Self-determination*. Cambridge, MA: MIT Press, 1986.

*Turing, A. M. (1936). 'On Computable Numbers, with an Application to the Entscheidungsproblem', *Proceedings of the London Mathematical Society*, series 2, 42: 230–65.

—— (1950). 'Computing Machinery and Intelligence', *Mind* 50: 433–60.

—— (1954). 'Solvable and Unsolvable Problems', *Science News* 31: 7–23.

*Twardowski, Kasimir (1894). *Zur Lehre vom Inhalt und Gegenstand der Vorstellungen. Eine psychologische Untersuchung*. Vienna: Alfred Hölder; tr. Reinhardt Grossmann as *On the Content and Object of Presentations: A Psychological Investigation*. The Hague: Martinus Nijhoff, 1977.

Tyler, Colin (2006). 'Green, Thomas Hill (1836–82)', in Grayling, Pyle, and Goulder 2006, II, pp. 1276–9.

—— (2011). 'Thomas Hill Green', *The Stanford Encyclopedia of Philosophy*, online at: <http://plato.stanford.edu/entries/green> [accessed 28 May 2012].

Uebel, Thomas (ed.) (1991). *Rediscovering the Forgotten Vienna Circle*. Dordrecht: Kluwer.

—— (1992). *Overcoming Logical Positivism from Within: The Emergence of Neurath's Naturalism in the Vienna Circle's Protocol Sentence Debate*. Amsterdam and Atlanta, GA: Rodopi.

—— (1999). 'Otto Neurath, the Vienna Circle and the Austrian Tradition', in O'Hear 1999, pp. 249–69.

—— (2000). *Vernunftkritik und Wissenschaft: Otto Neurath und der erste Wiener Kreis*. Vienna: Springer.

—— (2007). *Empiricism at the Crossroads: The Vienna Circle's Protocol-Sentence Debate*. Chicago: Open Court.

—— (2011). 'Vienna Circle', *The Stanford Encyclopedia of Philosophy*, online at: <http://plato.stanford.edu/entries/vienna-circle> [accessed 28 May 2012].

Urmson, J. O. (1956). *Philosophical Analysis: Its Development between the Two World Wars*. Oxford: Oxford University Press.

—— (1962). 'The History of Philosophical Analysis', together with discussion of the paper, in Rorty 1967, pp. 294–311.

—— (1965). 'J. L. Austin', *Journal of Philosophy* 62: 499–508; repr. in Rorty 1967, pp. 232–8.

—— (1969). 'Austin's Method', in Fann 1969, pp. 76–86.

van Atten, Mark (2011). 'Luitzen Egbertus Jan Brouwer', *The Stanford Encyclopedia of Philosophy*, online at: <http://plato.stanford.edu/entries/brouwer> [accessed 28 May 2012].

van Cleve, James (2001). 'C. D. Broad', in Martinich and Sosa 2001a, pp. 57–67.

van Fraassen, Bastiaan (1980). *The Scientific Image*. Oxford: Oxford University Press.

van Heijenoort, Jean (ed.) (1967a). *From Frege to Gödel: A Source Book in Mathematical Logic, 1879–1931*. Cambridge, MA: Harvard University Press.

—— (1967b). 'Logic as Calculus and Logic as Language', *Synthese* 17: 324–30.

van Inwagen, Peter (1990). *Material Beings*. Ithaca, NY: Cornell University Press.

—— (2006). 'What is Naturalism? What is Analytical Philosophy?', in Corradini, Galvan, and Lowe 2006, pp. 74–88.

Venturinha, Nuno (ed.) (2010). *Wittgenstein after his Nachlass*. Basingstoke: Palgrave Macmillan.

Verstegen, Ian (ed.) (2010). *Maurice Mandelbaum and American Critical Realism*. London: Routledge.

Vienne, J.-M. (ed.) (1997). *Philosophie analytique et Histoire de la Philosophie*. Paris: Vrin.

Viger, Christopher (2005a). 'Dennett, Daniel Clement, III (1942–)', in Shook 2005, II, pp. 615–22.

—— (2005b). 'Fodor, Jerry Alan (1935–)', in Shook 2005, II, pp. 817–24.

*Vlastos, Gregory (1954). 'The Third Man Argument in the *Parmenides*', *Philosophical Review* 64: 319–49.

—— (1991). *Socrates: Ironist and Moral Philosopher*. Cambridge: Cambridge University Press.

*von Wright, Georg Henrik (1941). *The Logical Problem of Induction*. Helsinki: Acta Philosophica Fennica; 2nd rev. edn. Oxford: Blackwell, 1957.

—— (1951a). 'Deontic Logic', *Mind* 60: 1–15.

—— (1951b). *An Essay in Modal Logic*. Amsterdam: North-Holland.

—— (1958). 'Biographical Sketch [of Wittgenstein]', in Malcolm 1958, pp. 1–22.

—— (1963a). *The Varieties of Goodness*. London: Routledge & Kegan Paul.

—— (1963b). *Norm and Action: A Logical Inquiry*. London: Routledge & Kegan Paul.

—— (1971). *Explanation and Understanding*. London: Routledge & Kegan Paul.

—— (1982). *Wittgenstein*. Oxford: Blackwell.

—— (1989). 'Intellectual Autobiography', in Schilpp and Hahn 1989, pp. 1–56.

—— (1993a). *The Tree of Knowledge and Other Essays*. Leiden: E. J. Brill.

—— (1993b). 'Analytical Philosophy: A Historico-Critical Survey', in von Wright 1993a, pp. 25–52.

Vrahimis, Andreas (2012). 'Is the Royaumont Colloquium the Locus Classicus of the Divide between Analytic and Continental Philosophy? Reply to Overgaard', *British Journal for the History of Philosophy* 20: 177–88.

Wagner, Pierre (ed.) (2009). *Carnap's Logical Syntax of Language*. Basingstoke: Palgrave Macmillan.

—— (ed.) (2012). *Carnap's Ideal of Explication and Naturalism*. Basingstoke: Palgrave Macmillan.

*Waismann, Friedrich (1936). *Einführung in das mathematische Denken*. Vienna; tr. Theodore J. Benac as *Introduction to Mathematical Thinking: The Formation of Concepts in Modern Mathematics*. New York: Frederick Ungar, 1951.

—— (1965). *The Principles of Linguistic Philosophy*, ed. Rom Harré. London: Macmillan.

—— (1979). *Ludwig Wittgenstein and the Vienna Circle*, ed. B. McGuinness, tr. J. Schulte and B. McGuinness. Oxford: Blackwell.

Walker, Jeremy (1965). *A Study of Frege*. Oxford: Blackwell.

Walsh, W. H. (1984). 'Bradley and Critical History', in Manser and Stock 1984, pp. 33–51.

Walton, Kendall L. (1990). *Mimesis as Make-Believe: On the Foundations of the Representational Arts*. Cambridge, MA: Harvard University Press.

Wang, Hao (1974). *From Mathematics to Philosophy*. London: Routledge.

—— (1985). *Beyond Analytic Philosophy: Doing Justice to What We Know*. Cambridge, MA: MIT Press.

—— (1987). *Reflections on Kurt Gödel*. Cambridge, MA: MIT Press.

Ward, James (1886). 'Psychology', *Encyclopedia Britannica*, 9th edn., Edinburgh, vol. 20, pp. 37–85.

Warnock, G. J. (1956). 'Metaphysics in Logic', in Flew 1956, pp. 39–76.

—— (1958). *English Philosophy since 1900*. Oxford: Oxford University Press; 2nd edn. 1969.

—— (1967). *Contemporary Moral Philosophy*. London: Macmillan.

—— (1969). 'John Langshaw Austin, a Biographical Sketch', in Fann 1969, pp. 3–21.

—— (1989). *J. L. Austin*. London: Routledge.

—— (1998). 'Ordinary Language Philosophy, School of', in Craig 1998, VII, pp. 147–53.

Warnock, Mary (1960). *Ethics since 1900*. Oxford: Oxford University Press; 2nd edn. 1966; 3rd edn. 1978.

—— (2000). *A Memoir: People and Places*. London: Duckworth.

*Watson, John B. (1913). 'Psychology as a Behaviorist Views It', *Psychological Review* 20: 158–77.

—— (1914). *Behavior: An Introduction to Comparative Psychology*. New York: Henry Holt; rev. edn. New York: Norton, 1930.

Watson, Richard (1993). 'Shadow History in Philosophy', *Journal of the History of Philosophy* 31: 95–109.

Weatherson, Brian (2009). 'David Lewis', *The Stanford Encyclopedia of Philosophy*, online at: <http://plato.stanford.edu/entries/david-lewis> [accessed 28 May 2012].

Weber, Michel (2006). 'Whitehead, Alfred North (1861–1947)', in Grayling, Pyle, and Goulder 2006, IV, pp. 3419–22.

Weblin, Mark (2006). 'Anderson, John (1893–1962)', in Grayling, Pyle, and Goulder 2006, I, pp. 100–5.

Wedberg, Anders (1966). *Filosofins historia, Vol. 3: Fran Bolzano till Wittgenstein*. Stockholm: Bonniers; tr. as *A History of Philosophy, Vol. 3: From Bolzano to Wittgenstein*. Oxford: Clarendon Press, 1984.

Weinberg, Julius (1936). *An Examination of Logical Positivism*. London: Kegan Paul.

Weiner, Joan (1990). *Frege in Perspective*. Ithaca, NY: Cornell University Press.

—— (2001). 'Theory and Elucidation', in Floyd and Shieh 2001, pp. 43–65.

—— (2005). 'On Fregean Elucidation' [rev. version of Weiner 2001], in Beaney and Reck 2005, IV, pp. 197–214.

Weininger, Otto (1903). *Geschlecht und Charakter*, tr. as *Sex and Character*. London: Heinemann, 1906.

Weiss, Bernhard (2002). *Michael Dummett*. Chesham: Acumen.

Weiss, Bernhard and Jeremy Wanderer (eds.) (2010). *Reading Brandom: On Making It Explicit*. New York: Routledge.

Weitz, Morris (1944). 'Analysis and the Unity of Russell's Philosophy', in Schilpp 1944, pp. 57–121.

—— (1953). 'Oxford Philosophy', *Philosophical Review* 62: 187–233.

—— (ed.) (1966). *Twentieth-Century Philosophy: The Analytic Tradition*. New York: The Free Press.

—— (1967). 'Analysis, Philosophical', in Edwards 1967, I, pp. 97–105.

Weldon, T. D. (1953). *The Vocabulary of Politics*. London: Penguin.

Wheeler, Michael (2011). 'Martin Heidegger', *The Stanford Encyclopedia of Philosophy*, online at: <http://plato.stanford.edu/entries/heidegger> [accessed 28 May 2012].

Wheeler, Samuel C. (2000). *Deconstruction as Analytic Philosophy*. Stanford: Stanford University Press.

White, Alan R. (1958). *G. E. Moore: A Critical Exposition*. Oxford: Blackwell.

—— (1975). *Modal Thinking*. Oxford: Blackwell.

—— (1990). *The Language of Imagination*. Oxford: Blackwell.

*White, Morton (1950). 'The Analytic and the Synthetic: An Untenable Dualism', in Hook 1950; repr. in Linsky 1952, pp. 272–86.

—— (ed.) (1955). *The Age of Analysis: Twentieth Century Philosophers*. Boston: Houghton Mifflin Co.; Vol. 6 of 'The Great Ages of Western Philosophy'.

—— (1956). *Toward Reunion in Philosophy*. Cambridge, MA: Harvard University Press.

—— (1965). *Foundations of Historical Knowledge*. New York: Harper & Row.

—— (1999). *A Philosopher's Story*. University Park, PA: University of Pennsylvania Press.

*Whitehead, A. N. (1898). *A Treatise on Universal Algebra*. Cambridge: Cambridge University Press.

—— (1925). *Science and the Modern World*. Cambridge: Cambridge University Press.

—— (1929). *Process and Reality: An Essay in Cosmology*. New York: Macmillan.

—— (1941). 'Autobiographical Notes', in Schilpp 1941, pp. 3–14.

Whitehead, A. N. and Bertrand Russell (1910–13). *Principia Mathematica*, 3 vols. Vol. 1 1910, Vol. 2 1912, Vol. 3 1913. Cambridge: Cambridge University Press; 2nd edn. Vol. 1 1925, Vols. 2–3 1927; abridged as *Principia Mathematica to *56*. Cambridge: Cambridge University Press, 1962.

Wicks, Robert (2011a). 'Arthur Schopenhauer', *The Stanford Encyclopedia of Philosophy*, online at: <http://plato.stanford.edu/entries/schopenhauer> [accessed 28 May 2012].

—— (2011b). 'Friedrich Nietzsche', *The Stanford Encyclopedia of Philosophy*, online at: <http://plato.stanford.edu/entries/nietzsche> [accessed 28 May 2012].

Wiener, Norbert (1948). *Cybernetics, or Control and Communication in the Animal and the Machine*. Cambridge, MA: MIT Press.

Wiggershaus, Rolf (2004). *Jürgen Habermas*. Reibeck bei Hamburg: Rowohlt.

*Wiggins, David (1967). *Identity and Spatio-Temporal Continuity*. Oxford: Blackwell.

—— (1976). 'Truth, Invention, and the Meaning of Life', *Proceedings of the British Academy* 62: 331–78; repr. in Wiggins 1987, pp. 87–137.

—— (1980). *Sameness and Substance*. Oxford: Blackwell.

—— (1987). *Needs, Values, Truth: Essays in the Philosophy of Value*. Oxford: Blackwell.

—— (2001). *Sameness and Substance Renewed*. Cambridge: Cambridge University Press.

*Williams, Bernard (1973). *Problems of the Self: Philosophical Papers 1956–1972*. Cambridge: Cambridge University Press.

—— (1978). *Descartes: The Project of Pure Inquiry*. London: Penguin.

—— (1981). *Moral Luck: Philosophical Papers 1973–1980*. Cambridge: Cambridge University Press.

—— (1985). *Ethics and the Limits of Philosophy*. London: Fontana.

—— (1996). 'Contemporary Philosophy—a Second Look', in Bunnin and Tsui-James 1996, pp. 25–37.

——(2002a). *Truth and Truthfulness: An Essay in Genealogy*. Princeton, NJ: Princeton University Press.

—— (2006a). *Philosophy as a Humanistic Discipline*. Princeton, NJ: Princeton University Press.

——(2006b). *The Sense of the Past: Essays in the History of Philosophy*. Princeton, NJ: Princeton University Press.

Williams, Bernard and Alan Montefiore (eds.) (1966). *British Analytical Philosophy*. London: Routledge & Kegan Paul.

Williams, D. C. (1953). 'On the Elements of Being', *Review of Metaphysics* 7: 3–18, 171–92.

Williams, Michael (1992). *Unnatural Doubts: Epistemological Realism and the Basis of Skepticism*. Oxford: Blackwell; 2nd edn. 1996.

——(2001). 'Richard Rorty (1931–)', in Martinich and Sosa 2001a, pp. 428–33.

Williams, S. G. (2006). 'Wiggins, David (1933–)', in Grayling, Pyle, and Goulder 2006, IV, pp. 3426–31.

Williamson, Timothy (2000). *Knowledge and Its Limits*. Oxford: Oxford University Press.

——(2004). 'Past the Linguistic Turn?', in Leiter 2004, pp. 106–28.

——(2007). *The Philosophy of Philosophy*. Oxford: Blackwell.

Wilshire, Bruce (2002). *Fashionable Nihilism: A Critique of Analytic Philosophy*. Albany: State University of New York Press.

Wilson, Adrian F. (2001). 'Collingwood's Forgotten Historiographic Revolution', *Collingwood and British Idealism Studies* 8: 6–72.

Wilson, Fred (2007). 'John Stuart Mill', *The Stanford Encyclopedia of Philosophy*, online at: <http://plato.stanford.edu/entries/mill> [accessed 28 May 2012].

*Wilson, John Cook (1926). *Statement and Inference*, 2 vols., ed., A. S. L. Farquharson. Oxford: Clarendon Press.

Wilson, Mark (2005). 'Ghost World: A Context for Frege's Context Principle', in Beaney and Reck 2005, III, pp. 157–75.

—— (2006a). *Wandering Significance: An Essay on Conceptual Behavior*. Oxford: Oxford University Press.

—— (2006b). 'Review of Scott Soames, *Philosophical Analysis in the Twentieth Century*', *Philosophical Review* 115: 517–23.

——(2010). 'Frege's Mathematical Setting', in Potter and Ricketts 2010, pp. 379–412.

Wimsatt, William K. and Monroe C. Beardsley (1946). 'The Intentional Fallacy', *The Sewanee Review* 54: 468–88.

Winch, Peter (1958). *The Idea of a Social Science and its Relation to Philosophy*. London: Routledge & Kegan Paul; 2nd edn. 1990.

——(ed.) (1969). *Studies in the Philosophy of Wittgenstein*. London: Routledge.

*Windelband, Wilhelm (1882). 'Was ist Philosophie?', in Windelband 1915, vol. I, pp. 1–54.

—— (1883). 'Kritische oder genetische Methode?', in Windelband 1915, vol. II, pp. 99–135.

—— (1884). 'Beiträge zur Lehre vom negativen Urtheil', in *Strassburger Abhandlungen zur Philosophie. Eduard Zeller zu seinem siebzigsten Geburtstage*. Tübingen: J. C. B. Mohr, pp. 167–95; repr. 1921.

—— (1915). *Präludien. Aufsätze und Reden zur Philosophie und ihrer Geschichte*, 5th edn. Tübingen: J. C. B. Mohr.

*Wisdom, John (1931). *Interpretation and Analysis in Relation to Bentham's Theory of Definition*. London: Kegan Paul.

—— (1931–3). 'Logical Constructions', Parts I–V, *Mind*, 40–2; Parts I–II, 40, pp. 188–216; Part III, 41, pp. 441–64; Part IV, 42, pp. 43–66; Part V, 42, pp. 186–202; Part I repr. in Copi and Beard 1966, pp. 39–65; repr. together as *Logical Constructions*, ed. J. J. Thomson. New York: Random House, 1969.

—— (1934a). *Problems of Mind and Matter*. Cambridge: Cambridge University Press.

—— (1934b). 'Is Analysis a Useful Method in Philosophy?', *Proceedings of the Aristotelian Society*, Supplementary Vol. 13: 65–89.

—— (1937). 'Philosophical Perplexity', *Proceedings of the Aristotelian Society* 37: 71–88; repr. in Wisdom 1953, pp. 36–50.

—— (1952). *Other Minds*. Oxford: Blackwell.

—— (1953). *Philosophy and Psycho-Analysis*. Oxford: Blackwell.

—— (1961). 'The Metamorphosis of Metaphysics', *Proceedings of the British Academy* 47: 37–59; repr. in Wisdom 1965.

—— (1965). *Paradox and Discovery*. Oxford: Blackwell.

Witherspoon, Edward (2003). 'Much Ado about the Nothing: Carnap and Heidegger on Logic and Metaphysics', in Prado 2003, pp. 291–322.

*Wittgenstein, Ludwig (1914–16). *Notebooks 1914–1916*, ed. G. H. von Wright and G. E. M. Anscombe, tr. G. E. M. Anscombe. Oxford: Blackwell, 1961; 2nd edn. Chicago: University of Chicago Press, 1979.

—— (1921). *Tractatus Logico-Philosophicus*, in *Annalen der Naturphilosophie* 14: 185–262; tr. C. K. Ogden. London: Routledge, 1922; also tr. D. F. Pears and B. McGuinness. London: Routledge, 1st edn. 1961; 2nd edn. 1974.

—— (1929). 'Some Remarks on Logical Form', *Proceedings of the Aristotelian Society*, Supplementary Vol. 9: 162–71; repr. in Copi and Beard 1966, pp. 31–7.

—— (1929–32). *Ludwig Wittgenstein and the Vienna Circle*, conversations recorded by Friedrich Waismann, ed. B. McGuinness, tr. J. Schulte and B. McGuinness. Oxford: Blackwell, 1979.

—— (1930). *Philosophical Remarks*, ed. R. Rhees, tr. R. Hargreaves and R. White. Oxford: Blackwell, 1975; orig. pub. in German 1964.

—— (1930–2). *Wittgenstein's Lectures, Cambridge 1930–1932*, ed. Desmond Lee. Oxford: Blackwell, 1980.

—— (1932–5). *Wittgenstein's Lectures, Cambridge 1932–1935*, ed. Alice Ambrose. Oxford: Blackwell, 1979.

—— (1933). *Philosophical Grammar*, ed. R. Rhees, tr. A. Kenny. Oxford: Blackwell, 1974.

—— (1933–5). *The Blue and Brown Books*. Oxford: Blackwell, 1958; 2nd. edn. 1969.

—— (1933–7). *The Big Typescript: TS 213*, ed. and tr. C. G. Luckhardt and M. A. E. Aue. Oxford: Blackwell, 2005.

—— (1937–44). *Remarks on the Foundations of Mathematics*, ed. G. H. von Wright, R. Rhees, and G. E. M. Anscombe, tr. G. E. M. Anscombe. Oxford: Blackwell, 1956; 2nd edn. 1967; 3rd edn. 1978.

—— (1938–46). *Lectures and Conversations on Aesthetics, Psychology and Religious Belief*, ed. Cyril Barrett. Oxford: Blackwell, 1966.

—— (1939). *Wittgenstein's Lectures on the Foundations of Mathematics: Cambridge, 1939*, ed. Cora Diamond. Ithaca, NY: Cornell University Press, 1975.

—— (1953). *Philosophical Investigations*, tr. G. E. M. Anscombe. Oxford: Blackwell; 2nd edn. 1958; 3rd edn. 2001; 4th edn. 2009, tr. rev. by P. M. S. Hacker and J. Schulte.

—— (1967). *Zettel*, ed. G. E. M. Anscombe and G. H. von Wright, tr. G. E. M. Anscombe. Oxford: Blackwell.

—— (1969). *On Certainty*, ed. G. E. M. Anscombe and G. H. von Wright, tr. D. Paul and G. E. M. Anscombe. Oxford: Blackwell.

—— (1971). *Prototractatus: An Early Version of Tractatus Logico-Philosophicus*, ed. B. F. McGuinness, T. Nyberg and G. H. von Wright, tr. D. F. Pears and B. F. McGuinness. London: Routledge & Kegan Paul.

—— (1977). *Remarks on Colour*, ed. G. E. M. Anscombe, tr. L. L. McAlister and M. Schättle. Oxford: Blackwell.

—— (1980a). *Remarks on the Philosophy of Psychology*, vol. 1, ed. G. E. M. Anscombe and G. H. von Wright, tr. G. E. M. Anscombe. Oxford: Blackwell.

—— (1980b). *Remarks on the Philosophy of Psychology*, vol. 2, ed. G. H. von Wright and Heikki Nyman, tr. C. G. Luckhardt and M. A. E. Aue. Oxford: Blackwell.

—— (1980c). *Culture and Value*, ed. G. H. von Wright, tr. Peter Winch. Oxford: Blackwell; orig. pub. in German as *Vermischte Bemerkungen*. Frankfurt am Main: Suhrkamp, 1977.

—— (1982). *Last Writings on the Philosophy of Psychology*, vol. 1, ed. G. H. von Wright and Heikki Nyman, tr. C. G. Luckhardt and M. A. E. Aue. Oxford: Blackwell.

—— (1984). 'Wittgenstein's Letters to Norman Malcolm', in Malcolm 1984, pp. 85–134.

—— (1992). *Last Writings on the Philosophy of Psychology*, vol. 2, ed. G. H. von Wright and Heikki Nyman, tr. C. G. Luckhardt and M. A. E. Aue. Oxford: Blackwell.

—— (2000). *Wittgenstein's Nachlass: The Bergen Electronic Edition*, ed. Wittgenstein Archives at the University of Bergen. Oxford: Oxford University Press.

—— (2004). *Gesamtbriefwechsel: Innsbrucker elektronische Ausgabe*, ed. M. Seekircher, B. McGuinness and A. Unterkircher. Charlottesville: InteLex Corporation.

—— (2008). *Wittgenstein in Cambridge: Letters and Documents 1911–1951*, ed. Brian McGuinness. Oxford: Blackwell.

Woleński, Jan (1989). *Logic and Philosophy in the Lvov-Warsaw School*. Dordrecht: Kluwer.

—— (ed.) (1990). *Kotarbiński: Logic, Semantics and Ontology*. Dordrecht: Kluwer.

—— (1999). *Essays in the History of Logic and Logical Philosophy*. Kraków: Jagiellonian University Press.

—— (2011). 'Lvov-Warsaw School', *The Stanford Encyclopedia of Philosophy*, online at: <http://plato.stanford.edu/entries/lvov-warsaw> [accessed 28 May 2012].

Woleński, Jan and Eckehart Köhler (eds.) (1999). *Alfred Tarski and the Vienna Circle: Austro-Polish Connections in Logical Empiricism*. Dordrecht: Kluwer.

Wolf, Susan (1982). 'Moral Saints', *Journal of Philosophy* 79: 419–39.

Wolff, Jonathan (2010). 'Karl Marx', *The Stanford Encyclopedia of Philosophy*, online at: <http://plato.stanford.edu/entries/marx> [accessed 28 May 2012].

Wollheim, Richard (1959). *F. H. Bradley*. Harmondsworth: Penguin; 2nd edn. 1969.

—— (1968). *Art and its Objects*. New York: Harper & Row; 2nd edn. with six supplementary essays. Cambridge: Cambridge University Press, 1980.

Wolters, Gereon (2000). 'Mach', in Newton-Smith 2000, pp. 252–6.

Wood, Alan (1957). *Bertrand Russell: The Passionate Sceptic*. London: Allen & Unwin.

Wood, Oscar P. and George Pitcher (eds.) (1970). *Ryle*. London: Macmillan.

Wright, Andrew (2006). 'Lakatos, Imre (or Liposchitz or Molnar: 1922–74)', in Grayling, Pyle, and Goulder 2006, III, pp. 1801–3.

*Wright, Crispin (1980). *Wittgenstein on the Foundations of Mathematics*. London: Duckworth.

—— (1983). *Frege's Conception of Numbers as Objects*. Aberdeen: Aberdeen University Press.

—— (ed.) (1984). *Frege: Tradition and Influence*. Oxford: Blackwell; orig. pub. in *Philosophical Quarterly* 34(136). special issue: Frege (July 1984): 183–430.

—— (1985). 'Facts and Certainty', *Proceedings of the British Academy* 71: 429–72.

—— (1987). *Realism, Meaning and Truth*. Oxford: Blackwell; 2nd edn. 1993.

—— (1992). *Truth and Objectivity*. Cambridge, MA: Harvard University Press.

—— (2001). *Rails to Infinity*. Cambridge, MA: Harvard University Press.

—— (2004). 'Warrant for Nothing (and Foundations for Free)?', *Proceedings of the Aristotelian Society*, Supplementary Vol. 78: 167–212.

Wrinch, Dorothy (1919). 'On the Nature of Judgment', *Mind* 28: 319–29.

*Wundt, Wilhelm (1874). *Grundzüge der physiologischen Psychologie*, 2 vols. Leipzig: Engelmann; tr. E. B. Titchener as *Principles of Physiological Psychology*. London: George Allen, 1893.

—— (1877). 'Philosophy in Germany', *Mind* 2: 493–518.

Yourgrau, Palle (ed.) (1990). *Demonstratives*. Oxford: Oxford University Press.

Zalabardo, José L. (ed.) (2012). *Wittgenstein's Early Philosophy*. New York: Oxford University Press.

Zeller, Eduard (1888). 'Die Geschichte der Philosophie, ihre Ziele und Wege', *Archiv für Geschichte der Philosophie* 1: 1–10.

PART 1

THE ORIGINS OF ANALYTIC PHILOSOPHY

CHAPTER 5

BOLZANO'S ANTI-KANTIANISM: FROM A PRIORI COGNITIONS TO CONCEPTUAL TRUTHS

MARK TEXTOR

5.1 INTRODUCTION

Kant begins his *Critique of Pure Reason* by stating that although all knowledge begins with experience, we have knowledge that does not depend on experience. Such knowledge, Kant explains, is a priori. (See Kant 1781/87, B2.) These claims provide the impulse for Bolzano's philosophical work.[1] Bolzano writes about himself in the third person:

> In Kant's *Critique of Pure Reason*, which he started to study in his 18th year, he immediately found the distinction between judgements a priori and a posteriori, between analytic and synthetic judgements, and the division of ideas into intuitions and concepts very appealing. However, he never managed to understand Kant's explanations of these distinctions and found it objectionable that the concept of experience was presupposed—the same goes for the concept of necessity—without a provisional explanation. (Bolzano 1836, 67–8)[2]

In his *Beyträge zu einer begründeteren Darstellung der Mathematik* (1810) Bolzano traces all problems with Kant's philosophy of mathematics to the lack of a proper articulation of the distinction between a priori and a posteriori:

---

[1] Bolzano's discussions of Kant's philosophy are collected in Franz Příhonský, *Neuer Anti-Kant oder Prüfung der Kritik der reinen Vernunft nach den in Bolzano's Wissenschaftslehre niedegelegten Begriffen* (1850). I take the title 'Anti-Kantianism' from this book.

[2] If not indicated otherwise the translations are mine.

Indeed if I am honest then all this seems to rest on an unclear understanding of the distinction between what in our knowledge is called a priori and what is called empirical. The *Critique of Pure Reason* begins with this distinction, but it [...] does not give a proper explanation of it. How can one compensate for this absence? (Bolzano 1810, 139; the page reference is to the original text)

Bolzano's criticism of Kant is constructive in that he tries to articulate the distinctions that Kant discovered, but did not explain satisfactorily. Bolzano's proposals are based on his distinction between judgements and propositions (*Sätze an sich*). His retrospective remark brings home the importance of this distinction:

In ten different places the value of this distinction reveals itself in the most surprising way because it enables the author to determine *objectively* a number of concepts which hitherto one could not explain at all or only incorrectly such as the concept of experience, the concept of a priori, the concepts of possibility, contingency and necessity, probability and many more. This brings us closer to a final decision of the most important philosophical issues. (Bolzano 1839, 123)

If one takes a priority, possibility, contingency, and necessity to be properties of propositions, one can give adequate definitions of these important concepts. If we take them to be properties of judgements, we can't. Propositions are therefore explanatorily fundamental in Bolzano's philosophy.

What are propositions? Bolzano shares with early analytic philosophers like Frege, Russell, and Moore the core conception of propositions as those things for which the question of truth and falsity arises. However, unlike these philosophers, he distinguished between two kinds of propositions: intuitive propositions (*Anschauungssätze an sich*) and conceptual propositions (*Begriffssätze an sich*).[3] A *conceptual* proposition is, roughly, a proposition that can be completely expressed by a sentence that contains neither indexicals nor demonstratives; an intuitive proposition, in contrast, can't. The distinction between conceptual and intuitive propositions is pivotal in Bolzano's metaphysics and epistemology. For instance, all the concepts listed in the quote above are explained on the basis of the distinction between conceptual and intuitive propositions. This move sets him apart from Frege and other early analytic philosophers who neither draw on nor attach philosophical importance to such a distinction.

In the next section I will introduce the main tenets of Bolzano's theory of propositions to prepare the ground for further discussion. I will then reconstruct Bolzano's criticism of Kant and his own constructive view of the a priori/a posteriori distinction.

---

[3] On this see Dummett 1991, 70.

5.2 BOLZANO ON PROPOSITIONS AND IDEAS

Bolzano's basic concept is that of a *proposition* (*Satz an sich*).[4] He helps his reader to grasp it by providing several non-definitional characterizations of it. Here is one:

> One will gather what I mean by *proposition* as soon as I remark that I do not call *proposition in itself* or an *objective proposition* that which the grammarians call a proposition, namely, the linguistic expression, but rather simply the *meaning* of this expression, which always must be be only one of the two; true or false [...]. (Bolzano 1833–44, 40; I have changed the translation)

This clue together with others, Bolzano hopes, will suffice to get his reader started. Bolzano argued in *Wissenschaftslehre* that the concept of a proposition is primitive by working through 24(!) proposed definitions. Let us have a brief look at three representative proposals discussed by Bolzano.

When one judges one thinks a proposition in a distinctive way. Propositions, Bolzano will say, are the content or matter (*Stoff*) of certain acts of thinking like judgements. Can one use this as the starting point of a definition of proposition? *Prima facie*, there are propositions no one has ever judged. Leibniz worked around this problem:

> [Leibniz] pointed out that not all sentences need to be thought, and he uses the two expressions: *propositio* and *cogitatio possibilis* as equivalent [*gleichgeltend*]. (WL 11, 1: 111)[5]

Hence, one might try to define:

$$(1)\ x \text{ is a proposition} = \text{df. } x \text{ is a possible thought } (Gedanke).$$

Bolzano uses 'thought' to refer to datable episodes of thinking or corresponding states. ('Today at 3 I had an interesting thought.') All propositions are indeed possible thoughts because God *actually* grasps every proposition and knows every truth (WL 11, 1: 104–5). But some possible thoughts are not propositions. Let us first note that a possible thought is not a particular kind of thought. Just as a possible father is not a particular sort of father (some possible fathers are non-actual fathers and hence, no fathers at all), a possible thought is a kind of possibility: x is a possible thought, if, and only if, it is possible that x is the content of an act of thinking (WL 11, 1: 118). The problem with (1) is that it

---

[4] For a comparison between Frege's and Bolzano's conception of a proposition see Künne 1997a. See also Textor 1996, 9–41. On Leibniz and Bolzano see Mugnai 1992.

[5] References to the *Wissenschaftslehre* (WL) give first the number of the volume of the *Gesamtausgabe*, followed by the page or paragraph reference.

is too wide: there are possible acts of thinking whose content are not propositions. It is possible that I think of Rome. My possible thought is not a proposition, but something Bolzano will call an *objective idea*. How can one characterize the right kind of mental acts? The only way to guarantee that a possible thought is a proposition is to require that that the relevant mental act has as its content a proposition. Hence, one goes in a tight circle (WL 11, 1: 118). The challenge for the Leibnizian is to find a characterization of what a *propositional* attitude is that does not use the notion of a proposition.

Bolzano consequently explores another definitional strategy:

(2) *x* is a proposition = df. *x* is either true or false, never both or neither.
(WL 11, 1: 103 and 119)

(2) is true and recognizing it is an important step in acquiring the concept of a proposition. But it does not yield a definition of this concept, says Bolzano. Why? Because the concept of a proposition is not disjunctive, but (2) is (WL 11, 1: 119). This reason will not convince everyone. But a better reason is available to Bolzano. (2) employed the concept of truth to shed light on the concept of a proposition. Bolzano goes on to explain truth as follows: A proposition p deserves the name 'a truth' if, and only if, things are as p says they are (WL 11, 1: 137). If this is right, the concepts of proposition and truth are intertwined. For truth, the absolute property we signify by 'true, is' essentially a property of propositions. Nothing else can have *it*. And we conceive of truth, on reflection, as a property only propositions have. This is a reason to take (2) not to be a reductive definition.

According to Bolzano, 'things are as the proposition says they are' is more properly rendered as follows:

A proposition is true if, and only if, every object represented by the subject-part of the proposition has a property represented by the predicate-part. (See Bolzano 1832–48, 61.)

For example, [Plato has Wisdom] is true if, and only if, everything denoted by [Plato] has a property denoted by [Wisdom].[6] Why *a* property? The subject- and predicate-ideas of a proposition can divide their reference over different objects. 'Wisdom' is not a singular term that denotes *one* property: it divides its reference over kinds of wisdom (WL 12, 1: 86–7). Bolzano requires for truth that *there is an* object denoted by the subject-idea and *all* the objects denoted by it have *some* property that belongs to the property kind denoted by the predicate-idea.[7]

---

[6] I will use square brackets to form designators of ideas and propositions by enclosing the words that express those ideas or propositions.

[7] See Simons 1999, 15f.; Künne 2003, 109.

Bolzano's definition of truth does not capture propositions that don't have the form [A has b]. In response he argues that although the great variety of natural language sentences ('If it is raining, I will stay home', 'John and Mary went home early', 'Possibly it will rain') suggests otherwise, all propositions have the required form. He aims to make the thesis of the uniform composition of propositions inductively plausible: so far it has been possible, says Bolzano, to paraphrase all sentences as 'A has b' sentences. Bolzano frequently says that the target-sentence of the paraphrase 'means essentially nothing else than' the start-sentence (WL 12, 2: 40). Target- and start-sentence express the same proposition, but they differ in grammatical structure. I will leave discussion of the question whether Bolzano's paraphrases slant the sense of the sentences paraphrased or not for another occasion.

If Bolzano can paraphrase every natural language sentence into the 'A has b' form, this suggests a further definition of proposition:

(3) x is a proposition = df. x is the combination of two ideas by the concept of having.
(WL 12, 2: 78)

All and only propositions are such combinations, but (3) is circular. According to (3), propositions are a particular kind of combinations of ideas. But while ideas are prior to propositions in the mereological order of composition, one explains what ideas are by presupposing the concept of a proposition:

(I) x is an objective idea = df. x is a constituent of a proposition & x is not a proposition.
(WL 11, 2: 28 and 12, 2: 78)

Some ideas represent an object; they are objectual (*gegenständlich*). Other ideas don't.

Bolzano says that there are reasons to accept (I) (WL 11, 2: 28 and 12, 2: 78). Unfortunately, he does not disclose them. (I) structures the architecture of the first volume of *Wissenschaftslehre*. Bolzano starts with propositions, goes on to show that there are (infinitely many) true propositions and that such truths can be known, and only then does he move to objective ideas. Later, one will find a similar manoeuvre in Frege. But the similarity is superficial. Frege argues at least in his early work that concepts cannot exist independently of judgeable contents (propositions).[8] But there is no such argument in Bolzano. For him ideas are building-blocks of propositions, but one cannot explain what an idea is independently of the concept of a proposition.

In the next section, I will introduce a traditional ingredient that sets Bolzano's doctrine of propositions apart from views developed at the end of the nineteenth century.

---

[8] See, for example, Frege PMC, 101.

5.3 The Kantian Heritage: Conceptual and Intuitive Propositions

Kant famously distinguished between intuitions and concepts. In his *Stufenleiter* of ideas he says:

> Objective perception is cognition [*Erkenntnis*]. This is either intuition or concept. The former relates to the object immediately and is singular, the latter, mediately, by means of a mark [*Merkmal*] which several things may have in common. (Kant 1781/87, A320/B376–7)

A concept like *red* can only relate to an object by subsuming it together with potentially many other objects. The concept relates to an object by means of an intuition if the intuition presents an object to which the concept is applied in a judgement. Intuitions seem therefore to be mental analogues of singular terms.[9]

Bolzano acknowledges that Kant made him aware of the distinction between concept and intuition, but he argues that Kant has not drawn this important distinction in a satisfactory way (WL 11, 2: 150–1). First and foremost, one needs a distinction between objective and subjective intuitions (concepts). Bolzano identified an objective intuition with an objective idea that represents one object and has no parts (WL 11, 2: § 72). An objective concept is an objective idea that neither is nor contains an objective intuition; an objective idea that contains an intuition is a mixed objective idea (*gemischte Vorstellung*) (WL 11, 2: 137). He goes on to raise the question how an objective simple idea can represent a single object *x* if it is not composed out of ideas of properties that only *x* has. (See Bolzano 1841, 42.) His answer exploits the idea that an objective intuition can be the content of a subjective intuition. An objective intuition *x* represents *y* if, and only if, *x* is the content of a subjective intuition *z* and *y* is the immediate cause of *z*. For example, a sharp pain will immediately cause in us an awareness of the pain. This awareness of the pain is a subjective intuition whose content is an objective intuition. Bolzano calls judgements that contain subjective intuitions *experiences* or *judgement of experience* (WL 13, 1: § 294).

According to Bolzano, only very few real things, that is, things that can enter causal relations, are represented by *singular ideas that are pure concepts*:

> [I]f we set ourselves the task to compose out of pure concepts a singular idea that is to represent exclusively a real object (e.g. this house, this tree, this person), we see that this is with very few exceptions impossible for us. (WL 11, 2: 139)

We have singular concepts of God, some of his attributes, and the universe. But neither finite substances nor complexes of such substances are represented by singular ideas that are concepts. If such an object is represented by a singular idea, the idea is either mixed, for example, [the man who lived in *this* house] or [the cause of this experience], or an

---

[9] This interpretation is controversial. For an overview over the discussion see Smit 2000, 237ff.

intuition. Natural kind terms often express mixed ideas (WL 11, 2: 143–4). For instance, 'man' can be used to express a pure concept of a rational sensory being or a mixed concept of a rational sensory being from *this* planet.

Why believe that singular conceptual representation is so restricted? Some pure concepts seem to represent finite substances or complexes of substances: consider [the first finite thinking being that ever set a foot on a planet on which it was not born]. Bolzano's argument seems too weak to rule out singular concepts of finite objects. It deals with *our ability to form* singular concepts of finite substances (complexes). Although we might not be able to form singular concepts of such things and their attributes, yet there are such concepts. Compare: the fact that we might not be able to define certain numbers is no reason to say that such numbers don't exist. Bolzano takes our ability to form such concepts to be limited because there are no singular concepts of finite substances and complexes (WL 11, 2: 140).[10] Why not? To assess Bolzano's reasons in detail would require a further paper. But in outline his idea is this: Take two complexes of substances, say two people A and B. If we attend to them long enough, we are able to find an intrinsic difference between them (WL 11, 3: 126). However, if there are infinitely many real objects there might for every pair of objects that can be so distinguished be a further object that cannot be distinguished from one object of the pair. Hence, if we have a pure concept that fits only A, not B, it is still possible that this concept also fits C (WL 11, 2: 140). Bolzano gives us no independent reason to believe that this possibility is actual. But our inability to compose singular concepts of real objects provides inductive support for the conclusion that there are no such singular concepts.

Bolzano goes on to use the distinction between objective concepts and intuitions to draw a distinction between different kinds of propositions. A proposition that contains no objective intuition is a *conceptual proposition*. An *intuitive proposition* is a proposition that is not a conceptual one (WL 12, 1: 95). He gives as examples of conceptual propositions the propositions that gratitude is a duty and that the square root of 2 is irrational. The distinction between conceptual and intuitive propositions straddles the divide between practical and theoretical propositions. The highest moral law is a conceptual truth. (See WL 12, 1: 164.) Examples of intuitive propositions are the proposition expressed by an utterance of the sentence 'This is flower' and the truth that Socrates was born in Athens. A full analysis of the latter truth will show that 'Socrates' and 'Athens' express mixed objective ideas.

5.4 THE THEORY OF THE A PRIORI: IMPROVING ON KANT

With these concepts in place we can return to Bolzano's criticism of Kant's conception of the a priori. Bolzano develops it in the appendix to WL § 133:

---

[10] For discussion see Textor 1996, ch. 6.

> I too take [the distinction between *a priori* and *a posteriori* judgement] to be sufficiently important to be retained forever. However, I believe that it ought not to replace another distinction that is not based on the mere relation of propositions to our knowledge faculty [*Erkenntnisvermögen*], but on their internal constitution, namely the distinction in propositions which are composed out of pure concepts and those that are not so composed; I even go as far as to claim that it is really only this distinction which one had in mind in making the other one without being clearly conscious of it. This goes to show that the fact whether a judgement is *a priori* or not is considered to be an *objective attribute* of the judgement itself and therefore it should be explained in an *objective way* that is independent of the mere relation of the judgement to our epistemic faculty. (WL 12, 1: 98; my emphasis)

He adds a revealing remark about Kant's criteria of a priority: strict universality, and necessity:

> Whether a proposition has strict universality or not, and whether one can say that the predicate which it ascribes to the subject, belongs to the latter necessarily or not, these are all facts that depend on the internal constitution [*innere Beschaffenheit*] of the proposition itself, and not on the accidental relation of the proposition to our epistemic faculty. (WL 12, 1: 98)

Why has Kant confused the epistemic distinction between a priori and a posteriori judgements and the non-epistemic compositional distinction between intuitive and conceptual propositions?

> [T]his distinction of our cognitions [*Erkenntnisse*] almost coincides with the distinction of propositions into conceptual and intuitive propositions in that the truth of most conceptual propositions can be decided by mere reflection without experience, while propositions which contain an intuition can only be known by experience [*nur aus Erfahrung*]. Because of this one took the essential difference between these propositions not to lie in the nature of their constituents, but rather in the way in which one can come to be convinced of their truth and falsity. Therefore one explained the first as ones which can be known without any experience and the latter as ones which are in need of experience and one introduced the corresponding terms: judgement *a priori* and *a posteriori*. (See the Introduction to Kant's *Critique of Pure Reason*). (WL 12, 1: 97–8)

To see Bolzano's point consider an example: Your judgement that 2 + 2 = 4 is justified by induction (whenever you have added two pairs their sum turned out to be 4); my judgement that 2 + 2 = 4 is justified by a proof. One can come to know that 2 + 2 = 4, the same truth, by relying on experience—perception and methods to acquire knowledge relevantly similar to perception—and without relying on experience. In contrast, one can *only* come to know that it is raining now by relying on experience. This suggests that some propositions can be the content of judgements a priori and a posteriori, while others can only be the contents of a posteriori judgements. Why is this so? Kant can't even formulate this question. Bolzano can and did. According to him, the fact that a proposition can be known in a particular way depends in part on its composition.[11]

Now things get tricky. Bolzano straightforwardly asserted:

(B1) That p is an intuitive proposition if, and only if, whether p or not-p can *only* be known a posteriori.

But he did not go on to say:

That p is a conceptual proposition if, and only if, whether p or not-p can be known a priori.

Bolzano takes the left-to-right conditional to be false (Bolzano 1833–41, 53). For example, some conceptual truths about primes are only known by mathematical induction. Mathematical induction is according to Bolzano a kind of experience (1833–41, 53). Hence, there are conceptual truths only known a posteriori. Why is mathematical induction a kind of experience? What perceptual and 'mathematical' experience seem to have in common is that we make educated guesses on the basis of our knowledge of particular cases. Bolzano therefore endorses only the weaker claim:

If that p is a conceptual proposition, whether p or not-p can be known *a priori in most cases.*

Now Bolzano's counterexample is not convincing: even if we don't know such truths a priori, they can still be know*able* a priori. Later in *Wissenschaftslehre* Bolzano formulated the connection between conceptual truth and knowability in terms of a deontic modality:

(B2) That p is a conceptual proposition if, and only if, whether p or whether not-p *ought* to be established without recourse to experience. (WL 12, 2: 202)

Take the conceptual proposition that p which we accept so far on the basis of mathematical induction. As we will see, Bolzano claims that if this proposition has grounds at all, these are conceptual truths. So if one aims to establish it 'according to its nature' one *ought* to try to establish it on the basis of these grounds. If it turns out that we can't so establish it, the blame is on us. Our cognitive faculties are too feeble to track every grounding relation.

In this section we have seen that Bolzano gives explanatory priority to propositions. This order of explanation is also reflected in his explanation of the central modal con-

---

[11] See also Dummett 1991, 28–9.

cepts of necessary existence and necessary predication. Bolzano says for example about necessary predication:

> Whenever a proposition 'A has b' is a purely conceptual truth, it is customary to say that the property b belongs necessarily to object A regardless of whether or not this object, and hence that property, is real. Thus we say that every equation of odd degree necessarily has a real root, although neither equations nor their roots are something that is real. (WL 12, 2: 57)

Bolzano arrives at the following objective explanation of necessary predication:

(B3)   If that p is a conceptual truth and that p is the combination [A has b], b belongs necessarily to A.

(B4)   If that p is an intuitive truth and that p is the combination [A has b], b belongs contingently to A.

I will focus on (B1) and (B2) now. They leave an explanatory gap. For one can with good reason raise the questions 'And why can most conceptual propositions be known a priori, while no intuitive propositions can? Why ought one to establish conceptual propositions without recourse to experience, why ought one to establish intuitive propositions with the help of experience?' Saying that conceptual propositions contain only concepts may be a starting point for an answer, but it is not the whole answer. In the next sections I will complete Bolzano's answer.

5.5 Grounded Conceptual and Intuitive Propositions Differ in Their Grounds

Already in 1810 Bolzano argued that a priori and a posteriori judgements have different grounds:

> The law of sufficient reason [*der Satz vom Grunde*] makes me search for a particular ground for each of my judgements. *The grounds of empirical judgements are completely different from the grounds of a priori judgements.* It is distinctive of the former or so-called *judgements of reality*, that I search for their ground always in what is— (in something real, in things); namely, depending on the circumstances, in part in what I call "the special nature of my perceptual ability", in part in particular "objects distinct from myself, that is outer objects that (as one says) impinge on my perceptual ability." — This is different when it comes to judgements a priori. Here I cannot look for the ground for which I ascribe the predicate to the subject anywhere else than in the subject itself (and in the distinct properties of the predicate). (Bolzano 1810, 142–3; my emphasis)

'Subject' and 'predicate' are here short for 'subject idea' and 'predicate idea'.

In his mature philosophy the concept of a ground is used to answer the question left open by (B1) and (B2):

> The most distinguished reason why I take the distinction between conceptual and intuitive propositions in the way it is made here to be of such importance is the following one. If one puts forth truths in a scientific treatise, truths that are merely composed out of concepts and truths which contain intuitions have to be treated completely differently, especially if one does not only ask for a truth to be made certain, but for the specification of its objective grounds. *We can find the ground of a pure conceptual truth always only in other conceptual truths; the ground of an intuitive truth can at least in part lie in the objects represented by the contained intuitions.* (WL 12, 1: 95; my emphasis)

Bolzano's objective conception of the a priori/a posteriori distinction can now be spelled out further as follows:

(B1*)   If that p is a conceptual proposition and *it has grounds at all*, its grounds are other conceptual truths. Therefore whether p or not-p ought to be established a priori.

(B2*)   If that p is an intuitive proposition and *it has grounds at all*, that contains the intuition [i], its grounds lie in part in the object represented by [i]. Therefore, whether p or not-p ought not to be established a priori.

The rider 'if the proposition has grounds at all' is necessary because some propositions have no grounds; they are *basic truths (Grundwahrheiten)*. Basic truth is not an epistemic notion. A truth may be self-evident and yet be grounded in another truth. For example, one may need no epistemic reason to be justified in believing that either 1 is prime or 1 is not prime. But this self-evident disjunction has a ground. 1 is prime or 1 is not prime *because* 1 is not prime. Bolzano therefore quotes Leibniz with approval when he says:

> It is one of my main maxims that it is good to look for the demonstrations even of axioms themselves. (Leibniz 1765, I §24; quoted by Bolzano 1833–44, 72)

A good example of a basic truth is the law of identity. Why is everything identical with itself? There is no explanatory answer to this question. I will come back to basic truth in due course.

(B1*) and (B2*) are progress over (B1) and (B2) because, intuitively, if one knows that p and that p is ground of that q, one can come to know that q. But (B1*) and (B2*) still need further work. So let us first have a closer look at the notion of a ground.[12]

---

[12] Tatzel 2002 gives an overview of Bolzano's theory of grounding. Grounding is reintroduced into the current philosophical discussion in for example Fine 2001, § 5. On the connections between Bolzano and Fine see Batchelor 2010.

We sometimes say that something is so-and-so *in virtue of* something else or that something exists *because* something else exists. Bolzano will use the notion of ground to systematize what we are trying to get at in such cases. Consider some examples:

(1.1) It is true that blood is red because blood is red.

(1.2) Blood is red because it is true that blood is red.

(2.1) The (functioning) thermometer shows 32 degrees because it is 32 degrees outside.

(2.2) It is 32 degrees outside because the (functioning) thermometer shows 32 degrees

We have strong intuitions about these sentence-pairs in each of which 'because' connects assertoric sentences. The first sentences of these pairs strike us as saying something true, the second as something false. Bolzano takes the 'because' in these sentence pairs to be univocal. It expresses one and the same concept. This idea makes it implausible to reduce the relation under consideration to other already understood relations. For example, our intuition that (2.1) is true while (2.2) is false is due to the fact that (2.1) gets the direction of causation right. This observation suggests that one should explain the concept under consideration via causation. Bolzano considers therefore the following explanation:

> The truth: God is, could be taken to be the ground of the truth: a world is, because God's existence is the cause, and the existence of the world the effect. (WL 12, 1: 166)

But this proposal is too narrow. The 'because' in (1.1) and (1.2) cannot be the 'because' of causal production. Bolzano goes on to turn the direction of explanation around:

> *A* causes *B* iff the truth that *A* is real is the ground or a ground of the truth that *B* is real. (WL 12, 2: 34)

In section 5.8 I will come back to the connection between grounding and causation.

Sometimes we use 'because' to express the logical connection between premises and conclusions. The conclusion is true *because* the premises are true. But just as 'because' cannot be a shorthand for the 'because' of causation, it cannot be short for this logical 'because'. Bolzano calls the relation between the premises of a good deductive argument and its conclusion deducibility (*Ableitbarkeit*). Roughly, Q is deducible from P if, and only if, the truth of P determines the truth of Q. Aristotle and others spelled out 'determines' modally: if the proposition P is true, the proposition Q *must* be true. Bolzano spells out determination in terms of variation:

> I say the propositions M, N, O…are deducible from the propositions A, B, C, D, with respect to the variable parts i, j,…[if and only if] every collection of ideas whose substitution for i, j, makes all of A, B, C, D, true, also makes all of M, N, O,…true. (WL 12, 1: 170)

Bolzano's deducibility is different from what is now called 'logical consequence'. However, Bolzano hints at a restricted notion of deducibility according to which all logical ideas are taken to be invariable. (See Bolzano 1833–44, 55. For discussion see Burke and Rusnock 2010, 18.) I will come back to the notion of deducibility in section 5.9. Now the truth *that blood is red* is deducible from the truth *that it is true that blood is red* and *vice versa* with respect to all non-logical ideas. But only the former is a ground for the latter (WL 12, 2: 174).[13] Hence, the grounding relation cannot be the relation of deducibility between true propositions.

The grounding relation is not, then, a particular species of deducibility or causation. It is rather linked to explanation. The ground of the truth that p is specified in a true answer to the question 'Why p?' Such an explanation of why p is sometimes causal, but often it is not. If I answer the question 'Why does 2 + 3 equal 3 + 2?' by asserting 'Because for all x and y: if x and y are natural numbers, $x + y = y + x$', I have given an explanation, but not a causal one. The broad sense of explanation operative here can be characterized by saying that in an explanation one subsumes a special case under laws. One makes the particular case intelligible by seeing it as an instance of a generality, either an empirical 'law' or a law like the law of commutativity.

Appealing to the notion of explanation helps us to understand distinctive features of grounding. I have only explained something if I have specified a *truth* which, broadly speaking, sheds light on it. Bolzano takes it therefore to be a basic principle that only truths can be grounds. He goes further and holds that only truths have grounds (WL 12, 2: 169–72). This makes it problematic that Bolzano says that intuitive truths are partially grounded in real objects. I will come back to this problem in section 5.8.

Our grasp of the grounding relation is manifest in the demand for an axiomatic system in science. Ideally, we organize scientific knowledge by providing a kernel of general truths that contain the basic concepts of the science. All other truths of the science can be deduced from this kernel. This suggests to Bolzano that the grounding relation is the ordering of truths such that the greatest number of complex truths can be deduced from the smallest number of simple truths (WL 12, 2: 202–3).

5.6 How the Constituents of a Proposition Determine its Grounds

Let us now expand (B1*) and (B2*) further. The pressing question is *Why should one believe that the grounds of a conceptual truth, if it has any, can only be other conceptual truths?* Bolzano outlines his explanatory strategy as follows:

> If [a] proposition [...] consists merely of *concepts*, as for example the proposition
> that virtue deserves respect, or that the sum of any two sides of a triangle is longer

---

[13] On this topic see Tatzel 2002, 7–9.

than the third, etc., then its truth or falsity will merely depend upon the properties of these concepts; and consequently, at least in many cases, nothing else is required to convince oneself of its truth than that one closely attends to the concepts the truth is composed of. Therefore you can come to know the truth that virtue deserves respect because you possess the concepts of virtue, being deserving and respect. One could not say that you possess a particular concept, if you would not distinguish it from another, that is, if you would not know that certain other concepts can be combined with it to a form a true sentence while they cannot be combined with another concept. Hence, one recognizes truths of this kind (pure conceptual truths) in virtue of knowing [*kennen*] the concepts they are composed of. It is different with judgements that contain intuitions of objects existing outside of your representation. These are either of the following kind: *this (what I see now) is red*, where the subject idea is a simple intuition and the predicate idea a concept (red); or they are of this kind: *the same object which causes in me intuition A is also the cause of the intuition B that I have.* [...] There is no possibility of error for judgements of the first kind such as the first one above; you form them immediately in virtue of the two ideas you have. However the truth of judgments of the second kind (I call them *empirical sentences* proper [*eigentliche Erfahrungssätze*]) does not merely depend upon your ideas. [...], but also upon the properties of the external objects which are represented by them. (WL 11, 1: 201–2)[14]

The passage just quoted is representative of Bolzano's general explanatory strategy that moves from (i) the composition of a proposition to (ii) its particular grounds to (iii) relations that the proposition potentially bears to our cognitive faculty.

Bolzano discussed the move from (i) to (ii) already in his *Beyträge*. There he asked 'How do we tell which propositions have grounds and can therefore be proved?' He started by arguing for the more specific thesis that every conceptual proposition that has a *complex* subject- or predicate-concept has grounds. Why?

> *Because it is obvious that the complex and its properties must depend on the properties of the simple things it is composed of.* If therefore a subject is a complex concept, its properties, that is, the predicates one can ascribe to it, must depend on the several concepts it is composed of, and their properties, that is, the judgements one can make about the simple concepts. (Bolzano 1810, 87; my emphasis)

Bolzano's starting point is:

(D)   The properties of a complex depend on the properties of its simple constituents.[15]

---

[14] This passage occurs in a dialogue between an anti-sceptic and a sceptic. The view outlined here is clearly Bolzano's own. Bolzano misleadingly suggests that intuitive judgements of the first kind have no ground. But this suggestion should be resisted. My judgement that this (what I see now) is red is true because what I see now is red.

[15] I take that Bolzano holds that 'properties of simple constituents' covers the relations between them, for example, their mode of combination.

What he says about this kind of dependence in the quote above strongly suggests that he explains dependence in terms of grounding:

(D-G)   The properties of a complex x depend on the properties of its simple constituents if, and only if, every truth that ascribes a property to x is grounded in truth ascribing properties to the simple parts of x.

Let Pc be a conceptual truth that has either a complex subject-concept or a complex predicate-concept. If we apply (D-G) to conceptual truth with complex subject- or predicate-concepts, we can infer:

(T-D)   The truth of Pc depends only on the properties of its constituent concepts if, and only if, the grounds of Pc are exhausted by truths that predicate properties of the concepts contained in Pc.

The truths that predicate properties of the concepts contained in Pc will be *conceptual* truths. (T-D) sets the agenda for much of Bolzano's work. In several of his writings he tries to give, as he puts it, objective groundings (*objective Begründungen*) of conceptual truths.

Bolzano has so far argued that conceptual truths with *complex* subject- or predicate-concepts are grounded in conceptual truths ascribing properties to their constituents. But what shall we say about conceptual truths whose subject- and predicate-concepts are simple? If Bolzano's argument is convincing, these truth have no grounds. Consequently, their truth cannot depend on the properties of their constituents.[16]

This consequence is a problem for Bolzano. To see this go back to Bolzano's examples of propositions whose truth only depends on the properties of their constituent concepts. I take it to be doubtful that the constituents of the proposition that virtue deserves respect are complex. Independently of the complexity of subject- and predicate-concept one still wants to say that the truth of this and other propositions like it only depends on properties of its constituents. Bolzano himself endorsed generally that the properties of a complex depend on the properties of its simple constituents (D-G). Now the proposition that virtue deserves respect is complex: it is a combination of objective concepts, whether these concepts are themselves complex or not. Hence, the truth of the proposition should depend on the properties of its constituents.

In response Bolzano should give up the explanation of dependence in terms of grounds. There are forms of dependence that do not consist in the obtaining of the grounding relation between truths. Bolzano himself takes philosophers to confuse the grounding relation with another one. (See WL 12, 2: 168.) For example, the Wolffian philosopher Ulrich explains that the ground of something x is the thing that *determines* (*bestimmt*) x. We have an intuitive idea of one thing determining another. For example, two numbers determine their sum: the numbers 'fix' which number is their sum.

---

[16]   This point is made in Rusnock 2012, 824ff. For a reply see Textor forthcoming.

Bolzano rejects Ulrich's explanation precisely because there are cases of determination that are not cases of grounding. Although more work needs to be done, this opens up the possibility of saying that the truth of a basic conceptual proposition depends on the properties of its constituent concepts in that truths ascribing these properties *determine* the truth of the proposition, without being its grounds.

5.7 FROM GROUNDS TO A PRIORI KNOWLEDGE

We have now seen how Bolzano moves from (i) the composition of a proposition to (ii) its grounds. How do we move from (ii) to a particular kind of knowability of the proposition? Take a conceptual truth Pc. If Pc has either a complex subject- or predicate-concept, its grounds are exhausted by truths attributing properties to its simple constituents. Hence, one should expect that one can come to know Pc if one knows its grounds and realizes that the grounding relation obtains. If Pc has a simple subject- and predicate-concept, its truth is only determined by truths about the simple concepts contained in it.

How does one come to know these truths about the simple concepts? Kant had asked: 'How can one be justified independently of experience to judge that A is b if [b] is not a constituent of [A]?' Bolzano replied:

> Nothing else is required than that the mind possesses and knows the concepts A and B. In order to merely possess some concepts, I hold, we need to be able to make judgements about them. Because saying that someone has certain concepts A, B, C,...means that he knows and distinguishes them. Saying that he knows and distinguishes them, in turn, only means that he asserts something of one of them which he would not assert of the other. And that means that he makes judgements about them. Since this holds generally, it holds for the special case of simple concepts. (WL 13, 1: 186)

Bolzano's assumption that possessing a concept C requires the ability to make judgements about C of the form 'The concept C is thus and so' is controversial. Many thinkers who intuitively seem to possess a concept will either not be able or not be disposed to make such judgements. Even if Bolzano could defend his view of concept possession, the pressing question remains whether one's knowledge of those truths that one knows merely by possessing the concepts that compose a conceptual truth Pc suffices to come to know Pc. To my knowledge Bolzano does not try to give an argument that this is so. He just tries to convince us on a case by case basis. In his work on the philosophy of mathematics and geometry, for instance, he tries to give proofs that only use conceptual truths that are the result of the analysis of the concepts that compose the truths to be proved.

As a by-product this consideration helps us to understand which properties of concepts Bolzano has in mind. There are a number of properties of concepts we can truly predicate of concepts *simply because we possess the relevant concepts*. For example, we know that the concept [bachelor] is nothing but the conjunction of [being male] and [unmarried] in virtue of grasping the concept. These and similar properties will be predicated in the truths that ground conceptual truths.

We can now sum up Bolzano's objective view of what he calls 'objective *a priori*' as follows:

1. Composition → Dependence: If that p is a conceptual proposition, its truth depends only on the properties of its constituent concepts.
2. Dependence → Grounding: If this dependence is a form of grounding, the grounds of that p are exhausted by conceptual truths that predicate properties of the concepts contained in it. If the dependence is a form of determination, that p has no grounds but its truth is determined by truths about its constituents.
   In either case, the truth of a conceptual proposition ought to be recognized by inferring it from the truths that either ground it or determine its truths.
3. Dependence/Grounding → Knowledge: The simple conceptual truths that ground or determine the truth of other conceptual truths can be recognized by reflecting on them.

5.8 WHY ARE INTUITIVE PROPOSITIONS ONLY KNOWABLE A POSTERIORI?

We have shown how Bolzano argues for the thesis that conceptual propositions should be established a priori. Now we need to complete the account by showing why intuitive propositions can only be recognized a posteriori.

Bolzano obviously assumes that if a proposition contains intuitions its truth does not depend *only* on properties of its constituents. However, if, in general, the properties of a complex depend on the properties of its simple constituents, the truth of every proposition, *whether conceptual or intuitive*, must depend on properties of its simple constituents. This consequence undermines Bolzano's explanatory strategy, but it follows directly from his assumptions. How can Bolzano prevent his assumptions from implying that *every* proposition is true in virtue of the properties of its constituents?

We have seen in section 5.7 that Bolzano argued that concept-possession requires knowledge of truths about the concept one possesses. Possessing the concept C is knowing truths about it. Hence, one cannot possess a concept without being aware of certain of its properties. These truths are available as grounds for the conceptual propositions that contain the concept C.

Subjective intuitions are different. One can have an intuition of an object without being in reflection inclined to make judgements about it. All that is required to have an intuition of *x* is the possession of a causal mechanism that is suitably triggered by *x*: one's 'cognitive architecture' must allow mental events to cause immediately simple ideas. (See WL 13, 1: 149.) There are therefore no truths ascribing properties to an intuition that one knows because one has the intuition. Positively, Bolzano claimed 'the ground of an intuitive truth can at least in part lie in the objects represented by the contained intuitions' (WL 12, 1: 95). Given that Bolzano has argued that only truths can be grounds this and similar passages cry out for an explanation.

The key to the explanation is the connection between causation and grounding in Bolzano's work. According to Bolzano, the basic intuitive judgements register the occurrence of a mental event. For example, when I judge that I experience this (feeling), my subjective intuition is immediately caused by the object represented by it. This object is therefore a partial cause of the judgement. Now Bolzano brings the connection between causation and grounding to bear. (See, for example, Bolzano WL 12, 2: 192–3.) If an event E is a *partial cause* of the judgement that I experience this, the truth that E occurred is a *partial ground* of the intuitive truth that I experienced this. Hence, every intuitive truth is partially grounded in a truth about a real object. This is, I think, what Bolzano has in mind when he misleadingly says that intuitive truths are grounded in real objects. (See section 5.5.) By contrast, no conceptual truth has its partial ground in a truth ascribing existence to an external object. A judgement that apprehends a basic conceptual truth containing [A] and [b] is often stimulated by perceiving instances of the concepts [A] and [b], but truths concerning these instances are not the grounds of the conceptual truth. (See WL 13, 1: 150.) My judgement that gratitude is a duty may be initiated by seeing and appreciating that you are grateful. But the fact that you are grateful is not a partial ground of the truth that gratitude is a duty.

5.9 INTUITIVE PROPOSITIONS AND THE DISCOVERY OF THE VARIATION METHOD

The distinction between intuitive and conceptual propositions serves to underwrite Bolzano's critique of Kant. Propositions and grounds are more fundamental than judgements and epistemic reasons. Reflection on properties of intuitive propositions leads also to one of Bolzano's main philosophical innovations: his method of variation.

Bolzano holds that every proposition is true or false, and that no proposition is neither or both:

> It is undeniable that every given proposition is only one of both [true or false] and this constantly, either true and then this then forever, or false and this then again forever (§ 125); *unless we change something in the proposition and therefore no longer consider the original proposition itself, but another proposition in its place. We do the latter often without being distinctly aware of it.* (WL 12, 1: 135; my emphasis)

Take Bolzano's example for illustration. I utter 'This smells pleasant' in the morning smelling a rose; in the evening I utter the same sentence, this time smelling a stapelia. My first utterance says something true, my second something false. Has the *same* proposition changed from truth to falsity? No, a proposition is true or false; not true or false at a time. He concludes that the two utterances express *different* propositions. However, these propositions share the predicate-idea and the copula; they differ in the intuitions, which are their subject-ideas:

[This$_1$ smells pleasant]

[This$_2$ smells pleasant]

[This$_3$ smells pleasant]

If one takes an intuitive proposition to be a member of such a group of similar propositions, one can describe the group as 'generated' from one member by holding a propositional fragment fixed, while varying other parts. Bolzano proposed that we systematically impose this description on propositions:[17]

> But if we, as these examples show, often take certain ideas in a proposition to be variable without being distinctly conscious of it, and then observe the behaviour of the proposition with respect to truth by filling in the place of the variable parts with any other ideas: it will be worth our while to do this in a distinct consciousness and with the determinate intention to improve our knowledge of the nature of certain propositions by observing this behaviour with respect to truth. If we not only observe whether a given proposition is true or false, but also which behaviour with respect to truth all those propositions exhibit that result from it if we take certain ideas contained in it to be variable and allow ourselves to replace these with any other ideas; this will lead us to the discovery of many notable properties of propositions. (WL 12, 1: 136)

This passage can be read epistemically: intentionally varying constituents in a proposition P is *a method of acquiring knowledge about the nature of P*. Bolzano is frequently read differently: many properties of a proposition P are ones *that consist in relations to other propositions that are generated from P by varying constituents*. Here are some examples of such properties and relations:

1. Logical Form: take the proposition [Socrates has Wisdom] and consider [Socrates] and [Wisdom] to be variable ideas. The class of all propositions that can be generated from varying these ideas in [Socrates has Wisdom] is a logical form. (See WL 11, 1: 78–9.) It will contain such propositions as:

   [Cajus has Mortality]

   [Helena has Beauty]

---

[17] See Proust 1989, 71 and Textor 1996, 144.

but not

[It is raining]

The same proposition can belong to different logical forms. A logical form is the class of propositions that can be generated by varying certain ideas in a proposition. In a derived sense 'logical form' is applied to a schematic expression like 'A has b' which can be used to describe the members of a species of propositions (WL 11, 2: 197).

2. Analytic versus synthetic propositions: there are propositions that contain at least one idea *i* such that every variation of *i* with arbitrarily chosen objectual ideas yields a proposition with the same truth-value as the original one. Bolzano calls such propositions *analytic* (WL 12, 1: 140). A proposition that is not analytic is *synthetic*. A proposition all of whose non-logical ideas can be changed without change in truth-value is called *logically analytic* (WL 12, 1: 141).[18]

3. Deducibility (*Ableitbarkeit*): If we vary ideas in a group of propositions, we can define the notion of deducibility as outlined in section 5.5.[19]

5.10 BOLZANO'S (NON-) INFLUENCE AND IMPORTANCE

Bolzano's work had considerable direct impact on several of Brentano's students. For instance, Brentano's Polish student Kazimierz Twardowski's *Zur Lehre vom Inhalt und Gegenstand der Vorstellungen* (1894) discusses Bolzano's distinction between the content and object of an idea. Bolzano also inspired Brentano's student Husserl to accept propositions into his ontology.[20] Another Brentano student, Benno Kerry, discusses in a series of papers (Kerry 1885ff.) Bolzano and Frege.[21]

However, Bolzano had little direct influence on the development of analytic philosophy. The topic of this chapter, the a priori/a posteriori distinction, is a good example. Russell (1912, 49) criticizes Kant's view of the a priori as, roughly speaking, too subjective. Russell's constructive proposal that propositions that contain only universals can be known a priori is very similar in spirit to Bolzano's. (See Russell 1912, 59.) But Russell does not engage at all with Bolzano's view.[22] The same goes for Frege's definition of the a priori/a posteriori distinction. Like Bolzano, Frege connects the notion of a priority to grounds of truth, and not epistemic reasons. According to Frege, a truth is a priori if, and

---

[18] For an overview of the development of this conception see Künne 2006.

[19] On Bolzano's notion of deducibility see Siebel 2002, sections II and III.

[20] Husserl discusses the influence of Bolzano on his own work in Husserl 1903, 152ff. Husserl's propositions are kinds of mental acts and differ from Bolzano's. See Husserl 1903, 156–7. For discussion see Textor 1996, 16–24.

[21] See Künne 2008, 326–30. Künne 1997b gives an overview of Bolzano's reception between 1848 and 1939.

[22] Russell knows Bolzano's work on the infinite and discusses it in his 1903, § 71 and § 285.

only if, no unprovable particular truth is among its grounds (Frege 1884, 4). Bolzano is neither discussed nor mentioned by Frege.[23]

Some of Bolzano's philosophical arguments and theories have been rediscovered by philosophers in the analytic tradition. The most discussed examples are Tarski's definition of logical consequence and Quine's definition of logical truth.[24] There are analogies between Bolzano's definition of deducibility and one of Tarski's proposals to define logical consequence in Tarski 1936.[25] Tarski (1936, 414 note) remarks that Bolzano's definition was only later brought to his attention. Quine defined a logical truth as a true sentence that contains only logical words *essentially*, that is, whose non-logical words can be *varied* without changing the truth-value (Quine 1936, 80–1). In a later paper Quine himself comments that 'substantially this formulation is traced back a century and a quarter, by Bar-Hillel, to Bolzano' (Quine 1954, 110).

These rediscoveries of Bolzano's ideas have led to a new interest in the rediscovered theories. For example, the idea of defining logical notions via the variation method now receives more attention. Kneale (1961) and Etchemendy (1990) have argued that Bolzano's explication leaves out the modal element of the consequence-relation: to say that every variation of [John] in [John dances and John sings] that makes it true, makes also [John sings] true, is weaker than saying that the [John sings] *must* be true if [John dances and John sings] is true.[26] Such arguments put pressure on the constitutive reading of Bolzano's remarks about variation. On this reading of Bolzano he argued that important logical properties have a relational nature. Consider, for instance, logical analyticity. The fact that a proposition *p* is logically analytic is nothing but the fact that every proposition that shares *p*'s logical ideas and their arrangement also shares its truth-value. But, intuitively, no change of non-logical ideas in *p* can generate a proposition with a different truth-value *because p* contains certain logical ideas combined in a certain way. Should one then not identify logical analyticity with this more fundamental property and take the variation method to be merely a method of discovery? Thinking about Bolzano's ideas makes us aware of this question and will, one hope, help us to answer it.[27]

REFERENCES

Batchelor, R. (2010). 'Grounds and Consequences', *Grazer Philosophische Studien* 80: 65–77.

Bolzano, B. (1810). *Beyträge zu einer begründeteren Darstellung der Mathematik*. Prague: Caspar Widtmann. Tr. S. Russ as 'A Better Grounded Presentation of Mathematics', in S. Russ (ed.), *The Mathematical Works of Bernard Bolzano*. Oxford: Oxford University Press, 2004, pp. 83–139.

[23] The question whether Frege, although he never mentions Bolzano, had read Bolzano's work has received recently some attention; see Sundholm 1999 and Künne 1997b, 330–45.

[24] For discussion of this, see the chapters by Reck and Shieh in the present volume.

[25] Siebel 2002, 594f. points out differences between Tarski and Bolzano.

[26] See Burke and Rusnock 2010 for a defence of Bolzano against this objection.

[27] I am grateful to Michael Beaney, John Callanan, and Wolfgang Künne for advice, comments, and criticism.

—— (1832–48). 'Zusätze und Verbesserungen zur Logik'. In *Vermischte philosophische und physikalische Schriften 1832–48 II*, ed. Jan Berg. Series 2A. Stuttgart-Bad Cannstatt: Frommann-Holzboog, 1978, vol. 12.2, pp. 53–184.

—— (1833–44). *Von der Mathematischen Lehrart*. Stuttgart-Bad Cannstatt: Frommann-Holzboog 1981. Tr. R. George and P. Rusnock as 'On the Mathematical Method', in *On the Mathematical Method and Correspondence with Exner*. Amsterdam and New York: Rodopi, 2004, pp. 39–83.

—— (1836). 'Zur Lebensbeschreibung'. In *Vermischte Philosophische und Physikalische Schriften 1832–1848 I*, ed. J. Berg. Bolzano Gesamtausgabe Series 2A. Stuttgart-Bad Cannstatt: Frommann-Holzboog, 1977, vol. 12.1, pp. 65–9.

—— (1837) *Wissenschaftslehre* [WL]. 4 vols. Sulzbach: Seidel. New edition ed. J. Berg, in *Bernard Bolzano Gesamtausgabe*, Series I, vols. 11.1–14.3. Stuttgart-Bad Cannstatt: Frommann-Holzboog, 1985–99.

—— (1839). *Dr. Bolzano und seine Gegner: Ein Beitrag zur neueren Literaturgeschichte*, ed. J. Louzil and E. Winter. In *Vermischte Schriften 1839–1840 I. Gesamtausgabe*, Series I. Stuttgart-Bad Cannstatt: Frommann-Holzboog 1989, vol. 16.1, pp. 7–155.

—— (1841). *Bolzanos Wissenschaftslehre und Religionswissenschaft in einer beurtheilenden Uebersicht*. Sulzbach: Seidelsche Buchhandlung.

Burke, M. and P. Rusnock (2010). 'Etchemendy and Bolzano on Logical Consequence', *History and Philosophy of Logic* 31: 3–29.

Dummett, M. (1991). *Frege: Philosophy of Mathematics*. London: Duckworth.

Etchemendy, J. (1990). *The Concept of Logical Consequence*. Cambridge, MA: Harvard University Press.

Fine, K. (2001). 'The Question of Realism', *Philosophers' Imprint* 1: 1–30.

Frege, G. (1884). *Die Grundlagen der Arithmetik*. Breslau: W. Koebner. Tr. J. L. Austin as *The Foundations of Arithmetic*. Oxford: Blackwell, 1950.

—— (1980). *Philosophical and Mathematical Correspondence* [PMC], ed. G. Gabriel *et al.*, abr. B. McGuiness, tr. H. Kaal. Oxford: Blackwell.

Husserl, E. (1903). Besprechung von: M. Palágyi, *Der Streit der Psychologisten und Formalisten in der modernen Logik*, Leipzig 1902. In Husserl, *Aufsätze und Rezension 1890–1910. Husserliana* 22. The Hague: Martinus Nijhoff, 1979, pp. 152–62.

Kant, I. (1781/87). *Kritik der reinen Vernunft, Gesammelte Schriften*. English tr. N. Kemp Smith. Basingstoke and New York: Palgrave Macmillan, 2007.

Kerry, B. (1885ff.). 'Über Anschauungen und ihre psychische Verarbeitung (I–VIII)', *Vierteljahrezeitschrift für wissenschaftliche Philosophie*, I: 9 (1885), 433–93; II: 10 (1886), 419–67; III: 11 (1887), 53–116; IV: 11 (1887), 249–307; V: 13 (1889), 71–124; VI: 13 (1889), 392–414; VII: 14 (1890), 317–53; VIII: 15 (1891), 126–67.

Kneale, W. (1961). 'Universality and Necessity', *The British Journal for the Philosophy of Science* 12: 89–102.

Künne, W. (1997a). 'Propositions in Bolzano and Frege', *Grazer Philosophische Studien* 53: 203–40. Reprinted in Künne (2008), pp. 157–95.

—— (1997b). '"Die Ernte wird erscheinen…" Die Geschichte der Bolzano-Rezeption (1839–1939)'. Expanded and corrected version in Künne (2008), pp. 305–405.

—— (2003). *Conceptions of Truth*. Oxford: Oxford University Press.

—— (2006). 'Analyticity and Logical Truth: From Bolzano to Quine'. In M. Textor (ed.), *The Austrian Contribution to Analytic Philosophy*. London: Routledge. Reprinted with changes in Künne (2008), pp. 233–303.

—— (2008). *Versuche über Bolzano/Essays on Bolzano*. St. Augustin: Academia Verlag.

Leibniz, G. W. F (1765). *Nouveaux Essais Sur L'Entendement Humain*. In French and German. Frankfurt am Main: Suhrkamp Verlag, 1992.

Mugnai M. (1992) 'Leibniz and Bolzano on the "Realm of Truths"'. In *Bolzano's Wissenschaftslehre 1837-1987. International Workshop*. Firenze: Leo S. Olschki 1992, pp. 207–20.

Příhonský, F. (1850). *Neuer Anti-Kant oder Prüfung der Kritik der reinen Vernunft nach den in Bolzano's Wissenschaftslehre niedergelegten Begriffen*. A. Weller: Bautzen.

Proust, J. (1989). *Questions of Form: Logic and Analytic Propositions from Kant to Carnap*. Minneapolis: University of Minnesota Press.

Quine, W. V. O. (1936). 'Truth by Convention'. In O. H. Lee (ed.), *Philosophical Essays for A. N. Whitehead*. New York: Longmans. Reprinted in Quine, *The Ways of Paradox and other Essays*. Cambridge, MA: Harvard University Press 1976, pp. 70–106.

—— (1954). 'Carnap on Logical Truth'. In P. A. Schilpp (ed.), *The Philosophy of Rudolf Carnap*. La Salle, Illinois: Open Court, 1963, pp. 385–406. Reprinted in Quine, *The Ways of Paradox and other Essays*. Cambridge, MA: Harvard University Press 1976, pp. 107–32.

Rusnock, P. (2012). 'Remarks on Bolzano's Conception of Necessary Truth', *British Journal for the History of Philosophy* 20 (2012): 817–37.

Russell, B. (1903). *The Principles of Mathematics*. Cambridge: Cambridge University Press. 2nd edn. 1937. Repr. London: Routledge, 1992.

—— (1912). *Problems of Philosophy*. London: Home University Library. Repr. Oxford: Oxford University Press, 1967.

Siebel, M. (2002). 'Bolzano's Concept of Consequence', *The Monist* 85: 580–99.

Simons, P. (1999). 'Bolzano Über Wahrheit'. In E. Morscher (ed.), *Bolzanos Geistiges Erbe für das 21. Jahrhundert*. St. Augustin: Academia Verlag, pp. 13–28.

Smit, H. (2000). 'Kant on Marks and the Immediacy of Intuition', *The Philosophical Review* 109: 235–66.

Sundholm, G. (1999). 'When, and Why, did Frege read Bolzano?' *The Logica Yearbook 1999*. Praga: Filosofia Publishers, pp. 164–74.

Tarski, A. (1936). 'The Concept of Logical Consequence'. Reprinted in Tarski, *Logic, Semantics, Metamathematics: Papers 1923-38*, ed. J. Corcoran, tr. J. Woodger. Indianapolis: Hackett Publishing, pp. 409–20.

Tatzel, A. (2002). 'Bolzano's Theory of Ground and Consequence', *Notre Dame Journal of Formal Logic* 43: 1–25.

Textor, M. (1996). *Bolzanos Propositionalismus*. Berlin and New York: Walter de Gruyter. Repr. 2010.

—— (Forthcoming). 'Bolzano on the Source of Necessity: A Reply to Rusnock', *British Journal for the History of Philosophy*.

Twardowski, K. (1894). *Zur Lehre vom Inhalt und Gegenstand der Vorstellungen—Eine psychologische Untersuchung*. Vienna: Alfred Hölder. Tr. R. Grossmann as *On the Content and Object of Presentations: A Psychological Investigation*. The Hague: Martinus Nijhoff, 1977.

CHAPTER 6

TIME, NORMS, AND STRUCTURE IN NINETEENTH-CENTURY PHILOSOPHY OF SCIENCE

DAVID HYDER

Und mit starren Fingern
dreht er, was er kann.

–Wilhelm Müller[1]

INTRODUCTION

Analytic philosophy is generally described as an Anglo-American movement, even though, with the exception of Russell, Moore, and Ramsey, most of the early figures were from Germany or Austria. Furthermore, the problems these philosophers dealt with did not emerge from the head of Zeus. They were the product of a long development over the nineteenth century. Finally, since early analytic philosophy is essentially philosophy of science and mathematics, that development took place only partially within philosophy departments. Many of the early analyticians' heroes were working scientists such as Helmholtz, Heinrich Hertz, Poincaré, and Einstein. What we know about these figures is usually filtered through the interpretations of their work given by their philosophical successors, for instance the Paul Hertz/Moritz Schlick edition of Helmholtz's epistemological writings (Helmholtz 1921, 1977).

---

[1] In memory of Catherine Liepins née Veiland, Kiev 1899–Toronto 1994 and Herbert Edward Liepins, Riga 1898–Toronto 1994.

But these interpretations are highly coloured, and it is fair to say that historians of philosophy have followed a pattern, beginning with Russell himself, of skipping the nineteenth century. Kant is seen as the last philosopher of note, and from him one jumps straight to Frege, perhaps with a glance at Helmholtz and Poincaré along the way. Doctrines from the late nineteenth century are often retrojected onto Kant, with the result that this century cannot happen, since all essential moves were made before it began. This chapter is an attempt to counter this long-standing approach, so that we may better appreciate the problems that actually confronted turn-of-the-century think-ers such as Frege, Russell, Wittgenstein, Reichenbach, and Carnap. The goal is therefore to restore our depth of field.

I will focus on the antecedents to a variety of approaches typical of twentieth- and twenty-first-century analytic philosophy, such as *formal logic, logical empiricism, conventionalism*, and the *semantic view*, as well as theories that invoke notions of *normativity*. All of these respond to Kant's philosophy of science; however, it is not my goal to show how they are present *in nuce* in Kant. On the contrary, I will argue they are all solutions to problems posed by his philosophy, problems which he caused as opposed to solving.

The paper has four main sections, devoted to Kant, Helmholtz, Hertz, and early analytic philosophy. I track the evolution of two 'deductive' strategies, one based on the structure of manifolds of representation, one which appeals to regulative conditions on objective experience. The two strategies are connected through a single prin-ciple of natural science, namely the law of inertia, which connects uniform rectilinear motion to force. *Every body perseveres in its state of rest, or of uniform motion in a right line, unless it is compelled to change that state by forces impressed thereon.* Different parts of the law correspond to different elements of Kant's *Critique*. The materials for the definition of uniform motion in a right line are given in the Transcendental Aesthetic (TA), whereas the dynamic element derives from the category of causality, whose applicability to experience must be given a different sort of justification. All the scientists and philosophers I discuss in this chapter were concerned with the status of this law, which they generally took to follow from the principle of sufficient reason. I should warn at the outset that, should one take the law to be a *definition*, one is stand-ing at the terminus of the movement I am describing, and not at the point of departure (on the evolving epistemological status of the law, see Hanson 1963 and, above all, DiSalle 2006).

Because this is history of long duration, ranging from works of Euler in the mid-eighteenth century to retrospective assessments by Einstein at the beginning of the twentieth, I cannot offer detailed systematic and textual support for all the connec-tions I draw. Thus I must ask for the reader's forbearance in cases where my treatment is too schematic. I have tried, whenever possible, to provide references to sources which provide some of the missing details. The scope necessarily means neglecting certain authors, most obviously Mach, Boltzmann, Poincaré, Frege, and Russell, but such omis-sions do not mean that I believe their work to be unimportant, merely that I lacked the space and time to deal with it here.

6.1 KANT

6.1.1 The Structural and Normative Deductions

Kant had two distinct approaches to the problem of demonstrating the validity of foundational principles in the sciences, for the *Critique of Pure Reason* contains *two* transcendental deductions, one for the pure concepts of the understanding (the categories), and one for those of space and time.[2] When we speak of the Transcendental Deductions, we typically mean the A- and B-versions of the deduction of the categories, but in its introductory sections Kant remarks that the need for a deduction is already familiar to his reader, for 'we have above traced the concepts of space and time back to their sources, as well as determining and explaining their objective validity *a priori*, by means of a transcendental deduction' (B119–20). I call this other transcendental deduction the Spatio-temporal Deduction (SD), in order to avoid any confusion with the Transcendental Deduction(s) (TDs) in the standard sense just explained. The Spatio-temporal Deduction has the same purpose as the Transcendental Deduction proper, but it achieves its goal by grounding a priori cognitions in structure, and is thus in a sense superior to the latter. In particular, it can satisfactorily answer the following question, whereas the Transcendental Deduction itself cannot: What guarantee have we that the a priori principles derived from the concepts being transcendentally deduced will be valid under all circumstances, that is to say at all places and times?[3]

This suggestion would seem to be confirmed by Kant's amplification that metaphysical concepts, such as substance and cause, pose a special problem when compared to the concepts of space and time. A transcendental deduction is supposed to explain how concepts can relate to objects a priori (B117), and here there is a dichotomy between 'mathematical' and 'regulative' concepts, which could be glossed in a number of ways, but which I will explain in terms of their relation to time. The concept of a cause, for instance (B122f.), involves a relation of necessitation between two states, but Kant allows that appearances 'can be given' which, while in conformity with the formal conditions imposed by space and time, nevertheless cannot be subsumed under a causal relation. So whereas the concepts of space and time are transcendentally deduced by grounding their validity in the *form* of all appearances, thereby ensuring that every presentation of an object will conform to these concepts (B125f.), such a deduction is not available in the case of (at least some of) the categories, because appearances 'can be given' which do not do so.

---

[2] See Merritt 2009.

[3] This question and its relation to Helmholtz, Hertz, and the picture-theory have recently been discussed in Patton 2009, which provides a useful overview of much of the literature. Patton's article deals with what she calls the problem of validity or *Gültigkeit*. 'The problem is a variant of the problem of induction, since establishing the validity of a principle of inference, based on regularity, involves making an inference beyond objects as experienced' (Patton 2009, p. 282).

Given that the result of the deduction of the categories will be that, in some sense, appearances not conforming to the categories *cannot* be given, it is helpful to understand in what sense they could. It is this: at least those categories which Kant terms *dynamic*—for instance the traditional categories of causality and substance—refer to relations between realities, that is to say bits of matter or 'beings in time' (B182). Such realities 'fill' time (as well as space), which means for Kant that they can mark definite locations and thereby *determine* time and space by setting limits to (terminating) regions of these otherwise empty 'continuous *quanta*'. But there is nothing in the naked form of intuition to preordain the distributions of beings in time and space. In this sense, appearances could be given that would not conform to the dynamic categories. Because categories such as causality or substance apply to patterns amongst spatio-temporal distributions of beings, the problem of showing the necessary validity of the dynamic categories is at heart the problem of showing how a temporal sequence can be shown to conform to a pattern *necessarily*, without making the pattern part of the structure of representation itself.

6.1.2 Experience

Kant's *Critique* is somehow concerned with what he calls 'conditions on possible of experience'. Much disagreement hinges on how the term experience should be understood. Was Kant talking about our mental life or about our scientific practice, and was he perhaps fallaciously arguing from facts concerning to the first to normative conclusions concerning the second? It is therefore useful to recall that the word experience has a participial form, *experiment*, which Kant's contemporaries sometimes call a 'prepared experience'. Prepared experiences differ from everyday experiences in a number of respects. First, experiments are repeated under varied conditions, with the aim of isolating the necessary and sufficient conditions for changing observables. Second, they often make use of mathematics, in particular algebraic equations, to describe these observables. The causal dependencies we identify can then be expressed algebraically as equations of condition. In consequence, before even considering the physical theories such experiments may support or refute, certain basic conditions on the objectivity of experiments must be met, without which they cannot be reproduced at other times and places. In today's language, we would say that our experimental activity rests on a suite of *metrological sciences*, which lay down norms of measurement. They do so in part by specifying classes of physical object that, using the terminology of contemporary metrological science, *realize* the ideal *representations* of *definitions* of units of measure. For instance, the physical lasers in standards laboratories realize imagined lasers, designed on paper to represent the definition of an SI-metre in terms of a relation between physical light and the second.

For Kant and his contemporaries, there are two fundamental a priori metrological sciences, namely *geometry* and *chronometry*. Without these sciences and the norms they ground, it would be impossible for scientists working at different times and places to swap and check each other's data. In this sense, these sciences are conditions on the objectivity of experimental data, on possible prepared experiences, and conditions for the formulation of algebraic laws. Because they must mediate between timeless formal objects and changing material bodies, metrological objects have a foot in both worlds. As a rule, they imperfectly realize the very quantities they represent, meaning that they must ultimately be normed with respect to an ideal, the first of which was Pythagoras' theorem for the *norma*, or set-square. This dual nature explains the repeated occurrence of metrological examples in the literature from Plato to Kripke.

It is this original sense of the term *norm* that underlies the much-discussed normative aspects of Kant's philosophy. It is only against the background of geometry and chronometry that scientific laws can be stated, confirmed, or refuted, and in this sense they are conditions for the possibility of scientific experiences, as well as conditions for the possibility of formulating causal laws mathematically. At the same time, however, the explanation and isolation of such principles are basic conditions for an open-ended project, that is to say a complete or 'architectonic' description of the natural world.

6.1.3 Geometry, Chronometry, and Phoronomy

While it is commonly observed that the term *geometry* reflects the Greek origins of this science in land-surveying, it is worth remembering that geometry did not become fully independent of this role until the end of the nineteenth century, when it was finally brought into the fold of pure analysis. For eighteenth-century scientists, geometry is a science for measuring bodies, and it is still extraordinary because it makes true empirical claims even though it is based on apparently a priori axioms. To take one prominent example, Gauss's research into the problem of mapping spherical relations onto Euclidean ones—the same research Riemann used as his point of departure—was directly connected to cartographic questions. And one of the main preoccupations of the Swiss mathematician and philosopher of science Johann Lambert, to whom Kant considered dedicating the *Critique*, concerned map projections, what we would today call projective geometry. In other words, while geometry plays an essential role in physics (the study of motion), this was far from being its only natural scientific application.

What is less well known is that since the early modern period a similar a priori science existed for measuring time. In contrast to geometry, however, the a priori principles at the basis of chronometry are exceedingly simple. It presupposes only a few basic 'axioms', such as that time has one dimension, that it is continuous, that its parts are not simultaneous, etc. (Lambert 1771; Schultz 1789). Taken together, chronometry and geometry give rise to a third fundamental a priori science, namely 'phoronomy' or kinematics, which articulates laws for the composition of speeds and accelerations, such as the parallelogram law, and thereby makes the quantification of motion possible.

Those familiar with Kant will easily recognize that each of these sciences has a direct counterpart in his work, and that each is given its own separate foundation or 'transcendental deduction'. The possibility of the sciences of geometry and chronometry is explained in the Transcendental Aesthetic's sections on time and space, but here Kant observes in conclusion that he has also thereby grounded the a priori cognition displayed by 'the general doctrine of motion', that is to say the Phoronomy of his *Metaphysical Foundations of Natural Science (MFNS)*. The latter science is *empirical* in the sense that it concerns matter and time; however, it is *pure* because it depends only on the structure of pure intuition. This pure kinematics will be central to our subsequent discussions of both Hertz and Helmholtz. In order to get at the connection, we need to consider briefly the status of this science in eighteenth-century physics and mathematics.

It is generally accepted that Kant abandoned continental relationalism at least in part because of arguments advanced by the mathematician Leonhard Euler, in particular his 'Reflections on Space and Time', where Euler sided with Newton against Leibniz and his rationalist followers such as Wolff.[4] Euler had argued that the law of inertia proved the existence of independently existing parts of space and time, which sustained intrinsic relations of equality and simultaneity. Since the law is incontrovertibly *true*, Euler argued, bodies must be 'regulating' their behaviour relative to something real. Thus we must be absolutists not only concerning the existence of space and time, but indeed concerning their metric.[5] The independent existence of such structures is forced on us by the law, which Euler, like many of his contemporaries, regarded as the fundamental principle of natural science.

Thus in saying that the Transcendental Aesthetic provides a transcendental deduction of the concepts of space and time, Kant follows Euler in arguing that the possibility of geometry, chronometry, and kinematics presumes the existence of these same

---

[4] See Janiak 2009 on this question.

[5] Euler actually has *two* laws of inertia, one for rest and one for uniform motion; however this distinction can be ignored for our present purposes. It is sometimes suggested that Euler was arguing the opposite, and that Kant followed him on this score. 'Kant there appears to follow §§ 20, 21 of Euler's paper in rejecting the idea that the equality of times can be rendered intelligible independently of the law of inertia. Instead, Kant appears to hold that the law of inertia *defines* the equality of times: equal times are those during which an inertially moving body traverses equal distances' (Friedman 1992, p. 20n30). In these sections, Euler does indeed call the equality of times into doubt, but not to suggest that it be defined in terms of the law, rather as the premise of a reductio: '...if time is nothing other than the order of successions, then how will one make the equality of times intelligible?... As this equality could not be explained by the order of successions, just as little as the equality of spaces can be so by the order of coexistants, and since it enters essentially into our principle of motion, one cannot say that bodies, when pursuing their motion, obey something that exists only in our imagination' (Euler 1750, pp. 332–3). That is to say, without assuming an independent metric of both space and time, conformity of motions to the law of inertia would be inexplicable. See the passage from B67 discussed below in the section on Helmholtz's theory of space as well as Timerding 1919 and Jammer 2006, pp. 82–3.

The reason for this misunderstanding is perhaps a series of errors in the standard English translation, e.g. 'Since this equality cannot be explained by the order of succession, so just as little can the equality of spaces be explained by the order of co-existent ones, and whether it enters essentially into the principle of motion...' (Euler 1967, pp. 125–6). A parallel, apparently deliberate, misreading is made in § 5: 'Thus it is certain, that if it is not possible to conceive the two principles adduced from mechanics without their being involved in the ideas of space and time...' (Euler 1967, p. 118), versus 'Il est donc certain, que s'il n'etoit pas possible de concevoir les deux principes allegués de la Mecanique, sans y mêler les idées de l'espace & du tems [*sic*]...' (Euler 1750, p. 326).

structures. For Kant, however, they must be inherent to human sensibility, for we could not otherwise explain our a priori knowledge of them. The Transcendental Aesthetic 'explains the possibility of as much synthetic knowledge *a priori* as the general theory of motion evinces' (B49), because it provides the materials for the definition and laws of uniform motion found in the Phoronomy of the *Metaphysical Foundations*. Since deviation from uniform motion counts as a state change, thus as something requiring a sufficient reason, the application of the a priori law of causality to these definitions results in the principle that any deviation from uniform motion has a sufficient reason, in other words in an a priori derivation of the law of inertia (*MFNS*, 4.541–2).

Nevertheless, the foundation provided for all three sciences is provisional, for Kant has not yet explained the possibility of *quantifying* space, time, and motion. All three sciences must also be arithmetized if we are to formulate laws of nature in terms of the pure concepts of quantity, that is to say by means of algebraic equations of condition.

6.1.4 Algebra, Quantification, and Change

As recent work by Longuenesse (1993, 2001) and Shabel (1998) suggests, we find a clean split in Kant's theory of mathematics between classical Euclidean geometry and the new analytic geometry typical of Galilean–Cartesian mechanism. The quantitative categories (unity, plurality, totality) allow us to think 'the concept of many in one', that is to say to conceive of phenomena as denumerated sets. I suggest that for Kant and his contemporaries, this is part of a larger project, which I will term the *quantification of nature*. The mathematicians Kant knew best—Lambert, Euler, Kästner—see it as the aim of natural science to describe physical change first by means of numbers, then in terms of 'equations of variable quantities', which can increase or decrease in time. In the *Critique*, this is reflected in Kant's claim that all pure concepts attach to experience by means of a temporal 'schema', where, in the case of the categories of logical quantity, this schema is *number*.

Just as geometry must be quantified in order to become analytic geometry, the same must be done for chronometry and phoronomy. The passage of time, the quantities of motions, the intensities of forces, and, eventually, quantities such as temperatures and pressures, must all be open to arithmetization if an algebraic science of nature is to be possible. This possibility is explained in the Axioms of Intuition and the Anticipations of Perceptions of the *Critique*, which argue that all perceptions are implicitly quantifiable because all perception occurs in time (B201f., 23.28). The Phoronomy of the *Metaphysical Foundations* confirms this hypothesis, since Kant's main concern there is to ground the additive properties of motions (the parallelogram law for velocities). But he does so under a peculiar constraint: the motions being added must be represented as occurring within a single unit of time, for otherwise the component motions would not literally be parts of their sum. In other words, Kant is giving an account of the additive properties of velocities, which correspond to what he calls 'intensive quantities', namely ones which do not contain parts, but can be quantified with respect to their increase or decrease in time. Once we have an account of these additive properties, we can describe arbitrary motions by synthesizing, that is to say integrating, these differentials in time.

6.1.5 Causality

As we have seen, the fundamental metrological sciences are grounded in our intuitive knowledge of the structure of time and space asserted in the Transcendental Aesthetic and extended in the Phoronomy of the *Metaphysical Foundations*. This intuitive knowledge of space gives rise to a priori propositions concerning lines and figures, for instance that two lines cannot enclose a space (B65, B204), which can only be synthetic because they do not follow from the law of non-contradiction (B268). When augmented by the temporal schema of quantity, namely number, it grounds analytic geometry. In all cases, the principles in question must rest on what Kant calls 'constructions' of the requisite objects in intuition, since they are not analytic.

But there are no corresponding objects in the case of time, because its parts are never simultaneously given and therefore cannot be compared. Memory may give an impression of elapsed time, but memories cannot provide a basis for the quantification of time. This presupposes cyclical or oscillatory motions such as those of heavenly bodies or, in the lab, chronometers. Because these involve directional change, they count as alterations subsumable under the concept of causation. So the doctrines of the Aesthetic, which ground the fundamental metrical characteristics of space, time, and motion, dictate laws of nature in the form of conditions on time-measurement. For this reason, the doctrine of time set out in the Transcendental Aesthetic is filled in by those long sections of the *Critique* concerned with 'time-determination' (the Schematism, the Analogies). In Kantian terminology, we would say that although the continuity, dimensionality, and ordering relations of time have already been grounded, its three *modes*—perdurance, succession, and simultaneity—prescribe the application of the relational categories, by connecting the parts of time sequentially through necessary causal connection, and 'ubiquitously' when objects at different places are bound together by reciprocal causal relations (for instance, gravitational or electrostatic forces), and can therefore be regarded as simultaneous or not.

Kant inverts the analytic sequence in his typical fashion. From the empirical point of view, the claim is that objective time-measurement can only occur when we possess physical objects such as clocks, whose laws of oscillation or 'continuous alteration' are known. For it is, Kant argues, only rotational, accelerated motion that is actual or real (*wirklich*, 4.142ff.). Transcendentally, the argument is that without applying the dynamic categories of substance, cause, and community (reciprocal action), we would have no way of drawing a division between subjective and objective time-flow. Whereas, as Kant's contemporary Lambert observes in 1771, in a sequence of elements ordered by a necessary and asymmetric logical relation, the elements are connected to one another 'like the wheels in a clock', and can serve to norm time.

Kant's argument is straightforward. Recall that the mere ordering relations posited in the Aesthetic do not ascribe to time either direction or flow, which involves the supplementary 'mode' of succession and its corresponding category, namely causation. By contrast, our experience of time as a succession of moments reveals an implicit and pre-conceptual modal structure (23.22), for each *momentum* entails its successor, a necessity we sometimes express by saying that we cannot go back in time, whereas we can go back in space. But even within the succession of time, a difference between coupled states that resist my will and those that do not can be discerned. Certain kinds of experiential successions are reversible, whereas others are not. I can choose the order in which I examine the various parts of a house, but not the order in which I experience the motion of a ship following the flow of a river (B238). I call this resistance to my will exhibited by certain successive phenomena an objective cause. It is with respect to such indefeasible regular connections that I norm the passage of objective time.

The cognitive relation of logical consequence must, therefore, be given a corresponding 'figurative' representation, a structure in pure sensibility that maps the intellectual concept of causation onto the material world. (Cf. B152, 7.191.) For, as Kant insists, there can be no formal or qualitative similarity between the categories and the spatio-temporal appearances they might represent. If there were such a connection, the possible (if problematic) applicability of the categories to non-spatial temporal appearances would be called into doubt, undermining a fundamental aim of the *Critique*. Each category has two such figurations: first a figuration in time, which Kant calls a *schema*, second a figuration in both space and time, which, in the case of the dynamic categories, he calls *analogies*. For instance, the logical concept if-then expresses the idea that when one thing is posited, another thing is posited of necessity. The temporal *figure* of causation is that of the content of a part of time (a moment) that necessitates its successor, and its spatio-temporal figure is that of a pattern of material appearances that are subject to a universal rule (cf. the schemata of causality and necessity at B184–5). In projecting the first sort of figure onto space and matter to produce the second, we 'legislate to nature' (B160).

6.1.6 The Transcendental Deductions

With these remarks in place, I will now turn to a brief discussion of the Transcendental Deduction proper, considering only its role in grounding a priori principles in the sciences. My claim will be that, precisely because there is no formal similarity between the categories and their subsumpta, there is also no obstacle to making categorical subsumptions, thus that we are justified in subsuming categorically to the extent that doing so is a condition for our grasping, or apprehending, the manifold of appearances.[6] We may do so even in the face of contrary evidence, for everyday phenomena constantly violate the law of causality.

The form of Kant's argument faithfully reflects his own characterization, namely that it is an 'original acquisition' of the *right* to employ the categories, which defers the

---

[6] See Anderson 2001, pp. 291f.

question of their alethic validity in favour of a deontic grounding (Henrich 1989). The acquisition is justified as a condition of the Cartesian *cogito*, in the same way that an individual's right to unowned property in the state of nature is created *ex nihilo* through the act of seizure itself, while it is *justified* as a condition of his survival, a so-called 'right of necessity'. The Deduction describes how I would acquire such a right were I to think categorically, by appropriating the external and making it *mine* (6.258, B131f.).

This form of deduction can be applied psychologically or science-theoretically. One could take Kant to be arguing the case of a noumenal subject, who spontaneously applies the categories to experience in securing his existence through time. Or one can read him as laying down conditions of objectivity, which must be observed in order to produce a unified account of nature. In either case, the categories are justified relative to an end—consciousness or, in Helmholtz's later version, the 'complete comprehensibility of nature'—but that end is not really a matter of deliberative choice. As Wittgenstein later put it, we follow the rules deriving from the categories blindly, but not without justification.

Kant contrasts this deductive method with two others. First, a 'despotic' or 'dogmatic' deduction such as is found both in traditional and Wolffian metaphysics, which grounds a priori truth through an appeal to authority, and may indeed presume insight into the mind of God himself. Second, a 'physiological' deduction such as provided by British empiricists, who explain a priori principles in terms of innate, hardwired dispositions, but thereby lose the ability to explain why such principles are binding on physical reality. Kant avoids the problem entirely with a promissory note. The law of causality provides nothing more than the germ of the completed tree of nature, by which I mean it provides principles on whose basis natural science *should* be constructed, but which will be alethically valid only once natural science is complete. Universalizing the category of causation across time and space produces a causal law that can thus be asserted, with justification, in the face of recalcitrant evidence.

The 'non-homogeneity' of the categories with experience—the fact that they have no formal similarity to phenomena—plays a dual role here. First, because the categories are not and cannot be *in* the data they subsume, we must explain and justify their applicability to experience. Such a justification would be straightforward in the case of an empirical concept such as *plate*, for I need appeal to nothing beyond the true statement 'I once saw a plate' to justify my talking about other plates, whether actual or possible. Furthermore, because the concept of a plate contains that of roundness, and roundness is a property of spatial forms, the latter concept is 'homogeneous' with the objects it can subsume (B176), which in turn means there can be a question of right or wrong subsumptions. But Hume made such a justification of causal concepts impossible, and Kant accepts his result: no finite series of observations ever contains the necessary connection which is a cause, meaning that no one ever has seen nor ever will see a cause. There will never be an experience that justifies my use of causal concepts in the way that my concept *plate* was justified.

Kant turns this difficulty to his advantage. Clearly I can be mistaken in any causal judgement, such as *the sun warms the stone* (*Prolegomena* 4.301), but this singular judgement is neither verified nor refuted by this single (positive) case. If I subsequently judge that the sun did *not* warm the stone, this will be because of other observations of other objects placed in the sun, not because I discovered that what I thought was present in the first warming event (Hume's necessary connection) was actually absent. The truth-conditions of this judgement are in other words intrinsically linked to the possible outcomes of other experiences or experiments elsewhere in space and time. Similar remarks apply to the relation between numerical concepts and the spatio-temporal objects they may subsume.

In both cases, the category in question relates to the phenomena only through the medium of time. Although nothing in sensory experience corresponds to a cause, the concept of a cause can be represented as the figure, 'moment which necessitates a subsequent moment in time', that is to say by ascribing a structure of directed entailment to time itself. Similarly, since every physical object can be partitioned in many ways, there is no direct relation of correspondence between numerical concepts and physical objects; rather these are mediated by the temporal schema of the logical quantities and forms of judgement (all, some, one). This is 'a representation that comprises the successive addition of one to one (of the same kind)' (B183), that is to say the concept 'one set [*Menge*, B112] with *some* (n) members of the set of *all* these things', where the value n is the result of an ideal measurement operation.

Kant makes this doctrine explicit at two points in the *Critique*, namely when he introduces the notion of a 'figurative synthesis' in the Transcendental Deduction, and when in the next chapter, the Schematism, he insists that there is no shared form between categories and sensibility. *Figurative representations* depict one kind of thing by means of things of another kind, as notes on a scale depict sounds. An extreme case of figuration is when the intellectual is represented by means of the sensible, where the figures are there only as a means for representing concepts (7.191, on the *facultas signatrix*). So a figurative representation can represent in the absence of any formal or qualitative resemblance, for instance as is done in algebra and symbolic logic.

When Kant says that the schemata provide the missing link between category and sensation, he means that the schemata are figurative representations of the categories, produced, as he explains, by an 'influence of the understanding on inner sense'. But these figures are not figures in space, they are figures in time. Kant calls such a purely temporal synthesis of possible experiential data the *transcendental synthesis of the imagination*, distinguishing it sharply from a subordinate *pure sensible synthesis* which generates forms in space, and which is usually identified by commentators with the transcendental temporal synthesis on which it depends.[7]

---

[7] B151f., B185, above all the list at 23.18–19, 'The productive imagination is 1. empirical in apprehension 2. pure but sensible with regard to an object of pure sensible intuition 3. transcendental with regard to an object in general. The first presupposes the second and the second the third.

The pure synthesis of the imagination is the ground of the possibility of the empirical one in apprehension thus also of perception. It is possible a priori and produces nothing but shapes. The transcendental synthesis of the imagination concerns only the unity of apperception in the synthesis of the manifold in general through imagination. Through this the concept of an object in general is thought according to the various types of transcendental synthesis. The synthesis occurs in time...'

In conclusion, we can see how the deductive grounding of the dynamic categories differs from that of the mathematical ones, and from the deduction of the concepts of space and time. Concepts and principles that concern the form of spatial intuition itself—line, area, contain—are based on direct intuition and construction of their objects by the pure sensible imagination, objects which give these concepts a 'sense and reference' (*Sinn und Bedeutung*, Letter to Tieftrunk 13.224, A240/B299). Similar constructions for motion are advanced in the Phoronomy of the *Metaphysical Foundations*. However, quantifying space, time, and motion means applying both the quantitative categories (all, some, one) and their correlated schema (number) to these constructions. Line segments are produced by the imagination through successive aggregation, or synthesis of their homogeneous parts, just as we imagine the successive addition of the parts of time. Both are *extensive* quantities that literally contain their parts (B202f.). In the case of an *intensive* quantitative concept such as speed, quantification involves ordering the intuitions according to their growth from zero to an arbitrary value (B207f., *MFNS* 4.490f.). We get analytic geometry in the case of space, and analytic kinematics (phoronomy) in the case of motion. Theorems such as Pythagoras', which involve applying quantities to geometrical objects, are verified by the constructions to which they refer, and without these constructions, there would be no way of proving such non-analytic principles. For the concept of a triangle is equally applicable to objects on the surface of a sphere, and yet these have quite distinct characteristics, which were well understood in the spherical trigonometry of Kant's day (4.285).

By contrast, the deduction of the dynamic category of causation does not produce a principle that is verified by the forms of space and time, which is why Kant says that it is merely regulative, and not constitutive. When we consider the structure of time as laid out in the TA, we have not only ordering relations, but also directional asymmetry, and succession (B67). The 'determination' of time by the category of causality describes the structure of directed necessitation that Kant calls 'succession' in terms of pure logic. The events that fill each part of time should necessitate their successors, like the states of a logical machine. If the simultaneous parts of space that correspond to a moment in time are conceived as subject to a rule that necessitates the next moment, then this rule will be deterministic. The states it regulates can be nothing other than distributions of material properties (intensive quantities) in the manifolds of space and time. But the law of causality that dictates this modal structure—every temporal event has a sufficient reason that precedes it—is at most a demand we place on phenomena, one that everyday phenomena violate every day.

While we 'legislate to nature' (B159, Schultz 1785, p. 299) by imposing this normative demand on the physical world, we do so with the knowledge that the laws will be violated. Only when the project of a complete science of nature is complete will we be in possession of a conceptual system in which this law is true. So the *Critique of Pure Reason* and its physical extension, *The Metaphysical Foundations of Natural Science*, lay the cornerstones of a project that extends through the nineteenth century, namely the construction of a system of rational mechanics that will allow us to acquire or apprehend all natural phenomena within a closed causal system. Such a demand could be fulfilled,

Kant and his contemporaries believed, by a mechanics of mass-points subject to central forces (Hyder 2009). For in such a mechanics, the sufficient reason of the future motions of a system is the current spatial disposition of its mass-points. Kant's successor, the physicist and physiologist Hermann von Helmholtz, called this regulative ideal the 'complete comprehensibility of nature'.

6.2 HELMHOLTZ

Now that we have outlined the two distinct deductive strategies used by Kant to justify foundational physical principles, we will consider how these justificatory strategies evolved in the nineteenth century. This means focusing on two developments: the onset of non-Euclidean geometry and its relation to kinematics, and the ongoing attempts to justify force-laws on a priori grounds, culminating in Heinrich Hertz's geometrization of force. We will begin with Helmholtz's reinterpretation of geometry as a kinematic science of rigid-body motion, which he termed 'physical geometry'.

Hilary Putnam once suggested that the overthrow of Euclidean geometry was 'the most important event in the history of science for the epistemologist' (Putnam 1979, p. x). If the epistemologist is a Kantian, then Hermann von Helmholtz is his beast. Active in most domains of nineteenth-century science, Helmholtz gradually developed a naturalistic epistemology in stark contrast to the Kantian approach of his youth, and this epistemology, when joined to his work in physiology, mathematics, physics, and medicine, was instrumental in establishing the naturalistic world-view taken for granted by most scientists today. Nonetheless, I am not going to approach Helmholtz's work from that point of view in what follows, because I am primarily interested in the fate of our a priori principles. Both as a young Kantian and an older empiricist, Helmholtz continued to work within this tradition of rationalist mechanics, combining it only partly with his empiricist epistemology.

6.2.1 Geometry and Kinematics

In a series of papers from 1868–78, Helmholtz attacked Kant's theories of space and time by arguing that (1) the purpose of geometry was to measure spatial forms, and that this could be achieved only under the condition that rigid bodies (rulers) were freely transportable in space, (2) since the transportation of rigid bodies is a material process, the underlying assumptions of geometry are empirical and kinematic. Furthermore, (3) the possibility of rigid-body displacements conforming to non-Euclidean laws meant that the question of which geometry to use was an empirical one. In particular, while a 'strict Kantian' might preserve the a priori validity of Euclidean geometry by *defining* rigidity in Euclidean terms, this would render it analytic, and not synthetic, as Kant had clamed. Finally, we cannot know in advance whether the equal parts of space thus defined would be 'physically equivalent', in the sense that the same processes would occur in them in the same period of time. Thus all our physical laws, starting with the law of inertia, might have to be altered to compensate for a bad conventional choice.

In light of our preceding discussion, we can summarize Helmholtz's criticisms of Kant simply: Geometrical propositions are not verified by the simultaneous parts of intuited geometrical objects. If motion lies at the basis of geometry, and motion takes time and involves matter, then the outcome of geometrical measurements lies in the future. Whereas Kant had argued exactly the other way around. He insisted that because the parts of the kinematic magnitude lie in the future, the laws for the composition of speeds must be proven on the basis of 'geometrical congruence', that is to say with respect to an intuited and instantaneous spatial object.

Helmholtz was immediately attacked in a number of publications, the most sophisticated of which appeared in 1871, while he was still publishing on geometry. The philosopher Hermann Cohen, founder of the Marburg school of neo-Kantianism, was developing a reading of Kant's philosophy purging it of all 'physiological' elements, and positioned Helmholtz's first papers on geometry accordingly. Helmholtz 'departs from an interest in psychology, he is led from problems of sense-physiology to the mathematical problem of space. He does not depart from the connection of mathematics and natural science...' (Cohen 1987 [1871], p. 295 [227]). According to Cohen, one reads Kant 'physiologically' when one does what Kant himself warned against in the Transcendental Deduction (B119). Kant suggested that British empiricists such as Locke give *quid facti*, physiological explanations or deductions when they ascribe the (apparently) binding character of a priori principles to innate physiological inclinations of the human organism. Whereas Kant's 'original acquisition' does not ground the necessity of the categories in hardwired dispositions, so that the necessity acquired is instead that of a *right*. Helmholtz, who did indeed base much of his work on geometry on his physiological research, was thereby guilty of this same physiological misunderstanding.

In consequence, Cohen and his neo-Kantian successors, including many sympathetic to Helmholtz, characterized the relation between the physicist and the philosopher as follows. Helmholtz, misled by his work in sense-physiology, mistakenly took Kant to be advancing a thesis about the innate structure of human perception, whereas what Kant actually gave was a theory explaining the presence of a priori components in existing physics. That is to say, Kant was not claiming that we knew a priori that the laws of geometry and kinematics were *true*. Indeed, it makes no sense to say that they are true or not independently of their role in physics. Physics requires some assumed geometry to get started, but since this is a matter of convention, our choice is irrefutable, so that Kant's claim is vindicated, albeit it in weakened form. Helmholtz's error therefore consisted in (1) his mistakenly affirming the empirical character of geometry, whereas Kant had seen that geometry is purely normative, and has no independent truth-makers, and (2) his failing to grasp, as Cohen says explicitly in the quotation above, the connection between the laws of geometry and the laws of physics.[8]

---

[8] See Cohen 1885, pp. 406ff., translated as Cohen 2015.

Thus it speaks strongly against Cohen's interpretation when we observe that the young Helmholtz, in his earliest writings on the foundations of physics, introduced his definition of congruence in terms of rigid-body displacement in conjunction with the law of inertia and the problem of quantifying spatial relations. In other words, Helmholtz was from the beginning concerned with the role of geometry in physics, and indeed with the same foundational a priori sciences as were Euler, Lambert, and Kant. In these manuscripts from the 1840s, shortly before his landmark *Conservation of Energy*, Helmholtz's approach is in most respects indistinguishable from Kant's. He argues, for instance, that natural science presupposes an a priori suite of 'general physical concepts' (*allgemeine Naturbegriffe*) corresponding exactly to the ones we discussed earlier:

> These physical concepts are derived in part from the simple fact that there are determinate perceptions at all, which are not produced by our self-activity, and in part from individual determinate empirical perceptions themselves. The system of the first of these yields the general or pure natural sciences (theory of time, geometry, pure mechanics), and the system of the second yields theoretical physics. The common feature of the general physical concepts will be that they and their consequences are the basis of all natural intuition [*Naturanschauung*], thus that they are in this regard the general and necessary form of natural intuition, thus also that the certainty of their propositions is an absolute one, whereas the certainty of the specific natural concepts only ever extends so far as to say that all facts known up until now agree to them. Furthermore, the general concepts, derived only from the possibility of any natural intuition, may not restrict the possibility of any empirical combination of perceptions, *i.e.* no empirical fact or law may be derivable from them, rather they can yield only a norm for our explanations. (Königsberger 1903, p. 127; Helmholtz 2015, p. 6).

But there are crucial differences with Kant. Helmholtz argues that geometry, because it involves determinations of congruence, is a science of the properties space must have not merely to contain bodies, but to contain bodies in motion. In other words, geometry is a theory of rigid body motion, and since it concerns matter and time, it concerns facts within what Kant called *perception*. Therefore, Helmholtz begins his analysis with the concept of perceptual change, defining equal times in terms of similar processes. He then defines 'straight' lines in terms of uniform motion, and equal distances in terms of similar processes in the same time.

Helmholtz had correctly seen that geometry and chronometry were intrinsically linked to kinematics. But the idea did not originate with him. He was following the approach of two prominent thinkers in Berlin, the philosopher and Aristotle scholar Friedrich Trendelenburg (with whom Cohen studied) and his friend and colleague, the psychologist and physiologist Johannes Müller (who taught Helmholtz). Both argued for a new science of psychology, which would study the motion of the human soul. But Trendelenburg took this to have consequences for physics. Against Kant, he held that motion, but only motion, was common to mind and world, and that a reborn Aristotelian psychology would take this internal motion as its object. In his *Logical Investigations*

(Trendelenburg 1840), he attacked Kant for anchoring kinematics in the structure of spatio-temporal intuition, since, he argued, one ought to begin with pure kinematics and then define the concepts of distance and duration in kinematic terms.[9] In consequence, the *Logical Investigations*' chapter on 'Space and Time' comes after the chapter on 'Motion', for according to Trendelenburg, the latter are merely 'factors of motion'.[10] The task of philosophy of science, as reflected in his chapter headings, is to produce 'A Priori Objects out of Motion and Matter' by relating 'Formal Logic' to empirical data through the intermediate concepts of motion and causation.

Twenty years later, in his 1868 papers on geometry, Helmholtz also defined geometrical magnitudes kinematically, except that he was now able to entertain the possibility of non-Euclidean rigid-body displacements. In both the early work and these later papers, Helmholtz takes it for granted that the purpose of geometry is to determine *physically equivalent* magnitudes, namely the ones in which the same processes take place in the same time. But in contrast to Kant and Euler, metrical structure in Helmholtz is not intrinsic to the manifolds, waiting to be revealed. Instead, Helmholtz inquires into the conditions under which space could be said to sustain metrical relations at all, a question he had already confronted in his work on the metric of the colour-space. Unlike those of Kant, Helmholtz's metrical relations are essentially linked to matter, time, and dynamics: first, because even the young Helmholtz takes congruence verification to depend on properties of space that it must have in order for bodies to move; second, because the purpose of these congruence relations is to determine physically equivalent parts of space for the purpose of formulating general laws. Insofar as geometry has a meaning, that meaning is extended in time, and the image of that extension in time is the image of future motion. But if rigid-body displacements that do not conform to Euclidean geometry are imaginable, that deals a fatal blow to the assumption that Euclidean geometry is necessarily true, in the sense that it can be relied upon to do physics.

Two years later, Helmholtz did turn to the epistemological questions concerning the 'Origin and Meaning of Geometrical Axioms' in his third, popular paper, which has served as the primary source for most philosophical discussion of his work since then (Helmholtz 1870). As a result, the fundamental insight that accompanied his earlier mathematical publications has been overlooked, usually being ascribed to Kant himself, despite the fact that this philosophical insight is intrinsically connected to his mathematical analysis in terms of transformations. In his first two papers on geometry, Helmholtz had argued against Kant that geometry was a kinematic science, but he had not claimed that it was inductive. But in the intervening period, he realized that pseudo-spherical geometries were consistent with his measurement axioms. He now

---

[9] Trendelenburg 1840, pp. 130f. See Gottfried Gabriel's contribution to this volume for a discussion of Trendelenburg's impact on Frege.

[10] In his *History of the Theory of the Categories* (Trendelenburg 1846), pp. 173ff., he highlighted a number of passages in the *Critique* (e.g. B154ff.) in which Kant had gestured in this direction, even though Kant still rigorously distinguished between 'pure' and 'empirical' motion. Cohen cites these same passages as evidence for his corrected reading discussed below.

argued epistemologically, suggesting that had we grown up with the appropriate set of stimulations, we would have opted for a pseudo-spherical over a Euclidean geometry. Geometry was now a logical refinement of inductive generalizations, constructed for the purpose of doing physics.

Helmholtz concluded his 1870 paper with a number of remarks that have caused puzzlement ever since, since he appears in one breath to anticipate the entire development of conventionalism—which most people regard as the proper rebuttal to his empiricism—only to reject it outright in the next. He points out that one could, if one wanted, lay down an arbitrary geometry, but that this would require changing at least the law of inertia. So you have a choice: base your temporally projected geometry, that is to say your kinematics, on what you have observed; or, stipulate it, but then you may have to fudge the law.[11] A 'strict Kantian' could still save Kant by interpreting Euclidean geometry as a 'transcendental' conceptual doctrine, that is to say by defining rigid body motion in its terms, so that all and only what conformed to Euclidean displacement laws would be called rigid. That would mean reinterpreting geometry and kinematics as purely conceptual, transcendental conventions. But this would involve a price the Kantian should be unwilling to pay, argued Helmholtz, for he would have to admit that the propositions of geometry were 'analytic', in that they followed from a definition of rigid-body motion given in the terms of analytic geometry, that is to say in terms of the pure theory of quantity.

Cohen developed these suggested improvements to Kant into the standard neo-Kantian view of his theory of geometry. In the second edition of his *Kant's Theory of Experience* (Cohen 1885, 2015), he sharpened his criticism of Helmholtz, while availing himself of the latter's analyses. Cohen argued that the metrical structure referred to in the Axioms of Intuition was conceptually stipulated and indissociable from kinematics, meaning that there was effectively no difference between pure and applied geometry. This is the sense in which Cohen's was an 'inverted' reading of Kant: he implemented Trendelenburg's proposed corrective by following the *analytic* method of the *Prolegomena*. Here one begins with true and existing science and backs out its 'constitutive' a priori principles, following a method Kant judged appropriate for the *Prolegomena*'s intended audience of schoolteachers. Cohen accordingly argued that the aim of Kant's philosophy was not to provide certain foundational principles for the future, even though that would indeed appear to be the aim of the *synthetic* presentation of the *Critique*. Rather, '[t]he goal of all transcendental investigation is…the explanation of the possibility of synthetic propositions *a priori* from the apriority of the synthetic principles'.[12] In the case of the mathematical principles,

---

[11] It has often been asked why Helmholtz never considers Riemannian geometries of non-constant curvature in these papers, although he was fully aware of them. The answer is that none of these could ground the law in the way Helmholtz's tradition expected, because the law requires a definition of uniformity. Non-constant curvature, as Einstein later observed, would entail 'milieu-dependent' effects, which would mean ascribing causal powers to space, a result which flatly contradicts the view that space is a mere form of intuition. Einstein 1924, p. 86. A translation is available in Saunders and Brown 1991.

[12] Cohen 1885, p. 407; Cohen 2015, p. 107.

which justify the application of numbers, thus of analytic geometry and kinematics, to appearances in space and time, the inversion means denying that pure mathematics underlies applied mathematics. Instead, Cohen denies there is a meaningful distinction between the two, and '[t]he dialectical opposition between applied and pure mathematics is dissolved from a transcendental point of view by means of this explicit and repeated emphasis on the necessity of producing space in successive synthesis' (Cohen 1885, p. 420).

This 'equivalence of applied and pure mathematics' became an essential tenet of the neo-Kantian movement up to and including authors such as Cassirer. A modern version can be found in the work of Michael Friedman, which rests on the following 'Marburg' planks: Kant's theory of geometry is essentially conceptual, in that his appeal to intuitions has only the function of filling the gaps in deductive inference that arise from the inability of traditional logic to describe infinitary structures (Friedman 1992, pp. 56ff). Geometrical propositions are not verified by constructions in intuition, rather we 'think the propositions of mathematics by ... *presupposing* the required constructions, and it follows ... that the true propositions of mathematics are then necessarily true' (127, emphasis in original). Thus geometry has a model only in empirical appearances (101). Furthermore, the figurative representation of the one-dimensional inner manifold of time (B50, 23.27) is 'a reference to inertial motion' (131), meaning that equal periods of time are defined in terms of inertial motion. Geometry is thus a conceptual, normatively imposed theory of the affine structure of neo-Newtonian space-time:

> we do not define inertial motion in terms of a pre-existing temporal metric; we do not conceive inertial trajectories as those rectilinear trajectories that traverse equal distances in equal times. Rather, we first pick out a class of privileged inertial trajectories (in modern terminology, we endow space-time with an 'affine structure'), and then define the notion of temporal equality in terms of these trajectories. (Friedman 1992, p. 131)

In other words, just as Trendelenburg and Helmholtz had demanded, spatial and temporal quantities are defined kinematically, not the other way round. As the terms *presuppose, pick out, endow,* and *define* suggest, the affine structure in question is imposed on the manifolds—Kant's theory is, one might say, a version of space-time conventionalism in which only one convention is conceivable. But it is easily seen that this cannot be correct. Had Kant been kinematically defining spatio-temporal quantities in any meaningful sense, the overarching constraint of the Phoronomy—that its constructions must be restricted to a single, yet finite interval of time (4.486), so that the relations in question are reduced to 'geometrical congruence'—would be redundant. Friedman has performed the invaluable service of refocusing discussion of Kant's theory of mathematics on the connection to physics. And, as I have suggested above, these correctives do indeed produce a logically more appealing Kant. But this is because they ascribe to Kant the key mathematical and philosophical theses of his most sophisticated critics.

6.2.2 Force

Turning to Helmholtz's treatment of causality, thus his concept of force, we will keep our attention focused on the law of inertia, that is to say on the connection between the definition of uniform motion and force. We should recall that Kant gave separate deductions for the principles of geometry and kinematics on the one hand, and for the laws of inertia and the equality of action/reaction on the other. The first set of principles concerns structures that do not vary with time (although one of those structures is that of time itself); the second concerns correlations of possible entities within these structures, relations among material beings in time. The first can be transcendentally grounded in structure, whereas the second cannot, and must instead be justified as essential conditions on the possibility of apprehending spatio-temporal data. The German physical community of the nineteenth century, in part due to Kant, and in part due to older commitments deriving from the rationalist tradition it shared with Kant, still regarded many, if not all of these principles as a priori. And so the young Helmholtz attempted to prove force-centrality and the parallelogram law on a priori grounds, just as he attempted to derive the law of inertia from sufficient reason and a definition of uniform motion.

In Kant's model of original acquisition, dynamic laws could be *made* alethically valid. For so long as we are idealists, nothing opposes our construing nature on their basis, supplying whatever missing elements we require to render it nomological. The concepts of force and substance are the key players here. Thus Helmholtz also provided a transcendental grounding for force-laws; indeed, his first major publication, what we know as the *Conservation of Energy*, was literally entitled the *Conservation of Force*. In its philosophical preamble, which develops quite naturally from the earlier manuscript on a priori physical principles discussed above, Helmholtz argues that nature would not be 'completely comprehensible' without assuming central forces, because only then are the future variations of these forces, and thus their future actions, attached to fully determinate properties in intuition.

> We saw above that natural appearances must be reduced to unchanging last causes. This requirement now requires that we find time-invariant forces corresponding to these last causes. In the sciences, we call species of matter with invariant forces (ineliminable qualities) chemical elements. But if we imagine the universe decomposed in elements with unchanging properties, then the only remaining possible changes in such a system are spatial, that is to say locomotions, and the external relations through which the actions of the forces are modified can only be spatial, thus the forces can only be locomotive forces which depend for their action only on the spatial relations. (Helmholtz 1847, p. 4)

Helmholtz goes on to argue that his energy conservation principle is equivalent to the assumption that all forces in nature are central. We must formulate our theories in terms of central forces, he concludes, for without this we would abandon the complete comprehensibility of nature. That principle asserts that we must aim for a physics in which all changes in nature can be univocally subsumed under unchanging universal laws.

I should emphasize that these philosophical considerations are attached to practical concerns, in particular the emergence of electromagnetism. Having derived centrality from comprehensibility, Helmholtz went on to argue against theories of electromagnetism that involve velocity- and acceleration-dependent forces, because these make physical causes depend on unobservable absolute space. A mathematician may invoke such forces 'on paper', Helmholtz argued in later publications; however, they are not 'transferrable to physical reality' because they cannot be determinately represented in intuition, that is to say they are not reducible to functions of the relative positions of mass-points.[13] So Kant's (by now highly modified) first principles are here brought to bear on the physical problems that eventually provoked special relativity, where the central concern is the determinability of motions and forces with respect to absolute space.[14]

6.3 Hertz

The problem of space in its various forms is one of the vectors leading from nineteenth-century Germany philosophy of science into the mainstream of analytic philosophy. This question was connected to Heinrich Hertz's 'picture-theory' of scientific representation, because Hertz's life work centred on the theory of electromagnetism. The picture-theory is the second major vector we will consider, one whose importance derives from its influence first on the German physical community,[15] and thereby also on the young Wittgenstein. Hertz was Helmholtz's star pupil, and both his physics and philosophy are rooted in Helmholtz's work. But Hertz's picture-theory differs from Helmholtz's sign-theory in a number of ways, most notably in its being closer to the rationalist physical constructions of his mentor's youth than to Helmholtz's later empirico-physiological model.

Shortly after Helmholtz began publishing on geometry, the physicist Carl Neumann published a lecture on the law of inertia and 'Body Alpha', which, by introducing the notion of an inertial frame, began a period of explicit reflection on the epistemological problems raised by the law in a relativistic framework.[16] In his concluding discussion, Neumann invoked Helmholtz's sign-theoretical account of scientific knowledge and his principle of the complete comprehensibility of nature to contextualize the problem:

> I hope at the same time that my exposition may contribute to putting the *very essence of mathematico-physical theories* in the appropriate light, in order to show that these theories must be seen as subjective formations that originate in our-

---

[13] See Bevilacqua 1993; Darrigol 1994; and Hyder 2009 for a detailed discussion of these topics.

[14] For a retrospective assessment of Helmholtz's point-mass reduction, see Einstein 1924, pp. 86–7, translated in Saunders and Brown 1991.

[15] See van Fraassen 2008 for a discussion of the reception of Hertz's theory among turn-of-the-century German physicists.

[16] I am much indebted here to DiSalle 2006, pp. 23ff.

selves, and which (derived from arbitrarily chosen principles, developed in strict mathematical fashion) are determined to yield as true a picture of appearances as possible.

In the same way as our visual nerves react constantly to all stimulations of the external world—whatever their nature—with light-sensations, so similarly our cognitive faculty answers to all observations made within the realm of inorganic nature with pictures composed of numbers, points and motions. Objective reality or at least general necessity could—as Helmholtz correctly observes—be ascribed to the general outline of such a picture, to the principles of such a theory, only once we could prove that *these* principles were *the only possible ones*, that besides *this* theory no *second* theory, which would correspond to the phenomena, is thinkable. That satisfying such a condition is beyond human capability requires no elucidation. (Neumann 1870, p. 23)

In Neumann's paper, the problem of determining an inertial frame is connected to the problem of determining kinematic magnitudes, to the notion of a phenomenological 'time-picture', and finally to the notion of a completely determinate description of nature. Much of the underlying concern was again the theory of electromagnetism, which continued to put pressure on the concept of absolute space. Both Helmholtz and Hertz would likely have read this paper, and several elements of Hertz's picture-theory answer the questions Neumann raised, namely whether there can be a uniquely determinate picture of nature, and how we might select among competing ones if equally good candidates present themselves.

Neumann viewed the problem of representing spatially underdetermined forces (ones not satisfying Helmholtz's 'complete comprehensibility' requirement) as one concerning the possibility of bringing natural science to a unique conclusion (Neumann 1870, pp. 23 n9, 31). And he rejected that requirement as unsatisfiable in principle. Here we see a number of the concerns motivating Hertz's picture-theory as presented in his posthumous work, *The Principles of Mechanics* (Hertz 1910 [1894], 2004): (1) we form intellectual mechanical pictures of the external world; because, (2) there can be no question of representing that world as it is in itself; thus, (3) a picture can represent the world only to the extent that the necessary thought-consequences of the picture (the *Denknotwendigkeiten*—the same term used by Frege to describe the laws of logic) mirror the necessary consequences in nature (the *Naturnotwendigkeiten*).[17] But there *can* be a question about which of a family of pictures is best suited for doing so—a question that, however, will have to be decided on grounds that are partly regulative, for instance the picture's simplicity. A central motive for investigating the problem of univocal description raised by Neumann remained the status of electromagnetism and of velocity-dependent forces, so that our two themes—the problem of space and the nature of force—remain intimately connected.

---

[17] The term *Denknotwendigkeit* may originally be due to Fichte. For the connection between Helmholtz and Fichte, see Heidelberger 1993.

Although he began his research programme in Helmholtz's lab in Berlin, Hertz was his own man with his own agenda. His initial work attempted to reconcile Helmholtz's central-force theory of electromagnetism to its competitors, above all Maxwell's. But Hertz quickly showed a preference for Maxwell over his mentor, as is shown by his early lectures *On the Constitution of Matter*.[18] Both here and in the *Principles of Mechanics*, Hertz suggests that the notion of distance forces is repugnant (the cogency of his objections is open to dispute), and that they should be banished from physics. His own picture-theory is therefore articulated within a particular physical context. It was to enable the reduction of the distance forces of classical mechanics to field-theoretical entities, which would in turn be reduced to kinematic connections amongst the hidden masses making up the ether.

But already early on, Hertz was bothered by the epistemological problems raised by the ether. It was supposed to be a different sort of substance from the atomic elements. Like today's dark matter, it interacted only partially with other matter, so that its existence was inferred as opposed to observed (Hertz 1999, p. 62). How should we conceive of this hidden matter, which, Hertz explained, we are required to assume in order to explain the 'changes in the state of space' (Hertz 1999, p. 62) supposed by Maxwell's theory? Hertz's physical project of reducing forces to ether-fields thus required a theoretical supplement in the form of a 'pure' theory of matter.

In the introductory sections of *On the Constitution of Matter*, Hertz answers an imaginary philosophical interlocutor, who reproaches the physicist for ascribing sensory qualities to microscopic objects, when these cannot have such properties by definition (34ff.). Such philosophical objections are justified, Hertz concedes, but they can be met with the earliest version of his picture-theory. The philosopher's objection is part and parcel of the problem Hertz sets himself in these lectures: what aspects of matter are essential to it, and which are not? He answers that,

> we can make clear to ourselves what in these properties is inessential, and a core will remain which contains the essential properties we have to deal with. What we add in are then not false representations, they are the conditions of any representation at all; we could not remove them and replace them with something better, rather we must add them in or give up on all representations in this domain. (Hertz 1999, p. 36)

These essential properties are simply 'time- and space-relations'. Only these, and nothing we add in, for instance the concept of causes or forces, are essential to representation, precisely because only these underwrite quantitative reasoning about reality. In other words Hertz's strategy, both in the *Constitution of Matter* and the later *Principles of Mechanics*, is to argue that physical theories are *mathematical pictures*. In both cases the essence of a scientific picture is the system of spatio-temporal magnitudes that connects its mathematics to the phenomena, which is why the first half of the *Principles* is, on

---

[18] Cf. Hertz 1999, § 1.2, pp. 51ff. on the properties of the ether.

Hertz's own account, purely a priori. It is that part of the picture of the *Mechanics* which lays out the basic structure of those magnitudes, namely the theory of pure kinematics. This is a conception we have now seen several times.

6.3.1 Geometry, Kinematics, and Force Reduction in Hertz's *Principles of Mechanics*

Hertz's last work, the posthumous *Principles of Mechanics* (*PM*), is divided into two books, the first of which develops a kinematics resting on a priori truths 'in the sense of Kant', the second of which contains Hertz's Fundamental Law, a version of the principle of least action which, as Mach immediately pointed out, can be regarded as a generalization of the law of inertia. This second part also contains the theory of hidden masses, that is to say a mechanical theory of the ether, whose matter underlies the changes in the state of space supposed by field theories. In the *Constitution of Matter*, Hertz had argued that we should reduce all distance forces to fields, which are here reduced to hidden rigid connections. So we can and should read the *Principles* as an attempt to eliminate the troublesome category of force from our ontology and to replace it with 'intuitively imaginable' rigid connections between mass-points in spatio-temporal intuition.

It can be fairly objected to this reading that it imports far too much philosophy into Hertz's undertaking, which was after all a work in theoretical physics. For instance, Hertz did not divide the book into a priori and a posteriori parts until late in the day, meaning that he might not have attached much importance to it (Lützen 2005). But I do not see that we are compelled to choose between philosophical and physical motivations, particularly in the case of a book that always opts for theoretical purity over practical utility. I would rather suggest that the philosophical division is in service of a physical concern. Hertz's division clearly reflects the split between kinematics and dynamics that we have been concerned with all along. But in Hertz, the problematic status of the causal law is finally eliminated, for what appear to be distance forces are reinterpreted as rigid connections in the ether. This ether, because it has a definite velocity through all space, supplies the one missing dynamic element—we can identify it with Neumann's Body Alpha—required to distinguish inertial from accelerated motion.[19] Although Hertz's Fundamental Law is introduced in Book II and is clearly labelled empirical, it can be viewed as an extension of the law of inertia into spaces of higher dimension. Helmholtz explained in the introduction to Hertz's book that, had the theory been adequate, his student would have succeeded where his teacher failed, by deriving the fundamental laws of mechanics from a single *Grundanschaaung*, or fundamental intuition.

---

[19] See Einstein on Hertz's work, Einstein 1920, pp. 6ff. A translation is available in Einstein 1922. A helpful discussion of Einstein 1920, 1924 can be found in Rynasiewicz 1996.

The project of reducing forces to rigid connections within an a priori structure pushes the structural deduction of fundamental physical principles begun by Kant to its limit. This technique, which came to be known as geometrization, reached fruition in the theory of general relativity. It can be contrasted with Helmholtz's central-force deduction and his attempted aprioristic derivation of the parallelogram law. Both are reactions to the problem of representing force-laws in a way that secures their necessity, the same problem Kant faced with his 'dynamic categories'. In Helmholtz's case, this still involved a normative appeal to complete comprehensibility: without central forces, there would be actions in nature that could not be given sufficient reasons, so we must think in terms of central forces. In Hertz's case, the reduction is structural (SD) and not normative (TD): there are no forces, only rigid connections among mass-points, some of which are hidden. Our belief in forces is therefore a reflection of our ignorance of the hidden masses. Although these come at a considerable algebraic cost, the move is paradoxically justified by an appeal to economy. It is preferable, Hertz argues, to introduce more elements of a kind we can clearly grasp, and which do not involve contradictory or occult properties, even if these elements may be in principle unobservable.

Although Hertz's physical pictures, as opposed to the perceptual pictures of Helmholtz's theory, are mathematical and intellectual, he shares the general representational theory with his mentor. They conceive of the picturing relation between internal and external representations as an isomorphism, a mapping between temporal sequences represented in manifolds, much as Trendelenburg argued that our mental representations are true if and only if internal motions are analogues of external ones. Hertz carries this conception to its completion in the *Principles*, where he argues that the 'pictures' we form of the external world stand in the relation of isomorphism definitive of what he calls dynamic models. When one system is a dynamic model of another, the degrees of freedom and equations of condition of the two systems correspond in such a way that every possible displacement of the one system corresponds to a possible displacement in the other. Their *dynamic possibilities* are mappings or pictures (*Abbildungen*) of one another.

6.4 Wittgenstein and the Analytic Tradition

Hertz's mature picture-theory represents the tip of one strand of Kant's transcendental grounding of the pure principles of natural science. This is the strand that favours a structural deduction over a normative or regulative one, seeking to tie a priori physical principles to structural relations in the space- and time-manifolds, thereby closing the gap opened at the outset of the Transcendental Deduction. The problems for Kant's approach were two: the first concerned the status of geometry and kinematics, the second that of forces, conceived as the sufficient reasons of accelerations. Together with Neumann's work on the law of inertia, Helmholtz's analysis of the kinematic foundations of geometry shook loose this structural derivation of uniformity. After them, there were only two possible answers to the problem of describing inertial paths: either to interpret them as defined in terms of material reference systems such as rulers and clocks, perhaps ideally normed, but not immune to correction (this was Helmholtz's option); or, instead, to take the statements of one or the other geometry as stipulations of what are to count as rigid bodies and inertial paths. The latter interpretation was quickly seen by neo-Kantians as the perfect vindication of Kant's views, since it shifted the justification from the structural to the normative, and thereby also inoculated Kant against non-Euclidean geometry. The family of philosophical theories engendered by this view is known as *conventionalism*. Although it can be described as a Kantian doctrine, it was not Kant's view of the matter.

The second problem just mentioned concerned force-laws and the general admissibility of forces in our physical ontology. They became a problem for our physicists the moment the nascent theory of electrodynamics introduced forces that seemed to depend on motive quantities, as opposed to ones depending only on the distances between mass-points. Relative to what will these speeds be defined? Sustained questioning into the fundamental presuppositions of an empirically closed theory, that is to say one in conformity with Helmholtz's 'complete comprehensibility' criterion, led to the desire among some physicists, among them Hertz, to entirely eliminate forces from physics. Hertz's approach to force elimination engenders the twentieth-century picture-theory, which is then developed in quite different ways by Wittgenstein in the *Tractatus*, and by the German physical community in general, for whom it becomes a common device (van Fraassen 2008).

Exploring these last connections in detail would take us beyond the scope of this chapter, but a few indications of the connection to Wittgenstein and the Vienna Circle are perhaps in order. These have been the subject of some commentary over the years; however, the connection between Hertz's conception of a dynamic model and the picture-theory of the proposition—one of the very few explicit references to any other theory in the *Tractatus*—needs to be taken more literally. The key point is that the *Tractatus*' theory of logic relies essentially on the notion of a logical space of *counterfactual possibilities*. A logical picture is not a formal copy of the facts, a painting so to speak. It is a model, image, or mapping (*Abbildung*) of possible states in logical space, where the connections between possible, non-actualized states are just as important as those between actual ones.

Without the unactualized connections, the book would and could not solve the central problem Wittgenstein had inherited from Frege and Russell, which was to draw a boundary between what is logically and what is merely universally true, that is to say between what Frege and Russell called the 'logical propositions' and those of natural science. Wittgenstein's semantic approach differed fundamentally from their axiomatic one. Logical propositions do not derive from 'laws of thought', conceived by Frege in (genuinely) despotic terms. Rather, they are necessarily valid because of their degenerate relation to an intensional space of possibilities, namely the set of possible atomic facts, which are grouped into intrinsic classes by the objects *in* these facts. Since the facts either obtain or do not, and since each 'molecular' proposition asserts dependencies between actual and non-actual atomic facts, reference to non-actual possibilities by means of real properties and objects is a necessary and intrinsic feature of the theory. These counterfactual situations may be depicted or mapped (*abgebildet*) by a proposition even when no corresponding facts obtain. The difference between a logically true proposition and one which is merely universally true can then be defined as follows: the logical proposition is true under all possible variations of the truth-values of its elementary propositions, whereas the same does not hold of the universally true scientific proposition.

Since Russell's and Frege's theories of logic were not capable of enunciating this distinction, their axiomatic method inevitably led to the same justificatory regress that necessitated the Transcendental Deduction. If the laws of logic are to be justified by appealing to foundational principles characterizable as laws or necessities of thought (Frege's and Hertz's *Denknotwendigkeiten*), then a justification of the binding character of these laws must be produced. For any candidates, including those of *PM* or the *Grundgesetze*, might turn out to be invalid, in which case the reduction of mathematics to logical propositions, and the larger goal of providing a universal scientific calculus, would fail. Frege's rhetoric of anti-psychologism, which appeals to the normative as opposed to merely empirical or psychological character of these laws, was an outgrowth of the second deductive strategy, namely the 'value-theoretic' neo-Kantianism discussed by Gottfried Gabriel in his contribution to this volume. But that approach leaves open, as it always must, whether the laws are true.

The *Tractatus* answers that question with what we would today call semantic tools. Wittgenstein does not 'dogmatically' derive the validity of logical propositions from basic laws; instead he defines them as ones that remain true under all possible variation. As in the structural deductions beginning with Kant and extending through to Hertz, the validity of the principles derives from their relation to a representational space in which empirical states of affairs manifest themselves in time (*Tractatus* 2.0251), and against whose background physical laws may be discerned. The relation between proposition and world is modelled on Hertz,[20] for whom the possible variations of the dynamic model are mappings of the possible variations of the modelled system. In the *Tractatus*' version, the possible variations are of the possible elementary facts making up the logical space, and the sense of a given picture is those 'rigid' connections amongst the possible elementary facts that are determined or excluded if the picture is, respectively, true or false. Universally valid propositions of physics assert contingently invariant connections between the elements of this space, and such propositions correspond, just as they did in Kant's version, to the physical necessity distilled in our concept of force (*Tractatus* 6.3ff.). Thus it is only against the background of such an *intensional space* that the propositions of natural science acquire a definite meaning.

The theoretical approach we now call the *semantic view* is an evolution of this Hertz–Wittgenstein picture-theory, itself an outgrowth of the structural deduction. It provides

---

[20] Another key figure here is Boltzmann, who developed a state-space picture-theory inspired by Hertz's, but modified in light of Boltzmann's own work in statistical mechanics.

a distinct answer to the question of validity from that given by conventionalists. The conventionalist explains the validity of a priori propositions by saying they are arbitrary norms. Only in the context of a larger system can they be said to have a meaning, thus even to be true. So they are not so much necessarily true as they are unfalsifiable. By contrast, the semantic approach initiated by Wittgenstein explains the necessity of logical propositions in terms of their relation to a Stone space.

As a result, the troika of philosophical views on geometry we have considered so far—structural, normative-conventional, and empirical—replay verbatim in twentieth-century debates on the foundations of logic and philosophy of language. When Carnap abandoned his syntactic account of logical truth and moved to semantics (Carnap 1946), he moved to a state-space model based on the *Tractatus'* logical space. However, he quickly abandoned the hope of providing a uniquely correct foundation for Russell's and Frege's logical propositions, reinterpreting the logical rules as constitutive conventions, which could be changed if expedient. Quine countered with Helmholtz's empiricist dilemma: if the conventions are interpreted, they can be falsified, whereas if they are uninterpreted, they are trivially necessary and thus 'analytic', but the same holds true for any formal system, for instance Newton's laws. It is simplest to interpret both logic and mathematics as highly abstract, but nonetheless empirical theories. These theories quantify over only the actual world, with the salubrious result that the licentious slum of non-actual situations—a breeding ground for disorderly elements—can finally be cleared (Quine 1963 [1948]).

Quine's hardcore extensionalism was not able to handle induction, however, as Goodman soon demonstrated, consciously modelling his argument on Kant's refutation of Hume. If past extensions are all that is given, we should be indifferent to *grue* or *green*, since predicates denote only the individuals to which they apply (Goodman 1983 [1955]; Goodman and Quine 1947, p. 42), and—so far—these predicates have been applied to only the same individuals. But since we do in fact induce, we are committed to intensional criteria such as (1) counterfactual-supporting laws, (2) the existence of real properties or kinds, or (3) *de facto* mental or social preferences. The necessity of acting inductively thus forces me to become a non-extensionalist, and some sort of intensional structure is thereby transcendentally required.

But if one continues to reject the possibility of a ranking of hypotheses based on metaphysical realism, or on physiological dispositions, the requisite structure can be found only in the social history of word-uses (Goodman 1983 [1955], pp. 96–7). This approach gave rise to another major strand of twentieth-century philosophy of language, which fuses Goodman's grue-paradox with Wittgenstein's rule-following arguments, arguing that the intensional space is determined by socially entrenched norms. Although he articulated many of the key arguments typical of this view, Kripke's own metaphysical response to the problem was entirely different. He resuscitated the possibility-space of the *Tractatus* as a possible-worlds semantics, and thus brought the developments we have been considering full circle.

We can indeed understand many trends in twentieth-century philosophy of language as more or less unconscious oscillations between the SD- and TD-approaches. To take one example, Wittgenstein scholarship in recent years has made much of a so-called 'resolute' reading of the *Tractatus*, focused on the concept of nonsense. We are encouraged to think of the *Tractatus* normatively, as '*laying down a requirement*...which [is] internal to a sentence's use', as in the later Wittgenstein.[21]

As I suggested in my earlier discussion of the Transcendental Deduction, the peculiar modal status of the justification Kant offered for our use of the dynamic categories is reflected in Wittgenstein's account of rules. Base-level Wittgensteinian rule-following, that of the rules we follow blindly and without justificatory regress, has the same transcendental structure. Those who cannot follow the basic rules have another form of life. But there is not—beyond that fact—anything to justify our acceptance of these rules, indeed we act on them without reflection. Such a block of justificatory regress, it may be argued, can be found in the *Tractatus* itself. Thus we should kick away the ladder, and with it the semantic theory of the book.

But from the perspective of this chapter, this is simply to reinterpret the structural deduction of the *Tractatus* as a normative deduction. That is to say, it is to replicate the reinterpretation of Kant's theory of geometry as a normative-conceptual theory that was suggested by Helmholtz and endorsed by Cohen. Both of these reinterpretations are historically inaccurate, and they come at a high price: we must abandon the fundamental claim to universal validity grounded in metaphysical structure in favour of conventional norms.[22] Russell, we may recall, was unimpressed, because he rightly suspected that appeals to normativity in the absence of a deduction are empty. For why should I care whether what you are saying is normative unless it can also be shown that it will not steer me wrong—that it is, in other words, true?[23]

REFERENCES

Anderson, R. Lanier (2001). 'Synthesis, Cognitive Normativity, and the Meaning of Kant's Question, "How are synthetic cognitions a priori possible?"' *European Journal of Philosophy* 9(3): 275–305.

Bevilacqua, Fabio (1993). 'Helmholtz's Über die Erhaltung der Kraft: The Emergence of a Theoretical Physicist'. In D. Cahan (ed.) *Hermann von Helmholtz and the Foundations of Nineteenth-century Science*. Berkeley: University of California Press, pp. 291–333.

Brann, Eva (1999). *What, Then, Is Time?* Lanham, MD: Rowman & Littlefield.

Carnap, Rudolf (1946). *Introduction to Semantics*. Cambridge, MA: Harvard University Press.

---

[21] Diamond 1991, pp. 18–19, quoted in Conant and Diamond 2004, pp. 81–2, italics in original. My account of their position is reconstructive.

[22] On the question of reading resolutely see Climacus 1846, pp. 53–4.

[23] My thanks to Lanier Anderson, Michael Beaney, William Boos, Xavier Corsius, Robert DiSalle, Stephen Gardner, Dennis Klimchuk, Masoud Karimi, Guido Komatsu, Brandon Look, Jesper Lützen, Lydia Patton, Konstantin Pollok, Paul Rusnock, Robert Rynasiewicz, Eric Schliesser, Lisa Shabel, Abraham Stone, Alasdair Urquhart, and Gereon Wolters for comments and suggestions. Above all, however, to Heinz Lübbig of the PTB, for decades of discussion on metrology and the Berlin physical tradition.

Climacus, Johannes (1846). *Afsluttende uvidenskabelig Efterskrift til de philosophiske Smuler. Mimisk-pathetisk-dialektisk Sammenskrift, Existentielt Indlæg*. Copenhagen: C. A. Reitzel.

Cohen, Hermann (1885). *Kants Theorie der Erfahrung*, 2nd edn. Berlin: Dümmlers.

——(1987 [1871]). *Kants Theorie der Erfahrung*, ed. H. Holzhey. *Werke*, vol. 1.1. Hildesheim: Olms.

—— (2015). 'The Synthetic Principles'. In S. Luft (ed.), *The Neo-Kantian Reader*. London: Routledge.

Conant, James and Cora Diamond (2004). 'On Reading the Tractatus Resolutely'. In M. Kölbel and B. Weiss (eds.), *Wittgenstein's Lasting Significance*. London: Routledge, pp. 46–99.

Darrigol, Olivier (1994). 'Helmholtz's Electrodynamics and the Comprehensibility of Nature'. In L. Krüger (ed.), *Universalgenie Helmholtz*. Berlin: Akademie Verlag, pp. 216–42.

Diamond, Cora (1991). *The Realistic Spirit*. Cambridge, MA: MIT Press.

DiSalle, Robert (2006). *Understanding Space-Time: The Philosophical Development of Physics from Newton to Einstein*. Cambridge: Cambridge University Press.

Einstein, Albert (1920). *Äther und Relativitätstheorie*. Berlin: Springer.

——(1922). *Sidelights on Relativity*, tr. G. B. Jeffery and W. Perrett. London: Methuen.

——(1924). 'Über den Äther', *Verhandlungen der Schweizerischen naturforschenden Gesellschaft* 105: 86–93.

Euler, Leonhard (1750). 'Reflexions sur l'espace et le tems [sic.]', *Histoire de l'académie royale des sciences de Berlin* 4: 324–33.

——(1967). 'On Absolute Space and Time'. In A. Koslow (ed.), *The Changeless Order: The Physics of Space, Time and Motion*. New York: G. Braziller.

Friedman, Michael (1992). *Kant and the Exact Sciences*. Cambridge, MA: Harvard University Press.

Goodman, Nelson (1983 [1955]). *Fact, Fiction and Forecast*. Cambridge, MA: Harvard University Press.

Goodman, Nelson and W. V. O. Quine (1947). 'Steps Toward a Constructive Nominalism', *Journal of Symbolic Logic* 12: 105–22.

Hanson, Norwood Russell (1963). 'The Law of Inertia: A Philosopher's Touchstone', *Philosophy of Science* 30(2): 107–21.

Heidelberger, Michael (1993). 'Force, Law and Experiment: The Evolution of Helmholtz's Philosophy of Science'. In D. Cahan (ed.), *Hermann von Helmholtz and the Foundations of Nineteenth-Century Science*. Berkeley: University of California Press, pp. 461–97.

Helmholtz, Hermann von (1847). *Über die Erhaltung der Kraft*. Berlin: Reimer.

—— (1868a). 'Über die tatsächlichen Grundlagen der Geometrie'. In *Wissenschaftliche Abhandlungen. 2. Band*. Leipzig: Johann Ambrosius Barth, pp. 610–17.

——(1868b). 'Über die Tatsachen, die der Geometrie zum Grunde Liegen'. In *Wissenschaftliche Abhandlungen. 2. Band*. Leipzig: Johann Ambrosius Barth, pp. 618–39.

——(1870). 'Über den Ursprung und Bedeutung der geometrischen Axiome'. In *Vorträge und Reden. 2. Band*. Leipzig: Johann Ambrosius Barth, pp. 1–31.

——(1921). *Schriften zur Erkenntnistheorie*, ed. P. Hertz and M. Schlick. Berlin: Springer.

——(1977). *Epistemological Writings: The Paul Hertz/Moritz Schlick Centenary Edition of 1921*, tr. M. F. Lowe. ed. R. S. Cohen and Y. Elkana. Boston Studies in the Philosophy of Science. Dordrecht: Reidel.

—— (2015). 'On General Physical Concepts'. In S. Luft (ed.), *The Neo-Kantian Reader*. London: Routledge.

Henrich, Dieter (1989). 'Kant's Notion of a Deduction and the Methodological Background of the First Critique'. In E. Förster (ed.), *Kant's Transcendental Deductions*. Stanford: Stanford University Press, pp. 29–46.

Hertz, Heinrich (1910 [1894]). *Die Prinzipien der Mechanik in neuem Zusammenhang dargestellt*, 2nd edn., vol. 3, *Gesammelte Werke von Heinrich Hertz*. Leipzig: Johann Ambrosius Barth.

——(1999). *Die Constitution der Materie*. Berlin: Springer.

—— (2004). *The Principles of Mechanics Presented in a New Form*. New York: Dover Publications.

Hyder, David (2009). *The Determinate World: Kant and Helmholtz on the Physical Meaning of Geometry*. Berlin and New York: Walter de Gruyter.

Jammer, Max (2006). *Concepts of Simultaneity: From Antiquity to Einstein and Beyond*. Baltimore: Johns Hopkins University Press.

Königsberger, Leo (1903). *Hermann von Helmholtz*, 3 vols., vol. 2. Braunschweig: Vieweg.

Lambert, J. H. (1771). *Anlage zur Architectonic, oder, Theorie des Einfachen und des Ersten in der philosophischen und mathematischen Erkenntniss*, 2 vols., vol. 1. Riga: Johann Friedrich Hartknoch.

Longuenesse, Beatrice (1993). *Kant et le pouvoir de juger: sensibilité et discursivité dans L'Analytique transcendantale de la Critique de la raison pure*. Paris: Presses Universitaires de France.

——(2001). *Kant and the Capacity to Judge*. Princeton: Princeton University Press.

Lützen, Jesper (2005). *Mechanistic Images in Geometric Form: Heinrich Hertz's Principles of Mechanics*. Oxford: Oxford University Press.

Merritt, Melissa (2009). 'Kant on the Transcendental Deduction of Space and Time', *Kantian Review* 14(2): 1–37.

Neumann, Carl (1870). *Über die Principien der Galilei-Newton'schen Theorie*. Leipzig: Teubner.

Patton, Lydia (2009). 'Signs, Toy Models, and the A Priori: From Helmholtz to Wittgenstein', *Studies in History and Philosophy of Science* 40(3): 281–9.

Putnam, Hilary (1979). *Philosophical Papers, Volume 1: Mathematics, Matter and Method*. Cambridge: Cambridge University Press.

Quine, W. V. O. (1963 [1948]). 'On What There Is'. In *From a Logical Point of View*. New York: Harper, pp. 1–19.

Rynasiewicz, Robert (1996). 'Absolute Versus Relational Space-Time: An Outmoded Debate?' *The Journal of Philosophy* 93(6): 279–306.

Saunders, S. and H. R. Brown (eds.) (1991). *The Philosophy of Vacuum*. Oxford: Clarendon Press.

Schultz, J. (1785). Review of Ulrich's *Institutiones Logicae*, *Allgemeine Literatur-Zeitung* 295: 297–9.

——(1789). *Prüfung der Kantischen Critik der reinen Vernunft*, 2 vols., vol. 1. Königsberg: G. L. Hartung.

Shabel, Lisa. (1998). 'Kant on the "Symbolic Construction" of Mathematical Concepts', *Studies in the History and Philosophy of Science* 29(4): 589–621.

Trendelenburg, Friedrich Adolf (1840). *Logische Untersuchungen*, vol. 1. Berlin: Bethge.

——(1846). *Geschichte der Kategorienlehre*, vol. 1, *Historische Beiträge zur Philosophie*. Berlin: Bethge.

van Fraassen, Bas C. (2008). *Scientific Representation: Paradoxes of Perspective*. Oxford: Oxford University Press.

CHAPTER 7

....

FREGE AND THE GERMAN BACKGROUND TO ANALYTIC PHILOSOPHY

....

GOTTFRIED GABRIEL

IT is easy to get the impression that the classic works of analytic philosophy have been written with the explicit intention to set themselves apart from certain continental traditions. This may be true of Bertrand Russell and G. E. Moore, but certainly not in the case of Gottlob Frege.[1] The understanding of Frege's thinking still suffers from a hermeneutic deficiency: the historical background leading up to Frege's philosophy has not been taken into consideration, and as a consequence, a distorted picture has been drawn of his systematic insights. The impression of independence or even isolation has been strengthened by the fact that Frege rarely makes explicit reference to other authors, except in cases of polemic argumentation. In fact, however, Frege's writings frequently react to contexts of argumentation and discussion offered by the 'Jena microcosm'—without explicitly mentioning them. One clear example of this is provided by Frege's essay 'Die Verneinung' ('Negation'), in which he deals extensively with the views of his philosophical colleague Bruno Bauch without mentioning him even once.[2] In order to reveal such influences and relations, we therefore need to reconstruct the historical context which served Frege as a background against which he developed his own position. Since the relevant texts are unfamiliar even to many German readers today, we will have to carry out some detective work so that eventually, we will be able to integrate the textual evidence into a plausible overall picture of Frege's position within German philosophy. It is my aim here to contribute some thematically arranged pieces to this puzzle which should identify the continental roots of Frege's analytic philosophy.

---

[1] Cf. Sluga 1980.

[2] A detailed account of Frege's implicit reference to Bauch is provided by Schlotter 2006.

7.1 THEORY OF SIGNS, CONCEPTUAL NOTATION, AND CONCEPT FORMATION

The philosophical approach from language analysis is older than Frege. Friedrich Adolf Trendelenburg, taking up Humboldtian ideas, had already emphasized the role language plays in thinking. At the very least, it is clear that Frege took over the term 'Begriffsschrift' ('Conceptual Notation') from Trendelenburg.[3] In the preface to his *Begriffsschrift* (1879, V/1997, 50), he compares his project to Leibniz's programme of 'a universal characteristic, a *calculus philosophicus* or *ratiocinator*', and in a footnote in the same passage refers to volume 3 of Trendelenburg's *Historische Beiträge zur Philosophie* (*Historical Contributions to Philosophy*). This volume contains two articles on Leibniz: 'Ueber Leibnizens Entwurf einer allgemeinen Charakteristik' ('On Leibniz's Project of a Universal Characteristic'; 1856/1867a) and 'Ueber das Element der Definition in Leibnizens Philosophie' ('On the Element of Definition in Leibniz's Philosophy'; 1859/1867b). Frege's note refers to the first of these articles. This reference is the only explicit mention of secondary literature in the whole of the *Begriffsschrift* and is noteworthy for that reason alone.

Frege very probably came to study Trendelenburg's text—which must be considered rather remote for him as a mathematician—through the philosopher Rudolf Eucken, who had been a pupil of Trendelenburg. Although their academic interests were very different, Frege and Eucken were on good terms throughout their lives and at times influenced one another in their research.[4] In the mid-1880s, the two even became neighbours. Their houses—Forstweg 22 (Eucken) and Forstweg 29 (Frege) in Jena—still exist and lie directly opposite one another. It is likely that Eucken called Frege's attention to Trendelenburg's discussion of Leibniz's logic and thus indirectly inspired the title '*Begriffsschrift*'. Trendelenburg had used this expression as a term for Leibniz's programme of a universal characteristic.[5] It is also known that Frege decided on the title '*Begriffsschrift*' comparatively late: this is indicated by the fact that the publisher (or the typesetter) labelled the printed sheets using the specification 'Frege, *Formelsprache* (formula language)', that is, they applied a word from the subtitle.[6]

---

[3] The term 'conceptual notation' (if not marked as a title) is used here to refer to the logic developed in Frege 1879. References to Frege use the pagination of the original publications. In most cases, translations of direct quotations follow the translations of Frege's texts in Frege 1997 or Frege 1979; references to pages in these collections are also provided.

[4] Cf. Dathe 1995, 246f.

[5] Trendelenburg 1856/1867a, 4. The term 'Begriffsschrift' had already been used by Wilhelm von Humboldt. Christian Thiel was the first to point this out, cf. Thiel 1995, 20.

[6] In the 1964 reprint of Frege 1879, this specification is only found on page 1 (on the bottom, left-hand corner), whereas the original publication displays it on the first page of *every* printed sheet (pages 1, 17, 33, 49, 65, and 81).

Frege does not directly deal with Trendelenburg, but he does take up the latter's discussion of Leibniz's logic in his *Begriffsschrift* and in some other early writings. For instance, we clearly find allusions to Trendelenburg in Frege's short essay 'Ueber die wissenschaftliche Berechtigung einer Begriffsschrift' ('On the Scientific Justification of a Conceptual Notation'). This article appeared in the *Zeitschrift für Philosophie und philosophische Kritik* (*Journal for Philosophy and Philosophical Critique*), one of the most well-known philosophical journals at the time. With this publication, the mathematician Frege attempted to reach philosophers, too, and to give them an understanding of his project. The theory of signs, which had also been discussed in Trendelenburg's essay on Leibniz, serves him as a link to their interests.[7]

Trendelenburg begins his critical appraisal of the universal characteristic with some considerations of a theory of signs which serve to explain the purpose of the whole project. He accurately highlights the strong connection between the use of signs and the knowledge of something: 'The advancing human mind owes no real *thing* as much as it owes the *signs* of things.' This is because 'through the sign, ideas—which otherwise would melt away—are separated and, as separate elements, become a constant possession which the thinking mind can command' (1856/1867a, 1). Next, Trendelenburg discusses the advantage that writing has over 'spoken signs': 'The audible sign, which is elusive like a moment in time, becomes visible and durable in writing' (2). Or, in more general terms: 'Hence the sign, in spoken as well as in written language, is more significant for men than anything else. All inventions and discoveries, all things that the human mind acquires or forms, are almost without exception built on the foundation of the intelligible sign' (2). In natural languages, Trendelenburg resumes, the sign mingles with the corresponding idea so strongly that the idea 'comes as soon as the sign calls'. However, a firm connection with the 'full content of the concept' is lacking (3). In addition, different languages have different signs for the same thing. The association of sign and idea arises *psychologically* 'through blind habituation', not *logically* 'through differentiating consciousness'. It is therefore necessary, particularly in the sciences, to create signs 'that represent the characteristics which are distinguished and combined in concepts in a distinguishing and combining way' (3). Trendelenburg here calls for the creation of a '*Begriffsschrift*' (!) as it can be found, in a rudimentary form, in arithmetic and algebra (4).

It is noteworthy that the philologist Trendelenburg models his view on language more strongly on scientific thinking and its discovering progress than the mathematician Frege—who explicitly acknowledges the value of both 'ordinary language' (1879, V/1997, 49) and the language of 'the poet or the speaker' (1892, 31/1997, 155). Trendelenburg does not take into consideration the more aesthetic and rhetorical functions of language, which are traditionally ascribed to the sound of oral language and the succinct character of images (cf. Baumgarten, Herder, Humboldt). Frege calls this domain the '*Färbung*' ('colouring') of sense—which is a translation of the ancient expression '*colores*

---

7 Cf. Sluga 1980, 51f.

rhetorici. In his conceptual notation, which is intended to serve scientific purposes, such elements of language have to be eliminated. Outside of science, however, Frege admits that they have communicative value. Apart from this admission, Frege takes over Trendelenburg's sequence from acoustic-sensual signs through optical-conceptual signs to logical-conceptual signs. Accordingly, signs for ideas serve to establish a 'firm centre' which then allows us to stop the constant change of perceptions by making it present (1882, 49). In using the same sign for different but similar things, we stress similarities and initiate concept formation (49f.). In contrast to the *emotive* advantages of the human voice, which, in its 'infinite flexibility' enables us to 'do justice even to the subtlest mixtures and modifications of feelings', Frege then emphasizes the *cognitive* advantage of written language. The signs of writing are 'sharply delimited and clearly distinguished' and hence assist the demand for a sharp delimitation of concepts (52f.), which Frege calls for repeatedly in other places.

Frege motivates the two-dimensionality of his conceptual notation on the basis of Trendelenburg's views on the role of signs: in making use of two dimensions, the advantages of writing are doubled, 'the spatial relations of written signs on a two-dimensional writing surface' enable us to adequately express the non-linear, complex logical relations (53f.). This peculiarity of Frege's formalism will not be considered further here. What is important is the fact that Frege makes use of Trendelenburg's theory of signs in order to philosophically justify his own project. In addition, he tries to fend off the reservations Trendelenburg has against the practicability of Leibniz's programme with regard to his own enterprise of a conceptual notation. While he agrees with Trendelenburg's objection that Leibniz's idea of a *universal* characteristic is 'too grandiose', he emphasizes that his own conceptual notation has a more modest aim mainly restricted to arithmetic (1879, V/1997, 50).[8] At the same time, Frege dispels a potential misunderstanding of the subtitle of his *Begriffsschrift—eine der arithmetischen nachgebildete Formelsprache des reinen Denkens* (*A Formula Language of Pure Thought Modelled on that of Arithmetic*)— through the following clarification: 'Any attempt to establish an artificial similarity [to the formula language of arithmetic] by constructing a concept as the sum of its marks [*Merkmale*] was far from my mind' (1879, IV/1997, 49).

This passage has baffled many Frege scholars. Some have considered it an early rejection of the algebra of logic (Boole, Schröder)—without noticing, though, that regarding concepts as the sum of their marks or properties presupposes an intensional view of concepts. The algebra of logic, however, is based on an extensional view according to which a logical sum is defined as the union (and a logical product as the intersection) of the *extensions* of concepts (classes).[9] Hence, Frege's passage must refer to another view, namely an intensional one. It is just such an intensional view that Trendelenburg criticizes in his discussion of Leibniz's calculating logic:

---

[8] Cf. also Trendelenburg 1856/1867a, 43: 'It is admittedly quite clear how far apart the fundamental idea and the goal lie in Leibniz's characteristic.'

[9] Cf. for example Frege's presentation in Frege 1883, 2.

What is problematic in this whole conception [of Leibniz] is calculation. All calculating can be traced back to addition and subtraction as the most basic mathematical operations. In a like manner, the application of calculation to the elements of concepts will always have to be based on such an extrinsic relation which can be traced back to plus and minus of the properties which, through their interaction, form the concept. This is the case whether the properties are related to the concept which they form like summands to a sum or like factors to a product. (1856/1867a, 23f.)

In his *Logische Untersuchungen* (*Logical Investigations*), Trendelenburg accuses what he calls 'formal logic' of just this kind of 'algebraic' understanding of concept formation (or definition): 'Without this view of composition, formal logic cannot apply its own principle' (1862, I, 20). Trendelenburg, by contrast, emphasizes the 'peculiar interrelation' of the properties of a concept. Their 'organic bond' is 'torn apart and transformed into a mere sum of extrinsic parts' (21). Here, Trendelenburg follows Goethe and his critique of formal logic centred on the concept of the organism—he even uses a similar wording.[10]

With this background, we can understand Frege's opposition to the calculation of marks as an implicit reference to Trendelenburg's critique of Leibniz. Frege wants to emphasize that this critique does not apply to his own conceptual notation. Trendelenburg's objection that formal logic regards concepts 'as given' (1862, I, 18) is taken over by Frege verbatim in his later critique of the extensional concept formation or class formation of Boole's logic: he criticizes this logic for assuming 'as given a system of concepts' (1983, 38/1979, 34). In this context it is noteworthy that Trendelenburg and Frege depart from the view that judgements are formed from given concepts and that both regard the doctrine of judgement as primary to the doctrine of concepts. Trendelenburg can justly invoke Aristotle when he speaks of judgement as 'the starting point of logic' (1876, 1; cf. 1862, II, 214).

The similarities between Frege's and Trendelenburg's doctrines of concepts are most prevalent in Frege's early writings from the time between the *Begriffsschrift* (1879) and *Die Grundlagen der Arithmetik* (*The Foundations of Arithmetic*, 1884)—a time at which the contact between Frege and Eucken was particularly intense. Both Trendelenburg and Frege embrace an organic model of concept formation which expressly opposes a 'mere juxtaposition' (Trendelenburg 1862, I, 21) or 'a conjunction of marks' (Frege 1884, § 88/1997, 122), a thought which both authors ascribe to Kant. While Trendelenburg (following the tradition of genetic definitions) relies on an 'organic connection' which gives new 'life' to the 'subtracted properties' (1862, I, 21), Frege realizes 'fruitful definitions' through the functional structure of his conceptual notation, which guarantees 'a more intimate, I would say more organic connection of defining elements' than the mere addition of marks or properties (1884, § 88/1997, 122).

Frege does not only embrace the model of the organism in the case of the theory of concept formation; he also transfers this model to the doctrine of judgement.

---

[10] Goethe 1808/1994, verses 1936–9.

According to this view, propositions which follow from mathematical axioms are contained in these axioms like a plant is contained in the 'seed'; and the basic logical laws are laws that '*potentially* imply all others' (1879, 25). Frege here takes up a formulation that Trendelenburg used in his translation of Aristotle (as the translation of '*dynámei*'): 'It seems that the general judgement is more significant, because when we have the [logically] prior of two judgements we also in a way know the [logically] posterior—we *potentially* possess it. For example, if we know that in every triangle the sum of the angles equals two right angles, we also *potentially* know that in an isosceles triangle, the angles equal two right angles, even if we do not know the exact shape of the isosceles triangle.'[11] In the corresponding comment Trendelenburg summarizes the passage from Aristotle as follows: we 'govern' the individual through the general, because the individual 'potentially' lies in the general, that is, it follows from the general through specification.[12]

Hence we can say that Frege, in his early writings, adopts an organic view of logic as it was propagated by Trendelenburg. Later, however, after 'Über Sinn und Bedeutung' ('On Sense and Reference'), he weakens the organic model (although he still uses the metaphor of the organism) and favours a compositional model instead, which has become known as Frege's principle of compositionality in current semantic debates. But regardless of these later developments, our results so far should already make us sceptical of the common view of the relation between traditional and modern logic. The relation is in fact much more complicated than it has been supposed. Frege makes use of Trendelenburg's critique of formal logic in order to justify his own conception of a logic which, although it proceeds formally, also has content. Frege cannot do without an understanding which credits logic its own content, if only because his programme of logicism claims to develop the content of arithmetic from logic. Accordingly, he emphasizes that logic is not really 'completely formal' (1906, 428) and backs this claim with the concept of negation as a concept peculiar to logic which, in connection with other logical concepts such as universality and conditionality, can yield 'scientifically fruitful' definitions (1983, 39/1979, 34).

7.2 Anti-Psychologism and the Theory of Validity

Frege's demand for a logic that is independent of psychology plays a central part in his philosophy. But Frege was not the first to adopt such an anti-psychologist logic. Herbart, for instance, emphasizes:

---

[11] Trendelenburg 1876, 9 (§ 6); translation of Aristotle's *Analytica posteriora* I 24. 86a22ff, my emphasis.

[12] Trendelenburg 1876, 12 (§ 6).

It is necessary in logic to ignore everything psychological, because proof is to be established only of those forms of possible connections of thought which the nature of thought itself allows. (1813/1912, § 34)

For Herbart as well as for Frege, the basis of the independence of logic from psychology is the distinction between the activity of thinking and its contents: 'All our thoughts can be considered in two ways: partly as activities of our mind, partly in regard to what is being thought through them' (1813/1912, § 34). The activity of thinking belongs to psychology; the contents of thought are studied by logic. What is expressed here is the distinction between content with its atemporal identity and the mental 'realizations' of this content at different times.

Based on the same distinction, Frege repeatedly emphasizes that mental contents (relations of ideas) cannot be the entities which we call true or false. That is to say mental contents cannot be ascribed truth-value. Why not? Because ideas are private: everyone has their own ideas. A dispute about the truth of a proposition, however, presupposes that *different* disputants are talking about the *same* thing, that they are referring to the *same* content. This content is represented differently by different people; it is different 'in' different subjects, but it has to be the same *inter*subjectively, or more precisely, *trans*-subjectively 'for' different subjects.

While Frege's anti-psychologism has a forerunner already in Herbart, in its concrete form Frege's position primarily follows the neo-Kantian theory of validity with its distinction between the context of discovery and the context of justification. Only this distinction affords an adequate understanding of the a priori, one which takes into account the foundation of validity. In principle, it is already present in Kant's famous words: 'Even as all our cognition begins *with* experience, this does not mean that it all springs *from* experience' (1787/1968a, 27). Lotze supplies the terminology decisive for those after him. In his early logic from 1843, he had praised Herbart for 'entirely separating the psychological origin of the logical from its validity' (1843, 8f.). Windelband elaborated the distinction in contrasting the 'genetic method' with the 'critical method' and thus made the concept of validity the key concept of neo-Kantianism (1883/1915b).

It is noteworthy that even Carnap's programme with its critical stance towards metaphysics, which aims at substituting philosophy by a logic of science, ultimately is a radicalization of the neo-Kantian position that logic, in Windelband's words, as 'the *philosophical doctrine of knowledge*', forms the 'epitome of all theoretical philosophy' (1912, 2). It is a radicalization because Carnap—influenced by the *Lebensphilosophie* movement—denies ethics and aesthetics their scientific character so that out of the three neo-Kantian 'basic philosophical sciences' (3), only logic remains. Logic is then identified with formal logic, with which Carnap—as a student of the neo-Kantian Bruno Bauch—became directly familiar in Jena when he attended Frege's lectures on the '*Begriffsschrift*'. Because Carnap, influenced by his time in Vienna and Wittgenstein's *Tractatus*, denies the possibility of synthetic a priori knowledge, the transcendental deduction of the categories from the forms of judgements is dropped. The role of transcendental logic is now taken by modern propositional and predicate logic. Its analytic forms become categories of a 'logical structure of the world'.[13]

Frege is more closely connected to neo-Kantianism both temporally and intellectually. Nevertheless, even this connection has long been concealed, because Frege hardly ever refers to neo-Kantian authors in his writings. A close comparison of texts, however, reveals many remarkable (sometimes even verbatim) parallels between Frege and neo-Kantian authors. Hermeneutically, we cannot therefore doubt that Frege is at least part of the neo-Kantian tradition. This is particularly clear with regard to the value-theoretic version of neo-Kantianism, which has its origins in Hermann Lotze and is further developed by Windelband, Rickert, and Bauch.[14] We can regard Lotze as the founder of this tradition due to his theory of validity. Frege's extensive agreement with the basic ideas of value-theoretic neo-Kantianism can be explained by the fact that he, too, was in many respects inspired by Lotze. This influence has long been denied by analytic authors, in particular by Michael Dummett. Those who are still sceptical should take notice of the following handwritten passage from Bauch's (literary) estate:

> I have heard it from our great mathematician Frege himself, that for his mathematical—and I may add what Frege in his modesty didn't say, epoch-making—investigations, the impulses he got from Lotze were of decisive significance.[15]

When Bauch speaks of 'mathematical investigations' here, this should be understood in the sense of Frege's functional representation of logic.[16]

Already with Lotze, anti-psychologism, with its foundation in the theory of validity, is characterized by a peculiar mixture of Kantian and Platonic elements. We are hence justified in speaking of a *transcendental Platonism*. Analogies—even in particular distinctions and arguments—can be found especially between Frege and Windelband. A prominent example is the recognition of the 'fundamentally twofold character of all logical laws', which have a 'validity in themselves' as well as a 'validity for us':

> Seen from 'our' point of view, the logical is an 'ought': but this ought has to have its ground in something which is valid in itself and which becomes an ought, or a rule for us, only in its relation to a consciousness which can err. (Windelband 1912, 18)

This means that a norm or a rule derives its normativity (for us) from its independent (of us) validity. We can find the same thought again in Frege's *Grundgesetze der Arithmetik* (*Basic Laws of Arithmetic*), where he says about the 'ambiguity (*Doppelsinn*)...of the

---

[13] Carnap 1928/1961. For Carnap's relation to neo-Kantianism see Friedman 2000.
[14] Cf. Gabriel 2002; see also Schlotter 2004, especially 91–108.
[15] I am grateful to Sven Schlotter (Jena) for pointing out this passage to me. Cf. Schlotter 2006, 45.
[16] Frege's functional representation has little in common with Lotze's functional conception of concepts. Above all, Lotze lacks Frege's idea of the 'incompleteness' of concepts. Cf. Schlotter 2004, 52f., n.198.

word "law"': 'In one sense it states what is, in the other it prescribes what should be' (1893, XV/1997, 202).[17] And Frege adds:

> Any law that states what is can be conceived as prescribing that one should think in accordance with it, and is therefore in that sense a law of thought.

In his later essay 'Der Gedanke' ('Thought'), Frege repeats the insight that the word 'law' is used 'in two senses', and again emphasizes that logic is primarily concerned with the 'laws of truth'. These laws are valid 'in themselves', that is, 'objectively', for Frege as well as for Windelband. Their 'validity for us' is expressed by Frege through the assertion that from these objective laws, there follow 'laws of thinking' in the sense of 'prescriptions about asserting, thinking, judging, and inferring' (1918a, 58/1997, 325).

Frege and Windelband thus agree with regard to the *status* of logical laws: the normativity of the logical laws is based on their validity (or their being true), not vice versa. Formulations of Windelband such as the following could just as well be found in Frege: 'The validity of a proposition is the ground of our believing it to be true, and not the other way round, as if our believing something to be true would make it valid' (1909, 25). Frege and Windelband also agree in the question of the *justification* of logical laws. For Frege, there is only one way to *logically* justify a logical law, which consists in deriving it from other logical laws. Where this is not possible, as in the case of *basic* logical laws, there is consequently no *logical* way to justify such a law. This does not mean, however, that we have to do without any justification at all. Thus, Frege notes (for the example of the law of identity):

> Leaving aside logic, one can say: we are forced to make judgements by our nature and external circumstances, and if we make judgements, we cannot reject this law… we must recognize it if we are not to throw our thought into confusion and in the end renounce judgement altogether. (1893, XVII/1997, 204)

Frege here makes use of a way of argumentation which, although it does not, as he says, provide a 'ground of being true', does afford us a ground of 'our holding as true'. Or, in Windelband's words, we are not concerned with grounds 'in themselves' but with grounds 'for us'. In this respect, Frege is exactly in line with Windelband's argumentation, which was offered ten years earlier.

We should further emphasize that both authors derive the normativity of the logical laws—or their validity 'for us'—from our 'will to truth'. For Frege, the laws of logic are 'authoritative for our thought if it wants to attain truth' (1893, XVI/1997, 203). Like Frege, Windelband makes clear that the validity (in the sense of being true) of basic logical laws (or 'axioms') cannot be proved with 'logical necessity'. Instead, we can establish the 'teleological necessity' of these laws by remembering 'that their validity absolutely

---

[17] Windelband, too, uses the term 'ambiguity' (*Doppelsinn*): 1912, 19 (the first line).

has to be accepted' if we want thinking to 'fulfil the purpose of being true' (1883/1915b, 109; my emphasis). The teleological necessity of the axioms is hence based on the aim of thinking 'to be true'. It is in this sense that truth is a value for us.

Both Frege and Windelband argue in a transcendental way here, in the sense that the acceptance of basic logical laws forms the condition of the possibility of our judging. Whenever we state something with a claim to its truth, the acceptance of such axioms is already implicitly presupposed. If we wanted to deny these axioms or even just abstain from accepting them, this would result, as one might nowadays say, in a pragmatic contradiction—it would be like 'trying to jump out of one's own skin', as Frege says (1893, XVII/1997, 204), or, in Windelband's words, like wanting to 'learn to swim before entering the water' (1883/1915b, 112). Frege's and Windelband's argumentations agree very strongly—they even apply similar metaphors.

It is also noteworthy that for Windelband, logic is independent not only of psychology but also of grammar. Early on, he notes that 'logical analysis' has to 'go beyond the linguistic form everywhere and must not cling to the system of grammatical forms' (1884, 195). Later, Windelband not only emphasizes that 'there may be logical principles of psychology (as in every science), but there are no psychological principles of logic' (1912, 7). Without forgetting the *actual* connection between language and knowledge, he adds: 'Surely there are logical principles of grammar, but there are no grammatical principles of logic' (13). Such statements are perfectly in line with the branch of analytic philosophy which, influenced by logic, is concerned with the development of an ideal language.

7.3 Existential and Number Statements— The Origins of Predicate Logic

It is one of Frege's most important insights to have recognized the concept of existence as a second-level concept. This recognition provides the basis for the understanding of logical quantifiers and hence for the development of predicate logic. Many of Frege's ideas in this respect can already be found in Herbart in a basic form. The first step towards Frege's insight is provided by Herbart's comparison of particular affirmative judgements with number statements:

> The particular affirmative judgement (some A are B) does not actually have the entire concept A as its subject, but instead a part of its extension is singled out. This part is not usually further determined; yet one can add a quantitative assessment like *many, few, most, fewest*, or a numerical determination like *ten, hundred*, etc. (1813/1912, § 56)

According to this passage, a particular judgement such as '*some* apples are green' is transformed into a number statement ('*ten* apples are green') when we substitute the *indefinite* indication of an extension ('some') by a *definite* indication ('ten'). A particular judgement can hence be described as an indefinite number statement, and a number statement as a definite particular judgement. Since Herbart further derives existential statements from particular judgements (§ 63),[18] there will also be a connection between number statements and existential statements. He goes on (with regard to number statements): 'Now every number refers... to the general concept of the counted,'[19] or, expressed in modern terms, to a sortal concept under which the counted objects are subsumed. Number statements are thus statements about concepts, and hence, as Frege later came to express it, second-level statements. The ensuing consequences are almost inevitable: if number statements are second-level statements, and if particular judgements are indefinite number statements, then—if we take into account the similarity between particular judgements and existential statements (cf. Frege 1983, 275)—existential statements must also be indefinite number statements and hence second-level statements. The argumentation indicated here is confirmed when Frege says that 'existence is similar to number', since both express properties of concepts (and thus themselves are second-level concepts): 'Affirmation of existence is indeed nothing other than denial of the number zero' (1884, § 53/1997, 103; cf. § 55).

Looking back on his life's work, Frege describes in his 'Aufzeichnungen für Ludwig Darmstaedter' ('Notes for Ludwig Darmstaedter') how he was led 'from mathematics to logic'. As a starting point, he mentions the insight that 'in stating a number... we are making a statement about a concept' (1983, 273/1997, 262). Yet his investigations were hindered by the 'logical imperfections of language', which he 'tried to overcome' through his conceptual notation. A case can be made that Frege, starting from the need to find a logically precise formulation of number statements as second-level statements, was led via the analogy between existential and number statements to the development of predicate logic. Although Frege ultimately did not introduce numbers as quantifiers but as logical objects (which as we know led to Russell's paradox), his predicate logic is not affected by this. Without doubt, the one who deserves credit for showing Frege his philosophical way in this respect is Herbart.

7.4 KANT'S FORMS OF JUDGEMENT

In the previous section, we did not distinguish between 'propositions' and 'judgements'. This is not in line with Frege's practice, who attaches great importance to the distinction between the *content* of a judgement and the *act* of judging. Frege's theory of judgement (not only in this point, but also in general) turns out to be the continuation of a reduction of Kant's forms of judgement. The beginnings of this reduction can be traced

---

[18] For more detail, see Gabriel 2005, 118f.

[19] Herbart 1825/1892, 111. Cf. also Herbart 1841/1902, 102, note 2, 2nd paragraph: 'Two does not mean two things, but duplication.' This sentence is quoted affirmatively in Frege 1884, III. For the influence that Herbart had on Frege, see Sullivan 1990.

back to traditional logic and authors such as Herbart, Lotze, Sigwart, and Windelband, who paved the way for Frege in their critical reflections on Kant's theory of judgement. It cannot be doubted that Frege's propositional and predicate logic must be regarded as more productive than traditional logic (as developed by Aristotle). Frege's logic, with its replacement of subject–predicate analysis of propositions by function–argument analysis, is technically superior and richer. However, we should emphasize that Frege—here as elsewhere—did not develop his system out of the blue or without the influence of traditional logic.

So let us first consider the situation in which Frege began to develop his logic. Within the discussion of the construction of logic, the critique of the table of judgements and its claim to completeness plays an important role. The objections raised against the table of judgements are significant because Kant aims at providing 'guidelines for the discovery of all pure concepts of the understanding' (1787/1968a, 91–106). C. F. Bachmann had already criticized Kant's table for not being 'a real classification', because it only contains 'mere aspects with regard to which judgements may be considered' (1828, § 78, 119). Bachman addresses 'the mutual crisscrossing of all headings', that is, the fact that a given judgement cannot be unequivocally assigned to one of the twelve forms but instead may belong to all four titles at the same time. This leads us to the question of how the different forms of judgement are related to one another.

The order in which Kant puts the four titles—'quantity', 'quality', 'relation', and 'modality'—already indicates that they are not of equal standing. Thus, modality plays a minor role because Kant does not define it logically (as a mere form), but epistemologically through the 'relation between the judgement as a whole and the faculty of cognition'.[20] In more general criticisms, the threefold character of all four titles has been felt to be artificial. Most notably, it has repeatedly been claimed that the third form of quality (the infinite judgement) cannot be regarded as an independent form (particularly as contrasted with the second form, the negative judgement).[21] Even Kant himself notes that this form is not relevant for formal logic, but only for transcendental logic. Frege's contemporary Windelband approvingly cites Lotze's harsh comment: 'In science, obvious whims do not even have to be replicated through too careful a refutation.'[22] Furthermore, as we have seen, the individual forms are in many cases not independent of one another. Leibniz had already pointed out that it is possible to represent the universal categorical judgement ('All S are P') as a hypothetical judgement ('If something is an S, then it is a P').[23]

Following such considerations, post-Kantian discussion had been concerned with a rearrangement of the forms of judgement. Herbart expanded Leibniz's insight to disjunctive judgements when he noted: 'The difference between categorical, hypothetical, and disjunctive judgements lies entirely in their linguistic forms' (1808/1887, 222). In the same spirit, Frege comments on the relation of judgements in a single sentence,

[20] Kant 1800/1968b, § 30. Cf. Kant 1787/1968a, 99–101 and 266.
[21] Kant 1800/1968b, § 22, note 2; Kant 1787/1968a, 97.
[22] Windelband 1884, 185, note 3. Cf. Lotze 1874, 62.
[23] Leibniz 1765/1882, book 4, chapter XI, § 14; 1978 reprint V, 427.

which sounds like a late echo of Herbart's wording: 'The distinction between categorical, hypothetical, and disjunctive judgements seems to me to have only grammatical
significance' (1879, § 4/1997, 55). Frege here refers to the general possibility of defining logical connectives through one another with the help of negation. He also thereby
answers an objection which had already been raised against Kant in traditional logic:
that other connectives besides hypothetical and disjunctive ones, such as conjunction,
are not taken into account (cf. Sigwart 1904, I, 283).

One point which played an important role in the development of nineteenth-century
views is the fact that Kant's classification does not distinguish the content of a judgement from the act of judging. This was at the root of Herbart's critique in speaking of
the '*complete inadequacy* of Kant's table of the logical functions of judgement'. He clearly
interprets judgements in the sense of judging assertions when he emphasizes: 'Every
judgement, as such and taken by itself, is assertoric' (1808/1887, 221f.). The further
development of such thoughts initially led to the adoption of affirmation and negation
as two opposed acts of assertion. The quality of judgement was hence reinterpreted
in terms of acts of judging. Frege, finally, reduces the forms of judgement to the act of
affirmation and hence to the assertoric judgement. This judgement is equivalent to the
acceptance of a content as true, which is expressed in his conceptual notation by the
judgement stroke. In the judgement stroke, the first form of quality and the first form
of modality merge. All the remaining traditional forms of *judgement* (beginning with
negation) are transformed, in Frege's analysis, to forms of *content*. Along the same
lines, Sigwart had earlier declared: 'What is usually understood as a difference in *forms*
of judgement is really a difference in *content*' (1904, I, 313). The only exception Frege
makes concerns the modalities 'possible' and 'necessary', which (quite in line with Kant)
are interpreted *epistemologically* (1879, § 4/1997, 55) and hence do not count as *logical*
modalities. For Frege, there cannot be a modal logic.

The primacy of the quality of judgement is established during the course of the nineteenth century and is eventually expressed in the thesis that affirmation and negation
constitute the very essence of judgement. Thus, Herbart notes: 'This classification
(according to what is called quality) is the only one relevant to judgement; all the others,
as a random collection, have to be regarded as secondary' (1813/1912, § 54). In Kant's
table of judgements, quality only takes second place after quantity (1787/1968a, 95).
This order indicates that 'judgement' does not refer to the act of judging, but rather to the
content of judgement—even if Kant says that the 'logical function of judgement' is 'the
act of the understanding through which the manifold of given representations (whether
intuitions or concepts) is first brought under an apperception' (1787/1968a, 143). This is
because that act aims at establishing the 'unity' of the content (cf. 1800/1968b, § 17) and
is therefore no act of judgement in the sense of a positive or negative response to such a
content; hence Kant's remark that the unity of judgement can only be thought 'problematically' (1800/1968b, § 30).

The understanding of judgements as acts goes back as far as scholasticism. William
of Ockham allows for a separate act of judgement (*actus iudicativus*) through which
the intellect reacts affirmatively or negatively (*assentit vel dissentit*) to a content of

judgement (*complexus*). Descartes, in turn, relocates this act away from '*intellectus*' to '*voluntas*'. Accepting or negating a content are, for him, '*modi volendi*' (1644/1964, I, §§ 32 and 34). This view, which makes the act of judgement a practical matter, is taken up by Windelband and thus by the value-theoretic version of neo-Kantianism. The starting point is Lotze's interpretation of the truth–untruth distinction as a 'distinction of values' (of relations of ideas; 1874, 4). Lotze defines the 'validity or invalidity…as objective predicates…which apply to the content of a judgement as a whole (as their subject)'. It is in this sense that he takes the affirmative judgement 'S is P' and the negative judgement 'S is not P' to be a double-judgement (he speaks of the 'splitting of every judgement in two parts'). The subject is 'the same connection of S and P' for both judgements, and it is subjected to 'two opposed subsidiary judgements' (1874, § 40, 61).

Windelband goes a step further when he regards the affirmative or negative evaluation of the truth (of a content) not as a *subsidiary*, but as the *main* element of judgement. In this context, he also introduces the term 'truth-value' ('*Wahrheitswert*') as an analogy to the common values and emphasizes that the logical 'truth-value…has to be coordinated with the other values' (1884, 173f.). The judgement itself is, for Windelband too, a double-judgement. In addition to a theoretical judgement (in the sense of the propositional content of judgement), there is a practical act of 'judging' which decides on the 'truth-value by affirmation or negation' (1882/1915a, 32). This interpretation of the act of judging as a decision about the truth-value of a propositional content introduces an evaluative element to the act of judgement—a typical feature of value-theoretic neo-Kantianism.

Windelband's approach was further developed by Heinrich Rickert. Rickert transfers the ethical terminology to the 'action' ('*Thathandlung*') of cognition: next to moral conscience, he allows for an 'intellectual conscience…which expresses itself in our feeling the necessity to judge and which guides our cognition just as moral consciousness guides our action' (1892, 89). The practical interpretation of judgement as an act of the will is in line with Fichte's conception of the primacy of practical reason. In contrast to Nietzsche, who regards judgement as based on a 'will to power', Rickert emphasizes that the 'acknowledgement of the truth-value' is the expression of a 'will to truth'. With a critical allusion to Nietzsche, he notes: 'A purely theoretical person may be "beyond good and evil", but he can never be beyond truth and falsehood' (1892, 90). Rickert thus highlights the transcendental character of the distinction between truth and falsehood.

As we have already mentioned, Frege reduces the two acts of judgement (affirmation and negation) to a single affirmative—or assertoric—act. This act is linguistically expressed in a statement, that is, a declarative sentence uttered with a claim to truth. The act of negation, in turn, is reinterpreted as the assertion of a negative content (or thought) (1918b, 154/1997, 357). Judging itself becomes a mental act which is performed in time by the subject as an 'agent' (1918b, 151, fn/1997, 354). The act of judging is the result of a 'choice' between two opposed thoughts:

> Rejecting the one and accepting the other is *one* and the same act. Therefore there is no need of a special name, or special sign, for rejecting a thought. (1983, 201/1979, 185)

With his distinction between 'judgement stroke' and 'content stroke' (the 'horizontal'), Frege has found an expression of the separation of the act of judging from the content of judgement in his logical notation (1879, § 2; 1893, 9/1997, 53; 215). In stressing the active character of the decision concerning the truth-value of a thought, he reveals the influence that value-theoretic neo-Kantianism with its emphasis on the practical dimension of judgement had on him. In line with this, Frege assigns the judgement stroke a special ('pragmatic') function as a sign that something is being stated: the judgement stroke does not denote anything, but instead indicates that the content following it is being 'asserted' (1891, 22, fn/1997, 142); it symbolizes 'the acknowledgement of the truth of a thought—the *act* of judgement' (1918a, 62/1997, 329, my emphasis).[24]

Frege's affinity to value-theoretic considerations is also expressed in his emphasis on the 'relatedness' of logic to ethics (1983, 4/1979, 4) and, more generally, in his affirmative reference to the neo-Kantian triad of values: 'Just as "beautiful" points the way for aesthetics and "good" for ethics, so do words like "true" for logic' (1918a, 58/1997, 325). The reduction of two acts of judging to a single act of assertion corresponds to the introduction of an additional truth value: 'truth' is now supplemented by 'falsehood'. In sum, Frege's theory of judgement can be regarded as a continuation of value-theoretic neo-Kantianism. The last step, however, Frege had to take alone: he did so when he generalized the mathematical concept of a function so that functions could take as their arguments *any* object, including truth-values, conceived themselves as objects. It is undoubtedly this generalization which accounts for the superiority of modern logic over traditional logic. Still, we must not forget—when praising these functional aspects—that 'truth-values' also have a value-theoretic dimension. In particular, Frege's identification of the meaning (or reference) of a sentence with its truth-value shows that he deliberately plays on the connotation of the German word '*Bedeutung*' as indicating 'significance' or 'having a value'. He thus specifically establishes the connection between *Bedeutung* and value: 'The thought loses value for us as soon as we recognize that the *Bedeutung* of one of its parts is missing' (1892, 33/1997, 157).[25] In the Anglo-Saxon tradition, where '*Bedeutung*' has often been translated as 'reference', these important aspects have been lost (a translation of '*Bedeutung*' as 'significance' may retain the relevant connotations better here). But it is these very aspects—hence the value-theoretic, not the functional interpretation of 'truth-values'—that justify the talk of 'truth-values' in the first place. This again demonstrates how important it can be to know the historical background of a philosophical position, even if we are concerned with a very systematic analytic philosopher.[26]

---

[24]   The neo-Kantians were well aware of the similarities between their view and Frege's. Cf. Goedeke 1928. Concerning Frege, Goedeke first notes that he cannot 'be considered a philosopher of value in the strict sense' (139), but concludes: 'The doctrine of acknowledgement, however, establishes a close connection between Frege and the Baden philosophy of values' (140).

[25]   Angelelli (1982) was probably the first to have noted this aspect.

[26]   I would like to thank Franziska Tropschug and Christian Kästner for translating this chapter.

References

Angelelli, I. (1982). 'Frege's Notion of "Bedeutung"'. In L. J. Cohen *et al.* (eds.), *Logic, Methodology and Philosophy of Science*, vol. IV. Amsterdam: North-Holland, pp. 735–53.

Bachmann, C. F. (1828). *System der Logik*. Leipzig: Brockhaus.

Carnap, R. (1961). *Der logische Aufbau der Welt* (1928), 2nd edn. Hamburg: Meiner.

Dathe, U. (1995). 'Gottlob Frege und Rudolf Eucken—Gesprächspartner in der Herausbildungsphase der modernen Logik', *History and Philosophy of Logic* 16: 245–55.

Descartes, R. (1964). *Principia philosophiae* (1644), *Oeuvres*, vol. VIII/1, ed. C. Adam and P. Tannery. Paris: Vrin.

Frege, G. (1879). *Begriffsschrift, eine der arithmetischen nachgebildete Formelsprache des reinen Denkens*. Halle a. S.: L. Nebert. Repr. in *Begriffsschrift und andere Aufsätze*, ed. Ignacio Angelelli. Darmstadt and Hildesheim: Olms, 1964.

—— (1882). 'Ueber die wissenschaftliche Berechtigung einer Begriffsschrift', *Zeitschrift für Philosophie und philosophische Kritik* 81: 48–56.

—— (1883). 'Ueber den Zweck der Begriffsschrift', *Jenaische Zeitschrift für Naturwissenschaft* 16, suppl.: 1–10.

—— (1884). *Grundlagen der Arithmetik*. Breslau: Koebner.

—— (1891). *Function und Begriff*. Jena: Pohle.

—— (1892). 'Über Sinn und Bedeutung', *Zeitschrift für Philosophie und philosophische Kritik* 100: 25–50.

—— (1893). *Grundgesetze der Arithmetik. Begriffsschriftlich abgeleitet*, vol. I. Jena: Pohle.

—— (1906). 'Über die Grundlagen der Geometrie III', *Jahresbericht der Deutschen Mathematiker-Vereinigung* 15: 423–30.

—— (1918a). 'Der Gedanke. Eine logische Untersuchung', *Beiträge zur Philosophie des deutschen Idealismus* 1: 58–77.

—— (1918b). 'Die Verneinung. Eine logische Untersuchung', *Beiträge zur Philosophie des deutschen Idealismus* 1: 143–57.

—— (1979). *Posthumous Writings*, ed. Hans Hermes, Friedrich Kambartel, and Friedrich Kaulbach. Oxford: Blackwell.

—— (1983). *Nachgelassene Schriften*, ed. H. Hermes, F. Kambartel, and F. Kaulbach, 2nd edn. Hamburg: Meiner.

—— (1997). *The Frege Reader*, ed. Michael Beaney. Oxford: Blackwell.

Friedman, M. (2000). *A Parting of the Ways: Carnap, Cassirer, and Heidegger*. Chicago and La Salle: Open Court.

Gabriel, G. (2002). 'Frege, Lotze, and the Continental Roots of Early Analytic Philosophy'. In E. H. Reck (ed.), *From Frege to Wittgenstein: Perspectives on Early Analytic Philosophy*. Oxford: Oxford University Press, pp. 39–51; also in M. Beaney and E. H. Reck (eds.), *Gottlob Frege: Critical Assessment of Leading Philosophers*, vol. I: *Frege's Philosophy in Context*. London and New York: Routledge, 2005, pp. 161–75.

—— (2005). 'Existential and Number Statements: Herbart and Frege'. In M. Beaney and E. H. Reck (eds.), *Gottlob Frege: Critical Assessment of Leading Philosophers*, vol. I: *Frege's Philosophy in Context*. London and New York: Routledge, pp. 109–23.

Goedeke, P. (1928). *Wahrheit und Wert. Eine logisch-erkenntnistheoretische Untersuchung über die Beziehung zwischen Wahrheit und Wert in der Wertphilosophie des Badischen Neukantianismus*. Köln: A. Weinrich & Komp.

Goethe, J. W. (1994). *Faust* (part I: 1808/part II: 1832), ed. A. Schöne. Frankfurt am Main: Deutscher Klassiker Verlag.

Herbart, J. F. (1887). *Hauptpuncte der Logik* (1808). In *Sämtliche Werke*, vol. II, ed. K. Kehrbach and O. Flügel. Langensalza: Beyer; repr. Aalen: Scientia, 1989.

—— (1892). *Psychologie als Wissenschaft. Zweiter, analytischer Teil* (1825). In *Sämtliche Werke*, vol. VI, ed. K. Kehrbach and O. Flügel. Langensalza: Beyer; repr. Aalen: Scientia, 1989.

—— (1902). *Umriß pädagogischer Vorlesungen* (2nd edn., 1841). In *Sämtliche Werke*, vol. X, ed. K. Kehrbach and O. Flügel. Langensalza: Beyer; repr. Aalen: Scientia, 1989.

—— (1912). *Lehrbuch zur Einleitung in die Philosophie* (1813); repr. ed. K. Häntsch. Leipzig: Meiner.

Kant, I. (1968a). *Kritik der reinen Vernunft* (2nd edn., 1787). In *Kants Werke*, Akademie-Textausgabe, vol. III. Berlin: Walter de Gruyter.

—— (1968b). *Logik* (1800). In *Kants Werke*, Akademie-Textausgabe, vol. IX. Berlin: Walter de Gruyter.

Leibniz, G. W. (1882). *Nouveaux essais sur l'entendement humain* (1765). In *Philosophische Schriften*, vol. V, ed. C. I. Gerhardt. Berlin: Weidmann; repr. Hildesheim: Olms, 1978.

Lotze, H. (1843). *Logik*. Leipzig: Weidmann.

—— (1874). *System der Philosophie, I: Drei Bücher der Logik*. Leipzig: Hirzel.

Rickert, H. (1892). *Der Gegenstand der Erkenntnis*. Freiburg: J. C. B. Mohr.

Schlotter, S. (2004). *Die Totalität der Kultur. Philosophisches Denken und politisches Handeln bei Bruno Bauch*. Würzburg: Königshausen & Neumann.

—— (2006). 'Frege's Anonymous Opponent in *Die Verneinung*', *History and Philosophy of Logic* 27: 43–58.

Sigwart, Ch. (1904). *Logik*, 2 vols. (1873/1878), 3rd edn. Tübingen: J. C. B. Mohr.

Sluga, H. D. (1980). *Gottlob Frege*. London, Boston, and Henley: Routledge.

Sullivan, D. (1990). 'Frege on the Statement of Number', *Philosophy and Phenomenological Research* 50: 595–603.

Thiel, Ch. (1995). '"Nicht aufs Gerathewohl und aus Neuerungssucht": Die Begriffsschrift 1879 und 1893'. In Ingolf Max and Werner Stelzner (eds.), *Logik und Mathematik. Frege-Kolloquium Jena 1993*. Berlin and New York: Walter de Gruyter, pp. 20–37. Tr. M. Beaney as 'Not Arbitrarily and Out of a Craze for Novelty: The Begriffsschrift 1879 and 1893', in M. Beaney and E. Reck (eds.), *Gottlob Frege: Critical Assessments of Leading Philosophers*. London: Routledge, 2005, vol. II, pp. 13–28.

Trendelenburg, Fr. A. (1862). *Logische Untersuchungen*, 2 vols., 2nd edn. Leipzig: Hirzel.

—— (1867a). 'Ueber Leibnizens Entwurf einer allgemeinen Charakteristik' (1856). In *Historische Beiträge zur Philosophie, vol. III: Vermischte Abhandlungen*. Berlin: Bethge, pp. 1–47.

—— (1867b). 'Ueber das Element der Definition in Leibnizens Philosophie' (1859). In *Historische Beiträge zur Philosophie, vol. III: Vermischte Abhandlungen*. Berlin: Bethge, pp. 48–62.

—— (1876). *Erläuterungen zu den Elementen der aristotelischen Logik*, 3rd edn. Berlin: Bethge.

Windelband, W. (1884). 'Beiträge zur Lehre vom negativen Urtheil'. In *Strassburger Abhandlungen zur Philosophie. Eduard Zeller zu seinem siebzigsten Geburtstage*. Tübingen: J. C. B. Mohr, pp. 167–95; repr. 1921.

—— (1909). *Der Wille zur Wahrheit*. Heidelberg: Winter.

—— (1912). 'Die Prinzipien der Logik'. In A. Ruge (ed.), *Encyclopädie der philosophischen Wissenschaften*, vol. I. Tübingen: J. C. B. Mohr, pp. 1–60.

——(1915a). 'Was ist Philosophie?' (1882). In *Präludien. Aufsätze und Reden zur Philosophie und ihrer Geschichte*, vol. I, 5th edn. Tübingen: J. C. B. Mohr, pp. 1–54.

——(1915b). 'Kritische oder genetische Methode?' (1883). In *Präludien. Aufsätze und Reden zur Philosophie und ihrer Geschichte*, vol. II, 5th edn. Tübingen: J. C. B. Mohr, pp. 99–135.

CHAPTER 8

....

ANALYTIC PHILOSOPHY, THE ANALYTIC SCHOOL, AND BRITISH PHILOSOPHY

....

JOHN SKORUPSKI

8.1 INTRODUCTION: 'ANALYTIC PHILOSOPHY' AND THE 'ANALYTIC SCHOOL'

The aim of this chapter is to assess the relations between analytic philosophy and the British philosophical tradition. That calls for some preliminary clarifying of tasks and terms. For the purpose of our discussion, we can make two rough and ready distinctions. The first is between *background* and *influence*. 'Background' will be understood broadly: it can cover any aspect of pre-analytic British philosophy which is interestingly similar to approaches or themes in analytic philosophy and which may or may not have influenced it. Influence, in contrast, is causal, and thus often very hard to establish. Then there are large possibilities in between: even where there is no causal influence of one work on another, both may spring from a common cast of mind, or some national continuity or persisting tradition. This kind of possibility is speculative; but a sufficient commonality of background themes or approaches may suggest quite strongly that it is there.

Consider, in particular, the case of Mill's *System of Logic*.[1] The whole of this work counts as background; Mill's concerns, his theses, and his methods are throughout readily recognizable to any analytic philosopher working today. What of its influence? Since it became for several decades a standard text in British universities it had an influence that was pervasive. However, influence can of course be negative—not least in the case

---

[1] Mill 1963–91, vols. VII and VIII (*A System of Logic, Ratiocinative and Inductive*, first published 1843).

of standard texts—and in the case of the *System* it often was, both in Britain and abroad. A particularly striking instance is Mill's empiricist account of logic and mathematics. Frege discusses and rejects it in his *Foundations of Arithmetic* (1884), arguing against Mill on the one hand and Kant on the other that arithmetic is analytic; that discussion was to have a lasting effect. The Vienna Circle empiricists lined up on Frege's side against Mill's radical empiricism, though their notion of analyticity was very different from that of Frege.

Another point is that negative influence can also work, and often does work, through misunderstanding. A reaction against something never actually said can produce a fresh impetus. Moore's 'naturalistic fallacy' is an example (see Moore 1903)—and also a very good example of how counter-suggestibility is a significant philosophical force. No one—not Mill or anyone else—had committed the so-called naturalistic fallacy till Moore named it[2]—but once he had done so it became tempting to affirm the very thing he called a 'fallacy'.

And yet, after all these vicissitudes, to read Mill's philosophy today—be it the *System* or *Utilitarianism*—is to be forcibly struck by the way its sober, humane naturalism represents one resilient strand in British thought, a stance which, if anything, exists more strongly than ever in current analytic philosophy. It is not implausible to see this stance as springing from a British tradition of thought, a persisting cast of mind. We shall return to this.

The second distinction we shall need is between *analytic philosophy* and what I shall call the *Analytic school*.

By the latter I mean a distinctive school of twentieth-century philosophy which focuses on the idea that the analysis of language is basic to philosophy as such: basic, moreover, in a particular way—as the route by which traditional philosophical questions can be revealed as pseudo-problems. Historically, Wittgenstein is central to it, with Carnap close behind.[3] The central and most influential thrust, as particularly represented by these two, was that analysis of language can dissolve philosophical questions; but around them we can group other independently important philosophers, such as Schlick in Vienna and Russell and Moore in Cambridge—philosophers who may not have propounded this central thesis or agreed with it but who were, so to speak, abreast of it, and contributed ideas that in one way or another affected it.

Taking the Analytic school in this way, we can say that its early phases were the Cambridge of Moore, Russell, and Wittgenstein, and the Vienna of Wittgenstein and the Vienna Circle. Its antecedents include Moore's and Russell's rebellion against idealism, the influence of philosopher-scientists such as Mach, Hilbert, and Einstein on the Vienna Circle, and of course the crucial impact of Frege, both in Cambridge and in Vienna.

---

[2] Divine law theories of morality might be proposed as an exception.

[3] Alberto Coffa rightly emphasized the role played by these two (Coffa 1991). It can be argued that Wittgenstein thought himself out of the Analytic school and in his later work started thinking against it, but that is compatible with recognizing his seminal influence on it.

The Analytic school continued in later stages through Oxford ordinary language phi-losophy and the Harvard of Quine and Putnam. It's fair to say that it no longer exists, any more than other distinctive modernist schools of philosophy of the first half or so of the twentieth century any longer exist. I do not mean, of course, that there is some clear-cut point at which it ceased to exist, or that philosophers can be straightforwardly placed in or outside it. Hilary Putnam, for example, can be seen both as a contributor to it and as a critic leading philosophy out of it. Nor do I mean that its ideas no longer have any influ-ence. Intellectual movements cannot be crisply defined in such ways. Still, the Analytic school appears now as a historical phenomenon with a beginning and an end, a closely related set of movements that flourished in a certain distinctive cultural context, a con-text in which the focus was on *language*, rather than the traditional triad of *self, thought,* and *world*.[4]

In contrast, 'analytic philosophy', as people use it now, is a very vague term. It is best characterized not by distinctive themes or methods but rather by institutions and to some extent by style. 'Analytic philosophy' no longer even denotes ancestry from the Analytic school. Take for example the tradition of Franz Brentano and his Austrian and Polish pupils.[5] It would now be normal to recognize that tradition, or at any rate large parts of it, as 'analytic philosophy', yet it is doctrinally distinct from the Analytic school and had only weak interactions with it. The same goes for the tradition of American pragmatism, which represented an independent source right through to the latter-day Harvard phase, when it got fused with the Analytic stance in the highly distinctive work of Quine. Thematically, analytic philosophy is now highly pluralistic, one might say highly balkanized. It has become possible to speak of 'analytic' Marxism or 'analytic' Thomism. Analytic Hegelianism is on its way.

If we characterize analytic philosophy in terms of institutions, then it is a matter of what department you're in and in what journals you publish. In terms of style, as against content or institution, there is little more to it than an emphasis (in theory!) on clarity and care, a certain lack of overt rhetorical devices—in favour of the more subtle rhe-torical device of flaunted literal-mindedness in one's formulation—and importantly, a more-or-less common stock of by-now familiar ideas, terms, and symbols from the enormous advances achieved in modern logic and semantics. The latter unquestionably mark a watershed between our ways of doing philosophy and previous ways. They are loosely associated with the Analytic school inasmuch as this school recognized their importance, included thinkers who made important contributions to them, and in the English-language world was instrumental in bringing them into philosophy.

In short, we should consider British background and influence on two dispa-rate things—the Analytic school, and something much broader and vaguer, 'analytic

---

[4] It could be said that the true inheritors of the Vienna Circle in recent times have not been the analytic philosophers, many of whom have returned to metaphysics, but those post-modern philosophers who take texts to have priority over subjects and objects. (Of this at least Neurath could have approved.)

[5] On the latter, often referred to as the 'Lvov–Warsaw School', see Wolenski 1989.

philosophy', with respect to which British background and influence is just one background among many.

8.2 THE ANALYTIC SCHOOL

The idea I have taken to lie at the core of the Analytic school is that philosophical, specifically metaphysical, questions can be shown to be pseudo-questions by analysis of language use. The most powerful basis for this idea was linguistic conventionalism: the claim that aprioricity, and hence a priori epistemic norms, are a matter of linguistic convention. Epistemology becomes syntax; ontology becomes semantics.

Or rather, within the Analytic school some combination of two views of 'ontology' is possible. On the one hand one can see it as the shadow cast by linguistic reference: we are 'ontologically committed' to what our theories turn out to refer to when their language is analysed. A corollary is that if more than one analysis is possible 'ontology' is relative to an analysis. Thus, according to Carnap's ontological neutralism in the *Aufbau*,[6] our theories of the world can be constructed in a language that refers only to sensations *or* in a language that refers only to physical objects. The question, is reality 'really' physical or 'really' mental, is a pseudo-question, along with such questions as which logic is 'really' correct, what if anything do we know about the world as it 'really' is, etc. We should simply make the rules of our preferred language clear. That being done,

> the indication of the nominatum [reference] of the sign of an object, consists in an indication of the truth criteria for those sentences in which the sign of this object can occur. (Carnap 1928a [1967], 256–7)

A similar line, though with emphasis on variables rather than singular terms, is famously taken in Quine's 'On What There Is' (1948).

A somewhat different, but related, approach urges that 'ontology' is a pseudo-science to be replaced by ordinary-language analysis of such words as 'real' and 'exists'. Take Austin on 'this little word "real"'. According to Austin,

> 'real' does not have one single, specifiable, always the same *meaning* [but]…Nor does it have a large number of different meanings—it is not *ambiguous*, even 'systematically'. (1962a, 64)

Carnap, Quine, and Austin could all have agreed that it makes no sense to ask, about the things we talk about, or say there are, which of them '*really* exist'. So long, that is, as

---

[6] Carnap 1928a. The writing of the *Aufbau* actually slightly pre-dated Carnap's espousal of verificationism (in *Pseudo-Problems in Philosophy*, written at the end of 1927, and translated together with Carnap 1928a and 1928b in Carnap 1967).

we take what we say to be *true*, we can ask no further and separate metaphysical question about whether what we are talking about exists, or about whether there are metaphysically distinct types of existence, being, etc. The difference is that for Carnap and Quine the question of what exists is to be answered by analysis of science, whereas Austin thinks the question has no 'single, specifiable' answer. Nonetheless on either approach—whether we proceed by logical construction, or by ordinary-language description—we reject traditional metaphysical questions about the nature of existence as empty.

We can call this Analytic approach to ontology *the semantic conception of existence*. (The idea that 'existence is not a predicate', derived from Fregean logic, goes with it.) It remained a leading Analytic doctrine throughout and is still highly influential, though nowadays by no means uncontested. It marks a dividing contrast with philosophers of the Brentano school, for whom questions about which among the objects we can think and talk about really exist were significant and important.[7]

Two other Analytic ideas should be mentioned. First, there is verificationism about meaning. This conception of meaning, entailing as it does rejection of the correspondence theory of truth, is a presupposition of conventionalism, in that it underwrites the conventionalist's essential device of implicit definition.[8] Second, the basic idea that a priori principles of logic and epistemology are simply conventions of a language implies a strong anti-psychologism in logic and epistemology.

In short we have meaning as verification, epistemology as syntax, ontology as semantics, and a strong anti-psychologism about the a priori.

However, while conventionalism is a dominant strain in the Analytic school, there is also another strain—*realism*: 'logical' realism about concepts, propositions, sets, or other abstract objects. It can be combined with logical or set-theoretic construction, so that here too ontology is heavily dependent on analysis of language. This realism is not as such incompatible with the conventionalist and verificationist position, for it can be combined with an appropriately non-realist account of truth. It only becomes incompatible if it is combined, instead, with a realist or correspondence conception of truth and an intuitionist epistemology of the a priori.[9] But whether or not it is developed in the latter way it too assumes that one cannot significantly ask, about the things we turn out on analysis to talk about, *which* of them really exist and in what sense. And since according to the realist, analysis shows that we really do talk about abstract objects, we are committed to their existence. So logical realism, whether or not combined with verificationism, endorses the semantic conception of existence and also leads to strong anti-psychologism. On other matters, such the status of truth and the epistemology of

---

[7] See especially Meinong's theory of objects, of 1904. The tradition is being revived; see for example Priest 2008.

[8] I discuss this connection between verificationism, implicit definition, and conventionalism in Skorupski 2005, and give a fuller account of Analytic conceptions of meaning and truth in Skorupski 1997.

[9] The former without the latter could be found, as many contemporary readers thought, in Wittgenstein's *Tractatus*.

the a priori, verificationists and realists about truth may disagree. But on these two they are at one. Pious horror at any form of psychologism, together with adherence to the semantic conception of ontology, were leading marks of the Analytic stance.

We do not need to pursue the fascinating question of how these two fundamental directions in the Analytic school—conventionalism and realism—interacted. But we should ask what background for them, and more generally for the Analytic school's distinctive preoccupations, can be found in British philosophy. The answer, it seems to me, is none at all. For the Analytic school, as much as for the school of Brentano, the background is essentially Austro-German.[10]

Of course, British philosophers were important *within* the Analytic school. Russell made a major contribution to the discovery and the interpretation of the paradoxes—a subject that remains puzzling and unresolved—and contributed an analysis of definite descriptions that became a much-discussed paradigm of 'analysis'. Moore's early conceptual monism (1899) played an important role as a weapon against idealism; moreover his discussions of knowledge and goodness were, and remain, seminal (1903, 1925, 1939). A later phase of the school—Oxford ordinary language philosophy—was in many ways distinctively English (Ernest Gellner's waspish description of its practitioners as the 'Narodniks of North Oxford' fits rather well).[11] It produced important original work, for example by Austin and Strawson[12] among others. In all these ways British philosophers made important contributions to the Analytic school.

But what of the British background, as against the British contribution?

The Vienna Circle paid tribute to Hume: his division of assertions into those which concerned 'matters of fact and existence' and those which concerned 'relations of ideas' seemed to them to prefigure their master-division into factual assertions and expressions of convention. But how much of an *influence* was Hume? For most of the nineteenth century in Britain Hume was in eclipse as a philosopher, as against a historian and essayist. When his work was revived by T. H. Green it was with a polemical purpose.[13] Green presented him as the most intelligent naturalist, able to see clearly that

---

[10]   For an interpretation of the influences on Moore and Russell leading to a similar conclusion, see Bell 1999.

[11]   Gellner 1959 [1979], p. 259. (Russell's foreword to this volume may read like a purely internal English social skirmish—but it interestingly shows just how out of sympathy he really was, not just to the Oxford style, but to the basic ideas of the Analytic school itself.)

[12]   Some examples: Austin 1962a, 1962b; Strawson 1950, 1952. (However in later work Strawson seems to me to go beyond the Analytic school.) Michael Dummett, while not exactly an 'Oxford ordinary language philosopher' is certainly a major figure in the Analytic school, both as interpreter and as contributor, for example in the essays collected in Dummett 1978.

[13]   See Green's lengthy introduction in Hume 1874. Around the same time Brentano and Meinong were taking an interest in British empiricism. Meinong's earliest publications, in 1877 and 1882, were on Hume; Brentano read and discussed Mill and other British philosopher/psychologists. Mill's side of their correspondence, quoted by Brentano in Brentano 1874 [1995], 220, concerning predication and existence, can be found in Mill 1963–91, XVII (*Later Letters*), 1934–5. Brentano also sent Mill a copy of his book on Aristotle (Brentano 1867). I come back to this line of influence (from Mill through Brentano) in the next section.

naturalism collapses into scepticism, and thus rendering futile subsequent naturalistic projects by philosophically shallower thinkers. Naturally that was not the opinion of the Vienna Circle. But that is not to say that Hume was an *influence*, whether negative or positive, either on the British idealists or the Analytic school. The real influence on the Analytic school—as on British idealism—was Kant. The Vienna Circle was particularly concerned to deny the doctrine of mathematics as synthetic a priori: in this respect at least, it was Kant who had the influence, and his influence was negative.[14] Hume's views on mathematics did not get the detailed response from any philosopher in the Analytic school that Mill's philosophy of mathematics got from Frege. It was simply that Hume could be held to be an empiricist who, unlike Mill, took mathematics to be analytic, and could thus symbolically carry the logical positivists' banner. Hume's great influence on analytic philosophy came later, mainly through his theory of motives and passions.

While Hume's influence was in abeyance in the nineteenth century, the leading schools in Britain were some combination of Reidian common sense mixed with Kant on the one hand, and on the other the empiricism of Bentham and the Mills. Neither party had any discernible influence on the Analytic school (as against the school of Brentano) in any of its phases, other than the negative influences already noted in the case of John Stuart Mill. And yet, with the passing of the Analytic school Bentham and Mill survive as strong influences within the broad and pluralistic domain of 'analytic philosophy'—just as Hume and Reid do.

That suggests a wider point about the rise and fall of the Analytic tide in British philosophy. To make it we must broaden our picture, taking into account the trajectory of some lasting questions and debates that have existed throughout the last 200 years or so independently of the Analytic school, and irrespective of any treatment the Analytic school gave of them. There are three areas we can notice:

A. Non-empirical knowledge
B. Science and consciousness
C. Moral and political philosophy.

8.3 NON-EMPIRICAL KNOWLEDGE

To the question whether and in what sense there is such a thing as non-empirical knowledge the Analytic school proposed some highly distinctive and historically important answers, which we have noted. But what do we find if we step back and put these answers into a wider historical context?

---

[14] Which is not to deny that Kant was also a positive influence in important ways—see e.g. Coffa, 1991; Friedman 1991; Stroud 1984.

Here we need to go back again to Mill. Indeed it is not too much to say that we shall not have a clear view of the nineteenth-century prehistory of analytic philosophy until Mill's positions in the *System* and in the *Examination*[15] are as well known and understood as the work of Frege and of the Brentano school.

The *System of Logic* is an assault on the notion that there is a priori knowledge. Consider how Mill carries this through. The *System* comprises six substantial books; of these the first ('Of Names and Propositions') is devoted to an analysis of language. Now language was not a wholly new concern of the philosophical radicals. Bentham had contributed the notion of paraphrasis and the connected idea that one should think of sentences, not terms, as the integer of meaning. Mill adds to this his distinction between connotation and denotation and uses it to analyse the analytic/synthetic distinction, giving a very restrictive account of analytic sentences (or, as he calls them, verbal propositions). That gives him a semantic basis for his radical empiricism about logic and mathematics.

Particularly relevant to the present discussion, however, is Mill's attack on three other positions about the status of logic: Conceptualism, Nominalism, and Realism. The first of these amounts to psychologism about logic: the view that judgements are about mental representations and that the laws of logic are psychological laws governing how we operate with these representations.[16] Mill's response is to distinguish between mental acts and their objects; his discussion clearly influenced the very similar response of both Brentano and Frege, as a somewhat extended quotation will show:

> All language recognises a difference between a doctrine or opinion, and the fact of entertaining the opinion; between assent, and what is assented to.
>
> Logic, according to the conception here formed of it, has no concern with the nature of the act of judging or believing; the consideration of that act, as a phenomenon of the mind, belongs to another science. (*Collected Works*, VII, 134)

But, Mill holds, that has not been the orthodox opinion hitherto:

> almost all the writers on Logic in the last two centuries, whether English, German, or French, have made their theory of Propositions, from one end to the other, a theory of Judgments. They considered a Proposition, or a Judgment, for they used the two words indiscriminately, to consist in affirming or denying one *idea* of another. To judge, was to put two ideas together, or to bring one idea under another, or to compare two ideas, or to perceive the agreement or disagreement between two ideas: and the whole doctrine of Propositions, together with the theory of Reasoning, (always necessarily founded on the theory of Propositions,) was stated as if Ideas, or Conceptions, or whatever other term the writer preferred as a name for mental representations generally, constituted essentially the subject matter and substance of those operations.

[15] Mill, 1963–91, vol. IX, *An Examination of Sir William Hamilton's Philosophy, and of the Principal Philosophical Questions Discussed in his Writings* (1865).

[16] Bizarrely, Mill was for some time himself accused of psychologism about logic. For more on this misinterpretation, which seems to have come from Husserl, see Skorupski 1989, ch. 5, appendix.

Now Mill's response:

> It is, of course, true, that in any case of judgment, as for instance when we judge that gold is yellow, a process takes place in our minds, of which some one or other of these theories is a partially correct account. We must have the idea of gold and the idea of yellow, and these two ideas must be brought together in our mind. But in the first place, it is evident that this is only a part of what takes place; for we may put two ideas together without any act of belief; as when we merely imagine something, such as a golden mountain; or when we actually disbelieve...To determine what it is that happens in the case of assent or dissent besides putting two ideas together, is one of the most intricate of metaphysical problems. But whatever the solution may be, we may venture to assert that it can have nothing whatever to do with the import of propositions; for this reason, that propositions (except sometimes when the mind itself is the subject treated of) are not assertions respecting our ideas of things, but assertions respecting the things themselves. In order to believe that gold is yellow, I must, indeed, have the idea of gold, and the idea of yellow, and something having reference to those ideas must take place in my mind; but my belief has not reference to the ideas, it has reference to the things. (*Collected Works*, VII, 134–5)[17]

Of course once these distinctions between mental acts and their objects have been made, the question of what I am thinking *about* when I think, or seem to think, about the golden mountain comes to the fore. Here Mill provides no answer: answers came later, in Meinong and in Russell.

Of the other two positions Mill rejects, 'Nominalism' is the view that logic and mathematics consist of merely 'verbal' truths—he takes it to be the view of Hobbes, and deploys against it his distinction between denotation and connotation. 'Realism', the view that they consist of truths about abstract entities, he hardly takes seriously at all. In fact Mill is himself a nominalist in the modern sense (which poses a problem for him when he tries to specify what it is that terms connote). Mill could not, of course, have considered modern versions of 'Nominalism' and 'Realism', as developed by the Analytic school. However it's easy to see from his basic ideas and analytic tools that he would have rejected them. That leaves him with the same two problems facing a contemporary, post-Analytic school, naturalist. The first is what account to give of the ontology of content if nominalism doesn't work—the question, one might say, of whether to go Meinongian or Quinean about abstracta. The second question, which is worth considering in a little detail, is about non-empirical knowledge.

While Mill rejects psychologism about logic and maths, seeing these rather as the most general truths of empirical science, his standpoint in epistemology may fairly be described as psychologistic. The *System* does a very good job of providing a naturalistic, internal vindication of the inductive process; but in the end Mill has to give some

---

[17] The first part of this passage, including the example of the golden mountain, is quoted by Brentano (Brentano 1874 [1995], 206).

account of the principles of reasoning, or acquisition of warrant, that he takes to be primitive. How then are these grounded? By observing the reasoning agent at work:

> Principles of Evidence and Theories of Method are not to be constructed *a priori*. The laws of our rational faculty, like those of every other natural agency, are only learnt by seeing the agent at work. (VIII 833)

In this approach to epistemology Mill does not differ from his Reidian opponents. For both sides the *epistemic* grounding of basic normative principles, whether in epistemology or ethics, lies in our primitive psychological dispositions. However, this is not a reductive kind of psychologism: it does not reduce epistemic and ethical principles to psychological propositions. Indeed *realism* about such principles, reductive or otherwise, is foreign to them. The main difference between Reid and Mill, at the meta-normative level, is that Reid's psychologism is phenomenological and innatist, whereas Mill's is behavioural ('seeing the agent at work') and associationist.[18] At the substantive level, of course, they differ much more. At this level the Reidian school was 'intuitionist' in Mill's sense, i.e. it made a phenomenological appeal to a large number of principles of common sense, whereas Mill wanted to reduce basic principles, whether in epistemology or ethics, to the smallest possible number. Nonetheless, at the meta-normative level they share a naturalistic, psychological approach to the normative.

Compare Wittgenstein at the end of his life:

> Giving grounds, however, justifying the evidence, comes to an end;—but the end is not certain propositions' striking us immediately as true, i.e. it is not a kind of *seeing* on our part; it is our *acting*, which lies at the bottom of the language game. (1969, §204)

This too sounds like psychologism in epistemology: we establish epistemic norms by describing 'the agent at work'. It contrasts with the conventionalism of the Analytic school in interesting ways, but even more decidedly with the normative realism which we shall come to in section 8.5. So how can description of 'natural', 'inartificial', or 'original' dispositions legitimately warrant our normative claims, whether in epistemology or ethics? No kind of realism can be the answer for any of these philosophers, since they take it for granted that there can be no receptive faculty by which we know of 'normative facts'.

8.4 CONSCIOUSNESS AND SCIENCE

In the nineteenth century the standpoint of phenomenal experience dominated philosophy; in the twentieth century, the dominating standpoint came to be that of physics.

---

[18] Mill described it as the contrast between the 'introspective method' (Reid) and the 'psychological method' (himself).

Then, the standard question was how to fit physics into experience; now, the standard question is how to fit experience into physics. This is one of the most striking developments in twentieth-century philosophy. In just a few generations it moved from widespread acceptance of the philosophical idea that physics must somehow reduce to the contents of consciousness, to a quite different intellectual context: the equally widespread acceptance that consciousness must somehow reduce to a set of local elements or processes within physics. Few transitions provide more food for thought about the way extra-philosophical developments determine philosophy. (To be sure, history of philosophy also warns against dogmatic acceptance that we are now at the end of this story, or that it is the only story there is to tell.)

The change has marched in step with another, the growth of scientific realism—and that in turn with acceptance of inference to the best explanation as not merely a heuristic device but a basis for warranted belief.

The nineteenth century largely took for granted (set aside German idealism here) that our own conscious states are all that we immediately know. Various positions in the philosophy of perception, which sounded as though they might be denying that, in fact still made this assumption—as Mill pertinaciously argued in the *Examination*. Further, and just as importantly, it was also widely assumed through most of the century that only enumerative induction from particular observations can warrant a posteriori generalizations. As Larry Laudan noted in 1981,

> The method of hypothesis, known since antiquity, found few proponents between 1700 and 1850. During the last century, of course, [i.e. the century up to the time at which Laudan was writing] that ordering has been inverted and—despite an almost universal acknowledgement of its weaknesses—the method of hypothesis (usually under such descriptions as 'hypothetico-deduction' or 'conjectures and refutations') has become the orthodoxy of the twentieth century. (1981, 1)

Now if what we can know consists solely of immediate consciousness, memory of previous consciousness, and the results of enumerative induction, as Mill thought, the outcome seems clear. What we can know is restricted to our sensory experience past and present, and law-like regularities within that experience. This was the view Mill called 'phenomenalism', and rightly described as an orthodoxy of his time.

Phenomenalism in Mill's sense holds that there can be no knowledge of entities distinct from and 'outside' experience. There are then, as Mill notes, two possibilities. One is to hold that there are or may be unknowable 'things in themselves', external causes of sensation. The other is his distinctive innovation: reductive phenomenalism. Famously, Mill held that statements about material objects are reducible to 'brute' counterfactuals about experience, i.e. counterfactuals not grounded in any categorical such as, in Berkeley's philosophy, the mind of God. This was new, and very close to twentieth-century 'linguistic phenomenalism'—although Mill also comes close to an error-theoretic view of our physicalistic language.[19] A somewhat different possibility, which emerged soon after Mill's defence of reductive phenomenalism, is the neutral monism of William James and Mach, among others. According to this rather mysterious doctrine the world consists of neutral elements which can be 'read' either phenomenalistically or physicalistically.

These two lines of thought—reductive phenomenalism and neutral monism— persisted well into the twentieth century. They were an influence on the Analytic school. Linguistic phenomenalism became popular among Analytic philosophers; equally one can see Carnap's ontological neutralism as a kind of (would-be) non-metaphysical successor to neutral monism.[20]

Now consider the hypothetical method. A shift in its fortunes started in the latter half of the nineteenth century, with the work of the Cambridge scientist and philosopher William Whewell. Whewell argued that the method of hypothesis can yield warranted conclusions about the nature of reality. Mill responded with an inductivist critique; Whewell in turn defended his view.[21]

This early debate goes to the heart of the issues. Why, after all, given his psychologistic epistemology, noted in the last section, does Mill reject Whewell's view of hypotheses? Doesn't observation of the 'agent at work'—not just scientists but all of us all the time—show that we constantly make inferences to the best explanation? Enumerative induction is taken by epistemic agents to yield warrants for belief, but so is the method of hypothesis. That was the lesson Whewell drew from his monumental history of the inductive sciences, and emphasized in his response to Mill. Given Mill's naturalistic stance, it seems the question cannot be, is inference to the best explanation a source of warrant, but only in what circumstances it is, and what our criteria of a good explanation are.

However, the basic point that Mill urges against the hypothetical method is that hypotheses can be underdetermined by data. He does not question Whewell's historical findings; he acknowledges the heuristic value of the hypothetical method as a source of useful models, fruitful lines of inquiry—but denies that it is a source of warrant in its own right. In reply, Whewell denies that there is underdetermination. And certainly it's not enough for Mill to make the simple point that there is always more than one hypothesis that is predictively adequate. The point has to be that *given all natural constraints* that we *actually* apply on what counts as a good explanation—simplicity, coherence with the totality of our beliefs about the world, etc.—there will or can be a plurality of best

---

[19] Linguistic phenomenalism is the view that physicalistic statements can be translated without remainder into a language of phenomenal experience, whereas Mill's view is that while what is true in our physicalistic statements is open to phenomenalist reduction, there remains a residue that must be explained as error.

[20] We should note Schlick as an exception to these trends: he was a defender of scientific realism and physicalism about the mental (Schlick 1918).

[21] Mill 1963–91, vol. VIII; Whewell 1860; see also Skorupski 1989, 197–202, 206–12.

explanations. It can certainly be questioned whether we have grounds in the history of science for believing such a strong underdetermination thesis. Yet as a matter of sheer logic there is no way to rule it out. Nothing in the data can show that there is only one optimal explanation of them overall.

How then can we claim that inference to the best explanation provides warrant for belief? Without metaphysical or theological backing, what could show that, in Peirce's phrase, inquiry is 'fated' to converge?[22]

These questions push powerfully, as they pushed Mill, towards an instrumentalist view of theory. That being so, it is striking that what in fact has happened is acceptance of the hypothetical method and scientific realism about its results. The philosophical response has not, typically, been 'metaphysical realism' combined with instrumentalism about science, but rejection of a metaphysical realist view of truth combined with 'internal' or 'empirical' realism about the objects postulated by science.[23] And that response, when combined with the possibility of strong underdetermination, seems to commit one to a kind of 'ontological relativism in principle'.

The long development we have just noted achieves a classic formulation in Quine. In this final phase of the Analytic school we still have verificationism, but now of a fully holistic kind, the 'integer of meaning' now being the theory not the sentence.[24] We have a deflationary, non-realist, conception of truth. We have the semantic conception of existence plus ontological commitment to abstract objects. But conventionalism is rejected,[25] and physicalism about experience is asserted.

It seems that the driver for these developments has simply been the success of science itself. It has become ever less disputable that modern scientific theory is hypothetical in its methods and inextricably holistic in its outcomes. Philosophers can argue about its implications, for example for truth, but they increasingly take scientific realism for granted. Science sets the parameters of belief, undermining other claims to knowledge of how things really are, making it ever more difficult to sustain an instrumentalist interpretation of scientific theory. In short, the decline of reductive phenomenalism and neutral monism in favour of physicalism went hand in hand with the growth of scientific realism, and that in turn arose from the development of science, rather than the development of philosophy.

The arc of development from the time of Mill to the time of Quine is singularly telling. My point, however, is not that realism about empirical 'mind-independent' objects depends on inference to the best explanation, or even that inference to the best explanation is a way of vindicating such realism. I don't believe that either of these claims is true. There is a further contrast to be drawn, which also has a history. In British terms it is the contrast between a common sense and a scientific stance in philosophy (in continental terms, between a phenomenological and a scientific stance).

---

[22] For Whewell's influence on Peirce see Fisch 1991, e.g. p. 110.
[23] These are Hilary Putnam's terms—e.g. Putnam 1981.
[24] Quine on Bentham: 'Five Milestones of Empiricism', in Quine 1981.
[25] Conventionalism required verificationism; but as Quine showed, the converse does not hold.

This contrast existed in British philosophy before the Analytic school, existed within the Analytic school, and exists in analytic philosophy today. In the nineteenth century, a tradition of philosopher-scientists represented the side of science, and the school of Reid represented common sense.[26] Its representatives in the Analytic school might be Schlick, Russell, Carnap, and Quine on the science side and Moore, Austin, and Strawson on the phenomenological or common sense side.

Now suppose we ask, why shouldn't a philosopher accept the hypothetical method and develop an account in which physics is derived by inference to the best explanation from subjective experience? Why hasn't this approach been more popular? The answer, it seems, is that it runs up against objections both from the side of science and from the side of common sense.

On the scientific stance, the physics you arrive at, with its closure principles, seems to leave no room for the very data from which, on this account, it has been inferred. From the standpoint of physics, it's very natural to marginalize the standpoint of subjective experience and take the data to be physical right from the start. From this standpoint, the earlier struggles by scientifically minded philosophers to reconcile science and phenomenology—linguistic phenomenalism, neutral monism, ontological neutralism such as Carnap's—seem redundant.

From the common sense side, they seem equally misplaced. Common sense accepts the realism of the natural attitude. We know the material world around us because we perceive it. This is the 'natural realism' that Sir William Hamilton contrasted with 'hypothetical realism',[27] i.e. the view that our knowledge of physical objects requires an inference from experience. Hamilton thought this latter view was incoherent; Mill objected that it provided the only possible basis for natural realism's idea that we know a material world around us. But that response arose from Mill's epistemological principles. A natural realist could argue that the principles were too narrow. After all, as Mill acknowledged, memory yields warrants for belief—so why shouldn't one say the same about perceptual claims?[28] That would be the common sense path.

The dualism of the scientific and the phenomenological or common sense standpoint persists. It plays to characteristically British preoccupations with the philosophy of perception on the one hand, and the philosophy of science on the other. It remains a continuous preoccupation from the nineteenth to the twenty-first century.

---

[26] Mill, elusively many-sided as ever, is not easy to place. By and large he represents the scientific stance. Yet there is much on the other side, though it is not so much Reidian as Coleridgean. And of course I'm not saying that any philosopher has to choose—presumably some reconciliation is to be hoped for.

[27] Hamilton 1859–60, *passim*. (Also 'hypothetical dualism', 'cosmothetic idealism'.)

[28] Mill's answer was that to explain our beliefs he needed to postulate a reliable memory mechanism, but not a reliable mechanism whereby we perceive mind-independent objects.

8.5 MORAL PHILOSOPHY

Of the two debates we have considered so far, the Analytic school played a leading role in the debate about non-empirical knowledge, putting forward distinctive and new ideas. In the second, concerning consciousness and science, philosophers of the Analytic school took a variety of positions: they were taking part in a complex, ongoing development, although some of them made attempts to treat it in terms of new ideas that were distinctively 'Analytic'—most notably in Carnap's *Aufbau*. In the area of ethics and politics the story is different again. Neither ethics nor political theory were significant ingredients in the philosophical activity of the Analytic school, but Analytic doctrines about apriority and factuality had a lasting, and arguably baneful, effect on meta-ethics.

True, both Moore and Wittgenstein had striking ethical ideas. At the very least, the last chapter of Moore's *Principia Ethica*, on 'The Ideal', and Wittgenstein's treatment of ethics in the *Tractatus* and the 'Lecture on Ethics'[29] are significant documents of their time. In a historical interpretation of the Analytic school as a phenomenon of modernism they would be among the prime, though not the only, evidence. Moore's quietist elitism, which finds the absolute good in beauty and friendship, and Wittgenstein's quietist mysticism of the ethical as inexpressible belong to the spirit of early modernism. Moreover, their ethical ideas feel integral to their whole philosophical outlook. They are part of what one has to grasp in grasping them as *philosophers*—and in grasping their attractiveness as philosophers. In contrast, the political engagements of Neurath, Carnap, and Russell did not form a part of their philosophical position in the same way (unless one sees Viennese socialist construction as going in some way with Viennese language construction). The ethical ideas of Moore and Wittgenstein are personally felt and philosophically worked-through contributions to the characteristic texture of early modernism, whereas in ethics and politics the other three feel like intelligent and aware people responding to prevailing ideas, rather than creating them.

It would be surprising if Moore's and Wittgenstein's ethical attitudes lost influence completely, since both forms of quietism express perennial attitudes towards life and world. At the moment, however, it must be said that they have little influence in analytic moral philosophy, though not none. In contrast, the importance of Analytic school doctrines for meta-ethics has been enormous, and traceable.

The conventionalist and realist strands in the Analytic school force a choice between non-cognitivism and realism about all normative claims. Wittgenstein's view both of tautologies and of the ethical is an unusual kind of non-cognitivism. Carnap's conventionalism about epistemic principles is another. Where cognitivists see us asserting true or false principles of epistemic warrant, the conventionalist sees us as expressing a rule, commitment, or decision that has no truth-apt content. The application of these ideas to

---

[29] Wittgenstein 1921, 1965; see also 1979, e.g. pp. 115–17.

ethical as well as epistemological principles has been obvious from the start. Equally, the possibility of transferring realism from mathematics to ethics is obvious: comparison with mathematical realism has been a major trope for moral realists.

I am sceptical whether either of these positions about normative claims, non-cognitivism or realism, can be attributed to any philosopher before the twentieth century. It was the Analytic school that produced the appearance of an exhaustive choice of non-cognitivism or realism about the normative. This could work either through the logical-positivist dichotomy between factual assertion and non-factual expression, or by way of realism about truth and propositionhood. But to interpret Kant, Mill, or Reid in terms of this dichotomy is anachronistic.[30] To clarify, we should distinguish cognitivism from realism. Cognitivism is the view that normative claims are truth-apt objects of belief. Realism is the view that they are factual claims: that what makes them true, when they are true, is the substantive fact, natural or non-natural, that they assert obtains.

Reid and Kant are cognitivists about epistemology and ethics, but it by no means follows that they are realists. They didn't focus on the issue in this way, nor were they working with the conceptual tools and the problematic that would cause them to do so. The same can be said for Mill. Insofar as one can impute meta-normative views to them at all, they have nothing to do with any of the common current options—expressivism, or naturalistic or non-naturalistic realism. The same can be said for Sidgwick, and indeed for the Moore of *Principia Ethica*.[31]

While these philosophers may have taken it for granted that normative claims are true or false assertions, it does not follow that they thought them to be *factual* assertions. And they may have been right about that. If their views run up against the realist conception of truth or the semantic conception of existence, then perhaps it is these Analytic ideas that have to go; in any case we should be cautious in attributing those ideas to them.

But let us turn back to normative ethics. If Moore's and Wittgenstein's conceptions of ethical life do not currently make much impact in analytic moral philosophy, nor do those of twentieth-century continental moral theorists. In contrast, the continuing influence of the British tradition is quite obvious. Once again it seems to me that one can see this in terms of the rise and fall of modernism. The most prominent ethical ideas of the twentieth century on the continent belong to the modernist culture of its first fifty or sixty years. British moral philosophy played no major role in this culture; rather it continued in the traditions that came before. That is not to say that it contained nothing new: the views of Moore, Ross, Ewing, and Prichard on the concepts of value and moral obligation were innovative, and have become much appreciated.[32] Still, the normative framework was largely set by continued discussion between utilitarians

---

[30] Equally, although one can see elements of non-cognitivism and of a dispositionalist realism in Hume, it seems to me too strong to attribute to him a clear endorsement of either of these positions.

[31] Moore is thought to have been a paradigm realist in *Principia Ethica*; in fact, however, his view of ethical predicates seems to have been cognitivist but not realist. He denies, for example, 'that "good" *must* denote some *real* property of things' (1903, 191). See Baldwin 2010.

[32] See e.g. Hurka 2011.

and moral intuitionists or pluralists: the debate that had also dominated the nineteenth century.

These British themes remain important in current ethical theory. And in political theory the influence of Hobbes, Locke, Burke, Mill, and Green remains. But since the 1960s new influences have arrived.

Above all there is the new interest in the ethics of Kant. This revival of Kantian ethics in the English-language world is a phenomenon of post-1960s American liberalism. The principal animator has been Rawls, though in political theory another important factor has been the recovery of Marx. But these movements are part of a great widening of horizons since the 1960s. Other revivals in normative ethics include Aristotle, Rousseau, Fichte, Hegel, and Nietzsche. The contrast with the virtual absence of normative ethics in the Analytic school is striking indeed.

8.6 CONCLUDING THOUGHTS

British nineteenth-century philosophy had little influence on the distinctive ideas of the Analytic school, even though Britain was home to some of its greatest twentieth-century figures. Equally, however, many of those ideas, in particular verificationism and the idea that philosophy consists of pseudo-problems, seem for the moment at least exhausted, indeed positively unfashionable, within analytic philosophy itself. In striking contrast, positions that have always been important in British philosophy, independently of the Analytic school, have returned as leading positions in analytic philosophy now. We can see that in all the three areas we have discussed—(A) the nature of non-empirical knowledge, (B) science, consciousness, and perception, and (C) ethics. Looked at from a British perspective we might see the main continuity in analytic philosophy as a continuity of British preoccupations in the face of an advancing, and then receding, modernist tide.

However, this would grossly underestimate just how big and pluralistic the world of analytic philosophy has come to be. Many other ideas inhabit its space. The British background is only one of the backgrounds to current analytic philosophy that need to be taken into account. A full review of nineteenth-century philosophy, continental as well as Anglo-American, is required to situate current philosophy properly in its historical background.

This is beyond our remit, but we can end by considering some limits of the British philosophical tradition, and some sources of reflection in current philosophy that come from outside those limits.

Just as in epistemology and metaphysics so in moral philosophy the British dialectic is a dialectic of common sense and science, or in the case of ethics, of common sense and theoretical perspectives that aim at a 'science of ethics'. That, in a way, is its true glory. Importantly however, in both areas spiritual questions about the meaning of life, whether humanistic, religious, or post-humanistic and post-religious, are relatively absent as determinants of philosophy.[33] Connectedly, distancing perspectives on both common sense and science, whether Critical in origin, or deriving from Absolute idealist rethinkings of religion, are relatively absent. (The brief period of British idealism is the exception.) Thus, for example, the fact that these perspectives are not missing from Wittgenstein's thought, however elusive or repressed they may be, is part of what distinguishes him from the British tradition, and indeed makes him as much a 'continental' as an 'analytic' philosopher.

In many ways one can say that the mainstream of analytic philosophy continues in these strengths and limits. At the same time, however, it is becoming less clear how much sense it makes to talk about a 'mainstream'. Analytic philosophy is thinning and widening thematically to a pluralism in which it is no longer very clear what the point of the word 'analytic' is, as we noted at the beginning of this discussion. And to a considerable extent this widening is a matter of bringing in Critical and idealist themes, and questions about how to live, what it means to live.

Who knows whether significant new directions in philosophy will emerge from this pluralism, or whether it will turn out to be a period of eclecticism and dissipation. Still, at least we live in interesting times, in which dogmatism and narrow-mindedness find it that much harder to flourish.

References

Austin, J. L. (1962a). *Sense and Sensibilia*. Oxford: Oxford University Press.
——(1962b). *How to Do Things with Words*. Oxford: Oxford University Press.
Baldwin, Thomas (ed.) (1993). *G. E. Moore: Selected Writings*. London: Routledge.
——(2010). 'The Open Question Argument'. In John Skorupski (ed.), *The Routledge Companion to Ethics*. London: Routledge, pp. 286–96.
Bell, David (1999). 'The Revolution of Moore and Russell: A Very British Coup?' In Anthony O'Hear (ed.), *German Philosophy since Kant*. Cambridge: Cambridge University Press, pp. 193–208.
Brentano, Franz (1867). *Die Psychologie des Aristotles*. Mainz: Verlag von Franz Kirchheim.
——(1874). *Psychologie vom empirischen Standpunkt*. Leipzig: Duncker & Humblot; 2nd edn. Leipzig: Felix Meiner, 1924. Tr. A. C. Rancurello, D. B. Terrell, and L. McAlister as *Psychology from an Empirical Standpoint*. London: Routledge, 1973; 2nd edn. 1995.
Capaldi, Nicholas (2004). *John Stuart Mill*. Cambridge: Cambridge University Press.
Carnap, Rudolf (1928a). *Der logische Aufbau der Welt*. Berlin-Schlachtensee: Weltkreis-Verlag; 2nd edn. Hamburg: Felix Meiner, 1961. Tr. Rolf A. George (together with Carnap 1928b) as Carnap 1967.

---

[33] As determinants of philosophy. I don't mean they are absent as such: one has only to consider Mill's openness to romantic influence and Sidgwick's existential worries about the 'dualism of the practical reason'. But Mill did not become a German idealist philosopher (*pace* Capaldi 2004), and Sidgwick did not solve his problems by a philosophical search for transcendence (as against empirical research into psychic phenomena).

—— (1928b). *Scheinprobleme in der Philosophie: Das Fremdpsychische und der Realismusstreit.* Berlin-Schlachtensee: Weltkreis-Verlag. Tr. R. A. George as *Pseudoproblems in Philosophy: The Heteropsychological and the Realism Controversy* and incl. in Carnap 1967.

—— (1967). *The Logical Structure of the World*, tr. Rolf A. George. Berkeley: University of California Press; repr. Chicago: Open Court, 2003.

Coffa, Alberto (1991). *The Semantic Tradition from Kant to Carnap: To the Vienna Station.* Cambridge: Cambridge University Press.

Dummett, M. (1978). *Truth and Other Enigmas.* London: Duckworth.

Fisch, Menachem (1991). *William Whewell, Philosopher of Science.* Oxford: Clarendon Press.

Frege, G. (1884). *Die Grundlagen der Arithmetik.* Breslau: W. Koebner. Tr. J. L. Austin as *The Foundations of Arithmetic.* Oxford: Blackwell, 1950; 2nd edn. 1953.

Friedman, Michael (1991). 'The Re-evaluation of Logical Positivism', *Journal of Philosophy* 10: 505–19.

Gellner, E. (1959). *Words and Things.* London: Routledge & Kegan Paul; rev. edn. 1979.

Hamilton, Sir William (1859–60). *Lectures on Metaphysics and Logic.* Edinburgh and London: Blackwood.

Hume, D. (1874). *A Treatise of Human Nature and Dialogues concerning Natural Religion*, ed. with preliminary dissertation and notes T. H. Green and T. H. Grose. London: Longmans, Green.

Hurka, Thomas (ed.) (2011). *Underivative Duty: British Moral Philosophers from Sidgwick to Ewing.* Oxford: Oxford University Press.

Laudan, L. (1981). *Science and Hypothesis.* Dordrecht: D. Reidel.

Meinong, A. (1904). 'Über Gegenstandstheorie'. In Meinong, *Untersuchungen zur Gegenstandstheorie und Psychologie*, Leipzig: Barth, pp. 1–51. Tr. as 'The Theory of Objects', in Roderick M. Chisholm (ed.), *Realism and the Background of Phenomenology.* Glencoe, IL: Free Press, 1960, pp. 76–117.

Mill, J. S. (1963–91). *Collected Works of John Stuart Mill.* London: Routledge.

Moore, G. E. (1899). 'The Nature of Judgement', *Mind* 8: 176–93; repr. in Baldwin (1993), pp. 1–19.

—— (1903). *Principia Ethica.* Cambridge: Cambridge University Press.

—— (1925). 'A Defence of Common Sense'. In J. H. Muirhead (ed.), *Contemporary British Philosophy* (2nd series). London: Allen & Unwin, pp. 193–223; repr. in Baldwin (1993), pp. 106–33.

—— (1939). 'Proof of an External World', *Proceedings of the British Academy* 25: 273–300; repr. in Baldwin 1993, pp. 147–70.

Priest, G. (2008). 'The Closing of the Mind: How the Particular Quantifier Became Existentially Loaded Behind our Backs', *Review of Symbolic Logic* 1: 42–55.

Putnam, H. (1981). *Reason, Truth and History.* Cambridge: Cambridge University Press.

Quine, W. V. O. (1948). 'On What There Is', *Review of Metaphysics* 48: 21–38.

—— (1981). *Theories and Things.* Cambridge, MA: Harvard University Press.

Schlick, M. (1918). *Allgemeine Erkenntnislehre.* Berlin: Springer; 2nd edn. 1925. Tr. A. Blumberg as *General Theory of Knowledge.* La Salle, IL: Open Court, 1985.

Skorupski, John (1989). *John Stuart Mill.* London: Routledge.

—— (1997). 'Meaning, Verification, Use'. In Bob Hale and Crispin Wright (eds.), *The Blackwell Companion to the Philosophy of Language.* Oxford: Blackwell, pp. 29–59.

—— (2005). 'Later Empiricism and Logical Positivism'. In Stewart Shapiro (ed.), *The Oxford Handbook to the Philosophy of Mathematics.* Oxford: Oxford University Press, pp. 51–74.

Strawson, P. F. (1950). 'On Referring', *Mind* 59: 320–44.

—— (1952). *Introduction to Logical Theory*. London: Methuen.

Stroud, Barry (1984). *The Significance of Philosophical Scepticism*. Oxford: Oxford University Press.

Whewell, William (1860). *On the Philosophy of Discovery*. London: Parker & Son.

Wittgenstein, L. (1921). *Tractatus Logico-Philosophicus*. In *Annalen der Naturphilosophie*, tr. D. F. Pears and B. McGuinness. London: Routledge, 1961.

—— (1965). 'A Lecture on Ethics', *The Philosophical Review* 74: 3–12.

—— (1969). *On Certainty*, ed. G. E. M. Anscombe and G. H. von Wright, tr. D. Paul and G. E. M. Anscombe. Oxford: Blackwell.

—— (1979). *Ludwig Wittgenstein and the Vienna Circle: Conversations Recorded by Friedrich Waismann*, ed. B. McGuinness, tr. J. Schulte and B. McGuinness. Oxford: Blackwell.

Wolenski, Jan (1989). *Logic and Philosophy in the Lvov–Warsaw School*. Dordrecht and London: Kluwer.

CHAPTER 9

....

THE MATHEMATICAL AND LOGICAL BACKGROUND TO ANALYTIC PHILOSOPHY

....

JAMIE TAPPENDEN

9.1 INTRODUCTION

....

THIS chapter surveys the logical and mathematical background to 'analytic philosophy'. For this to be feasible I'll need to pass quickly over complicated material, referring to further reading in footnotes.[1] Also I'll need to circumscribe the topic. 'Analytic philosophy', as here understood, regards mathematics, and especially mathematical logic as a central contributor to philosophical progress and an indispensable component of philosophical reasoning. (I'll only count 'logic' as within the scope of this study if it is the mathematical tradition of Boole, Frege, Russell, and Peano.) On the philosophical side, I'll count as 'analytic philosophy' the work in the stream tracing back to and back from the Vienna Circle and subsequently 'Logical Positivism', or to Bertrand Russell.

This excludes J. L. Austin and the Ordinary Language philosophers, as well as Gilbert Ryle and P. F. Strawson. It would be hard to do them justice without studying non-mathematical formal logic. England at the turn of the twentieth century saw W. E. Johnson's *Logic*, Bernard Bosanquet's influential translation of Lotze's *Logic*, and Lewis Carroll's *Symbolic Logic*, for example. These contributed to the context in which Cook Wilson, critic of mathematical logic and of Russell, developed his views. Wilson in turn influenced Austin and others, and coloured the Oxford environment in which these parts of the broader analytic tradition emerged. Despite the richness of (say) Strawson's

---

[1] Two indispensable selections of original sources translated (when necessary) into English are van Heijenoort 1967a and Ewald 1996. Primary sources in their original languages are now in the public domain, and can easily be found online.

Introduction to Logical Theory, it differs in fundamental respects from what I explore here.

There were many reasons for mathematics and mathematical logic to become prominent, and considerations were weighed differently by different actors. A crucial factor was the advances in logic from mathematical analysis. Kant declared logic so obviously finished that its purported completeness could be taken as a datum. But he was speaking of a system of inferences that are, to contemporary eyes, quite meagre. Advances in logic supported the hope of foundations of arithmetic and (mathematical) analysis via formal logic. From the other direction, advances in mathematics generated, as part of ordinary research practice, concepts and resources that later were used to deepen the analysis of reasoning, and put pressure on the idea that mathematics could be grounded in spatial intuition. Once discovery in logic began to pick up momentum, it became a somewhat autonomous research programme itself.

9.2 GEOMETRY AND SPACE

9.2.1 Projective Geometry

The algebraic geometer Federigo Enriques in 1929 and the methodologist of science Ernest Nagel in 1939 (apparently independently) made a neglected observation: The development of projective geometry played a crucial role in shaping the emergence of formal logic.[2] Philosophical issues arose directly out of advances in ordinary, non-foundational mathematics. For example, the idea that a concept might be undefinable in a framework was presented by the undefinability of 'distance' in projective terms. The introduction of points at infinity presented questions about patterns of definition and the interaction of (what we would now call) the ontology of a theory and its ideology. In the 1860s, work by Plücker (e.g. Plücker 1868) and then Lie developed the idea that it was possible to construct, in ordinary spatial intuition, models of other geometries by interpreting expressions like 'point' as referring to lines or spheres. Thus a rudimentary idea of interpretation joined the geometer's tool-set.

Enriques and Nagel devote special attention to the *principle of duality* in projective geometries: substitution of terms can match up theorems in pairs. The simplest example: In the projective plane, with other vocabulary formulated properly, taking any theorem and uniformly replacing 'point' with 'line' and 'line' with 'point' results in another projective theorem. This striking fact not only demanded explanation in itself, which was a contributing factor to the (broadly speaking) 'syntactic' research discussed in 9.2.4 but also placed the puzzle of explaining the contribution of logical form to mathematical theoremhood right before the eyes of geometers working in the late nineteenth century.

---

[2] See Enriques 1929 and Nagel 1939. A valuable recent presentation of nineteenth-century geometry covering figures like von Staudt and Plücker in addition to the more familiar non-Euclidian geometry, is Gray 2007.

Indeed, mathematicians had duality literally before their eyes: Textbooks on projective geometry had each page divided into two columns with coordinated lines of reasoning. The columns were paired line-by-line, theorem-by-theorem, and even diagram-by-diagram, each with its projective dual.[3]

9.2.2 Non-Euclidean Geometry: Riemann, Grassmann, and the Abstract Conception of Space

Though projective geometry isn't Euclidean, the label 'non-Euclidean geometry' suggests in the popular imagination alternatives to the Parallels Postulate, and to a lesser extent spaces of higher dimension. The early nineteenth century saw hints from Gauss and synthetic developments by Bolyai and Lobachevsky, but the work only came before a wide audience when Riemann's lecture (Riemann 1854/1868b) appeared.[4] This put two ideas in play: that a principle of space previously regarded as self-evident might fail even to be true, and that the theory of space might not best be developed in intuition, but rather within what Frege called 'conceptual thought'.[5] A different presentation of abstract geometry (Grassmann 1844) was influential in complementary ways, though the effect on logic and philosophy was more indirect.[6]

Non-Euclidean geometries were taken mostly in stride by mathematicians. But many philosophers reacted negatively to the proposed alternate geometries.[7] (Somewhat surprisingly, since, as Otto Liebmann observed, the thesis that space is synthetic a priori *entails* that the *logical* development of alternative geometries should be possible.)[8] *Some* philosophers on the continent were enthusiastic: Hermann Helmholtz is a prominent example.[9]

---

[3] I discuss projective duality in connection with Frege in Tappenden 2005b.

[4] The importance of this lecture to logic and philosophy is often underestimated. See Ferreirós 2006 and Ferreirós 1999.

[5] 'Conceptual thought can after a fashion shake off this yoke [of intuitive constraints on geometry] when it assumes, say, a space of four dimensions or of positive curvature ... For purposes of conceptual thought we can always assume the contrary of one or another of the axioms without involving ourselves in any contradictions when we proceed to our deductions ...' (Frege 1953/1884, § 14). Frege's overall attitude to non-Euclidean geometry is quite puzzling: despite the openness to exploring non-Euclidean geometry 'as a matter of conceptual thought', he did not view abstract presentations as capturing all the content of true geometry, and held Euclidean geometry to be evidently true of actual space as late as the 1920s, for unknown reasons.

[6] I discuss Grassmann's effect on some parts of nineteenth-century German mathematics relevant to the history of analytic philosophy in Tappenden 2011.

[7] Hermann Lotze was the most renowned (Lotze 1879, Book II, ch. 2 §§ 131–7). Russell's discussion of Lotze on geometry in Russell 1897 is useful.

[8] Liebmann 1880. Otto Liebmann's son Heinrich, a mathematician who attended Frege's lectures, played an important role in the popularization of non-Euclidean geometry.

[9] See Helmholtz 1868. For further discussion, see Hyder's chapter in the present volume.

The polished version of the idea of model developed by Tarski would not be rigorously formulated for decades but rudimentary forms and parts of the puzzle appeared here and there.[10] For example, the idea that non-Euclidean geometry presented an example of logical independence, understood in terms of *consequence* appeared well before the twentieth century. In 1873 Felix Klein produced an interpretation of non-Euclidean geometry and commented:

> The examination of non-Euclidean geometry is in no way intended to decide the validity of the parallel axiom but only to address this question: is the parallel axiom a mathematical consequence of the other axioms of Euclid? To this question these investigations provide a definite *no*.[11]

The impact in England differed, in part because Euclid's *Elements* was embedded in the school curriculum as the paradigm of rational thought.[12] The debate was galvanized by an article in English by Helmholtz in 1870.[13] There were some supporters (notably William Clifford), but overall the reception was negative.[14] The mathematical reaction in England was channelled along a course scouted by Arthur Cayley. In 1859 Cayley had explored algebraic representations of non-Euclidean geometries within a general algebraic projective geometry.[15] Cayley devised a way of introducing different representations of distance within projective geometry and closed the essay with a ringing statement about the extent of the geometrical: 'Metrical geometry is thus a part of [projective] geometry, and [projective] geometry is all geometry, and reciprocally' (Cayley 1859, p. 92). Cayley was not by temperament inclined to philosophy, but he believed that there were philosophical issues implicit in the new geometrical developments, and in 1883 he urged English philosophers (largely unsuccessfully) to wrestle with them (Cayley 1884).

It wasn't until Russell's *An Essay on the Foundations of Geometry* of 1897 that a British philosopher would engage recent geometry systematically, and there Cayley's viewpoint is presupposed. With an odd blend of neo-Hegelian and Kantian principles, Russell defends the view that 'Projective Geometry, in so far as it deals only with

---

[10] For example, even when producing his representation of non-Euclidean geometry in 1868, Beltrami didn't see a relative consistency proof or a proof of independence. But Christian Houel saw it and soon had convinced Beltrami in correspondence. Once again see Gray 2007 for an overview, or the thorough scholarly treatment in Voelke 2005 for further details. For a more philosophical perspective see Stump 2007 and Webb 1995.

[11] Klein 1873, p. 314. Philosophers too drew this moral: Wundt speaks of the work of Klein as establishing 'the independence of the parallels axiom from the remaining axioms of geometry' (Wundt 1880, p. 442) and it is similarly characterized in Erdmann 1877.

[12] See for example the defence of Euclid in Dodgson 1879. See Richards 1988, ch. 4.

[13] Helmholtz 1870.

[14] The exchanges between Helmholtz and Land were typical of the ensuing debate. Helmholtz 1876; Land 1877. See Richards 1988, ch. 2.

[15] Cayley 1859.

the properties common to all spaces, will be found ... to be wholly *a priori*, to take nothing from experience, and to have, like Arithmetic, a creature of the pure intellect for its object.'[16] Russell's essay is decently informed about, but disengaged from, the mathematics it discusses: philosophical conclusions are drawn from research observed from outside, rather than driven by the process of developing the mathematics. There were disengaged commentaries across the channel too, but the deepest philosophical insight emerged (sometimes only implicitly) from the mathematicians, or from mathematically active philosophers like Helmholtz. Russell himself shifted direction, when G. E. Moore helped persuade him to abandon the idealism colouring Russell (1897).[17]

9.2.3 Other Stresses and Strains

Additional developments pressed on the question of the relationship between intuitive geometry and abstract mathematics, such as pathological functions that admitted of analytic definitions but seemed bizarre if imagined in space. Examples are the everywhere continuous, nowhere differentiable real-valued function on $\mathbb{R}$, and Peano's space-filling curve.[18] Though examples from real analysis attracted attention, more profound foundational pressures were arising for functions of a *complex* variable that made paring off the role of intuition necessary. A salient problem for complex analysis was the adjudication of the 'extent of validity' of the so-called 'Dirichlet principle', which Riemann used in a central way to support function-existence proofs in his new approach to problems in complex analysis.[19] The principle is evidently true in physical situations but untrue in general. A research target in the nineteenth century was a provably correct formulation general enough to support Riemann's proofs: this was finally accomplished in Hilbert (1901) and Hilbert (1904). The uncertainty over the Dirichlet principle was especially relevant to logicians like Frege who based his logic on functions, since some mathematicians—even some otherwise sympathetic to Riemann—viewed uncertainty about the Dirichlet principle to arise from Riemann's appeal to an uncontrolled concept of function (see Tappenden 2006).

---

[16] Russell 1897, p. 117. Russell adds that if the project is successful, it will fulfil the promise of (his words) the 'beautiful failure' of Grassmann 1844.

[17] On Moore's and Russell's rejection of idealism, see Griffin's chapter in the present volume.

[18] Archibald 2008 is an accessible brief treatment of the historical ramifications of these functions. For Peano's curve see Peano 1890; a contemporary perspective is Sagan 1994.

[19] Variations on the phrase 'ascertain extent of validity [*Gültigkeitsgrenzen*]' often appeared in discussions of what was needed for the Dirichlet principle, as well as in Frege's description of his foundational objectives in his *Grundlagen*. See Tappenden 2006, p. 118.

9.2.4 Pasch, Hilbert, and Deductive Relations Among Geometric Principles

That Euclid's proofs contained foggy inferences here and there was common knowledge among geometers in the nineteenth century. The first successful effort at an axiomatization in broadly Euclidean style (as opposed to the transformation-based investigations of Klein, Lie, and Helmholtz) was in Pasch (1882). Pasch did not explicitly declare rules of inference, or craft his proofs in a formal language, but his disciplined work set the standard for future efforts.

Independently of Pasch, there was an effort to establish a fine classification of fundamental geometric principles according to their deductive relations. It was noted in 9.2.2 that in 1873 Klein viewed the independence of the parallel axiom as settled. Less glamorous from a popular standpoint, but more important, was research into the dependence and independence of building block principles. Following a lecture on one such discovery—that the Fundamental Theorem of Projective Geometry depends on the Pappus and Desargues theorems—Hilbert is said to have made a (possibly apocryphal) remark 'One must always in the position of "point, line, plane" to be able to say "table, chair and beermug".'[20]

Hilbert explored the deductive structure of geometry in careful lectures over a decade (Hilbert 2004), culminating in his 1899 *Foundations of Geometry*.[21] His concern for deductive relations led him to produce long lists of axioms, the better to finely dissect what depended on what. Hilbert laid bare some astonishing connections and disconnections. One example was a striking link between deductive structure and the structure of space: Beginning with minimal incidence axioms for a plane and for a three-dimensional space, requiring that the classical Desargues theorem holds in the plane is equivalent to requiring that the plane be embeddable in the space. For more on Hilbert's results in this vein, see Hallett 2008. For the theorem about space and the plane see Arana and Mancosu 2012. The Arana/Mancosu article compellingly explores how purely mathematical investigations led naturally to a study of deduction.

Hilbert's study of deductive relations was driven by the mathematical questions he faced: he had at that point no concern for traditional philosophical issues like answering sceptics. His understanding of consequence was informal—he didn't state explicit rules of inference or formation rules for sentences, and he treated his axioms as sentences with not-necessarily interpreted primitives. The second represented a departure from Pasch, who held that deductive relations should be unaffected by uniform substitutions of primitives, but for whom primitives were interpreted and axioms meaningful.

---

[20] The proof appears in Weiner 1892. For more of these investigations into the deductive relations of fundamental geometric principles see Toepell 1986. This research was not the province of a small cadre of researchers: it appeared in elementary textbooks. For example, a textbook by Frege's colleague Thomae on conics reflects extensively on which basic principles entail which others (Thomae 1894, pp. 24–5).

[21] See Hilbert 1899 and Hilbert 1902.

9.3 'Conceptual Thought', Rigour, and the 'Arithmetization of Analysis'

In the mid-to-late ninteenth century, mathematicians often spoke of a movement toward 'arithmetization'. But the label meant different things to different people.[22] The goals differed as well: arithmetization was seen as a way to increase trustworthiness of proofs, or to increase clarity for teaching, or to diagnose the range of application for the result proved, or to provide a canonical proof method, or as answering the question 'When is a theorem proven in basic terms?' and more.

The precise form in which 'arithmetization' was manifested interacted with an issue from 9.2.2: mathematics as properly done via 'conceptual thought'.

9.3.1 Göttingen and the Conceptual Approach

The mathematics of the eighteenth century strikes contemporary mathematicians as overwhelmingly computational. Recognizably modern patterns of definition and proof appeared early in the nineteenth century, and were developed self-consciously in the second half of the century, notably by mathematicians from Göttingen.[23] Early inspiration came from Gauss:

> And Waring confessed that the proof seemed the more difficult, since one cannot imagine any *notation* to express a prime number. But in our opinion, however, such truths should be extracted from concepts (*notio*) and not notations (*notatio*). (Gauss 1801, art. 76)

Another early tone-setter was Dirichlet who remarked in his 1852 obituary of computational master Jacobi that there was in recent analysis a trend 'to put thoughts in place of computations' (Dirichlet 1852). Of course, such vague orienting remarks can be taken many ways. What gave them substance was that specific mathematical projects, definitions, and proof techniques were taken to exemplify the trend. The most important exemplar for our purposes is the approach to complex analysis pioneered by Riemann, especially as developed by Dedekind.[24]

---

[22] A discussion of the diversity of 'arithmetization' is Petri and Schappacher 2007. Also illuminating is Ferreirós 2007.

[23] Ferreirós 1999 is a canonical secondary source on this history from a philosopher's perspective. Stein 1988 is also valuable. For a mathematician's view see Laugwitz 1999.

[24] Concerning the Dedekind–Riemann connection in a philosophical context see Tappenden 2008b.

Here are some features of the 'conceptual approach' relevant to the evolution of logic. 'Function' (understood as 'mapping') was usually accepted as basic. There was an orientation toward 'defining functions with internal characteristic properties' rather than 'external' properties such as potential linguistic (broadly speaking) representations (f.x. power series). The distinction wasn't sharply defined, but specific definitions and methods were cited as exemplifying it. A proof text came from expansive remarks of Riemann interpreting his method of studying functions in a methodological commentary within his Ph.D. thesis:

> A theory of these functions on the basis provided here would determine the presentation of a function (i.e. its value for every argument) independently of its mode of determination by operations on magnitudes, because one would add to the general concept of a function of a variable complex magnitude just the attributes necessary for the determination of the function, and only then would one go over to the different expressions [for] the function. (Riemann 1851, pp. 38–9)

In the following lines, he states that the 'operations on magnitudes' are just the familiar $+, -, \times, \div$, and that the 'necessary attributes' are properties like the location and type of the zeros and discontinuities, behaviour at specific crucial points ('branch points'), etc. (To consider one particularly simple illustration: an elliptic function is determined (up to a constant multiple) by the location and types of its zeros and poles—any further information about values need only be ground out when it is specifically needed.) A few years later, he speaks of this style as bearing fruit in Riemann (1857b) by reproducing earlier results about functions definable by series 'nearly without computing' (*fast ohne Rechnung*) (Riemann 1857a, p. 85). In the paper itself, Riemann says his methods have produced 'almost immediately from the definition' results about series obtained earlier, partly by 'tiresome computations' (*mühsame Rechnungen*) (Riemann 1857b, p. 67).

The methodological principle was extended and interpreted by Dedekind in his theory of ideals, which would be the cornerstone of his unification of the theory of algebraic numbers with Riemann's theory of algebraic functions. Alluding to Riemann in a way that any mathematician of the time would have recognized immediately, Dedekind sees 'almost all areas of mathematics' as requiring the choice between essential ('internal') and accidental ('external') so that the formulation 'based immediately on fundamental characteristics' will support the effective *anticipation* of the results of as yet unfinished computations:

> One notices, in fact, that the proofs [by Kummer] of the most important propositions depend on the representation of an ideal by the *expression* ... and on the effective realization of multiplication, that is on a *calculus* ... If we want to treat fields of arbitrary degree in the same way, then we shall run into great difficulties, perhaps insurmountable ones. Even if there were such a theory, based on calculation, it still would not be of the highest degree of perfection, in my opinion. It is preferable, as

in the modern theory of [complex] functions to seek proofs based immediately on fundamental characteristics, rather than on calculation, and indeed to construct the theory in such a way that it is able to predict the results of calculation ... Such is the goal I shall pursue in the chapters of this memoir that follow. (Dedekind 1877/1996, p. 102 italics in original)

The distinction fit with an attitude toward the way to identify fundamental concepts. Rather than see them as fixed at the outset (by, for example, taking as obvious in advance that + and × should be primitive) the determination of basic concepts was seen as part of the problem to be solved. The appropriate fundamental concepts were those that made it possible to find solutions easily and 'practically without computing'. Also there was a novel attitude toward existence arguments: to discuss an object or function there need not be a canonical way to refer to it, or calculate its values. It suffices to prove it exists.

The development of rigour in analysis is often associated with the foundations of real analysis, which by the second half of the nineteenth century was largely freed from apparent need to appeal to intuition. But in Riemann's stream of research, *complex* analysis suddenly became *more* apparently geometrical rather than less, paradigmatically through the use of Riemann surfaces to represent multi-valued functions and studying the functions via the properties of the surfaces. Riemann died young, before he worked out the ramifications, so it was left to others. There were many paths from Riemann to twentieth-century descendants: some mathematicians embraced the apparent intuitive character of Riemannian complex analysis, some treated it as in essence a computational analytic geometry of curves and surfaces, some regarded Riemann surfaces as mere devices for visualizing complex functions and not part of fundamental mathematical arguments. All of these led to important mathematical developments. The lack of a rigorous definition of 'Riemann surface' until the second decade of the twentieth century contributed to the multifurcation.

Most relevant to the historian of analytic philosophy is the substream that embraced Riemann's methods but regarded the geometric component—the apparent appeal to spatial intuition—as a foreign element to be pared off: the most profound mathematician was Dedekind and the most profound philosopher Frege, considered in 9.3.2.1 and 9.3.2.2.

9.3.2 Logic and Freedom from Intuition

Contemporaneous with the gradual progress on alternative geometries (9.2.2) the nineteenth century saw other substantial debates concerning space. It wouldn't be unreasonable to conjecture that the mathematical developments interacted with work of figures more traditionally regarded as 'philosophers' (Kant, Lotze, Fries, Herbart, Helmholtz ...), and occasionally that happened. One salient historical antecedent—Kant's theory of space as empirically real but transcendentally ideal—is often mentioned by historians of philosophy as influential, either negatively by holding back non-Euclidean geometry or as driving the effort to demonstrate the logical character of arithmetic and analysis.[25] To be sure, Kantian accounts of space played a role, but as just one of a cluster of interacting forces pressing for a case that reasoning in arithmetic is (or could be and ought to be) free of intuition, most arising naturally in mathematical practice. Among them were the currents aimed at showing arithmetic and analysis to be in some sense logical, and hence free of anything 'foreign to arithmetic'.

A conceptual problem for the use of analytic geometry was partly solved in the mid-nineteenth century: the assignment of coordinates seems to require Euclidean distance, so how can coordinates be used non-circularly for research into foundations, for example with alternative geometries? The breakthrough came with von Staudt (1847) and von Staudt (1856). Exploiting solely projective methods, von Staudt showed (with some soft spots) that coordinates could be assigned throughout the projective plane without presupposing distance.[26]

It took time for von Staudt's techniques to propagate. But by 1870 Klein used them as a basis for the interpretation of non-Euclidean geometry mentioned in 9.2.2, thus dodging the objection that Euclidean distance had been question-beggingly assumed. In an ensuing debate, Klein identified von Staudt's tacit appeal to what we would now call the *completeness* of the line as a hole to be patched.[27] But by the final paper in the series Klein passed the burden to papers that had appeared in 1872 (Klein 1874 pp. 346–7). One—Dedekind (1872/1901)—is taken up in 9.3.2.1 and another—Cantor (1872)—in 9.4.1.

9.3.2.1 Dedekind

By the mid-twentieth century, analytic philosophy had internalized a picture of 'Logic' as what had come to be called 'Symbolic Logic', representing inference patterns via symbols, with formal definitions of valid inference (either via rules of proof based on the formal structure of sentences or structured contents, or a semantic definition of truth, or both). This leaves the status of what Kreisel famously called 'informal rigour' unclear (Kreisel 1967). What of reasoning that is as disciplined as a cogent, non-formal proof in a mathematics journal, but is not formally regimented? Perhaps because there is this prejudice in place, we count Russell, Frege, and Peano as attempting a 'logicist reduction', a type of *philosophical* analysis, while Dedekind's disciplined non-formal work is not so counted.

---

[25] The idea that Kant's philosophy was a substantial obstacle for mathematicians pursuing non-Euclidean geometry was suggested in Bonola 1906/1955 (pp. 64, 92, 121), a history of these events whose 1912 translation was for years the most widely available English resource on non-Euclidean geometry. Coffa 1991 conveys the impression that the effort to prove Kant wrong about space and the a priori was the dominant engine driving the development of logical semantics.

[26] Von Staudt's argument is sometimes spoken of as a proof of 'the equivalence of synthetic and analytic projective geometry': Rota 1997, p. 147.

[27] Klein's side of the debate appeared in Klein 1871, Klein 1873, and Klein 1874.

But this was not how things were regarded from the mid-nineteenth century to its end. Dedekind viewed his account of number as a contribution to the thesis that reasoning in arithmetic is logical[28] and by 1899 for Hilbert it needs no further elaboration:

> It is of importance to establish precisely the starting point of our investigation. *As given, we take the laws of pure logic and in particular all of arithmetic.* (On the relationship between logic and arithmetic see Dedekind, *Was Sind und was Sollen die Zahlen?*) [Hilbert 2004, p. 303. Emphasis in original][29]

Already in 1849 Gauss recognized a tension between new techniques in mathematics and the apparently inadequate use of intuition, in a paper of 1849 cited by Riemann as one of the few sources for the lecture on abstract magnitudes noted in 9.2.2.

> The demonstration is presented using expressions borrowed from [projective geometry] for in this way, the greatest acuity and simplicity is obtained. Fundamentally, the essential content of the entire argument belongs to a higher domain, independent from space, in which abstract general concepts of magnitudes, are investigated as combinations of magnitudes connected by continuity, a domain, which, at present, is poorly developed, and in which one cannot move without the use of language borrowed from spatial images. (Gauss 1849, p. 79)

The need for clarification became more acute as the conceptual style developed. Not just for the Dirichlet principle (9.2.3) but in many other respects, discoveries outpaced what could be addressed in terms that Dedekind, Hilbert, and those who shared their attitudes would call logical.

In excluding from arithmetic and analysis elements judged 'foreign to it' (Dedekind 1872/1901, p. 5) Dedekind created many of the foundational tools we now take for granted. Among these: an axiomatic treatment of arithmetic (the Dedekind–Peano Axioms), a clear analysis of the structure of proof by induction and definition by

---

[28] 'In speaking of arithmetic (algebra, analysis) as a part of logic I mean to imply that I consider the number-concept entirely independent of the notions or intuitions of space and time, that I consider it an immediate result from the laws of thought' (Dedekind 1888/1901, p. 31).

[29] Frege's name is conspicuous by its absence. We can be confident Hilbert was aware of Frege's work at the time, if only because the Hilbert assistant, Hans von Schaper, who compiled the lecture notes from which this quote is taken attended several Frege courses during the years 1894–6 including one on Frege's logic. From the viewpoint of mathematics Frege wasn't even in the equation in 1899, since he had to that point only treated a small fragment of arithmetic and scattered illustrative sentences of analysis (and even that was done with a system soon learned to be inconsistent in a rather simple way). When Johannes Thomae issued a second edition of his textbook on complex analysis (Thomae 1898) he tried to raise the profile of his Jena colleage by including in the section on foundations a reference to Frege 1953/1884 along with Dedekind 1888/1901. Stackel, reviewing the volume in *Jahrbuch über die Fortschritte der Mathematik* tut-tuts Thomae, since in Stäeckel's view 'The uninformed reader would take from this that Frege treats irrational numbers' so reference to Dedekind 1872/1901 was called for instead (or perhaps in addition).

recursion, and (picking up from Riemann, in this case) a clear recognition of the value of the concepts of set and function, understood extensionally, in the foundations of mathematics.[30] His characterization of the continuity displayed by the structure of the real numbers is given by the 'Dedekind cut', a division of the rational numbers into sets A and B, with all elements of A less than all elements of B, and A having no greatest element.[31]

The Dedekind cut is an algebraist's characterization, geared to ensure directly that a set bounded above relative to < has a least upper bound. However, it is an 'algebraist's characterization' in a distinctly twentieth-century sense of 'algebraist' that appears for the first time in Dedekind. On this understanding, algebra is the study of *structure*.[32] It is no hyperbole to call this reorientation revolutionary. Prior to Dedekind, 'algebra' was understood as it is presented in a textbook like Chrystal (1886): the manipulation of symbols. With Dedekind, the contemporary conception appears. Through the mathematicians influenced by Dedekind, principally Emmy Noether, it has become the background understanding of algebra that 'goes without saying'.[33]

Dedekind's conception of mathematics is also on display in Dedekind and Weber (1882). Dedekind and his co-author produce a structural interpretation of work which seemed inescapably geometric: Riemann's complex analysis, including the concept of a Riemann surface.[34] Dedekind unites work he had done earlier in number theory with a structural/algebraic interpretation of Riemann surfaces to produce a *unified* theory of algebraic numbers and one-variable algebraic functions.[35]

Dedekind signals allegiance to the conceptual orientation in many places as far back as Dedekind (1854), where he explores the attitude that a significant part of mathematical investigation is defining concepts in terms of central properties and that a sign of having identified those properties is that the discovery of proofs and fruitful conjectures is facilitated. In other words, an identifying mark of a proper definition is its fruitfulness.[36]

---

[30] On Dedekind's foundations see Sieg and Schlimm 2005.

[31] Today we take the real number to *be* the sets A and B. Dedekind himself took the real number (if non-rational) to be an entity posited in thought to fill a gap between A and B. Dedekind came in for criticism for this, and it is unclear why he thought it important, since in other settings he had no misgivings about identifying the 'object corresponding to a set' with the set itself, for example in his treatment of ideals in algebraic number theory.

[32] Depending on how the vague 'structure' is made precise one might want to argue for the priority of Grassmann.

[33] For discussion of some philosophical dimensions of Dedekind's structuralism, see Reck 2003. For a historical map of the way Dedekind's influence propagated through one part of twentieth century mathematics, see McLarty 2008.

[34] Dedekind was not forced to interpret Riemann's work in terms of a new structural conception of algebra simply by mathematical necessity, *faute de mieux*. There *were* other ways to rigorously approach Riemann's innovations without appeal to intuition. For example, Riemann's successor at Gottingen, Clebsch (Clebsch and Gordon 1868) interpreted Riemann's work as an algebraic theory of curves and surfaces (in the pre-Dedekind sense of 'algebraic').

[35] The basic secondary sources for information about Dedekind on ideals are the papers of Harold Edwards. Edwards 1980 is a good place to begin.

[36] For details and more discussion of Dedekind's methodology see Avigad 2006 and Tappenden 2008b.

Of course, this may sound like an empty truism, but in Dedekind's hands (developing Riemann's insights) it displayed a profound shift in problem solving: In mathematics and reasoning generally the best solution strategy may require identifying and properly defining the best vocabulary to state the problem. In the effort to find connections between apparently disparate and remote facts, crucial resources for discovery, explanation, and clarification can be lost if we rest content with the basic terms handed down to us, with no rationale but tradition. The attitude is displayed not only in Dedekind's algebraic and number theoretic research, but also in his approach to foundations: Why stick with traditional logical ideas like 'concept' and 'extension' rather than 'set' and 'mapping' when the former have only tradition to recommend them rather than demonstrated value in rigorous investigation?

9.3.2.2 *Frege*

There are profound affinities between Frege and Dedekind, beginning with agreement in the objective, and even the language, of excluding from arithmetic and analysis elements 'foreign to it', with Frege explicitly expressing the hope of thereby establishing the 'extent of validity' of arithmetic and analysis.[37] This is not altogether unexpected, since both of them were trained and immersed in the Göttingen style of mathematics.[38] Though Frege did prove substantial foundational results, his strength was the power and permanence of the tools and point of view he introduced (see 9.5.1).[39] Though Frege too falls short of a systematic discussion, he has more to say about his background epistemology and conception of logic. Frege's 'gapless' proofs were aimed at tracing theorems back to the most basic support—the 'sources'—of the knowledge. Logic was the source of knowledge supporting the most general investigation, spatial intuition was more limited.[40]

Frege was of one mind with Dedekind on identifying basic ideas: Don't take those that are at first blush most appealing, but rather those of proven fruitfuless in reasoning:[41]

> To those who feel inclined to criticise my definitions as unnatural, I would suggest that the point here is not whether they are natural, but whether they go to the heart of the matter and are logically beyond criticism. (Frege 1953/1884), p. xi)
>
> All these concepts have been developed in science and have proved their fruitfulness. For this reason what we may discover in them has a higher claim on our attention than anything that our everyday trains of thought might offer. For fruitfulness is the acid test of concepts, and scientific investigation logic's true field of observation. (Frege 1979/1880, p. 33)

---

[37] See for example Frege 1953/1884, § 103 for such a use of 'foreign to it'. On Frege's views of the geometry/arithmetic + analysis relationship, see Demopolous 1994 and Tappenden 1995b.

[38] On this dimension of Frege's background see Tappenden 2006.

[39] For a reconstruction of some of the mathematical content of Frege's foundational writings see Heck 2011.

[40] Two efforts to reconstruct this epistemology are Kitcher 1979 and Weiner 1990, though Frege's sparse remarks leave much room for dispute.

[41] On fruitfulness as a methodological concept for Frege, see Tappenden 1995a.

Drawing from the scientific 'field of observation' around Frege, his logic took the concept of function as basic, plus generality (the universal quantifier). Symbols for generality and negation yielded the existential quantifier, supporting a treatment of the logical structure of existence arguments. Frege's indifference to logical tradition showed itself in another way. In *Grundlagen der Arithmetik*, a work aimed at a broad audience, Frege had employed what were treated as logical ideas in textbooks of the time: 'concept' and 'extension of a concept'.[42] But soon he set the traditional ideas to one side: 'concept', rather than taken as primitive, was defined as a kind of function, and 'extension of a concept' was set aside in favour of the new coinage 'value-range' of a function.[43]

Frege's contributions have had a more lasting influence on philosophy and logic than any area of mathematics besides foundations, so further discussion is deferred to 9.5.1.

9.3.2.3 Berlin and Weierstrassian rigour

The mathematical centre most popularly associated with rigour in the late nineteenth century was the University of Berlin, where both Leopold Kronecker and Kurt Weierstrass taught. Weierstrass was regarded as upholding the highest standards of disciplined argument, and the phrase 'Weierstrassian rigour' came into wide use. Weierstrass' style continues today to be regarded as a gold standard, partly because the $\delta - \varepsilon$ type of definition associated with him is usually the first glimpse of mathematical rigour to greet a beginning student.[44] Though this was not presented in a formal logical costume, it was of the utmost importance in unmasking the structure of key concepts (continuity, for example, or uniform convergence) that require quantification theory to be represented.[45] Consider, for example, his familiar definition of the continuity of a function: rather than appeal to infinitesimals or intuitive limits, Weierstrass uses quantification and inequalities: A function $f \colon \mathbb{R} \to \mathbb{R}$ is *continuous at a point* $c \Leftrightarrow_{def}$ $(\forall \epsilon > 0)(\exists \delta > 0)(\forall x \in \mathbb{R})(|x - c| < \delta) \to (|f(x) - f(c)| < \epsilon)$.[46]

---

[42] In an odd footnote (§ 68) he disavows the need for the latter, without explanation.

[43] The value-range of a function is the collection of argument-value pairs for every argument. Value ranges were introduced by axioms, including the ill-fated inconsistent Basic Law V; the inconsistency of the axioms introducing the concept naturally put a limit on the extent to which it can be exactly characterized. 'Value-ranges' have plausibly been suggested to have been introduced by Frege as an adjustment of his logical system needed to reconstruct a proof in Dedekind 1888/1901. See Sundholm 2001, with a critical rejoinder in Heck 2011, pp. 66–7.

[44] This has generated the argot 'epsilontics' for rigour in this style (sometimes used perjoratively for a perceived excess of rigour obscuring central ideas).

[45] This was observed in Grattan-Guinness 1975. The choice of definition illustrates the slipperiness of the distinction between definition and factual assumption: The $\delta - \epsilon$ statement that was taken to define continuity had been earlier stated by Dirichlet as a theorem that needed to be *proved* (Bottazzini 1986, p. 216). Weierstrass similarily transformed a provable principle into his definition of 'analytic function' (Manning 1975).

[46] The importance for problem-solving of the Weierstrass definitions of continuity of a function, and the distinction of uniform and pointwise convergence of functions is clearly presented in Kitcher 1984.

Like Dedekind (and Frege) Weierstrass sought to separate the concepts of analysis from those of geometry or mechanics.[47] But unlike Dedekind who took Riemann's methods in their original (at least superficially) geometric guise and attempted a non-geometric but otherwise faithful rigorous reconstruction, Weierstrass viewed Riemann's approach as fundamentally misguided, and to be avoided when it was time to give proofs in canonical form. (Though Weierstrass conceded that Riemann's methods could be valuable for inspiring discoveries.) There were other deep-rooted differences. Dedekind and Riemann stated explicitly that proper technique called for mathematical objects to be studied via their 'essential' or 'inner characteristic properties' as noted in 9.3.1 rather than through the properties of specific linguistic presentations of them, such as power series.[48] For Weierstrass, the study of the properties of *representations* of functions (paradigmatically, power series) was the 'ultimate goal'.[49]

Weierstrass was slow to publish, so his foundational efforts appeared later, typically in works by other writers.[50] Despite the mathematical conservativeness that set him at odds with the conceptual stance, he nonetheless displayed some reformist instincts. He wanted plus and times to be the basic operations for representations of the objects of analysis, but he accepted infinite sums. He accepted infinite aggregates in his theory of the real numbers. Both of these would lead to tension with Kronecker. But the significance of an equally profound milestone in mathematical reasoning would only become evident later: in the theorem (today called the Bolzano–Weierstrass theorem) indispensable to his approach—that every infinite, bounded sequence of real numbers has a convergent subsequence—Weierstrass introduces into his foundations a result that we now recognize can only be proven by non-constructive methods. As early as 1870, this was noticed by his colleague Kronecker, who called it an 'obvious sophism' (Ferreirós 1999, p. 141).

9.4 THE ANALYSIS OF THE INFINITE

9.4.1 Cantor

Cantor's set theory arose from problems in representation with trigonometric series, that is, series (real or complex) of the form:

$$f(x) = a_0 + \sum_{n=1}^{\infty} (a_n \cos nx + b_n \sin nx)$$

---

[47] Bottazzini 1986, pp. 260–2 and *passim*. Bottazzini's book is an excellent source on Weierstrass' foundations.

[48] For more on this aspect of Riemann and Dedekind's approach, see Tappenden 2008b. For general reflections on mathematical definition broadly in this spirit, see Tappenden 2008a.

[49] The passage in which Weierstrass makes this remark (Weierstrass 1886/1988, p. 176) includes an explicit contrast with Riemann. See also Laugwitz 1999, especially pp. 82–4.

[50] Readers of Frege can easily misidentify his rhetorical targets, since his references to Weierstrass are often references to Kossak 1872 and Biermann 1887, which were for years the only available presentations of much of Weierstrass' foundations.

A restricted class of these equations (*Fourier series*), with coefficients given by certain integrals, had been developed and studied in the late eighteenth century in connection with problems of heat flow. Subsequent research was motivated by two questions: When does such a series define a function? Does a series that defines a function *uniquely* define it?[51] In retrospect clearer understanding and definition of 'function' and 'integral' was needed. Dirichlet published some papers pressing the topic forward in the years 1829–37.[52] Subsequently, in a landmark paper on trigonometric series (Riemann 1854/1868a), Riemann defined (in $\delta - \varepsilon$ style) the Riemann integral, and defined 'function' in the modern way as an arbitrary correspondence. As late as 1870, Riemann's student Hankel cited trigonometric series as prompting the persistent interest in the concept of function, and he criticized the unclarity in various definitions of function.[53] His paper explored how many discontinuities a function defined by a trigonometric series could tolerate and still be continuous at the other points. He discovered that there could be infinitely many discontinuities, if they are nowhere dense on the line.[54]

Soon after, Georg Cantor proved that a trigonometric series defining a function f is unique if the series converges (pointwise) to f for all x but *finitely many* exceptional points. This prompted Cantor to ask: 'What is the most general exception set for which this result holds?' The following year Cantor wrote a review (Cantor 1871) exploring Hankel (1870/1882). Drawing on Hankel's ideas, Cantor indicated that uniqueness could hold even with *infinitely many* exceptional points, but he needed a framework to express the ideas.

This brings us to Cantor (1872): The framework needed a precise definition of real numbers. Furthermore, it needed to be an analyst's definition, ensuring the convergence of sequences. Cantor didn't execute the idea with perfect logical hygiene, but with subsequent cleaning up it became the definition used (along with Dedekind's) in introductory textbooks today: A real number is an equivalence class of Cauchy sequences from $\mathbb{Q}$.[55] Liberally using the non-constructive Bolzano–Weierstrass theorem (9.3.2.3), Cantor finds a way to measure how clustered an infinite subset of $\mathbb{R}$ is, and proves that

---

[51] The second, uniqueness question is implicit in Riemann 1854/1868a, § 38.4.

[52] Indeed these papers are often credited with introducing the contemporary idea of function as 'arbitrary correspondence', but Bottazzini 1986, sect. 5.3 compellingly argues that this is an over-creative interpretation of Dirichlet's words. It would not be until Riemann 1854/1868a that this further step would be taken.

[53] See Hankel 1870/1882. Hankel's paper indicates the extent to which 'function' was still controverted in 1870. In fact, the concept would remain a topic of dispute into the twentieth century, as we see in 9.4.2. For the development of the function concept up to and including Hankel 1870/1882 see Youskevich 1976. For the interactions between the evolution of the concept of function and the study of trigonometric series see Bottazzini 1986, ch. 5. Riemann 1854/1868a itself contains a clear survey of preceding work.

[54] A set S is *dense* in $\tilde{S} \subseteq \mathbb{R}$ if for any $b \in S$ and arbitrarily small $\varepsilon \in \mathbb{R}$ there is some $a \in \tilde{S}$ in the interval $(b - \varepsilon, b + \varepsilon)$. A set S is *nowhere dense* if there is no interval $(a, b) \subseteq \mathbb{R}$ in which the points of S are dense.

[55] A *Cauchy sequence* is a sequence $a_0, a_1, a_2, \ldots, a_n, \ldots$ in which (roughly) as the subscripts get larger, the a_i's get closer together. More exactly: $(\forall \varepsilon > 0)(\exists N > 0)(\forall i, j)(i, j > N \rightarrow |a_i - a_j| < \varepsilon)$. Cantor's definition was a small variation.

the uniqueness theorem holds with an even more intricate infinite set of exceptions, as long as they are not too densely packed.[56]

This discovery prompted several more in quick succession to further clarify how the reals as ordered on the line are richer than the rationals. In Cantor (1874) he proved that $\mathbb{R}$ could not be put in 1–1 correspondence with $\mathbb{N}$ —that, loosely speaking, there are 'more' elements of $\mathbb{R}$ than $\mathbb{N}$ or $\mathbb{Q}$.[57] In Cantor (1879) he defined *cardinality*: Two sets have the same cardinality if one can be mapped 1–1 onto the other. He explored successively more complicated constructions of derived sets, which required what we can recognize as a makeshift, jerry-rigged theory of cardinal and ordinal numbers.

Finally Cantor (1883) presented that background as a theory of sets, cardinals, and ordinals. A defining feature of the ordinals is that they are *well-ordered*: Any set of ordinals has a least element. The natural numbers (order type ω) were the base, with further ordinals generated by successor and limit: $\omega, \omega + 1, \omega + 2, \ldots, \omega + n, \ldots; \omega + \omega, \omega + \omega + 1 \ldots$ (limit indicated with ';'). The arithmetic of transfinite ordinals was worked out. Cantor's approach uses ordinals as canonical examples of *cardinals*, a stance that is asserted without fanfare in contemporary set theory textbooks: The cardinal number of a set is the ordinal of the shortest well-ordering of that set. Thus representing cardinals by ordinals presumes that a given set can be well-ordered, which leads to the complications of 9.4.2.

Cantor's last two important papers were Cantor (1893) and Cantor (1895). In these he introduces the now standard $\aleph$ notation for ordinal numbers (setting $\omega = \aleph_0$) and explores the possibilities of generating larger sets by iterating the operation of taking the set of all subsets (the *powerset* $P(S)$). This led straightforwardly to paradoxes: what is the size of the set of all sets, given that it would need to contain its own (demonstrably larger) powerset? (A similar problem arose for ordinals [revisited in 9.4.3].) Cantor recognized this, but his response was unconvincing: 'inconsistent multiplicities' containing (for example) all sets, are not sets. There remained work to do: For the theory of cardinals and ordinals it had to be ascertained whether all sets admit a well-ordering, and the variety of principles Cantor appealed to needed to be gathered into a compact axiomatic framework, which leads us to 9.4.2.[58]

---

[56] More exactly: Cantor considers the *accumulation points* of a set S of reals: the set of points $a \in S$ with other members of S arbitrarily close to a. He called the set of *all* accumulation points of S its *derived set S'*. One can obviously take the derived set S'' of that derived set S', and continue arbitrarily many times. If S'' is non-empty, then S is densely packed around the members of S' but not necessarily elsewhere. If S'' is non-empty, then there are points in S around which the places where S is densely packed are densely packed. Cantor then calls a set $\bar{S}$ a *set of the first species* if for some n, $\bar{S}^n$ is finite, and hence $\bar{S}^{n+1}$ is $\varnothing$. Cantor's result was that the uniqueness theorem holds if the set of exceptions is of the first species.

[57] The proof did not exploit his famous 'diagonal argument', which was not published until 1891. Details of that argument appear in many places, for instance Boolos *et al.* 2007, pp. 18–20.

[58] For further reading on Cantor, three good sources are Dauben 1979/1990, Hallett 1984, and Ferreirós 1999. Some of Cantor's work has been translated and reprinted in Cantor 1915/1955, easily available as an inexpensive Dover edition.

9.4.2 Zermelo's Axioms, the Iterative Conception of Set, and the Axiom of Choice

There was little work on set theory in the 1890s, but the field was revitalized when the continuum hypothesis (9.4.4), and as a sub-problem whether $\mathbb{R}$ could be well-ordered, appeared on Hilbert's list of 23 mathematical problems.[59] Young Göttingen lecturer Ernst Zermelo took up the question. In Zermelo (1904) he published a proof that any set could be well-ordered, but since he introduced what we now call the Axiom of Choice (AC) to do it, the question was not put to rest. AC states, in one simple form, that if you have a family $\left\{S_i \mid i \in I\right\}$ of non-empty sets, then there is a function $f : \left\{S_i \mid i \in I\right\} \to \cup_{i \in I} \left\{S_i\right\}$ such that $f(S_i) \in S_i$. (f selects one element from each set.)

We now know AC and the proposition that any set can be well-ordered to be provably equivalent, so Zermelo could not have avoided AC or an equivalent. Several mathematicians—saliently the French mathematicians Baire, Borel, and Lebesgue—regarded AC as less evident than the theorem it was introduced to prove.[60] The perceived problem with AC is its non-constructiveness.[61] It states that a function exists, but not which function it is. Objections interacted with antecedent reservations about a broad concept of function noted above.

Zermelo also needed to address the paradoxes that can result with overly broad set theoretic principles deployed unreflectively. The simplest and best known is the Russell paradox. Any development of set theory will need some connection between properties (or predicates, or functions …) and sets, since we'll want to treat sets satisfying various conditions. The simplest intuitively compelling candidate is *Naive Comprehension*: For any property P, there is a set S, so that for any object a, a has P if and only if a is in S. (In symbols: $(\forall P)(\exists S)(\forall x)(Px \leftrightarrow x \in S)$.) But with no restriction on sets or properties, the paradox Russell conveyed to Frege (9.5.1) is an almost immediate consequence.[62]

---

[59] On the Hilbert problems see Gray 2000, or for more mathematical detail Browder 1974.

[60] For the interchanges between Zermelo and his French ally Hadamard with Baire, Borel, and Lebesgue see Moore 1982. The exchanges raise questions about self-evidence, evidence through introspection, and tacit knowledge. A motif repeated itself several times: Despite their explicit rejection of AC, proofs published by one or another of the French trio were discovered to implicitly appeal to it. On one occasion when this was pointed out, the revised proof turned out to appeal to it as well! As we now know, some signature results from this group, like the countable additivity of Lebesgue measure, are equivalent to restricted versions of AC.

[61] The point is tricky, because a consistent constructivism need not conflict with AC. It often happens that constructive accounts validate AC because not only are the possible choice functions restricted, but also the families $\{S_i \mid i \in I\}$. It can be that a constructive f will be available for *constructive* families, depending on the sense of 'constructive'.

[62] The idea is simple, and probably will be familiar to most readers. Choose P to be the property of a set that it is not a member of itself: $x \notin x$. Instantiating on our choice of P, we have $(\exists S)(\forall x)(x \notin x \leftrightarrow x \in S)$. Say that S_R (the Russell set) is the set we have just proven to exist: $(\forall x)(x \notin x \leftrightarrow x \in S_R)$. Since this statement holds for all x, it holds for S_R, so we obtain: $(S_R \notin S_R \leftrightarrow S_R \in S_R)$, a contradiction.

Zermelo had discovered Russell's paradox independently in Göttingen, sometime after 1897 and demonstrably no later than April 1902 when Husserl's papers record that Zermelo informed him about it (Ebbinghaus and Peckhaus 2007, pp. 45–7). So, when Zermelo crafted axioms systematizing the maelstrom of ideas in Cantor, he crafted them to avoid it. In addition to AC the axioms include some that are uncontentious: the existence of unions of given sets for example. More contentious axioms assert the existence of a countably infinite set (Axiom of Infinity) and the set of all subsets of a set (the Powerset Axiom). One axiom—the Axiom of Foundation—rules out the existence of infinite descending set-membership chains $\ldots \in a_i \in a_{i-1} \in \ldots a_3 \in a_2 \in a_1$. Foundation also forms the backbone of a conception of set called the 'iterative conception' that is now standard in mathematics. It was later articulated explicitly by Zermelo and Gödel, but it is already implicit here. The idea of the iterative conception is to begin with some given collection (possibly only the empty set) and build a larger and larger cumulative heirarchy of sets by iterating the powerset operation as many times as there are ordinals to index iterations.[63]

Rather than seek a set that collects *everything in the universe* with a property P, Zermelo ensures that *given any set* S, there is a *subset of* S containing exactly the things in S with P. This motivates the *Separation Axiom*: $\forall\phi\,\forall X\exists Y\forall u(u \in Y \leftrightarrow u \in X \wedge \phi(u))$. With adjustments, this Separation Axiom, and indeed Zermelo's axioms *en bloc* have proven to be a rich and fruitful framework, adequate to almost every mathematical problem that touches on set theory. One adjustment concerns the interpretation of '$\forall\phi$' in the axiom. What are the ϕ's? To Zermelo, they were 'definite properties'—an idea that Frege expressed as 'sharply defined': for every object there is a definite fact of the matter as to whether or not that object has ϕ.[64] Skolem argued that the idea of definite property lacked the clarity needed for mathematical reasoning, and should stand aside for the sharp replacement 'definable in first-order logic'.[65] By the mid-twentieth century logic had adopted Skolem's suggestion removing the '$\forall\phi$' and treating the rest as a *scheme*: *any* sentence resulting from replacing 'ϕ' with an appropriate first-order formula in the language of set theory is an axiom.[66]

---

[63] For more detail on these axioms, and an intuitive picture of the iterative conception of set as motivating them, see Boolos 1971 and Schoenfield 1977.

[64] Felgner 2010 (§ 5) argues plausibly that the idea and the terminology 'definite property' were taken from Edmund Husserl, who had lectured on the topic at Göttingen during Zermelo's time there. One would expect Zermelo to take Husserl's opinion seriously, since Zermelo had attended mathematics lectures by Husserl while Zermelo was a student in Berlin and they subsequently corresponded for many years. Zermelo's 1894 Berlin Ph.D. thesis addressed problems in the calculus of variations, Husserl's area of mathematical research in the 1890s.

[65] For references to Skolem's papers, and a clear and perceptive discussion of Zermelo's and Skolem's reasoning, see Benacerraf 1985. This paper also contains a philosophically minded account of Skolem's theorem mentioned in the next paragraph and his evolving attitudes toward it.

[66] For more on Zermelo's axiomatization see Moore 1982 and Felgner 2010. The scientific biography Ebbinghaus and Peckhaus 2007 is indispensable for the broader philosophical and scientific context of Zermelo's work.

Skolem proved that the gain in clarity had a striking technical consequence which we now call the Löwenheim–Skolem theorem.[67] Any first-order theory with infinite models has a model in which the domain has the cardinality of $\mathbb{N}$. This gives rise to a puzzle—sometimes called 'Skolem's paradox'—whose significance continues to be debated: how can we be said to understand the idea 'uncountable set' if our theory can always be satisfied by a countable set? (A popular stance in the debate is the deflating suggestion that the appearance of paradox is illusory.)[68]

9.4.3 Von Neumann, the Burali–Forti Paradox, and 'limitation of Size'

Recall the structure of the ordinal numbers from (9.4.1):

$$0, 1, \ldots; \omega, \omega + 1, \omega + 2, \ldots; \omega + \omega \ldots; \omega \times \omega \ldots; \omega^{\omega} \ldots; \aleph_1, \aleph_1 + 1 \ldots; \aleph_2 \ldots;$$

Any set $\mathcal{O}$ of ordinals is itself ordered. If, whenever $\alpha \in \mathcal{O}$ and $\beta < \alpha$ then $\beta \in O, O$ will have an ordinal number larger than any in $\mathcal{O}$. For example $\{0, 1, 2, 3, \ldots, n, \ldots\}$ has ordinal number ω and $\{0, 1, 2, 3, \ldots, n, \ldots; \omega, \omega + 1, \omega + 2\}$ has ordinal number $\omega + 3$. The Burali–Forti paradox arises from this pattern. Let Ω be the set of *all* ordinals. As a well-ordered set it must have an ordinal, and since it satisfies the condition given, that ordinal must be *greater* than any in the set. So Ω is not, after all, the set of all ordinals.

The Burali–Forti paradox seems to turn on a different principle from Russell's: that certain aggregates are just 'too big' to be sets.[69] Zermelo's axiomatic approach incorporates this idea indirectly, in that the 'too big' sets cannot be generated at all. A more explicit codification of 'limitation of size' is the Axiom (Scheme) of Replacement, originally proposed by Skolem and Abraham Fraenkel independently: given a two-free-variable expression $\phi(x, y)$ associating a unique y with every x in a set A there is a set containing all the y's that are matched with some $x \in A$ by ϕ. Loosely: anything the same size as a set is also a set.

Current nomenclature calls Zermelo's axioms minus AC plus Replacement Zermelo–Fraenkel set theory (ZF). Adding AC yields Zermelo–Fraenkel set theory with Choice (ZFC). One crucial effect of Replacement is conceptual clarity and symmetry in the theory of ordinal numbers. One would like to choose some straightforward canonical sets

---

[67] Since the canonical status of first-order logic has been a widely shared, rarely defended assumption for some time, it may not be obvious what a significant step Skolem's restriction was. Even in the early 1930s, only authors with a constructivist bent like Skolem and Weyl thought first-order logic was the proper choice of framework for representing mathematical reasoning. Ferreirós 1999, pp. 357–64.

[68] Two attempts to use the Löwenheim–Skolem theorem as a springboard to ambitious conclusions about the metaphysics of properties, reference, and truth are Lewis 1984 and Putnam 1980.

[69] The classic scholarly work on the early career of 'limitation of size' is Hallett 1984.

to represent the ordinals: but without Replacement there would be no guarantee of a canonical ordinal as long as a given well-ordering.

A more ambitious use of the limitation of size idea was proposed in von Neumann (1925). His theory treats collections that are not sets—proper classes—as genuinely existing, rather than as a *façon de parler*, with the sole restriction (adequate to block the paradoxes) that proper classes may not be members of anything. This is accompanied by a *global* limitation of size principle: Anything (for example the aggregate of ordinals) that can be mapped 1–1 onto the universe V is a proper class. Replacement is an immediate consequence and so is the Well-Ordering Theorem and hence AC.

Von Neumann introduced the currently canonical representation of ordinals. 0 is associated with the empty set $\emptyset$, the successor to a given ordinal α is $\alpha \cup \{\alpha\}$, and the limit ordinal of a gapless sequence $\emptyset, \{\emptyset\}, \{\emptyset, \{\emptyset\}\}, \ldots$ is the union $\{\emptyset, \{\emptyset\}, \{\emptyset, \{\emptyset\}\}, \ldots\}$. For orientation it is useful to consider a contrasting construction: Zermelo's representation of $\mathbb{N}$, which takes each finite ordinal to be the unit set of its predecessor. (Which produces the sequence: $\emptyset, \{\emptyset\}, \{\{\emptyset\}\}, \ldots, \underbrace{\{\{\{\& \{\emptyset\} \ldots\}\}\}}_{n \text{ times}}, \ldots$.) There is a mini-tradition in contemporary analytic philosophy, initiated by Benacerraf (1965), that regards the choice between the finite von Neumann and Zermelo ordinals as a representation of $\mathbb{N}$ to be a clear example of a mathematical choice that is undetermined by any possible mathematical reasoning. But this suggestion is plausible only on a bloodlessly narrow construal of what mathematical research and reasoning consists in, such as, perhaps, solely articulating sharply stated conjectures and spitting out rigorous proofs. In fact, the mathematical community has securely settled on the von Neumann numbers, not as an arbitrary choice made for the sake of making one, but rather for compelling mathematical reasons. The simplest is that von Neumann's numbers generalize immediately to all ordinals, finite and infinite, without changing the uniform generating principle (every ordinal is the set of its predecessors).

9.4.4 The Continuum Problem and Independence Arguments

In 9.4.1 we noted $|\mathbb{N}| < |\mathbb{R}| = |P(\mathbb{N})|$. Are there subsets of $\mathbb{R}$ that are smaller than $\mathbb{R}$ but larger than $\mathbb{N}$? Could it be that $\aleph_1$ is wedged in there (i.e. $|\mathbb{N}| = \aleph_0 < \aleph_1 < \aleph_2 = |\mathbb{R}|$)? The proposition that this is *not* the case—that in fact $\aleph_1 = |\mathbb{R}|$—is called the *Continuum Hypothesis* (CH). Cantor expended considerable effort to prove CH, but it turned out to be unprovable from the axioms of ZFC.

A loose thread at the end of 9.4.1 was the relationship of two procedures for producing larger cardinal numbers. One could proceed up the $\aleph$'s, generating new cardinal numbers by taking the ordinal of all ordinals of given cardinalities. The other path is to iterate the power set operation: Cantor introduced additional notational conventions for this case. (I'll give modern definitions.) The cardinality of the powerset of $P(S)$ is written $2^{|s|}$. Cantor used the Hebrew letter $\beth$ for the hierarchy of cardinalities generated by iterated powerset beginning with $\aleph_0 = \beth_0$. For every successor ordinal $\beth_\alpha$, $2^{\beth_\alpha} = \beth_{\alpha+1}$. For limit ordinals β, $\beth_\beta = \cup_{\alpha<\beta} \beth_\alpha$. We can thus write CH as $\beth_1 = \aleph_1$. The generalized continuum hypothesis (GCH) is that for every ordinal α, $\aleph_\alpha = \beth_\alpha$.

CH and GCH became marquee examples of naturally arising, important conjectures that likely will never be proven in terms of 'obvious, self-evident' axioms (though considerations that are taken to give evidence one way or another have been put forward).[70] Gödel (1940) proved that ¬GCH cannot be proven from ZFC (assumed to be consistent) and ¬*AC* cannot be proved from ZF assuming ZF is consistent. Nearly a quarter-century later, Cohen (1963) proved the rest: GCH cannot be proven from ZFC assuming ZFC is consistent, and AC cannot be proven from ZF assuming ZF is consistent.[71] Modifications of Cohen's technique prove that if ZFC is assumed to be consistent, there are surprisingly fewer $\aleph$'s than one would think that demonstrably *cannot* be $2^{\aleph_0}$. The latitude left by the codified parts of Cantor's original conception leaves a swath of uncertainty.

9.5 Early Mathematical Logic

The epistemological picture of Logical Positivism treated it as established, or nearly established, or bound to be established by next Tuesday that mathematics is ultimately just logic and definitions. Consequently arithmetic and analysis did not represent a counterexample to the thesis that knowledge of the world must be grounded in empirical verification. But there was a certain softness in this stance. A powerful argument for the logical character of arithmetic and analysis had been made by the nineteenth-century mathematicians culminating in Dedekind, if arguments meeting the standard of rigor set by Dedekind's non-formal arguments were enough. But generally something more ambitious and formal was intended by the Logical Positivists, and though the details differed from case to case, none of the attempts at *formal* derivation had been successful.[72]

---

[70] In Gödel 1947/1983, an article generally to be recommended for its reflections on mathematical argument and evidence, Gödel discusses some mathematical facts he regards as supporting the suggestion that CH is false. The topic of mathematical evidence short of compelling proof is often discussed in the writings of Penelope Maddy. In connection with GCH see Maddy 1988.

[71] Cohen 1966 is a more detailed presentation of the argument, though not something a beginner is likely to find illuminating. The textbook presentation in Kunen 1980 is clearer but will still be a book with seven seals to untrained readers without guidance.

[72] Most of the material in this section has been extensively studied in connection with the development of analytic philosophy, so brief surveys supplemented with references will suffice. I omit discussion of Hilbert's post-1900 foundations, as well as the intuitionist reaction of Brouwer since an excellent survey is already available (Mancosu *et al.* 2009). For more detail, an indispensable reference is Mancosu 1998 which makes available translations of otherwise unavailable key papers. The editor's commentary corrects many surprisingly tenacious misimpressions about Hilbert and Brouwer. I'll also pass over in silence the tradition of Boole and Schroeder. See Peckhaus 1999 and Peckhaus 2004.

9.5.1 Frege

Frege's efforts to derive arithmetic and analysis with his logic were by the strictest accounting a failure—his *Begriffsschrift* in its most developed version incorporated a naïve comprehension axiom and produced the Russell paradox. Frege never corrected the flaw in a way that would not violate one or another of his philosophical principles. But as noted in 9.3.2.2, Frege's enduring contribution lay less in what he managed to derive, and more in the clarity, explicitness, and sharpness of his logic. Contributing to this paradigmatic clarity are innovations in the logical works Frege (1967/1879), Frege (1893), and Frege (1903), which include:

1. Inferences are analysed in a quantified logic of propositions. Logical inferences are not restricted to sentences in subject-predicate form but extend to sentences incorporating relations. We would today describe Frege's system (with the anachronism that any such century-backward look will involve) as a higher-order predicate calculus.[73]
2. Syllogistic forms (such as 'All A's are B') are interpreted as quantified conditionals ('For all x, if x is an A then x is a B'). This analysis has become so entrenched that it is hard to imagine it once represented a novelty. This presents the philosophical point that the logical grammar of a sentence may differ from its surface grammar.
3. The syntax of a logical language must be presented explicitly, so whether or not a string of symbols is a sentence of the language can be ascertained from the rules of syntax alone.
4. Consequence and the material conditional are distinguished, and the distinction is written into the syntax. Rules of inference and axioms are distinguished, with inferences carried out according to explicitly stated formal rules.
5. The universal quantifier ('the representation of generality') is incorporated into the syntax, as is negation, so the existential quantifier can be defined as well. Iteration of quantifiers is allowed, so the logic can reflect the quantifier patterns noted in 9.3.2.3.
6. 'Function' is an undefined primitive, with principles of reasoning governing universal function quantification. With a defined existential function quantifier, this provides a tool for representing the logic of function existence.

---

[73] One respect in which Frege differs from contemporary logicians is that, like Pasch, he insisted on an *interpreted system*, and viewed the study of systems of uninterpreted symbols as contributing only indirectly to logic. A puzzling correspondence with Hilbert played out over this issue. (See the letters to and from Hilbert, and to Liebmann, in Frege 1980.) The classic article on Frege's emphasis on interpreted languages is van Heijenoort 1967b. A scholarly tradition, initiated by Burton Dreben in his Harvard seminars, holds Frege's insistence on interpreted languages for logic to have been bound up with a commitment to rejecting what would now be called 'metatheory', though this is controversial. The Dreben interpretation has been most recently articulated in Goldfarb 2001 and Ricketts 1997. Critical evaluation of this point of view, and discussion of the Hilbert–Frege exchange is in Tappenden 2005b and Tappenden 2000.

In addition to the technical treatises just mentioned, Frege published *Die Grundlagen der Arithmetik*, an informal exposition for a broad audience. (A beautifully written but occasionally unreliable translation [Frege 1953/1884, first edn. 1950] by J. L. Austin had a significant influence on subsequent English-language analytic philosophy.) In the core sections of the book Frege gives a definition of 'number belonging to a concept' grounded in a relation of 'likenumberedness' between two concepts, fixed by a 1–1 correspondence pairing up all objects possessing each concept. The core transition 'If A and B are likenumbered then (the number of A's = the number of B's)' may be taken to be the *logical* introduction of an *object* based on a relationship between concepts, and as such may be argued to be a counterexample to the Kantian thesis that logic cannot by itself demonstrate the existence of objects. Frege himself sets this definition aside in favor of an explicit definition: 'The number of F's is the extension of the concept "likenumbered with F"'. Frege's reasons for setting this definition aside are not easy to understand, and we now can recognize the definition he gives runs into 'limitation of size' problems (9.4.3).[74] In recent decades, largely inspired by the influential Wright (1983), efforts have been made to revive the first definition.[75]

9.5.2 Peano

The Italian Giuseppe Peano made his early reputation with work in analysis and differential equations, including the 'space-filling curve' mentioned in 9.2.3. Like Dedekind and Frege, he sought to clarify the foundations of arithmetic and analysis (and, in Peano's case, also Grassmann's abstract geometry [9.2.2]). Peano also pursued the late nineteenth-century idealistic quest to develop artificial languages to promote international communication, developing a scientific language he called *Latino sine Flexione*.[76]

His major project was the *Formulario*, an effort over many years and several completely reworked editions (the first four written in French and titled first *Formulaire de Mathematiques* [the first three] then *Formulaire Mathématique*, the last called

---

[74] Frege's argument is called 'The Julius Caesar problem' because he objects that the first definition does not fix whether an arbitrary object—Frege's example is Julius Caesar—is a number or not. The definition seems only to settle the question for objects presented in a specific way. This may be connected with the debates in the wider context about the introduction of mathematical objects and functions noted in 9.3.1, 9.3.2.1, and 9.3.2.3, though this suggestion is speculative. See Tappenden 2005a.

[75] An indispensable reference on Frege's philosophy of mathematics is Dummett 1991, though it predates most of the neo-Fregean work. Good sources for the technical study of Frege's derivations of arithmetic are Burgess 2005 and Heck 2011.

[76] The language is sometimes called *Interlingua*, after the *Academia Pro Interlingua* that adopted it as their scientific language. As the twentieth century progressed, Peano came to be occupied with the language project to the point of leaving aside his foundational research (Kennedy 1980, pp. 134–5 and *passim*). Drawing from work of Grassmann and apparently independently of Dedekind, he proposed the Dedekind–Peano axioms (often simply called the Peano Axioms) of arithmetic (Peano 1889; Peano cites Dedekind 1888/1901 but saw it for the first time as his booklet was heading to press. Kennedy 1980, pp. 25–6).

Formulario Mathematico, in *Latino sine Flexione*).[77] A goal was to produce an internationally accessible presentation of mathematics using symbolic notation, with the hope of facilitating scientic collaboration. The system mixes set theory and logic in a way that can strike contemporary eyes as written in a foundational pidgin language. Peano's reputation as a mathematician won the logical project credibility in the formative period before 1900, and he was an early inspiration to Russell. His logical/foundational writings have not so far received the attention devoted to those of Russell, Frege, Hilbert, or Dedekind in recent years, so there may be treasures still to be unearthed.[78]

9.5.3 Russell

Unlike the other logicians discussed here, Russell was not engaged in mathematical research when he took up foundations.[79] He is also the only philosopher or logician discussed here who wrote in English and engaged with English-language analytic philosophy so his influence is more easily discerned.

Exposure to Peano's project at the 1900 International Congress of Philosophy influenced Russell profoundly, and directed him to symbolic logic. He was a superhumanly energetic correspondent, and quickly established lines of communication among participants in the project of logical foundations. (Notably, he communicated to Frege the paradox that has come to bear Russell's name [9.4.2].)

9.5.3.1 Principles of Mathematics *and* Principia Mathematica *with* Whitehead

In 1903 Russell finished a first pass at deriving arithmetic and analysis: *Principles of Mathematics*. There are a few divergences from his later views, notably that he held arithmetic and logic to be synthetic (Russell 1903, p. 457), and what he takes his logic to be is often unclear. He gives a definition of number similar to Frege's (pp. 114–15), he critically discusses the work of Cantor, Weierstrass, and Dedekind on the definition of $\mathbb{R}$ and Cantor's on transfinite cardinals and ordinals, and in two appendices presents

---

[77] The *Formulario* project was a collaboration, drawing on the contributions of many other talented Italian mathematicians, including Alessandro Padoa and Mario Pieri.

[78] Writing on Peano in English is not easy to come by. The biography Kennedy 1980 is informative, but out of date and limited in ambition. Useful discussions of Peano are throughout Mancosu *et al.* 2009. Kennedy 1973 contains translations of Peano papers and extracts from the *Formulaire/Formulario*.

[79] The logic of *Principia Mathematica* has been studied extensively and many good introductions are available. Two sources stand out as indispensable, not as scholarly treatments *per se* but as engagements with Russell's logic by profound and influential members of a subsequent generation: Gödel 1944 and Quine 1941. The Quine article, though principally about Whitehead, discusses in addition ramified type theory and other areas of *Principia Mathematica* that were Russellian contributions. Also valuable is Quine's introduction (Quine 1967) to Russell 1908. A systematic, cleaned-up presentation of the technical details of Russell's ramified theory of types is in Church 1976.

the work of Frege to his English-speaking audience, and sketches the theory of types (9.5.3.2).

Russell (1905) unveiled the theory of descriptions, which, in it's final form, analysed 'The ϕ is ψ' as $(\exists x)$ $(x$ is a ϕ & $(\forall y)(y$ is a $\phi \to y = x)$ & x is a $\psi)$. This was enormously influential in early analytic philosophy both as a tool of analysis and (as Frank Ramsey famously called it) 'that paradigm of philosophy' (Ramsey 1931, p. 263 fn.)[80] The theory contributed the concept of 'incomplete symbols' to the conceptual framework of *Principia Mathematica*. Incomplete symbols are those like 'The F' in the theory of descriptions that are meaningful only in the context of a sentence. Sentences containing the defined expressions are assigned meaning *as a whole* by other sentences not containing them.

Principia Mathematica was released in three volumes in 1910, 1912, and 1913. It was a watershed as the first relatively successful working out of a relatively formal derivation of a significant body of mathematics from definitions and what could not implausibly be argued to be 'logic'. The work has flaws. As Gödel dryly puts it: 'It is to be regretted that this first comprehensive and thorough-going presentation of a mathematical logic and the derivation of mathematics from it [should be] so greatly lacking in the foundations (contained in *1-*21 of *Principia*) that it presents in this respect a considerable step backwards as compared with Frege' (Gödel 1944, p. 126). To name just three: The syntax of the system is not adequately stated, the derivations sometimes appeal to more than the axioms and rules given, and persistent use/mention ambiguity leaves Russell's analogue of a property ('propositional function') obscure. The authors use an axiom of infinity and the Axiom of Choice. Yet neither were plausibly described as 'logical', in any of the ways 'logic' was traditionally understood. An axiom discussed in 9.5.3.2—the 'Axiom of Reducibility'—was almost uniformly judged non-logical, and it was unclear if it was even *true*, yet it was necessary for *Principia*'s proofs of central principles of analysis. But despite the flaws, it was a monumental accomplishment and the reference point of subsequent discussion of the foundations of mathematics. The work brought into bold relief the conceptual knots that would have to be untied to maintain that mathematics is logic while providing a general solution to paradoxes.

9.5.3.2 *Theories of Types*

Russell tried several ways to evade paradoxes including a limitation of size theory, before settling on the ramified theory of types (RTT), articulated in Russell (1908) and incorporated into *Principia*. The diagnosis was natural enough: paradoxes arise from violations of what Russell called the Vicious Circle Principle (VCP):

> An analysis of the paradoxes to be avoided shows that they all result from a kind of vicious circle [footnote: Russell cites Poincaré 1906, p. 307] [arising] from supposing

---

[80] A more general study of the theory of descriptions is in Bernard Linsky's contribution to this volume.

that a collection of objects may contain members which can only be defined by means of the collection...

The principle which enables us to avoid illegitimate totalities may be stated as follows: Whatever involves all of a collection must not be one of the collection; or, conversely: If, provided a certain collection had a total, it would have members only definable in terms of that total, then the said collection has no total. (Whitehead and Russell 1910, pp. 39–40)[81]

The structuring idea is that a formula with a variable place only can take a restricted collection of arguments, which Russell calls a 'type'. *Principles of Mathematics* outlined a simple type theory, stratifying the universe into levels of individuals, classes of individuals, classes of classes of individuals, ..., with statements of the form $v \in u$ meaningful only if u is one level higher than v.[82] But even in 1903 Russell suggested that an adequate solution would need to be more intricate (Russell 1903, p. 523). One reason was Russell's ambitions for a *unified* solution dissolving both the set theoretic and semantic paradoxes such as the liar by consistently unfolding a single principle. In addition to the types ensuring non-contradictoriness of set membership, Russell stratifies classes into *orders*, in accordance with what needs to be presupposed to define the classes, producing a two-dimensional hierarchy.[83]

But the resulting framework was *too* restrictive. For example, a property generally put forward in axiomatic presentations of the theory of $\mathbb{R}$ is the *least upper bound property*: Any $S \subseteq \mathbb{R}$ that is bounded above has a least upper bound. This property, or some equivalent, is indispensable: its presence distinguishes $\mathbb{R}$ and $\mathbb{Q}$.

But because the least upper bound is itself in the set of upper bounds, the definition of least upper bound violates the VCP in the strong form Russell builds into RTT. To make the derivation of analysis possible, Russell adopted an additional axiom, called the Axiom of Reducibility, which had the triple disadvantages of (i) striking everyone as unjustified and possibly even false, (ii) not appearing to be 'logical' in any recognized sense of the term, and (iii) wiping away one dimension of the RTT framework, leading some to ask, as Ramsey (1925) did, why Russell hadn't just made do with simple type theory to begin with.

---

[81] As Gödel 1944 observes, Russell's vague terminology ('involves', 'defined by means of', ...) presents several distinct principles mushed into one, with subsequent discussions sometimes playing crucially on the ambiguity.

[82] It is similar to the Zermelo heirarchy (9.4.2): self-referential paradoxes are blocked by well-foundedness of the $\in$ relation, though simple type theory lacks the cumulative character of the Zermelo hierarchy. Also, the Zermelo hierarchy is defined internally within the theory rather than written into the syntax.

[83] This compressed description makes the two dimensions sound independent, and makes the 'unified solution' appear as the gluing of two distinct solutions together rather than a unified diagnosis. But as Quine 1941 spells out, Russell's analysis begins just with the orders, and spins the hierarchy of types out in a non-*ad hoc* way.

9.5.4 Russell's Filter: *Introduction to Mathematical Philosophy*

Principia Mathematica was the first important work on foundations in English, and Russell, who handled the philosophical and earliest foundational parts, was not a research mathematician. As a consequence the foundational work of Frege, Dedekind, etc. was introduced to English speakers through the work of a gifted amateur with no research interest in non-foundational mathematics. We've noted Russell's research contributions, but it is also worth noting the importance for subsequent philosophy of a slender volume Russell published in 1919: *Introduction to Mathematical Philosophy* (2nd edn.: Russell 1920).

For generations of English-speaking students, this was a first introduction to the foundations of mathematics. Russell covers technical details, but only a narrow band of the spectrum of research, and motivates it solely by narrowly philosophical concerns. He presents Dedekind's characterization of the reals divorced from its mathematical context, as the capstone of a programme motivated by epistemological and ontological concerns. His sole point of critical engagement with Dedekind is over Dedekind's admittedly puzzling talk of creating objects in thought, to which he issues a famous harumphing rejoinder:

> The method of 'postulating' what we want has many advantages; they are the same as the advantages of theft over honest toil. Let us leave them to others and proceed with our honest toil. (Russell 1920, p. 71)

Limits and continuity are afforded context-free conceptual analysis omitting mathematical reasons why one definition might be preferred to another, apart from bloodless appeals to 'rigour'. The Axiom of Choice (9.4.2) (Russell calls it the 'multiplicative axiom') is explored without reference to any mathematical connections other than the well-ordering theorem that it was introduced to prove. Infinite ordinals and cardinals appear as an exercise in abstract concept-castle-building with no mention of the continuum problem (9.4.1), or other mathematical needs.

For half a century, the outlook of this book seemed to inform nearly every philosophical discussion of foundations in English-language philosophy, contributing to a widely shared tacit assumption informing the analytic tradition that philosophical-logical work is by nature disengaged from mathematical practice. This chapter has emphasized the opposite, that the scrutiny of deductive relations and progressive isolation of workable conceptions of logical consequence, the choice of function-argument as a building block for logic, the production of an intuition-free analysis and an abstract conception of space, the characterization of the real numbers in terms of abstract structure rather than measurement, ZFC as an adequate foundation for mathematics, and so on arose organically in the mathematical context in response to problems confronted there. Though philosophical insight may well have been generated in other connections by disengaged projects of first philosophy like Russell's, they conferred only meagre insight into the fruits of genuine mathematical research. To borrow a rejoinder from Paul Benacerraf: 'At least with theft you come away with the loot' (Benacerraf 1973, p. 679).

9.6 CONCLUSIONS FROM THE ABOVE CONCEPTS

A casual distinction is often made by philosophers discussing mathematically informed philosophy: mathematicians produce 'technical results' which are sometimes useful in the distinct activity of 'philosophy'. The message informing this survey is that this framing of the situation can artificially distort and undervalue the mathematical investigation. Philosophical critique often arises and is resolved in the natural course of mathematics.[84] Consider as an illustration Zeno's paradoxes. Two millennia of conceptual stumbles resulting from drastically inadequate conceptualization of the possible structures of space and time were banished with the work of Cantor and Dedekind. Of course, there were other stumbling blocks besides clarification of dense and complete orders, convergence, etc. But beginning with Tannery (1885) and continuing through Russell (1903) and Russell (1929) to today, the analysis of the structure of the continuum, the behaviour of convergent series, etc, has become a cornerstone of what could now be called the standard solution. The structural puzzles were dispatched via the mathematical confrontation; with that accomplished, drawing the explicit connection to the Zeno paradoxes was, so to speak, a matter of simple technique.

For another illustration, consider the suggestion of Michael Friedman that Kant's view that geometry is grounded in spatial intuition was induced by the absence of a logic adequate to represent the generation of infinite structures (Friedman 1992, ch. 1). This is a valuable observation, but perhaps it also overestimates the role of explicit formal codifications of logic, in a manner reminiscent of Russell's famous (notorious?) opinion that the philosophies of Spinoza and Hegel took the form they did due to an absence of a logic of relations.[85] Well before Frege produced a formal logic that could represent the informal reasoning of Bolzano, Dedekind, Weierstrass, Riemann, Grassmann, etc. there were mathematicians who maintained that arithmetic and analysis are logical and that a representation of space grounded in concepts rather than intuition is possible. There is, of course, no question that mathematical developments in formal logic from Frege onward presented a magnificent advance in knowledge, opening up breathtaking possibilities for more, but we shouldn't be blinkered by the richness of this stream of research into

---

[84] I am here borrowing a turn of phrase from my colleague Larry Sklar, who argues a similar point in connection with foundational physics in Sklar 2000. The picture informing this survey also has much in common with Penelope Maddy's 'Second Philosophy' (Maddy 2007) and, in different connections, with the attitude toward Cantor and Dedekind as philosophers in Tait 1997.

[85] Russell 1929, Lecture 3: 'Logic as the Essence of Philosophy'.

forgetting that the formal and informal investigations reinforce each other. Which is to be expected for those who hold with Frege and Dedekind that 'fruitfulness is the acid test of concepts, and scientific investigation logic's true field of observation' (9.3.2.2).

REFERENCES

Arana, A. and P. Mancosu (2012). 'On the Relationship between Plane and Solid Geometry', *Review of Symbolic Logic* 5(2): 294–353.

Archibald, T. (2008). 'The Development of Rigor in Mathematical Analysis'. In T. Gowers (ed.), *The Princeton Companion to Mathematics*. Princeton, NJ: Princeton University Press, pp. 117–29.

Avigad, J. (2006). 'Methodology and Metaphysics in the Development of Dedekind's Theory of Ideals'. In J. Ferreirós and J. Gray (eds.), *The Architecture of Modern Mathematics*. Oxford: Oxford University Press, pp. 159–86.

Benacerraf, P. (1965). 'What Numbers Could Not Be', *The Philosophical Review* 74(1): 47–73.

—— (1973). 'Mathematical Truth', *The Journal of Philosophy* 70(19): 661–79.

—— (1985). 'Skolem and the Skeptic', *Proceedings of the Aristotelian Society,* Supplementary Volume 59: 85–115.

Biermann, O. (1887). *Theorie der Analytischen Funktionen*. Liepzig: Teubner.

Bonola, R. (1906/1955). *Non-Euclidean Geometry*, tr. H. Carslaw. New York: Dover Publications. 1955 reprint of 1912 Chicago: Open Court edition. Italian original pub. 1906.

Boolos, G. (1971). 'The Iterative Conception of Set', *The Journal of Philosophy* 68(8): 215–31.

Boolos, G., R. Jeffrey, and J. Burgess (2007). *Computability and Logic*, 5th edn. Cambridge: Cambridge University Press.

Bottazzini, U. (1986). *The Higher Calculus: A History of Real and Complex Analysis from Euler to Weierstrass*. Berlin: Springer.

Browder, F. (ed.) (1974). *Mathematical Developments arising from the Hilbert Problems*. De Kalb: AMS Series Proceedings of Symposia in Pure Mathematics.

Burgess, J. (2005). *Fixing Frege*. Princeton, NJ: Princeton University Press.

Cantor, G. (1871). Review of Hankel 1870/1882, *Literarisches Centralblatt* 7: 150–1.

—— (1872). 'Über die Ausdehnung eines Satzes aus der Theorie der trigonometrischen Reihen', *Mathematische Annalen* 5: 123–32.

—— (1874). 'Über eine Eigenschaft des Inbegriffes aller reelen algebraischen Zahlen', *Journal für die reine und angewante Mathematik* 77: 258–62. Repr. in Cantor's *Gessammelte Abhandlungen*, pp. 115–18.

—— (1879). 'Über unendlich, lineare Punktmannigfaltigkeiten I', *Mathematische Annalen* 15: 1–7. Repr. in Cantor's *Gessammelte Abhandlungen*, pp. 139–45.

—— (1883). *Grundlagen einer allgemeinen Mannifaltigkeitslehre. Ein mathematisch—philosophischer Versuch in der Lehre des Unendlichen*. Leipzig: Teubner. Partial tr. W. B. Ewald in Ewald (ed.), *From Kant to Hilbert: A Source Book in the Foundations of Mathematics*. Oxford: Clarendon Press, 1996, vol. 2, pp. 878–920.

—— (1893). 'Beiträge zur Begründung der transfiniten Mengenlehre', *Mathematische Annalen* 46: 481–512. Repr. in *Contributions to the Founding of the Theory of Transfinite Numbers*, ed. and trans. P. Jourdain. Chicago: Open Court, 1915; repr. New York: Dover, 1955.

—— (1895). 'Beiträge zur Begründung der transfiniten Mengenlehre', *Mathematische Annalen* 49: 207–46. Repr. in *Contributions to the Founding of the Theory of Transfinite Numbers*, ed. and trans. P. Jourdain. Chicago: Open Court, 1915; repr. New York: Dover, 1955.

—— (1915/1955). *Contributions to the Founding of the Theory of Transfinite Numbers*, ed. and trans. P. Jourdain. Chicago: Open Court, 1915; repr. New York: Dover, 1955.

Cayley, A. (1859). 'Sixth Memoir on Quantics', *Philosophical Transactions of the Royal Society* 149: 61–90. Page references to reprint in *The Collected Works of Arthur Cayley*. Cambridge: Cambridge University Press, 1889–97, vol. 2.

—— (1884). *Presidential Address. Report of the Fifty-third Meeting of the BAAS held at Southport in September 1883*, pp. 3–37. Page references to reprint in *The Collected Works of Arthur Cayley*. Cambridge: Cambridge University Press, 1889–97, vol. 9.

Chrystal, G. (1886). *Algebra: An Elementary Textbook for the Higher Classes of Secondary Schools and for Colleges*, vol. I. Edinburgh: A. & C. Black.

Church, A. (1976). 'Comparison of Russell's Resolution of the Semantical Antinomies with that of Tarski', *Journal of Symbolic Logic* 41: 747–60.

Clebsch, A. and P. Gordon (1868). *Theorie der Abelschen Funktionen*. Leipzig: Teubner.

Coffa, A. (1991). *The Semantic Tradition from Kant to Carnap: To the Vienna Station*, ed. Linda Wessels. Cambridge: Cambridge University Press.

Cohen, P. J. (1963). 'The Independence of the Continuum Hypothesis', *Proceedings of the National Academy of Sciences of the United States of America* 50(6): 1143–8.

—— (1966). *Set Theory and the Continuum Hypothesis*. New York: W. A. Benjamin.

Dauben, J. (1979/1990). *Georg Cantor: His Mathematics and Philosophy of the Infinite*. Princeton, NJ: Princeton University Press. 1990 reprint of 1979 Harvard University Press publication.

Dedekind, R. (1854). 'Über die Einführung neuer Funktionen in der Mathematik', Habilitation lecture, Göttingen, 30 June. Repr. in *Gessammelte mathematische Werke I–III*. Braunschweig: Vieweg, 1930–2, vol. 3, pp. 428–38.

—— (1872/1901). *Continuity and Irrational Numbers*. Chicago: Open Court. Original published 1872, tr. W. Behman 1901. Page references to Dover reprint of *Essays on the Theory of Numbers*, 1963.

—— (1877/1996). *Theory of Algebraic Integers*, ed. and tr. John Stillwell. Cambridge: Cambridge University Press 1996 (orig. pub. 1877).

—— (1888/1901). *The Nature and Meaning of Numbers*. Chicago: Open Court. Original published 1888, trans. W. Behman 1901. Page references to Dover reprint of *Essays on the Theory of Numbers*, 1963.

Dedekind, R. and H. Weber (1882). 'Theorie der algebraischen Funktionen einer Veränderlichen', *Journal für die Reine und Angewante Mathematik* 92: 181–290. Repr. in *Werke*, vol. 1, pp. 248–349.

Demopolous, W. (1994). 'Frege and the Rigorization of Analysis', *Journal of Philosophical Logic* 23: 225–45. Page references to the reprint in William Demopolous (ed.), *Frege's Philosophy of Mathematics*. Cambridge, MA: Harvard University Press, 1995.

Dirichlet, P. G. L. (1852). 'Gedächtnissrede auf Karl Gustav Jacob Jacobi', *Abhandlungen der Koniglich Preussischen Akademie der Wissenschaften* 8: 1–27. Page references to the reprinting in *G. Lejeune Dirichlet's Werke vol. 2*, ed. L. Kronecker. Berlin: George Reimer 1897, pp. 225–53.

Dodgson, C. (1879). *Euclid and his Modern Rivals*. London: Macmillan.

Dummett, M. (1991). *Frege: Philosophy of Mathematics*. Cambridge, MA: Harvard University Press.

Ebbinghaus, H.-D. and V. Peckhaus (2007). *Ernst Zermelo: An Approach to his Life and Work*. Berlin: Springer.

Edwards, H. (1980). 'The Genesis of Ideal Theory', *Archive for History of Exact Sciences* 23: 321–78.

Enriques, F. (1929). *The Historic Development of Logic*. New York: Henry Holt.

Erdmann, B. (1877). *Die Axiome der Geometrie. Eine Philosophische Untersuchung der Riemann-Helmholzschen Raumtheorie*. Leipzig: Leopold Voss.

Ewald, W. (ed.) (1996). *From Kant to Hilbert: A Source Book in the Foundations of Mathematics*, 2 vols. Oxford: Clarendon Press.

Felgner, U. (2010). 'Comment on 1908b' [Introductory note on Zermelo, *Untersuchungen über die Grundlagen der Mengenlehre*, vol. I, orig. referred to as dated 1908b]. In H.-D. Ebbinghaus, A. Kanamori, and C. G. Fraser (eds.), *Collected Works/Gesammelte Werke* [of Ernst Zermelo], vol. I. Berlin: Springer, pp. 160–87.

Ferreirós, J. (1999). *Labyrinth of Thought: A History of Set Theory and its Role in Modern Mathematics*. Boston: Birkhäuser Verlag.

—— (2006). 'Riemann's Habilitationsvortrag at the Crossroads of Mathematics, Physics and Philosophy'. In J. Ferreirós and J. Gray (eds.), *The Architecture of Modern Mathematics: Essays in History and Philosophy*. Oxford: Oxford University Press, pp. 67–96.

—— (2007). 'The Rise of Pure Mathematics as Thought with Gauss'. In *The Shaping of Arithmetic after C. F. Gauss's Disquisitiones Arithmeticae*. Berlin: Springer, pp. 235–68.

Frege, G. (1893). *Grundgesetze der Arithmetik*, vol. I. Jena: Verlag Hermann Pohle. Partial English translation in *Basic Laws of Arithmetic: Exposition of the System*, tr. M. Furth. Berkeley: University of California Press, 1964. References to translation for passages that occur in the translation, to original otherwise.

—— (1903). *Grundgesetze der Arithmetik*, vol. I. Jena: Verlag Hermann Pohle.

—— (1953/1884). *The Foundations of Arithmetic*, trans. J. L. Austin, 2nd edn. Evanston, IL: Northwestern University Press. Original published 1884, 1st edn 1950.

—— (1967/1879). 'Begriffsschrift, a Formula Language Modeled on that of Arithmetic, for Pure Thought', tr. Stephan Bauer-Mengelberg. In J. van Heijenoort (ed.), *From Frege to Godel*. Cambridge, MA: Harvard University Press, pp. 1–82.

—— (1979/1880). 'Boole's Logical Calculus and the Concept-Script'. In H. Hermes, F. Kambartel, and F. Kaulbach (eds.), *Posthumous Writings*. Chicago: University of Chicago Press, pp. 9–46.

—— (1980). *Philosophical and Mathematical Correspondence*, ed. G. Gabriel, H. Hermes, F. Kambartel, C. Thiel, and A. Veraart; abridged from the German edition by B. McGuinness, tr. H. Kaal. Chicago: University of Chicago Press.

Friedman, M (1992). *Kant and the Exact Sciences*. Cambridge, MA: Harvard University Press.

Gauss, C. F. (1801). *Disquisitiones Arithmeticae*. Leipzig: G. Fleischer. Repr. as vol. I of Gauss' *Werke*, tr. with a preface by Arthur A. Clarke. New Haven, CT: Yale University Press, 1966.

—— (1849). 'Beiträge zur Theorie der algebraischen Gleichungen'. In *Lecture of 1849*, page references to printing in Gauss' *Werke, Nachrichten der Königlichten Gesellschaft der Wissenschaften der Göttingen*, vol. 3, pp. 71–102.

Gödel, K. (1940). *The Consistency of the Continuum Hypothesis*. Princeton, NJ: Princeton University Press. Annals of Mathematics Studies, vol. 3.

—— (1944). 'Russell's Mathematical Logic'. In P. Schilpp (ed.), *The Philosophy of Bertrand Russell*. Chicago: Open Court, pp. 123–53. Repr. with a minor addition in *Kurt Gödel: Collected Papers*, vol. II, ed. Solomon Feferman *et al.* Oxford: Oxford University Press, 1990, pp. 119–41.

—— (1947/1983). 'What is Cantor's Continuum Problem?' *The American Mathematical Monthly* 54(9): 515–25. Revised edition with supplementary comments printed in Paul Benacerraf and Hilary Putnam (eds.), *The Philosophy of Mathematics: Selected Readings*, 2nd edn. Cambridge: Cambridge University Press, pp. 470–85.

Goldfarb, W. (2001). 'Frege's Conception of Logic'. In J. Floyd and S. Shieh (eds.), *Future Pasts: The Analytic Tradition in Twentieth-Century Philosophy*. Oxford: Oxford University Press, pp. 25–41.

Grassmann, H. (1844). *Die Lineale Ausdehnungslehre ein neuer Zweig der Mathematik, dargestellt und durch Anwendungen auf die übringen Zweige der Mathematik, wie auch auf die Statik, Mechanik, die Lehre vom Magnetismus und die Krystallonomie erläutert*. Leipzig, 1844. Tr. Lloyd C. Kannenberg in H. Grassmann, *A New Branch of Mathematics: The Ausdehnungslehre of 1844 and other works*. Chicago: Open Court, 1995.

Grattan-Guinness, J. (1975). 'Preliminary Notes on the Significance of Quantification and of the Axioms of Choice in the Development of Analysis', *Historia Mathematica* 2: 475–88.

Gray, J. (2000). *The Hilbert Challenge*. Oxford: Oxford University Press.

——(2007). *Worlds out of Nothing: A Course in the History of Geometry in the 19th Century*. London: Springer.

Hallett, M. (1984). *Cantorian Set Theory and Limitation of Size*. Oxford: Oxford University Press.

——(2008). 'Reflections on the Purity of Method in Hilbert's *Grundlagen der Geometrie*'. In P. Mancosu (ed.), *The Philosophy of Mathematical Practice*. Oxford: Oxford University Press, pp. 198–255.

Hankel, H. (1870/1882). *Untersuchungen über die unendlich oft oscillierenden und unstetigen Functionen*. Tübingen: Ludwig Fues. Repr. in *Mathematische Annalen* 22 (1882): 63–112 and in the Ostwalds Klassiker series 1905.

Heck, R. (2011). *Frege's Theorem*. Oxford: Oxford University Press.

Helmholtz, H. (1868). 'Über die Tatsachen die der Geometrie zu Grunde liegen', *Abhandlungen der Koniglichen Gesellschaft der Wissenschaften zu Göttingen* 9: 193–231.

——(1870). 'The Axioms of Geometry', *The Academy* 1: 128–31.

——(1876). 'The Origin and Meaning of Geometrical Axioms', *Mind* 1(3): 301–21.

Hilbert, D. (1899). 'Die Grundlagen der Geometrie'. In *Festschrift zur Feier der Enthullung der Gauss-Weber Denkmals in Gottingen*. Leipzig: Teubner.

——(1901). 'Über das dirichletsche prinzip', *Jahresbericht der Deutschen Mathematiker-Vereinigung* 8: 184–8.

——(1902). *Foundations of Geometry*, tr. E. Townsend. Chicago: Open Court. Translation of a minor revision of Hilbert (1899).

——(1904). 'Über das dirichletsche prinzip', *Mathematische Annalen* 59: 161–86.

——(2004). *David Hilbert's Lectures on the Foundations of Geometry 1891–1902*, ed. M. Hallett and Ulrich Majer. Berlin: Springer-Verlag.

Kennedy, H. (ed.) (1973). *Selected Works of Giuseppe Peano*. Toronto: University of Toronto Press.

——(1980). *Peano: Life and Works of Giuseppe Peano*. Dordrecht: D. Reidel.

Kitcher, P. (1979). 'Frege's Epistemology', *Philosophical Review* 88: 235–62.

——(1984). *The Nature of Mathematical Knowledge*. Oxford: Oxford University Press.

Klein, F. (1871). 'Über die sogenannte nicht-Euklidische Geometrie (erster aufsatz)', *Mathematische Annalen* 4: 573–625. Page references to reprint in Klein's *Gess. Math. Abh.* vol. I, pp. 254–310.

——(1873). 'Über die sogenannte nicht-Euklidische Geometrie (zweiter aufsatz)', *Mathematische Annalen* 6: 112–45. Page references to reprinting in Klein's *Gess. Math. Abh.* vol. I, pp. 311–43.

——(1874). 'Nachtrag zu dem "zweiten Aufsatz über nicht-Euklidische Geometrie"', *Mathematische Annalen* 7: 531–7. Page references to reprinting in Klein's *Gess. Math. Abh.* vol. I, pp. 344–50.

Kossak, E. (1872). *Die Elemente der Arithmetik*. Berlin: Nicolai'sche Verlagsbuchhandlung.

Kreisel, G. (1967). 'Informal Rigour and Completeness Proofs'. In I. Lakatos (ed.), *Problems in the Philosophy of Mathematics*. Amsterdam: North-Holland Publishing Company, pp. 138–57.

Kunen, K. (1980). *Set Theory: An Introduction to Independence Proofs*. Amsterdam: North-Holland Publishing Company.

Land, J. P. (1877). 'Kant's Space and Modern Mathematics', *Mind* 2(5): 38–46.

Laugwitz, D. (1999). *Bernhard Riemann: 1826–1866. Turning Points in the Conception of Mathmatics*, tr. Abe Shenitzer. Boston: Birkhäuser.

Lewis, D. (1984). 'Putnam's Paradox', *Australasian Journal of Philosophy* 62: 221–36. Repr. in Lewis, *Papers in Logic and Epistemology*. Cambridge: Cambridge University Press, 1999, pp. 56–77.

Liebmann, O. (1880). *Zur Analysis der Wirklichkeit*, 2nd edn. Strassburg: Trübner.

Lotze, H. (1879). *Metaphysik*. Leipzig: Hirzel.

McLarty, C. (2008). 'Emmy Noether's "Set Theoretic" Topology: From Dedekind to the Concept of Functor'. In J. Ferreirós and J. Gray (eds.), *The Architecture of Modern Mathematics: Essays in History and Philosophy*. Oxford: Oxford University Press, pp. 187–208.

Maddy, P. (1988). 'Believing the Axioms I', *Journal of Symbolic Logic* 53(2): 481–511.

——(2007). *Second Philosophy*. Oxford: Oxford University Press.

Mancosu, P. (ed.) (1998). *From Hilbert to Brouwer*. Oxford: Oxford University Press.

Mancosu, P., R. Zack, and C. Badesa (2009). 'The Development of Mathematical Logic from Russell to Tarski'. In L. Haaparanta (ed.), *The Development of Modern Logic*. Oxford: Oxford University Press, pp. 318–470.

Manning, K. R. (1975). 'The Emergence of the Weierstrassian Approach to Complex Analysis', *Archive for History of the Exact Sciences* 14: 297–383.

Moore, G. (1982). *Zermelo's Axiom of Choice: Its Origins, Development and Influence*. New York: Springer.

Nagel, E. (1939). 'The Formation of Modern Conceptions of Formal Logic in the Development of Geometry', *Osiris* 7: 142–224. Repr. in *Teleology Revisited and Other Essays*. New York: Columbia University Press, 1979, pp. 195–259.

Pasch, M. (1882). *Vorlesungen über neuere Geometrie*. Leipzig: Tübner.

Peano, G. (1889). *Arithmetices principia ova methodo exposita*. Turin: Bocca. Translation in *Selected Works of Giuseppe Peano*, tr. and ed. Hubert Kennedy. Toronto: University of Toronto Press, 1973, pp. 101–34. Page references to translation.

——(1890). 'Sur une courbe, qui remplit toute une aire plane', *Mathematische Annalen* 36: 157–60. Translation (with supplementary remarks from 1908) in *Selected Works of Giuseppe Peano*, tr. and ed. Hubert Kennedy. Toronto: University of Toronto Press 1973, pp. 143–9. Page references to translation.

Peckhaus, V. (1999). '19th Century Logic between Philosophy and Mathematics', *Bulletin of Symbolic Logic* 5: 433–50.

——(2004). 'Schröder's Logic'. In D. Gabbay and J. Woods (eds.), *Handbook of the History of Logic. Vol. 3: The Rise of Modern Logic: From Leibniz to Frege*. Amsterdam: North-Holland Publishing Company, pp. 557–609.

Petri, B. and N. Schappacher (2007). 'On Arithmetization'. In N. S. Goldstein, Catharine and J. Schwermer (eds.), *The Shaping of Arithmetic after C. F. Gauss's* Disquisitiones Arithmeticae. Berlin: Springer, pp. 343–74.

Plücker, J. (1868). *Neue Geometrie des Raumes gegründet auf die Betrachtung der geraden Linie als Raumelement*, vol. 1 ed. A. Clebsch, vol. 2 ed. F. Klein (1869). Leipzig: Teubner.

Poincaré, H. (1906). 'Les matématiques et la logique', *Revue de Métaphysique* 14: 294–317. English translation in William Ewald (ed.), *From Kant to Hilbert: A Source Book in the Foundations of Mathematics*. Oxford: Clarendon Press, 1996, pp. 1038–52.

Putnam, H. (1980). 'Models and Reality', *Journal of Symbolic Logic* 45(3): 464–82.

Quine, W. V. O. (1941). 'Whitehead and the Rise of Modern Logic'. In P. Schilpp (ed.), *The Philosophy of Albert North Whitehead*. Chicago: Open Court, pp. 125–64. Reprinted in W.V.O. Quine, *Selected Logic Papers*. New York: Random House, 1966, pp. 1–36.

—— (1967). 'Introduction' to Bertrand Russell, 'Mathematical Logic as Based on the Theory of Types'. In J. van Heijenoort (ed.), *From Frege to Gödel: A Source Book in Mathematical Logic, 1879–1931*. Cambridge, MA: Harvard University Press, pp. 150–2.

Ramsey, F. (1925). 'The Foundations of Mathematics', *Proceedings of the London Mathematical Society* Series 2 25(5): 338–84..

—— (1931). 'Philosophy'. In R. Braithwaithe (ed.), *Foundations of Mathematics and Other Logical Essays*. New York: Harcourt, Brace, pp. 263–9.

Reck, E. (2003). 'Dedekind's Structuralism: An Interpretation and Partial Defence', *Synthese* 137: 369–419.

Richards, J. (1988). *Mathematical Visions: The Pursuit of Geometry in Victorian England*. San Diego: Academic Press.

Ricketts, T. (1997). 'Frege's 1906 Foray into Metalogic', *Philosophical Topics* 25: 169–87.

Riemann, B. (1851). 'Grundlagen für eine allgemeine Theorie der Functionen einer veränderlichen complexen Grösse'. Inauguraldissertation, Göttingen, 1851. Reprinted in *Bernhard Riemann's Gesammelte Mathematicsche Werke und Wissenschaftlich Nachlass*, R. Dedekind and H. Weber with Nachträge ed. M. Noether and W. Wirtinger, 3rd edn., ed. R Narasimhan. New York: Springer, 1990, pp. 3–45. 1st edn. ed. R. Dedekind and H Weber. Leipzig: Teubner 1876.

—— (1854/1868a). 'Ueber die Darstellbarkeit einer Function durch eine Trigonometrische Reihe'. *Abhandlungen der Koenigliche Gessellschaft der Wissenschaft zu Göttingen*, XIII. Habilitation paper, published posthumously. Reprinted in *Werke*, pp. 272–87..

—— (1854/1868b). 'Ueber die Hypothesen, welche der Geometrie zu Grunde liegen'. *Abhandlungen der Koenigliche Gessellschaft der Wissenschaft zu Göttingen*, XIII. Reprinted in *Werke*, pp. 272–87. English tr. W. Clifford (rev. Ewald) in W. Ewald (ed.), *From Kant to Hilbert: A Source Book in the Foundations of Mathematics*. Oxford: Clarendon Press, 1996, vol. 2, pp. 652–61. Page references to translation.

—— (1857a). Abstract of (1857b). *Gottinger Nachrichten* 1. Reprinted in *Werke*, pp. 84–5.

—— (1857b). 'Beiträge zur Theorie der durch die Gauss'sche Reihe $f(\alpha, \beta, \gamma, x)$ darstellbaren Functionen'. *Abhandlungen der Koenigliche Gessellschaft der Wissenschaft zu Göttingen*, VII. Reprinted in *Werke*, pp. 67–83.

Rota, G.-C. (1997). *Indiscrete Thoughts*. Boston: Birkhäuser.

Russell, B. (1897). *An Essay in the Foundations of Geometry*. Cambridge: Cambridge University Press.

—— (1903). *The Principles of Mathematics*. Cambridge: Cambridge University Press.

—— (1905). 'On Denoting', *Mind* 14: 479–93. Reprinted in B. Russell, *Essays in Analysis*. London: Allen & Unwin, 1973, pp. 103–19.

—— (1908). 'Mathematical Logic as Based on the Theory of Types', *American Journal of Mathematics* 30(3): 222–62.

—— (1920). *Introduction to Mathematical Philosophy*, 2nd edn. London: George Allen & Unwin. 1st edn. 1919.

—— (1929). *Our Knowledge of the External World as a Field for Scientific Method in Philosophy*. New York: W. W. Norton. 1st edn. 1914.

Sagan, H. (1994). *Space-Filling Curves*. Berlin: Springer.

Schoenfield, J. (1977). 'The Axioms of Set Theory'. In J. Barwise (ed.), *Handbook of Mathematical Logic*. Amsterdam: North-Holland Publishing Company, pp. 321–44.

Sieg, W. and D. Schlimm (2005). 'Dedekind's Analysis of Number: Systems and Axioms', *Synthese* 147: 121–70.

Sklar, L. (2000). *Theory and Truth: Philosophical Critique within Foundational Physics*. Oxford: Oxford University Press.

Staudt, K. G. C. von (1847). *Geometrie der Lage*. Nürnburg: Bauer and Raspe.

—— (1856). *Beiträge der Geometrie der Lage*. Nürnburg: Bauer and Raspe.

Stein, H. (1988). 'Logos, Logic, Logistiké: Some Philosophical Remarks on the 19th Century Transformation of Mathematics'. In P. Kitcher and W. Aspray (eds.), *History and Philosophy of Modern Mathematics*. Minneapolis: University of Minnesota Press, pp. 238–59.

Stump, D. (2007). 'The Independence of the Parallel Postulate and the Development of Consistency Proofs', *History and Philosophy of Logic* 28(1): 19–30.

Sundholm, G. (2001). 'Gottlob Frege, August Bebel, and the Return of Alsace-Lorraine: On the Dating of the Distinction between Sinn and Bedeutung', *History and Philosophy of Logic* 22(1): 57–73. Issue date 2001, actually appeared 2002.

Tait, W. (1997). 'Frege versus Cantor and Dedekind: On the Concept of Number'. In W. Tait (ed.), *Early Analytic Philosophy*. Peru, IL: Open Court, pp. 213–48.

Tannery, P. (1885). 'Le concept scientifique du continu: Zenon d'Élée et Georg Cantor', *Revue Philosophique de la France et de l'Étranger* 20: 385–410.

Tappenden, J. (1995a). 'Extending Knowledge and "Fruitful Concepts": Fregean Themes in the Foundations of Mathematics', *Noûs* 29: 427–67.

—— (1995b). 'Geometry and Generality in Frege's Philosophy of Arithmetic', *Synthese* 102: 319–61.

—— (2000). 'Frege on Axioms, Indirect Proof, and Independence Arguments in Geometry: Did Frege Reject Independence Arguments?' *Notre Dame Journal of Formal Logic* 41(3): 271–315.

—— (2005a). 'The Caesar Problem in its Historical Context: Mathematical Background', *Dialectica* 59 (fasc. 2): 237–64.

—— (2005b). 'Metatheory and Mathematical Practice in Frege'. In M. Beaney and E. Reck (eds.), *Gottlob Frege: Critical Assessments of Leading Philosophers*, vol. II. London: Routledge, pp. 190–228. Revised version of Tappenden, 'Metatheory and Mathematical Practice in Philosophy', *Philosophical Topics* 25(2) (1997): 213–64.

—— (2006). 'The Riemannian Background to Frege's Philosophy'. In J. Ferreirós and J. Gray (eds.), *The Architecture of Modern Mathematics: Essays in History and Philosophy*. Oxford: Oxford University Press, pp. 97–132.

—— (2008a). 'Mathematical Concepts and Definitions'. In P. Mancosu (ed.), *The Philosophy of Mathematical Practice*. Oxford: Oxford University Press, pp. 256–75.

—— (2008b). 'Mathematical Concepts: Fruitfulness and Naturalness'. In P. Mancosu (ed.), *The Philosophy of Mathematical Practice*. Oxford: Oxford University Press, pp. 276–301.

—— (2011). 'A Primer on Ernst Abbe for Frege Readers', *Canadian Journal of Philosophy* Supplementary Volume: *Truth and Values: Essays for Hans Herzberger*: 31–118.

Thomae, J. (1894). *Die Kegelschnitte in rein Projectiver Behandlung*. Halle: Louis Nebert.

—— (1898). *Elementare Theorie der analytischen Functionen einer complexen Veranderlichen*, 2nd edn. Halle: Louis Nebert.

Toepell, M. (1986). *Über die Entstehung von David Hilberts 'Grundlagen der Geometrie'*. Göttingen: Vandenhoeck und Ruprecht.

van Heijenoort, J. (ed.) (1967a). *From Frege to Gödel: A Source Book in Mathematical Logic*. Cambridge, MA: Harvard University Press.

—— (1967b). 'Logic as Language and Logic as Calculus', *Synthese* 17: 324–30.

Voelke, J. D. (2005). *Renaissance de la géometrie non Euclidienne entre 1860 et 1900*. Bern: Peter Lang.

von Neumann, J. (1925). 'Eine Axiomatisierung der Mengenlehre', *Journal für die Reine und Angewante Mathematik* 154: 219–40. English translation in J. van Heijenoort (ed.), *From Frege to Godel: A Source Book in Mathematical Logic, 1879–1931*. Cambridge, MA: Harvard University Press, 1967, pp. 393–413.

Webb, J. (1995). 'Tracking Contradictions in Geometry: The Idea of a Model from Kant to Hilbert'. In J. Hintikka (ed.), *Essays on the Development of the Foundations of Mathematics*. Dordrecht: Kluwer Academic Publishers, pp. 1–20.

Weierstrass, K. (1886/1988). *Ausgewalte Kapitel aus der Funktionenlehre. Vorlesung, gehalten in Berlin. Mit der akademischen Antrittsrede, Berlin 1857 uns drei weiteren Originalarbeiten von K. Weierstrass aus den Jahren 1870 bis 1880/86*. Leipzig: Teubner. Collection of Weierstrass lectures edited and annotated by R. Siegmund-Schultze, 1988.

Weiner, H. (1892). 'Über Grundlagen und Aufbau der Geometrie', *Jahresbericht der Deutschen Mathematiker-Veireinigung* 1: 45–8.

Weiner, J. (1990). *Frege in Perspective*. Ithaca, NY: Cornell University Press.

Whitehead, A. and B. Russell (1910). *Principia Mathematica*. Cambridge: Cambridge University Press.

Wright, C. (1983). *Frege's Conception of Numbers as Objects*. Aberdeen: Aberdeen University Press.

Wundt, W. (1880). *Logik. Eine Untersuchung der Principien der Erkenntniss und der Methoden wissenschaftlicher Forschung*. Vol. I: *Erkenntnislehre*. Stuttgart: Ferdinand Enke.

Youskevich, A. P. (1976). 'The Concept of a Function up to the Middle of the Nineteenth Century', *Archive for History of Exact Sciences* 7: 37–85.

Zermelo, E. (1904). 'Beweis, dass jede Menge wohlgeordnet werden kann (aus einem an Herren Hilbert gerichteten Briefe)', *Mathematische Annalen* 59: 514–16. English translation in J. van Heijenoort (ed.), *From Frege to Godel: A Source Book in Mathematical Logic, 1879–1931*. Cambridge, MA: Harvard University Press, 1967, pp. 139–41.

CHAPTER 10

GOTTLOB FREGE: SOME FORMS OF INFLUENCE

TYLER BURGE

THE products of great philosophical minds are often seminal in two interestingly different ways. One is to contain prima facie opposing elements or emphases that influence contrary developments, each feeding off the original. The other is to contain ideas that are initially neglected or rejected, but that come to seem lasting. Their fruitfulness can derive either from providing an exemplar that deepens understanding of later ideas or from opening possibilities that come to seem viable only after substantial philosophical changes have occurred.

A dramatic example of the first sort of seminal fruitfulness is Kant's providing resources for both empiricist and rationalist views. Twentieth-century logical positivists took up his empiricist emphases. They did so both in their rejection of logic as a source of genuine knowledge and in their looking to natural science as inspiration for formulating a principle to distinguish cognitively worthwhile enterprises from philosophical delusion. Kant's rationalist emphases were influential both in the twentieth-century development of a sharp distinction between pure and applied geometry and in more recent accounts of constitutive conditions on thought.

A dramatic example of the second type of influence is Aristotle's doctrine that the forms of physical objects reside in perceptual or intellectual states, only in a 'different way'. This conception of psychological states and their representational powers had, from the early modern period onward, been widely regarded as quaint and nearly worthless. It came to be seen in late twentieth-century philosophy as the ur-ancestor of anti-individualism.

These points have implications for doing history of philosophy. The history of philosophy is both a resource for materials to build with and an instructive limit on temporal parochiality. To preserve the former sort of value, one must study the history of philosophy with contemporary philosophical projects and interests firmly in mind. To preserve the latter, one must avoid anachronism and respect historical context—do genuine history, not simply engage in scavenging hunts in the temples of the dead.

Preserving each value is enhanced by taking seriously the other. Given that the older philosophical projects are not incommensurable with our own, approaching historical work with a keen sense of difficulties and possibilities inherent in our own projects sharpens an understanding of the great minds' earlier points of view. Given the richness, depth, and *historical foreignness* of the great minds, an understanding of exactly what they meant by their claims is likely to yield richer, more subtle building materials than if one treated the claims as issuing from the mind of a contemporary interlocutor.

In this chapter, I discuss some aspects of Gottlob Frege's influence on philosophy during the last hundred and twenty-five years. Frege (1848–1925) is the undisputed father of 'analytic philosophy', or of what I prefer to call the mainstream tradition in twentieth-century philosophy.[1] I discuss seven respects in which Frege influenced subsequent philosophizing. The last five illustrate one or the other of the just cited ways in which a great philosopher can be seminal. The first two constitute a different, more unusual form of philosophical influence.

10.1 DEVELOPMENT OF LOGIC

Frege's greatest intellectual contribution was his development and nearly flawless formulation of first- and second-order logic.[2] His logic is what is used in logic texts today. Frege did not produce a model theory. But his semantical construal of his logic formed the basis for more modern treatments; and the syntax of his logic, though not his symbolism, is almost identical to modern versions.

Frege's logicism was one of the earliest of what became a number of attempts to provide a 'foundation' for mathematics. Dedekind, Hilbert, Russell, and Zermelo—the latter building on the set theory of Cantor—and others offered various basic principles from which all, or substantial parts, of mathematics could be derived.[3] Frege's own

---

[1] For a discussion of the term 'analytic philosophy' and this preference for the term 'mainstream philosophy', see my *Truth, Thought, Reason: Essays on Frege* (Oxford: Clarendon Press, 2005), pp. 6–14.

[2] Gottlob Frege, *Begriffsschrift* (1879), in *Begriffsschrift und Andere Aufsätze*, ed. Ignacio Angelelli (Hildesheim: Georg Olms Verlag, 1977); reprinted and translated in *From Frege to Gödel*, ed. Jean van Heijenoort (Cambridge, MA: Harvard University Press, 1981).

[3] Richard Dedekind, *Was Sind und Was Sollen die Zahlen?* (Minneapolis: University of Minnesota Press, 1988); David Hilbert, *Grundlagen der Geometrie* (1899); 'On the Foundations of Logic and Arithmetic' (1904), reprinted in *From Frege to Gödel*; Bertrand Russell, 'Mathematical Logic as Based on the Theory of Types' (1908), reprinted in *From Frege to Gödel*, Ernst Zermelo, 'Investigations in the Foundations of Set Theory I' (1908), reprinted in *From Frege to Gödel*. For more recent attempts to defend a neo-Fregean conception of logicism (with which I believe Frege would have had scant sympathy), see Bob Hale and Crispin Wright, *The Reason's Proper Study: Essays Toward a Neo-Fregean Philosophy of Mathematics* (New York: Oxford University Press, 2001).

foundational effort attempted to reduce the mathematics of *number* to *logic*.[4] Because the logic that he proposed relied on a defective principle that cannot be included in first- and second-order logic (which he otherwise correctly formulated), his attempt failed. But his was one of the most influential attempts at establishing foundations for mathematics. More specifically, his work provided a paradigm for subsequent attempts to reduce substantial parts of mathematics to logic, notably Russell's attempt.[5] More broadly, the rigor and depth of Frege's thinking established a paradigm for all work in the new branch of mathematics—mathematical logic—whether reductive or not.

Frege's first influence on *philosophy* was on the philosophy of mathematics, especially the epistemology and proof structure of mathematics. The initial conduit of this influence was Russell.[6] But Frege's work on logic had a much wider effect on philosophy. Russell himself used Frege's logical techniques in metaphysics and epistemology.[7] The early Wittgenstein constructed a metaphysics using Frege's work in logic.[8] Carnap offered his own metaphysics using Frege's logical apparatus, and later applied Frege's logic in rejecting metaphysics and in attempting to understand the logical structure of natural science.[9] Church steadily advocated the relevance of Frege's logic to the philosophy of language.[10]

Frege's logic provided a versatile tool for thinking about a great variety of philosophical problems. This tool brought with it new standards of rigor in doing philosophy. Frege's use of and reflection on logic for philosophical purposes suggested both new approaches to old problems, and a new set of philosophical problems. These problems figured very prominently in twentieth-century philosophy.

Thus Frege's largest impact on philosophy was to connect philosophy more closely to the explicit use of logic, and to direct philosophical inquiry to problems suggested by and tractable to the application of logic. For example, Frege's attempt to find the structure of inference in the logical structure of language, and his attempt to understand the structure of thought through an underlying deep structure of language, helped create

---

[4] Gottlob Frege, *Begriffsschrift*; *The Foundations of Arithmetic* (1884), tr. J. L. Austin, with German text, 2nd edn. (Oxford: Blackwell 1953); *Grundsetze der Arithmetik*, vols. I–II (1893, 1903) (Hildesheim: Georg Olms, 1962); Preface, Introduction, and parts of vol. I translated as *The Basic Laws of Arithmetic*, tr. M. Furth (Berkeley: University of California Press, 1967). Frege took geometry to be *non*-logical.

[5] See note 3. Also A. N. Whitehead and Bertrand Russell, *Principia Mathematica*, vol. I (1910), vol. II (1912), vol. III (1913) (Cambridge: Cambridge University Press, 1910, 1912, 1913).

[6] Bertrand Russell, *The Principles of Mathematics* (Cambridge: Cambridge University Press, 1903); *Introduction to Mathematical Philosophy* (London: Allen & Unwin, 1919).

[7] Bertrand Russell, 'On Denoting', *Mind* 14 (1905): 479–93; *The Problems of Philosophy* (Oxford: Oxford University Press, 1912).

[8] Ludwig Wittgenstein, *Tractatus Logico-Philosophicus* (1922), tr. D. F. Pears and B. McGuinness (London: Routlege, 2001).

[9] Rudolf Carnap, *The Logical Structure of the World* (1928), tr. R. George (Berkeley: University of California Press, 1967); *Meaning and Necessity* (1947) (Chicago: University of Chicago Press, 1956).

[10] Alonzo Church, 'The Need for Abstract Entities in Semantic Analysis', *Proceedings of the American Academy of Arts and Sciences* 80 (1951): 100–12; reprinted in *The Philosophy of Language*, ed. A. P. Martinich (New York: Oxford University Press, 1985); *Introduction to Mathematical Logic*, vol. I (Princeton, NJ: Princeton University Press, 1956).

the philosophy of language and produced a new way of thinking about the philosophy of mind. His reflection on types of 'meaning' encouraged philosophers to reflect on the nature and meaning of their own subject, to clarify the basis for their claims, and to connect them to clear logical structures. Stated so abstractly, the point seems rather bloodless. But in application, all subdisciplines in philosophy, from philosophy of mathematics to ethics, took on a greater commitment to clarity, explicitness, and self-criticism which in turn furthered philosophical communication and progress. Moreover, Frege's attempt to understand the basis for mathematics and his emphasis on the public, communal nature of scientific claims, revived a concern to ally philosophy with the sciences that had been muted in philosophy since Kant.

The influence on philosophy of Frege's development and application of logic is unusual. The form of influence is unlike the two types discussed in the preamble. It was unitary, pervasive, and steady, from Russell's initial recognition of Frege as a great philosopher onward. It is not too much to say that this influence was the largest factor in initiating a new era of philosophy. The new era was marked by a shared understanding of techniques and problems, a distaste for vague, grandiose claims, and a consequent openness of discussion to communal development.

10.2 Taking Propositional Structures as the Basis for Understanding Language, Thought, and Ontology

The most specific application of Frege's use of logic in philosophy was his taking propositional structures to be the basis for theorizing about logic, language, thought, and ontology. Like the first form of influence, this specific instance is unusual in being unitary, pervasive, and constant, from the beginning.

In the Introduction to *Foundations of Arithmetic* (1884), Frege stated a context principle: (a) 'Never ask for the denotation (*Bedeutung*) of a word in isolation, but only in the context of a proposition.' Later in the book, he associates, either implicitly or explicitly, this methodological recommendation with two substantive claims: (b) Only in the context of a proposition does a word have denotation (*Bedeutung*), and (c) It is sufficient for a word to have a denotation (*Bedeutung*) that it occur in certain positions in true propositions.[11]

When Frege wrote *Foundations of Arithmetic*, he had not drawn his ground-breaking distinction between sense (*Sinn*) and denotation (*Bedeutung*) (1891–2).[12] Later Frege

---

[11] *The Foundations of Arithmetic*, Introduction, p. x, and sections 60, 62, 106.

[12] Gottlob Frege, 'On Function and Concept' (1891); 'On Sense and Denotation' (1892), the latter translated as 'On Sense and Reference', in *Translations of the Philosophical Writings of Gottlob Frege*, 2nd edn., tr. P. Geach and M. Black (Oxford: Blackwell, 1966); also in *Collected Papers*, ed. B. McGuinness (Oxford: Blackwell, 1984), and in *The Frege Reader*, ed. M. Beaney (Oxford: Blackwell, 1997).

recognized that in *The Foundations of Arithmetic* he had used '*Bedeutung*' sometimes to mean what he later meant by '*Bedeutung*' and sometimes to mean what he later meant by '*Sinn*'. Each of (a), (b), and (c) can be taken with either reading of '*Bedeutung*'—yielding six principles. Frege accepted all six principles. Even with this sharpening, the specific meanings of (b) and (c) are, of course, not transparent. What does it mean to be 'in the context' of a proposition? What is meant by 'certain positions' in true propositions? I say a little in response to this latter question in what follows. But most of the discussion will not depend on answering these questions.[13]

A key to Frege's revolutionary influence in the study of logic, language, and the structure of thought lay in his focus on patterns of valid *inference* and in his focus on understanding conditions under which the primary function of *judgment* (to connect to truth) is fulfilled. Frege had discovered and formulated modern logic by considering what propositional structures underlie formal, deductively valid inference. His methodological point in (a) was that one can best understand structural and certain functional aspects of language and thought by reflecting on how formal, deductively valid inferences hinge on parts of propositional structures, and how parts of propositional structures connect with a subject matter (the world, broadly construed) and with one another in determining their truth or falsity.

Frege showed how to follow his own methodological advice in his analysis of the logical/grammatical structure of numerical statements,[14] and in his brilliant discussion in 'On Sense and Denotation' of the structure of numerous constructions in ordinary language. Frege's method contrasts with previous approaches to language that focused on definitions of words, or on the association of words with perceptual images, or on ideas in individuals' minds. By contrast, Frege inferred the structural nature of propositional components from their behavior in inferential activity. And he inferred the semantic functions of propositional components from explanations of their contributions to determining conditions whose fulfillment constitutes propositional truth.

Russell took up Frege's approach. He developed it in a competing theory of the structure of thought, especially in his theory of descriptions.[15] The logical positivists concentrated on the cognitive meaning of propositional statements. By mid-century the approach had become the basis for understanding semantics not only in philosophy but in linguistics. Indeed, the focus on the structural behavior of whole sentences, a methodology closely connected to Frege's more semantically oriented (a), became the methodological basis for the study of syntax in linguistics.

The key idea behind both interpretations of the methodological claim (a) and both interpretations of claim (b) is to focus on the way words or thought components contribute to truth conditions and inferential potential. Such focus is impossible unless words and thought components are considered in relation to propositional structures

---

[13] I discuss these principles at somewhat greater length in *Truth, Thought, Reason*, pp. 15–16, 87–90, 108–11, 307.

[14] *The Foundations of Arithmetic*, sections 29–54.

[15] Russell, 'On Denoting'.

that could contain them. Although there are other aspects of language and thought besides structural ones, many of even these other aspects are best understood in relation to the structural ones.

For example, referential aspects of words—their being connected representationally to subject matters—are best understood in the context of the grammatical roles of the words and the ways the words contribute to truth conditions. Similarly, tonal or pragmatic aspects of language use are best understood in contrast with truth-conditional aspects of the words' meaning and reference. Over the last century and a quarter, these points have been borne out through the fruitfulness of their application in linguistics, formal semantics, and applied mathematical logic. Similar points apply, I think, to understanding the nature of propositional thought.

A second way in which Frege's focus on propositional structure and truth conditions influenced twentieth-century philosophy lay in its contribution to ontology—the metaphysics of being, or of what is. The key source of influence is the principle obtained from the denotational interpretation of (c). Frege's use of the principle, as distinguished from his formulation of it, shows the principle to be that if, under semantic analysis, a word's (or thought component's) having a denotation is entailed by the semantics of a true proposition's truth, then the word (or thought component) has a denotation. The truth of a proposition and its semantic analysis are sufficient for determining that a word or symbol has a denotation: no further considerations are relevant.

Frege appealed to this principle in his defense of taking numbers and functions to be entities in the subject matters of the mathematical sciences.[16] His idea was that there could be no better ground to believe in entities than that the entities are needed to be the denotations of expressions in order to explain the semantics of propositions known to be true—particularly in the sciences. According to his logical-semantical analysis, the explanation of the known truth of propositions of arithmetic appeals (i) to numbers as denotations of singular numerical expressions, and (ii) numerical functions as denotations of predicates (*is a natural number*) and functors (*the successor of*). So he concluded that numbers and numerical functions *are* denotations, and figure in the ontology of mathematics—in mathematics' subject matter.

Frege's principle (c), interpreted in the denotational way, served to undermine extraneous ontological requirements. For example, empiricists might claim that because one cannot be in perceptual or other causal relations to numbers, one should doubt that there are any numbers, or one should claim that numbers are just convenient fictions. Physicalists or nominalists might claim that because numbers lack causal powers or are not in space or time, one should disallow them in ontology. Frege took such views to be undermined by his context principle.[17]

---

[16] *The Foundations of Arithmetic*, esp. section 60.

[17] For a discussion, somewhat removed from Frege's texts, but in Frege's spirit on this matter, see Michael Dummett, 'Nominalism' (1956) in *Truth and Other Enigmas* (Cambridge, MA: Harvard University Press, 1978). See also Michael Dummett, *Frege: Philosophy of Mathematics* (Cambridge, MA: Harvard University Press, 1991), chapter 16; and my 'Frege on Truth' in *Truth, Thought, Reason*.

Of course, the context principle (c), interpreted in the denotational way, is not self-evident. Some philosophers have flouted or ignored it—citing the intuitive force of their own intuitions. For example, a few philosophers still deride the assumption of abstract entities like numbers. Other philosophers have tried to limit the scope of Frege's principle, or to interpret it differently from the way Frege interpreted it. For example, Quine took predicates and functors not to have denotations. And he revised Frege's principle—focusing on the range of first-order quantifiers rather than the denotations of terms.[18]

Despite such controversy, the relevant principle associated with (c) has been almost as influential in ontology as principles (a) and (b) have been in the study of structural aspects of language and thought. Two forms of this influence can be distinguished. One is that Frege used the principle in conjunction with his deep analysis of propositional structure and truth-conditional semantics. Thus his assertion of the principle provided a methodological ground rule for thinking about ontology that was vastly clearer than anything that had come before. Quine's criterion for ontological commitment (alluded to in the previous paragraph) has been justly influential for precisely this contribution. From a broad historical perspective, Quine's contribution is simply a turn on Frege's.

The second, much deeper form of Frege's influence on ontology lay in the methodology that stands behind his use of the context principle (c). Frege's reflection on ontology occurred within his reflection on the structure and nature of the science of mathematics. In effect, he took ontology not to be an independent discipline. He allied it with other disciplines that yield truths. So his ontology is very closely allied with mathematics. He started with propositions known in the sciences—or otherwise known, but not through some special discipline of ontology. Then he determined what entities the semantical explanation of their truth requires. Frege's approach influenced the practice of Russell, Carnap, and Quine. Quine's pragmatic approach to ontology has been justly influential for grounding metaphysics in epistemologically more sound enterprises, principally scientific enterprises.[19]

Quine was less pragmatic than Frege in some ways. Without any serious justification, he confined 'science' to natural science—as distinguished from logic and mathematics.

---

[18] W. V. Quine, *Word and Object* (Cambridge, MA: MIT Press, 1960), sections 20–5; and 'On What There Is' (1948) in *From a Logical Point of View*, 2nd edn. (Cambridge, MA: Harvard University Press, 1961); also reprinted in *Quintessence*, ed. R. F. Gibson (Cambridge, MA: Harvard University Press, 2004). For more on Frege's notion of predicate denotation, see Montgomery Furth, 'Two Types of Denotation', in *Studies in Logical Theory*, American Philosophical Quarterly Monograph Series 2 (Oxford: Blackwell, 1968). For a defense of a similar view, see my 'Predication and Truth', *The Journal of Philosophy* 104 (2007): 580–608. For a lucid discussion of issues that are associated with ontological commitment through first- and second-order quantifiers, and through predicates, see Charles Parsons, *Mathematical Thought and Mathematical Objects* (Cambridge: Cambridge University Press, 2008), chapter 1.

[19] Quine, *Word and Object*, chapters 1 and 7, esp. section 48.

He took mathematics, I think without justification, to be entirely parasitic for its scientific status on its applications within natural science. Moreover, he showed no openness to or interest in non-natural-scientific sources of knowledge—for example self-knowledge or knowledge through semantics or psychology—as Frege did. Further, Quine placed extensionalist ontological strictures on his investigation that have not accorded with the actual development of the sciences. Natural science is committed to properties, and the human sciences are committed to perceptions, intentions, and beliefs. Quine's strictures on extensionalist explanations have been justly ignored in the sciences. (See also section 10.7 below.) Still, in its primary motivations, Quine's approach to ontology—like the approaches of Russell, Carnap, Church, Strawson, and many others—is rooted in Frege's precept and example.

The approach to ontology that flows from Frege deepens Kant's attempt to make theoretical philosophy concrete by associating it closely with scientific practice, and with other non-metaphysical cognitive enterprises. Although appeals to independent ontological principles ('no abstract objects', 'no entities without causal powers', 'no intensional entities') are perennially tempting, they have not led to progress or agreement in philosophy, much less science. Frege's more pragmatic, scientifically grounded approach to ontology put the subject on a stronger footing.

As noted, both the influence of Frege's use of logic in philosophy and, more specifically, the influence of his context principles in semantics, linguistics, applied logic, epistemology, and ontology were unitary and powerful from the beginning. This type of influence is rare in the history of philosophy. Arguably, such massive and unitary influence is possible in philosophy only because it centers in method, not doctrine. Understanding it requires sensitivity to the many ways in which Frege's logic and his contextualist principles have been applied—or, in the case of the latter, developed, refined, and re-directed in philosophy and in the sciences.

10.3 THE LANGUAGE OF SCIENCE VS. ORDINARY NATURAL LANGUAGE

Throughout his career, Frege took the language of science, principally mathematical science, to be the evidential basis for insight into epistemology, semantics, and ontology. He aimed at discovering a language that was ideal for expressing scientific thought perspicuously. The method of discovery was to reflect on the structure of sentences as revealed through patterns of propositional inference. Thus in *Foundations of Arithmetic* he reflects on ordinary expressions of arithmetic to find their underlying logical structure. In 'On Sense and Denotation' and 'On Function and Concept', he extends this logical analysis to natural language. He extends his analysis partly to understand ordinary reasoning, whether scientific or not, but mainly, I think, to develop a language for sciences beyond mathematics—including the natural sciences and psychology.[20]

Frege's own experience of his relation to natural language was one of hostile struggle. He wrote,

> If it is one of the tasks of philosophy to break the domination of the word over the human spirit by laying bare the misconceptions that through the use of language often almost unavoidably arise concerning the relations between concepts and by freeing thought from that with which only the means of expression of ordinary language, constituted as they are, saddle it, then my ideography, further developed for these purposes, can become a useful tool for the philosopher.[21]

Natural language was both a necessary route to insight and an annoying obstruction. Frege was interested in the subtleties of natural language because he thought that he had to be, in order to understand the underlying structures that support reasoning in the sciences. He gave natural language serious attention only intermittently—pre-eminently in the great articles of the 1890s—'On Sense and Denotation' and 'On Function and Concept'—and in the article 'Thought', published in 1918, but itself begun in the late 1890s.[22]

Frege had a genius-level feel for the structure and nuances of natural language. His success derived partly from his bringing his understanding of logic and his contextualist principles to bear on natural language, but partly from his subtle distinctions between structural and non-structural elements of language. His work harbors materials for two very different types of philosophical development. Both types mined Frege's work.

One type continued Frege's quest for an ideal scientific language. The aim of this quest was both to make the structure, epistemology, and ontology of science perspicuous, and to provide a basis for philosophical reflection on problems raised by such language. As noted, Russell built on Frege's work in the foundations of mathematics. The logical positivists, notably Carnap and Hempel, shifted attention from the logical structure of mathematics to the logical structure of natural science, but retained Frege's interest in an ideal language for science. Quine discarded positivist principles, but presented in *Word and Object* a detailed theory of an ideal, regimented language for natural science. Current philosophy of science concerns itself less with the logical structure of language than the work of Carnap, Hempel, and Quine did. But the continuing focus on scientific reasoning in actual scientific theory owes much to Frege.

---

[20] See Gottlob Frege, 'Über das Trägheitsgesetz' ('On the Law of Inertia') (1891) in *Kleineschriften*, I. ed. I. Angelelli (Hildesheim: Georg Olms, 1967); and Letter to Russell 28/12/1902 in *Philosophical and Mathematical Correspondence*, ed. G. Gabriel *et al.* (Chicago: University of Chicago Press, 1980).

[21] *Begriffsschrift*, Preface.

[22] 'Thought' in *Collected Papers*, and in *The Frege Reader*.

The second type of philosophical development centered on the matter that Frege took to be secondary. Beginning with work by Grice, Strawson, and Austin on ordinary language in the mid-twentieth century and exploding in the work of Donnellan, Kripke, Putnam, Davidson, Montague, Kaplan, Searle, T. Parsons, Kamp, Higginbotham, Schiffer, Stalnaker, Evans, Burge, and others, the use of Fregean ideas in understanding the semantics and logical form of natural language became a central area of philosophy. Some of this work fed into theories of meaning and reference in linguistics, especially from the last two decades of the century to the present. Therein, philosophy again played the role of midwife, indeed parents, of a science. Some of the work provided the basis for philosophical work on philosophy of mind and philosophy of psychology—for example, in work by Kripke, Fodor, Evans, and Burge.

In numerous ways Frege set the questions for serious work on semantics, both of ideal scientific language and of natural language: How is one to distinguish reference from various notions of meaning? How is one to distinguish meaning from use, coloring, implicature, presupposition? What is the logical form of various sentences? What logical resources are needed to capture the contribution of the underlying logical form of a sentence in inference? What are the roles, respectively, of communication and thought in understanding meaning and reference? What are the correct semantical accounts of names, demonstratives, and indexical devices? What is the structure of pronomial cross-reference? How should prima facie intensional contexts be construed semantically and structurally?

The fact that philosophical contributions taking such very different directions—with foci on ideal and ordinary language—could be inspired by different aspects of Frege's philosophy is a tribute to the richness and power of his semantical views and logical tools.

10.4 COMMUNAL LANGUAGE VS. IDIOLECT

Frege's concern with an ideal scientific language was a concern with the language of a community of scientists. In reflecting on natural language, Frege sometimes centered on a communal language, but other times theorized about idiolects. *Idiolects* are the particular languages spoken by specific individuals, with vocabulary, construals of words, and so on that are specifically the individual language user's—perhaps partly idiosyncratic to that individual.

When Frege first introduces the notion of *sense* (see section 10.5 below) in 'On Sense and Denotation', he remarks that the sense of a specific word ('Bucephalus') 'may be the common property of many'. In the next paragraph, clearly thinking of idiolects, he writes that 'one man can associate this sense and another that sense' with a given word.[23] He contrasts senses with *ideas* by saying that different people are 'not prevented from grasping the same sense; but cannot have the same idea'. (He regards ideas as tokens in

---

[23] 'On Sense and Denotation', p. 29 in the original pagination, marked in nearly all translation editions. The issues in this paragraph are discussed in much greater detail in *Truth, Thought, Reason*, pp. 37–9.

individual minds.) In this discussion, Frege clearly has idiolects in mind. Some have taken this last quotation to count as stating a constitutive condition on senses—that senses *must* be shareable. In 'Thought', however, Frege writes that language users can on occasion think first-person thoughts that involve cognitive values that only they can grasp. Although he does not state that they can attach a *sense* to the word 'I' that can be grasped only by themselves, the passage strongly implies that he believes that they can. At the very least, a thought component associated with a person's use of 'I' can on occasion be graspable only by the speaker/thinker.[24] If the interpretation that holds that senses are *constitutively* graspable by different people were correct, the passage in 'Thought' would seem to contradict Frege's own doctrine. I believe that the interpretation is mistaken.[25] Frege clearly believed that the senses of many expressions are in fact shared among different language users. I think Frege maintained that *nearly* all senses— and *all* senses usable in a science—are graspable by different people, whereas no ideas are graspable by different people. But I think that he allowed certain exceptions. In any case, Frege's remarks about constitutively idiosyncratic senses of 'I' are not central to his main philosophical work.

Frege argues that senses can be grasped by different people, claiming 'mankind has a common store of thoughts that is transmitted from one generation to another'.[26] Laid out more fully: Different people have the same thoughts. Such thoughts are transmitted through language. So different people understand language as expressing the same thoughts. Thoughts expressed by declarative sentences just *are* propositional senses. So senses—some senses, at least ones involved in thoughts understood in common through language—are understandable (graspable) by different people.

Frege's focus on idiolects is most prominent when he discusses indexicals, demonstratives, and ordinary proper names.[27] He regarded such devices as largely or entirely absent from an ideal scientific language, at least one used to state the basic principles of a science. With respect to such linguistic devices, he notes that different people associate different senses with the same words. For example, he writes that in uses of 'now' by

---

[24] 'Thought' in *Collected Papers*, and in *The Frege Reader*. The passage occurs on p. 66 in the original pagination. See also pp. 71–2. Frege makes it clear that he thinks that a language user can attach senses to 'I' that are graspable by others. But he implicates that in solitary thought expressed in language, the user can also, on occasion, think thoughts in which the thinker is presented to him- or herself in a way in which he/she is presented to no one else, and which he or she alone can grasp.

[25] Some commentators have charged Frege with inconsistency or outrageous error on this point. See P. T. Geach, Preface to G. Frege, *Logical Investigations*, tr. P. T. Geach and R. H. Stoothoff (New Haven: Yale University Press, 1977), p. viii; J. Perry, 'Frege on Demonstratives', *The Philosophical Review* 86 (1977), p. 474, reprinted with postscript in J. Perry, *The Problem of the Essential Indexical and Other Essays* (Oxford: Oxford University Press, 1993). But nothing in Frege's texts convicts him of inconsistency. And I believe that his idea that each person has a special cognitive access to himself, which could be an idiolectal sense or cognitive value, is obviously true. If sense is properly understood as cognitive mode of presentation, rather than as linguistic meaning in a garden variety sense, Frege's claim seems simply commonsensical.

[26] 'On Sense and Denotation', p. 29 in the original pagination.

[27] 'On Sense and Denotation', pp. 27–32 in the original; 'Thought', pp. 64–7 in the original; I intend *ordinary* proper names to contrast with canonical names, like numerals.

different people at different times, or by the same person at different times, the sense of 'now' changes. Clearly, the ordinary linguistic meaning of 'now' does not change so easily. Frege also sometimes elaborates the possibility of failures of communication in cases in which different people associate different senses with the same symbol, even though the symbol has the same reference for the different people.

In making these points, Frege is not claiming that the words have different *meanings* for different people. His notion of *sense* is very specifically associated with the thoughts that people associate with their uses of language. His notion of 'expressing a sense' is specifically part of the project of understanding thought and knowledge conveyed, engaged in, or attained through language. His notion of sense is thus not as separated from epistemic and psychological issues as modern notions of meaning commonly are. I shall return to this matter in section 10.5.

I think that Frege's views about the *senses* of proper names are not correct. I think that he probably underrates the role of context-dependent linguistic devices in making possible an ideal scientific language. But I think that his view that one might think specific thoughts in using demonstrative-infused sentences that are not shared or easily understood by interlocutors is clearly correct. His view that there is room for context dependence and a variety of thoughts 'expressed' when demonstratives are used seems to me to target a still under-developed feature of linguistic communication.

On the other hand, Frege carried out most of his work, even his work on natural language, on the assumption that senses (thought components) are commonly shared when words are used. Much of his impact on philosophy lay in emphasizing the shared aspects of language use, and their role in communicating knowledge. Frege is interested in natural language inasmuch as it is the basis for development of a communal scientific language. He is primarily interested in those aspects of natural language that might be worked into, or toward, scientific language. These aspects are shareable, and largely shared, among different natural language users. Indeed, he associates *objectivity* not only with law but with common use by different individuals.[28] Despite the fact that in 'On Sense and Denotation' he writes with idiolects almost constantly in mind, that work led to a widespread focus in philosophy on a common, public, communal language— dialects of English, German, or the like. The reason for this influence lay in Frege's effective and insightful emphasis on shared senses and a 'common store' of thoughts.

Most subsequent work in the philosophy of language assumed that the language being analyzed was a public, shared language. Some even claimed that the notion of an idiolect is suspect, and that it is at best an artificial abstraction from the more basic communal language.[29] On the other hand, a few philosophers took idiolects to be basic and doubted the respectability of the notion of a common language. Such philosophers

---

[28] *Foundations of Arithmetic*, sections 26–7; 'On Sense and Denotation', p. 30 in the original.

[29] Michael Dummett, 'The Social Character of Meaning', in *Truth and Other Enigmas*; 'Indexicality and *Oratio Obliqua*', chapter 6 of *The Interpretation of Frege's Philosophy* (Cambridge, MA: Harvard University Press, 1981), pp. 113–14; 'Language and Communication', in *Reflections on Chomsky*, ed. A. George (Oxford: Blackwell, 1989); 'Thought and Language', chapter 13 in *Origins of Analytic Philosophy* (Cambridge, MA Harvard University Press, 1994).

tended to model linguistic understanding within a community on interpreting a foreigner.[30] Or they rejected the notion of a communal language because they deemed it unscientific. They regarded a notion of language as a branch of individual psychology as the only legitimate one.[31]

These issues are extremely complex. I believe that neither of the extreme views just sketched is tenable. Frege would certainly have accepted neither of them. He took idiolects seriously, but emphasized and tried to understand the elements of common understanding in scientific and natural-language communities.

10.5 SENSE AND DENOTATION

So far I have emphasized sources of Frege's influence that derive from his methodology or from areas of focus in his work. His most famous and influential *substantive* contribution is his distinction between sense and denotation (*Bedeutung*).[32] Frege's isolating a

[30] W. V. Quine, 'Speaking of Objects', in *Ontological Relativity and Other Essays* (New York: Columbia University Press, 1969); *Word and Object,*, chapter 2; Donald Davidson, *Inquires into Truth and Interpretation* (Oxford: Clarendon Press, 1984), especially 'Radical Interpretation' and 'Communication and Convention'; 'A Nice Derangement of Epitaphs', in *Truth, Language, and History* (Oxford: Clarendon Press, 2005). For criticism of these views, see my 'Comprehension and Interpretation', in *The Philosophy of Donald Davidson*, ed. Lewis Hahn (Chicago: Open Court, 1999).

[31] Noam Chomsky, *Aspects of the Theory of Syntax* (Cambridge, MA: MIT Press, 1965); *Rules and Representations* (Oxford: Blackwell, 1980); *Knowledge of Language: Its Nature, Origin, and Use* (New York: Praeger, 1986). For engagement with Chomsky's view from a different standpoint, see my 'Wherein is Language Social?' in *Reflections on Chomsky*, ed. George.

[32] The translation of '*Bedeutung*' is controversial. Some translators leave the term untranslated. Although the normal translation of the term into English is 'meaning', I believe that this translation is a very bad one for helping to understand Frege. Frege's understanding of '*Bedeutung*' is, in numerous ways, deeply different from ordinary understandings of the term 'meaning'. I prefer 'denotation' to 'reference' as a translation because '*Bedeutung*' is a more technical term than 'reference' is, and because 'reference' (like '*nominatum*', another prominent translation) is strongly associated with representation by singular or plural noun phrases. Frege applied '*Bedeutung*' to a representational relation (or the entity represented in such a relation) that is associated with *predicates* and *functional expressions*—a representational relation that I call 'indication' below—as well as to a representational relation associated with noun phrases. It is at best awkward to speak of the referents of predicates or functors. Moreover, Frege takes sentences to have a '*Bedeutung*'—which he took to be their truth value. Speaking of the reference of sentences is very odd to most ears. Frege himself saw his claim that sentences have a *Bedeutung* as a technical usage that exploited theoretically important analogies between the semantical behavior of sentences, on one hand, and the semantical behavior of singular terms and predicates, on the other. (For discussion, see my 'Frege on Truth' in *Truth, Thought, Reason*.) So a translation that lacks heavy ordinary-language associations and that is amenable to special, technical usage is desirable. 'Denotation', my choice of translation, has the mild disadvantage of being associated with Russell's famous 'On Denoting', which takes denoting phrases to be noun phrases. But a broader usage in which denotation is contrasted with connotation, and in which that pair is closely associated with the pair *extension* and *intension*, is present in the history of logic—for example, in the work of William Hamilton (1788–1856) and J. S. Mill (1806–73). This usage takes predicate expressions as well as noun phrases to have denotations. Of course, Frege's particular theory of *Sinn* and *Bedeutung* differs from any earlier theory. My translation follows that of Alonzo Church in 'A Formulation of the Logic of Sense and Denotation', in P. Henle, *et al.* (eds.), *Structure, Method, and Meaning* (New York: Liberal Arts Press, 1951). I regard '*designatum*' as another viable translation of '*Bedeutung*'.

clear notion of denotation is an accomplishment almost as pervasively and beneficially influential as his methodological concentration on propositional structure and truth conditions.

The notion of denotation is integral to his explanation of how truth conditions figure in inferential structure. For the truth value of a proposition depends only, on his view, on the denotations of the proposition's component parts, given their arrangement in the logical form of the proposition.

Denotation for singular propositional components is reference. Thus the denotation of a singular term, or singular thought component, is its *referent*. For names, the referent is the named object, if any. For definite descriptions, the referent is the entity, if any, that is uniquely described. The denotation of a predicate is the attribute (which Frege took to be a function) that is predicated of the (purported) referent of a singular expression. Let us call the denotation relation between predicates and the functions (or attributes) that they predicate *indication*. Let us call the denotations of predicates *indicants*. Frege assimilated predication to functional application. So the denotations (indicants) of both predicates and functors are functions. First-order functions take the referents of singular expressions as their arguments or inputs. Higher-order functions take lower-order functions as their arguments or inputs.[33]

The details of Frege's ontology—and his literal assimilation of predication to functional application—are less important than his isolation of denotation as a distinctive aspect of semantics, his identification of singular denotation with reference, and his recognition of a distinction between functional (including predicative) denotation and singular denotation. The key explanatory roles of denotation are two-fold. One is a role in understanding the connection of language and thought to a subject matter. The other is a role in explaining how the truth value of propositional entities—whether sentences or thought contents—depends structurally (for Frege, literally functionally) on the semantical values of propositional sub-parts.

Frege's use of the notion of denotation in these two enterprises constituted the birth of modern semantics. Although there has been controversy over both Frege's ontology of denotation and the details of his explanation of how truth values depend on the semantical values of propositional sub-parts, the influence of this side of his sense–denotation distinction has been pervasive and broadly unitary.

The effect of his notion of sense has been less unified, although nearly all philosophers have recognized some role for something like his notion of sense in explaining cognitive aspects of language use.

Frege used the notion of sense to fulfill four explanatory roles: (a) to mark certain thoughts and thought components that figure in linguistic usage—roughly, to constitute the ways denotations (or purported denotations) are understood or cognitively thought (as) of in uses of language; (b) to mark the determination of denotation by thought components; (c) to be the denotations of expressions that report thoughts; and (d) to

---

[33] 'Function and Concept'. The terminology of 'indication' derives from my 'Predication and Truth'.

constitute what is understood in language use, especially what is shared in much successful linguistic communication.[34]

Frege's notion of sense has been much more controversial than his notion of denotation.

Much of the controversy has, I think, stemmed either from philosophical ideology that has largely lost its steam or from misunderstandings of the point of Frege's notion. Thus I believe that much of the controversy has been pointless, or at least beside Frege's point.

Russell tried to avoid invoking any notion of sense in his analysis of language. He attempted to get by with a variant of Frege's notion of denotation. Russell confronted Frege on his own terms—*attempting to explain the cognitive and epistemic aspects of language use*. Russell's attempt to explain thought and knowledge purely in terms of the psychological analog of a denotation relation rested on his theory that individuals are *acquainted* with every component of a proposition.[35] All knowledge was supposed to rest on acquaintance. Empirical knowledge was supposed to rest partly on acquaintance with sense-data. Mathematical knowledge was supposed to rest entirely on acquaintance with universals (propositional functions). Acquaintance was supposed to be an infallible, omniscient, perspective-free relation to an object or propositional function. Russell's notion of acquaintance, his theory of thought, and his theory of knowledge are all nearly universally recognized to be naïve and unacceptable. His attempt to do the explanatory work that Frege's notion of sense was supposed to do, without appealing to any notion of sense, was a failure.

Russell's animus against sense was followed in later twentieth-century philosophy by a broader hostility to abstract entities. This animus was initiated by logical positivists and was continued by the later Wittgenstein and ordinary language philosophers, such as Austin, and behaviorist philosophers, such as Ryle. The animus was further backed by the idea that the explanatory roles of *sense* (as an epistemic notion, or a notion marking psychological competence and cognitive value) and of *meaning* (as a notion capturing communal linguistic understanding) could be filled by notions of *procedure* or *use*. Hostility to abstraction was thus combined with a broad anti-mentalism. Although in mid-career Quine dropped his earlier hostility to abstraction *per se*, he retained the anti-mentalism and more broadly an opposition to any conceptions that could not be explained in 'extensionalist' language.

All these post-Russellian philosophical movements have run out of steam. None of them justified animus toward abstract entities, mentalistic explanations, or non-extensionalist explanations. The particular attempts to reduce notions of sense (cognitive value) to use or methods of confirmation have all failed. Moreover, unlike

---

[34] For further discussion of these roles, see *Truth, Thought, Reason*, pp. 31–5.

[35] 'On Denoting'; 'Knowledge by Acquaintance and Knowledge by Description', in *The Problems of Philosophy*; 'On the Nature of Acquaintance', in *Logic and Knowledge*, ed. R. Marsh (London: Hyman, 1956).

Russell, few of these sources of hostility to Frege's notion of sense confronted the legitimate explanatory tasks that he introduced his notion of sense to carry out.

Science appeals freely to abstractions in its mathematical explanations—for example, sets, functions, numbers. It also appeals to properties and other attributes (relations, kinds). These latter are entities that clearly do not meet extensionalist strictures. Psychological explanations that do not meet extensionalist strictures are now part of rigorous mathematicized scientific explanation in psychology (especially perceptual psychology) and semantics. The philosophical ideologies that were dominant in post-Russellian opposition to Frege's notion of sense have not only failed to endure. They have shown themselves to be unscientific.

Since mid-century, misunderstanding, not just principled hostility, has tended to fuel controversy over Frege's notion of sense. The key error has been to construe sense as linguistic meaning. The notion of linguistic meaning became prominent in philosophical discussions of a communal language. In particular, the notion was meant to apply to *what is understood in common by all competent users of a communal natural language by virtue of being competent users*. Given such a construal, it is certainly plausible to say that the meaning of a proper name, if it has one, is very minimal; and the meaning of demonstratives and indexicals is what is understood context-independently. Thus, for example, the restriction to a time that is contextually contemporaneous with an occurrent use is roughly all there is to the linguistic meaning of 'now'. Similar points apply for the demonstrative pronouns 'she' and 'this'.

It is plausible that the linguistic meaning of a proper name, if any, does not suffice to determine its referent. It is even questionable whether most proper names have any linguistic meaning. It is *obvious* that the linguistic meanings of demonstratives and indexicals do not suffice to determine denotation. One needs a context of use, and strictly I think, a use in a context. In some cases, one needs further contextual factors, such as the intentions of the speaker—for example, in many uses of demonstratives. So Frege's claim (b) about sense does not hold true for the linguistic meanings of these devices. And clearly linguistic meaning in these cases does not even approximate a full account of how a denotation is thought of when these demonstrative or indexical devices are used in sentences. So Frege's claim (a) about senses does not hold true of the linguistic meanings of these devices. Similar difficulties can be thought to arise for the third explanatory role, (c), that Frege gives to senses, if senses are thought of as linguistic meanings.[36]

Criticisms, in this vein, of Frege's use of his notion of sense rest on misunderstanding. As noted in section 10.4, Frege's notion of sense is simply not the notion of linguistic meaning.[37] It cannot be over-emphasized that Frege took senses to figure in explanations of thought and knowledge. Every passage in which he employs the notion of sense

---

[36] These criticisms are frequently part of the exposition of so-called 'direct reference' views of the reference of proper names, demonstratives, and indexicals. Direct reference views focus on linguistic reference and meaning, not cognitive value or sense. But the assumption that sense is just ordinary communal linguistic meaning also permeates the historical work on Frege of Michael Dummett. See, for example, 'Indexicality and *Oratio Obliqua*', chapter 6 of *The Interpretation of Frege's Philosophy*.

[37] See 'Sinning Against Frege'; 'Sense and Linguistic Meaning', both in *Truth, Thought, Reason*; 'Living Wages of *Sinn*', *The Journal of Philosophy* 109 (2012), 40–84.

centers on these psychological and epistemic matters. The criticisms just discussed do not measure Frege's theories against their own objectives. Usually the linguistic issues that are at stake are not sharply specified. Usually they appear to be concerned with what is minimally understood by all competent speakers of a communal natural language. They certainly do not attempt to explain language users' ways of thinking about denotations or the knowledge that they associate with linguistic usage, thought, or knowledge. Thus the criticisms do not apply to Frege. They apply only to thinking that Frege's notion of sense solves problems that it was not meant to solve.

Frege held that senses, which are components of possible thoughts, are independent for their natures of anything in space or time, although their being senses (being expressed by some linguistic expression) *does* depend on the competence and usage of individual thinkers in space or time.[38] I believe that Frege's eternalistic ontology of sense can be reasonably doubted. There are two general difficulties. One is that Frege's Ontological Platonism about senses appears to be completely general. *Ontological Platonism* about a given entity, as I understand it, is the view that the entity is not only abstract (not localizable in space or time), but completely independent for its existence and nature from anything in space or time. Frege seems to have maintained a completely general Ontological Platonism about senses.[39] Senses that determine contingently existing denotations— denotations that are themselves not eternal or even everlasting—are not plausibly construed as independent of entities in time. The idea that a thought component that is a way of thinking as of pianos or horses is completely independent of anything in space or time for its existence and nature (including minds, artifacts, and biological organisms) is simply not credible. Certainly, Frege's arguments for such a view do not succeed.[40] Whether senses that are certain ways of thinking of numbers, functions, or logical operations are eternal and independent of anything in space or time seems to me less obvious.

The second, more basic difficulty for Frege's ontology of senses is that he used the notion to cover significantly different types of cognitive contents, some of which are not context-independent in the way that the thought components that are senses were supposed to be. Some thought components determine denotations by their natures. Others, contrary to Frege, represent what they represent by virtue of irreducibly occurrent mental applications.[41] Thus a thought as of a perceived solidly red ball on a solidly white background depends irreducibly for its referring to the red ball on perceptual

---

[38] 'Thought'. Frege's idea is that thought contents and their components are independent for their existence and nature of anything in space and time, but that their being senses is a role that they take on through being related appropriately to the capacities and uses of language users. Thus being a sense is not part of the nature of thought contents, but is a relation that they bear to individuals in time.

[39] 'Thought'.

[40] I discuss Frege's Ontological Platonism and Frege's arguments for it in 'Frege on Knowing the Third Realm', in *Truth, Thought, Reason*, and in 'Introduction', *Truth, Thought, Reason*, pp. 50–4.

[41] I discuss these matters with particular reference to Frege in 'Belief *De Re*', *The Journal of Philosophy* 74 (1977): 338–62, also in *Foundations of Mind* (Oxford: Clarendon Press, 2007); and more generally, independently of reference to Frege, in 'Postscript: Belief *De Re*', in *Foundations of Mind*; 'Disjunctivism and Perceptual Psychology', *Philosophical Topics* 33 (2005): 1–78; and 'Five Theses on *De Re* States and Attitudes', in *The Philosophy of David Kaplan*, ed. J. Almog and P. Leonardi (Oxford: Oxford University Press, 2008).

interaction with the ball on a particular occasion. No eternal thought content can plausibly single out that red ball from other ones that have similar appearances and backgrounds. The thought requires an occurrent perceptual application in the psychology of the thinker. Such applications cannot determine their denotations by virtue of abstract, time-independent natures. The applications do not type-identify general patterns or abilities. They determine their denotations contextually, through particular, actual occurrences (acts or other events) in time.

Despite these difficulties, Frege's identification of an explanatory role for sense endures. The notion of sense is an aspect of Frege's theory that was long neglected and seen as fruitless. After the fall of behaviorism and the rise of mentalistic explanations in science, issues regarding thought in the use of language re-emerged as worthy of attention. This development, together with a better understanding of what Frege's real explanatory objectives were, has enabled his notion of sense to be recognized as a significant contribution, relevant to contemporary philosophical concerns. Although perhaps no one now conceives of senses, or modes of presentation in thought, in just the way Frege did, the power and explanatory advantages of his notion have become a source of challenge and inspiration to contemporary thinking about language and mind.[42]

10.6 Individual vs. Extra-Individual Factors in Determining a Term's Sense and Denotation

Frege's uses of his notion of sense illustrate the way a rich vein of thought can be neglected or lost, only to be rediscovered. By contrast, his reflection on individual and communal aspects of language (see section 10.3) *as they bear on determining the sense and denotation of an individual's terms* (see section 10.4) illustrates how different strands in a great philosopher's work can inspire very different directions of theorizing.

In understanding how an individual's terms come to be associated with senses and denotations, one must consider both factors that are under the individual's psychological control and factors that are outside that control, including perhaps such factors as the individual's dependence on others in a linguistic community. I will discuss Frege's views on this matter in two areas of his work. I will also discuss the later impact of these views.

The first area again concerns demonstratives and proper names. Frege thinks that the individual's psychology *on an occasion of use* is the primary factor in determining what

---

[42] See, for example, the work of Gareth Evans, *Varieties of Reference* (Oxford: Clarendon Press, 1982); Christopher Peacocke, *Truly Understood* (Oxford: Oxford University Press, 2007); Burge, *Foundations of Mind.*

senses proper names and demonstratives have, and through such senses (see claim (b) in section 10.5), what denotations such devices have.

It is hard to see a strong basis for doubting Frege's view on this matter with respect to *demonstratives*. An individual's psychology—intentions, perceptions, and so on—determines the cognitive value (sense) associated with demonstratives used in context. That is, when an individual thinks a true thought of the form *that ball is red* on a particular occasion, the individual's thought succeeds in picking out a particular ball and predicating redness of that ball. Different psychological states can be determinative on different occasions in uses of the same demonstrative. For example, an individual's perceptually based way of thinking about a ball—marking different types of psychological states— might vary on different occasions on which the individual uses the demonstrative 'that'. Seen from straight-on, the ball might be presented in a different way than if it were seen at an angle or from a greater distance.

On the other hand, Frege's view that the senses, or cognitive values, associated with *proper names* are determined on occasions of use by the individual's associating, with the name, descriptions or representational devices other than the name itself is, I think, mistaken. It remains mistaken even if one clearly distinguishes sense from meaning. An individual may associate a definite description d or perception-governed representational content p with a name a when the individual thinks a thought of the form Fa. The individual may think Fa, Fd, and Fp all at the same time. It does not follow that the sense (cognitive value) of a is that of d or p. In fact, the thought that $a = d$ or $a = p$ will nearly always be a non-logical truth for the individual on the occasion of use, even if it is true. So the thought Fa cannot in those cases be the same thought as the thought Fd or Fp. Proper names almost *never* have the cognitive value (sense) of associated definite descriptions, or any other type of representation that is not cognate with the name itself.[43]

Frege's view of names influenced Russell. Russell followed Frege in thinking that the thought content of names should be explained in other terms, and that the other terms depend on what other terms the individual associates with the name on an occasion of use. In fact, Russell states a doctrine about names (that they are, for purposes of expressing thought, covert definite descriptions) that is much more specific than any doctrine that Frege states.[44]

Wittgenstein, Strawson, and Searle rejected the view that the individual's associations with the name determine a name's sense or denotation.[45] They maintained that certain relations that hinge on the individual's belonging to a wider linguistic community, together with the descriptions actually available in the wider community, determine the

---

[43] Saul Kripke, *Naming and Necessity* (Oxford: Blackwell, 1980); Keith S. Donnellan, 'Proper Names and Identifying Descriptions', *Synthese* 21 (1970): 335–58.

[44] Russell, 'On Denoting'; 'The Philosophy of Logical Atomism', in *Logic and Knowledge*.

[45] Ludwig Wittgenstein, *Philosophical Investigations*, tr. G. E. M. Anscombe (Oxford: Blackwell, 1958), section 79; John Searle, 'Proper Names', *Mind* 67 (1958): 166–73; P. F. Strawson, *Invididuals* (1958) (London: Routledge, 2002), pp. 26–9.

sense and reference of a name. Kripke and Donnellan retained the role for social relations, postulated by Wittgenstein, Strawson, and Searle. But they showed that the individual's linguistic community need not contain sufficient descriptions to determine the name's denotation. Hence relevant language users need not have access to descriptions sufficient to determine the name's denotation. They showed that a chain of causal connections through shared usage connects a name back through history to its bearer.[46]

This development is usually portrayed as anti-Fregean. It is indeed opposed to his apparent view that the individual's psychology controls the referent of a name by associating it with other cognitive devices independent of the name. But often the lesson has been drawn that proper names lack senses. This lesson depends on conflating sense with linguistic meaning. Names clearly *do* contribute to the cognitive content of thoughts. Thus they are or have cognitive values. Different names commonly contribute different contents, different cognitive values, even when they have the same denotation. What Kripke and Donnellan showed was that these cognitive values are ordinarily not definite descriptions and normally cannot be regarded as independent of the name itself. Moreover, they showed that the denotation of a name is fixed by social-historical relations that are normally *not* represented in the individual's psychology. The right conclusion is that these social-historical relations help determine the nature of the individual's way of thinking with the name. So again, Frege's eternalistic conception of sense is mistaken. In determining what it is that an individual thinks of in using the name—what the denotation is—these social-historical relations help determine the nature of the individual's way of thinking, the cognitive value or sense associated with the name. An individual thinks of Jonah as Jonah even if neither the individual nor anyone in his community can describe Jonah specifically enough to single him out from all other individuals. The individual's way of thinking of Jonah (as Jonah) is what it is partly because the individual is connected to Jonah through a historical chain of uses of the name, a chain that the individual need not be able to describe.[47]

Although Frege did not anticipate this revolutionary development, he provided the basis for it in two ways. First, he delineated the notions of sense and denotation. He posed the question of what the sense (cognitive value) of a name is, and the question of how it determines a name's denotation. Second, through his deeply original focus on shared elements of language, he provided a climate and a source of influence, primarily I think through affecting Wittgenstein, that invited serious thinking about how one individual's linguistic usage and thought might interlock with and depend on others'. The resources for the social-historical turn, in philosophical thinking about proper names, were discovered and articulated by Frege, even though the development of these resources told against his particular views on proper names.[48]

---

[46] Kripke, *Naming and Necessity*; Donnellan, 'Proper Names and Identifying Descriptions'.

[47] The example is Kripke's, *Naming and Necessity*, pp. 67–8, 87, 160.

[48] Frege's views on indexicals, such as 'now', 'here', 'today', 'I', are not completely explicit. But he appears to believe that frequently, the senses are partly determined by the context—for example, the actual time—not descriptions or other modes of cognition that are completely under the control of the speaker. See 'Thought', p. 64 in the original.

A second area in Frege's work that bears on the relative contributions of individual and extra-individual factors in determining a term's sense and denotation is his reflection on the sense and denotation of number expressions. In *Foundations of Arithmetic*, Frege famously stated, 'To obtain the concept of number, one must fix (*feststellen*) the sense of a numerical identity' by articulating a 'recognition proposition', a 'criterion' (*Kennzeichen*) for the identity of numbers.[49]

Frege's requirement of a criterion of identity and recognition for numbers exerted a huge influence on subsequent philosophy. Demands for criteria for the meaning or denotation of a wide range of terms in a wide range of philosophical projects became commonplace. The logical positivists made and answered such a demand in their general criterion for cognitive meaning and in their attempts to supply specific methods of confirmation associated with specific terms. Wittgenstein and, later, Strawson and Wiggins demanded criteria for identity and recognition for various categories of entities as a requirement on the meaningfulness of discourse about such entities.[50] Quine articulated a completely general principle, 'no entity without identity'. He meant that in the absence of a specific criterion for identity and difference, one could not reasonably believe in the existence of a type of entity.[51] The common theme of these calls for criteria was that the very meaningfulness or reasonability of the use of a type of expression that purports (functions) to apply to a subject matter depends on the individual language user's associating the expression with a *principle* that determines the meaning or application of a term.

Frege's call for a criterion that 'fixes' the sense of number words was thus extended well beyond his own use of it. Indeed, demands for criteria were used for philosophical ends antithetical to Frege's own. In the first place, Frege's remarks were later applied as a general principle about sense, denotation, or reasonable use. In fact, he made the demand strictly within his project to *reduce* the mathematics of number to pure logic. The demand was part of his project of *explaining* uses of numerical expressions as covert uses of logical expressions. He needed to explain use of numerical expressions in a way that made it clear that that use could be taken to be a use of pure logic. There is no evidence that Frege intended the requirement as part of a general theory of language or ontological commitment.

In the second place, and more importantly, Frege's remarks were interpreted—or at least employed—as conditions on *giving* a term sense, denotation, or reasonable use.

---

[49] *The Foundations of Arithmetic*, sections 62, 106, 109.

[50] Wittgenstein, *Philosophical Investigations*; P. F. Strawson, *Individuals*, pp. 2006ff.; 'Entity and Identity', in *Entity and Identity and Other Essays* (Oxford: Clarendon Press, 1997); David Wiggins, *Sameness and Substance* (Oxford: Blackwell, 1980); see the moderation of his views on criteria in *Sameness and Substance Renewed* (Cambridge: Cambridge University Press, 2001), p. xiii.

[51] W. V. Quine, 'Speaking of Objects' (1958) in *Ontological Relativity and Other Essays*, p. 23; 'On the Individuation of Attributes' (1975) in *Theories and Things* (Cambridge, MA: Harvard University Press, 1981), p. 102: 'We have an acceptable notion of class, or physical object, or attribute, or any other sort of object, only insofar as we have an acceptable principle of individuation for that sort of object. There is no entity without identity.'

In fact, Frege's claims occurred against a background assumption that number words already have a sense, denotation, and reasonable use. His requirement of a principle of identity was part of an attempt to understand and state clearly a principle that explicates or explains sense, denotation, and reasonable use that are already in place.

One source of this latter employment of Frege's idea was that the logical positivists and Wittgenstein demanded criteria within projects that started from doubt that certain uses of terms in philosophy have cognitive meaning or reasonable use.

A second source of the use of Frege's idea for ends other than his own may have been Austin's misleading translation of Frege's remarks. Austin translated '*feststellen*' as 'fix'. The German term is at best unspecific between giving a sense and explaining a sense that is already in place. '*Feststellen*' can standardly mean 'state' or 'ascertain'. And the context in which Frege demands the principle of identity for number words makes it clear that he intended such a reading. In *Foundations of Arithmetic*, section 106, he paraphrases '*den Sinn einer Zahlengleichung festzustellen*' ('to state the sense of a numerical identity') as '[*den Sinn*] *auszudrücken*' ('to express the sense').

Austin also repeatedly translates Frege's word '*erklären*' as 'define', whereas it means *explain* or *explicate*.[52] This translation allows the reader to take Frege to be thinking of *Erklärungen* as stipulations, as *givings* of meaning. Frege sometimes regards his attempt at producing a new ideal language of arithmetic in this way. But he sees stipulation as a momentary act in clarifying a purportedly ideal language. The definitions resulting from stipulations can, however, be evaluated as fruitful or not, and as true or not. His underlying view is that his explanations (*Erklärungen*) of terms attempt to explicate senses that are already in place in mathematical science. Prior to the explanations, the senses are just dimly understood and expressed.[53] They are in need of being associated more perspicuously with expressions (like 'number') newly embedded in an ideal language. Thus his notion of definition is fundamentally one of *real definition*. Real definitions attempt to express an important antecedent truth, rather than to give sense to a neologism, or provide a sense to an old term whose sense is doubtful or non-existent.

The effect of these misinterpretations was to present Frege's call for a principle or criterion of numerical identity as part of a general theory of sense, denotation, and reasonable usage that takes individuals to have cognitive and even stipulative control over the senses of their terms. The idea was that the individual *gives* sense to an expression by being able to state a general principle or criterion for the use of that expression. A consequence of such a view is that if one lacks a principle for a term, the term lacks sense. Another consequence is that if one gives up or otherwise changes a principle, the term changes sense (and perhaps denotation).

There is ample evidence that Frege did not regard sense, denotation, or reasonable usage in mathematics in these ways at all. He saw his logicist project as attempting to

---

[52] See, for example, *Foundations of Arithmetic*, section 62. For related discussion of the point, see *Truth, Thought, Reason*, p. 116 n13.

[53] Cf. Frege, 'Logic in Mathematics', 228, in *The Frege Reader*, pp. 317–18.

clarify the natures of the sense and denotation of numerical words—natures that had been only dimly understood. He explicitly construes mathematical progress as coming to better understand numerical concepts. He states that what is commonly known as the history of concepts is really a history of our knowledge of concepts or of our knowledge of the *Bedeutungen* of words.[54] His view is that the sense and denotation of numerical words had been fixed all along. That is, the senses and denotations of numerical words had always been attached to the words or symbols that were in mathematical theory and practice—even though those senses and denotations may not have been clearly understood. Our stating principles of identity are, when successful, discoveries or clarifications of basic principles long implicitly associated with those senses and denotations. Frege's logicist project was an attempt to clarify a structure and content of thought that was present in mathematics all along.

Frege's view of cognitive values (including senses) associated with mathematics is exactly opposite to the view of much of twentieth-century philosophy. The post-Fregean view maintained that the cognitive value, denotation, and reasonable usage of an individual's terms constitutively depends on the individual's being able to produce definitions or criteria—principles—that govern such use. Frege's view is that the human mind has a basic capacity to track the subject matters of its thought.[55] Thus the sense and denotation of an individual's terms is, for Frege, assured by the individual's root ability to make true judgments about an antecedent and mind-independent subject matter. The individual need not be able (even in principle) to provide principles under which these true judgments are made. The growth of an ability to provide principles constitutes growth in the capacity to understand clearly what was already minimally, but dimly or incompletely, understood in the making of the judgments in the first place.

Obviously, this picture is closely associated with Frege's context principles. Understanding sufficient to carry out mathematics resides in a capacity to understand mathematical truths and a capacity to make inferences from those truths. Understanding the basic principles on which the truths rest, and understanding the exact form of the inferences that one competently carries out, come later. Thus what thoughts an individual thinks—the cognitive values of those states, the senses minimally understood in using terms—is to be explained in terms of judgments and inferential capacities that are explained in terms of their tracking a mind-independent subject matter. A capacity to abstract and understand the basic *principles* governing those inferences comes later. Such a capacity constitutes a deepening and refining of the minimal understanding needed to think the thoughts in the first place.

---

[54] *Foundations of Arithmetic*, Introduction pp. vii–viii. See also 'Über das Trägheitsgesetz', pp. 157–61. For extensive discussion of this view, including further passages in Frege, see 'Sinning Against Frege', 'Frege on Sense and Linguistic Meaning', 'Frege on Knowing the Foundations', and 'Frege on Apriority', all in *Truth, Thought, Reason*.

[55] See, for example, *The Foundations of Arithmetic*, Introduction, p. viii and section 105.

This type of explanation is anti-individualistic. Anti-individualism is the view that the nature of many of an individual's mental states is constitutively determined by relations between the individual and a reality beyond the individual.[56] The natures of the individual's states are in effect constitutively dependent on relations to the reality that is the subject matter of the individual's psychological states. Frege's anti-individualism was obscured for almost a century because his remarks on sense were systematically misunderstood and misappropriated for projects very different from his own. His anti-individualism came to be recognized only when anti-individualism itself had been developed and articulated.[57] Although Frege's anti-individualism centered on thoughts about mathematics, there is reason to believe that he held the view about empirical thought as well.[58]

Frege's anti-individualism is compatible with his recognition of the role of an individual's psychology in determining the sense and denotation of demonstratives *on particular occasions of use*. His anti-individualism is also compatible with his exaggeration of individual control in determining the sense of names on occasions of use. Anti-individualism is primarily concerned with constitutive conditions under which an individual has certain psychological capacities. Even if an individual's intentions or perceptions determined what senses are associated with names on particular occasions of use, the understanding of the associated senses, including understanding of alleged descriptive senses of names, would be determined partly by the individual's relations to a reality that is independent of the individual. (In the empirical case, these include causal relations as well as representational tracking relations.) Anti-individualism is primarily, though not entirely, concerned with patterns of relations between subject matters and individuals that determine individuals' abilities—relation types, not particular occurrences of relations.

Similarly, Frege's anti-individualism is compatible with both his focus on communal languages and his focus on idiolects. Anti-individualism concerns the ways individuals' mental states and capacities constitutively depend on relations to a wider reality. The wider reality can be physical, abstract, or social. Even the thoughts expressed in individuals' idiolects can depend on such relations, including relations to the idiolects of others. Individuals' understanding of senses in idiolects is not constitutively sealed off from social connections, simply by virtue of being idiolectal understanding. Frege's focus on idiolects is compatible with his generalized anti-individualism.

Frege's anti-individualism has philosophical value beyond just being a late-recognized antecedent of more modern work. It has contemporary philosophical interest in its own right. First, Frege's extreme Ontological Platonism about all thought components that

---

[56] See my *Foundations of Mind*, Introduction, pp. 1–27.

[57] See my 'Frege on Extensions of Concepts: From 1884 to 1903', *The Philosophical Review* 93 (1984): 3–34, reprinted with 'Frege on Sense and Linguistic Meaning' in *Truth, Thought, Reason*. See also Introduction, *Truth, Thought, Reason*, pp. 56–9.

[58] Frege, 'Über das Trägheitsgesetz', pp. 157–61. For further discussion see *Truth, Thought, Reason*, pp. 262–3, 297–8.

are senses brings home the importance of understanding anti-individualism as a doctrine about the natures of mental states, not the natures of mental contents or senses. It is natural, and I think correct, to regard at least empirical mental contents (and where these are associated with linguistic expressions, senses) as *constitutively* type-identifying individuals' conceptual abilities. The very content of basic empirical cognitive modes of presentation depends on perceptual capacities of individuals in time. Regardless of this ontological issue about the nature of thought contents, Frege regarded the *understanding of* and *thinking with* such contents as constitutively dependent on relations between individuals and a subject matter, including temporal subject matters. Despite his extreme Platonism about the nature of thought components (which senses *are*—see note 38), Frege was an anti-individualist. Anti-individualism concerns the natures of mental states, not the natures of mental contents. The natures of mental contents themselves is a further matter.

Second, Frege's anti-individualism about mathematical thought provides one source for broadening anti-individualism beyond the focus on *empirical* thought that marked the initial modern development of anti-individualism. Anti-individualism is not to be understood as confined to contingencies of twin-earth thought experiments. The fundamental idea is that the natures of mental states are constitutively determined by their relations to a wider reality, the subject matter of the individual's thought. Frege shows one way in which anti-individualism regarding logical and mathematical thought can be supported, without arguing that differences in mental states depend on possible differences in contingent subject matters. Features of minds can be explained in terms of *necessary* features of a mind-independent reality—for example, logical or mathematical reality.[59]

10.7 Rationalism

Frege's rationalism was fundamental to his work in philosophy of logic and philosophy of mathematics. He was primarily a theorist of knowledge. He regarded justification or warrant for knowledge of logic and mathematics to be fundamentally independent of sense experience—fundamentally an exercise of reason.[60] Frege took rationalism in these areas to be natural and relatively obvious. But he defended it through devastating criticisms of the best-known types of empiricism in his day—formalism and Millian empiricism.[61]

---

[59] *The Foundations of Arithmetic*, pp. vii–viii and section 105; *The Basic Laws of Arithmetic*, vol. I, Introduction, p. xvi. See 'Frege on Knowing the Foundations' and 'Frege on Sense and Linguistic Meaning' in *Truth, Thought, Reason*.

[60] *The Foundations of Arithmetic*, sections 2–3, 5, 8–11, 64, 90, 105; *The Basic Laws of Arithmetic*, vol. I, p. 253 in the original; vol. II, section 60. See also 'Frege on Knowing the Foundations' and 'Frege on Apriority' in *Truth, Thought, Reason*.

[61] *Foundations of Arithmetic*, sections 7–10.

Frege's rationalism contained both traditional and original elements. It was traditional in taking mathematical knowledge to rest fundamentally on a set of axioms that were to be discovered, not stipulated or laid down. Axioms had to be true, fundamental, rationally certain, and self-evident, to *be* axioms. The structure of mathematical knowledge was for him fundamentally the structure of mathematical proof. With such predecessors as Euclid and Leibniz, Frege regarded this structure as a natural one. Thus proofs were taken to be not just any valid derivations. They were derivations that started with the *real* axioms and followed an order that *explained* the truth of the theorems—a natural order.

This way of looking at axioms, proof, and mathematical knowledge came, even in Frege's time, to be regarded as outmoded. Already in the first decade of the twentieth century, Zermelo was arguing for axioms that he did not think of as self-evident. Hilbert's attitudes toward proof and modelling of axiomatic systems were antithetical to regarding mathematical systems as resting on natural, self-evident axioms.[62] In foundation studies, mathematicians were more interested in what could be derived from what than in the springs of mathematical knowledge, or natural, 'correct' starting points for mathematical reasoning. The very idea of a natural, correct starting point began to lose favour in a mathematics less allied to philosophy than it was in the work of Leibniz, Frege, and Russell.[63]

Frege was deeply serious about the idea that self-evidence was not a psychological feature of fundamental mathematical truths. That is, he took 'evidence' for believing a fundamental mathematical truth to reside in the truth itself. The evidence could be fully appreciated through and only through fully understanding the proposition. He thought that an axiom could be self-evident but, because of a mathematician's incomplete understanding, unobvious. Conversely, he thought that a proposition that seemed obvious could be false. Ironically, one of Frege's own proposed logical axioms (the notorious Law V) turned out to be false. He did *not* regard the proposition to be obvious. In fact, he feared—correctly as it turned out—that he did not sufficiently understand it and its implications, even though he took it to be self-evident.[64]

This much of Frege's rationalism was in accord with traditional views. What was original in Frege's rationalism was that he combined these views with a thoroughly original conception of understanding that features the role of inference, as opposed to reflective insight, in understanding, and that incorporates a conception of inference that is informed by his original development of logic. The original conception of understanding is part of what is expressed in the sense-version of his methodological context principle

---

[62] Ernst Zermelo, 'Proof that Every Set Can Be Well-Ordered' (1904) and 'Investigations in the Foundations of Set Theory I' (1908), both reprinted in *From Frege to Gödel*; Hilbert, 'On the Foundations of Logic and Arithmetic' (1904), reprinted in *From Frege to Gödel*.

[63] I have no doubt that freeing mathematical investigation from difficult traditional issues about what principles are epistemically basic was pragmatically liberating for opening a variety of valuable approaches to mathematical logic and foundations studies. But I believe that these traditional issues have not disappeared; nor are they pointless.

[64] See my 'Frege on Extensions of Concepts: From 1884 to 1903'.

(a): only by understanding how a proposition fits into a system of deductive derivations can one fully understand the sense expressed by the proposition. Thus Frege's theory of understanding helped articulate, in his own terms, the practice of Zermelo and others who argued for axioms by discussing their fruitfulness in yielding interesting mathematical consequences. For genuine axioms, he would have regarded the inferences from them as part of understanding them, but not part of the fundamental justification for them.[65]

Frege's rationalism was also original in that it was developed in conjunction with his deep understanding of mathematical practice. His epistemology was rooted in an understanding of actual reasoning in mathematics. Thus his epistemology was in effect a philosophy of mathematical science.[66]

In criticizing Mill's empiricism, Frege articulated a strong pragmatic ground for rejecting the more sophisticated Quinean form of empiricism (developed well after Frege's death). The Quinean form maintains that logic and mathematics are justified exactly inasmuch as they have explanatory roles in *empirical science*. Quine's idea is that mathematics is warranted only through its contributing to empirical explanation.[67] In criticizing Mill, Frege articulated the principle that statements of number are aposteriori or apriori 'according as the general laws on which their proofs depend are so'.[68] The implication is that one should look to the types of justification or warrant used *in mathematical science* to decide the nature of mathematical warrant or justification.

Quine's empiricism imposes an external standard (mathematics' role in empirical science) as the sole determiner of the epistemic status of mathematical principles. Quine imposed this standard without offering any criticism of the epistemic methods actually employed within mathematics. Such an empiricist philosophy appears dogmatic and poorly connected to scientific method. In fact, Frege's implicit criticism of Quinean empiricism is analogous to his use of his context principles in ontology. In both cases, Frege points out that philosophy—whether epistemology or ontology—is stronger when it looks for guidance to the substance and practice of science, rather than imposing 'principles' that are not grounded in well-established cognitive procedures. This is not to say that a science is beyond criticism from the outside. It is rather to say that to be credible, any such criticism must find an epistemic basis that is at least as strong as the epistemic basis of the science being criticized. Quine's empiricism does not meet this standard.

Frege's rationalism is another aspect of his work that was neglected or laid aside for much of the twentieth century. Just as Russell shared Frege's interest in the cognitive

---

[65] See 'Frege on Sense and Linguistic Meaning', in *Truth, Thought, Reason*, especially pp. 262–3, and 'Frege on Knowing the Foundation', in *Truth, Thought, Reason*, especially pp. 297–8.

[66] For further discussion of how Frege's rationalism relates to the classical conceptions of Kant and Leibniz, see 'Frege on Apriority', in *Truth, Thought, Reason*.

[67] Quine, *Word and Object*, chapter 1; W. V. Quine and J. S. Ullian, *The Web of Belief* (New York: Random House, 1970).

[68] *The Foundations of Arithmetic*, section 7.

and epistemic aspects of language use, so he shared his rationalism.[69] But after Russell's early work, rationalism fell into disfavor or neglect. The logical positivists were aggressively empiricist. Austin and Strawson took philosophical analysis to be recovering a largely empirical wisdom embedded in common sense conceptions.[70] Neither British philosopher had much to say about mathematics. Although Quine rejected the empiricism of logical positivism, he replaced it with his own version (see note 67). Except for Quine's empiricism and the empiricism of Sellars, which is even less oriented to discussion of mathematical practice,[71] after the mid-twentieth century, epistemology receded to being a specialized sub-field, rather than one of philosophy's driving sources. For all these reasons, Frege's rationalism came to be seen as mistaken, or at best old-fashioned and irrelevant, to contemporary philosophical concerns.

With gradual loosening of the stranglehold that empiricism maintained on philosophy through much of the twentieth century, Frege's rationalism is being rediscovered as a valuable resource. His combination of pragmatism and contextualism with a recognition of the deep difference between methods of coming to know in mathematics and logic, on one hand, and empirical science, on the other, provides materials for better understanding the nature and place of apriori knowledge. It remains to be seen how this rediscovered strength in Frege's work will fructify contemporary philosophy.

[69] Russell, 'On Our Knowledge of General Principles', in *The Problems of Philosophy*.

[70] J. L. Austin, 'A Plea for Excuses', in *Philosophical Papers*, ed. J. O. Urmson and G. J. Warnock (Oxford: Oxford University Press, 1961); Strawson, *Individuals*, chapter 1; *The Bounds of Sense* (1966) (London: Routledge, 1989), e.g. p. 42.

[71] W. S. Sellars, 'Is There a Synthetic *A Priori?*' in *Science, Perception, and Reality* (London: Routledge, 1963).

CHAPTER 11

RUSSELL AND MOORE'S REVOLT AGAINST BRITISH IDEALISM

NICHOLAS GRIFFIN

11.1 BRITISH NEO-HEGELIANISM

During the last quarter of the nineteenth century British philosophy was dominated by a kind of idealism which owed its original inspiration to Hegel. Though the British turn towards Hegel had begun in 1865 with the publication of J. H. Stirling's *The Secret of Hegel* (Stirling 1865), what came to be known as neo-Hegelianism did not emerge clearly as a movement until 1883, when the publication of *Essays in Philosophical Criticism* (Seth and Haldane 1883) provided it with a manifesto centred loosely around the ideas that had been promulgated at Oxford by T. H. Green, to whom the *Essays* were dedicated. After Green's early death in 1882, leadership of the movement passed to F. H. Bradley. With three books, *Ethical Studies* (1876), *The Principles of Logic* (1883), and *Appearance and Reality* (1893), each more influential than its predecessor, Bradley established himself as the most important philosopher working in Britain at the end of the nineteenth century.

As its title suggests, *Appearance and Reality* is divided into two parts. The first seeks to show, via a series of *reductio ad absurdum* arguments, that most of what we ordinarily take to be real—space and time, the self, matter, motion, change, causation—is in fact mere appearance. This task is accomplished swiftly because much of Bradley's case depends upon a series of prior and now famous *reductio* arguments purporting to show that the fundamental concept of a relation is incoherent. Once this is established to Bradley's satisfaction, he has little trouble showing that all the concepts under attack depend in essential ways on relations and thus share the incoherence of the latter. The second part of the book is concerned with reality, or the Absolute. Although it is much longer than the first, there is actually much less to say, and most of that is negative. The Absolute, more or less, is whatever cannot be dismissed as mere appearance. Since relations belong to appearance, it follows that the Absolute is relationless, a single, indivisible whole. But since thought is inherently relational, any attempt to capture the nature of the Absolute by thought distorts and falsifies it: no thought of the Absolute is simply and exactly true. Little wonder, then, that *Appearance and Reality*, often thought of by those unfamiliar with it as the high-water mark of British metaphysical speculation, was seen by Bradley himself as a 'sceptical study of first principles' (Bradley 1893, p. xii).

Not all neo-Hegelians were content to follow Bradley to this rather bleak conclusion. The most significant metaphysical division among the neo-Hegelians was between the absolute idealists, who (like Bradley) maintained the monistic doctrine that the Absolute was a single indivisible spirit, and the personal idealists, who held that it consisted of a plurality of interrelated spirits, a form of monadism. Since Bradley's scepticism was predicated upon his monism, the personal idealists were under no compulsion to take his scepticism seriously.[1] The most important of the personal idealists was the Cambridge philosopher, J. M. E. McTaggart, who was beginning his philosophical career at the time Bradley's was approaching its peak. In the year that *Appearance and Reality* was published, McTaggart produced his first philosophical work, a small, privately printed pamphlet called 'A Further Determination of the Absolute' (McTaggart 1893a). In it he outlined a three-part programme for neo-Hegelianism. The first task was to refute naturalism, and the second was to establish that only spirit, the Absolute, was real. McTaggart maintained that these tasks had already been accomplished.[2] The third part of the programme, however, remained—to determine the nature of the Absolute. McTaggart, unlike Bradley, was optimistic that this could be done and, with rare singleness of purpose, devoted his entire career to the task: his magnum opus, *The Nature of Existence* (1921) remained incomplete at his death. It is, as Passmore (1957, p. 77) said, 'almost unique in English philosophy... in attempting to work out a deductive metaphysics, which deduces its conclusions rigorously from indubitable first principles'.

11.2 RUSSELL AND NEO-HEGELIANISM[3]

Russell's early philosophical development recapitulated that of the neo-Hegelian movement itself, at least as McTaggart presented it, and McTaggart himself, though

---

[1] In fact, not even all the absolute idealists followed Bradley in this respect. Bosanquet, for example, whose work was in most respects closely linked to Bradley's, differed from him on this point. In the terms in which they framed the debate, Bosanquet maintained that thought was identical to reality, Bradley that it was not. See, for example, Bosanquet 1885a, 1885b.

[2] Bradley tended to get most of the credit for these two achievements, but some belongs to T. H. Green, who, as co-editor of the main nineteenth-century edition of Hume's philosophical works, had demolished Hume's empiricism in a long and unrelentingly critical introduction—few philosophers have ever been so ferociously assailed by their editor. Green argued that Hume, by fearlessly deducing the consequences of his empirical premises, had produced a *reductio ad absurdum* of empiricism—a view that Russell, for all his later differences with Green, essentially shared (*HWP*, p. 685).

[3] The material in this section is treated at much greater length in Griffin 1991.

he was never Russell's teacher, was instrumental in getting Russell to take the first step. When Russell went up to Cambridge in 1890, his philosophical views were derived largely from J. S. Mill—although, even then, he could not bring himself to accept Mill's inductive account of mathematics (MMD, p. 8).[4] At that time McTaggart was the dominant figure in the Cambridge Apostles, the secret debating society to which Russell was elected early in 1892,[5] and it was there that Russell was first exposed to neo-Hegelianism.[6] McTaggart quickly persuaded Russell that empiricism was crude and old-fashioned (*MPD*, p. 38), but it took quite a bit longer for him to take the second step and accept the existence of the Absolute. Though Russell gives the impression that McTaggart was the chief influence here as well, it was G. F. Stout's classes on the history of philosophy in the spring of 1894 that actually provided him with an argument for the existence of the Absolute, at which point Russell regarded himself as a neo-Hegelian (cf. Spadoni 1976). What remained to be done thereafter was the further determination of the Absolute.

Russell, unlike McTaggart, did not propose to tackle the Absolute head-on, deducing its nature from metaphysical first principles. Nor was he content with Bradley's negative dialectics. Unusually for a neo-Hegelian, Russell began with particular scientific theories. Throughout his entire career he held that the special sciences were the most reliable source of knowledge, and thus the appropriate starting point for any metaphysics. Metaphysical principles and, even worse, common sense (the metaphysics of the stone age, in Russell's view) were, respectively, too remote from the empirical data and too dependent upon human prejudice to be reliable, while hard empirical data on its own was too fragmentary to yield much information about the world so that a thoroughgoing empiricism would result in the sterile scepticism which, on Green's account, had engulfed Hume.

Russell's plans—sometimes called the Tiergarten Programme (Griffin 1988) because they were first formulated in the Tiergarten in Berlin in the spring of 1895—were nothing if not ambitious. He intended to re-do Hegel's encyclopaedia of the sciences, complete with dialectical supersessions from science to science, and culminating in a metaphysical science of the Absolute, but this time getting the science right. Each special science, Russell held, tackled the Absolute from its own vantage point, applying a limited number of concepts to treat particular aspects of the Absolute in abstraction

---

[4] Works by Russell and Moore are cited by means of acronyms, a list of which is given at the end of the chapter.

[5] For more on the Cambridge Apostles during this period see Levy 1979. For their influence on Russell, see Griffin 1991, pp. 45–61.

[6] Russell studied mathematics for his first three years as an undergraduate at Cambridge, switching to philosophy for his final year (1893/4). He chose mathematics with a philosophical agenda in mind—he sought certainty in knowledge and thought to find it, if anywhere, in mathematics. But the mathematics syllabus at Cambridge was hardly suited to inquiries of this kind: it left no time for topics not on the exam syllabus and shunned even the degree of rigour that had become commonplace in nineteenth-century mathematics as taught elsewhere. The proofs offered for theorems were, Russell said, 'an insult to the logical intelligence' (*MPD*, p. 38). It was with relief that he switched to philosophy in 1893. For further details on Russell's mathematical education see Lewis and Griffin 1990 and Griffin 1991, pp. 16–25.

from the rest.[7] But abstraction, as Bradley repeatedly emphasized, was always false abstraction: that things were thus-and-so under conditions of abstraction provided no ground for thinking that they were thus-and-so when those conditions were removed.[8] 'I accepted', Russell wrote, 'the Hegelian view that none of the sciences is quite true, since all depend upon some abstraction, and every abstraction leads, sooner or later, to contradictions' (*MPD*, p. 42). Bradley himself found little of philosophical interest in scientific abstractions, but for Russell they were the key to the Absolute. Although the inspiration for Russell's programme was broadly Hegelian, the methods he used to carry it out were Kantian. The special sciences were to be analysed by a series of transcendental arguments designed both to identify the principles which made the science possible and the principles which were necessary for experience of the subject matter with which the science dealt. If all went to plan, the two sets of principles should be identical, though, as I have argued elsewhere (Griffin 2003b, pp. 92–4), Russell had little reason to suppose that this would invariably be the case.

But this analysis of the special sciences was only part of the Tiergarten Programme. The main task of philosophy (in particular, of metaphysics) was to amalgamate the individual sciences into a single comprehensive system of the world (EPI, p. 121). This was to be achieved by adding to each science concepts dealing with aspects of the world which had been abstracted out in order to create the original science. In the process, a new, broader science would be created, one which did better justice to the complexity of the Absolute. Russell started with geometry because he was already working on it for his Trinity Fellowship dissertation at the time he formulated the Tiergarten Programme, and, not surprisingly, it is in connection with geometry, the only science for which he completed a neo-Hegelian treatment, that he explains his project most fully:

> [W]e abstract the spatial qualities of things, not only from all other qualities, but also from the things themselves, leaving, as the matter of our Science, a subject totally devoid of what may be called Thinghood... The set of relations among things, which in presentation are distinguished as spatial, are abstracted from the things and set in a continuum, called space, whose only function is to allow the creation, *ad lib.*, of these relations. (OSG, pp. 93–4)

Such abstraction, though legitimate, is ultimately falsifying:

> Of course such an abstraction cannot give us metaphysical truth—we know, all the while, that space would be meaningless if there were not things from which to abstract it—still, as the subject of a special Science, the abstraction is as legitimate as any other. (OSG, p. 93)

---

[7] '[E]very Science may be regarded as an attempt to construct a universe out of none but its own ideas' (NLS, p. 5).

[8] 'Every science deals necessarily with abstractions: its results must therefore be partial and one-sided expressions of truth' (EPI, p. 121).

To remove the falsification inherent in geometry, it is necessary to make a transition to physics, which reintroduces those 'things' from which spatial relations are abstracted. Russell also mentions the need for a subsequent transition from physics to psychology, for physics abstracts matter from perception, even though matter 'wholly apart from perception is an absurdity' (OSG, p. 94). Only when metaphysics is reached does this process stop. Metaphysics alone constitutes 'independent and self-subsistent knowledge' (NLS, p. 5).

It is not clear from this why Russell thought that abstraction would lead to contradiction, rather than to mere incompleteness, and thus why the transition from one science to another would be dialectical. As we shall see, this was more than mere lip-service to Hegel. To understand it, we have to understand the individual contradictions which infested the special sciences. They are, at first sight, a rather heterogeneous collection. Some of them are quite familiar from elsewhere: for example, a batch of antinomies in geometry arising from the continuity of space whose antecedents go back to Zeno. Though these would be important for Russell's work in the philosophy of mathematics after he abandoned neo-Hegelianism (see OKEW), they were not of special importance for his work as a neo-Hegelian. More relevant was a much more unlikely type of antinomy which he came to call 'the contradiction of relativity' (AMR, p. 166) and of which he found at least one exemplar in each of the sciences he considered.

The first and simplest example of the contradiction of relativity is 'the antinomy of the point': all points are identical, yet each is distinct. Geometry presupposed the existence of abstract points as the required relata of spatial relations. These points are all intrinsically exactly alike, yet each is distinct from all the others (EFG, p. 189). It is easy to see how this results from the abstraction by which the concept of a spatial point was arrived at, but less easy to see why Russell regards it as a contradiction. All it means, surely, is that each point is numerically distinct from, though exactly similar to, all the others; that they are differentiated by their differing relations. In fact, there are reasons, deeply bound up with Russell's neo-Hegelianism, which prevented him from viewing it in this way, and I shall come back to them shortly.

Further examples emerged from Russell's work on arithmetic in 1897. At that time, he thought of arithmetic (as was then common) as the science of continuous and discrete quantity. He treated numbers as ratios: in the case of discrete quantity (counting), they give the ratio between the class being counted and a single element of it; in the case of continuous quantity (measurement) they give the ratio between the quantity to be measured and an arbitrarily chosen unit (RNQ, pp. 70–82). In arithmetic an antinomy exactly analogous to the antinomy of the point arises because, in counting, the differences between the members of the class being counted are ignored—each element, arithmetically, is exactly like any other, yet each is distinct. Similarly with units in the case of measurement: each unit-quantity differs from all others, but all are qualitatively exactly alike. Russell stated the antinomy of quantity with a certain Hegelian panache: between two quantities there is a conception of difference, but no difference of conception (VN, p. 24; RNQ, p. 81). What he means is that we have a conception of the difference between the two quantities, i.e. we conceive of them as being distinct; but exactly the same conceptions apply to both, so there is no difference of conception. This became the basis for Russell's general formulation of the contradiction of relativity; namely, 'the contradiction of a difference between two terms, without a difference in the conceptions applicable to them' (AMR, p. 166).

Russell dealt with the antinomy of the point by a transition from geometry to kinematics. Following Boscovich (1758), he adopted a theory of unextended, *kinematic* point-atoms, and individuated spatial points by reference to the atoms which occupied them (*EFG*, pp. 190–2). The trouble was that point-atoms merely reproduce the problems of geometrical points, with kinematic relations replacing spatial ones. There was nothing intrinsic to a point-atom, any more than to a spatial point, to distinguish it from any other—another example of the contradiction of relativity. To solve this problem, Russell introduced forces as properties of point-atoms, thereby transiting to dynamics. Forces introduced not only causal relations into physics, but also, in Russell's view, 'active principles' and even 'self-assertion' (VN, p. 12), features which already hint at the idealistic monadology towards which he was tending. But, once more, the contradiction of relativity re-emerged, in the form of what Russell called the 'essential relativity of force'. Dynamical atoms can be distinguished in principle by their causal powers, but these powers can be exhibited only by their effects, and their effects consist in the relative motions of matter (VN, pp. 18–19). Matter was introduced in order to resolve the problems of the relativity of space, but it seems now as if absolute space is required in order to resolve the problems of the relativity of matter.

In itself, this was no cause for alarm: Russell was, after all, an idealist and did not expect a purely material world to pass muster metaphysically. His solution to the problem of the relativity of force was to turn point-atoms into monads, thereby transiting to psychology in the hope that the mental states of monads might provide the intrinsic properties needed to ground the whole system. However strange it may seem, this is no more than Russell taking his idealism seriously and expecting the spirits which form the ultimate basis of reality actually to do some explanatory work. Few idealists took the courage of their convictions quite this far. Russell obviously faced enormous problems in extracting the necessary physics from the psychology of monads. He had, in fact, no clear idea of how this was to be done, and left only a few fragmentary speculations on the topic (*CPBR2*, pp. 12, 16, 34). But, more fundamentally, he still had no real guarantee that the mental states of monads would be any less relative than the forces of atoms. Indeed, the best psychological theories of the day gave grounds for thinking that they would not. Act-object psychology, which dominated psychological thought at Cambridge, embraced Brentano's intentionality thesis: that what distinguished mental states from others was that they were directed towards an object.[9] If this was correct, then mental states were by their nature relational and Russell's dialectic of the sciences was doomed.

---

[9] Act-object psychology began with Brentano 1874; the best-known statement of the intentionality thesis is at p. 88. In Britain, its two most important proponents were Russell's teachers, James Ward and G. F. Stout. Cf. Ward 1886 and Stout 1896. Stout's contributions to this development and his influence on Russell and Moore (especially the latter) are examined in van der Schaar 1996, Bell 1999, and Preti 2008.

Within the framework of Russell's dialectic, the only way out was to return to Bradley's monism. The need was to find an item which did not depend for its identity on relations to other items and could be individuated by means of its own intrinsic features alone, and Bradley's Absolute filled the bill admirably. Bradley's Absolute, if anything, could stand on its own feet as independently real, because there was nothing else for it to depend on. The progress of Russell's dialectic from arithmetic to psychology had equipped the items under consideration with progressively richer sets of properties, in the hope of reaching items that were independently real. Bradley's Absolute had *all* the properties which had been abstracted away in the first place; it was both unique and all-encompassing. The contradiction of relativity is thus eliminated: there is no conception of difference. The trouble is, according to Russell and many other neo-Hegelians including Bradley himself, the conception of difference is essential for thought, without it thought is confined to the realm of appearance. Russell's explorations had led him to the conclusion that the only way to be a consistent neo-Hegelian was to embrace a strict monism, as Bradley had done. But this rendered the Absolute unthinkable, a form of scepticism so thoroughgoing as to constitute a *reductio* of the position.

By 1898, therefore, Russell's dialectic had reached an impasse. One of the remarkable things about it was the precision with which Russell located the contradiction of relativity as the fundamental problem of the entire system and the exactness with which he formulated it. But once he had got the contradiction in sharp focus it did not take him long to realize it could be solved only by abandoning neo-Hegelianism. This move, he said, was the one real revolution in his thought: 'so great a revolution as to make my previous work, except such as was purely mathematical, irrelevant to everything I did later.... [S]ubsequent changes have been of the nature of an evolution' (*MPD*, p. 11). The conceptual origins of this revolution came, oddly enough, from his early work on projective geometry in *An Essay on the Foundations of Geometry*.

Russell had thought that arithmetic was the science of quantity. But he never shared the widespread view that mathematics as a whole was to be so defined, because he acknowledged that projective geometry was a branch of mathematics in which the concept of quantity did not figure at all: it was a purely qualitative science, logically presupposed by any quantitative science. In Russell's analysis of projective geometry, the central concept was an harmonic (or cross) ratio, a device by means of which numerical coordinates can be introduced into projective space. The concept was important for the development of Russell's philosophy because it drew his attention to the concept of order, so that by 1898 he had come to think that order was the fundamental concept in mathematics.[10] Though Russell was still more than two years away from embracing logicism, his mature

---

[10] Despite this, even five years later in *POM*, quantity precedes order in the presentation; though, as Russell makes clear, this is only for ease of exposition. 'Quantity', he writes, 'has lost the mathematical importance which it used to possess, owing to the fact that most theorems concerning it can be generalized so as to become theorems concerning order. It would therefore be natural to discuss order before quantity... [though] I shall follow the more traditional course, and consider quantity first' (*POM*, p. 158).

philosophy of mathematics, this move was an important step in the right direction, for order was a concept eminently amenable to a purely logical analysis in terms of relations. As order was the key to mathematics, so relations were the key to order. By 1898 Russell had come up with what is essentially the modern formal classification of relations as reflexive, symmetrical, and transitive—though he did not use these terms in quite the modern way (VN, pp. 26–7; COR, pp. 138–9).[11] Equally important, Russell had discovered that order depended upon asymmetrical relations (NOO, p. 353).

This work on relations was an essential preliminary to solving the contradiction of relativity. But, so far, we have still not seen why this was a genuine contradiction. The reason is to be found in the neo-Hegelian doctrine of relations which, up to 1898, had been an unexamined part of Russell's philosophy. Central to neo-Hegelianism of all kinds was the doctrine that relations, insofar as they are admissible at all, are internal; that is, they are 'grounded' (to use the vague but then-fashionable phrase) upon the qualities of their terms.[12] Different relations require different intrinsic qualities in their terms,[13] and asymmetrical relations require different qualities in each term. These three theses—(i) that relations are grounded on intrinsic qualities; (ii) that different relations are grounded on different qualities; (iii) that an asymmetrical relation is grounded on different qualities in each term—constitute Russell's doctrine of internal relations. Effectively, relations supervene upon qualities, though Russell, of course, did not state it thus. It is this doctrine that makes the contradiction of relativity a genuine contradiction. For if different points, for example, are to be distinguished by their relations, they must have different relations, and thus (by (ii)) must have different qualities. But all points have the same qualities.

In 'An Analysis of Mathematical Reasoning' Russell first explains the point using the relation of cause and effect as an example:

> To be a cause is not, so far as can be discovered, an adjective [quality] of a thing *per se*: nothing can be discovered by analysis which will reveal, apart from the relation of causality, a conceptual difference between what can be a cause and what can be an effect... Thus the relation of causality gives a conception of difference—namely the difference of cause and effect—without giving, apart from this conception of difference, any difference of conception. (AMR, p. 224)

---

[11] I shall use the words in their modern sense here. The respects in which Russell's usage differed make little difference at the level of generality at which the present discussion is conducted. For more detail (though, in some respects, still not enough), see Griffin 1991, pp. 331–4.

[12] In fact Russell (AMR, p. 224; *POM*, p. 221) distinguishes two versions of the doctrine of internal relations—a monadistic theory (stated above) and a monistic theory (in which the relations are grounded on the qualities of the whole comprised of their terms). Because Russell's neo-Hegelian system was a monadology only the first of these theories concerns us here. Russell refutes both theories in *POM*. Subsequent scholars (e.g. Watling 1970, pp. 40–1; Sprigge 1979, pp. 151–9) have questioned whether Russell's refutation applies to Bradley's theory. In Griffin 1998a I argue that it does.

[13] Russell did not explicitly state this thesis, no doubt thinking it too obvious to need stating. If two different relations could be grounded on exactly the same qualities, then the qualities (or the grounding) would seem to serve no explanatory purpose.

But causality is an asymmetrical relation and therefore each causal relation must (by (iii)) be grounded on the different qualities of its two terms; so there must, after all, be a difference of conception between the terms. Russell then goes on to provide a general argument that *all* relations which are grounded on different qualities in the two terms, a class which includes all asymmetrical relations, produce such a contradiction (AMR, pp. 225–6). The argument concludes:

> Thus we have a difference without a point of difference, or, in the old formula, a conception of difference without a difference of conception. This contradiction belongs, therefore, to all relations of our fourth type [asymmetrical relations]; and relations of this type pervade almost the whole of Mathematics, since they are involved in number, in order, in quantity, and in space and time. The fundamental importance of this contradiction for Mathematics is thus at once proved and accounted for. (AMR, p. 225)

The contradiction of relativity, therefore, is a direct consequence of Russell's neo-Hegelian theory of relations. It pervades mathematics because the type of relation which gives rise to it is the type on which the concept of order depends, and the concept of order is the fundamental concept of mathematics.

Ironically the passage I've just referred to survives only because Russell transferred the page on which it occurs from the typescript of 'An Analysis of Mathematical Reasoning' (most of which has been lost) into an early draft of *The Principles of Mathematics*, which Russell started in 1899 and subsequently preserved. Now, in the draft of the *Principles* there is no trace of the contradiction of relativity nor of the dialectic of the sciences. As one would expect from the published book, the draft is a thoroughly, even aggressively, anti-Hegelian work.

What happened was this: Russell simply changed the argument from *modus ponens* to *modus tollens*. Instead of arguing, as he did in 'An Analysis of Mathematical Reasoning', from the doctrine of internal relations to the contradiction of relativity, in the 1899–1900 draft of the *Principles* he used the fact that it entails the contradiction of relativity as a *reductio* argument against the doctrine of internal relations. No doubt with well-justified pride in his own cleverness, he preserved the wording of the argument intact through the transition, and deleted merely the concluding sentence. In its place, he started the next paragraph with the sentence: 'We cannot hope, therefore, so long as we adhere to the view that no relation can be "purely external", to obtain anything like a satisfactory philosophy of mathematics' (POM/D, p. 93). In what amounts to a Gestalt shift, Russell saw that his previous problems depended upon his neo-Hegelian theory of internal relations, rejected this theory, and thereby ceased to be a neo-Hegelian.

Michael Dummett (1993) notoriously proposed that analytic philosophy began with Frege's writing § 62 of the *Grundlagen* (Frege 1884), in which Frege switches his immediate attention from the numbers themselves to sentences in which number words occur, thereby taking what Dummett sees as a decisive 'linguistic turn'. I find it hard to take seriously the claim that something like analytic philosophy had a precise moment of conception,[14] but if one had to propose such an event I think Russell's *volte-face* on internal relations late in 1898 has a much better claim. It was, for one thing, a far more self-conscious rejection of previous ideas than Frege's supposed linguistic turn, and it was a turn about which Russell (unlike Frege) expressed no subsequent misgivings.

11.3 MOORE AS A NEO-HEGELIAN

Moore went up to Cambridge two years after Russell, in 1892, to study classics. Unlike Russell, he had no prior philosophical agenda; indeed he said, doubtless with some hyperbole, that when he went up he had 'hardly known that there was such a subject as philosophy' (A, p. 13). Nor did he feel the sort of antipathy for classics at Cambridge that Russell came to feel for mathematics: he seemed content with his course of study, 'learning more of the same kind of things' (p. 12) that he had learnt in school and 'look[ing] forward with pleasure' to a career 'teaching Classics to the Sixth Form of some Public School' (A, p. 13). Like Russell, however, he switched to philosophy for Part II of his Tripos. Russell, who had recognized Moore's philosophical ability at meetings of the Apostles, was an important influence in this decision. Moore's approach to philosophy was markedly different from Russell's. Russell, as we've seen, found the sciences bristling with philosophical problems. Moore, by contrast, did not find philosophical problems ready to hand: 'I do not think', he said, 'that the world or the sciences would ever have suggested to me any philosophical problems. What has suggested philosophical problems to me is things which other philosophers have said about the world or the sciences' (A, p. 14). He gave as an example McTaggart's view that time is unreal (cf. McTaggart 1893b), which struck him when he first heard it as a 'perfectly monstrous proposition' against which he argued as best he could. It was occasions such as this, he thought, that led Russell to think he had 'some aptitude for philosophy' (A, p. 14).

Despite his 'perfectly monstrous' propositions, it was McTaggart who shaped Moore's earliest philosophical views. Unlike Russell, Moore had McTaggart as a teacher: he took his course on the history of modern philosophy, which included an extended study of Hegel.[15] He was clearly the most influential of Moore's teachers, partly due to the fact that Moore saw a lot of him outside the lecture hall at the Apostles, but also due to his

---

[14] There are many other things wrong with Dummett's account, including his use of the linguistic turn as a demarcation criterion for analytic philosophy. See Monk 1996, 1997; Griffin 1998b.

[15] Most British neo-Hegelians were not much interested in Hegel's own views. McTaggart was an exception: he produced three volumes of Hegelian exegesis (McTaggart 1896, 1901, 1910), though, as C. D. Broad (1967, p. 101) famously said, McTaggart's interpretation of Hegel made orthodox Hegelians blush all over. Russell had taken the same history of philosophy course two years earlier, though on that occasion it was taught by Stout and Hegel wasn't covered. Russell did not read much Hegel until 1897, when he tackled the *Wissenschaft der Logik* on the calculus and was suitably appalled—it was hardly Hegel's finest hour.

intellectual ability. To Moore, he appeared 'immensely clever and immensely quick in argument' (A, p. 18). 'I think what influenced me most', Moore wrote, 'was his constant insistence on clearness—on trying to give a precise meaning to philosophical questions, on asking the question "What does this mean?"' (A, p. 18). At all events, Moore became another of McTaggart's converts to neo-Hegelianism.

For several reasons, it is not easy to make out Moore's position as a neo-Hegelian. First, he did not write very much as a neo-Hegelian and the most extensive piece he did write—his Trinity Fellowship dissertation of 1897[16]—has only recently been published.[17] Since he abandoned neo-Hegelianism the following year, we have, apart from the first dissertation, only two articles and two reviews to go on. Second, Moore never subsequently said very much about the views he held during his brief period as a neo-Hegelian. But thirdly, and perhaps most importantly, Moore's way of doing philosophy makes it difficult to see the big picture. Most of what he published as a neo-Hegelian is taken up with a detailed and very critical exegesis of quite isolated remarks by other philosophers which are indeed very puzzling. While Moore may make it clear what he thinks of the remark in question, that does not necessarily reveal much of his overall philosophical position.

Ironically, it was McTaggart's perfectly monstrous claim that time was unreal that Moore defended in his first publication, a contribution to an Aristotelian Society symposium with Bernard Bosanquet and Shadworth Hodgson on the topic, 'In What Sense, If Any, Do Past and Future Time Exist?' Most of the paper is taken up, in typical Moorean fashion, with detailed criticisms of remarks made by his fellow symposiasts (e.g. criticizing an ambiguity in Bosanquet's use of 'continuity'), not all of which are directly germane to the question at hand. Nonetheless, his conclusion is clear, albeit rather reluctantly drawn:

> If I need...to give a direct answer to our question, I would say that neither Past, Present, nor Future exists, if by existence we are to mean the ascription of full Reality and not merely existence as Appearance. On the other hand I think we may say that there is more Reality in the Present than in Past or Future, because, though it is greatly inferior to them in extent of content, it has that co-ordinate element of immediacy which they entirely lack. Again...I think we may distinguish in this respect between Past and Future. The Past seems to be more real than the Future, because its content is more fully constituent of the Present, whereas the Future could only claim

---

[16] Moore wrote two dissertations, one in 1897 (D97), which failed to win him a Fellowship, and one in 1898 (D98), which was successful. (In those days, it was the exception rather than the rule to win a Fellowship on one's first attempt.) It was in the course of writing the second that Moore came to reject neo-Hegelianism. Nonetheless, the first contains important intimations of his later philosophy. For example, he identifies a 'fallacy involved in all empirical definitions of the good' which is a special case of the naturalistic fallacy presented in PE, pp. 10ff (cf. Baldwin 1990, pp. 3–4).

[17] Both dissertations are now published in EPW but appeared too late for me to be able to consult them for this chapter. For more information about their contents see Miah 1997 and the editors' introduction to EPW. Research in progress by Consuelo Preti, which makes full use of the unpublished materials, will give us a much fuller account of Moore's early philosophical development.

a superiority over the Past, if it could be shown that in it Appearance would become more and more at one with Reality. (T, p. 24)[18]

From the point of view of Moore's subsequent views, however, this conclusion is less interesting than a distinction he draws, in response to Hodgson, 'between the process of thinking and the content of the thought'. 'Because I cannot think without taking some time about it,' Moore says, 'I cannot see it follows that what I think about need also be in time' (T, p. 22). Moore's point is straightforward, clearly put, and hard to deny, but what is worth noting for future reference is the implication that the content of a thought is identical to what the thought is about. This is the first intimation of Moore's and Russell's early direct realist theory of propositions, which was a key part of their rebellion against neo-Hegelianism.

'Freedom', the second paper that Moore published as an idealist, is much more substantial. It was taken from Moore's first Fellowship dissertation. Moore described the first dissertation as 'an attempt to make sense' of Kant's 'extremely mysterious assertions' about freedom. He says that he 'found something which seemed to me at the time to give them an intelligible meaning' (though he subsequently doubted whether it was Kant's intended meaning) and wrote it up in an article in *Mind*. By 1942, he had not looked at the article for many years and had 'no doubt that it was absolutely worthless' (A, p. 21). Once again, the unreality of space and time is central to his position:

According to [Kant] Freedom means not only that each part of Nature is necessarily connected with all the other parts in respect of its form as well as in respect of its existence; but also that all these different forms, considered in themselves, together with their differences and the laws of their connexion, must be taken into account in explaining the world as a whole: and since the world as a whole is an impossible conception, if the objects of experience be taken to be its ultimate constituents, since they are necessarily conceived as in the infinite forms of space and time, the complete reason for all that appears must be placed in a supersensible reality. This supersensible reality is the world as a whole, and is the reason of everything that appears; and, as such, it has Freedom. (F, p. 44)

While appearances are determined, supersensible reality is free. But this, as Moore points out (F, p. 46), applies to 'any natural object whatever' and the question of whether human volition is free in any special sense has still to be addressed. Kant argues that it is because human volition is determined by reason.[19] Moore counters that this depends

---

[18] Moore's argument owes more to Bradley that to McTaggart, who isn't mentioned in the paper. In another paper published the following year Moore says '[T]he arguments by which Mr Bradley had endeavoured to prove the unreality of Time appear to me perfectly conclusive' (F, p. 53). More general debts to Bradley, to whom Moore owes his 'conception of the fundamental problems of metaphysics', are acknowledged in D97 (quoted in Baldwin 1990, p. 3).

[19] I follow Baldwin's formulation here (1990, p. 7). It is both clearer and more concise than either Kant's or Moore's.

upon a crucial ambiguity: either Kant means by 'reason' an abstract reason ('a logical reason', 'a mere conception', 'a universal', F, p. 47) or else he means the presentation of such a reason. While the former transcends the naturalistic realm of appearance, it is utterly implausible to think of the will as determined by reason in that sense. On the other hand, the *presentation* of an abstract reason may well determine the will, but the presentation of the reason (as distinct from the reason itself) is an appearance and thus the determination involved is that of 'natural causality' and 'freedom would be no more than that aspect of every mechanical process' (F, p. 48). Kant's claim that reason determines human volition gets its plausibility from reading 'reason' in the second way; it gets its philosophical significance from reading it in the first way.

Moore's argument here is an adaptation of a powerful line of argument that Bradley had used against associationist psychology. The associationists treated ideas naturalistically as mental occurrences and hoped by means of them to explain logical matters such as judgement and inference. But Bradley maintained that the ideas which might explain judgement and inference ('logical ideas') were altogether different from mere mental occurrences; logical ideas had to be understood non-naturalistically as 'signs of an existence other than themselves' (Bradley 1883, p. 2).[20] This line of argument is especially important for Moore, for he returns to it in his second Fellowship dissertation and there turns it against Bradley himself. The argument was presented in Moore's next paper, 'The Nature of Judgment' (*Mind*, 1899), which was drawn from the successful dissertation of 1898.[21] Moore starts 'The Nature of Judgment' with Bradley's argument against the associationists, but goes on to argue that 'Mr Bradley himself does not remain true to this conception of the logical idea as the idea *of* something' (NJ, p. 59), for he goes on to treat the logical idea, not as that which symbolizes, but as what is symbolized. '[I]n predication', Bradley writes, 'we do not *use* the mental fact, but only the meaning' (1883, p. 8). Rather than treat the idea as a symbol which means something, 'it is better to say, the idea *is* the meaning' (1883, p. 6). Moore comments caustically: 'The question is surely not of which is "better to say", but which is true' (NJ, p. 60). But Moore's objection is not just that Bradley's terminology is muddled, but that his concept of the meaning as 'a part of the content . . . cut off, fixed by the mind, and considered apart from the existence of the sign' which is 'neither given nor presented, but . . . taken' (Bradley 1883, pp. 4, 7) is fundamentally mistaken. 'It will be our endeavour', Moore writes, 'to show, on the contrary, that the "idea used in judgment" is not part of the content of our ideas, nor produced by any action of our minds' (NJ, p. 60). The remainder of his paper undertakes

---

[20] Bradley was not the first to make this distinction; it appears (along with a parallel distinction between propositions as thought and propositions as they are in themselves) in Bolzano 1837, vol. I, §§ 48ff. I do not know if Bradley was aware of Bolzano's work.

[21] D98 included most of its predecessor with the addition of a chapter on Reason. Only fragments of this new chapter remain with the ms of the dissertation; many pages are missing and others exist only in part (having been cut up and parts removed). Moore himself said that the 'substance' of the chapter had been published as 'The Nature of Judgment' (A, p. 22) and detailed textual work by Preti 2008 not only confirms this but suggests that the chapter was not extensively rewritten.

to do just that. It was, Russell said, 'the first published account of the new philosophy' (*MPD*, p. 54).

11.4 THE NEW PHILOSOPHY

The philosophy with which Russell and Moore replaced neo-Hegelianism was a drastic form of direct realism.[22] The first intimation of it comes in a letter from Moore to Desmond MacCarthy: 'I have arrived at a perfectly staggering doctrine.... An existent is nothing but a proposition: nothing *is* but concepts.... I am pleased to believe that this is the most Platonic system of modern times.'[23] At this stage Moore still wanted to keep the Absolute, though he didn't know what to do with it.[24] A month later, immediately after submitting his second dissertation, Moore broke the news to Russell, adding more details:

> a proposition is not to be understood as any thoughts or words, but the concepts + their relation of which we think. It is only propositions in this sense, which can be true, and from which inference can be made. Truth therefore does not depend upon any relation between... concepts and reality, but is an inherent property of the whole formed by certain concepts and their relations... True existential propositions are those in which certain concepts stand in a specific relation to the concept existence; and I see no way of distinguishing such from what are commonly called 'existents'.... Existents are in reality only one kind of proposition. The ultimate elements of everything that is are concepts, and a part of these, when compounded in a special way, form the existent world. With regard to the special method of composition I said nothing. There would need, I think, to be several kinds of ultimate relation between concepts—each, of course, necessary. (11 September 1898)

Russell, though he thought it 'needlessly paradoxical' to say that an existent was a proposition, nonetheless responded enthusiastically on 13 September, saying that he thought the discovery of the several different kinds of relation between concepts was 'the true business of Logic'. He went on to outline his own formal classification of relations which he had developed earlier in the year. By 1 December, however, having just finished reading Moore's dissertation, he was eagerly pressing Moore for further details.

---

[22] Nelson 1967, p. 373 called it absolute realism in contrast to Bradley's absolute idealism, its most salient competitor. The term 'analytic realism' is often used, but this is more generic and applies equally well to Russell's position long after most of the doctrines of 1898–9 had been rejected.

[23] 14 August 1898. I am grateful to Sajahan Miah for bringing this letter to my attention.

[24] Preti, in a personal communication, has suggested that this does not represent a serious commitment to a Bradleian metaphysic so much as to something objective and supersensible to give ethical propositions the right kind of nature.

The philosophy here intimated at appeared in print for the first time in 'The Nature of Judgment' where it received little attention. Even the first generation of historians of analytic philosophy dismissed it as 'bizarre' (Nelson 1967, p. 373) and 'so extraordinary [as to seem] hardly worth...exhuming' (Ayer 1971, p. 190).[25] In 'The Nature of Judgment', Moore uses 'judgment' synonymously with 'proposition' (NJ, p. 63), and uses 'concept' for what Bradley had called a 'universal meaning' (p. 61). Concepts, thus understood, are fundamental to Moore's position both in the sense that they are 'irreducible to anything else' (p. 62) and in the sense that everything is a concept, 'the world [is] formed of concepts' (p. 67). A concept is 'not a mental fact, nor any part of a mental fact' (p. 62), nor is it an abstraction from ideas or things (p. 67), nor is it produced by the mind (p. 60). A proposition 'is composed not of words, nor yet of thoughts, but of concepts' (p. 63); it is 'nothing other than a complex concept' (p. 64).

> The difference between a concept and a proposition, in virtue of which the latter alone can be called true or false, would seem to lie merely in the simplicity of the former.... A proposition is constituted by any number of concepts, together with a specific relation between them; and according to the nature of this relation the proposition may be either true or false. What kind of relation makes a proposition true, what false, cannot be further defined, but must be immediately recognized. (p. 64)

A proposition is 'to be understood, not as anything subjective—an assertion or affirmation of something—but as the combination of concepts which is affirmed' (p. 67). Concepts are 'the only objects of knowledge' (p. 67); they are 'possible objects of thought' though '[i]t is indifferent to their nature whether anybody thinks them or not' (p. 63). This last remark is an implicit rejection of the neo-Hegelian notion of internal relations and, as such, it was attacked at length by Joachim in the first substantial critique of the new philosophy (Joachim 1906, ch. 2). It was also the only one of these early views of Moore's that Russell in old age continued to endorse, as (he thought) Moore did also (*MPD*, p. 54).

None of Moore's doctrines in 'The Nature of Judgment' has occasioned more difficulty for subsequent commentators than his doctrine that judgements (or propositions) are neither mental nor linguistic but are complex combinations of the simple concepts which make up the world. But the difficulty arises because subsequent commentators have anachronistically assumed that Moore (and Russell) were using 'proposition' in the way philosophers (including Moore and Russell) generally used it in the 1920s and after. If we avoid this misreading, and think of propositions circa 1899 as possible combinations of concepts (like Tractarian *Sachverhalten*), the main difficulty disappears,

---

[25] Though Gilbert Ryle, who to his credit devoted a late paper to it, described it as the '*De Interpretatione* of early twentieth-century Cambridge logic' and correctly traced its influence to Wittgenstein's *Tractatus* (Ryle 1970, pp. 89–90).

although a subsidiary difficulty concerning the distinction between true and false propositions remains.[26] The direct realism of Moore's and Russell's early analytic philosophy derives from this account of propositions. In making a judgement the mind grasps a proposition which actually contains the mind-independent concepts themselves about which the judgement is made. It was on account of this direct realism that Russell found the new philosophy so bracing—like escaping from 'a hot-house on to a wind-swept headland' he said (*MPD*, p. 61). Elements of this direct realism remained in Russell's philosophy for the rest of his career, but the sort of face-value direct realism to be found in *The Principles of Mathematics*—where (roughly) every word in a sentence indicated some constituent term in the proposition expressed by the sentence—did not survive the theory of descriptions of 1905.

One other claim from 'The Nature of Judgment' deserves mention, namely Moore's claim that 'A thing becomes intelligible first when it is analysed into its constituent concepts' (NJ, p. 67). This is the only hint Moore gives of a new philosophical method, but it is the method to which the new philosophy—analytic philosophy—owes its name. As practised at this time by Moore and Russell, philosophical analysis is to be understood as analogous to chemical analysis, in which complex substances are broken down into their elementary constituents, though philosophical analysis is, of course, intellectual rather than physical. Moreover, the analysis is, at least in Russell's opinion, always provisional, in the sense that there is (and can be) no guarantee that the products of analysis are genuinely simple and thus incapable of further analysis. This is what Michael Beaney (2002, 2003) has usefully called 'decompositional analysis'. Since complex concepts are propositions, analysis is the analysis of propositions. Russell espoused the same view in print the following year in his book on Leibniz, where his argument begins brashly with the claim: 'That all sound philosophy should begin with an analysis of propositions, is a truth too evident, perhaps, to demand a proof' (*POL*, p. 8).

Moore elaborated these views further, with some modification, in two subsequent papers: 'Necessity', and 'Identity', as well as in a series of short entries in Baldwin's *Dictionary of Philosophy* (Baldwin 1902). Though these early writings have received relatively little attention,[27] the philosophy they propound, at least in broad outline, underlies Moore's best-known work, *Principia Ethica* (1903). At the time that Moore was writing his second dissertation, Russell was writing 'An Analysis of Mathematical Reasoning' and starting to come to very similar conclusions. In Russell's case, however, the theory was worked out in considerably more detail and went through a number of rapid changes in successive works—the unpublished *Fundamental Ideas and Axioms of Mathematics* (1899), an unpublished draft of *The Principles of Mathematics* (1899–1900),

---

[26]   Russell offered some awkward reflections on it (*POM*, pp. 48–9; MTCA, pp. 472–4). There is no space to examine it here, but, as Moore's comments above indicate, the correspondence theory of truth must be rejected in favour of an identity theory (cf. Baldwin 1990, pp. 43, 55–6; Baldwin 1991).

[27]   The best commentary to date is Baldwin 1990, chs. 1 and 2. But see also Hochberg 1962, 1969a, 1969b, 1978, ch. 4; Nelson 1962; Ryle 1970; Pettit 1973; Bradford 1981; O'Connor 1982, ch. 2; Hylton 1990, pp. 117–52; Cartwright 2003.

and the important book on Leibniz (1900), as well as many shorter writings—before it emerged in the form which is (more or less) familiar in *The Principles of Mathematics* (1903). The detailed study of this development is still rather patchy[28] and there is no space here to elaborate on it here, but at least one point is worth making.

Russell is much more interested in the details of the new theory—especially logical details—than Moore. Moore's 'The Nature of Judgment' offers a sketch of a theory rather than the theory itself. By contrast, in all Russell's major works in the 1898–1903 period (with the arguable exception of his book on Leibniz) it is obvious that, whatever gaps and inconsistencies there may be (and there are serious gaps even in the published version of the *Principles*), Russell has at least the makings of an elaborate theory to propound. Each work was a serious attempt to do philosophy without promissory notes. In this, Russell was certainly influenced by practices in the sciences, and in particular by the newly rigorous practices in nineteenth-century mathematics. Thus, while Moore went only so far as to say that propositions must be complexes of concepts united by a relation, Russell, even in 1898, was already identifying different types of proposition, the different types of term (the word Russell used in preference to Moore's 'concept') which made them up, and (most important) the different types of relation which related them. In all these respects, Russell sought precise criteria to differentiate the different categories of item.[29] For example, he gives a formal characterization of a term as whatever is capable of being a logical subject, an account which remains constant from AMR (p. 167) to *POM* (p. 43). In addition, Russell drew a distinction, important for his mathematical concerns, between complexes the constituent terms of which were united by a relation (propositions) and complexes where the constituent terms were not related (e.g. classes, called 'aggregates' in AMR). It is obvious that Russell's elaboration of the new philosophy is driven by his primary concern, which was to find a philosophically satisfactory account of mathematics. As this account edged slowly towards logicism, a position he did not finally adopt until 1901 (cf. LOR), it was inevitable that he needed to go more deeply into logical matters than did Moore, whose main concern from 1897 to 1903 was with ethics. In fact, it is somewhat surprising that Moore went as far into logic as he did. But, given how much of the logical development was due to Russell rather than to Moore, it is even more surprising that Russell, for several years, continued to think of it as 'Moore's logic'.[30] This connects to a number of historical puzzles about Russell and Moore's rebellion against neo-Hegelianism, which I take up in the next section.

---

[28] But see Rodriguez-Consuegra 1991. Hylton 1990, pp. 152–66 deals with *POL*, and Griffin 1991, ch. 7 with AMR.

[29] It would be slightly anachronistic to describe this as 'defining' the items in question, for Russell held that philosophical definition was actually philosophical analysis and thus only possible if the *definiendum* was complex. Russell did, however, recognize what he called 'mathematical definition' in which a simple term might be identified by its relations to other terms (AOG, p. 410; *POM*, p. 27).

[30] See, for example, BR letter to Moore, 1 December 1898; to Louis Couturat, 2 July 1899 (*SLBR1*, pp. 191; 194–5). On 11 February 1904 he told Bradley that he planned, when he had completed the work which became *Principia Mathematica*, 'to attempt something on the more purely philosophical side of Logic', but that, hitherto, he had put this off in the hope that Moore would do it 'better than I could' (*SLBR1*, p. 274).

11.5 RUSSELL AND MOORE

From what has just been said about their relative contributions to the new philosophy, Russell's acknowledgements to Moore must seem excessive. He says that he was led to his new views 'largely under Moore's guidance' (*Auto.* vol. I, p. 135) and that 'Moore led the way, and I followed closely in his footsteps' (*MPD*, p. 54). Moore's account was characteristically more modest, though not necessarily inconsistent with this: 'I do not know that Russell has ever owed to me anything except mistakes' (A, p. 15). Russell expanded on his indebtedness in *The Principles of Mathematics*:

> On fundamental questions of philosophy, my position, in all its chief features, is derived from Mr. G. E. Moore. I have accepted from him the non-existential nature of propositions (except such as happen to assert existence) and their independence of any knowing mind; also the pluralism which regards the world, both that of existents and that of entities, as composed of an infinite number of mutually independent entities, with relations which are ultimate, and not reducible to adjectives of their terms or of the whole which these compose. Before learning these views from him, I found myself completely unable to construct any philosophy of arithmetic, whereas their acceptance brought about an immediate liberation from a large number of difficulties which I believe to be otherwise insuperable. (*POM*, p. xviii)

Russell may have got these views from Moore, but he didn't get them from reading Moore's second dissertation, for they are already to be found (in broad outline, at any rate) in AMR which was finished in July 1898, and Russell did not read Moore's dissertation until the following November. In fact, Russell had finished AMR well before Moore finished his dissertation,[31] so while Moore was the first to publish the new philosophy, Russell was the first to get it down on paper. If it were not for Russell's acknowledgement of Moore's priority, the surviving documentary record would suggest that it was Russell who led and Moore who followed.

Moore's influence on Russell took place mainly through meetings.[32] Three relevant meetings are recorded, there may have been others. The first occurred on 11 March 1898, just before Russell started to write AMR, when Russell read a paper which led to a long debate with Moore about existence.[33] Unless there were some other source now

---

[31] We don't know exactly when in July AMR was finished, but as of 19 June Moore had only written 'about six pages' of D98 (GEM, letter of that date to Desmond MacCarthy, quoted in Preti, 2009). Nor, apparently, did Moore read AMR while writing D98, even though Russell sent him Book I on 20 July 1898 and told him on 13 September that he could get a copy of Books II–IV from Whitehead. There is no evidence that Moore made use of them in writing his dissertation.

[32] This is confirmed by Moore (A, p. 15) and Russell (letter to Ellis Edwards, 30 July 1904 and *Auto.*, vol. I, p. 64; LA, p. 162).

[33] BR to Alys Russell, 12 March 1898. Unfortunately, no other details of this paper have survived.

lost without trace, this must have been the occasion on which Russell first heard of Moore's ontology of mind-independent concepts, for that part of the new philosophy seems to have been built into AMR from the very beginning. The other two meetings (mid-May and late June 1898) occurred while AMR was being written. Of the first, Russell merely reported that Moore 'seemed on the whole inclined to assent to what I had to say' (BR to Alys Russell, 10 May 1898), but of the second he said that Moore had recommended starting with 'a dogmatic definition, instead of indulging [Russell's] scepticism' (to Alys Russell, 28 June). It seems very likely that Russell took this advice, and proceeded to replace an earlier version of Book I of AMR (of which a very few sheets survive: cf. *CPBR2*, pp. 239–42), by a new one which states, directly and without exploring alternatives, the principles of the new philosophy which were already beginning to emerge.[34]

This meeting, however, may have had more important consequences. On 3 June, Russell had told Couturat that AMR was intended to answer the Kantian question 'How is pure mathematics possible?' and that he expected to give a 'purely Kantian' answer. On 5 July, however, a week after the discussion with Moore, Russell told his wife that he had 'discovered what was the question I had been asking myself for the last month'. Evidently, then, the question was not the old Kantian question. What the new question was is probably indicated in a further letter to Couturat on 18 July, where Russell said that he was trying to discover 'the fundamental ideas of mathematics and the necessary judgments (axioms) which one must accept on the basis of these ideas'. In the light of what he wrote subsequently, this suggests a marked change of method for Russell. Transcendental arguments, which had been the mainstay of the Tiergarten Programme from its inception, were abandoned in favour of an axiomatic analysis of theories and a decompositional analysis of terms, methods which characterized early analytic philosophy. This change took place *during* the writing of AMR and is securely established the following year in Russell's next major attempt to write a book on the philosophy of mathematics, the very title of which, 'The Fundamental Ideas and Axioms of Mathematics', reflects the wording of his letter to Couturat. This agenda remained constant through *The Principles of Mathematics*.

Reflecting on their initial break from neo-Hegelianism, Russell said that he was most concerned to reject monism while Moore was most concerned to reject idealism (*MPD*, p. 54). This seems entirely accurate. We have already seen how Russell came to reject the neo-Hegelian theory of relations in order to save himself from a (literally) unthinkable monism and how Moore turned arguments Bradley had deployed against the psychologism of the associationists against Bradley's own position. Now rejection of psychologism does not imply a rejection of idealism, as Bradley's own philosophy indicates, and Russell himself had been opposed to psychologism even while

---

[34] Too little survives of the early version of Book I to permit any firm conclusions, but what there is does indicate a more exploratory, tentative approach.

he was an idealist (cf. RH).[35] On the question of psychologism, Moore thought that Russell, like Bradley, had not gone far enough. The most critical review that Russell's *Essay on the Foundations of Geometry* received was from Moore (REFG) and the chief criticism he had to make was that Russell had not successfully avoided psychologism. The most important case in point was Russell's use of transcendental arguments, which Russell claimed to use in a 'purely logical' way 'without any psychological implication' (*EFG*, p. 3). Moore argued that he had failed to live up to this requirement, and by the time Moore's review appeared Russell agreed with him (letter to Couturat, 2 July 1899, *SLBR1*, p. 195).[36] What connected Moore's radical anti-psychologism with the rejection of idealism (and, ultimately, with Russell's rejection of monism) was his direct realism, which took both the world and propositions to be entirely composed of concepts. By adding to this the radically anti-psychologistic doctrine that concepts were entirely independent of the mind, he arrived at a position that was not just anti-psychologistic, but incompatible with metaphysical idealism. Russell, on the other hand, driven (even before Moore's rebellion against neo-Hegelianism) to reject monism in order to permit any genuine knowledge, was forced, in his attempt to find a philosophically viable account of mathematics, to acknowledge the importance of relations. By identifying relations with the mind-independent concepts Moore required for the combination of concepts into propositions, Russell was able to link his research programme to Moore's—and the new philosophy was born.

References

I Works by Russell and Moore

A   Moore, 'An Autobiography' (1942), in P. A. Schilpp (ed.), *The Philosophy of G. E. Moore*. La Salle, IL: Open Court, 1968, pp. 3–39.

AMR   Russell, 'An Analysis of Mathematical Reasoning' (1898), *CPBR2*, pp. 163–222.

AOG   Russell, 'On the Axioms of Geometry' (1899), *CPBR2*, pp. 394–415; first published in *Revue de métaphysique et de morale* 6: 759–76.

Auto   *The Autobiography of Bertrand Russell*, 3 vols. (London: Allen & Unwin, 1967–9).

COR   Russell, 'The Classification of Relations' (1899), *CPBR2*, pp. 138–46.

CPBR1   *The Collected Papers of Bertrand Russell*, I. *Cambridge Essays, 1888–99*, ed. Kenneth Blackwell, *et al.* London: Allen & Unwin, 1983.

CPBR2   *The Collected Papers of Bertrand Russell*, II. *Philosophical Papers, 1896–99*, ed. Nicholas Griffin and Albert C. Lewis. London: Unwin Hyman, 1990.

---

[35] By the end of the nineteenth century, opposition to psychologism stretched broadly—across different philosophical positions—from Frege to Bradley to the neo-Kantians to Husserl. Kusch 1995 offers a partial history, along with alleged philosophical morals according to the dogmas of the 'strong programme' in the sociology of science.

[36] In KI Moore argues forcefully for the much more general claim that it was impossible to free Kant's treatment of the a priori from psychologism.

CPBR3   *The Collected Papers of Bertrand Russell*, III. *Toward the 'Principles of Mathematics',*
          1900–02, ed. Gregory H. Moore. London and New York: Routledge, 1993.
CPBR4   *The Collected Papers of Bertrand Russell*, IV. *Foundations of Logic, 1903–05*, ed. Alasdair
          Urquhart with the assistance of Albert C. Lewis. London and New York: Routledge,
          1994.
CPBR9   *The Collected Papers of Bertrand Russell*, IX. *Essays on Language, Mind and Matter,*
          1919–26, ed. John G. Slater with the assistance of Bernd Frohmann. London, Boston,
          Sydney, Wellington: Unwin Hyman, 1988.
CPBR11   *The Collected Papers of Bertrand Russell*, XI. *Last Philosophical Testament, 1943–68*, ed.
          John G. Slater with the assistance of Peter Köllner. London and New York: Routledge,
          1997.
D97   Moore, 'The Metaphysical Basis of Ethics' (1897), first fellowship dissertation (Moore
          Papers, Cambridge University Library, Add. Mss, A247), published in *EPW*, pp.
          3–94.
D98   Moore, 'The Metaphysical Basis of Ethics' (1898), second fellowship dissertation
          (Moore Papers, Cambridge University Library, Add. Mss, A247), published in *EPW*,
          pp. 117–242.
EE   Moore, *The Early Essays*, ed. Tom Regan. Philadelphia: Temple University Press,
          1986.
EFG   Russell, *An Essay on the Foundations of Geometry*. New York: Dover, 1956; 1st edn.,
          1897.
EPI   Russell, 'Paper on Epistemology, I' (1893), *CPBR1*, pp. 121–3.
EPW   Moore, *Early Philosophical Writings*, ed. Thomas Baldwin and Consuelo Preti.
          Cambridge: Cambridge University Press, 2011.
F   Moore, 'Freedom' (1898), *EE*, pp. 25–57; first published *Mind* NS 7: 179–204.
FIAM   Russell, 'The Fundamental Ideas and Axioms of Mathematics' (1899), *CPBR2*,
          pp. 265–305.
HWP   Russell, *A History of Western Philosophy*. London: Allen & Unwin, 1965; 1st edn.,
          1946.
I   Moore, 'Identity' (1900), *EE*, pp. 121–45; first published *Proceedings of the Aristotelian*
          Society NS 1: 103–27.
KI   Moore, 'Kant's Idealism' (1904), *EE*, pp. 233–46; first published *Proceedings of the*
          Aristotelian Society 4: 127–40.
LA   Russell, 'Logical Atomism' (1924), *CPBR9*, 162–79; first published in *Contemporary*
          British Philosophy: Personal Statements, ed. J. H. Muirhead. London: Allen & Unwin,
          pp. 357–83.
LOR   Russell, 'The Logic of Relations: With Some Applications to the Theory of Series'
          (1901), *CPBR3*, 314–49; first published in Peano's *Revue des mathématiques* 7: 115–48.
MMD   Russell, 'My Mental Development' (1944), *CPBR11*, 5–18; first published in P. A. Schilpp
          (ed.), *The Philosophy of Bertrand Russell*. Evanston and Chicago: Northwestern
          University Press, pp. 3–20.
MPD   Russell, *My Philosophical Development*. London: Allen & Unwin, 1959.
MTCA   Russell, 'Meinong's Theory of Complexes and Assumptions' (1904), *CPBR4*, 21–76;
          first published in *Mind* 13: 204–19, 336–54, 509–24.
N   Moore, 'Necessity' (1900), *EE*, pp. 81–99; first published *Mind* NS 9: 289–305.
NJ   Moore, 'The Nature of Judgment' (1899), *EE*, pp. 59–80; first published *Mind* NS 8:
          176–93.

NLS   Russell, 'Note on the Logic of the Sciences' (1896?), *CPBR2*, p. 5.

NOO   'Note on Order' (1898), *CPBR2*, pp. 341–58.

OKEW   *Our Knowledge of the External World*. Chicago: Open Court; 2nd edn., 1926.

OSG   Russell, 'Observations on Space and Geometry' (1895), unpublished ms, RA 210.006551.

PE   Moore, *Principia Ethica* (1903). Cambridge: Cambridge University Press.

POL   Russell, *A Critical Exposition of the Philosophy of Leibniz*. London: Allen & Unwin, 1975; 1st edn., 1900.

POM   Russell, *The Principles of Mathematics*. London: Allen & Unwin, 1964; 1st edn., 1903.

POM/D   Russell, Draft of *The Principles of Mathematics* (1899–1900), *CPBR3*, pp. 13–180.

REFG   Moore, Review of Russell *EFG* (1899), *Mind* NS 8: 397–405.

RH   Russell, Review of Heymans, *Die Gesetze und Elemente des wissenschaftlichen Denkens* (1895), *CPBR1*, pp. 251–5; first published in *Mind* 4: 245–9.

RNQ   Russell, 'On the Relations of Number and Quantity' (1897), *CPBR2*, pp. 70–82; first published in *Mind* 6: 326–41.

SLBR1   *The Selected Letters of Bertrand Russell*, vol. I, *The Private Years, 1884–1914*, ed. Nicholas Griffin. London: Allen Lane, 1992.

T   Moore, 'In What Sense, If Any, Do Past and Future Time Exist?' (1897), *EE*, pp. 17–24; first published *Mind* NS 6: 235–40.

VN   Russell, 'Various Notes on Mathematical Philosophy' (1896–98), *CPBR2*, pp. 11–28.

II Works by other authors

Ayer, A. J. (1971). *Russell and Moore: The Analytical Heritage*. London: Macmillan.

Baldwin, J. Mark (1902). *Dictionary of Philosophy*, 2 vols. London: Macmillan.

Baldwin, Thomas (1990). *G. E. Moore*. London: Routledge.

—— (1991). 'The Identity Theory of Truth', *Mind* 100: 35–52.

Beaney, Michael (2002). 'Decompositions and Transformations: Conceptions of Analysis in Early Analytic and Phenomenological Traditions', *The Southern Journal of Philosophy* 40 (suppl. vol.): 53–99.

—— (2003). 'Analysis', *Stanford Encyclopedia of Philosophy*, online at <http://plato.stanford.edu/entries/analysis/> (accessed 26 June 2006).

Bell, David (1999). 'The Revolution of Moore and Russell: A Very British Coup?' In A. O'Hear (ed.), *German Philosophy Since Kant*. Cambridge: Cambridge University Press, pp. 193–208

Bolzano, Bernard (1837). *Wissenschaftslehre*, 4 vols. Sulzbach: Seidel.

Bosanquet, Bernard (1885a). 'Mr. Bradley on Fact and Inference', *Mind* 10: 256–65.

—— (1885b). *Knowledge and Reality: A Criticism of Mr. F. H. Bradley's 'Principles of Logic'*. London: Kegan Paul, Trench.

Boscovich, R. J. (1758). *A Theory of Natural Philosophy*, tr. J. M. Child, 1922. Cambridge, MA: MIT Press, 1966.

Bradford, Dennis E. (1981). 'Moore, Russell, and the Foundations of Analytic Metaphysics', *Philosophy Research Archives*: 553–81.

Bradley, F. H. (1876). *Ethical Studies*. Oxford: Oxford University Press; 2nd edn., 1970.

—— (1883). *The Principles of Logic*, 2 vols. Oxford: Oxford University Press; 2nd edn., 1967.

—— (1893). *Appearance and Reality*. Oxford: Oxford University Press; 2nd edn., 1969.

Brentano, Franz (1874). *Psychology from an Empirical Standpoint*, tr. L. McAlister. London: Routledge, 1973.

Broad, C. D. (1967). 'Some Personal Impressions of Russell as a Philosopher'. In R. Schoenman (ed.), *Bertrand Russell: Philosopher of the Century*. London: Allen & Unwin, pp. 100–8.

Cartwright, Richard L. (2003). 'Russell and Moore, 1898–1905'. In Griffin (ed.) (2003a), pp. 108–27.

Dummett, Michael (1993). *The Origins of Analytical Philosophy*. London: Duckworth.

Frege, Gottlob (1884). *The Foundations of Arithmetic*, tr. J. L. Austin. Oxford: Blackwell, 1950.

Griffin, Nicholas (1988). 'The Tiergarten Programme'. In Ian Winchester and Kenneth Blackwell (eds.), *Antinomies and Paradoxes: Studies in Russell's Early Philosophy* (*Russell: The Journal of the Bertrand Russell Archives* 8). Hamilton, ON: McMaster University Library Press, pp. 19–34.

—— (1991). *Russell's Idealist Apprenticeship*. Oxford: Clarendon Press.

—— (1998a). 'Did Russell's Criticisms of Bradley's Theory of Relations Miss Their Mark?' In Guy Stock (ed.), *Appearance versus Reality: New Essays on Bradley's Metaphysics*. Oxford: Clarendon Press, pp. 153–62.

—— (1998b). 'Dummett and the Origins of Analytic Philosophy', *Philosophy and Progress* (Dhaka), 24–5: 1–22.

—— (ed.) (2003a). *The Cambridge Companion to Bertrand Russell*. Cambridge: Cambridge University Press.

—— (2003b). 'Russell's Philosophical Background', in Griffin (ed.) (2003a), pp. 84–107.

Hochberg, Herbert (1962). 'Moore's Ontology and Non-Natural Properties', *The Review of Metaphysics* 15: 365–95; revised version printed in Klemke (ed.) (1969), pp. 95–127.

—— (1969a). 'Moore and Russell on Particulars, Relations and Identity'. In Klemke (ed.) (1969), pp. 155–94.

—— (1969b). 'Some Reflections on Mr Nelson's Corrections'. In Klemke (ed.) (1969), pp. 141–54.

—— (1978). *Thought, Fact, and Reference: The Origins and Ontology of Logical Atomism*. Minneapolis: University of Minnesota Press.

Hylton, Peter (1990). *Russell, Idealism and the Emergence of Analytic Philosophy*. Oxford: Clarendon Press.

Joachim, H. H. (1906). *The Nature of Truth*. Oxford: Clarendon Press.

Klemke, E. D. (ed.) (1969). *Studies in the Philosophy of G. E. Moore*. Chicago: Quadrangle.

Kusch, Martin (1995). *Psychologism: A Case Study in the Sociology of Knowledge*. New York: Routledge.

Levy, Paul (1979). *Moore: G. E. Moore and the Cambridge Apostles*. London: Weidenfeld & Nicolson.

Lewis, Albert and Nicholas Griffin (1990). 'Bertrand Russell's Mathematical Education', *Notes and Records of the Royal Society* 44: 51–71.

McTaggart, J. M. E. (1893a). 'A Further Determination of the Absolute'; reprinted in McTaggart (1934), pp. 210–72.

—— (1893b). 'Time and the Hegelian Dialectic', *Mind* NS 2: 490–504.

—— (1896). *Studies in the Hegelian Dialectic*. Cambridge: Cambridge University Press.

—— (1901). *Studies in Hegelian Cosmology*. Cambridge: Cambridge University Press.

—— (1910). *A Commentary on Hegel's Logic*. Cambridge: Cambridge University Press.

—— (1921). *The Nature of Existence*, 2 vols. Cambridge: Cambridge University Press, 1921–7.

—— (1934). *Philosophical Studies*, ed. S. V. Keeling. London: E. Arnold; Freeport, NY: Books for Libraries, 1968.

Miah, Sajahan (1997). 'Moore's Influence on Russell: Transition from Idealism to Realism', *Philosophy and Progress* (Dhaka), 22–3: 61–80.

Monk, Ray (1996). 'Bertrand Russell's Brainchild: Analytical Philosophy—Its Conception and Birth', *Radical Philosophy* 78: 2–5.

—— (1997). 'Was Russell an Analytic Philosopher?' In H. J. Glock (ed.), *The Rise of Analytic Philosophy*. Oxford: Blackwell, pp. 35–50.

Nelson, J. O. (1962). 'Mr Hochberg on Moore: Some Corrections', *The Review of Metaphysics* 16: 119–32; reprinted in Klemke (ed.) (1969), pp. 128–40.

—— (1967). 'Moore, George Edward'. In Paul Edwards (ed.), *The Encyclopedia of Philosophy*. New York: Macmillan, vol. V, pp. 372–81.

O'Connor, David (1982). *The Metaphysics of G. E. Moore*. Dordrecht: Reidel.

Passmore, John (1957). *A Hundred Years of Philosophy*. Harmondsworth: Penguin, 1980.

Pettit, Philip (1973). 'The Early Philosophy of G. E. Moore', *Philosophical Forum* 4: 260–98.

Preti, Consuelo (2008). 'On the Origins of the Contemporary Notion of Propositional Content: Anti-Psychologism in Nineteenth-Century Psychology and G. E. Moore's Early Theory of Judgment', *Studies in the History and Philosophy of Science* 39: 176–85.

—— (2009). '"He was in those days beautiful and slim": Bertrand Russell and G. E. Moore, 1894–1901', *Russell: The Journal of Bertrand Russell Studies* 28: 101–26.

Roberts, G. W. (ed.) (1979). *Bertrand Russell Memorial Volume*. London: Allen & Unwin.

Rodriguez-Consuegra, Francisco A. (1991). *The Mathematical Philosophy of Bertrand Russell: Origins and Development*. Basel: Birkhäuser.

Ryle, Gilbert (1970). 'G. E. Moore's "The Nature of Judgment"'. In A. Ambrose and M. Lazerowitz (eds.), *G. E. Moore: Essays in Retrospect*. London: Allen & Unwin, pp. 89–101.

Seth, Andrew and R. B. Haldane (eds.) (1883). *Essays in Philosophical Criticism*. London: Longmans Green; New York: Franklin, 1971.

Spadoni, Carl (1976). 'Great God in Boots!—The Ontological Argument is Sound', *Russell: The Journal of the Bertrand Russell Archives* 23–4: 37–41.

Sprigge, T. L. S. (1979). 'Russell and Bradley on Relations', in Roberts (ed.) (1979), pp. 150–70.

Stirling, J. H. (1865). *The Secret of Hegel*. Edinburgh: Oliver & Boyd, 1898.

Stout, G. F. (1896). *Analytical Psychology*, 2 vols. London: Sonnenschein.

van der Schaar, Maria (1996). 'From Analytic Psychology to Analytic Philosophy: The Reception of Twardowski's Ideas in Cambridge', *Axiomathes* 7: 295–324.

Ward, James (1886). 'Psychology'. In *Encyclopedia Britannica*, 9th edn. Edinburgh: A. & C. Black, Vol. XX, pp. 37–85.

Watling, John (1970). *Bertrand Russell*. Edinburgh: Oliver & Boyd.

CHAPTER 12

RUSSELL'S THEORY OF DESCRIPTIONS AND THE IDEA OF LOGICAL CONSTRUCTION

BERNARD LINSKY

12.1 RUSSELL AND ANALYSIS

In a posthumously published paper written in 1929, Frank Ramsey described Bertrand Russell's theory of definite descriptions as a 'paradigm of philosophy'.[1] It is clear that Ramsey meant the then new analytic philosophy. The theory of definite descriptions is still taken as the model of a certain method for analytic philosophy, which is thought to be called for when ordinary language is misleading and gives rise to philosophical problems that can only be resolved by a proper analysis of that language, and which results in a correct account of the 'semantics' of that language. According to this picture of analysis, an expression in ordinary language which includes a definite description such as 'The present King of France is bald' suggests a problematic ontology of non-existent entities, if one follows a superficial analysis into a subject term 'The present king of France' and predicate 'is bald'. Instead, the theory of definite descriptions proposes a superior analysis of such sentences, one which helps to free us from a tempting Platonic or Meinongian ontology that includes either an abstract or non-existent King of France.[2] The contribution of the theory of descriptions, on this view, is to show how a correct analysis of ordinary language sentences will aid philosophers dealing with problems about ontology.

[1] In the first footnote to the paper called 'Philosophy' (Ramsey 1931, p. 263).
[2] This view of the significance of the theory of descriptions is presented by Gilbert Ryle as one of Russell's chief contributions to philosophy, in a memorial note to the Aristotelian Society in 1970 (Ryle 1979).

In fact this view of philosophy, which finds a paradigm case of analysis in the theory of definite descriptions, did not even appear in Russell's writings until later in his philosophical career, and when it did, it was attributed to Wittgenstein's *Tractatus*, rather than claimed as his own project. In Russell's early works between 1905 and 1918 there is little mention of language. Instead we find the analysis of putative entities of various categories; numbers, classes, propositions, judgments, and then facts. Recent scholarship has convincingly shown that it was in fact Russell's own earlier theory of non-linguistic 'denoting concepts' that was the main target of criticism in 'On Denoting'.[3] The notion of logical construction also made a late appearance in Russell's thought. It was only in the 1918 'Philosophy of Logical Atomism' lectures that Russell introduced the term 'logical construction' for the method to be used to solve 'the problem of matter', for his theory of matter and space, and in retrospect, identified his earlier definitions as examples of this project. Along the way these variously defined notions had come to be described by the seemingly very different notions of 'incomplete symbol' and 'logical fiction'. It is not surprising, then, that by the early 1930s Susan Stebbing and John Wisdom were charging that Russell did not properly understand his own project. Stebbing (1933, p. 502), for example, says that the sentence 'This table is a logical construction' is 'systematically ambiguous', having, as well as an ordinary reading on which it confusingly expresses what later came to be known as a category mistake, also a metaphysical reading on which it says something about how sentences and inferences about the table may be replaced by sentences about sense-data. It is not to be taken as an ordinary sentence like 'This table is brown'. When Gilbert Ryle described his project of analysis in 'Systematically Misleading Expressions' (1931), he seemed to be describing this same project of analysing ordinary language, but wanted to disavow any association with the doctrine of 'logical constructions' which had become a technical project at the hands of John Wisdom in his five-part series of articles with that title from 1931 to 1933. Thus, the import of the theory of definite descriptions and logical construction and the relation of both to 'philosophical analysis' was never clear, from soon after their appearance and after, despite the importance of both for the later history of analytic philosophy.

This chapter will trace a series of definitions and projects that Russell identified in 1924 as logical constructions. These begin with the theory of definite descriptions, appearing first in 'On Denoting' (1905), followed by the 'no-classes' theory of classes, and then the definition of numbers as equivalence classes that first appeared in *Principles of Mathematics* (1903), but was fully worked out in *Principia Mathematica* (1910). Only after Russell had turned from logic and mathematics to problems in epistemology and metaphysics do we finally see the 'construction' of space, time, and matter in *Our Knowledge of the External World* (1914) and *The Analysis of Matter* (1927). In addition to these works, which contain technical logical details, Russell also described his method in more popular books and essays: 'The Philosophy of Logical Atomism' lectures (1918),

---

[3] See the papers from before 1905 in Russell (1994) and the discussion of the theory of denoting concepts they contain in Makin (2000).

Introduction to Mathematical Philosophy (1919), and then 'Logical Atomism' (1924). Together they present a series of related yet distinct technical logical projects. In hindsight the projects can be seen to emphasize different aspects of 'analysis' which came to be more clearly distinguished in later analytic philosophy. Thus, the theory of definite descriptions was designed to capture the logical properties of propositions that contained definite descriptions. It came to be seen as a model of analysis as revision of misleading ordinary language in order to reveal an underlying logical form. The 'no-classes theory of classes' was also introduced for technical purposes, but came to be seen as the model of the project of ontological reduction by proclaiming putative entities to be 'logical fiction'. The apparent element of free choice among alternative possible formal definitions of numbers as equivalence classes of classes was later seen by Carnap as illustrating the 'explication' of vague ordinary notions which replaces them with exact, formalized, notions. Finally, the 'logical construction' of matter was interpreted as a model of a distinctive, new, logical kind of ontological reduction, by Susan Stebbing and John Wisdom, and much later, as a precursor of the 'structuralist realist' project in the philosophy of science.[4] The review of these various definitions and projects which follows will show both the main logical purpose that each served for Russell, as well as the element of each of these aspects of 'analysis' which later analytic philosophers found in what Russell had done.

12.2 THE THEORY OF DEFINITE DESCRIPTIONS

Russell's theory of definite descriptions first appeared in print in a short paper, 'On Denoting', in the journal *Mind* in 1905. The paper limits itself to the logical analysis of certain particular linguistic constructions, namely, the determiner phrases 'a man, some man, every man, all men...', which Russell called 'indefinite descriptions', and then, seemingly only as another special case, 'definite descriptions' such as 'the present King of England, the present king of France, the centre of mass of the solar system at the first instant of the twentieth century, the revolution of the earth round the sun, the revolution of the sun round the earth' (1905, p. 479). While quite narrow in scope, the theory of definite descriptions introduces the notion of 'incomplete symbols' and with that the germs of all the ideas that were to be developed into the proposal that classes are 'logical fictions', and then the notion of logical constructions that was central to Russell's later work on space, time, and matter.

The first of this series of new ideas were the notions of 'incomplete symbol' and 'contextual definition', which emerge in accounts of both indefinite and definite descriptions. The theory of definite descriptions is presented as a proposal about how to analyse

---

[4] The project of 'constructing matter' has also been, more justifiably, discussed as a precursor to Carnap's project in his *Der Logische Aufbau der Welt* (1928), although Richardson (1988), and others, argue that Carnap's project is not as close to Russell as has been thought.

sentences that contain definite descriptions 'in context'. It is the entire proposition which includes a definite description that is provided with a definition. To use Russell's own example: 'Thus "the father of Charles II was executed" becomes: "It is not always false of *x* that *x* begat Charles II and that *x* was executed" and that "if *y* begat Charles II, *y* is identical with *x*" is always true of *y*' (1905, p. 482). In 'On Denoting' Russell was clearly struggling to avoid the use of logical symbols, which for any later analytic philosophers who had taken an elementary course in symbolic logic actually make the theory quite simple to state. If one represents '*x* is father of Charles II', or equivalently, '*y* begat Charles II' as 'ϕy' and '*x* was executed' by 'ψx', then the sentence 'the father of Charles II was executed' is of the form 'The ϕ is ψ', or '$\psi(\imath x)(\phi x)$', using the 'inverted iota' description operator that Russell had inherited from Peano's symbolism. What this formal expression becomes, according to the analysis in 'On Denoting', is presented in this definition:

$$\psi(\imath x)(\phi x) =_{df} \sim \forall x \sim [(\phi x \,\&\, \psi x) \,\&\, \forall y\,(\phi y \supset y = x)]$$

Given that what 'is not always false' is 'sometimes true' and so amounts to an instance of the existential quantifier, a proposition of the form 'The ϕ is ψ' is defined in *Principia Mathematica* with a logically equivalent expression: 'There is an *x* such that for any *y*, *y* is ϕ if and only if *y* is identical with *x*, and that *x* is ψ':

$$\psi(\imath x)(\phi x) =_{df} \exists x\,[\forall y\,(\phi y \equiv y = x) \,\&\, \psi x]$$

Three technical features of this definition stand out, and appear in various ways in the different sorts of analyses we will examine below. First, the definition makes possible the derivation of various logical properties of definite descriptions, as was later carried out in *14 of *Principia Mathematica*. Indeed the theory is justified solely by its ability to deal with various logical puzzles involving definite descriptions. Russell asks that the theory should be judged by its logical consequences, rather than by how accurately it reports what we may think we mean by expressions of this form: 'This may seem a somewhat incredible interpretation; but I am not at present giving reasons, I am merely *stating* the theory.' He concludes the essay with a repetition of this point:

> I will only beg the reader not to make up his mind against the view—as he might be tempted to do, on account of its apparently excessive complication—until he has attempted to construct a theory of his own on the subject of denotation. This attempt, I believe, will convince him that, whatever the true theory may be, it cannot have such a simplicity as one might have expected beforehand. (1905, p. 493)

The theory is to be judged by its logical consequences, not by an appeal to intuition or some intuition of what we were have been saying all along. The second point follows from this. We have seen that the theory of descriptions is presented with distinct, though logically equivalent, definitions. Russell was interested in finding the ultimate constituents of propositions, and among those constituents could be entities represented by the quantifiers 'all' and 'some', and the sentential connectives 'if and only if', 'and', 'if then', etc.[5] It appears that for one of the purposes, namely to allow the efficient derivation of logical theorems involving descriptions, one of these definitions is chosen over the other for use in *Principia Mathematica*. This does seem to anticipate the kind of analysis that Carnap called 'explication'. Some ordinary concept or expression, in this case the definite descriptions of natural language 'The ϕ is ψ', is given a precise meaning or definition from among several perhaps equally good alternatives, just so that it has a fixed meaning for the purposes at hand. Russell can't insist that the detailed analysis in terms of negation and quantifiers of 'On Denoting' captures what we intend by using definite descriptions, for he offers a different definition in *Principia Mathematica*.[6] Unlike 'explication', however, the various alternative precise symbolizations of propositions containing definite descriptions are logically equivalent. They do not make a vague notion precise in alternative ways, but instead capture the logical form of the proposition in logically equivalent ways.

A third feature of this definition of great significance for the later notion of logical construction is the novel form that the definition takes, namely what came to be called a 'contextual' definition. The definition does not provide an equivalent for the phrase 'The ϕ' by itself, by proposing some other expression that can be substituted for any occurrence of the definite description. Russell says, 'According to the view which I advocate, a denoting phrase is essentially *part* of a sentence, and does not, like most single words, have any significance on its own' (1905, p. 488). Rather, the proposal is to replace occurrences of the description in context, so that the entire expression 'The ϕ is ψ' is replaced by a rather complex sentence involving quantifiers, identity, equivalence, and both 'ϕ' and 'ψ'. Russell describes definite descriptions as consequently being 'incomplete symbols'. Incomplete symbols are contrasted with (logically proper) names, which do have a 'meaning' on their own. For a genuine name, i.e. one that is not to be analysed as a disguised description, the meaning of the name is the object that it denotes, its reference. For definite descriptions, however: 'The phrase per se has no meaning, because in any proposition in which it occurs the proposition, fully expressed, does not contain the phrase, which has been broken up' (1905, p. 488). Russell's account of classes also makes use of a contextual definition, so that, later, when he referred to numbers and matter using interchangeably the terms 'incomplete symbols' and the very different sounding 'logical fictions' and 'logical constructions', it is this aspect of those accounts that he was emphasizing.

---

[5] See the discussion of 'negative' and 'general' facts in the 'Philosophy of Logical Atomism' (1918), lectures II and III. *Principia Mathematica* defines all the other connectives in terms of 'not' and 'or' using only the universal quantifier as primitive. It is not claimed that this is the unique, proper, set of primitive logical operations.

[6] Although the notion that descriptions are more like quantifiers than singular terms is now common in contemporary philosophy of language following Neale (1990). Neale focuses on the contribution of descriptions to the truth conditions of sentences in which they occur, separating this part of the theory from the aspects involving acquaintance with constituents. He avoids the issue of whether there is more to logical form for Russell than an account of truth conditions.

While the theory of definite descriptions does provide an analysis of propositions in which they occur, the primary notion of *analysis* in Russell's epistemology and metaphysics comes from this search for the proper representation of propositions, in which all the primitive terms do have some meaning. The meaning of these logically proper names can only be known through *acquaintance*, which is a direct mental relation, contrasted with 'knowledge by description'. To know an object by acquaintance is to be directly aware of it rather than to only know it as the object 'that is so and so'. That, Russell says, is to know it only indirectly, 'by description'. Grasping a proposition is made possible by our acquaintance with its constituents. 'On Denoting' contains the first statement of a claim that is repeated variously through Russell's writings: 'Thus in every proposition that we can apprehend (i.e. not only those whose truth or falsehood we can judge of, but in all that we can think about), all the constituents are really entities with which we have immediate acquaintance' (1905, p. 492). The ultimate constituents of propositions are discovered by analysis. These are entities with which we are acquainted, and that acquaintance makes possible the 'apprehension', or understanding, of the proposition. Russell later makes a distinction between a definition which provides an analysis into objects of acquaintance, and the 'definition' of a word like 'red' as 'the colour with the greatest wave-length'. The latter is really a description rather than a definition by analysis. 'In the sense of analysis, you cannot define "red"' (1918, p. 174), he says:

> Analysis is not the same thing as definition. You can define a term by means of a correct description, but that does not constitute an analysis. It is analysis, not definition, that we are concerned with at the present moment, so I will come back to the question of analysis.
> We may lay down the following provisional definitions: That the components of a proposition are the symbols we must understand in order to understand the proposition; That the components of the fact which makes a proposition true or false, as the case may be, are the *meanings* of the symbols which we must understand in order to understand the proposition. (1918, pp. 174–5)

Beyond the familiar explicit definitions that Russell considers to allow the replacement of defined symbols as simply an abbreviation for their definition, and the contextual definition of definite descriptions, this is another new sort of definition. According to this notion, the process of definition consists of identifying what is being talked about by description in contrast with acquaintance. Thus a definition such as that suggested by Russell does not suffice for the sort of direct acquaintance that really provides the meaning of the term 'red'. The definition of an expression by description, as Russell suggests in the case of 'red', does not produce the result of an analysis of a proposition expressed with the word 'red'. That would require uncovering our acquaintance with the colour, which is found as the result of analysis proper.

The process of analysing a proposition consists in discovering those entities with which we must be acquainted in order to understand that proposition. Rewriting definite descriptions using the contextual definition is a part of this process on the way to discovering the real constituents of the proposition. In the case of a definite description 'the ϕ is ψ', it will be the constituents of the equivalent proposition 'There is one and only one φ and that thing is ψ'. The constituents of that proposition will then be the logical expressions, and the properties expressed by φ and ψ. Russell includes 'certain abstract logical universals' among the things with which we can be acquainted (1912, p. 109). The result of applying the definitions of the theory of descriptions, by reformulating sentences, is a stage in the process of analysing expressions that do not 'mean' entities with which we can be acquainted. It is unclear, however, if there are in fact distinct 'logical objects' associated with the logical expressions which are discovered by the analysis of descriptions, because of the seeming indifference to the precise choice of logical expressions to use in the analysis. The important lesson that we learn from the analysis of definite descriptions is that that an expression 'the φ is ψ' does not have a constituent corresponding to 'the φ' but rather only to 'φ' and 'ψ' and some logical notions involving generality. The details of the rest of the analysis seem to be a matter of choice.

12.3 The Multiple Relation Theory of Judgment and Propositions

While the notion of the constituent of a proposition has an important role in Russell's thinking about objects and names, by 1910 those propositions were themselves rejected as independent entities, and the 'phrases' which represent them relegated to the role of incomplete symbols:

> a judgment does not have a single object, namely the proposition, but has several interrelated objects. That is to say, the relation which constitutes judgment is not a relation of two terms, namely the judging mind and the proposition, but is a relation of several terms, namely the mind and what are called the constituents of the proposition. That is, when we judge (say) 'this is red', what occurs is a relation of three terms, the mind, and 'this,' and red. (1910, p. 43)

This is the 'multiple relation theory of judgment' that Russell first considers in *The Problems of Philosophy*, and which he continues to explore through the logical atomism period, up to the proposal of the very different theory of belief sentences in Appendix C of the second edition of *Principia Mathematica* in 1925. Using his example from *The Problems of Philosophy*, when Othello judges (or believes) that Desdemona loves Cassio, what occurs is a complex four-place relation of judging or believing which relates Othello, Desdemona, Cassio, and the relation of loving.[7] The entire complex is a *fact*, something that occurs in the world, whether or not its supposed object, the *proposition*

---

[7] One can also have a judgment like 'this is red' above, which relates three items, the judger, the referent of 'this', and red. This possibility is the source of the description 'multiple relation' for the theory. The judging relations in these two cases will differ, in each case having as many arguments as there are constituents of the supposed proposition, four in the first case, three in the second.

that Desdemona loves Cassio, or that 'this is red', is true or not. What is important for our purposes is to see the result of this analysis, the analysis of judgments according to the multiple relation theory:

> Owing to the plurality of objects of a single judgment, it follows that what we call a 'proposition' (in the sense in which this is distinguished from the phrase expressing it) is not a single entity at all. That is to say, the phrase which expresses a proposition is what we call an 'incomplete symbol'; it does not have meaning in itself, but requires some supplementation in order to acquire a complete meaning. (1910, p. 44)

Like definite descriptions such as 'the ϕ', the expressions for propositions such as 'that Desdemona loves Cassio', are themselves incomplete, and only occur as part of the sentences that express judgments, such as 'Othello judges that Desdemona loves Cassio.' As was the case for definite descriptions, an account is only given for complete sentences in which the apparent expressions for propositions occur as apparent constituents. But unlike the case of definite descriptions there is no possibility of providing contextual definitions to account for the incompleteness of these expressions, for propositions do occur as basic entities in the logic in which the analysis would be presented. Still, there is definitely a sense of ontological elimination in the 'multiple relation theory', or at least a feeling of getting by without requiring certain entities, which results from this analysis of judgments. This is yet another form of analysis, a theory that results in a proposal about the correct logical form of a proposition. A proposition which apparently contains a two-place relation between a judger and a judged proposition actually reports a fact involving several arguments which are the constituents of the seeming proposition. The multiple relation theory is like the analysis of propositions containing definite descriptions in this regard. A proposition which seems to have a certain form, with certain constituents, in fact has a very different form, indeed one in which an apparent constituent is represented by an 'incomplete' symbol which does not stand for a constituent of the proposition at all.[8]

12.4 THE NO-CLASSES THEORY OF CLASSES

The account of classes in *Principia Mathematica* *20, which enables Russell's resolution of his paradox of the class of all classes that are not members of themselves had been driving his logical investigations since 1901. It is, like the theory of definite descriptions, a series of contextual definitions of occurrences of apparent singular terms. In

---

[8] Wrinch (1919) proposes an account of the 'logical form' of quantified propositions that represents their constituents while observing the denial of propositions that is part of the 'multiple relation' theory of judgment. It seems that Russell had not completely abandoned the theory despite the well known criticisms by Wittgenstein. See Griffin (1985), and more recently, Carey (2007) for a presentation of Wittgenstein's criticisms of Russell's theory.

this case the eliminated symbols include the form '$\hat{x}\phi x$', Whitehead and Russell's notation for 'the class of x which are ϕ' which in modern notation is '$\{x: \phi x\}$'. The theory acquired the name 'no-classes theory of classes' because it provides, like the theory of definite descriptions, a contextual definition of all occurrences of expressions '$f\{x: \phi x\}$', where the class term '$\{x: \phi x\}$' occurs in a context 'f':

$$f\{x: \phi x\} =_{df} \exists \psi \, [\forall y \, (\phi y \equiv \psi y) \, \& \, f\psi]$$

Subject to the technical condition imposed by the theory of types that ψ must be a predicative function, this says that 'The class of ϕs is f' is defined as 'There is a (predicative) propositional function ψ, such that for any y, y is ϕ if and only if it is ψ, and that ψ is f'. That ϕ and ψ are true of all the same things y is the condition that ϕ and ψ are coextensive, so the definition replaces the apparent predications f of the class of ϕs by a distinct proposition saying that there is some (predicative) function ψ which is coextensive with ϕ, and that ψ is f. The two distinctive features of the theory of definite descriptions equally characterize the no-classes theory. The definitions allow for the derivation of various logical properties of classes, as is carried out in *20 of *Principia Mathematica* and later numbers. Secondly, the no-classes theory also consists of contextual definitions which allow the elimination of apparent reference to classes.

Consider, for example, the most characteristic feature of classes, their *extensionality*, that is the property that the class of ϕs is identical with the class of θs if any x is a member of the class of ϕs if and only if it is a member of the class of θs. To be a member of a class of θs, when θ is a predicative function, is simply to be θ in virtue of another definition that is part of the no-classes theory. The principle of extensionality which is assumed as one of the fundamental axioms in the alternative account of axiomatic set theory can be proved as a theorem from these definitions quite directly. Other familiar principles of unions and intersections and other theses of the theory of classes which are assumed as axioms in axiomatic set theory, are proved as theorems in *20 of *Principia Mathematica* and some of the later chapters. Notoriously, of course, the 'multiplicative axiom' (the axiom of choice) and the axiom of infinity, both standard axioms in ZFC (Zermelo–Frankel with Choice) and other axiomatic systems, cannot be proved with just definitions of the no-classes theory. Whitehead and Russell present them as hypotheses to qualify theorems upon which they depend, although others have taken these as signs of the ultimate failure of the logicist project of *Principia Mathematica*. The question of the place of axioms in logicism is especially acute given what Russell says famously in the *Introduction to Mathematical Philosophy* (1919):

> The method of 'postulating' what we want has many advantages; they are the same as the advantages of theft over honest toil. Let us leave them to others and proceed with our honest toil. (1919, p. 71)

To the extent that 'postulating' is to take as an axiom what otherwise could be proved from definitions and logic, such as the 'honest toil' of deriving principles such as extensionality from the definitions of the no-classes theory, then what Russell says here amounts to finding fault with the account of classes in *Principia Mathematica* which has to postulate the axioms of choice and infinity.

The second feature that the no-classes theory shares with the theory of definite descriptions is that it also consists primarily of a contextual definition which eliminates the term 'the class of φs' from a context *f* in which it occurs. Expressions for classes are also incomplete symbols, which Russell sometimes carelessly expresses by saying that classes themselves are 'incomplete symbols' and indeed 'logical fictions'. The contextual definitions of the theory of classes have a more direct ontological import than those of the theory of descriptions. While much is made, by Russell himself, of the way in which his account of 'the present king of France' avoids ontological commitment to 'Meinongian' non-existent entities, other cases of the theory, such as the very example of 'the present King of England' which Russell used in 'On Denoting', do not have any such ontological import. Sentences involving the description 'the present King of England' are made true by the properties of Edward VII, who was the King of England in 1905. All such sentences using definite descriptions are made true by the properties of existing individuals. There is no need for Meinongian individuals who do not exist, but there is no general reduction of talk of individuals to quantification over some other category. In contrast, the no-classes theory replaces apparent talk of classes, including singular terms such as 'the class of things *x* such that *x* is φ', to a general proposition which expresses features of a propositional function ψ, which is coextensive with φ, but certainly of the same sort, and specifically same *logical type*, as φ. Unlike the case of definite descriptions, where the commitment to kings is in no way eliminated by the proper analysis of 'the present King of France', the analysis of 'the class of φs' involves no commitment to classes, but only to propositional functions.

One of Russell's first reactions to the paradox he discovered in 1901 was to conclude that classes must not be objects. The paradox of 'the class of all classes that are not members of themselves' in fact arose from Russell's consideration of Cantor's theorem:[9]

> We are met then with the necessity, therefore, of distinguishing between classes and particulars. You are met with the necessity of saying that a class consisting of two particulars is not itself in turn a fresh particular, and that has to be expanded in all sorts of ways; i.e. you will have to say that in the sense in which there are particulars, in that sense it is not true to say there are classes. (1918, p. 227)

Russell's solution to his paradox thus can be described as finding, via the no-classes theory, a way to avoid classes altogether, and to paraphrase talk of classes in terms of other expressions about propositional functions. The paradox, in particular, will be found to be resolved then in the details of the definition combined with the theory of types for propositional functions which forbids the sort of talk of self-membership that

---

[9] Cantor proved that there are more subsets of a set than members of the set. The proof when applied to 'the set of all sets' leads directly to Russell's paradox. Russell suggests that he was led to his paradox by looking for a mistake in Cantor's argument, likely by trying to show that it led to absurdity when applied to 'the set of all sets'.

leads to the paradox in the first place. It is with this theory that the notion we have been following comes to be identified by the expression 'logical fiction', in addition to the characterization in terms of 'incomplete symbols':

> We must seek a definition along the same lines as the definition of descriptions, i.e. a definition which will assign a meaning that altogether eliminates all mention of classes from a right analysis of such propositions. We shall then be able to say that the symbols for classes are mere conveniences, not representing objects called 'classes', and that classes are in fact, like descriptions, logical fictions, or (as we may say) 'incomplete symbols'. (1919, p. 182)

12.5 The Definition of Numbers as Classes of Classes

The familiar 'Frege–Russell' definition of numbers as classes of equinumerous classes precedes both the theory of definite descriptions and the no-classes theory in Russell's thinking. It appears that Russell rediscovered the account after seeing a criticism of the idea by Peano, who was likely reacting to the proposal originally made by Frege (see Russell 1903, p. 115). The account of numbers as classes certainly preceded the discovery of Russell's paradox, and so the motivation to give an account of denoting expressions which included terms for classes, the theory of types, and the no-classes theory which reduced classes to propositional functions. Consequently, when Russell speaks of entities as classes of sense-data, and hence 'nothing' in the Philosophy of Logical Atomism lectures, we must take this as the result of the two-stage analysis, of numbers as classes, and then classes as propositional functions.

The definition of the number 2 at *54·02 of *Principia Mathematica* makes use of notions from the theory of classes, defined earlier using the no-classes theory. In particular, the definition uses the notion of the *singleton* class of x, '$\{x\}$' in modern notation, and of the *union* of two classes. The union $\alpha \cup \beta$ of two classes α and β is the class of all things x such that x is in α or x is in β. It is a class that collects into one class the members of both. The definition is then an *explicit definition*, allowing each occurrence of the numeral '2' to be replaced by an expression in the theory of classes:

$$2 =_{df} \{\alpha : \exists x \, \exists y \, (x \neq y \, \& \, \alpha = \{x\} \cup \{y\})\}$$

Thus the number 2 is the class of all classes that are the union of pairs of distinct objects x and y, in other words, 2 is the class of all pairs.[10] This kind of definition, often

---

[10] This is a *proper class*, in the terminology which distinguishes *classes* and *sets*, because there will be no *set* of all pairs. There are simply too many, for there will be a one to one mapping from the elements of the universe to the class of pairs, and the range of any such mapping is too large to be a set.

described as a 'construction', is common in the elementary portions of axiomatic set theory in which various mathematical entities are defined as sets of a particular sort. This begins with the notion of the ordered pair of two things x and y, $\langle x, y \rangle$, which is defined standardly as $\{\{x\}, \{x,y\}\}$, that is, the set containing the singleton of x and the pair of x and y. There are alternative definitions of pairs, indeed the original proposal by Norbert Wiener in 1914 was the alternative $\{\{\{x\}, \Lambda\}, \{\{y\}\}\}$, where Λ is the empty class, the one class that has no members. A third definition, due to Kuratowski, is also used: $\{\{x,y\}, x\}$, which is a pair of two classes: the pair of x and y as one member and x as its second member. The alternative definitions each contain what is essential for an adequate definition, namely, they enable one to recover the members of an ordered pair from an unordered class that is selected in the right way. The existence of such alternatives argues against this as an analysis in the primary sense, however, for the alternatives are chosen almost arbitrarily from equally good alternatives. No amount of analysis of what one means by a proposition about the ordered pair $\langle x, y \rangle$ will reveal one that is correct.[11]

Whitehead and Russell's definition of the number 2 is not arbitrary in this way. If one looks to propositions that include 2, such as the famous theorem *110·643 in Volume II, $1 + 1 = 2$, and replace numbers and the addition sign by their definitions in terms of classes, and then apply the no-classes account of the results, we do in fact find a proposition that only uses logical terminology. Other 'constructions' of the natural numbers within set theory select particular sets as the numbers, say $\{\{\Lambda\} \Lambda\}$, and then other pairs, which by Whitehead and Russell's definition are *members* of 2, become in set theory simply *equinumerous* with 2, in the sense that their members can be mapped one to one onto the members of $\{\{\Lambda\} \Lambda\}$. The choice of which definition to use seems to be a matter of convention, and so the definition of the numbers takes on the role of settling on one of several equally good ways of fixing the meaning of a term for theoretical purposes. The original definitions of numbers, however, which are preserved in *Principia Mathematica* do not share that arbitrariness. As such, the definition of number can be seen to be an analysis of the standard sort which reveals the ultimate constituents of propositions of arithmetic.

The idea of choosing from among equally adequate technical substitutes for ordinary notions is yet another sort of analysis which emerged as a clear alternative later in the history of analytic philosophy under Carnap's name of 'explication'.[12] Indeed, Carnap

---

[11] Indeed, Quine (1960, p. 257) titles a section 'The ordered pair as philosophical paradigm'. The Kuratowski proposal is taken by Quine as a consequence of the observation that 'ordered pair' is a 'defective noun' and so the proposal is a paradigm of analysis, alternatively 'explication', which can be characterized with the slogan 'explication is elimination'. All of these ideas have their origins in Russell's views of analysis and construction.

[12] The existence of different sets with which numbers can be identified with no way of saying which is right is taken by Benacerraf (1965) to show that numbers are not sets, and therewith introducing a new, non-reductionist 'structuralist' approach in analytic philosophy of mathematics. See the articles on structuralism in Shapiro (2005).

describes the Frege–Russell 'definition' of numbers as a prime example of his method of 'explication' at the beginning of *Meaning and Necessity* (1947).[13]

> The task of making more exact a vague or not quite exact concept used in everyday life or in an earlier stage of scientific or logical development, or rather of replacing it by a newly constructed, more exact concept, belongs among the most important tasks of logical analysis and logical construction. We call this the task of explicating, or of giving an **explication** for, the earlier concept; this earlier concept, or sometimes the terms used for it, is called the **explicandum**; and the new concept, or its term, is called an **explicatum** of the old one. Thus, for instance, Frege and, later, Russell took as explicandum the term 'two' in the not quite exact meaning in which it is used in everyday life and in applied mathematics; they proposed as an explicatum for it an exactly defined concept, namely, the class of pair-classes...other logicians have proposed other explicata for the same explicandum. (Carnap 1947, p. 8)

It does not seem that this is just how Russell saw his method of 'tasks of logical analysis and logical construction', at least not in the case of the definition of the term 'two'. While the definition does take the form of a replacement of one expression by another, the replaced expression is not an expression of inexact meaning from 'everyday life and applied mathematics', but rather a term from the exact science of arithmetic, to be reduced to the new exact science of symbolic logic. There is some element of choice of the specific definition to be used, but this is because of the goal of allowing for the proof as theorems of what would otherwise have to be hypothesized with axioms. As we will see next with Russell's 'construction' of matter, any accounting for applied science, much less 'everyday life' was not part of Russell's projects of logical analysis and logical construction.

12.6 THE CONSTRUCTION OF SPACE, TIME, AND MATTER

Russell's philosophy from somewhat before 1912 until at least 1927 is appropriately called 'logical atomism', even though components of these views changed during the period. In the essay 'Logical Atomism' (1924, pp. 164–6) from 1924 Russell looks back on this series of definitions and theories as all examples of this new technique. 'The first instance I came across was what I have called "the principle of abstraction" or rather "the

---

[13] See the discussion of the definition of number and the comparison with Frege, in Reck (2007). Reck suggests that Frege's explication is closer to the original informal explicandum in that it treats numbers as objects, or 'individuals' while Russell treats them as entities of higher type. Russell starts in agreement with Frege in treating the number 2, for example, as a class of classes, but then differs in deciding that classes are not individuals at all, but instead to be eliminated via the 'no-classes theory'.

principle which dispenses with abstraction"'. Russell here means substituting equivalence classes for a common quality, such as a magnitude. 'A very important example of
the principle', he says, is 'Frege's definition of the cardinal number of a given set of terms
as the class of all sets that are "similar" to the given set...'. Then we have '...classes
themselves can be dispensed with by similar methods'. This is clearly a reference to the
no-classes theory. Another 'important example', he says, are definite descriptions. We
are referred to *14 of *Principia Mathematica*. Russell follows this with a list of further
cases and then, at the end, a turn to the construction of notions beyond mathematics. 'There are many other examples of the substitution of constructions for inferences
in pure mathematics, for example series, ordinal numbers, and real numbers....But
I pass on now to the examples in Physics.' Russell gives two examples of these constructions from physics: 'Points and instants are obvious examples: Dr. Whitehead has
shown how to construct them out of sets of events all of which have a finite extent and
a finite duration. In relativity theory, it is not points or instants that we primarily need,
but event-particles...'. Finally the example that others have focused on most: 'Similar
considerations apply to a particle of matter...'. Looking back, Russell sees each of the
definitions and analyses that have been discussed above as species of one genus, 'logical constructions', to which his new proposals to analyse space, time, and matter are
the latest instalment. In fact, construction is a new sort of analysis, and attention to
its details will reveal new features not common to what preceded. Nevertheless Russell
continues to use his old expressions, with the result that we find matter described as
'incomplete symbols', echoing the structure of the theory of descriptions, and as 'logical fictions', from the avoidance of commitment to classes of the no-classes theory, and
finally as 'constructions' like the numbers, when matter is proposed to consist of classes
of sense-data.

These examples of the notions of instants, locations, and particles are introduced
along with this new terminology of 'logical construction', despite Russell's claim to have
been engaged in the same project all along. In the 1924 essay Russell gives credit for the
project to Whitehead:

> One very important heuristic maxim which Dr. Whitehead and I found, by experi-
> ence, to be applicable in mathematical logic, and have since applied in various other
> fields, is a form of Ockham's razor. When some set of supposed entities has neat
> logical properties, it turns out, in a great many instances, that the supposed entities
> can be replaced by purely logical structures composed of entities which have not
> such neat properties. In that case, in interpreting a body of propositions hitherto
> believed to be about the supposed entities, we can substitute the logical structures
> without altering any of the detail of the body of propositions in question. This is an
> economy, because entities with neat logical properties are always inferred, and if the
> propositions in which they occur can be interpreted without making this inference,
> the ground for the inference fails, and our body of propositions is secured against
> the need of a doubtful step. The principle may be stated in the form: 'Whenever
> possible, substitute constructions out of known entities for inferences to unknown
> entities.' (1924, p. 164)

This certainly describes the no-classes theory of classes. Some 'supposed entities', in this case, classes, have certain 'neat logical properties', namely the properties described in the algebra of classes and in elementary set theory. For these objects we can 'substitute' certain logical constructions, in this case the definitions of the no-classes theory, and so the basic properties of classes can be directly proved from logic, rather than 'inferred' from hypotheses or axioms. In the case of matter, the inference to entities which is replaced is of a different sort. In *The Problems of Philosophy* (1912), Berkeley's arguments against matter are answered by showing that the existence of matter is a reasonable 'inference' from the patterns of experience, or sense-data, which we encounter. Acquaintance is an important notion in Russell's epistemology going back to the early appearance of the distinction between knowledge by acquaintance and knowledge by description in 'On Denoting'. At the time of *Problems*, Russell identifies the sense-data with which we are acquainted as the source of the direct or immediate knowledge we have of the world. The notion of sense-data as the *given*, namely, as a source of certain knowledge of sensory experience is part of the standard interpretation of Russell's epistemology, and certainly the target of much later criticism of the notion of sense-data, as in J. L. Austin's *Sense and Sensibilia* (1962).[14] Russell is taken as holding that through experience we come to have knowledge originally of just our sense-data, for example, when we are experiencing a patch of red at a certain place in our visual field. The problem presented by sense-data, then, is how we make inferences from our knowledge of experience, our sense-data, to knowledge of the external world, other minds, and all other aspects of the world that we do not directly experience. We start with the experience of sense-data, of which we have *knowledge by acquaintance*. That inference from sense-data leads us to knowledge 'by description'. We refer to a table before us, for example, as 'the cause of such and such sense-data I am now experiencing' and that description provides the content of our *knowledge by description*. This purported identification of immediate knowledge with acquaintance, and inferred knowledge with descriptions, however, is not explicitly made by Russell, nor is the epistemology that is supposed to accompany it presented in any detail. To begin with, acquaintance seems too thin and of the wrong sort to provide all immediate knowledge from experience. Acquaintance is a direct, unmediated mental relationship in which the self is related to an object, in our case, some sense-datum. Using terminology that developed later, we might say that acquaintance seems only to give us knowledge 'of' an object, not 'knowledge that' it is so and so. Thus Russell says in *Problems of Philosophy* that in sensing a table we may have acquaintance with a particular shade of colour:

> The particular shade of colour that I am seeing may have many things said about it. I may say that it is brown, that it is rather dark, and so on. But such statements, though they make me know truths *about* the colour, do not make me know the colour itself any better than I did before: so far as concerns knowledge of the colour

---

[14] The connection between acquaintance and the epistemology of the 'given' is explored by Peter Hylton in his contribution to this volume.

itself, as opposed to knowledge of truths about it, I know the colour perfectly and completely when I see it, and no further knowledge of it itself is even theoretically possible. (1912, p. 47)

Thus acquaintance gives us 'complete and perfect' knowledge *of* the colour, but less complete and perfect knowledge of such properties it may have such as being of a dark brown shade. Yet it would seem that if acquaintance is to give us immediate knowledge from which the rest of our knowledge from experience is to be derived, then what we ought to be 'given' are truths of the form 'this is dark brown', or 'I am experiencing dark brown.' These look more like the incorrigible reports of experience that are traditionally associated with an epistemology of sense-data. While knowledge by acquaintance may provide only the first step in an account of the sensory 'given', the notion of knowledge by acquaintance adds little detail to an account of knowledge inferred from that given. The descriptions of material objects as 'the causes of such and such sense-data' only provide a mechanism by which we can have beliefs, and then perhaps knowledge, about objects with which we are not acquainted. A proposition can denote, or be about, an entity that satisfies a definite description even though it is not a constituent of the proposition that contains that description. But that a belief can be about an object with which we are not acquainted does not say anything to explain how we can have knowledge that the object is such and such, based only on the occurrence of some acquaintance with sense-data.

Seen this way, the role of definite descriptions in Russell's epistemology is very different from the later examples of logical constructions. With *Our Knowledge of the External World* (1914) and lasting to thirteen years later, in *The Analysis of Matter* (1927), inference to what is known by description is replaced by construction:

The central problem by which I have sought to illustrate method is the problem of the relation between the crude data of sense and the space, time, and matter of mathematical physics. I have been made aware of the importance of this problem by my friend and collaborator Dr Whitehead, to whom are due almost all the differences between the views advocated here and those suggested in *The Problems of Philosophy*. I owe to him the definition of points, the suggestion for the treatment of instants and 'things', and the whole conception of the world of physics as a *construction* rather than an *inference*. (1914, pp. vii–viii)

It might seem that Russell has here proposed a new epistemology of physical objects that will avoid the necessity of giving an account of the inference from experience to the nature of the objects we experience. It would be simply to deny that there are such objects, or at least that we can have knowledge of them, and then to replace these objects with constructions from objects of acquaintance of which we can have knowledge. This would be a move from a realist view of material objects in the world, in addition to sense-data, to one according to which objects are rather constructions from sense-data. This looks like phenomenalism, the view that material objects are nothing but 'bundles' of perceptions, or perhaps J. S. Mill's 'permanent possibilities of sensation'. As Omar Nasim has recently discussed, there was indeed a controversy among several prominent 'Edwardian' realist philosophers such as G. F. Stout and T. P. Nunn about just these issues, into which Russell entered with his construction of matter in *Our Knowledge of the External World* in 1914.[15] The dispute was about the nature of the direct objects of perception. It was agreed among these 'New Realists' that perceptions are not of our own ideas, and thus we do perceive extra-mental objects. The dispute, however, was over the relation of these sensory objects, called 'sense-data' following Russell, to the material objects that they might seem to represent. In *Problems of Philosophy* Russell had proposed that material objects are *inferred* from the patterns of sense-data that we directly observe. The other 'New Realists' spoke of material objects as psychological or social 'constructions' which guide our thinking about the world, but which are not the extra-mental objects of our perception. As Nasim presents the controversy, Russell entered the discussion by abandoning his 1912 view of matter as 'inferred' and replacing it with his own, technical, notion of 'logical construction'.

But just as it is erroneous to see Russell's notion of acquaintance as providing his account of the 'given' knowledge of propositions from experience, it is incorrect to read logical constructions as simply a new account of what would ordinarily be inferred to exist, as thought by the other participants in the New Realist debates. It is this mistake which led Stebbing (1933) to question the view as seeming to be one on which tables are now to be asserted to be nothing but logical constructions. Although Russell may have entered a debate about the classic 'problem of the external world' and the nature of the ordinary, physical, objects of perception, he seems to have backed away from it with his own notion of the 'logical construction' of matter. With his emphasis on the analysis of physics and science, Russell seems to leave the epistemology of ordinary objects just where it was, as inferred from knowledge directly obtained from experience. Rather, it seems that there is another project at work here, that of giving an account of 'the matter of mathematical physics', and an account of the logically 'neat' properties attributed to matter in mathematical physics, which Russell feels must be logical properties.

What are the 'neat logical properties' of matter that might be analogous to the 'neat' properties of the theory of classes? If one looks at the details of *The Analysis of Matter* one does not find definitions, whether contextual or any other sort, for expressions about ordinary physical objects. Indeed, the term 'logical construction' is not used. Instead it is simply 'construction', although what is found are described as 'logical structures', so some of the old terminology persists. It is the abstract properties of matter and its location in space and time that is described in terms of the structural relationships of sense-data which reveal that structure to us.

---

[15] See Nasim (2008). Nasim's 'controversy' was published primarily in the *Proceedings of the Aristotelian Society*, and begins with Stout (1904) and Nunn (1906) and continues past the famous symposium with Moore and Stout (1914).

> What we mean is this: Given a set of terms having properties which suggest certain general mathematical (or logical) properties, but are subject to exceptions in regard to these properties, it is a mistake to postulate other terms, logically homogeneous with the original set, and such as to remove the exceptions; the proper procedure is to look for logical structures composed of the original terms, and such that these structures always have the mathematical properties in question. (1927, p. 291)

It is the structural features of the physical world, that matter occupies locations in space and time, and 'logically neat properties' of those locations, such as no two physical objects being in the same place at the same time, and other 'neat' properties explored in mathematical physics, which are supposed to be provable with logic alone, given the logical construction of matter from sense-data. It is not particular properties of particular material objects that are 'constructed' but rather the structural features of the world are derivable from the constructions. Indeed this feature of the logical construction of matter has led recent interpreters, Demopoulos and Friedman (1985), to find an anticipation of the later 'structural realist' view of scientific theories in Russell's work on the 'analysis' of matter. On this interpretation the notion of construction plays a role in the inference of the objective properties of space and matter from the patterns of sense-data as they occur in us. We may sense patches of colour next to each other in our visual field, but what that tells us about the causes of those sense-data, about matter, is only revealed by the structure of those relationships. The intrinsic properties of matter are not revealed by the intrinsic properties of our sense-data, as the tradition of distinguishing primary and secondary qualities had long held. The colour of a patch in our visual field tells us nothing about the intrinsic properties of the table which causes that experience. Instead it is the structural properties of our experiences, their order in time, and which are between which in the visual field, that gives us a clue as to the structural relationships of time and space within the material world that causes the experience. The contemporary version of this account, called 'structural realism', holds that it is only the structural properties and relations that a scientific theory attributes to the world about which we should be scientific realists. It is all we can know of the world which is objective. The version of this attributed to Russell, then, is that he held that from the patterns and relations between the sense-data with which we are acquainted, we can only infer that the world has some structure in common with that pattern. If, then, the project of replacing inference with construction is to find, for every pattern of sense-data, some logical construction which bears isomorphic structural relations, then there is still an inference from the given in experience, but only to a rather impoverished, structural reality causing those experiences.

It seems that in fact Russell's construction of matter project was indeed taken in this way by others, and led, in 1927, to G. H. Newman's apparently devastating objection to the whole project. Newman objected to Russell's project, as he saw it, by pointing out that there is always a structure of arbitrarily 'constructed' relations with any given structure if only the number of basic entities, in this case sense-data, is large enough. There must be more, Newman is read as saying, to scientific theories than just asserting that matter has some structural properties isomorphic to those of the 'construction' of matter that Russell proposes. In this interpretation of Russell's project, 'logical construction' has changed from being a technique for defining apparent referring expressions with contextual definitions, to instead finding actual set theoretic structures which are to represent the isomorphic, real structures of the world. It is not at all the proposal to give an 'analysis' of apparent objects to show that they aren't real after all, of the sort of Stebbing's example 'This desk is a logical construction.' Russell's response to Newman is puzzling if he is taken as having had this as the whole of his project. Russell simply acknowledged that Newman was right. 'It was quite clear to me, as I read your article, that I had not really intended to say what in fact I did say, that nothing is known about the physical world except its structure.'[16] This nonchalant response to a devastating criticism suggests that in fact the 'structural realist' account of physics was not Russell's main goal with his construction project. Rather, the project makes sense if we remember that the 'neat' logical features of mathematical physics, which were to be accounted for by the logical construction of matter, are only some of the properties we attribute to matter. They are the properties that matter has in mathematical physics rather than those involved in our everyday knowledge of material objects, including the table right in front of her which so concerned Stebbing.

Russell's project of constructing the basic notions of mathematical physics comes from a view of scientific theories that is now lost to us. Writing before Tarski, Russell's account is purely 'syntactic', there is no notion of a scientific theory as a set of sentences which has set theoretic models. The structures that concern Russell are not that of relations in extension, which are how set theoretic models would appear in the no-classes theory, but rather structures of genuine relations which hold between things in the world. The structures described in mathematical physics are not discovered by theorizing about the 'observation sentences' delivered by empirical science, for their properties are too 'neat' to have come from experience. In the later view of scientific theory developed by the Logical Empiricists and then Quine, the theoretical part of physics must be continuous with sentences about ordinary physical objects. The points and particles constructed by Russell's account are rather part of an abstract 'model' in a more popular sense, like the Bohr 'model' of the atom as consisting of small particles, electrons, orbiting around a central nucleus. Antecedents of the later accounts of scientific theories, from the 'model theoretic' view to 'structural realism', can be seen jumbled together in Russell's views, just as the different projects of analysis and explication can be seen in the earlier mathematical constructions. Perhaps Russell's response to Newman should be seen as a moment when Russell realized that there were in fact different projects that he might have been engaged in, only one of which had been demolished.

---

[16] Letter from Bertrand Russell to Newman of 24 April, 1928 (1968, p. 176) quoted in Demopoulos and Friedman (1988, pp. 631–2).

12.7 Descriptions, Constructions, and the Analysis of Ordinary Language

That Russell meant to be providing an analysis of ordinary language, to say what we really mean by certain expressions, and to claim that apparently ordinary objects are in fact 'logical constructions' and so not genuine, is in fact an interpretation imposed by others. This interpretation arose soon after these writings, and was proposed by philosophers who worked with Russell, namely Wittgenstein and Ramsey. In the *Tractatus Logico-Philosophicus* (1922), Wittgenstein develops the view that ordinary language sometimes hides the real logical form of the propositions which it is nevertheless able to express. And it was Russell who is given credit for starting this project:[17]

> 4.0031 All philosophy is a 'critique of language' (though not in Mauthner's sense). It was Russell who performed the service of showing that the apparent logical form of a proposition need not be its real one.

It is this theme of 'analysis' as revealing the real logical form of propositions which is hidden by the superficial structures of ordinary language, combined with what Carnap would call 'explication', which is repeated by Ramsey in the essay which refers to the theory of descriptions as a paradigm of philosophy:

> Also sometimes philosophy should clarify and distinguish notions previously vague and confused, and clearly this is meant to fix our future meaning only. [footnote: But in so far as our past meaning was not utterly confused, philosophy will naturally give that too. E.g. that paradigm of philosophy, Russell's theory of descriptions.] (1931, p. 263)

Susan Stebbing (1933, Appendix B), describing John Wisdom's series of five articles in *Mind* with the title 'Logical Constructions' (1931), repeats the charge that Russell has confused the notions of incomplete symbol and logical fiction with the further suggestion that a table might be a logical construction. She cites as a better example of a logical construction the proposal to treat statements about a council or committee or nation acting as reducible to statements about the actions of individuals. For Wisdom and Stebbing, logical construction was a method of analysis which reduced statements about entities of one category to statements about entities

---

[17] Although it is Russell, in his 'Introduction' to (1922), that identifies Wittgenstein's project as resolving philosophical problems by translating ordinary language into a 'logically perfect language'. Russell had introduced the notion of a logically perfect language in his lectures (1918). See Hylton's contribution to this volume.

of another, thus combining the themes of ontological reduction and the notion of category mistake.[18]

After the 'linguistic turn' in analytic philosophy, by which one of the main methods of philosophy is to be this project of discovering the proper analysis of vague or mis-leading sentences of ordinary language, the project of logical construction looks very different in retrospect. In the paper 'Systematically Misleading Expressions' (1931), in which Gilbert Ryle proposes this as the primary method of analysis, he concludes with a disclaimer about antecedents of this view in the project of logical construction:

> In this paper I have deliberately refrained from describing expressions as 'incom-plete symbols' or quasi-things as 'logical constructions'. Partly I have abstained because I am fairly ignorant of the doctrines in which these are technical terms, though in so far as I do understand them, I think that I could re-state them in words which I like better without modifying the doctrines. But partly, also, I think that the terms themselves are rather ill-chosen and are apt to cause unnecessary perplexities. But I do think that I have been talking about what is talked about by those who use these terms, when they use them. (1931, p. 100)

Although it is likely that by 'technical terms' he means the theories of Stebbing and Wisdom, it is also clear that Ryle thinks that the basic idea of his new proposal about the nature of philosophy has its antecedents in Russell's theory of definite descriptions and notion of logical construction. It is my contention that many of the later distinct uses of the notion of analysis find their antecedents in different aspects of Russell's defini-tions and constructions. In fact there are several different ideas under the notions of 'incomplete symbol', 'definition', and 'logical construction' in Russell's thinking, which were only clearly distinguished and named more accurately later in the history of ana-lytic philosophy.

References

Austin, J. L. (1962). *Sense and Sensibilia*, ed. G. J. Warnock. Oxford: Oxford University Press.

Benacerraf, Paul (1965). 'What Numbers Could Not Be', *Philosophical Review* 74: 47–73.

Carey, Rosalind (2007). *Russell and Wittgenstein on the Nature of Judgement*. New York: Continuum.

Carnap, Rudolf (1928). *Der Logische Aufbau der Welt*. Tr. Rolf A. George as *The Logical Structure of the World*. Berkeley: University of California Press, 1967.

—— (1947). *Meaning and Necessity*. Chicago: University of Chicago Press.

Demopoulos, William and Michael Friedman (1985). 'Bertrand Russell's *The Analysis of Matter*: Its Historical Context and Contemporary Interest', *Philosophy of Science* 52(4): 621–39.

---

[18] In his later obituary notice for Russell, Ryle (1979) credits the source of the idea of category mistakes to Russell's theory of types. Statements with expressions of the wrong types would be meaningless.

Griffin, Nicholas (1985). 'Russell's Multiple Relation Theory of Judgment', *Philosophical Studies* 47: 213–48.

Makin, Gideon (2000). *The Metaphysicians of Meaning: Russell and Frege on Sense and Denotation*. London: Routledge.

Moore, George E. (1914). 'Symposium: The Status of Sense-Data', *Proceedings of the Aristotelian Society* 14: 335–80.

Nasim, Omar (2008). *Bertrand Russell and the Edwardian Philosophers: Constructing the World*. Basingstoke: Palgrave Macmillan.

Neale, Stephen (1990). *Descriptions*. Cambridge, MA: MIT Press.

Quine, Willard Van Orman (1960). *Word and Object*. Cambridge, MA: MIT Press.

Ramsey, Frank P. (1931). 'Philosophy'. In *The Foundations of Mathematics and Other Logical Essays,* ed. R. B. Braithwaite. London: Routledge & Kegan Paul, pp. 263–9.

Reck, Erich (2007). 'Frege–Russell Numbers: Analysis or Explication?' In Michael Beaney (ed.), *The Analytic Turn: Analysis in Early Analytic Philosophy and Phenomenology*. New York and London: Routledge, pp. 33–50.

Richardson, Alan (1998). *Carnap's Construction of the World: The Aufbau and the Emergence of Logical Empiricism*. Cambridge: Cambridge University Press.

Russell, Bertrand (1903). *The Principles of Mathematics*. Cambridge: Cambridge University Press.

—— (1905). 'On Denoting', *Mind* 14: 479–93. Reprinted in *Foundations of Logic 1903–05, The Collected Papers of Bertrand Russell, Volume 4,* ed. Alasdair Urquhart. London and New York: Routledge, 1994, pp. 415–27.

—— (1912). *The Problems of Philosophy*. Home University Library of Modern Knowledge. London: Williams and Norgate. Repr. Oxford: Oxford University Press, 1997.

—— (1914). *Our Knowledge of the External World*. London: George Allen & Unwin. Repr. London: Routledge, 1993.

—— (1918). 'The Philosophy of Logical Atomism', *The Monist*, 28 (October 1918): 495–527; 29 (January, April, July 1919): 32–63, 190–222, 345–80. Page references to reprint in *The Philosophy of Logical Atomism and Other Essays 1914–19, The Collected Papers of Bertrand Russell, Volume 8,* ed. John G. Slater. London: George Allen & Unwin, 1986, pp. 157–244.

—— (1919). *Introduction to Mathematical Philosophy*. London: George Allen & Unwin; New York: Macmillan. Repr. London: Routledge, 1993.

—— (1924). 'Logical Atomism'. In J. H. Muirhead (ed.), *Contemporary British Philosophy: Personal Statements*. London: George Allen & Unwin, pp. 357–83. Page references to reprint in *Essays on Language, Mind and Matter 1919–26, The Collected Papers of Bertrand Russell, Volume 9,* ed. John G. Slater. London: Unwin Hayman, 2001, pp. 160–79.

—— (1927). *The Analysis of Matter*. London: Kegan Paul, Trench, Trubner & Co.; New York: Harcourt, Brace & Company. Repr. London: Routledge, 1992.

—— (1968). *The Autobiography of Bertrand Russell*. New York: Little, Brown.

—— (1994). *Foundations of Logic 1903–1905*, ed. Alasdair Urquhart. London and New York: Routledge.

Ryle, Gilbert (1931). 'Systematically Misleading Expressions', *Proceedings of the Aristotelian Society* 32 (1931–2): 139–70. Page references to Richard M. Rorty (ed.), *The Linguistic Turn: Essays in Philosophical Method*. Chicago: University of Chicago Press, 1992, pp. 85–100.

—— (1979). 'Bertrand Russell: 1872–1970'. In George W. Roberts (ed.), *Bertrand Russell Memorial Volume*. London: George Allen & Unwin, pp. 15–21.

Shapiro, Stewart (ed.) (2005). *The Oxford Handbook of Philosophy of Mathematics and Logic*. Oxford: Oxford University Press.

Stebbing, L. Susan (1933). *A Modern Introduction to Logic*, 2nd edn. London: Methuen.

Stout, G. F. (1904). 'Primary and Secondary Qualities', *Proceedings of the Aristotelian Society* 4 (1903–4): 141–60.

—— (1914). 'Symposium: The Status of Sense-Data', *Proceedings of the Aristotelian Society* 14 (1913–14): 381–406.

Whitehead, A. N. and B. A. Russell (1910). *Principia Mathematica*. Cambridge: Cambridge University Press. 3 vols., 1st edn, 1910–13, 2nd edn., 1925–7.

Wiener, Norbert (1914). 'A Simplification of the Logic of Relations', *Proceedings of the Cambridge Philosophical Society* 17: 387–90.

Wisdom, John (1931–3). 'Logical Constructions', *Mind*, I: 40 (1931): 188–216; II: 40 (1931): 460–75; III: 41 (1932): 441–64; IV: 42 (1933): 43–66; V: 42 (1933): 186–202.

Wittgenstein, Ludwig (1922). *Tractatus Logico-Philosophicus*, tr. C. K. Ogden and F. P. Ramsey, with an introduction by Bertrand Russell. London: Routledge & Kegan Paul.

Wrinch, Dorothy (1919). 'On the Nature of Judgment', *Mind* 28: 319–29.

CHAPTER 13

....

G. E. MOORE AND THE CAMBRIDGE SCHOOL OF ANALYSIS

....

THOMAS BALDWIN

13.1 INTRODUCTION

....

In his 1931 *Mind* paper 'Logical Constructions (1)' John Wisdom wrote:

> Philosophy is concerned with the analysis of facts—a doctrine which Wittgenstein
> has lately preached and Moore long practised. (Wisdom 1931: 195 n. 2)

Alluding to this passage in a paper given in 1932 at the Aristotelian Society, Susan
Stebbing commented:

> It is from the writings of Prof. Moore that I have learnt the importance of the method
> of metaphysical analysis.* He has not explicitly dealt with the problem of method,
> but he has shown clearly the necessity of analysis, and has indicated some presup-
> positions of the use of the method.
>   * I do not wish to suggest that Moore uses this expression, nor that he would
> agree with what I say. But if what I say is correct, then I think it could have been
> derived from a study of his writings (Cf. J. Wisdom, *Mind*, April, 1931, p. 195 *n*.)
> (Stebbing 1932–3: 76)

In a similar way Austin Duncan-Jones wrote in his contribution to a 1937 Joint Session
symposium 'Does Philosophy Analyse Common Sense?'

> The question asked in this title relates, of course, to philosophy as understood and
> practised by a particular limited group of philosophers; primarily, the contempo-
> rary philosophy of the people in this country who have commonly been called ana-
> lytic philosophers.

Ever since G. E. Moore published his 'Defence of Common Sense,' the idea has been current that the main activity of these philosophers consists of taking propositions which are known to be true, and which are matters of common sense, and discovering what their correct analysis is. (Duncan-Jones 1937: 139–40)

These passages exemplify what one can call 'the Cambridge School of Analysis' and the role of G. E. Moore in inspiring this 'school'. John Wisdom and Austin Duncan-Jones had studied philosophy with Moore in Cambridge during the 1920s when he was the dominant influence there. Susan Stebbing had also studied at Cambridge, but at an earlier time when Moore was absent. She recounts how she first encountered Moore in 1917 when he took control of the discussion of her paper at a meeting of the Aristotelian Society, and how she became converted there and then to his approach to philosophy (Stebbing 1942: 530). One point worth noting in the passage by Duncan-Jones is his use of the phrase 'the contemporary philosophy of the people in this country who have commonly been called analytic philosophers'. This indicates that talk of 'analytic philosophers' (and, by implication, 'analytic philosophy') was by then (1937) common, and raises the question of what was then understood by this talk. In his introduction to *Problems of Mind and Matter* (Wisdom 1934b) John Wisdom had presented one conception of 'analytic philosophy':

An introduction to a science, such as chemistry, will contain a selection of the easier and more fundamental chemical truths. In my opinion there cannot be such an introduction to analytic philosophy. For there is no special set of analytic truths. Analytic philosophy has no special subject-matter. You can philosophise about Tuesday, the pound sterling, and lozenges and philosophy itself. This is because the analytic philosopher, unlike the scientist, is not one who learns new truths, but one who gains new insight into old truths. (Wisdom 1934b: 2)

As we shall see later, the contrast between the 'new insights' of the analytic philosopher and the 'new truths' of a science such as chemistry is not straightforward. But Wisdom's account does, I think, capture the general sense at the time of what was distinctive about analytic philosophy.

13.2 MOORE AND ANALYSIS

Duncan-Jones alluded to Moore's paper 'A Defence of Common Sense' (Moore 1925). This was Moore's contribution to the second series of invited essays by British philosophers edited by J. H. Muirhead and published as *Contemporary British Philosophy*. Muirhead's aim had been 'to give the contributors an opportunity of stating authentically what they regard as the main problem of philosophy and what they have endeavoured to make central in their own speculation upon it' (Muirhead 1924: 10). In the passage which Duncan-Jones had in mind, Moore writes:

> I am not at all sceptical as to the *truth* of such propositions as 'The earth has existed for many years past', 'Many human bodies have each lived for many years upon it', i.e. propositions which assert the existence of material things...But I am very sceptical as to what, in certain respects, the correct *analysis* of such propositions is.... [I] hold also that no philosopher, hitherto, has succeeded in suggesting an analysis of them, as regards certain important points, which comes anywhere near to being certainly true. (Moore 1993b: 127)

In the light of Muirhead's invitation, therefore, Moore is here identifying 'the correct *analysis*' of common sense propositions as 'central in [his] own speculation upon' these propositions. But what does Moore here mean by this talk of 'the correct *analysis*'? And why does he regard this as central to his own philosophical 'speculation' (though this is not a term Moore would have applied to his own work)?

Moore does not address these questions explicitly in his essay, but he discusses one case in sufficient detail to indicate the direction of his thought. The case is that of the analysis of 'This is a hand', concerning which Moore writes:

> Two things only seem to me to be quite certain about the analysis of such propositions...namely that whenever I know, or judge, such a proposition to be true, (1) there is always some *sense-datum* about which the proposition is a proposition—some sense-datum which is *a* subject (and, in a certain sense, the principal or ultimate subject) of the proposition in question, and (2) that, nevertheless, *what* I am knowing or judging to be true about this sense-datum is not (in general) that it is *itself* a hand. (Moore 1993b: 128)

Moore proceeds to elucidate his first point, concerning the role of a 'sense-datum' as subject of this proposition, by inviting his reader to look at his own hand; the reader is invited to participate, not in a typically philosophical thought-experiment, but in an apparently simple visual experiment:

> And, in order to point out to the reader what sort of things I mean by sense-data, I need only ask him to look at his own right hand. If he does this he will be able to pick out something (and, unless he is seeing double, *only* one thing) with regard to which he will see that it is, at first sight, a natural view to take that that thing is identical, not, indeed, with his whole right hand, but with that part of its surface which he is actually seeing, but will also (on a little reflection) be able to see that it is doubtful whether it can be identical with the part of the surface of his hand in question. Things *of the sort* (in a certain respect) of which this thing is, which he sees in looking at his hand, and with regard to which he can understand how some philosophers should have supposed it to *be* the part of the surface which he is seeing, while others have supposed that it can't be, are what I mean by 'sense-data.' (Moore 1993b: 128–9)

One point that is immediately clear is that the analysis in this case starts from a reflective analysis of visual experience: the reader is invited to 'pick out something' (visually) concerning which, as Moore puts it, the reader will recognize 'on a little reflection' that is doubtful whether it is identical to 'that part of [his hand's] surface which he is actually seeing'. Moore proceeds to give two grounds for this doubt: first, that this part of the surface of the hand will look very different when viewed through a microscope, which suggests that this part of the hand's surface cannot be the thing, the 'sense-datum', he picks out visually now unless the sense-datum does not need to have the qualities, e.g. the colour and texture, which it appears to have. Moore is prepared to accept this; but he takes it that there is a second ground for doubt which is 'a far more serious objection' (Moore 1993b: 131) to the sense-datum's being part of the hand's surface. This concerns a case of double vision, where we have a 'double image' of our right hand: Moore holds that in a case of this kind 'we certainly have *two* sense-data' which cannot both be one and the same part of the hand's surface; and from this he infers that 'every sense-datum is, after all, only "representative" of the surface *of* which it is a sense-datum' (Moore 1993b: 131).

There is much here that might be questioned, but the key inference is that from there being a 'double image', and thus two images, to there being '*two* sense-data'. This inference may seem uncontentious, but in fact it is easy to reject. If the basic conception of a visual sense-datum is just that of something which, on reflection, we are able to pick out visually when looking at our right hand, something which seems at first to be part of the surface of our hand, etc., there is no compelling reason to deny that in a case of double vision we are still able to pick out just one such sense-datum, since Moore's argument assumes that each sense-datum is 'of' one and the same part of the surface of our hand. Moore's contrary confidence that two sense-data are involved implies that he is individuating visual sense-data not just by what we pick out visually, but also by reference to the ways in which something we pick out visually is presented to us: his view seems to be that in a case of double vision 'we certainly have *two* sense-data' because, given that the situation involves an experience in which there is an unresolved difference in visual perspective, there are two ways in which part of the surface of our right hand is visually presented to us, namely a left-eye way and right-eye way. Officially, therefore, Moore holds that a sense-datum is just something that, on reflection, we can pick out within experience and which need not be as it appears to be; but his discussion implies that he takes that which is thus picked out to include the way in which it is presented to us in experience, so that where visual experience involves two such ways, two sense-data are involved. His official account of sense-data is intended to be neutral concerning their metaphysical status; but his discussion implies that they are individuated on a subjective basis.

In an assessment of Moore's philosophy of perception more would obviously need to be said about this issue and its significance (see Bouwsma 1942 for a famous discussion of Moore's 'theory of sense-data' based around the passage discussed here). But I have introduced this sense-datum analysis here primarily because Moore himself selects it as an example of analysis, and we need now to return to this aspect of Moore's discussion of it. As I have indicated, the analysis seems to be a reflective analysis of visual experience, comparable to that which Moore employs when he introduces his conception of sense-data in his 1910–11 lectures *Some Main Problems of Philosophy* where he writes 'the occurrence which I mean here to analyse is merely the *mental* occurrence—the act of consciousness—which we call seeing' (Moore 1953: 29). This analysis fits into a long-standing tradition of providing a psychological analysis of mental states which Moore encountered when studying at Cambridge; a notable example of this tradition is G. F. Stout who writes in his *Analytic Psychology* of the 'analysis of consciousness' as 'largely introspective' (Stout 1896: 35–6). Moore certainly knew this book well, although he did not accept Stout's analyses of perception and judgement.

Yet once one turns back to 'A Defence of Common Sense' it is striking that Moore no longer writes of providing an analysis of mental states such as seeing but of *propositions*, and not even propositions such as 'I am looking at my right hand', but, instead, propositions such as that expressed by 'This is a hand' which includes no explicit reference to perception. In 'Some Judgments of Perception' (Moore 1918) Moore had called the judgement 'This is a hand' a judgement of perception, and we need to consider why this description is appropriate since, on the face of it, the truth that 'this' (whatever it is) is a hand (if it is true) does not depend on any perception of it. The answer is that, for Moore, perception (and thus sense-data) come in via the role of the demonstrative, 'This'. Moore takes it we use this demonstrative precisely to refer to something which we can 'pick out' in our current sensory field, a sense-datum, though he then adds that, in judging 'This is a hand' we are not judging that this sense-datum is itself a hand; instead we are judging that it is '*of*' a hand, where the '*of*'-relation remains to be further analysed. One way to present this position would be as a descriptive analysis of demonstratives according to which 'This' abbreviates 'the thing which is currently presented to me'. Such an account would readily show why it is appropriate to call that judgement that this is a hand a 'judgement of perception'; but the resulting position would be vulnerable to familiar objections concerning the truth of the proposition in counterfactual situations in which other things are presented to me. Moore, however, standardly uses a demonstrative when presenting his position in a way which is alien to this descriptive approach, as in the following passage from 'Some Judgments of Perception':

> That is to say, when I make such a judgment as 'This inkstand is a good big one'; what I am really judging is: 'There is a thing which stands to *this* in a certain relation, and which is an inkstand, and that thing is a good big one'—where '*this*' stands for the presented object. (Moore 1922: 234)

So Moore's position is, I think, better understood as a direct reference account of demonstratives combined with the further thesis that the object referred to by a demonstrative is always 'the presented object'; and it is this further thesis which leads him to describe the judgement 'This is a hand' as a judgement of perception. To use David Kaplan's terminology (Kaplan 1989), for Moore the role of 'this' is to 'load' the 'presented object', the relevant sense-datum, into the proposition we affirm or judge as the 'principal or ultimate subject' of this proposition.

The implication of this is that Moore's (partial) analysis of the proposition expressed by 'This is a hand' is a hybrid: he employs a semantic analysis of the demonstrative which he expresses in terms of 'sense-data' as the objects referred to in experience, and this latter aspect is then developed by means of a reflective analysis of perception. One way to think about the resulting position is to view it as the result of applying Russell's fundamental principle that '*Every proposition which we can understand must be composed wholly of constituents with which we are acquainted*' (Russell 1912: 91) to judgements of perception, on the assumption that it is sense-data with which we are primarily acquainted in perception. So it is worth considering whether Moore was guided to his sense-datum analysis by Russell's principle. I think the answer to this is negative: not only does Moore never invoke Russell's principle, there is also a discussion of memory in *Some Main Problems of Philosophy* (Moore 1953: 245–7) in which Moore undermines Russell's principle for the case of memory. Suppose, Moore argues, that you now remember some past sense-datum, such as the appearance yesterday of your right hand; clearly you are not now 'directly perceiving' that sense-datum (Moore's 'direct perception' is equivalent to Russell's 'acquaintance'). Moore recognizes that the obvious response is that you are directly perceiving a memory image of that sense-datum and that it is in virtue of this image that you remember the earlier sense-datum, and for the sake of the argument he accepts this hypothesis. However, he now invites you to suppose in addition that you are aware that this image differs from the previous sense-datum. In being aware of this, Moore argues, it cannot be that you are merely directly perceiving the image of the sense-datum; instead you are remembering the original sense-datum without directly perceiving either it or another image of it. So it constitutes a clear counterexample to Russell's principle, and, Moore continues, once this counterexample involving memory is admitted, 'why should it not be what normally occurs, whenever we remember' (Moore 1953: 246; Moore's argument anticipates Wittgenstein's famous critical discussion in 'The Blue Book' of the role of images in the imagination in which we are invited to 'consider the order "*imagine* a red patch"'—see Wittgenstein 1958: 3). Moore acknowledges that he cannot provide a positive account of 'this obscure sort of consciousness' which is characteristic of memory; but he has already said enough to undermine Russell's fundamental principle—though Russell appears not to have agreed since he persisted in affirming the principle despite having attended Moore's lectures.

Moore's emphasis on the importance of questions of analysis is prominent throughout his writings. He opens *Principia Ethica* (Moore 1903) with the following bold declaration:

> It appears to me that in Ethics, as in all other philosophical studies, the difficulties and disagreements, of which its history is full, are mainly due to a very simple cause: namely to the attempt to answer questions, without first discovering precisely *what* question it is you desire to answer. (Moore 1993a: 33)

Moore then proceeds to explain that the way to achieve the requisite clarity concerning the meaning of philosophical questions is through 'the work of analysis and distinction' (Moore 1993a: 33; Moore's emphasis on the importance of identifying the questions one seeks to answer is emphasized by Stebbing in her description of 'Moore's Influence' (Stebbing 1942); and there is a sense in which this aspect of Moore's method anticipates Collingwood's influential later emphasis on the logic of question and answer—see Collingwood 1938: 31–4). Thus in ethics he takes it that the fundamental distinction is that between the questions 'What kind of things ought to exist for their own sake?' (i.e. have intrinsic value) and 'What kind of actions ought we to perform?' (i.e. are duties), and the importance of this distinction is that answers to the first question are self-evident and not susceptible of justification, whereas answers to the second require justification by evidence, for example concerning the results of action (Moore 1993a: 33–4). So, for Moore, the fundamental error in ethics is not ethical error concerning which things which have intrinsic value, nor moral error concerning one's duty; instead it is *philosophical* error, the 'error of confusion' (Moore 1993a: 35) concerning the kinds of evidence, if any, appropriate to different ethical questions. And, he maintains, once such confusion is corrected, the answers to ethical questions are obvious:

> Indeed, once the meaning of the question is clearly understood, the answer to it, in its main outlines, appears to be so obvious, that it runs the risk of seeming to be a platitude. By far the most valuable things, which we can know or can imagine, are certain states of consciousness, which may be roughly described as the pleasures of human intercourse and the enjoyment of beautiful objects. (Moore 1993a: 237)

Analysis is therefore central to Moore's ethics since he uses it to distinguish fundamental ethical and moral questions and thereby identify the considerations which are relevant to answering them. Indeed, this is the aspect of Moore's approach to ethics which, in retrospect, is so striking—the fact that he devotes the first four chapters of his book, which has only six chapters in total, to an extended discussion of what we now call 'metaethics'. In embarking on this project Moore takes it that the distinctions between ethical and moral questions arise from the properties involved, and thus that what is required are definitions of these properties where they are available. Further, he maintains, definition is not a matter of 'verbal definition' concerning the proper use of a word; instead it is a matter of identifying the 'parts' which compose some complex property considered as a 'whole' (Moore 1993a: 60); and analysis is involved because 'we cannot define anything except by an analysis' (Moore 1993a: 61), namely an analysis of a complex property into those simple parts which are themselves among 'the ultimate terms of reference by reference to which whatever *is* capable of definition must be defined' (Moore 1993a: 61).

Moore is here operating with a conception of analysis which is basically metaphysical. In his early paper 'The Nature of Judgment' (Moore 1899) he had sketched a metaphysics in which concepts, the constituents of propositions, are the fundamental substances, somehow giving rise to ordinary things via the identity of reality with truth in such a way that 'A thing becomes intelligible first when it is analysed into its constituent concepts'

(Moore 1993b: 8). A version of this metaphysics is implicit in *Principia Ethica*, both in Moore's account of definition and then in his fundamental claim that goodness—'that quality which we assert to belong to a thing, when we say that the thing is good'—is 'simple, unanalysable, indefinable' (Moore 1993a: 89). One feature of this position is a deliberate blurring of the distinction between, as we would put it, properties and concepts: concepts, the constituents of propositions, are, we would say, ways of characterizing properties, which are the constituents of things. But Moore's position in 'The Nature of Judgment' precisely rejects this distinction, and as a result Moore's discussion of goodness in *Principia Ethica* also does not take account of it in a way which affects the significance of his claim that goodness is unanalysable.

Moore's main argument for this claim is of course the 'open question' argument which takes the form of a critical thought experiment concerning a proposed analysis of goodness such as that it is what we desire to desire (Moore 1993a: 67). Moore's argument is that the analysis implies that the question 'is anything which we desire to desire something which is good?' means the same as the question 'is anything which we desire to desire something which we desire to desire?' since the phrasing of the questions differs only in that where the first has the phrase 'is good' the second has the phrase 'is something which we desire to desire', which should not alter its meaning if the proposed analysis of goodness in terms of desire is correct. But, Moore objects, these questions obviously differ in meaning: the former raises a substantive ethical question concerning the value of what we desire to desire whereas the latter is manifestly trivial. To equate these questions is to hold that doubts concerning the value of the objects of desire can be swept aside with the comment: 'This is not an open question: the very meaning of the word decides it: no one can think otherwise except through confusion' (Moore 1993a: 72). Since nothing here depends on the example chosen, Moore suggests, this line of argument suffices to undermine any proposed analysis of goodness.

The merits of this argument remain disputed and this is not the place for a detailed examination of it. But there are aspects of it that are important for an understanding of Moore's conception of analysis. One concerns the distinction between the analysis of concepts and the analysis of properties. As I have indicated, Moore rejects this distinction, but since his argument primarily concerns the distinctive meaning of questions concerning what is good it looks as though it can really only support a conclusion concerning the unanalysability of the *concept* goodness. After all, as it is often said, the fact that it was no part of the meaning of the word 'water' that water = H_2O does not show that this chemical definition of water is incorrect (Putnam 1981: 206–8). So it remains appropriate to ask whether the argument has any purchase against a proposed 'synthetic' definition of the property goodness. This question cannot be settled here; but my own view is that since a successful definition of this kind transforms our understanding of the phenomenon defined (such as water), especially by providing new ways to determine whether some substance is water, a successful definition of goodness of this kind is vulnerable to an extension of Moore's argument (Baldwin 2003).

The other aspect of Moore's open question argument that merits attention here concerns 'the paradox of analysis'. Moore's argument called into question a proposed analysis of goodness by means of the substitution of the *analysans* for the *analysandum*, which should be legitimate if the analysis is correct. The paradox of analysis arises from the application of this line of argument, involving the substitution of *analysans* for *analysandum* within analyses themselves; for it seems to imply that an analysis must be either trivial or incorrect. This 'paradox' had been noted in some form by several philosophers, such as Husserl, but it was only in the context of reflection on Moore's method of philosophical analysis that the issues to which it gives rise were clearly addressed (so far as I am aware, the phrase 'paradox of analysis' first occurs in print in Wisdom 1933: 197, but it may well have been used in earlier discussion). These issues are best considered in the context of an example: so consider Moore's suggestion that an agent acts freely where she could have acted otherwise if she had so chosen (Moore 1966a: 113). This can be regarded as offering an analysis of free action which, following Moore (Moore 1942: 667), we can express as the claim that to say that an agent acts freely is just to say that she could have acted otherwise if she had so chosen. The 'paradox' arises where we use this analysis to make a substitution within the analysis itself to generate a further analysis of the analysis, so as to infer that anyone who propounds the analysis that to say that an agent acts freely is to say that she could have acted otherwise if she had so chosen is just propounding the analysis that to say that an agent acts freely is to say that an agents acts freely. This result is clearly wrong, since the proposed analysis is substantive, not trivial. But the line of argument involved seems directly comparable to that of Moore's own open question argument.

In fact, there is a way out here: one can allow that analyses license substitutions within first-order propositions or questions but not within iterated second-order propositions or questions, such as questions about the identity of putative analyses. To back this up one needs something like a Fregean theory of indirect sense (as Church proposed in Church (1946), though it suffices to stop Church's hierarchy of senses at the second level), so that within these second-order contexts what is important is not just the meaning of the expressions in question (e.g. 'acts freely') but the 'mode of presentation' of this meaning, i.e., typically, the expressions themselves—as Moore himself in effect maintained:

> in order to explain the fact that, even if 'To be a brother is the same thing as to be a male sibling' is true, yet nevertheless this statement is *not* the same as the statement 'To be a brother is to be a brother', one *must* suppose that both statements are in *some* sense about the expressions used as well as about the concept of being a brother. (Moore 1942: 666)

So far I have discussed Moore's use of analysis in his accounts of perception and in his ethical theory. In both cases Moore's discussion starts from a familiar type of analysis, psychological in one case, metaphysical in the other; but the discussion also turns out to require further, semantic, considerations, for example concerning demonstratives or the type of substitutivity licensed by an analysis. This complexity is indicative of the development of a linguistic component, often only implicit, in Moore's practice of analysis. This new sensitivity to language owes much to Russell and when Moore discussed analysis in the course of his lectures (Moore 1966b) he frequently alluded to Russell's contributions to logical theory and thus to the analysis of propositions provided by theories such as Russell's theory of definite descriptions (though he also noted the non-Russellian generic use of definite descriptions, as in 'The right arm is often slightly longer than the left one'—Moore 1966b: 162). I say more about Russell's 'logical-analytic' programme below, but it is worth saying a little here about Moore's influential reaction to it.

Moore's attitude was basically one of deferential, but not uncritical, admiration. He was not a formal logician himself but he was able to appreciate Russell's achievements even when he could not follow all the details of Russell's mathematical theories. His comments are largely directed at the philosophical points which Russell attached to his logical theories and often draw on informal considerations which are apparent in ordinary language. A good example of Moore's informal logical analysis is provided by his 1936 paper 'Is Existence a Predicate' (Moore 1993b; 134–46), in which Moore compares our use of sentences such as 'Tame tigers exist' and 'Tame tigers growl' in order to elucidate the differences between 'exist' and 'growl' and thus the sense in which 'exist' is not a predicate comparable to 'growl'. Thus far Moore's discussion can be seen as a way of elucidating Russell's thesis that, unlike growling, existence should be predicated of propositional functions, not individuals, i.e. that it is a second-order, not a first-order, concept. But at the end of the paper, Moore undermines Russell's position by observing that we do also want to be able to judge, concerning particular, basic, individuals (Moore of course instances sense-data), 'This might not have existed', and argues that such a claim makes sense only if 'This exists' also makes sense, i.e. only if there is a first-order concept of existence. Moore does not bring these two lines of argument in his paper into a single coherent account of existence, but there can be little doubt that Moore demonstrates the need for a first-order concept of existence of the kind that Russell had hoped to banish.

My examples of Moorean philosophical analysis have been heterogeneous, and they exemplify the fact that although he regarded analysis as a central method of philosophical argument, he never signed up to any of the powerful programmes of philosophical analysis which dominated much philosophical debate during the first half of the twentieth century. As I have indicated, Moore rejected Russell's principle which called for an epistemological analysis of propositions in terms of constituents with which we are acquainted. Moore also rejected the logical atomism of Wittgenstein's *Tractatus Logico-Philosophicus* which called for an analysis of propositions based on the thesis that the basic objects named in a language are objects whose existence is necessary (Wittgenstein 1922: 2.0271). For Moore this assertion of the necessity of substance was as incredible as the assertion by the British Hegelians that all relations are internal.

Finally, Moore rejected the logical empiricist programme of the Vienna Circle and its followers such as A. J. Ayer. Although he never argued explicitly against this programme, and indeed helped it by publishing important papers by leading figures of this movement in *Mind* (of which he was editor from 1925 until 1947), it is clear from his writings on perception, ethics, and metaphysics that he did not endorse the empiricist assumptions of the movement. In his 1908 paper 'Professor James' Pragmatism' (Moore 1907–8) Moore had argued that William James's verificationist conception of meaning does not deal adequately with meaningful claims about the past for which there is now no evidence (Moore 1922: 101–4); and although he does not return explicitly to this argument in later writings, it could have led him to adopt a critical attitude to a philosophical movement whose basic approach to meaning is vulnerable to much the same objection.

The fact that Moore's use of analysis was not tied to any of these analytic programmes helps to explain his emphatic protest at John Wisdom's use of the phrase 'Moore's account of philosophy as analysis' in his paper 'Moore's Technique' (Wisdom 1942: 425). In response to Wisdom Moore wrote:

> But it is not true that I have ever either said or thought or implied that analysis is the only proper business of philosophy. (Moore 1942: 675–6)

As the examples discussed here show, for Moore analysis was always just a part, albeit a central part, of more general philosophical discussion. Insofar as these discussions aim to provide answers to philosophical questions, the preliminary work of 'analysis and distinction' required to identify these questions was an essential component of philosophical inquiry. But although in some cases analysis may imply that familiar questions are so confused that they do not merit further consideration, Moore certainly did not think that this is always the case. The sense-datum analysis belongs within a general account of perception which also requires an account of what it is for a sense-datum to be '*of*' a hand or something similar; and insofar as it concerns the 'principal or ultimate subject' of a proposition, it also connects with both logic and metaphysics. The metaethical analysis of ethical concepts is intended to identify the fundamental questions of ethics and show what types of consideration are relevant to answering them, but not to settle these questions. And Moore's contributions to the philosophy of logic help to identify the basic categories of logical theory such as existence and entailment without supplanting the need for logical theory itself. So for Moore analysis was an essential ingredient of philosophical argument; but other considerations, such as the appeal to common sense he employs in 'A Defence of Common Sense' (Moore 1925), were also appropriate. The primary aim of analysis was not to dissipate philosophical confusion, though Moore did attempt (not always successfully) to use it in this way when discussing F. H. Bradley's absolute idealism; instead the main role of analysis was to advance discussion concerning traditional 'problems of philosophy', such as those addressed in his 1910–11 lectures on 'Some Main Problems of Philosophy' (Moore 1953).

13.3 THE 'CAMBRIDGE SCHOOL'—THE GREAT GENERATION

As I indicated at the start of this chapter, in the 1930s there was group of young philosophers whose approach to philosophy was much influenced, for a time at least, by their contact with Moore in Cambridge in the 1920s, so much so that they came to think that the main task of philosophy was analysis, especially the analysis of 'common sense', such as the propositions Moore had identified in his paper 'A Defence of Common Sense'. But if one is to think of there being a 'Cambridge School of Analysis' during the 1920s and '30s, one needs also to attend to the work of other major Cambridge philosophers of the period. Obviously the two major figures are Bertrand Russell and Ludwig Wittgenstein, though it is important to bear in mind that while they had both been in Cambridge during the 1910s, and Wittgenstein returned during the 1930s, neither of them was in Cambridge during the 1920s, which no doubt explains Moore's influence on the younger group. I shall not attempt here to describe the work of Russell and Wittgenstein in any detail; my aim is only to sketch those aspects of it which contribute to the broader range of approaches to philosophy which one can still think of as fundamentally involving analysis.

I have already mentioned Russell's fundamental principle which connects understanding to acquaintance. As Russell was aware this principle motivates a programme of analysis that is dependent upon the range, and limits, of acquaintance. In Russell's work this programme intersects with the programme of logical analysis that he developed in the context of his work on the foundations of logic and mathematics which led up the ramified theory of types of *Principia Mathematica*. In some of his writings he presents this programme of logical analysis as an all-encompassing way of doing philosophy; thus he begins his 1914 lecture 'Logic as the Essence of Philosophy' with the bold claim:

> every philosophical claim, when it is subjected to the necessary analysis and purification, is found to be not really philosophical at all, or else to be, in the sense in which we are using the word, logical. (Russell 1914: 33)

But it should be added that in the preface to the text of these lectures he adds:

> The following lectures are an attempt to show, by means of examples, the nature, capacity, and limitations of the logical-analytic method in philosophy. (Russell 1914: v)

and these 'limitations' become evident in the lectures, for example in his discussion of our knowledge of 'other minds' (Russell 1914: 93–7). The technique which Russell generally used to combine his two analytic programmes was that of 'logical construction'; the idea was to use techniques of logical analysis developed within his theory of classes in such a way that propositions which appear to concern things with which we are not acquainted, such as other minds, can be 'constructed' in such a way that they deal only with classes of things with which we are acquainted, such as our own sense-data. This technique is central to Russell's new account of the physical world, as in his 1914 paper 'The Relation of Sense-Data to Physics' (Russell 1986: 11), and his 1917–18 lectures on 'The Philosophy of Logical Atomism' (Russell 1986: 160–244): the 'atoms' are objects of acquaintance, and logical construction is used to provide on their basis an account of the world (Russell 1986: 240). As the case of other minds indicates, it is far from clear that the technique of logical construction is really able to achieve what was needed, but the basic idea was an important contribution to the analytic programme.

Russell's philosophical work was interrupted by his political activities during 1917–18, and when he returned to philosophy his approach to philosophy and analysis was somewhat different, although he still used the term 'analysis' in the titles of his two major new books, *The Analysis of Mind* (Russell 1921) and *The Analysis of Matter* (Russell 1927). The main change was that he now abandoned acquaintance, and with it the fundamental principle concerning the understanding of propositions which had dictated a programme of analysis guided by epistemological concerns, and adopted instead a programme of metaphysical analysis based on a form of 'neutral monism', according to which 'sensations' are supposedly neutral basic atoms which provide the basis for two different analyses, one of mind and the other of matter, both guided, as before, by the technique of logical construction (for further details, see Baldwin 1995). The details of this new analytic programme are not important here and it attracted little support; but there is one feature of Russell's new approach which is manifest in his contribution to the first volume of Muirhead's collections of essays *Contemporary British Philosophy* (Russell 1924). Russell called his essay 'Logical Atomism', where the atoms are now his neutral 'sensations'; but the important point is the central epistemological role that Russell now gives to science within philosophy: 'we shall be wise to build our philosophy upon science' (Russell 1924: 377), he writes, not because science is infallible, but because scientific methods of inquiry are less prone to error than other methods, especially those of a priori philosophy. The contrast between this endorsement of science and Moore's defence of common sense in their respective contributions to Muirhead's volumes shows clearly the difference between these two 'Cambridge analytic philosophers'.

Turning now to Wittgenstein, and in particular to his *Tractatus Logico-Philosophicus* (Wittgenstein 1922; the title was suggested by Moore), we also find a programme of logical analysis based on a kind of logical atomism. But in this case the atomism is neither epistemological (as implied by Russell's acquaintance doctrine) nor metaphysical (as implied by Russell's neutral monism); instead it is conceived by Wittgenstein as a purely *logical* atomism, though in truth it seems to be driven by a semantic doctrine, the Fregean doctrine that sense must be determinate (3.23). Wittgenstein takes this to imply that there must be a fundamental level of reference at which simple signs occur in statements in such a way that they refer to objects whose existence is necessary and that the relationships between these signs in a statement represent relationships between the objects named, relationships which actually obtain where the statement is true. These 'atomic' statements are the foundation of meaningful language and all other meaningful statements must be susceptible of a 'complete analysis' in terms of these atomic statements, though we may well not be able to complete this analysis because of the complexity of ordinary language (4.002), which often disguises the logical form of a statement (Wittgenstein here alludes to Russell, presumably with his theory of descriptions in mind, as 'showing that the apparent logical form of a statement need not be its real one'—4.0031).

Where then does philosophy come into this programme? It is clear that for Wittgenstein analysis is *just* logical analysis, since all complexity is logical complexity, either the logical complexity of the statements of ordinary language or the complexity of simple signs within an atomic statement. So there is no place for philosophical analysis in Wittgenstein's programme. Nonetheless there is a role for philosophy—as an activity of 'clarification' (4.112) whose aim is not to establish any distinctively 'philosophical propositions' but to clear away the misconceptions which lead us to attach importance to what are, in fact, nonsensical questions (4.003). And since the basic method to be employed here is one of showing how language in fact works, it follows that 'All philosophy is a "critique of language"' (4.0031).

Wittgenstein was understandably annoyed at Russell's misunderstanding when he attributed to Wittgenstein a 'concern with the conditions for a logically perfect language' in his introduction to the book (Russell 1922: 8), since Wittgenstein had been quite explicit that his discussion concerns any language. Nonetheless because Wittgenstein's book is written in a way that is both captivating and mesmerizing, it is no great surprise that it was not well understood when it was published, especially given his failure to provide any examples of atomic statements. The issue for us here is how far it contributed to the development of 'analytic philosophy'. As I indicated above, for Wittgenstein analysis is exclusively logical, whereas philosophy is a different activity, 'clarification', whose main aim is to exhibit traditional philosophical questions as disguised nonsense so that they can be cleared away. In practice, however, it is easy to see how these two activities can be combined: Russell used his logical analysis of descriptions to clear away what he took to be Meinongian nonsense about the *Sosein* of round squares; and Moore used his informal open question argument to establish what he took to be the logical basis of ethics, the unanalysability of goodness. So it is not surprising to find Wisdom coming close to Wittgenstein's conception of philosophy, but using the language of 'analysis' in the description of analytic philosophy I quoted earlier (Wisdom 1934b: 2). And it was then in this way that a loose understanding of Wittgenstein's *Tractatus* became part of the 'Cambridge' conception of analytic philosophy.

In addition to Russell and Wittgenstein, two other philosophers should be mentioned as important contributors to the 'Cambridge School', C. D. Broad and Frank Ramsey. Broad had studied at Cambridge with Russell at the same time as Wittgenstein but never became caught up in the enthusiasm of Russell and Wittgenstein for logical analysis. Instead Broad initially directed his attention to the foundations of science, to studies of causation, induction, and the philosophy of space and time, though he also wrote extensively on perception, the philosophy of mind, metaphysics, and ethics. Broad's capacity for constructive insights is exemplified by his early papers on induction and probability in which he argues persuasively that the merits of inductive inference do not depend on the uniformity of nature. Instead, he argues, what is crucial is the existence of substances which belong to natural kinds and possess clusters of characteristic causal powers, so that the value of inductive inference within some domain of inquiry depends on our capacity to identify appropriate natural kinds for that domain (see Broad 1918, 1920). Broad's book *Scientific Thought* (Broad 1923) is a more characteristic example of his work. In Part I he provides what is still one of the best introductions to the special and general theories of relativity ever written. But then in Part II he attempts to provide an account of this relativistic space-time on the basis of sensible appearances ('sensa') whose existence is conceived as logically independent of the physical world. At first this part looks rather disappointing—yet another attempt at a scientific representative theory of perception. Yet once Broad gets going his discussion becomes reminiscent of Husserl's phenomenology, for example in his account of the special status for each of us of the spatiality of our own body (Broad 1923: 437ff.); and interpreted this way, as a phenomenological inquiry into the basis within ordinary experience of the relativistic conception of space-time, the virtues of Broad's discussion become apparent.

In many ways Broad's writings display what we have come to think of as the characteristic virtues of analytic philosophy, in particular in respect of the work of 'analysis and distinction', though sometimes he can take things too far, as when he identifies seventeen types of theory concerning the relation between mind and matter in the final chapter of *The Mind and its Place in Nature* (Broad 1925: 607ff.). Yet Broad does not enjoy much of a reputation as a major contributor to analytic philosophy. In part this is because although he provides careful critical discussions of many philosophical issues he does not advance many distinctive and original positions of his own. But it is also because he did not think of his way of doing philosophy as primarily an exercise of critical analysis. He held that philosophy can make its own contributions to knowledge and understanding, so that although analysis is an essential ingredient of worthwhile philosophical discussion, it is not as important as Russell, Wittgenstein, and indeed Moore took it to be.

Frank Ramsey first achieved recognition as the main translator of Wittgenstein's *Tractatus* and the successful critic of Russell's ramified theory of types. Russell, Moore, and even Wittgenstein all admired his work, and he seemed likely to become the next great Cambridge analytic philosopher, had he not died in 1930 at the age of 26. Nonetheless in his short brilliant career he achieved a great deal. His redundancy theory of truth prefigured subsequent deflationary conceptions of truth; and he rightly saw that once the issue of truth is in this way set to one side, the misguided pragmatist theory of truth can be reworked as a pragmatist theory of content which has much to be said in its favour (Ramsey 1931: 142–4). Indeed, one of his insights was his recognition of the merits of pragmatist approaches to traditional philosophical debates: he argued that the problem of induction can be solved by taking a pragmatist attitude to the justification of belief, which 'judges mental habits by whether they work' (Ramsey 1931: 197), and he proposed the pragmatist hypothesis that degrees of belief be measured by reference to the odds at which people would be prepared to bet on the truth of the belief. In the light of this hypothesis he was able to show how a rational individual's subjective degrees of belief need to satisfy the probability calculus on pain of making that individual vulnerable to betting at odds on which she is bound to lose money (Ramsey 1931: 174–84), thereby providing the basis for a subjectivist interpretation of probability. Finally he challenged the presumption inherent in the logical theories of Frege, Russell, and Wittgenstein that the logic of conditionals is to be determined by treating conditionals as judgements with truth-conditions. Instead, Ramsey argued, conditionals of the form 'if A then B' should be regarded, not as judgements at all, but as 'rules for judging' (Ramsey 1931: 241), i.e. such that in accepting the conditional one acquires a disposition to judge B when one judges A. Ramsey's position implies that when considering how to understand contested concepts such as causation and responsibility which involve conditionals, it will be appropriate to investigate, not just the truth-conditions of judgements involving these concepts, but also the complex dispositions inherent in accepting them—which brings with it a rather different approach to philosophical inquiry, in which one considers what it is to have some attitude—e.g. to hold someone responsible for an action—rather than merely the content of the attitude, e.g. what it is to be responsible for an action. Thus while subsequent discussions of conditionals have refined Ramsey's approach, he helped to make it legitimate to approach philosophical issues in a new way.

13.4 THE NEXT GENERATION

When one turns from the Cambridge philosophers of the 1920s to the next generation, to those whose comments I cited at the start of this essay, Wisdom, Stebbing, and Duncan-Jones, there is a clear sense that they felt that analytic philosophy had come of age, that it was the 'main activity' (in Duncan-Jones's phrase) of those philosophers who had been taught by Moore and read Russell, Wittgenstein, and others. Furthermore, it was no longer confined to Cambridge. The journal *Analysis*, which was founded in 1933 with the policy of publishing 'short discussions...concerned, as a rule, with the elucidation or explanation of facts, or groups of facts, the general nature of which is, by general consent, already known' (*Analysis* 1933: 1), was edited by Austin Duncan-Jones with the help of Susan Stebbing, C. A. Mace, and Gilbert Ryle, none of whom held positions at Cambridge; and the journal immediately attracted papers from all over Britain, and indeed from the USA and elsewhere. The 'Cambridge School' had, in effect, become part of a more general movement of analytic philosophy. Indeed, at the same time in Cambridge itself analytic philosophy was being called into question by the new approach to philosophy propounded by Wittgenstein, who returned there in 1930 and quickly dominated philosophical discussion. Although Wittgenstein's new approach evolved out of the positions he had developed in his *Tractatus*, it was quite different in style and substance from the questions of analysis which were debated in *Analysis* and elsewhere.

Moore was perhaps unique in being both a resolute practitioner of philosophical analysis and someone who was able to keep in contact with Wittgenstein's new way of doing philosophy, which had some similarities with his own respect for common sense and increasing attention to the complexities of ordinary language. Russell, by contrast, was unable to see any value in Wittgenstein's new approach to philosophy, and denounced it in extravagant terms (see Russell 1959: 159).

Thus if one looks for major contributions to analytic philosophy during the 1930s, Cambridge does not provide anything comparable to the great works of the period 1910–30 except for Moore's late papers such as his 1939 'Proof of an External World' (Moore 1993b: 147–70). Instead, as far as analytic philosophy is concerned, there is no question that the most productive debates were taking place in Vienna and Prague between the members of the Vienna Circle and its associated groups. Nonetheless there was an interesting strand of reflection concerning the nature and value of analysis in philosophy that is apparent in British debates of the period and which is well exemplified by the 1934 Aristotelian Society symposium on the question 'Is Analysis a Useful Method in Philosophy?' between Max Black, John Wisdom, and Maurice Cornforth. Max Black had studied mathematics and philosophy at Cambridge during the 1920s, and then taught mathematics at Newcastle Grammar School during the 1930s before moving to the USA in 1940, where he eventually became a professor of philosophy at Cornell in 1946. I have already mentioned John Wisdom; having studied in Cambridge during the 1920s he returned to Cambridge in 1934 where he became Professor of Philosophy in 1952. As we have already seen, his early work included a series of five papers with the Russellian title of 'Logical Constructions' but which are in fact based on themes from Wittgenstein's *Tractatus*; later he wrote another series of papers, on 'Other Minds' (Wisdom 1952), which was much influenced by aspects of Wittgenstein's later philosophy, and further papers on philosophy and psychoanalysis. Maurice Cornforth, the third symposiast, had studied philosophy with Wittgenstein after the latter's return to Cambridge in 1930, but by 1934 he had become a Marxist critic of analytic philosophy, a stance which he then retained throughout his long career.

In the first paper of the symposium Black was mainly concerned to differentiate 'logical' analysis from 'philosophical' analysis (Black 1934: 53–65). Logical analysis is the analysis of statements and, Black maintained, respects the meaning of the statements analysed, whereas philosophical analysis is the analysis of facts, and aims to elucidate these facts by identifying the basic categories whose elements constitute the facts in question. Philosophical analysis, Black maintained, takes one from a higher-level description of a fact to a lower-level description of it which does not need to preserve the meaning of the first description since it provides a more determinate specification of the fact in question. Some such distinction between 'same level' and 'new level' analysis was a commonplace of discussions of analysis at this time (see Stebbing 1932–3; Black 1932–3; Ewing 1935). But, as Black recognizes at the end of his paper, the key to distinguishing philosophical from logical analysis lies with the grounds for determining the basic categories whose elements are referred to in a philosophical analysis. Disappointingly, however, Black himself does not offer any suggestions concerning these grounds.

In his paper (Wisdom 1934a: 65–89) Wisdom continues much the same line of thought, retaining Black's conception of 'philosophical analysis' as an analysis which 'more explicitly displays the structure of the fact' (Wisdom 1934a: 70) by providing an 'ultimate description' of the unique set of elements of the fact in question (Wisdom 1934a: 84). At this point, Wisdom turns to address the question raised by Black at the end of his paper, but not there answered: 'how is the system of basic categories used in analysis determined?' Wisdom's answer is surprising:

> In so far as we may speak of *the* system of categories, it is determined by the accidents determining the development of language. (Wisdom 1934a: 87)

In elucidating this further, Wisdom appeals to the use of language. To support the claim that '*Nations are of a less ultimate category than individuals* i.e. *Nations are reducible to individuals*,' he remarks that *Nations are reducible to individuals* 'though apparently a fact about nations is really about the relative usage of "nation" and "individual"' (Wisdom 1934a: 88). Thus what we are offered here is a linguistic conception of metaphysics. Wisdom does not explain here how the relative usage of these words determines which is the 'less ultimate category' of being. But in his first 'Logical Constructions' paper he had proposed a position explicitly modelled on that of the *Tractatus* according to which the 'ultimate' elements of a fact are those aspects of it which are indicated by the logically simple terms of a sentence which provides a 'sketch' of the fact (Wisdom 1931: 212–14). Given this approach, and further assumptions about the relationship between talk of nations and of individuals, such that the former can be treated as logical constructions of the latter, one can understand how facts about the relative use of the terms 'nation' and 'individual' might be deployed to imply that individuals are more ultimate than nations.

As we have seen, however, this *Tractatus*-inspired line of thought is dependent on questionable assumptions about the simple terms of language which are in the end metaphysical themselves. Moore's early rejection of the key assumption that there is a category of basic necessary existents was endorsed by Wittgenstein in §§55–60 of his *Philosophical Investigations* (Wittgenstein 1953), and the line of thought he advances here can be seen in the notes from his Cambridge lectures (e.g. in his critical discussion of atomic propositions in his 1932–3 lectures: Wittgenstein 1979: 10–12) which Cornforth may well have attended. Cornforth's paper (Cornforth 1934: 90–118) is a combination of scientific pragmatism and Marxist criticism of analytic philosophy as 'the most highly developed form of this philosophical speculation of the bourgeoisie' (Cornforth 1934: 95). Stripped of its Marxist rhetoric, Cornforth provides an intelligent discussion of the way in which analytic philosophers have used their conception of philosophical analysis to preserve a domain of metaphysical speculation from scientific inquiry. While, as we have seen, this is a far from fair account of the work of Russell, Broad, and Ramsey, it is not an unfair judgement on the conception of metaphysics implicit in the conception of philosophical analysis employed by Black and Wisdom in their contributions to the symposium, though Cornforth does not explore its basis in the conception of language Wisdom had earlier set out.

Cornforth's paper showed the danger that analytic philosophy faced if it did not renew itself by moving beyond the logical atomist conception of analysis. Cornforth recommended drawing on the resources of the sciences, and this was of course the direction taken by the Vienna Circle and also by philosophers such as Richard Braithwaite who came closest to being Ramsey's successor at Cambridge (see especially Braithwaite 1953). An alternative resource was provided by the distinctions identified through reflective study of ordinary language, as Moore had already recognized and others such as Gilbert Ryle increasingly advocated (see Ryle 1931–2 and 1946), and which was brilliantly exploited by J. L. Austin (see Austin 1956–7). And during the 1950s it appeared that 'analytic philosophy' was indeed divided between supporters of these two methodologies. But as it became clear that neither methodology could hope to provide a satisfactory and all-encompassing way of doing philosophy, the practice of analytic philosophy has evolved into a piecemeal willingness to take advantage of analyses of any kind—semantic, logical, metaphysical, epistemological, phenomenological, and so on—just as long as these analyses are intrinsically persuasive and contribute something worthwhile to the resolution of philosophical debates. As such, the methodology of contemporary analytic philosophy has returned to that exemplified by Moore's work, whose unprogrammatic and heterogeneous nature I emphasized earlier. To that extent, therefore, the founding spirit of the 'Cambridge School of Analysis' remains active in contemporary analytic philosophy. [1]

References

Austin, J. L. (1956–7). 'A Plea for Excuses', *Proceedings of the Aristotelian Society* 57: 1–30.

Baldwin, Thomas (1995). 'Introduction' to reprint of Russell (1921). London: Routledge.

——(2003). 'The Indefinability of Good', *The Journal of Value Inquiry* 37: 313–28.

Black, Max (1932–3). 'Philosophical Analysis', *Proceedings of the Aristotelian Society* 33: 237–58.

——(1934). 'Is Analysis a Useful Method in Philosophy?', *Proceedings of the Aristotelian Society, Supplementary Volume* 13: 53–64.

Bouwsma, O. K. (1942). 'Moore's Theory of Sense-Data', in Schilpp (1942), pp. 201–22.

Braithwaite, Richard (1953). *Scientific Explanation*. Cambridge: Cambridge University Press.

Broad, C. D. (1918, 1920). 'On the Relation between Induction and Probability (I), (II)', *Mind* 27: 389–404; 29: 29–45.

——(1923). *Scientific Thought*. London: Kegan Paul.

——(1925). *The Mind and its Place in Nature*. London: Kegan Paul.

Church, Alonzo (1946). 'Review of Morton White and Max Black', *Journal of Symbolic Logic* 4: 132–3.

Collingwood, R. G. (1938). *An Autobiography*. Oxford: Oxford University Press.

Cornforth, Maurice (1934). 'Is Analysis a Useful Method in Philosophy?', *Proceedings of the Aristotelian Society, Supplementary Volume* 13: 90–118.

[1] I am very much indebted to the editor for helpful comments on earlier drafts of this chapter.

Duncan-Jones, Austin (1937). 'Does Philosophy Analyse Common Sense?', *Proceedings of the Aristotelian Society, Supplementary Volume* 16: 139–61.

Ewing, Alfred (1935). 'Two Kinds of Analysis', *Analysis* 2: 60–4.

Kaplan, David (1989). 'Demonstratives', in J. Almog *et al.* (eds.), *Themes from Kaplan*. Oxford: Oxford University Press, pp. 481–564.

Moore, G. E. (1899). 'The Nature of Judgment', *Mind* 8: 176–93. Reprinted in Moore (1993b), pp. 1–19.

——(1903). *Principia Ethica*. Cambridge: Cambridge University Press.

——(1907–8). 'Professor James' Pragmatism', *Proceedings of the Aristotelian Society* 8: 33–77. Reprinted in Moore (1922), pp. 97–146.

——(1918). 'Some Judgments of Perception', *Proceedings of the Aristotelian Society* 19: 1–29. Reprinted in Moore (1922), pp. 220–52.

——(1922). *Philosophical Studies*. London: Kegan Paul.

——(1925). 'A Defence of Common Sense', in J. H. Muirhead (ed.), *Contemporary British Philosophy: Personal Statements* (second series). London: George Allen & Unwin, pp. 192–233. Reprinted in Moore (1993), pp. 106–33.

——(1942). 'A Reply to my Critics', in Schilpp (1942), pp. 535–677.

——(1953). *Some Main Problems of Philosophy*. London: George Allen & Unwin.

——(1966a). *Ethics*. London: Oxford University Press.

——(1966b). *Lectures on Philosophy*, ed. C. Lewy. London: George Allen & Unwin.

——(1993a). *Principia Ethica*, revised edition, ed. T. Baldwin. Cambridge: Cambridge University Press.

——(1993b). *Selected Writings*, ed. T. Baldwin. London: Routledge.

Muirhead, J. H. (1924). 'Editor's Preface', in J. H. Muirhead (ed.), *Contemporary British Philosophy: Personal Statements* (first series). London: George Allen & Unwin, pp. 9–12.

Putnam, Hilary (1981). *Reason, Truth and History*. Cambridge: Cambridge University Press.

Ramsey, Frank (1931). *The Foundations of Mathematics*. London: Kegan Paul.

Russell, Bertrand (1912). *The Problems of Philosophy*. London: Williams and Norgate.

——(1914). *Our Knowledge of the External World*. London: George Allen & Unwin.

——(1921). *The Analysis of Mind*. London: George Allen & Unwin.

——(1922). 'Introduction' to Wittgenstein (1922), pp. 7–23.

——(1924). 'Logical Atomism', in J. H. Muirhead (ed.), *Contemporary British Philosophy: Personal Statements* (first series). London: George Allen & Unwin, pp. 359–83.

——(1927). *The Analysis of Matter*. London: George Allen & Unwin.

——(1959). *My Philosophical Development*. London: George Allen & Unwin.

——(1986). *The Philosophy of Logical Atomism and Other Essays, 1914–19: The Collected Papers of Bertrand Russell, Volume 8*, ed. J. G. Slater. London: George Allen & Unwin.

Ryle, Gilbert (1931–2). 'Systematically Misleading Expressions', *Proceedings of the Aristotelian Society* 32: 139–70.

——(1946). *Philosophical Arguments*. Oxford: Oxford University Press. Reprinted in Ryle (1971), pp. 194–211.

——(1971). *Collected Essays 1929–1968, Collected Papers*, Vol. 2. London: Hutchinson.

Schilpp, P. A. (ed.) (1942). *The Philosophy of G. E. Moore*. La Salle, IL: Open Court.

Stebbing, Susan (1932–3). 'The Method of Analysis in Metaphysics', *Proceedings of the Aristotelian Society* 33: 65–94.

——(1942). 'Moore's Influence', in Schilpp (1942), pp. 517–32.

Stout, G. F. (1896). *Analytic Psychology*. London: Kegan Paul.

Wisdom, John (1931). 'Logical Constructions (1)', *Mind* 40: 188–216.

—— (1933). 'Logical Constructions (V)', *Mind* 42: 186–202.

—— (1934a). 'Is Analysis a Useful Method in Philosophy?', *Proceedings of the Aristotelian Society Supplementary Volume* 13: 65–89.

—— (1934b). *Problems of Mind and Matter.* Cambridge: Cambridge University Press.

—— (1942). 'Moore's Technique', in Schilpp (1942), pp. 421–50.

—— (1952). *Other Minds.* Oxford: Blackwell.

Wittgenstein, Ludwig (1922). *Tractatus Logico-Philosophicus*, tr. C. K. Ogden. London: Kegan Paul.

—— (1953). *Philosophical Investigations*, tr. G. E. M. Anscombe. Oxford: Blackwell.

—— (1958). *The Blue & Brown Books*, ed. R. Rhees. Oxford: Blackwell.

—— (1979). *Wittgenstein's Lectures: Cambridge 1932–5*, ed. A. Ambrose. Oxford: Blackwell.

CHAPTER 14

THE WHOLE MEANING OF A BOOK OF NONSENSE: READING WITTGENSTEIN'S *TRACTATUS*

MICHAEL KREMER

WITTGENSTEIN'S *Tractatus Logico-Philosophicus*, a monograph of less than 100 pages, has perhaps generated the highest ratio of commentary and controversy to text of any philosophical book of the past century. Wittgenstein recognized the difficulty his work would present to his readers. The only debts he cites in the Preface to the *Tractatus* are to 'the great works of Frege and the writings of my friend Bertrand Russell',[1] yet Wittgenstein concluded that neither of these understood his book.[2] In a famous letter to Ludwig von Ficker, whom he was trying to persuade to publish the *Tractatus*, Wittgenstein admitted that 'You won't—I really believe—get too much out of reading it. Because you won't understand it—the content of the book will be strange to you.' But he added, 'In reality, it isn't strange to you, for the point of the book is an ethical one' ('Letters to Ficker', 94). It is doubtful that Ficker found this last remark comforting, for it must have appeared completely mysterious to him how this book, which seems to consist almost entirely of a discussion of issues in philosophy of logic tied to the then still fairly obscure systems of symbolic logic of Frege and Russell, with only a few cryptic remarks about ethics in its closing pages, could have an ethical point. Nonetheless, Wittgenstein was completely serious in making this remark, and I hope to explain how a book with the title *Logisch-Philosophische Abhandlung* could yet be conceived as having an ethical point by the end of this essay.

---

[1] Quotations from the *Tractatus* are generally from the Ogden and Ramsey translation. Occasionally I will make silent emendations in the light of the Pears and McGuinness translation. Citations from the body of the *Tractatus* will be by numbered proposition.

[2] *Wittgenstein in Cambridge*, 103, 118, 119–20.

Wittgenstein provided Ficker with a suggestion as to how to understand the book: 'For the time being I'd recommend that you read the *foreword* and the *conclusion* since these express the point most directly' ('Letters to Ficker', 95). I will begin by following this advice, discussing the Preface and final numbered propositions of the *Tractatus*, with an eye to understanding the general approach to philosophy that these passages suggest. I will then build on my reading of these passages to interpret key moments in the main body of the work, returning at the end to the ethical point of the book as a whole.

14.1 THE WHOLE MEANING OF THE *TRACTATUS*: A FIRST APPROACH

In the second paragraph of the Preface, Wittgenstein provides a statement of the 'whole meaning' of the book which 'could be summed up somewhat as follows: What can be said at all can be said clearly; and whereof one cannot speak thereof one must be silent.' This summation has two parts; and a contrast is implied between the two, between 'what can be said' and that 'whereof one cannot speak'. Both parts reoccur in the main body of the work. The second half corresponds to the last numbered proposition, 7; whereas the first half is close to a proposition in the middle of the work, 4.116: 'Everything that can be thought at all can be thought clearly. Everything that can be said can be said clearly.'

This first branch of the contrasting pair seems relatively easy to understand: it expresses an ideal of clarity, shared by Wittgenstein with Frege and Russell—whenever we use language so as to make sense, what we mean can be expressed in a totally perspicuous manner. Frege and Russell held that the way to achieve such clarity was to employ a symbolism designed expressly for this purpose, a notation in which clarity would be built into the structure of the language—a *Begriffsschrift* or symbolic logic. Wittgenstein shared with his predecessors the project of clarifying our thought; we will see below in what sense Wittgenstein shared also their approach to realizing this project.

The second half of Wittgenstein's contrast has proved much more difficult to understand, and has generated a great deal of scholarly controversy. Wittgenstein seems to speak here of *that* 'whereof one cannot speak' and to say that about *it* 'one must be silent'. This suggests the following reading:[3] there are ineffable truths, things we can know, but which cannot be expressed in words. These truths, once recognized, can only be

---

[3] One *locus classicus* of this kind of reading is Hacker, *Insight*. It was fairly standard in the literature until the advent of the 'resolute reading' or 'new Wittgenstein' championed by Cora Diamond and James Conant (see for example 'Throwing Away the Ladder' and 'The Method of the *Tractatus*'). My reading of the book is in the general family of 'resolute readings', so-called because they attempt to resolutely accept Wittgenstein's claim that his propositions are nonsensical and convey no ineffable truths; readings such as Hacker's are sometimes characterized as 'ineffability' (or, less sympathetically, 'irresolute') readings.

appreciated in a respectful silence. The *Tractatus* aims to get us to recognize these truths. However, since they are inexpressible, the book must do this in an indirect way: it communicates these truths which cannot be spoken *through* the failed attempt to speak them.

An example can help to clarify the thought that is here being attributed to Wittgenstein: Frege's difficulty in conveying the categorial distinction between concept and object that is fundamental to his conception of logic. Frege found that any attempt to put this distinction into words inevitably misrepresented it—in saying something like 'concepts are not objects' he ended up treating concepts as if they were objects, as if the same things could meaningfully (if falsely) be said of concepts as could be said of objects. Yet Frege insisted that his distinction reflected a truth, 'founded deep in the nature of things.'[4] One could *see* that the distinction held, and one could bring others to see this as well, though the words one would use to do this would inevitably 'miss my thought' ('Concept and Object', 54). On the present suggestion, Wittgenstein's view of philosophical matters in general is a kind of analogous extension of this thought of Frege's about fundamental logical distinctions.[5]

This way of reading the *Tractatus* draws support from its famous closing paragraphs, the 'conclusion' which Wittgenstein mentioned to Ficker. Immediately before the final proposition Wittgenstein writes at 6.54:

> My propositions are elucidatory in this way: he who understands me finally recognizes them as nonsense, when he has climbed out through them, on them, over them. (He must so to speak throw away the ladder, after he has climbed up on it.)
>   He must surmount these propositions; then he sees the world rightly.

According to the present suggestion, Wittgenstein's propositions are nonsensical because they attempt to express in words ineffable truths. Sometimes, this is put using a distinction that Wittgenstein draws between 'saying' and 'showing':

> 4.1212 What *can* be shown *cannot* be said.

Writing to Russell in 1919, Wittgenstein called this distinction both his 'main contention', and 'the cardinal problem of philosophy' (*Wittgenstein in Cambridge*, 98). According to the reading I am sketching here, the nonsensical propositions of the *Tractatus* result from the attempt to say what can only be shown—but those unsayable truths can be *seen*, by one who 'sees the world rightly'. One who sees them overcomes the attempt to express them—and appreciates them in silence.

---

[4] 'Function and Concept', 41. (Frege is there referring to his distinction between first- and second-level functions but clearly would take the same view of his distinction between first-level functions, including concepts, and objects.)

[5] An early and influential exploration of this idea is found in Geach, 'Saying and Showing'.

This is *not* the reading of the *Tractatus* that I am going to develop in this essay. However, it has been a widely popular reading, and it has a definite advantage—it offers a way of accounting for the ethical dimension of the work. Towards the end of the *Tractatus*, Wittgenstein makes some brief remarks about ethics, which, like logic, is 'transcendental' and 'cannot be expressed' (6.421, 6.13). If 'transcendental' here refers to that which transcends expression, we might take it that ethics, like logic, consists in a body of ineffable truths. There is an ethics, then, that Wittgenstein is trying to communicate. The ethical point of the book is both to get the reader to see this, and also to see the ineffable ethical truths that the book fails to express directly. This ethical point is subsumed under the whole meaning of the book, here understood as follows: whatever we can say can be said clearly; but there is a realm of unsayable truths, including both logic and ethics. We have to be brought to *see* this realm of truths, and then stop talking about it. In his letter to Ficker, trying to explain the ethical point of the book, Wittgenstein says that his work consists of two parts, what he has written, on the one hand, and 'everything that I have *not* written' on the other—with the latter 'the important one' ('Letters to Ficker', 94). Here we might take the part he has not written to consist precisely in those logical and ethical truths that cannot be expressed, but must be *seen* and then recognized in silence.

Thus we have a reading of the whole meaning of the book which helps to give an account of how the book has an ethical point. Nonetheless I think this account is mistaken. To begin to see why, we should return to the summary of the whole meaning in the Preface, and place it in its immediate context.

14.2 DRAWING LIMITS: THOUGHT, SENSE, AND NONSENSE

Immediately *after* summing up its whole meaning, Wittgenstein states an aim for his work: 'the book will, therefore, draw a limit to thinking'. He adds that this limit will be drawn '*in language*' by limiting 'the expression of thoughts'—but as he later equates what can be thought with what can be said[6] this does not seem to make much difference. So it might appear that when we draw the limit to thought (or to the expression of thought) this will amount to drawing a line, on the other side of which will be the ineffable truths that we have to recognize but cannot put into words.

However, Wittgenstein in fact does see a significant difference between drawing a limit to thought and drawing a limit to the expression of thoughts in language. He explains that in order to draw a limit to thought he would have had to *think* both sides of the limit, which is, he says, impossible. In contrast, we can limit the *expression*

---

[6] 4: 'The thought is the significant proposition'—compare the parallelism between what can be thought and what can be said in 4.116, corresponding to the first half of the whole meaning, cited above.

of thoughts, because 'what lies on the other side of the limit will be simply nonsense'. Here it is useful to consider another form of the summation of the whole meaning of the work, given in the motto Wittgenstein chose as an epigraph for the book: 'Whatever a man knows, whatever is not mere rumbling and roaring that he has heard, can be said in three words'.[7] Here the contrast is between what can be expressed succinctly and clearly ('in three words') and 'mere rumbling and roaring'. 'Nonsense' for Wittgenstein is mere *noise*—not deep but inexpressible truths. When we draw the limit to the expression of thoughts, for each thought that we can think clearly there will be a corresponding proposition that can be said clearly, but to the putative ineffable truths of logic and ethics there will correspond nothing but noise. Therefore, when Wittgenstein tells us that to understand *him* we need to recognize his propositions as nonsensical, all we are to recognize is that his putative propositions are simply so much meaningless 'rumbling and roaring'. But this threatens to make it even more mysterious how writing such a book can have an ethical point, or indeed any point at all.

To shed further light on this, consider a claim Wittgenstein makes just *before* introducing his summation of the meaning of the *Tractatus*. He says that his book 'deals with the problems of philosophy', which, at the end of the Preface he claims to have 'in essentials ... finally solved' thereby showing 'how little has been done when these problems have been solved'. The key to the solution of these problems involves recognizing 'that the method of formulating these problems rests on the misunderstanding of the logic of our language'. This claim, like many other key points in the Preface, is taken up in the body of the book, and linked to the idea of nonsense:

4.003 Most propositions and questions, that have been written about philosophical matters, are not false, but nonsensical. We cannot, therefore, answer questions of this kind at all, but only state their nonsensicality. Most questions and propositions of the philosophers result from the fact that we do not understand the logic of our language.

Wittgenstein concludes that 'it is not to be wondered at that the deepest problems are really *no* problems'. If we *properly* understand the logic of our language, we will see that the problems of philosophy are, really, no problems, but mere rumbling and roaring.

Commenting at 4.0031 on this account of the questions and propositions of philosophy, Wittgenstein says that 'all philosophy is "Critique of language"' and credits Russell with having shown that 'the apparent logical form of a proposition need not be its real form'. This 'merit' of Russell's derives from his theory of descriptions, first presented in 'On Denoting' (1905). Russell there analyses the logical form of a sentence like 'The present king of France is bald' as very different from its apparent, subject-predicate form. Its true logical form is represented as:

$$(\exists x)(Kx \,\&\, (y)(Ky \supset y = x) \,\&\, Bx).[8]$$

---

[7] From Ferdinand Kürnberger; I follow the Pears and McGuinness translation here.

[8] 'On Denoting', 482 (although Russell does not use logical notation to express his analysis there, as he later does in *Principia Mathematica*).

This contrasts sharply with the logical form of a simple predication like 'Nuel Belnap is bald', represented as '*Bn*'. But more importantly, Russell *uses* this theory to solve logical puzzles, by showing how they arise from *confusion* about logical form.

For example, if we focus on 'The present king of France is *not* bald', a logical puzzle is generated if we fail to distinguish two possible logical forms corresponding to this sentence: the primary occurrence (wide scope) reading,

$$(\exists x)(Kx \,\&\, (y)(Ky \supset y = x) \,\&\, {\sim}Bx)$$

and the secondary occurrence (narrow scope) reading,

$${\sim}(\exists x)(Kx \,\&\, (y)(Ky \supset y = x) \,\&\, Bx).^{[9]}$$

If we assume that 'The present king of France is not bald' is *both* the logical opposite of 'The present king of France is bald' *and* of the same basic type as 'The present king of France is bald'—two simple predications, one positive and one negative—we can be puzzled about the status of these sentences, given that there is no present king of France. But analysis reveals that these two roles cannot be combined: on the primary occurrence reading, 'The present king of France is bald' and 'The present king of France is not bald' are of the same basic logical type, and both imply that there is a present king of France, but they are not logical opposites; on the secondary occurrence reading, they are logical opposites, but are not of the same basic logical type, and the second does not imply that there is a present king of France. The puzzle simply disappears, and is shown to rest on a confusion about logical form.[10]

14.3 SIGN AND SYMBOL, CONFUSION
AND CLARIFICATION

According to Wittgenstein, this kind of confusion pervades philosophical discourse. He writes that the 'whole of philosophy is full' of 'the most fundamental confusions', deriving from particular forms of equivocation in language (3.324). He explains the origin of these confusions in terms of a fundamental distinction between *sign* and *symbol*, expounded in the 3.31s and 3.32s as part of his commentary on his version of Frege's 'context principle'[11] (3.3): 'Only the proposition has sense; only in the context of a proposition has a name meaning.' A proposition expresses its sense; but we must distinguish between the 'sensibly perceptible' propositional *sign*, and the proposition proper, 'the

---

[9] 'On Denoting', 485, 490.
[10] I discuss Wittgenstein's debt to Russell's treatment of puzzles at length in my 'Russell's Merit'.
[11] *Foundations*, x.

propositional sign in its projective relation to the world' (3.1–3.14). Propositional signs are *facts*, and therefore *articulate*: 'Only facts can express a sense, a class of names cannot' (3.141–2). Therefore, we can distinguish within any proposition the *symbols* or *expressions*, the logical working parts which 'characterize its sense' (3.31). These too have a sensibly perceptible aspect: 'The sign is the part of the symbol perceptible by the senses' (3.32).

A symbol is thus a sensibly perceptible sign put to use in language, and according to Wittgenstein's context principle (3.3, 3.314) the use we make of signs as symbols is use in propositions that make sense, that say something. Consequently 'in order to recognize the symbol in the sign we must consider the significant (*sinnvollen*) use' (3.326)—use in a proposition that makes sense. Outside of such use, we do not have symbols or meaning at all.

Wittgenstein uses his distinction between sign and symbol to account for the confusions that he says permeate philosophy. The fundamental point here is that 'two different symbols can … have the same sign … in common—they then signify in different ways' (3.321). More generally, 'in the language of everyday life it very often happens that the same word signifies in two different ways—and therefore belongs to two different symbols—or that two words, which signify in different ways, are apparently applied in the same way in the proposition' (3.323).

Wittgenstein here mentions two forms of equivocation. We may have one sign used in two ways, functioning as two different symbols; or we may have two signs governed by the same grammatical rules, so that they appear to have the same logical form, yet realizing symbols with distinct logical forms. He provides examples of both kinds: 'the word "is" appears as the copula, as the sign of equality, and as the expression of existence' and ' "to exist" [appears] as an intransitive verb like "to go" ' (3.323).

Take the first case, and compare the three propositions:

(a) Obama *is* American
(b) Obama *is* (=) Barack
(c) There *is* a president.

These have the sign 'is' in common, but logically they are different and would be represented in logical notation by

(a') Ao
(b') $o = b$
(c') $(\exists x)Px$

respectively.

A confusion between the first and second meanings of 'is' seems to be involved in F. H. Bradley's puzzlement about 'substantive and adjective' (*Appearance and Reality*, chapter 2). Bradley begins with the example of a lump of sugar which is 'white, and hard, and sweet'. He remarks: 'The sugar, we say, *is* all that; but what the *is* can really mean, seems doubtful. A thing is not any one of its qualities, if you take the quality by itself ...'—and so we are off to the philosophical races (Bradley, *Appearance and Reality*, 19). If we represent 'the lump of sugar is sweet' along the lines of (a′), and distinguish this from 'the lump of sugar is (identical to) its sweetness', Bradley's puzzlement simply does not arise. In his puzzlement he has mistakenly confused these two distinct meanings.

Wittgenstein's second example does *not* involve one sign being used in two symbols. Rather, two signs that realize logically different symbols are used in the *same* way. Consider the sentences

(d) Cars go.
(e) Cars exist.

These *appear* to have the same form. That this is misleading is revealed by their representations in logical notation:

(d′) $(x)(Cx \supset Gx)$
(e′) $(\exists x)Cx.$

The confusion exhibited in Russell's puzzle about the present king of France is a complex instance of this latter sort. The difficulty with 'The present king of France is not bald' does not arise from any single sign being used equivocally as part of two symbols; rather the whole grammatical form 'The *CN* is not *A*' is structurally equivocal—it can be used to represent fundamentally distinct logical forms.

Wittgenstein holds that the problems of philosophy are generated by similar kinds of confusion: confusion about how language works, logically. Russell used a logical notation to represent the distinct logical forms that can be confused in 'The present king of France is not bald', and we have used such a notation to distinguish the logical forms that the different uses of 'is', or the related uses of 'to go' and 'to exist', might lead us to muddle together. In the *Tractatus*, Wittgenstein sees here the general remedy to the sorts of confusions he is warning against, 'misunderstandings of the logic of our language'. 'In order to avoid these errors, we must employ a symbolism that excludes them, by not applying the same sign in different symbols and by not applying signs in the same way which signify in different ways'—for example 'the logical symbolism [*Begriffsschrift*] of Frege and Russell' (3.325).

Logical symbolism therefore provides a tool for an activity of clarification. In the propositions leading up to the reiteration of the first half of the summation, at 4.116, Wittgenstein says that 'philosophy is not a theory, but an activity', whose object is 'the logical clarification of thoughts' and whose result is 'not a number of "philosophical propositions", but to make propositions clear' (4.112). Using a properly designed logical symbolism, we can clearly express what can be said, and we can unmask the confusions that everyday language makes possible. We will then discover that the problems of philosophy are no longer there. We can delimit what can be said clearly within language, not by drawing a line outside of language, but simply by saying everything that can be said, clearly. Thus philosophy will 'limit the thinkable and thereby the unthinkable', will 'limit the unthinkable from within through the thinkable' (4.114). In other words, philosophy 'will mean the unspeakable by clearly displaying the speakable' (4.115). By expressing clearly what can be thought and what can be said, we delimit what can be thought and said, and thereby also what cannot be thought and cannot be said. But what we thereby delimit is not a realm of ineffable truths; we simply indicate cases in which language-users have failed to make sense. It is in *this* way that philosophical problems arise.

We can now begin to see the ethical point of the book, which is meant in some sense to be liberating.[12] Near the end of the book, Wittgenstein writes 'For an answer which cannot be expressed the question too cannot be expressed. *The riddle* does not exist. If a question can be put at all then it *can* also be answered' (6.5). Philosophical problems involve questions that it seems *can* be *put* but *cannot* be *answered*—but then they aren't real questions, either. The same is true of the 'problems of life':

> We feel that even if *all possible* scientific questions be answered, the problems of life have still not been touched at all. Of course there is then no question left, and just this is the answer. The solution of the problem of life is seen in the vanishing of the problem. (6.52–6.521)

The seeming intellectual problem of how to live vanishes when we realize that there is nothing there to be said, since there is nothing left to ask. Delimiting what can be said clearly from within, we simply exclude the problems of life and are thereby freed up to go ahead and live. 'Is not this the reason why men to whom after long doubting the sense of life became clear, could not then say wherein this sense consisted?' asks Wittgenstein (6.521), and one can imagine that among those men is the author of the *Tractatus*. Yet this way of thinking about the ethical significance of the book is perhaps not entirely satisfactory, and I will return to this question at the end of this essay.[13]

14.4 SENSE AND NONSENSE, MEANING AND SUPERFLUITY

So far, I have emphasized the idea that the nonsensical problems of philosophy arise from confusions, trading on the equivocal use of words. This may seem like an implausible

---

[12] The liberating impetus of the *Tractatus* is a fundamental theme of Ostrow, *Wittgenstein's Tractatus*.

[13] Two interrelated concerns in particular arise here: (1) is there a right and a wrong way to live? (2) how can we communicate how to live, if not through ethical propositions? The *Tractatus* teaches us how to live by engaging in an activity of clarification which can free us from confusions and ethical illusions which distort our lives. But it is further possible to derive ethical guidance from stories, parables, and poems, which *show* something about human life without trying to *say* how to live. Famously, Wittgenstein admired works such as Tolstoy's novella, *Hadji Murad*, for their capacity to show something ethical.

claim—one which could hardly be supported by the kinds of examples adduced above. Russell, after all, only used his theory of descriptions to solve—or 'dissolve', as it is often said—a toy puzzle of his own invention, not a real 'problem of philosophy'. Shortly, I will turn to examples drawn from Wittgenstein's critical discussions of Frege and Russell, and then consider the claim that the propositions of the *Tractatus* itself are similarly to be discarded as nonsensical. But first I must consider a possible objection to my reading, developing out of some further Wittgensteinian remarks about nonsense that I have so far neglected.

At 5.4733, Wittgenstein says: 'Every possible proposition is legitimately constructed, and if it has no sense this can only be because we have given no *meaning* to some of its constituent parts.' Hence, nonsense results from a failure on our part to determine a meaning for the signs that make up our failed attempts at making sense. Wittgenstein relies on a similar thought when he says, just before the conclusion of the book, that 'the right method of philosophy would be this: To say nothing except what can be said ... and then always, when someone else wished to say something metaphysical, to demonstrate to him that he given no meaning to certain signs in his propositions' (6.53). This would be, according to 5.4733, to demonstrate to him that he had failed to make sense. But how is all this related to the idea that nonsense results from forms of equivocation?

To answer this let us first consider how we might demonstrate to another that they have given no meaning to some of their signs. Clearly, it will not be convincing simply to *assert* that we do not understand their words. They would reasonably ask us to try harder. The above discussion suggests a better way: if we can convince them that they have equivocated, sliding between two different possible meanings of their signs, we will make clear to them that they have failed to *determine* a meaning for their signs in *this* context, and so have failed to make sense. And here a symbolic notation can function as a tool for exhibiting distinct possible meanings of their words, making explicit their confusion.

But Wittgenstein appears to indicate another way in which someone can fail to have given meaning to their words: by using words that are logically superfluous, which do no logical work. Wittgenstein associates this idea with 'Occam's razor' and presents it twice, in contexts that are highly significant for the reading we have been developing. Just *after* discussing the forms of equivocation that yield philosophical confusion he writes 'If a sign is *not necessary* then it is meaningless. That is the meaning of Occam's razor' (3.328). And just *before* explaining that if a possible proposition has no sense, this must be because we have given no meaning to some of its parts, he repeats this idea: 'Occam's razor ... simply says that *unnecessary* elements in a symbolism mean nothing.... signs which serve *no* purpose are logically meaningless' (5.47321).

Once again, the question arises how one might demonstrate to another that one of their signs is unnecessary, logically superfluous, and so meaningless—and that consequently they have failed to make sense. Wittgenstein's first step here is to construct an *alternative notation* in which nothing corresponds to the sign in question. Consider the example (a) above, 'Obama is American'. In the symbolic representation (a′), '*Ao*' there is a sign corresponding to 'Obama' and a sign corresponding to 'American' but apparently none corresponding to 'is'. The representation of 'Obama is American' is of exactly the same form in our symbolic logic as the representation of 'Obama talks' ('*To*'). So this representation seems to show that the copula 'is' is superfluous, and can be dispensed with.

Yet this point has to be handled with care. For of course one should not conclude that, as 'Obama is American' contains a meaningless (since superfluous) word, this sentence lacks a sense. The way we show that 'is' is superfluous, is to construct a notation in which *the sense* of 'Obama is American' is expressed without anything corresponding to 'is' among the logical working parts of the proposition. There is, after all, no philosophical confusion in asserting that Obama is American. Confusion arises, rather, from treating the word 'is' as a separable part of the entire proposition, rather than recognizing that it forms only a part of the predicate. Such confusion might lead one to wonder about the *meaning* of the copula 'is' and thereby to generate philosophical problems about the relation of being uniting subject and predicate.

Yet where does this confused idea come from? I suggest that it is fostered by the presence in the language of relation words expressed through transitive verbs, resulting in the grammatical similarity of 'Obama is American' and 'Obama eats pizza'. This exemplifies the sort of structural equivocation we saw above with 'to exist' and 'to go', fostering the illusion that 'is' must be treated as a logically separable sentential constituent whose meaning we can then ask after. The ambiguity of 'is' itself, pointed out by Wittgenstein, may also contribute to the confusion—we can be tempted to muddle the 'is' of predication and the 'is' of identity, as we saw F. H. Bradley do.

Consequently the relation between the two sources of meaninglessness, equivocation and superfluity, is complex and intricate. One could say the following: in presenting an alternative notation in which no sign corresponds to a particular sign of our everyday language (such as the 'is' of predication), we see how to do *the* logical work that that sign helped to accomplish, in a different way. At the same time we see how *no* logical work is done by certain uses of the original sign that we were tempted to think must be meaningful. The temptation to think of these uses of the original sign as making sense is generated by forms of ambiguity and equivocation involving the sign. This dynamic is played out in some of Wittgenstein's criticisms of Frege and Russell, discussed below.[14]

As I intimated above, this account of the nonsensical status of philosophical propositions and of the activity of clarification that shows their nonsensicality may seem completely unconvincing. In what follows I will flesh it out with examples drawn from the main body of the *Tractatus*.[15] These examples will help to introduce some of the main themes of the work, and to show why Wittgenstein thought that he had such a potent tool for philosophical clarification in the idea of a perspicuous logical notation. They will also, eventually, help us to understand both the self-destructive conclusion of the book and its claim to have an ethical aim.

[14] My discussion of Wittgenstein's criticisms of Frege and Russell is indebted to Ricketts, 'Wittgenstein against Frege and Russell'.

[15] At 4.003, Wittgenstein provides as an example of a philosophical problem, the question whether the Good is more or less identical than the Beautiful. It is an interesting exercise to try to trace out what kind of confusion might be involved in this question. I address this example in my 'Russell's Merit'.

I will begin with a very simple observation. Wittgenstein says that the correct method in philosophy would be to demonstrate to anyone who wished to say something metaphysical that 'he had given no meaning to certain signs in his propositions'. This will be immediately puzzling to anyone who has been reading the book from the beginning. For, if anyone ever wished to say something metaphysical surely it was Ludwig Wittgenstein, whose book begins with the pronouncements 'The world is everything that is the case. The world is the totality of facts, not of things'—and so on (1–1.1). Here Wittgenstein seems to present a metaphysics of logical atomism—the world is analysed into facts, the facts into atomic facts, and the atomic facts into combinations of objects (1.2, 2). Yet if this is metaphysical, according to Wittgenstein's own lights he must have failed to give a meaning to at least some of the words in these opening remarks.

Of course, this is connected to the thought that anyone who understands him will recognize his propositions as nonsensical (6.54). Ultimately we must come to see that the propositions of the *Tractatus* themselves exhibit confusions from which we need to be relieved. But it will be helpful to first outline how Wittgenstein applies this sort of 'critique of Language' to the works of his great predecessors, Frege and Russell.

14.5 THE CRITIQUE OF FREGE AND RUSSELL: LETTING LOGIC TAKE CARE OF ITSELF

As we saw, at 3.325 Wittgenstein suggests that we can avoid the confusions of philosophy by employing a symbolism that 'obeys the rules of *logical* grammar', 'by not applying the same sign in different symbols and by not applying signs in the same way which signify in different ways'. He adds, parenthetically, that 'the logical symbolism [*Begriffsschrift*] of Frege and Russell is such a language, which, however, does still not exclude all errors'. While praising the logical notations of his predecessors, Wittgenstein criticizes them as potentially encouraging confusions, by 'applying the same sign in different symbols' and 'applying signs in the same way which signify in different ways'. How do their symbolisms do this, and what problems result?

Frege and Russell devised their logical notations in order to establish the epistemological status of mathematics, and in particular to demonstrate that the truths of arithmetic are reducible to logic. This required a symbolism in which the truths of arithmetic could be clearly expressed, and proofs of these truths could be given from logical laws and definitions alone. Frege, in particular, sought a way to ensure that all proofs were free of 'gaps' where an appeal to something extra-logical might be hidden. He therefore set up precise *rules* governing inferences from one or more propositions to the next. Given a putative inference in his notation, it is possible to check whether the inference is correct or not by consulting the rules. The rules separate the good inferences from the bad ones and thereby also *justify* the good inferences.

This conception comes under criticism at *Tractatus* 5.13: 'That the truth of one proposition follows from the truth of other propositions, we perceive from the structure of the propositions.' Wittgenstein continues (5.131–2):

> If the truth of one proposition follows from the truth of others, this expresses itself in relations in which the forms of these propositions stand to one another, and we do not need to put them in these relations by first connecting them with one another in a proposition; for these relations are internal, and exist as soon as, and by the very fact that, the propositions exist....
>
> The method of inference is to be gathered from the ... propositions alone.
>
> Only they themselves can justify the inference.
>
> Laws of inference, which—as in Frege and Russell—are to justify the conclusions, are senseless and would be superfluous.

Consider a typical rule of inference, *modus ponens*:

$$p \supset q$$

$$p$$

$$\therefore q$$

Adding this rule to our symbolism adds nothing, according to Wittgenstein. If we understand the symbols involved, we already know that this inference is correct without being told so, and being told so won't make the inference correct if it is not already correct.

This is an instance of a more general theme in the *Tractatus*: 'Logic must take care of itself' (5.473). This is the first sentence in Wittgenstein's wartime notebooks, where he calls it 'an extremely profound and important insight'. He immediately draws a consequence: 'If syntactical rules for functions can be set up *at all*, then the whole theory of things, properties, etc. is superfluous'—just what he says about rules of inference in the *Tractatus*. This insight puts into question the conception of philosophy he had held up to that point: 'How is it reconcilable with the task of philosophy, that logic should take care of itself?' (*Notebooks*, 2).

He goes on to question the meaningfulness of 'philosophical questions' such as 'whether "A is good" is a subject-predicate proposition; or whether "A is brighter than B" is a relational proposition', asking '*How can such a question be settled at all?*' He gives an example of a 'simpler and more fundamental' such question, 'Is a point in our visual field a *simple object*, a *thing*?' He remarks 'Up to now I have always regarded such questions as the real philosophical ones' but now worries that there is 'a mistake in the formulation[16] here' since 'it looks as if I could say definitively that these questions could never be settled at all'.

---

[16] 'Formulation' translates '*Fragestellung*', the word translated 'method of formulating' in the *Tractatus*.

Consider from this point of view Frege's distinction between concepts and objects.[17] Frege's logical language is based on replacing a subject–predicate analysis of sentences with a function–argument analysis (*Begriffsschrift*, Preface, in *Conceptual Notation*, 107). He represents sentences like (a) above, 'Obama is American', by writing things like (a′), '*Ao*', conceiving of this as composed of two parts, the 'complete' object-expression '*o*' and the 'incomplete' (or functional) concept-expression '*A*( )'. The latter has a *gap* which must be filled by an object-expression. The importance of this function–argument analysis comes out in Frege's representation of quantified sentences like 'Every president is an American', which would be represented as '$(x)(Px \supset Ax)$'. Here, Frege says, the distinction between function and argument becomes essential to the *content* (*Begriffsschrift* §9, in *Conceptual Notation*, 128).

Frege conceives of object and concept-expressions as standing for ontologically distinct entities, objects and concepts; the former are 'self-subsistent' and complete whereas the latter require completion by an argument. As we saw, Frege insists that this is an *ontological* distinction of the deepest importance. Here we seem to have a metaphysical theory about the nature of objective reality: it consists of 'unsaturated' concepts, and 'complete' objects which saturate those concepts. From Wittgenstein's point of view, this looks like an attempt to provide an ontological *grounding* for Frege's logic. The logical distinction between concepts and objects, reflected in his distinction between names and concept-expressions, must be accepted because it is 'founded deep in the nature of things'. But this is to deny that logic can 'take care of itself': logic is made to depend on a metaphysical view about features of reality. For Wittgenstein, any such metaphysical view must be *superfluous*. Consequently, our language here *has no meaning*, according to the interpretation of Occam's razor advanced in the *Tractatus*.

Similarly, Wittgenstein tells us that laws of inference are superfluous and therefore senseless. We can illuminate Wittgenstein's point through a parable, adapted from Lewis Carroll's famous 1895 paper 'What the Tortoise said to Achilles'.[18] Achilles and the Tortoise (characters drawn from one of Zeno's paradoxes of motion) are tired out from running, and take a break to discuss logic. Achilles sets up an argument, which we can think of as having the form of *modus ponens*:[19]

$$p \supset q$$

$$p$$

$$\therefore q$$

---

[17] The importance of Frege's difficulties concerning the expressibility of the concept–object distinction for understanding Wittgenstein's early philosophy is stressed in Geach, 'Saying and Showing'. For a very illuminating discussion, see Jolley.

[18] Russell discusses Carroll's paper in *Principles* (1903), in the context of discussing rules of inference (35). I do not adhere strictly to Carroll's discussion.

[19] Carroll begins with an argument from Euclid's *Elements*; but this is inessential to the point I am using this parable to make.

Achilles wants to use this argument to convince the Tortoise that q, but the Tortoise, who is rather slow, accepts the premises, $p \supset q$ and p, but refuses to accept the conclusion q. Achilles now makes a fatal mistake—he gets the Tortoise to agree to the *conditional* $((p \supset q) \,\&\, p) \supset q$. Achilles having made the rule of inference, *modus ponens*, explicit in the form of this additional proposition, adds it to his argument as an additional premise, in an attempt (as it were) to catch up to the Tortoise. But the Tortoise is still one step ahead—he accepts this new premise along with the first two, but still refuses to accept the conclusion. So, Achilles gets the Tortoise to agree to yet another conditional: $(((p \supset q) \,\&\, p) \supset q) \,\&\, ((p \supset q) \,\&\, p)) \supset q)$, trying to assert that the conclusion follows from the three premises the Tortoise has already acceded to. But still the Tortoise keeps ahead, refusing to accept the conclusion—and it is evident that this can go on forever without the Tortoise ever conceding.

Of course, if the Tortoise isn't willing to draw the conclusion from the initial premises, there is nothing that can be done for him, logically. Adding rules as further explicit premises will not force the Tortoise to accept the conclusion. If the Tortoise accepts the *initial* premises but not the conclusion, this shows that the Tortoise did not really understand either the premises or the conclusion in the first place. At 4.024, Wittgenstein tells us that 'To understand a proposition means to know what is the case, if it is true.' This is to grasp its sense: 'The proposition *shows* its sense. The proposition *shows* how things stand, if it is true. And it *says* that they do so stand' (4.022). Anyone who *understands* $p \supset q$ and p, and accepts both of them, already *knows* that they are in a circumstance in which q is also true. No rule of inference is needed to show that the inference is valid. Logic has to take care of itself; we can't take care of logic.

14.6 THE *GRUNDGEDANKE* AND THE LOGIC OF DEPICTION

As we saw, Wittgenstein claims that the problems of philosophy arise from confusions occasioned by forms of equivocation which obscure for us the logic of our language. We can avoid such confusions by employing a logical symbolism designed to eliminate the equivocations that foster them. The logical notations of Frege and Russell can play this role; but, Wittgenstein adds, their symbolisms do not eliminate all possible confusions. As he sees it, these confusions generate the philosophical problems facing Frege and Russell. We can now add: the temptation to fall into these confusions is largely generated by the desire to 'take care' of logic—to not let logic take care of itself.

At 4.0312, Wittgenstein states his 'fundamental thought' (*Grundgedanke*): 'that the "logical constants" do not represent. That the *logic* of the facts cannot be represented.' By the 'logical constants' Wittgenstein means such signs of Frege and Russell's logic as '$\supset$',

'~', '∃', '=',[20] as well as the forms of proposition expressible in that logic, such as the form of simple predication exhibited in examples like (a') ('Ao') above.[21] Such signs—and such forms—'do not represent'. Here he *contrasts* the logical constants with signs that *do* represent. The first half of the remark in which the 'fundamental thought' occurs, 4.0312, reads: 'The possibility of propositions is based on the principle of the representation of objects by signs.' The contrast is between the logical constants and names like 'Kremer', which represent objects (here, the author of this essay)—and perhaps also predicates like 'essay' and 'author of', which represent properties and relations.[22]

Wittgenstein's claim that the possibility of propositions depends on signs representing objects harks back to the opening sections of the book, which present an account of what he calls 'pictures'. A picture 'represents a possible state of affairs' (2.202) and 'the elements of the picture stand, in the picture, for the objects'—objects which are combined in the state of affairs (2.131, 2.01, 2.014). He applies this account to propositions, which are 'pictures of reality', indeed 'logical pictures' (4.01, 4.021, 4.03).

This conception of propositions as pictures involves a parallelism between language and the world, which appears from the very first sentences of the *Tractatus*: 'The world is everything that is the case. The world is the totality of facts, not of things' (1–1.1). These parallel 4.001: 'The totality of propositions is the language' and 4.11: 'The totality of true propositions is the total natural science (or the totality of the natural sciences).' In these first sentences, there is a contrast, as fundamental for the *Tractatus* as the contrast between concepts and objects is for Frege. But Wittgenstein's contrast is not between concepts and objects, but between *facts* and things. Facts are what correspond to true propositions (*Wittgenstein in Cambridge*, 98). 'The world divides into facts' (1.2), and these in turn into atomic facts—where 'an atomic fact is a combination of objects (entities, things)' (2.01). Atomic facts correspond in turn to true 'elementary propositions' (*Wittgenstein in Cambridge*, 98); every proposition is a truth-function of elementary propositions (5), just as facts consist in the existence and non-existence of atomic facts (2, 2.06).

True propositions, then, state facts. To say that the world is the totality of facts, and not things, is to say that to list all the things in the world is not yet to describe the world. To do that, one has to say how things stand with these things—and this is to state the facts. Atomic facts are combinations of objects, and Wittgenstein gives a lovely image for this: 'In the atomic fact, objects hang in one another like the links of a chain' (2.03). Objects are made to go with one another, they fit together.[23]

---

[20]   Throughout the chapter I use a modernized form of Russell's notation rather than Frege's.

[21]   On this see McGuinness, '*Grundgedanke*'.

[22]   There is dispute in the secondary literature about what the objects of the *Tractatus* are—whether they include properties and relations as well as particulars, whether they include ordinary objects or only elements out of which other objects are to be constructed, and whether such elements would be sense-data, physical atoms, or 'logical' atoms. I intend what I say here to be neutral on these topics.

[23]   This image can be contrasted with Frege's image of 'incomplete' concepts, with gaps that need to be filled, forming unities with 'complete' objects, which fill the gaps. Links in a chain both have a hole to be filled, and fill the holes in other links. They hang together without any asymmetry like the asymmetry between concept and object.

Facts divide into atomic facts, which cannot be further subdivided: this means, for Wittgenstein, that the atomic facts are logically independent (2.061).[24] For example, the fact that Kremer is older than Obama is independent of the fact that Obama is president. The fact that Kremer is older than Obama is not independent of the fact that Obama is younger than Kremer, but Wittgenstein would regard these as the *same* fact, the same combination of objects. Perhaps the fact that Obama is president is not independent of the fact that Obama is an American—but this shows that at least one of these facts is *not* atomic, but can be further analysed.

Objects too are independent, in the sense that how things stand with one object is independent of how things stand with the others. 'The thing is independent in so far as it can occur in all *possible* circumstances, but this form of independence is a form of connexion with the atomic fact, a form of dependence' (2.0122). To know an object one must know 'its internal qualities', 'all the possibilities of its occurrence in atomic facts' (2.0122–3). An object *is* essentially a potential for combining with other objects in atomic facts; more precisely, 'the possibility of its occurrence in atomic facts is the *form* of the object' (2.0141, my emphasis).

Against this apparently metaphysical background, Wittgenstein introduces the idea of pictures: 'We make to ourselves pictures of facts' (2.1). Pictures have a *sense*— what they represent, 'a possible state of affairs in logical space', that is 'the existence and non-existence of atomic facts' (2.221, 2.202, 2.11).[25] Pictures are true or false, according as their sense agrees or disagrees with the reality they depict (2.21, 2.222). All of this applies to propositions, for propositions *are* pictures—*logical* pictures.

What is a logical picture, though? And *how* do pictures represent possible states of affairs? Let's begin with more ordinary pictures, spatial pictures for example—but we must think of even a spatial picture as representing a possible state of affairs. So the sort of picture to have in mind is not just a picture of Kremer, or of Obama, but a picture representing *that* Obama is taller than Kremer. Such a picture might involve an image of Obama and an image of Kremer, with the first image longer in the vertical dimension than the second. The image of Obama stands for Obama, and the image of Kremer for Kremer; but the way in which they are combined is also significant: the fact that one image is longer than the other, vertically, represents *that* Obama is taller than Kremer.

Wittgenstein says that the picture must have a *form* in common with the reality it depicts (2.17–2.171). The form of an object consists of the possibility of its occurrence in atomic facts, and the form of a picture is equally explained in terms of possibility. A picture has a *structure*, the 'connexion of the elements of the picture'—the 'definite way' in which 'its elements are combined with one another' (2.14, 2.141, 2.15). The *form* of the picture is 'the possibility of this structure' (2.15). This might seem to involve only the possible arrangements of the elements of the picture, but Wittgenstein asserts that the

---

[24] Compare 1.21: 'Any one can either be the case or not be the case, and everything else remains the same.' This remark applies to the facts *into which the world divides* (1.2)—atomic facts—since facts in general are not independent in this way.

[25] Where Ogden and Ramsey have 'facts' in 2.11 they should have 'states of affairs' ('*Sachlage*').

form of the picture is 'the possibility that the things are combined with one another as are the elements of the picture' (2.151), and comments '*Thus* the picture is linked with reality; it reaches up to it' (2.1511).

So for the picture *to be* a picture, it must share form with the reality it depicts—picture and reality must share the same *possibility of structure*. Consider a spatial picture depicting Kremer as taller than Obama—contrary to reality. In such a picture, the image representing Kremer will be vertically longer than the image representing Obama. Here the picture has a spatial structure which is not the same as that of the reality it represents. But there is nonetheless a shared *form*, insofar as it is *possible* for Kremer to be taller than Obama. This form is actualized in the structure of the picture, but not in the structure of reality, and so the picture depicts a possible state of affairs that does not exist. The picture is false—it does not 'agree with reality' (2.21). But the possibility of this judgement depends on the sharing of form between picture and reality.

Wittgenstein claims that even a *proposition* like 'Obama is taller than Kremer' is a picture—a *logical* picture. Although it does not share spatial form with the reality it depicts, it shares *logical* form with that reality—'what every picture, of whatever form, must have in common with reality in order to be able to represent it at all' (2.18). One name is not vertically longer than the other, so we do not have a spatial representation of Obama being taller than Kremer. Nonetheless the two names *are* placed in relation by the *words* 'is taller than'. In this way the *possibility* that Obama is taller than Kremer is contained in the proposition. In this case the proposition is true, agrees with reality, since this possibility is also actualized in the structure of reality. But in the false proposition, 'Kremer is taller than Obama', while the structure of the proposition is not duplicated in reality, its form is shared with the reality, insofar as it is possible for Kremer to be taller than Obama.

At 3.1432, Wittgenstein says: 'We must not say, "The complex sign '*aRb*' says that *a* stands in relation *R* to *b*"; but rather, "*That* '*a*' stands in a certain relation to '*b*' says *that* *aRb*"'. *What* says that Kremer is taller than Obama, is *that* the name 'Kremer' stands in a 'certain relation' to the name 'Obama', a relation realized through the presence of the words 'is taller than' between the two names.[26] This point is reiterated in remarks leading up to the fundamental thought that 'the *logic* of facts cannot be represented' (4.0312)— 'The proposition communicates to us a state of affairs, therefore it must be *essentially* connected with the state of affairs. And the connexion is, in fact, that it is its logical picture.... In the proposition a state of affairs is, as it were, put together for the sake of experiment.... One name stands for one thing, and another for another thing, and they

---

[26] It is misleading to say (as is often said) that the 'certain relation'—unspecified by Wittgenstein— between the two names is simply that of flanking 'is taller than' on the left and the right. That spatial relation is merely the 'sensibly perceptible' aspect of the relation doing the symbolizing work in the proposition—it is merely the sign, not the symbol. The symbol is the relation that holds between the names, such that *that* this relation holds *says that* Kremer is taller than Obama. This 'certain relation' cannot be specified independently of this symbolizing work. I owe this point to the dissertation work of my student Daesuk Han.

are connected together. And so the whole, like a living picture, presents the atomic fact'
(4.03, 4.031, 4.0311).

14.7 SAYING, SHOWING, AND LOGICAL FORM

Against this background we can understand Wittgenstein's claim that the logical constants 'do not represent' (4.0312). They are not depicting elements in the logical pictures, the propositions, in which they occur. Why does he think that? What a picture must share with the reality it depicts is logical form—the possibility of structure. But, Wittgenstein argues, 'the picture … cannot represent its form; it shows it forth [*es weist sie auf*]' (2.172). To represent the logical form of a picture, one would have to step outside this picture and make another picture about that logical form (2.173–4). Clearly, the picture itself cannot do this, but Wittgenstein holds that the logical form of a picture cannot be represented *at all*, not even in some 'meta-proposition'. He generalizes his argument: 'Propositions … cannot represent what they must have in common with reality in order to be able to represent it—the logical form. To be able to represent the logical form, we should have to be able to station ourselves with the propositions outside logic …' (4.12). Consequently, 'propositions cannot represent the logical form: this mirrors itself in the propositions.… The propositions *show* the logical form of reality. They exhibit it. [*Er weist sie auf.*] … What *can* be shown *cannot* be said' (4.121, 4.1212).

It can look as if Wittgenstein is telling us here about something we would like to, but cannot, do—represent the logical form of reality—as if logical form were an item we can see there in the proposition, alongside the names that are combined in it, but when we try to depict this item we find we just cannot. But that attempt to describe what we cannot do is itself a nonsensical attempt to represent logical form, to 'station ourselves outside of logic'. What is wrong with such an attempt and why are drawn to it?

Part of the problem is that the purported 'meta-proposition' representing the logical form is, like rules of inference, superfluous and so lacks sense. To understand a proposition is to grasp its logical form; there is no need of a different proposition to say what that form is. If one understands the proposition 'Kremer is taller than Obama' one knows what possible situation is depicted, what possibility of structure is projected. 'The proposition *shows* its sense. The proposition *shows* how things stand, *if* it is true.… To understand a proposition means to know what is the case, if it is true' (4.022, 4.024). That is: to understand a proposition is to know how to compare it to reality, to recognize the possible structure it projects and to know how to tell whether that structure is realized. This is not to know an additional fact about the proposition, such as 'it is the case that Kremer is taller than Obama, if "Kremer is taller than Obama" is true'. Such an attempt to *say* under what conditions a proposition is true ends up in empty self-repetition. In fact, knowledge of the logical form of a proposition is simply the ability to use the proposition to say something, to make sense. We cannot represent the logic of facts, because the logic of facts is not some additional fact or piece of information; grasping the logic of facts is knowing how to speak and think. But then why might anyone be tempted to try to represent the logic of facts in a proposition? This temptation stems from the desire not to let logic take care of itself—to provide a ground for logic in some super-fact about the nature of reality—'founded deep in the nature of things', in Frege's words.

14.8 THE CRITIQUE OF FREGE AND RUSSELL: VIOLATING THE *GRUNDGEDANKE*

According to Wittgenstein, Frege and Russell's logical symbolisms fail to 'exclude all errors', all 'fundamental confusions' which pervade philosophy. Their notations still contain forms of equivocation that foster such confusions. But these confusions might be harmless, if they did not at the same time fit the mistaken desire to take care of logic. This is shown by Frege and Russell's violations of the 'fundamental thought' that the logic of facts cannot be represented.

Consider such propositional connectives as '~' and '⊃'. There is a danger of assimilating these to ordinary property and relation signs. This confusion is encouraged in Russell's notation by the grammatical similarity between '~p', and 'Ao' ('Obama is American'), and '$p \supset q$' and 'oTk' ('Obama is taller than Kremer'). Russell reads '$p \supset q$' as 'p implies q' (*Principia*, 6–7), and treats '~' and '⊃' as denoting *propositional functions*, just like 'x is American' and 'x is taller than y'. Frege, the pioneer of function–argument analysis in logic, thinks of sentences as expressing thoughts and referring to truth-values (the True or the False). He understands concepts (like ξ *is American* or ξ *is taller than* ζ) as functions from objects to truth-values. Thus 'ξ is American' refers to that function whose value is the True whenever the argument is American, and whose value is the False otherwise, and 'ξ is taller than ζ' refers to that function whose value is the True whenever the first argument is taller than the second, and false otherwise. Frege treats his negation and conditional signs as referring to concepts of exactly this sort: '~ξ' refers to that function whose value is the True when the argument is any object other than the True, and whose value is the False when the argument is the True, so that ~ξ is 'a concept under which falls every object with the sole exception of the True' (*Basic Laws*, §6, 39). Similarly '$\xi \supset \zeta$' refers to that function whose value is the False whenever the first argument is the True and the second argument is any object other than the True, and whose value is the True whenever the first argument is other than the False, or the second argument is the True; so $\xi \supset \zeta$ is a special kind of relational concept (*Basic Laws*, §12, 51).

According to this Fregean conception the True and the False are objects which sentences stand for, and negation and the conditional are concepts under which these objects fall or fail to fall. Wittgenstein comments on this conception at 4.431: 'Frege's explanation of the truth-concept is false: if "the true" and "the false" were real objects and the arguments in ~p etc., then the sense of ~p would by no means be determined by Frege's determination.'

Wittgenstein sees Frege's 'determination' of 'the sense of $\sim p$' as meant to fix the 'truth-conditions of the proposition' (4.431), 'what is the case, if it is true' (4.024; cf. Frege, *Basic Laws*, §32, 89). This is determined by setting that $\sim p$ is true when p is false and vice versa—Wittgenstein agrees with *that*. But if the True and the False are *objects*, our preference for one of these two makes no sense: why should one of them be privileged, tied to agreement of a proposition with the facts, while the other has the opposite role? There is nothing that can force this in the nature of the objects themselves; within Frege's logic the two could switch roles, or be replaced by any two other distinct objects, and nothing would change.

From Wittgenstein's perspective, the treatment of sentences as names of special objects, the truth-values, and of logical signs like negation and the conditional as referring to concepts under which these objects can fall or fail to fall, rests on a confusion fostered by the notation of Frege's logic—a confusion of propositions and names, facts and things (1.1, 3.14, 3.142, 3.3, etc.). But why is this confusion tempting? I suggested above that the appeal of such confusions rests on the desire to take care of logic, not to let logic take care of itself. Consider once again in this connection rules of inference like *modus ponens*. In the *Basic Laws of Arithmetic*, Frege appears to offer a *justification* for *modus ponens* grounded in the nature of the concept expressed by the conditional sign: 'From the propositions "$\vdash \Delta \supset \Gamma$" and "$\vdash \Delta$" we may infer "$\vdash \Gamma$"; for if Γ were not the True, then since Δ is the True, $\Delta \supset \Gamma$ would be the False' (§14, 57). Wittgenstein, in contrast, holds that 'The method of inference is to be understood from the ... propositions alone. Only they themselves can justify the inference' (5.132). This is one instance of the more general principle that logic has to take care of itself.

14.9 DISTINGUISHING LOGICAL CONSTANTS FROM REPRESENTATIONAL ELEMENTS

Wittgenstein distinguishes logical signs like '$\sim$' and '$\supset$' from depicting elements, such as 'Obama', 'Kremer', and 'taller than' in 'Obama is taller than Kremer'. He points to disanalogies between logical signs and ordinary concept-expressions or propositional functions, in support of this point of view. For example, logical signs can cancel themselves: '$\sim\sim oTk$' says the same thing as 'oTk', for example—the first is just a more complicated way of saying what the second says, that Obama is taller than Kremer.[27] But if the '$\sim$' sign were a depicting element, the possible state of affairs represented by '$\sim\sim oTk$' would involve some further item, and would be a different state of affairs than that represented by 'oTk' (4.0621, 5.44).

---

[27] The same point can be made for '$\supset$'—'$((oTk \supset oTk) \supset oTk)$' says the same thing as 'oTk'.

But Wittgenstein not only offers such negative arguments (several of which are scattered through the *Tractatus*) to distinguish logical signs from ordinary concept-expressions. He also provides a positive alternative: a different notation to express what we use '~' and '⊃' to express, designed to avoid the confusions encouraged by Frege and Russell's symbolism. This alternative notation makes use of the idea of truth-tables, but not in the familiar form taught in logic classes today. Wittgenstein does not use truth-tables to test the validity of arguments written in the familiar notation of propositional logic. Rather, he uses truth-tables to *rewrite* this notation. For Wittgenstein, a proposition like '~o Tk' can be expressed as (compare 4.4–4.442):

oTk	
T	F
F	T

Similarly, '*Po* ⊃ *Ao*' ('if Obama is President, then Obama is American') can be rewritten as (4.4–4.442):

Po	Ao	
T	T	T
F	T	T
T	F	F
F	F	T

These truth-tabular notations, Wittgenstein says, are 'propositional signs' (4.442). But they have no depicting elements over and above those contained in the elementary propositions '*oTk*', '*Po*', and '*Ao*': 'It is clear that to the complex of the signs "F" and "T" no object (or "complex of objects") corresponds; any more than to the horizontal or vertical lines or to brackets. There are no "logical objects"' (4.441). Just as one would not be tempted to think of the lines making up the truth-tables, or the '(' and ')' in '~(*Po* ⊃ *Ao*)', as having a representative function, Wittgenstein's truth-tabular notation should disabuse one of the temptation to think of the letters 'T' and 'F' as standing for special logical objects (the truth-values), and so also of the temptation to think of negation and the conditional as representing special concepts, properties of propositions and relations between propositions, or properties of truth-values and relations between truth-values.

Wittgenstein's symbolism displays negation and the conditional as *operations*. An operation takes one or more propositions as its base, and yields a further proposition as its result. Displaying one proposition as the result of an operation on other propositions expresses an 'internal relation' between the base propositions and the resultant proposition. For example, '~kTo' does not express a property *of* the proposition (or the truth-value) kTo. Rather, an internal relation *between* the propositions 'kTo' and '~kTo' is set up—the two have opposite sense, because the latter is a truth-function of the former, and agrees with reality exactly when the former does not (5.2–5.22). This internal relation is displayed explicitly in the truth-tabular notation introduced by Wittgenstein. But it is not a further element to be depicted in a separate proposition; it is an aspect of the logical form of both propositions, which cannot further be represented (4.122ff.). To grasp this relation is part of what is required to *understand* both propositions, to locate them in logical space (3.4); and that is just to know how to use them logically, to make sense with them and to reason with them.

In a certain sense, then, Wittgenstein's alternative notation shows that the apparent 'logical constants' of Frege's and Russell's notations are *superfluous*—an alternative notation can be constructed which does the same expressive work but without using individual logical signs that correspond to '~' and '⊃'. As we saw above, this does not mean that the propositions of Frege and Russell's logic are meaningless—quite the contrary. But the logical signs of their symbolism are revealed not to be doing the kind of work they might appear to be doing, when we see how the work they do can be accomplished in another way. They are shown to be, as Wittgenstein colourfully puts it, 'punctuation signs' (5.4611).[28]

It is instructive to see how this alternative notation relates to the two logical points introduced in our discussion of the logical signs for negation and the conditional: *modus ponens* and the self-cancelling of negation. Consider first an instance of *modus ponens*, as expressed in Russell's notation: $Po ⊃ Ao, Po ∴ Ao$. Wittgenstein says that 'the method of inference' should 'be understood from the … propositions alone' (5.132), but this is not perspicuously displayed in Russell's symbolism. If we rewrite the conditional premise in the truth-tabular form given above, it may not seem we have achieved greater perspicuity. But it is also possible to rewrite the second premise, and conclusion, in this form, even though they are elementary propositions—for 'propositions are truth-functions of elementary propositions', and 'an elementary proposition is a truth-function of itself' (5). Hence the *modus ponens* inference can be written:

---

[28] Wittgenstein makes a similar set of moves concerning the identity sign of Frege and Russell's logic. He shows that it is a confusion to treat the identity sign as a real relation sign, by constructing an alternative notation in which 'identity of the object' is expressed 'by identity of the sign and not by a sign of identity'. For discussion of this, see my 'The Cardinal Problem of Philosophy' and 'Russell's Merit'.

Po	Ao	
T	T	T
F	T	T
T	F	F
F	F	T

Po	
T	T
F	F

∴

Ao	
T	T
F	F

One needs only to compare the T's and F's in these displays to see that 'the truth-grounds that are common to [the premises]' (namely Po and Ao assigned T) 'are also truth-grounds of [the conclusion]' so that 'the truth of [the conclusion] follows from the truth of [the premises]' (5.11).

Similarly, consider how to represent a double negation like '∼∼oTk' in Wittgenstein's tabular notation. Since 'every truth-operation creates from the truth-functions of elementary propositions another truth-function of elementary propositions, i.e. a proposition', Wittgenstein argues, 'the propositional sign in No. 4.42'—that is, the truth-tabular representation of 'p ⊃ q'—'expresses one truth-function of elementary propositions even when "p" and "q" are truth-functions of elementary propositions' (5.3–5.31). Applying this to the truth-tabular representation of negation, we should be able to write the double negation '∼∼oTk' as:

∼oTk	
T	F
F	T

or, fully explicitly, as:

oTk	
T	F
F	T
T	F
F	T

If we compare this to the representation of 'oTk' as a truth-function of itself, we imme-diately see that these are two ways of writing the same thing, expressing the same sense:

oTk	
T	T
F	F

So here the logical relations can be read off of the signs, and do not need to be written down in additional rules. Logic is allowed to take care of itself.[29]

This case study illustrates Wittgenstein's method for exposing confusions made pos-sible by the logical symbolisms of Frege and Russell. But how does this help us to appre-ciate the ethical significance of the *Tractatus*? I will approach this question from two directions, which I hope will converge on a coherent conception of the ethical vision of Wittgenstein's early work. The first line of thought begins with Wittgenstein's infa-mous pronouncement, that to understand *him* is to recognize his propositions as non-sensical, a ladder to be thrown away once one has climbed up on it to a proper vantage point (6.54). The second line of thought is inspired by some remarks in the *Tractatus* not about ethics, but about science, put beside some remarks about ethics that he made in the period immediately after his return to philosophy in the early 1930s.

14.10 RECOGNIZING NONSENSE
IN THE *TRACTATUS*

To begin with the first line of thought: Wittgenstein tells us that we are to recog-nize the propositions of the *Tractatus* as nonsensical. According to the argument of this chapter, we should therefore expect some combination of the two factors to be

[29] Whether logic, as understood by Frege and Russell, can be said to take care of itself in this way, when we include expressive resources such as multiple quantification and relational predicates, that we now know not to be amenable to decision procedures analogous to truth-tables, is a question I will not address in this chapter.

at work in his propositions: forms of equivocation and confusion, on the one hand, and a kind of superfluousness on the other. Consider in this light Wittgenstein's own repeated talk about *logical form*—which any proposition must have in common with the reality it represents, in order to represent it correctly or incorrectly (4.12). Wittgenstein's discussions of logical form are clearly problematic, given his thesis that logical form can't be represented by propositions (4.12). As we saw above, any attempt to represent logical form in language, as if it were an additional element of propositions and the reality they represent, would be superfluous and so meaningless. Yet Wittgenstein's statements about logical form—that it is the possibility of structure (2.15), that it is shared by any picture and the reality it depicts (2.18), and so on—certainly seem as if they involve representing logical form and characterizing it in some way.[30] 'Propositions', Wittgenstein tells us, '*show* the logical form of reality' (4.121), and 'What *can* be shown *cannot* be said' (4.1212)—but as Russell points out in the Introduction to the *Tractatus*, 'What causes hesitation is the fact that, after all, Wittgenstein manages to say a good deal about what cannot be said …' (p. 22). In the immediate context of 4.1212, Wittgenstein provides examples of things that can be shown, all of them aspects of logical form: that the object *a* occurs in the sense of the proposition *fa*; that two propositions *fa* and *ga* are about the same object; that two propositions contradict one another; that one proposition follows from another (4.1211); that internal properties and relations hold of objects (4.122, 4.124); that one blue colour is brighter or darker than another (4.123); and that an object falls under a formal concept (4.126)—only to declare such seeming propositions nonsensical (4.124, 4.1241, 4.1272). Here we have what Peter Geach colourfully calls 'Ludwig's self-mate' ('Assertion', 265).

But why are we tempted into this self-undermining discourse? Consider the association Wittgenstein repeatedly draws between *form* and *possibility*: the form of an object is 'the possibility of its occurrence in atomic facts' (2.0141), the form of an atomic fact is 'the possibility of structure' (2.033), and the form of representation of a picture is also 'the possibility of [its] structure' (2.15). Frege's and Russell's philosophies of logic make it almost inevitable that these propositions will be read as follows:

> Objects come in various logical types.[31] Each type brings with it principles that determine possibilities of combination with objects of other types. For example, there is a type of individuals (or Fregean objects). A relation between individuals is of a different logical type—it takes as arguments two individuals and cannot combine in the same way with two relations. The form of a relation R is something like $\xi R \zeta$; the letters 'ξ' and 'ζ' indicate the need for arguments of the individual type. There are possibilities of combination—the combination

---

[30] The ultimate incoherence of Wittgenstein's account of picturing and of the notions of pictorial form and possibility on which it depends is discussed in Goldfarb, 'Metaphysics and Nonsense', 65–6, and is a major theme of Ricketts, 'Pictures, Logic, and the Limits of Sense', from which I draw inspiration here.

[31] I set aside complications due to the ramification of Russell's theory of logical types.

aRb is possible—and impossibilities—if *S* and *T* are relations one cannot combine them with *R* to yield *SRT*. Our language needs to conform to these possibilities and impossibilities of combination that characterize the logical types
of objects.

As Russell put it in a letter to Wittgenstein: 'the theory of types … is a theory of correct
symbolism … a symbol must have the same structure as its meaning' (*Wittgenstein in
Cambridge*, 98).

But Wittgenstein sees this as yet another attempt to take care of logic. He replies:
'That's exactly what one can't say. You cannot prescribe to a symbol what it *may* be used
to express. All that a symbol *can* express, it *may* express. This is a short answer but it is
true!' (*Wittgenstein in Cambridge*, 98). This 'short answer' is given in the *Tractatus* as
the follow-through on the claim that 'logic must take care of itself' at 5.473, which continues: 'A *possible* sign must also be able to signify. Everything which is possible in logic
is also permitted.' At 5.4733 the same point is made against Frege: 'Frege says: Every
legitimately constructed proposition must have a sense; and I say: Every possible proposition is legitimately constructed, and if it has no sense this can only be because we have
given no *meaning* to some of its constituent parts.' One cannot consult the meanings of
the signs to determine which combinations of those meanings are possible and which
impossible, and then ensure the 'legitimate construction' of one's propositions by guaranteeing that the possible modes of combination of one's symbols mirror the possible
modes of combination of their meanings.

But the picture that associates Wittgenstein's talk of form with attempts to take care of
logic by ensuring that our symbolisms respect logical type distinctions rests on a confusion about what Wittgenstein is referring to when he identifies form with the possibility of structure. This confusion can be elucidated by considering Wittgenstein's
characterization of modal categories of possibility and necessity as themselves *logical*.
According to the *Tractatus*, 'there is only *logical* necessity' and 'so there is only a *logical* impossibility' (6.37, 6.375). That is—there is only the necessity of *tautologies* like
'*oTk* ⊃ *oTk*', propositions which are 'true for all the truth-possibilities of elementary
propositions'; and there is only the impossibility of *contradictions* like '*oTk* & ~*oTk*',
propositions which are 'false for all the truth-possibilities' (4.46).[32] Therefore, there is
also only *logical* possibility—the possibility of 'significant propositions', propositions
with sense—propositions which are true for some truth-possibilities and false for others. 'The truth of tautology is certain, of propositions possible, of contradiction impossible' (4.464). In contrast, on the type-theoretic reading of logical form, the logical form of
elementary propositions depends on a range of possibilities and necessities that cannot
be accounted for in terms of the truth-possibilities of elementary propositions, since it
is presupposed by the very ability of those elementary propositions to be true or false,
to represent the world correctly or incorrectly. It is no solution to this difficulty to push

---

[32] 6.3751 makes clear that 'logical impossibility' in 6.375 refers to the impossibility of contradictions.

these fundamental possibilities and necessities into the realm of what can only be shown and not said. If these underlying modal facts are nonetheless *there*, even if they cannot be said, they give the lie to the claim that there is only *logical* modality.

The solution is to recognize that when Wittgenstein associates form with the 'possibility of structure' he intends simply the possibility that an atomic fact, represented by an elementary proposition, exists. The form of the proposition '*kTo*' ('Kremer is taller than Obama') is simply the possibility that Kremer is taller than Obama, the possibility that this atomic fact exists. To what is this possibility opposed? In one sense, it is opposed to the *opposite possibility*, the possibility that Kremer is not taller than Obama, that ~*kTo*. In another sense it is opposed to the impossibility of contradiction, the impossibility of *kTo* & ~*kTo*. What it is *not* opposed to is the supposed impossibility of a faulty combination like '*OTO*'—'older than is taller than older than'. There is no impossibility there, only meaningless nonsense—in this combination of signs we have given *no* meaning to some of the constituent parts. The type-theoretic reading of Wittgenstein's talk of possibility embodies the confused attempt to speak about *possibility and impossibility of form*—or what one might call a *form of form*—as if there were a more fundamental level of possibility and impossibility determining which combinations are *candidates* for possibility in the logical sense.

It might seem, then, that we have rescued a meaning for Wittgenstein's talk of possibility and logical form after all. This is simply talk of the possibility of propositions with sense, as opposed to the necessity of tautologies and the impossibility of contradictions. Yet such talk is ultimately *superfluous*, according to the *Tractatus*. For 'The picture contains the possibility of the state of affairs which it represents' (2.203) and 'the thought contains the possibility of the state of affairs which it thinks' (3.02) so nothing is added in trying to *state* the possibility of this state of affairs.[33] Consequently this too is relegated by Wittgenstein to the realm of what is shown, and so cannot be said. 'The proposition *shows* its sense' (4.022), and while 'the proposition shows what it says, the tautology and the contradiction [show] that they say nothing' (4.461).[34] Yet this solution is itself unstable. We rescue our conception of logical form—of the 'possibility of structure'—only by *saying what it is* that supposedly can only be shown.

---

[33] 3.13 puts the point somewhat differently: 'In the proposition ... its sense is not yet contained, but the possibility of expressing it.' But 3.13 goes on to say 'In the proposition the form of its sense is contained, but not its content.' Since form is the possibility of structure, what this shows is that the possibility of expressing a state of affairs is not distinct from the possibility of that state of affairs (the form of the sense). Picture and state of affairs share a form—that is there is one possibility that governs them both.

[34] It is sometimes thought that the first part of 4.461 contradicts the claim that what can be shown cannot be said (4.1212). This rests on a mistaken reading of the remark that 'the proposition shows what it says'. This is just another way of saying that the proposition 'shows its sense'. It is not that the proposition '*kTo*' 'shows what it says' in the sense that it *both* says and shows that Kremer is taller than Obama, in contradiction with 4.1212. Rather the proposition shows what it says in the sense that it *shows that it says that* Kremer is taller than Obama. This is the only reading to make sense of the parallel between the first and second parts of 4.461.

Moreover, the very claim that 'there is only *logical* necessity', on which we relied to diagnose the confusion of the type-theoretic reading of logical form, is itself deeply problematic.[35] As long as we hold onto this sentence, we set it up in opposition to the alternative view: that there are, in addition to logical necessity and impossibility, substantive forms of necessity and impossibility. We then see ourselves as defending the correct view of the matter against a false conception. But this requires us to recognize the *intelligibility* of that alternate view. Yet to hold onto the idea that the view of modality as logical is correct, as opposed to the false but intelligible view of modality as substantive, is to admit again a higher-order sense of modality in which both these views are in some sense possible—both represent possible ways in which the modal facts might be structured. We then ground the logical character of necessity in a super-fact about the world, a fact which cannot be depicted in our propositions because it is the presupposition of our making sense with propositions of this sort (propositions that are constructed as truth-functions of logically independent elementary propositions). In this way we again refuse to let logic take care of itself.

14.11 SAYING, SHOWING, AND THE DESIRE TO TAKE CARE OF LOGIC

Clearly Wittgenstein's difficulties here are connected to the crucial distinction between saying and showing, and the way in which Wittgenstein deploys that distinction in his talk of logical form, possibility, necessity, and impossibility, as that which is *shown*. Wittgenstein described this distinction to Russell as both 'my main contention' and 'the cardinal problem of philosophy'. This should strike us as strange—how can Wittgenstein's 'main contention' also be a '*problem* of philosophy'? Bearing in mind that 'the method of formulating these problems [of philosophy] rests on the misunderstanding of the logic of our language', I suggest that the distinction between saying and showing must at least sometimes be deployed in a way that involves philosophical confusion—a confusion we seize upon because it seems to let us satisfy our desire to take care of logic.

Our temptation, in other words, is to give a justification, or grounding, for logic.[36] This is the temptation one is in danger of falling into when one embraces the idea of ineffable proposition-like insights into the nature of reality, insights which reveal the structure our language must conform itself to in order to be meaningful. This idea can be tempting insofar as it makes it possible for us to conceive of a grounding for logic which cannot itself be subject to a further demand for justification, an 'internal' grounding, which we can appreciate through an insight that cannot be expressed—close enough

---

[35] Here I follow Cora Diamond in 'Throwing Away the Ladder', 198ff.

[36] The following argument is elaborated at greater length in my 'The Purpose of *Tractarian* Nonsense' and 'The Cardinal Problem of Philosophy'.

to a proposition to serve as a justification, yet different enough to escape the demand for further justification. But this idea rests on a confusion, which is fostered by the very word 'show' that is so crucial to Wittgenstein's self-confessedly problematic distinction between saying and showing. We use this one verb, 'to show', in a variety of ways. Suppose you are going to take care of my cat while I am away. I show you my cat, I show you how much food to give her, I show you where I keep the food, and I show you that there is enough food in the cabinet to last until I get back. Finally, I show you how to make her purr by rubbing her under her chin. All of these uses of 'show' are related, but they do not have the same meaning, or even the same logical function—this one sign is shared by many symbols.

Of particular interest here is the final pair of senses of 'show' illustrated above: a propositional sense of 'showing *that*' and a practical sense of 'showing *how*'. We can now see the thought that there are ineffable quasi-propositional truths which can be shown but cannot be said as involving a subtle equivocation between these two senses of 'showing', propositional and practical. Thinking of the practical sense of 'showing how', we expect that what is shown can't be said; slipping towards the propositional sense of 'showing that', we think of this 'what' as something like a fact. That something like this confusion is involved in the *Tractatus*'s talk of 'showing' is suggested by the fact that showing is connected by Wittgenstein to *sense* and so also to *understanding*. At 4.02 Wittgenstein says that 'we understand the sense of the propositional sign, without having had it explained to us'. He comments on this at 4.022 that 'the proposition *shows* its sense'. Yet sense is something that we make: 'We make to ourselves pictures of facts' (2.1). And 'to understand a proposition', 'to know what is the case if it is true' (4.024), is simply to know how 'reality is compared with the proposition' (4.06). Similarly, inferential relations are said to be shown in the *Tractatus*: 'if two propositions contradict each other, this is shown by their structure; similarly if one follows from another, etc.' (4.1211). Yet we *draw* conclusions and *make* inferences: 'if *p* follows from *q*, I can conclude from *q* to *p*; infer *p* from *q*. The method of inference is to be understood from the two propositions alone' (5.132). In understanding the propositions, grasping their sense, we know *how* to reason with them.

So, the idea that 'logical form', as something *shared* by propositions and the reality they depict, is *shown* by those propositions but cannot be represented by them, exploits the equivocation we have found in 'show'. We slip back and forth between the idea of a feature of reality, the world which we represent, and the idea of an aspect of our making sense by representing that world, an activity which we engage in and which depends on abilities we possess. We confusedly think of these features both as having to do with how reality *is, and* as having to do with how language is to be *used*. We *willingly* fall into this confusion to the extent that we are moved by the desire that it seems to allow us to fulfil: the desire to take care of logic by providing the ineffable ground of all our saying and making sense. In recognizing that the *Tractatus* itself involves this kind of philosophical confusion, in recognizing its propositions as nonsensical, we understand its author as showing to us the groundlessness of logic: logic has to take care of itself. At the same time we recognize the superfluousness of the ground we sought to provide for logic. If logic *has* to take care of itself, then it *does* take care of itself and needs no caretaker, external or internal.[37]

14.12 The *Tractatus* as an Ethical Work

Now, to conclude, how does all of this relate to the ethical point of the *Tractatus*? That some connection is intended here is evident from the deep parallel set up in the *Tractatus* between ethics and logic, both of which are called 'transcendental' (6.13, 6.421). I will develop this parallel beginning with a point that Wittgenstein makes about neither logic nor ethics, but rather science. In the *Tractatus*, Wittgenstein discusses natural science in the 6.3s, just before his brief explicit remarks about ethics in the 6.4s and 6.5s. Near the end of his discussion of science, Wittgenstein says this:

> 6.37 A necessity for one thing to happen because another has happened does not exist. There is only *logical* necessity.
> 6.371 At the basis of the whole modern view of the world lies the illusion that the so-called laws of nature are the explanations of natural phenomena.
> 6.372 So people stop short at natural laws as at something unassailable, as did the ancients at God and Fate.
> And they both are right and wrong. But the ancients were clearer, in so far as they recognized a clear terminus, whereas the modern system makes it appear as though *everything* were explained.

Wittgenstein's thought here can be understood in terms of (one form of) the cosmological argument for the existence of God. Beginning with the contingent events that we observe in the world, we seek an explanation for why *these* events occur, and not others. We can trace each event to a preceding cause, but insofar as that cause is equally contingent, we remain unsatisfied. So, the argument goes, there must be a *necessary* being which is the cause of the entire sequence of causally interrelated contingent events, a being that itself could not have been otherwise. For the ancients, this is 'God and Fate'. The modern view puts in place of God (and Fate) the laws of nature, thought of as necessary ('unassailable') truths that determine how contingent events are related to one other as cause and effect.

Wittgenstein says that the ancients and moderns 'both are right and wrong'. They are right in recognizing that 'explanations come to an end somewhere', as Wittgenstein later put it (*Philosophical Investigations*, §1). But they are wrong in thinking that this stopping point is somehow *necessary*—for 'there is only *logical* necessity'. Nonetheless, there is something preferable to the ancients' view over the moderns, according to Wittgenstein. The latter rests on a misconception of the laws of nature and 'makes it appear as though

---

[37] I argue for the plausibility of this reading in some detail in 'The Cardinal Problem of Philosophy'.

everything were explained'. The laws of nature are not explanations of natural phenomena at all. They do not ground phenomena in some metaphysical necessity. Rather, they are a way of organizing our description of the facts that we have observed in reality. Wittgenstein uses the metaphor of a net with a particular mesh, in which we can capture facts (6.341–2). The ancients, who stopped at God and Fate, did not conceive of these as explanatory hypotheses on a par with the contingent causes in the chain of explanations within the world—by appealing to some source from out of this world, they really expressed the point that explanations had come to an end in 'one clear terminus'.

After his return to philosophy, in the early 1930s, Wittgenstein made some interestingly similar remarks about ethics, and these can shed light on the ethical point of the *Tractatus*. On 17 December 1930, in a conversation with members of the Vienna Circle, Wittgenstein took up the question raised in Plato's *Euthyphro*, whether the good is good because the gods command it, or the gods command it because it is good. He said:[38]

> Schlick says that in theological ethics there used to be two conceptions of the essence of the good: according to the shallower interpretation the good is good because it is what God wants; according to the profounder interpretation God wants the good because it is good. I think that the first interpretation is the profounder one: what God commands, that is good. For it cuts off the way to any explanation 'why' it is good, while the second interpretation is the shallow, rationalist one, which proceeds 'as if' you could give reasons for what is good.
>
> The first conception says clearly that the essence of the good has nothing to do with the facts and hence cannot be explained by any proposition. If there is any proposition expressing precisely what I think, it is the proposition 'What God commands, that is good.'

Here, the profounder interpretation corresponds to the view of the ancients about the explanation of natural phenomena. Like that view, it 'recognizes a clear terminus'—'it cuts of the way to an explanation'. In a diary entry written about five months later, Wittgenstein wrote: '"It is good because God commanded it" is the correct [*richtige*] expression for groundlessness [*die Grundlosigkeit*]'.[39] So the proposition 'expressing precisely what I think' is also the correct way to express the *groundlessness* of ethics. Saying 'it's good because God commanded it' is really just a way of saying 'it's good—period'. There is nothing more to say. In sum, we could say: 'ethics has to look after itself'.[40] Ethics is not some body of ethical theory, but a way to live. The ethical point of the *Tractatus* is to get us to see that logic and ethics are *groundless*—that we cannot provide justifications

---

[38] *Ludwig Wittgenstein and the Vienna Circle*, 115. Wednesday, 17 December 1930. The connection of this passage to the *Tractatus*'s treatment of the laws of nature is illuminatingly discussed by James Klagge, '*Das erlösende Wort*'.

[39] 'Movements of Thought', 82–3. I have modified the translation. The link between this remark, the discussion with the Vienna Circle, and *Tractatus* 6.372, is made by the original editor, Ilse Somavilla—see fn. g, p. 82—and is also discussed by Klagge, '*Das erlösende Wort*'.

[40] This formulation is given in James Conant, 'What Ethics in the *Tractatus* is Not', which discusses the parallels between logic and ethics in the *Tractatus* in more depth than I have been able to here.

for them in any kind of theorizing—or even in the grasping of ineffable insights into the nature of reality, or the 'higher'. This is why those who 'to whom after long doubting the sense of life became clear, could not then say wherein this sense consisted'. The clarity they have achieved is not a clarity about anything like a theoretical proposition, even an ineffable one. It is rather a clarity about how to live. The ethical point of the *Tractatus* is to free us from the need for justification, to enable us to live. Understanding *this* we see the world rightly (6.54).[41]

References

Bradley, F. H. *Appearance and Reality*. 1st edn. London: Swan Sonnenschein & Co., 1893.

Carroll, Lewis. 'What the Tortoise Said to Achilles', *Mind* 4 (1895): 278–80.

Conant, James. 'The Method of the *Tractatus*'. In E. Reck (ed.), *From Frege to Wittgenstein: Perspectives on Early Analytic Philosophy*. Oxford: Oxford University Press, 2002, pp. 374–462.

——'What Ethics in the *Tractatus* is Not'. In D. Z. Phillips and M. von der Ruhr (eds.), *Religion and Wittgenstein's Legacy*. Aldershot: Ashgate, 2005, pp. 39–88.

Diamond, Cora. 'Throwing Away the Ladder: How to Read the *Tractatus*'. In *The Realistic Spirit: Wittgenstein, Philosophy, and the Mind*. Cambridge, MA: MIT Press, 1995, pp. 179–204. Dated 1984–5 in *The Realistic Spirit*; first published in *Philosophy* 63 (1988): 5–27.

Frege, Gottlob. *The Basic Laws of Arithmetic: Exposition of the System*, tr. and ed. M. Furth. Berkeley and Los Angeles: University of California Press, 1967. Partial translation of *Grundgesetze der Arithmetik*, vols. 1 and 2. Jena: Hermann Pohle, 1893 and 1903.

——*Conceptual Notation*. In *Conceptual Notation and Related Articles*, tr. and ed. T. W. Bynum. Oxford: Clarendon Press, 1972. Translation of *Begriffsschrift*. Halle: Louis Nebert, 1879.

——*Conceptual Notation and Related Articles*, tr. and ed. T. W. Bynum. Oxford: Clarendon Press, 1972.

——*Foundations of Arithmetic*. tr. J. L. Austin. Evanston: Northwestern University Press, 1980. Translation of *Die Grundlagen der Arithmetik*. Breslau: Wilhelm Koebner, 1884.

——'Function and Concept'. In *Translations from the Philosophical Writings of Gottlob Frege*, tr. and ed. Peter T. Geach and Max Black. Oxford: Blackwell, 1952; 2nd edn. 1960; 3rd edn. 1980, pp. 21–41. Translation of *Funktion und Begriff*. Jena: Hermann Pohle, 1891.

——'On Concept and Object'. In *Translations from the Philosophical Writings of Gottlob Frege*, tr. and ed. Peter T. Geach and Max Black. Oxford: Blackwell, 1952; 2nd edn. 1960; 3rd edn. 1980, pp. 42–55. Translation of '*Über Begriff und Gegenstand*'. *Vierteljahrsschrift für wissenschaftliche Philosophie* 16 (1892): 192–205.

Geach, Peter. 'Assertion'. In *Logic Matters*. Berkeley and Los Angeles: University of California Press, 1972, pp. 254–69. First published in *Philosophical Review* 74 (1965): 449–65.

——'Saying and Showing in Frege and Wittgenstein'. In J. Hintikka (ed.), *Essays on Wittgenstein in Honour of G. H. von Wright*, *Acta Philosophica Fennica* 28 (Amsterdam, 1976), pp. 54–70.

[41] Portions of this material were presented to the Philosophy Department at Georgetown University and discussed in a 'Master Class' there on the *Tractatus*, and also at a Workshop on Wittgenstein and the Literary, the Ethical and the Unsayable at the University of Chicago. I am indebted to these conversations for several clarifications and improvements in this essay.

Goldfarb, Warren. 'Metaphysics and Nonsense: On Cora Diamond's *The Realistic Spirit*', *Journal of Philosophical Research* 22 (1997): 57–73.

Hacker, P. M. S. *Insight and Illusion: Themes in the Philosophy of Wittgenstein*, 2nd revised edn. Oxford: Clarendon Press, 1986; 1st edn. 1972.

Jolley, Kelly. *The Concept 'Horse' Paradox and Wittgensteinian Conceptual Investigations: A Prolegomenon to Philosophical Investigations*. Aldershot: Ashgate, 2007.

Klagge, James. *'Das erlösende Wort'*. 32nd International Wittgenstein Symposium, August, 2009. Online at <http://www.phil.vt.edu/JKlagge/ALWSTalk09.pdf> accessed 29 November 2012.

Kremer, Michael. 'The Cardinal Problem of Philosophy'. In A. Crary (ed.), *Wittgenstein and the Moral Life*. Cambridge: MIT Press, 2007, pp. 143–76.

—— 'The Purpose of Tractarian Nonsense', *Noûs* 35 (2001): 39–73.

—— 'Russell's Merit'. In J. Zalabardo (ed.), *Wittgenstein's Early Philosophy*. Oxford: Oxford University Press, 2012, pp. 195–240.

McGuinness, Brian. 'The *Grundgedanke* of the *Tractatus*'. In *Approaches to Wittgenstein: Collected Papers*. New York: Routledge, 2002, pp. 103–15. First published in G. Vesey (ed.), *Understanding Wittgenstein*. London: Macmillan, 1974, pp. 49–61.

Ostrow, Matthew. *Wittgenstein's Tractatus: A Dialectical Interpretation*. Cambridge: Cambridge University Press, 2002.

Ricketts, Thomas. 'Pictures, Logic and the Limits of Sense in Wittgenstein's *Tractatus*'. In H. Sluga and D. Stern (eds.), *The Cambridge Companion to Wittgenstein*. Cambridge: Cambridge University Press, 1996, pp. 59–99.

—— 'Wittgenstein against Frege and Russell'. In E. Reck (ed.), *From Frege to Wittgenstein: Perspectives on Early Analytic Philosophy*. Oxford: Oxford University Press, 2002, pp. 227–51.

Russell, Bertrand. 'On Denoting'. *Mind* 14 (1905): 479–93.

—— *Principles of Mathematics*, 2nd edn. New York: W. W. Norton, 1938; 1st edn. Cambridge: Cambridge University Press, 1903.

Whitehead, Alfred North and Bertrand Russell. *Principia Mathematica*. 3 vols. 2nd edn. Cambridge: Cambridge University Press, 1927; 1st edn. vol. 1 1910, vol. 2 1912, vol. 3 1913.

Wittgenstein, Ludwig. 'Letters to Ludwig von Ficker', tr. B. Gillette, ed. A. Janik. In C. G. Luckhardt (ed.), *Wittgenstein: Sources and Perspectives*. Ithaca: Cornell University Press, 1979, pp. 82–98.

—— *Ludwig Wittgenstein and the Vienna Circle: Conversations recorded by Friedrich Waismann*, ed. B. McGuinness, tr. J. Schulte and B. McGuinness. Oxford: Basil Blackwell, 1979. Translation of *Friedrich Waismann: Wittgenstein und der Wiener Kreis*, ed. B. McGuinness. Oxford: Basil Blackwell, 1967.

—— 'Movements of Thought: Diaries 1930–1932, 1936–1937'. In *Public and Private Occasions*, ed. J. C. Klagge and A. Nordmann. London: Rowman & Littlefield, 2003, pp. 3–255. Translation of *Denkbewegungen: Tagebücher 1930–1932, 1937–1937*, ed. I. Somavilla. Innsbruck: Haymon-Verlag, 1997.

—— *Notebooks: 1914–1916*, ed. G. H. von Wright and G. E. M. Anscombe, tr. G. E. M. Anscombe, 2nd edn. Chicago: University of Chicago Press, 1979; 1st edn. Oxford: Basil Blackwell, 1961.

—— *Philosophical Investigations*, ed. and tr. G. E. M. Anscombe, P. M. S. Hacker, and J. Schulte. Revised 4th edn. Chichester: Wiley-Blackwell, 2009. Translation of *Philosophische Untersuchungen*; earlier editions ed. G. E. M. Anscombe and R. Rhees, tr. G. E. M. Anscombe, 1953, 1958, 2003.

——*Tractatus Logico-Philosophicus*, tr. C. K. Ogden. London: Routledge & Kegan Paul, 1985; 1st edn. London: Routledge & Kegan Paul, 1922. Reprinted with corrections 1933. Translation of *Logische-Philosophische Abhandlung*. First published in *Annalen der Naturphilosophie* 14 (1921): 185–262. Also tr. D. Pears and B. McGuinness. London: Routledge & Kegan Paul, 1981. First published in 1961.

——*Wittgenstein in Cambridge: Letters and Documents, 1911–1951*, ed. B. McGuinness. Oxford: Blackwell, 2008.

PART 2

THE DEVELOPMENT OF ANALYTIC PHILOSOPHY

CHAPTER 15

···

OXFORD REALISM

···

CHARLES TRAVIS AND MARK KALDERON

THIS is a story of roughly a century of Oxford philosophy told from the outside. It is highly selective. We mean to trace the unfolding, across roughly the last century, of one particular line of thought—a sort of anti-idealism; also a *sort* of anti-empiricism. By focusing in this way we will, inevitably, omit, or give short shrift to, more than one more than worthwhile Oxford philosopher.

Our story begins with a turn away from idealism. Frege's turn began in 1882, his definitive case made in 'Der Gedanke' (1918). The main elements of Oxford's realism, or anti-idealism, were probably in Cook Wilson's lectures by 1904, and certainly in his student, H. A. Prichard's 1909 *Kant's Theory of Knowledge*. It would be misleading to suggest that either philosopher held unwaveringly throughout to the realism in question. Indeed, some of Prichard's later work is, in the light of the earlier, somewhat puzzling. But within the first decade of the last century a view had emerged which overlaps Frege's at many key points, and which continued on in the main lines of thought at Oxford for the rest of the century.

Idealism, Frege argued, abolishes truth. A main evil in it is that it places the objects of experience beyond the reach of *judgement*. In doing so, it leaves us *nothing* to judge about. Perception's main role is to make the *world* bear for the perceiver on what he is to think. If what one experiences belongs, in Frege's term, to 'the contents of his consciousness', then, Frege argues, this is something perception cannot do. There is *no* judging of (again Frege's terms) what requires a bearer, and admits of no two bearers. Such is *one* point Prichard retained throughout, directing it late on against those *he* called 'sense datum theorists'. It is a point Cook Wilson directed, around 1904, against Stout. There is a positive side to the coin: *all* there is for us to judge about—all there is which, in being as it is might *be* a way we could judge it to be—is that environment we all cohabit; to be a thought is, intrinsically, to be sharable and communicable. All these are central points in Cook Wilson's, and Prichard's, Oxford realism. So, as they both held (early in the century), perception *must* afford awareness of, and relate us to, objects in our cohabited environment.

There is another point which Prichard, at least, shared with Frege. As Prichard put it,

> There seems to be no way of distinguishing perception and conception as the apprehension of different realities except as the apprehension of the individual and the universal respectively. (1909: 44)

Compare Frege:

> But don't we see that the sun has risen? And don't we also thereby see that this is true? That the sun has risen is no object which emits rays which arrive in our eyes…That the sun has risen is recognised as true on the basis of sensory input. (1918: 61)
>
> But don't we see that this flower has 5 petals? One can say that, but then does not use the word 'see' in the sense of bare experiences of light, but means by it a thought, or judgement connected with this. (1897: 149)

For the sun to have risen is a way for things to be; that it has risen is the way things are according to a certain thought. A way for things to be is a generality, instanced by things being as they are (where the sun has just risen). Recognizing its instancing is recognizing the truth of a certain thought; an exercise of a faculty of thought. By contrast, what instances a way for things to be, what makes for that thought's truth, does not itself have such generality—any more than, on a different level, which Frege calls 'Bedeutung', what falls under a (first-level) concept might be the sort of thing things fall under. What *perception* affords is awareness of the sort of thing that *instances* a way for things to be. Perception's role is thus, for Frege, as for Prichard, to bring the *particular*, or individual, in view—so as, in a favourable case, to make recognizable its instancing (some of) the generalities it does.

For all this agreement, there is difference in focus. Where, for Frege, the main ill of idealism was that it made no room for *truth*, so nor for judgement, for Cook Wilson and Prichard the main ill was that it made no room for knowledge. Ideas (Frege), or appearances (Prichard) are not (Frege) things one can *judge* to be some way; nor, equally, and for the same reason, are they (Prichard) things one can *know* anything about. No way of standing towards *them* would *be* knowledge. It is in this version that the shared view continued to shape Oxford philosophy throughout the last century.

Oxford realism coincided roughly with several other rejections of idealism. Frege's has been mentioned. There was also, at Cambridge, Moore's and Russell's celebrated revolution, begun in 1899 with Moore's 'The Nature of Judgement', and continued with his 'The Refutation of Idealism' of 1903, and with various papers by Russell (see notably 'The Nature of Truth', 1906). Russell's focus was a bit different from either Moore's or Cook Wilson's and Prichard's. As Russell puts it, 'I think that Moore was most concerned with the rejection of idealism, while I was most interested in the rejection of monism' (1959: 42). Specifically, Russell spent a good deal of time campaigning against a 'doctrine of internal relations', held by Bradley and others. But, as Russell also said, both he and Moore were concerned to insist on 'the doctrine that fact is in general independent of experience' (1959: 42).

Russell reports finding it exhilarating to reject idealism:

> I felt it…a great liberation.…In the first exuberance…I became a naïve realist and rejoiced in the thought that grass is really green…I have not been able to retain this pleasing faith in its pristine vigour, but I have never again shut myself up in a subjective prison. (1959: 48)

A subjective prison, though, is just what Russell entered eagerly in his atomism of 1917, one of whose virtues is, he tells us, making objects of judgement out of what are precisely *Vorstellungen* in Frege's sense. Neither Russell, nor Moore, nor (later) Prichard was able to hang onto that realism with which they began. Prichard always opposed what *he* called 'sense data'. But by 1938 he had become convinced that, in the nature of the case, an object of perception was always sole property of its perceiver. The fragility of their realisms has a systematic ground: lack of the tools needed for disarming the argument from illusion. Austin first introduced those, as will emerge below.

In addition to the 'realism' just sketched, Cook Wilson also contributed to Oxford philosophy a new conception of philosophical good faith (certainly new relative to Hume, to Hegel, and to most of the post-Cartesian tradition). It is a conception perhaps better known as later championed by Moore. Cook Wilson expressed it thus:

> The actual fact is that a philosophical distinction is *prima facie* more likely to be wrong than what is called a popular distinction, because it is based on a philosophic theory which may be wrong in its ultimate principles.… There is a tendency to regard [the second] as the less trustworthy because it is popular and not due to reflective thought. The truth is the other way. (1926: 875)

A philosopher's claims must be answerable to something. If they are, say, claims about seeing, there is nothing better to which they may be answerable than the way the verb 'see' is actually used. This is one way of putting the foundations of what came to be known as 'ordinary language philosophy'—some decades before there was any. This, though, is a point about philosophic methodology. It does not yet identify the main focus of twentieth-century Oxonian interest in language.

15.1 LANGUAGE

Though for Cook Wilson and Prichard knowledge came first, the present exposition begins with language. The most significant Oxford views of language did *not* persist throughout the century. Rather, with their roots firmly in Cook Wilson, they flowered from the late 1940s until the early '60s, largely thanks to J. L. Austin, then more or less disappeared from the Oxford scene. But these distinctive views of language were borne mostly of necessity. More specifically, they were (or were seen as) what was necessary in order to keep afloat those very views of knowledge and perception which not only bear the Oxford mark, but, moreover, persisted into this millennium. It is a nice question how it was thought those views on knowledge and perception could stand alone, without Austin's view of language.

Austin's linguistic legacy has two parts. One is a particular conception of the relation of language to thought—thus, too, of truth. The other is a methodological strategy. One concerns the relation between mind and language, the other the strategy of minding one's language. We do not normally attend to the ways our words work; rather to what we hope to work with them. But, the idea is, in philosophy words can all too easily block our view of the phenomena; clarity as to *words'* workings is often the best way to see through them to the objects of our study. Both these views are rooted in Cook Wilson, though in somewhat different ways.

As to the first, there is a line of thought in Cook Wilson's notion of logic which adumbrates, perhaps inspired, a main line in Austin's view of language. Cook Wilson was, roughly, a contemporary of Frege. So it is fair to compare the two. On first reading, Cook Wilson—precisely in his concern for the ordinary use of words—may seem to be missing all Frege's best insights. He probably did miss some. But both agreed in finding a *grammatical* distinction between subject and predicate—a distinction as generated by English or German syntax—of little or no relevance to logic. Frege writes,

> Our logic books still drag in much—for example, subject and predicate—that really does not belong to logic. (1897: 60, and cf. *Begriffsschrift* vii; section 3)

Rejecting that distinction, he gives fundamental importance to another, that between *object* and *concept*. Cook Wilson writes,

> The above analysis [of a statement, or proposition] would make the distinction of subject and predicate, one not of words but of what is meant by the verbal expression. We may call this the strict logical analysis, and the distinction of the words of the sentence into 'subject words' and 'predicative words' may be called the grammatical analysis. (1926: 124)

Thus, for example, in 'That building is the Bodleian', 'that building' is the grammatical subject; in 'Glass is elastic', 'glass' is the grammatical subject. But in the first either 'that building' or 'the Bodleian' may identify the *logical* subject, depending on the use being made of that sentence on an occasion. In the second, either 'glass' or 'elastic' may identify the logical subject on a use. *Mutatis mutandis* for logical predicates. An instance of the *sentence* 'Glass is elastic', while meaning just what it does, having precisely the syntax and semantics it does, so while having the same grammatical subject and predicate, might have either of two pairs of strict (or true) logical subject and predicate. So the well-formed part, 'glass', in the sentence, 'Glass is elastic', might, on two different uses of that sentence to state something, make either of two different contributions to the stating of what is thus stated. Similarly for other sentences and their grammatical subjects and predicates.

Two different uses of the sentence 'Glass is elastic', each to say something to be so, may thus form a minimal contrasting pair: in the one member of the pair, but not the other, 'glass' is the logical subject in what is said; there is a corresponding difference in logical predicates. What each says differs in no way not entailed by these differences. Accordingly, Cook Wilson tells us, each use, or what is said on it, requires a different 'logical analysis' (see 1926: 125). The first use thus says something which admits of the first but not of the second analysis, and *mutatis mutandis* for the second. Thus, each differs in what is thus said. Perhaps there is something to be said which admits of either analysis, just as for Frege a given thought admits of many different analyses. But here each member of the pair requires an analysis which what the other says does not admit of. So neither member is a thought analysable in either of these two ways. Whether 'glass' figures as a logical subject contributes to determining what it is that is thus said.

Does each member of the pair thus express a different thought in Frege's sense? That depends on whether the different analysis each requires—a 'logical' analysis in Cook Wilson's sense of this term—is an analysis of the thought expressed. For Frege, to bear on the thought expressed is to bear on how some question of truth would be decided. So the minimal difference between each member of the pair would make for a different thought expressed in each if, but only if, whether 'glass' was the logical subject mattered to when, or on what condition, the relevant whole would be true. It is not evident that whether something is a logical subject does so matter. For the moment we leave this question open.

To a Fregean, two or three things may seem to have gone wrong already. One of these lies in something Cook Wilson stresses about the just-mentioned 'logical' distinction:

> Subject and predicate mean not the idea or conception of an object, but the object which is said to be an object of the idea or conception. But, while the things called subject and predicate are objects without anything that belongs to our apprehension of them or our mode of conceiving them, the distinction of them as subject and predicate is entirely founded on our subjective apprehension of them, or our opinion about them, and on nothing in their own nature as apart from the fact that they are apprehended or conceived. It may be said that the distinction is not in them, but in their relation to our knowledge or opinion of them, and so not a relation between what they are in themselves apart from their being sometimes apprehended. (1926: 139)

Logical subject and *logical predicate* may thus seem mere psychological notions, which, for Frege, could have no bearing on logic. Whereas Frege's distinction between *concept* and *object* precisely *is* a distinction between the sorts of things we designate in expressing the thoughts we do.

Cook Wilson's logical subjects and predicates need be no more psychological than Frege's thoughts. A thought, for Frege, identifies a commitment there is for one to make in his stance towards the world; one by which a thinker exposes himself to some definite risk of error (as Frege puts it). Stances, commitments taken, are part of a thinker's psychology. But what stances there are to take—how it is possible to stand towards things—need not be, and for Frege is not, a psychological matter. Nor is the way those stances, as such, relate, e.g., whether by relations which preserve truth. For Cook Wilson, two statements, otherwise as alike as possible, but differing in whether such-and-such is their logical subject, accordingly differ in what question(s) they are to be understood to answer; and, accordingly, in to what one is committed in making them. What questions there *are* thus to answer, and how the answers to one relate to those to another, need be no more a psychological matter than those parallel issues, above, about thoughts. Of course, that there *are* different questions for statements with different logical subjects to answer is a substantial thesis which needs to be made out. Such is the really important issue.

In dismissing the subject-predicate distinction, as in many other contexts, Frege insists,

> Thus we will never forget that two different sentences can express the same thought; that as to the content of a sentence, what concerns us is only what can be true or false. (1897: 60)

One sentence, perhaps, can express many thoughts (each on some occasion). But what concerns Frege here is that many sentences can express *one* thought. As he often stresses, the same thought can be articulated, now this way, now that, so that now this, now that, appears as predicative in it. The same thought can be structured in many different ways out of many different sets of concepts and objects. Intuitively, we can see how we would, in some sense, understand 'That building is the Bodleian' differently depending on whether it was an answer to the question what that building is, or an answer to the question which building is the Bodleian. But what we have not seen—and what Cook Wilson has done little towards showing—is that *that* difference in understanding makes for different thoughts expressed—or, again, exploiting Frege's above framework, that such a difference could make any difference to when the thought thus expressed would be true.

Frege's object/concept distinction falls on one side of another distinction, equally fundamental for him, between sense and 'Bedeutung'. One might think of this *Bedeutung*, on Cook Wilson's lines, as what we speak of, on some understanding of *speaking of*. But it is not the sort of object of discussion that Cook Wilson has in mind. Rather, it is, so to speak, a distillate from things at the level of sense, notably thoughts, of what matters for the sorts of calculations, or relations, of concern to logic, most notably truth-preservation. Frege begins a discussion of his main essay on the sense–reference distinction by remarking,

> The fundamental logical relation is that of an object falling under a concept; all relations between concepts reduce to this. (1892–5: 128)

He goes on to observe that, waiving some niceties, there is considerable justice in the view of extensionalist logicians. Having first explained how attempts to ascribe features to concepts generally misfire, ending up speaking of *objects* where the intention was to speak of concepts, he goes on to remark:

If we keep all this in mind, we are indeed in a position to say, 'What two concept-words denote is the same just in case the associated extensions of the concepts coincide.' And with this, I think, an important concession is made to the extensionalist logicians. (1892–5: 31)

If logic is concerned with, as Frege puts it, the laws of being true (*Wahrsein*), then logic is concerned with thoughts, since, for Frege, thoughts just *are* that which raise questions of truth (see 1918: 59–60). But the business of logic reduces, for most purposes, at least, to operations on the level of *Bedeutung*. The first sentence here is all that is needed, and really all that Cook Wilson demands, to honour his insistence that logic is, in some sense, about thought. The second *seems* entirely consistent with his views on the role of relations between things as opposed to our manners, on occasion, of apprehending them.

So though, for several reasons, Frege is not prepared to say just what a concept is (here see his 1904), one can think of what is at the level of *Bedeutung* as including such things as mappings from some range of things to others; as the taking on of such-and-such range of values for such-and-such range of arguments. What corresponds to objects and concepts at the level of sense is, to use one of Frege's terms for this, modes of presentation of them: ways of thinking of some object, or some concept, in thinking things to be some given way. One may, e.g., speak of fauns as gambollers. To do so is to make truth turn, first, on how fauns are—so which concepts assign them the value true—and what gambols—so what *this* concept assigns the value true. Such sets the stage for logic's calculations. Speaking of being a gamboller is *one* way, of many, of bringing *that* concept into play; one way of presenting it.

What there is not at the level of sense, on Frege's conception of things, is anything corresponding to logical subjects and predicates, or more pertinently, since something would *be* a logical subject, or predicate, within some given proposition, or something of that form, there is, for Frege, nothing at the level of sense which *has* logical subjects and predicates. Certainly thoughts do not. Thoughts, for Frege, articulate into elements only relative to an analysis. If we were to decompose a thought so that its elements were being about the Bodleian, and being about being in the Broad, what we would thus have would be *one* way of presenting, or regarding, *that thought*. We would have a mode of presentation of a mode of presentation of whatever, at the level of *Bedeutung*, thoughts present. If sense just is what fixes reference, there is no room at either level for a distinction between subject and predicate.

As noted, there is *something* in Cook Wilson corresponding to Frege's level of *Bedeutung*. Its denizens are the things we talk *about*, on an ordinary understanding on which this includes, for example, the Bodleian, glass, being in the Broad, and being elastic, and by 'real relations' between them. So it is not quite inhabited by the same things which belong to Frege's *Bedeutung*. But it might be seen as inhabited by Cook Wilson's candidates for the things which really matter to the concerns of logic—notably truth-preservation. For he insists that when we say, 'That building is the Bodleian', no matter what the grammatical, or even logical, subject may be, what we *speak of* is just that building being the Bodleian. Which, one might well think—and Cook Wilson seems sometimes to think—leaves nothing for truth to turn on but whether that build-ing *is* the Bodleian. But then, why is there *any* interest in the notions of (strict) logical subject and predicate, at least if one's concern is with that to which laws of logic apply? How can whether such-and-such is the logical subject of one's statement matter to when what one stated would be true?

Here is one approach to answering these questions. Frege restricts sense (*Sinn*) in his sense to what bears on *truth*, which he takes to exclude much in the understandings our words bear. It is under this restriction that no features such as logical subject or predicate seem to distinguish any given sense from any other. If such is *mere* appearance, it is most straightforwardly dispelled by pairs of statements (or thoughts) which differ in when each would be true, in a way that difference in logical subject would precisely mark. Such would place Cook Wilson's distinction within Frege's conception of sense. Such an idea seems to have inspired Austin. His essay, 'How To Talk (Some Simple Ways)' (1952) is, in effect, a more refined elaboration of Cook Wilson's idea; its object (or one of them) is to show that features of this kind do bear on truth.

Austin's distinctions carve the field more finely that do logical subject and predicate. But the drift is the same. Suppose the problem is to come up with samples to show what *crimson* is. Then sample A may be ill-suited for the job. But suppose, rather, that the problem is to say what colour A is. Then, perhaps, 'crimson' is as well suited for the job as anything. Now the problem is to show that, where someone says A to be crimson, the purpose for which this is to be taken to be done—the job so speaking of A is meant to do on that occasion—is something that *can* matter to whether what is thus said is true. Austin works towards making this plausible. To what extent he succeeds is another question we leave open. For it turns out not to matter all that much.

In the end, its answer does not matter much. If Austin began from the above ques-tion, his investigation led him to a more general point about what is relevant to ques-tions of truth. It is that what words mean in their language, so far as that goes, does not fully determine when what one says in saying what *they* say would be true. It does not fix for *them* a truth-condition. Rather, what is said to be so in using words as meaning what they do is, in general, compatible with saying any of indefinitely many things to be so, each differing from the others in when it would *be* so. Accordingly, what one says of something in calling it a dahlia, or hexagonal, is liable to depend on whether, *in those circumstances*, such-and-such would be called *being a dahlia (hexagonal)*. Austin puts the point thus:

> [T]he question of truth and falsehood does not turn only on what a sentence *is*, nor yet on what it *means*, but on, speaking very broadly, the circumstances in which it is uttered. Sentences are not *as such* either true or false. (1962: 110–11)

Whether one speaks truth in saying that cloth to be crimson, or that fossil a dahlia, depends on how truth is to be decided on *that* occasion. One may, on one occasion, speak truly, and on another falsely, in saying the very same thing, in the very same con-dition, to be the very same way (e.g., crimson). What being crimson, or a dahlia, might be admits of understandings. One speaks truly, or falsely, in calling something a dahlia only where enough is to be understood as to what would *then* so count. On different occasions for speaking of something as a dahlia, or as crimson, different ranges of cases would count as something so being. What being a dahlia is as such does not by itself pick out any one such range. Such is the form into which, in Austin's hands, Cook Wilson's seminal idea had sprouted by mid-century.

Not that the idea was even then ubiquitous in Oxford. The most significant dissenter in Austin's lifetime was H. P. Grice. His counter-view first appeared in Grice (1961), then, more fully, in his 1967 William James lectures. The focus is on one corollary of Austin's view. Suppose that, as per that view, words (e.g., 'Fauns gambol') *underdetermine* what would be said in using them as meaning what they do. Circumstances of a speaking must then do *work* if something true *or false* is to be said then in using them. In those circumstances, there must be something which *would* be understood by *gambolling*; enough for gambolling so understood to be something fauns do, or not, full stop. Circumstances are not obliged *per se* to do this work. Which means that one *might* say 'Fauns gambol', assertively, while neither saying something true nor saying something false. Or if the ways of fauns should rule *that* out, such might happen for some speaking of, say, 'Sid tried to lift his pen', or 'Pia did it voluntarily.' Grice focuses on this corollary of Austin's point.

Grice's case against Austin centres on the truism that in *saying* given things one may also *suggest*, or imply, others. If I say, 'Pia became pregnant and married', I (often, not inevitably) at least suggest that pregnancy preceded marriage. It is not yet shown, Grice insists, that this is part of what was *said*. Grice introduces the technical term 'implicate' for all those ways in which, in stating, things may be communicated which were not stated.

The core idea to be used against Austin is to be: where Austin sees the possibility of *saying* a variety of things in given (unambiguous) words (while meaning what they do), Grice will argue that the variety here is only in what is implicated; that just *one* thing, either true or false, was said in all Austin's envisaged cases. Or rather, this is what Grice needs to argue. He tends, instead, to focus on the corollary, arguing only that if, in certain circumstances, one would not say, e.g., 'Sid tried to lift his pen', this may be, not because what one thus said would not be true, but rather because one would implicate something unwanted. It is not clear that Grice really grasped Austin's point. If not, this may be because of an unfortunate choice of words by Austin. We will come to that shortly. In any case, the idea of implicature is arguably ill-suited for impeaching Austin's view. The idea to be countered is: a sentence, say, 'That painting is crimson', may be used of a given painting, in a given condition, to say different things, some true, some false, where there is no limit, in principle, to the new things new occasions may make available thus to say. The counter would be: these different things are merely implicated. But then, what is implicated on any such occasion is, on some possible understanding of being crimson, that the painting is crimson. Now what, in addition to *that*, is to be the thing which is *said* throughout all those cases? Surely something to the effect that the painting is crimson. Each use of those words *implicates* that the painting is crimson, as being crimson would *then* be understood. In addition, each use *says* the painting to be crimson on some understanding of being crimson which is the *same* throughout all these uses. What understanding is *that*?

Austin's possibly unfortunate phrasing, of which Grice makes much, appears in his rendering of Cook Wilson's second methodological point:

> Our common stock of words embodies all the distinctions men have found worth drawing, and the connexions they have found worth making, in the lifetimes of many generations: these surely are likely to be more numerous, more sound, since they have stood up to the long test of the survival of the fittest, and more subtle, at least in all ordinary and reasonably practical matters, than any that you or I are likely to think up in our armchairs of an afternoon...
>
> ...When we examine what we should say when, what words we should use in what situations, we are looking again not *merely* at words...but also at the realities we use the words to talk about: we are using a sharpened awareness of words to sharpen our perception of, though not as the final arbiter of, the phenomena. (1956–7/1979: 182)

A Cook Wilsonian idea applied. Do we ever see tomatoes? When would it be *seeing* that this question is about? When would it be what *we* are prepared to recognize as seeing that was spoken of? Are tomatoes the kind of thing one might *so* relate to? Well, how *is* the verb 'see' used? Just what might make a relation one could *not* bear to a tomato recognizable as what we thus speak of? Attention to the details of this might, the idea is, spare us much fruitless philosophy. Again, if one is inclined to say that causation is mere appearance, he might ask (on the right occasion) whether, then, no one (really) spilled his beer.

But Austin's vocabulary here, specifically, 'what we should say when', can be misread. Supposing that there are things words are *for* saying, it would be natural to read this as: 'If you (one) were to use *these* words of *this*, or in *these* circumstances, what would you say?' What one thus asks after is how words in fact work. Austin clearly hears things this way. Grice insists on a different reading. On it, 'what we would say' merely reports our customs, mores, manners: 'One wouldn't say, "What's the vigorish?" when the neighbour asks to borrow a cup of milk', 'One shouldn't say, "That's just autobiography" to your small niece when she says she wants another biscuit'. But asking what one would say when *can* be a way of asking what the words one uses in fact apply to, or describe *truly*—what they *are* for in their language. If one is moved primarily by Austin's view of language and thought—that it is not, e.g., English words, but rather their use on an occasion, which determines how things are thus represented to be—one will so read it.

15.2 KNOWLEDGE

Germs of Austin's view of language are found in Cook Wilson. So is pressing need for it. At Oxford the view did not long survive Austin himself. It was lost in what is known as 'the Davidsonic boom', if not sooner. Whether need for it survived is another matter. One Cook Wilsonian idea which lasted out the century at Oxford concerns knowledge (most centrally). It appears later in the guise of *disjunctivism* (a term derived from J. M. Hinton;

see section 15.3), and its various applications. Austin saw his view of language as essential to the viability of Cook Wilson's *insight* here. Later Oxonians seem to disagree. This section will set out the insight and raise the question which Oxonian was right on this.

The idea about knowledge, simply stated, is: knowing is no less than having proof. *Having* proof here is, *inter alia*, appreciating what one has as the proof it is. For it to be *proof* is, *inter alia*, for it to exclude absolutely P not being so—as the pig before you excludes any possibility that there is none (it remaining only to recognize its doing so). Having proof need not be having *a* proof. Cook Wilson expresses this idea as follows:

> In knowing, we can have nothing to do with the so-called 'greater strength' of the evidence on which the opinion is grounded; simply because we know that this 'greater strength' of evidence of A's being B is compatible with A's not being B after all.... Belief is not knowledge and the man who knows does not believe at all what he knows; he knows it. (1926: 100)

Prichard insists that knowledge is 'certainty'. Here certainty that P is not a feeling, but a standing conferred by one's access to the world: there being no room for what one is aware of to fall short of it being so that P. (See 1950: 103–4.) For Prichard and Cook Wilson, to know is to have *proof* in the present sense. For Prichard, being *certain* as to P excludes *intelligible* doubt whether P.

Let us apply this view to the question whether knowledge might rest on evidence. One might think so. Has Sid been drinking? That loopy expression is some evidence for this, his slurred speech a bit more. Now he comes close, and we smell his breath. Now we *know*. What has happened? One story might be: Sid's expression is a bit of evidence, his slurred speech a bit more. With his breath the evidence mounts so high that we *know*. Good enough evidence amounts to knowledge. Cook Wilson and Prichard reject this story. On their view, if all we have is evidence, even very strong evidence (but still, evaluable as to strength), its presence leaves open the possibility that Sid has not been drinking. The question, 'But *has* he?' makes sense. Where one knows that Sid has been drinking, *not* for all one knows not. So having *evidence* does not amount to knowing. This is not to deny that one can come to know that Sid has been drinking by smelling his breath. But where one does this, one is aware of, as Prichard puts it, some fact of nature: Sid could have breath like that only if he had been drinking. In which case, his breath smelling as it does is not evidence, but proof.

Cook Wilson refers to knowing as a 'frame of mind'. One *could* say 'mental state'. But, as both stress, to see whether you know that P, attend, not to what sort of state you are in, but rather to the question whether P. What you need to ask is whether *that* question is settled, beyond *any* doubt, by what you are aware of. *Has* Sid been drinking? *Is* there a largest prime? Is there *proof*? Sid's breath *tells* me he has been drinking only if I see how *that* breath can only so mean. Looking elsewhere to see whether I know that P would be self-defeating. (See Prichard 1950: 92–3.) If that one knows showed itself only in some other mark distinguishing such frames of mind, then to see that I know I would need to see that my frame of mind had that mark, thus that it had the mark of knowing that it had that mark. A malign regress would have begun. If knowing *is* a mental state, one sees whether he is in it *in re* P only by directing attention to its object, P. This idea, in more general form, has enjoyed a long life at Oxford. (See, e.g., Evans 1982: 223–9.)

For Cook Wilson and Prichard, knowledge is not a variety of belief. In Prichard's words,

> Knowing is not something which differs from being convinced by a difference of degree...as being more convinced differs from being less convinced...Knowing and believing differ in kind as do desiring and feeling, or as do a red colour and a blue colour....To know is not to have a belief of a special kind, differing from beliefs of other kinds; and no improvement in a belief and no increase in the feeling of conviction which it implies will convert it into knowledge....It is not that there is a general kind of activity, for which the name would have to be thinking, which admits of two kinds, the better of which is knowing and the worse believing. (1932/1950: 87–8)

Part of the point is that knowledge is not *analysable* in terms of belief (or of anything). It is not believing (or any other non-factive stance) with such-and-such further features added. Such is now a widely held view, at Oxford, and beyond. But Cook Wilson also holds that when you know that P, you do *not* believe it. This is, to say the least, less widely held. It may *seem* to be controverted by obvious facts—e.g., if Sid stands as he does towards Pia being the new dean, then it can be (depending on how he thus stands) that I, knowing that she is, may say, truly, 'Sid knows that Pia is dean', while you, doubting that she is, may say, also truly, 'Well, Sid *thinks* that Pia is dean'. Each of us, it seems, states a truth about Sid's condition; truths which hold simultaneously, and, it seems, may hold of the same frame of mind, or mental state. Austin's view of language makes this less convincing. Cook Wilson's thesis may then be seen as a not-implausible disjunctivism, denying a certain sort of common factor in standing as one might towards a thought both in knowing, and in merely judging it. (See Hinton 1967.) However, this remains here only a suggestion.

Cook Wilson and Prichard stress a further feature of their view. Given their conception of a frame of mind, it seems to them simply to follow from the above conception of knowledge. Cook Wilson sets up the inference by considering the possibility that there are two frames of mind—one knowing, the other merely being under the impression of knowing—which were such that if you were in the one, you might be unable to tell that you were in it rather than the other, so that, as he puts it,

> the two states of mind in which the man conducts his arguments, the correct and the erroneous one, are quite indistinguishable to the man himself. But if this is so, as the man does not know in the erroneous state of mind, neither can he know in the other state. (1926: 107)

So a state of knowing cannot be indistinguishable to someone in it from an 'erroneous' state—one of merely seeming to have proof; nor vice versa. Prichard puts the conclusion this way:

We must recognize that whenever we know something we either do, or at least can, by reflecting, directly know that we are knowing it, and that whenever we believe something, we similarly either do or can directly know that we are believing it and not knowing it. (1950: 86)

We will refer to this point as *the accretion*.

Not that one can *always* tell his frame of mind just by reflection. Nor does Cook Wilson, or Prichard, hold some general form of semantic internalism. The point turns specifically on what *knowledge* is. Suppose that I cannot see, just by reflection, that I *could not* be mistaken as to whether P. Then I cannot, in fact, have proof. For whatever *my* grounds are for taking it that P, these are *not* incompatible, or I cannot see them to be, with P failing to obtain. So, so far as I can see, perhaps not P. Such is not knowledge. Having proof is, necessarily, what one can see oneself to do.

At which point, the conception begins to crumble. Suppose you now, in fact, see a pig before you. A genetically engineered ovine ringer pig, or a fleshapoid mechanical one, are at least conceivable. So are tricks with mirrors and lasers. Things might then be just as they are now, for all *you* could see. You cannot tell *by mere reflection* that no such thing is so. If it were you would not know there was a pig before you, since there would be none. So you do not meet Cook Wilson's standards for knowing there is a pig before you. So, it seems, no one ever would. Again, you may have, clearly in mind, what is in fact a perfectly good proof of the Pythagorean theorem. You may in fact appreciate how the proof proves. But one does, sometimes, suffer illusions of proof. Can reflection alone rule out *all* possibility of your now being in such a position? So, it seems, the conception plus accretion make knowledge collapse, or at least contract beyond plausibility.

Preserving the conception thus means treating the accretion. Enter Austin. For Austin's way with the accretion, we start from the question whether knowledge could be based on evidence. On this he says,

The situation in which I would properly be said to have *evidence* for the statement that some animal is a pig is that, for example, in which the beast itself is not actually on view, but I can see plenty of pig-like marks on the ground outside its retreat. If I find a few buckets of pig-food, that's a bit more evidence, and the noises and the smell may provide better evidence still. But if the animal then emerges and stands there plainly in view, there is no longer a question of collecting evidence; its coming into view doesn't provide me with more *evidence* that it's a pig, I can now just *see* that it is, the question is settled. (1962: 115)

Evidence contrasts with proof. Unlike proof, it is liable to be weaker or stronger, better or worse—as with the noises and smell in Austin's case. For it to be so liable is for evidence that P to be compatible with P not being so. So having evidence cannot be knowing on Cook Wilson's conception (accretion or not). Austin suggests that seeing a pig can give one *proof*, so knowledge, that a pig is about; and thus *not* mere evidence. Suppose that Sid, approaching Pia's farm, sees a pig in the pen. That pig's presence in the pen is as incompatible with it failing to be so that there is a pig there as a proof that there is no largest prime is incompatible with there being one. Accordingly, Austin insists, seeing the pig *can* (sometimes) provide *proof* in the strongest sense. By contrast, in the case Austin imagines, the sounds and smells are compatible with no pig about. They are thus merely evidence.

But let us adjust cases. Pia, a country girl, arrives on Sid's farm, sniffs, and says, 'So he keeps pigs.' *Must* what she sniffs provide her something less than knowledge? Sid, on Pia's farm, sees a pig in the pen. *Must* this supply him knowledge? We can distinguish between, on the one hand, things smelling as they do, and, on the other, Pia's then smell-ing what she does; on the one hand, the pig's being in the pen, and, on the other, Sid's seeing the pig in the pen (or, for a closer parallel, the pen's being as it is, and Sid's seeing what he does of this). Things smelling as they do is compatible with Sid keeping no pigs: other things *could* have made the smell. Whether Pia's smelling what she did is compat-ible with no pigs about is another matter. That pig's presence in the pen leaves no room for there being none. Whether Sid's seeing it gives *him* proof is another matter. Austin's idea is that answers to things like the second member of each pair are liable to depend on further factors. This is what allows him both to reject the idea of knowledge on evidence and to insist that seeing the pig *may* furnish one proof.

Austin endorses a further feature of Cook Wilson's view. He writes,

> Saying 'I know'...is *not* saying, 'I have performed a specially striking feat of cognition, superior, in the same scale as believing and being sure, even to being merely quite sure': for there *is* nothing in that scale superior to being quite sure. (1946/1979: 99)

What, then, *is* the difference between knowing and merely being sure? For Cook Wilson and Prichard, these are different 'frames of mind', distinguishable on 'reflection'. Austin puts things differently:

> When I say 'I promise', a new plunge is taken: I have not merely announced my intention, but, by using this formula...I have bound myself to others...Similarly, saying 'I know' is taking a new plunge.... When I say 'I know', I *give others my word*; I *give others my authority for saying* that 'S is P'.
>
> When I have said only that I am sure...I am not liable to be rounded on in the same way as when I have said 'I know'. I am sure *for my part*, you can take it or leave it...that's your responsibility. But I don't know 'for my part', and when I say 'I know' I don't mean you can take it or leave it (though of course you *can* take it or leave it). (1946/1979: 99–100)

This idea has attracted much criticism. There are two main complaints. First, the verb 'know' has other uses in the first person than that Austin has in mind—e.g., 'It's hard to park near the beach in August'; 'I know, I know.' Second, even if 'I know' often marks a special force attaching to 'I know that P', to describe that force is not yet to tell us what knowledge is, or how to understand 'know' in all its occurrences.

How telling are such objections? Austin's idea is that saying 'I know that P' is offering oneself as authoritative as to whether P; offering relief from the burden of settling this oneself, on grounds that the work needed has already been done. Suppose there is an identifiable use for 'I know' of which this is so. Then that it is so may be *part* of what knowledge is. Suppose this much. Now suppose that Vic says Pia to know that a finch is on the branch. What Vic said may then be to be understood in terms of that use just mentioned: for Pia to be as thus said is for her to be in a position to invoke that use in making *good* offers of the sort just sketched; that is, to *be* authoritative. Austin's insight can thus offer entry into a more general understanding of the workings of 'know', and thereby of knowledge.

One might still ask what the *point* is of putting things this way. A start of an answer: authority is a *status* one might enjoy or fail to, gain or lose—notoriously, not just by increase or decay in one's credentials, but by change in the circumstances in which one is to enjoy it. 'Sid was the fastest draw in town until The Kid arrived.' Sid's trigger finger remained unchanged. Now we are close to Austin's main idea:

> The question of truth and falsehood does not turn only on what a sentence *is*, nor yet on what it *means*, but on...the circumstances in which it is uttered. Sentences are not *as such* either true or false. But it is really equally clear...that for much the same reasons there could be no question of picking out from one's bunch of sentences those that are evidence for others, those that are 'testable', or those that are 'incorrigible'. (1962: 110–11)

So whether A is (or counts as) evidence for B, as opposed to *no* evidence, or as opposed to proof, depends not just on what A and B are, but on the circumstances of so saying (or so counting things). Correspondingly for proof. Which allows us to say: *Pia's then* smelling what she did may rule out any possibility of absence of pigs, depending on what counts as compatible with that very historic event having taken place. And Sid's seeing what, in fact, was a pig in the pen *may* fail to give him proof, depending on whether he counts as then able to recognize what he sees for what it thus is, so, *inter alia*, on what his ability to tell pigs at sight would then need to be. Whether N has proof or merely evidence thus depends on the circumstances in which he is to be so credited. With that, Cook Wilson's conception of knowledge lines up, near enough, with what, when it comes to cases, we *recognize* knowledge to be. The question raised by subsequent Oxford philosophy is whether there is any alternative way of accomplishing this.

What thus emerges is an application of Austin's view of language to the special case of epistemic notions—as portrayed here, the case of assigning epistemic status. The general view applies equally, e.g., to talk of things being blue. There are, on the view, various things to be said in calling the sky blue, some true, some false. *What* one would say in so speaking varies with the circumstances of his doing so. Whether the sky is blue or not independent of any such circumstances—whether it is *really* blue—is thus an ill-formed question. The idea is: *mutatis mutandis* for knowledge.

Pia watches the pig emerge from its shelter and approach her. In *her* circumstances, does she know that a pig approaches? There are many occasions on which to say her to, or not to, each one for reckoning her an authority as to whether this is so or not. These may differ in what, on them, would merit such recognition. Pia might, thus, qualify as an authority on some, not on others. First, then, there are different things to be said, on different such occasions, in saying Pia to know that a pig approaches. Second, some such things to be said might be true, while others are false. There may be truths and falsehoods thus to be expressed. Third, there is *nothing* either true or false to be said in saying Pia to know this *other than* what there is to be said on some such occasion. So there is nothing true, or false, to be said which *is* so said throughout. Such is knowledge on Austin's view.

What, then, of evidence? Is Sid's breath proof, or mere evidence, that he has been drinking? The question, as thus asked, might well leave us at a loss. On Austin's view, so asked (as such questions are asked in philosophy) it need have no answer. On some occasions, whether Sid has been drinking counts as more than can be settled by smelling his breath. His breath is, for those purposes, merely evidence. (One's smelling what he *thus* does, perhaps, does not settle whether Sid swallowed.) In others it might. The breath then counts as proof. The breath remains the same. What varies is what proof would be. What it varies across is occasions for counting that breath as evidence rather than proof, or vice versa.

Pia stares at the approaching pig. Does she know that a pig approaches? Nothing in *her* circumstances answers that question. So far there is no determinate enterprise of settling whether a pig approaches which she has thus accomplished (or is in a position to) or not. There may now be occasions for counting her as knowing this, or as not—as authoritative, or not, on that subject. On some of these she may so count, on others not. Changing example, suppose the pig is a *bísaro*—a certain breed—and the question is whether Pia knows this. If she can tell a *bísaro* by sight, then, perhaps, yes. But *can* she tell a *bísaro* at sight? For a start, from what else need she be able to distinguish a *bísaro* to count as having this ability? Such is not the sort of thing fixed independent of some occasion for the question. This summarizes Austin's core idea.

What now of the accretion? By it, one who knows that P must, on reflection, be able to answer a certain question. The question is, in effect, whether he has *proof* that P, or rather whether, so far as he can see, it is possible for P to be false—for him to be in error. As Pia, wandering by the pen, notes the pig therein, whether she knows that there is a pig in the pen, the idea is, turns on whether, on reflection, she could find the answer to *the* question whether she has proof of this. But if Austin's idea is right, there *is* no such question. There are questions to raise on particular occasions for raising one, and that is all. That Pia is strolling by the pen does not automatically make for any such occasion, or none providing a question that has answers. Just *seeing* a pig does not fix a determinate question as to whether one has proof of this. Whatever it does, it leaves countless further occasions on which to ask whether Pia *knew* there was a pig—thus, on the conception in common to Austin and Cook Wilson, whether she had proof. Whatever the answer to some supposed question raised just by her strolling by, it would not settle these further ones, each of which would be to be settled in its own distinct way, and, thus, if some in the affirmative, others not. On Austin's view, the accretion is simply senseless.

On the other hand, dropping the 'on reflection', when Pia sniffs the air in the fore-court of Sid's farm and says to herself, 'So. He keeps pigs', if the question is whether she can see what she smells to rule out things being otherwise, and if it is a determinate one, there is no general obstacle to the answer being 'Yes'. Being able to appreciate the proof at one's disposal *can* consist, e.g., in seeing the pig and being able to tell what one is seeing.

At Oxford Austin's view of language did not long outlive his death. Cook Wilson's conception of knowledge (usually minus accretion) survived, most notably in two landmark essays by John McDowell (1982, 1995). McDowell's main concern there is to resist a 'hybrid' view of knowledge, that is, the idea that this is a construct out of some non-factive attitude of a subject towards the world (e.g., belief) and some further condition of the world, not guaranteed by the first factor, where the subject need take no attitude towards that condition obtaining. His view of what knowledge is lines up, accordingly, with Cook Wilson.

With Austin, McDowell sees that such a view can stick only if the argument from illusion can be resisted. But he does not accept Austin's view of language. He sees that the argument might break down with the right stress on particular cases—Pia's then seeing the pig approaching (an historical event), rather than Pia seeing the pig approaching (something that might happen). One can then insist that there are two kinds of histori-cal event. There are those where Pia, seeing the pig approaching, thereby sees that the (a) pig approaches. She then knows this on grounds of what she sees. (A good case.) And there are those where, e.g., it seems to Pia just as though a pig approached, but none does. She is merely under the illusion of having seen that this is so. (A bad case.) That there are bad cases does not mean, on this idea, that there are not, or even not recogniz-ably, good ones. The power of ringers is thus broken.

Occasions for McDowell are thus ones on which a candidate knower finds himself—e.g., facing a pig; whereas for Austin they are ones for ascribing epistemic statuses. Which leads McDowell to write,

> Whether we like it or not, we have to rely on favours from the world...that on occa-sion it actually is the way it appears to be. But that the world does someone the nec-essary favour, on a given occasion, of being the way it appears to be is not extra to the person's standing in the space of reasons....once she has achieved such a stand-ing, she needs no extra help from the world to count as knowing. (1995: 406)

One may be under the illusion of being in a good case. If not, that is a favour from the world. For all of which, viewing someone in a good case, we may say of him, truly, that he knows.

How, then, is the distinction between good cases and bad ones to be drawn? There is the case where no pig approaches, but Pia suffers an illusion. That, of course, is a bad case. But, for familiar reasons, and others, it cannot be that every case in which a pig does approach is, by contrast, a good one. As McDowell himself puts it, 'the uncon-nected obtaining of' (e.g., that a pig approaches) cannot 'have any intelligible bear-ing on an epistemic position' (1995: 403). If a pig does approach, this makes available something for Pia to appreciate as to how things stand (and how she does). But to see *that* a pig approaches (or to know this on grounds of what she sees) she must take up what is thus on offer. Which requires that she have, and exercise, a certain capacity: one to tell, in a situation such as hers, *whether* a pig approaches. So drawing the right distinction between good and bad cases means saying when she has such a capacity.

Now Austinian considerations re-enter. Most of us *often* count as able to tell a pig when we see one. But suppose we are in a region rife with tapirs, and suppose that (though these are distinguishable from pigs by sight) one of us might easily mistake a tapir for a pig. In such circumstances, we might not count (so easily) as being able to tell a pig when we see one. On what, then, does our having or lacking the capacity turn? Does it turn on whether there *are* tapirs about (or some other sort of obstacle to our identifying correctly)? Or is it rather that whether we would *count* as having such a capacity turns on whether *it is to be supposed* that there very well might be tapirs about (or is some other obstacle)—supposed, that is, on some occasion for counting us as with, or without, capacity? For Austin, it is this last. For McDowell, it must be the first, on pain of accepting Austin's core idea about language. Can one make a go of this? We leave this topic here.

15.3 PERCEPTION

A concern for realism motivates a fundamental strand of Oxford reflection on perception. Begin with the realist conception of knowledge. The question then will be: What must perception be if it can, on occasion, afford us with *proof* concerning a subject matter independent of the mind? The resulting conception of perception is not unlike the conception of perception shared by the Cambridge realist. Roughly speaking, perception is conceived to be a fundamental and irreducible sensory mode of awareness of mind-independent objects, a non-propositional mode of awareness that enables those with the appropriate recognitional capacities to have propositional knowledge concerning that subject matter.

The difference between Oxford and Cambridge realism concerns the extent of this fundamental sensory mode of awareness. Whereas Oxford realists maintained that perception affords us this sensory mode of awareness, Cambridge realists maintained that this mode of awareness has a broader domain. Let sense experience be the genus of which perception is a species. Cambridge realists maintained that *all* sense experience, and not just perception, involves this non-propositional mode of awareness. Cambridge realists are thus committed to a kind of *experiential monism* (in Snowdon's 2008 terminology). Specifically, all sense experience involves, as part of its nature, a non-propositional mode of awareness. Even subject to illusion or hallucination, there is something of which one is aware. And with that, they were an application of the argument from illusion, or hallucination, or conflicting appearances away from immaterial sense-data and a representative realism that tended, over time, to devolve into a form of phenomenalism.

Framing the discussion is the fundamental realist commitment common to Cook Wilson and Moore—that the objects of knowledge are independent of the act of knowing. This is a thesis about knowledge, not perception. What connects this thesis to perception is a doctrine that perception makes the subject *knowledgeable* of its object. In being so aware of an object, the subject is in a position to know certain things about it, depending, of course, on the subject's possession and exercise of the appropriate recognitional capacities in the circumstances of perception. The subject is knowledgeable of the object of perception in the sense that knowledge is *available* to the subject in perceiving the object, whether or not such knowledge is in fact activated (in Williamson's 1990 terminology).

Suppose, then, that perception makes the subject knowledgeable of its object. The objects of perception are then at least potential objects of knowledge. If, in addition, knowledge is always knowledge of a mind-independent subject matter, then it follows that the objects of perception are themselves mind-independent and so independent of the act of perceiving. In this way the doctrine that perception is a form of knowing allows the realist conception of knowledge to have implications for how perception is properly conceived in light of it.

Working out the demands of the realist conception of knowledge on the nature of perception was subject to internal and external pressures.

Internally, the core features of the realist conception of knowledge get differently conceived by different authors, in a process of refinement and extension, and so the demands that conception of knowledge places on the nature of perception are themselves reconceived. Importantly, an independent aspect of Cook Wilson's conception of knowledge, *the accretion*, an aspect endorsed by Prichard and rejected by Austin, turns out to be inconsistent with the idea that perception makes the subject knowledgeable of a mind-independent subject matter. So the development of the realist conception of knowledge involved not merely refinement and extension, but elimination as well.

Externally, Oxford reflection on perception is subject to alien influences, in particular, Cantabrigian and Viennese influences. Thus Price comes to Oxford from Cambridge where he was Moore's student. Paul comes to Oxford from Cambridge as well but studied with Wittgenstein. And Ayer, given Ryle's encouragement, studied for a time with the logical positivists in Vienna. Incorporating the insights and resisting the challenges posed by these alien influences play an important part in the development of philosophy of perception in Oxford.

The main source of Cook Wilson's (1926: 764–800) views on perception is a letter of July 1904 criticizing Stout's (1903–4) 'Primary and Secondary Qualities'. To highlight the connections between his realist conception of knowledge and his views about perception, it is useful to begin, however, with Cook Wilson's (1926: 801–8) earlier letter of January 1904 to Prichard. There, Cook Wilson discusses two variants of a fundamental fallacy concerning knowledge or apprehension.

The first variant is the idealist attempt to understand knowledge as an activity. If knowledge is an activity, then in knowing something a subject must *do* something to the object known. But this, Cook Wilson claims, is absurd. The object of knowledge must be independent of the subject's knowing it, if coming to know is to be a discovery:

> You can no more act upon the object by knowing it than you can 'please the Dean and Chapter by stroking the dome of St. Paul's'. The man who first discovered that equable curvature meant equidistance from a point didn't supposed that he 'produced' the truth—that absolutely contradicts the idea of truth—nor that he changed the nature of the circle or curvature, or of the straight line, or of anything spatial. (Cook Wilson 1926: 802)

The second variant is the representative realist's attempt to understand knowledge and apprehension in terms of representation. Whereas the idealist attempts to explain apprehension in terms of *apprehending*, the representative realist attempts to explain apprehension in terms of *the object apprehended*, in the present instance, an idea or some other representation. The problem is that this merely pushes the problem back a level:

> The image itself has still to be *apprehended* and the difficulty is only repeated. (Cook Wilson 1926: 803)

How are the fallacies of explaining apprehension in terms of apprehending and in terms of the object of apprehension variants of the same fallacy? Both attempt to *explain* knowledge or apprehension:

> Perhaps most fallacies in the theory of knowledge are reduced to the primary one of trying to *explain* the nature of knowledge or apprehending. We cannot *construct* knowing—the act of apprehending—out of any elements. I remember quite early in my philosophic reflection having an instinctive aversion to the very expression 'theory of knowledge'. I felt the words themselves suggested a fallacy—an utterly fallacious inquiry, though I was not anxious to proclaim <it>. (Cook Wilson 1926: 803)

This is a clear statement of the anti-hybridism or anti-conjunctivism about knowledge that McDowell (1982) and Williamson (2000) will later defend. So conceived, knowledge is not a hybrid state consisting of an internal, mental state and the satisfaction of some external conditions. Cook Wilson's aversion to the 'theory of knowledge' is just an aversion to explaining knowledge by constructing it out of elements, and this scepticism will be echoed by Prichard, Ryle, and Austin and in precisely these terms.

Does Cook Wilson himself endorse anti-hybridism about perception? In his letter to Stout he does defend a conception of perception as the direct apprehension of objects spatially external to the perceiving subject. And in the letter to Prichard he does at one point speak indifferently of knowledge, apprehension, and perception. Neither consideration is decisive. More telling, however, is that the variant fallacies are echoed in the letter written later that year to Stout on perception. In particular, both idealist and representative realist accounts of perception are criticized in line with the two variant fallacies concerning knowledge or apprehension. Let's consider these in turn.

First, like Moore (1903), Cook Wilson emphasizes the distinction between the act of perceiving and the object of perception. In perceiving an object, the object appears to the subject, and so the subjective act of perceiving is sometimes described as an *appearance*. Given the act–object distinction, an appearance, so understood, is necessarily distinguished from the object. However, Cook Wilson warns against a misleading 'objectification' of appearing:

> But next the *appearance*, though properly the appear*ing* of the object, gets to be looked on as itself an object and the immediate object of consciousness, and being already, as we have seen, distinguished from the object and related to our subjectivity, becomes, so to say, a mere subjective 'object'—'appearance' in that sense. And so, as *appearance* of the object, it has now to be represented not as the object but as the phenomenon caused in our consciousness by the object. Thus for the true appearance (= appearing) to us of the *object* is substituted, through the 'objectification' of the appearing as appearance, the appearing to us of an *appearance*, the appearing of a phenomenon caused in us by the object. (Cook Wilson 1926: 796)

If perceptual appearances are 'the appearing of a phenomenon caused in us by the object', then it would be impossible for a subject to come to know about the mind-independent object on the basis of its perceptual appearance and hence impossible to discover how things stand with a mind-independent subject matter by perceiving:

> It must be observed that the result of this is that there could be no direct perception or consciousness of Reality under any circumstances or any condition of knowing or perceiving: for the whole view is developed entirely from the fact that the object is distinct from our act of knowing it or recognizing it, which distinction must exist in any kind of knowing it or perceiving it. From this error would necessarily result a mere subjective idealism. Reality would become an absolutely unknowable 'Thing in Itself', and finally disappear altogether (as with Berkeley) as an hypothesis that we could not possibly justify. (Cook Wilson 1926: 797)

This straightforwardly parallels the fallacy of explaining apprehension in terms of apprehending.

Second, Cook Wilson criticizes Stout's (1903–4) representative realism. The basis of his criticism involves negative and positive claims about the nature of representation. The negative claim is that nothing is intrinsically representational: 'Nothing has *meaning in itself*' (Cook Wilson 1926: 770). The positive claim is put as follows: 'Representation is our subjective act. . . . It is *we* who mean' (Cook Wilson 1926: 770). According to Cook Wilson, then, representation is something that the subject does.

How, according to Stout (1903–4: 144), might the sensation of extension 'represent, express, or stand for' extension? Plausibly in two ways: by resembling extension or by necessarily co-varying with the presence of extension. However, the natural relations of mimesis and necessary co-variation are *impersonal*—they obtain independently of anything that the subject does. And since they are *symmetric*, this has the surprising consequence that external qualities represent sensations. However, if representation is something that a subject does, then the natural relations of mimesis and necessary co-variation could not make a sensation represent an external quality (let alone make an external quality represent a sensation, for plausibly nothing does). At most, mimesis and necessary co-variation are natural relations that *incline* us to represent things by means of them:

> It is we who make the weeping willow a symbol of sorrow. There may of course be something in the object which prompts us to give it a meaning, e.g., the resemblance of the weeping willow to a human figure bowed over in the attitude of grief. But the willow in itself can neither 'mean' grief, nor 'represent' nor 'stand for' nor 'express' grief. *We* do all that. (Cook Wilson 1926: 770)

In using the willow to represent grief, the subject must apprehend the content of that representation. And that, according to Cook Wilson, is what prevents representation from figuring in an explanation of perceptual apprehension. This straightforwardly parallels the fallacy of explaining apprehension in terms of the apprehension of a representation.

Thus the two fallacies of explaining apprehension in terms of apprehending and in terms of the object apprehended (a representation) arise in the perceptual case as well. This raises the question whether in the perceptual case these fallacies are variants of the fundamental fallacy of trying to *explain* perception in more fundamental terms. Just as knowledge cannot be explained in terms of belief that meets further external conditions, perhaps perception cannot be explained in terms of, say, experience or appearance that meets further external conditions. Cook Wilson expresses his scepticism about such explanations in the case of knowledge by denying that there is any such thing as a theory of knowledge. Farquharson in the postscript to *Statement and Inference* reports a similar attitude in the perceptual case: 'He came to think of a theory of Perception as philosoph-ically preposterous' (Cook Wilson 1926: 882).

Even if Cook Wilson accepted an anti-hybridist conception of perception, we remain unclear why the realist conception of knowledge requires this. A reason begins to emerge with later Prichard's case *against* the idea that perception is a form of knowing. While later Prichard opposes the doctrine that links the realist conception of knowledge with the nature of perception, his discussion reveals some of what is required if one were to retain the doctrine that perception makes us knowledgeable of a mind-independent subject matter.

The central argument occurs in Prichard's (1938) 'Sense Datum Fallacy'. His main target is the sense-datum theory of Cambridge realists. Like their Oxford counter-parts, the Cambridge realists held that the object of knowledge is independent of the act of knowing, and that perception makes the subject knowledgeable of its object. Cambridge realism departs from Oxford realism in its adherence to a further thesis: that there is something of which a subject is aware in undergoing sense experience whether perceiving or no. According to the theories of Moore (1953 [1910–11]), Russell (1912), and Price (1932), sense-data are whatever we are aware of in sense experience. This characterization of sense-data is *neutral* in the sense that it assumes nothing about the substantive nature of objects that play this epistemic role. We have already noted how the sense-datum theory is committed to an experiential monism—all experience involves, as part of its nature, a non-propositional sensory mode of awareness. A further commitment is presently important. For so conceived, sense-data are objects whose substantive nature is open to investigation independent of our acts of awareness of them. It is this consequence of the conjunction of the realist conception of knowledge, the conception of the objects of perception as potential objects of knowledge, and the sense-datum theory that is Prichard's primary target. And Prichard's central thought is that perception could not make one knowledgeable of its object, since the object of perception depends on the subject's experience of it in a way that the object of knowledge could not.

Much of Prichard's case is a variant of Berkeley's (1710; 1713) critique of Locke (1690). However, two arguments go beyond the familiar Berkeleian critique. Both present important morals for Oxford realism. The moral of the first argument is that the accretion must be abandoned if Oxford realism is to be sustained. The moral of the second argument is that the realist conception of knowledge and the conception of the objects of perception as potential objects of knowledge together require abandoning the Cambridge realist's commitment to experiential monism (though it will take the work of Austin 1962 and Hinton 1973 to begin to vindicate this).

The first argument can seem like a variant of the argument from illusion though it really has a very different character:

> ...if perceiving were a kind of knowing, mistakes about what we perceive would be impossible, and yet they are constantly being made, since at any rate in the cases of seeing and feeling or touching we are almost always in a state of thinking that what we are perceiving are various bodies, although we need only to reflect to discover that in this we are mistaken. (Prichard 1938: 11)

Suppose a pig is in plain view of Sid, and Sid can recognize as a pig the animal that he sees. It might seem that what Sid is thus aware of is incompatible with there not being a pig before him. In which case, perception affords Sid something akin to proof of a porcine presence. In this way, perception can seem to make the subject knowledgeable of a mind-independent subject matter. Prichard's insight is that this picture is incompatible with a further feature of Cook Wilson's conception of knowledge, *the accretion*. Knowledge admits of no ringers—a state indiscriminable upon reflection from knowledge just is knowledge. What would it take for perception to make us knowledgeable of a mind-independent subject matter if there are no ringers for knowledge? If Sid's seeing the pig makes him knowledgeable of the pig's presence, then Sid must recognize that what he is aware of in seeing the pig is incompatible with the pig's absence. But is Sid in seeing the pig in a position to recognize that? After all, there are situations indiscriminable upon reflection from seeing a pig that do not involve the pig's presence. Sid's hallucination of the scene would be indiscriminable upon reflection from his perceiving it. If what Sid is aware of in seeing the pig is not discriminable upon reflection from what, if anything, he is aware of in hallucinating the pig, then it could seem that he is not in a position to recognize that what he is aware of in seeing the pig is incompatible with the pig's absence. He would lack proof of a pig before him. Since perception admits of ringers, it could not be a source of ringerless knowledge.

This argument reveals a tension within the Oxford realism of Cook Wilson and early Prichard. If Cook Wilson and early Prichard were right in claiming that the objects of knowledge are mind-independent objects, and the objects of perception are at least potential objects of knowledge, then these claims can only be sustained by abandoning the accretion.

Prichard's second argument derives from Paul (1936). Arguably it has ancient roots as well. At the very least, it is a variant of Berkeley's interpretation of the *Theaetetus* (*Siris* §§ 253, 304–5). On the Berkeleian interpretation, the objects of perception are in a perpetual flux of becoming. In perception, every subject is aware of the sensible qualities whose coming and going constitute the flux since every subject is the 'measure' of what they perceive. Though perception affords us with awareness of its objects, this mode of awareness could not constitute knowledge since knowledge pertains to *being*, not *becoming*. More prosaically, the objects of perception could not have a continuing identity through time, if every feature they manifest is relativized to a perceiver at a time. Nor could the objects of perception be publicly accessible to different perceivers. But this would preclude the objects of perception from being objects of knowledge if knowledge is to have a mind-independent subject matter (see Burnyeat 1990, for further discussion). Paul's discussion of sense-data is of a piece. Paul, and Prichard following him, emphasize our inability to decide key questions about the persistence and publicity of sense-data. If sense-data are meant to be objects open to investigation independent of our awareness of them, then such questions should be settled by looking to the sense-data themselves. But our inability to decide such questions belies this thought. At best, sense-data are shadows cast by experiences that can be elicited by suitably affecting the mind. So conceived, open questions about the nature of sense-data are resolved not by investigation but by linguistic decision.

Suppose that sense-data do not have a substantive nature open to investigation independent of our awareness of them in sense experience. There are at least three alternative morals:

1. One might claim that sense-data constitutively depend on our awareness of them in sense experience. Sense-data would be in this regard like Berkeleian ideas. (Though neither deploy the sense-data vocabulary, Berkeley and later Prichard endorse this alternative.)
2. One might deny that there are any substantive facts about the nature of sense-data that are open to investigation independent of our awareness of them in sense experience. (Wittgenstein, Paul, and Ayer endorse this alternative.)
3. One might retain the conception of perception as a sensory mode of awareness that makes one knowledgeable of a mind-independent subject matter by abandoning the fundamental claim of the sense-datum theory—that there is an object of which we are aware whenever we undergo sense experience—and the experiential monism that came in its wake. (Austin and Hinton endorse this alternative.)

There have been relatively few takers for the Berkeleian alternative (though see Foster 2000 for a recent defence). We will set it aside and focus, instead, on the second and third alternatives, as represented by the work of Ayer and Austin respectively.

In *The Foundations of Empirical Knowledge*, Ayer (1940) takes over from the logical positivists the general idea that there is no substantive metaphysics and that metaphysical disagreements are better understood as practical disagreements about what language to adopt. Ayer applies this idea to sense-data and suggests that talk of sense-data is just an alternative way of talking about facts that all of us can agree about, namely, facts about appearances.

Ayer understands the argument from illusion to establish not that there are sense-data, distinct from material objects, that are the objects of sensory awareness, if this is to be understood as a substantive metaphysical claim; rather, the argument from illusion highlights the practical need to regiment our perceptual vocabulary. According to Ayer, 'see', 'perceive', and their cognates have readings that implicate the existence of the object seen or perceived *and* readings that fail to so implicate. Sense-datum theorists, as Ayer understands them, simply regiment in favour of the existential reading. The practical need for talk of immaterial sense-data arises in the context of an epistemological project:

> For since in philosophizing about perception our main object is to analyse the relationship of our sense-experience to the propositions we put forward concerning material things, it is useful for us to have a terminology that enables us to refer to the contents of our experiences independently of the material things they are taken to present. (Ayer 1940: 26)

That project involved two central claims:

1. Sentences about material objects are empirically testable but do not admit of conclusive verification, while
2. Sentences about sense-data are *observation* sentences—they furnish evidence for other sentences and are themselves incorrigible.

Each claim is an instance of a more fundamental commitment that is independent of Ayer's positivism. Moreover, each stands opposed to fundamental claims in Cook Wilsonian epistemology and philosophy of language, at least as extended and refined by Austin.

The first claim involves a commitment to a Lockean conception of knowledge:

> I believe that, in practice, most people agree with John Locke that 'the certainty of things existing *in rerum natura*, when we have the testimony of our sense for it, is not only as great as our frame can attain to, but as our condition needs'. (Ayer 1940: 1)

The Lockean conception of knowledge is opposed to the Cook Wilsonian conception of knowledge as proof. If knowledge only requires as much certainty as our frame can attain to and as our condition needs, then such certainty can, and most certainly will, fall short of proof (as Ayer acknowledges in conceding that material sentences do not admit of conclusive verification.) In this way, this dispute replays key elements of the early modern dispute between Hobbes and Boyle on the epistemic status of experimental philosophy (see Shapin and Schaffer 1985, for discussion).

The second claim involves a commitment to a form of foundationalism according to which there is a subclass of sentences (sentences about sense-data) that can be incorrigibly known to be true. Moreover, these sentences can serve as the basis of an inferential transition to less certain sentences (sentences about material objects) that can nevertheless be known to be true on the basis of the evidence they provide. However, foundationalism, so conceived, conflicts with a fundamental claim in Cook Wilsonian philosophy of language, at least as extended and refined by Austin.

Suppose that Sid sees a pig in plain view. The pig that Sid sees is a material object, and for Ayer statements about material objects do not admit of conclusive verification. His thought seems to be this. Contrast Sid seeing a pig in plain view with Sid seeming to see a pig but where there is no pig to be seen and where the Sid's seeming to see a pig is, at least in this instance, indiscriminable upon reflection from seeing a pig. While the statement 'There's a pig' is true in the good case, it is false in the bad case. Since from Sid's perspective the bad case is a ringer for the good case, Ayer concludes that the possibility of Sid's mistakenly judging that a pig is before him in the bad case means that he cannot be certain that there is a pig before him in the good case. At most, he can have inconclusive evidence for there being a pig. But there is an incorrigible judgement that Sid can make in both cases, a judgement about how things appear to Sid in his experience. (For Ayer, this a judgement about sense-data, but even philosophers who deny that there are sense-data can, and do, accept the more general claim.) And this incorrigible knowledge of appearances constitutes the evidence for the truth of material object sentences.

Ayer is supposing that there is a type of sentence, an observation sentence that represents how things appear in Sid's experience, that can be incorrigibly known to be true by Sid independently of the occasion of his expressing this knowledge. Against this claim, Austin insists that the truth of a claim is only determined by the standards in play on the occasion of utterance. Thus, there could be no sentence that is true independent of an occasion of utterance, and, hence, no such sentence could be incorrigibly known to be true.

While no sentence can be incorrigibly known to be true independent of an occasion of utterance, that's not to say that there are no occasions of utterance where Sid can speak with certainty. But recognizing that there are occasions where things can be incorrigibly known undermines the thought that what can be incorrigibly known is restricted to reports about how things appear in sense experience. If circumstances are propitious, Sid can just know that there is a pig before him by seeing the pig and can express this knowledge by saying 'There's a pig'. This is not undermined by there being other circumstances or other occasions where the very same sentence could be used to say something false and so fail to express knowledge. That there are other possible circumstances where Sid would speak falsely and fail to express knowledge is consistent with Sid, in the present circumstances, speaking truly and expressing knowledge of a pig before him. (It is on these grounds that Austin rejects the accretion.)

We are now in a position to appreciate the emerging need for an anti-hybridist conception of perception. Nothing short of Sid's encounter with a pig in sight could make Sid knowledgeable of the pig if this is akin to the availability of proof. It is the presentation of the pig in perceptual experience, an object whose existence is incompatible with there not being a pig, that makes Sid knowledgeable. The relation to the object of perception that makes a subject knowledgeable of that object simply couldn't be present in a case of hallucination. This is at the very least in tension with the idea that the subject could be so related in part by undergoing an appearance that can obtain independently of the material object that it is taken to present.

Anti-hybridism about perception is a thesis about the nature of perception—that perception cannot be reductively explained in terms of a hybrid state consisting of an internal mental component and an external non-mental component. Experiential monism, in contrast, is a thesis about the nature of sense experience understood as the genus of which perception is a species—that sense experience has a unitary nature. Despite being conceptually distinct in this way, the emerging debate reveals a tension between these doctrines, at least when set against a concern for realism. Oxford and Cambridge realists share a conception of knowledge where the objects of knowledge are independent of the act of knowing and a conception of perception where perception makes the subject knowledgeable of its object by affording sensory awareness of it. Cambridge realists, however, further held that the sensory mode of awareness was not distinctive of perception but characterized sense experience more generally. If the non-propositional mode of awareness characterizes sense experience generally, and if the arguments from illusion, hallucination, or conflicting appearances lead one to conclude that the objects of awareness are not ordinary material things like pigs, then it would be increasingly difficult to retain a common-sense realism according to which Sid's seeing the pig puts him in a position to know that there is a pig before him. While Austin is not explicitly committed to the denial of experiential monism, he may be implicitly committed to its denial insofar as experiential monism is in tension with the common sense realism that he sought to defend with anti-hybridist conceptions of perception and knowledge. It will take the work of Hinton (1973), specifically his reflections on the semantics and epistemology of perception–illusion disjunctions, to make the denial explicit. Disjunctivists are experiential pluralists. Part of the point of such pluralism is to acknowledge what's distinctive about perception. And according to the present tradition, adequately conceiving of perception requires acknowledging what's distinctive about perceptual experience if it can make us knowledgeable of a world without the mind.

References

Austin, J. L. (1946/1979). 'Other Minds'. In *Philosophical Papers*, 3rd edn., ed. J. O. Urmson and G. J. Warnock. Oxford: Clarendon Press, 1979, pp. 76–116; first pub. in *Proceedings of the Aristotelian Society, Supplementary Volume* 20 (1946).

—— (1956-7/1979). 'A Plea For Excuses', In *Philosophical Papers*, 3rd edn., ed. J. O. Urmson and G. J. Warnock. Oxford: Clarendon Press, 1979, pp. 175–204; first pub. in *Proceedings of the Aristotelian Society* 56 (1956–7).

—— (1952/1979): 'How To Talk: Some Simple Ways'. In *Philosophical Papers*, 3rd edn., ed. J. O. Urmson and G. J. Warnock. Oxford: Clarendon Press, 1979, pp. 134–51; first pub. in *Proceedings of the Aristotelian Society* 52 (1952–3).

—— (1962). *Sense and Sensibilia*. New York: Oxford University Press.

Ayer, A. J. (1940). *The Foundations of Empirical Knowledge*. London: Macmillan.

Berkeley, George (1710). *Treatise concerning the Principles of Human Knowledge*.

—— (1713). *Three Dialogues between Hylas and Philonous*.

—— (1744). *Siris: A Chain of Philosophical Reflexions and Inquiries Concerning the Virtues of Tar Water and divers other Subjects connected together and arising from another. A New Edition with Additions and Emendations*.

Burnyeat, Myles (1990). *The Theaetetus of Plato*. Indianapolis: Hackett Publishing Company.

Cook Wilson, John (1926). *Statement and Inference*. Oxford: Oxford University Press.

Evans, Gareth (1982). *The Varieties of Reference*. Oxford: Oxford University Press.

Frege, Gottlob (1892–5). 'Ausführungen über Sinn und Bedeutung'. In Frege (1983), pp. 128–36.

—— (1897). *Logik*. In Frege (1983), pp. 137–63.

—— (1918). 'Der Gedanke. Eine logische Untersuchung', *Beiträge zur Philosophie deutschen Idealismus* 2 (1918–19): 58–77; reprinted in *Logische Untersuchungen*, ed. G. Patzig. Göttingen: Vandenhoeck and Ruprecht, 1966, pp. pp. 30–53.

—— (1983). *Nachgelassene Schriften*, ed. H. Hermes, F. Kambartel, and F. Kaulbach. Hamburg: Felix Meiner Verlag (2nd, expanded, edition).

Foster, John (2000). *The Nature of Perception*. Oxford: Oxford University Press.

Grice, H. P. (1961). 'The Causal Theory of Perception', *Proceedings of the Aristotelian Society, Supplementary Volume* 35: 121–53.

Hinton, J. M. (1967). 'Visual Experiences', *Mind* 76(302): 217–27.

—— (1973). *Experience: An Inquiry into Some Ambiguities*. Oxford: Clarendon Press.

Locke, John (1690). *An Essay Concerning Human Understanding*. Oxford: Oxford University Press.

McDowell, John (1982). 'Criteria, Defeasibility and Knowledge', *Proceedings of the British Academy* 68: 455–79. Reprinted in *Meaning, Knowledge and Reality*. Cambridge, MA: Harvard University Press, 1998, pp. 369–94.

—— (1995). 'Knowledge and the Internal', *Philosophy and Phenomenological Research* 55(4): 877–93. Reprinted in *Meaning, Knowledge and Reality*. Cambridge, MA: Harvard University Press, pp. 395–413.

Moore, G. E. (1903). 'The Refutation of Idealism', *Mind* 12: 433–53.

—— (1953). *Some Main Problems in Philosophy*. The Muirhead Library of Philosophy. London: George Allen & Unwin; lectures originally given in 1910–11.

Paul, G. A. (1936). 'Is There a Problem about Sense-Data?' *Proceedings of the Aristotelian Society, Supplementary Volume* 15: 61–77.

Price, H. H. (1932). *Perception*. London: Methuen.

—— (1909). *Kant's Theory of Knowledge*. Oxford: Oxford University Press.

—— (1938). 'The Sense-Datum Fallacy', *Proceedings of the Aristotelian Society* 17: 1–18.

—— (1950). 'History of the Theory of Knowledge'. In *Knowledge and Perception: Essays and Lectures*, ed. W. D. Ross. Oxford: Clarendon Press, pp. 69–199.

Russell, Bertrand (1906). 'The Nature of Truth', *Mind* 15(60): 528–33.

—— (1912). *The Problems of Philosophy*. London: Home University Library; repr. Oxford: Oxford University Press, 1967.

—— (1959). *My Philosophical Development*. London: George Allen & Unwin.

Shapin, Steven and Simon Schaffer (1985). *Leviathan and the Air-Pump*. Princeton, NJ: Princeton University Press.

Snowdon, Paul (2008). 'Hinton and the origins of disjunctivism'. In Adrian Haddock and Fiona Macpherson (eds.), *Disjunctivism: Perception, Action, Knowledge*. Oxford: Oxford University Press, pp. 35–56.

Stout, G. F. (1903–4). 'Primary and secondary qualities', *Proceedings of the Aristotelian Society* 4: 141–60.

Swartz, Robert J. (ed.) (1965). *Perceiving, Sensing, and Knowing*. Berkeley: University of California Press.

Williamson, Timothy (1990). *Identity and Discrimination*. Oxford: Blackwell.

——(2000). *Knowledge and its Limits*. Oxford: Oxford University Press.

Wittgenstein, Ludwig (1958). *The Blue and Brown Books*. Oxford: Blackwell, 2nd edn. 1969.

CHAPTER 16

EARLY LOGICAL EMPIRICISM AND ITS RECEPTION: THE CASE OF THE VIENNA CIRCLE

THOMAS UEBEL

LOGICAL empiricism—sometimes also called 'logical positivism'—was a considerably more complex philosophical movement, possessing a much greater heterogeneity and far more sophisticated motivation, than it is customarily credited with. Yet while the lines of its developments as well as its failures and achievements are much clearer now than they were in its heyday, the question of its legacy remains a controversial one. Even among those who deny that it represents a modernist cul-de-sac, there is disagreement as to whether its legacy has yet been fully exhausted or not. Here the view will be defended that, in any case, it is a mistake to think of logical empiricism in terms of a set of doctrines fixed at the start, of its history in terms of a series of attritions and of its long-term reception as wholesale rejection. It is the trajectories of developments within logical empiricism that hold the greatest interest and attention to them is likely to pay the greatest dividend if we are concerned to assess its role in the history of analytical philosophy. Too often, very early positions are portrayed as representative and dismissed as mistakes characteristic for the movement—leaving unrecognized that work on their correction took centre stage in subsequent periods.[1] Rather than as purveyors of hopeless reductionisms, logical empiricists are better understood as early (and so not always wholly happy) pioneers of philosophical deflationism.

---

[1] A textbook example of the strategy of distortion by selective attention to early doctrines is the anti-reductionist argument, directed against Carnap, of Quine (1951). Putnam's claim that for the logical positivists 'a "fact" is just a sensible "impression"' (2002, 22) is but one recent version on the theme.

Here I must limit the argument to examples from early logical empiricism, its pre-Second World War mainly European stage. I begin by outlining the doctrinal constants that characterize all logical empiricisms before giving examples of the heterogeneity and sophistication in its early stages of development (§§ 16.1–16.3). Then I discuss A. J. Ayer's version of logical positivism (§ 16.4), the difference between the Berlin and the Vienna versions of early logical empiricism (§ 16.5), and differences within the Vienna Circle itself (§ 16.6). I close by considering the potential of the conception of philosophy developed on the left wing of the Vienna Circle (§ 16.7).

16.1 THE HETEROGENEITY OF EARLY LOGICAL EMPIRICISM

Basic to all logical empiricisms is the assumption that only those propositions are cognitively meaningful whose truth or falsity makes a difference that is discernible, at least in principle and however fallibly, by scientific means. (From the start, cognitive meaning was understood as entailing the truth-evaluatability of statements; other sorts of meaning were recognized but held to be irrelevant for scientific discourse.) Metaphysics and unconditional normative ethics were ruled out of court as neither analytic nor empirically testable. The correct formulation of the empiricist meaning criterion, however, proved difficult and its status remained controversial.[2] Within the sciences, a sharp division was drawn between the empirical sciences (physics, biology, sociology, etc.) and the formal sciences (logic, mathematics). To this corresponded the sharp and exclusive distinction between statements that were of a synthetic nature whose assertion was justifiable a posteriori and statements analytic in nature and justifiable by a priori reasoning. Unlike the knowledge claims of the empirical sciences, those of logic and mathematics were justified on purely formal grounds, by proof of their derivability by stated rules from stated axioms and premises which in turn were considered merely linguistic rules and determined by convention. Thus in logical empiricism, empiricism itself underwent change by shedding some of its traditional ambitions: to account for logical and mathematical knowledge as well as for the very possibility of knowledge in general. For the logical empiricists, philosophy was to become 'scientific' by becoming, first of all, an entirely second-order inquiry, reflecting upon the first-order sciences. And, unlike

---

[2] See Hempel (1950, 1951) for a classic diagnosis of, in turn, classic proposals for a criterion of empirical significance; see Creath (1976) for an assessment of Carnap's proposal in (1956) and Ayer (1992b, 302) for comments on the proposal in Wright (1986 which became 1993a and 1993b). It would appear that despite their popularity, global statements about 'the' empiricist meaning criterion are mistaken. It is important to be clear about the type of target language for the criterion (formal or natural languages) and the standard of adequacy demanded by the philosophical approach taken (formal definitions or pragmatic explication): while definitions require that necessary and sufficient conditions be determined, explications can get away with exemplar-based understandings of the principle.

traditional empiricist epistemology, this version did not reserve for itself even a very last domain of its own by disputing philosophical scepticism. Sceptical doubts that were not themselves scientific doubts, in principle allayable by scientific means, lay beyond its brief.

So much for the bare basics.[3] The complexity and sophistication of logical empiricism are particularly evident in its early, post-First World War European phase (despite its undeniable share of enthusiasms). For instance, two 'Continental' features reflecting its background must be acknowledged. First, this particular empiricism was not only distinguished by its novel way of dealing with the problem of accounting for knowledge of logic and arithmetic, but also by its ambition to safeguard the objectivity of natural knowledge. (Even though Kant's solution was rejected, his problematic was faced squarely.) Besides the well-known influences on logical empiricism of Frege, Russell, and the early Wittgenstein—and Hume—also the complex legacy of the Kantian tradition must be recognized. Second, this empiricism was also tempered by the influence of the French conventionalism of Poincaré, Duhem, and Rey, all of whose major philosophical works had been available in German translations long before the outbreak of the First World War.

Internally early logical empiricism also possessed great heterogeneity. First we must note the existence of two cooperating but largely independent centres, the so-called Vienna Circle (around Schlick) and the Berlin Society for Empirical (from 1932, Scientific) Philosophy (around Reichenbach). Compared to the Vienna Circle, the Berlin Society functioned more as a forum for interdisciplinary scientific discussion and less as a group working out a comprehensive philosophy (which Reichenbach thought was best left for later stages). Within the Vienna Circle we must distinguish two factions, a more traditionalist grouping around the leader (with Waismann and Feigl) and a so-called left wing (comprising Carnap, Frank, Hahn, and Neurath) and we must note an additional philosophical influence feeding into the latter (the Austrian tradition starting from Bolzano) and its further differentiation between a formalist (Carnap, Hahn) and a pragmatist camp (Neurath, Frank). (Within the left wing we may further distinguish Frank, Hahn, and Neurath as former members of a pre-First World War discussion group, the so-called First Vienna Circle.) With any one of these distinctions came a different emphasis in their broadly shared philosophical programme. (I'll return to these differences below.)

Given the differences of philosophical temperament and outlook that hide under the heading of early logical empiricism, it is tempting to suspect that what united its practitioners was their joint opposition to the established philosophies of their day, the ongoing 'chaos of systems', as Schlick (1930 [1959, 54]) put it. What spurred them on, moreover, were what they perceived as deplorable states of affairs not only in the

---

[3] More detailed overviews are given of logical empiricism generally in Creath (2011), of the Vienna Circle in particular in Uebel (2006/2011), and of Ayer in Macdonald (2005/2010). For recent collections of detailed discussions of specific topics pertaining to logical empiricism not covered here see Friedman and Creath (2007) and Richardson and Uebel (2007).

rarified fields of academia, but in public discourse generally. What was needed, given the deep sense of crisis that had engulfed the entirety of social and cultural life in post-First World War Germany and Austria, were the means to distinguish genuine knowledge claims—and distinguish them not only from false ones, but above all from claims possessing great emotive power but no factual content at all. Only then could a meaningful reconstruction of social and cultural life begin. While all the early logical empiricists shared this view to some extent, differences soon emerged in the degree of militancy of their opposition against the traditional philosophies which had failed to counteract (if not fostered) this intellectual malaise and in the degree to which they tended to associate their philosophy with political movements. Behind all these differences, however, stood the shared conviction that for philosophy to restore itself as a proper discipline both capable of making truth claims and of benefiting public life generally, it had to emulate the example of science in some form.[4]

Much of this broader context remained long unknown in the English-speaking world due to the complex history of the logical empiricist movement. Driven into exile by the threat to its members of racial and political persecution by the German National Socialist and Austro-fascist parties that had assumed power in 1933 and 1934, most surviving representatives like Reichenbach, Carnap, Hempel, and Feigl found themselves in an entirely different cultural setting in the United States. At the end of the Second World War, with their doctrines partially de-radicalized and themselves situated in more congenial professional surroundings, they largely seemed to converge on the type of formalist philosophy that the anti-positivists of the 1960s attacked as out of touch with real science and its real history. Much of their early socio-political Enlightenment radicalism as well as many of the early discussions about what it meant for philosophy to be scientific were simply forgotten in the process.[5]

16.2 THE PARADIGMATIC STATUS OF SCIENTIFIC KNOWLEDGE

Whatever the differences of the early logical empiricists' ideas about how to render philosophy scientific, one central tenet of theirs was that a new understanding of science itself was required. This made logical empiricism primarily a philosophy of science.

---

[4] This may mean attempting the solution of at least some traditional philosophical problems by scientific means (Reichenbach) or the strict adherence to an ontologically neutral second-order of analysis of scientific languages and/or practices (Carnap, Neurath) or the elucidatory determination of the meaning of scientific propositions (Schlick).

[5] For explorations of the socio-political dimension of the logical empiricists' resettlement in North America, see Howard (2003) and Reisch (2005) and the symposium about the latter edited by Douglas (2009).

Certainly some of its doctrines fed into general philosophy and demonstrated their wider implications, but the concern with science took centre stage. Moreover, the knowledge claim of science was no longer in question. This stance testifies to the modernist convictions that propelled the theorists of the Vienna Circle and the Berlin Society in their early days but it also is easily misunderstood nowadays.

One way of misunderstanding it is to read it as uncritical science worship. It is true, of course, that the early logical empiricists took scientific knowledge to be the paradigm of human knowledge generally and that some even centred it nearly exclusively on mathematical physics (though others warned of the dangers of this exclusivist approach).[6] But when they did so, they did not expect science to fulfil the philosophical dreams of old: they did not import traditional views of knowledge into science (certainty) nor deny that in some respects science was continuous with everyday cognition. Their belief in science was tempered by a deep appreciation of the complexities of scientific knowledge, of its fallibility and forever provisional, open-ended nature.

Another way of misunderstanding the centrality of science for the early logical empiricists is to read it as indicative of belief in inevitably cumulative progress. To be sure, they shared the Enlightenment's belief that evidence-based reasoning was superior to the acceptance of doctrines on the basis of tradition, secular or religious. But most of them saw clearly that historical development rarely was linear and that overstraining the bow of reason led to pitfalls that undermined the Enlightenment project itself.[7] That some of their programmatic statements undoubtedly overshot the mark (like their early verificationism) does not indicate the naïve scientism that some critics foist on them. Rather, it is best explained by the urgency that the defence of scientific reason by means of its proper analysis possessed at a time when irrationalist tendencies were on the rise in popular and educated culture and sinister political forces stood ready to exploit them. If anything was naïve about early logical empiricism, it also was not the idea that philosophy mattered—it clearly did—but how much rational discourse about it could be made to count in social and cultural life generally. Some were more aware than others of the limited reach of reason in the socio-political domain.[8]

Yet another misunderstanding hides a deep metaphilosophical disagreement. Though the early logical empiricists most emphatically denied philosophy the role of lording over science and accepted for it the role of the under-labourer, they did not renounce its critical role. It is important to note that from what appeared to them as the paradigms of scientific achievement they derived non-trivial criteria which contenders to the status of scientific knowledge had to meet: by no means any theory qualified.[9]

---

[6] See the explicit comment in Neurath (1936a [2004, 506]). Already his (1932a) was written to counteract what he saw as an undue concentration on the best developed natural sciences.

[7] See Neurath (1913) and (1930).

[8] See Stadler (1997 [2001, 498–507]) for an analysis of the relevant contrast between Schlick and Neurath.

[9] Vitalistic biology and Nazi race theories were thus ruled out, though Neurath stressed that ruling out the latter, for instance, was not merely a matter of matching formal requirements (1944, 19).

Philosophy was to act as critical conscience, not from an eternal standpoint but on the basis of reflection of the methods and aims of current science.

16.3 EARLY LOGICAL EMPIRICIST PHILOSOPHY OF SCIENCE

Instead of a top-down approach to science, the early logical empiricists took a far more reflexive stance. Consider their view that a new understanding of science was required before philosophy could become properly scientific, while they also held that the existing philosophies of science had failed their subject. When the early logical empiricists looked to science as a knowledge ideal to emulate, they found that the Einsteinian revolution demanded that a new philosophy be created that was adequate to its new physics. As they perceived it, there did not exist as yet a theory of scientific knowledge that combined strict accountability to experience with the recognition of the need for bold theoretical invention. The facility with which formal and natural science working in conjunction in the theory of general relativity had overthrown what had been presumed to be one of the external truths of reason—the nature of physical space—was left entirely unaccounted for. What were the conceptual conditions of this scientific development?

Our understanding both of science and of philosophy had to be corrected, they concluded. First, it had to be accepted that scientific theories of sufficient generality contained principles that could not by themselves be tested by experiment; since they bear on experience only in conjunction with other principles and auxiliary hypotheses, their conjunction could be tested, however. This underdetermination of theory by data and the resultant epistemological holism illustrated the freedom that the space of scientific reason granted to theorists. Then it had to be realized that the space of philosophical reason was not significantly bigger than that of scientific reason in its formal and empirical varieties. (Counterfactual reasoning in science already demanded facility with the modalities of nomological and logical necessity.) Rejecting both the rationalist claim that reason alone can tell us about the world and the transcendental idealist idea that pure reason can prescribe how we must conceptualize our experience while the world 'in itself' should forever remain unknown to us, the early logical empiricists returned to the strict separation of knowledge claims into empirical ones justified a posteriori and logico-linguistic ones justified a priori. Their denial of the synthetic a priori left them free to regard the principles of high theory either as linguistic conventions (and so as analytic) or as very general hypotheses (and so as synthetic) that are valid either universally or only locally (like the principle of causality): it depended on the case at hand. Either way, the second-order inquiry that philosophy had become did not possess types of resources beyond those of the sciences that were its objects (though their metatheoretical deployment allowed new perspectives).

A distinction is often drawn nowadays between philosophies of science that approach their subject matter with agendas external to it and impose seemingly alien categories and distinctions, and philosophies of science that arise out of the clarification of conceptual issues and the resolution of methodological quandaries of scientific practice itself. Not uncommonly, logical empiricism is classified among the former. While it may hold to some degree of the orthodox logical empiricism that is remembered to have dominated philosophy of science from the early 1950s to the later 1960s—by which time the criticisms of Kuhn, Feyerabend, and Hanson had found a responsive audience—it is false for early logical empiricism. Nearly all of its representatives of note had at least some training in one of the sciences at university, be it the natural, social, or formal ones; many had even gained their doctorates there and only later turned to philosophy prompted by issues in their own disciplines. Given their varied scientific backgrounds this means that early logical empiricism arose and developed in response not only to radical innovations in natural science (the inception and expansion of relativity theory and the development of quantum physics), but also to the ongoing crisis in the foundations of arithmetic (prompting the stand-off between logicism and formalism and later intuitionism) and to the methodological confusions that marked much of the social science of its day.

Whether their claim to have been the first to have faced up coherently to the challenge that relativity theory posed to traditional conceptions of scientific knowledge is accepted or not, that and the task to comprehend quantum physics was the central aim of their efforts in philosophy of natural science.[10] Schlick's early essays on relativity theory (1915, 1917–22) from an empiricist-conventionalist perspective quickly gained him Einstein's support, while Reichenbach's first book (1920) still sought to compatibilize relativity theory with a Kantian perspective (a position dropped in his later works on the topic [1924, 1928]) and Carnap's doctoral dissertation (1922) aimed to distinguish and defend, relative to their distinct frameworks, different conceptions of space. Frank meanwhile, the physicist among the members of the so-called First Vienna Circle and Einstein's successor in Prague in 1912, worked actively on relativity-related physics at the time; his later main philosophical work concerned the notion of causality after the advent of quantum physics (1932), a topic that also attracted Schlick (1931, 1937) and especially Reichenbach (1944).

Likewise, whatever one's judgement of Carnap's attempt in *Logical Syntax of Language* (1934) to overcome the foundational dispute between logicism, formalism, and intuitionism in the light of Gödel's incompleteness result by conventionalizing basic axioms and embracing logical pluralism and by stratifying mathematics into a hierarchy of ever stronger languages (each with their own Gödel-sentences), there can be little doubt that—following on from Hahn's long-standing interest in and explorations of the matter (e.g. 1931, 1933)—it represents a major development in the history of logic. This interest in formal science finds its complement in the Berlin Society in Grelling's early and late work on the logical paradoxes (e.g. 1908, 1936) and Dubislav's on definition (1931). Later Carnap helped pioneer both extensional and intensional semantics with his *Meaning and Necessity* (1947) functioning as one

---

[10] For doubts both about the primacy of the response and its coherence, see Ryckman (2005).

of the conduits for Frege's bipartite theory of meaning into post-Second World War analytic philosophy.

Finally, whatever one might make of Neurath's views on sociology (1931a) and economics (1935a), it is clear that they reflect his close familiarity with and partial involvement in the methodological debates in the social sciences in the late nineteenth and early twentieth centuries.[11] And though Zilsel did not publish on his large project of the socio-economic roots of modern science until later, already during his association with the Vienna Circle he published on the socio-economic roots of the ideal of the individualistic genius (1926) and on the distinctive nature of the concept of tradition for history and sociology in opposition to biology (1931). (There seems to exist no complement to these social scientific outputs in the Berlin Society.)[12]

So the stereotype of armchair-philosophers regimenting the variety of the sciences by the imposition of a priori determinations does not apply to the early phase of the logical empiricist movement. However relentless especially Neurath's pursuit of the ideal of the unity of science may appear, it must be noted that his conception of it (1935b) was remarkably liberal in forsaking (like his conception of physicalism) the reductionism that is often associated with it and nowadays gives cause for its rejection.[13] It was the early logical empiricists' familiarity with the sciences of their day that prompted their clear recognition of the need for posits or conventions in theory-building and of the holistic nature of theory-testing. Even though the solutions which the early logical empiricists offered to the problems that arise from such a position may no longer be acceptable, it is simply false to claim that they were not even aware of them: many of the problems that contemporary philosophy of science still struggles with were first confronted by the logical empiricists. For example, already in the Vienna Circle's protocol sentence debate Neurath problematized the notion of observation on which empirical science was built (1932a, 1932b) and around the close of that debate Carnap first unveiled the doctrine of the linguistic incommensurability between scientific successor theories (1936). In Berlin meanwhile, Reichenbach pressed relentlessly for the thorough probabilization of all knowledge claims (1931).[14]

16.4 AYER'S PHENOMENALIST REDUX

Recognition of the variety and relative vitality of early logical empiricism prompts the question to what the current one-dimensional picture of its practitioners as rabid reductionists

[11] For details, see Uebel (2004).

[12] The later Frank returned to the investigation of extra-theoretical determinants of theory choice previously explored by Neurath; see Uebel (2000).

[13] That reductionism was still affirmed in Oppenheim and Putnam (1958).

[14] Probability theory came increasingly to the fore as a subject in later years, but had always been a main topic for Reichenbach (1916, 1935) and already a large part of the 1929 Prague Conference on the Epistemology of the Exact Sciences was dedicated to it (see *Erkenntnis* 1 (1930/31, 158–287). For a detailed analysis of the Viennese protocol sentence debate see Uebel (2007).

and simplistic foundationalists may be owed. Part of the rather complex reason for this must lie in the plain fact that caricatures work best for pedagogical as well as for propagandistic purposes: where quick instruction or sharp self-definition are the issue, differentiation only gets in the way. (The latter motive appears to have played a significant role in the so-called positivism dispute in 1960s German sociology which set the pattern of response for self-styled 'critical theorists' everywhere ever since.)[15] Another part surely lies in aspects of the reception of particularly the Vienna Circle in the English-speaking world before the Second World War. Two widely read books can be charged with having played a pivotal role in this respect, especially so since they were fully supportive of 'logical positivism' and/or 'logical empiricism'.

The first of these is A. J. Ayer's *Language, Truth and Logic* (1936). Slim, breezily written, and cheerfully controversial, it proved a remarkable publication success.[16] Given the relative paucity of publications in English by logical empiricists up to that date—what little there was mostly appeared in specialist journals[17]—Ayer very much helped to set the scene for them in the Anglophone world, especially Britain.[18] (Susan Stebbing's explorative British Academy lecture [1933] was directed to the cognoscenti only and Julius Weinberg's scholarly and critical volume [1936] attracted considerably less attention.) Liberally citing writings by members of the Vienna Circle and occasionally engaging critically with some of their pronouncements, Ayer spoke with some authority.[19] The philosophical views he presented, however, owed more to the tradition of British empiricism than to the Vienna Circle. 'Logical positivism', he once stated, 'is a blending of the extreme empiricism of Hume with the modern logical techniques developed by people like Bertrand Russell.'[20] Taking Ayer as a guide to the views of early logical empiricism in general and the Vienna Circle in particular thus results in significant distortions.

The differences that matter pertain not so much to the detail of the doctrines that Ayer defended as to his overall perspective. Consider first the means by which the elimination

---

[15] See Adorno *et al.* (1969) for the original documentation, Dahms (1994) for a thorough analysis.

[16] Published in January 1936, the book went through three impressions in the year of publication alone—albeit none 'exceeded five hundred copies' (Ayer 1992a, 18)—saw another one before the war, and appeared in a second edition in 1946, with frequent higher volume reprintings since.

[17] The exceptions were Carnap (1934) and (1935).

[18] In the United States, logical empiricism did not receive a book-length treatment until Reichenbach (1938). Previously the *Journal of Philosophy* featured reports on and overviews of the movement by Hook (1930), Blumberg and Feigl (1931), Nagel (1936), and Reichenbach (1936).

[19] He had attended meetings of the Vienna Circle between December 1932 and April 1933 but did not say so in the book. Reichenbach is not mentioned once.

[20] Magee (1971, 68). See also the discussion in Hung (1992) and Ayer's reply conceding that his outlook was 'closer to that of the Cambridge School of Analysis than that of the Vienna Circle' (1992b, 301) as well as his admission that *Language, Truth and Logic* was 'no more than Hume in modern dress' (1987, 24). It is questionable, therefore, whether it is correct to speak of the 'brilliant advocacy' which the Vienna Circle's 'leading ideas' received from Ayer, as the editors of a collection of essays commemorating the 50th anniversary of *Language, Truth and Logic* still did (Macdonald and Wright 1986a, 1). Failure to distinguish the logical positivisms at issue persists, however, and allows a recent two-volume history of analytic philosophy to deal exclusively with Ayer's volume (but for two short footnotes) when discussing 'logical positivism' (Soames 2003).

of metaphysics was to be effected. As always, the principle of verification placed a premium on observability, but with Ayer this notion turns on his version of phenomenalism according to which 'sense-contents' are neither mental nor physical but instead are what all mental and physical objects are 'logical constructions' of (1936 [1946, 123]). To be sure, while no one in the Vienna Circle embraced the neutral monism of Mach, it is the case that Carnap's *Aufbau* of 1928 was erected on a phenomenalist base. Moreover, around 1930 many members endorsed a psychologized version of the *Tractatus* (following Wittgenstein's suggestions in conversation) according to which the states of affairs pictured by elementary propositions concerned phenomenal experiences.[21] But that was by no means a settled view but merely the starting point for one of several phases of a long and complex debate in the Vienna Circle about the content, the form, and the epistemological status of the evidence statements for science (the so-called protocol sentence debate). Ayer's position entailed that these ultimate evidence statements spoke of sense-contents 'private to single self' (1936 [1946, 128]). All talk of material objects and other people was to be reduced to or 'translatable into' (1936 [1946, 123]) talk about these sense-contents. Ayer did not, however, ascribe to these basic statements the property of certainty, for 'any description of the content of any sense-experience is an empirical hypothesis of whose validity there can be no guarantee' (1936 [1946, 121]). Moreover, at this time Ayer was something of an epistemological holist.[22]

Ayer's position was original—and short-lived[23]—in that it matched none of those taken in the Viennese debate, for it married holistic fallibilism with phenomenalism. The question arises whether this phenomenalism is a good guide to the Vienna Circle's philosophies. One may wonder, for instance, what definition of 'metaphysics' is entailed by Ayer's assertion 'that in order to avoid metaphysics we are obliged to adopt a phenomenalist standpoint' (1936 [1946, 121]): apparently what's metaphysical is whatever resists his form of empiricism. This clearly was not Carnap's understanding of the matter even though Ayer took his *Aufbau* (1928) as the blueprint for his own reduction.[24] (For Carnap, the basic experiences were not more real than the objects constituted thereof.) But it is even more uncharacteristic of Vienna Circle views to base the idea of the unity of science on the contention that 'all empirical hypotheses refer ultimately to our sense-contents' (1936 [1946, 151]). Ayer's reductive phenomenalism represents a position that by 1935 none of the major participants in the Viennese protocol sentence debate held to.[25]

---

[21] Ayer independently had adopted the same reading; see his (1987, 25).

[22] He held that 'the "facts of experience" can never compel us to abandon a hypothesis' (1936 [1946, 95]).

[23] Already soon after in his (1936/7 [1959, 243]) he granted 'basic propositions' Moorean 'incorrigibility' such that only errors of linguistic classification are possible. This position was retained, now speaking of indubitability except for the possibility of verbal error, in (1940 [1969, 82–4]) and (1950, 72); see also (1956, 66–8).

[24] See Ayer (1936 [1946, 130n.]). In retrospect Ayer held that Carnap 'somewhat disingeniously' chose the term 'methodological solipsism' for his procedure in the *Aufbau* (1992a, 16).

[25] Ayer refers to some major papers from that debate in footnotes at (1936 [1946, 90–1]).

Second, consider Ayer's thesis of the 'apodeictic certainty of logic and mathematics' (1936 [1946, 85]). As regards mathematics, this represents a straight contradiction of assertions by the two leading mathematicians of the Vienna Circle, Hans Hahn and Karl Menger. In an essay cited by Ayer, Menger clearly stated that 'mathematics has no safeguard against the occurrence of contradictions' (1933 [1979, 41]).[26] Logical certainty was not to be had in mathematics either. As regards logic, Ayer's claim fails to incorporate the central lesson of Carnap's *Logical Syntax*: logical pluralism. Contrary to Ayer's claim (1936 [1946, 81]), we can never tell of an isolated logical principle whether it is valid or not, only of a system of such principles. Even if analyticity is defined as a proposition's 'validity depend[ing] solely on the definitions of the symbols which it contains' (1936 [1946, 78]), we can never tell of a proposition that it is analytic or not in the absence of knowing which logical principles hold. Whatever else may be said of Ayer's account of a priori knowledge, it fails to give any indication of the relativity of all proofs of non-contradiction and of the relativity of analyticity to particular logical frameworks.[27] Ayer tautologized what used to be called 'truths of reason' but, since he failed to relativize them, their unconditionality remained unchallenged.

These differences matter because two doctrines that are recognizably logical positivist of sorts, the verificationist rejection of metaphysics and the analyticity of mathematics, were given a philosophical slant by Ayer that they did not have in early logical empiricism generally. With Ayer, they became the central pillars of an empiricism that remained remarkably traditionalist in its conception of experience and reason. But not only is it the case that Ayer's logical positivism presented a reductionist phenomenalism and conception of analyticity that leading members of the Vienna Circle by then had already successfully left behind.[28] What is perhaps most remarkable is that his thoroughly British empiricism remained wholly unresponsive to the worry that animated the one early Vienna Circle work that his epistemology closely resembled in some other respects, Carnap's *Aufbau*. Ayer's inadequate response to the worries previously expressed by Susan Stebbing that phenomenalism leads to solipsism contrasts sharply with Carnap's explicit concern to attain objectivity in the face of his purely subjective starting point by requiring the thoroughgoing transformation of all empirical statements into pure structure descriptions.[29] While Carnap did not succeed, he

---

[26] Hahn likewise declared that 'an absolute proof of freedom from contradiction is probably unattainable; every such proof is relative' and that 'in every field of thought, the demand for absolute certainty of knowledge is an exaggerated demand: in no field is such certainty attainable' (1934 [1980, 121]).

[27] Since Ayer thought he could dispense with the logicist reduction and derive the certainty of mathematical knowledge from its analyticity as following from definitions (1936 [1946, 82]), the latter argument also applies to his account of mathematical knowledge.

[28] His later concern with scepticism still further distanced him from them.

[29] Compare Carnap (1928, § 16) with Ayer (1936 [1946, 128–30]); for forthright criticism of what she took to be the position shared by Wittgenstein, Schlick, and Carnap, see Stebbing (1933, 70–9). Later Ayer admitted the inadequacy: 'What I had done was to conjoin a mentalistic account of statements made in the first person with a physicalistic or behavioural account of statements made in the second

did at least recognize that reducing other minds to physical behaviour and then to sense-data alone did not solve the problem. In sum, Ayer's logical positivism did not only represent (despite his short-lived anti-foundationalism) a relapse into a very early and already long discarded phenomenalist form of logical empiricism, but also a falsifying simplification since the central problem at the heart of empiricism was not recognized at all.

16.5 REICHENBACH AND THE VIENNA CIRCLE

Reichenbach's influential *Experience and Prediction* also presented Vienna Circle philosophy as a reductionist phenomenalist enterprise and so also focused attention only on one of its earliest phases of development. Unlike Ayer, however, Reichenbach did so in order to draw a sharp contrast between his own and the Viennese philosophy. This was also not without consequences, for unlike Carnap whose most famous self-styled disciple owed a considerable part of his fame to arguing against him, Reichenbach inspired fierce loyalty to his perspective among his American students. This extends in the present day to upholding the sharp distinction that Reichenbach first drew in the middle and later 1930s between the 'logical positivism' of the Vienna Circle and the 'logical empiricism' of the Berlin Society.[30] The former was identified with the phenomenalist foundationalism and anti-realism often associated with Carnap's *Aufbau* (and Mach before him), whereas the latter was represented by Reichenbach's own inductivist probabilism and realism.[31]

There certainly existed a fault line between the philosophies emerging from the Vienna Circle and the Berlin Society, but it is doubtful whether this amounts to the distinction between phenomenalist positivism and empirical realism that it is advertised as. To begin with, already by the time Reichenbach drew the distinction, no one in the Circle any longer held to the views Reichenbach ascribed to them. (Even Schlick, who still insisted on retaining a significant function for the phenomenal given, happily conceded the fallibilism of scientific protocol statements.)[32] Secondly, even when a certain foundationalist mood temporarily held sway (*ca.* 1930) it was never the case that all members of the Circle fell under it. (Neurath always presented a vigorous if sometimes

or third.…if the ascription of conscious states to others, on a par with my ascription to myself, was unintelligible to me, I could not intelligibly affirm that they ascribed them to themselves' (1987, 30–1). That's of course just where the purely 'methodological' nature of Carnap's phenomenalism makes a difference.

[30] See Reichenbach (1936) and (1938); compare Salmon (1985) and Rescher (2006).

[31] It is notable that already Reichenbach's (rather late) review of Carnap's *Aufbau* ascribed to it the desire to establish 'an epistemological basis of maximum certainty' (1933 [1978, 407]), whereas certainty was not a concern for Carnap.

[32] 'Thus *all* propositions occurring in the sciences have the character of hypotheses' (Schlick 1935 [1979b, 406, orig. emphasis]).

unpersuasive opposition.)[33] Thirdly, though the name 'logical positivism' was coined by a Circle member for propagandistic purposes in America, it failed to gain universal acceptance back in Vienna where Neurath was already championing the name 'logical empiricism'.[34] Fourthly, even though the Vienna Circle can also call on the Austrian tradition for genealogical purposes, it is by no means the case that the philosophy emerging from the Berlin Society was more strongly rooted in mainstream German philosophy: not only the young Reichenbach but also the early Carnap were deeply influenced by neo-Kantian ideas (as was, to a lesser degree, Schlick). The anti-Kantian radicalism of both groups was not a function of their ignorance of 'critical philosophy'.[35] Then there is the close (though not always friction-free) cooperation between the two groups in organizing the two conferences on the 'epistemology of the exact sciences' (Prague 1929, Königsberg 1930) and in the running of the journal *Erkenntnis* from 1930 until its publication ceased in 1939. Finally, there is the rather fluid movement of C. G. Hempel between the two groups already as a student of Reichenbach, later as close associate of Carnap.

Wherein then did the fault lines between these groups lie? Besides differences in emphasis on different subject matters (where Carnap pursued philosophy of logic and mathematics, Reichenbach pursued philosophy of physics) and differences of orientation in shared areas of interest (Reichenbach's frequentist interpretation of probability compared to Carnap's logical one), the difference lies mainly in metaphilosophical matters. Whereas many (though not all) members of the Vienna Circle revelled in declaring a revolutionary break between them and the philosophical tradition (some like Neurath even abjuring the term 'philosophy'), members of the Berlin Society, particularly Reichenbach himself (but not Dubislav), were more concerned to retain traditional affiliations, both institutionally and doctrinally.

A striking instance is provided by the difference between Carnap's 'logic of science' and Reichenbach's 'analysis of science'. Whereas Reichenbach allowed into the analysis of science not only the problems of logic and probability theory but also 'all the basic problems of traditional epistemology' (1938 [2006, 8]), Carnap stressed that to designate his logic of science as 'theory of knowledge (or epistemology)' is 'not quite unobjectionable, since it misleadingly suggests a resemblance between the problems of our logic of science and the problems of traditional epistemology; the latter, however, are always permeated by pseudo-concepts and pseudo-questions, and frequently in such a way that their disentanglement is impossible' (1934 [1937, 280]). Thus when Carnap declared that 'the logic of science takes the place of the inextricable tangle of problems which is known as philosophy' (1934 [1937, 279]), he also announced a much sharper break between traditional philosophy and his logic of science than did Reichenbach for his analysis of science. Scepticism, be it about the external world generally or specifically about induction, was not an issue that stirred most members of the Circle (Feigl was an

---

[33] See Uebel (2007, chs. 4, 6–9).

[34] See Blumberg and Feigl (1931) and Neurath (1931b [1983, 52]).

[35] As has sometimes been suggested or implied, e.g. by Popper (1974, 82–3).

exception). Carnap's post-1932 position, moreover, was not an anti-realism towards theoretical entities that directly contradicted Reichenbach in the usual fashion, but a position that opposed both realism and anti-realism: it theoreticized the given as much as it instrumentalized the theoretical and withheld categorial existence claims from both.[36]

These differences, though significant, are not fruitfully conceptualized along the positivism–realism divide. They indicate rather differences about what needs explaining by philosophy or, better, how such philosophical explanations are to proceed. If naturalism were not associated with the denial of the distinctions between analytic and synthetic statements and a posteriori and a priori knowledge and a robust materialism, it would come more naturally than it now does to ascribe to the Vienna Circle—or rather to its left wing in particular—a naturalistic attitude. For them, explaining objective knowledge consisted in showing its actuality from within by spelling out the logico-linguistic workings of scientific reason in getting and building on empirical evidence and investigating the notion and nature of evidence itself. It did not consist in rendering plausible claims to such actuality by means of disarming traditional sceptical doubts—even less, of course, did it consist in establishing the possibility of objective knowledge from without by transcendental arguments. Put differently, for Reichenbach 'scientific philosophy' was still primarily philosophy, a philosophy that emulated scientific ideals, whereas for theorists of the Circle it had become a form of science itself, a metatheory that aimed to sort out conceptual and methodological issues of first-order science by formal and empirical means.

Another distinguishing term here is 'and'. Consider the use both parties made of something like the distinction between the contexts of discovery and justification.[37] Reichenbach introduced it under this name—previously Carnap had distinguished logically perspicuous 'rational reconstructions' from psychologically realistic descriptions of cognitive processes (1928, § 100)—by way of two distinctions. First, that between matters 'internal' and 'external' to the domain of knowledge: philosophy of science was only concerned with the former in that 'epistemology concerns the internal structure of knowledge and not the external features which appear to an observer who takes no notice of its content' (1938 [2006, 4]). This excluded sociology. Reichenbach then added 'a second distinction which concerns psychology' (1938 [2006, 4]). Thereby he excluded concerns with how a given knowledge claim was actually arrived at from what would in principle justify it. Reichenbach's context distinction thus separated sociological and psychological questions as of merely causal import from any concern with the normative standing of knowledge claims such that the former could not possibly have a bearing on the latter. In effect Reichenbach's understanding of the context distinction de-contextualized the knowledge claims it investigated and the justifications it provided by focusing purely on logical relations of evidential support between propositions. (In this respect, Reichenbach's analysis of science resembled Carnap's logic of science.) But by no means all in the Vienna Circle understood the distinction of the contexts in this way

[36] For a mature expression of this position see Carnap (1950a).
[37] On the long history of the family of related distinctions, see Hoyningen-Huene (1987).

even though they accepted the need to separate descriptive from normative concerns: Frank and Neurath were much concerned with social determinants of theory choice.[38] Most importantly, perhaps, Carnap's own exclusion of concerns with social influences or institutional practices was only a function of the division of labour: he worked on the formal logic of science, but colleagues working on the empirically informed 'pragmatics of science' were free to provide what are in effect rational reconstructions of institutional scientific practices (like Neurath's proposal for protocol statements as rule-governed testimonies [1932b]) alongside his own. Reichenbach's understanding of the context distinction, by contrast, precludes the quasi-naturalization of philosophical concerns in the form of a bipartite metatheory for science as it was being developed on the left wing of the Vienna Circle (namely as comprehending both logical and empirical investigations of first-order theories).

In sum, like Ayer's, Reichenbach's portrayal of Vienna Circle philosophy as phenomenalist foundationalism conjoined with certain aspects of his own version of early logical empiricism effectively obscured a radically new form of philosophy taking shape within the Vienna Circle. What was obscured was different in each case, however. While Ayer's traditionalism neglected the new conception of analyticity that was being developed, Reichenbach failed to give recognition to the development of a deflationary and multidisciplinary conception of philosophy as metatheory.

16.6 INSIDE THE VIENNA CIRCLE: TOWARDS OBJECTIVITY WITHOUT METAPHYSICS

Let's explore some aspects of the Circle's non-realist version of early logical empiricism. The first point to note here is one of principled agreement with Reichenbach (and only temporarily with Ayer). Central among the philosophical preconceptions of the nature of knowledge that had to be abandoned if one wanted to do justice to the then latest advances in the empirical and the formal sciences was the criterion of certainty (which Russell had still accepted in the 1910s). Early logical empiricism had no ambition of replacing the lost certainties of pure reason by claims built on the certainties of sense experience. It is a striking misreading of Carnap's *Aufbau*, for example, to read it as the most thorough attempt ever at the realization of the old empiricist programme of placing science on the secure basis of sense experience.[39] To be sure, Carnap's genealogy of scientific concepts pursued a strategy of phenomenalist reductionism, but it did so only for the purpose of illustrating the use of the particular method—the employment of

---

[38] See n. 12 above.

[39] Reichenbach did so repeatedly: see his (1933 [1978, 407]) and (1936, 149). In *Experience and Prediction* he claimed more obliquely that 'it was the intention of modern positivism to restore knowledge to absolute certainty' (1938 [2006, 344]).

definite structure descriptions (ultimately quasi-analysis)—by means of which Carnap sought to pursue his real goal. That was to show how science can attain to objectivity even though the sense experiences upon which it builds are ineluctably private and ultimately non-communicable. It is perhaps one of the most significant but also most unrecognized features of early logical empiricism that some of its representatives explored to breaking point the then extant conceptions of objectivity and then moved beyond them. Ultimately, the winning idea was to recast objectivity itself as testable intersubjectivity. That insight, however, proved to be difficult to formulate correctly. A look at some stations of the Vienna Circle's protocol sentence debate can shed light on some of the complexities involved.

The traditional conception of the objectivity of knowledge may be dubbed 'the view from nowhere'.[40] This conception employed a correspondence theory of truth such that objective knowledge portrayed matters as they were 'in themselves' with no addition or distortion whatsoever. Kant took steps away from this correspondence conception of objectivity by delineating the conditions of its possibility in the a priori forms of pure intuition and pure reason. Conformity to these forms, held to be necessary for all human cognition, was a precondition for objective knowledge: their employment makes objective knowledge possible, their correct employment on a given occasion makes it actual. The price of grounding objectivity in this way was the unknowability of noumena (things-in-themselves) and the restriction of human knowledge to mere phenomena. Logical empiricism dropped the noumena as metaphysical phantoms, but some of its early theorists engaged with Kant's conception all the same: Schlick and Carnap stripped Kant's conditions of their apodicity but retained the idea that objectivity rests in the form of cognition alone. Their key idea was that only the form or structure of the known was communicable, whereas subjective qualitative content was not. What led to difficulties, however, was how the form of the known was here conceptualized.

Carnap's answer in the *Aufbau* to the question of what allowed science its objectivity was that it uses essentially only structure descriptions (definite and indefinite, as required) that are communicable and therefore intersubjectively testable (1928, § 16). (All non-structural purely qualitative descriptions were held to be eliminable.) Given the empiricist starting point, objectivity was to be safeguarded by the possibility to describe the given in purely formal terms (by way of the method of 'quasi-analysis') and establishing that all the concepts of empirical science could be 'rationally reconstructed' step by step on the basis of just one basic relation, remembered similarity, holding between as yet unanalysed experiential wholes. All non-basic concepts were defined by reduction chains featuring only the basic relation concept in various logical permutations and so were purely structurally defined relative to it. But what about the basic concept itself? Carnap was unable to define it structurally further than up to isomorphism. This meant, of course, that he was unable to single out one and only one such relation as a definite description should. To complete his structuralist project, Carnap required that

---

[40] The phrase is taken from Thomas Nagel (1986), but it aptly describes what Bernard Williams called 'the absolute conception of knowledge' and ascribed to Descartes (1978). For discussion see Fine (1998).

the second-order concept 'founded relation extensions' (which applied to the relation of remembered similarity), a concept which made reference to empirical conditions, be counted a logical one. The idea was to save both the generality and the uniqueness of his reconstruction by insisting that the theory is true over every domain which is 'founded' (presuming that there is only one such founded domain). Given that mathematical logic as we know it does not contain this concept, Carnap himself had to note that this constituted 'an unresolved problem' (1928, § 155). Recent commentators tend to agree that his structuralist project unravels at just this point—at least as he conceived of it at the time.[41]

But suppose that Carnap's quasi-analysis, somewhat updated and improved, could overcome the problems with which it has been charged, among them the problem just reviewed.[42] This would show that there exists a way of describing the given in purely formal terms such that out of its basic relation(s) all scientific concepts, including those for the physical world, other minds, and cultural objects, can be constructed and that it is possible, for different subjects, using those rules of concept construction, to create an intersubjective world, i.e. that their representation of the world is mirrored in the representation of the world by others. What this would show is that it is possible in principle for a science that refers to the given as the final court of adjudication to be objective, but it would not show that our science is (for our science does not refer to the phenomenal given under any description). There is no reason to believe that our everyday discourse about physical objects is understood only because its statements are amenable to a phenomenalistic reconstruction. This kind of reconstruction is wholly optional and as such, naturalistically speaking, idle. The in-principle objectivity of a constitution system built on the given does not underwrite our science—that is the price of de-transcendentalizing the thesis that objectivity rests in the form of our cognition

Now consider Schlick. Having replaced the traditional correspondence theory of truth already in his habilitation dissertation by the idea that truth consisted in unique one-to-one coordination of judgements and facts (1910), Schlick motivated the idea that objectivity consisted in the formal nature of cognition by drawing a sharp distinction between experience (*Erleben*) and cognition (*Erkennen*) (1918, § 11/1925, § 12, 1927). Just as the objects of cognition were of a structural nature (the hanging together of facts as reflected in interrelated judgements), so cognition itself depended on vehicles whose structure was intersubjectively discernible (like public signs or speech), whereas experience was of and depended on uncommunicable subjective qualities. In his London lectures 'Form and Content' (1932–8) Schlick explored this long-held thesis of the purely structural nature of all communicable meaning in the Tractarian idiom where meaning consisted in the isomorphism of the logical structure of proposition and fact and truth consisted in the correspondence of the logical structure of the proposition expressed with that of the fact which it sought to designate. Now it was the logical structures of

---

[41] See, e.g., Friedman (1987) and (1992) and Richardson (1998, 89).

[42] On refashioning the *Aufbau* project with contemporary means, see Mormann (2004) and (2009) and Leitgeb (2011).

individual propositions that constituted the forms that were the objects of knowledge. Schlick's trouble arose with the analysis of the process of verification. His own earlier holism required (unique) coordination between networks of judgements and facts; Tractarian atomism, however, required coordination between individual propositions and facts. How can it be determined that such a structural correspondence between the logical form of a proposition and that of fact obtains?

According to the Tractarian scheme, the structure of molecular propositions was revealed by their reduction to the atomic propositions out of which they were truth-functionally composed, yet how were we to determine the logical structure of facts? Schlick's answer was that that was not necessary.[43] Verification was effected on the elementary level at which concepts were defined by ostensive reference to elements of the given. Given knowledge of their meaning, the correspondence of elementary propositions with atomic facts was easily established, he claimed. Unlike Carnap, however, Schlick gave no indication of how the reduction of molecular to atomic propositions and of complex to primitive concepts was to be accomplished. His Tractarian belief that the logical structure which true propositions shared with the facts they pictured could not itself be described by language (on pain of self-referential paradoxes, this form could only 'show' itself) disallowed further questions. (Presumably, even examples like 'red here now' served at best as illustrative proxies.) Whatever other problems beset Schlick's conception of verification, this alone left the matter utterly mysterious and rendered unconvincing his rescue of objectivity by logical form.

What went wrong? It fell to Neurath to argue that Carnap and Schlick looked for the relevant notion of form in the wrong places. The form of the given was ultimately as intersubjectively inaccessible as its content. Both Carnap's and Schlick's accounts were rational reconstructions without any claim on scientific practice. One had to attend to intersubjectively discernible forms of the vehicles of actual scientific communication. Put differently, confronting the problem of objectivity required that empiricists began to think of experience in new and different ways: not primarily as something essentially private in nature but as something mostly about public states of affairs. In still other words, empiricists had to stop worrying about what experience is in order to concentrate on what experience is of and to stop expecting that what experience is of be neatly reflected in what is private about experience. This ultimately was the point of Neurath's early and pre-Wittgensteinian use of a private language argument. By means of it he motivated his advocacy of statements of the everyday language of physical objects as basic and his rejection of even only methodological phenomenalisms.[44]

Unlike Schlick who insisted on the unchallengeable authority of the individual subject over the given as the cornerstone of empiricism, Carnap did, after considerable hesitation, follow Neurath into the consistently physicalist camp. Even so, they still ended up with different conceptions. For both the objectivity of science was guaranteed by the intersubjective

---

[43] That was just as well, for he would have been unable to solve the mystery by defining facts as true propositions since the definition of truth is at issue.

[44] See Uebel (2007, chs. 6–8).

confirmability of its statements. Yet while for Carnap this rested on the direct intersubjective testability of the predicates of its evidence statements (where only intersubjectively observable predicates were allowed), for Neurath this rested on a set of procedures establishing the acceptability of scientific testimony (of evidence statements which were allowed to employ predicates that were only intersubjectively confirmable but not intersubjectively observable).[45] Schlick meanwhile remained caught in the unhappy dilemma of admitting the fallibility of scientific evidence statements while insisting on the foundational status of his certain and phenomenal 'affirmations'. Once again, the point and purpose of the latter remained deeply mysterious (unless it be thought that Schlick sought to use them to ground the objectivity of science still more deeply than in its surface evidence).

What can be seen from this brief review of some stations of the Vienna Circle's protocol sentence debate is that far from promulgating foundationalist doctrines, its main theorists were concerned to develop conceptions of objectivity that confronted the Kantian challenge to empiricism and that some of them attempted to ground objectivity in intersubjective scientific discourse. Their lesson was to complete the moves towards a tenable conception of objectivity that had been taken so far. Beyond the moves from qualitative correspondence between knowledge and the known as characteristic of objectivity to the apodictic pure forms of intuition and reason as grounds of the possibility of objectivity, and beyond the move from there to characterizing objectivity as the correspondence of the logical form of true statement and fact, another move was required to find a stable non-metaphysical position: precisely that of locating objectivity squarely in the conditions of intersubjective scientific discourse. Whatever one may think of the details of their proposals—or of their treatment of specific aspects of scientific theories more generally, or indeed of the entire relation between theory and experimental practice—it should be conceded that on this very point of locating objectivity in testable intersubjectivity these early logical empiricists have not been bettered to this day.[46]

16.7 ON THE LEFT WING OF THE VIENNA CIRCLE

It should also be readily intelligible now why Carnap divided the Circle into separate wings (1963, 57) and on which of them the most striking pioneering efforts towards philosophical deflationism are to be sought.

---

[45] For the analysis of Neurath's proposal for so-called protocol sentences, see Uebel (2009). For the difference between Neurath's and Carnap's proposals from the latter's perspective, see the discussion in Carnap (1936–7, 9–14). Importantly, Neurath's relaxed condition allowed for first-person mental state ascriptions in the evidence base of social scientific discourse.

[46] Note that the radically new conception of objectivity that Daston and Galison (2007, 382–415) see emerging in the nano-sciences seems limited in its applicability to precisely these nano-domains.

But why, it might be asked, distinguish just two wings? Given the differences between Carnap's and Neurath's physicalisms and their difference from Schlick's position, it is clear that three different positions were defended in the Vienna Circle's protocol sentence debate which (like also Reichenbach's realist Berlin variant) reflected different conceptions of the new philosophy of science. Roughly, in competition were Schlick's Wittgenstein-inspired non-formal activity of determining the meaning of scientific discourse, Carnap's reconstructive formalist logic of science, and Neurath's naturalist-pragmatist interdisciplinary empirical investigations of science. What combined Carnap and Neurath (after the former's conversion to physicalism without methodological solipsism) into one (not always fully harmonious) wing (which included also Frank and, until his untimely death, Hahn) was not only that they occupied positions that were increasingly critical of Wittgenstein's *Tractatus*-views as adhered to by the Schlick–Waismann wing, but also that, at least on a certain level of abstraction, Carnap's formalist logic of science and Neurath's and Frank's empirical pragmatics of science were readily combinable.

First, what did their opposition to Wittgenstein amount to? While Carnap's opposition was couched in technical disagreements with Wittgenstein's Tractarian philosophy of logic and language—ultimately he rejected the conception of a universal logic underlying all languages and the alleged impossibility of metalinguistic discourse—Neurath's was expressed bluntly: he objected to its metaphysics of correspondence. Neurath's objection focused first on how the process of verification was conceived of in the psychologized version of logical atomism that around 1930 even Carnap appears to have subscribed to temporarily but gradually abandoned again, starting with his rejection of strict verificationism in 1931. By late 1932, when Carnap also had abandoned methodological solispsism for practical reconstructive purposes and first embraced the Principle of Tolerance (the recognition of the legitimacy of logical pluralism and freedom in linguistic reconstruction),[47] his conversion to Neurath's opposition to correspondence truth was complete. It was this opposition that most strongly united the left wing in the 1930s (having long been shared by Frank and Hahn)—just as Neurath's failure to appreciate Carnap's disquotational approach to semantics split it during their later years in exile.[48]

With their opposition to correspondence truth came a conception of the office of philosophy that differed from Schlick's of making clear what our statements really mean. This conception was no less language-oriented but considerably less beholden to the idea that at least in language there were essence-like things for the philosopher to uncover. Instead, what philosophers like Carnap did was to make proposals for speaking about phenomena in certain ways. (In later years Carnap called such proposals

---

[47] 'Everyone is at liberty to build up his own logic, i.e. his own form of language, as he wishes. All that is required of him is that, if he wishes to discuss it, he must state his methods clearly and give syntactical rules instead of philosophical arguments' (Carnap 1934/1937, § 17). Not yet so called this principle was invoked with regard to protocol languages already in Carnap (1932).

[48] See Mancosu (2008) for details of the unfortunate Neurath–Carnap dispute about semantics.

'explications.')[49] Making proposals for reconceptualizations of certain phenomena is not the same as revising views of what these things really are. The former is not just a more careful and non-committal version of the latter. Whereas claims about what and how things really are engage in metaphysics (however much rooted in the ontological commitments of favoured scientific theories), claims about how it would be helpful to think about certain phenomena abstain from it (being both guided and limited by pragmatic criteria). Significantly, the two kinds of logico-linguistic and procedural proposals are evaluated not for their truth but for their utility in rendering problems amenable. (Carnap's characterization of empiricism in 'Testability and Meaning' [1936-7, 33-35] and Neurath's proposal for protocol sentences [1932b], respectively, may serve as examples.).

Second, note that another distinctive doctrine of the left wing appears to have been the shared understanding, rarely made explicit, of the nature of the second-order inquiry that philosophy had become. Already in 1932 Neurath had sharpened an earlier claim of the manifesto to state that 'within a consistent physicalism there can be no "theory of knowledge", at least not in the traditional form. It could only consist in defense actions against metaphysics, i.e. unmasking meaningless terms. Some problems of the theory of knowledge will perhaps be transformable into empirical questions so that they can find a place within unified science' (1932a [1983, 67]).[50] Two tasks were here assigned to whatever was to be philosophy's successor discipline and both represented different aspects of the higher-order theory of science comprised of logical inquires as well as empirical ones. From late 1932 onwards, Carnap saw the logic of science as replacing traditional philosophy because its methods of inquiry remained the same: empirical concerns did not play into the exploration of the consistency of various logics and of the expressive power of various logico-linguistic frameworks. What Carnap added to Neurath's 'defensive' task for the logic of science was his conventionalist constructivism concerning alternative frameworks. This was a widening of the scope of the logical part of metatheory that Neurath accepted. That Carnap's position in turn did not banish all naturalistic concerns from metatheory is made clear by his remark that the logic of science is itself but part of a still more comprehensive inquiry, the 'theory of science', which comprises also 'empirical investigation of scientific activity', namely, 'historical, sociological and, above all, psychological inquiries' (1934 [1937, § 72]). It is precisely this empirical field of investigation that Neurath differentiated from the logic of science as 'the behavioristics of scholars' in which he located his own concerns with protocol statements (1936b [1983, 169]) and that Philipp Frank later called the 'pragmatics of science' (1957 [2004, 360]) and in which he investigated external determinants of theory choice. So both Carnap and Neurath (and Frank) recognized the need for both logical and empirical branches of scientific metatheory, but they pursued their own detailed work in different branches.

---

[49] See Carnap (1950b, §§ 3-5) and Carus (2007) and Creath (2009) for discussion.
[50] Compare Carnap, Hahn, and Neurath (1929 [1973, 306]).

Carnap's and Neurath's considered proposals concerning protocols reflect this. As noted, for Neurath, protocols were complex statements containing repeated embeddings of clauses meant to indicate different sets of conditions which the acceptance of scientific observation reports is subject to. By treating protocol statements as testimony whose acceptance is circumscribed in particular ways, Neurath moved away from any concern one might have—and Schlick did have (1934)—about the 'foundation of knowledge' in one's own first-hand experience. First-person authority was, if not wholly undermined, then radically subverted: in principle, one's own protocol carried no more weight than another's. Carnap likewise was no longer concerned with personal beliefs but knowledge claims and their objective evidence. Where Neurath sought to outline canons of report acceptance, Carnap's work concentrated on isolating the logical relations of deductive and inductive support that protocols afforded to more theoretical statements. Yet note that despite their different tasks, both accounts of protocols can readily be combined: Carnap's preferred protocol statements form a proper part of Neurath's (i.e. their inner-most clause). The seeming tension between the formalist logic of science and the more naturalistic pragmatics of science thus finds a resolution in the conception of philosophy's successor discipline as bipartite metatheory here ascribed to the left wing.[51]

Now whatever its virtues in embracing the potential of both purely logical and multi-disciplinary empirical inquiries for improving our understanding of science, it is clear that certain traditional questions—like scepticism and the realism/anti-realism issue—remain outside the reach of this bipartite conception of philosophy of science. To call certain Vienna Circle theorists 'philosophical deflationists' does not merely redescribe their well-known opposition to metaphysics, therefore, but also draws attention to the explicationist bent of their metatheory. Rather than render the veil of transcendent reality, they sought to provide tools for managing manifest phenomena: in principle, no job was too small for these conceptual handymen.

Just as scientific realists may look to Reichenbach as a pioneering thinker, so philosophical deflationists may cite the left Vienna Circle as pioneers of their approach to philosophy of science. Either party has reason to appreciate early logical empiricism—albeit different factions thereof—for important work in their spirit. Since both of these parties represent 'live' options on the contemporary scene, it is clearly misleading to think of logical empiricism in terms of a set of doctrines fixed at the start, of its history in terms of a series of attritions, and of its long-term reception as wholesale rejection.

REFERENCES

Adorno, T. W., et al. (1969). *Der Positivismusstreit in der deutschen Soziologie*. Neuwied/Berlin: Luchter. Tr. as *The Positivist Dispute in German Sociology*. London: Heinemann, 1976.

Ayer, A. J. (1936). *Language, Truth and Logic*. London: Gollancz, 2nd edn. 1946.

[51] The role of the bipartite metatheory conception in the thinking of Carnap and Frank is further explored in Uebel (2011a) and (2011b).

—— (1936/7). 'Verification and Experience', *Proceedings of the Aristotelian Society*, New Series 37. Repr. in Ayer (1959), pp. 228–43.

—— (1940). *The Foundations of Empirical Knowledge*. London: Macmillan, repr. 1969.

—— (1950). 'Basic Propositions'. In M. Black (ed.), *Philosophical Analysis*. Ithaca: Cornell University Press, pp. 60–74.

—— (1956). *The Problem of Knowledge*. Harmondsworth: Pelican.

—— (ed.) (1959). *Logical Positivism*. New York: Free Press.

—— (1987). 'Reflections on *Language, Truth and Logic*'. In B. Gower (ed.), *Logical Positivism in Perspective: Essays on Language, Truth and Logic*. London: Croom Helm, pp. 23–34.

—— (1992a). 'My Mental Development'. In Hahn (1992), pp. 3–40.

—— (1992b). 'Reply to Tscha Hung'. In Hahn (1992), pp. 301–7.

Blumberg, A. E. and H. Feigl (1931). 'Logical Positivism', *Journal of Philosophy* 28: 281–96.

Carnap, R. (1922). 'Der Raum. Ein Beitrag zur Wissenschaftslehre', *Kant Studien Ergänzungshefte* 56. Tr. as 'Space: A Contribution to the Theory of Science', in Carnap, *Collected Works Vol. 1: Early Writings,* ed. A. W. Carus, M. Friedman, W. Kienzler, and S. Schlotter. Chicago: Open Court, in press.

—— (1928). *Der logische Aufbau der Welt*. Berlin: Bernary. Tr. as *The Logical Structure of the World*. Berkeley: University of California Press, 1967, repr. Chicago: Open Court, 2003.

—— (1932). 'Über Protokollsätze', *Erkenntnis* 3: 215–28. Tr. as 'On Protocol Sentences', *Noûs* 21 (1987): 457–70.

—— (1934). *Logische Syntax der Sprache*. Vienna: Springer. Rev. edn. tr. A. Smeaton as *The Logical Syntax of Language*. London: Kegan, Paul, 1937, repr. Chicago: Open Court, 2002.

—— (1935). *Philosophy and Logical Syntax*. London: Kegan, Paul.

—— (1936). 'Wahrheit und Bewährung', *Actes du Congres Internationale de Philosophie Scientifique, Sorbonne, Paris 1935*, Facs. IV, 'Induction et Probabilité'. Paris: Hermann & Cie., pp. 18–23. Tr. with additions as 'Truth and Confirmation', in H. Feigl and W. Sellars (eds.), *Readings in Philosophical Analysis*. New York: Appleton-Century-Crofts, 1949, pp. 119–27.

—— (1936–7). 'Testability and Meaning', *Philosophy of Science* 3: 419–71, 4: 1–40.

—— (1950a). 'Empiricism, Semantics and Ontology', *Revue International de Philosophie* 4: 20–40. Repr. in Carnap, *Meaning and Necessity*, 2nd edn. with supplementary essays. Chicago: University of Chicago Press, 1956, pp. 205–21.

—— (1950b). *Logical Foundations of Probability*. Chicago: University of Chicago Press.

—— (1956). 'The Methodological Character of Theoretical Concepts'. In H. Feigl and M. Scriven (eds.), *The Foundations of Science and the Concepts of Psychology and Psychoanalysis*. Minneapolis: University of Minnesota Press, pp. 38–76.

—— (1963). 'Intellectual Autobiography'. In P. A. Schilpp (ed.), *The Philosophy of Rudolf Carnap*. La Salle: Open Court, pp. 3–84.

Carnap, R., H. Hahn, and O. Neurath (1929). *Wissenschaftliche Weltauffassung. Der Wiener Kreis*. Vienna: Wolf. Tr. (without bibliography) in Neurath (1973), pp. 299–318.

Carus, A. W. (2007). *Carnap and Twentieth-Century Thought: Explication as Enlightenment*. Cambridge: Cambridge University Press.

Creath, R. (1976). 'Kaplan on Carnap on Significance', *Philosophical Studies* 30: 393–400.

—— (2009). 'The Gentle Strength of Tolerance: *The Logical Syntax of Language* and Carnap's Philosophical Programme'. In P. Wagner (ed.), *Carnap's Logical Syntax of Language*. Basingstoke: Palgrave Macmillan, pp. 203–16.

—— (2011). 'Logical Empiricism'. In *Stanford Encyclopedia of Philosophy* online at: <http://plato.stanford.edu/entries/logical-empiricism/>; accessed 10 January 2013.

Dahms, H.J. (1994). *Positivismusstreit. Die Auseinandersetzungen der Frankfurter Schule mit dem logischen Positivismus, dem amerikanischen Pragmatismus und dem kritischen Rationalismus*. Frankfurt am Main: Suhrkamp.

Daston, L. and P. Galison (2007). *Objectivity*. New York: Zone Books.

Douglas, H. (ed.) (2009). *Politics and Philosophy of Science*. Special issue of *Science & Education* 18(2): 157–220.

Dubislav, W. (1931). *Die Definition*, 3rd edn. Hamburg: Meiner, repr. 1981.

Fine, A. (1998). 'The Viewpoint of No-One in Particular', *Proceedings and Addresses of the American Philosophical Association* 72: 9–21.

Frank, P. (1932). *Das Kausalgesetz und seine Grenzen*. Vienna: Springer. Tr. as *The Causal Law and its Limits*. Dordrecht: Kluwer, 1998.

—— (1957). *Philosophy of Science: The Link between Science and Philosophy*. Englewood Cliffs, NJ: Prentice-Hall, repr. New York: Dover, 2004.

Friedman, M. (1987). 'Carnap's *Aufbau* Reconsidered', *Noûs* 21: 521–45. Repr. in Friedman (1999), pp. 89–113.

—— (1992). 'Epistemology in the *Aufbau* Reconsidered', *Synthese* 93: 15–57. Repr. in Friedman (1999), pp. 114–51.

—— (1999). *Reconsidering Logical Positivism*. Cambridge: Cambridge University Press.

Friedman, M. and R. Creath (eds.) (2007). *The Cambridge Companion to Carnap*. Cambridge: Cambridge University Press.

Grelling, K. (1936). 'The Logical Paradoxes', *Mind* 45: 480–6.

Grelling, K. and L. Nelson (1908). 'Bemerkungen zu den Paradoxien von Russell und Burali-Forte', *Abhandlungen der Friesschen Schule*, Neue Folge 2: 301–34.

Hahn, H. (1931). '[Beitrag zu] Diskussion zu Grundlagenfragen der Mathematik', *Erkenntnis* 2: 135–41. Tr. as 'Discussion about the Foundations of Mathematics' in Hahn (1980), pp. 31–8.

—— (1933). *Logik, Mathematik und Naturerkennen*. Vienna: Gerold. Tr. as 'Logic, Mathematics, and Knowledge of Nature' in McGuinness (1987), pp. 24–45.

—— (1934). 'Gibt es Unendliches?' In H. Mark *et al.*, *Alte Probleme—neue Lösungen in den exakten Wissenschaften. Fünf Wiener Vorträge*. Zweiter Zyklus, Leipzig/Vienna: Deuticke, pp. 93–116. Tr. as 'Does the Infinite Exist?', in Hahn (1980), pp. 73–102.

—— (1980). *Empiricism, Logic, Mathematics*, ed. B. McGuinness. Dordrecht: Reidel.

Hahn, L. E. (ed.) (1992). *The Philosophy of A. J. Ayer*. La Salle, IL: Open Court.

Hempel, C. G. (1950). 'Problems and Changes in the Empiricist Criterion of Meaning', *Revue International de Philosophie* 11: 41–63..

—— (1951). 'The Concepts of Cognitive Significance: A Reconsideration', *Proceedings of the American Academy of Arts and Sciences* 80: 61–77. .

—— (1965). 'Empiricist Criteria of Cognitive Significance: Problems and Changes', in Hempel, *Aspects of Scientific Explanation*. New York: Free Press, pp. 101–23.

Hook, S. (1930). 'A Personal Impression of Contemporary German Philosophy', *Journal of Philosophy* 27: 141–60.

Howard, D. (2003). 'Two Left Turns Make a Right: On the Curious Political Career of North American Philosophy of Science at Midcentury'. In G. Hardcastle and A. Richardson (eds.), *Logical Empiricism in North America*. Minneapolis: University of Minnesota Press, pp. 25–93.

Hoyningen-Huene, P. (1987). 'Context of Discovery and Context of Justification', *Studies in History and Philosophy of Science* 18: 501–15.

Hung, T. (1992). 'Ayer and the Vienna Circle'. In Hahn (1992), pp. 279–300.

Leitgeb, H. (2011). 'New Life for Carnap's *Aufbau?' Synthese* 180: 265–99.

Macdonald, G. (2005). 'Alfred Jules Ayer'. In *Stanford Encyclopedia of Philosophy* online at: <http://plato.stanford.edu/entries/ayer/>. Revised 2010; accessed 10 January 2013.

Macdonald, G. and C. Wright (1986a). 'Introduction'. In Macdonald and Wright (1986b), pp. 1–7.

———— (eds.) (1986b). *Fact, Science and Morality: Essays on A. J. Ayer's* Language, Truth and Logic. Oxford: Blackwell.

McGuinness, B. (ed.) (1987). *Unified Science.* Dordrecht: Kluwer.

Magee, B. (1971). *Modern British Philosophy.* St. Albans: Paladin.

Mancosu, P. (2008). 'Tarski, Neurath and Kokoszyńska on the Semantic Conception of Truth'. In D. Patterson (ed.), *New Essays on Tarski and Philosophy.* Oxford: Oxford University Press, pp. 192–224.

Menger, K. (1933). 'Die neue Logik', in H. Mark *et al., Krise und Neuaufbau in den exakten Wissenschaften.* Fünf Wiener Vorträge. Leipzig/Vienna: Deuticke, pp. 93–122. Rev. and tr. as 'The New Logic', *Philosophy of Science* 4 (1937): 299–36; 2nd rev. in Menger, *Selected Papers in Logic and Foundations, Didactics, Economics.* Dordrecht: Reidel, 1979, pp. 18–45.

Mormann, T. (2004). 'A Quasi-Analytical Constitution of Physical Space'. In S. Awodey and C. Klein (eds.), *Carnap Brought Home: The View From Jena.* Chicago: Open Court, pp. 79–100.

—— (2009). 'New Work for Carnap's Quasi-Analysis', *Journal of Philosophical Logic* 38: 249–82.

Nagel, E. (1936). 'Impressions and Appraisals of Analytic Philosophy in Europe', *Journal of Philosophy* 33: 5–24 and 29–53.

Nagel, T. (1986). *The View from Nowhere.* Oxford: Oxford University Press.

Neurath, O. (1913). 'Die Verirrten des Cartesius und das Auxiliarmotiv (Zur Psychologie des Entschlusses)', *Jahrbuch der Philosophischen Gesellschaft an der Universität zu Wien 1913,* pp. 45–59. Tr. as 'The Lost Wanderers and the Auxiliary Motive (On the Psychology of Decision)' in Neurath (1983), pp. 1–12.

—— (1930). 'Wege der wissenschaftlichen Weltauffassung', *Erkenntnis* 1: 106–25. Tr. as 'Ways of the Scientific World Conception' in Neurath (1983), pp. 32–47.

—— (1931a). *Empirische Soziologie. Der wissenschaftliche Gehalt der Geschichte und Nationalökonomie.* Partly tr. as 'Empirical Sociology' in Neurath (1973), pp. 391–421.

—— (1931b). 'Physikalismus', *Scientia* 50: 297–303. Tr. as 'Physicalism' in Neurath (1983), pp. 52–7.

—— (1932a). 'Soziologie im Physikalismus', *Erkenntnis* 2: 393–431. Tr. as 'Sociology and Physicalism' in Ayer (1959), pp. 282–320, and 'Sociology in the Framework of Physicalism' in Neurath (1983), pp. 58–90.

—— (1932b). 'Protokollsätze', *Erkenntnis* 3: 204–14. Tr. as 'Protocol Sentences' in Ayer (1959), pp. 199–208, and 'Protocol Statements' in Neurath (1983), pp. 91–9.

—— (1935a). *Was bedeutet rationale Wirtschaftsrechnung?* Vienna: Gerold. Tr. as 'What is Meant by Rational Economic Theory?' in McGuinness (1987), pp. 67–109.

—— (1935b). 'Einheit der Wissenschaft als Aufgabe', *Erkenntnis* 5: 16–22. Tr. as 'The Unity of Science as a Task' in Neurath (1983), pp. 115–20.

—— (1936a). 'Soziologische Prognosen', *Erkenntnis* 6: 398–405. Tr. as 'Sociological Predictions' in Neurath (2004), pp. 506–12.

—— (1936b). 'Physikalismus und Erkenntnisforschung', *Theoria* 2: 97–105, 234–7. Tr. as 'Physicalism and the Investigation of Knowledge' in Neurath (1983), pp. 159–71.

—— (1944). *Foundations of the Social Sciences.* Chicago: University of Chicago Press.

—— (1973). *Sociology and Empiricism,* ed. M. Neurath and R. S. Cohen. Dordrecht: Reidel.

—— (1983). *Philosophical Papers 1913–1946,* ed. R. S. Cohen and M. Neurath. Dordrecht: Reidel.

—— (2004). *Economic Writings: Selections 1904–1945,* ed. T. Uebel and R. S. Cohen. Dordrecht: Kluwer.

Oppenheim, P. and H. Putnam (1958). 'Unity of Science as a Working Hypothesis'. In H. Feigl, M. Scriven, and G. Maxwell (eds.), *Concepts, Theories and the Mind–Body Problem.* Minneapolis: University of Minnesota Press, pp. 3–36.

Popper, K. (1974). 'Intellectual Autobiography'. In P. A. Schilpp (ed.), *The Philosophy of Karl Popper.* La Salle, IL: Open Court, pp. 3–181. Repr. separately as *Unended Quest.* La Salle, IL: Open Court, 1976.

Putnam, H. (2002). *The Collapse of the Fact/Value Dichotomy and Other Essays.* Cambridge, MA: Harvard University Press.

Quine, W. V. O. (1951). 'Two Dogmas of Empiricism', *Philosophical Review* 60: 20–43. Repr. in Quine, *From a Logical Point of View,* rev. edn. 1980. Cambridge, MA: Harvard University Press, pp. 20–46.

Reichenbach, H. (1916). *Bedeutung der Wahrscheinlichkeit für die mathematische Darstellung der Wirklichkeit,* PhD Thesis, University of Erlangen. Tr. as *The Concept of Probability in the Mathematical Representation of Reality.* Chicago: Open Court, 2008.

—— (1920). *Relativitätstheorie und Erkenntnis A Priori.* Berlin: Springer. Tr. as *The Theory of Relativity and A Priori Knowledge.* Los Angeles: University of California Press, 1965.

—— (1924). *Axiomatik der relativistischen Raum-Zeit-Lehre.* Braunschweig: Vieweg. Tr. as *Axiomatization of the Theory of Relativity.* Berkeley: University of California Press, 1969.

—— (1928). *Philosophie der Raum-Zeit-Lehre.* Berlin: De Gruyter. Tr. as *Philosophy of Space and Time.* New York: Dover, 1958.

—— (1931). 'Der physikalische Wahrheitsbegriff', *Erkenntnis* 2: 156–71. Tr. as 'The Physical Concept of Truth' in Reichenbach (1978), pp. 343–56.

—— (1933). 'Besprechung: Carnap, *Der logische Aufbau der Welt*', *Kantstudien* 38: 199–201. Tr. as 'Review of Carnap's *Aufbau*' in Reichenbach (1978), pp. 405–8.

—— (1935). *Wahrscheinlichkeitslehre.* Leyden: Sijthoff. Tr. as *The Theory of Probability.* Berkeley: University of California Press, 1949.

—— (1936). 'Logistic Empiricism in Germany and the Present State of its Problems', *Journal of Philosophy* 33: 141–60.

—— (1938). *Experience and Prediction.* Chicago: University of Chicago Press, repr. Notre Dame: University of Notre Dame Press, 2006.

—— (1944). *Philosophical Foundations of Quantum Mechanics.* Berkeley: University of California Press.

—— (1951). *The Rise of Scientific Philosophy.* Berkeley: University of California Press.

—— (1978). *Selected Writings 1909–1953, Vol. 1,* ed. M. Reichenbach and R. S. Cohen. Dordrecht: Reidel.

Reisch, G. (2005). *How the Cold War Transformed Philosophy of Science: To the Icy Slopes of Logic.* Cambridge: Cambridge University Press.

Rescher, N. (2006). 'The Berlin School of Logical Empiricism and its Legacy', *Erkenntnis* 64: 281–304.

Richardson, A. (1998). *Carnap's Construction of the World.* Cambridge: Cambridge University Press.

Richardson, A. and T. Uebel (eds.) (2007). *The Cambridge Companion to Logical Empiricism*. Cambridge: Cambridge University Press.

Ryckman, T. A. (2005). *The Reign of Relativity: Philosophy in Physics 1915–1925*. Oxford: Oxford University Press.

Salmon, W. (1985). 'Empiricism: The Key Question'. In N. Rescher (ed.), *The Heritage of Logical Positivism*. Lanham, MD: University Press of America, pp. 1–21.

Schlick, M. (1910). 'Das Wesen der Wahrheit nach der modernen Logik', *Vierteljahresschrift für wissenschaftliche Philosophie und Soziologie* 34: 386–477. Tr. as 'The Nature of Truth According to Modern Logic' in Schlick (1979a), pp. 41–103.

—— (1915). 'Die philosophische Bedeutung des Relativitätsprinzips', *Zeitschrift für Philosophie und philosophische Kritik* 159: 129–75. Tr. as 'The Philosophical Significance of the Principle of Relativity' in Schlick (1979a), pp. 153–89.

—— (1917). 'Raum und Zeit in der gegenwärtigen Physik', *Die Naturwissenschaften* 5: 161–7, 177–86. Also pub. separately in enlarged version, Berlin: Springer. Trans. of 4th edn. (1922) in Schlick (1979a), pp. 207–69.

—— (1918). *Allgemeine Erkenntnislehre*. Berlin: Springer, 1918, 2nd rev. edn. 1925. Tr. H. Feigl and A. Blumberg as *General Theory of Knowledge*. La Salle, IL: Open Court, 1974.

—— (1927). 'Erleben, Erkennen, Metaphysik', *Kantstudien* 31: 146–58. Tr. as 'Experience, Cognition, Metaphysics' in Schlick (1979b), pp. 99–111.

—— (1930). 'Die Wende in der Philosophie', *Erkenntnis* 1: 4–11. Tr. as 'The Turning Point in Philosophy' in Ayer (1959a), pp. 53–9, and in Schlick (1979b), pp. 154–60.

—— (1931). 'Die Kausalität in der gegenwärtigen Physik', *Die Naturwissenschaften* 19: 145–62. Tr. as 'Causality in Contemporary Physics' in Schlick (1979b), pp. 176–209.

—— (1932–8). 'Form and Content'. In Schlick, *Gesammelte Aufsätze 1926–1936*. Vienna: Gerold, 1938, pp. 151–250. Repr. in Schlick (1979b), pp. 285–369.

—— (1934). 'Über das Fundament der Erkenntnis', *Erkenntnis* 4: 79–99. Tr. as 'The Foundation of Knowledge' in Ayer (1959a), pp. 209–27, and in Schlick (1979b), pp. 370–87.

—— (1935). 'Introduction'. In Schlick, *Sur le Fondament du Connaissance*. Paris: Heinman & Cie. Tr. as 'Introduction' in Schlick (1979b), pp. 405–7.

—— (1937). 'Quantentheorie und Erkennbarkeit der Natur', *Erkenntnis* 6: 317–26. Tr. as 'Quantum Mechanics and the Intelligibility of Nature' in Schlick (1979b), pp. 400–10.

—— (1979a). *Philosophical Papers Vol. 1 (1909–1922)*, ed. H. L. Mulder and B. van de Velde-Schlick. Dordrecht: Reidel.

—— (1979b). *Philosophical Papers Vol. 2 (1925–1936)*, ed. H. L. Mulder and B. van de Velde-Schlick. Dordrecht: Reidel.

Soames, S. (2003). *Philosophical Analysis in the 20th Century*, 2 vols. Princeton, NJ: Princeton University Press.

Stadler, F. (1997). *Studien zum Wiener Kreis. Ursprung, Entwicklung und Wirkung des Logischen Empirismus im Kontext*, Frankfurt am Main: Suhrkamp. Tr. as *The Vienna Circle: Studies in the Origins, Development and Influence of logical Empiricism*. Vienna and New York: Springer, 2001.

Stebbing, S. (1933). 'Logical Positivism and Analysis', *Proceedings of the British Academy* 19: 53–87.

Uebel, T. (2000). 'Logical Empiricism and the Sociology of Knowledge: The Case of Neurath and Frank', *Philosophy of Science* 67 (Proceedings): S138–S150.

—— (2004). 'Introduction: Neurath's Economics in Critical Context', in Neurath (2004), pp. 1–108.

—— (2006). 'Vienna Circle'. In *Stanford Encyclopedia of Philosophy* online at: <http://plato. stanford.edu/entries/vienna-circle/>. Revised and updated 2011; accessed 30 November 2012.

——(2007). *Empiricism at the Crossroads: The Vienna Circle's Protocol Sentence Debate*. Chicago: Open Court.

——(2009). 'Neurath's Protocol Statements Revisited: Sketch of a Theory of Scientific Testimony', *Studies in History and Philosophy of Science* 40: 4–13.

—— (2011a). 'Carnap and Kuhn: On the Relation between the Logic of Science and the History of Science', *Journal for General Philosophy of Science* 42: 129–40.

—— (2011b). 'Beyond the Formal Meaning Criterion: Phillip Frank's Later Anti-Metaphysics', *HOPOS* 1: 47–72.

Weinberg, J. (1936). *An Examination of Logical Positivism*. London: Kegan, Paul.

Williams, B. (1978). *Descartes: The Project of Pure Enquiry*. Harmondsworth: Pelican.

Wright, C. (1986). 'Scientific Realism, Observation and the Verification Principle'. In Macdonald and Wright (1986b), pp. 247–74.

—— (1993a). 'Scientific Realism, Observation and Verificationism' in Wright (1993c), pp. 279–99.

——(1993b). 'The Verification Principle' in Wright (1993c), pp. 300–20.

——(1993c). *Realism, Meaning and Truth*, 2nd edn. Oxford: Blackwell.

Zilsel, E. (1926). *Die Entstehung des Geniebegriffs. Ein Beitrag zur Ideengeschichte der Antike und des Frühkapitalismus*. Tübingen: Mohr, repr. Hildesheim: Olms, 1972.

——(1931). 'Geschichte und Biologie, Überlieferung, und Vererbung', *Archiv für Sozialwissenschaft und Sozialpolitik* 65: 475–524. Repr. in Zilsel, *Wissenschaft und Weltanschauung: Aufsätze 1929–1933*, ed. G. Mozetic. Vienna: Bohlau, 1992.

CHAPTER 17

··

DEVELOPMENTS IN LOGIC: CARNAP, GÖDEL, AND TARSKI

··

ERICH H. RECK

ANALYTIC philosophy and modern logic are intimately connected, both historically and systematically. Thinkers such as Frege, Russell, and Wittgenstein were major contributors to the early development of both; and the fruitful use of modern logic in addressing philosophical problems was, and still is, definitive for large parts of the analytic tradition. More specifically, Frege's analysis of the concept of number, Russell's theory of descriptions, and Wittgenstein's notion of tautology have long been seen as paradigmatic pieces of philosophy in this tradition. This close connection remained beyond what is now often called 'early analytic philosophy', i.e., the tradition's first phase. In the present chapter I will consider three thinkers who played equally important and formative roles in analytic philosophy's second phase, the period from the 1920s to the 1950s: Rudolf Carnap, Kurt Gödel, and Alfred Tarski.

Undoubtedly, Gödel and Tarski were two of the greatest logicians of the twentieth century, indeed of all time. Their influence on mathematical logic can hardly be exaggerated. However, they also exerted a significant influence on philosophy, especially analytic philosophy, as we will see. Carnap, in turn, is widely recognized as one of the most important and influential analytic philosophers of the twentieth century. Yet he also played an under-appreciated role in the history of modern logic. For a number of reasons it makes sense to treat these three figures together: they were all born and educated in Central Europe (in Germany, Austria, and Poland, respectively); they knew each other personally, from early on in their careers; they interacted frequently and influenced each other's views directly; and all three emigrated to the United States, within a few years of each other, so as to exert their main influence there.

In briefly surveying the contributions of three such seminal figures it is impossible to be comprehensive; thus my discussion will have to be selective. My main objective will be to establish the major role their contributions to logic played in the development of analytic philosophy (as opposed to, say, the development of mathematical logic). Thus, I will focus on their philosophically most influential results. Various technical details will be suppressed and a wide range of their other achievements only mentioned in passing. My discussion will revolve around the following related topics: the transformation of modern logic, especially the rise of meta-logic; logicism and its relation to formal axiomatics; the notions of truth, logical truth, and logical consequence; formal semantics, metaphysics, and epistemology; and philosophical methodology. A recurring theme will be Carnap's, Gödel's, and Tarski's continued interactions, which will reveal many shared interests, but also some striking differences in their philosophical convictions.

17.1 FIRST ENCOUNTERS AND INITIAL INTERACTIONS

The first time all three of our protagonists met was in Vienna in February 1930. The occasion was Tarski's first visit to the city. On the invitation of the mathematician Karl Menger, Tarski was to give three talks at the University of Vienna. Their topics were: (i) set theory, (ii) methodology of the deductive sciences, (iii) the sentential calculus. A main motivation for Menger's invitation had been to establish closer ties between the Vienna Circle, of which he was a member, and the Lvov–Warsaw school of logic, for which Tarski served as a kind of emissary. These two groups (as well as the Berlin group around Hans Reichenbach) shared a preference for 'scientific philosophy'. This meant: the rejection of grand, speculative system building and its replacement by more specific, detailed analyses of concepts; the focus on philosophical questions arising out of the exact sciences; and the application and further development of modern logic. Tarski's Vienna talks exemplified all of these features, but especially the third.

Alfred Tarski (1901–83) had received his Ph.D. in mathematics from the University of Warsaw in 1924, with a dissertation on logic under Stanisław Leśniewski. Among his other teachers were: Tadeusz Kotarbiński in philosophy, Jan Łukasiewicz in logic, and Wacław Sierpiński in set theory. Tarski was, in fact, their star student, which is why he had been selected to represent 'Polish logic' in Vienna. By the late 1920s he had already arrived at important results in several subfields of mathematical logic, including: set theory (on uses of the Axiom of Choice, especially the well-known Banach–Tarski Paradox), general axiomatics (new axiomatizations for geometry), on the decision problem (decision procedures for elementary geometry and algebra), and on the topic of definability (concerning definable sets of reals). Tarski had also started to investigate the 'methodology of the deductive sciences' more generally; and indeed, this served as the theme of his second talk in Vienna. This is the talk that attracted Carnap's attention the most, and it was soon after it that the two had their first substantive discussion.[1]

Ten years older than Tarski, Rudolf Carnap (1891–1970) had received a Ph.D. in philosophy from the University of Jena in 1921, with a dissertation on geometry (published, as *Der Raum*, in 1922). Besides his dissertation adviser Bruno Bauch and the writings of other neo-Kantian philosophers, there had been further formative influences on Carnap: in 1910–14, while at Jena, he took classes in logic and the foundations of mathematics from Gottlob Frege; in the early 1920s, after finishing his dissertation, he read Bertrand Russell's logical works in detail, including Whitehead and Russell's *Principia Mathematica*; and in 1921–2, he took classes with Edmund Husserl at the University of Freiburg. Carnap arrived at the University of Vienna in 1926, hired as a senior lecturer (*Privatdozent*) and with a draft of *Der Logische Aufbau der Welt* in hand (his *Habilitation*, published in 1928), the text that established him as a major thinker among 'scientific philosophers'. He started to take part in activities of the Vienna Circle right away, but continued other projects as well. Two results were: *Pseudoprobleme in der Philosophie* (also published in 1928) and *Abriss der Logistik* (1929).[2]

Kurt Gödel (1906–78), finally, was the youngest of our three thinkers, five years younger than Tarski and fifteen years younger than Carnap. (In 1930, they were 24, 29, and 39 years old.) At the time of Tarski's arrival he had just finished his Ph.D. in mathematics at the University of Vienna, under Hans Hahn. In addition to working with Hahn, Menger, and the number theorist Philipp Furtwängler, Gödel had taken classes in the philosophy of mathematics and logic from Moritz Schlick and, especially, from Carnap, which awakened his interest in foundational studies. He had also been drawn into the activities of the Vienna Circle more generally, although he remained quietly independent in his philosophical convictions. Gödel's dissertation, accepted in 1929, already contained a major result in logic: a proof of the completeness of first-order logic. It answered a question posed by David Hilbert, in an influential lecture in Bologna (1928) and in Hilbert and Ackermann's *Grundzüge der theoretischen Logik* (1928). It was also directly connected with Carnap's work in logic (as we will see more below). During Gödel's and Tarski's first meeting in Vienna, this is the result they discussed.[3]

After their initial meeting, in February 1930, there would be many further interactions between the three thinkers, later that year and subsequently. For example, in October 1930 Carnap and Gödel attended the well-known Königsberg conference on the foundations of mathematics together. At that occasion, Carnap gave a talk on logicism; Gödel presented his completeness result, and to everyone's surprise, he also announced his incompleteness theorem for *Principia Mathematica* and related systems. Actually, Gödel had already told Carnap about the latter in August 1930, during

---

[1] For more on Tarski's life and his (early as well as later) works, cf. Feferman and Feferman (2004). For details concerning his publications, see the references.

[2] For more on Carnap's background and early works, cf. Reck (2004), the first half of Creath and Friedman (2007), and Carus (2007). Concerning his publications, see again the references.

[3] For Gödel's background, life, and (early as well as later) works, cf. Dawson (1997). For his relevant publications, see again the references.

conversations in Vienna. He informed Tarski, who was not present in Königsberg, of its details in a letter in January 1931. As another example, Tarski invited Carnap to come to Warsaw in November 1930, as an emissary of the Vienna Circle, to present three talks at the university there in turn. But it was the first meeting of the three of them that set the stage for many of their later interactions. To understand better how and why, let us briefly review the development of logic and related issues up to 1930.

17.2 LOGIC, LOGICISM, AND AXIOMATICS UP TO 1930[4]

Modern logic is often taken to start with Frege's *Begriffsschrift* (1879). In it, both propositional and quantificational logic are presented systematically for the first time, in the form of a simple theory of types (a form of higher-order logic). They are also used to analyse a core part of the foundations of arithmetic, the principle of mathematical induction, thus inaugurating Frege's logicism—his project of reducing arithmetic to logic alone. He motivated this project further in *Die Grundlagen der Arithmetik* (1884), and he expanded on both his technical machinery and its application in *Grundgesetze der Arithmetik*, Vols. I–II (1893/1903). In the latter, he added a theory of classes ('extensions of concepts') to his logic that, as is well known, falls prey to Russell's antinomy. Partly for that reason, Frege's work was largely ignored for a while, although not entirely, as Carnap learned about it in his Jena classes. A few other thinkers were directly influenced by his contributions as well, most crucially Russell and Wittgenstein.

Nevertheless, it was Bertrand Russell's subsequent writings on logic, and especially A. N. Whitehead and B. Russell's *Principia Mathematica*, Vols. 1–3 (1910–13), that had a much more widespread influence. Indeed, virtually everyone concerned about modern logic in the first half of the twentieth century studied *Principia*, including Carnap, Gödel, and Tarski. As in Frege's case, Russell's logical system contained a theory of classes (at least indirectly, in the form of a 'no-classes theory of classes'). The general framework was a ramified theory of types (a more complex version of higher-order logic), introduced to avoid a whole range of antinomies discovered by then (not just 'set-theoretic', but also 'semantic' antinomies such as Richard's). In addition, Russell's logicist aspirations were more far-reaching than Frege's: he saw logic as the foundation for all of mathematics, not just arithmetic. Suitably supplemented, it was even to form a framework for all scientific knowledge, as sketched in Russell's *Our Knowledge of the External World* (1914).

Another crucial development for our purposes, initially separate from Frege–Russell logic, is the emergence of modern axiomatics. It grew out of the investigation of various non-Euclidean geometries in the nineteenth century, but led to a reconsideration of

---

[4] In the next three sections, I draw heavily on Awodey and Carus (2001), Awodey and Reck (2002a), Reck (2004), and Reck (2007). For mathematical details, cf. also Mancosu, Zach, and Badesa (2009).

Euclidean geometry as well, culminating in Hilbert's *Grundlagen der Geometrie* (1899). There were also related novel treatments of arithmetic by Dedekind and Peano, of analysis by Dedekind and Hilbert, and of set theory by Zermelo (the latter along Cantorian and Dedekindian lines, in contrast to Frege's and Russell's logicist theories of classes). This intense focus on axioms, together with Hilbert's 'formalist' rethinking of them, led to questions about the independence, consistency, and completeness of the main axiom systems. These were investigated in Hilbert's Göttingen, earlier also by the 'American Postulate Theorists', E. Huntington, O. Veblen, etc.[5] Another issue that became prominent during this period was the mechanical decidability of the corresponding parts of mathematics (the '*Entscheidungsproblem*').

In pursuing such issues, it gradually became clear that one has to be mindful of the logical system in which one works. For one thing, there is a difference between the completeness of a mathematical axiom system (the issue of whether it 'decides' all relevant sentences), and the completeness of the logic in the background (whether it allows for formal, syntactic proofs of all semantic consequences). For another, while Russellian ramified type theory was used initially as the proper logical framework, this is not the only option; e.g., one can use Fregean simple type theory instead (stripped of its inconsistent theory of classes, as Frege had done in the lectures Carnap attended). Indeed, the simplicity of Frege's version of higher-order logic seemed preferable for various purposes, as Frank Ramsey and others began to argue. Along such lines, Carnap's early logic textbook, *Abriss der Logistik* (1929), abandoned Russellian ramifications; similarly for Hilbert and Ackerman's *Grundzüge der theoretischen Logik* (1928), at least in its later editions. Moreover, within simple type theory certain self-contained subsystems can be isolated and studied profitably, especially propositional logic and first-order logic. With this proliferation of logical systems and subsystems, the question arose: Which of them, if any, should be seen as 'the correct' logic?

Already in the 1910s, special attention to propositional logic led to proofs, by Paul Bernays (1918) and Emil Post (1921), of its completeness.[6] The natural next step concerned the completeness of first-order logic (the 'lower functional calculus', as it was called at the time)—as established in Gödel's dissertation, 'Über die Vollständigkeit des Logikkalküls' (1929). After that, the completeness of the simple theory of types as a whole remained as a question.[7] Parallel to these developments in logic, various systems of mathematical axioms were investigated in more detail, either as formulated in first-order or higher-order logic. The case of first-order axiomatic set theory, based on suggestions by Skolem, Weyl, and Fraenkel (but resisted by, e.g., Zermelo), attracted much attention, from the 1920s on. Axiom systems for the natural numbers, the real numbers, and various parts of geometry were studied in novel ways as well.

---

[5] For more on the rise of 'formal axiomatics' and 'postulate theory', see Awodey and Reck (2002a).

[6] In the case of propositional logic, completeness amounts, more explicitly and precisely, to the existence of an adequate (strong enough) deduction system relative to truth-value semantics.

[7] For first- and higher-order logic, including simple type theory, completeness means here the existence of an adequate (strong enough) deduction system relative to standard set-theoretic semantics.

In Hilbert's school the consistency of such axiomatic theories was explored with great vigour. The topic of decidability was seen as closely related, as some decision procedures, applicable in restricted contexts, were discovered. Concerning set theory, there were also questions about the legitimacy of specific axioms, particularly the Axiom of Choice (after its explicit formulation by Zermelo in 1904). All of this fed into Hilbert's 'meta-mathematical' and 'proof-theoretic' programs, which took shape in the late 1910s and early 1920s.[8] The strong focus on consistency was partly a response to the antinomies already mentioned, which were widely seen as leading to a 'foundational crisis'. Additional pressure came from intuitionistic or constructivist mathematicians, especially Brouwer and (for a while) Weyl, who rejected both a formal axiomatic approach and highly non-constructive principles such as the Axiom of Choice. The opposition between the classic schools of logicism, formalism, and intuitionism resulted. In connection with formalism, Hilbert was led to 'finitist' restrictions of the means by which consistency proofs were to be given, so as to convince even intuitionists of their cogency.[9]

Concerning logicism, two further issues arose in the 1920s. The first involves a controversial aspect of *Principia Mathematica*: its reliance on the axioms of infinity and reducibility, introduced somewhat *ad hoc* so as to be able to derive all of classical mathematics. Neither of them could easily be accepted as logical, which led to the question of how to justify their use. Second, there was Wittgenstein's new notion of tautology, introduced in his *Tractatus Logico-Philosophicus* (1921). It was presented as filling a gap in Frege's and Russell's works: to provide a precise, general characterization of logical laws. In Wittgenstein's and others' eyes, this notion had the additional advantage of providing a deflationary account of logical truth (as a tautology is true in virtue of its form alone, no matter what other facts obtain). And that led to the question of how far such an account could be extended, since its only clear application was to propositional logic (pace Wittgenstein's further claims). Both of these issues were much discussed at the time, including in the Vienna Circle of the 1920s.

17.3 CARNAP'S AND TARSKI'S EARLY FORAYS INTO META-LOGIC

The developments just described indicate that the 1920s were an extremely fertile period in the history of logic. (Together with the 1930s, they formed modern logic's 'Golden Age'.) This is further confirmed if we add Carnap's and Tarski's contributions to the mix. It should be evident that much of Tarski's early work, as mentioned above (on the Axiom of Choice, new axiomatizations for geometry, decision procedures for

---

[8] For more on the early development of Hilbert's program, or programs, cf. Sieg (1999); see also Zach (1999).

[9] For a relatively recent comparison of the three main schools, cf. George and Velleman (2002).

elementary geometry and algebra, etc.), fits squarely into these developments. The same holds for some of Carnap's works from the 1920s, especially *Abriss der Logistik*, but also *Der Logische Aufbau der Welt*, a book motivated by Russell's suggestion (as well as related neo-Kantian and, to some degree, Husserlian ideas) to logically reconstruct scientific knowledge in general.[10] But the main focus of Carnap's and Tarski's initial conversation in Vienna, in 1930, was somewhat different. It concerned what Tarski liked to call 'the methodology of the deductive sciences', what was called 'meta-mathematics' in the Hilbert school, and what often goes under the name of 'meta-logic' today.

Carnap was led to meta-logical considerations in at least four ways (against the background of the general developments already mentioned). First, from early on in his career he was not only exposed to Frege–Russell logic, but also to Hilbertian axiomatics. Especially relevant among Hilbert's writings, in addition to *Die Grundlagen der Geometrie*, was the article 'Axiomatisches Denken' (1918), which advocated a wide-ranging application of the axiomatic method. Second, while in Frege's logic classes at Jena, as well as in Russell's writings, Carnap had been confronted with their critical, even dismissive attitude towards axiomatics, he did not take over that attitude. Instead, his reaction was to strive for a reconciliation and synthesis, i.e., he wanted to combine Frege–Russell logic with a Hilbertian axiomatic approach. Third, both logic and the axiomatic method played a prominent role in the broader discussions of scientific knowledge in the Vienna Circle, as illustrated by Schlick's remarks on 'implicit definitions' in *Allgemeine Erkenntnislehre* (1918, second edition 1925) and Carnap's response in 'Eigentliche und Uneigentliche Begriffe' (1927). Fourth, in the mid-1920s Carnap encountered Abraham Fraenkel's work on axiomatics, which suggested a potentially fruitful way of approaching crucial logical and meta-logical issues in all of these connections.[11]

The text by Fraenkel that influenced Carnap the most was his *Einleitung in die Mengenlehre*, especially its second edition (published in 1923) to which a novel section on 'general axiomatics' had been added. This section contained a probing discussion of the notion, or of several related notions, of completeness for axiomatic systems. Carnap quickly started a correspondence with Fraenkel about this topic. One result of it, as evident from the third edition of Fraenkel's book (1928), was the sharper differentiation and characterization of three notions of completeness that had often been confused or simply identified so far, namely: 'syntactic completeness', 'semantic completeness' (being 'non-forkable', as Carnap called it), and 'categoricity' (being 'monomorphic').[12]

---

[10]   For more on the big role Carnap's *Aufbau* played in the history of analytic philosophy, cf. Richardson (1998), Friedman (1999), the relevant pieces in Creath and Friedman (2007), and Carus (2007, chs. 5–6).

[11]   Concerning the first, second, and fourth aspects, compare Reck (2004) and (2007). Concerning the third—which deserves more attention than it has received so far and than I can give it here—cf. Goldfarb (1996), several of the articles in Friedman (1999), Awodey and Carus (2001), and Carus (2007, ch. 7).

[12]   Briefly, an axiom system is syntactically complete if, for each sentence in the given language, either it or its negation is deducible from the axioms (i.e., follows syntactically from them); it is semantically complete if, for each such sentence, either it or its negation is true in all models of the axioms (i.e., follows semantically); and it is categorical if all models of the axioms are isomorphic. Compare Awodey and Carus (2001), Awodey and Reck (2002a), and Reck (2007) for further discussion and background.

As Fraenkel also stressed, the relationships between these three notions were in need of further exploration. In order to make progress with that task one had to go beyond the informal setup of Fraenkel's book—one had to make explicit the logical framework in which one intended to work. Realizing that, Carnap had a specific suggestion: use the simple theory of types, as spelled out in his *Abriss der Logistik*.

At this point Carnap had a new research project at hand and started to compose another book, with the working title *Untersuchungen zur Allgemeinen Axiomatik*. Pretty quickly he produced a partial manuscript, which he then, from 1928 on, circulated among friends—including Gödel. Carnap actually thought he had arrived at substantive results already, i.e., proved several core theorems in general axiomatics. Specifically, he believed he had proved that, within simple type theory, all three notions of completeness just distinguished were equivalent. He also believed that, within the same context, any consistent axiom system was satisfiable (has a model)—a version of the completeness of simple type theory. He was mistaken on both counts, and there were other, more basic problems with his approach. It was exactly those basic problems he was confronted with in his first meeting with Tarski, in February 1930. And Gödel's incompleteness theorem, of which he heard in August 1930, confirmed that something fundamental was amiss. Right after realizing that he gave up the *Allgemeine Axiomatik* project, but only after having interacted significantly with both Gödel and Tarski on its basis.[13]

In the next section I will explain how exactly Gödel's surprising theorem undercuts Carnap's project. To close off this section, let me say a bit more about the problems of which Tarski made him aware. Basically, what Carnap had done in his *Allgemeine Axiomatik* manuscript was to work within one logical system and define all the relevant notions internal to it. (He was still a Fregean or Russellian 'universalist' in that respect.) But what the situation really called for was to work at two distinct logical levels and with two different languages: the level of the given axioms and of the deductive system in the background, as formulated in an 'object language'; and the level at which results about them were established, in a 'meta-language'. That is to say, Carnap was learning the hard way, through his failures, that the issues he was interested in could only be captured adequately, and investigated properly, by proceeding 'meta-logically'. Tarski had already achieved considerable clarity on such matters in his seminars at the University of Warsaw in the 1920s, but this was little known beyond Poland at the time. And indeed, these were exactly the kinds of achievements to be disseminated more widely in Tarski's second Vienna talk, on 'the methodology of the deductive sciences'.

While the details of Tarski's talk seem not to have been preserved, one can get a sense of its content from articles he published around the same time, such as: 'Fundamentale Begriffe der Methodologie der deduktiven Wissenschaften' (1930a) and 'Über einige fundamentale Begriffe der Metamathematik' (1930b). His general topic in them is

---

[13] Carnap's corresponding manuscript was not published until seventy years later, as Carnap (2000). It should be added that, as his project led to some partial results, it was not a complete failure; cf. Awodey and Reck (2002a) and Reck (2007). Tarski addressed closely related issues in Tarski and Lindenbaum (1934–5).

the 'deductive method', and the main goal is to clarify how best to organize 'deductive theories', including mathematical theories, so as to study their properties more precisely. This involves distilling out basic concepts and axioms, but also making explicit—along meta-logical lines—the notions of definition, sentence, consequence, theory, etc. On that basis, Tarski was able to establish results about definability, axiomatizability, independence, consistency, and completeness. The connections to Hilbertian meta-mathematics, on the one hand, and to the general axiomatics pursued by Fraenkel and Carnap, on the other, are clear. It should be added that, while Tarski was ahead of Carnap in various respects, his approach would require later modifications as well. Both were working at the cutting edge of logic, where things were still in flux.[14]

17.4 GÖDEL'S INCOMPLETENESS THEOREMS

I already mentioned that Gödel's first major result in logic, his completeness theorem for first-order logic, was answering a question prominently raised by Hilbert. His second result, the incompleteness theorem (or theorems), can also be seen as a response to Hilbert, specifically to his goal of proving the consistency of classical mathematical theories by restricted means. Indeed, this is how the result is typically discussed in the literature. We are now in a position to recognize, however, that the theorem can equally well be seen as a response to Carnap's work in logic from the 1920s, of which Gödel knew first-hand. (Not only did he get a copy of *Allgemeine Axiomatik* in 1928, he read *Abriss der Logistik*, a text circulated in Vienna from 1927 on, and he attended lectures on logic and the foundations of mathematics by Carnap during the period.) It was no accident, then, that Carnap was one of the first people to be told about this discovery by Gödel, even before he announced it publicly at the Königsberg conference.

The title of Gödel's famous paper on the subject, 'Über formal unentscheidbare Sätze der *Principia Mathematica* und verwandter Systeme I' (1931), points towards Russellian ramified type theory as the relevant logical framework. But in fact, Gödel worked with the simple theory of types in this paper—in line with Carnap. What he showed was that any axiomatic theory formulated in simple type theory that contains (a moderate amount of) arithmetic does not allow one to decide, by formal deductions from its axioms, all the sentences in its language; there is always a sentence such that neither it nor its negation is deducible (assuming consistency). In other words, any such theory is syntactically incomplete. And this result applies quite widely: to arithmetic; to analysis; to simple and ramified type theory with a theory of classes; to Zermelo–Fraenkel set theory; etc. Moreover, if one tries to amend things by adding new axioms to the theory (while meeting a minimal condition

---

[14] For more on Tarskian 'methodology of the deductive sciences', see Blok and Pigozzi (1988). For the sense in which Tarski and Carnap were at the cutting edge of logic, cf. Awodey and Reck (2002a).

of adequacy, namely their recursive enumerability, as before), the same situation recurs: there will again be a sentence that is neither deducible nor refutable within the enlarged system. This is, basically, the content of Gödel's 'first incompleteness theorem'. According to his 'second incompleteness theorem', which follows from the first, the consistency of such theories can also not be proven by elementary means (on pain of inconsistency).[15]

Another way in which Gödel's first incompleteness theorem is often put is that no formal system (that satisfies certain minimal conditions, including consistency) can capture all of arithmetic—arithmetic is 'inexhaustible'. And consequently, mathematics as a whole is inexhaustible in the same sense. Gödel's first incompleteness theorem also implies that higher order logic, either in the form of simple or ramified type theory, is not complete in the sense in which propositional logic and first-order logic are complete.[16] For anyone working with an axiomatic approach along Hilbertian lines these are striking results, to say the least. The same holds for logicists working along Fregean or Russellian lines. Gödel's second incompleteness theorem adds that Hilbert's goal of establishing the consistency of central mathematical theories by restricted means is futile. In particular, no consistency proof for arithmetic can be given that doesn't employ resources stronger than arithmetic itself; likewise for set theory, etc.

Gödel's results undermine Carnap's *Allgemeine Axiomatik* project in two ways. First, Carnap thought he had proved the completeness of simple type theory, which, as just noted, cannot be the case (and his supposed proof was, in fact, flawed). Second, he believed he had established that, within simple type theory, the syntactic completeness of any axiomatic theory is equivalent to the theory's semantic completeness. Now, it is a standard theorem, and one that was well known at the time, that the higher-order axioms for arithmetic—the Dedekind–Peano axioms as formulated within simple type theory, say—are semantically complete, since categorical. Yet according to Gödel's first incompleteness theorem these axioms are not syntactically complete, as there are formally undecidable sentences in its language. But then, Carnap's equivalence 'theorem' could not be correct either (and its proof was, again, flawed).

The main significance of Gödel's incompleteness results lies in these implications. In addition, they were important because of certain notions and techniques introduced in proving them. For instance, Gödel provided an explicit characterization of 'primitive recursive' and 'recursive functions', notions later central for computability

---

[15] This brief summary glosses over several details, e.g., the fact that Gödel worked with ω-consistency, not with consistency, at a crucial point (a detail amended by Rosser soon thereafter). Moreover, a proof of the second incompleteness theorem was not included in Gödel's 1931 paper; it was supposed to appear in 'Part II', which was never published. Hilbert and Bernay's *Grundlagen der Mathematik, Vols. I–II* (1934, 1939) filled that gap in print. For a recent, technical, and detailed treatment of Gödel's theorems, see Smith (2007). For more background, cf. again Mancosu, Zach, and Badesa (2009), also George and Velleman (2002).

[16] More precisely again, for higher-order logic no deductive system exists that is adequate relative to standard set-theoretic semantics. (The situation changes if one allows for other kinds of semantics, e.g., those provided by Henkin models or by category theory; for the latter, cf. Awodey and Reck 2002b.)

theory.[17] His ingenious way of talking about expressions indirectly (in terms of 'Gödel numbers'), together with the technique of 'coding' proof-theoretic facts within arithmetic (the 'arithmetization of syntax'), also proved useful more generally. Tarski recognized quickly that they could be employed to establish a result he had conjectured before: the indefinability of the set of (Gödel numbers of) true sentences in arithmetic. More generally, Tarski and Carnap were among the first to be aware of the revolutionary character of Gödel's results. They also helped with their dissemination—Tarski by lecturing on them in Warsaw right after receiving Gödel's letter in January of 1931, Carnap by discussing them in his next book, *Logische Syntax der Sprache*.

17.5 Carnap and the Logical Syntax of Language

After learning about the fundamental problems with his 1920s approach, Carnap quickly regrouped and began working on a new project in logic. This project incorporated several big changes in his outlook. Some of them were prompted directly by Tarski and Gödel: he now worked self-consciously with the distinction between object-level and meta-level; his new approach was in line with the incompleteness theorems; and he used Gödel's technique of arithmetizing syntax at certain points. But there were other, more original, and quite radical changes as well. The two most important ones, for present purposes, are: First, Carnap explicitly abandoned the idea of working within just one (privileged, universal) logical system; instead, a whole range of such systems was to be explored. Second, none of these systems was seen as even potentially 'the correct' one, in any metaphysical or strong foundational sense; they were all just more or less useful. Taken together, what Carnap thus adopted was a kind of 'pluralistic pragmatism', a distinctive move.

The two changes just mentioned are closely related. In *Logische Syntax der Sprache* (1934) they were also tied to a third feature, already flagged in the title of the work: Carnap's 'syntactic' methodology. The guiding idea here was that philosophical disputes could be addressed in a productive way, and many of them resolved, by switching from the 'material mode of speech', in which they had traditionally been formulated, to the 'formal mode of speech'. The latter was not only seen as less misleading, but also as amenable to logical, and especially syntactic, analysis. This idea was not entirely without precedents. In fact, it was influenced by Hilbert's meta-mathematics, in which a central goal was to turn vague philosophical debates about the foundations of mathematics

---

[17] In a more encompassing survey of the development of modern logic and its connections to analytic philosophy, several other contributions to computability theory would deserve to be covered as well, especially those by Alan Turing and Alonzo Church (the notion of Turing machine, the λ-calculus, corresponding technical results, etc.). See again Mancosu, Zach, and Badesa (2009) for details.

into precise mathematical questions. What *Logische Syntax* added was to apply this idea much more widely—philosophy in general was to be done by studying the 'logical syntax of language' (in the pluralistic and pragmatist manner indicated above).

While Carnap promoted a 'syntactic' approach quite generally, his main application in *Logische Syntax* was more specific. He used it to mediate in the debates about the foundations of mathematics raging at the time, i.e., the disagreements between logicists, formalists, and intuitionists. For that purpose Carnap distinguished two languages, simply called 'Language I' and 'Language II'. Language I is a version of primitive recursive arithmetic, devised to capture the neutral core of mathematics acceptable even to intuitionists. Language II, much stronger and intended to be sufficient for all of 'classical mathematics', is a version of simple type theory superimposed on unrestricted arithmetic. Along Carnap's lines, both languages could be studied 'syntactically'. Prior philosophical arguments about them were to be put aside and, instead, their pragmatic merits weighed. To repeat, neither language was supposed to be 'the correct' one; they were just more or less useful, relative to whatever goal or goals one was pursuing.[18]

Besides this comparison of Languages I and II, *Logische Syntax* contains several other details worth noting in our context. For instance, during Carnap's discussion of Gödel's first incompleteness theorem in the book he simplified the theorem's proof in a now standard way (by introducing what has come to be called the 'Fixed Point Lemma'). In his attempt to capture the notion of 'analyticity' syntactically, Carnap partly anticipated Tarski's later analysis of logical truth (in semantic terms). And in his reflections on the relationship of logical and mathematical notions, Carnap touched on an issue that was to play an explicit role in Tarski's later investigations, namely: '[A] precise clarification of the logical symbols in our sense into logical symbols in the narrower sense and mathematical symbols has so far not been given by anyone' (p. 327). (We will come back to the latter two issues below, in Sections 17.6 and 17.8, respectively.)

With the position adopted in *Logische Syntax*, Carnap had moved far away from the logicism promoted by Frege and Russell earlier. Most crucial is his explicit rejection of the view that there is a 'correct logic' in which all reasoning is to be reconstructed; instead, there are various such systems, all to be evaluated pragmatically. This makes Carnap's position much more conventionalist and deflationist than Frege's and Russell's. At the same time, he continued to think of himself as a 'logicist' in some sense. Besides pursuing the general goal of reconstructing scientific notions logically, what made him hold on to this label was a preoccupation he took himself to share with Frege and Russell, namely: to consider logico-mathematical languages not in isolation, but to keep their application in the sciences firmly in view.[19] The main goal in this connection was to

---

[18] This is the main point of Carnap's 'Principle of Tolerance', first stated at the end of § 17 of *Logische Syntax*: 'In logic there are no morals. Everyone is at liberty to build up his own logic, i.e., his own form of language, as he wishes. All that is required of him is that, if he wishes to discuss it, he must state his methods clearly, and give syntactical rules instead of philosophical arguments' (Carnap 1937, p. 52).

[19] Concerning Carnap's logicism, cf. Bohnert (1975), the chapter by Steve Awodey in Creath and Friedman (2007), and, for a somewhat different interpretation, the chapter by Thomas Ricketts in the same volume.

clarify the role logic plays in scientific reasoning; and the specific form this now took for Carnap was to incorporate languages such as Language I and II into more encompassing frameworks, ones that contain not just 'analytic', but also 'synthetic' sentences.

So far I have only mentioned the notion of analyticity in passing. The attempt to capture this notion, and with it those of logical and mathematical truth, in 'syntactic' terms is often seen as the central legacy of *Logische Syntax* (especially after Quine's criticisms of it). Yet Carnap's turn to pluralist pragmatism is arguably more significant, especially in retrospect. Nevertheless, a few more remarks about analyticity are in order. On this issue Carnap was strongly influenced by Wittgenstein's notion of tautology. The question was, again, how to generalize it so as to cover all of mathematics. The core of Carnap's answer was to characterize logico-mathematical truths as truths based just on the formation rules of the language at issue (as 'L-truths'). But he knew that, because of Gödel's results, he could not spell this out in terms of syntactic derivability. He started to explore a variety of alternatives, in *Logische Syntax* and later, including rudimentary semantic ideas, infinitary logic, modal logic, etc. In spite of all his efforts, he never arrived at a satisfactory solution.[20] Still, these attempts led to some fruitful outcomes, including Carnap's openness to Tarski's work on truth and logical consequence.

17.6 TARSKI ON TRUTH AND LOGICAL CONSEQUENCE

We already considered Tarski's metalogical work from the 1920s briefly. This work came to further fruition, and started to be more widely influential, in the 1930s. Most central in this connection is Tarski's well-known essay on truth: 'Der Wahrheitsbegriff in den Formalisierten Sprachen' (published 1935 in German, 1933 in the original Polish). In it, the following question is addressed head on: Is it possible to define the notion of truth for a formalized language, such as the languages of arithmetic or geometry, in precise terms? For some time now, Dedekind, Peano, Hilbert, and others had used it (the notion of truth in a mathematical structure) in their axiomatic investigations implicitly, as had Fraenkel and Carnap in the 1920s. Thus it was not a matter of introducing the notion for the first time; nor was it a matter of correcting widespread mistakes in its earlier uses. Rather, the task was to reconstruct explicitly the implicit understanding that was already there, and by doing so, to set the stage for corresponding mathematical theorems (such as Tarski's theorem about the indefinability of arithmetic truth).

---

[20] For more on these failed attempts, see again the chapter by Awodey in Creath and Friedman (2007); for the connection to Wittgenstein's notion of tautology, cf. Awodey and Carus (2007); and for a helpful further analysis of Carnap's use of rudimentary semantic ideas in *Logische Syntax*, cf. de Rouilhan (2009).

Tarski's approach to this issue had three basic components: to correlate the non-logical symbols of the language with specific objects, properties, and relations (as their 'interpretation'); to use the notion of satisfaction, on that basis, for defining truth at the bottom level (for atomic sentences); and then to exploit the recursive structure of the formal language (the way in which its sentences are build up, step-by-step, out of atomic ones). Together this provides, basically, what is known today as 'truth-under-an-interpretation'. But there are a few noteworthy differences, especially the following two: The main logical framework within which Tarski still operates is a version of the simple theory of types, not first-order logic. And the now standard idea of considering various different domains over which the variables range is not used yet, as Tarski is still working with one fixed (universal) domain.[21] As a consequence, what we get is not quite the 'model-theoretic' notion of truth, only something close to it. (Tarski seems to have been aware of the latter in the 1930s, but didn't adopt it fully until later; cf. Section 17.8.)

In addition to the definition of truth itself, Tarski's paper contains other noteworthy contributions. He starts by considering general desiderata for any theory of truth, which leads to the formulation of his 'T-schema': S is true if and only if P, where 'P' can be replaced by any statement of one's language and 'S' by any name for that statement. (Standard example: 'Snow is white' is true if and only if snow is white.) This allows Tarski to note, next, that his own definition satisfies this desideratum. Two classical laws of logic also become provable: the law of non-contradiction and the law of the excluded middle. He takes that fact to speak in favour of his approach as well. Moreover, both a diagnosis and a solution for various 'semantic' paradoxes are provided, including Richard's Paradox and, especially, the Liar Paradox. The core of the diagnosis is that ordinary languages are 'semantically closed', in the sense of containing their own meta-language (which makes it possible to form paradoxical sentences). Tarski's solution is to make sure that this is not the case for formalized languages, by distinguishing the object language one studies, a meta-language for it, a meta-meta-language, etc. With such a hierarchy of languages in place, semantic notions such as truth can always be defined 'one level up', as indicated above, but never at the same level.

Yet another aspect of Tarski's treatment of truth turned out to be the most controversial, especially within philosophy. It concerns the question of whether the formal account given in 'Wahrheitsbegriff' should be seen as neutral between traditional theories of truth (correspondence theories, coherence theories, pragmatic theories, etc.) or not. Sometimes its neutrality seems to be implied by Tarski. But at other times—including in a later, more informal, and often anthologized essay, 'The Semantic Conception of Truth and the Foundations of Semantics' (1944)—he claims that what has been provided is an analysis, indeed a defence, of a traditional 'realist' conception of truth.[22]

---

[21] Along such lines one can simulate domain variation to some degree (by restricting variables, via conditionalizing, to relevant predicates). The additional step, or steps, from such an approach to the later model-theoretic one is still in need of further attention, it seems to me. (Both Tarski's and Carnap's writings from the 1930s to the 1950s might be worth reconsidering in this connection.)

[22] Already in his 1935 essay, Tarski quotes Aristotle in this connection: 'To say of what is that it is not, or of what is not that it is, is false, while to say of what is that it is and of what is not that it is not, is true' (*Metaphysics* 1011b 26).

The latter caused strong reactions, starting with the conference in Paris in 1935 where Tarski presented his definition of truth for the first time to a large audience. Several people present at that occasion, including Otto Neurath and other members of the Vienna Circle, rejected the whole approach, since they objected to the apparent reintroduction of metaphysics along such lines. Others endorsed the new treatment of truth quickly, while interpreting it in a more neutral way. The latter group included, most prominently, Carnap.

Another essay by Tarski published in the mid-1930s, besides 'Wahrheitsbegriff' (1935), is widely seen as very significant philosophically too, namely: 'Über den Begriff der logischen Folgerung' (1936). While the former provides an explicit account of truth for formalized languages, what the latter adds is a parallel account of logical consequence (in the semantic sense). Here again, Tarski formulates a precise, mathematically exploitable definition of a notion implicitly understood before. Also again, his account comes close to, but is not identical with, the current model-theoretic account (formulated explicitly in the 1950s, as we will see more below). The core idea common to both is this: A sentence A is the semantic consequence of a set of sentences $\{B_1, B_2, \ldots, B_n\}$ if and only if every interpretation that makes all the B_i ($1 \leq i \leq n$) come out true also makes A true. Two differences are, like before: In the 1936 essay Tarski still works with simple type theory, not first-order logic; and he doesn't vary the domain underlying his interpretations yet. Finally, the notion of logical truth, or 'logical validity', can now be defined as a limiting case of logical consequence, as follows: A is logically true if and only if it is a logical consequence of the empty set, i.e., comes out true under all interpretations. (This is what Carnap anticipated, partly and somewhat indirectly, in his 1934 book.)

Tarski's treatments of truth and logical consequence proved hugely influential. In mathematical logic, they would soon provide the foundation for the new subdiscipline of model theory (especially in the modified forms these treatments assumed in the 1950s). And it is in that subdiscipline that the results in axiomatics discussed earlier, from Dedekind and Hilbert to Fraenkel and Carnap, can be spelled out in full precision and pushed even further. In philosophy, Tarski's accounts were taken to be highly significant as well, even if their precise and full significance remained controversial, as already indicated.[23] Perhaps most importantly, they came to be seen as paradigmatic examples of the logical analysis of concepts, thus reinforcing Frege's, Russell's, and Wittgenstein's influence and shaping 'analytic philosophy' in a deep way. More specifically again, Tarskian semantics—as promoted and developed further by Carnap—became extremely influential in the philosophy of language and related fields.[24]

---

[23] Not only Tarski's treatment of truth but also that of logical consequence has elicited controversy, although the latter started later; cf. Etchemendy (1988, 1990), more recently the essays by Etchemendy and M. Gómez-Torrente in Patterson (2008). Concerning truth, cf. the essays by S. Feferman, M. David, and P. Mancosu in Patterson (2008), also general surveys in books such as Kirkham (1995).

[24] For its influence in the philosophy of language, see Miller's chapter in the present volume.

17.7 CARNAP ON SEMANTICS, MODAL LOGIC, AND INDUCTIVE LOGIC

Tarski's work on truth and logical consequence became widely available in 1935–6, through his publications and his participation in international meetings. Carnap's *Logische Syntax* had come out shortly before that, in 1934. However, the reception of both was thwarted for a while, especially in Europe, because of political events. The rise to power of the Nazis drove many Central European philosophers and scientists into exile—including our three protagonists, who all ended up in the United States. Carnap was the first to arrive, already in 1936, taking up a position at the University of Chicago, later another at UCLA. Tarski, who followed in 1939, eventually settled down at the University of California at Berkeley. Gödel made it to the US in 1940 and became a member of the Institute for Advanced Studies in Princeton.[25] After their relocation, all three began to publish in English, as illustrated by the (expanded) English edition of Carnap's *Logische Syntax* (1937) and by Tarski's textbook, *Introduction to Logic and the Methodology of the Deductive Sciences* (1941, translated from Polish). Partly for that reason, their ideas became most influential in the English-speaking world.

Upon his arrival in the US, Carnap continued to write on topics he had investigated before, e.g., the well-known article 'Testability and Meaning' (1936), also his contribution to the International Encyclopedia of Unified Science, the booklet *Foundations of Logic and Mathematics* (1939). However, his main attention had turned to issues in semantics by now, largely under Tarski's influence (but also building on related ideas in his own earlier writings). Carnap's focus on semantics became fully manifest in the 1940s, with publications such as *Introduction to Semantics* (1942) and *Formalization of Logic* (1943). These books were intended to establish Tarskian ideas more firmly and to make them available more widely. Carnap also integrated these ideas into his own philosophical perspective, which thus broadened beyond his previous, narrower focus on 'syntax'. As a general result, Tarskian semantics—or a combination of syntax and semantics along Tarskian and Carnapian lines (also building on Frege, Russell, Hilbert, Gödel, etc.)—became a standard part of textbooks in logic.

Carnap expanded his perspective in other respects as well, as his next book, *Meaning and Necessity* (1947), shows. The title already indicates how he intended to proceed: first, by paying systematic attention to the notion of 'meaning' (or 'intension', as opposed to 'extension'), thereby picking up on things he had learned from Frege long ago (related to Frege's notion of 'sense'); and second, by reconsidering the notions of necessity and

---

[25] Being Jewish, Tarski was most in danger. He escaped, almost accidentally, by attending a conference at Harvard in 1939. Neither Carnap nor Gödel was Jewish, but both had many Jewish friends, including some who did not manage to escape. Carnap was also politically active on the left. And by 1940, even Gödel, who was largely apolitical, was driven out by the social and political climate in Central Europe.

possibility, thus developing a novel approach to modal logic. Concerning the former, Carnap's work was parallel to and made fruitful contact with studies by Alonzo Church (on the 'logic of sense and denotation', themselves influenced by Frege). Concerning the latter, it should be noted that, while some work on modal logic had been done before, for example by C. I. Lewis at Harvard, this part of logic was still relatively marginal at the time. That started to change with Carnap's work (and soon led to major contributions by Ruth Barcan Marcus, Saul Kripke, David Lewis, and others).

Besides extending the scope of logic, Carnap's books had a strong influence on the study of natural language, thus adding to Tarskian ideas in yet another way. In his essays from the 1930s, Tarski had indicated that, while it is impossible to formalize a language such as English in its entirety (on pain of inconsistency), significant fragments of it are amenable to such treatment. Carnap's new investigations went further—they suggested ways in which one could deal with aspects of ordinary language that had proven recalcitrant to formalization so far, especially ones involving 'intensional contexts'. (His particular suggestions were soon found wanting, however, as in other cases.) Carnap's and Tarski's contributions led to 'formal semantics'. More specifically, they set the stage for possible world semantics, Montague grammar, and somewhat later, Donald Davidson's 'truth-conditional' theory of meaning. All of this had a strong impact on the nascent field of philosophy of language, but also beyond philosophy, on fields such as linguistics and computer science.[26] By focusing on language as a main topic for inquiry, it also contributed to, and built on, the 'linguistic turn' in analytic philosophy.[27]

To round off this section, let me briefly mention three further contributions in Carnap's works from the 1940s and 1950s that are still influential today: his investigations of probability and inductive logic, in *Logical Foundation of Probability* (1950b) and *The Continuum of Inductive Methods* (1952); the refinement of his deflationary views concerning metaphysics, in 'Empiricism, Semantics, and Ontology' (1950a); and the further development of his general methodology, both in *Meaning and Necessity* (1947) and *Logical Foundations of Probability* (1950). With his writings on inductive logic, Carnap contributed to yet another extension of logic, now beyond deductive logic. Its strong impact can still be felt in 'formal epistemology' (epistemic logic, Bayesian models of scientific reasoning, etc.), and more generally, in 'formal philosophy'.[28] The refinement of Carnap's deflationary approach to metaphysics—his distinction between 'internal' and 'external' questions and related suggestions—was, among others, a response to W. V. O. Quine's previous resurrection of ontology. Quine's less deflationary position dominated analytic philosophy over the next few decades, especially in the US; and together with the rise of modal logic, it led to a revival of metaphysics. Yet Carnap's

---

[26] For a survey of formal semantics that emphasizes Tarski's and Carnap's influence, cf. King (2006). In computer science, I have in mind topics such as the syntax and semantics of programming languages.

[27] On the linguistic turn, see Hacker's chapter in the present volume.

[28] Cf. Hendricks (2007) as well as Hendricks and Simons (2005), respectively. Here and elsewhere, Carnap's work in logic shades over into the philosophy of science, to which he made various other contributions as well; cf. the contributions by Mormann, Demopoulos, and Zabel in Creath and Friedman (2007).

reaction to the latter has found defenders again today. Finally, the articulation of Carnap's mature methodology in terms of the notion of 'explication'—which expands on his pluralistic pragmatism—is starting to attract attention again as well.[29]

17.8 FURTHER CONTRIBUTIONS BY TARSKI AND GÖDEL

While Carnap held positions in philosophy departments after his move to the US, Tarski's and Gödel's new professional homes were in mathematical or mathematics-oriented institutes. This reflects the main impact of their later works. From the mid-1940s on, Tarski became a major force in the mathematics department at Berkeley, gradually assembling around himself the most impressive and influential group of mathematical logicians in the world.[30] One result of their joint work, already alluded to above, was the formation and consolidation of model theory as a subdiscipline of mathematical logic in the 1950s and '60s. It was here that the notions of interpretation, truth-in-a-model, and logical consequence were all reconceived in now standard ways: by focusing on first-order logic, allowing for variations of the domain of discourse, and working in ZF set theory as the general framework.[31] While Tarski continued pursuing many of his older, philosophically rooted projects at Berkeley as well—from set theory and the foundations of geometry to decision procedures and general methodological questions—there was a general tendency to move logic away from philosophy and more in the direction of mathematics.[32] This was a self-conscious move. A main goal was to break down the barrier between logic and advanced mathematics, not the least to convince mainstream mathematicians of logic's significance. For better or worse, this contributed to a gradual drifting apart of mathematical logic and philosophy.

There were and are exceptions to this tendency, no doubt. A good example, provided by Tarski himself, is a talk he gave in 1966, entitled 'What are Logical Notions?' (Tarski 1986b). In it, he returned to a question that had been raised in connection with Frege's and Russell's works, as well as mentioned in Carnap's *Logische Syntax*, namely: Is there a principled way of distinguishing the notions of modern logic from all other notions,

---

[29] For metaphysics, cf. the chapters by Chalmers, Eklund, Hirsch, Hofweber, and Price in Chalmers *et al.* (2009). For Carnap's mature methodology, cf. Carus (2007) and, more critically, Reck (2012). As Carus makes clear, the later Carnap has moved far away from the positivistic stereotype often associated with his work.

[30] Counting colleagues, students, and regular visitors, the list includes: Addison, Chang, Craig, Feferman, Henkin, Keisler, Monk, Montague, Robinson, Scott, Vaught, and many others.

[31] For more on Tarski and model theory, cf. Vaught (1986), also again Feferman and Feferman (2004).

[32] Here I have in mind Tarski's development of algebraic approaches to logic, his exploration of connections to measure theory, topology, etc.; cf. again Feferman and Feferman (2004), earlier also two special issues of *The Journal of Symbolic Logic* on Tarski: Vol. 51 (1986) and Vol. 53 (1988).

including mathematical ones? Another way to ask this question is: What, if anything, is special about the 'logical constants' (negation, conjunction, the existential and universal quantifier, etc.)? Tarski proposed an intriguing answer (inspired by the Erlangen Program of Felix Klein): The logical constants are distinctive in being invariant under all 1–1 mappings of the universe of discourse onto itself (under all relevant automorphisms). A philosophically interesting but controversial aspect of this proposal is that it doesn't just cover the constants of first-order logic, but also, for example, those of the simple theory of types, thus leading to an inclusive view of 'logic'. The proposal's further exploration, including suggested amendments to it, has continued until today.[33]

Like Tarski's, Gödel's works published after his immigration to the US had their biggest impact in mathematical logic, although Gödel remained motivated by philosophical concerns throughout. Already in the 1930s, he had turned towards axiomatic set theory as a research focus, and it was in this area that he made his next major contribution. It concerned both the Axiom of Choice and the Continuum Hypothesis. The latter (a conjecture about the cardinality of the set of real numbers) had been formulated by Cantor, in the late nineteenth century, and then highlighted by Hilbert, in 1900, as one or the main open problem in mathematics. Yet nobody had been able to prove or disprove it. Gödel's approach—presented in *The Consistency of the Axiom of Choice and of the Generalized Continuum Hypothesis* (1940)—was, once more, strikingly original. He showed, not that AC and CH are provable, but that they are at least consistent relative to the usual Zermelo–Fraenkel axioms. His method was to construct an 'inner model' of the latter in which both AC and CH hold (the model *L* of 'constructible sets'). Doing so opened up a whole new dimension for axiomatic set theory. In 1966, Gödel's result was complemented by Paul Cohen's proof that the negations of AC and CH are also relatively consistent. Together this shows that they are independent of the ZF axioms.

Such independence results raise fundamental questions. To begin with, how should the situation in set theory now be viewed? Is it akin to geometry, where Euclidean geometry (including Euclid's Fifth Postulate) and various non-Euclidean geometries (with some form of its negation) have come to be seen as equally legitimate? In that case, neither 'Cantorian' set theory (with CH) nor 'non-Cantorian' set theories (with forms of its negation) would be true or privileged in any absolute sense. Or is such a pluralistic, relativistic view about set theory to be rejected? More basically, how could a principled decision be reached in this connection? Gödel himself suggested a direction in which to go: the study of additional axioms to decide CH, especially so-called 'large cardinal axioms' (concerning the existence of large infinities). The idea was that some of them might have a special justification, thus blocking set-theoretic relativism.

A related, more basic move by Gödel was to establish close ties between axiomatic set theory, now usually framed in first-order logic, and simple type theory (by iterating the latter's types into the transfinite, parallel to the iterative conception of set). This allowed subsuming the study of type theory under advanced set theory. It thus

---

[33] See Sher (1991), more recently also Bonnay (2008) and the chapter by Sher in Patterson (2008).

reinforced a general shift in logic, present in Tarski's works from the period as well: away from a Fregean or Russellian perspective rooted in higher-order logic, and towards seeing first-order logic and axiomatic set theory as the main foundational theories for mathematics. Gödel made various other contributions to mathematical logic that influenced its development too. Still concerning set theory, he played a role in formulating the 'Von Neumann–Bernays–Gödel' (NBG) axioms, as an alternative to the Zermelo–Fraenkel axioms, which allows for a systematic treatment of (proper) classes. He also contributed to the development of proof theory, especially in two ways: by showing that classical arithmetic can be embedded in intuitionistic arithmetic (thus establishing that certain views about their relationship were untenable); and by suggesting how Hilbert's 'finitist' standpoint might be modified and extended in a fruitful way (thus possibly circumventing his own supposed 'refutation' of Hilbert's proof-theoretic program).[34]

Yet another side of Gödel's later works concerned philosophy more directly. From the 1940s on, he published a number of overtly philosophical essays, such as 'Russell's Mathematical Logic' (1944) and 'What is Cantor's Continuum Problem?' (1947). In them (also in related lectures and unpublished notes), he endorsed a 'Platonist' or 'realist' position, to the effect that questions like the Continuum Hypothesis have objectively true answers. Such answers were to be found by a kind of 'intuitive insight', informed by rational inquiry. This went hand in hand with Gödel's study of the works of G. W. Leibniz and, from the 1950s on, those of Edmund Husserl, whose rationalist and phenomenological approaches seemed congenial to him. Gödel's Platonist remarks provoked strong and often critical reactions, while his interest in phenomenology helped to bring Husserl back to the attention of analytic philosophers.[35]

17.9 CONTINUED INTERACTIONS AND CLASHING CONVICTIONS

Carnap's, Gödel's, and Tarski's paths continued to cross after their moves to the US, both in person and in their writings. To mention just three examples of personal contacts: In 1940–1, shortly after his arrival in the US, Tarski spent a year as a research fellow at Harvard where Carnap was also visiting at the time. In 1941–2, Tarski was a year-long visitor at the Institute of Advanced Studies in Princeton, not long after Gödel had arrived

---

[34] For more on Gödel's strong influence on set theory, see Floyd and Kanamori (2006) and Kanamori (2007); for proof theory, cf. Avigad and Feferman (1995) and Tait (2006). While at Princeton, where Einstein was his colleague, Gödel even contributed to mathematical physics, by finding a surprising solution to Einstein's field equations for gravitation; see Vol. II of his collected works.

[35] For both Gödel's Platonism and his interest in Husserl, see, e.g., Parsons (1995), Tieszen (1998), Van Atten and Kennedy (2003), and Hauser (2006). For more on his unpublished writings, cf. Tait (2001).

there. And during 1952–4, Carnap spent time at the Institute in Princeton while Gödel was there. In each case, this provided the opportunity for direct interactions. One example of a crossing of paths in writing is this: When a volume on Carnap for the *Library of Living Philosophers* series was in preparation, in the mid-1950s, Gödel was invited to contribute. He spent a considerable amount of energy on preparing an essay for it, although it was not included in the end.

An interesting aspect of these later interactions is that they reveal a considerable amount about the philosophical convictions of our three protagonists. This is noteworthy especially in the case of Tarski, who generally avoided expressing philosophical views in his publications; but Gödel too had been reluctant to do so until the 1940s. What comes to the fore, moreover, is a striking divergence of philosophical outlooks. The basic contrast between Gödel's Platonist views, as expressed in his essays from the 1940s, and Carnap's deflationary position on metaphysics should be clear. Beyond that, Gödel's planned contribution to the Carnap volume—a paper entitled 'Is Mathematics Syntax of Language?'—was to contain a direct refutation of Carnap's syntax-based approach to mathematics (which Gödel never managed to formulate in a satisfactory form, thus withholding it). During Carnap's and Tarski's discussions at Harvard, in 1940–1, a different but similarly stark contrast emerges. As we know now, Tarski had nominalist convictions (partly inherited from his Polish teachers) and he expressed them forcefully on that occasion, although this did not make Carnap change his mind. Then again, Tarski's nominalism appears to have had a significant impact on two younger philosophers also present at the Harvard discussions: Quine (of that period) and Nelson Goodman, the co-authors of 'Steps Toward a Constructive Nominalism' (1947).[36]

Carnap's, Gödel's, and Tarski's many contributions to logic were thus grounded in, and partly guided by, radically different metaphysical views. Evidently these differences did not prevent them from taking each other seriously and interacting fruitfully. In Tarski's case there also seems to have been an odd disconnect between his nominalist leanings and the free use of set-theoretic methods in his meta-logical work. (Unlike Hilbert, he never restricted the means to be used at the meta-level.) Gödel always formulated his mathematical results in a way that was philosophically as neutral as possible so as not to restrict their reception. (His careful formulations of the incompleteness theorems are a good example.) Nevertheless, he was clearly motivated by philosophical convictions in his research, probably from early on. Carnap, finally, seems to have valued the mathematical expertise of both Gödel and Tarski so much that he was able to put aside their metaphysical views (as he had done with the Platonism of his teacher Frege). He also usually tried to mediate between opposed viewpoints by focusing on formal aspects, thus navigating around metaphysical quagmires.

---

[36] For Gödel's aborted criticism of Carnap in the 1950s, see Vol. 3 of Gödel's collected works. For Carnap's and Tarski's discussions at Harvard, including Tarski's nominalism, cf. Mancosu (2005, 2008). For Tarski's more general engagement with philosophy, cf. Woleński (1993) and Mancosu (2009).

17.10 CONCLUDING REMARKS

There can be no doubt about the importance of Gödel's and Tarski's contributions to the development of modern logic. They proved theorems that are among the most famous and influential in the field. They also played decisive roles in reorienting, or even creating, entire subfields of logic, such as set theory and model theory. In contrast, Carnap is seldom acknowledged as a major contributor to logic. As no specific results in mathematical logic can be connected with his name, this is understandable. Nor did any of his systematic projects in logic work out fully or result in definitive treatments, the way in which Gödel's and Tarski's did. Carnap clearly didn't have their mathematical abilities. He also wasn't as good an expositor of logic as Gödel or Tarski, both of whom were masters at it, although he still promoted logic effectively. All of this applies especially to the core areas of mathematical logic: set theory, model theory, and proof theory. But if one includes modal, intensional, and inductive logic as well, Carnap's role in the history of logic is harder to ignore. And even with respect to the core areas he played an important historical role, since he influenced Tarski and, especially, Gödel directly.

With respect to philosophy the perception tends to be the opposite. Carnap has to be covered in any respectable history of twentieth-century philosophy. His pluralistic pragmatism and his notion of explication are lasting contributions to philosophical methodology (although crude stereotypes of him as a 'positivist' still sometimes prevent their recognition). He also influenced formal semantics, metaphysics, and epistemology in profound ways. Then again, Gödel and Tarski played important roles in the development of analytic philosophy too, as we saw. In Gödel's case, this was ensured already by his incompleteness theorems, which establish something crucial about the limits of formal reasoning (perhaps also about the limits of the mind, although that is controversial).[37] In addition, his Platonist views provoked strong reactions, mostly of a critical kind. In the case of Tarski, three kinds of philosophical influence deserve highlighting: his reshaping of our views on logic, along meta-theoretic lines; his thorough impact on the philosophy of language; and the fact that his accounts of truth and logical consequence came to be seen as paradigms of logical analysis.

Overall, our conception of logic was transformed profoundly in the period from the 1920s to the 1950s. This includes the rise of meta-logic, with its sharp distinction between syntactic and semantic notions and techniques. There was also the separation and further exploration, not only of type theory (simple and ramified), first-order logic, propositional logic, and axiomatic set theory, but also of intuitionistic logic, intensional logic, modal logic, and inductive logic. Logic came into its own as a subfield of mathematics, with the rise of proof theory, model theory, and advanced set theory. Several classic positions in the philosophy of mathematics were reconceived and refined: logicism, formalism, and intuitionism, also Platonism, nominalism, and

---

[37] For controversies concerning the broader implications of Gödel's famous results, cf. Franzén (2005).

deflationism. Finally, logical tools found innovative and far-reaching applications in various branches of philosophy, as well as in linguistics and related fields, thereby affecting methodology greatly. Both individually and as a group, Carnap, Gödel, and Tarski played central roles in all of these developments. In fact, it is hard to even imagine what modern logic and much of analytic philosophy would look like without their contributions.[38]

References

Avigad, J. and S. Feferman (1995). 'Gödel's Functional ('Dialectica') Interpretation'. In S. Buss (ed.), *Handbook of Proof Theory*. Elsevier: Dordrecht, pp. 337–406.

Awodey, S. and A. Carus (2001). 'Carnap, Completeness, and Categoricity: The Gabelbarkeitssatz of 1928', *Erkenntnis* 54: 145–72.

—— —— (2007). 'Carnap's Dream: Gödel, Wittgenstein, and Logical Syntax', *Synthese* 159: 23–45.

Awodey, S. and E. Reck (2002a). 'Completeness and Categoricity, Part I: Nineteenth-Century Axiomatics to Twentieth-Century Metalogic', *History and Philosophy of Logic* 23(1): 1–30.

—— —— (2002b). 'Completeness and Categoricity, Part II: Twentieth-Century Metalogic to Twenty-first-Century Semantics', *History and Philosophy of Logic* 23(2): 77–94.

Blok, W. and D. Pigozzi (1988). 'Alfred Tarski's Work on General Metamathematics', *The Journal of Symbolic Logic* 53: 36–50.

Bohnert, H. (1975). 'Carnap's Logicism'. In J. Hintikka (ed.), *Rudolf Carnap, Logical Empiricist*. Dordrecht: Reidel, pp. 183–216.

Bonnay, D. (2008). 'Logicality and Invariance', *The Bulletin of Symbolic Logic* 14: 29–68.

Carnap, R. (1922). 'Der Raum: Ein Beitrag zur Wissenschaftslehre', *Kant-Studien*, Ergänzungsheft 56, Berlin: Reuther & Reichard.

—— (1927). 'Eigentliche und Uneigentliche Begriffe', *Symposium* 1: 355–74.

—— (1928a). *Der logische Aufbau der Welt*. Berlin: Weltkreis-Verlag; English tr., *The Logical Structure of the World*. Berkeley: University of California Press, 1967.

—— (1928b). *Scheinprobleme in der Philosophie: Das Fremdpsychische und der Realismusstreit*. Berlin: Weltkreis-Verlag; English tr., *Pseudoproblems in Philosophy*. Berkeley: University of California Press, 1967.

—— (1929). *Abriss der Logistik*. Vienna: Springer.

—— (1934/7). *Logische Syntax der Sprache*. Vienna: Springer; English tr., with additions, *The Logical Syntax of Language*. London: Kegan, Paul.

—— (1936). 'Testability and Meaning', *Philosophy of Science* 3: 419–71, and 4: 1–40.

—— (1942). *Introduction to Semantics*. Cambridge, MA: Harvard University Press.

—— (1943). *Formalization of Logic*. Cambridge, MA: Harvard University Press.

—— (1947). *Meaning and Necessity: A Study in Semantics and Modal Logic*. Chicago: University of Chicago Press.

[38] I am grateful to Michael Beaney for inviting me to contribute a chapter to this volume. I would also like to thank Jeremy Avigad, André Carus, Georg Schiemer, and Clinton Tolley for helpful comments. All the remaining problems are, as usual, my responsibility.

—— (1950a). 'Empiricism, Semantics, and Ontology', *Revue Internationale de Philosophie* 4: 20–40.

——(1950b). *Logical Foundations of Probability*. Chicago: University of Chicago Press.

——(1952). *The Continuum of Inductive Methods*. Chicago: University of Chicago Press.

——(2000). *Untersuchungen zur allgemeinen Axiomatik*, ed. T. Bonk and J. Mosterin. Darmstadt: Wissenschaftliche Buchgesellschaft.

——(forthcoming). *Collected Works, Vols. 1–13*, ed. R. Creath *et al.* Chicago: Open Court.

Carus, A. (2007). *Carnap and Twentieth-Century Thought: Explication as Enlightenment*. Cambridge: Cambridge University Press.

Chalmers, D., D. Manley, and R. Wasserman (eds.) (2009). *Metametaphysics: New Essays on the Foundations of Ontology*. Oxford: Oxford University Press.

Creath, R. and M. Friedman (eds.) (2007). *The Cambridge Companion to Carnap*. Cambridge: Cambridge University Press.

Dawson, J. W. (1997). *Logical Dilemmas: The Life and Work of Kurt Gödel*. Wellesley, MA: A. K. Peters.

Etchemendy, J. (1988). 'Tarski on Truth and Logical Consequence', *The Journal of Symbolic Logic* 53: 51–79.

—— (1990). *The Concept of Logical Consequence*. Cambridge, MA: Harvard University Press; repr. Stanford: CSLI Publications, 1999.

Feferman, A. and S. Feferman (2004). *Alfred Tarski: Life and Logic*. Cambridge: Cambridge University Press.

Floyd, J. and A. Kanamori (2006). 'How Gödel Transformed Set Theory', *Notes of the American Mathematical Society* 53: 419–27.

Franzén, T. (2005). *Gödel's Theorem: An Incomplete Guide to its Use and Abuse*. Wellesley, MA: A. K. Peters.

Friedman, M. (1999). *Reconsidering Logical Positivism*. Cambridge: Cambridge University Press.

George, A. and D. Velleman (2002). *Philosophies of Mathematics*. Oxford: Blackwell.

Gödel, K. (1929). 'Über die Vollständigkeit des Logikkalküls', Ph.D. thesis, University of Vienna; English tr., 'On the Completeness of the Calculus of Logic'. In Gödel (1986–2005), Vol. 1, pp. 60–100.

—— (1931). 'Über formal unentscheidbare Sätze der Principia Mathematica und verwandter Systeme I', *Monatshefte für Mathematik und Physik* 38: 173–98; English tr., 'On Formally Undecidable Propositions of *Principia Mathematica* and Related Systems I'. In Gödel (1986–2005), Vol. 1, pp. 144–95.

——(1940). *The Consistency of the Axiom of Choice and of the Generalized Continuum Hypothesis with the Axioms of Set Theory*. Princeton: Princeton University Press.

——(1944). 'Russell's Mathematical Logic'. In P. Schilpp (ed.), *The Philosophy of Bertrand Russell*. Evanston, IL: Northwestern University Press, pp. 123–53; repr. in Gödel (1986–2005), Vol. II, pp. 119–41.

——(1947). 'What is Cantor's Continuum Problem?', *American Mathematical Monthly* 54: 515–25; repr. in Gödel (1986–2005), Vol. II, pp. 176–87.

——(1986–2005). *Collected Works, Vols. I–V*, ed. S. Feferman *et al.* Oxford: Oxford University Press.

Goldfarb, W. (1996). 'The Philosophy of Mathematics in Early Positivism'. In R. Giere and A. Richardson (eds.), *Origins of Logical Empiricism*. Minneapolis: University of Minnesota Press, pp. 213–30.

Hauser, K. (2006). 'Gödel's Program Revisited Part I: The Turn to Phenomenology', *The Bulletin of Symbolic Logic* 12: 529–90.

Hendricks, V. (2007). *Mainstream and Formal Epistemology*. Cambridge: Cambridge University Press.

Hendricks, V. and J. Symons (eds.) (2005). *Formal Philosophy*. London and New York: VIP Press.

Hilbert, D. (1918). 'Axiomatisches Denken', *Mathematische Annalen* 78: 405–15.

Hilbert, D. and W. Ackermann (1928). *Grundzüge der theoretischen Logik*. Berlin: Springer.

Hilbert, D. and P. Bernays (1934–9). *Grundlagen der Mathematik, Vols. I–II*. Berlin: Springer.

Kanamori, A. (2007). 'Gödel and Set Theory', *The Bulletin of Symbolic Logic* 13: 153–88.

King, J. (2006). 'Formal Semantics'. In E. Lepore and B. Smith (eds.), *The Oxford Handbook of Philosophy of Language*. Oxford: Oxford University Press, pp. 557–73.

Kirkham, R. (1995). *Theories of Truth: A Critical Introduction*. Cambridge, MA: MIT Press.

Mancosu, P. (2005). 'Harvard 1940–1941: Tarski, Carnap, and Quine on a Finitistic Language of Mathematics for Science', *History and Philosophy of Logic* 26: 327–57.

—— (2008). 'Quine and Tarski on Nominalism'. In D. W. Zimmerman (ed.), *Oxford Studies in Metaphysics, Volume IV*. Oxford: Oxford University Press, pp. 22–55.

—— (2009). 'Tarski's Engagement with Philosophy'. In S. Lapointe *et al.* (eds.), *The Golden Age of Polish Philosophy*. New York: Springer, pp. 131–72.

Mancosu, P., R. Zach, and C. Badesa (2009). 'The Development of Mathematical Logic from Russell to Tarski: 1900–1935'. In L. Haaparanta (ed.), *The Development of Modern Logic*. Oxford: Oxford University Press, pp. 318–470.

Parsons, C. (1995). 'Platonism and Mathematical Intuition in Kurt Gödel's Thought', *The Bulletin of Symbolic Logic* 1: 44–74.

Patterson, D. (ed.) (2008). *New Essays on Tarski and Philosophy*. Oxford: Oxford University Press.

Reck, E. (2004). 'From Frege and Russell to Carnap: Logic and Logicism in the 1920s'. In S. Awodey and C. Klein (eds.), *Carnap Brought Home: The View from Jena*. Chicago: Open Court, pp. 151–80.

—— (2007). 'Carnap and Modern Logic'. In Creath and Friedman (2007), pp. 176–99.

—— (2012). 'Carnapian Explication: A Case Study and Critique'. In P. Wagner (ed.), *Carnap's Ideal of Explication and Naturalism*. Basingstoke: Palgrave Macmillan, pp. 96–116.

Richardson, A. (1998). *Carnap's Construction of the World: The Aufbau and the Emergence of Logical Empiricism*. Cambridge: Cambridge University Press.

Rouilhan, P. de (2009). 'Carnap and Logical Consequence for Languages I and II'. In P. Wagner (ed.), *Carnap's Logical Syntax of Language*. Basingstoke: Palgrave Macmillan, pp. 147–64.

Russell, B. (1914). *Our Knowledge of the External World*. London: George Allen & Unwin; repr. London: Routledge, 1993.

Schlick, M. (1918). *Allgemeine Erkenntnislehre*. Berlin: Springer; 2nd edn. 1925; tr. A. Blumberg as *General Theory of Knowledge*. La Salle, IL: Open Court, 1985.

Sher, G. (1991). *The Bounds of Logic: A Generalized Viewpoint*. Cambridge, MA: MIT Press.

Sieg, W. (1999). 'Hilbert's Programs: 1917–1922', *The Bulletin of Symbolic Logic* 5: 1–44.

Smith, P. (2007). *An Introduction to Gödel's Theorems*. Cambridge: Cambridge University Press.

Suppes, P. (1988). 'Philosophical Implications of Tarski's Work', *The Journal of Symbolic Logic* 53: 80–91.

Tait, W.W. (2001). 'Gödel's Unpublished Papers on Foundations of Mathematics', *Philosophia Mathematica* 9: 87–12.

—— (2006). 'Gödel's Correspondence on Proof Theory and Constructive Mathematics', *Philosophia Mathematica* 14: 76–111.

Tarski, A. (1930a). 'Fundamentale Begriffe der Methodologie der deduktiven Wissenschaften'. In *Monatshefte für Mathematik und Physik* 37: 361–404; English tr., 'Fundamental Concepts of the Methodology of the Deductive Sciences'. In Tarski (1956), pp. 60–109.

—— (1930b). 'Über einige fundamentale Begriffe der Metamathematik', *Comptes Rendue des sciences de la Société des Sciences* 23: 22–9; English tr., 'On the Fundamental Concepts of Metamathematics'. In Tarski (1956), pp. 30–7.

—— (1935). 'Der Wahrheitsbegriff in den formalisierten Sprachen', *Studia Philosophica* 1: 261–405; English tr., 'The Concept of Truth in Formalized Languages'. In Tarski (1956), pp. 152–278.

—— (1936). 'Über den Begriff der logischen Folgerung', *Actes du Congrès International de Philosophie Scientifique III* (Paris: Hermann): 1–8; English tr., 'On the Concept of Logical Consequence'. In Tarski (1956), pp. 409–20.

—— (1941). *Introduction to Logic and the Methodology of the Deductive Sciences*. Oxford: Oxford University Press.

—— (1944). 'The Semantic Conception of Truth and the Foundations or Semantics', *Philosophy and Phenomenological Research* 4: 341–76.

—— (1956). *Logic, Semantics, and Metamathematics*. Oxford: Oxford University Press; 2nd rev. edn. ed. J. Corcoran. Indianapolis: Hackett, 1983.

—— (1986a). *Collected Papers, Vols. 1–4*, ed. S. Givant and R. McKenzie. Basel: Birkhäuser.

—— (1986b). 'What are Logical Notions?', ed. J. Corcoran, *History and Philosophy of Logic* 7: 143–54.

Tarski, A. and A. Lindenbaum (1934–5). 'Über die Beschränktheit der Ausdrucksmittel deduktiver Theorien', *Ergebnisse eines mathematischen Kolloquiums* 7: 15–22; English tr., 'On the Limitations of the Means of Expression of Deductive Theories'. In Tarski (1956), pp. 384–92.

Tieszen, R. (1998). 'Gödel's Path from the Incompleteness Theorems (1931) to Phenomenology (1961)', *The Bulletin of Symbolic Logic* 4: 181–203.

Van Atten, M. and J. Kennedy (2003). 'On the Philosophical Development of Kurt Gödel', *The Bulletin of Symbolic Logic* 9: 425–76.

Vaught, R. (1986). 'Alfred Tarski's Work in Model Theory', *The Journal of Symbolic Logic* 51: 869–82.

Wittgenstein, L. (1921). *Tractatus Logico-Philosophicus*. In *Annalen der Naturphilosophie*, 14, pp. 185–262; tr. C. K. Ogden, London: Routledge, 1922; also tr. D. F. Pears and B. McGuinness, London: Routledge, 1st edn. 1961; 2nd edn. 1974.

Woleński, J. (1993). 'Tarski as Philosopher'. In F. Coniglione *et al.* (eds.), *Polish Scientific Philosophy: The Lvov–Warsaw School*. Amsterdam: Rodopi, pp. 319–38.

Zach, R. (1999). 'Completeness before Post: Bernays, Hilbert, and the Development of Propositional Logic', *The Bulletin of Symbolic Logic* 5: 331–66.

CHAPTER 18

WITTGENSTEIN'S LATER PHILOSOPHY

HANS-JOHANN GLOCK

DURING his lifetime, Ludwig Wittgenstein (1889–1951) only published one significant philosophical work, the *Tractatus*. Nevertheless, some 60 years after his death many regard him as the greatest philosopher of the twentieth century. A fairly comprehensive bibliography covering the period up to 1995 has in excess of 9,000 entries (Philipp 1996), and the stream of publications has not abated since then. Wittgenstein is the only philosopher to have made it onto the *Time Magazine* list of the '100 most important people of the [twentieth] century' <http://www.time.com/time100/scientist>. In a recent poll among professional philosophers in North America, the *Philosophical Investigations* was ranked as the most important philosophical work of the twentieth century, while the *Tractatus* came in fourth (Lackey 1999: 331–2).

As this suggests, the contribution of Wittgenstein's later work to analytic philosophy is no less significant than that of his early work. My aim is to chart that contribution, against the background of a discussion of the development of Wittgenstein's thought after the *Tractatus*. I start with a summary of that work and of Wittgenstein's 'wilderness years'. In the next section I survey the changes of mind that led Wittgenstein to abandon many of his early positions during the so-called transition period. Section 18.3 presents Wittgenstein's philosophy of mathematics and section 18.4 the main threads of the *Investigations*. Section 18.5 is devoted to Wittgenstein's last writings and the nature of his philosophical progression. Section 18.6 discusses the legacy of the later work within analytic philosophy. At the same time, that work has also inspired non-analytic philosophers. For that reason I end by addressing the question of whether the later Wittgenstein is a *bona fide* member of the analytic tradition.

18.1 THE STARTING-POINT OF THE LATER PHILOSOPHY

The *Tractatus* revolves around the relation between *thought* and *language* on the one hand and *reality* on the other (see Glock 2006; and Kremer, this volume). But its perspective on that relation reflects the philosophical problems bequeathed by the revolution of formal logic through Frege and Russell, problems that mark both an important starting-point and an abiding concern of the analytic tradition. Wittgenstein's focus is not on the epistemological worries that dominated modern philosophy after Descartes, but on logical or semantic questions that are in some respects prior to those of epistemology and metaphysics. The issue is not: How can we represent reality accurately, i.e. arrive at beliefs that are true and justified? It is rather: How can we represent reality *at all*, whether truly or falsely? What gives content to our beliefs and sense to our sentences? What enables them to be about something?

For Wittgenstein, the essence of *representation* or *intentionality* is intimately connected with the nature of *logic*, since logic comprises the most general preconditions for the possibility of representation. We represent reality through thought. But the *Tractatus* breaks with the traditional view that language is merely a medium for transmitting pre-linguistic thoughts. Thought is intrinsically linked to the linguistic expression of thought. The *Tractatus* features a striking account of the essence of symbolic representation—the picture theory of the proposition—which at the same time furnishes a metaphysical account of the basic constituents of reality—logical atomism—together with a novel understanding of logic and a revolutionary conception of philosophy itself. All meaningful propositions can be analysed into logically independent 'elementary propositions'. The ultimate constituents of such propositions are unanalysable 'names' (the simplest components of language). These names have as their meaning, i.e. stand for, indestructible 'objects' (the simplest components of reality). An elementary proposition depicts a possible combination of objects—a possible 'state of affairs'—by arranging the names of those objects in a certain manner. If that possible state of affairs actually obtains, the elementary proposition is true.

Empirical propositions have sense by virtue of depicting possible states of affairs. They are bipolar—capable of being true but also capable of being false. All propositions with a sense share a 'general propositional form': they all purport to state how things are (as a contingent matter of fact). By contrast, logical propositions are vacuous 'tautologies', since they combine empirical propositions in such a way that all factual information cancels out. 'It is raining' says something about the weather—true or false—and so does 'It is not raining'. But 'Either it is raining or it is not raining' does not. The necessity of tautologies simply reflects the fact that they make no claims whose truth-values depend on how things actually are. The pronouncements of metaphysics, finally, are not just 'senseless' but 'nonsensical'. They try to say what could not be otherwise, e.g. that red is a colour. What they seem to exclude—e.g. red being a sound—contravenes logic, and is hence nonsensical. But the attempt to refer to something nonsensical, even if only to exclude it, is itself nonsensical. What such pseudo-propositions try to *say* is instead *shown* by the structure of genuine propositions properly analysed (e.g. that 'red' can combine only with names of points in the visual field, not with names of acoustic pitch). As a result, the final propositions of the *Tractatus* condemn the preceding pronouncements as nonsensical themselves. These pronouncements serve a *propadeutic* purpose, in that they lead one to appreciate the essence of symbolic representation and thereby enable one to analyse linguistic expressions. Once this is achieved, however, one must throw away the ladder up which one has climbed. Philosophy cannot be a 'doctrine', since there are no meaningful philosophical propositions. It is an 'activity', a 'critique of language' by means of logical analysis. Positively, it elucidates the meaningful propositions of science; negatively, it reveals that metaphysical statements are nonsensical (4.0031, 4.112, 6.53f.).

With engaging modesty, Wittgenstein thought that the *Tractatus* had solved all the fundamental problems of philosophy. After its publication (1921) he therefore withdrew from academic life and took up various improbable vocations in Austria. However, Wittgenstein never lost touch with philosophy completely. Between 1923 and 1930 he had sporadic discussions with F. P. Ramsey, who, along with other Cambridge analysts, was heavily influenced by the *Tractatus*. That book had also come to the attention of the Vienna Circle. Moritz Schlick made contact with Wittgenstein, and although the latter did not take part in the weekly meetings of the Circle, he met a select few (Schlick, Waismann, Carnap, and Feigl). These discussions (recorded in WVC),[1] together with the *Tractatus*, were formative influences on the development of logical positivism in the interwar years. (For Wittgenstein's influence on analytic philosophy between the wars see Hacker 1996: chs. 3–4; for Ramsey see Glock 2005.)

In the course of these discussions, Wittgenstein developed the now notorious principle of verification, according to which the meaning of a proposition is the method of its verification. This idea has its roots in a claim which informs contemporary truth-conditional semantics, namely that 'to understand a proposition means to know what is the case if it is true' (TLP 4.024). Now Wittgenstein operationalizes this idea by maintaining that to understand a proposition is to know not just what is the case if it is true, but to know *how one establishes* whether it is true (WVC 47, 53, 79; PR 66–104, 174, 200).

Wittgenstein combined this verificationist conception of meaning with an obscure version of phenomenalism. He distinguished three different types of propositions according to whether and how they can be verified (see WVC 100–1, 159, 210–11; PR 192, 200, 282–97; PG 361). The only 'genuine propositions' are sense-data statements, which are verified by direct comparison with the subject's experience. Other empirical propositions are 'hypotheses', which can never be completely verified but only made more or less probable. Finally, mathematical propositions are not verified at all, since they neither agree nor disagree with reality. But their sense is given by their proofs, that is, by how they are justified.

---

[1] All references to Wittgenstein's works employ abbreviations explained at the beginning of the References section.

18.2 WITTGENSTEIN IN TRANSITION

His philosophical interest revived, Wittgenstein returned to Cambridge in 1929. The original intention had been to elaborate and modify some of the thoughts of the *Tractatus*. But it soon became clear that a radical rethink was required. Between 1929 and 1934, the so-called *transition period*, Wittgenstein's thought underwent a series of rapid transformations. These can be classified under five headings.

Philosophy of logic. The initial difficulty which led to the unravelling of the *Tractatus* system was the colour-exclusion problem. Colour statements like 'A is red all over' and 'A is green all over' are incompatible not just as a matter of fact but as a matter of logic. Hence, according to the *Tractatus*, they would have to be analysed further into logically independent elementary propositions (6.3751). Now Wittgenstein realized that this cannot be done, and that the same problem arises for all propositions attributing a determinate property out of a determinable range (if a stick is precisely 1 metre long, it cannot also be precisely 2 metres long). As a result he abandoned the requirement that elementary propositions are logically independent, holding instead that they form propositional systems of mutual exclusion and implication (RLF; PR ch. VIII).

However, the thesis of independence was the linchpin of the *Tractatus* philosophy of logic. Without it, Wittgenstein had to acknowledge that there are logical relations which are not the result of truth-functional composition. 'A is red' and 'A is green' are logically incompatible even though their conjunction is not a contradiction that could be displayed by a truth-table. The idea that all meaningful propositions are the result of truth-functional operations on logically independent elementary propositions thus collapses, as does the idea that there is a single propositional form (see WVC 73–4, 91–2; PG App. 4). At best there can be characteristic logical forms for the members of specific propositional systems, for example for propositions ascribing colours or lengths.

Metaphysics of logical atomism. At much the same time, Wittgenstein relinquished logical atomism. The world does not consist of facts rather than things, since facts are not concatenations of objects, and cannot be located in space and time (PG App. 2). The atomist notion of indecomposable objects is equally confused. For one thing, the distinction between simple and complex is not absolute. Standards of complexity must be laid down separately for each kind of thing, and even then they are relative to different purposes. The squares of a chess-board, for example, are simple for the purpose of playing the game, but may be complex for the purpose of producing the board (PG 221; PI § 59; Z § 338). For another, the role of simple objects is in fact occupied by the samples of ostensive definitions. What looked like metaphysical atoms are the humdrum things we point to in explanations such as 'This ☞ colour is called "red"'. Ostensively defined terms would indeed lose their meaning if all possible samples by reference to which they could be explained were destroyed. Contrary to the *Tractatus*, however, the sense of a form of words, its potential to be used to say certain things, may depend on certain contingent facts such as the existence of samples or our ability to perceive these samples (WVC 43; AWL 120; PG 208–9; BB 31; PI §§ 48–57).

Picture theory of the proposition. The collapse of logical atomism also undermines the picture theory of the proposition. If there are no ultimate constituents of facts (objects) which are simple in an absolute metaphysical sense, then there are no corresponding constituents of propositions (names) which are simple in an absolute semantic sense.

The picture theory provided a partially correct account of the intentionality of thought and language. It was right to insist on the 'pictorial' nature of propositions, insofar as the relation between a proposition ('*p*') and the fact that verifies the proposition if it is true (the fact that *p*) is logical rather than contingent, i.e. a relation that could not fail to obtain. But it went wrong in explaining that relation by holding that propositions and facts share an arcane logical form, or that a shadowy entity (a possible state of affairs) mediates between them. The mysterious 'harmony between language and reality' (the harmony between a proposition and the fact that verifies it) is simply a distorted reflection of linguistic conventions, conventions which specify, for instance, that 'The proposition that *p*' = 'The proposition which is verified by the fact that *p*' or that 'the desire, that *p* may be the case' = 'the desire which is satisfied by it being the case that *p*' (in such contexts Wittgenstein uses '=' to express semantic equivalence, sameness of meaning or role in the language). Furthermore, linguistic representation does not presuppose a one-to-one correlation between words and things, but rather that words have an established use (see PR 57, 63–71; PG 162–3, 212; PI §§ 428–65, 519–21).

Metaphysics of symbolism. A guiding principle of the *Tractatus* had been that the rules of logical syntax mirror the structure of reality (see 5.511, 6.13). Wittgenstein now held that language is 'autonomous'. 'Grammar'—the constitutive rules of language—is not responsible either to empirical reality or to a Platonic realm of abstract entities (PG 88, 184–94; PI §§ 371–3). Grammatical rules do not somehow *follow* from 'meanings', they *constitute* them. Signs *in themselves* don't have meanings; we *give* them meaning by explaining and using them in a certain way (BB 27–8).

There is not a single logical syntax shared under the surface between all meaningful sign-systems, but a genuine plurality of forms of representation. 'One symbolism is as good as the next; no one symbolism is necessary' (AWL 22). Unlike propositions, concepts cannot be true or false, correct or incorrect, but only more or less useful. While Wittgenstein rejected the idea that grammar has metaphysical foundations, he acknowledged that grammar is subject to pragmatic constraints. But he also embraced a conceptual relativism according to which no conceptual framework, no 'form of representation', is intrinsically superior to any other. Through Winch (1958), this conceptual-cum-cultural relativism had an abiding influence on post-war philosophy of social science.

Analysis and philosophy. Wittgenstein continued to hold that because of their a priori character, philosophical problems must be clarified by reference to linguistic rules. But he came to reject logical analysis as a means of achieving this clarity. There are no logically independent elementary propositions or indefinable proper names for analysis to terminate with. More fundamentally, the very idea that analysis yields unexpected discoveries about language is misguided. It does not take logical analysis to find out what our humdrum propositions mean (LWL 34–5, 90; M 113; WVC 129–30; PI §§ 60–4).

By the same token, the argument that, appearances notwithstanding, natural languages must possess the features of formal calculi is based on 'dogmatism' and 'grammatical prejudices'. In particular, ordinary language is not 'a calculus according to definite rules' that we operate when we communicate. The rules of language cannot be 'hidden', as many linguists and philosophers assume (PG App. 4; PI §§ 81, 126–8). Rather, competent speakers must be capable of recognizing these rules as the normative standards which guide their linguistic practice. To fight the 'bewitchment of our understanding through the means of our language' we require not logical analysis, but a description of our linguistic practices, which constitute a motley of 'language-games' (BB 16–7; PI § 23, 108).

The result of these transformations was a fundamentally new conception of language and of the proper procedures of philosophy. Perhaps partly as a result of reading Spengler and of discussions with the Marxist economist Pierro Sraffa, Wittgenstein adopted a more 'anthropological' perspective. Thus language is no longer seen as a self-sufficient abstract system, but as part of human practice, part of a form of life (PI § 23; RPP I § 630). Wittgenstein's new outlook contained many ideas of the *Tractatus*, yet in a framework which completely changed their significance. Indeed, the *Tractatus* was seen as 'the symptom of a disease', as Wittgenstein wrote in Schlick's copy of the book. Immediately after his return, he decided to write a new book, at first to continue, later to correct his earlier work. But he constantly changed his mind and was never satisfied with the result of his efforts. In the course of his labours he frequently selected and pruned remarks from his notebooks, and worked them into more polished and structured typescripts. None of them were intended for publication, yet some of them mark important stages in the development of his thought.

Thus the *Blue Book* contains Wittgenstein's most sustained attack on the solipsism of his verificationist phase. In both his early and middle writings, Wittgenstein had suggested that the world is simply what is represented by the subject, but that the subject of representation, like the eye of the visual field, cannot itself be represented. On the linguistic plane, this corresponds to the suggestion that the first-person pronoun 'I' can be eliminated, because being possessed by me is not a contingent feature that experiences could possibly lack. At the heart of these views lie certain peculiarities of the first-person pronoun, in particular its immunity to referential failure and to misidentification. Wittgenstein now approaches these peculiarities in a more down-to-earth fashion, and also investigates related problems about personal identity (see BB 61–7; PI §§ 398–417; II 187–92).

As early as 1932, Wittgenstein had abandoned the view that sense-data propositions provide the foundations of language, or that they can be verified by comparison with immediate experiences. Between 1934 and 1936 he lectured on private experience and sense-data. This marks the beginning of his interest in philosophical psychology, which crystallized in the private language argument, and of the idea that first-person psychological statements are avowals rather than descriptions of an inner realm.

18.3 Philosophy of Mathematics

About half of Wittgenstein's writings between 1929 and 1944 were devoted to the philosophy of mathematics—the most important of them are collected in *Remarks on the Foundations of Mathematics*—and shortly before he abandoned the topic he stated that his 'chief contribution' had been in the philosophy of mathematics. He gave various lecture courses on the subject, and during the course of one of these (recorded in LFM) was confronted with orthodox objections from the brilliant logician Alan Turing. Wittgenstein's conception of mathematics is as original as the rest of his work, and even more provocative. It views mathematics not as a body of truths about abstract entities, but, from an anthropological perspective, as a part of human practice serving a multitude of purposes (RFM 61, 92–3, 176, 182, 399). Wittgenstein rejects logicism, formalism, and intuitionism alike, and claims that the very project of providing foundations for mathematics, and the fear of 'hidden contradictions' which fuels it, is misguided (WVC 119–20; RFM 204–19, 254–6, 370–8, 400–10; LFM 209–30).

The *Tractatus* had already indicated that although mathematical equations appear to describe relations between abstract entities they are, *au fond*, rules for the transformation of empirical propositions (6.211). From 1929 onwards, Wittgenstein developed this suggestion into a radical solution to Kant's problem of how mathematical propositions can seem to hold true of empirical reality in spite of being a priori. The explanation is that they do not describe a super-empirical reality, as Platonism has it, but express *rules* for talking about empirical reality. More specifically, arithmetical equations are rules for the transformation of empirical propositions about quantities and magnitudes. For example, '$2 + 2 = 4$' licenses one to pass from 'There are *two pairs* of apples in the bucket' to 'There are *four* apples in the bucket'. Similarly, the propositions of geometry are not descriptions of the properties of space, but rules for describing the shapes of and relations among material objects (e.g. WVC 61–3, 153–63; RFM 98–9, 163–4).

By the same token, a mathematical proof is not a demonstration of truths about the nature of numbers or geometrical forms, but a piece of concept-formation (e.g. AWL 185–91; RFM 221, 309–10, 363). It stipulates a new rule for the transformation of empirical propositions. Thus, once we accept Pythagoras' theorem we have a new criterion for a figure being a right-angled triangle, namely that the square over its largest side equals the sum of the square over its two smaller sides.

Wittgenstein also freed his earlier account of logical truth from the early metaphysics of symbolism—the idea that logic arises out of the essence of linguistic representation. He thereby created a form of conventionalism, albeit one which differs substantially from that of logical positivism. Necessary propositions do not *follow* from meanings or conventions, but are *themselves* rules, norms of representation which partly determine the meaning of words. They function as or are linked to 'norms of description' or of 'representation' (see PI §§ 122, 50, 104, 158; AWL 16; OC §§ 167, 321) which lay down what counts as an intelligible description of reality, establish internal relations between concepts (e.g. between 'bachelor' and 'unmarried'), and license transformations of empirical propositions (e.g. from 'Wittgenstein was a bachelor' to 'Wittgenstein was unmarried'). It is this special, normative role, and not the abstract nature of their alleged referents which accounts for their non-empirical character. As norms of representation grammatical rules 'antecede' experience (RFM 96). It is logically necessary and is knowable a priori that bachelors are unmarried, simply because we would not *call* anybody both married and a bachelor.

18.4 *PHILOSOPHICAL INVESTIGATIONS*: A CURE FOR THE DISEASE OF THE UNDERSTANDING

In 1937 Wittgenstein started those manuscripts which eventually led to his second masterpiece, *Philosophical Investigations* (Part I). In 1939, he was appointed to succeed Moore in the chair of philosophy at Cambridge. But he suspended his appointment between 1941 and 1944 and resigned from the chair in 1947. In the same year he stopped work on the *Investigations*. Although he never finished the book completely, it was as complete as he could make it, and he authorized its posthumous publication (which was to follow in 1953).

Philosophical Investigations was meant to be read against the backcloth of the *Tractatus*. However, its critique applies not just to Wittgenstein's earlier work, but to the whole logico-metaphysical tradition to which it belongs. It is often indirect, since it confronts not specific doctrines, but the *general presuppositions* that inform them. Thus it starts with a quotation from the *Confessions* in which Augustine describes how he learned to speak (PI §§ 1–4, 21–7, 32). Wittgenstein regarded this passage as expressing a picture of the essence of language which, at least tacitly, informs a multitude of philosophical theories: words are names, their meanings are the objects for which they stand, and words are correlated with these meanings by ostension. Sentences are combinations of names which describe how things are. The essential functions of language are naming and describing, and it is linked with reality by means of word–world connections.

This seemingly innocuous referential conception of meaning is wrong in several respects. Not all words refer to objects, and there is no such thing as *the* name-relation (PI §§ 15, 37; BB 172–3). Moreover, even in the case of referring expressions, it is a misuse of the term 'meaning' to treat a word's meaning as the object for which it stands. The meaning of a word is *not* an object of any kind, but its *use* according to 'grammatical rules' (see PI §§ 43, 432, 454; BB 69). Finally, ostensive definitions do not provide an inexorable foundation of language in reality: the objects pointed at are samples, which provide standards for the correct use of words, and *in that respect* they are part of grammar (PI §§ 27–36).

Not all words are, or need to be, sharply defined by reference to conditions which are individually necessary and jointly sufficient for their application. Analytic definition is only one form of explanation among others. Many philosophically important concepts are united by 'family-resemblances' rather than by a common characteristic mark (PI §§ 65–88). In particular, propositions are not united by a common essence, a general propositional form. When we 'look and see', we shall notice that they are united not by a single common defining feature, but by a complex network of overlapping and criss-crossing similarities. Contrary to the *Tractatus*, not all propositions describe states of affairs, and even among those that do, one must distinguish different kinds. The meanings of words and the senses of sentences can only be elucidated by attending to their use within our various 'language-games' (PI § 23).

Like Frege, the *Tractatus* had invoked anti-psychologism to dismiss the question of how we understand utterances as irrelevant to logic, while tacitly relying on an obscure mentalist conception of linguistic understanding. Now Wittgenstein recognizes the importance of the concept of understanding, and provides an account of understanding which avoids both mentalism and materialism. Understanding an expression is neither a mental nor a physical state or process, but akin to an *ability*. Mental imagery may accompany linguistic understanding, and as a matter of biological fact neurophysiological processes are prerequisites of our ability to understand linguistic expressions. But as regards our *concept* of understanding, neither mental images nor neural processes are *necessary or sufficient* for understanding. Whether someone understands an expression depends on whether he can use and explain it correctly, and whether he can respond appropriately to its use by others (PI §§ 143–84).

In this context, Wittgenstein also first clarified a concept which had been central to his conceptions of language, logical necessity, and philosophy from the word go, namely that of a linguistic rule (PI §§ 185–242). There is a difference between *following a rule* and merely *acting in accordance* with a rule, otherwise planets would follow rules in conforming to Kepler's laws. If an agent follows a rule in Φing, she must Φ intentionally, and the rule must be part of her *reason* for Φing. This excludes the idea of rules which are completely unknown to the agent (such as those invoked by the model of language as a calculus of hidden rules which is common to the early Wittgenstein, contemporary theories of meaning for natural languages, and Chomskian linguistics). But how does a rule determine what counts as a correct or incorrect application? Wittgenstein rejects various tempting answers. He shows that a rule cannot be a (physiological) mechanism, since statements about mechanisms and dispositions to behave lack the *normative* dimension characteristic of rules. He also undermines the Platonic picture of rules as abstract entities, logical machines which churn out their applications independently of us. Finally, he demonstrates that connecting a rule with its application cannot always presuppose an 'interpretation' of the rule, since this would simply lead to the vicious regress of replacing one formulation of the rule by another (its interpretation). Instead, rule-following is a practice. What conforms with or violates a rule is determined by what we call 'following the rule' or 'going against it'.

In *Philosophical Investigations* the discussion of linguistic understanding leads to an examination of mental concepts in general. A concept which is closely related to that of understanding is that of thinking (see BB 24–5; PI §§ 316–62; Z §§ 100–30). According to a prevailing view, epitomized by Locke and Fodor, thinking is a mental *process* which accompanies speech and endows it with meaning. Wittgenstein attacks this natural idea. If thoughts are to give meaning to sentences they must themselves have *symbolic content*, which leads to a vicious regress. This becomes obvious if one replaces the mental accompaniment of our utterances by a physical one: a sentence plus a painting is no less capable of different interpretations than the sentence by itself. To suppose that the mind 'could do much more in these matters' because of its occult qualities is a 'mythology of psychology' (PG 99; Z § 211). Speaking with thought is not like singing and accompanying it by playing the piano, but more like 'singing with expression' (PI § 332). The difference with speaking without understanding lies in *how it is done*, and in what the speaker is *capable of doing* (notably by way of explaining and defending his utterance). 'Thinking' has an *adverbial character*: it signifies not a process that accompanies our overt activities, but how the latter are performed.

Wittgenstein adopts a similar strategy with respect to the will (PI §§ 587–94, 611–29; RPP I §§ 840–52, 897–902). Like thinking, willing is not an act or process which accompanies our overt actions. Willing is not a phenomenon that 'simply *happens*' to us, and which we observe 'from outside', but something 'we *do*'; it consists in our being 'in the action', as its true 'agent' (PG 143–50). Wittgenstein aims to undermine both the empiricist idea—prominent in James—that 'willing too is merely an experience', and the 'transcendental' idea of willing as an 'extensionless point', an ineffable mental force, an idea which derives from Schopenhauer, and which plays an obscure role in the *Tractatus* (6.373f., 6.423ff.). What distinguishes an intentional action from a mere bodily movement is not a mental act of 'volition' (an idea also criticized by Ryle), but the degree to which the action is under the agent's control, and perhaps also on the context of the action. Though often cryptic, Wittgenstein's remarks on agency and the will helped to create what we now call the theory of action, in particular through the 'analytic hermeneutics' developed by Anscombe and von Wright (see Candlish, this volume).

Philosophical Investigations tackles not just specific mental concepts, but also the mind in general. Running through the mainstream of modern philosophy is the idea that a person can be certain about his inner world of subjective experiences, yet can at best infer how things are outside him. Subjective experience was conceived not only as the foundation of empirical knowledge, but also as the foundation of language: the meaning of words seems to be fixed by naming subjective experiences (impressions, sense-data, qualia, preconceptual contents), for example through inner ostension ('"pain" means *this*'). Wittgenstein's famous private language argument undermines this assumption (PI §§ 243–314; LPE). Only if it *can* be understood by others can a ceremony of naming lay down standards for distinguishing between correct and incorrect uses of a term 'S', and hence provide that term with meaning.

Wittgenstein explicitly allows for the possibility of a language spoken or even invented by a *single speaker*; he only rules out a language which *cannot* be understood by others because its 'meanings' are private in principle. The fulcrum of his argument is neither a stipulation according to which the term 'language' is confined to sign-systems suitable for communication, nor scepticism about memory. At issue is not whether the private linguist can remember what he means by 'S', but whether he has managed to endow 'S' with meaning in the first place. To this end, the putative naming ceremony would have to lay down a rule for the correct use of 'S'. But there is no such thing as a *non-operational* rule, one which cannot even in principle be used to distinguish between correct and incorrect applications (LPP 247). Yet the putative definition of the private linguist is non-operational. The private linguist's application of 'S' at t_1 is incorrigible not just at t_1: it cannot even be corrected by him at t_2. For at t_2 nothing distinguishes the private linguist's *rectifying a mistake* by reference to a prior rule from his *adopting a new rule*. Justification consists in 'appealing to something independent', and this kind of calibration is *ab initio* precluded in the case of a private language (PI § 265). Hence there can be no private ostensive definition in which a subjective impression functions as a sample (for an alternative interpretation see Schroeder 2006: ch. 4.7).

The private language argument militates not just against a venerable conception of the foundations of language, but also against the inner/outer picture of the mind, which has dominated Western philosophy since Descartes. This picture is the main theme of Wittgenstein's last reflections on philosophical psychology (RPP II; LW I & II; PI II 222–4; RPP I 563–86, 903–22, 927–39). According to this picture, the mind is a private domain to which its subject enjoys privileged access by means of introspection, an inner gaze. What is private, my own mind, is better known than the public world of material phenomena and the minds of others. I can know for certain that I am in pain, but not that others are in pain. Wittgenstein turns this reasoning on its head. On the one hand, we often know that others are in pain on the basis of their behaviour. The behavioural criteria for the application of mental terms are partly constitutive of their meaning. Although they are defeasible, in the absence of defeating conditions it is senseless to doubt whether someone displaying them is in pain. On the other hand, to say 'I know that I am in pain' is either an emphatic avowal of being in pain or a nonsense, since knowing that one is in pain would presuppose that one can be ignorant, mistaken, or in doubt, which makes no sense (for a partial criticism of this position see Glock 1996: 304–9).

The later Wittgenstein transformed rather than abandoned his earlier methodological ideas (see PI §§ 89–133; BT 406–35). Philosophy is not a cognitive discipline—there are no propositions expressing philosophical knowledge—and cannot emulate the methods of science. But this is not a form of obscurantism. Wittgenstein stands firmly in the tradition of critical philosophy inaugurated by Kant, although his anthropological stress on human practice and his Schopenhauerian sympathy for an anti-rationalist voluntarism are at odds with Kant's intellectualism. Wittgenstein's methodological views are based on the conviction that, unlike science, philosophy is concerned not with truth, or matters of fact, but with meaning or concepts. Philosophical problems are conceptual confusions which arise out of the misapprehension of words with which we are perfectly familiar outside philosophy. These problems should not be answered by constructing theories, but *dissolved* by describing the rules for the use of the words concerned. Hence, if there were theses in philosophy, everyone would agree with them, because they would be truisms, reminders of grammatical rules (PI § 128), for example that we tell whether someone is in pain from his behaviour.

18.5 LAST WRITINGS

Having resigned his chair, Wittgenstein spent the rest of his life with various friends and disciples in Ireland, the USA, Oxford, and Cambridge. In some respects his work after the completion of *Philosophical Investigations* Part I marks a break. In that work mental concepts—intentionality, understanding, thinking—play an important role because of their connection with the main theme, the nature of language and meaning. Now philosophical psychology is discussed in its own right; indeed, between 1945 and 1949 it is the predominant theme of his writings and lectures. Whereas *Philosophical Investigations* is mainly concerned with attacking misconceptions, these works make steps towards a positive overview of mental concepts. But the emerging picture remains tentative.

Partly in reaction to Köhler's Gestalt psychology, Wittgenstein sought to dissolve the paradoxical appearance of aspect-dawning. When looking at a picture like that of the duck-rabbit, we can come to *see* it differently, although we also *see* that the object itself remains *unchanged*; it seems to have changed and yet seems not to have changed. His solution is that aspect-perception lies between thinking and interpreting on the one hand, and immediate perception on the other. Wittgenstein also reflected on the philosophical significance of aspect-blindness, in particular on 'meaning-blindness', the inability to associate words with certain characteristic experiences. During his final years Wittgenstein also worked briefly on colours (ROC) and, more intensively, on epistemology in *On Certainty*. Though only a collection of notes, this last work is among his finest. As in the areas of mathematics and of other minds, Wittgenstein tries to show that sceptical doubts about our knowledge—in this case, our knowledge about the material world—and foundationalist attempts to meet these doubts are equally misguided. G. E. Moore had maintained that there are empirical truths which he can know with certainty, for example that he was a human being, that the object he was pointing to was his hand, or that the earth has existed for many years. According to Wittgenstein, these are not cases of sceptic-proof *knowledge*. Nevertheless, the propositions highlighted by Moore constitute the 'scaffolding' or 'foundations' of our language-games and of our 'world-picture'. Sceptical doubt about them is futile, because our whole system of beliefs depends on them, including the beliefs which any doubt must take for granted. In recent years these ideas have inspired diverse attempts to undermine sceptical challenges (Stroll 1994; McManus 2004).

Although Wittgenstein's main contributions lie in central areas of theoretical philosophy, the *Nachlass* and his lectures and conversations also feature intermittent reflections on aesthetics, ethics, religion, and other cultural issues (see Cottingham 2009; Oberdiek 2009; Glock 1996: 107–11, 320–3). Wittgenstein was a cultural conservative who felt at odds with the 'spirit of the main current of European and American civilization' (CV 6–7). He detested in particular its veneration for science and its faith in progress. The early Wittgenstein believed that aesthetics, ethics, and religion feature ineffable revelations. In his later writings he adopted a more plausible view, which continues to inspire current debate. The propositions of aesthetics, ethics, and religion are not nonsensical attempts to express the unsayable. But neither are they unfounded factual claims about some kind of reality. Rather, they express certain fundamental attitudes, either of individuals or of whole communities. These attitudes are not irrational, as scientistic philosophers would have it, because they antecede matters of rational debate. These suggestions are often denigrated as 'Wittgensteinian fideism', yet they continue to fuel one of the main currents of contemporary philosophy of religion, epitomized by the work of D. Z. Phillips (1993).

The first readers of *Investigations* were struck by the sharp contrast with the *Tractatus*. Together with Wittgenstein's 'wilderness years' (1921–9) this even gave rise to the postulation of two literary *personae*—early Wittgenstein, author of the *Tractatus*, and later Wittgenstein, author of the *Investigations* (Pitcher 1964). Against this dichotomy, scholars like Kenny (1973) pointed to a whole catalogue of ideas that run through Wittgenstein's entire work, notably his conviction that philosophy is *toto caelo* different from science, and that it has to do with problems of language rather than matters of fact. Their hand was strengthened by the increasing availability of the *Nachlass*, and in particular of the manuscripts Wittgenstein composed after his return to Cambridge in 1929. However, instead of unifying Wittgenstein's *oeuvre*, these discoveries led to the idea of a distinct 'transition' or 'middle period' (see Pitcher 1964: v–vi; Arrington 1983; Stern 2005). Even more recently, the idea of a 'Wittgenstein' postdating the *Investigations* has been launched (Moyal-Sharrock 2004), on the grounds that *On Certainty* adopts a distinct outlook.

The alternative tack has been to deny any fundamental change. Thus Hintikka (1996) has maintained that Wittgenstein continued to hold on to the ineffability of semantics and the privacy of experience, merely switching from a phenomenological to a physicalist language grounded in our everyday language-games. An even greater continuity is assumed by the so-called 'New Wittgensteinians', who deny that the *Tractatus* was ever committed to any metaphysical claims from which the later Wittgenstein could have distanced himself. In my judgement, it is best to steer a middle course between the Scylla of multiplying Wittgensteins *sine necessitatem* and the Charybdis of 'Mono-Wittgensteinianism' (Conant 2007). Wittgenstein's explicit pronouncements, most notably in the Preface of *Philosophical Investigations*, support the impression one gets from reading his manuscripts and typescripts in sequence: there was a single major, though gradual and multifaceted, change in philosophical outlook, namely from the logico-metaphysical vision of the *Tractatus* to its dialectic demolition in the *Investigations*. By contrast, the other changes concern mainly the manner of representation or the focus of attention. Thus Wittgenstein's writings after 1945 nowhere contradict *Philosophical Investigations* substantially, but rather complement it and extend it to new areas.

18.6 WITTGENSTEIN'S LEGACY

Wittgenstein continued working right up to his death. His last words were 'Tell them I've had a wonderful life!' This would be startling as a comment on his personal life, which was dominated by torment and self-obsession. But it is unsurprising as a comment on his philosophical life, which was one of momentous achievements. If, philosophically speaking, the seventeenth century was the age of science, the eighteenth century the age of reason, and the nineteenth century the age of history, the twentieth century was the age of logic and language. Logic would have loomed large without Wittgenstein, due to Frege and Russell. But it was Wittgenstein who provided a powerful methodological rationale for its prominent role, and who brought language decisively into the equation. Finally, I suspect that the current century will be that of philosophical anthropology, and in that case Wittgenstein's anthropological perspective with its emphasis on the social and cultural nature of human beings will play an important part.

His main contributions lie in five areas: philosophy of language, philosophy of logic and mathematics, philosophical psychology, epistemology, and philosophical methodology. In each of them his views were original and revolutionary.

Many philosophers of the past have disparaged the theories of their predecessors as false, unfounded, or pointless. But according to Wittgenstein, metaphysical theories suffer from a more basic defect, namely that of being nonsensical. It is not just that they provide wrong answers; rather, the questions they address are misguided. The idea of rejecting the assumptions underlying long-standing philosophical problems and disputes goes back to Kant's Transcendental Dialectic. But it is also a fundamental—though currently under-appreciated—theme of analytic philosophy. Moore's tactic of *questioning the question* attempts to *dissolve* rather than answer those questions which lead to misguided philosophical alternatives (1903: vi). Similarly, Russell's theory of types introduces a systematic dichotomy between propositions which are true or false and statements which are not even truth-apt, although they may be impeccable as regards vocabulary and syntax. The strategy of questioning underlying assumptions was also endorsed by Ramsey (1931: 115–16), presumably under Wittgenstein's influence. At any rate, it is in Wittgenstein that this *critique of (non-)sense* comes to fruition. He eschewed received positions and rejected traditional alternatives (realism/idealism; Cartesianism/behaviourism; Platonism/formalism), demonstrating his unique ability to bring to light the most fundamental unchallenged presuppositions. In subjecting these assumptions to critical scrutiny he combined dialectical acuity and imaginative analogical thought.

Through the mediation of Carnap, the *Tractatus* shaped much subsequent philosophy of language, in particular the project of a theory of meaning for natural languages. Ironically, after his return to philosophy, Wittgenstein himself attacked various fundamental assumptions of this project, such as the referential conception of meaning and the calculus model of language. He also developed the most sustained and sophisticated attack ever on the inner/outer picture of the mind, which has dominated modern philosophy since Descartes. In all these respects he was a major force in analytic philosophy between the 1930s and 1970s (for Wittgenstein's influence on post-war analytic philosophy see Hacker 1996: chs. 6–8 and Glock 2008a; for different interpretations of his work see Glock 2007). The initial impact of Wittgenstein's later ideas was through teaching, lecture notes, and dictations. As a result it was largely confined to his colleagues and pupils at Cambridge—Malcolm, Anscombe, and von Wright pre-eminent among them.

This influence through hearsay was decisively superseded by the publication of the *Investigations*, and later of parts of the *Nachlass*. The later Wittgenstein was a guiding force behind so-called 'Oxford ordinary language philosophy', especially the work of Ryle and Strawson. They themselves preferred labels such as 'conceptual analysis' or 'linguistic philosophy'. For they regarded philosophical problems as conceptual and concepts as embodied in language.

Since the 1960s, Wittgensteinian scholarship and interest in his work has flourished. But the influence of Wittgenstein's thought on the mainstream of analytic philosophy has waned. This is due partly to the dominance of Quine's naturalistic, or scientistic, conception of philosophy; partly to the rise of essentialist metaphysics in the wake of the realist semantics of Kripke and Putnam. Furthermore, the conception of language presented by the *Investigations* lost out to Tractarian theories of meaning—as developed by Davidson and Dummett—complemented by Chomskian linguistics. Finally, Wittgenstein's philosophical psychology was replaced by materialist theories fuelled by neurophysiology and functionalist theories fuelled by computer science. But many of the arguments which are widely agreed to have refuted Wittgenstein and conceptual analysis more generally in these areas are either based on misunderstanding or are inconclusive at best (see Glock 2008a).

In any event, one should not exaggerate the decline of Wittgenstein's influence. Thus Wittgenstein was an important inspiration behind the historicist revolution led by Kuhn that continues to shape contemporary history and philosophy of science (see Kindi 2006; Preston 2008). Furthermore, in recent years the naturalistic assimilation of philosophy to natural science has increasingly been challenged and conceptual analysis has been rehabilitated, not least through recourse to Wittgenstein. While some contemporaries maintain that Wittgenstein's distinction between conceptual and factual (grammatical and empirical) problems and propositions does not fall prey to Quine's attacks on the analytic/synthetic distinction (Baker and Hacker 2009), others have tried to rehabilitate that distinction, partly by appeal to his ideas (e.g. Glock 2003: ch. 3; Schroeder 2009). Similarly, the essentialist claim that there are *de re* necessities has been challenged on Wittgensteinian grounds (Hanfling 2000).

Several contemporary Wittgensteinians are not just accomplished interpreters, they have also made seminal and high-profile contributions to current debates in the philosophy of mind, neurophilosophy, the philosophy of language, and epistemology. This holds true in particular of Kenny (1989) and Hacker (Bennett and Hacker 2003), who attack contemporary 'neurophilosophy' and challenge both Cartesianism and materialism by combining Wittgenstein's and Ryle's attacks on the inner/outer model of the mind with Aristotelian-cum-Thomistic explorations of mental abilities.

Moreover, there is a small but distinguished group of leading analytic philosophers who are neither specialist scholars nor card-carrying Wittgensteinians, yet who have drawn on his ideas in various important ways. Thus the semantic anti-realism of Dummett and Wright is inspired both by Wittgenstein's verificationism and by his rule-following considerations. And Putnam came to recognize affinities with Wittgenstein as part of his more general move towards a kind of neo-pragmatism (e.g. Putnam

1995). Indeed, even philosophers who are generally regarded as hostile to Wittgenstein have acknowledged important intellectual debts to him. Thus Wittgenstein's attack on the inner/outer model and the notion of behavioural patterns in a social form of life are important sources both for Dennett's instrumentalism and for Burge's anti-individualism. *Mutatis mutandis* for Searle's (e.g. 1987) scepticism about strong artificial intelligence and 'deep unconscious' rule-following and his claim that even the most evolved mental life presupposes a background of non-representational and non-theoretical capacities and dispositions.

Another important strand of contemporary philosophy is indebted to Wittgenstein's later work in a more comprehensive way. McDowell's attempt to undermine both empiricism and rationalism not only grows out of the suggestion that perception is non-inferential, it is also an avowed exercise in Wittgensteinian therapy (McDowell 1994). McDowell's combination of Kantianism and Wittgensteinianism has strong affinities to Sellars, who had coined the dismissive phrase 'myth of the given' for sense-data empiricism. Sellars is also the founding father of a semantic approach inspired by Wittgenstein that is highly influential at present (see Sellars 1963: chs. 7 and 11; also Brandom, this volume). Conceptual or inferential role semantics starts out from Wittgenstein's slogan that meaning is use. Unfortunately, that slogan suffers from the fact that the notion of meaning is highly unspecific. Conceptual role semantics therefore refines it by identifying a more narrowly specified kind of use, namely the role of expressions in inferences. By contrast to some versions of conceptual role semantics, the one initiated by Sellars and further developed by Brandom also goes back to Wittgenstein in another respect, namely, its emphasis on the normative dimension of language. An expression has a meaning only insofar as it is subject to conditions for its correct application. Linguistic behaviour is guided by rules of a specifically semantic (Wittgenstein would have said 'grammatical') kind. These are only implicit in our practices and need to be made explicit (as in the title of Brandom 1994; for a similar approach see von Savigny 1983).

Rules and rule-following are also the topic of Kripke's stimulating discussion of Wittgenstein's so-called 'rule-following considerations'. Kripke does not purport to provide an accurate account of the primary texts, but to propound 'Wittgenstein's argument as it struck Kripke' (1982: 5). As regards its content, Kripke's interpretation is characterized by two features. First, like Fogelin (1976) before him, he portrays Wittgenstein as constructing a sceptical paradox in the style of Hume, one which questions the possibility of distinguishing between following and violating a rule, and thereby casts doubt on the very phenomenon of meaning. Secondly, he adopts a *communitarian* reading according to which rule-following and language are inherently social. Kripke's book was the starting-point for a debate about 'Kripkenstein' on rule-following, a debate which is now conducted largely in blissful disregard for Wittgenstein's own writings (see Miller and Wright 2002). Kripke's quasi-interpretation provoked hostile reactions from several scholars (e.g. Baker and Hacker 1984). Nevertheless, it placed rule-following at the centre of attention and helped to revive interest in Wittgenstein's philosophy of mathematics. And while the sceptical interpretation of Wittgenstein is wrong and the community interpretation contentious at best, as regards the *normativity of meaning*, Kripke has highlighted and ably defended a genuinely Wittgensteinian idea.

Norms are also central to what is currently the most pertinent legacy of the later Wittgenstein. I am thinking of attempts to avoid *both* epistemological naturalism, the view that there is no knowledge outside of natural science, *and* ontological supernaturalism, the view that there are supernatural entities such as God, Platonic forms, or Cartesian souls (see Glock 2008b: 137–46). The basic idea is that human beings are special not because they are connected to a reality beyond the physical world of space, time, and matter, but because language and human practice more generally can only be adequately understood from a normative perspective alien to the natural sciences. For this reason, there is knowledge outside of natural science, knowledge of meaning and of necessary truths, for example, even though it does not deal with supernatural entities.

This 'third way' goes back to Wittgenstein's comparison of language to a game like chess. On the one hand, a chess-piece is a piece of wood whose constitution can be described by physics. On the other hand, one cannot explain what a chess-piece or what the game of chess is in purely physical terms. Yet the difference between a chess-piece and a simple piece of wood is not that the former is associated with an abstract entity or with a process in a separate mental realm. Rather, it is that the chess-piece has a role in a rule-guided practice (PI § 108).

That practice in turn presupposes agents with special and distinctively human capacities. Yet while these capacities cannot be adequately characterized in physical terms, they do not transcend the natural world. They are perfectly intelligible features of animals of a unique kind; and their causal prerequisites and evolutionary emergence can be explained by science.

18.7 The later Wittgenstein and Analytic Philosophy

Although the *Tractatus* is an exotic work by any standards, it is indisputably a classic of analytic philosophy, and indeed the source of its linguistic turn (see Glock 2008b: 34–9, 121–34, and Hacker, this volume). Wittgenstein's later *oeuvre*, by contrast, is a contested case. While some regard it as the crowning achievement of the analytic tradition, others fervently deny this, and yet others claim it for what is known under the misleading label 'continental philosophy' (see Glock 2004). Thus according to Cavell's influential approach, the *Investigations* manifests existential tensions typical of the modern subject. Wittgenstein is torn between the deep human need to transcend the limitations of the ordinary and the realization that such attempts are ultimately futile (1969, 2001; see also Mulhall 2001).

What one makes of this issue naturally depends on one's construal of analytic philosophy. In *What is Analytic Philosophy?* I have argued at length that analytic philosophy cannot be defined by reference to specific doctrines, topics, methods, or even a distinctive style. Instead it is a loose historical movement that is held together by ties of influence on the one hand and various family resemblances on the other. From that perspective, the later Wittgenstein's membership of the analytic tradition becomes evident. He was mainly influenced by analytic philosophers (Frege, Russell, Moore, and of course the author of the *Tractatus*), and he in turn mainly influenced analytic philosophers (Moore, Wittgensteinians and conceptual analysts in general, post-positivism). This is not to deny that he was also influenced by non-analytic philosophers (Schopenhauer, James, Spengler) and that he in turn influenced movements outside of the analytic tradition (hermeneutics, post-modernism). But these influences are less extensive, and they are rarely crucial to the all-important details of his reflections.

This verdict is reinforced by looking at the features which run through different parts of the analytic family. As regards the linguistic turn and the demarcation of philosophy from science, which characterizes a main strand of analytic philosophy between the *Tractatus* and the ascendancy of Quine, Wittgenstein passes with flying colours.

Even the method of analysis is not as alien to the later work as one might suppose. Philosophical problems are resolved by explaining expressions and by establishing the status and inferential powers of the statements in which they occur. In this context Wittgenstein continued to endorse a liberal conception of analysis, which is very close to what Ryle calls logical geography and Strawson calls connective analysis (for diverse conceptions of analysis within the analytic tradition see Beaney 2003; Glock 2008b: chs. 2 and 6.1).

> A sentence is completely logically analysed, when its grammar is laid out completely clearly. (BT 417; see also PI § 90)

We analyse a sentence (proposition) by describing its implications, compatibilities, and incompatibilities. And we analyse a term (concept) by describing the conditions and circumstances of its use, the way it is explained, and the criteria for understanding it. What survives the rejection of logical and reductive analysis is conceptual analysis and linguistic paraphrase.

There have always been 'irrationalist' interpretations of Wittgenstein's later work, which distance it from the ideal of rational argument that is dear to most analytic philosophers (for a critical discussion see Glock 2007). And it must be conceded that there are passages in which Wittgenstein stresses the therapeutic aspirations of his enterprise (e.g. PI §§ 133, 254–5), or suggests that philosophy might proceed exclusively through jokes and questions (RFM 147; Malcolm 1984: 27–8). On the other hand, he insisted that philosophy should provide arguments that are 'absolutely conclusive', and he described his own thought as the 'rejection of wrong arguments', an avenue open to those feeling a need for 'transparency of their own argumentation' (MS 161: 3; BT: 408, 421). Wittgenstein's work contains or at least intimates plenty of powerful and profound arguments of an elenctic or dialectic rather than demonstrative type. It is just that, because of his idiosyncratic style, these arguments need to be spelled out by painstaking exegesis.

The rational line for *interpreters* is to acknowledge that Wittgenstein's work combines rationalist and irrationalist elements. The rational line for *philosophers* is to explore the arguments, insights, and instructive errors it has to offer. This exhortation presupposes, of course, that philosophy is an enterprise based on reasoning. But since one cannot reason against this presupposition without self-refutation, it is one to which we should commit.[2]

References

I Wittgenstein's published works in order of composition

The date of composition is specified in square brackets where appropriate.

TLP   *Tractatus Logico-Philosophicus*, tr. D. F. Pears and B. F. McGuinness. London: Routledge and Kegan Paul, 1961. References are to numbered sections. *Tractatus Logico-Philosophicus* [German–English Parallel text], tr. C. K. Ogden. London: Routledge, 1990. First published 1922. *Logisch-Philosophische Abhandlung*, Kritische Edition, ed. B. McGuinness and J. Schulte. Frankfurt: Suhrkamp, 1989.
      First German edition in *Annalen der Naturphilosophie*, Vol. 14 (1921), 185–262.

RLF   'Some Remarks on Logical Form', *Proceedings of the Aristotelian Society*, suppl. vol. 9 (1929): 162–71.

CV   *Culture and Value* [German–English Parallel text], ed. G. H. von Wright in collaboration with H. Nyman, tr. P. Winch. Oxford: Blackwell, 1980.
      Vermischte Bemerkungen. Frankfurt: Suhrkamp, 1984.

PR   *Philosophical Remarks* [1929–30], ed. R. Rhees, tr. R. Hargreaves and R. White. Oxford: Blackwell, 1975.
      Philosophische Bemerkungen. Frankfurt: Suhrkamp, 1984.

PG   *Philosophical Grammar*, ed. R. Rhees, tr. A. J. P. Kenny. Oxford: Blackwell, 1974.
      Philosophische Grammatik. Frankfurt: Suhrkamp, 1984.

BB   *The Blue and Brown Books* [1933–5]. Oxford: Blackwell, 1958.

RFM   *Remarks on the Foundations of Mathematics* [1937–44], ed. G. H. von Wright, R. Rhees, G. E. M. Anscombe, tr. G. E. M. Anscombe, rev. edn. Oxford: Blackwell, 1978.
      Bemerkungen zu den Grundlagen der Mathematik. Frankfurt: Suhrkamp, 1984.

PI   *Philosophical Investigations* [German–English Parallel text], ed. G. E. M. Anscombe amd R. Rhees. Oxford: Blackwell, 1958; 1st edn. 1953. References are to sections of Part I (except for footnotes), and to pages of Part II.

RPP I   *Remarks on the Philosophy of Psychology* [1945–7, German–English Parallel text], Volume I, ed. G. E. M. Anscombe and G. H. von Wright, tr. G. E. M. Anscombe. Oxford: Blackwell, 1980.

RPP II   *Remarks on the Philosophy of Psychology* [1948, German–English Parallel text], Volume II, ed. G. H. von Wright and H. Nyman, tr. C. G. Luckhardt and M. A. E. Aue. Oxford: Blackwell, 1980.
      Bemerkungen zur Philosophie der Psychologie. Frankfurt: Suhrkamp, 1984.

Z   *Zettel* [1945–8, German–English Parallel text], ed. G. E. M. Anscombe and G. H. von

---

[2] For comments and corrections I should like to thank Mike Beaney, David Dolby, and Peter Hacker.

Wright, tr. G. E. M. Anscombe. Oxford: Blackwell, 1967.

LW I   *Last Writings on the Philosophy of Psychology* [1948–9, German–English Parallel text], Volume 1, ed. G. H. von Wright and H. Nyman, tr. C. G. Luckhardt and M. A. E. Aue. Oxford: Blackwell, 1982.
Letzte Schriften zur Philosophie der Psychologie. Frankfurt: Suhrkamp, 1984.

LW II   *Last Writings on the Philosophy of Psychology* [1949–51, German–English Parallel text], Volume 2, ed. G. H. von Wright and H. Nyman, tr. C. G. Luckhardt and M. A. E. Aue. Oxford: Blackwell, 1992.

OC   *On Certainty* [1951, German–English Parallel text], ed. G. E. M. Anscombe and G. H. von Wright, tr. D. Paul and G. E. M. Anscombe. Oxford: Blackwell, 1969.
Über Gewißheit. Frankfurt: Suhrkamp, 1984.

ROC   *Remarks on Colour* [1951, German–English Parallel text], ed. G. E. M. Anscombe, tr. L. L. McAlister and Margarete Schättle. Oxford: Blackwell, 1980; 1st edn. 1977.

II Wittgenstein's lectures and conversations

WVC   *Wittgenstein and the Vienna Circle* [1929–32], shorthand notes recorded by F. Waismann, ed. B. F. McGuinness. Oxford: Blackwell, 1979.*Ludwig Wittgenstein und der Wiener Kreis.* Oxford: Blackwell, 1967 and Frankfurt: Suhrkamp, 1984.

M   'Wittgenstein's Lectures in 1930–33', in G. E. Moore, *Philosophical Papers.* London: George Allen & Unwin, 1959. References are to the reprinted version in PO.

LWL   *Wittgenstein's Lectures, Cambridge 1930–32*, from the notes of J. King and D. Lee, ed. Desmond Lee. Oxford: Blackwell, 1980.

AWL   *Wittgenstein's Lectures, Cambridge 1932–35*, from the notes of A. Ambrose and M. MacDonald, ed. A. Ambrose. Oxford: Blackwell, 1979.

LPE   'Wittgenstein's Notes for Lectures on "Private Experience" and "Sense Data"' [1936], ed. R. Rhees, *Philosophical Review,* 77 (1968): 275–320.

LFM   *Wittgenstein's Lectures on the Foundations of Mathematics, Cambridge 1939*, from the notes of R. G. Bosanquet, N. Malcolm, R. Rhees, and Y. Smythies, ed. C. Diamond. Sussex: Harvester Press, 1976.

LPP   *Wittgenstein's Lecture on Philosophy of Psychology 1946–7*, notes by P. T. Geach, K. J. Shah, A. C. Jackson, ed. P. T. Geach. Sussex: Harvester Press, 1988.

PO   *Philosophical Occasions* [German–English Parallel texts where appropriate], ed. J. Klagge and A. Nordmann. Indianapolis: Hackett 1993. Unless otherwise specified, writings in this anthology are cited after the original paginations, which are given in brackets.

III Works of other authors

Arrington, R. L. (1983). 'Representation in Wittgenstein's *Tractatus* and Middle Writings', *Synthese* 56: 181–98.

Baker, G. P. and P. M. S. Hacker (1984). *Scepticism, Rules and Language.* Oxford: Blackwell.

—— (2009). *Rules, Grammar and Necessity,* 2nd edn. Oxford: Blackwell.

Beaney, M. (2003). 'Analysis'. *The Stanford Encyclopedia of Philosophy* (Summer 2003 Edition), ed. E. N. Zalta. Online at: <http://plato.stanford.edu/archives/sum2003/entries/analysis/>.

Bennett, R. and P. M. S. Hacker (2003). *The Philosophical Foundations of Neuroscience.* Oxford: Blackwell.

Brandom, R. (1994). *Making it Explicit*. Cambridge, MA: Harvard University Press.

Cavell, S. (1969). *Must We Mean What We Say?* New York: Scribner.

——(2001). 'The *Investigations'* Everyday Aesthetics of Itself'. In T. McCarthy and S. C. Stidds (eds.), *Wittgenstein in America*. New York: Oxford University Press, pp. 250–66.

Conant, J. (2007). 'Mild Mono-Wittgensteinianism'. In A. Crary (ed.), *Wittgenstein and the Moral Life*. Cambridge, MA: MIT Press, pp. 31–142.

Cottingham, J. (2009). 'The Lessons of Life: Wittgenstein, Religion and Analytic Philosophy'. In H. J. Glock and J. Hyman (eds.), *Wittgenstein and Analytic Philosophy*. Oxford: Oxford University Press, pp. 203–27.

Fogelin, R. F. (1976). *Wittgenstein*. London: Routledge, 2nd edn. 1987.

Glock, H. J. (1996). *A Wittgenstein Dictionary*. Oxford: Blackwell.

——(2003). *Quine and Davidson*. Cambridge: Cambridge University Press.

——(2004). 'Was Wittgenstein an Analytic Philosopher?' *Metaphilosophy* 35: 419–44.

——(2005). 'Ramsey and Wittgenstein: Mutual Influences'. In M. J. Frápolli (ed.), *F. P. Ramsey: Critical Reassessments*. London: Continuum, pp. 41–68.

——(2006). '*Tractatus Logico-Philosophicus'*. In J. Shand (ed.), *Central Works of Philosophy* Vol. 4. Chesham: Acumen, pp. 71–91.

—— (2007). 'Perspectives on Wittgenstein: An Intermittently Opinionated Survey'. In G. Kahane, E. Kanterian, and O. Kuusela (eds.), *Wittgenstein and His Interpreters*. Oxford: Blackwell, pp. 37–65.

——(2008a). 'Analytic Philosophy: Wittgenstein and After'. In D. Moran (ed.), *The Routledge Companion to Twentieth Century Philosophy*. London: Routledge, pp. 76–117.

——(2008b). *What is Analytic Philosophy?* Cambridge: Cambridge University Press.

Glock, H. J. and J. Hyman (eds.) (2009). *Wittgenstein and Analytic Philosophy*. Oxford: Oxford University Press.

Hacker, P. M. S. (1996). *Wittgenstein's Place in Twentieth Century Analytical Philosophy*. Oxford: Blackwell.

Hanfling, O. (2000). *Philosophy and Ordinary Language*. London: Routledge.

Hintikka, J. (1996). *Ludwig Wittgenstein: Half-Truths and One-and-a-Half Truths*. Dordrecht: Kluwer.

Kenny, A. (1973). *Wittgenstein*. Harmondsworth: Penguin.

——(1989). *The Metaphysics of Mind*. Oxford: Oxford University Press.

Kindi, V. (2006). 'The Relation of History of Science in the *Structure of Scientific Revolutions* and Kuhn's Later Philosophical Work', *Perspectives on Science* 13: 495–530.

Kripke, S. (1982). *Wittgenstein on Rules and Private Language*. Cambridge, MA: Harvard University Press.

Lackey, D. (1999). 'What are the Modern Classics? The Baruch Poll of Great Philosophy in the Twentieth Century', *Philosophical Forum* 4: 329–46.

McDowell, J. (1994). *Mind and World*. Cambridge, MA: Harvard University Press.

McManus, D. (ed.) (2004). *Wittgenstein and Scepticism*. London: Routledge.

Malcolm, N. (1984). *Ludwig Wittgenstein: A Memoir*. Oxford: Oxford University Press.

Miller, A. and C. Wright (eds.) (2002). *Rule-Following and Meaning*. Chesham: Acumen.

Moore, G. E. (1903). *Principia Ethica*. Cambridge: Cambridge University Press.

Moyal-Sharrock, D. (ed.) (2004). *The Third Wittgenstein: The Post-Investigations Works*. Aldershot: Ashgate.

Mulhall, S. (2001). *Inheritance and Originality: Wittgenstein, Heidegger, Kierkegaard*. Oxford: Oxford University Press.

Oberdiek, H. (2009). 'Wittgenstein's Ethics: Boundaries and Boundary Crossings'. In H. J. Glock and J. Hyman (eds.), *Wittgenstein and Analytic Philosophy*. Oxford: Oxford University Press, pp. 175–202.

Philipp, P. (1996). *Bibliographie zur Wittgenstein-Literatur*. Bergen: Wittgenstein Archives.

Phillips. D. Z. (1993). *Wittgenstein and Religion*. New York: St. Martin's Press.

Pitcher, G. (1964). *The Philosophy of Wittgenstein*. Englewood Cliffs: Prentice-Hall.

Preston, J. (2008). *Kuhn's* The Structure of Scientific Revolutions. London: Continuum.

Putnam, H. (1995). *Pragmatism*. Oxford: Blackwell.

Ramsey, F. P. (1931). *The Foundations of Mathematics*. London: Routledge & Kegan Paul.

Savigny, E. von (1983). *Zum Begriff der Sprache*. Stuttgart: Reclam.

Schroeder, S. (2006). *Wittgenstein: The Way out of the Fly-Bottle*. Cambridge: Polity Press.

——(2009). 'Analytic Truths and Grammatical Propositions'. In H. J. Glock and J. Hyman (eds.), *Wittgenstein and Analytic Philosophy*. Oxford: Oxford University Press, pp. 83–108.

Searle, J. (1987). 'Wittgenstein'. In B. Magee (ed.), *The Great Philosophers*. Oxford: Oxford University Press, pp. 320–47.

Sellars, W. (1963). *Science, Perception and Reality*. London: Routledge & Kegan Paul.

Stern, D. (2005). 'How Many Wittgensteins?' In A. Pichler and S. Säätelä (eds.), *Wittgenstein: The Philosopher and his Works*. Bergen: Wittgenstein Archives, pp. 164–88.

Stroll, A. (1994). *Moore and Wittgenstein on Certainty*. New York: Oxford University Press.

Winch, P. (1958). *The Idea of a Social Science and its Relation to Philosophy*. London: Routledge & Kegan Paul.

CHAPTER 19

QUINE, KRIPKE, AND PUTNAM

MARIA BAGHRAMIAN AND
ANDREW JORGENSEN

19.1 INTRODUCTION

The emergence of semantic externalism and its dominance is undoubtedly one of the most significant philosophical developments of the past fifty years. Saul Kripke and Hilary Putnam's rejection of Fregean and Russellian accounts of names introduced profound changes not just in philosophy of language, but also in our thinking about mind, metaphysics, epistemology, and even ethics. Their key ideas—rigid designators, aposteriori necessity, division of linguistic labour, the twin earth thought experiment, etc.—have become the common tools of how we think about our discipline and conduct our craft. This momentous development, however, was preceded by an earlier and equally significant challenge to philosophical orthodoxy: Quine's attempt at naturalizing philosophy, which centrally involved his questioning of the very idea of analyticity and hence the possibility of having a coherent conception of meaning as traditionally construed. The broad outline of these tectonic changes is well known and discussions of their significance abound. What, at least until recently, have been neglected are the metaphilosophical consequences of the changes these philosophers had wrought and their impact on philosophical methodology. In this chapter we examine the connections between these dual shifts in philosophy of language and explore a concern about the methodological assumptions underlying the externalist takeover in philosophy of language.[1]

---

[1] The first wave of externalism about meaning has been followed by a second where Tyler Burge and others attempted to externalize not just meaning but mental content. For an account of Frege's influence in this story, see Burge's chapter in the present volume.

For much of the twentieth century, philosophy of language was dominated by what is commonly known as 'descriptivism'—the approach to meaning adopted by the founders of analytic philosophy, Gottlob Frege and Bertrand Russell.[2] The views that in any way associate reference with conceptual content or descriptions have also come to be known as internalist theories of meaning. In these theories, with a few exceptions such as logically proper names for Russell, the meaning of a word is a quite separate matter from its reference. Our utterances about the world are mediated by ideas that we have in our head, where the relevant sense of 'idea' is spelled out quite differently, varying for example, from the straightforwardly Lockean mental images of Wittgenstein (1921), to more sophisticated construals invoking representational intentional states, as in Searle (1983).

19.2 QUINE'S TROUBLES WITH SAMENESS OF MEANING

Frege famously distinguished between two aspects of the pre-theoretical notion of the meaning of an expression: its sense and reference. He argued that names do not refer directly to their bearers, rather their reference is given to them through a mode of presentation of the object he called the 'sense' of a name.[3] Russell's Theory of Descriptions, while it was developed as a critique of Frege's idea of sense, made descriptions the medium linking names with their bearers. In Russell's version of descriptivism, ordinary names are disguised definite descriptions and these descriptions determine what names refer to, e.g. the name 'Scott' may be shorthand for 'the author of Waverley' and the referent of 'Scott' would be the object, whatever it is, that wrote Waverley. According to Russell only logically proper names such as 'this' and 'I', used under appropriate circumstances, can refer directly. What the two theories have in common is the positing of semantic intermediaries between the referent of a name and that name.

Putnam and Kripke's revolutionary move is rightly seen as a reaction to this model of meaning, but what is frequently neglected in the telling of this familiar story is the role of another revolution in twentieth-century philosophy, Quine's attempt at dismantling the traditional notion of analyticity and hence meaning.[4]

---

[2] The story of Frege and Russell's descriptivism is much more complicated than it is commonly presented, however, but a detailed discussion of their position is beyond the scope of this chapter.

[3] Michael Dummett has questioned this interpretation. He thinks that Frege did not necessarily identify sense with descriptions or see them as intermediaries between thinker and the object of reference. But Dummett does admit that Frege's examples of the sense of a name are definite descriptions (Dummett 1973: 110).

[4] Morton White, a sometime colleague of Quine at Harvard, had also produced criticisms similar to Quine's in 1950.

Frege distinguished between the sense and reference of an expression by drawing our attention to the cognitive difference between identity statements containing two occurrences of the same name and those containing two different names of the same thing (Frege 1892). The cognitive value of 'Hesperus is Hesperus' differs from the cognitive value of 'Hesperus is Phosphorus'. Both sentences are true, but while the first, at least on the standard account, appears to be a tautology, the second represents an astronomical discovery. In Frege's account, the truth of identity statements depends on the reference of the names involved and the difference in cognitive value is due to the different sense attached to the names. Frege's distinction is grounded in a difference, but arguably it takes more than that to introduce a new notion. To make sense of the distinction, we also have to know when the sense of one expression is the same as the sense of another, i.e. to say when two coextensive expressions mean the same thing or to give a criterion of synonymy. One way to see Quine's 'Two Dogmas of Empiricism' is as a challenge to the possibility of providing this criterion of sameness of sense. If his challenge succeeds, those seeking an explanation of Frege's distinction must return to square one.

The distinction between analytic and synthetic judgements was explicitly introduced by Kant in the *Critique of Pure Reason*, where Kant defines analytic statements as those where 'the predicate B belongs to the subject A, as something which is (covertly) contained in this concept'. Analytic judgements, e.g. 'bachelors are unmarried men' are 'explicative', while synthetic ones, e.g. 'Kant is a bachelor', are 'ampliative'. Kant also believed that analytic truths are logically necessary because their denial leads to contradiction ([1781/1787] 1965: 48). The distinction came to play an important role in Frege's logicist programme, albeit with different definitions, especially of analyticity; it also became central to the logical positivists' criterion of cognitive significance. In this sense, it is a formative idea of the analytic tradition of philosophy in the twentieth century. Frege characterizes analytic judgements as those that can be reduced to general logical truths and definitions only. Truths which are not of a general logical nature, but belong to the sphere of some special science, are synthetic (Frege 1884: § 3). Carnap, who was the primary target of Quine's article, follows Frege's lead and identifies analytic truth with truth by definition and logical truth (Carnap 1937, 1947) but also adds a more explicit semantic dimension by identifying analyticity with truth by semantical rule (Carnap 1947).

Quine's general strategy is to show that none of the attempts to characterize the analytic/synthetic distinction, including Kant's but most notably Carnap's, manages to give a non-circular or non-question-begging account of the distinction. He concludes that the belief 'That there is such a distinction to be drawn at all is an unempirical dogma of empiricists, a metaphysical article of faith' (Quine 1953: 37).

Quine's official target in 'Two Dogmas of Empiricism', in the first instance, was not so much the notion of sameness of meaning as that of truth in virtue of meaning and independently of fact, that is, the very idea of an analytic truth, which in its traditional rendering relies on the notion of meaning. He notes that the statements people take to be analytic fall into two general classes: logical truths and statements that become logical truths when we substitute synonyms for synonyms within them. He uses the statements

1. No unmarried man is married
2. No bachelor is married

as examples of the first and second kind respectively. Statement 2 becomes the logical truth 1 when 'unmarried man' is substituted for 'bachelor' in 2. Quine grants that we have an acceptable account of what makes a statement a logical truth: given a fixed set of logical vocabulary ('if', 'then', 'and', 'not', etc.), a sentence is a logical truth if it is true and remains true under all reinterpretations of the sentence's non-logical vocabulary. So, the good standing of the notion of analyticity will be assured if what it is for expressions to be synonyms of each other can be made clear. Unfortunately, Quine thinks, the notion of synonymy is just as much in need of clarification as analyticity itself. The reason, it later appears, for finding synonymy unclear is that we lack an independent criterion for when two expressions are synonymous. That two words apply to exactly the same things is not sufficient for synonymy, but we can say what more is required only by employing the notion of analyticity.

Quine next considers whether statements like 2 can be reduced to logical truths by definitions. There are three cases to consider. First, there are dictionary definitions of the kind put together by lexicographers. These, he claims, rely on the pre-existing belief in the synonymy of the *definiendum* and *definiens*. They don't provide any independent support for the notion of synonymy, as presumably the 'definitions' will have to be reconceived as something else if the notion of synonymy is unclear. The second case concerns explicative definitions of the kind often provided by philosophers. Here, the philosopher fixes on a number of favoured cases in which the *definiendum* is employed, finds an apparently synonymous *definiens*, and extrapolates on that basis to provide the *definiendum* with a precisified and sharpened usage in those further contexts. While this form of definition does not presuppose synonymy across the whole range of the word's employment, it does rely on the belief in a pre-existing synonymy for the initially favoured cases. As with dictionary definition, then, it doesn't offer independent support for synonymy. Lastly, Quine considers the introduction of novel notation for the purposes of abbreviation. In this case, the new vocabulary is synonymous with the old because it has been expressly created for the purpose of being synonymous with the old. Quine grants that here we do have a case of synonymy established by definition, but denies that the lessons carry over to the general case. Quine's admission, with the last case, that there are genuine examples of synonymous expressions is inconsistent with his overall conclusion, since his concern is not how synonymies get created but what synonymy is (Soames 2003: 364n8; the tension is also noted by Boghossian 1997). If his arguments derail the notion, then it applies to nothing, so the status of these 'definitions' will also have to be reconceived.

The heart of Quine's critique is a discussion of the following necessary and sufficient condition for synonymy:

> S   x is synonymous with y if and only if x and y may be substituted for each other wherever they occur *salva veritate* (without affecting the truth value of the sentences concerned).

This is immediately qualified to exclude substitution within words or phrases (to forbid, for example, the substitution of 'puss' for 'cat' in the word 'cattle') and within quotes (to forbid, for example, the substitution of 'unmarried man' for 'bachelor' in 'the word "bachelor" starts with a "b"'). Quine also specifies that the synonymy in question need not be perfect, encompassing all aspects of a word's meaning including poetic and psychological associations or those aspects which a Fregean might call tone (*Färbung*). No two expressions are perfectly synonymous in this sense. But this does raise the question of precisely what 'grade' of synonymy is at issue. Quine elects to specify the relevant sense indirectly.

> The sort of synonymy needed [here is] merely such that any analytic statement could be turned into a logical truth by putting synonyms for synonyms. Turning the tables and assuming analyticity ... we could explain cognitive synonymy of terms as follows (keeping to the familiar example): to say that 'bachelor' and 'unmarried man' are cognitively synonymous is to say no more nor less than that the statement 'all and only bachelors are unmarried men' is analytic. (1953: 28–9)

In other words, the synonyms we are after are intersubstitutables such that the statement of their equivalence is an analytic truth.

Now the necessity of this condition is not disputed, but the question is whether it provides a strong enough condition for, as he calls it, cognitive synonymy. This is the heart of Quine's argument. Quine claims that the strength of the condition depends on what sorts of contexts are covered by the 'wherever they occur'. He says two things. If the 'everywhere' where the two terms are intersubstitutable encompasses only extensional contexts, then the condition is not strong enough for synonymy. For in these cases, any two terms with the same extension, that is, any two terms that correctly apply to exactly the same things, will be intersubstitutable without affecting the truth-value of the resultant sentences. And there are plenty of examples to show that such pairs are not synonyms. For example, the phrases 'creature with a heart' and 'creature with kidneys' have the same extension. So they are intersubstitutable in an extensional context like the sentence fragment 'For all x, if x is a —— then x has blood'. If the sentence is true when the blank is filled in by one of the pair, it is also true when filled in by the other. But no one takes these phrases to be synonyms.

On the other hand, if the 'everywhere' where the two terms are intersubstitutable encompasses modal contexts, such as that formed by prefixing sentences with the modal operator 'necessarily', then Quine concedes that the condition is strong enough. That is, Quine believes only terms which intuitively really are synonyms could satisfy the criterion. How could we show that only intuitive synonyms pass the test? We could assume that two terms are intersubstitutable and then ask whether they are synonyms in the relevant sense, allowing their status as synonyms to be settled by whether the statement of their equivalence or identity is an analytic truth.

Indeed this is how Quine argues: The statement 'Necessarily all and only bachelors are bachelors' is true. If 'bachelor' and 'unmarried man' are everywhere intersubstitutable, then this sentence is also true: 'Necessarily all and only bachelors are unmarried men.' And for Quine this last statement says all of and no more than that the statement 'All and only bachelors are unmarried men' is analytically true. So, the mutually intersubstitutable terms can transform an analytic sentence of the second class into a logical truth, so they are synonyms in the relevant, cognitive, sense.

Before evaluating the argument, consider what it would show if it is successful. If successful, it shows that intersubstitutivity everywhere up to and including modal contexts is sufficient for synonymy (if two terms are so intersubstitutable, then they are synonyms). Quine has rested his case on the unclarity of synonymy, so once a necessary and sufficient condition for synonymy is provided, his case falls. The argument, however, does not withstand scrutiny for long. For Quine the problem lies with the adverb 'necessarily', which is 'so construed as to yield a truth when and only when applied to an analytic statement' (29/30), and consequently, 'intelligible only in so far as the notion of analyticity is already understood in advance' (31). In other words, Quine objects that this explanation of synonymy in terms of necessity and analyticity is circular.

Nowadays, however, circularity isn't always seen as a fatal defect. Especially where the *explanandum* and *explanans* enjoy strong intuitive support, as the notions of analyticity and synonymy do, circular explanations can be seen as perspicuously displaying mutually supportive relationships among concepts. But the work of Kripke and Putnam, to follow, provides independent reason to reject the explanation of synonymy in terms of analyticity and necessary truth. Kripke and Putnam argue that the domain of analytic truths and the domain of necessary truths are not coextensive. If this is right, modal contexts aren't themselves strong enough to test for cognitive synonymy.

The intersubstitutivity criterion poses particular problems in the contexts of belief ascription. As Quine himself has pointed out, coextensive terms such as 'creature with a heart' and 'creature with a kidney' are not intersubstitutable *salva veritate* in belief contexts, which might suggest that only genuine synonyms will be. It was the observed differences in cognitive significance and in behaviour of terms in belief contexts that led Frege to distinguish meaning as sense from meaning as reference in the first place. Belief contexts, then, are an especially appropriate venue for examining the intersubstitutability criterion and can afford a more direct specification of the kind of synonymy at issue. If two expressions are intersubstitutable in belief contexts they are equivalent in what matters for meaning as sense. They are therefore synonyms.

Two questions arise: are putative synonyms intersubstitutable in these contexts, and is anything else also intersubstitutable? These are rather delicate questions. But the following considerations seem to show that any reading of 'belief' context that would permit the intersubstitutivity of putative synonyms would also permit the intersubstitutivity of necessarily coextensive terms, like 'water' and 'H_2O', that are not synonyms. In his subsequent discussions of the topic, Quine distinguished between referentially transparent and referentially opaque senses of belief (1956 and 1960: §§ 30, 31). A belief, or more generally, a sentential context, is referentially transparent if and only if co-referring expressions can be substituted for each other without affecting the truth-values of the resultant sentences (and opaque otherwise). The opaque sense of belief, that disallows substitutions, seems called for by the fact that someone who believes Superman can fly may deny that Clark Kent can fly (if they're unaware that Clark Kent and Superman are one and the same man). If we take their sincere avowals and denials as circumscribing the extent of their beliefs, we must say they don't believe that Clark Kent can fly. The transparent sense of belief, on the other hand, seems to be required by the fact that it is also true that the man they believe can fly is Clark Kent. So they do, in another sense, believe he can fly.

Given the above, it seems that the two senses of belief dictate different answers as to whether putative synonyms are intersubstitutable in belief contexts. On the transparent sense, if John believes that all bachelors are bachelors, then he *ipso facto* believes that all bachelors are unmarried men. Of course the recognition that certain terms pass the intersubstitutivity criterion given a transparent sense of belief still doesn't establish that the terms are synonyms unless we can make the connection between transparent belief sentences and analytic truths (a move analogous to the move we rejected between necessity and analyticity). But we can say for sure that the move should be rejected because other terms besides synonyms are intersubstitutable in transparent, *de re*, belief contexts. For exactly the same reasons motivate saying that anyone who believes that (liquid) water is wet *ipso facto* believes that liquid H_2O is wet. Intersubstitutivity in transparent belief contexts isn't sufficient proof that the intersubstitutables are synonyms.

On the referentially opaque, *de dicto*, sense, we cannot automatically infer from 'John believes that all bachelors are bachelors' to 'John believes that all bachelors are unmarried men' because John might for some reason not believe this. He might think there are exceptions, or he may just be unsure. Given that the extent of his beliefs is settled by what he is disposed sincerely to avow, he simply may not have the latter belief. A defender of synonymy might be tempted to hold that if someone such as John fails to believe that all bachelors are unmarried men, it can only be because they don't really understand the expressions in question. If John believes that all bachelors are bachelors and understands the meaning of 'bachelor' and of 'unmarried man' then the inference must go through. Recent work by Timothy Williamson undermines this suggestion (2005 and 2007).[5] John might, consistent with understanding them, believe that both 'bachelor' and 'man' are vague terms with borderline cases. Indeed they are vague terms. No one would call a young boy a bachelor no matter how raucous he was. John could hold that in such cases 'all bachelors are bachelors' is true, but that 'all bachelors are unmarried men' is indeterminate for want of a guarantee that the vaguenesses of the terms exactly match. And the inference fails because truth is not preserved. If

---

[5] Tyler Burge anticipated Tim Williamson's point in his 1978 article.

the Williamsonian counterexample is accepted, the intersubstitutability criterion once more fails to sort synonyms from non-synonyms. Even putting the apparent counterexample to the side, it would seem that the only reason to insist that someone who believes that all bachelors are bachelors must for that reason also believe that all bachelors are unmarried men, if they understand it, is a pre-existing belief in the synonymy of the words in question. For that reason the criterion, even if it provides an acceptable statement of what it is to be a synonym, doesn't provide an independent test of whether there are any pairs of synonyms (and consequently any analytic truths). Making an exception in the case of alleged synonyms to taking a subject's sincere avowals as indicative of their beliefs deprives the criterion of its original simple clarity. What someone believes is no longer a matter of what they would be inclined to say. 'The thinks idiom,' as Quine would say, 'is heir to all the obscurities of the notion of synonymy … and more' (Quine 1986: 9).

Quine's dismantling the traditional view of analyticity had wide-ranging consequences, not least of which was the dethroning of logical positivism as the dominant philosophical position of the 1930s and 1940s. A further, and more damaging, consequence was his questioning of the very possibility of a theory of meaning. Our inability to give a non-circular or empirically backed meaning to the notion of meaning undermined the very idea of philosophy of language. Quine's positive proposal was to offer an account of meaning, which would be in line with his behaviourist naturalism. He tells us,

> we now have before us the makings of a crude concept of empirical meaning. For meaning, supposedly, is what a sentence shares with its translation; and translation at the present stage turns solely on correlations with non-verbal stimulation. (Quine 1960: 32)

Quine bases his argument from the outset on behaviouristic premises and thinks of problems about meaning as problems of disposition to behaviour; as he puts it, 'There is nothing in linguistic meaning, then, beyond what is to be gleaned from overt behaviour in observable circumstances' (Quine 1987: 5). Meaning is to be explicated in terms of manuals of translation constructed by observing the stimulus-responses of speakers engaged in verbal behaviour. 'We can take the behavior, the use, and let the meanings go' (Quine 1979: 1). But even this pared down empirical approach was beset with problems, most notably the indeterminacy of translation and the inscrutability of reference. Quine's thesis of indeterminacy, possibly his most controversial philosophical position, states that 'manuals for translating one language into another can be set up in divergent ways, all compatible with the totality of dispositions, yet incompatible with one another' (1960: 27). The doctrine, however, is not about mere translation, but applies to attempts at interpreting a 'home' language as well. Language is irredeemably indeterminate and the indeterminacy permeates even the level of singular putatively referential terms. Neither meaning nor reference can be pinned down. All we are left with is with language as

[A] social art which we all acquire on the evidence of other people's overt behavior under publicly recognizable circumstances. Meanings, therefore, those very models of mental entities, end up as grist for the behaviorist's mill. Dewey was explicit on this point: 'Meaning [...] is not a psychic existence, it is primarily a property of behavior'. (1969: 26–7)

Moreover, Quine's naturalism further solidified the dismissive attitude taken towards metaphysics by the logical positivist. Philosophy was no more than science conducted at higher levels of abstraction. As with the positivists, the autonomy of philosophy as a discipline was once again denied.

The next big revolution in philosophy of language challenged the two main assumptions of this Quinean picture, while simultaneously calling into question the prevailing descriptivist views of reference. The changes it brought about also revolutionized the thinking about the proper domain of philosophy.

19.3 KRIPKE AND PUTNAM

The outline of Kripke and Putnam's arguments for externalism about meaning is well known. Quine had argued for an essential gap between meaning and reference. According to him,

> When the cleavage between meaning and reference is properly heeded, the problems of what is loosely called semantics become separated into two provinces so fundamentally distinct as not to deserve a joint appellation at all. They may be called the *theory of meaning* and the *theory of reference*. (1953: 130)

Even earlier, in the 'Two Dogmas of Empiricism', he had relied on Frege's discussion of sense and reference to argue that meaning is not to be identified with naming or reference. The Evening Star is the planet Venus, and so is the Morning Star. The two singular terms name the same thing. But the meanings must be treated as distinct, since the identity 'Evening Star = Morning Star' is a statement of fact established by astronomical observation. If 'Evening Star' and 'Morning Star' were alike in meaning, the identity 'Evening Star = Morning Star' would be analytic (Quine, 1953: 21). Kripke makes essentially the same argument the centrepiece of his new non-descriptivist position.

> If 'Aristotle' meant *the man who taught Alexander the Great*, then saying 'Aristotle was a teacher of Alexander the Great' would be a mere tautology. But surely it isn't; it expresses the fact that Aristotle taught Alexander the Great, something we could discover to be false. So, *being the teacher of Alexander the Great* cannot be part of [the sense of] the name. (1980: 30)

Where Quine thought of meaning and reference as 'so fundamentally distinct as not to deserve a joint appellation at all', Kripke drew a dramatically different conclusion. He, and Putnam, sought to establish the contrary, Millian view that, at least in some crucial cases, meaning involves a direct relationship between names and their objects of reference and more generally, that we can give sense to the idea of meaning by looking at the relationship between language and the natural and social world.

Kripke offers three key arguments against the theory that names are disguised descriptions. First, many names are not, in general, associated with any uniquely identifying descriptions. For example, many people would be hard pressed to associate anything more descriptive than 'a famous physicist' with the name 'Richard Feynman'. Second, it is perfectly possible to use a proper name in appropriate circumstances without being aware of the descriptions that others have associated with it. It does not seem like a case where we should want to say the name literally has a different meaning for speakers with different associations. Third and most significantly, proper names and natural kind terms act as rigid designators, expressions that refer to the same object in all possible worlds in which those objects exist, whereas descriptions can be satisfied by different objects in different possible worlds.[6] For example, it seems intuitive to say 'Aristotle', as *we* use it, refers to Aristotle in the actual world and continues to refer to him when we consider him in various counterfactual situations, whereas the description 'Plato's greatest pupil' needn't always refer to him (such as when we imagine Plato had an even greater pupil).

Kripke's arguments regarding the meaning and reference of names often rely on thought experiments or possible world scenarios as test cases for deciding between the two competing philosophical hypotheses of descriptivism and his preferred option of names acting as rigid designators,[7] and the plausibility of his account of them is established, not just through testing their consistency and coherence, but ultimately by reliance on shared intuitions or our common sense. To take a favourite example, we could envisage possible worlds where Aristotle was not the teacher of Alexander, but there cannot be a possible world in which Aristotle is not Aristotle. Later we consider the role of intuition in these arguments more closely.

---

[6] At least retrospectively, this last of the three arguments offered by Kripke has become less significant as post-Kripkean descriptivists, including two-dimensionalists, now employ rigidified descriptions using the modifier 'actually'.

[7] Possible worlds, for Kripke, are not obscure metaphysical objects but ways the world might have been. In the preface to *Naming and Necessity*, he explains: 'I will say something briefly about "possible worlds".... In the present monograph I argued against those misuses of the concept that regard possible worlds as something like distant planets, like our own surroundings but somehow existing in a different dimension, or that lead to spurious problems of "transworld identification". Further, if one wishes to avoid the *Weltangst* and philosophical confusions that many philosophers have associated with the "worlds" terminology, I recommended that "possible state (or history) of the world", or "counterfactual situation" might be better. One should even remind oneself that the "worlds" terminology can often be replaced by modal talk—"It is possible that . . . " ' (15).

According to semantic externalism, objects, as well as persons, are named through acts of linguistic baptism, which also fix their reference. Names are introduced into a linguistic community for the purpose of referring to an individual and they continue to refer to that individual as long as their uses are linked to the original act of dubbing or 'baptism' via a social historical chain of continuous use. Each new user acquires the name from others, who in turn have acquired it from their predecessors, and so on, up to the first user who introduced the name to refer to a specific individual. The reason that the name 'Aristotle', to revert to our previous example, picks out or refers to the man Aristotle is that there exists a long chain of connections between the name and the person Aristotle. Kripke explains,

> Someone, let's say, a baby, is born; his parents call him by a certain name. They talk about him to their friends. Other people meet him. Through various sorts of talk the name is spread from link to link as if by a chain. A speaker who is on the far end of this chain, who has heard about, say Richard Feynman, in the market place or elsewhere, may be referring to Richard Feynman even though he can't remember from whom he first heard of Feynman or from whom he ever heard of Feynman. (1980: 90)

Kripke's social-historical picture of the fixation of reference for names has come to be known as the causal account of reference.[8] Kripke applies it both to proper names and natural kind terms (names for kinds or types of things that occur in nature, e.g. 'water', 'tiger', 'lemon', 'gold'). In this approach, natural kind terms are also rigid designators and they pick out certain objects through causal, communicative ties between the term and the object to which it refers rather than through a cluster of descriptions that may be associated with the term. Semantic externalism is motivated by an underlying metaphysics whereby the essential properties of each natural kind object are seen as microstructural rather than phenomenal. For instance, gold is anything which has the atomic number 79 and not whatever looks like gold. As we'll see, the view has important consequences not just for theories of meaning but also for our understanding of the modalities of necessity, the a priori, etc.

Shortly after Kripke's first statement of semantic externalism, Hilary Putnam set out to refute what he called a 'grotesquely mistaken' view of language (1975b: 271), a mistake rooted in our propensity to ignore the social nature of language and to neglect the contribution of external reality to meaning. In this, Putnam's externalism has a wider scope than Kripke's, which had little to say about the social determinants of meaning, or so-called social externalism. Putnam, like Kripke, argued that the description theory does not capture what our words mean because for proper names and natural kind terms the

---

[8] We refer to Kripke's preferred picture of naming as his 'social-historical' account, and not the 'causal account of reference', as is conventional, because what is distinctive about the view is the transmission of knowledge of reference from one speaker to another, which is certainly social and historical, but only causal in so far as social and historical connections are causal. The initial baptism by which the reference of the name is fixed may, though it need not, indeed be causal in a more direct way.

reference of a name is determined by a causal interaction between objects in the world and the speakers using those names. For both these philosophers, even in cases where a proper name has been introduced to language by means of a description, the description will not give the meaning of the name. Traditional theories of meaning, chiefly descriptivism, have tended to make two incompatible assumptions about language. First, that to know the meaning of a term is to be in an appropriate psychological state and second, that meaning determines reference. The obvious consequence was that speakers in the same mental state uttering the same word token would share both the intension and the extension of that word. Putnam argues against this conclusion, by pointing out that since he is unable to differentiate between a beech and an elm, his conception of the two trees is the same, while the meaning and the reference of 'elm' and 'beech' are quite different in his idiolect. Putnam, or any other speaker in a similar predicament, does refer to an elm when using the term 'elm' even if he is not able to identify an elm. Successful reference is possible because of what Putnam calls 'the division of linguistic labour'. Experts, horticulturalists in this instance, can distinguish an elm from a beech just as metallurgists can distinguish gold from fool's gold, etc. Ordinary users of language defer to these experts in deciding the cases where 'elm' and 'beech' should be used. Shared meaning does not require that every member of a linguistic community should have the ability to identify accurately the objects of reference for a given name. What is needed is a stereotype associated with the object of reference and shared by the members of that linguistic community.

Naming and Necessity and 'The Meaning of "Meaning"' not only provided trenchant criticisms of the then-prevailing descriptivist views of meaning but also ran counter to Quine's scepticism about the possibility of a theory of meaning. Quine, as we saw, in addition to questioning the legitimacy of the division between analytic and synthetic statements also doubted the related distinction between necessary and contingent truths. Kripke and Putnam break from the traditional conception of necessity, making space for both a theory of meaning and a re-engagement with metaphysics, even in the context of a naturalist conception of philosophy.[9] What they, in effect, try to show is that there can indeed be such a thing as a theory of meaning, but a correct theory will have to take the formative role of the world into account. Furthermore, while their view of meaning does not give analyticity quite the role formulated and criticized by Quine, necessity and identity, recast in terms of possible world semantics, do become central.

19.4 NECESSITY AND THE ANALYTIC/ SYNTHETIC DISTINCTION

Since Kant it has become common practice to assume that a priori and necessary truths are coextensive, that analytic truths are both a priori and necessary, and that contingent

---

[9] A move that, as Putnam admits, turned him, in the eyes of the ardent Quinean Burton Dreben, into a Girondist to Quine's revolutionary aspirations (Putnam 2002).

truths are known only a posteriori, while necessary truths are known a priori. Quine, like the logical positivists, particularly Carnap who was the prime target of his arguments, identifies analyticity with necessity and by denying the legitimacy of the analytic/synthetic distinction also undermines the necessary/contingent distinction. To take one example, the true premises, 'necessarily 9 is odd' and '9 = the number of planets' gives us the outrageous conclusion, 'necessarily the number of planets is odd' (Quine 1943, 1947).[10] Quine blames the problem on the ill-defined operators of non-truth-functional logic and particularly the modal operator 'necessarily' which does not permit the substitution of coextensive expressions within its scope, thus delegitimizing any attempt at quantifying into their scopes (Quine, 1953, 1960). But once the core ideas of analyticity and necessity are called into question, given the context of Quine's strong naturalism, the very possibility of a priori knowledge also becomes problematic. The rethinking of these core philosophical ideas underpins Putnam and Kripke's revolutionary approach to meaning. The point at stake is most explicitly made in Putnam's ' "Two Dogmas" Revisited' (1976), where Putnam affirms the historic importance of Quine's original paper while pointing out its main failure: the failure to distinguish between analyticity and the a priori. Quine, Putnam maintains, targets two different accounts of analyticity. On the first account, the Kantian account, analytic truth is a true statement derived from a tautology by putting synonyms for synonyms. The second account, however, has a more epistemic thrust. Analytic truth here is defined as a truth confirmed come what may. This account, according to Putnam, is closer to the traditional account of the a priori. Putnam further argues that while the first four sections of Quine's 'Two Dogmas' focus on analyticity in the first sense discussed above, the last two concern the a priori. The accuracy of the above interpretation is not at stake here, rather, the point we are making is that the externalist revolution was not only an attack on descriptivism but also a rethinking of the then prevailing views of the triumvirate analyticity/necessity/apriority.

Putnam, more explicitly than Kripke,[11] sees a role for a rehabilitated version of the analytic/synthetic distinction. He insists that there is little doubt that Quine is wrong in rejecting the distinction out of hand. 'This is not a matter of philosophical argument', he says, for there is 'as gross a distinction between "All bachelors are unmarried" and "There is a book on this table" as between any two things in the world, or, at any rate, between any two linguistic expressions in the world' (Putnam 1975a: 36). However, Putnam is also in agreement with Quine's concern about the over-use of the ill-defined notion of analyticity and believes that 'overworking the analytic–synthetic distinction has created serious distortions in the logical positivists' writing about

---

[10] At the time Quine was writing, Pluto was considered a planet in its own right. So there were considered to be nine solar planets.

[11] What does not emerge from our focus on Quine, Putnam, and Kripke is that Kripke's work, unlike Putnam's, is part of a significant tradition of formal intensional semantics going back to Carnap, through people like Montague and David Lewis, and now flourishing in linguistics as well as philosophy. We owe this point, and many more than we could mention, to Tim Williamson.

science' (1975a: 33). The distinction, he argues, could have a role provided that it is not treated as a sharp dichotomy but a continuum. Statements, in his approach, range from the clearly analytic ('bachelors are unmarried men') to the clearly synthetic ('this piece of chalk is white'). For specific purposes and in specific contexts we may find it useful or appropriate to distinguish between analytic and synthetic sentences, but such situational distinctions are not fixed for all times and contexts and sentences don't fall neatly under one or other rubric.

In his earlier writing on the topic, Putnam delineates a small group of concepts; he calls them 'one-criterion concepts', which have a single criterion for application. For instance, the only criterion for the application of 'bachelor' is that of being an unmarried man and we cannot abandon this criterion without depriving 'bachelor' of its use, hence the analyticity of 'all bachelors are unmarried men'. A majority of concepts, on the other hand, are 'law cluster' concepts where 'any one law can be abandoned without destroying the identity of the … concept involved' (Putnam 1975a: 52). It is wrong to think of such concepts as being analytic or sentences containing them as true by virtue of the meaning of their terms, because the link between the term picking out this type of concept and the cluster of laws associated with it is contingent, contextual, and malleable. The Quinean arguments against analyticity apply to this type of statement.

Putnam also agrees with Quine that in principle, all our claims to knowledge are open to revision. Even laws of logic, he has argued, could be revised in order to accommodate evidence from quantum mechanics; indeed there could be purely theoretical reasons for abandoning beliefs that were previously treated as true a priori or necessary (1975a: 48). Yet, his position is markedly different from Quine's in that Putnam is prepared to allow for the possibility of necessary statements in the empirical domain, such as physics, that are nevertheless open to revision in the light of new information. This was the situation with Euclidean geometry, a favourite example, where 'a statement that was necessary relative to a body of knowledge later came to be declared false in science' (1962: 662).

In his later work, Putnam draws an even sharper distinction between necessity and the a priori, and thus makes room for the synthetic a priori truth. He divides necessary truths into three main sub-areas: the analytic, the logical and mathematical truths, and the 'synthetic apriori' (Putnam 1975a). Quine's arguments against a particular view of meaning applies to analytic sentences, but it is possible for some feature of a natural kind to be part of the meaning of a term by being part of the stereotype associated with that term, without rendering the definition of the term 'analytic'. For instance, being striped is part of the meaning of 'tiger' as it is one of the stereotypes associated with tigers. However, albino tigers will still be tigers and upon their discovery, being striped will cease to be a stereotype associated with the name, without the meaning of the name changing. Some features are seen as central to our thinking about a particular natural kind but centrality is not the same thing as analyticity. All this would be in agreement with Quine who also explains our 'intuitions' regarding analyticity in terms of the centrality of certain beliefs. But Putnam, more controversially, also argues that although 'all tigers are animals' is not analytic it is necessary because the natural kind term 'tiger' is a rigid designator—it refers to tigers in all the possible worlds where tigers exist. However, this necessary truth is discovered empirically and is not known a priori. Moreover, even though no single empirical example will refute 'all tigers are animals', it would be falsified if it turned out all tigers were robots sent by aliens.

The gap between Kripke and Quine on the issues of necessity and the a priori is even wider than the one separating Putnam from Quine. Quine's worries about the legitimacy of the analytic/synthetic distinction extended to the related issues of the a priori and necessity, since for Quine, the necessity operator depended on a clear sense of analytic truth. Kripke, on the other hand, not only allows for the a priori necessities of logic but also for a posteriori necessities such as 'water is H_2O' which is not merely verbal or conventional but straightforwardly empirical. As with Putnam, rejecting Quine's approach to the a priori and necessity has consequences for theories of meaning. In the Frege–Russell theory, names are abbreviated descriptions. As we saw, Kripke's key idea is that names are rigid designators and not non-rigid descriptions. Descriptions attach themselves to objects contingently, while rigid designators refer to the same object in every possible world. The description 'teacher of Alexander' is true of Aristotle, but it could have been false. Aristotle may have chosen a different career. There is no possible world in which Aristotle is not Aristotle, while there are possible worlds where Aristotle is not a teacher. What is more, necessities can be established empirically. As Frege noted, the identification of Hesperus with Phosphorus was an empirical discovery, but once the identity was established then we are in possession of an a posteriori necessary truth as identity statements involving rigid designators are necessarily true.[12] The same point holds with other frequently used examples of a posteriori necessities such as water is (=) H_2O and temperature is (=) mean kinetic molecular energy. Kripke also argues that there are some contingent truths that are known a priori. For instance, we have stipulated that a certain platinum/iridium rod, kept in Paris, is the standard measure for 'one metre'. Once we accept this stipulation, then we know a priori that particular rod in Paris is a metre long. But the claim is not necessary, the definition of a metre—one/ten-millionth of the distance from the equator to the north pole along a meridian through Paris—and the rod that was originally picked could have been different. Thus, contrary to the assumption dominating philosophy since Kant, the a priori/a posteriori distinction does not track the *necessary/contingent* distinction. And most significantly, while Quine runs apriority and necessity together, Kripke lays bare an essential difference between them showing that some kinds of necessity are metaphysical, rather than logical, while the a priori is epistemic. Moreover, contrary to Quine, genuine a priori knowledge is not limited to necessary truths. Kripke explains:

---

[12] Identity statements involving rigid designators are necessarily true, if true. Simplifying things a little, suppose 'a' and 'b' are rigid designators for the same individual. Then a = b is true (in the actual world). But since the names both refer to the same individual and that individual continues to be that same individual wherever they are, the names refer to the same individual in every possible world. So the identity is necessary.

Philosophers have talked ... [about] various categories of truth, which are sometimes called 'apriori', 'analytic', 'necessary' ... these terms are often used as if whether there are things answering to these concepts is an interesting question, but we might as well regard them all as meaning the same thing.

... First the notion of aprioricity is a concept of epistemology. I guess the traditional characterization from Kant goes something like: apriori truths are those which can be known independently of any experience.... The second concept that is in question is that of necessity.... what I am concerned with here is a notion, which is not a notion of epistemology, but of metaphysics ... We ask whether something might have been true, or might have been false. Well, if something is false, it's obviously not necessarily true. If it is true, might it have been otherwise? Is it possible that, in this respect, the world should have been different than the way that it is? ... This in and of itself has nothing to do with anyone's knowledge of anything. It's certainly a philosophical thesis, and not a matter of obvious definitional equivalence, either that everything apriori is necessary or that everything necessary is apriori.... at any rate they are dealing with two different domains, two different areas, the epistemological and the metaphysical. (Kripke 1980: 33–5)

He goes on to point out that that even if the a priori and the necessary are conceptually distinct, it does not follow that they are extensionally distinct. There could indeed be truths that are necessary but knowable only a posteriori as well as a priori truths that are not necessary. Almost paradoxically, Kripke's arguments could help to undermine analyticity. Kripke stipulates that 'an analytic statement is, in some sense, true by virtue of its meaning and true in all possible worlds by virtue of its meaning. Then something which is analytically true will be both necessary and apriori' (Kripke 1980: 39). But as Tim Williamson has noted, after Kripke distinguished necessity from apriority, it's not clear what work is left for the concept of analyticity to do (2007: 51ff.). But putting aside this particular caveat, it is widely accepted that Kripke's novel treatment of necessity rescues meaning, at least when it comes to names and natural kind terms, from Quinean despair.

Kripke and Putnam's role in shifting the debate on questions of language is well known. What is less frequently discussed, at least until recently, are the metaphilosophical changes that their approach to meaning and reference generated. Their work, Kripke's in particular, not only led to a resurgence of interest in metaphysical questions but also gave new rigour to the view that philosophy could be an autonomous discipline, independent of the natural sciences.

19.5 THE ROLE OF INTUITION

One significant and influential feature of both Kripke's and Putnam's approaches is their use of thought experiments in driving their arguments. Putnam's Twin-Earth water and XYZ thought experiment, the aluminium–molybdenum science fiction story, and the less other-worldly elm–beech illustration, and Kripke's Gödel/Schmidt and the biblical Jonah stories are by now classics in discussions of meaning and reference. The thought experiments attempt to show that descriptions associated with a name are not sufficient for establishing its reference, rather it is features of the environment that determine both the meaning and reference of proper names and natural kind terms.[13] Kripke and Putnam used these thought experiments to demonstrate that our intuitive judgements about meaning and reference give us verdicts that are inconsistent with traditional descriptivism. Since then a growing number of philosophers of language, including most anti-externalists, have come to share Putnam and Kripke's intuitions, finding them convincing enough to try to accommodate within a more sophisticated descriptivist framework (e.g. Evans 1973; Jackson 1998). Over the last thirty years it has become well entrenched that our semantic intuitions support the social-historical view; however, while logicians, mathematicians, linguists and philosophers rely heavily on *intuitions* in the justification of their theories, at least in philosophical debates, not much justification is provided for the authority assigned to such intuitions.

The prominence and respect philosophers ascribe to intuitions have ebbed and flowed, partly because of developments in sciences and cognate fields. The discovery of non-Euclidean geometries undermined what were once seen as strong spatial intuitions; the same is true of the theory of relativity and the revisionary views of time and motion it introduced. Furthermore, not all philosophers have advocated the use of intuitions as a methodological device. For example, John Stewart Mill in discussing theologians and other religious commentators says, 'So they either dislike and disparage all philosophy, or addict themselves with intolerant zeal to those forms of it in which intuition takes the place of evidence, and internal feeling is made the test of objective truth' (Mill 1874/2008: 72). Frege and Russell also mistrusted common intuitions in questions of mathematics and logic and Russell particularly disparaged any reliance on our stock of common-sense beliefs. Quine too is suspicious of over-reliance on them. On the role of intuitions in establishing the legitimacy of the analytic/synthetic distinction he says:

> The intuitions are blameless in their way, but it would be a mistake to look to them for a sweeping epistemological dichotomy between analytic truths as by-products of language and synthetic truths as reports of the world. (Quine 1960: 67)

The question of the role intuitions in philosophy is thorny, to say the least. At its most extreme, the appeal to intuitions in philosophy of language assumes that language users have an implicit theory of reference that becomes the sources of speaker's intuitions on the connections between names and their objects (Mallon *et al.* 2009). Such appeals to intuitions about reference are frequently conceived by analogy to Chomsky's project

---

[13] For instance, in the case of the Twin Earth thought experiment—the most celebrated of all of them—through the telling of a science fiction story, we are led to the conclusion that what tastes, smells, or looks like water would not be correctly labelled water unless it has the underlying molecular structure of H2O.

in linguistics. Chomsky, as is well known, maintains that all language users rely heavily upon 'intuitions' of grammaticality, or the innate linguistic abilities to make instant judgements about correct syntax in sentences such as 'Who did you speak to Noam and?' *vs.* 'Who did you and Noam speak to?' Ordinary speakers of language simply know what a well-formed linguistic expression is and any native or even non-native but competent speaker of English, including very young children who have had very little exposure to language, would be able to see (intuit) the difference between the two sentences and pick the grammatical one. To have intuitions about the correct use of language is constitutive of being a language user. Linguists, on the other hand, make use of these intuitive judgements as data for their theories, but also rely on their own intuitions to further these theories.

There may indeed be a historical connection between the use of intuitions in linguistics and philosophy of language. Hintikka (1999) points out that the use of the term 'intuition' in contemporary philosophy became much more common as philosophers became acquainted with Chomsky's work in linguistics. The thought was that theories of reference could be constructed in analogy with the Chomskyan project in linguistics and philosophers of language would be able to rely on ordinary people's intuitions about reference in their reconstruction of the implicit theories that were part of speakers' cognitive endowment (Mallon *et al.* 2009: 339). Interestingly, Chomsky believes that there is no such thing as 'philosophical intuitions' about language and that linguistic intuitions and the so-called 'philosophical intuitions' are not comparable.

> A good part of contemporary philosophy of language is concerned with analyzing alleged relations between expressions and things, often exploring intuitions about the technical notions 'denote', 'refer', 'true of', etc., said to hold between expressions and something else. But there can be no intuitions about these notions, just as there can be none about 'angular velocity' or 'protein'. These are technical terms of philosophical discourse with a stipulated sense that has no counterpart in ordinary language. (Chomsky 2000: 130)

Chomsky's objections, however, have not had much impact on the use of intuitions as a methodological tool. Devitt and Hanley's *Blackwell Guide to the Philosophy of Language*, confirms that:

> The dominant method in semantics is to consult 'intuitions' about what an expression means, refers to, and so on, intuitions that are usually elicited in 'thought experiments'.... Whichever account of intuitions one adopts, there is almost uniform consensus on the role of intuitions in philosophy. (Devitt and Hanley 2006: 1–2)

One problem with the official ideology is a lack of consensus on what philosophical intuitions are and what role they play in philosophical argument. Are semantic intuitions expressions of our a priori knowledge of concepts, or simply unreflective first judgements with the same evidential status as the type of empirical intuitions scientists use in building and assessing their theories? Indeed at times, the official ideology seems more akin to a sleight of hand than a reliable methodology. As Tim Williamson puts it,

> When contemporary analytic philosophers run out of arguments, they appeal to intuition. Intuitiveness is supposed to be a virtue, counter-intuitiveness a vice. It can seem, and is sometimes said, that any philosophical dispute, when pushed back far enough, turns into a conflict of intuitions about ultimate premises: 'In the end, all we have to go on is our intuitions'. Yet analytic philosophy has no agreed or even popular account of how intuition might work, no accepted explanation of the hoped-for correlation between our having an intuition that P and its being true that P. Since analytic philosophy prides itself on its rigour, this blank space in its foundations looks like a methodological scandal. (2004: 109)

Accounts of intuitions range from apriorist views, on which intuition is a *sui generis* intellectual faculty (Bealer, 1992), to those that compare intuitions to perception—a strategy that has it roots in Kant where one 'sees' the force of a philosophical argument (Sosa 1999), to comparisons with imagination (Chalmers 2002), to the so-called naturalist view of intuitions where intuitions are seen as judgements reached quickly (Devitt 2006; Williamson 2004).

In *Naming and Necessity* Kripke appeals to philosophical intuitions in a number of fundamental ways. Intuitions are used to decide the connection between names and their referents, they are also arbiters of meaning, but even more importantly they are aids for establishing the general plausibility of an argument. For instance, he writes: 'When you ask whether it is necessary or contingent that *Nixon* won the election, you are asking the intuitive question whether in some counterfactual situation, *this man* would in fact have lost the election' (1980: 41). Furthermore, he thinks that meaningful sentences have 'intuitive content', which is evident to the 'ordinary man' and not just to philosophers. He goes on to add,

> Some philosophers think that something's having intuitive content is very inconclusive evidence in favor of it. I think it is very heavy evidence in favor of anything, myself. I really don't know, in a way, what more conclusive evidence one can have about anything, ultimately speaking. (Kripke 1980: 42)

Such a stance assumes people don't have conflicting intuitions (individually and between themselves). If one's direct intuition in one case clashes with the consequences of one's intuitions about other cases, as is arguably the case in the semantics of names, it's not clear which should win out.

In addition to the central role assigned to intuitions in general, Kripke, more specifically, seems to be relying on two types of intuitions. The first are conceptual or linguistic intuitions—or what Margolis and Laurence (2003) have called 'Socratic intuitions', which are pretheoretical dispositions to apply concepts to some particular cases and scenarios and refuse to apply them to others. The second are so-called 'modal intuitions', which seem to boil down to a direct or unmediated knowledge of metaphysical necessity and possibility. It is this second form of intuition, in particular, that creates serious philosophical worries.

In arguing for names as rigid designators, Kripke relies on modal and counterfactual reasoning, but he seems to believe that the 'ordinary man' is as well placed to grasp the intuitive content of propositions as any philosopher. He argues,

> Suppose that someone said, pointing to Nixon, 'that's the guy who might have lost'. Someone else says 'Oh no, if you describe him as "Nixon", then he might have lost; but, of course, describing him as the winner, then it is not true that he might have lost.' Now which one is being the philosopher, here, the unintuitive man? It seems to me that obviously the second. The second man has a philosophical theory. (1980: 41)

It is not clear why the famous 'man on the street' should possess any modal intuitions, but if his intuitions do have special evidential value, surely this would require a move away from the philosophical armchair in favour of the polling and sampling methods common in the rest of social science. Especially since, as we shall see, these intuitions are readily contested by both philosophers and non-philosopher.

Putnam, on the other hand, assigns a more modest scope to philosophical intuitions. In mathematics and science, intuition, he tells us, is a fallible but valuable guide, and a fallible guide is better than no guide at all. In particular, intuition plays a significant but not decisive role in mathematics and natural sciences to help with the formation of hypotheses (Putnam 1979b: 67). In 'Possibility and Necessity' and 'Is Water Necessarily H_2O?' (1990) he expresses his initially implicit and then more clearly articulated reservations about Kripke's view that, in addition to linguistic intuitions, there could be such a thing as metaphysical intuitions. What Putnam initially had done, he now confesses, was try to give a 'minimalist' (re)interpretation to Kripke's fuller conception of intuitions by assimilating his '*metaphysical* intuitions to the *linguistic* intuitions, intuitions about how we speak, that other analytic philosophers talk about' (Putnam 1990: 64). But this is what he now thinks cannot be done. According to Putnam, Kripke's notion of metaphysical intuition points to a fundamental capacity of reason to discover metaphysical necessities. This is the view of intuition that Putnam now fully rejects but initially, he confesses, he was trying to whitewash out of Kripke's text. For Putnam, intuitions, in general, are a mode of access to a culture's inherited picture of the world. And linguistic intuitions could be understood in terms of 'sortal identity' which gives speakers criteria for substance-identity, person-identity, table-identity, and so on. To decide on questions of identity regarding these categories, what we need to do is 'to consult our intuitions and lay down a set of conventions which seem reasonable in the light of those intuitions' (Putnam 1990: 64). The convention could vary in different contexts, and so would be context-dependent; it could also vary depending on the 'point' of the counterfactuals under consideration. Putnam explains:

> When philosophers disagree about what are reasonable criteria of, say, person-identity across possible worlds, then (unless one of them thinks the other has a 'tin ear,' that is, no ear for the way we actually speak at all) they may well agree 'one can do it either way.' In this view, the criteria for person-identity across possible worlds are, to some extent, to be *legislated* and not *discovered*. (Putnam 1990: 64)

Kripke, as we saw, argued that there could be empirically discovered identities that hold necessarily or in all the possible worlds where the entities exist. The thought experiments Kripke has used to elicit common intuitions on behalf of causal external-ism relate to proper names such as 'Gödel' and 'Jonah'; he then extends the argument to natural kind terms and empirically discovered identities. As Putnam points out, Kripke is a realist about identity conditions across possible worlds. Yet, it is not at all clear that common-sense intuitions follow his on this matter. Kripke is aware of the discrepan-cies and conflicts of intuitions in this area. He attempts to explain the contrary intuition that empirically discovered, but necessary, identities might not have held, by propos-ing the idea of 'qualitatively identical epistemic situations' or situations that produce the 'same sensory evidence' and yet which are connected with different natural kinds. For instance, there could be entities that produce gold type sensory evidence, the experi-ence of shininess, yellowness, etc., but are not causally linked to gold. The metaphysical possibility of such a scenario explains our intuition that necessary a posteriori identities might not have held. But Kripke's defence of this appeal to intuitions, in this particular case, demonstrates the weakness of his approach. Kripke is introducing a complex theo-retical apparatus in order to overcome what seems intuitively appealing. And once we allow that intuitions are trumped by more theoretical constructs in one domain then it behoves us to question their authority in others.

What is at stake between Quine and Kripke, in particular, is not just a question of the very possibility of a theory of meaning, but the much more significant and profound issue of the nature and scope of philosophy as a discipline. Kant famously had restored philosophy to its supposedly rightful place as an autonomous and even foundational subject by arguing that the domains of analytic and synthetic are separate, that a priori truths belong uniquely to the domain of philosophy, and that metaphysics is made possi-ble by our having access to the domain of synthetic a priori truths. Quine's rejection of the legitimacy of these categories was a direct challenge to this loftier conception of knowl-edge and his naturalism reinstates philosophy as continuous with the empirical sciences. Kripke reassigns a unique role to philosophy by allowing for metaphysical intuitions;[14]

---

[14] Putnam's role in this story is more complicated, at least partly because of his willingness to rethink his philosophical positions. As we saw, Putnam is to some extent in agreement with Quine on the analytic/ synthetic distinction, or so Quine thought. He also rejects the Kripkean talk of metaphysical intuitions, but Putnam in his later work reintroduces the role of intuition in philosophy by giving pride of place to 'common sense.'

by introducing the idea of metaphysical necessity, and through his emphasis on the central role of intuitions, once again he makes it possible for philosophers to think seriously about their discipline as both rigorous and independent of the natural sciences.

The accuracy of our intuitive or common-sense judgements has been questioned in various arenas; for instance, we now know a great deal about the systematically irrational features of our instantaneous judgements concerning probability (see Tversky and Kahneman 1974). The role of intuitions has also come under considerable scrutiny recently through the work of so-called experimental philosophers who through empirical experiments, using test cases from philosophy, have attempted to cast doubt on the use of intuitions in philosophy.[15] Their attack on the established view of intuitions by now covers large areas of philosophy. We will concentrate only on those that touch directly on the work of Quine, Kripke, and Putnam on the topic of meaning.

19.6 THE ANALYTIC/SYNTHETIC DISTINCTION AND INTUITIONS

Philosophers who acknowledge the authority of intuitive evidence find a straightforward justification for the necessary/contingent distinction: we have a very wide range of robust modal intuitions (for example, the intuition that it is contingent that the number of planets is greater than seven—there could have been fewer), and when such intuitions are taken as evidence, the best theory is one which accepts the distinction at face value. Early criticism of Quine appealed to this idea of widespread agreement over which sentences were analytic. Grice and Strawson claimed:

> We can appeal, that is, to the fact that those who use the terms 'analytic' and 'synthetic' do to a very considerable extent agree in the applications they make of them. They apply the term 'analytic' to more or less the same cases, withhold it from more or less the same cases, and hesitate over more or less the same cases. This agreement extends not only to cases which they have been taught so to characterize, but also to new cases. In short, 'analytic' and 'synthetic' have a more or less established philosophical use; and this seems to suggest that it is absurd, even senseless, to say that there is no such distinction. For, in general, if a pair of contrasting expressions are habitually and generally used in application to the same cases ... this is a sufficient condition for saying that there are kinds of cases to which the expressions apply; and nothing more is needed for them to mark a distinction. (1956: 143)

Similarly, J. J. Katz claimed that empirical tests would demonstrate the presence of the distinction (1967: 50). He suggested compiling lists ABCD comprising analytic, synthetic, contradictory, and anomalous sentences respectively. Subjects were to be shown

---

[15] For instance see Knobe and Nichols, 'An Experimental Philosophy Manifesto' (2008).

a classification of initial range of cases into ABCD and told to classify further sentences. Katz did not carry out the procedure but he was as confident as Grice and Strawson that it would reveal habitual and general uniformity in usage. Putnam also thinks that Strawson and Grice are right to claim that those who use the terms 'analytic' and 'synthetic' do to a very considerable extent agree in the applications they make of them, but believes that the weakness of their argument is in not providing a positive account of what that distinction is: 'It is the task of the methodologist to explain this special status, not to explain it away' (Putnam 1979a: 92).

Rather surprisingly, this may have been a mistake. Geoffrey Sampson (1980: 70–1, 2001: 203–4) reports the results of an experiment by Morley-Bunker (1977), to determine the consistency of judgements of analyticity between and within groups of philosophically trained and untrained subjects. Morley-Bunker's results did not support Katz's or Grice and Strawson's contentions that speakers by and large draw the distinction in the same way. If Morley-Bunker's work is correct, then to the extent to which expectations of the distinction were based on a philosophical intuition, such intuition and the intuitions driving analyticity judgements themselves are shown to be fallible.[16]

In recent years, experimental philosophers have challenged the universality of Kripkean intuitions regarding rigid designators.[17] One such experiment makes use of the

---

[16] The experiment has not been published so it is worth giving a slightly more detailed summary than is conventional. Morley-Bunker's subjects, 28 non-philosophy students and faculty and 10 philosophy faculty, were given cards displaying clear cases of analytic and synthetic sentences respectively and asked to sort these into piles. Their allocation was corrected by the experimenter as necessary, according to the generally perceived status of the sentences as analytic or synthetic. Thereafter, the subjects were asked to sort 18 further samples. The experiment assumed no fact of the matter as to the status of these further sentences. The goal was simply to determine the consistency of the different groups. Sampson reports the results in detail:

> The results were as would be expected by sceptics of the analytic/synthetic distinction, in that neither group was internally consistent. Two sentences were assigned to a single category by a highly significant majority ($p < 0.005$) of each group of subjects, and for each group there were three more sentences on which a consistent classification was imposed by a significant majority ($p < 0.05$) of members of that group; on ten sentences neither group deviated significantly from an even split between those judging it analytic and those judging it synthetic. (To give examples: *Summer follows Spring* was judged analytic by highly significant majorities in each group of subjects, while *We see with our eyes* was given near-even split votes by each group.) Overall, philosophers were somewhat more consistent than the non-philosophers. But the global finding conceals results that manifested the opposite tendency. Thus *Thunderstorms are electrical disturbances in the atmosphere* was judged analytic by a highly significant majority of non-philosophers, while a (non-significant) majority of philosophers deemed it synthetic. [...] *Nothing can be completely red and green all over* was judged analytic by a significant majority of philosophers but only by a non-significant majority of non-philosophers. (2001: 203)

[17] Similarly there have been claims that there are gender differences in intuitive responses to Putnam's Twin Earth thought experiments between men and women and that women are more likely to believe that Oscar and Twin-Oscar mean different things when they say 'water'. The results, however, are controversial and have been questioned by Jennifer Nagel (2012), among others.

Gödel/Schmidt story in cross-cultural contexts. Here is a brief account of the thought experiment:

> Suppose that Gödel was not in fact the author of [Gödel's] theorem. A man called 'Schmidt' ... actually did the work in question. His friend Gödel somehow got hold of the manuscript and it was thereafter attributed to Gödel. On the [descriptivist] view in question, then, when our ordinary man uses the name 'Gödel', he really means to refer to Schmidt, because Schmidt is the unique person satisfying the description 'the man who discovered the incompleteness of arithmetic'.... But it seems we are not. We *simply* are not. (1980: 83–4; emphasis added)

Kripke assumes that most readers of the passage would agree with his intuition that the name 'Gödel' refers to the man Gödel regardless of the descriptions associated with the name. He tells us that our externalist judgements regarding the correct assignment of a name are 'simple' and straightforward. However, experimental data collected by Machery *et al.* (2004) indicate that this is not the case. They claimed to have shown that Westerners are significantly more likely to respond to Kripke's thought experiment in accordance with social-historical accounts of reference, while East Asians are more likely to respond in accordance with descriptivist accounts of reference.[18] Their data were strongly supported by experiments that Maria Baghramian conducted in Guiyang University in China in August 2010.[19] The 2004 experiment, its methodology, and the accuracy of the results have been questioned in a number of ways;[20] however, regardless of their shortcomings, what the results obtained by experimental philosophers, and the extensive discussion arising out of them demonstrate is that the reliability of philosophical intuition could not simply be assumed but ought to be justified.

A major difficulty in taking intuition as an essential component of the methodology of philosophy is that the term 'intuition' in effect acts as a placeholder for a number of vaguely defined moves in philosophy. What the different intuitive gambits in ethics, epistemology, metaphysics, philosophy of language, etc., have in common is the absence of well-specified steps in reasoning and the largely unreflective character of the resulting judgements. Intuitions are often the starting point of philosophical arguments, because

---

[18] Machery *et al.* (2004) found that 56.5% of Western participants gave a causal historical response compared to 31.5% of East Asian participants. The difference between the scores for the two groups is statistically significant, and Machery *et al.* conclude that there is cross-cultural variation in the responses to this probe.

[19] In a repeat of this experiment in Guangzhou University in China Maria Baghramian obtained even more dramatic results than those reported by Machery *et al.* Ninety-two per cent of the participants in the experiment, consisting of Ph.D. students and lecturers with some familiarity with philosophy of language, opted for a descriptivist, Russellian account of meaning and reference (Baghramian forthcoming).

[20] For instance, the experiment has been criticized by Genoveva Marti and others for inadequacies in its design and methodology. Marti argues that the experiment tests 'people's intuitions about *theories* of reference, not about the *use* of names' (2009: 43). I believe Marti misstates the aim of the experiment, but will not argue the point here. For a discussion of various criticisms of the experiment see Maitra *et al.* 2012.

arguments have to start somewhere. This is the role of intuition emphasized by Devitt and Williamson. They are also the ultimate tribunal where we seem to come to the end of explicit procedure for philosophical argumentation. They are used as handy and easy decision procedures for some of the most important and all-embracing philosophical questions, realism vs. anti-realism, for instance, as well as detailed issues in sub-areas of philosophy, e.g. the trolley problem or the innocent person hooked up to the famous violinist (Thomson 1971). It is a common experience that some statements or philosophical positions just seem right to us. But the metaphor of seeming should not be taken too seriously. It is not so much a particular faculty of mind's eye that gives us the impression that we have a deep and immediate philosophical insight, but our inability to spell out some crucial steps of the argument clearly or carefully. Faced with such a situation, the use of the term 'intuition' should carry a warning sign as it signals an inability rather than providing a short cut to philosophical truth.

And yet, intuitions played a formative role in the revolution in philosophy of language wrought by Putnam and Kripke. If the experimental philosophers are correct in their view that our intuitions vary with cultural and socio-economic background or gender then the authority assigned to them by Kripke and other philosophers of his ilk begins to flounder. Putnam's more modest position, which attempts to stay clear of metaphysical aspirations, fares better. His advocacy of a more context sensitive and changeable conception of both analyticity and necessity, where they are seen as contextual or relative to a particular body of belief, could accommodate the worries raised by experimental philosophers. Above all, the increasing willingness of philosophers to subject premises supplied by intuition to empirical examination harkens back to Quine's call for a 'naturalized epistemology' and his vision of a profound rapprochement between philosophy and the other sciences. Such a trend, if fully established, could ultimately give rise to an empirically informed conception of meaning and the a priori.[21]

REFERENCES

Baghramian, Maria (forthcoming). 'Semantic Intuitions Chinese Style'.

Bealer, George (1992). 'The Incoherence of Empiricism', *Proceedings of the Aristotelian Society, Supplementary Volume* 66: 99–138.

Boghossian, Paul (1997). 'Analyticity'. In Bob Hale and Crispin Wright (eds.), *A Companion to the Philosophy of Language*. Oxford: Blackwell, pp. 331–68.

Burge, Tyler (1978). 'Belief and Synonymy', *Journal of Philosophy* 75(3): 119–38.

Carnap, Rudolf (1937). *The Logical Syntax of Language*, tr. A. Smeaton. London: Kegan, Paul. Originally published in German in 1934.

——(1947). *Meaning and Necessity*. Chicago: University of Chicago Press.

Chalmers, David J. (2002). 'Does conceivability entail possibility?'. In Tamar S. Gendler & John Hawthorne (eds.), *Conceivability and Possibility*. Oxford: Oxford University Press.

[21] We would like to thank Tim Williamson and Michael Beaney for their extensive and very helpful comments on earlier drafts of this chapter.

Chomsky, N. (2000). *New Horizons in the Study of Language and Mind*. Cambridge: Cambridge University Press.

Devitt, M. (2006). 'Intuitions in Linguistics', *British Journal for the Philosophy of Science* 57(3): 481–513.

Devitt, M. and R. Hanley (eds.) (2006). *The Blackwell Guide to the Philosophy of Language*. Oxford: Blackwell.

Dummett, M. (1973). *Frege: Philosophy of Language*. London: Duckworth.

Evans, G. (1973). 'The Causal Theory of Names', *Proceedings of the Aristotelian Society, Supplementary Volume* 47: 187–208.

Frege, G. (1884). *Die Grundlagen der Arithmetik*. Breslau: W. Koebner. Tr. J. L. Austin as *The Foundations of Arithmetic*. Oxford: Blackwell, 1950.

——(1892). 'Über Sinn und Bedeutung', *Zeitschrift für Philosophie und philosophische Kritik* 100: 25–50. Tr. in M. Beaney (ed.), *The Frege Reader*. Oxford: Blackwell, 1997, pp. 151–71.

Grice, H. P. and P. F. Strawson (1956). 'In Defence of a Dogma', *Philosophical Review* 65(2): 141–58.

Hintikka, J. (1999). 'The Emperor's New Intuitions', *Journal of Philosophy* 96: 127–47.

Jackson, F. (1998). *From Metaphysics to Ethics*. Oxford: Oxford University Press.

Kant, I. (1781/1787). *Critique of Pure Reason*, tr. Norman Kemp Smith. Basingstoke: Macmillan, 1965.

Katz, J. (1967). 'Some Remarks on Quine on Analyticity', *Journal of Philosophy* 64(2): 36–52.

Knobe, J. and S. Nichols (2008). 'An Experimental Philosophy Manifesto'. In J. Knobe and S. Nichols (eds.), *Experimental Philosophy*. Oxford: Oxford University Press, pp. 3–16.

Kripke, S. (1980). *Naming and Necessity*. Oxford: Basil Blackwell.

Machery, E., R. Mallon, S. Nichols, and S. Stich (2004). 'Semantics, Cross-Cultural Style', *Cognition* 92: B1–B12.

Maitra, I., B. Weatherson, and J. Ichikawa (2012). 'In Defense of a Kripkean Dogma', *Philosophy and Phenomenological Research* 85(1): 56–68.

Mallon, R., E. Machery, S. Nichols, and S. Stich (2009). 'Against Arguments from Reference', *Philosophy and Phenomenological Research* 79: 332–56.

Margolis, E. and S. Laurence (2003). 'Should We Trust Our Intuitions? Deflationary Accounts of the Analytic Data', *Proceedings of the Aristotelian Society* 103(3): 299–323.

Marti, G. (2009). 'Against Semantic Multi-Culturalism', *Analysis*, 69(1): 42–8.

Mill, J. S. (1874). 'The Utility of Religion'. In *Three Essays on Religion*. New York: Cosimo, 2008, pp. 69–124.

Morley-Bunker, N. (1977). 'Speaker's Intuitions of Analyticity', unpublished BA dissertation, University of Lancaster. Available online at: <http://experimentalphilosophy.type-pad.com/experimental_philosophy/2011/06/xphi-before-xphi-was-cool.html>, accessed 3 December 2012.

Nagel, J. (2012). 'Intuitions and Experiments: A Defense of the Case Method in Epistemology', *Philosophy and Phenomenological Research* 85(3): 495–527.

Putnam, H. (1962). 'It Ain't Necessarily So', *Journal of Philosophy* 59(22): 658–71.

—— (1975a). 'The Analytic and the Synthetic'. In *Mind, Language and Reality: Philosophical Papers, Volume 2*. Cambridge: Cambridge University Press, 1979, pp. 33–69.

—— (1975b). 'The Meaning of "Meaning"', *Minnesota Studies in the Philosophy of Science*, 7: 131–93; repr. in *Mind, Language and Reality: Philosophical Papers, Volume 2*. Cambridge: Cambridge University Press, 1979, pp. 215–71.

—— (1976). '"Two Dogmas" Revisited'. In G. Ryle (ed.), *Contemporary Aspects of Philosophy*. London: Oriel Press, pp. 202–13.

—— (1979a). 'Philosophy of Physics'. In *Mathematics, Matter, and Method: Philosophical Papers, Volume 1.* Cambridge: Cambridge University Press, pp. 79–92.

—— (1979b) 'What is Mathematical Truth?' In *Mathematics, Matter, and Method: Philosophical Papers, Volume 1.* Cambridge: Cambridge University Press, pp. 60–78.

—— (1990). 'Is Water Necessarily H_2O?' In *Realism with a Human Face.* Cambridge, MA: Harvard University Press, pp. 54–79.

—— (2002). 'Quine', *Common Knowledge* 8(2): 273–9.

Quine, W. V. O. (1943). 'Notes on Existence and Necessity', *Journal of Philosophy* 40(5): 113–27.

—— (1947). 'The Problem of Interpreting Modal Logic', *Journal of Symbolic Logic* 12(2): 43–8.

—— (1953). *From a Logical Point of View.* Cambridge, MA: Harvard University Press; 2nd edn. 1961.

—— (1956). 'Quantifiers and Propositional Attitudes', *Journal of Philosophy* 53; repr. in *The Ways of Paradox and Other Essays.* New York: Random House, 1966, pp. 185–96.

—— (1960). *Word and Object.* Cambridge, MA: MIT Press.

—— (1969). *Ontological Relativity and Other Essays.* New York: Columbia University Press.

—— (1979). 'Use and its Place in Meaning', *Studies in Linguistics and Philosophy* 3: 1–8.

—— (1986). *Philosophy of Logic.* Cambridge, MA: Harvard University Press.

—— (1987). 'Indeterminacy of Translation, Again', *Journal of Philosophy* 84(1): 5–10.

Sampson, G. (1980). *Making Sense.* Oxford: Oxford University Press.

—— (2001). *Empirical Linguistics.* London: Continuum.

Searle, J. R. (1983) *Intentionality: An Essay in the Philosophy of Mind.* Cambridge: Cambridge University Press.

Soames, S. (2003). *Philosophical Analysis in the Twentieth Century*, 2 vols. Princeton, NJ: Princeton University Press.

Sosa, E. (1999). 'Minimal Intuition'. In M. R. DePaul and W. Ramsey (eds.), *Rethinking Intuition: The Psychology of Intuition and its Role in Philosophical Inquiry.* Lanham, MD: Rowman & Littlefield, pp. 257–69.

Thomson, J. J. (1971). 'A Defense of Abortion', *Philosophy and Public Affairs* 1(1): 47–66.

Tversky, A. and D. Kahneman (1974). 'Judgment Under Uncertainty: Heuristics and Biases', *Science* 185: 1124–31.

White, M. (1950). 'The Analytic and the Synthetic: An Untenable Dualism'. In *John Dewey: Philosopher of Science and Freedom.* New York: Dial Press; repr. in Leonard Linsky (ed.), *Semantics and the Philosophy of Language.* Urbana: University of Illinois Press, 1952, pp. 272–86.

Williamson, T. (2004). 'Philosophical "Intuitions" and Scepticism about Judgement', *Dialectica* 58(1): 109–53.

—— (2005). 'Armchair Philosophy, Metaphysical Modality and Counterfactual Thinking', *Proceedings of the Aristotelian Society* 105(1): 1–23.

—— (2007). *The Philosophy of Philosophy.* Oxford: Blackwell.

Wittgenstein, L. (1921). *Tractatus Logico-Philosophicus*, tr. B. F. McGuinness and D. Pears. London: Routledge and Kegan Paul, 1975.

CHAPTER 20

THE MYTH OF LOGICAL BEHAVIOURISM AND THE ORIGINS OF THE IDENTITY THEORY

SEAN CRAWFORD

THE identity theory's rapid rise to ascendancy in analytic philosophy of mind during the late 1950s and early 1960s is often said to have constituted a sea change in perspective on the mind–body problem. According to the standard story, logical or analytical behaviourism was analytic philosophy of mind's first original materialist-monist solution to the mind–body problem and served to rein in various metaphysically extravagant forms of dualism and introspectionism. It is understood to be a broadly logico-semantic doctrine about the meaning or definition of mental terms, namely, that they refer to dispositions to engage in forms of overt physical behaviour. Logical/analytical behaviourism then eventually gave way, so the standard story goes, in the early 1960s, to analytical philosophy's second original materialist-monist solution to the mind–body problem, the mind–brain identity theory, understood to be an ontological doctrine declaring states of sensory consciousness to be physical states of the brain and wider nervous system. Of crucial importance here is the widely held notion that whereas logical behaviourism had proposed an identity between the meanings of mental and physical-behavioural concepts or predicates—an identity that was ascertainable a priori through conceptual analysis—the identity theory proposed an identity between mental and physical properties, an identity that could only be established a posteriori through empirical scientific investigation. John Searle (2004) has recently described the transition thus:

> [logical behaviourism] was gradually replaced among materialist-minded philoso-
> phers by a doctrine called 'physicalism', sometimes called the 'identity theory'. The
> physicalists said that Descartes was not wrong, as the logical behaviourists had
> claimed, as a matter of logic, but just as a matter of fact.... The identity theorists

were anxious to insist on the contrast between their view and behaviourism. Behaviourism was supposed to be a logical thesis about the definition of mental concepts. The identity thesis was supposed to be a factual claim, not about the analysis of mental concepts, but rather about the mode of existence of mental states. The model for the behaviourists was one of definitional identities. Pains are dispositions to behaviour in a way that triangles are three-sided plane figures. In each case it is a matter of definition. The identity theorists said no, the model is not definitions, but rather empirical discoveries of identities in science. (pp. 54–5)

Searle cites Gilbert Ryle and C. G. Hempel as 'famous' logical behaviourists (he could easily have added Rudolf Carnap as another) and U. T. Place, J. J. C. Smart, and Herbert Feigl as identity theorists. The alleged insight of the great triumvirate of identity theorists is that materialism, if true, cannot be an a priori knowable semantic thesis about the meanings of mental and physical terms, but must take the form of an empirical ontological thesis about the mental and physical realms.

While there is a grain of truth in this very familiar historical take on the transition from logical behaviourism to the identity theory—it was indeed a shift away from a focus on language and concepts characteristic of analytic philosophy's more general 'linguistic turn', to a focus on ontology—the story is much more an instance of what Richard Watson (1993) calls 'shadow history of philosophy':

> The shadow history of philosophy is a kind of received view consisting of stories of philosophy that most philosophers accept even though they know that these stories are not really quite precisely right.... The presumption is that they are basically right, that the pictures they present display the important logical or conceptual guts of history like a medical diagram, in an ideal way, without the mess of the real thing.... They are important as the bases from which philosophers derive their systems, either by development or opposition.... These shadow positions ... are at least as substantial and influential in the development of philosophy as the 'true' positions they are shadows of. Shadow histories provide indispensible foundations for philosophy. (pp. 97, 107–108, 109)

The received view of logical behaviourism just outlined is a shadow position and the story of its overthrow by its successor, the mind–brain identity theory, is shadow history in Watson's sense—at least so I shall argue. More specifically, I will argue that the difference between one form of what is misleadingly called 'logical behaviourism'—namely, the logical positivists' logical behaviourism—and the identity theory, has been misunderstood and its significance consequently overrated and exaggerated. I will try to demonstrate this in detail in the next section by looking closely at some of the works of the logical positivists, Carnap's in particular, and by placing these works in the larger system of their thought. After setting the historical record straight, I will go on to explore in the following section the origins of the identity theory, which I trace to Moritz Schlick's pre-positivist philosophy, and the seldom discussed difference between the two different versions that succeeded logical behaviourism. I will focus on Herbert Feigl's less familiar and rather puzzling identity theory because it is derived directly from Schlick and explicitly against the background of Feigl's earlier logical positivism. Moreover, while it has received very little critical commentary, attention to its striking difference from Place's and Smart's theory is illuminating, I believe, because it reveals a deep and seemingly perennial opposition in modern philosophy of mind, one that we are witnessing today in the debate over the so-called hard problem of phenomenal consciousness.[1]

20.1 THE MYTH OF LOGICAL BEHAVIOURISM

20.1.1 Two Logical Behaviourisms

According to the shadow history of philosophy of mind, retold to generations of undergraduates, and reported in countless textbooks, anthology introductions, and encyclopaedias, there was something called 'logical behaviourism' and it was overthrown at the end of the 1950s by the mind–brain identity theory. Carnap's 'Psychology in Physical Language' (1933), Hempel's 'The Logical Analysis of Psychology' (1935), and Ryle's *The Concept of Mind* (1949) are taken virtually universally to be the three canonical texts of logical behaviourism. Now, to begin with, it should be obvious on reflection that the idea that there was a single doctrine known as logical behaviourism and that it was an early twentieth-century form of materialism is obviously a shadow position. For logical behaviourism was in fact associated with two very different movements in analytic philosophy, ordinary language philosophy and logical positivism. Moreover, in neither form was it a type of materialism. In the eyes of both movements, the mind–body problem is a pseudo-problem to be dissolved or replaced by linguistic analysis. All traditional '-ism' solutions to it—dualism and materialism alike—are metaphysical pseudo-doctrines. So logical behaviourism is not really a form of materialism at all, at least not in the traditional sense. To be sure, it was for the logical positivists a form—or more accurately, an application—of what they called 'Physicalism'.[2] But, again, the Physicalism of the logical positivists is not a metaphysical doctrine—on the contrary, it is an anti-metaphysical doctrine. The logical positivists were explicit and adamant about this, repeating it tirelessly in an often vain effort to avoid misunderstandings. 'Physicalism', Carnap (1935/1963) tells us, '... has nothing to do with any such theses as monism, dualism or parallelism'; and although Physicalism 'is allied to that of *Materialism* ... the agreement extends only as far as the logical components of Materialism; the metaphysical components, concerned with the question of whether the essence of the world is material or spiritual, are completely excluded from consideration' (p. 459). Physicalism is a doctrine

---

[1.] My scope in this chapter is thus very limited. More comprehensive recent surveys of the history of analytic philosophy of mind, covering much more than the mind–body problem, can be found in Burge (2007) and Patterson (2008).

[2] The term was coined by Neurath (1931).

about the language of science. It is the thesis that the only kind of language known to be capable of providing the necessary inter-subjective, inter-sensory, and universal confirmation base for empirical science is physical language. So understood Physicalism (with a capital 'P') is crucially part of the 'Unity of Science' movement initiated by the logical positivists in the early 1930s, the central aim of which was to which ensure that all of the theories and hypotheses of all empirical sciences were subject to rigorous inter-subjective confirmation or testing.[3] In effect, logical behaviourism for the logical positivists is simply Physicalism applied to the empirical science of psychology. The fact that the logical behaviourism of the logical positivists was simply one part of their grand goal of constructing a 'Unified Science'—and hence was no different in principle from the corresponding 'physicalization' of biology and other special sciences—indicates that it must have a very different character from the logical behaviourism of the anti-scientistically inclined ordinary language philosophers—and, more importantly, a very different character from the received view that it proposed analytic meaning equivalences between mental and physical-behavioural statements.

In the hands of the logical positivists, logical behaviourism is strongly reductive; for the ordinary language philosophy, especially Ryle, it is strongly non-reductive. The former reductive version explicitly attempts to describe behaviour in purely 'physical language', hence in non-mentalistic terms, while the non-reductive version does not. As the most cursory browsing in *The Concept of Mind* amply demonstrates, Ryle makes no attempt whatsoever to purge his behavioural-dispositional analyses of psychological terms. His analyses of mentalistic discourse are saturated with mentalistic terminology.[4] Moreover, very early on in *The Concept of Mind*—in the most reprinted chapter, 'Descartes's Myth'—he explicitly states his agreement with the view that 'a person's thinking, feeling and purposive doing cannot be described solely in the idioms of physics, chemistry and physiology' (p. 18).[5] In contrast to this, there is no question but that the logical positivists explicitly intended a person's psychological phenomena to be described precisely in the idioms of physics, chemistry, and physiology—that just is the thesis of Physicalism applied to psychology.

Although this difference between the two versions of logical behaviourism—that the one is reductive and the other non-reductive—has been noted by commentators less inclined to shadow history, its full significance has still not been appreciated. For just as it is the very non-reductive nature of Ryle's logical behaviourism that allows it to be

---

[3] As Hardcastle (2007) has rightly emphasized, the Unity of Science movement was also a reaction against the prevailing view of the time in Germany that there is a fundamental difference between the methods of the *Naturwissenschaften* (natural sciences) and those of the *Geisteswissenschaften* (human sciences). This point is made very forcefully in the first early statements of Physicalism by Neurath (1931), Carnap (1932), and Hempel (1935).

[4] Something Burge (2007) fails to appreciate, including as he does Ryle among those philosophers he alleges 'shared a tendency to think that theorizing in psychology or philosophy of mind should dispense with mentalistic vocabulary, or interpret it in nonmentalistic terms, as far as possible' (p. 441).

[5] In agreeing with this part of the Cartesian Myth, Ryle's central point is of course that it does not follow from this truth that a person's thinking, feeling, and purposive doing are to be described in a 'counterpart idiom' referring to 'occult processes' running in parallel to physical processes.

logical or 'analytical' in character, so too it is the very reductive nature of the logical posi-tivists' logical behaviourism that prevents it from being logical or analytical (see § 20.1.4 below). But before we turn to this, let us have before us some prominent examples of the shadow understanding of logical behaviourism.

20.1.2 Shadow (Analytic) Behaviourism

In his highly influential and often anthologized critique of logical behaviourism, 'Brains and Behaviour' (1963), Hilary Putnam writes that 'The Vienna positivists in their "physi-calist" phase (about 1930) ... [produced] the doctrine we are calling *logical behaviourism*— the doctrine that, just as numbers are (allegedly) logical constructions out of *sets*, so *mental events* are logical constructions out of actual and possible *behaviour events*' (p. 326). He goes on to say that logical behaviourism so understood 'implies that all talk about mental events is translatable into talk about actual or overt potential behaviour' (p. 326). Putnam's aim is not to praise but to bury logical behaviourism (once and for all). But since he consid-ers the Vienna Circle's version too extreme to need burying, he purports to inter a weaker and more plausible form, according to which 'There exist entailments between mind-state-ments and behaviour-statements; entailments that are not perhaps analytic in the way that "All bachelors are married" is analytic, but that nevertheless follow (in some sense) from the meanings of mind words.' Putnam says that he 'shall call these *analytic entailments*' (p. 327).[6]

Along similar lines, Jerry Fodor, in a well-known book, states that 'To qualify as a behaviourist in the broad sense of that term that I shall employ, one need only believe that the following proposition expresses a necessary truth: For each men-tal predicate that can be employed in a psychological explanation, there must be at least one description of behaviour to which it bears a logical connection' (1968, p. 51).[7] Furthermore, claims Fodor, 'one of the more important differences between ... behaviourism and ... materialism [is] that while both maintain the identity of each mental state with some nonmental [*sic*] states, the propositions that enunciate the ... behaviouristss's reductions of mental to behavioural predicates are supposed to be ana-lytic.... By contrast, the materialist's identifications of mental with physical states are presumably enunciated by contingent propositions' (p. 155 n6). Since analytic truths and entailments are supposed to be knowable a priori, it follows that the analyses or translations or entailments in question between psychological statements and behav-ioural statements proposed by logical behaviourists are—according to Putnam and Fodor—supposed to be knowable a priori. Moreover, *pace* the logical behaviourists,

---

[6] Putnam does not cite a single work of the Vienna Circle, or indeed of any logical positivist, in which is to be found an endorsement of even an approximation of this, let alone of the previous extreme version of logical behaviourism. This is not surprising since, as I shall argue, no such semblance is there to be found.

[7] Cf. Cornman (1971), pp. 132ff., esp. p. 140, and Kim (1971), p. 328.

the materialists, that is, the identity theorists, maintain that any link between the mental and the physical must be empirical in character, not conceptual or semantic, and hence knowable only a posteriori.

20.1.3 The Real (Synthetic) Behaviourism of the Logical Positivists

When one turns to the two canonical logical positivist texts of logical behaviourism, however, one finds a very different story. We can begin by noting a curious and rather blatant tension in standard accounts of the logical positivists' logical behaviourism. It is common for critics to maintain both that the logical positivists' thesis of logical behaviourism claims that the links between mind and behaviour are analytic and that such meaning links are forged by the logical behaviourists' verificationism. It is rarely noticed that in order for these two tenets to be true together, the statements of the conditions of verification (or confirmation) for psychological sentences must be analytically linked to them and hence determinable a priori. But when one turns to the texts one finds appeals to verification, confirmation, or test conditions that cannot possibly be known a priori and are in no way analytically connected with psychological sentences.

Take Hempel's (1935/1972) oft-quoted and much-derided attempt at a logical behaviourist 'translation' of the psychological statement 'Paul has a toothache'. According to Hempel, the conditions under which this statement would be verified include not only Paul's verbal utterances, gestures, and other overt behaviour, but also his internal physiological and neurological states, such as 'Paul's blood pressure, digestive processes ...' and 'such and such processes occur[ring] in Paul's central nervous system' (p. 122). Now, it is obvious—and it was surely obvious to Hempel—that any connection between Paul's toothache and his blood pressure, digestive and neural processes is empirical and established a posteriori; hence that it cannot be conceptual or analytical. At best, it will be a lawful empirical correlation and hence clearly synthetic.

Turning now to Carnap's (1933/59) very similar example of the sentence 'Mr. A is now excited' (P_1), Carnap asks *what does sentence P_1 mean?* and answers as follows:

> The viewpoint which will here be defended is that P_1 has the same content as a sentence P_2 which asserts the existence of a physical structure characterized by the disposition to react in a specific manner to specific stimuli. In our example, P_2 asserts the existence of that physical structure (*micro-structure*) ... of Mr. A's body (*especially of his central nervous system*) that is characterized by a high pulse and rate of breathing, which, on the application of certain stimuli, may even be made higher, by vehement and factually unsatisfactory answers to questions, by the occurrence of agitated movements on the application of certain stimuli, etc. (p. 172, my emphasis)

Very few of these physical-behavioural characterizations—if any—can be considered analytically linked with excitement. One year earlier Carnap had claimed, in the 'formal mode', that 'all psychological statements can be translated into physical language' (1932/34, p. 28), adding that the equivalent claim in the misleading and dangerous 'material mode' is that all psychological statements 'refer to physical events (viz. physical events in the body, *especially the central nervous system* ...)' (p. 71, my emphasis). Five years later he wrote:

> Let us take as an example the term 'angry'. If for anger we knew a sufficient and necessary criterion to be found by a physiological analysis of the nervous system or other organs, then we could define 'angry' in terms of the biological language. The same holds if we knew such a criterion to be determined by the observation of the overt, external behaviour. But a physiological criterion is not yet known. And the peripheral symptoms known are presumably not necessary criteria because it might be that a person of strong self-control is able to suppress these symptoms. If this is the case, the term 'angry' is, at least at the present time, not definable in terms of the biological language. But, nevertheless, it is reducible to such terms. (1938/91, p. 401)

We shall return to Carnap's distinction between definition and reduction below (§ 20.1.5.5) as misunderstandings of it seem to have played a key role in corrupting the logical positivists' logical behaviourism into the received shadow position. The point for present purposes is that both physicalist definition and physicalist reduction statements of psychology are synthetic.

It is true that shadow histories sometimes draw attention to the fact that both Hempel and Carnap, in their canonical statements of 'logical behaviourism', go well beyond, or rather behind, overt behaviour and curiously include internal neurophysiological conditions in what are allegedly supposed officially to be overt-behavioural translations of psychological sentences. The typical reaction to this surprising discovery is to conclude that Hempel's and Carnap's translations are faulty because no such internal conditions could possibly be analytically linked to any psychological terms or sentences.[8] Others refrain at the outset from describing the logical positivists as behaviourists at all and characterize them rather as holding a 'semantic' or 'logical' or 'translation' form of materialism according to which psychological statements are translatable a priori on the basis of conceptual analysis into physical *simpliciter* statements rather than into physical *behavioural* ones.[9] David Rosenthal, for example, has described a strong form of materialism that he calls the 'translation view', associated with the thesis of the unity of science, which 'could be established without a detailed study of psychological beings' and which 'could be shown [to be true] by examining simply what we mean by the words we use'. He notes how strange this view is, as it seems to follow from it that 'it would then be possible to defend the unity of science, which is a claim about the results of future scientific investigation, without appealing to any such results'. In contrast, a

---

[8] See, e.g., Patterson (2008,) p. 532 and Kim (2011), p. 70. But cf. Kim (2003) where the opposite and correct conclusion is drawn, namely, that Hempel and Carnap were operating with very different notions of translation, definition, and meaning.

[9] See, e.g., Rosenthal (1971/87), Beckermann (1992), and Stoljar (2010).

weaker form of materialism, of which the identity theory is one variety, 'does not result in peculiarities of this sort … [for it] can only be established on the basis of results from future scientific study'.[10] While the recognition that the logical positivists' Physicalistic translations were never intended to be restricted to overt behavioural terms is salutary, it is unfortunately accompanied by the erroneous view that the translations in questions are still meant to provide analytical equivalences between mental and physical statements.

Throughout his early writings of the 1930s, Carnap speaks of the 'rules of inference', 'rules of transformation', and 'rules of translation' of the physical language in which the analyses or reductions are to be carried out. Although he is not always entirely explicit about it, it is pretty clear even in the earliest of these writings that not all of these 'rules' are laws of logic and that some of them are intended to be laws of nature. For example, in 'Unity of Science' (1932) he wrote of the 'the rules of transformation inside the physical language (*including the system of natural laws*)' (p. 88, my emphasis; cf. p. 92). This became much clearer in *The Logical Syntax of Language* (1934) and 'Testability and Meaning' (1936–7) in which Carnap explicitly distinguishes between the L-rules and the P-rules of a scientific language on the basis of which inferences or 'transformations' may be validly carried out: the former are logical laws and the latter physical laws. (Carnap also defines various correlative notions, such as L-validity and P-validity, L-equipollence and P-equipollence, and L- and P-synonymy.) Both kinds of 'translation' 'rules' are to be employed in physicalistic analysis or reduction.

In *Philosophy and Logical Syntax* (1935/1963), which was based on lectures delivered at the University of London in 1934, Carnap claims that 'every sentence of any branch of scientific language is equipollent to some sentence of the physical language, and can therefore be translated into the physical language without changing its content' (p. 455; cf. *The Logical Syntax of Language* § 82). Carnap is very clear in this work (as well as in *The Logical Syntax of Language* § 51) that there can be two concepts of equipollence, that is, equivalence, in the physical language: logical equipollence (L-equipollence) and physical equipollence (P-equipollence). Two sentences are L-equipollent when they are mutually derivable solely on the basis of logical laws; two sentences are P-equipollent when they are mutually derivable only on the basis of physical laws as well. Carnap explicitly allowed a psychological sentence, Q_1, and a physical translation of it, Q_2, to be P-equipollent, as Q_1 could be transformed into Q_2 on the basis of 'a scientific law, that is, a universal sentence belonging to the valid sentences of the scientific language-system' (1935/1963, p. 456). Carnap took pains to point out that, in his view, this universal sentence 'need not be analytic; the only assumption is that it is valid. It may be synthetic, in which case it is P-valid' (1935/1963, p. 456). In a letter he wrote to Herbert Feigl in 1933 Carnap is more committal and expressly states that the two sentences are not analytic. His example is 'N. has a visual image of a house' (A) and he offers two translations: 'The

---

[10] Rosenthal (1971/87), p. 4. Beckermann (1992) seems to misinterpret Carnap's Physicalism in essentially the same way on pp. 2–7, as does Stoljar (2010) on pp. 117–18.

organism of N. is in the state of house-imagining' (B_1) and 'In the organism of N. there is an electrochemical condition of such a kind (described in terms of electrochemistry)' (B_2). Carnap's comments on this are highly instructive:

> Both B_1 and B_2 are translations of A. According to my recently adopted terminology, I assert: A is equivalent ('*gehaltgleich*') to both statements ... ; viz., L-equivalent (*logically* equivalent) with B_1; but P-equivalent (*physically* equivalent) with B_2, i.e., mutually translatable (derivable) using besides the logical laws also natural laws as rules of inference, incorporated as transformation rules in the scientific language. You are therefore right in saying that B_2 is only synthetically equivalent with A. (Feigl, 1963, p. 255n28)

It is noteworthy that while B_1, unlike B_2, is claimed by Carnap to be L-equivalent to A, it is not behavioural[11]—in fact, it is not even physical. I would conjecture that it is intended as an adverbial analysis of (A) intended to avoid commitment to the intentional object apparently designated by the phrase 'visual image of a house', and hence to avoid intentional language, thus paving the way for the ultimate physical translation into B_2. Such adverbial techniques were sometimes employed by Russell in order to avoid commitment to intentional objects (and by some of the American New Realists in a quasi-behaviourist spirit) and Russell of course had a great influence on Carnap.[12] At any rate, it should by now be clear that the real logical behaviourism of the positivists was in fact far less extreme than even Putnam's two-decades older weakened version. For it never claimed mental events to be logical constructions of overt behaviour and never claimed to offer analytically true logical constructions of 'mind talk' into either (overt or covert) 'behaviour talk' or 'physical talk'.

20.1.4   Analytic Behaviourism vs. Synthetic Behaviourism/Materialism

The philosophical behaviourism of those ordinary language philosophers who were behaviourists, Ryle in particular, is properly called 'analytic', since it did indeed attempt to give a priori conceptual analyses of (some) mentalistic sentences in behavioural-dispositional terms. Such behavioural 'definitions' or 'hypotheticals' were supposed to give the ordinary meaning of mentalistic sentences. Moreover, the behaviour they adverted to was indeed of the 'outer' and 'overt' variety; it was purely behaviouristic. And it was so because it was on the basis of overt behaviour, not on the basis of internal neurophysiological states, that ordinary mentalistic language was learned and applied in everyday situations by ordinary language users. But this pure overt behaviour was described

---

[11] Cirera (1993) also notes this.

[12] Such adverbial strategies for avoiding intentional language are strongly criticized by Chisholm (1955–6).

using an abundance of mental terms and so the logical behaviourism produced was fla-grantly non-reductionist. On reflection, this should not be very surprising. For if there are going to be analytically true behavioural analyses of psychological sentences, these are bound to contain mental terminology, as they will draw out conceptual connections between mental states and behaviour described as *intentional action*. (If we had to have a name for it, we might call this kind of Rylean ordinary-language logical behaviourism *pure non-reductive analytic behaviourism*: 'pure' because it adverts to overt behaviour only; 'non-reductive' because it employs mentalistic terms in its *analysans*; and 'ana-lytic' because the connections between the mental and the behavioural are supposed to be analytically true and knowable a priori.) In contrast, the logical positivists' vari-ous 'definitions', 'reductions', 'transformations', and 'translations' were indeed explicitly couched—or intended to be so in a programmatic spirit—in non-mentalistic termi-nology and so were (supposed to be) truly reductive. But very few—perhaps none—of these translations were supposed to be analytic but rather were intended to be synthetic, arrived at empirically, in fact experimentally in many cases.[13] Moreover, they did not advert only to purely overt behaviour ('peripheral states') but made explicit reference to inner neurophysiological processes and structures ('central states'). (Again, if we needed a name, perhaps *impure reductive synthetic behaviourism* or, given the last mentioned fact, *synthetic semantic materialism*, would do.)

20.1.5 Origins of the Shadow Doctrine

How, then, did the idea that the logical positivists endorsed the shadow doctrine that there are analytic entailments between psychological sentences and either behavioural sentences or physical sentences couched in non-mentalistic vocabulary (*pure reductive analytic behaviourism* or *analytic semantic materialism*, as we might put it) get started? Perhaps many philosophers simply ran the two versions together producing a home-less and unstable fusion that was easy to refute and that served as a foil for their own allegedly superior positions. In other words, as Watson suggests, shadow history pro-vided the necessary opposition by which to define and build one's own position. While there must be some truth in this, I think that there are more concrete and interesting reasons.

20.1.5.1 *The Extensionality of Translation*

We can trace the origin of the shadow position partly to the positivists' highly techni-cal and, especially for us today, counter-intuitive use of the expressions 'translation',

---

[13] I am grateful to my colleague Thomas Uebel for pointing out after reading an earlier draft of this chapter that Cirera (1993), of which I was unaware, independently makes this crucial point. When following up citations of Cirera's work, I was subsequently led to Kim (2003), who also makes the point independently.

'meaning', 'synonymy', 'definition', and their cognates.[14] None of these terms is used today in anything like the way the positivists, especially Carnap and Hempel, were using them in the 1930s and even to some extent in the 1940s. Many of these terms and their cognates have strong modal implications for us now that they did not have back then for the positivists. Indeed, Carnap and Hempel were working with a background extensional logic. When they claim that 'mind talk' can be *translated* into 'physical talk', what they mean is that one can construct material bi-conditionals—or Carnap's (1936–7) later 'reduction sentences', of which more presently—with mind talk on the left-hand side and physical-thing-language talk on the right-hand side. These material bi-conditional 'translations' were just that—*material* bi-conditionals, containing the straightforward truth functional connective symbolized by the horseshoe. These material bi-conditionals (and reduction sentences) were clearly understood at the outset to be synthetic statements of lawful correlations discovered by empirically through scientific investigation.[15] From the very beginning, Carnap fully acknowledged the empirical character of the proposed physical definitions of psychological concepts and the translations of psychological sentences into physical sentences. As he says,

> Sentence P_1, 'A is excited' cannot, indeed, today be translated into a physical sentence P_3 of the form 'such and such a physico-chemical process is now taking place in A's body' (expressed by a specification of physical state-coordinates and by chemical formulae). Our current knowledge of physiology is not adequate for this purpose. (1933/59, p. 175)

Physical 'translation' draws on the empirical knowledge available at the time.

20.1.5.2 *Empirical Physicalization*

Indeed, in both 'Unity of Science' and 'Psychology in Physical Language'—which are among Carnap's earliest treatments of psychology and considered as canonical texts of logical behaviourism—Carnap outlines an empirical, experimental procedure he calls 'physicalization'. A primary example of physicalization occurs when a non-physicalistic sentence reporting a quality (e.g., a colour or sound) is correlated with a physicalistic sentence reporting a measurable quantity (light or sound wave frequency). For example, one can physicalize a protocol (observation) sentence reporting a 'qualitative determination', such as a statement about colour ('Green here now'), by correlating it with a sentence reporting a 'quantitative determination' (wavelength of such and such frequency). The procedure involves an experimenter varying various physical conditions (e.g., wave

---

[14] Actually, the technical use ran against the grain even during the first half of the twentieth century. Ducasse (1941), ch. 7, e.g., complains that what Carnap (1935/1963) calls translation is not truly translation.

[15] Carnap (1956) is especially clear about this. Philosophers of science, including Carnap (1936–7), soon began to realize, of course, that natural laws, disposition statements, and the counterfactual conditionals associated with them cannot be formalized using an extensional logic. See Carnap (1956), Hempel (1954), and Suppe (1977) for some discussion of this.

frequencies and oscillations) in order to discover which ones correlate with a subject's utterance of a protocol sentence. Carnap gives an interesting, if rather quirky, example of how this might work in the psychological subfield of graphology, which is the study of the relation between handwriting and personality. Carnap describes the third stage of the physicalization of graphology as follows:

> the basic empirical task of graphology ... consists of the search for the correlations which hold between the properties of handwriting and those of character.... The problem of systematization here is to determine the degree of correlation of the two properties by a statistical investigation of many instances of script of the type in question and the characters of the corresponding writers. (1933/1959, p. 189)

He also believes the same kind of physicalization can be carried out on psychological sentences describing actions: 'The class of arm-movements to which the protocol-designation "beckoning motion" corresponds can be determined, and then described in terms of physical concepts' (p. 182). The interesting point for present purposes is not that Carnap thinks such physicalization is plausible or even possible in principle. No doubt it is not and Carnap was characteristically overly optimistic here. As many have pointed out time and again, it is most unlikely that all the arm movements constituting the class of beckoning or waving have anything purely physical in common, and hence most unlikely that such a class of actions can be correlated with any single physical property picked out (non-trivially, that is, non-disjunctively) by any purely physical concept. The interesting point is that the physicalization of actions proposed by Carnap is entirely empirical in character and a matter of painstaking experimental work. Moreover, granted that the physicalization in question is empirically highly unlikely, it seems no more unlikely than an identity theory's proposed type-identification of a raw feel with a brain state.

20.1.5.3 *Physicalization vs. Identity*

It is worth dwelling briefly on this last point. In his recent survey of contemporary physicalism, Daniel Stoljar discusses 'the semantic version of physicalism associated with Carnap and Neurath', which he characterizes as the thesis that 'every statement or predicate is synonymous with some physical statement or predicate' (2010, p. 117). One of the many reasons for denying the 'semantic view', according to Stoljar, is that there will be many meaningful predicates that are not synonymous with any physical predicate. His example is the predicate 'has no soul' in the sentence 'Otto has no soul'. Stoljar claims that in order for the semantic view of Carnap and Neurath to be true, this sentence 'would have to be equivalent in meaning to a physical statement' and that 'this is extremely unlikely' (p. 118). He then presses a further 'simple-minded objection' that 'translation is a singularly difficult business'—justifying this by noting that 'translating Proust into English is something that people are still arguing about, and while Proust might be a special case, it remains advisable that one should not associate physicalism with translation too closely' (p. 118). He continues by stating that 'It was for these and similar reasons that many philosophers in the 1950s and 1960s turned from a semantic to a non-semantic formulation of physicalism (e.g., Smart 1959)' (p. 118).

Although he is not explicit about it, it is clear that by 'synonymy' and 'translation' Stoljar has in mind a strongly modalized notion, according to which the bi-conditional translation of 'Otto has no soul' into some candidate physical sentence is analytic and therefore knowable a priori—translators of Proust, after all, argue with each other from the armchair, as it were, and not from laboratories. In other words, in Carnap's terminology, Stoljar is assuming that Carnap and Neurath claim that 'has soul' is L-synonymous with a physical predicate and 'Otto has no soul' is L-equipollent (L-equivalent) with a physical sentence. Stoljar is undoubtedly correct that any such analytic translation is indeed extremely unlikely. But there are a couple of problems with Stoljar's account here. First, neither Carnap nor Neurath nor Hempel ever held the shadow doctrine of semantic physicalism; as we have seen, Carnap's claim is that 'has soul' is P-synonymous with a physical predicate and 'Otto has no soul' P-equipollent with a physical sentence. Consequently, Stoljar has mischaracterized the difference between the physicalism of the logical positivists and the physicalism of the identity theory. Second, once it is recognized that the logical positivists' translations and synonymies are synthetic, the claim that the psychological predicate 'has soul' is 'synonymous' with a physical predicate—that is, *nomologically co-extensive* with some physical predicate—is no less plausible than a type identity theorist's claim that the property of having soul is *identical* with some physical property. Indeed, one might maintain that the logical positivists' claim is in fact more plausible than the identity theorists', as it rests with a simple correlation between predicates, which is much weaker than a claim of identity between the properties designated by the predicates, and all that can arguably be established empirically—while the identity theorist must somehow convert the predicate-correlation into an property-identity on non-scientific, or at least non-empirical, grounds (of parsimony, say, or abduction).[16]

20.1.5.4 *The Term 'Logical Behaviourism'*

Returning to our question of the origin of shadow logical behaviourism, we should note that the term 'logical behaviourism' was coined by Hempel in passing, parenthetically, in 'Logical Analysis of Psychology' (so far as I know, Carnap never used the term to describe his position, and of course neither did Ryle). To our contemporary ears the expression 'logical behaviourism' irresistibly suggests a doctrine according to which mind talk is logically or conceptually or analytically equivalent to behaviour talk, and hence necessarily linked with it, in contrast to being merely contingently connected with it. The suggestion is only exacerbated by the occurrence of the terms 'translation', 'meaning', and 'definition'. But the sense of 'logic' that both Carnap and Hempel had in mind was that of *logical analysis*, specifically the logical analysis of science, or simply 'logic of science', as Carnap called it. Logic of science is the analysis and study of the linguistic expressions of science, their kinds and relations, and how they are ordered and

---

[16] One original point of disagreement between Place (1956) and Smart (1959) was that Smart considered the conversion of a correlation into an identity at least partly a philosophical and not completely scientific matter.

structured into systems known as scientific theories, all abstracted from the psychological and social conditions of working scientists. There are two important terminological points here. First, a 'logical' investigation or study of science is intended to contrast with a psychological and sociological study (and a philosophical study, presumably, if philosophy is understood as speculative metaphysics). Second, since many of the relations between scientific sentences studied by the logical analysis of science, particularly between the theoretical sentences and the protocol or observation sentences that confirm them, will be contingent and empirically established, the 'logic' of science includes the study of synthetic sentences—in particular the synthetic sentences that describe the 'translations' of sentences of the empirical sciences (as opposed to mathematics) into the physicalistic sentences that constitute the inter-subjective confirmation basis of a unified science. Hempel's parenthetical coinage was intended further to contrast the logical positivist's physicalization of psychology, essentially a logico-linguistic affair, with the psychological behaviourism of J. B. Watson and his followers, which was a thesis about the methods and aims of the empirical science of psychology.

The 'logical behaviourism' of the logical positivists is simply part of their overall project of the physicalization of all of empirical science, which in turn is an implication of the goal of unified science. When combined with the claim that a physicalistic language is the only known inter-subjective (as well as inter-sensory and universal) language—not as a matter of necessity, but only contingently, something Carnap took pains to point out from the very beginning[17]—the unity of science thesis becomes 'Physicalism'. The doctrine's emphasis on language is characteristic of the early days of analytic philosophy. When applied to the science of psychology, Physicalism, understood as the linguistic doctrine that only a physicalistic language is capable of serving as an inter-subjective confirmation base for empirical science, becomes the 'logical behaviourism' of Hempel and Carnap. It is in this light that one must view Carnap's general thesis that 'all statements of Science can be translated into physical language' and the relevant sub-thesis for psychology that 'all psychological statements can be translated into physical language'. This sub-thesis is no different, in principle, from the relevant sub-thesis for biology, namely, that 'every statement of Biology can be translated into physical language' (1932/1934, p. 70) and not many philosophers are tempted to view the physicalization of biology as a project in a priori conceptual meaning-analysis.

20.1.5.5 *The Confusion of Definition/Reduction with Analytic/Synthetic*

I would like to suggest, however, that the chief source of confusion has to do with the already mentioned orthodox understanding of the transition from logical behaviourism to the identity theory, a confusion that again turns on not appreciating the extensionalism of Physicalism (§ 20.1.5.1), in particular the extensionality of Physical definition. The confusion seems to originate or at least stem primarily from Feigl—ironically, as we shall see, given his letter from Carnap quoted above—and is (I think) perpetuated and

---

[17] *Pace* Smith (1986), p. 60, who erroneously claims that Carnap did not view Physicalism as contingent. Carnap (1932/34), pp. 60ff. and 96, contradicts Smith's claim.

carried into contemporary philosophy of mind's self-image through the Feigl–Putnam–Fodor line of influence. Early on in 'The "Mental" and the "Physical"', Feigl makes clear the famous *anagnorisis* of the identity theorists:

> A most important *logical* requirement for the analysis of the mind–body problem is the recognition of the *synthetic* or *empirical* character of the statements regarding the correlation of psychological to neuro-physiological states. It has been pointed out time and again that the early reductionistic logical behaviorism failed to produce an adequate and plausible construal of mentalistic concepts by explicit definition on the basis of purely *behavioral* concepts.... I was tempted to identify, in the sense of *logical* identity, the mental with the neurophysiological ...
>
> But if this theory is understood as holding a *logical translatability* (analytic transformability) of statements in the one language into statements in the other, this will certainly not do....
>
> [T]he question which mental states correspond to which cerebral states is in *some* sense ... an empirical question. If this were not so, the intriguing and very unfinished science of psychophysiology could be pursued and completed by purely a priori reasoning....
>
> ... Subjective experience ... cannot be *logically* identical with states of the organism; i.e., phenomenal terms could not explicitly be defined on the basis of physical$_1$ or physical$_2$ terms. (1958, pp. 389–90)

Aside from encouraging the erroneous shadow view that early reductionistic logical behaviourism was purely overt-behavioural, excluding reference to inner neurophysiological states, while his own early view included them, Feigl runs together two crucially different things: *analyticity* and *definability*. He assumes that an explicit definition cannot be synthetic but can only be analytic and consequently assumes that abandoning the idea of explicit definition is tantamount to embracing the idea that the connection between what was originally the *definiendum* and *definiens* is synthetic.[18] But both of these assumptions are mistaken.

According to Carnap and Hempel, if a non-primitive expression, the *definiendum*, is explicitly definable in terms of primitive expressions, then it can be eliminated and replaced by its *definiens*, by the primitive expressions. Such explicit definitions were understood by Carnap and Hempel to be the specification of necessary and sufficient conditions for the *definiendum*; that is, the construction of a material bi-conditional whose right-hand side, the *definiens*, contains only undefined primitive terms.[19] (For the logical positivists, of course, the defined expressions will be so-called 'theoretical' terms and the primitive expressions the 'observation' terms.) Now, Carnap (1936–7) very early on saw that the search for explicit definitions of all empirical scientific terms in the physical-thing language, on the basis of which physical translation could be carried

---

[18] Cf. Feigl (1958), pp. 427, 447, as well as Feigl (1963), p. 251 and Feigl (1971), p. 302. Pap (1952, p. 210) and Smith (1986), p. 53 also seem to hold these mistaken assumptions.

[19] This is an oversimplification: strictly speaking, only the ultimate definition in a definition chain will have only undefined primitive terms in the *definiens*. See Carnap (1936–7) and Hempel (1952).

out, was misconceived—especially and famously in the case of dispositional terms—
and consequently weakened the project to one of providing what he called 'reduction
sentences', which were either material conditionals with further material conditionals
as consequents or material conditions with material bi-conditionals as consequents.[20]
These reduction-sentence conditionals linked the empirical term in question to physical
conditions only under certain test circumstances. Since these physical reduction sentences were not definitions of the terms they were reducing—they were only incomplete
'conditional definitions'—they did not allow the terms to be eliminated and replaced
and hence they could not form the basis for translations.[21]

The important point to notice about this shift from definition to reduction (or partial
or conditional definition) is that, with respect to the physicalization of psychology and
other empirical sciences, it is not a shift from the category of analytic truths knowable
only a priori to the category of synthetic truths knowable only a posteriori. Rather, it is a
shift *within* the single category of synthetic truths knowable only a posteriori from complete or explicit definability (which permits elimination of the defined term) to incomplete or conditional definability (which does not permit elimination of the partially
defined term). Recall Carnap's statement quoted earlier (in § 20.1.3) about the lack of
necessary and sufficient physiological conditions for anger preventing the latter's definition. The majority of these material bi-conditionals are not analytic, they are neither conceptually true purely in virtue of meaning nor a priori knowable, but are supposed to be
physical laws discovered on the basis of experimental investigations.[22] Thus, contrary to
what Feigl and others seem to suppose, the failure of explicit definition and hence translation is not at all tantamount to the failure of a priori analytic definition and translation.[23]

The mistaken assumption that explicit definitions are analytic seems to have been
abetted by misinterpretations of the addenda that Carnap and Hempel added to later
reprintings of their respective articles. The addenda to Carnap (1933) and Hempel
(1935) state that the two philosophers no longer hold the strict definability thesis and
have replaced it with the more flexible reducibility thesis.[24] In his 1977 'prefatory note' to

---

[20] See Carnap (1936–7), §10 and Hempel (1952).

[21] Contrary to Suppe's (1977) assertion that reduction sentences were claimed to be analytic sentences
(p. 23), Carnap (1936–7, §8) explicitly states that some reduction sentences may be analytic and some may
be P-valid. Indeed, it can be formally proved that some reduction sentences are synthetic (see note 26
below).

[22] Cf. Cirera (1993) and Kim (2003).

[23] A fuller treatment of this issue would need to discuss the distinction between analyticity in the narrow
sense, viz., logical truth, and analyticity in the broader all-bachelors-are-married sense. The problem is
that the shadow understanding of logical behaviourism requires the broader notion of analyticity but it
seems that (unlike ordinary language philosophers) the logical positivists during this period, Carnap in
particular, understood analyticity only in the narrow sense. Obviously no one thinks, or ever thought, that
the physical-behavioural translations of logical behaviourism are supposed to be logical truths.

[24] See Carnap's 1961 addenda to the reprinting of Carnap (1932) in Alston and Nakhnikian (1963)
and Hempel's 1977 prefatory note in Block (1980). As Hempel notes in his addendum, physicalization
was liberalized even further with the later introduction of 'hypothetical constructs' connected to the
observation language via 'correspondence rules'. See also Carnap's 1957 addendum to the reprinting of
Carnap (1933) in Ayer (1959) and Carnap (1956) and Hempel (1954).

the reprinting in Block (1980), Hempel tells us that he had reservations about agreeing to the reprinting because he no longer held the 'narrow translationist form of physicalism [there] set forth' but 'yielded to Dr. Block's plea that it offers a concise account of an early version of logical behaviourism' (p. 14). On Jaegwon Kim's interpretation, this implies that 'Hempel was in agreement with Block's assessment that logical behaviourism was the position advocated in his 1935 paper' (2003, p. 266). Since Kim understands logical behaviourism as the thesis that psychological sentences analytically entail physical-behavioural sentences, Kim is claiming that Hempel is implying that he (Hempel) advocated the latter thesis in his original article. Kim goes on to point out how problematic Hempel's note is *so interpreted* because hardly any of Hempel's proffered physical-behavioural conditions are analytically entailed by his sample psychological sentence 'Paul has a toothache' (as we saw in § 20.1.3 above). But there is no such implication. There is absolutely nothing in Hempel's note to suggest he understood early logical behaviourism as the thesis that psychological sentences analytically entail physical-behavioural sentences. Kim's interpretation can be arrived at only on the assumption that explicit definitions are analytic. But Hempel was never under any such illusion. On the contrary, he is clear that he understands his early version of logical behaviourism to be the claim that psychological concepts are explicitly definable in physical terms and his point is that he has now moved to the more liberal thesis of reduction. Carnap's addendum makes exactly the same point.[25]

20.1.6 Purely Behavioural Translations

It is important to acknowledge, however, despite the impression that might have been given in § 20.1.3 above, that Carnap does countenance behaviouristic reductions that are explicitly only about overt molar behaviour. It might be thought that at least these were intended by Carnap to be analytic. Here is a relevant passage:

> The logical nature of the psychological terms becomes clear by an analogy with those physical terms which are introduced by reduction statements of the conditional form. Terms of both kinds designate a state characterized by the disposition to certain reactions. In both cases the state is not the same as those reactions. Anger is not the same as the movements by which an angry organism reacts to the conditions in his environment, just as the state of being electrically charged

---

[25] Another source of shadow logical behaviourism, which space limitations prevent me from discussing here, is probably the often-drawn analogy with phenomenalism. If one thinks of phenomenalism as the doctrine that material-object statements are analytically equivalent to sense-data statements, and one thinks logical behaviourism is like phenomenalism, then one will likely arrive at a shadow understanding of logical behaviourism. But, as Goodman (1963, p. 555n5) has pointed out, 'The avowed extensionalism of so outstanding a monument of phenomenalism and constructionism as the *Aufbau* would seem to confute Quine's recent charge [in 'Two Dogmas'] that the notion of analyticity is a "holdover of phenomenalistic reductionism".' Phenomenalism, in other words, cast its own influential shadow. But that is another story.

is not the same as the process of attracting other bodies. In both cases, that state sometimes occurs without these events which are observable from outside; they are consequences of the state according to certain laws and may therefore under suitable circumstances be taken as symptoms for it; but they are not identical with it. (1938/91, p. 402)

But even here, with a purely overt-behavioural proposal, Carnap does not say that such a molar-behaviouristic reduction sentence for anger will be analytic. Indeed, the 'laws' referred to, connecting inner states with outer behavioural reactions or symptoms, are obviously intended to be empirical physical laws. Notice also that Carnap here takes the inner state to *cause* the outer behavioural reaction, and so anticipates and pre-empts by more than two decades both Putnam's celebrated 'Super-Spartan' objection to shadow logical behaviourism (effectively voiced by Carnap himself in the quotation from 'Foundations' in § 20.1.3 above), which formed the basis of its internment in 'Brains and Behaviour', as well as Putnam's distinction between an inner state and its outer symptoms, backed by his well-known polio analogy. It is further noteworthy that Carnap here anticipates both the causal critique of behaviourism pressed by Fodor and David Armstrong (that mental states are not identical with behaviour but are the causes of behaviour) and the causal-functional analysis of mental concepts. This latter point has been noted by Patterson (2008, p. 531) and Kim (2003, p. 275), but it needs to be handled carefully lest we wrongly re-foist shadow logical behaviourism onto Carnap. Contrary to what Kim says, it would be incorrect to associate Carnap with (David Lewis style) analytic functionalism, which is a development of Rylean logical/analytical behaviourism, according to which the functional definitions of mental terms are specified a priori by conceptual analysis of commonsense psychology, and the only role for empirical science is to discover a posteriori which inner states are the actual realizers of the definitions. Carnap's proto-functionalism is more akin to an empirical psycho-functionalism (see Block (1978)), in which empirical science is involved at the first stage; that is, the functional definitions of mental terms are themselves specified a posteriori by scientific theory. This fits the texts and the spirit of 'Logical Foundations' and 'Psychology in Physical Language' better, makes better sense of the strong analogy Carnap draws between concept formation in the physical sciences and in the sciences of psychology, and gels better with Carnap's procedure of 'physicalization' (discussed above in §20.1.5.2). It is also confirmed by Hempel, who later wrote that for Carnap behavioural symptoms are determined empirically 'rather than by an aprioristic reflection upon the meaning of the psychological terms in question' (Hempel 1969, p. 180).[26]

---

[26]   Moreover, as Hempel (1952, 1954) and Pap (1958, ch. 11) point out, if there is more than one conditional definition (e.g., a set of two or more bi-lateral reduction sentences) for a given term, as Carnap clearly expected there to be in many cases, including psychology, then one can derive a non-analytic empirical statement from them, from which it follows that at least one of the conditional definitions must be non-analytic and hence empirical or synthetic.

20.1.7 The Physicalism of Logical Positivism vs. the Physicalism of the Identity Theory

What, then, is the real nature of the shift from the physicalism of the logical positivists to the physicalism of the identity theory, if both in fact proposed empirical, contingent connections between the mental and the physical? The simple answer is that for the logical positivists physicalism was essentially a linguistic doctrine about the language of science, or about the language of the inter-subjective confirmation basis of science, combined with the view that the mind–body problem was a metaphysical pseudo-problem to be ignored and replaced by a logico-linguistic analysis of the place of psychology in a unified physical science. This is one strand in the great period of the 'linguistic turn'. The identity theorists' physicalism (or materialism), in contrast, was an ontological doctrine and they certainly did not view the mind–body problem as a pseudo-problem. I suggest therefore that the real change in approach to the mind–body problem that occurred in the 1950s and '60s was simply the rejection of the earlier view, shared by both logical positivists and ordinary language philosophers, that it was a pseudo-problem.[27] The radical difference of approach is succinctly summed up in Carnap's response to Feigl's identity theory:

> The identity statement mentioned [that a certain psychological process *P* is identical with a certain neurophysiological process *N*] is a sentence of the object language; this fact may mislead the reader into believing that the controversy about the identity view concerns a question of fact.... It seems preferable to me to formulate the question in the metalanguage, not as a factual question about the world, but as a question concerning the choice of language.... Those facts Feigl proposes as evidence for the identity view are perhaps better regarded as reasons for preferring a monistic language ... in this language the predicates '*P*' and '*N*', though not L-equivalent, are P-equivalent ... I am willing to call my position an identity conception in the following sense: in agreement with Feigl I prefer the monistic language, and like him I believe that the evidence available today provides good reasons for the assumption that this language will also function well in the future. (Carnap 1963, pp. 885–6)

Although Carnap wrote (or at least published) this statement in 1963, this was his position from the very beginning, thirty years earlier in the heyday of logical positivism. In 1935 Carnap had said that the 'pseudo-object' identity-sentence of the material mode, 'The evening-star and the morning-star are identical' is to be replaced by the syntactical formal-mode sentence 'The words "evening-star" and "morning-star" are synonymous' (1935/63, p. 447); and in the earlier more rigorous treatment (1934/2002, § 75), it is clear that he means P-synonymous. Throughout his life, Carnap remained committed to his radical positivistic empirico-pragmatic view that the only legitimate philosophical problems that were not straightforward empirical scientific questions were questions

---

[27] Cf. Feigl (1960).

of language choice. But according to Carnap himself, his position on the mind–body problem can, and always could, be expressed in the misleading material mode as a synthetic identity theory.

Kim, however, has questioned whether Carnap's and Hempel's 'overly generous' notion of translation 'can underwrite the kind of physicalism/behaviourism that these philosophers wanted to formulate and defend' (2003, p. 273). He argues that it cannot because a nomological correlation between two predicates does not license the claim that they designate the same property. Such correlations are consistent with a variety of dualisms and 'Physicalism, however it is formulated, must exclude dualisms' (p. 268). But this criticism assumes that physicalism is a metaphysical doctrine and so flatly begs the question against Carnap and Hempel. To be sure, lawful correlations between mental and physical predicates are not sufficient to establish the kind of metaphysical physicalism that Kim and the identity theorists wish for. But the question is whether they are sufficient to establish physicalism as Carnap and Hempel understood it, namely, as anti-metaphysical Physicalism; and whether, if so, the anti-metaphysicalism of Physicalism is a better approach to the mind–body problem than Kim's preferred metaphysical physicalism. Neither question can be treated in detail here. Suffice it to say, with respect to the first question, that it is not at all clear that Physicalism cannot be underwritten merely by lawful correlations between the predicates of the various special sciences and the predicates of a physical language. Physicalism is, after all, intended to be a contingent thesis, indeed, a working empirical hypothesis. With regard to the second question, Kim offers no argument for the superiority of physicalism to Physicalism. Carnap and Hempel reject the call for an explanation of psychophysical correlations because on their view any such alleged explanation would be metaphysical, hence impossible to verify or confirm, hence unscientific. One might even argue that Carnap's anti-metaphysical instincts have been spectacularly borne out by the subsequent history of failed attempts to establish metaphysical physicalism as a solution to the mind–body problem. Place, Feigl, and Smart, for example, all argued for the identity theory on the basis of psychophysical correlations; but there remains little consensus and much scepticism about whether these arguments are successful. Whether it is possible to convert psychophysical correlations into identities remains a highly controversial question and various arguments based on simplicity and abduction have so far garnered few adherents. Kim (2011) himself has offered devastating criticisms of several arguments that attempt to derive identities from correlations. The second wave of identity theorists, in particular David Armstrong (1968) and David Lewis (1966), offered different and stronger, but no less controversial, arguments for psychophysical identity. Many more recent attempts again rely on controversial and undefended claims about the 'causal closure (or completeness) of the physical domain'.[28] Or take the concept of supervenience, introduced into philosophy of mind in the early 1970s by Davidson (1970) as a possible position on the relation between the mental and the physical. For a time it was

---

[28] An admirable exception is David Papineau (2001), who defends causal completeness at length.

thought that supervenience offered a significant (non-reductive) materialist solution to the mind–body problem. But a decade of intensive research showed that most, if not all, mental–physical supervenience relations were consistent with various different and incompatible metaphysical positions on the mind–body relation, including even substance dualism![29] I dare say Carnap would not have been the least surprised by these developments. None of this proves of course that the anti-metaphysic of Physicalism is to be preferred to the metaphysic of physicalism. But it does suggest, I think, that the when the logical positivists' anti-metaphysic is applied to the mind–body problem, it is not to be lightly dismissed.

20.2 TWO IDENTITY THEORIES AS A REFLECTION OF TWO PHILOSOPHIES

20.2.1 Introduction

The late 1950s and early 1960s saw the rise to prominence of the celebrated mind–brain identity theory propounded by Place, Feigl, and Smart, in their respective classic articles 'Is Consciousness a Brain Process?' (1956), 'The "Mental" and the "Physical"' (1958), and 'Sensations and Brain Processes' (1959).[30] The theory was actually knocking around at least a decade earlier—in fact, as we shall see, several decades earlier. Putnam remarked in print a year before Feigl's article and two years before Smart's that

> 'Physicalism', expressed as a working hypothesis, amounts to this: subjective experience (e.g., a particular feeling of anger) is a particular kind of physical state of the organism. This is of course a synthetic identity, if true (as Feigl has very well pointed out). Philosophers are quite right in saying that 'the sensation blue' cannot *mean* a physical state. But they are wrong when they maintain that it cannot *be* a physical state. (Thus, 'the morning star' cannot *mean* 'the evening star'. But the morning star *is* the evening star—for both are identical with the planet Venus, to use the familiar example.) (Putnam 1957, p. 97)

The work by Feigl that Putnam refers to is a 1950 article entitled 'The Mind–Body Problem in the Development of Logical Empiricism', in which Feigl defends a proposal according to which there is an identity between the mental and the physical, an identity to be established empirically, like other scientific identifications. He too uses

---

[29] See Kim (1998, ch. 1).

[30] While Smart was following Place's lead—the two were colleagues at the time at the University of Adelaide in Australia—Feigl was working independently at the University of Minnesota. Feigl's long essay was reprinted as a book with an accompanying postscript written a decade later: *The 'Mental' and the 'Physical': The Essay and a Postscript* (1967).

Frege's famous example as an analogy, as well as other examples of 'theoretical identities' that have entered into the mainstay of analytic philosophy of mind, such as heat's being (identical with) molecular motion and visible light's being a certain frequency of electromagnetic waves.

As Putnam makes clear, the mind–brain identity theory in question was in fact a more restricted identification of sensory consciousness with physical states. Place and Smart, having studied at Oxford, were under the influence of Gilbert Ryle's *The Concept of Mind* (1949) and so were largely sympathetic to a behaviourist-dispositional view of intentional mental states, such as beliefs, wants, fears, and expectations. But they were concerned that the so-called qualitative mental states associated with sensory consciousness, the having of after-images and sensations of pain, for example, were not dispositional in nature, but were occurrent episodes, and so were unlikely to yield to behavioural analyses.[31] They proposed to identify this non-dispositional 'mental residue' of sensory consciousness with neural events and processes in the brain. Interestingly, Feigl too independently wished to identify only sensory consciousness with brain states. But this was not owing to any reservations about the possibility of dispositional analyses of it. Rather, he viewed the idea of a physical reduction of intentional mental states to brain states as confused, a kind of category mistake, since the intentionality of intentional mental states was properly a logico-semantic problem and was to be dealt with by theories of reference and designation in philosophy of language.[32] More importantly, however, Feigl was coming out of a very different empiricist tradition that viewed the phenomenal elements of conscious awareness as both the paradigm of the mental and as the epistemological foundation for empirical knowledge. This empiricist tradition included the phenomenalism of the early days of logical positivism (especially Carnap's *Aufbau*) and the epistemologically oriented neutral monism of William James and Bertrand Russell.[33] Both can be traced back to the phenomenalism of the physicist-philosopher Ernst Mach and ultimately of course to the phenomenalistic empiricism of Mill and Hume. Most crucial of all for Feigl, however, was the virtually unknown 1918 identity theory of Moritz Schlick, which was itself part of the nineteenth-century German and Austrian tradition of psychophysical parallelism (Heidelberger 2003).

It has sometimes been noted there were really two different identity theories originally developed in the 1950s, the Austrian Schlick–Feigl version and the Australian

---

[31] *Pace* Livingston (2004, ch. 4), neither Place nor Smart thought that Ryle himself claimed that sensations were behavioural dispositions. They just noticed that his behavioural analyses could not be extended to sensations.

[32] The view that intentionality was ultimately a semantic phenomenon to be explained linguistically was defended at the same time by Feigl's colleague Wilfrid Sellars against the contrary view of Roderick Chisholm. See the debate between Sellars and Chisholm in the Appendix to *Minnesota Studies in the Philosophy of Science*, vol. 2 (1958).

[33] This early period of analytic philosophy of mind, roughly 1900–30, which was much more epistemologically centred than philosophy of mind is today, has received little scholarly attention. For some edifying discussion of it, see Hatfield (2002, 2004) and Hatfield's chapter in the present volume.

Place–Smart version, and that the latter is more materialistic and reductionistic—even eliminativistic—than the other.[34] In a recent article Leopold Stubenberg argues that 'The Australian approach to the problem of identifying mind and body represents a stunning reversal of the Austrian approach' (1997, p. 136). He adds that 'Whether [it] be idealism or panpsychism is not clear to me. But it is clear to me that this view is deeply antimaterialistic in spirit' (p. 143). Stubenberg goes on to argue for the superiority of the Schlick–Feigl version. His valuable discussion brings out an important and deep rift running through post-1950 analytic philosophy of mind—a rift which has begun to widen even more under contemporary analytic philosophy of mind's turn-of-the-millennium obsession with phenomenal consciousness. The Schlick–Feigl version of the identity theory is, however, at least as problematic as the Place–Smart version and there is in fact a more fundamental rift between them than that recognized by Stubenberg.

20.2.2 Schlick and the Origins of the Identity Theory

Most of the crucial elements of Feigl's theory are in fact derived directly from Schlick, who had proposed in his *General Theory of Knowledge* (1918; 2nd edition 1925) what seems to be truly the first twentieth-century mind–brain identity theory, as Feigl (1958, p. 80n) notes. Kim has disputed this, claiming—contrary to the editors of the English translation, one of whom is Feigl—not to be able to find in this work a 'reasonably clear and unambiguous statement of the mind–brain identity theory' (2003, p. 276), and that it is anyway doubtful that Schlick could have worked out an identity theory at this time, because it is only after 1930 that the Vienna Circle adopted physicalism. Kim thus suggests that it is in Schlick's later article 'On the Relation between Psychological and Physical Concepts' (1935), written during his positivist period, that we find a genuine psychophysical identity theory—though even here, apparently, it is a psychobehavioural, and not a psychoneural, identity theory. But all this is, I think, a confusion, stemming again from Kim's failure to appreciate that physicalism for the logical positivists—that is, Physicalism—is not a metaphysic and hence does not purport to offer a metaphysical solution to the mind–body problem, *a fortiori* not a materialist one. Schlick's (1935) 'physicalism' is simply Physicalism, as he makes clear: 'every psychological proposition can be translated into an expression in which physical concepts alone occur' (1935, p. 399). On the contrary, it is precisely because Schlick's *General Theory of Knowledge* is written before his positivist period that it can enunciate an identity theory. We can in any case settle the matter by turning directly to the text. I submit that in §§ 33–5 Schlick does indeed propound an identity theory. Here is one of the crucial passages:

> The … relation between immediately experienced reality and the physical brain process is [not] one of causal dependency but of simple *identity*. What we have is one and the same reality, not 'viewed from two different sides' or 'manifesting itself

---

[34] Cornman (1971), pp. 30, 125, Armstrong (1993), p. xiii, and Borst (1970), p. 20. Cf. Feigl (1975), p. 15.

in two different forms', but designated by two different conceptual systems, the psychological and the physical.' (p. 299, italics in original; cf. pp. 310–12)

If this is a statement of the mind–brain identity theory, or rather, a statement of *a* mind–brain identity theory, as it certainly seems to be, it follows that Place (n.d.) too is mistaken when he claims that 'The earliest statement of the identity theory under the title was in the psychologist E. G. Boring's book *The Physical Dimensions of Consciousness* published in 1933.'[35] Assuming Boring was the first to state the identity theory back in 1933, Place offers a plausible explanation for why it was not accepted more widely until the 1950s. First, as far as psychologists go, psychology is dominated by behaviourism during this period; second, when it comes to the philosophers, Frege's logical work on identity statements, with its central claim that two expressions which differ in meaning (sense) can nevertheless be discovered empirically to refer to the same thing, is not yet well known among philosophers, but is a crucial part of any defensible identity theory.

It is certainly true that Feigl and Smart in their presentations of the identity theory both invoke Frege's idea that expressions with different meanings can have the same referent and that it may take an empirical discovery to reveal this. But, as we have seen, Carnap was well aware of Frege's works and the distinction between sense and reference and redescribed it with his own L- and P-concepts in the 1930s. Carnap had in fact attended Frege's lectures in Jena during 1910–14, and his lecture notes for the Winter Semester of 1910–11 contain Frege's famous astronomical example and his explanation of the distinction between sense and reference.[36] Moreover, given that Schlick had already formulated an identity theory at least a decade earlier, and did not draw on Frege's work on sense and reference at all in order to do so, the question remains why, given Schlick's prominence and influence in philosophical circles at the time in Vienna, it still took another thirty years for it to make any significant impact. The answer must be that Schlick came under the strong spell of Wittgenstein and Carnap, and other members of the Vienna Circle, all of whom, while well aware of Frege's distinction between sense and reference, were wont to dismiss the mind–body problem as a metaphysical pseudo-problem to be replaced by the project of constructing a Physicalistic language into which to translate psychological sentences.[37] In short, Schlick became a logical positivist, took the linguistic turn, and ascended to the formal mode, leaving his original material-mode metaphysical identity theory behind. Any hopes (however vain) of Schlick returning to his original pre-positivist position were dashed by his murder in 1933. It was left to Feigl to carry the torch to the United States and refine the theory into a more sophisticated version, using some of the tools from the rapidly developing

---

[35] Carnap uses the phrase 'identity theory' in §22 of the *Aufbau* (1928).

[36] See Reck and Awodey (2003), p. 71 (p. 24 of Carnap's notes for the Winter Semester 1910–11).

[37] While Wittgenstein and the Vienna Circle shared the view that traditional metaphysical problems were pseudo-problems, the relationship between the Vienna Circle (especially Carnap), Wittgenstein, and Physicalism is much more controversial. For discussion, see Uebel (1995).

philosophies of logic and science—but only after liberating himself from the strictly positivist position vis-à-vis the mind–body problem.[38]

20.2.3 The Schlick–Feigl Identity Theory

When thus liberated Feigl came to employ Russell's distinction between knowledge by acquaintance and knowledge by description to articulate and update Schlick's identity solution to the mind–body problem:

> the physical sciences consist of knowledge-claims-*by-description*. That is to say that the objects (targets, referents) of such knowledge claims are 'triangulated' on the basis of various areas of observational (sensory) evidence. What these objects are acquaintancewise is left completely open as long as we remain within the frame of *physical* concept formation and theory construction. But, since in point of empirical fact, *I* am directly acquainted with the qualia of my own immediate experience, I happen to know (by acquaintance) what the neurophysiologist refers to when he talks about certain configurational aspects of my cerebral processes. (p. 450)

It is here, in connection with Feigl's idea that we are directly acquainted with the qualia of our own experiences that the peculiar nature of his identity theory emerges. It is perhaps the peculiar nature of the Schlick–Feigl theory that led Kim to claim that Schlick never articulated such a theory. There is, at any rate, a certain tension in Feigl's formulations of his identity theory that is a clue to its peculiar nature. On the one hand, Feigl offers fairly straightforward statements of identity; for example, he writes that 'The identity thesis which I wish to clarify and to defend asserts that the states of direct experience which conscious human beings "live through" … are identical with certain … aspects of the neural processes in those organisms' (p. 446). Along the same lines, he speaks of 'The identification of raw feels with neural states' and how the identification in question 'identifies the referents of subjective terms with the referents of certain objective terms' (p. 448). But on the other hand, he curiously tends to prioritize the mental side of the identity, as in: 'The "mental" states or events (in the sense of raw feels) are the referents (denotata) of both the phenomenal terms of the language of introspection, as well as of certain terms of the neurophysiological language' (p. 447). And in a later paper, he writes that 'I take these referents [of mental and neurophysiological terms] to be the immediately experienced qualities' (1960, p. 38; cf. 1963, pp. 262, 257). Now, one might think that these latter formulations are not to be taken too seriously and that they are just incautious ways of restating the identity thesis. But Feigl is careful never to engage in the opposite prioritization of the physical over the mental and say such things as 'neurophysiological processes are designated by raw feel terms' or that 'the common referents of both neurophysiological terms and raw feel terms are neurophysiological processes'.

---

[38] Feigl (1958) claims that Feigl (1934) defends a typical form of unity-of-science Physicalism.

That there can be no mistake is evident, I think, from the following statement: 'According to the identity thesis the directly experienced qualia and configurations are the realities-in-themselves that are denoted by the neurophysiological descriptions' (1958, p. 457; cf. p. 474). So Feigl appears to hold a mentalistic form of the identity theory.

Unfortunately, it is not clear that such a position is coherent. Identity, after all, is a symmetric relation: if a given mental phenomenon is strictly identical with some physical phenomenon then surely that phenomenon can be no more mental than it is physical. To claim that a given psychophysical identity theory is mentalistic or idealistic would be like saying that a Hesperus–Phosphorus identity theory is 'Phosphoristic' in that it somehow gives prominence to the 'Phosphorus side' of the identity; or like saying that while heat is identical with molecular motion, one less reductive version of the identity favours the 'heat side', while the other more reductionist version promotes the primacy of the 'molecular' side of the identity. None of this makes any sense.

Perhaps a psychophysical identity theory could be said to be more mentalistic than a materialistic rival if it were a form of panpsychism, that claimed that everything in existence, including things we do not ordinarily think of as mental in any way, were also mental, such as plants and stones and sub-atomic particles. And it is here indeed that we seem to come to the difference between Feigl's identity theory and Smart's and Place's. Strikingly, for Feigl, 'sentience (qualities experienced, and in human beings knowable by acquaintance) and other qualities (unexperienced and knowable only by description) [are] the basic reality' (1967, p. 107). The concepts of theoretical physics 'denote realities which are unknown by acquaintance, but which may in some way nevertheless be not entirely discontinuous with the qualities of direct experience' (1967, p. 40; cf. 1971, p. 308). According to Feigl's own understanding of the doctrine, however, it is not strictly speaking panpsychism, 'for the simple reason that nothing in the least like a psyche is ascribed to lifeless matter' (1960, p. 39). Stones do not have 'selves' then. This is fair enough but it is potentially misleading. For Feigl is prepared to apply the label 'pan-quality-ism' to his view that the phenomenal qualities we are directly acquainted with may well be instantiated throughout all of nature—not just in brains and nervous systems. Russell (1956) similarly viewed the question of 'pan-quality-ism' as wide open: 'since we know nothing about the intrinsic quality of physical events except when these are mental events that we directly experience, we cannot say either that the physical world outside our heads is different from the mental world or that it is not'.[39] Feigl very consciously drew inspiration from both Schlick and Russell in this regard.[40]

Nevertheless, while pan-quality-ism expands the range of physical things that are mental, it does not make this universal class of mental beings any more mental than they are physical. Identity is a symmetric relation. There remains the possibility that the 'identity' at stake in the Schlick–Feigl identity theory is intended to be, like Place's (1956) was, the so-called 'identity of composition'. As Stubenberg notes, Feigl 'seems to say that matter is made of qualia' (p. 143). Since composition is an asymmetric relation

---

[39] See also Russell (1927).
[40] Feigl (1975) explores the similarity between the two philosophers.

perhaps it is a way to make sense of Feigl's claim that phenomenal qualities are the 'basic reality'. It is not clear, however, that this interpretation sits very well with Schlick's and Feigl's Fregean way of stating their identity theory, that is, with the claim that physical and mental terms refer to the same things. Suffice it to say that if this puzzle at the heart of the Schlick–Feigl theory remains unresolved, the Austrian version of the identity theory is in danger of lapsing into incoherence or collapsing into its Australian rival.

20.2.4 Reconceiving the Physical

As Stubenberg emphasizes, the two versions of the identity theory target different sides of the mind–body problem as the source of the difficulty of accepting the identification. The Australian version—as well as its radicalized offspring, the Feyerabend–Rorty eliminativism and the later deflationary, neo-Rylean behaviouristic instrumentalism of Daniel Dennett—finds the mind-side of the dichotomy to be the culprit and seeks to deflate it, either by exposing its committal of phenomenological fallacies, its involvement in conceptual incoherence, or by reinterpreting it in a 'neutral' (usually causal-functional) form more amenable to physicalist reduction. In contrast, the material or physical is relatively unproblematic. The Austrian version, however, sees the physical side of the dichotomy as the villain and is accordingly more prepared to question conceptions of the physical. As Feigl remarks, 'I am convinced that it is primarily the concept of the "physical" that requires reinterpretation and reconstruction' (1967, p. 142).

The problem, in Feigl's eyes, is that we wrongly think of the physical in misleadingly 'intuitive' terms, by which he appears to mean primarily in terms of images, usually visual ones. The physical states, events, and processes with which the identity theory identifies phenomenal states, events, and processes should not be thought of imagistically or pictorially as literally grey brain matter or nervous tissue. We are not acquainted with the physical; we have only theoretical knowledge by description of it. Schlick had already offered precisely this diagnosis: 'The worst mistake that can be made in viewing the psychophysical problem—a mistake that, strangely enough, is made time and again—is, without noticing it, to substitute for the brain processes themselves, which are to be regarded as identical with the mental processes, the perceptions or images of the brain processes' (1925/1974 p. 300; cf. pp. 311–13). This too is Feigl's view:

> even sophisticated analytic philosophers tend to confuse the meaning of physical concepts with the perceived or imaged appearance of physical things. No wonder then that we are told that the identity of certain neurophysiological states (or features thereof) with raw feels is a logical blunder. If the denotatum of 'brain process (of a specified sort)' is thus confused with the appearance of the gray mass of the brain as one perceives it when looking into an opened skull, then it is indeed logically impossible to identify this appearance with … raw feels. (p. 454; cf. 1963, p. 258)

According to Feigl, then, the mind–body problem—more accurately, the sentience-body problem—is to be solved by realizing that the physical is nothing like what we intuitively think it is. To suppose that the identity theory implies that one person could literally see the 'raw feels' of another person, their pains and experiences of red, because the first person can see the brain states of the second person they are identical with, is to confuse the data of sensory experience, which serves as the evidentiary confirmation base for physical theory, with what the data are evidence *for*, namely, the *true referents* of neurophysiological terms, which can only be conceived of abstractly and theoretically by description and not visualized on the basis of acquaintance. Feigl's view thus seems to be that the alleged features of the physical that make it problematic to identify raw feels with, are not really features of the physical at all. They are the sensory evidence for the physical; hence they are in fact mental features—in short, they are the raw feels, the qualia of which we are directly aware. Once the physical has been thus 'thinned out' (in Stubenberg's nice phrase) there can no longer be any objection to identifying 'its referents with something directly given and knowable by acquaintance' (Feigl 1958, p. 454).

So on Feigl's view, what happens is something like this. We look at a subject's exposed brain, or at some of his nervous tissue under a microscope, and see what we take to be its various features: its grey colour, spatial expanse, bumpy and folded texture, etc. An identity theorist then says that the subject's experiences of redness when he looks at a ripe tomato, his pains and after images and other raw feels, are in fact the very physical processes in his brain that we are now looking at. We balk at this, wondering how a pain or experience of red could be a brain process, an occurrence in the grey, bumpy, moist object we are looking at: the subject's experience is red but his brain is grey, after all—to identify them is a logical blunder! Feigl, following Schlick, replies that we have confused sensory evidence for brains with brains themselves. Brains and other neurophysiological phenomena—indeed, the entire physical realm—do not really have these features: they are not grey, they are not bumpy, they are not moist; on the contrary, these are mental features mistakenly projected by us onto the true referent of the neurophysiological term 'brain', which has none of these features. The mistake we have made is to try to identify one raw feel, a visual experience of red say, with another, a visual experience of grey, which we take to be a feature of the brain we are looking at. But now that the true physical nature of the brain has been sufficiently abstracted, by relocating its problematic and 'identification-resistant' features to the mind, there is no problem with identifying all the raw feels in question with processes going on in the brain, that is, with processes going in the unvisualizable and unintuitable real physical brain.[41]

20.2.5 Austria vs. Australia: Nil, Nil

In Stubenberg's view, 'It is the Austrian Version's ability to better satisfy the requirement of phenomenological adequacy that makes it more deserving of our acceptance [than the Australian]' (p. 143). According to him, the view 'combines a profound

---

[41] Cf. Schlick (1925/1974), pp. 311–13.

respect for phenomenology with an unconditional acceptance of a rational, scientific view of the world. And nothing less will do. For all theories that slight phenomenology are simply false, and we know that.' He concludes that 'if we want to avoid blatant falsity and lunacy we must, somehow, combine phenomenology with science without short-changing either. And Schlick and Feigl have shown us how to do just that' (p. 144).[42]

I am not so sure. Perhaps Schlick and Feigl have shown how to reconcile phenomenology with the deeply counter-intuitive nature of fundamental theoretical physics at its quantum and cosmological scales. Indeed, for Feigl, there do appear to be two exhaustive categories of being: the mental as phenomenal and whatever is described by theoretical physics (Feigl 1971, p. 309). But the status and nature of the subject matter of the higher-level special sciences, such as biology and psychology, is rather harder to ascertain on the Austrian model. Phenomenology and physics may have been saved and reconciled. But we seem to have lost the world of ordinary experience in which we live and breathe. According to Schlick and Feigl, it is a grave mistake to think of brains and other macro-physical objects as actually possessing the features they appear to possess when we are looking at them and touching them (this is what blocks acceptance of the identity theory by creating logical blunders). The visual and tactual qualities of the brain are merely the brain surgeon's sensory *evidence* for the real brain, the 'thing-in-itself', whose true nature is only to be revealed by the theoretical descriptions of micro-physics. Now, while the phenomenology of after-images, floaters, and double-vision clearly presents them as subjective features of our individual consciousnesses, colours, sounds, textures, and the rest of the so-called secondary properties certainly are presented as 'out there' on the surfaces of macro-physical objects—at least the majority of the time. Perceptual reference, in other words, is more often than not to ordinary macro-physical objects, such as brains, sofas, and mountains. It is very hard to see how the Schlick–Feigl view can accommodate the mundane intentionality of phenomenology. So it is not immediately clear that phenomenology has not in fact been at least a little short-changed on the Schlick–Feigl view.

I think that despite his avowed rejection of the kind of phenomenalism associated with the early days of logical positivism, Feigl retained a quasi-phenomenalistic, or perhaps quasi-Kantian philosophy.[43] Kantian language pervades both Schlick's and Feigl's writings on the mind–body problem. They often invoke the phrase 'things-in-themselves', even if contrary to Kant, they think 'things-in-themselves' are knowable, knowable, that is, only by highly abstract and mathematized theoretical description and inference. It is clear that ordinary macro-objects, such as brains, are not things-in-themselves. It is not clear what has become of them. Moreover, both Feigl and Schlick seem to view not just the traditional secondary qualities of classical phenomenalism

---

[42] Cf. Hatfield (2004) who admires the 'respect for the phenomenal' found in Russell, William James, and various theoretical physicists in the first two decades of the twentieth century, while deploring the disrespect for it found in Smart and company.

[43] Aune (1966) critically discusses Feigl's phenomenalism in the context of his identity theory.

as mind-dependent but the space within which these qualities exist too.[44] According to them, part of the solution to the mind–body problem necessarily involves distinguishing between two different kinds of space, physical space, effectively a metric space, and phenomenal space, effectively a field of qualities. It quite unclear what these spaces are ontologically speaking and especially how they are related. Even aside from the Kantianism, Feigl's phenomenalistic tendencies are evident in his unquestioning acceptance of Russell's view that the only things we can be acquainted with are the sensory qualities present in immediate experience. Everything else, including what we take to be ordinary physical objects, we know only by description, and by a highly abstracted and mathematized theoretical description, presumably only understood by physicists, at that. It is very hard to make room in Feigl's view for the idea that we might be acquainted with ordinary physical objects too; that we can make perceptual reference to brains and other macro-physical objects. On the Australian version of the identity theory, if a person's feeling of pain is literally identical with a certain neural event or process in his brain, and one were small enough to observe that neural process, then one would literally be seeing that person's feeling of pain.[45] Rather than bite the bullet and accept the consequence that we can literally see another person's raw feels, because we can see the brain processes they are identical with, Feigl ends up in the equally (if not more) counter-intuitive position that we do not ever really see brains or any rate that brains are nothing like what we take them to be. To my mind, it is not at all clear that the Austrian theory has, as Stubenberg maintains, avoided 'blatant falsity and lunacy'.

20.2.6 Two Perennial Philosophies

Whether or not this is a faithful account of Feigl's view, there can be little doubt that crucial to the Austrian view is a particular epistemology, associated with certain forms of Cartesian empiricism: we are directly and indubitably aware of data presented to us in conscious experience (Feigl 1958, *passim*, 1975, p. 15; Schlick, 1916/79, p. 197). Phenomenal properties are simply given to us in experience. This is a first principle beyond dispute. It is something we know before we engage in science and philosophy and it cannot be overthrown by subsequent scientific or philosophical theorizing. Phenomenal qualities exist, pure and simple, and this datum is non-negotiable. This Austro-Cartesian tradition, according to which the phenomenal is unproblematically given to us in experience, and our focus must fall on reconceiving the nature of the physical in order to accommodate it, is continued to this day in the work of several contemporary philosophers, all united by the idea that, in the face of the undeniable existence of phenomenal qualities, the key to solving the mind–body problem may be to reconceive

---

[44] Schlick (1916/79). Kim (2003) discusses this peculiar idealistic feature of Schlick's view.
[45] A consequence embraced and made much of by Perry (2001).

the physical.[46] These latter-day Feiglians have no truck with any lingering phenomenal-istic epistemology and thus, I believe, make an advance on the earlier Austrian tradition. Crucially, however, like the Austrians, they maintain that the physical, but not the phe-nomenal, is allowed to be reconceived because, unlike the phenomenal, it is not some-thing whose intrinsic nature we are directly acquainted with and can therefore claim to know.

Smart's and Place's background philosophy is very different and I think that at least in the case of Smart, it would be fair to describe it as a kind of pure untainted scientism, influenced by Quine's extreme scientism. From Smart's point of view, there is no 'first philosophy' prior to scientific theorizing; certainly there is no legitimate Cartesian-style epistemological–phenomenological prioritizing of philosophy over science. According to Quine and Smart, there is only shifting and ever-developing theory—no pre-theoretic or pre-scientific intuitions that must be preserved at all costs. Contrary to the Austrian tradition, the Australian tradition has it that our current conception of the physical is in fine working order and the problem lies with the mental, in particular with various phe-nomenological fallacies and conceptual incoherencies we are prone to succumb to when we think of it and try to describe it. The flames of this profoundly anti-Cartesian phi-losophy-as-continuous-with-science approach, which seeks to inflate the physical and deflate the mental, were fanned and taken to the limit by Richard Rorty's Wittgenstein-and Sellars-inspired view that the so-called philosophical 'intuition' that we are pre-sented with immediately given phenomenal qualities—'respect for the phenomenal', in Hatfield's (2002) phrase—is nothing more than a collection of deeply ingrained lin-guistic habits we acquired when we were taught the language-game of incorrigible sen-sation reports.[47] The tradition is expanded in scope to include propositional attitudes as well as sensory consciousness in the work of the later eliminative materialists of the 1980s.[48] The most sophisticated development of this tradition is found in the work of Daniel Dennett (1969, 1979), work which combines speculative empirical theorizing simultaneously with ingenious attempts to expose alleged conceptual incoherencies in our ordinary mentalistic notions.[49]

The disagreement between the two identity theories over the viability of a materi-alism based on our current conception of the physical is thus the product of a deeper

---

[46] Maxwell (1978), Lockwood (1981), Chalmers (1996), Unger (1999), Stoljar (2001), Strawson (2006). It is interesting to note in this regard that Sellars (1981), a close collaborator of Feigl's, and the famous enemy of the 'the given' in experience, was squarely on Feigl's side in this respect, positing phenomenal qualities as a basic and irreducible part of reality.

[47] See Rorty (1965, 1970, 1979, 1981).

[48] For example, Churchland (1981) and Stich (1983).

[49] Rorty (1981) discusses the opposition between the Wittgenstein–Ryle–Sellars–Dennett tradition, according to which we have 'no intuitions, no "initial facts"', which all theorizing must always respect, about the mind' (p. 343), and the Descartes–Broad–Nagel–Searle tradition, according to which we do have such intuitions. The two identity theories are also a reflection of this opposition and the recent revival of panpsychic forms of materialism, such as Strawson (2006), and their opponents, is the latest manifestation of this opposition.

disagreement about the nature, status, and role of pre-theoretical phenomenological intuitions in philosophical theorizing about the mind. It is unlikely that we will see in our lifetimes a victor in this great battle in contemporary analytic philosophy of mind between Cartesian phenomenology and deflationary scientistic naturalism—or indeed in the lifetimes of the next few generations of philosophers of mind.

REFERENCES

Achinstein, Peter and Stephen F. Barker (eds.) (1969). *The Legacy of Logical Positivism: Studies in the Philosophy of Science*. Baltimore: Johns Hopkins University Press.

Alston, William and George Nakhnikian (eds.) (1963). *Readings in Twentieth Century Philosophy*. New York: The Free Press of Glencoe.

Armstrong, D. M. (1968). *A Materialist Theory of the Mind*. London: Routledge & Kegan Paul.

—— (1993). 'Preface to the Paperback Edition', *A Materialist Theory of the Mind*, revised edn. London: Routledge, pp. xiii–xxiii.

Aune, Bruce (1966). 'Feigl on the Mind–Body Problem'. In Pauk K. Feyerabend and Grover Maxwell (eds.), *Mind, Matter, and Method: Essays in Philosophy and Science in Honor of Herbert Feigl*. Minneapolis: University of Minnesota Press, pp. 17–39.

Ayer, A. J. (ed.) (1959). *Logical Positivism*. New York: Glencoe.

Beckermann, Ansgar (1992). 'Introduction—Reductive and Non-Reductive Physicalism'. In A. Beckermann, Hans Flohr, and Jaegwon Kim (eds.), *Emergence or Reduction? Essays on the Prospects of Nonreductive Physicalism*. Berlin: Walter de Gruyter, pp. 1–21.

Block, Ned (1978). 'Troubles with Functionalism'. In C. Savage (ed.), *Perception and Cognition: Minnesota Studies in the Philosophy of Science*, vol. 9. Minneapolis: University of Minnesota Press, pp. 261–326. Reprinted in Block (1980), pp. 268–306.

—— (ed.) (1980). *Readings in the Philosophy of Psychology, Volume 1*. Cambridge, MA: Harvard University Press.

Borst, C. V. (1970). 'Editor's Introduction'. In Borst (ed.), *The Mind/Brain Identity Theory*. New York: St. Martin's Press, pp. 13–39.

Burge, Tyler (2007). 'Philosophy of Mind: 1950–1990'. In *Foundations of Mind*. Oxford: Oxford University Press, pp. 440–64.

Carnap, Rudof (1932/1934). 'Die physikalische Sprache als Universalsprache der Wissenschaft', *Erkenntnis* 2: 432–65; tr. Max Black as *The Unity of Science*. London: Kegan, Paul, 1934.

—— (1933/1959). 'Psychology in Physical Language', tr. George Shick in Ayer (1959), from the original German article 'Psychologie in physikalischer Sprache', *Erkenntnis* 3 (1933): 102–42.

—— (1934/2002). *The Logical Syntax of Language*, tr. Amethe Smeaton. Chicago: Open Court, 2002, a reprinting of the original 1937 translation of the 1934 German original.

—— (1935/1963). *Philosophy and Logical Syntax*. London: Routledge & Kegan Paul. Reprinted, with addenda added by Carnap and terminological improvements suggested by him, in Alston and Nakhnikian (1963), pp. 424–60

—— (1936–7). 'Testability and Meaning', *Philosophy of Science* 3 (1936): 419–71 and 4 (1937): 1–40.

—— (1938/1991). 'Logical Foundations of the Unity of Science'. In Otto Neurath, Rudolf Carnap, and Charles W. Morris (eds.), *International Encyclopedia of Unified Science*, vol. 1, no. 1.

Chicago: University of Chicago Press, 1938. Repr. in Richard Boyd, Philip Gasper, and J. D. Trout (eds.), *The Philosophy of Science*. Cambridge, MA: MIT Press, 1991, pp. 393–404.

—— (1956). 'The Methodological Character of Theoretical Concepts', *Minnesota Studies in the Philosophy of Science*, vol. 1. Minneapolis: University of Minnesota Press, pp. 38–76.

—— (1963). 'Herbert Feigl on Physicalism'. In Schilpp (1963), pp. 882–6.

Chalmers, David (1996). *The Conscious Mind*. New York: Oxford University Press.

Chisholm, Roderick (1955–6). 'Sentences about Believing', *Proceedings of the Aristotelian Society* 56: 125–48.

Churchland, Paul (1981). 'Eliminative Materialism and the Propositional Attitudes', *The Journal of Philosophy* 78: 67–90.

Cirera, Ramon (1993). 'Carnap's Philosophy of Mind', *Studies in the History and Philosophy of Science* 24: 351–8.

Cornman, James (1971). *Materialism and Sensations*. New Haven and London: Yale University Press.

Davidson, Donald (1970). 'Mental Events'. In Lawrence Foster and J. W. Swanson (eds.), *Experience and Theory*. London: Duckworth, pp. 79–101.

Dennett, Daniel (1969). *Content and Consciousness*. London: Routledge.

—— (1979). *Brainstorms*. Cambridge, MA: MIT Press.

Ducasse, Curt (1941). *Philosophy as a Science: Its Matter and its Method*. New York: Oskar-Piest.

Feigl, Herbert (1934). 'Logical Analysis of the Psychophysical Problem: A Contribution to the New Positivism', *Philosophy of Science* 1(4): 420–45.

—— (1950). 'The Mind–Body Problem in the Development of Logical Empiricism', *Revue de Internationale de Philosophie* 4: 64–83. Repr. in H. Feigl and M. Brodbeck (eds.), *Readings in the Philosophy of Science*. New York: Appleton-Century Crofts, 1953, pp. 612–26.

—— (1958). 'The "Mental" and the "Physical"', *Minnesota Studies in the Philosophy of Science*, vol. 2. Minneapolis: University of Minnesota Press, pp. 370–497.

—— (1960). 'Mind–Body, *Not* a Pseudo-Problem'. In Sydney Hook (ed.), *Dimensions of Mind*. New York: Collier Books, pp. 24–36.

—— (1963). 'Physicalism, Unity of Science and the Foundations of Psychology'. In Schilpp (1963), pp. 227–68.

—— (1967). 'Postscript After Ten Years'. In Feigl, *The 'Mental' and the 'Physical'*. Minneapolis: University of Minnesota Press, 1967, pp. 133–60.

—— (1971). 'Some Crucial Issues of Mind–Body Monism', *Synthese* 22: 295–312.

—— (1975). 'Russell and Schlick: A Remarkable Agreement on a Monistic Solution of the Mind–Body Problem', *Erkenntnis* 9: 11–34

Feyerabend, Paul (1963). 'Materialism and the Mind–Body Problem', *Review of Metaphysics* 17: 49–66.

Fodor, Jerry (1968). *Psychological Explanation*. New York: Random House.

Goodman, Nelson (1963). 'The Significance of *Der Logische Aufbau Der Welt*'. In Schilpp (1963), pp. 545–58.

Hardcastle, Gary L. (2007). 'Logical Empiricism and the Philosophy of Psychology'. In Alan Richardson and Thomas Uebel (eds.), *The Cambridge Companion to Logical Empiricism*. Cambridge: Cambridge University Press, pp. 228–49.

Hatfield, Gary (2002). 'Sense-Data and the Philosophy of Mind: Russell, James and Mach', *Principia* 6(2): 203–30.

—— (2004). 'Sense Data and the Mind–Body Problem'. In Ralph Schumacher (ed.), *Perception and Reality: From Descartes to the Present*. Paderborn: Mentis, pp. 305–31.

Heidelberger, Michael (2003). 'The Mind–Body Problem in the Origin of Logical Empiricism'. In Parrini *et al.* (2003), pp. 233–62.

Hempel, Carl G. (1935/1972). 'The Logical Analysis of Psychology'. Repr. in Ausonio Marras (ed.), *Intentionality, Mind, and Language*. Urbana, IL: University of Illinois Press, 1972, pp. 115–31. Tr. Wilfrid Sellars from the French original in *Revue de Synthese* (1935), in H. Feigl and W. Sellars (eds.), *Readings in Philosophical Analysis*. New York: Appleton Century Crofts, 1949. Repr. with prefatory note in Block (1980).

—— (1952). *Fundamentals of Concept Formation in Empirical Science*. Chicago: University of Chicago Press.

—— (1954). 'A Logical Appraisal of Operationism', *Science Monthly* 79: 215–20.

—— (1969). 'Logical Positivism and the Social Sciences'. In Achinstein and Barker (1969), pp. 163–94.

Kim, Jaegwon (1971). 'Materialism and the Criteria of the Mental', *Synthese* 22: 323–45.

—— (1998). *Mind in a Physical World*. Cambridge, MA: MIT Press.

—— (2003). 'Logical Positivism and the Mind–Body Problem'. In Parrini *et al.* (2003), pp. 263–78.

—— (2011). *Philosophy of Mind*, 3rd edn. Oxford: Westview Press.

Lewis, David (1966). 'An Argument for the Identity Theory', *Journal of Philosophy* 63: 17–25.

Livingston, Paul M. (2004). *Philosophical History and the Problem of Consciousness*. Cambridge: Cambridge University Press.

Lockwood, Michael (1981). 'What Was Russell's Neutral Monism?', *Midwest Studies in Philosophy* 6(1): 143–58.

Maxwell, Grover (1978). 'Rigid Designators and Mind–Brain Identity'. In C. Savage (ed.), *Perception and Cognition: Minnesota Studies in the Philosophy of Science*, vol. 9. Minneapolis: University of Minnesota Press, pp. 365–404.

Neurath, Otto (1931). 'Physicalism: The Philosophy of the Viennese Circle', *The Monist* 41: 618–23.

Pap, Arthur (1952). 'Semantic Analysis and Psycho-Physical Dualism', *Mind* 61: 209–21.

—— (1958). *Semantics and Necessary Truth*. New Haven: Yale University Press.

Papineau, David (2001). 'The Rise of Physicalism'. In Carl Gillett and Barry M. Loewer (eds.), *Physicalism and its Discontents*. Cambridge: Cambridge University Press, pp. 3–36.

Parrini, Paolo, Wesley C. Salmon, and Merrilee H. Salmon (eds.) (2003). *Logical Empiricism: Historical and Contemporary Perspectives*. Pittsburgh: University of Pittsburgh Press.

Patterson, Sarah (2008). 'Philosophy of Mind'. In Dermot Moran (ed.), *The Routledge Companion to Twentieth Century Philosophy*. London: Routledge, pp. 525–82

Perry, John (2001). *Knowledge, Possibility, and Consciousness*. Cambridge, MA: MIT Press.

Place, U. T. (1956). 'Is Consciousness a Brain Process?', *British Journal of Psychology* 47: 44–50.

—— (n.d.). 'Identity Theories'. In *A Field Guide to the Philosophy of Mind*. Online at: <http://host.uniroma3.it/progetti/kant/field/>, accessed 3 December 2012.

Putnam, Hilary (1957). 'Psychological Concepts, Explication, and Ordinary Language', *The Journal of Philosophy* 54: 94–100.

—— (1963/1975). 'Brains and Behavior'. In R. Butler (ed.), *Analytical Philosophy, Second Series*. Oxford: Blackwell, 1963. Repr. in Putnam, *Mind, Language and Reality: Philosophical Papers, Volume. 2*. Cambridge: University of Cambridge Press, 1975, pp. 325–41.

Reck, Erich H. and Steve Awodey (eds. and trs.) (2003). *Frege's Lectures on Logic: Carnap's Student Notes 1910–14*. La Salle, IL: Open Court.

Rorty, Richard (1965). 'Mind–Body Identity, Privacy, and Categories', *Review of Metaphysics* 19: 24–54.

——(1970). 'Incorrigibility as the Mark of the Mental', *The Journal of Philosophy* 67: 399–424.

——(1979). *Philosophy and the Mirror of Nature*. Princeton, NJ: Princeton University Press.

——(1981). 'Contemporary Philosophy of Mind', *Synthese* 53: 323–48.

Rosenthal, David M. (1971/1987). 'Introduction'. In Rosenthal (ed.), *Materialism and the Mind–Body Problem*. Indianapolis: Hackett, 1987, pp. 1–17. 1st edn. Englewood Cliffs: Prentice-Hall, 1971.

Russell, Bertrand (1927). *Analysis of Matter*. London: Routledge & Kegan Paul.

——(1956). 'Mind and Matter'. In Russell, *Portraits from Memory and Other Essays*. London: George Allen & Unwin, pp. 145–65.

Ryle, Gilbert (1949). *The Concept of Mind*. London: Hutchinson.

Schilpp, P. A. (ed.) (1963). *The Philosophy of Rudolf Carnap*. La Salle, IL: Open Court.

Schlick, Moritz (1916/1979). 'Ideality of Space, Introjection and the Psycho-Physical Problem', in Schlick, *Philosophical Papers*, vol. 1. Dordrecht: Reidel, pp. 190–206.

——(1925/1974). *General Theory of Knowledge*, tr. Albert E. Blumenberg. New York: Springer-Verlag. Translated from the 2nd original German edition of *Allgemeine Erkenntnislehre* (1925). 1st edition published in 1918.

——(1935/1949). 'On the Relation Between Psychological and Physical Concepts'. In H. Feigl and W. Sellars (eds.), *Readings in Philosophical Analysis*. New York: Appleton-Century Crofts, pp. 393–407. Translation from the French original 'De la relation entre les notions psychologiques et les notions physiques', *Revue de Synthese* (1935).

Searle, John (2004). *Mind: A Brief Introduction*. Oxford: Oxford University Press.

Sellars, Wilfrid (1981). 'Is Consciousness Physical?', *Monist* 64: 66–90.

Smart, J. J. C. (1959). 'Sensations and Brain Processes', *Philosophical Review* 68: 141–56.

Smith, Laurence D. (1986). *Behaviorism and Logical Positivism: A Reassessment of the Alliance*. Stanford: Stanford University Press.

Stich, Stephen (1983). *From Folk Psychology to Cognitive Science: The Case Against Belief*. Cambridge, MA: MIT Press.

Stoljar, Daniel (2001). 'Two Conceptions of the Physical', *Philosophy and Phenomenological Research* 62: 253–81.

——(2010). *Physicalism*. London: Routledge.

Strawson, Galen (2006). 'Realistic Monism: Why Physicalism Entails Panpsychism', *Consciousness Studies* 13: 3–31.

Stubenberg, Leopold (1997). 'Austria vs. Australia: Two Versions of the Identity Theory'. In K. Lehrer and J. C. Marek (eds.), *Austrian Philosophy, Past and Present: Essays in Honour of Rudolf Haller*. Dordrecht: Kluwer, pp. 125–46.

Suppe, Frederick (1977). 'The Search for Philosophic Understanding of Scientific Theories'. In Suppe (ed.), *The Structure of Scientific Theories*, 2nd edn. Urbana, IL: University of Illinois Press, pp. 1–241.

Uebel, Thomas (1995). 'Physicalism in Wittgenstein and the Vienna Circle'. In K. Gavrolgu *et al.* (eds.), *Physics, Philosophy, and the Scientific Community: Essays in the Philosophy of Science and Mathematics in Honor of Robert S. Cohen*. Dordrecht: Kluwer, pp. 327–56.

Unger, Peter (1999). 'The Mystery of the Physical and the Matter of Qualities: A Paper for Professor Shaffer', *Midwest Studies in Philosophy* 23: 75–99.

Watson, Richard (1993). 'Shadow History in Philosophy', *Journal of the History of Philosophy* 31: 95–109.

CHAPTER 21

THE DEVELOPMENT OF THEORIES OF MEANING: FROM FREGE TO MCDOWELL AND BEYOND

ALEXANDER MILLER

THE phrase 'theory of meaning' can mean a number of things in the history of analytic philosophy of language. It may denote an attempt to 'analyze, elucidate, or determine the empirical content of, the concept of meaning in general' (Sainsbury 1979: 127). This we can call an *informal* theory of meaning. Alternatively, it may denote a particular kind of *formal* theory concerning a specific language. If the language is L, a theory of meaning in this second sense is a theory capable of generating, for each well-formed sentence s of L, a theorem that in some way gives the meaning of s.[1] This we can call a *formal* theory of meaning. Many of the main figures in analytic philosophy of language have attempted to construct both informal and formal theories of meaning, and in some cases have seen the construction of formal theories of meaning for natural languages as the only—or at least best—way to achieve the elucidatory aims of an informal theory of meaning. This viewpoint is captured well by John Foster:

> [T]he point of investigating the conditions for an adequate [formal] theory of meaning is to gain philosophical insight into the *nature* of language and meaning, to bring the semantic character of language into the right philosophical perspective. This perspective is not provided by a [formal] theory of meaning itself, which only purports to give the meanings of expressions in some particular language. The idea is rather that if we put the right constraints on what giving-the-meanings involves, then characterizing the general method by which such [formal] theories can

---

[1] This distinction roughly corresponds to Jane Heal's distinction between 'seeking a concept analysis' and 'constructing a calculus' (Heal 1978: 359). Note that in this essay the focus is on the work of truth-conditional theorists as opposed to what Strawson (1971) dubbed 'theorists of communication intention' (although it should also be noted that the distinctions between the two approaches are not always sharp: see Davidson 1990: 309).

be constructed and verified reveals what meaning-in-language really amounts to. By showing what for certain purposes counts as a [formal] theory of meaning, we show what meaning is. (Foster 1976: 4)

A full survey of the development of theories of meaning—in both the formal and informal senses—would require a full history of analytic philosophy itself. Hence, this essay makes no claim to be comprehensive. Instead, we focus primarily on one issue, and even then only sketchily: the capacity of formal theories of meaning to shed light on our ability to understand novel utterances. In §§ 21.1–21.2, we set the scene with a brief outline of Frege's views on meaning; this is followed in § 21.3 with an account of Davidson's critique of Frege and his idea that Tarskian truth-theories can serve as formal theories of meaning for natural languages. A critical look at Davidson in § 21.4 is followed in §§ 21.5–21.6 by an exposition and critical discussion of the debate between Dummett and McDowell concerning 'modesty' and 'full-bloodedness' in theories of meaning. We then argue in §§ 21.7–21.10 that a non-reductionist view capable of going hand in hand with McDowell's modest approach can and must be developed in a way that allows it to view implicit knowledge of theories of meaning as potentially explanatory of our capacity to understand novel utterances. In § 21.11 we conclude with some brief remarks on the importance of the theory of meaning within the history of analytic philosophy.

21.1 FREGE

The usual starting point for a discussion of theories of meaning is the mature work of Gottlob Frege (1848–1925). The key papers are Frege 1891, 1892a, 1892b, 1892c, 1914, and 1918.

For Frege, the *Bedeutung* of a linguistic expression is that feature that determines whether sentences in which it occurs are true or false.[2] Expressions from different syntactic categories are assigned different kinds of *Bedeutung*. The *Bedeutung* of a sentence is its truth-value (true or false, or for Frege, The True or The False, both of which he takes to be objects of a special sort). A proper name, such as 'Hugo Chavez', has an object as its *Bedeutung*. According to Frege, so does a definite description, such as 'the Venezuelan president in 2009'. Indeed, these have the same *Bedeutung*, and the substitution of one for the other in a sentence preserves that sentence's truth-value. A predicate, such as '… is red', has as its *Bedeutung* a first-level function from objects to truth-values (Frege calls these 'concepts'). Thus, the *Bedeutung* of '… is red' is a function that maps the Chinese flag onto The True and the Scottish flag onto The False. Sentential connectives, such as '~' or '&', have first-level functions from truth-values to truth-values as their *Bedeutungen*. The *Bedeutung* of '~' maps The True onto The

---

[2] For a discussion of issues concerning the translation of 'Bedeutung', see Beaney 1997: 36–46. I will follow Beaney's practice of leaving 'Bedeutung' untranslated.

False and vice versa; while the *Bedeutung* of '&' maps the pair (The True, The True) onto The True, and all other pairs of truth-values onto The False. The universal and existential quantifiers have second-level functions from concepts to truth-values as their *Bedeutungen*. The first-level concept denoted by '… is self-identical' maps all objects onto The True, so the second-level function denoted by '∀' maps this concept onto The True. The concept denoted by '… is a philosopher' maps some but not all objects onto The True, so the second-level function denoted by '∀' maps this concept onto The False while the second-level function that is the *Bedeutung* of '∃' maps it onto The True. Since the concept denoted by '… is not self-identical' maps no objects onto The True, the *Bedeutung* of '∃' maps it onto The False. The extension of a function is the set of objects that it maps onto The True, and 'concepts differ only insofar as their extensions are different' (Frege 1892b: 173). Despite having extensional identity conditions, functions, unlike the *Bedeutungen* of names, are incomplete or unsaturated, since the expressions that stand for them require the insertion of a further expression—a name for first-level functions or a concept-word for second-level functions—in order to generate a truth-value. Frege holds a *principle of compositionality* with respect to *Bedeutungen*: whether a sentence stands for The True or The False is determined by the *Bedeutungen* of its constituents.[3]

Frege introduces the notion of *Sinn* (or 'sense') in addition that of *Bedeutung*. Since 'The Morning Star is The Morning Star' and 'The Morning Star is The Evening Star' are both true, they have the same *Bedeutung*. But the first expresses an obvious truism, whereas the second expresses a non-obvious piece of astronomical information, and Frege accounts for this via the claim that the two sentences express different senses. The sense of a sentence is the thought that it expresses, where thoughts are conceived not as subjective psychological items but as truth-conditions: for a given sentence, the condition whose obtaining is necessary and sufficient for its truth. The sense of a sentence, unlike its *Bedeutung*, is grasped by someone who understands it. 'The Morning Star is The Morning Star' and 'The Morning Star is The Evening Star' express different thoughts because their constituents have different senses: 'The Morning Star' and 'The Evening Star' have the same celestial object as *Bedeutung*, but present that object in different ways, perhaps in one case as the object that appears in such and such a place in the morning firmament and in the other as the object that appears in such and such a place in the evening firmament. The sense of an expression determines its *Bedeutung*: that a particular object appears in such and such a place in the morning firmament determines it as the *Bedeutung* of 'The Morning Star', and that 'The Morning Star is The Evening Star' expresses the thought that the object that appears in such and such a place in the morning firmament is identical to the object that appears in such and such a place in the evening firmament determines, together with the relevant

---

[3] Note that this paragraph concerns only extensional contexts. Frege holds that in intentional contexts, such as e.g. 'Wittgenstein believes that Hugo Chavez is the Venezuelan president in 2009', the *Bedeutung* of 'Hugo Chavez' is its customary sense (the sense it has in extensional contexts). See Dummett 1973: ch. 9.

astronomical fact, that the *Bedeutung* of 'The Morning Star is The Evening Star' is The True. Frege holds a *principle of compositionality* with respect to sense: the sense of a sentence is determined by the senses of its constituents. Thus, someone who grasps the sense of the sentence can be viewed as doing so in virtue of their grasp of the sentence's constituents.

In addition to sense and *Bedeutung*, Frege also distinguishes the notions of *force* (concerned with distinctions between assertions, orders, questions, and other kinds of speech-act) and *tone* (concerned with those aspects of the meaning of 'and' that distinguish it from 'but' even though the two expressions have the same sense).

In analysing the pre-theoretical notion of meaning into the four aspects of sense, *Bedeutung*, force, and tone, Frege thus contributes to the development of an informal theory of meaning. In addition, he *inter alia* provides resources for the beginnings of a formal theory of meaning for a natural language.[4]

21.2 FREGEAN FORMAL THEORIES OF MEANING

A Fregean formal theory of *Bedeutung* for a language would consist of a finite set of axioms detailing the *Bedeutungen* of its primitive expressions plus compositional axioms governing the *Bedeutungen* of complex expressions.[5] For example, if we have a simple language L consisting of 5 names and 5 predicates, such a theory will have axioms for each name, predicate, and the subject-predicate mode of construction. If an object or function is the *Bedeutung* of an expression, we'll say that the expression *refers* to that object or function. So we might have:

- (i) 'a' refers to Socrates
- (ii) 'b' refers to Plato
- (iii) 'c' refers to Hume
- (iv) 'd' refers to Kant
- (v) 'e' refers to Marx
- (vi) 'F' refers to f( ), where $\forall x\, f(x) = $ The True $\leftrightarrow$ x is Greek
- (vii) 'G' refers to g( ), where $\forall x\, g(x) = $ The True $\leftrightarrow$ x is Scottish
- (viii) 'H' refers to h( ), where $\forall x\, h(x) = $ The True $\leftrightarrow$ x is German
- (ix) 'I' refers to i( ), where $\forall x\, i(x) = $ The True $\leftrightarrow$ x is a philosopher
- (x) 'J' refers to j( ), where $\forall x\, j(x) = $ The True $\leftrightarrow$ x is female

---

[4] Although Frege had severe doubts about the applicability of his views of meaning to natural languages, there are reasons to believe that these have been somewhat overstated in the literature. See Segal 2006: 190–3. Note that below we simply prescind from considering issues relating to the notion of force and the presence of force-indicators in natural languages.

[5] It would also have to contain a *syntax*: a specification of rules for the admissible combination of items from the language's vocabulary.

The extension of a concept is the set of objects that yield The True as value when presented to the function as argument. Given this, we can complete the formal theory by adding a *compositional axiom*:

(xi) Where Φ is a one-place predicate and α is a name: ^Φα^ is true ↔ the referent of α belongs to the extension of the referent of Φ[6]

Given the above, we can generate truth-values for sentences from the referents of their constituents together with the relevant worldly facts. For example, the sentence 'Fa' is true if and only if the referent of 'a' (Socrates) belongs to the extension of f( ). The extension of f( ) is {Socrates, Plato}, and it follows that 'Fa' is true. Using Frege's idea that logical connectives and quantifiers have, respectively, functions from truth-values to truth-values and second-level functions from concepts to truth-values as *Bedeutungen*, the Fregean formal theory of *Bedeutung* could be extended in the obvious way if logical connectives and quantifiers were added to our simple language.

What are the prospects for a Fregean formal theory of sense for a language? Given that, for Frege, senses are *entities*,[7] such a theory would appear to have the same general shape as his formal theory of *Bedeutung* for that language. It would have axioms associating senses with primitive expressions together with compositional axioms governing their concatenation. This would substantiate Frege's claim that the sense of a semantically structured sentence is determined by the senses of its constituents and mode of construction. Given that the sense of an expression is what a competent user of that expression grasps, we would have the makings of an explanation of semantic creativity: a speaker would be able to grasp the sense of an unfamiliar sentence that consists of familiar constituents in virtue of his grasp of the senses of the latter.

So how do we go about constructing a formal theory of sense of this type? According to Gareth Evans (1946–80), the prospects of success are dim:

> Frege nowhere appears to have envisaged a theory which would entail, for any sentence of the language, S, a theorem of the form,
> The sense of S is …,
> derived from axioms which would state the sense of the primitive words of the language. Frege had no more idea of how to complete a clause like
> The sense of 'and' is …
> than we do. (Evans 1982: 25–6)

---

[6] Here we say that L is the *object-language*. The sentence (xi) itself belongs to the *meta-language*, the language in which the theory of meaning for L is couched. The Greek characters are meta-linguistic variables that range over expressions belonging to the object-language. '^Φα^' is to be read as 'the result of concatenating Φ and α in that order'.

[7] For Frege, a thought—the sense of a sentence—is an abstract object: 'A thought belongs neither to my inner world as an idea, nor yet to the external world, the world of things perceptible by the senses' (Frege 1918: 342) and the sense of a sub-sentential expression is *a part* of the thought expressed by the sentence (Frege 1914: 320).

A way out of this impasse is suggested by the following reflection. In the formal theory of *Bedeutung* sketched above for our simple language we were able to derive the truth-value of 'Fa' from facts about the world together with facts about the *Bedeutungen* of its constituents. As a step in this process we derived:

(a) 'Fa' is true if and only if the referent of 'a' (Socrates) belongs to the extension of f( )

Since Socrates belongs to the extension of f( ) if and only if he is Greek, we have in effect:

(b) 'Fa' is true if and only if Socrates is Greek

Recall from above that for Frege the sense of a sentence is a thought, where this is conceived of as a truth-condition. Given that (b) tells us what condition—Socrates being Greek—has to obtain in order for 'Fa' to be true, it effectively gives us the truth-condition—and hence sense—of 'Fa'.

What this suggests is that a theory of *Bedeutung* might be used as a theory of sense, so that we can have a theory of sense without viewing senses as entities or embarking on the search for a theory of sense of the sort castigated by Evans. This suggestion is the departure point for the key claim about theories of meaning pioneered by Donald Davidson (1917–2003):

> Frege held that an adequate account of language requires us to attend to three features of sentences: reference [*Bedeutung*], sense, and force. [I argue] that a theory of truth patterned after a Tarski-type truth-definition tells us all we need to know about sense. Counting truth in the domain of reference [*Bedeutung*], as Frege did, the study of sense thus comes down to the study of reference [*Bedeutung*]. (Davidson 1979: 109)

21.3 DAVIDSON'S CRITIQUE OF FREGE

Davidson's famous 1967 paper 'Truth and Meaning' can be viewed as making a number of criticisms of the Fregean theories of sense and *Bedeutung* adumbrated in the previous section. Two of the criticisms concern the formal theory of *Bedeutung* and two concern the theory of sense:

(i) To explain the compositionality of *Bedeutung* it is not sufficient to assign functions—or any other entities—as the *Bedeutungen* of predicates and quantifiers.[8]

(ii) To explain the compositionality of *Bedeutung* it is not necessary to assign

---

[8] To say that *Bedeutung* is compositional is just to say that the *Bedeutung* of a complex expression is determined by the *Bedeutungen* of its constituents together with its structure.

functions—or any other entities—as the *Bedeutungen* of predicates and quantifiers.

(iii) Positing senses as entities corresponding to linguistic expressions is not sufficient to explain the compositionality of sense.

(iv) It is not necessary to posit senses as entities corresponding to linguistic expressions in order to explain the compositionality of sense.

Criticisms (ii) and (iv) will be explained shortly when we describe how Davidson's idea that Tarskian truth-theories can do duty as theories of sense allows him to explain the compositionality of *Bedeutung* and sense without assigning *Bedeutungen* to predicates and quantifiers or viewing senses as entities associated with expressions. Before then, though, we'll briefly consider criticisms (i) and (iii), as outlined in the opening pages of Davidson (1967).

Davidson argues that in the Fregean formal theory the unsaturated entities assigned to, e.g., predicates play no genuine explanatory role. He writes:

> We might assign Theaetetus to 'Theaetetus' and the property of flying to 'flies' in the sentence 'Theaetetus flies'. The problem then arises how the meaning of the sentence is generated from these meanings. Viewing concatenation as a significant piece of syntax, we may assign to it the relation of participating in or instantiating; however, it is obvious that we have here the start of an infinite regress. Frege sought to avoid the regress by saying that the entities corresponding to predicates (for example) are 'unsaturated' or 'incomplete' in contrast to the entities that correspond to names, but this doctrine seems to label a difficulty rather than solve it. (Davidson 1967: 17)

Davidson's argument is that if we hold that 'Theaetetus flies' is true if and only if Theaetetus instantiates the property of flying, then we make the truth-value of the sentence dependent on the truth-value of 'Theaetetus instantiates the property of flying', which is then true if and only if Theaetetus instantiates the property of instantiating the property of flying, and so on, *ad infinitum*, so that no truth-value is determined. Or, if we hold that 'Socrates is Greek' is true if and only if Socrates belongs to the extension of f(), then we make the truth-value of the sentence dependent on the truth-value of 'Socrates belongs to the extension of f()', which is then true if and only if Socrates belongs to the extension of 'belongs to the extension of f()', and so on, *ad infinitum*. Preventing the regress from getting started by labelling the property of flying and the function f( ) 'unsaturated' is no real solution, but just a terminological manoeuvre.[9] This is Davidson's argument for (i).

Davidson then considers whether Frege might be aided by turning 'for help to the distinction between meaning [sense] and reference [*Bedeutung*]' (1967: 19). He argues that this does not help:

> The switch from reference [*Bedeutung*] leads to no useful account of how the meanings [senses] of sentences depend upon the meanings [senses] of the words (or other structural features) that compose them. Ask, for example, for the [sense] of 'The-

---

[9] See also Segal 2006: 194 n13.

aetetus flies'. A Fregean answer might go something like this: given the [sense] of 'Theaetetus' as argument, the [sense] of 'flies' yields the [sense] of 'Theaetetus flies' as value. The vacuity of this answer is obvious. We wanted to know what the [sense] of 'Theaetetus flies' is; it is no progress to be told that it is the [sense] of 'Theaetetus flies'. This much we knew before any theory was in sight. In the bogus account just given, talk of the structure of the sentence and of the [senses] of words was idle, for it played no role in producing the given description of the [sense] of the sentence. (1967: 20)

This is Davidson's argument for (iii).

Davidson argues that we can utilize the work of Alfred Tarski (1901–83) on the definition of truth for formal languages (Tarski 1956a) to explain the compositionality of *Bedeutung* and sense in a manner that does not involve the assignment of functions as the *Bedeutungen* of predicates and quantifiers or entities as the senses of natural language expressions. Take the simple language L discussed in the previous section and augment it with the existential quantifier, brackets, and a stock of variables. As before, we assign referents to the proper names via axioms (i) to (v). We then have five further axioms spelling out the *satisfaction* conditions for L's predicates:

(6) $\forall x$ [x satisfies 'F' $\leftrightarrow$ x is Greek]
(7) $\forall x$ [x satisfies 'G' $\leftrightarrow$ x is Scottish]
(8) $\forall x$ [x satisfies 'H' $\leftrightarrow$ x is German]
(9) $\forall x$ [x satisfies 'I' $\leftrightarrow$ x is a philosopher]
(10) $\forall x$ [x satisfies 'J' $\leftrightarrow$ x is female]

We then let X, Y, Z … range over infinite ordered sequences of objects, and A, B, C … range over open sentences of L. We let X_i denote the ith member of the sequence X, and continue the axioms as follows:

(11) $\forall X$: X satisfies $^\wedge\Phi\alpha^\wedge$ $\leftrightarrow$ the referent of α satisfies Φ
(12) $\forall X$: X satisfies $^\wedge\Phi x_i^\wedge$ $\leftrightarrow$ X_i satisfies Φ
(13) $\forall X$, A: X satisfies '$(\exists x_i)$A' if and only if there is a sequence Y, differing from X in at most the ith place, such that Y satisfies 'A'.

We then give a definition of what it is for a closed sentence to be true-in-L:[10]

(14) A closed sentence is true-in-L if and only if it is satisfied by all sequences

---

[10] To see why we have 'true-in-L' note Davidson's comment: 'Tarski showed how to define a truth predicate for each of a number of well-behaved languages, but his definitions do not, of course, tell us what these predicates have in common. Put a little differently: he defined various predicates of the form "s is $true_L$", each applicable to a single language, but he failed to define a predicate of the form "s is true in L" for variable "L"' (Davidson 1990: 285).

The truth-value of e.g. 'Fa' can be derived as follows:

'Fa' is true-in-L if and only if it is satisfied by all sequences (from (14)).
'Fa' is satisfied by all sequences if and only if it is satisfied by an arbitrary sequence X.
An arbitrary sequence X satisfies 'Fa' if and only if the referent of 'a' satisfies 'F' (from (11)).
The referent of 'a' satisfies 'F' if and only if Socrates satisfies 'F' (from (i)).
Socrates satisfies 'F' if and only if Socrates is Greek (from (6)).

Thus

(A) 'Fa' is true-in-L if and only if Socrates is Greek

and since Socrates is in fact Greek, the sentence 'Fa' is true.

The truth-value of '$\exists x[Fx_1]$' can be derived in similar fashion, using the fact that a closed sentence is satisfied by all sequences if and only if it is satisfied by at least one sequence (see Miller 2007: 287):

'$\exists x[Fx_1]$' is true-in-L if and only if it is satisfied by all sequences (from (14)).
'$\exists x[Fx_1]$' is satisfied by all sequences if and only if it is satisfied by at least one sequence.
'$\exists x[Fx_1]$' is satisfied by a sequence X if and only if there is a sequence Y, differing from X in at most the 1st place, such that Y satisfies 'Fx_1'.
For a given sequence X, there is a sequence Y, differing from X in at most the 1st place, such that Y satisfies 'Fx_1', if and only if someone is Greek (if there is someone suitable—Socrates, say—we can replace the 1st member of X with him; if there is no one suitable, there will be no suitable Y_1 and hence no suitable sequence Y).

Thus

(B) '$\exists x[Fx_1]$' is true-in-L if and only if someone is Greek

and it follows, given the obvious worldly fact, that the sentence '$\exists x[Fx_1]$' is true.

Now, if we recall that the sense of a sentence is given by its truth-condition, we can see that (A) and (B) give us, respectively, the truth-conditions of 'Fa' and '$\exists x[Fx_1]$'. Moreover, we have derived these specifications of truth-conditions on the basis of axioms detailing the semantic properties of the constituents of the relevant sentences in a way that makes no use of senses as entities and that does not require functions as *Bedeutungen* of the predicate 'F' or the existential quantifier.

Tarski writes:

We shall call any equivalence of the form
   (T) s is true if and only if p
(with 'p' replaced by any sentence of the language to which the word 'true' refers, and 's' replaced by a name of this sentence) an 'equivalence of the form (T)' ... [W]e

are able to put into a precise form the conditions under which we will consider the usage and the definition of the term 'true' as adequate from the material point of view: we wish to use the term 'true' in such a way that all equivalencies of the form (T) can be asserted, and we shall call a definition of truth 'adequate' if all these equivalencies follow from it. (Tarski 1944: 344)

This expresses Tarski's 'Convention T' or condition of material adequacy on definitions of 'true'. Davidson's insight is that if we have a formal theory of *Bedeutung* that satisfies Convention T—and some additional empirical constraints (see below)—in effect we will have a theory that explains the compositionality of *Bedeutung* and that is capable of doing duty as a theory of sense, all without senses as entities or functions as *Bedeutungen* of predicates and quantifiers. Davidson's grand project is thus to take a natural language (or a fragment thereof), formalize it into a formal language amenable to Tarskian treatment, and then construct a formal theory satisfying Convention T that displays the compositionality of both *Bedeutung* and sense.[11]

The quote from Tarski in the preceding paragraph applies to the case where the meta-language contains the object-language. In the general case where the meta-language and object-language are distinct Tarski requires the sentence 'p' to be a *translation* of the sentence on the left-hand side of (T). Since a correct translation is effectively a *meaning-preserving* translation, Davidson, unlike Tarski, cannot simply help himself to the notion, since Davidson is attempting to construct a formal theory of meaning, whereas Tarski was attempting to define truth-in-a-language:

> What I propose is to reverse the direction of explanation: assuming translation, Tarski was able to define truth; the present idea is to take truth as basic and to extract an account of translation or interpretation. (Davidson 1973: 134)

Davidson 'extracts' the notion of translation by imposing further constraints—in addition to Convention T—on the formal theories that serve as theories of meaning. He requires that they allow us to correctly interpret the speakers of the relevant language, and he lays down constitutive principles governing the process of interpretation whose satisfaction presupposes no facts about correct translation, the most important of which is the *principle of charity*. A formal theory can serve as a theory of meaning if—given the assumption that the speakers of the language have beliefs that are intelligible by the lights of the interpreter—taking the right-hand sides of the T-theorems to give the meanings of the sentences mentioned on the left-hand sides makes maximal sense of what the speakers of the language say and do (see Miller 2007: 292–302).[12]

---

[11] Note that Tarski himself was pessimistic about the possibility of rendering natural language amenable to formal treatment (see e.g. Tarski 1956b: 403). For Davidson's more optimistic outlook, see Davidson 1967: 35.

[12] In addition to the idea that T-sentences give the meanings of the sentences named on their left-hand sides only if the overall theory to which they belong satisfies the principle of charity, Davidsonians also typically require that they be derived from the axioms of the theory via a *canonical* route. See Kölbel 2002: ch. 5, for references and some stimulating discussion.

The execution of this project of constructing a formal theory that satisfies Convention T and the principle of charity in effect constitutes Davidson's extended argument for claims (ii) and (iv) above.

21.4 WRIGHT'S CRITIQUE OF DAVIDSON

Davidson clearly thinks that the construction of formal theories satisfying Convention T, the principle of charity, and so on, can contribute to the explanation of how speakers of natural language are able to understand novel utterances:

> [T]he speakers of a language can effectively determine the meaning or meanings of an arbitrary expression (if it has a meaning), and ... it is the central task of a theory of meaning to show how this is possible. I have argued that a characterization of truth [along Tarskian lines] describes the required kind of structure. (Davidson 1967: 35)

We would have the materials for such an explanation if speakers of the language could be viewed as *implicitly knowing* the formal theory in question, but this is not how Davidson chooses to proceed. In a well-known paper, John Foster writes:

> Rather than ask for a statement of the knowledge implicit in linguistic competence, let us ask for the statement of a theory whose knowledge would suffice for such competence. Instead of demanding a statement of those metalinguistic facts which the mastery of a language implicitly recognizes, let us demand a statement of those facts explicit recognition of which gives mastery. What we are then demanding is still a theory of meaning, but without the questionable assumption that one who has mastered the language has, at some deep level, absorbed the information which it supplies. The theory reveals the semantic machinery which competence works, but leaves undetermined the psychological form in which competence exists. (Foster 1976: 2)

Although Davidson, in his reply to Foster, goes on to tackle the objections that Foster went on to develop, he signals agreement with the conception of the aims of a theory of meaning that Foster expresses in the passage just quoted:

> I think Foster is right in asking whether a proposed theory explicitly states something knowledge of which would suffice for interpreting utterances of speakers of the language to which it applies. (Davidson 1976: 171)

The inadequacy of the view shared by Davidson and Foster has been forcefully highlighted by Crispin Wright. Wright argues that at least in the case where the metalanguage contains the object-language, the Foster–Davidson view of the aim of the theory of meaning fails to connect the project of explaining semantic creativity with the construction of axiomatic theories of the sort described in the previous section. Wright argues:

> Provided we have a recursive specification of the syntax of the (declarative) part of the language, and provided we are content with the disquotational form of meaning-delivering theorem for which theories of truth are famous, Foster's project is well-enough served by a semantic 'theory' which merely stipulates as an axiom every instance of the schema
>
> A is T if and only if P
>
> where 'P' may be replaced by any declarative sentence of the object-language and 'A' by the quotational name of that sentence. (Wright 1986: 211)

What is the problem? On the Davidson–Foster view, the theory's capacity to explain semantic creativity is not a consequence of what the theory does (captures knowledge, explicit possession of which would yield linguistic competence), since what it does can be done just as well by a theory consisting of an infinitary axiom schema as described by Wright, which manifestly does not contribute to the explanation of semantic creativity. Davidson's conception of what the theory of meaning does is thus uncoupled from his conception of what the theory of meaning is capable of explaining. And this is unsatisfactory: in order for the theory to have genuine explanatory power, it should be in virtue of what it does that it explains what it explains. (Compare this with the implicit knowledge view. Whatever other problems it faces, on the implicit knowledge view that the theory explains what it explains (semantic creativity) is a direct consequence of what it does (captures what speakers implicitly know).) The Davidson–Foster view thus provides no satisfactory account of *how* the construction of formal theories of meaning contributes to the explanation of semantic creativity.[13]

21.5 DUMMETT: 'A THEORY OF MEANING IS A THEORY OF UNDERSTANDING'

On the Davidson–Foster view, a theory of meaning should tell us what speakers know, but there is no requirement that it should tell us what their having that knowledge consists in. In contrast, Michael Dummett (1925–2011) demands that a formal theory of

---

[13] Wright also suggests that the reference to autonomous 'semantic machinery' in Foster's outline of what the theory does vis-à-vis speakers' knowledge puts it in danger of generating 'an intolerable divide between the concepts of meaning and understanding' (Wright 1986: 210), a divide which is unsatisfactory because 'truths about meaning have to be, ultimately, constituted by facts about understanding' (Wright 1986: 210). Barry Smith archly expresses the suspicion that the Davidsonian view fails to do justice to the idea that a theory of meaning is a theory of understanding (Smith 1992: 124).

meaning 'must give an explicit account, not only of what anyone must know in order to know the meaning of a given expression, but of what constitutes having such knowledge' (Dummett 1975: 22). In other words, a theory of meaning should be a 'theoretical representation of a practical ability' (Dummett 1976: 36), in line with Dummett's guiding dictum that 'philosophical questions about meaning are best interpreted as questions about understanding' (Dummett 1976: 36).[14]

What does Dummett mean when he says that a theory of meaning should be a theoretical representation of a practical ability? Dummett writes:

> A theory of meaning will, then, represent the practical ability possessed by a speaker as consisting in his grasp of a set of propositions; since the speaker derives his understanding of a sentence from the meanings of its component words, these propositions will most naturally form a deductively connected system. The knowledge of these propositions that is attributed to a speaker can only be an implicit knowledge. In general, it cannot be demanded of someone who has any given practical ability that he have more than an implicit knowledge of those propositions by means of which we give a theoretical representation of that ability. (Dummett 1976: 36)

Wright (understandably) reads this passage as expressive of a commitment to the idea that 'the explanatory ambitions of a theory of meaning [are] entirely dependent upon the permissibility of thinking of speakers of its object language as knowing the propositions which its axioms codify and of their deriving their understanding of (novel) sentences in a manner mirrored by the derivation, in the theory, of the appropriate theorems' (Wright 1986: 207). However, this cannot be what Dummett intends, as in the paragraph immediately following that quoted above he goes on to say:

> A theory of meaning of this kind is not intended as a psychological hypothesis. Its function is solely to present an analysis of the complex skill which constitutes mastery of a language, to display, in terms of what he may be said to know, just what it is that someone who possesses this mastery is able to do; it is not concerned to describe any inner psychological mechanisms which may account for his having those abilities. (Dummett 1976: 37)[15]

If the theory of meaning is not a psychological hypothesis, in what sense can it be said to contribute to an explanation of a speaker's capacity to understand novel utterances?

---

[14] Elizabeth Fricker suggests that the dictum and the idea that a theory of meaning should be a theoretical representation of speakers' ability both flow from a rejection of the idea that meaning facts have the kind of autonomy mentioned in the previous footnote. See Fricker 1983: 55. Of course, Dummett's views here are pivotal in his conception of the debate between realists and their opponents. Realism about an area of discourse is identified as the view that the meaning of some sentences in that discourse is constituted by their possession of potentially evidence-transcendent truth-conditions, and it is then argued that a theory of meaning couched in terms of such truth-conditions cannot deliver an accurate representation of speakers' linguistic abilities. See Miller 2002.

[15] Note that in contrast to Wright, McDowell in some places takes Dummett's talk of implicit knowledge in his 1976 paper to be 'a mere *façon de parler*, replaceable without loss by talk of practical capacities' (McDowell 1987: 97n29).

Dummett here appears to face a dilemma. If he is in the market for such an explanation, his eschewal of the idea that a theory of meaning might describe the workings of a psychological mechanism in speakers appears to leave him with only the Davidson–Foster view of the relationship between speakers and theories of meaning: a view the inadequacy of which was described in the previous section. On the other hand, if he is not in the market for such an explanation, and limits himself to a purely descriptive *account* of the ability constitutive of linguistic competence, he faces a different worry. Wright suggests that 'No matter what ability we are concerned to describe, and however complete our characterization of its ingredient abilities, the description is incomplete if the ingredients have certain causal interrelations about which it keeps silent' (Wright 1986: 212), and one might take this to justify the construction of finitely axiomatized and compositional theories of meaning in the sense that the derivational structure of the theory provides the necessary information about the causal relationships between the various sub-abilities the totality of which constitutes linguistic mastery.[16] But this seems unsatisfactory. Whether a description of an ability is complete or incomplete is not a context-independent matter, but is determined by the *purposes* we have in framing the description. If those purposes don't include the explanation of semantic creativity, in the absence of some further story, the requirement that the theory of meaning convey information about the causal structure of speakers' abilities appears to be completely unmotivated.[17]

Thus, Dummett's conception of the nature of a theory of meaning either collapses back into the Davidson–Foster view with its attendant difficulties, or leaves the construction of finitely axiomatized and compositional theories of meaning looking curiously unmotivated.[18]

21.6 McDowell on Modest and Full-Blooded Theories of Meaning

In the previous section, we saw that for Dummett, a theory of meaning is supposed to be a theory of understanding, in the sense that it provides a theoretical representation of the practical capacity in which linguistic mastery consists. John McDowell (1942–) agrees that a theory of meaning should be a theory of understanding in this sense, but disagrees with Dummett over the issue of whether the theory of meaning

[16] Wright is not actually discussing Dummett when he makes this remark, but this doesn't matter for our present purposes.

[17] Note that settling the debate between realism and anti-realism (on Dummett's conception) appears to be independent of the issue about the causal structure of speakers' abilities.

[18] Note that my discussion is here limited to the views expressed in Dummett (1975) and (1976). In the preface to his 1993a collection, Dummett distances himself from the view of a theory of meaning as a representation of a practical ability (see e.g. p. x).

should be 'full-blooded' or 'modest'. A 'full-blooded' theory of meaning with respect to a given concept is one which provides a theoretical representation of the ability in which competence with that concept consists, but without using that concept within the scope of a content-specifying that-clause (in other words, without displaying that concept in its role as a determinant of content).[19] A 'modest' theory of meaning would be one that describes the ability in a way that involves using that concept within the scope of a content-specifying that-clause. Dummett requires theories of meaning to be full-blooded with respect to all concepts expressed by the words of the object language, whereas McDowell argues that modesty is both harmless and unavoidable. Why?

McDowell argues that in Dummett's writings on the theory of meaning an aspiration to avoid the twin evils of psychologism ('the view of language as a code for thought, independently endowed with content' (1987: 94)) and behaviourism ('a view that leaves out of account the involvement of mind in meaningful speech' (1987: 94)) is at work. According to McDowell, the rationale for Dummett's introduction of the notion of implicit knowledge is that it apparently allows him to steer clear of both. The theoretical representation of the practical ability in which linguistic competence consists—i.e. a theory of meaning—is taken by Dummett to specify something *implicitly known* by speakers: 'knowledge which shows itself partly by manifestation of the practical ability, and partly by a willingness to acknowledge as correct a formulation of what is known when it is presented' (Dummett 1978a: 96). Dummett avoids psychologism, since the implicit knowledge in question is manifested in speakers' behaviour (as opposed to lying behind and guiding behaviour), but behaviourism is avoided too 'because the implicit knowledge is … capable of acknowledgement by speakers as what guides their practice' (McDowell 1987: 95).

McDowell gives two arguments against Dummett's attempt to avoid both psychologism and behaviourism. These relate to the kind of description Dummett offers of the abilities constitutive of linguistic competence.

What is it to mean *square* by 'square'? Dummett writes:

> At the very least, it is to be able to discriminate between things that are square and those that are not. Such an ability can be ascribed only to one who will, on occasion, treat square things differently from things that are not square; one way, among many other possible ways, of doing this is to apply the word 'square' to square things and not to others. (Dummett 1978a: 98)

In the description of the ability, 'square' never appears within the scope of a that-clause, so that a theory of meaning that described it in these terms would be full-

---

[19] This definition is taken from the opening pages of McDowell 1987. As McDowell notes, in this definition concepts are 'determinants of the thoughts expressible by sentences containing the associated words' (1987: 87) and so belong to the level of sense rather than the level of *Bedeutung*. So 'concept' here means something different from what it meant in the exposition of Frege in § 21.1 above.

blooded. But the fact that the word 'square' is nevertheless used here means that we cannot view the competent speaker's use of 'square' as guided by implicit knowledge of the description:

> Comprehension of this object of acknowledgement would be an exercise of the very capacity we were trying to see as guided by the implicit knowledge that the acknowledgement supposedly reveals. If we needed guidance in our overt practice, we would need it just as much in our understanding of the supposed guide. (McDowell 1987: 95)

McDowell's second objection is that if the behaviour that manifests the ability constitutive of meaning *square* by 'square' is described in accordance with Dummett's insistence on full-bloodedness—and therefore described in terms that don't exploit the notion of content—we will be prone to a virulent form of meaning-scepticism.[20] Someone who has applied 'square' only to square things may manifest implicit knowledge of the clause

(a) $\forall x[x \text{ satisfies 'square'} \leftrightarrow x \text{ is square}]$

But this behaviour is also consistent with the hypothesis that the speaker is manifesting implicit knowledge of the clause

(b) $\forall x [x \text{ satisfies 'square'} \leftrightarrow x \text{ is square or } ...]$

If the speaker's behaviour is described in accordance with the demand for immodesty, we get radical indeterminacy in the implicit knowledge that it is supposed to manifest, and with the demand in place the indeterminacy is irremovable:

> If we assume a stable propensity, guided by an unchanging piece of implicit knowledge, we can use further behaviour to rule out some of these competing candidates [e.g. such as (b)]. But no finite set of performances would eliminate them all; and finite sets of performances are all we get. (McDowell 1987: 96)

McDowell's preferred way of avoiding the indeterminacy that plagues Dummett's ascriptions of implicit knowledge to speakers is to adopt what is essentially a form of *non-reductionism* about content. In line with his adherence to modesty, McDowell allows 'square' to appear within the scope of a content-specifying that-clause in the description of the ability possessed by a speaker who means *square* by 'square': it is the ability to use 'square' so as to be understood by speakers of English to be expressing

---

[20] Although McDowell doesn't say so explicitly in this context, the scepticism is akin to that propounded by the sceptic who takes centre stage in Kripke's presentation of the rule-following considerations (Kripke 1982).

the thought that such-and-such is square (see McDowell 1987: 102). McDowell's antipathy to Dummett's invocation of implicit knowledge is an instance of a more general aversion to the notion:

> There is no merit in a conception of the mind that permits us to speculate about its states, conceived as states of a hypothesised mechanism, with a breezy lack of concern for facts about explicit awareness. Postulation of implicit knowledge for such explanatory purposes sheds not scientific light but philosophical darkness. (McDowell 1977: 180)

McDowell's non-reductionist view of meaning deserves an extended treatment not possible in the present essay (see Miller 2007: 234–43 for some elementary exposition and pointers). In the remainder of the essay we will argue (i) that McDowell himself needs to invoke something like implicit knowledge of a theory of meaning if he is to have a satisfactory account of compositionality and semantic creativity, and (ii) that McDowell *can* invoke the notion of implicit knowledge of a theory of meaning in an explanation of semantic creativity without doing violence to the non-reductionist view of meaning he adopts as a moral of the rule-following considerations.

21.7 CAUSAL-INFORMATIONAL STRUCTURE AND LINGUISTIC COMPETENCE

In order to do this, we'll sketch—but not defend—a particular picture of linguistic competence in which a notion of implicit knowledge is invoked in an explanation of semantic creativity. We'll then refer to this picture in our arguments for (i) and (ii).

On this picture, linguistic competence is a causally structured ability—an ability which consists of a set of causally interrelated sub-abilities. To simplify matters, let L1 be the language that results when quantifiers and so on are dropped from L, and take the following to be a formal theory of meaning for L1:

(1) 'Socrates' refers to Socrates
(2) 'Plato' refers to Plato
(3) 'Hume' refers to Hume
(4) 'Kant' refers to Kant
(5) 'Marx' refers to Marx
(6) $\forall x$ [x satisfies 'Greek' $\leftrightarrow$ x is Greek]
(7) $\forall x$ [x satisfies 'Scottish' $\leftrightarrow$ x is Scottish]
(8) $\forall x$ [x satisfies 'German' $\leftrightarrow$ x is German]
(9) $\forall x$ [x satisfies 'Philosopher' $\leftrightarrow$ x is a philosopher]

(10) $\forall x$ [x satisfies 'Female' $\leftrightarrow$ x is female]
(11) A subject-predicate sentence is true-in-L1 if and only if the referent of the name satisfies the predicate

A speaker S of language L1, for example, will have the ability to use the sentence 'Socrates is Greek' so as to be understood by L speakers to be expressing the thought that Socrates is Greek (note that this characterization of the ability is modest). This ability may stand in a particular causal relationship to those that constitute competence with other of L's sentences. For example, a speaker who has never heard or used 'Socrates is Greek' before but who has the relevant abilities to use 'Socrates is Scottish' and 'Marx is Greek' may have come, without further training, to have the ability constitutive of understanding 'Socrates is Greek'. Likewise, a competent speaker who loses the ability constitutive of understanding 'Socrates is Greek' may lose the abilities associated with sentences containing the name or sentences containing the predicate (or both).

Suppose that S is such a speaker. Corresponding to S's ability to use 'Socrates is Greek' so as to be understood as expressing the thought that Socrates is Greek will be a state of implicitly knowing that 'Socrates is Greek' is true-in-L1 if and only if Socrates is Greek. This is a causal-informational state that will be implicated in explaining S's competent use of 'Socrates is Greek'. We can explain the fact that S was able to understand the utterance of 'Socrates is Greek' the first time he heard it in terms of his implicit knowledge of the formal theory for L1 outlined above. The causal-informational state associated with competence with 'Socrates is Greek' is the causal upshot of causal informational states associated with 'Socrates', 'Greek', and the subject-predicate mode of concatenation. Since these causal-informational states are states of implicit knowledge of either theorems or axioms in the formal theory of meaning for L1, we can explain the causal relationships between the relevant abilities by adverting to the derivational structure of the theory: the causal route from competence with 'Socrates', 'Greek', and so on to sentential understanding is mirrored by the fact that in the theory we can derive a theorem specifying the truth-condition of 'Socrates is Greek' on the basis of axioms (1), (6), and (11). Thus, if we view the derivational structure of a formal theory of meaning as mirroring the causal relationships between the set of causal-informational states underlying the practical abilities constitutive of linguistic competence, there is a clear sense in which implicit knowledge of such a theory can yield an explanation of semantic creativity.[21]

---

[21] Those familiar with the literature on implicit knowledge will recognize the picture of linguistic competence outlined in this section as that associated with the 'mirror constraint' on formal theories of meaning. See Evans 1981 and Davies 1987. Note that on Evans's view theories of meaning satisfying the mirror constraint don't contribute to the explanation of semantic creativity. The explanatory use of the mirror constraint in the text is closer to that proposed by Davies. For more on Evans and Davies, see Wright 1986 and Miller 1997.

21.8 McDowell on Modesty and Semantic Structure

In this section, we'll argue that McDowell has a need that the picture of linguistic competence sketched in the previous section would satisfy.

McDowell considers Dummett's worry that a modest theory of meaning fails to display the meaning of a sentence as dependent on the meaning of its constituents. McDowell writes:

> [I]n order to claim that a modest theory effects no segmentation of the ability to speak a language into component abilities, Dummett must disallow as irrelevant a segmentation effected 'as from inside' the contents expressible in the language, by specifications of practical abilities in such forms as 'the ability to use 'NN' so as to be understood by speakers of the language to be expressing thoughts about NN'. Here, too, it is tendentious to equate the thesis that the capacity to speak a language should be articulated 'from inside' content, on the one hand, with a picture of that capacity as wholly devoid of structure, on the other. (McDowell 1987: 102)[22]

Is the segmentation of the ability to speak a language offered by a modest theory of meaning intended to contribute to an explanation of speakers' capacities to understand novel utterances? It is difficult to see how it can. Suppose that a speaker can understand sentences containing 'NN' and also sentences containing 'flies'. Can a modest theory explain how it is that such a speaker can understand a novel utterance of 'NN flies' without the need for further training? According to the modest theory the ability constitutive of understanding 'NN flies' is: the ability to use 'NN flies' so as to be understood by speakers of the language to be expressing the thought that NN flies; while the abilities constitutive of understanding 'NN' and 'flies' are, respectively, the ability to use 'NN' so as to be understood to be expressing thoughts about NN and the ability to use 'flies' to be expressing thoughts about flying. Clearly, on its own, this tells us nothing informative about how it is possible for a speaker to have the ability to understand 'NN flies' on the basis of the abilities associated with 'NN' and 'flies'. As such, it yields no explanation of semantic creativity.

Might McDowell respond that this objection can be thwarted via reflection on the platitudinous connection between linguistic understanding and grasp of truth-conditions? He writes:

> There is a truistic connection between the notion of the content of an assertion and a familiar notion of truth ... the connection guarantees, as the merest platitude,

---

[22] A theory that describes linguistic practice 'as from inside' content is simply a modest theory of meaning (so that a full-blooded theory is one that offers such descriptions 'as from outside' content).

that a correct specification of what can be asserted, by the assertoric utterance of a sentence, cannot but be a specification of a condition under which the sentence is true. (McDowell 1981: 319)

Mimicking Wright (1993: 18), it is easy to show that this entails that to understand a sentence is to know its truth-condition. Take any declarative sentence 'P' and competent speaker S who understands 'P'. Then, trivially, S knows what 'P' says. What 'P' says is that a particular state of affairs, P, obtains. By the 'truistic connection', the obtaining of state of affairs P is necessary and sufficient for the truth of 'P'. So S understands the assertoric content of 'P' to be that a particular state of affairs, necessary and sufficient for its truth, obtains. So S 'knows the truth-condition' of 'P'. Given that the truth-condition will be derivable, in the theory of meaning, from axioms governing its constituents, might we here have the makings of an explanation of semantic creativity? It seems not. Even if we were able, by a similar manoeuvre, to redescribe understanding of the constituents of a sentence in terms of knowledge of the relevant axioms of a theory of meaning, it is clear that we would not have enough material for an explanation of creativity: from platitudes only platitudes flow, so we would have at most the platitude that if someone understands the vocabulary and syntax of a sentence then they understand the sentence. As Wright points out, this platitude 'need only be regarded as describing a feature of the "grammar" of *misunderstanding*; nobody may properly be regarded as misunderstanding a sentence unless guilty of some more specific misunderstanding, either of the words deployed within it or its syntax' (Wright 1986: 208). A speaker's understanding of the vocabulary and syntax of a sentence would not be taken 'to describe an ulterior state of information which *enables* a subject to understand the sentence' (Wright 1986: 208). As such, the materials provided by McDowell are not sufficient for an explanation of semantic creativity.[23]

This is perhaps a reflection of the fact that McDowell, like Dummett and Davidson before him, eschews the idea that there might be a substantial epistemic relation between speakers of a language and the axioms of a theory of meaning for that language. McDowell writes, of knowledge of the truths expressed by such axioms, 'that we are concerned with these states of knowledge, not as actually possessed by all competent speakers, but as such that someone who possessed them would be able to use them in order to arrive by inference at the knowledge about particular speech acts that a fluent hearer acquires by unreflective perception' (McDowell 1977: 182). We saw above (§21.4)

---

[23] In his response to Dummett 1987, McDowell rejects the idea that 'no articulation of mastery of a language is effected by saying things like, in effect: 'agile' is used in this language to predicate agility of things' (McDowell 1997: 119). He continues: 'That exemplifies a kind of statement that is specifically about a single atom of the language, but could be exploited, together with suitable similar statements about other expressions, so as to display how what can be done with whole utterances containing the atom—as characterized, of course, in terms of what thought is expressed, perhaps in some specific mode—depends on the presence of that atom in the form of words uttered' (McDowell 1997: 119). This may be so, but it is unclear that anything McDowell offers us here takes us beyond describing 'a feature of the grammar of misunderstanding' in the sense mentioned in the text.

that the Davidson–Foster view of the aims of a theory of meaning faces insurmountable difficulties, and also (§21.5) that despite advertisements to the contrary, Dummett was unable to improve on it. In a way, it is unsurprising that McDowell takes us no further. He shares Dummett's view of the aims of a theory of meaning, with the only difference being that he loosens Dummett's restrictions on the description of the abilities in which linguistic understanding is said to consist. As such, it is no surprise that his account succumbs to similar objections—and this is underlined by the fact that his talk of 'segmentation' of abilities is of no explanatory value.

Given that the picture sketched in §21.7 does promise an explanation of semantic creativity in terms of a substantial epistemic relation between a speaker and a formal theory of meaning, we can say that that picture would satisfy a need left unsatisfied by McDowell's account. But can a non-reductionist picture of meaning inspired by the rule-following considerations embrace such a picture? We'll now argue that it can.

21.9 JUDGEMENT-DEPENDENCE, IMPLICIT KNOWLEDGE, AND MEANING

In order to do this, we'll first show that the non-reductionist view of meaning that Crispin Wright (1942–) proposes in his judgement-dependent account of meaning is consistent with the kind of explanation of semantic creativity that would be delivered by a view along the lines of that sketched in § 21.7. We'll then suggest that McDowell's non-reductionist position can be viewed as a modified form of Wright's judgement-dependent view, and that it too can thus live side-by-side with the position sketched in § 21.7.

According to Wright, there is a good case to be made for the claim that our optimal judgements about the colours of middle-sized objects *constitutively determine* the truth about the colours of those objects. This case consists in showing that in a provisional equation such as

(α) Conditions C obtain → (S judges that an object x is red ↔ x is red)

we can elaborate conditions C on optimal judgement and the notion of a suitable subject in such a way that (α) is *a priori, non-trivial*, and satisfies two further conditions that Wright calls the *independence* condition (roughly that whether in a given context the prevailing conditions are optimal and a given subject suitable must be logically independent of facts about the extension of redness) and the *extremal* condition (that the claim that optimal judgements constitutively determine the truth about colour is the best explanation of (α)'s satisfying the a prioricity, non-triviality, and independence conditions). In contrast, according to Wright, no such case can be made in the case of a provisional equation for shape such as (β) Conditions C obtain → (S judges that an object x is square ↔ x is square)

so that optimal judgements about shape must be viewed as merely *tracking* or *detecting*—as opposed to constitutively determining—the facts about shape (see Wright 1988).

For our present purposes, the important point about the judgement-dependent view of colour—on which optimal judgements about colour constitutively determine the truth about colour—is the following. Take

    (χ) It is because certain objects are red that they are judged to be red by a suitable subject S in optimal conditions C

and

    (δ) It is because they are judged to be red by a suitable subject S in optimal conditions C that certain objects are red.

On the face of it, it might look as if (χ) and (δ) are inconsistent, so that the judgement-dependent account of redness, which via (α) is committed to (δ), must rule out the idea that the colour judgements of suitable subjects in optimal conditions can be empirically explained in terms of facts about the colours of objects. However, Wright points out that there is no inconsistency so long as the 'because' in (χ) is that of *empirical explanation* and the 'because' in (δ) is that of *conceptual determination*. (α) and (δ) are

> quite consistent with the belief that, *as it happens*, there are interesting underlying physical characteristics in common among the objects which best opinions determine as, say, red; characteristics which are involved in the aetiology of, inter alia, those very opinions, and which, by—as it happens—being common to and distinctive of red things, have a case to be regarded as physically constitutive of redness. (Wright 1992: 132)

The difference between judgement-dependent and judgement-independent views of colour emerges when we reflect on their respective implications vis-à-vis counterfactual scenarios in which it turns out that objects that are deemed to be red by optimal judgements share no interesting underlying physical characteristics. In this kind of scenario—where the physical properties implicated in the aetiology of optimal judgement about redness are wildly heterogeneous—judgement-independent views are committed to the claim that it has been discovered that nothing is red, while judgement-dependent views are committed only to the weaker claim that although some things are red, it has been discovered that redness is not a causally unified kind. (Compare this with a natural kind concept such as *gold*: substances that according to visually determined optimal judgement are gold may not in fact be gold—they may be *fool's gold*. So a judgement-dependent account of gold is ruled out. This contrasts with colours: there could be no such thing as *fool's redness*.) So, judgement-dependent views of colour are consistent with the legitimacy of *colour physics*, the empirical investigation of the physical states that are implicated in the aetiology of optimal judgement about colour. All that judgement-dependent accounts entail is that the possibility of colour physics is not delivered courtesy of the *semantics* of colour terms in conjunction with the fact that some ascriptions of colours are true. If colour physics is possible, that is an *empirical* fact about us and the world that we happen to occupy that is additional to what is implied by the semantics of colours terms and the truth of some ascriptions of colours.

The main conclusions Wright draws from the rule-following considerations are that a judgement-independent view of meaning is untenable and that a judgement-dependent account promises an epistemologically satisfying form of non-reductionism about meaning (see e.g. Wright 1989). According to Wright, we can specify conditions C and the notion of a suitable subject in such a way that

> (α1) Conditions C obtain → (S judges that he means addition by '+' ↔ he means addition by '+')

can be seen to comply with the a prioricity, non-triviality, independence, and extremal conditions.[24] For present purposes, the important point to note is that this is consistent with both

> (χ1) It is because suitable subjects mean addition by '+' that in optimal conditions C they judge themselves to mean addition by '+'.

and

> (δ1) It is because suitable subjects in optimal conditions C judge themselves to mean addition by '+' that they mean addition by '+'

so long as the occurrence of 'because' in (χ1) is that of empirical explanation and the occurrence in (δ1) that of conceptual determination. As in the colour case, that (χ1) is an empirical truth is consistent with (α1)'s satisfying the various conditions on judgement-dependence. So, the judgement-dependent account of meaning is consistent with the idea that understanding 'Socrates is Greek' to mean that Socrates is Greek is as a matter of empirical fact a causally efficacious kind. Arguably, there is nothing in the judgement-dependent account of meaning inconsistent with the idea that the causally efficacious kind that is as a matter of fact understanding 'Socrates is Greek' to mean that Socrates is Greek is a causal-informational state of the sort described in § 21.7: a state of implicitly knowing that 'Socrates is Greek' is true if and only if Socrates is Greek. And there is nothing in the judgement-dependent account that is inconsistent with the idea that it is because speaker S of language L1 implicitly knows axioms (1), (6), and (11) of the theory

---

[24] For ease of exposition we are here oversimplifying Wright's account, but for present purposes the infelicities that this entails are not to the point.

of meaning for L1 outlined in § 21.7 that he implicitly knows that 'Socrates is Greek' is true-in-L1 if and only if Socrates is Greek. The fact that the derivational route from (1), (6), and (11) to the theorem specifying the truth-conditions of 'Socrates is Greek' mirrors the empirical route from the causal-informational states underlying S's competence with the constituents of the sentence to the causal-informational state underlying his competence with the sentence provides the material for an empirical explanation of S's capacity to understand a novel utterance of 'Socrates is Greek'. Thus, just as a judgement-dependent account of colour is consistent with the legitimacy of an empirical inquiry into the physics of colour, the judgement-dependent account of meaning which Wright takes to be the upshot of the rule-following considerations is consistent with the empirical, cognitive-psychological investigation of the causal-informational states implicated in the explanation of a speaker's capacity to understand novel utterances.[25]

21.10 McDowell, Implicit Knowledge, and Anti-Psychologism

In the previous section, we saw how Wright's non-reductionist view of meaning can be rendered consistent with a cognitive-psychological approach towards explaining semantic creativity. We'll now see, very briefly, how this story can be extended to include the non-reductionist view of meaning that goes along with McDowell's insistence on modest rather than full-blooded formal theories of meaning.

One way of interpreting McDowell's non-reductionism is as follows. Wright's distinction between judgement-independent and judgement-dependent accounts of particular subject matters is tied to a specific view of the conditions under which it is appropriate to think of optimal judgement as merely detecting, tracking, or accessing the facts about that subject matter. As we saw above, Wright thinks that it is only appropriate to view optimal judgement as merely detecting the facts if a provisional equation such as

(ε) Conditions C obtain → (S judges that an object x is F ↔ x is F)

fails to satisfy the a prioricity, non-triviality, independence, or extremal conditions. In cases where (ε) does satisfy the four conditions, optimal judgement must be view as *constitutively determining* the facts about F-ness as opposed to merely tracking, detecting, or accessing them. Wright argues that since

(α1) Conditions C obtain → (S judges that he means addition by '+' ↔ he means addition by '+')

---

[25] For Wright's own—different and arguably less attractive—account of how a judgement-dependent account of meaning can coexist with a cognitive-psychological explanation of semantic creativity see Wright 1989: 200–1.

satisfies the four conditions, we must accept an *anti-realist* view of meaning on which it is constitutively determined by optimal judgement.

McDowell regards his non-reductionist view of meaning as a *realist* view of meaning, and one way to make sense of this is as follows. McDowell uses the rule-following considerations, not to place meaning on one side of a divide between cases where optimal judgement merely detects the facts and cases where it constitutes them, but rather to undermine the very notion of detection that underlies Wright's conception of the contrast between judgement-independence and judgement-dependence. Arguably, McDowell can be viewed as jettisoning the independence and extremal conditions, and as proposing a conception of detection on which the non-trivial aprioricity of (α1) is consistent with the idea that optimal judgement merely tracks or detects the facts about meaning. It is impossible to do more than merely advertise this interpretation of McDowell's non-reductionism here (for more, see Miller 1998). If it could be sustained and defended, it would yield a view that was non-reductionist (and therefore consistent with modesty in the theory of meaning), realist (since optimal judgement is no longer viewed as playing a constitutive role), and explanatory of the first-person epistemology of meaning (via the provision of an account of the conditions under which semantic judgements in an unexceptionable sense detect the facts about what we mean by the expressions of our language). Since the independence condition has been jettisoned, the view avoids a number of worries about the plausibility and coherence of Wright's anti-realism (Miller 1989; Boghossian 1989; Johnston 1993). Since the view involves a constructive account of a philosophically unexceptionable notion of detection, it avoids the strong form of quietism that renders McDowell's position philosophically unsatisfying for many. Finally, since none of the differences between Wright's view of (α1) and the view attributed to McDowell matter to the argument of the previous section, the view here attributed to McDowell can simply co-opt that argument to show that it too is consistent with the project of seeking a cognitive-psychological explanation of speakers' capacities to understand novel utterances.

Suppose we adopt such a hybrid view: a commitment to McDowell-style modesty in the theory of meaning that coexists with a cognitive-psychological explanation of semantic creativity utilizing the notion of implicit knowledge as described above. Would such a view be a form of 'psychologism' in the pejorative sense used by McDowell? As we saw above (§21.6), psychologism is for McDowell the view of language as a code for thought, with the latter viewed as independently endowed with content. Elsewhere McDowell characterizes psychologism as the view that linguistic understanding is 'something ulterior, lying behind and governing the various performances that … we conceive as its at best partial manifestations, with its existence at best a hypothesis as far as an observer of those performances is concerned' (1981: 322) and also as 'involving hypotheses about inner states of the speaker lying behind the behaviour' (1981: 331). Avoiding psychologism, according to McDowell, requires the thought that 'there can be facts that are overtly available (so that the conviction that they obtain need not be a matter of speculation as to something hidden behind what is overtly available), but awareness of which is an exercise of a perceptual capacity that is not necessarily universally shared' (1981: 331–2). There is nothing in the view we are currently considering that rules out the anti-psychologistic thought referred to by McDowell. Understanding 'Socrates is Greek' in the normal way is, on this view, a matter of having the ability to use the sentence 'Socrates is Greek' so as to be understood by speakers of English to be expressing the thought that Socrates is Greek. The fact that a causal-informational state of implicitly knowing that 'Socrates is Greek' is true-in-English is implicated in exercises of that ability, and that that state itself is the causal product of states of implicit knowledge of semantic axioms, in no way implies that in manifesting the ability a speaker cannot make what he means—that Socrates is Greek—directly available to another speaker. I can hypothesize—if I am struck by curiosity about your capacity to understand novel utterances—about the causal-informational states underlying your linguistic abilities, but I do not need to form such hypotheses in order to know what you say.[26, 27]

21.11 THE PLACE OF THE THEORY OF MEANING IN ANALYTIC PHILOSOPHY

At the outset of this discussion, we noted that a full survey of the development of theories of meaning would require a full history of analytic philosophy itself. The reason for

[26] Given that the hybrid view is consistent with modesty, if McDowell is right that immodesty 'can only be justified on the basis of the psychologism rejected [by Frege]' (1977: 195), it is also consistent with Frege's anti-psychologism. This is interesting, given Frege's remark: 'It is astonishing what language can do. With a few syllables it can express an incalculable number of thoughts, so that even if a thought has been grasped by an inhabitant of the Earth for the very first time, a form of words can be found in which it will be understood by someone else to whom it is entirely new' (quoted in Beaney 1997: 320 n6). Frege goes on to suggest that we can understand this and 'how a few parts of sentences can go to make up a great multitude of sentences' if 'we distinguish parts in the thought corresponding to the parts of a sentence, so that the structure of the sentence can serve as the picture of the structure of the thought' (Beaney 1997: 320 n6). Is Frege here hankering after the sort of explanation of semantic creativity whose possibility is left open by the hybrid view?

[27] One objection that would need to be addressed in a fuller presentation turns on the fact that the argument of § 21.9 that prepares the way for the hybrid view appears to imply that the causal structure of a speaker's capacity to speak a language is a *contingent* feature of that capacity. The issue here is related to 'the doctrine of essential linguistic structure'. Sainsbury 1980 and Davies 1986 both argue that the structure of a language is a contingent feature of the language, which on the hybrid view amounts to the claim that the causal structure of a speaker's linguistic ability is a contingent feature of that ability; two speakers might speak the same language despite having linguistic abilities with different underlying causal structures. In contrast, Fricker 1983 argues for a position that appears to be less congenial to the hybrid view: the semantic structure of a language is one of its *essential* features, so that speakers with abilities with different underlying causal structures could not be said to be speaking the same language. I hope to address in future work the delicate question of how this debate impacts on the plausibility of the hybrid view: for some initial thoughts see section 4 of Miller 2011. (Thanks to Ali Saboohi for raising this issue.)

this is that historically, the theory of meaning has been viewed, not just as one important area of philosophy amongst others in which analytic philosophers have taken an interest, but as occupying a *foundational* role within philosophy. This view is most clearly expressed by Dummett, who describes Frege as 'the fountain-head of analytical philosophy' (Dummett 1978b: 440), and continues:

> Only with Frege was the proper object of philosophy finally established: namely, first, that the goal of philosophy is the analysis of the structure of *thought*; secondly, that the study of *thought* is to be sharply distinguished from the study of the psychological process of *thinking*; and, finally, that the only proper method for analysing thought consists in the analysis of *language*. (1978b: 458)

On this view, philosophy is ultimately grounded in the 'analysis of language', or in the terms we adopted earlier, in the informal theory of meaning. It is a view which Dummett himself shares:

> [T]he theory of meaning is the fundamental part of philosophy that underlies all the others. Because philosophy has, as its first if not its only task, the analysis of meanings, and because, the deeper such analysis goes, the more it is dependent upon a correct general account of meaning, a model for what the understanding of an expression consists in, the theory of meaning, which is the search for such a model, is the foundation for all philosophy, and not epistemology as Descartes misled us into believing. Frege's greatness consists, in the first place, in having perceived this.... We can, therefore, date a whole epoch in philosophy as beginning with the work of Frege, just as we can do with Descartes. (Dummett 1973: 669)

Frege was not alone in attributing a fundamental status to the theory of meaning, as Colin McGinn points out:

> However much interpreters of Wittgenstein's philosophy may disagree, there is one point on which no dispute is to be expected: that Wittgenstein held that the proper way of understanding and resolving philosophical problems lies in arriving at a correct conception of language. Both the *Tractatus* and the *Investigations* are concerned first and foremost with the topic of meaning. So the philosophy of language is not, for Wittgenstein, merely one department of the subject, its results bearing in no essential way upon enquiry in other areas of philosophy; it is, rather, to be conceived as anterior and foundational. (McGinn 1984: xi)

For example, in the *Tractatus* Wittgenstein writes:

> Most of the propositions and questions of philosophers arise from our failure to understand the logic of our language. (Wittgenstein 1921: 4.003)

This view of philosophy is still in place three decades later in the *Philosophical Investigations*:

[Philosophical problems] are, of course, not empirical problems; they are solved, rather, by looking into the workings of our language, and that in such a way as to make us recognize those workings: *in despite of* an urge to misunderstand them. The problems are solved, not by giving new information, but by arranging what we have always known. Philosophy is a battle against the bewitchment of our intelligence by means of language. (Wittgenstein 1953: §109)

On the issue about how best to proceed in the theory of meaning or philosophy of language, Frege and Dummett both subscribe to the view expressed in the passage from Foster quoted at the start of this chapter: that we investigate the nature of meaning via reflecting on what is involved in the construction of formal theories of meaning. As Dummett puts it:

A satisfactory account of the form which such a theory [a formal theory of meaning] would take would answer the fundamental questions of the philosophy of language: what meaning is, and what it is for words and sentences to have the meanings they do. (1993b: 176)

How do traditional philosophical problems appear when seen through the prism of this view of philosophy and the place of the theory of meaning within it? A classic example is provided by Dummett's treatment of the debate between realism and its opponents. Dummett argues that any attempt to construe realism in purely metaphysical terms results at best in *metaphor* or *pictures* (see e.g. the opening chapter of Dummett 1991 for a clear summary of this view). Instead, realism about a particular region of thought and talk has to be construed as the view that our understanding of the sentences in that region consists in grasp of potentially evidence-transcendent truth-conditions, or in other words, that the central concept used in the construction of a formal theory of meaning for that region is an epistemically unconstrained notion of truth. As is well known, Dummett attacks semantic realism using arguments in the philosophy of language such as the 'acquisition argument' and 'manifestation argument'. Whether these arguments succeed needn't concern us here (see Miller 2002, 2003a for a critique). Instead, we can ask: would Dummett's approach to the realism debate survive rejection of the idea that the theory of meaning is foundational and that the literal content of realism about an area is the claim that linguistic understanding consists in grasp of potentially evidence-transcendent truth-conditions? Various philosophers have argued that it can. Although there are other ways of being a realist, embracing semantic realism is 'one way of laying the essential semantic groundwork' for realism in certain areas (Wright 1992: 4); semantic realism is a consequence of the inclusion, as semantic component, of the truth-conditional conception of understanding, in a worldview that incorporates a certain sort of realist metaphysic (Miller 2003b); and 'the attempt to provide a semantic theory that coheres with a given metaphysical claim can ... constitute a searching test of the latter claim, even though semantics and metaphysics are distinct' (Williamson 2006: 182). For example, a metaphysical realist about arithmetic who gave expression to the idea that arithmetical facts are mind-independent via the claim that the nature of arithmetical reality might outrun our best attempts at proof construction would, if Dummett's arguments against semantic realism were convincing, have the task of finding an alternative account of linguistic understanding to that provided by the truth-conditional conception. Although some realists attempt to defuse the Dummettian arguments (e.g. McDowell 1981), others adopt the more radical approach of rejecting the idea that sentential understanding is a matter of *knowledge* of truth-conditions at all (e.g. Devitt 1991, 2006).[28]

We can see, then, that the Frege–Dummett approach to the theory of meaning can remain relevant to metaphysical debate, even if Dummett was wrong to claim that metaphysics is literally *part* of the theory of meaning.

A deeper challenge to the Frege–Dummett approach to the theory of meaning comes from contemporary descendants of what Dummett once called 'particularism' (Dummett 1978b: 448). Recall from § 21.1 that according to Frege, we need to distinguish between *sense* and *force*. As Dummett puts it:

> Those constituents of the sentence which determine its sense associate a certain state of affairs with the sentence; that feature of it which determines the force with which it is uttered fixes the conventional significance of the utterance in relation to that state of affairs (i.e., according as the speaker is asserting that the state of affairs obtains, asking whether it obtains, commanding that it should obtain, expressing a wish that it obtain, etc.). (Dummett 1978b: 449–50)

Dummett thinks that the possibility of constructing a formal theory of meaning for a language requires the good standing of Frege's distinction between sense and force, and that this imposes a shape on formal theories:

> Any theory of meaning … will fall into, broadly, two parts: a core theory, which determines the conditions for the application, to sentences of the language, of some meaning-relevant property (candidates being, for instance, truth or warranted assertibility); and a supplementary part, the theory of force, which gives an account, in terms of the central notion of the core theory, of what it is to effect each of the various types of speech-act. (McDowell 1981: 317–18)[29]

If we could not distinguish between sense and force

> [O]ur theory of meaning must, for each individual sentence, issue in a direct account of the conventional significance of an utterance of that sentence, rather than

---

[28] And, of course, the option favoured by Wright and Dummett themselves is a view on which the truth-conditional conception is retained and the worries about acquisition and manifestation avoided via the imposition of epistemic constraints on the notion of truth. See in particular the Preface to Dummett (1978b) and the Introduction to Wright (1993).

[29] McDowell is here outlining Dummett's view. McDowell goes on to reject Dummett's view of the relationship between the theory of sense and the theory of force, and uses this as part of a defence of realism against Dummett's manifestation argument.

one derived from a general description of the use of sentences of some general category to which it belongs. (Dummett 1978b: 450)[30]

Dummett thinks that this would amount to the repudiation of the very idea of a systematic theory of meaning for a language, and associates the rejection of Frege's distinction between sense and force with the Oxford 'ordinary language' school of philosophy led by J. L. Austin. Although 'ordinary language' philosophy has long been out of fashion, and assumed by many to be dead and buried, in recent years a number of philosophers of language have developed forms of contextualism about meaning that appear to have the same anti-Fregean implications as the rejection of the sense–force distinction by the ordinary language philosophers. We saw in § 21.1 that for Frege the sense of a sentence is the thought that it expresses, where this is taken to be its truth-condition, the condition whose obtaining is necessary and sufficient for its truth; and the truth-condition of a sentence is determined by the senses of its constituents and their mode of syntactic combination. On the view described in § 21.2, in which a formal theory of *Bedeutung* can be made to do duty as a formal theory of sense, this comes down to the view that the truth-condition of a sentence is determined by the *Bedeutungen* of its parts and the way they are put together. An example of a contemporary philosopher who attempts to undermine this view is Charles Travis. Travis writes that according to the later Wittgenstein 'What words name (by way of concepts and objects), and the structured way they do *that*, does *not* determine, uniquely, when they would be true' (Travis 2006: 2–3). For example, 'when, in given circumstances, one speaks of a thing (my car, say) in given terms (one calls it blue, say), what one thus *says* as to how things are, so when one would have spoken truly, is determined by what it is reasonable to expect of that particular describing' (Travis 2006: 30–1). If, for example, in asking you to help find my car in a garage I tell you that it is blue, the fact that it has black upholstery doesn't mean that I spoke falsely, given what it is reasonable to expect of my describing it so in that particular situation (although there are other language games in which that fact would mean that I had spoken falsely). Similarly, if I say of Lake Michigan on a sunny morning, 'The water is blue', on some ways of using those words I may speak truly, but on others not ('where water drawn from the lake would have to look blue—perhaps as minerals, or dye, might make it look' (2006: 32)). The moral that Travis draws is: 'Content is inseparable from point. What is communicated in our words lies, inseparably, in what we would expect of them. How our words represent things is a matter of, and not detachable from, their (recognizable) import for our lives' (2006: 33), and the upshot is the rejection of the Fregean view that 'the fact of a word naming what it does … determines all that is so as to when one would speak truth in using it of something' (2006: 16) and also of the view that *knowledge* of what the parts of an expression of a complete thought name imparts knowledge of the truth-condition of the whole.

---

[30] This explains why Dummett dubs the view that he opposes here 'particularism'.

Can the phenomena highlighted by Travis be accommodated within the Fregean approach favoured by Dummett via the distinction between what a sentence literally says and 'what, in particular circumstances, someone might seek to convey by uttering it' (Dummett 1978b: 445)? The plausibility of the hybrid view sketched in § 21.10 would appear to depend upon the provision of an affirmative answer to this question.[31, 32]

References

Beaney, M. (ed.) (1997). *The Frege Reader.* Oxford: Blackwell.

Boghossian, P. (1989). 'The Rule-Following Considerations'. Repr. in A. Miller and C. Wright (eds.), *Rule-Following and Meaning.* Chesham: Acumen 2002, pp. 141–87.

Davidson, D. (1967). 'Truth and Meaning'. Repr. in Davidson (1984), pp. 17–36.

—— (1973). 'Radical Interpretation'. Repr. in Davidson (1984), pp. 125–40.

—— (1976). 'Reply to Foster'. Repr. in Davidson (1984), pp. 171–9.

—— (1979). 'Moods and Performances'. Repr. in Davidson (1984), pp. 109–21.

—— (1984). *Inquiries into Truth and Interpretation.* Oxford: Clarendon Press.

—— (1990). 'The Structure and Content of Truth', *Journal of Philosophy* 87: 279–328.

Davies, M. (1986). 'Tacit Knowledge and the Structure of Thought and Language'. In C. Travis (ed.), *Meaning and Interpretation.* Oxford: Blackwell, pp. 127–58.

—— (1987). 'Tacit Knowledge and Semantic Theory: Can a 5% Difference Matter?', *Mind* 96: 441–62.

Devitt, M. (1991). *Realism and Truth,* 2nd edn. Princeton, NJ: Princeton University Press.

—— (2006). *Ignorance of Language.* Oxford: Clarendon Press.

Dummett, M. (1973). *Frege: Philosophy of Language.* London: Duckworth.

—— (1975). 'What is a Theory of Meaning? (I)'. Repr. in Dummett (1993), pp. 1–33.

—— (1976). 'What is a Theory of Meaning? (II)'. Repr. in Dummett (1993), pp. 34–83.

—— (1978a). 'What Do I Know When I Know a Language?' Repr. in Dummett (1993), pp. 94–105.

—— (1978b). *Truth and Other Enigmas.* London: Duckworth.

—— (1987). 'Reply to John McDowell'. In B. Taylor (ed.), *Michael Dummett: Contributions to Philosophy.* Dordrecht: Nijhoff, pp. 252–68.

—— (1991). *The Logical Basis of Metaphysics.* Cambridge, MA: Harvard University Press.

—— (1993a). *The Seas of Language.* Oxford: Oxford University Press.

—— (1993b). *Origins of Analytical Philosophy.* Cambridge, MA: Harvard University Press.

Evans, G. (1981). 'Semantic Theory and Tacit Knowledge'. In S. Holtzman and C. Leich (eds.), *Wittgenstein: To Follow a Rule.* London: Routledge, pp. 118–37.

—— (1982). *The Varieties of Reference.* Oxford: Oxford University Press.

Foster, J. (1976). 'Meaning and Truth Theory'. In G. Evans and J. McDowell (eds.), *Truth and Meaning: Essays in Semantics.* Oxford: Clarendon Press, pp. 1–32.

---

[31] As would the idea that the plausibility or otherwise of an epistemically unconstrained notion of truth's playing a central role in formal theories of meaning might provide some leverage in debates between realists and their opponents.

[32] For many stimulating conversations related to the topics covered in this essay, I am grateful to Ali Saboohi. Thanks also to Mike Beaney, Nicholas Melville, and Reza Mosmer.

Frege, G. (1891). 'Function and Concept'. In Beaney (1997), pp. 130–48.

—— (1892a). 'On *Sinn* and *Bedeutung*'. In Beaney (1997), pp. 151–71.

—— (1892b). 'Comments on *Sinn* and *Bedeutung*'. In Beaney (1997), pp. 172–80.

—— (1892c). 'On Concept and Object'. In Beaney (1997), pp. 181–93.

—— (1914). 'Letter to Jourdain'. In Beaney (1997), pp. 319–21.

—— (1918). 'Thought'. In Beaney (1997), pp. 325–45.

Fricker, E. (1983). 'Semantic Structure and Speakers' Understanding', *Proceedings of the Aristotelian Society* 83: 49–66.

Heal, J. (1978). 'On the Phrase "Theory of Meaning"', *Mind* 87: 359–75.

Johnston, M. (1993). 'Objectivity Refigured'. In J. Haldane and C. Wright (eds.), *Reality, Representation and Projection*. Oxford: Oxford University Press, pp. 85–130.

Kölbel, M. (2002). *Truth Without Objectivity*. London: Routledge.

Kripke, S. (1982). *Wittgenstein on Rules and Private Language*. Oxford: Blackwell.

Lepore, E. and Smith, B. (eds.) (2006). *The Oxford Handbook of the Philosophy of Language*. Oxford: Oxford University Press.

McDowell, J. (1977). 'On the Sense and Reference of a Proper Name'. Repr. in McDowell (1998), pp. 171–98.

—— (1981). 'Anti-Realism and the Epistemology of Understanding'. Repr. in McDowell (1998), pp. 314–43.

—— (1987). 'In Defence of Modesty'. Repr. in McDowell (1998), pp. 87–107.

—— (1997). 'Another Plea for Modesty'. Repr. in McDowell (1998), pp. 108–31.

—— (1998). *Meaning, Knowledge and Reality*. Cambridge, MA: Harvard University Press.

McGinn, C. (1984). *Wittgenstein on Meaning*. Oxford: Blackwell.

Miller, A. (1989). 'An Objection to Wright's Treatment of Intention', *Analysis* 49: 169–73.

—— (1997). 'Tacit Knowledge'. In B. Hale and C. Wright (eds.), *A Companion to the Philosophy of Language*. Oxford: Blackwell, pp. 146–74.

—— (1998). 'Response-Dependence, Rule-Following, and McDowell's Debate with Anti-Realism', *European Review of Philosophy* 3. Stanford: CSLI, pp. 175–97.

—— (2002). 'What is the Manifestation Argument?', *Pacific Philosophical Quarterly* 83: 352–83.

—— (2003a). 'What is the Acquisition Argument?' In A. Barber (ed.), *Epistemology of Language*. Oxford: Oxford University Press, pp. 459–95.

—— (2003b). 'The Significance of Semantic Realism', *Synthese* 136: 191–217.

—— (2007). *Philosophy of Language,* 2nd edn. London: Routledge.

—— (2011). 'Judgement-Dependence, Tacit Knowledge and Linguistic Understanding'. In P. Stalmaszczyk (ed.), *Philosophical and Formal Approaches to Linguistic Analysis*. Frankfurt: Ontos, pp. 405–28.

Sainsbury, M. (1979). 'Understanding and Theories of Meaning', *Proceedings of the Aristotelian Society* 80: 127–44.

Segal, G. (2006). 'Truth and Meaning'. In Lepore and Smith (2006), pp. 189–212.

Smith, B. (1992). 'Understanding Language', *Proceedings of the Aristotelian Society* 92: 109–42.

Strawson, P. F. (1971). 'Meaning and Truth'. In Strawson, *Logico-Linguistic Papers*. London: Methuen, pp. 131–46.

Tarski, A. (1944). 'The Semantic Conception of Truth', *Philosophy and Phenomenological Research* 4: 341–75.

—— (1956a). 'The Concept of Truth in Formalized Languages'. In Tarski, *Logic, Semantics, Metamathematics,* ed. and tr. J. H. Woodger. Oxford: Clarendon Press, pp. 152–278.

—— (1956b). 'The Establishment of Scientific Semantics'. In Tarski, *Logic, Semantics, Metamathematics,* ed. and tr. J. H. Woodger. Oxford: Clarendon Press, pp. 401–8.

Travis, C. (2006). *Thought's Footing: A Theme in Wittgenstein's Philosophical Investigations*. Oxford: Oxford University Press.

Williamson, T. (2006). 'Must Do Better'. In P. Greenough and M. Lynch (eds.), *Truth and Realism*. Oxford: Oxford University Press, pp. 177–87.

Wittgenstein, L. (1921). *Tractatus Logico-Philosophicus*, tr. D. Pears and B. McGuiness. London: Routledge & Kegan Paul 1961.

—— (1953). *Philosophical Investigations*, tr. G. E. M. Anscombe. Oxford: Blackwell.

Wright, C. (1986). 'Theories of Meaning and Speakers' Knowledge'. Repr. in Wright (1993), pp. 204–38.

—— (1988). 'Moral Values, Projection and Secondary Qualities'. Repr. in Wright (2003), pp. 155–82.

—— (1989). 'Wittgenstein's Rule-Following Considerations and the Central Project of Theoretical Linguistics'. Repr. in Wright (2001), pp. 170–213.

—— (1992). *Truth and Objectivity*. Cambridge, MA: Harvard University Press.

—— (1993). *Realism, Meaning and Truth*, 2nd edn. Oxford: Blackwell.

—— (2001). *Rails to Infinity*. Cambridge, MA: Harvard University Press.

—— (2003). *Saving the Differences*. Cambridge, MA: Harvard University Press.

CHAPTER 22

....

REASONS, ACTIONS, AND THE WILL: THE FALL AND RISE OF CAUSALISM

....

STEWART CANDLISH AND NIC DAMNJANOVIC

22.1 INTRODUCTION

....

At the time that Donald Davidson published his influential article 'Actions, Reasons and Causes' (1963), many of his contemporaries were convinced that reasons for action could not be causes of anything, so that even an explanation such as 'Gilbert knelt *because* he had decided to propose to Gertrude' did not work by citing Gilbert's decision as a cause of his kneeling. Davidson was mainly responsible for demolishing that consensus and reinstating causalism—the thesis that psychological or rationalizing explanations of human behaviour are a species of event-causal explanation—as the dominant view in the philosophy of action, so that it is now often regarded as an obvious truth.

Davidson's advocacy of causalism had a profound effect on twentieth-century philosophy. Not only did it reshape the philosophy of action, it also contributed directly to forming the new consensus view in the philosophy of mind that psychological events or states are physical, spatially internal, and capable of standing in causal relations. More generally again, by re-establishing the doctrine that explanations of intentional human behaviour are a species of causal explanation, Davidson invigorated the project of providing a complete naturalistic account of the mind. Indeed, this project caught the attention of a generation of philosophers, and gave a characteristic profile to the entire philosophical landscape of the latter half of the twentieth century.[1]

---

[1] Interesting in this regard is A. J. Ayer's *Man as a Subject for Science* (1964), which supported the naturalistic project in part by dismissing many of the same arguments against causalism that Davidson had attacked a few months before. As John Heil (2009) makes clear, another seminal figure in the rise of causalism was C. B. Martin.

A common account of the growth of the new consensus presents it as a synthesis of the thesis of dualism and the antithesis of behaviourism.[2] In the philosophy of action, the dualist position was represented by volitionism—the idea that intentional actions are caused by (or contain as a causally active component) mental states or processes of a certain sort: generically, 'volitions', a special sort of mental state or process 'by means of which a mind gets its ideas translated into facts' (Ryle 1949: 63); they might be acts of will, intentions, tryings, decidings, or ...[3] With rare exceptions, the truth of volitionism was casually assumed by philosophers until Ryle's 1949 attack on it in *The Concept of Mind*.[4] After this attack, its *falsehood* was just as casually assumed and, according to the story standardly retailed in textbooks in the philosophy of mind, it was replaced by philosophical behaviourism, according to which psychological terms like 'intention' or 'motive' do not refer to inner mental states and instead are to be analysed in terms of publicly observable behaviour or dispositions for behaviour. The story associates this view with Ryle and other so-called 'neo-Wittgensteinians',[5] and displays Davidson's role in establishing physicalistic realism as demolishing the (alleged) behaviourism of the neo-Wittgensteinians by exposing their sloppy arguments against causalism. More positively, it continues, he suggested that causalism, unlike its contemporary rivals, provided the only clear and scientifically respectable account of psychological explanation.[6]

The usual story is unfortunate in several ways. It treats the 'neo-Wittgensteinians' (already a diverse group) as one and all behaviourists, when in fact few were. It also ignores the fact that they were not alone in rejecting causalism. Several philosophers in the mid-twentieth century defended agent-causation—the position that *agents* (not events) are the causes of actions—and also attacked causalism.[7] (Probably, Davidson's

---

[2] The Hegelian talk is Armstrong's (1968: 129), but the underlying idea is common.

[3] Volitionism's central idea is not essentially dualist, since volitions might be physical. However, the label is now generally reserved for dualist versions. Sometimes the terms 'conationism' and 'internalism' are employed. These have the advantage of covering dualist versions which eschew the term 'volition', and materialist forms of the idea too.

[4] Traditional volitionists (though this label conceals a very mixed bag of fine distinctions) include Descartes, Hobbes, Locke, Berkeley, Hume, Reid, Bentham, and Mill. In the twentieth century, the main proponent of the view prior to Ryle's attack was H. A. Prichard (1932, 1945), perhaps the first modern philosopher to have focused intensely on the topic.

[5] Two prominent examples of such an attribution: Armstrong (1968: 54–5) calls both Wittgenstein and Ryle behaviourists, even while acknowledging their refusals of the label; Danto (1973: 46 and 205n21) calls the later Wittgenstein and also the 'Wittgensteinians' Anscombe, Kenny, and Melden behaviourists. Another influential voice here is that of Fodor (1968).

[6] Davidson's position here has much in common with Fodor's (1968). One odd feature of this story is already apparent, however, since the 'neo-Wittgensteinian' alternative to causalism was a teleological form of explanation which was also dismissed by psychological behaviourists as being unscientific. For a detailed response to the claim that teleological explanations are unscientific see Taylor (1964). Also interesting is Anscombe's short review of Taylor (Anscombe 1965).

[7] Collingwood (1940) was an early proponent of agent-causation. At the start of his *Action and Purpose* (1966: ix), Richard Taylor acknowledged the influence of Melden, Ryle, and Anscombe, before going on to defend the notion of agent-causation and deny that reasons are causes. Recent defenders of agent-causation who deny that reasons are causes include Timothy O'Connor (2000) and E. J. Lowe (2008).

defence of causalism itself was partly responsible for this position's fading from view, since it is widely believed that agent-causation is inconsistent with naturalism.) Most importantly, however, it misses the fact that Davidson's critique of the 'neo-Wittgensteinian' arguments against causalism ignored the most powerful arguments offered by Wittgenstein himself and two of the most famous of the group, Ryle and Anscombe.[8] Without committing themselves to a denial of mental causation of action, each of these philosophers argued that the causalist picture of action leads to one or other of a range of unpalatable consequences. Unsurprisingly, Davidson ended up committed to some of these consequences, about which he had been warned. Or so we shall argue.

We proceed by outlining the arguments of Wittgenstein (§ 22.2), Ryle (§ 22.3), and Anscombe (§ 22.4) against causalism and the related doctrine that intentional actions are caused by interior mental events. In § 22.5 we turn to Davidson's defence of causalism.

22.2 WITTGENSTEIN

Wittgenstein's discussion of the will, intention, and action in *Philosophical Investigations* is as suggestive as it is difficult. In particular, his treatment of the will is so condensed that its argument is barely visible and it is hard to believe that on its own it exerted much direct influence at the time.[9] Nevertheless, Wittgenstein's lectures and conversations had a powerful subterranean impact, and it is worth outlining this treatment as an indication of what lay behind the anti-causalism that Davidson attacked. Its main theme is the rejection of the conception of acts of will as originating causes of our bodily actions. He argues for this by exploring the two versions this conception inevitably takes: an empiricist form (found in the writings of James and Russell), in which acts of will are supposed to be phenomena, discernible in experience; and a transcendental form (inherited by the author of the *Tractatus* from his reading of Schopenhauer) in which they are thought of as lying outside the realm of phenomena. He suggests that thinking of the will in this way binds one into a permanent oscillation between these two unsatisfactory versions, each a response to an unsolvable problem with the other, the only escape being to abandon the underlying causal conception. That is, his main target is not volitionism, but a deeper picture that motivates the volitional view, as well as many other accounts of intentional action. The deeper picture is not quite causalism either, but something more general again. It is the idea that the will is the *executive function* of the mind.[10]

---

[8] It is striking that Davidson, in his seminal paper, despite mentioning by name 'many recent writers' (Davidson 1963: 3), singles out for detailed and documented treatment only Melden, probably the weakest of an anyway motley group. Melden's total reliance upon a Humean conception of causation made him particularly vulnerable. It seems to us that subsequent philosophers have tended to assume that Davidson thereby did for the lot of them.

[9] Its most obvious influence is on the work of Brian O'Shaughnessy, culminating in his *The Will* (1980).

[10] Given constraints of space, we have suppressed most of the detail of, and justification for, our interpretation of Wittgenstein. For the fuller story see Candlish (1991, 2001).

Wittgenstein's treatment of the will in *Philosophical Investigations* begins at § 611 with this strange remark from an interlocutor: "'Willing too is merely an experience", one would like to say ... I cannot bring it about.' The source of this remark is the empiricist perspective we just mentioned. From that perspective, our fairly strong first-person authority about action—when something happens involving me, I can usually say whether or not it's something I've *done*—is bound to suggest that willing is a kind of experience. But we can't *do* an experience, so willing is not something we 'bring about'.[11]

There is more than just an empiricist assumption pushing in this direction, though. Working through it is the executive picture of the will. Wittgenstein attributes (§ 613) his use of the wrong expression 'cannot bring about' to a 'misleading analogy', that is, thinking of willing in terms of causally connected mechanisms that can be exploited as means (as one might press a button to ring a bell). On this conception, willing is the primary action which is the origin of our outwardly perceptible acts. Then, when faced with the obvious fact that we do not in the ordinary cases employ indirect means of moving our bodies (§§ 614–16), we are forced to think of willing as a peculiarly direct bringing about (a kind Wittgenstein misleadingly labels 'non-causal'—but all he means by this here is 'not working indirectly through a mechanism'). Then we note that there can be no such direct bringing about of willing itself: so we are obliged to conclude that our own actions are beyond the reach of our own powers!

But if willing is not a phenomenal doing, then what might it be? As long as we maintain the 'misleading analogy', there seems to be only one option: willing is a non-phenomenal, ineffable, or transcendental doing, and the willing subject must be non-phenomenal, a 'motor which in itself has no inertia to overcome. So it is only mover, not moved' (§ 618). This idea is given free rein in § 620:

> *Doing* itself seems not to have any volume of experience. It seems like an extension-less point, the point of a needle. This point seems to be the real agent. And the phenomenal happenings only to be consequences of this acting. 'I *do* ...' seems to have a definite sense, separate from all experience.

Yet with his very next sentence, 'But let us not forget this: when "I raise my arm", my arm goes up' (§ 621), Wittgenstein brings us immediately back to earth by reminding us that our doings include real, physical events.[12]

The famous question of § 621 follows immediately: 'And the problem arises: what is left over if I subtract the fact that my arm goes up from the fact that I raise my arm?' This question has occasionally been put to perverse use by being removed from the context of

---

[11] Compare '[W]hatever phenomenon you take is something that *simply happens*, something we undergo, not something we *do*' (Wittgenstein 1974: § 97).

[12] The crucial word 'But', which should open § 621, was omitted from Anscombe's translation, so that the point, which is to remind us that there *are* phenomena involved in action, has been lost. Once it is restored we can easily see the connection between the last sentence of § 620 above and the first of § 621.

§ 620 and treated as one which arises in its own right, with the talk of subtraction made to look straightforward.[13] But it is clear that what is being asked is, given that 'I *do* ...' *seems* to have a sense separate from all experience but that action does involve experiential phenomena, are these phenomena merely consequences of that doing? What do we find if we attempt to subtract the seemingly non-active consequential phenomena from the total action? The earlier and rather easier discussion at *Philosophical Grammar* § 97 helps:

> Very well; but there's no doubt that you *also* have experiences when you voluntarily move your arm; because you *see* (and feel) it moving whether or not you take up the attitude of an *observer*. So just for once try to distinguish between *all the experiences* of acting plus the doing (which is not an experience) and *all* those experiences without the element of doing. Think over whether you still need this element, or whether it is beginning to appear redundant.

Here, as in *Philosophical Investigations* §§ 620–1, only the metaphysical answer is under consideration. Responding to § 621's question with 'Nothing is left over in experience' is not a proof that there is something left over which is *not* in experience, an 'extensionless point' which is the real doing.

Wittgenstein is trying to guide us between two poles: one, that willing is an interior phenomenal experience; the other, that the will is transcendental. What the two poles have in common is the 'misleading analogy' of the will as a mechanism, the executive function of the mind. Moreover, when we try unsuccessfully to fulfil our intentions, the willing must also be identified with the *trying*. The problem is that the misleading analogy suggests that if, in the case of failure, willing is trying, then since willing is a mechanism, the same mechanism must be in operation when we succeed. Thus, even when we succeed, what we do immediately is try. When we see the act of willing as something lying behind the act, we are led to the view that there must be actions that we do immediately, with no gap between the willing and the acting. But since, with any ordinary act, failure is possible, we are also led to the conationist view that there must be some common factor found in all actions and willings, and the trouble is identifying this infallible commonality. Wittgenstein has already argued against this view, but there is another worry that has now arisen, since, according to him, when we succeed the willing is the act (of walking or speaking, etc.) itself (§ 615).

Wittgenstein's overall strategy has been to try to show that all the views consistent with the idea that the will is an executive relation between us and our physical acts are hopeless. But he also offered more direct reasons for doubting the 'causal' model of intentional action. He pointed out that when we intend to do something, and do it, we are not surprised by the fact that the appropriate events take place. Yet this lack of surprise is not at all like when we have earlier predicted that something will come to pass.

---

[13] For example, McCann (1974).

'I am going to take two powders now, and in half-an-hour I shall be sick.' ... It was
not on grounds of observation of my behaviour that I said I was going to take two
powders. The antecedents of this proposition were different. I mean the thoughts,
actions and so on which led up to it. (§ 631)

As the surrounding discussion makes clear, Wittgenstein intends to distinguish
between prediction based on observation and our knowing that we will do something. We are not first acquainted with some thoughts or actions which cause (or more
loosely 'bring about') certain physical results and from which we predict those results.
'Intention' does not belong alongside those causal-explanatory concepts we deploy in
predicting future events.

What, then, is the right picture of intentional action? The discussion is frustratingly
incomplete, but the broad outlines of an account are discernible. An action is intentional
not in virtue of some intention or doing lying behind it, but by being embedded in the
surrounding circumstances in certain ways. For example:

'I am not ashamed of what I did then, but of the intention which I had.'—And didn't
the intention lie *also* in what I did? What justifies the shame? The whole history of
the incident. (§ 644)

Although this is suggestive, we don't get much more. At best, Wittgenstein has provided some ingredients for a better picture of intentional action. Some of these ingredients are: the importance of the place of the action in its context, the special epistemic
access we have both to our intentions and our intentional actions, and the unimportance
of interior mental events.[14] What other ingredients are required and how we should
combine them is left unspecified. We are also left with other questions. For example,
does Wittgenstein's hostility to interior acts of intention amount to some form of behaviourism?[15] Did he mean to deny the seemingly obvious truth that our intentions or reasons for action *bring about* our intentional actions? These are hard interpretative and
historical questions, which we cannot further explore here. Instead, we examine how
Wittgenstein's remarks were interpreted and developed by those who shared his hostility to causalism.

22.3 RYLE

In *The Concept of Mind*, Ryle launched an attack on what he labelled 'the official doctrine', the idea that human beings are made up of two things, a physical body and
a mind which is the subject of all psychological predicates. His basic target was a

---

[14] There is some (but not much) filling out of the picture in *Zettel* (1967) §§ 577–99.

[15] Wittgenstein quite clearly wanted to distance himself from behaviourism. See § 308, for example.

para-mechanical, causal conception of the mind that led to thinking of it as hidden, interior, and non-spatial; he tried to dismantle both the central doctrine itself and its particular manifestations, including the view of intentional actions as being 'brought about' by interior acts of intention. Ryle termed this view the 'doctrine of volitions', thus using the vocabulary of certain versions of the theory in mounting a sweeping attack on all of its forms by rejecting the governing idea that physical actions are those amongst physical movements which are *caused* by mental volitions (1949: ch. VI).

Of Ryle's various arguments, one, a kind of trilemma which bears a striking resemblance to Wittgenstein's two-poles treatment, was particularly compelling. It begins by noting that the point of the doctrine of volitions is to distinguish those movements which are actions from those which are not—or, as Ryle puts it, voluntary from involuntary movements. It does this by postulating a distinctive causal background for the voluntary movements: they are those, and only those, which are preceded and caused by volitions. If my arm goes up without this being caused by a prior volition, then this is a mere arm-rising; but if the volition causes the arm-rising, then we have a case of arm-raising. Now volitions, on this theory, are mental events. But, Ryle points out, the distinction between voluntary and involuntary applies to mental events as well as to physical ones—for example, something can just remind me of my sister, so that I think of her involuntarily, or I can deliberately start to think of her. In the latter case, but not in the former, a volition must have occurred, because it is itself a voluntary mental event. So of any mental event, just as of any physical event, it can be asked whether it was voluntarily or involuntarily produced. Hence we can ask this question of a volition too. But this possibility is fatal to the doctrine.

Why is it fatal? If a volition is involuntary, it cannot do its supposed job of bestowing voluntariness upon an external movement. But if it is voluntarily produced, then, because of the volitionist account of the nature of voluntariness, it must have this character of voluntariness because of its being caused by a prior volition. The same question, 'voluntary or not?', can then be asked of the prior volition, with the same range of possible answers. Thus either we stop the posing of the questions by resting the voluntary upon the involuntary, which seems to destroy the voluntariness we are trying to explain, or we embark upon an infinite regress of volitions in which we end up having to do an infinite number of things before we can succeed in doing anything at all. That is, either action turns out to originate with something inactive, merely passive, or we have to be infinitely active to be active at all.

If we try to escape between the horns of this dilemma by holding volitions to be special, being neither voluntary nor involuntary, then—quite apart from the puzzling character this seems to give them—this would enable us to escape moral responsibility for our volitions, since we are morally responsible only for what we do voluntarily. This would be an intolerable consequence, however, for it would mean that if, for example, I performed a volition which would normally have resulted in someone's murder, but for some reason the volition did not produce the usual result, then I would be completely blameless. Yet clearly I am morally blameworthy in such a case. Any theory which prevents moral predicates from being applied to volitions must be mistaken. Furthermore, if volitions are not the sort of thing we produce 'at will', and yet are necessary causal conditions for acting, then it appears we must wait for them to arise before we can do anything.[16]

So, no matter whether volitions are held to be voluntary or involuntary or neither—and this surely exhausts the possibilities—the consequences are unacceptable. Hence any theory of action which works in terms of volitions must be wrong. Moreover, if the argument works at all, it undermines all versions of causalism. For as long as any type of event causes our voluntary actions we can ask of it, 'Is it voluntarily produced, involuntary, or neither?'

In terms of its negative programme, Ryle's discussion has much in common with Wittgenstein's. But what about his positive discussion? As we mentioned, Ryle is often, indeed typically, characterized as a 'logical behaviourist'. And it is not hard to see how this attribution came to be made, despite his protestations in *The Concept of Mind*. In outlining what it is to act from a motive like vanity, Ryle famously suggested that 'The statement "He boasted from vanity" ... is to be construed as saying "he boasted on meeting the stranger and his doing so satisfies the law-like proposition that whenever he finds a chance of securing the admiration and envy of others, he does whatever he thinks will produce this admiration and envy"' (1949: 89). And in explaining voluntary action he argued that one who acts voluntarily does something (e.g. breaks a window) even though they had the capacity (the know-how) to do otherwise. Our attributions of voluntary action rely on ascertaining that the agent had the relevant capacities and the opportunity to employ them. All of this is done, of course, by appeal to publicly observable behaviour.

Nevertheless, Ryle should not be characterized as a logical behaviourist. For one thing, he did not shrink from talk of inner mental processes.[17] For another, logical behaviourism is an attempt to fit the mind in general, and intentional action in particular, into the physical realm by reducing mental properties to physical properties (or dispositional properties) of a certain sort—namely publicly observable behaviour. Yet Ryle saw physicalism as the other side of the coin of the 'official doctrine' and counselled us not to turn the coin over, but to throw it away. Like Wittgenstein, for Ryle the mistake of both behaviourists and dualists was to treat mental concepts as if they were causal-explanatory concepts that referred to properties whose nature stands in need of explication.[18]

Throughout *The Concept of Mind*, Ryle argued that it was a mechanistic view of the universe that led to dualism, since it was the search for inner, mechanistic causes of outer behaviour that led to that position. And it is clear that Ryle is opposed not just to dualism, but to the mechanistic view that he thought motivates it. In other words, explanations of behaviour in terms of reasons, intentions, and motives should not be seen

---

[16] Compare Wittgenstein (1953: § 612).

[17] P. M. S. Hacker (2007: 26n14) reminds us of the following remark from Ryle (1962: 189): 'we employ for saying things about the mental life of people many active verbs which do signify acts of mind ... correctly list[ing] calculating, pondering and recalling to mind as mental acts or processes'.

[18] In talking about intelligent behaviour for instance, Ryle says that 'Our inquiry is not into causes (and *a fortiori* not into occult causes), but into capacities, skills, habits, liabilities and bents' (1949: 45).

as causal-mechanistic explanations, but instead explanations of another sort. But what other sort?

Ryle compares explanations of actions by appeal to motives with explanations by appeal to dispositions. Moreover, he explicitly contrasts the latter with causal explanations.

> So when we say that that the glass broke when struck because it was brittle, the 'because' clause does not report a happening or a cause; it states a law-like proposition. People commonly say of explanations of this second kind that they give the 'reason' for the glass breaking when struck. (1949: 89)

Ryle's account of disposition statements is well known, and leaves us with a number of equally well-known questions. In particular, in what does a person's (or thing's) having a disposition consist? Don't we need a categorical base to serve as truth-maker for dispositional statements? And, if we do, doesn't this mean that the categorical base could serve as the cause of action?[19] Even if the answers to either of these last two questions are 'no', there are other reasons we might wish to say that explanations by appeal to dispositions are at least sometimes causal explanations. Here is Kenny on this point:

> For if to offer X as a causal explanation of Y is roughly to say that whenever X then Y, then Ryle's explication of 'he boasted from vanity' as 'whenever an opportunity for boasting arrives, he takes it' construes 'he boasted from vanity' as a causal statement. His theory differs from the one he rejects only in that it offers public circumstances, instead of private impulses, as the cause of the boasting. (Kenny 1963: 79)

Or, again, if one disagrees with this account of causation in terms of laws, Ryle also speaks of dispositional explanations as counterfactual-supporting. 'How does the law-like general hypothetical proposition work? It says, roughly, that the glass, *if* sharply struck or twisted, etc. *would* not dissolve or stretch or evaporate but fly into fragments' (Ryle 1949: 89, emphasis original). Thus, even on a counterfactual account of causation, it seems that explanations by appeal to dispositions would count as causal explanations.

Thus Ryle supplied us with a compelling argument *against* causalism, and a positive account of action from motives which appears to *imply* causalism. There may be a way of resolving this tension, but the prospects seem dim. We turn instead to another influential development of Wittgensteinian ideas.

---

[19] There is room here to say that the explanations are not causal—because in using disposition terms we are not talking about or referring to a categorical base for them—while also allowing that, metaphysically, there must always be a categorical basis which is the cause of the action. There has been much discussion in the recent metaphysics literature of whether (in general) dispositions need a non-dispositional categorical basis (e.g. G. Strawson 2008).

22.4 ANSCOMBE

Elizabeth Anscombe too opposed the idea that intentional action should be understood as bodily movements caused by some inner occurrence. In fact, her penetrating book *Intention* (1957) can profitably be read as a sustained critique of the idea that intentions are interior acts or events.

Anscombe begins her book by pointing out three important, and importantly different, uses of the concept of intention: (i) we express our intentions to do certain things; (ii) we describe actions as intentional; (iii) we ask with what intention an act was performed. Anscombe's preferred approach is through the second use of the concept.

To a first approximation, Anscombe offers the following characterization of intentional action (cf. 1957: 15, 24–5):

> An act is intentional only if we can know without observation that we are doing it, and what caused us to do it.

Thus bodily movements that we merely observe as taking place, and those whose causes we must discover, such as hiccups, are not intentional. Anscombe calls those things that we know without observation are the causes of our own actions 'mental causes', and so maintains that all intentional actions must have mental causes.[20] However, the relation between mental causes and intentional actions is complicated. First, some actions with mental causes aren't intentional. Second, actions are only intentional if we can give our reasons for acting *without* merely citing a mental cause. And, third, somewhat confusingly, and despite the common belief that Anscombe held that reasons can't be causes, she says that for some intentional actions the reason for action *is* a mental cause.[21]

Anscombe's point in all of this is that intentional actions are those which have a mental cause, and which we can explain by doing *more* than citing a mental cause. What we primarily must be able to do is make the act intelligible by placing it in its appropriate context, including locating it in, to use Sellars' phrase, the 'space of reasons' for our action. Establishing that this is the key to understanding the notion of intention requires breaking the hold of the notion that intentions are interior mental events that cause actions (or bodily movements). Her main strategies are (a) to remove various motivations we may have for thinking that intentions are interior events or mental states and (b) deriving unpalatable consequences from the view that there are interior acts of intention. There

---

[20] Mental causes need not be mental events, since they can include external physical events. But in order to be a mental cause an event must be perceived by the agent, so Anscombe is happy to allow us to speak as if mental causes were always mental events (1957: 17–18). Significantly, she holds the notion of a mental cause to be of very little importance, making it clear that she does not think of action in terms of event-causation (1957: 17–18).

[21] For all three points see Anscombe (1957: 23–4).

are two examples of these strategies worth considering in the context of Davidson's causalism. The first is Anscombe's argument for what has since become known as the Identity Thesis. The second is her discussion of knowledge by observation.

The Identity Thesis, roughly expressed, is the claim that one action can have many descriptions. Stated as baldly as this, however, it is hard to see who would disagree with it—my action of kicking a cat could be described as such, or as my favourite action. More precisely, then, the Identity Thesis is the idea that when I make my opponent sad by scoring a goal by kicking a ball by swinging my leg, there is only one action, and not four, of which we have four descriptions. What gives the thesis substance is that the differences between the descriptions are not *trivial* (e.g. involving synonymy).

Anscombe's discussion of these issues (1957: 37–47) is an attempt to remove our temptation to say that there is always one description 'which is *the* description of an intentional action' (37). If we succumb to this temptation, then we are quickly led to the idea that what we do, primarily, or what gives *the* description of an intentional action, is always some bodily movement, or perhaps muscle contractions, or some other interior act, which then causes further 'external' events to take place. Consider her famous example: a man is pumping poisoned water into a cistern that supplies the drinking water to a house in which several party chiefs and their families are staying. There are (at least) four descriptions of what the man is doing: he is moving his arm up and down, pumping water, replenishing the water supply, and poisoning the inhabitants. Which of these descriptions is the best candidate for *the* description? Surely it is the first, since the rest are only contingently correct descriptions of what went on—suppose, for example, there was a hole in the pipe between the pump and the cistern. Similar reasoning would push the description further and further inside the agent, until we are left with some interior act of intention.

If we think that there is one correct description of each action, and there are four correct descriptions of what our man did, then there must be four distinct actions here, each of which has one of the descriptions as *the* description of them. But if we think this way, then we are thinking of the circumstances in which the action takes place as *external* to the action—the man moves his arm up and down and luckily there happens to be a pump in the way and so he also pumps water. Anscombe reminds us (1957: 41–5) that the surrounding circumstances at least partly *determine* which intentional action occurs. Once we acknowledge the circumstances are part of what makes an act the intentional act it is, we can say that 'moving his arm up and down with his fingers round the pump handles *is*, in these circumstances, operating the pump; and, in these circumstances, it *is* replenishing the house water-supply; and, in these circumstances, it *is* poisoning the household' (1957: 46). And this amounts to the Identity Thesis. There are many, equally good, descriptions of the one action. So there is no one primary action, and we have removed one temptation for postulating interior acts of intention.

However, the next section (1957: § 27) begins immediately with the question 'Is there ever a place for an interior act of intention?' and we are plunged back into further temptations towards the view. Anscombe considers a variety of alternatives which are each dismissed, but for our purposes it is the motivation for these views that she identifies that is most important.[22] The motivation comes from the idea, which Anscombe endorses, that we can know of our intentional actions without observation. If intentional actions are as dependent on external circumstances as Anscombe suggests, how can we know them without observation? There is another problem too, arising from the modern prejudice that knowledge is 'incorrigibly contemplative':

> For if there are two knowledges—one by observation, the other in intention—then it looks as if there must be two objects of knowledge; but if one says the objects are the same, one looks hopelessly for the different *mode of contemplative knowledge* in acting, as if there were a very queer and special sort of seeing eye in the middle of the acting. (1957: 57)

Here Anscombe presents us with a dilemma. We might say that there are two objects to match our two modes of knowing—an action and an interior intention. Or, since we subscribe to the Identity Thesis, we might say that there is just one object. On the latter option, though, we can't think what this other mode of contemplative knowledge might be. So we are forced back to the idea of two acts, one of which is an interior intention which we know without observation.

This option has disastrous consequences, according to Anscombe. For if we know what we are doing without observation, then the content of our intentions must be such that we can know it is satisfied without observation. Since we can't know what is happening external to our bodies without observation, it seems the content of our intentions must be pushed back inside us: 'first to the bodily movement, then perhaps to the contraction of the muscles, then to the attempt to do the thing, which comes right at the beginning' (1957: 53). Anscombe takes all of these options to be hopeless, since in exercising certain skills, I can describe what I am doing in terms of external 'consequences', but not in terms of internal states: 'The only description that I clearly know of what I am doing may be of something that is at a distance from me' (1957: 53). For example, some physiologist might want to observe some nerve impulses in my arm and so trains me to move my arm in a particular way. The way he trains me is to teach me to throw a ball through a hoop: this is the only way to move my arm in just the way in which he is interested. I could then say precisely what I was doing in terms of aiming at the hoop, without being able to say exactly how I was moving my arm or what muscles I was contracting. And if we try to internalize this description by turning it into a thought, the thought will not count as an intention unless it too is intended (1957: 52).

Since interior intentions are no good, and since we have no idea what the required strange mode of contemplative knowledge of our actions could be, we need a way around the dilemma Anscombe poses. The way forward that she suggests is to treat our 'knowledge without observation', at least when it comes to intentional action, as a form of practical rather than theoretical knowledge. Anscombe's account of 'practical knowledge' is hard to interpret, however, and so it is difficult to see the alternative to either

---

[22] The views and their critiques are in §§ 27, 29, and 30. The motivation first emerges in § 28.

interior acts of intention or causalism that she has in mind. As with Wittgenstein and Ryle, Anscombe gave several powerful arguments against interior acts of intention and causalism, but gave no clear alternative to the standard, and commonsensical, position that treats intentions as interior causes of intentional actions.

22.5 DAVIDSON

Wittgenstein, Ryle, and Anscombe were not alone in their rejection of causalism. If there was a uniting theme in the philosophy of action in the 1950s and early 1960s, particularly at Oxford, it was the rejection of causalism. Philosophers taking this stance included Hampshire (1959), Hart and Honoré (1959), Kenny (1963), Melden (1961), and Taylor (1964). These and others developed their own arguments against causalism as well as accepting some we have already considered, and offered positive accounts of intentional action.

It is unfortunate that this group are so often lumped together with Ryle and Anscombe and communally labelled 'neo-Wittgensteinians'. For one thing, 'neo-Wittgensteinian' is typically associated with 'behaviourist', and so the label suggests that all these philosophers were behaviourist sympathizers. Yet however close some may have come to behaviourism, most of the 'neo-Wittgensteinians' were explicitly opposed to it, especially (as in Ryle's case, for instance) in its reductive, anti-teleological forms. Most obviously, Taylor's *The Explanation of Behaviour* is a sustained and meticulous *attack* on behaviourism. This unfortunate labelling also had another important, and detrimental, consequence. Davidson's justly lauded 'Action, Reasons and Causes' launched a powerful and influential counter-attack on anti-causalism, and included decisive criticisms of a number of 'neo-Wittgensteinian' arguments for the conclusion that reasons can't be causes. As we have seen, Davidson himself encouraged the idea that he had destroyed the anti-causalist case altogether. But his discussion left the central arguments of Wittgenstein, Ryle, and Anscombe against causalism largely untouched.

Davidson set out to defend the view that explanations of action in terms of reasons (including intentions) are a form of causal explanation. His best, and most influential, argument in favour of causalism simply appealed to the fact that we regularly say that agents acted as they did *because* of some reason or intention, and there is no clear alternative to treating this 'because' as causal.[23] While *prima facie* this is a forceful argument, it certainly doesn't clinch the case. In particular, if there are powerful general arguments against causalism, we might still prefer an unclear alternative position, which might at least be profitably developed, to a clear and likely false one.[24]

---

[23] 'But I would urge that, failing a satisfactory alternative, the best argument for a scheme like Aristotle's is that it alone promises to give an account of the "mysterious connection" between reasons and actions' Davidson (1963: 11). Goldman develops this idea further (1970: 78–9).

[24] For the clearest development of a non-causalist position, see Wilson (1989), especially ch. 7.

So Davidson's positive views dialectically depend upon his criticisms of arguments against causalism.

One argument that Davidson dismissed was a familiar line of thought in the 1950s, traceable to Ryle: explanations that appeal to reasons or intentions work by attributing dispositional properties, and dispositions cannot be causes. Interestingly, at the time of 'Actions, Reasons and Causes' Davidson *agreed* that intentions are not events, or any other sort of thing that can be a cause, but maintained that they aren't dispositions either.[25] How can reason explanations then be causal? Because there are events closely related to intentions which *can* do the relevant causing, including the *onset* of states, the *noticing* of certain external situations, and the *forming* of intentions. This does not require the volitionist claim, whose phenomenological inaccuracy was emphasized by Wittgenstein, Anscombe, and Melden, that every act of hand-raising, say, requires the same 'internal' cause. This mistake only follows if we think that each act of hand-raising is caused by an intention to raise one's hand, and this is what Davidson denied.

A related line of argument Davidson considered claims that reasons for actions are not logically distinct from the actions they 'bring about' and so, since causes must be distinct from their effects, reasons can't be causes. For example, the intention to drink is not logically distinct from the act of drinking since any description of the intention involves an account of the act intended.[26] His devastating response was that we need to distinguish between events and our descriptions of them. Once we do this, we realize that we can describe events in terms of their causes. For example, we can describe my action of turning on the light switch as the event caused by the sudden onset of my desire to turn on the light switch. The fact that one event can be described as the effect of another event does not show that the two events are not causally related. Otherwise, no event could be the cause of any other.

A more difficult argument to dismiss came from Hart and Honoré (1959). They argued that, contra Ryle, reason explanations do *not* involve an appeal to covering laws, and it is for this reason that they cannot be causal explanations. Davidson agreed that reason explanations do not involve laws. Indeed, he famously argued that the entire psychological realm is *anomalous* (not law-governed). Nevertheless, this does not imply that psychological events cannot be causes. According to Davidson's now well-known 'anomalous monism' (1970), token psychological events are identical with token physical

---

[25] He said that 'intention' 'cannot be taken to refer to an entity, state, disposition, or event' (1963: 8). In 1963, Davidson largely ignored intentions and instead posited 'primary reasons' as the causes of intentional action. Primary reasons are a combination of beliefs and desires. In 1978, he came to treat intentions as irreducible mental states.

[26] See Melden (1961: 52) in particular; without going to the trouble of detailed citation, Davidson (1963: 13) also attributes the argument to Kenny, Hampshire, Peters, and Winch, suggesting that an argument of this sort can be traced back to Ryle's discussion of explanation by appeal to motives. Presumably, Davidson has in mind Ryle's treatment of motives as dispositions, together with his claim that dispositional explanations are not causal explanations. But what does this have to do with Melden's argument? Probably the idea is that dispositional properties, like being vain, are logically connected to the manifestations of the disposition, like acting vainly. This may be the answer to our earlier question, as to why Ryle claimed that dispositional explanations cannot be causal explanations.

events. Described in psychological vocabulary, there are no laws linking internal events with actions. However, described in physical vocabulary there may, indeed, he thought, must, be laws linking causally related physical events.

Davidson's response had much in common with the views of those he criticized. Specifically, he accepted the idea that there are two types or 'levels' of explanation that need to be carefully distinguished. He also accepted that only one level contains, properly speaking, causal explanations. For there can be no psychological laws, and, for Davidson, laws are essential to causation. This way of thinking is strikingly similar to Taylor's in *The Explanation of Behaviour* (1964). Taylor distinguished teleological from mechanistic explanation and argued that teleological explanations were indispensable in explaining behaviour, did not involve appeals to laws, and yet were properly scientific. He also agreed that intentions 'bring about' behaviour. However, unlike Davidson, Taylor denied that teleological explanation is causal.

> [W]e could not say that the intention was the causal antecedent of the behaviour. For the two are not contingently connected in the normal way. We are not explaining the behaviour by the 'law', other things being equal, intending X is followed by doing X, for this is part of what we mean by 'intending X', that, in the absence of interfering factors, it is followed by doing X ... (1964: 33; cf. Malcolm 1968)

This argument that teleological explanation is not causal has much in common with the second argument we mentioned above, which Davidson took himself to have defeated. More specifically, it appears as if Taylor is relying on the idea that the only 'law' that might 'explain' behaviour by appeal to intention is analytic, and therefore incapable of being used in a causal explanation. To this, Davidson had said: 'The truth of a causal statement depends on *what* events are described; its status as analytic or synthetic depends on *how* the events are described' (1963: 14, emphasis original).

Davidson's point is important, and many philosophers at the time were confused in the way he suggests. Yet the point faces an obvious rejoinder, and his response to it highlights how his critique of the anti-causalist arguments begs an important question. The rejoinder is this: whether an explanation of behaviour works, whether it is really an *explanation*, does depend on how the events are described, and not just on which events are described. Davidson's response is not entirely clear, but one line of thought that can be extracted from his discussion is that even if explanations in psychological terms are analytic, they contain place-holders for terms that would yield more informative explanations. The comparison he offers is to explanations that appeal to water-solubility. The notion of water-solubility is a place-holder for an account of the relevant microphysical structures that interact with water molecules in such a way as to dissolve. An explanation that appeals to water-solubility only involves an analytic 'law' (water-soluble things dissolve in water), but this doesn't rule it out as a causal explanation since there are more informative explanations that replace this analytic truth with contingent physical laws.

We can flesh this line of thought out in a way that has since become familiar. Davidson's opponents ran together the idea that a claim like 'water-soluble things dissolve in water' is a priori with the claim that it is necessary—they did this by referring to them merely as 'analytic'. Yet, at least on one reading, 'water-soluble things dissolve in water' is a contingent truth, since the substances which are water-soluble in this world are not water-soluble in worlds in which the laws of physics are different. On this reading we have a contingent a priori truth. Such truths are susceptible to deeper explanations in terms of contingent laws, as in this case. And these deeper explanations make it clear that explanations that appeal to the a priori truth can still be causal.

Davidson's response thus relies on a close analogy between psychological terms and 'theoretical' and 'causal-explanatory' terms like 'water', 'water-soluble', or 'gold'. For our model of a contingent, a priori truth is one in which the reference of at least one term contained in the truths is fixed by a sort of description or functional role specification. But this analogy begs perhaps the crucial question against many of his opponents, including especially Wittgenstein, Ryle, and Anscombe. As we have seen, they thought that treating psychological terms in this way led inevitably to implausible theories of action. And Davidson hasn't given us any reason to doubt their claims.

In particular, Davidson ignored Ryle's trilemma argument (a development of Wittgenstein's 'two-poles' discussion) which, though directed at volitionism, applies to causalism more generally. Later, he did respond to something very similar to the trilemma. Without referring to Ryle, he presented a problem for causalism concerning whether a causal analysis is consistent with free action. If intentions (willings, choosings …) are distinct from our actions, then we can ask whether the intention (willing, choosing …) was freely chosen, and we are off on Ryle's regress. But if the intention is not distinct from the action, then it cannot be a cause of it. Davidson says:

> The only hope for the causal analysis is to find states or events which are causal conditions of intentional actions, but which are not themselves actions or events about which the question whether the agent can perform them can intelligibly be raised. (1973: 72)

This manoeuvre certainly blocks the sort of regress with which Ryle was concerned. But it simply ignores the reasons Ryle gave for avoiding it, namely, that if the reasons we acted on are neither voluntary nor involuntary, then we cannot be held to be morally blameworthy for having them. It also raises the question as to how we can control when we act, if one of the causal conditions for acting is some event which we do not bring about at will.[27]

Another consequence of causalism about which Wittgenstein and Anscombe warned us is that it leads to the idea of primitive (or basic) actions, and on to an unworkable account of interior acts of intention.[28] Primitive actions are those actions we perform directly, those by doing which we perform non-primitive actions.[29]

---

[27] Davidson's response to Ryle's trilemma has much in common with Armstrong's (1968: 136–7).

[28] The notion of a basic action was introduced by Danto (1963, 1965). Although it was subject to a great deal of discussion for twenty-odd years, it has since largely faded from view.

[29] There is a careful definition in Candlish (1983).

It is thus interesting that Davidson came to endorse the idea of primitive action. His main argument for the existence of primitive actions is the following (1971: 56–9). Suppose we perform an act of moving our arm that results in the poisoning of a party chief. Have we performed two actions, an arm moving and a poisoning, or one? Suppose there were two. What is the relation between them? It cannot be event causality, since then we would have to say that by moving our arm we caused ourselves to poison someone. Moreover, all we needed to *do* to poison the party chief was move our arm. If the relation can't be event causality, it also can't be the relation of part to whole. For then the poisoning would consist of the arm-moving plus one of its consequences. Yet in moving our arm we did something which caused the poisoning of the party chief, and to do something which causes the poisoning of someone is to poison someone. According to Davidson, the right thing to say is that we did not perform two actions, a poisoning and an arm-moving, but just one, the arm-moving, which can also be described as a poisoning. In describing it as a poisoning, we are describing it in terms of one of its effects. This reasoning generalizes and so suggests that whenever we act, we only do one thing, a primitive action, which potentially has many consequences. More specifically, primitive actions, he thought, are always movings of our bodies. 'We never do more than move our bodies: the rest is up to nature' (1971: 59).

There are several things worth noticing about this argument. First, the sub-conclusion of this argument is clearly the Identity Thesis.[30] However, Davidson's argument for this thesis is very different from Anscombe's. Her strategy was to point out that by treating the poisoning of the party chiefs as external to what we do (a mere contingent consequence), we are forced to push back what we do to some interior event such as a muscle contraction, an act of willing or a brain event. Since Davidson wants to say that primitive actions are bodily movements, he obviously can't endorse this argument. His own argument, however, seems to come close to begging the question. Against the idea that there are two causally related actions, an arm-moving and a poisoning, he says the only thing we need *do* to poison someone is move our arm. Against the view that the arm-moving is a part of the action of poisoning he says that doing something which causes a poisoning *is* a poisoning. But both of these remarks seem to simply assume the Identity Thesis. Even if Davidson could establish this thesis, however, he cannot move, as he tries to, from it to the thesis of primitive actions. All he is entitled to claim is that the arm-moving and the poisoning are the same action, and this does not entail that what we primarily do is move our bodies. Why not say instead, as Anscombe does, that the act of poisoning 'swallows up' the act of moving the arm?

We suggest that the real reason Davidson leant towards primitive actions is that his causalist theory faces pressure from another direction—the problem of deviant causal chains. As Davidson himself noted (1973: 79), it is not enough to intentionally act (kill the party chief) that we merely have an intention to do so and this intention causes the appropriate result (the death of the party chief). Our intention (or primary reason) must

---

[30] He acknowledges Anscombe for this thesis (1971: 59 n19).

cause the result in the *right sort of way*—if our water pumping enrages a passing local who then murders the party chief, we haven't intentionally killed the party chief. This problem can be avoided if there are primitive actions we perform directly with no intermediaries between our intentions (primary reasons) and the result, which for Davidson is always a bodily movement. This line of thought is just what Wittgenstein had in mind, we suggest, when he urged that the executive, mechanistic model leads to a picture of the will as an *immediate* sort of bringing about.

Of course, one of Wittgenstein's complaints about such a view is that it in turn leads to internalism, whereby our primary actions are not bodily movements, but internal actions such as efforts of will, tryings, or muscular contractions. Anscombe, too, argued that the causalist picture leads us to think of our 'nested' actions on the model of a causal chain, and from there to the idea that what we primarily do is some interior action. As we have just seen, Davidson's adoption of causalism led him to the notion of primitive actions in just the way Wittgenstein and Anscombe predicted. Moreover, as later conationists like Hornsby noted, Davidson's argument for primitive actions, including the adoption of the Identity Thesis, gives better support to the view that primitive actions are conations than to the view that they necessarily involve gross muscular events. The reasoning, in a kind of unintentional *reductio*, leads to the conclusion that 'bodily movements [where 'move' is understood as a transitive verb] take place even before the muscles contract' (Hornsby 1980: 28) and are thus in the brain (1980: 106).[31] We thus end up with a kind of Cartesian materialism, which, by a move now familiar from our discussion of Anscombe, Ryle, and Wittgenstein, is only one step away from volitionism: as such events are *phenomena*, we can ask whether they themselves were willed/intentional/voluntary.

Here we see the attraction of volitionism, for any materialist account seems to render our doing subject to the vagaries of nature: not merely 'the rest', but everything in our acts is 'up to nature'. This has seemed intolerable to philosophers: 'The will itself cannot be paralysed!', cried O'Shaughnessy (1980). Here we see how illuminating, after all, Wittgenstein's discussion is: we are left, it seems, with a stark choice between an empiricist volitionism, whose need to avoid the possibility of failed attempts at volitions requires its causally basic events not to admit a distinction between a doing and a mere happening (e.g. McCann 1974), and in reaction against that, a transcendental form, where the will becomes an 'extensionless point'.

These days the issue of primitive or basic actions is rarely discussed, perhaps because of the realization that the notion involves such consequences. But as we've just seen, this is only half of the story, since the causalist picture, which remains dominant in contemporary philosophy of action, leads to the notion of primitive actions. There may, of course, be ways of escape, perhaps by spelling out the difference between deviant and non-deviant ways for intentions to cause behaviour. Since this project has not yet succeeded, and there remain other arguments against causalism that Davidson did

---

[31] For a fuller account of this transition from Davidson's account of basic actions to internalism see Candlish (1983).

not address, we hope our historical story has at least provided a few more reasons for doubting that causalism is the obvious truth it is often taken to be in the philosophy of action.[32]

REFERENCES

Anscombe, G. E. M. (1957). *Intention*. Oxford: Blackwell.

—— (1965). 'Mechanism and Ideology', *New Statesman*, February: 206.

Armstrong, D. (1968). *A Materialist Theory of Mind*. London: Routledge & Kegan Paul.

Ayer, A. J. (1964). *Man as a Subject for Science*. London: Athlone Press.

Candlish, S. (1983). 'Inner and Outer Basic Action', *Proceedings of the Aristotelian Society* 84: 83–102.

—— (1991). '"Das Wollen ist auch nur eine Erfahrung"'. In R. L. Arrington and H.-J. Glock (eds.), *Wittgenstein's Philosophical Investigations: Text and Context*. London and New York: Routledge, pp. 203–26.

—— (2001). 'The Will'. In H.-J. Glock (ed.), *Wittgenstein: A Critical Reader*. Oxford: Blackwell, pp. 156–73.

Collingwood, R. G. (1940). *An Essay on Metaphysics*; rev. edn. Oxford: Clarendon Press, 1998.

Danto, A. (1963). 'What We Can Do', *Journal of Philosophy* 60: 435–45.

—— (1965). 'Basic Actions', *American Philosophical Quarterly* 2: 141–8.

—— (1973). *Analytical Philosophy of Action*. Cambridge: Cambridge University Press.

Davidson, D. (1963). 'Actions, Reasons and Causes', *Journal of Philosophy* 60: 685–700. Repr. in Davidson (1980), pp. 3–20. Page references are to the latter.

—— (1970). 'Mental Events'. In L. Foster and J. W. Swanson (eds.), *Experience and Theory*. London: Duckworth, pp. 79–101. Repr. in Davidson (1980), pp. 207–25. Page references are to the latter.

—— (1971). 'Agency'. In R. Binkley, R. Bronaugh, and A. Marras (eds.), *Agent, Action, and Reason*. Toronto: University of Toronto Press, pp. 3–25. Repr. in Davidson (1980), pp. 43–62. Page references are to the latter.

—— (1973). 'Freedom to Act'. In T. Honderich (ed.), *Essays on Freedom of Action*. London: Routledge & Kegan Paul, pp. 137–56. Repr. in Davidson (1980), pp. 63–82. Page references are to the latter.

—— (1978). 'Intending'. In Y. Yovel and D. Reidel (eds.), *Philosophy of History and Action*. Jerusalem: Magnes Press, pp. 41–60. Repr. in Davidson (1980), pp. 83–102. Page references are to the latter.

—— (1980). *Essays on Actions and Events*. Oxford: Clarendon Press.

Fodor, J. A. (1968). *Psychological Explanation*. New York: Random House.

Ginet, C. (1990). *On Action*. Cambridge: Cambridge University Press.

Goldman, A. (1970). *A Theory of Human Action*. New York: Prentice Hall.

Hacker, P. M. S. (2007). *Human Nature*. Oxford: Blackwell.

Hampshire, S. (1959). *Thought and Action*. London: Chatto & Windus.

Hart, H. L. A. and Honoré, A. M. (1959). *Causation in the Law*. Oxford: Clarendon Press.

Heil, J. (2009). 'Obituary: C. B. Martin', *Australasian Journal of Philosophy* 87(1): 177–9.

---

[32] Other reasons can be found in Wilson (1989), Ginet (1990), Tanney (1995, 2008), and Lowe (2008).

Hornsby, J. (1980). *Actions*. London: Routledge & Kegan Paul.

Kenny, A. (1963). *Action, Emotion and Will*. London: Routledge & Kegan Paul.

Lowe, E. J. (2008). *Personal Agency: The Metaphysics of Mind and Action*. Oxford: Oxford University Press.

McCann, H. J. (1974). 'Volition and Basic Action', *The Philosophical Review* 83: 451–73.

Malcolm, N. (1968). 'The Conceivability of Mechanism', *The Philosophical Review* 77: 45–72.

Melden, A. I. (1961). *Free Action*. London: Routledge & Kegan Paul.

O'Connor, T. (2000). *Persons and Causes: The Metaphysics of Free Will*. Oxford: Oxford University Press.

O'Shaughnessy, B. (1980). *The Will*, 2 vols. Cambridge: Cambridge University Press.

Prichard, H. A. (1932). 'Duty and Ignorance of Fact'. Repr. in Prichard (1949), pp. 18–39.

——(1945). 'Acting, Willing and Desiring'. Repr. in Prichard (1949), pp. 187–98.

——(1949). *Moral Obligation*. Oxford: Clarendon Press.

Ryle, G. (1949). *The Concept of Mind*. London: Hutchinson.

—— (1962). 'Phenomenology versus "The Concept of Mind"'. Repr. in Ryle, *Collected Papers, Vol. 1*. London, Hutchinson, 1971, pp. 179–98.

Strawson, G. (2008). 'The Identity of the Categorical and the Dispositional', *Analysis* 68(4): 271–82.

Tanney, J. (1995). 'Why Reasons May Not Be Causes', *Mind & Language* 10: 103–26.

—— (2008). 'Reasons as Non-Causal, Context-Placing Explanations'. In C. Sandis (ed.), *New Essays on the Explanation of Action*. Basingstoke: Palgrave Macmillan, pp. 94–111.

Taylor, C. (1964). *The Explanation of Behaviour*. New York: Humanities Press.

Taylor, R. (1966). *Action and Purpose*. Englewood Cliffs, NJ: Prentice-Hall.

Wilson, G. (1989). *The Intentionality of Human Action*. Stanford: Stanford University Press.

Wittgenstein, L. (1953). *Philosophical Investigations*, tr. G. E. M. Anscombe. Oxford: Blackwell.

——(1967). *Zettel*, ed. G. E. M. Anscombe and G. H. von Wright, tr. G. E. M. Anscombe. Oxford: Blackwell.

——(1974). *Philosophical Grammar*, ed. R. Rhees, tr. A. Kenny. Oxford: Blackwell.

....

CHAPTER 23

METAPHYSICS IN ANALYTIC PHILOSOPHY

....

PETER SIMONS

23.1 INTRODUCTION: LOSS AND RESTITUTION

Among those with an outdated or partial conception of analytic philosophy, the whole movement is associated with the rejection of metaphysics. But such rejection, however motivated and justified, was never the sole prerogative of analytic philosophy, nor was it ever the majority view within that movement. Early analytic philosophers engaged in metaphysics without compunction, and it was only during the 'middle period' of the 1930s–1950s that, under the influence of logical positivism and ordinary language philosophy, metaphysics was first rejected and later marginalized. It is this publicity-catching period that is often taken *pars pro toto*. We shall chart the origins, critique, and re-establishment of metaphysics within analytic philosophy.

Whichever philosophers are taken to be the parents or progenitors of analytic philosophy, whether Russell and Moore, Frege, Bolzano, or even Leibniz, all of them were fully engaged in metaphysics. In Leibniz and Bolzano we have a monadology of mental or physical atomic substances, in Bolzano and Frege we have a timeless Platonic realm of abstract objects guaranteeing the objectivity of logic and meaning, in Moore and Russell we have a world of many material objects existing independently of minds.

As analytic philosophers grappled with the problems in the foundations of mathematics and engaged in consolidating the new logic, attention shifted to the language medium and the metaphysical dimension faded from attention. Wittgenstein's trenchant prohibitions on nonsense found resonance with continental European logicians and philosophers of science whose suspicion of metaphysics derived from empiricist tendencies in Germany and France, and these crystallized in the Vienna Circle's attempts to demonstrate the senselessness of metaphysics.

These efforts quickly emerged as self-defeating, but a general suspicion of metaphysics as reactionary and backward-looking lingered through analytic philosophy's establishment as a dominant movement. Never completely extinguished even in the analytical movement, metaphysics began to re-emerge to prominence in the 1950s with the work of Quine, Strawson, and others, and the increasing importance of logical and linguistic semantics afforded a ready avenue for the re-establishment of metaphysics as the ontic counterpart to language, as it had been among the early analytics.

The rediscovery of genuine and unsolved metaphysical problems at the hands of several analytic philosophers gradually led to a de-emphasis on the linguistic and semantic approach to metaphysics, and in a reverse of the linguistic turn, metaphysics was pursued in wide circles in relative autonomy. As the new millennium dawned, it was clear not only that metaphysics was no longer dead, but that its resurrection as analytic metaphysics was one of the more remarkable developments in philosophy in general and in its analytic strain in particular.

23.2 FREGE AND LOGICAL OBJECTIVITY

We start with Frege. Never a philosopher by avocation, still less a metaphysician, Frege's mission was to prove Leibniz right against Kant that the concepts of arithmetic and analysis are purely logical, and that the laws of arithmetic have the same objectivity and certainty as those of logic, being logical themselves. This was logicism. Unburdened by the weight of logical tradition, Frege reinvented logic for this purpose, introducing an astonishing range of innovations including modern quantification, truth-functions, and the functional analysis of sentential complexity, yielding in passing a treatment of relations and the development of a logical system of unprecedented precision and clarity.

On the face of it this appears relatively remote from metaphysical speculation. But Frege's insightful analyses rested on certain key assumptions that turned out to be ontological in nature, in particular his view that proper names such as numerals and other mathematical constants designate abstract individuals, that function names stand for abstract functions, and that clauses designate two special entities called the True and the False.

Frege's assumptions about the harmony between the grammatical categories of expressions and the categories of entities they designate appear to be, and in some respects are, naïve, but he held to them in order to secure logic's objectivity against what he construed as the twin diseases of his time: psychologism and formalism. Psychologism, which was a particular embodiment of the Humean naturalism and empiricism then dominant in Germany, claimed that the laws of logic are to be taken in scientific manner as the laws of thought, that is, the contingent empirical laws governing actual thought-processes. Frege saw that this would lead to logical relativism, allowing alternative thought-processes to have their own, equally legitimate 'logics', undermining the Western tradition of the objectivity of knowledge from Plato onwards. It would also give the laws of logic, which

Frege saw as normative, an inferior status as mere empirical generalizations and undermine the distinctness of arithmetic and other non-geometric parts of mathematics he considered as analytic. Frege's position and arguments, seconded more ponderously but more influentially by Edmund Husserl, soon pushed psychologism aside.

Formalism on the other hand treated mathematics as a mere game with symbols, having no reference to any objects and having at best incidental usefulness in application. Since many games are possible, the certainty of mathematics is undermined because the applicability of mathematics is left unexplained, or regarded as mere good fortune, or a matter of convention or convenience. In dispute with the more advanced formalism of David Hilbert, however, Frege's trenchantly ontological interpretation of mathematical concepts and axioms failed to emerge as a clear winner. This undecided outcome was to affect later philosophy of mathematics and influence the metaphysics debate.

In the course of consolidating his position in logic and mathematics, Frege incidentally developed a powerful and still widely influential philosophy of language, distinguishing in meaning between sense and designation, and upholding the objectivity of the contents of thought as abstract propositions or 'thoughts'. Like the numbers and other mathematical entities, such propositions and their parts were construed Platonistically as neither material nor mental, but of a 'third realm', thus involuntarily reprising the forgotten position and arguments of Bolzano more than half a century earlier. Like Bolzano before him and Popper after him, Frege faced the metaphysical difficulty of explaining how the mind could 'grasp' such transcendent abstract senses, a problem he never satisfactorily resolved.

Another problem that Frege left to others to resolve was how to deal with contradictions that emerged in his logic and were highlighted by Bertrand Russell. These concerned Frege's assumption of 'value ranges', special abstract objects corresponding to functions, which were to be the designations for numerical and other terms. In his later work Frege dropped value ranges without replacement, but persisted with the general Platonistic framework for logic and his three-way metaphysics of the material, the mental, and the abstract.

23.3 Moore, Russell, and Realism

It was Bertrand Russell who first notified Frege of the inconsistency in his system, discovered when Russell was grappling with the foundations of mathematics from a similar and independently formulated logicist standpoint. Unlike Frege, however, Russell came to his Platonism through a struggle, the struggle against the absolute idealism of Bradley and others then dominant in English-language philosophy. Bradley was the dominant British philosopher of the day, and his Victorian update of Parmenides, Spinoza, and Hegel in a monism in which the only true object is the Absolute was the staple of Cambridge philosophy when Russell and his contemporary G. E. Moore were studying there under the idealist John McTaggart. Bradley's monism was an unabashedly metaphysical position, motivated by logical considerations and supported by arguments attempting to show the inconsistency of diversity. The incredible epistemological consequences of this idealism, surfacing also in McTaggart's arguments against the reality of time, pushed Moore into rebellion and rejection with several papers, notably his 1899 'The Nature of Judgment' and his 1903 'The Refutation of Idealism'. The former rejected Bradley's absolute idealism by distinguishing between objects and concepts, though in a way that is hard to credit today, while the latter rejected Berkeleian subjective idealism. This led Moore into a greater respect for unsophisticated opinions, coming to imbue his subsequent philosophy with its twin characteristics of common-sense realism and a tendency to indulge in copious and minute analysis of the terms in which philosophical problems are expressed. Of these, the former has generally (though not universally) survived, while the latter has tended to be preserved in spirit but sidelined in practice by logico-linguistic analysis more akin to that of Frege or Russell.

Fired by Moore's rebellion, Russell thankfully embraced a luxuriant realism, allowing every name or term to stand for something, often in many and varied ways. Along the way Russell discovered a kindred spirit in the Austrian philosopher Alexius Meinong, and for a while their positions were close. But Russell never agreed with Meinong's acceptance of objects with inconsistent characteristics, and sought ever more refined ways to show that Meinong's assumptions led to logical contradiction. In this first enthusiasm for realism, Russell was able to treat mathematical objects as equally existent alongside more familiar material ones, while Moore was happy to construe objective values such as goodness as something indefinable outside us, to be grasped by a special kind of intuition. In so doing, Moore and Russell were not only working in partly recognized parallel to continental thinkers such as Brentano, Meinong, and Husserl: they were also storing up again the access problems of prior Platonists.

After the long dominance of idealism in Britain and America, the turn to realism in the early 1900s brought about a seemingly permanent shift away from the Hegel–Bradley line. It was not only the principal analytic philosophers who contributed here: apart from the Austrians previously mentioned, a similar movement among the American New Realists reacted against American idealism, and older contemporaries such as Samuel Alexander, C. D. Broad, and G. F. Stout also influentially promoted various versions of realism. Of these the most considerable was Alexander, whose work influenced not only Whitehead but also later generations of Scottish and Australian analytic philosophers.

23.4 Logicism and Logical Atomism

Russell's pursuit of logicism led him not only to his mathematical Platonism but to a decisive engagement with the new logic, apprehended by him first through Peano, but soon diverted through detailed if fallible study of Frege. The years of struggle to find a solution to the logical paradoxes dominated a decade of Russell's life, during which time he completed his early masterpiece *The Principles of Mathematics* and embarked on the more ambitious realization of logicism in collaboration with his former teacher

Alfred North Whitehead, resulting in the three-volume (and yet incomplete) monument *Principia Mathematica* (1910–13).

Russell's favoured solution to the paradoxes was his theory of types, sketched in a crude version for classes in 1903 but fully developed for propositional functions in an article of 1908. Like Frege, Russell realized that his paradox arose through an uncritical acceptance of all singular terms for classes as actually designating such a class. While the theory of types undercut this assumption by restricting the meaningful phrases that could enter into such expressions, Russell went further and looked to treat all expressions for classes as only appearing to designate. This 'no class' theory became the official version in *Principia*, but the way had been prepared by Russell's twin preoccupations with Meinong on the one hand and Frege on the other. Rejecting both terms for impossible objects like the round square and Frege's two-layered theory of meaning as sense and designation, Russell contrived to find a new way to account for descriptive terms like 'the author of *Waverley*' as entering into truths without standing for (denoting) objects. The resulting theory of definite descriptions had a threefold effect. Despite the obscurity of its initial exposition, it came to serve as Ramsey's 'paradigm of philosophy'. Secondly, it did serious work in *Principia*, in that nominal terms for classes were used but taken as not fundamental, being analysed as more or less elaborate quantifier phrases. Finally, in the hands of Russell's collaborator Whitehead, where as part of a Grassmann-influenced method of 'extensive abstraction' it was used in a crusade against imperceptible geometrical entities like points, lines, and surfaces, it inspired Russell to go on to 'expose' ever more singular terms as not really designating expressions, but as overt or covert descriptions to be 'paraphrased away'. The result was that the exuberant realism of Russell's early years was progressively pared back as more and more kinds of entity such as people and cities were 'replaced' by *Principia*-inspired logical constructions out of a more limited range of entities such as sense-data and Platonic universals. The logical method was now functioning as the cutting edge of Ockham's Razor, which Russell wielded with relish to simplify his ontology.

From 1911, Russell's logico-philosophical investigations came increasingly under the influence of the young Austrian engineer Ludwig Wittgenstein, whom Frege had advised to study with Russell. Imbued with linguistic and aesthetic puritanism alien to Russell's English liberalism, Wittgenstein persuaded Russell to let him take over development of the philosophy of logic, which Wittgenstein, in common with others, found imperfectly, perhaps incoherently stated in *Principia*. His austere account of the world and the role logic plays in our knowledge and understanding of it emerged as Wittgenstein grappled in largely solitary struggle with questions of the nature of representation, truth, and the proper nature of logic. The early *Notes on Logic*, dictated for Russell's sake, state many of Wittgenstein's positions in clear form, and Russell let them work on his views. Cut off from contact by the war, Russell and Wittgenstein independently developed similar but importantly divergent visions of the world and logic's role, Russell in the sparklingly readable 1918–19 *Lectures on Logical Atomism* (a name he had invented in 1911), Wittgenstein in the painstakingly formulated and painfully published but ultimately more influential *Tractatus Logico-Philosophicus* of 1921.

While both works, the latter in particular, lay massive stress on language and logic, they share a broad metaphysical viewpoint and plan. The world consists primarily not of objects but *facts*, and it is facts that correspond to true propositions and by existing make these propositions true. Whereas an object like Socrates is named by a name, a fact is the ontological counterpart of a true statement or its associated that-clause, e.g. that Socrates taught Plato. Some apparent names do not in fact name at all, as in the theory of descriptions, while not all true statements correspond to their own facts, for example the truths of logic and mathematics. In such cases the truth is to be explained by the role of logical connectives like negation and conjunction, which are truth-functions, and do not stand for anything, whereas for Frege they stood for logical functions.

Beyond this convergence, however, there are notable disparities between Russell's and Wittgenstein's versions of logical atomism, with metaphysical implications. Russell accepts negative, conjunctive, and general facts, corresponding to true negations, conjunctions, and universal quantifications. Wittgenstein rejects all facts as constituents of reality apart from those corresponding to true atomic propositions, which consist in what Wittgenstein calls the existence of a state of affairs. Russell takes sense-data and universals as the designata of genuine singular and general terms respectively, while Wittgenstein steers clear of such internal differentiation among the components of states of affairs. Pursuing a trenchant and ultimately confused notion of analysis, Wittgenstein pronounces a priori that all objects (nameables) in the world are atomic, or lacking in proper parts, and exist independently of what is the case, thus coming close to ancient and Leibnizian atomism.

Most importantly for the sequel, Wittgenstein has a radically more austere conception of what a meaningful language can be like. Language serves the representation of empirical reality, the facts, or natural science, and any form of expression that is neither doing this nor (like logic) is a by-product thereof, is literally meaningless. This includes, by a disconcerting reflexive move, the statements of the *Tractatus* itself, which are incoherently understood as 'enlightening' nonsense by comparison with the unenlightening nonsense that Wittgenstein dubs 'metaphysics'. Russell never bought this deflationary analysis, and suggests in his published Introduction that languages might come in a hierarchy whereby we can talk about one language using another, thereby anticipating metalogical moves initiated by Leśniewski and Tarski shortly afterwards. Nevertheless, Wittgenstein's insistent opposition to such a way out led him not only into disagreement with Russell but also to conceive of himself as having finally solved the problems of philosophy, or rather, showing that there are no real philosophical problems, and leading to his (temporarily) abandoning philosophy.

23.5 THE RISE AND FALL OF LOGICAL POSITIVISM

The most famous clash between metaphysics and analytic philosophy occurred in and around the Vienna Circle of logical positivists and associated thinkers. Logical positivism, as manifest most prominently in interwar Vienna but echoed with varying emphasis in other parts of Europe, notably in Berlin, did not emerge *ex nihilo*. Three streams fed it. One was Wittgenstein. A second stream, generally underemphasized in English-language depictions of positivism, was the background of scientific approaches to the human and social sciences, as advocated by Mill, Comte (from whom the word 'positivism' was taken), and Marx. The third was a general enthusiasm of German-speaking philosophers for a form of empiricism inspired by Hume and other British empiricists. This arose initially in reaction to Kant, Hegel, and other German idealists and the anti-scientific tendencies of German romanticism. While later eclipsed in academic philosophy by the rise of German neo-Kantianism, it informed the work of German scientists such as Weber, Helmholtz, Kirchhoff, and Boltzmann, whose philosophical education tended to be better than their counterparts elsewhere, and was bolstered outside the physical sciences by the enthusiastic take-up of Darwinism in Germany by Haeckel and others. Such scientists tended towards a metaphysically low-key, instrumentalist understanding of their work, emphasizing the procedures of observation and measurement and regarding theories as regulative instruments rather than as depictions of reality.

The most prominent philosopher–scientist representing this position was the Austrian physicist–physiologist–philosopher Ernst Mach. Mach pursued a metaphysically deflationary phenomenalism, treating theories as ways to streamline the move from observation to prediction, and disallowing them any ontological import. Mach carried his position forward in print, formulating a version of Newtonian mechanics lacking Newton's 'occult' forces and imperceptible space and time, and thereby inspiring the young Albert Einstein. Appointed to a chair of the History and Philosophy of the Inductive Sciences in Vienna, Mach soon retired due to ill health, remaining as a radical member of the Austrian Parliament's Upper House, and through the strong influence of his non-Marxist radicalism in Russia inspiring a furious *ad hominem* critique by Lenin.

Mach's influence in Vienna extended to local scientists and from 1911 a trio consisting of mathematician Hans Hahn, physicist Philipp Frank, and social theorist Otto Neurath met regularly in Viennese cafés to discuss Mach and the foundations of science. After the First World War Mach's chair was filled by the German philosopher Moritz Schlick, who had trained as a physicist with Max Planck and shared many of the trio's views. It was the socially adept and urbane Schlick who initiated regular Thursday meetings in Vienna that became known as the Vienna Circle.

Not himself a logician, Schlick moved to bolster logical competence in Vienna by appointing a rising young German logician, Rudolf Carnap, who like himself had worked on the borders between philosophy and physics. Carnap had studied with Frege and Husserl and was well versed in the new logic. Carnap's first major book, *The Logical Construction of the World* (usually called by its short German title, the *Aufbau*) was an heroic attempt to marry the logical methods of Frege and Russell with the phenomenalism of Mach and the first-person constructive perspective of Husserl and in the process scientifically 'recover' the world, no less.

Having read and been forcibly struck by the *Tractatus*, Schlick arranged for the Circle to study the book. The closing remarks on metaphysical nonsense struck a resonant chord with Neurath and Carnap, and Schlick undertook to introduce the socially extremely inept Wittgenstein to the Circle. His persuasive powers brought the two sides together but the meetings were not a social success and soon Wittgenstein restricted his contact to Schlick and Waismann. Nevertheless the combination of the Circle's scientistic attitude and Wittgenstein's dismissive attitude towards metaphysics resulted in the first attempt since Hume to formulate a clear principle by which bad metaphysics (which in their view was all of metaphysics) could be exposed as such. This was the much-vaunted verification criterion of meaning, according to which a statement is meaningful if and only if some observation could count as verifying it. Setting logical truths and falsehoods aside in Wittgensteinian fashion as marginal cases, it proceeded to lay waste to all other forms of discourse, including theology, ethics, and aesthetics, as well as traditional metaphysics.

One important fact about this criterion is that it works with the whole sentence or statement as a unit of meaningfulness, this a legacy of Frege's and Wittgenstein's insistence on the priority of sentences over names. Another is that the verifiability is clearly one in principle, not restricted by mere practical limitations. Neurath, who was opposed to all metaphysics in principle as an anti-democratic hangover from feudal and bourgeois societies, seized on verifiability, as did Carnap. The latter expounded metaphysics in Wittgensteinian fashion, but more systematically, as resulting from misuses of language that produce pseudo-statements that look like statements of fact but in reality are not. These would include statements of value, of theology, and of metaphysics. Philosophical problems are pseudo-problems that arise precisely through such a misuse of scientific language. Carnap in particular identified the practice of speaking about language misleadingly as though it were about the things designated rather than the words, as a source of ready misunderstanding. His remedy was always, when in doubt, to perform 'semantic ascent', the move to talking about language rather than its objects.

The verifiability criterion did not, some renderings to the contrary, debar scientists, or indeed logical positivists, from meaningfully using terms that have ontological import. Someone who states in biology for instance that such and such is a recessive gene is thereby implying that among the things that exist in the world are genes. Nor did its adoption rule out ontological disagreements among positivists. Ever the Marxist, Neurath interpreted scientific statements as being about material bodies rather than the collections of sense-data that phenomenalists such as Mach or Russell thought made up the world. Neurath also persuaded Carnap that this was the best way to treat the basic statements of science. Nevertheless 'victory' over Carnap in an ontological dispute was not a heavy metaphysical matter, because Carnap took the alternatives of materialist (physicalist) and phenomenalist languages to be a matter for convenience and pragmatic decision rather than finding out which one correctly depicted the world. There is some evidence that this kind of light-touch attitude to what the basic names designated also represented Wittgenstein's view at the time he was interacting with the Vienna Circle.

A generally scientific attitude to philosophy was shared not only by the logical empiricists around Hans Reichenbach in Berlin, but also by various groups in France, Britain, Scandinavia, and Poland. Contacts between Warsaw and Vienna proceeded mainly at the level of logic, involving Carnap, Tarski, and Gödel. The Lvov–Warsaw school of philosophy and logic never bought the Vienna Circle's anti-metaphysical stance: their philosophy can best be described as anti-irrationalist, and involved respect for logic, language, and science rather than a rejection of metaphysics. While metaphysical positions among Polish analysts varied widely, from the extreme reism of Kotarbiński via the Husserlian moderatism of Ajdukiewicz to the lush Platonism of Łukasiewicz, they were prepared to disagree metaphysically and regard such disputes as substantive rather than as a matter of linguistic choice. In this way they resisted the excesses of positivism and pointed the way forward to the post-war revival.

The positivist criterion of meaningfulness was attacked almost immediately by Ingarden and others as reflexively self-defeating, since it was itself unverifiable but supposedly meaningful. The effects of this critique can be observed at painfully close range in the tortuously backtracking Foreword to the second edition of the English positivist A. J. Ayer's influential *Language, Truth and Logic*, a work which for many Anglophones encapsulated the excitement and ultimately the failure of the positivist anti-metaphysical crusade. In 1934 Karl Popper proposed his alternative falsifiability criterion, not of meaningfulness but of scientificity: scientific statements are falsifiable; unscientific ones, including metaphysical statements, are not. Like mathematics, metaphysics is assigned by Popper a potentially constructive 'framework' role. Like the verifiability criterion, but for different reasons, Popper's criterion is unsuccessful, but that did not stop him vehemently opposing Carnap's stance on induction and probability, nor did it inhibit him later from subscribing to a three-realm ontology like those of Bolzano and Frege.

Two incidental disadvantages of the attempt to find a blanket recipe for disallowing metaphysics, both already painfully apparent in Wittgenstein's own formulation, but endemic to the enterprise, were that the purveyors of the criterion would be tacitly making metaphysical assumptions while claiming not to do so, and that such a blunt instrument was powerless to discriminate bad metaphysics from good. The former worry was addressed in part by Quine. The latter may be illustrated by two contemporary works that both put forward revisionary metaphysical positions, but which stand the test of subsequent scrutiny to different extents. On the one hand there is Heidegger's *Being and Time* of 1927, proposing a new ontology of humanity, and on the other hand there is Whitehead's *Process and Reality* of 1929, which puts forward a panpsychic cosmology of interrelated events. Both are difficult works to interpret, but whereas Heidegger's later prose grew in opacity, Whitehead's was elsewhere more translucent. Carnap had little difficulty in lampooning Heidegger's 'Das Nichts nichtet' as syntactic nonsense, but much of Whitehead's prose, while grammatical, is at least as tough to interpret. Yet neither is a priori nonsensical.

23.6 ORDINARY LANGUAGE AND DESCRIPTIVE METAPHYSICS

The re-entry of Wittgenstein into philosophy in England, his growing influence, and the parallel development of linguistically oriented philosophy in Oxford under Ryle and Austin kept the focus in British philosophy of the 1930s–1950s on the role of language in formulating and solving or dissolving philosophical problems. Wittgenstein's reluctance both to theorize systematically and to make general statements about what exists kept attention diverted from metaphysical questions, while Ryle's attempts to linguistically undercut Cartesian dualism and Austin's examination of the minutiae of the English lexicon likewise kept attention on matters of language and methodology. It was principally during this period that the myth of a permanent revolution in philosophy, eloquently supported by Russell's dramatizations of his intellectual development, gained sway as a reading of the previous half-century.

However, there were indications for those with an eye to see that metaphysics had not disappeared completely even in these circles. Ryle was after all denying the existence of souls, and proposing that the mental be given a dispositional–behavioural explanation. Austin recommended a phenomenology of language as a preliminary, not the be-all-and-end-all of philosophical theory, and in his theory of truth opposed Strawson's deflationary performative account of truth in upholding a subtle and sophisticated version of the correspondence theory, returning to Russellian facts. With the publication in 1959 of Strawson's *Individuals*, subtitled *An Essay in Descriptive Metaphysics*, stressing the categories of body, person, space, and time, it would appear that metaphysics was making a comeback. Both the appearance and the subtitle were subtly deceptive. Strawson's metaphysics, like that of his mentor Kant, is retained within an epistemological straitjacket. We are constrained to refer to bodies in space and time because that provides a framework for identifiable reference: the argument is transcendental, not ontological. Likewise Strawson's characterization of the useful distinction between descriptive and revisionary metaphysics is a distinction between two different kinds of conceptual scheme: one consonant with everyday common sense and linguistic usage, the other attempting to replace that scheme with another. His preferences clearly on the side of the descriptive, Strawson refuses in Kantian fashion to propose the question which scheme might be correct of the world. This is Königsberg with an Oxford accent, Metaphysics Lite rather than full-strength. The implicit target of Strawson's insistence on the ahistoricity of descriptive metaphysics is his predecessor Robin Collingwood, who had not only embraced metaphysics against the trend of the time, but had insisted that the ultimate presuppositions that make up metaphysics may and will shift as science and human culture develop.

23.7 SCIENTIFIC LANGUAGE AND ONTOLOGICAL COMMITMENT

Although the word 'metaphysics' largely remained taboo in analytical circles, the notion of *ontology* began to be cautiously used, particularly in the context of the discussion launched by W. V. Quine of ontological commitment. Quine had visited the Vienna Circle and other European centres of scientific philosophy. He was especially impressed by Carnap, whose *Logical Syntax of Language* he had seen in preparation in Prague, and by Tarski, whose lectures he had attended in Warsaw. A student of Whitehead and a staunch proponent of the merits of formal logic in philosophy, Quine initially worked on streamlining the logic of *Principia* by new interpretations and a new set theory. The ontological side of his work emerged in the 1930s, probably as a result of his visit to Warsaw in 1933. A dominant logician there was Leśniewski, whose lectures Quine attended. Leśniewski, who had taken his understanding of quantification from Peirce and Schröder, regarded it as acceptable to quantify any variables in logic, while still believing that only individuals exist. Quine, whose understanding of quantification came from Whitehead and Russell, on the contrary took variables, after the semantic fashion he had newly learnt from Tarski, as varying over a domain of objects, different sorts for different kinds of variable. While sympathizing with Leśniewski's view that only individuals exist, Quine disagreed that quantifying sentential and predicate variables was an innocent procedure. Quine later took Leśniewski to be proposing a substitutional interpretation of quantifiers. This verdict is both anachronistic, since the distinction between substitutional quantification, where the quantifier ranges over expressions, and objectual quantification, where they vary over what the expressions designate, was at that time inchoate, and it also misrepresents Leśniewski's view, albeit that this too was then semantically unarticulated.

The upshot was that Quine formulated his principle of ontological commitment: that a theory formulated in the language of predicate logic is committed to those entities that the bound variables of the theory have to range over in order for sentences in the theory to be true. So individual variables range over individuals, sentential variables range over propositions, predicate variables over properties and relations, and set variables over sets. Thus Quine's most famous slogan: 'To be is to be the value of a variable.'

Thus equipped, a scientifically minded philosopher may scan a properly regimented scientific theory and discern to what it commits its proponent, ontologically. Ever inclined towards nominalism, Quine put aside all but nominal variables, but finding the expressive powers of a purely reistic theory too impoverished, he 'embraced' sets, in order to give his scientific language sufficient expressive power to encode the mathematics needed to do modern science. Sets he preferred to properties, propositional functions, propositions, and possibilia because they have clear criteria of identity: sets are the same whose elements are the same. This second principle, 'No entity without identity', became Quine's second slogan and a watchword for scientifically minded philosophers.

It is worth contrasting Quine's views with those of his admired mentor Carnap. Carnap always took the choice of a scientific language to be one of expediency rather than externally mandated principle. For some purposes, it might be beneficial to quantify variables apparently designating mere possibilia, or states of affairs, or numbers. No such choice has the strong metaphysical consequences that Quine's criterion appears to entrain, because we are always able to swap this language for another. Convenience, not the world, dictates the choice. While within a particular language we can say what exists according to that point of view, which is an internal question, there is no saying what exists from a language-external point of view: that is an external question, and in logic, a principle of tolerance reigns, which means that no metaphysical conclusion is to be taken seriously. Carnap's earlier concession to Neurath over physicalism was thus a matter of decision rather than principle, and his parting advice to his students at the end of his career remained uncompromisingly anti-metaphysical.

Quine's advocacy of ontological commitment seems to place ontology on a firmer footing than Carnap's utter rejection, but this appearance also turned out to be deceptive. Because Quine, rejecting both the Vienna Circle and Popper, regarded scientific theories as confronting reality as a whole, rather than sentence-by-sentence, the ultimate test of a scientific theory is its general fit with our experience rather than its correspondence to a supposedly independently existing linguistically unformulated reality. All we know about the world is what our best scientific theories tell us: there is no higher court of appeal, no metaphysics that can trump a scientific result. Metaphysics does not deal with a higher realm and is not a priori: it deals with the same domain of experience as everyday and scientific life, and its concepts are distinguished solely by their greater generality. No statement, not even one of logic, let alone one of metaphysics, is guaranteed forever immune from revision. Admittedly it would take a lot more to persuade someone to give up the law of contradiction than to give up the belief in, say, dark matter, but the principle is the same.

Not all terms in a theory function alike: some are more remote from sensory experience than others. This is where Quine's holism undermines his ontology. We imagine a world exactly like ours, except that the objects that the basic names denote are permuted one-to-one. Provided this permutation remains undetected, as it must if properties and relations are left invariant by the permutation, it makes no difference to science. In other words, which objects are which is not a scientifically determinate affair. This, supported collaterally by the underdetermination of theory by observation and measurement, is ontological relativity. All that remains invariant are the numbers of objects to which a theory may be committed and the relational role they play within the theory. They have no 'identity' beyond this. So there is for example no fact of the matter as to which atom was the first to split in the explosion of the Hiroshima bomb. Quine ends up closer to the Vienna Circle than the ontological terminology would suggest. One way to see this result is that it is the extension of the indeterminacy of identity from a realm where it makes *prima facie* sense, namely pure mathematics, to science in general, where it is less clear. Since Quine denies that there is a difference in principle between mathematical and empirical theories, this is wholly acceptable for him.

The remoteness of ontology from ordinary as well as scientific language was reinforced by Quine's famous doctrine, expounded in his 1960 *Word and Object*, of the indeterminacy of translation, according to which different semantic interpretations may be placed on a corpus of utterances without one being correct at the expense of the others. By compensatory readjustments, my surprised shout of 'There goes a rabbit' may be interpreted variously as 'It rabbiteth yonder' or 'Rabbitish processes are locally concrescent', with differing ontologies, yet equally apt as responses to the scene, and no one will be any the wiser.

23.8 RE-EMERGENCE

We have seen that despite Quine's terminology, his use of the term 'ontology' and its cognates does not constitute a full-on revival of metaphysics in the classical style. While differing in various respects from the 'atheistic' position of Carnap, it remains like Strawson's a very light-touch form of metaphysics, as would be expected from the pragmatist that Quine was. A heavier-duty approach to metaphysics, returning it to the kind of central status it had during ancient, medieval, and early modern philosophy, emerged from different currents of analytic philosophy, starting in the 1950s and continuing to the present.

The first of these was, ironically, logical semantics. This developed from modern logic in the 1930s. Its principal architect was Alfred Tarski, whose seminal work *The Concept of Truth in the Languages of the Deductive Sciences* appeared in Polish in 1933, in German in 1935/6, and finally in English in 1956. In this, the most important work on truth since Aristotle, Tarski showed how to provide a paradox-free delimitation of the true sentences from certain formalized languages, starting a debate about the correct account of truth that continues unabated to this day. Central to Tarski's theory is the idea that we need a number of objects, of type varying according to the language, to provide the raw materials for names to name, predicates to be true of, and for quantification to be interpreted over. The details are not important: what is important is that we need objects, and that they play a role in fixing truth. Neurath immediately and presciently recognized this as the Trojan Horse by which metaphysics could re-enter scientific philosophy via the back door of semantics, and vehemently if unsuccessfully opposed it. Tarski's teacher Leśniewski opposed it for the quite different ontological reason that it makes use of objects Leśniewski rejected, namely sets.

As the limitations of Tarski's languages began to be widely felt, and as the model theory which his work had initiated was more fully developed by himself and other mathematicians, it began to be mooted that ordinary language, with all its complications and non-mathematical features, might be susceptible to the same sort of treatment. Carnap had already initiated such wider work on logical semantics in the 1940s, and this work, especially his 1947 *Meaning and Necessity*, encouraged Tarski's student Richard Montague to broaden the semantic treatment to ever more ambitious parts and features of English and other natural languages, resulting in Montague Grammar, where a wide variety of entities are invoked as the semantic values of expressions such as indexicals like 'I', 'here', and 'yesterday' and modals like 'possibly'.

Modal logic also provided the motor for developing the notion of a possible world, as a 'hidden' index accounting for the truth-values of modal propositions as distinct from merely categorical ones. Inspired by Leibniz, the idea of a possible world, mooted by Arthur Prior and others, came to full prominence in the semantics for modal logics developed by Saul Kripke. Kripke's *Naming and Necessity* (1972) offered a semantic account of proper names at variance with the then standard descriptivist view, proposing that proper names designate the same individual in every possible world (in which they designate anything at all). Reinforced by this powerful semantic vision, and gaining support for their ability to do semantic work, possible worlds soon entered the vocabulary, and in some cases also the ontology, of many analytic philosophers.

The semantic route to metaphysics was not the only one that philosophers took, though it was numerically the most influential. Even during the heyday of positivism and its aftermath, pockets of metaphysical research could be found in analytic philosophy. One such was in Poland, where the pre-war prominence of exact philosophy was eradicated neither by Nazism nor by communism. Another was in Iowa, where a former Vienna Circle member, Gustav Bergmann, reflecting on the failure of positivism, suggested that logical positivism's failure showed in its poor implicit metaphysics of phenomenalism. Inspired by earlier metaphysical Europeans such as Brentano, Meinong, Husserl, Frege, and Russell, Bergmann and his students returned to a face-to-face confrontation with metaphysical issues such as the existence of universals, the nature of facts, and how conscious beings differ ontologically from inanimate objects. A further centre of metaphysics from the 1950s was Australia. The founder of Australian analytical empiricism, the Scot John Anderson, had heard Alexander and had rejected both positivism and Oxford analysis. Anderson's student David Armstrong joined with Scot Jack Smart, Englishman Ullin T. Place, and American Charles B. Martin to debate Ryle's behaviouristic reduction of consciousness, and to reject it in favour of a metaphysical thesis: the identity theory of mind, according to which conscious mental processes simply are processes in the brain. Ironically or not, this is a view adopted in 1916 by the first Australian philosopher of note, Samuel Alexander. While this view sparked a massive and ongoing debate on mind and body, and spawned a host of ever diverging positions, its frank and direct adherence to a metaphysical thesis provided a clarion example to other would-be metaphysicians struggling to lift themselves clear of the ties of semantics.

Of these so-called Australian materialists, the one true Australian amongst them, David Armstrong, continued his metaphysical work in other areas, upholding an Aristotelian realism of universals, whose interrelations account for laws of nature, subscribing to a Russellian ontology of states of affairs, which are given the important semantic task of making sentences true, and construing possible worlds reductionistically via the recombinability of the components of our actual world. Taken together, Armstrong's various treatises constitute a systematic metaphysics in the same general vein as that of Alexander or Whitehead.

23.9 CONSOLIDATION AND FLOURISHING

It is hard to pinpoint a time when metaphysics re-emerged triumphant as a fully paid-up member of the Philosophical Disciplines Club. Quine, Strawson, and Kripke all have claims to have rendered metaphysics acceptable in polite society, while Bergmann and Armstrong offered a new old-fashioned directness in their approach to metaphysics. However, if a single work can be identified that got almost all theoretical philosophers discussing metaphysics again, it was David Lewis' 1986 treatise *On the Plurality of Worlds*, a trenchant and articulate defence of modal realism in the face of 'the incredulous stare', blank ontological inability to accept alternative worlds as real as our own. While making few total converts, Lewis' realism and the vocabulary of counterparts, haecceitism, and intrinsic duplicates that he deploys to defend it, have had philosophers 'doing' metaphysics with little thought for the linguistics. While Lewis' ultimate motivation is that of Montague or Kripke, to provide a proper semantics for modal logic, he is eager to recommend his solution for its own metaphysical sake, and as part of a systematic vision of the world as a Humean mosaic of independent particulars. Around that work Lewis also wove a dense tissue of metaphysical discussion involving properties and relations, structures, sets, states of affairs, persistence and change, all of which instructs subsequent philosophers that it is both profitable and acceptable to engage in metaphysical speculation, which of course is what his view is.

At the same time as Lewis was getting incredulously stared at, other metaphysicians were broaching topics either untouched for generations or wholly new. From this point, some time in the 1980s, analytic metaphysics was a going concern and could be pursued unaccompanied by shamefaced apologies or reference to the positivist past of analytic philosophy. Indeed as historical concerns began to inform analytical philosophy, both in discovering its own lengthening past and in discerning themes pursued in common with previous traditions and epochs, from fourth-century Greece to thirteenth-century Paris to nineteenth-century Vienna, the sense of analytic philosophy as archetypically antithetic or indifferent to metaphysics was replaced by a sense of the positivist era itself as atypical and aberrant.

As our story approaches the present, it becomes harder to pick out enduringly salient works and figures, so we shall confine our attention to some prominent topics, problems, and positions that have been discussed in more recent analytic metaphysics.

One concern, voiced by Lewis in passing, has been to account consistently for the idea of intrinsic change in a persisting individual, as when a leaf changes from green to yellow, or a man changes from sitting to standing. Five solutions have been proposed to this problem, three of them discussed by Lewis, two by others. The first is that a temporary feature like redness in a leaf is not an intrinsic property but a relation to a time. Lewis rejects this out of hand, though it implicitly informs much of the 'at t' style of analysis: the leaf is green at t_1 but red at t_2. A related approach, but subsumed by Lewis under this heading, denies that the indexing of a property to a time makes it into a relation. Lewis also rejects out of hand the extreme idea that only the present exists, so there is no inconsistency to worry about. Perhaps surprisingly, this view, known as presentism, has enjoyed much discussion and some popularity in the philosophy of time, where it contrasts both with eternalism, the idea that all times are equally real, and other views whereby the past grows or the future shrinks. Lewis' preferred solution is that the leaf, the man, and other persisting things have temporal parts or phases as well as spatial parts, so the redness and the greenness belong to different temporal parts of the same temporally extended thing, much as a chessboard has some black spatial parts and some white spatial parts. Defenders of a neo-Aristotelian ontology of substances deny that these have temporal parts, and look for alternative explanation along the lines of the indexing solution.

A fifth option, deriving largely but not exclusively from earlier work of Donald C. Williams, is to take properties not as universals but as dependent individuals, *tropes*, so that change consists merely in the replacement of one colour-trope, of the green kind, by another of the red kind. This view consciously invokes ancient and medieval theories of individual accidents as its forebear. Trope theories of individuals, their properties and kinds have grown in popularity as offering a nominalistically acceptable alternative to Aristotelian theories of properties and change, making fewer ontological commitments than their realist alternatives.

In the assessment of the ontological commitments made by a theory or even a sentence, while Quine's criterion continues to be popular, another criterion widely invoked is that of the required *truth-makers* of a proposition. The idea of a truth-maker, any object which by existing makes some proposition true, is explicit in Russell and Whitehead's logical atomism but already present in medieval philosophy. A truth-maker is any object whose existence is sufficient for a truth: the truth is conversely ontologically committed to such truth-makers as are necessary for it to be true. A lively debate among proponents of this view, first arising in the Australian discussion of Rylean dispositions, has ensued as to what kinds of entities play the truth-maker role, for example whether it is necessary to invoke states of affairs for this purpose, and whether every truth must have a truth-maker.

The Lewisian temporal-part account of persistence, anticipated earlier by Bolzano, Carnap, Whitehead, Leśniewski, and others, draws attention to the notion of a temporal part, and the metaphysical importance of the part–whole relation and its formal theory, mereology, has steadily risen, returning it again to levels found among earlier philosophers from Anaximander to Russell, before the positivist deluge and the hegemony of predicate logic and its standard set-theoretic semantics blunted ontological sensibilities among analytic philosophers. Mereology has not remained a neutral tool, however: like set theory itself it has served as a springboard to further metaphysical controversy. In particular the question has been raised, most notably by Peter van Inwagen, as to when a collection of objects go to compose or make up a further object. This composition question has given rise to two surprisingly extreme answers, namely 'always' and 'never'. The associated metaphysical theories, called composition universalism and compositional nihilism respectively, have commanded much support and even more attention despite their lack of consonance with standard ways of speaking and thinking, an indication that large numbers of metaphysicians are unafraid to be revisionist in their views in support of satisfyingly rounded metaphysical theory. Among the many possible compromise positions between these two extremes, one still uncompromising one is van Inwagen's organicism, according to which the only mereologically complex objects are organisms. Ants exist, tables do not: apart from organisms, there are only simples (mereological atoms). The extent to which such a view comports with science, including not just biology but modern physics, is a moot point.

It has become apparent that philosophers, whether 'straight' metaphysicians or philosophers of science, have become increasingly prepared to let metaphysical considerations enter into their assessment of the nature and status of science and its theories and objects. Metaphysics has to this extent 'gone applied'. For example a seemingly parochial debate among various brands of evolutionary biologist as to the nature of species and the unit of evolutionary selection has both informed and been informed by considerations of set theory, mereology, and other seemingly esoteric metaphysica. In mathematics as well as physics one form of realism about their respective subject matters, entertained for different reasons in each case, is structural realism, according to which the objects dealt with by mathematics (or physics) have no intrinsic properties or natures and no identity apart from their position in relational structures. The extent to which such a position is both coherent and mandated by considerations of the nature of the subject is a matter of ongoing debate, with some proponents of mathematical structuralism insisting their considerations are a priori and a modern kind of logicism, while proponents of physical structuralism claim their position insulates them against the pessimistic meta-induction, the idea that in the long run all scientific theories are false. Structures are precisely what survive scientific change invariantly, is the claim.

While moves to apply ontology and metaphysics to various disciplines have come only sporadically from philosophers, a more urgent requirement for sophisticated ontological analysis is posed by the burgeoning of large databases in medicine, engineering, automated language processing, and the world-wide web, where initial models drawn directly from computer science proved incapable of reflecting the ontological complexity both of the domain and of the knowledge of practitioners in the discipline. While what data modellers call 'ontologies' are implementation-independent conceptual models with implementable interfaces rather than philosophical theories of what there is, their adequate design calls for just the kind of considerations that metaphysicians have been deploying in the name of their discipline since Aristotle, so the equivocation is more than a mere pun.

Metaphysics never remains cut off from other philosophical problems, and one of the most persistent of these has been the mind–body problem in all its forms. While attention has shifted from the identity or otherwise of neural processes with mental processes, problems of interpreting the two marked characteristics of the mental, namely consciousness and intentionality, have provoked a rash of metaphysical speculations of variable generality. While attempts to reduce or eliminate consciousness and intentionality in favour of physicalistically construed processes have met with little success and less acceptance, philosophers keen to stake out a solution have not only formulated the concept of *supervenience*, or covariance across domains, as a potential way to bridge the differences, but have returned more recently to G. H. Lewes' concept of *emergence*, last prominent in Alexander and other philosophers of the 1920s, as a way forward. As with all debates in the area, it is wise not to hold one's breath for a resolution. The difficulties of explaining the emergence of consciousness from matter have prompted a revival not just of mind–body dualism but also of the Leibnizian idea of panpsychism, that all beings, down to fundamental particles, have the germ of consciousness in them. Thus in metaphysics no theory from the past appears to be so conclusively rejected as to be inconceivable for future use. Even the monistic holism of Hegel and Bradley exerts some pull, as does the Leibnizian rejection of relations as genuine constituents of reality.

The question as to what genuinely or fundamentally compromises the world appears to be at the heart of metaphysics, but it too has given rise to two different kinds of controversy. One is whether there is a difference between two kinds of existence, real or genuine existence on the one hand and mere or ordinary existence on the other. Once again, this is a view that seemed to have faded into the past in the wake of Quine's criticisms, but has acquired a new lease of life. As analytical metaphysicians comes to grips with a lengthening tradition of largely unresolved controversies, a second and more fundamental issue gives rise to what has come to be called *metametaphysics*, which discusses the question whether the ontological disagreements to which metaphysics is prone are genuine disagreements at all, and whether there is a right and a wrong answer as to which if either of two disagreeing parties is correct. This raises, in a new key, the disquiet that gives positivism its attraction, namely the idea that metaphysical disputes are somehow not genuine disagreements, but constitute a kind of shadow-boxing. As before, there are the relativists who recapitulate Carnapian tolerance, and there are the strict neo-positivists who instruct metaphysicians to restrict their activity to interpreting the results of corroborated science. As to which science is corroborated and what kinds of ontological commitment it displays, that is either left to the long run, or is shrugged off as a pseudo-problem. This may sound familiar.

23.10 Ways Forward

The plethora of metaphysical theories and concepts that has come to prominence in recent analytical metaphysics invites more than the standard piecemeal treatment of problem after problem characteristic of earlier analytical philosophy. It invites systematization, as practised by all the great metaphysicians. As reliance on predicate logic and its semantics has diminished, it becomes more important to formulate anew and set in connection with one another the system of *categories* which inform such a metaphysics. The source, number, nature, and justification of such categories remains as controversial in metaphysics as it has always been, but one possible way forward in the increasing diversity of metaphysical speculation may be to pay greater attention to the systematic coherence of the system of categories used. An increasing number of analytic metaphysicians are framing questions about the interconnections of their theories via the system of categories deployed. That is just one possible way forward.

Through its development in analytic philosophy, metaphysics has arisen again to the kind of prominence and variety that it enjoyed in medieval and early modern Europe.

Some of the problems it faces are new; many are old, and still unresolved. The course that metaphysics will take in analytic philosophy is largely unclear: it is even unsure whether its present prominence will continue. Perhaps the metametaphysical imponderables will discourage philosophers from pursuing metaphysics and their attention will turn elsewhere. But whether the present Golden Age of metaphysics continues or fades, metaphysical problems will persist, and the concepts and theories proposed by analytical philosophers in the recent phase will take their deserved place in the history of the subject.

REFERENCES

These are the works mentioned and alluded to in the chapter, given in their most definitive or accessible English-language editions.

Alexander, S. (1920). *Space, Time and Deity*. London: Macmillan.

Armstrong, D. M. (1978). *Universals and Scientific Realism*. Cambridge: Cambridge University Press.

—— (1989). *A Combinatorial Theory of Possibility*. Cambridge: Cambridge University Press.

—— (1997). *A World of States of Affairs*. Cambridge: Cambridge University Press.

—— (2004). *Truth and Truthmakers*. Cambridge: Cambridge University Press.

Anderson, J. (2007). *Space, Time and the Categories*. Lectures on Metaphysics, 1949–50. Sydney: Sydney University Press.

Austin, J. L. (1970). *Philosophical Papers*. Oxford: Oxford University Press.

Ayer, A. J. (1936). *Language, Truth and Logic*. London: Gollancz; 2nd edn. 1946.

Ayer, A. J. et al. (1956). *The Revolution in Philosophy*. London: Macmillan.

Bergmann, G. (1954). *The Metaphysics of Logical Positivism*. New York: Longmans, Green & Co., 1954; 2nd edn. Madison: University of Wisconsin Press, 1967.

—— (1967) *Realism: A Critique of Brentano and Meinong*. Madison: University of Wisconsin Press.

Carnap, R. (1947). *Meaning and Necessity: A Study in Semantics and Modal Logic*. Chicago: University of Chicago Press.

—— (1967). *The Logical Construction of the World and Pseudoproblems in Philosophy*. Berkeley: University of California Press. First pub. in German, 1928.

Chalmers, D., D. Manley, and J. Wasserman (eds.) (2009). *Metametaphysics: New Essays on the Foundations of Ontology*. Oxford: Oxford University Press.

Clayton, P. and P. Davies (eds.) (2006). *The Re-Emergence of Emergence*. Oxford: Oxford University Press.

Collingwood, R. G. (1940). *An Essay on Metaphysics*. Oxford: Clarendon Press.

Frege, G. (1984). *Collected Papers on Mathematics, Logic, and Philosophy*. Oxford: Blackwell.

Kim, J. (1993). *Supervenience and Mind*. Cambridge: Cambridge University Press.

Kripke, S. (1980). *Naming and Necessity*. Cambridge, MA: Harvard University Press. First pub. 1972.

Lewis, D. K. (1986). *On the Plurality of Worlds*. Oxford: Blackwell.

Mach, E. (1960). *The Science of Mechanics: A Critical and Historical Account of its Development*. La Salle, IL: Open Court. First pub. in German, 1883.

—— (1984). *The Analysis of Sensations and the Relation of the Physical to the Psychical*. La Salle, IL: Open Court. First pub. in German, 1886.

Montague, R. (1974). *Formal Philosophy: Selected Papers of Richard Montague*, ed. R. H. Thomason. New Haven: Yale University Press.

Moore, G. E. (1993). *Selected Writings*, ed. T. Baldwin. London: Routledge.

Munn, K. and B. Smith (eds.) (2008). *Applied Ontology: An Introduction*. Frankfurt am Main: Ontos.

Passmore, J. (1966). *A Hundred Years of Philosophy*, 2nd edn. Harmondsworth: Penguin. First pub. 1957.

Popper, K. R. (1959). *The Logic of Scientific Discovery*. London: Hutchinson. First pub. in German, 1934.

——(1972). *Objective Knowledge: An Evolutionary Approach*. Oxford: Clarendon Press.

Quine, W. V. (1953). *From a Logical Point of View*. Cambridge, MA: Harvard University Press.

——(1960). *Word and Object*. Cambridge, MA: MIT Press.

——(1969). *Ontological Relativity and other Essays*. New York: Columbia University Press.

Russell, B. (1903). *The Principles of Mathematics*. Cambridge: Cambridge University Press.

——(1959). *My Philosophical Development*. London: Allen & Unwin.

——(1986). *The Philosophy of Logical Atomism and Other Papers, 1914–1919*. Collected Papers, Vol. 8. London: Allen & Unwin.

——(1994). *Foundations of Logic, 1903–1905*. Collected Papers, Vol. 6. London: Routledge.

Ryle, G. (1949). *The Concept of Mind*. London: Hutchinson.

Simons, P. M. (1987). *Parts: A Study in Ontology*. Oxford: Clarendon Press.

Strawson, P. F. (1959). *Individuals. An Essay in Descriptive Metaphysics*. London: Methuen.

Tarski, A. (1956). *Logic, Semantics, Metamathematics*. Oxford: Clarendon Press; 2nd edn. Indianapolis: Hackett, 1983.

van Inwagen, P. (1990). *Material Beings*. Ithaca: Cornell University Press.

Whitehead, A. N. and B. Russell (1910–13). *Principia Mathematica*. Cambridge: Cambridge University Press.

Williams, D. C. (1966). *Principles of Empirical Realism*. Springfield: Thomas.

Wittgenstein, L. (1963). *Tractatus Logico-Philosophicus*. London: Routledge & Kegan Paul. First pub. in German, 1921.

Woleński, J. (1989). *Logic and Philosophy in the Lvov–Warsaw School*. Dordrecht: Kluwer.

CHAPTER 24

META-ETHICS IN THE TWENTIETH CENTURY

JONATHAN DANCY

META-ETHICISTS do not concern themselves directly with what one would think are the most important questions of moral philosophy, namely which actions, or sorts of action, should be done or avoided. Meta-ethics is the study of the nature of moral thought and judgement. This involves attention to the following issues:

Moral metaphysics: are there distinctively moral or evaluative facts, or properties?

Moral epistemology: if there are such facts, how do we come to know them, and if there are such properties, how do we come to discern them?

Moral psychology: what is the nature of moral judgement? In particular, is it the recognition of a fact, or is it the adoption of an attitude? Is there such a thing as moral experience?

Moral motivation: what is the relation between moral judgment and motivation?

The pattern of events in the last century is simple enough in outline. The first forty years were dominated by forms of ethical intuitionism, which were supplanted by Stevenson's emotivism and Hare's universal prescriptivism. These reigned in turn until the early 1970s, at which point Hare's dominance suffered a sudden eclipse. The situation for the last thirty years of the century was much more fluid, with new positions emerging but none of them achieving the sort of paradigm status that intuitionism enjoyed at the outset. In what follows I attempt to document these events and to offer such explanations for them as can be found.

24.1 THE HEYDAY OF ETHICAL INTUITIONISM

The British intuitionists were H. A. Prichard, W. D. Ross, E. F. Carritt, and H. W. B Joseph at Oxford, and C. D. Broad and A. C. Ewing at Cambridge. Prichard was the acknowledged leader of this group, though he published by far the least.

If one wants an account of what drove the intuitionists, I think the best one is that they wanted to make sense of the relevant phenomena (moral debate, disagreement, judgement, belief, and reasoning) just as they appear to the practitioner. Moral thought seems to be an attempt to find out a certain sort of truth—a truth about how to act. Moral debate seems to be an attempt to determine which of two competing views to accept, and the prize that the views are competing for is truth. The intuitionists thought there was no reason to suppose these appearances to be misleading, or to suspect that things are other than they seem.

It is best to think of intuitionism in terms of a series of marks, as follows.

Mark 1: *realism*. Intuitionists assert that there are facts of the matter in ethics as elsewhere.

Mark 2: *cognitivism*. Intuitionists take moral judgement to be a cognitive state. (If challenged, they would probably say that this is a straight consequence of the first mark, since belief is the appropriate attitude to a fact.)

Mark 3: *non-naturalism*. Intuitionists assert that the facts at issue are non-natural facts, not merely that they can be properly characterized using non-natural concepts.

Mark 4: *metaphysical quietism*. Intuitionists show little interest in the metaphysical issues that are so often pressed against them because of their non-naturalism.

Mark 5: *epistemology*. Intuitionists think that at least some of these normative facts are self-evident, and known a priori. (This is the point at which the term 'intuition' makes its appearance.)

Mark 6: *pluralism in the theory of the right*. Intuitionists are suspicious of artificially architectonic theories, and especially of the idea of a Supreme Ethical Principle; they assert several equipollent principles if they deal in principles at all, and if they don't they assert that there are many distinct ways of getting to be right or wrong.

Mark 7: *the independence of the right*. Intuitionists think that the right has a certain independence from the good. So they do not think that every action that is right is so because of the values of its consequences, even if some are. This is why they are not consequentialists.

It is important to realize that one can be an intuitionist without accepting all of these things. The people I listed above did accept them all, with the possible exception of the seventh mark, about which there was debate. But it might be worth classifying as intuitionists thinkers who don't accept everything on my list. There is, for instance, no reason why an intuitionist should not show more interest in metaphysical issues than Prichard and Ross did, and more recent intuitionists have certainly done so.

The intuitionist school was remarkably unified, and in addition to the things I have listed as marks they also agreed on some things that are not themselves distinctive of intuitionism, and may be accepted by proponents of other meta-ethical positions. The main one of these is the general structure of Ross' theory of prima facie duties (1930: ch. 2). There was still debate about the best terminology to employ in the expression of Ross' insight. Most thinkers now accept that the term 'pro tanto' used by Broad in a slightly different connection (1930: 282) would have been a better choice than 'prima facie', with which Ross himself was less than happy. Prichard suggested 'claims'; Carritt offered 'responsibilities'. But the general idea was agreed; indeed Ewing called it 'one of the most important discoveries of the century in moral philosophy' (1959: 126).

Of course the intuitionists did not agree about everything. The most interesting disagreement concerned the sort of independence at issue in the seventh mark. Prichard is hard to read on the point. The difficulty arises because it is possible to deny that all right actions are right because of the value of their consequences while allowing that wherever there is a duty there will be some relation to value. The latter, much weaker and vaguer claim seems to have been allowed by Prichard; in doing so he does not thereby turn himself into a maximizing consequentialist. The question is whether it could ever be our duty to do less good than we might. Ross and Prichard thought that this could and indeed did often happen. Joseph and Ewing argued to the contrary. Joseph asked 'Why ought I to do that, the doing which has no value ... and which being done causes nothing to be which has value? Is not duty in such a case irrational?' (1931: 26; cf. Ewing 1959: 105, 188). In taking this line, Joseph and Ewing of course weaken their defences against consequentialist conceptions of rightness.

24.2 MOORE AND THE OPEN QUESTION ARGUMENT

I have started this chapter with a section on intuitionism, but in a way this distorts the actual passage of events, for the twentieth century started with the publication of G. E. Moore's extraordinarily influential *Principia Ethica* (1903), and Moore is often contrasted with the British intuitionists. But in fact he accepted almost all the marks I listed above, as indeed did Sidgwick before him. The main reason for excluding him from the list of intuitionists is the view expressed in *Principia Ethica* that rightness can be analysed as the property of having the best consequences. This is at odds with the seventh mark; classic intuitionists are not consequentialists. Moore later (1912) changed his mind, asserting only that right actions are those which have the best consequences; but even this is more than intuitionists would accept. Still, in other respects Moore fits pretty well. (It is worth asking similar questions about more recent thinkers such as John McDowell, David Wiggins, Joseph Raz, and Thomas Scanlon; see below.)

For present purposes what makes Moore stand out is his famous argument for the third mark, the Open Question Argument, whose conclusion is that naturalism involves an inevitable fallacy—or better, perhaps, error. This argument has been extraordinarily influential, despite its manifest defects. It is appealed to by the intuitionists, by the emotivists, by Hare, by the expressivists—pretty well everyone seems to feel the need to acknowledge its importance.[1]

---

[1] For recent confirmation of this, see the early pages of Darwall, Gibbard, and Railton 1992, and of Gibbard 2003.

Other writers have documented the influence of the Open Question Argument. But they have not agreed on how best to understand Moore's argumentation, which is hardly surprising given the many acknowledged faults in the presentation in *Principia Ethica*. Some people abandon the attempt to make sense of Moore and simply provide their own argument; the one Hare provides (1952: ch. 5) is not in fact a version of the Open Question Argument at all, but a rather good version of what Derek Parfit has called the Triviality Objection, which is itself an elaboration of a single footnote in Sidgwick's *Methods of Ethics* (1907: 26 n1).

The best version of Moore's actual argument, in my view, was that there is a difference between two questions:

1. Is being good being what we desire to desire?
2. Is being what we desire to desire being what we desire to desire?

The first question is 'open' in a way that the second is not. Moore concluded from this that being good is not being what we desire to desire—and then generalized this conclusion to all possible candidate 'definitions' of being good, or of goodness, in natural terms. Sometimes the conclusion is expressed in terms of properties. The property of goodness is not definable in natural terms, because all possible definitions fall to the distinction between open and closed questions; they render closed a question that should be open.

There are two achievements in general analytic philosophy that are relevant to the success of this argument. The first is Frege's distinction between sense and reference (1892). The second is Kripke's discovery of the possibility of a posteriori necessary truths (1980). I start with Frege. This is a hard place to start because of the contentiousness of any account of what Frege meant by the referent of a predicate. I will be using David Wiggins' account (1984), according to which Frege's distinction between sense and reference applies to predicates as well as to names. The sense of a name is the mode of presentation of the object that is the referent of the name. The sense of a predicate is the mode of presentation of a concept, which is the referent of the predicate.

Let us now apply this to Moore's argument. In Fregean terms, Moore's conclusion is that the concept of being what we desire to desire is not the concept of being good. But this is not the conclusion that Frege would have drawn from the same premises. Frege's conclusion would have been that the sense of the predicate 'is good' is not the sense of the predicate 'is what we desire to desire'. There are two modes of presentation here, not one; but all this is perfectly compatible with there being only one concept differently presented, not two. So those familiar with Frege's distinction should already have rejected Moore's argument.

This is important because the standard response to Moore's argument nowadays is that Moore is only capable of establishing a distinction between concepts, not between properties. Different concepts can still pick out the same property, and there might be two ways of picking out the property of goodness, the natural way (via the predicate 'is what we desire to desire', for example) and the non-natural way (via the predicate 'is good'). We will see claims of this sort shortly. But Frege would say that Moore has not even established a distinction between concepts. And he can say this without even entering into a debate about how many properties are at stake. (Though probably the Fregean picture is that there is no need for properties in addition to concepts and their instantiations.)

Why then was Moore's argument so influential? One possible answer is that the version of Frege's distinction between sense and reference that I have been working with is contentious. If one understands Frege differently, as saying that the sense of a predicate is a concept, and the referent a property (or an extension), things would look different. Moore's argument would then give us the more familiar result that there are two concepts, leaving it open whether there are two properties. But it remains a mystery why Frege's views had no impact on Moore's argument for so long.

I now turn to Kripke. I remember thinking, when the text of 'Naming and Necessity' first appeared (1972), that it was directly relevant to Moore's argument. But one has to work to see what that relevance was. A quick way of making the point is by saying that Kripke showed us that necessarily true property identities could be a posteriori, and so could be surprising; competence with the relevant concepts could not be expected to yield knowledge of the identity of the properties. This is the point about properties and concepts in the previous paragraph. If Moore's argument is that competence with the concepts will not tell us whether the identity is true or false, and that therefore the properties involved are not identical, Kripke has an answer. But one has to be careful here. Kripke's starting point was a distinction between rigid and non-rigid designators. He argued that, when one is dealing with two rigid designators, a true identity statement would be necessarily true, but might still be a posteriori. When one is dealing with non-rigid designators, any identity would be contingent. Now Kripke's main examples of a posteriori necessary identities concern events; the event of my suffering pain is to be necessarily identical with the event of my C-fibres firing. But Moore's argument does not concern events; it concerns such things as being good, and the application of Kripke's approach in this new context is not straightforward.

At first blush we might think that if it is true that being good is being what we desire to desire, it is so only contingently, because the things we desire to desire vary across worlds—and from this we would conclude, I imagine, that it is not true, since those who we imagine making that claim presumably intend it as a necessary truth if true at all. But this would be a mistake. 'Being what we desire to desire' is a rigid designator. What it designates is a property, and it designates the same property in all possible worlds. It is irrelevant that the things that in one world we desire to desire we might, in another, not desire to desire at all.

24.3 EMOTIVISM

It is often supposed that emotivism arose as an offshoot of logical positivism. The reason for this is the *éclat* that greeted the appearance of Ayer's *Language, Truth and Logic*

(1936), which offered, or perhaps one should say preached, an emotivist understanding of moral thought and language as the only one consistent with positivism's basic claim that all propositions are either analytic (and therefore tautologies) or synthetic (and therefore empirically testable and confirmable). Since moral propositions are neither the one nor the other, the only recourse is to say that there are no such things at all. And this is indeed what Ayer did say. But the same suggestion had been made earlier on different and more respectable grounds. The possibility that there are no moral propositions to be known, believed, doubted, asserted, or denied had been mooted two years earlier by Austin Duncan Jones, the first editor of *Analysis*. But his reasons (as reported by Broad 1934: 107–9) were that if we abandon the moral proposition we get good explanations of two things: why no natural analysis can be given of a moral term, and why it is nonetheless possible (though not, of course, uncontentious) to analyse some moral words in terms of others. The only reason for sticking to the moral proposition is the assertoric appearance of sentences such as 'Killing is wrong', which do indeed look very like sentences such as 'Golf is fun'. If we allow ourselves to be influenced by surface similarities, we will be driven to accept the existence of moral propositions, capable of truth and falsity, and of being believed, asserted, and so on. But analytic philosophers were well used to the idea that the surface structure of a sentence may be no guide to the logical form of the proposition expressed. And we already know that some utterances which share the form of 'Killing is wrong' are not what they appear to be. Barnes' example (1948; see also his 1934) is 'Full academic dress will be worn', which he says is not an assertion but a command; this is perhaps not quite the right point, since it concerns speech acts rather than propositional form. But we might argue that 'Full academic dress will be worn' is not a prediction, since its contradictory is not 'Full academic dress will not be worn' but something like 'Full academic dress is not required'. Again, consider the structure of the sentence 'That is a dog'. It is apparently the same as that of the sentences 'That is a shame', and 'That is a relief'. But we all know that this appearance is misleading. 'That is a relief' seems to say much the same as the simple 'Whew!'. So in the light of the evident philosophical advantages of doing without the moral proposition, that is the way we should go.

What are those advantages? The emotivists eventually fixed on two weaknesses in the intuitionists' general position, weaknesses that are common to all versions. The first of these is the familiar metaphysical worry about the addition of distinct normative facts and properties to a world that is characterizable in physical terms. The second, which emerged later (in Stevenson 1948, a piece written in 1941) but proved more effective, concerns motivation. The intuitionists supposed that there were, as one might put it, practical facts. But the facts that they discerned by intuition, though they were no doubt about actions, were still theoretical facts; an action's being wrong is apparently the same sort of fact as its being done on Sunday. And this leads us to say that people might be perfectly capable of discerning these facts without thinking of them as in any way relevant to their choices and decisions. Only those people who already mind about doing the right and avoiding the wrong are going to think of the right/wrong distinction as relevant in this way, just as only those who care about Sundays take it that its being, or not being, Sunday might be a reason for acting or abstaining from action. But this conclusion seems untenable. Somehow we have to make sense of the way in which facts about what is right and wrong are facts about how to act. They seem to have an intrinsic, not an extrinsic, practical relevance. But intuitionism seems not to have the resources to make sense of this.

When it comes to constructing an alternative to intuitionism, various ways of understanding what is going on when people engage in moral debate and deliberation were proposed, compatible with the rejection of the moral proposition. Moral utterances can be thought of as commands, exhortations, expressions of feeling or emotion or attitude, and so on. All these possibilities were debated within the emotivist camp. In the only full-scale presentation of an emotivist position, *Ethics and Language* (1944), C. L. Stevenson's preference was for attitude. For him, moral utterances express the attitude of the speaker and are attempts to affect the attitude of the hearer. Moral disagreements are not disagreements in belief, but differences of attitude.

Stevenson was well aware, however, that many evaluative utterances had what he called 'descriptive meaning' as well as 'emotive meaning'. When I say that you did wrong to take a second slice of cake, there is a mixture of description and evaluation going on. It is also true that, even if I just say 'you were wrong to do that' I represent myself as disapproving of your action, in a way that is close to describing myself as disapproving. Now Stevenson is keen to avoid any understanding of emotive language purely as description of the speaker's attitudes. The intuitionists had succeeded in refuting accounts of 'this is wrong' as identical in meaning to 'I disapprove of this', understood as a self-description. But he wants to allow for an element of description in an utterance that is mainly emotive. He offers us therefore two 'patterns of analysis' of an utterance of 'this is good'. On the first pattern, it is synonymous with 'I approve of this; do so as well'. In this pattern, the description present is self-description. But on the second pattern, ' "This is good" has the meaning of "This has qualities or relations X, Y, Z ...," except that "good" has as well a laudatory emotive meaning which permits it to express the speaker's approval, and tends to evoke the approval of the hearer' (1944: 207). Here the description is not of the speaker but of the object of the attitude. Stevenson thinks it possible to offer two patterns of analysis of the 'same' utterance because, as he puts it, ethical terms are vague, and 'whenever a term is vague there is no sharp distinction between its strict descriptive *meaning* and what it *suggests*' (p. 206). The first pattern understands the speaker's approval as part of the descriptive meaning, while the second understands it more as a suggestion; by contrast, the relevant features of the object are no more than suggested in the first pattern, but supposedly part of the descriptive meaning of the utterance on the second pattern.

In his second book (1939), Ross had attempted to see off emotivism in general by attacking positivism as a theory of meaning. Emotivists replied, correctly, that their position had its own advantages and did not need to be grounded on dubious positivistic doctrine. But Stevenson's emotivism did make its own appeal to a theory of meaning, namely the causal theory developed by Ogden and Richards in *The Meaning of Meaning* (1923). On this theory the meaning of a term was understood as the difference its presence makes to the effect produced in the audience. Stevenson argued that this theory is too simple, since responses vary while the meaning is supposed to remain the same. But he offered a causal theory of his own, according to which the meaning of a sign is 'a dispositional property ... where the response, varying with various attendant circumstances, consists of psychological processes in a hearer, and where the stimulus is his hearing the sign' (54).

As one might imagine, this causal theory did not attract many adherents, largely because it increased the sense that emotivism undermined the rational nature of moral debate. This comes out especially strongly in Stevenson's eventual announcement that a reason is any consideration likely to affect the hearer in the way intended. Hare singles this aspect out for criticism in the first chapter of his first book, insisting that there is a difference between telling someone that something is so, or to do something, and trying to get them to believe it to be so, or to do it. The causal theory of meaning cannot draw this distinction.

24.4 PRESCRIPTIVISM

R. M. Hare's Universal Prescriptivism is not a form of emotivism, but it does share with emotivism the view that there are no moral facts. For Hare, there is no such thing as the right answer to the question 'should I do this?' There are only answers to such questions as 'can I consistently assent to an imperative enjoining me to do this?' The answer to this question may be different for different people. On this point, Hare and the emotivists might have agreed. But in other respects Hare was keen to distance himself from emotivism. For the reasons given at the end of the previous section, Hare thought that on the emotivist picture moral thought was a non-rational process, and wanted to present himself as a moral rationalist.

Hare understands moral utterances as entailing (but not as being) imperatives addressed to everyone. 'Lying is wrong' entails 'Let me not lie' as an instance of the universal imperative 'Let nobody lie'. As Hare sees things, there are no antecedent constraints on the moral attitudes one adopts, and hence on the imperatives one commits oneself to, but there are considerable consistency constraints thereafter, and it is on these that the rationality of moral thought and the possibility of moral argument depend. Hare developed a post-Kantian system under which insisting that others should not treat one in a certain way commits one to not treating others in that way oneself. If I say 'you should not hold me to my promise', I commit myself to a principle of the form 'in such circumstances as we find ourselves, let the promisor not hold the promisee to his promise'. So I cannot consistently prescribe that you treat me kindly without committing myself to treating others kindly in similar circumstances.

This strategy offers a kind of rational leverage that we can bring to bear on inconsistent moralizers, those who expect to get the protection of morality without being willing to accept its constraints. But Hare had larger aims; he wanted to revive a version of Kant's

Golden Rule. This version does not say 'You should treat others as you think they should treat you'. It says 'You should treat others as you wish to be treated'. In Hare's hands, this becomes 'You cannot prescribe that you should be treated, in certain circumstances, in ways to which you are now averse'. The target of this argument is someone who is tempted to treat others in certain ways, but would object strongly if he were treated in that way himself. He may think that those others have certain features (Hare's examples are a hooked nose or a dark skin) that make the difference. But Hare asks 'what do you say now, with your present preferences, about a hypothetical case in which you are in your victim's position (with his nose or skin)?' His claim is that someone who strongly prefers not to suffer discrimination cannot consistently assent to a certain singular prescription (let me, if my skin is dark, suffer discrimination) and so cannot assent to the universal prescription (let those with dark skin suffer discrimination) that entails it (1963: 108–9).

In this way Hare hopes to establish the rationality of moral thought and argument. Since the appeal is always to consistency and to logic, the leverage Hare is applying is rational leverage—hence the 'Reason' in the title of his second book. The 'Freedom' in the title refers to the logical possibility of wanting anything at all (1963: 110). There are no antecedent constraints on what can be wanted and so prescribed; consistency constraints only get a bite once one has committed oneself to something.

Hare's system was extraordinarily influential, and dominated analytic moral philosophy between 1955 and the mid-1970s (roughly). Though it had a meta-ethical core, Hare argued that that core in effect led to Preference Utilitarianism. I think it is fair to say that most people found this argument very unconvincing. But the main objections to Hare's position as a whole were those of Philippa Foot (1958) and Elizabeth Anscombe (1958), who maintained that the freedom from which Hare started was a myth. There are antecedent constraints on what can be wanted, and the content of moral requirements is to some extent given in advance. It makes no sense to say 'it is morally wrong to wear blue trousers' unless some comprehensible reason can be given for this—and only certain sorts of reason are comprehensible as such.

It is generally agreed that Hare's dominance in the subject suffered a dramatic eclipse in the mid-1970s. Reading his work, one gets the impression that his main target was the dreaded intuitionist, who bases everything on certain moral truths, or principles, that are somehow endorsed by intuition and thereby magically validated. In this he was far from being alone: Warnock wrote that intuitionism was 'a confession of bewilderment got up to look like an answer' (1967: 7).[2] Hare's pride was in having constructed a system in which there was no appeal to moral intuitions at all; everything is done by logic. Further, there is no sign of metaphysics, since there are no moral facts to be slotted into the world of physics, and no moral properties to be discerned; there are only assentings and prescribings, which are things that we do, and which raise no metaphysical or

---

[2] For a far more trenchant assessment of intuitionism, I offer this: 'Intuitionism and, more generally, all forms of non-naturalism from Plato to Ross, have fundamentally had one and only one purpose: to help support the morality of self-denial and sin ... the moralities of the fuddy-duddies and sour-pusses' (Edwards 1955: 240).

epistemological difficulties. But by the end of the 1970s all these topics, so recently and so effectively banned, were back on the philosophical agenda. There is a question how this sudden reversal of fortune came about. Certainly Hare himself was quite bewildered by the change, and I think it would be fair to say that he never came to terms with it.

If one looks for ways of explaining what happened, various hypotheses present themselves. Though there were serious arguments against Hare's views, these had been around for some time and it is not plausible to say that they eventually had their effect; for the effect was sudden rather than gradual. One thought is that philosophy is as subject to fashion, boredom, and the desire for change as is any other area of human endeavour. The idea here is that people just got fed up and moved on. Another possibility is to appeal to something in the general intellectual climate in the late 1960s—and there are certainly things there to appeal to.

There are two further things to be mentioned. The first is the appearance of John Rawls' *A Theory of Justice* in 1971. This book had an enormous impact in the United States, though rather less in the UK, where it was treated mainly as a very significant contribution to political philosophy but not so much as a contribution to moral philosophy, in particular meta-ethics. Hare wrote a notorious two-part review of it (1973) in which he complained at great length about Rawls' philosophical methodology, which he saw as nothing more than the juggling of intuitions to get the desired answer. Hare insisted yet again that the only way to make genuine progress in moral philosophy is to start from the logic of 'ought', because here there is no sign of pernicious and unfounded intuitions. The fact that Rawls sought an equilibrium between general intuitions, intuitions of principles, and judgements about particular cases (which for Hare are still intuitions) was for Hare no defence. So a contributing factor to Hare's eclipse might be the way in which Rawls showed that a different sort of methodology, the search for reflective equilibrium with no *fixed* starting points, either of logic or of intuition, could yield apparently significant conclusions; and that moral philosophers seized on this with relief. (See also Rawls 1951, where the elements of his methodology first appeared.)

This explanation seems to me to apply more to the United States than in Britain. In Britain the emerging position was not Rawlsian in inspiration, but far more like the intuitionism that Hare (and others) had supposedly seen off. And the main alternative to that intuitionism was a form of expressivism, advocated by Simon Blackburn, that appeared to owe much more to Stevenson than to Hare.

The leading figures in the return of intuitionism to centre stage were David Wiggins (1976) and John McDowell (1978, 1979, 1981). Now if one is looking for an explanation of the sudden eclipse of Hare, one attractive suggestion is to look at other significant shifts in philosophy at around the same time that can be linked to these two thinkers, and one, at least, suggests itself. This is a concern with Davidson's work on truth and meaning, which emerged in the late 1960s, and was extraordinarily influential in Britain during the next decade.[3] A book published by Mark Platts in 1979, *Ways of Meaning*, is

---

[3] See Miller's chapter in the present volume.

some evidence that there is a connection to be drawn between the latter and the revival of intuitionism. This book is a presentation of Davidsonian theory of meaning, but ends with two chapters on moral realism. (Platts taught at University College, Oxford, where McDowell also taught; Wiggins moved there from London in 1981.) And I remember thinking even in 1970, when as a postgraduate student in Oxford I first read Davidson's 'Truth and Meaning' (1967), that it would make a significant difference to moral philosophy. What then was the connection? One answer is that Davidson showed that there was no need, indeed no room for, Hare's distinction between prescriptive and descriptive meaning. The whole thing is to be done in terms of Tarski-style T-sentences, denotation, and satisfaction, and this applies to moral language just as to the rest; we don't need what we might call compliance-conditions in addition to truth-conditions.[4] The second and perhaps less influential thought was that Davidson showed us how there could be truth without metaphysics. A Tarski-style truth theory runs perfectly well without any appeal to facts that true sentences are to correspond to, even though a full truth-theory will specify, for each true sentence, some truth-condition.

So there are connections between aspects of the Davidsonian programme and the neo-intuitionism that supplanted Hare. It would be nice to be able to say that the revival of moral intuitionism in Britain was a side-effect of the explosion of interest in Davidson that characterized the 1970s there—but nothing like so much in the US. That explosion was just as striking at the time as was the suddenness of Hare's fall from grace, and a link between the two would be explanatory. (And to add a mild autobiographical note, I too was a minor part of the Davidsonian surge, have my Aristotelian side—who from Oxford does not?—and was involved early in the revival of intuitionism.) But I have not been able to persuade either Wiggins or McDowell that there is much in this idea. In private communications, they have both said that it just didn't seem like that to them. This may not be conclusive, but is hard to challenge. And it is to be noted that the attractions of truth without metaphysics, of predicates without properties, which should be evident to those versed in the intuitionist tradition, have not made much impact on McDowell, who takes metaphysical worries as seriously as any.

24.5 THE NEW INTUITIONISM

Intuitionism had collapsed under the pressure of two challenges. The first of these was the metaphysical worry about how the world can have a normative nature in addition to a physical nature. The second, and more damaging, was the motivational challenge. How could intuitionism explain the practical nature of moral judgement, or the practical nature of the facts judged? The dominant theory of motivation was Humean, and this

---

[4] But there is an interesting footnote in Hare's third book *Moral Thinking* (1981: 67) on exactly this point.

led the intuitionists to admit that since moral judgement is belief, there is no intrinsic, or internal, connection between moral judgement and motivation. Those who care about that sort of thing will be motivated, and those who don't will not, even though they are perfectly capable of telling the difference between right and wrong. But this seems plain wrong.

The new intuitionism tackled both of these challenges. McDowell and others produced alternative, cognitive theories of motivation under which certain facts, or beliefs in those facts, can motivate in their own right. (There are traces of such a view in Prichard's early work (1912), but he seems to have abandoned the idea later.) Though it would be wrong to say that these theories of motivation have attracted universal assent, they have at least shown that Humeanism in the theory of motivation is not the only possibility. There is also the point that Humeanism in the theory of motivation is not an independent input, one by appeal to which significant metaphysical conclusions can be imposed on us. For the idea that the world is, as McDowell puts it, 'motivationally inert' is just the same idea as the idea that motivation requires both belief and desire.

On the more metaphysical front, intuitionists have divided into those who stick to the quietism characteristic of Prichard and Ross, and those who take the worry seriously and try to respond. The quietists include Joseph Raz, Thomas Scanlon, and David Wiggins (though Wiggins said to me that he thinks of himself as an aggressive quietist); the non-quietists are led by John McDowell. McDowell has reworked Wilfrid Sellars' distinction between the 'space of reasons' and the 'space of causes', as a distinction between the realm of reasons and the realm of law. This is really a contrast between two forms of explanation: some explanations work by characterizing the events they explain as instances of some law, and others work by showing that the event is an instance of approximation to a rational ideal. For McDowell (1994: 71 n2), this is not a distinction between the causal and the non-causal; he wants to leave it open whether reasons can be causes, taking a flexible attitude to what is allowed to count as a cause. (There might be causes without causal laws.) He also denies that explanations that appeal to law are somehow primary, in a way that would demand 'scientific' validation of explanations that appeal to reasons. Our rational nature, something we grow into with education—which McDowell calls 'second nature'—cannot be and does not need to be explained or grounded from outside in this sort of way (1996). There is nothing quietistic about all this.

A further aspect of the new intuitionism is a general suspicion of the supposedly central role of moral principles. The earlier intuitionists had no problem with principles. But McDowell inveighed early on against conceptions of rationality that see it as the ability to respond to the guidance of formulable universal principles. He preferred to talk about responding to the particularities of the situation at hand. The 'must' that drives one from case to case ('if I disapprove of this, I must also disapprove of that') is not a logical must but a moral must. It appeals not to a logical contradiction, nor to subsumption under a principle, but to a sense of similarity—the sort of sense that underpins all use of language—and that sense of similarity is one into which we are inducted as we become members of a moral community. The richness of McDowell's work here, inspired by Wittgenstein, is partly lost in my later attempts to develop the same general approach in more detail (Dancy, 1993, 2004).

24.6 OTHER APPROACHES

24.6.1 American Naturalism

Moore showed, at the most, that moral concepts are distinct from natural concepts; this is all that the 'autonomy of the moral' amounts to. But this leaves it open to us to maintain that moral properties are natural properties, and that moral facts are natural facts. If they are, we can expect there to be two ways of expressing these facts, the moral way and the natural way. It may be, for instance, that the fact that his action was wrong is the same fact as the fact that actions of that sort tend to reduce human well-being. The concepts involved will not tell us whether this is so or not, of course. But we would establish the identity of property, or of fact, in the same sort of way that we have established other identities now accepted in the scientific community, such as that between heat and mean molecular motion. Here again we have two concepts, but only one property, supposedly. And our identification is reductive in the sense that it goes one way. It is more true to say that heat is mean molecular motion than that mean molecular motion is heat. Similarly, it is more true to say that being wrong is being an act of a sort that tends to reduce well-being than that being an act of that sort is being wrong. As we might put it, being wrong is just being of that sort, but being of that sort is not just being wrong. On this approach, wrongness has been *reduced* and being of a sort that tends to reduce well-being has not.

This approach, largely promoted in the United States (Boyd 1988; Brink 1989; Railton 1986; Sturgeon 1985) has obvious metaphysical advantages, since it finds moral properties and facts a straightforward location within the physical world studied by the sciences (not necessarily the natural sciences, of course). It also provides an easy epistemology. We can discover that an action is wrong by discovering that actions of that sort tend to reduce welfare (to continue with the example). There is no need to appeal to intuition here, any more than we did so to establish the relevant identity.

The influence of Kripke is visible here. These identities are necessary, but a posteriori, just like the scientific identities that they are modelled on. It is not a conceptual truth that being wrong is being of this natural sort; armchair contemplation will not reveal whether it is so or not. Nonetheless, it might be so, and if it is so, the relevant identity proposition expresses a necessary truth.

What happens to the idea that moral judgement necessarily motivates the judger? The intuitionists thought that moral judgement was the recognition of a fact of a special practical sort, one that had some sort of intrinsic connection with action; but they found it difficult to say how that could be. The American naturalists announce straight out that moral facts are just natural facts, and admit that as such they have no intrinsic link to motivation.

24.6.2 Expressivism

The difference between the American naturalists and the intuitionists lay in the nature of the supposed moral properties and the supposed moral fact. The intuitionists maintained that these are stubbornly non-natural, being normative; the naturalists insisted that something could be both normative and natural at once. But each side had difficulty with the practical nature of moral thought and judgement, that is, the way in which such judgements seem to commit the judger to act in one way rather than another. Maybe it is not *impossible* to think sincerely that an act is wrong and still do it, as Hare supposed. But someone who does so seems to have a question to answer. On the naturalist account, what such a person is thinking is (to continue with the example from the previous section) that the act is of a sort that reduces welfare, and it seems quite possible for someone to think this and not to care about it at all. But there seems to be something incoherent about thinking both that an act is wrong and that this is literally irrelevant to one's choices. The naturalists could not explain this; nor, it seems, could the intuitionists.

Expressivism in general is the view that the two sides are both wrong; they differ about the nature of the supposed moral fact, but there are no such facts to differ about. Moral utterances are not attempts to provide information about some peculiar matter of fact, but to express a stance or attitude (and also perhaps to influence people). As such, they have an obvious link with motivation, because someone who has the attitude that a sort of action is wrong is someone who is against it, and their being against it is (pretty well) bound to come out in how they behave. Being against has the sort of inherent practicality that no believing could ever have.

Expressivism is the modern successor of emotivism, and like the emotivists, expressivists are capable of differing about what the moral judgement actually expresses. For Simon Blackburn (1993) it is an attitude; for Allan Gibbard (1990) it is acceptance of a norm. Of course, the intuitionists could have agreed, so far as this goes. But they thought that when we express an attitude (that of approval, say), we do this by saying something about the action, that it is right. The expressivists want to do without this last bit. But they do think, in one way or another, that there is something going on that used to be called 'dynamic', namely a call on the audience to join in. As Blackburn put it recently, one is not merely letting people know that one has the attitude. One is doing this, but the attitude is put forward as one 'to be adopted' (2006: 151). This is analogous to what is going on when one expresses an opinion on some matter of fact. One is indeed letting people know that one holds that opinion, but one is also putting that opinion forward as one to be adopted by one's audience. Actually in the moral case Blackburn should have said that there are three stages: one expresses one's attitude, one *thereby* lets people know that one holds that attitude, and one also presents the attitude as one to be adopted by others. The intermediate autobiographical element is a mere by-blow in this.

Two very different difficulties have been raised for expressivism. The first is the notorious Frege–Geach problem (Geach 1960), which starts from the point that when I say, 'Stealing is wrong', I express disapproval of stealing, whereas when I say 'If stealing is wrong, it should be punished', I do not. This may not look like much of a problem until one asks how to display the validity of modus ponens in cases where the antecedent is 'stealing is wrong'. The argument is:

> Stealing is wrong
> If stealing is wrong, it should be punished
> So stealing should be punished.

And the problem is that the expressivist account of the first premise does not apply to the antecedent of the second premise; no attitude is being expressed there. But it is important to the validity of the inference that the very same thing that is somehow put on the table by the first premise should reappear as the antecedent of the second. Intuitionists have no difficulty here, since on their account the same moral proposition appears in both premises. Can expressivists somehow manage to say something similar within the confines of their approach (that is, without reintroducing the moral proposition)?

The second difficulty was very different. Expressivism is in the business of offering very different accounts of fact-stating discourse (and thought) and of evaluative discourse (and thought, again). Of course it could be allowed that some actual discourse contains elements of both, as when I say 'That was stealing, and so wrong'. But the expressivist programme requires that the fact-stating (or 'descriptive') element should be in principle disentanglable from the evaluative one in every case. No doubt this can often be achieved, as in the case above. But the new intuitionists argued that it is very implausible to suppose that fact and value can always be disentangled in this way (McDowell 1981). The discussion focused on the so-called 'thick concepts', such as 'honest', 'cruel', 'elegant', and 'tactful', but the same point could have been made about the thin concepts such as 'right' and 'wrong'. The point was that expressivists seem to have to suppose that instances of such concepts must share a common 'descriptive' nature; consistency in the use of the concept will amount to the adoption of the same attitude to all the things that share that descriptive nature. So there would have to be such a common nature to all wrong actions, and in principle that nature could be discovered by creatures who had no idea whatever of the point of the distinction between right and wrong. Such creatures could predict our approvings and disapprovings without having any understanding of the moral distinctions we are drawing. But all this seems very improbable. Actions can get to be wrong in all sorts of ways, and those ways need not display any 'natural' similarity at all; the similarity they display is a moral one, and it is only discernible by those who have a grasp on the point of the concept, which is not itself visible at the descriptive level.

There was a third point made against expressivism in general. This was that the disentangling of descriptive and evaluative required that in each case there be a separately discernible attitude. The idea was that actions can be sorted in descriptive terms, and we adopt attitudes to actions so sorted—and then we are led to try to turn the nature of our attitude into a property of the action. So we are interested in an action, and we award the action a property of 'being interesting'; we are appalled by an action and we award it a property of 'being appalling'. In both cases we are thinking of the action as being such as to merit a certain response—the response we give it, in fact. Now all this works well in some cases, where there is a distinct and recognizable response to start from. But not all evaluative terms are lucky enough to have one of those. Suppose we start from the idea of the elegant, in aesthetics. There just doesn't seem to be a distinct response to elegance that can be characterized in any other terms than 'recognizing elegance'. So the idea that we make a property out of an attitude doesn't seem to be very convincing in this, and many other cases (Wiggins 1975).

There is a fourth criticism of expressivism, which is that it does not take sufficiently seriously the assertoric nature of evaluative discourse. We see no difficulty in talk of truth and falsehood in ethics, of people who make mistakes, of reasons for believing an action to be wrong, and so on. Realists pounce on these things as evidence that moral discourse is factual discourse, which is what the expressivist denies. Simon Blackburn's quasi-realism (1993) is a form of expressivism that tries to show how a discourse expressivistically conceived might still display the features that tempt people to realism. These features include our sense that we might be wrong in our own moral beliefs and that there is a right answer if we could only find it.

I commented above on the fact that Blackburn's expressivism seemed to owe more to Stevenson than to Hare. Gibbard's most recent book, *Thinking How to Live* (2003), is, by contrast, astonishingly and explicitly close to Hare, especially in the early chapters. But then Gibbard has shown much more willingness to admit something like the moral proposition (for instance, in the way he has tried to resolve the Frege–Geach problem), and in this he resembles Hare. For Hare maintained that moral judgements are not imperatives but entail imperatives. And it seems impossible for them to do so if they have no propositional content. So it would not be true to say that Hare's influence effectively ended in the 1970s, and that subsequent thinkers took their lead rather from Stevenson. Some did, and some didn't.

Before leaving expressivism, it is worth asking whether later expressivists have managed to improve on Stevenson's account of a reason as any consideration that might lead one's interlocutor to agree with one. My own suspicion is that they have not. Hare prided himself on doing better, but on his account there are no such things as reasons not to do an action, or reasons why an action is wrong. There cannot be reasons why an action is wrong because there are no such things as wrong actions. There are only actions that are universally proscribed (as opposed to prescribed), and 'universally proscribed' does not mean 'proscribed by all': it means rather 'proscribed for all', and this just raises the question who is doing the proscribing. I may proscribe this sort of action universally, saying 'Let nobody do this'. You may not. There is no question which of us is right.

Hare can allow that a person who prescribes actions of a certain sort will do so for a reason. The reason will consist in the features of the action that led that person to prescribe it. And once one has prescribed actions of a certain sort universally, one has a reason—a reason of consistency—to do actions of that sort when the opportunity arises. But this is as far as Hare can go.

Blackburn and Gibbard have attempted to make expressivist sense of the notion of a reason for action. Doing this must involve saying what one is expressing when one says, or thinks, 'there is some reason to do this action'. Blackburn's *Ruling Passions* (1998: 257) offers the suggestion that a reason is 'a feature that prompts concern'. This does not look very promising, because something might very well prompt concern without deserving to. If we were to read 'prompt' as 'ought to prompt', things look better. But either the 'ought' in this phrase is itself a contributory ought, which is the same thing as a reason and so would leave us no further forward, or it is an overall ought, in which case the analysis (if such it is) would be plain wrong.

Gibbard writes (1990: 163):

> To say that R is some reason for S to Φ in C is to express acceptance of a system of norms that direct us to award some weight to R in deciding whether to Φ in C.

The obvious question is how to understand the notion of weight in this. I don't see any way of avoiding the idea that to award weight to a consideration is to treat it as a reason, in which case the analysis makes covert appeal to the notion of which it is intended as an expressivist explication.[5]

24.6.3 Post-Kantian Constructivism

Constructivists maintain that moral principles and values are in a certain sense constructed. They tend to have little time for expressivism, and contrast their position mainly with that of the intuitionists, who are their official opponents. What the intuitionists get wrong, supposedly, is that they think of rightness and wrongness as properties that exist out there in a sort of independent order, knowable by intuition, and prior to and independent of any procedures that we might employ to determine which sorts of action have such properties. The constructivist, by contrast, thinks that rightness and wrongness, if they are to be defensible at all, must be in some way constructed out of the procedures we employ to determine which actions are right and which wrong.

This general statement leaves open three forms of constructivism. On the first form, the properties of rightness and wrongness are themselves somehow constructed. An example of such a view might be attributed to Kant if we suppose him to have held that what it is for an action to be wrong is for it to be impossible for its maxim to be willed as a universal law for all rational beings. Wrongness is, as it were, made out of what can and what cannot be willed. Such a view would be realist, as I am using the term,[6] since there are facts about what can and what cannot be willed, and such facts are facts about what

---

[5] Gibbard tries to do better in his 2003 (pp. 189–90).

[6] Though it should be noted that Kantians tend to oppose their forms of constructivism to any realist position; see e.g. Korsgaard 2003 and O'Neill 2003.

is wrong and what is not. But it is not intuitionistic, because intuitionists don't think that rightness and wrongness need to be *made* in this sort of way.

A different view of the same sort—one that gave a constructive account of the moral properties themselves—would be that of Thomas Scanlon (1998), if we take him to have suggested that what it is for an action to be right is for it to be required by moral principles that no reasonable person could reject.

There are different forms of constructivism, however, under which the properties of rightness and wrongness are not themselves constructed, but still the procedures that Kant or Scanlon have in mind are centrally relevant to the way in which actions get to have those properties. In Scanlon's case, we might say that wrongness is just the property of being 'not to be done' (in Parfit's phrase), and then we ask how it is that an action can get to have that property. Two sorts of answer emerge, generating two further forms of constructivism. The first is that actions get to have that property by being such that their performance is forbidden by principles to which no reasonable person could object. On this approach, all wrong actions are wrong for the same reason: they have what we might call the Scanlonian property. The question would then be how an action could get to have *that* property, and the answer might be that there are lots of ways: by being a vicious killing, for instance, or by being the sort of way that banks have recently been behaving. This three-level picture would be worth calling constructivist. Kant's account could be reworked in this way. What makes an action wrong is that its maxim cannot be willed as a universal law for all rational beings. What makes *that* the case might be all sorts of things, and Kant himself gives a range of examples.

Myself, I don't find the structure of this form of constructivism very convincing, because I don't feel the pressure to announce that all wrong acts are wrong for the same reason. But there remains another way of running a position that is still recognizably constructivist. This announces that the sorts of thing that make an action wrong are the ordinary features of being a vicious killing, of being thoughtlessly careless with other people's money, and so on. The constructivist element would come in when we ask how it is that some features can make an action wrong and others cannot. Our explanation of why it is that *this* feature is a wrong-maker would appeal, say, to the fact that principles forbidding actions of that sort are ones to which no reasonable person would have an objection, or to the fact that maxims permitting actions of that sort could not be willed as universal laws for all rational beings. So there is still a central place for the Scanlonian property (or for the Kantian one), but it is a different place.

Intuitionists would say that there is no need for this sort of explanation. Constructivists are distinguished by their sense that the wrongness of a wrong act is a peculiar sort of property and needs a special sort of explanation, while the intuitionists see no need for any such thing. So as we have seen, this contrast between constructivism and intuitionism can emerge in three different ways, or at three different places.

Rawls is a constructivist about justice. He held that a just society is one whose basic arrangements would be endorsed by persons in the Original Position. The Original Position is defined in terms of what such persons do not know. Roughly, they know general facts about the society they are in (such as the proportion of rich to poor) but they do not know particular facts about themselves (such as whether they are rich and talented or poor and prospectless).

Rawls is not a constructivist about the right and the wrong. His view seems to be that an action is wrong if it is forbidden by the best view we can come to about which sorts of actions are right and which wrong, that is, by the most defensible set of moral principles. The most defensible set of principles is that set which best fits our considered moral judgements about particular cases and any other general views and theories we might accept (e.g. in sociology and psychology). This is not a form of constructivism, as I see it, because it holds that an action is right if it is right according to the best overall view about which sorts of action are right. Rightness itself is not constructed here, nor is there any sign of the other forms of constructivism outlined above. (But see O'Neill 2003.)

24.7 BRIEF SUMMARY

The twentieth century began with what was a broadly intuitionistic consensus on meta-ethical issues. After the Second World War this was supplanted by forms of anti-realism, of which the most dominant was expressivist. Intuitionism managed eventually to claw its way back into the picture, but only as one among several live options, none of which enjoys any sort of dominance.

REFERENCES

Anscombe, E. (1958). 'Modern Moral Philosophy', *Philosophy* 33: 1–19.

Ayer, A. J. (1936). *Language, Truth and Logic*. London: Gollancz.

Barnes, W. H. F. (1934). 'A Suggestion about Values', *Analysis* 1: 45–6.

—— (1948). 'Ethics without Propositions', *Proceedings of the Aristotelian Society, Supp. Vol.* 22: 1–30.

Blackburn, S. (1993). *Essays in Quasi-Realism*. Oxford: Oxford University Press.

—— (1998). *Ruling Passions*. Oxford: Oxford University Press.

—— (2006). 'Antirealist Expressivism and Quasi-Realism'. In D. Copp (ed.), *The Oxford Handbook of Ethical Theory*. Oxford: Oxford University Press, pp. 146–62.

Boyd, R. (1988). 'How to be a Moral Realist'. In G. Sayre-McCord (ed.), *Essays on Moral Realism*. Ithaca, NY: Cornell University Press, pp. 181–228.

Brink, D. (1989). *Moral Realism and the Foundations of Ethics*. Cambridge: Cambridge University Press.

Broad, C. D. (1930). *Five Types of Ethical Theory*. London: Kegan Paul, Trench, Trubner & Co.

—— (1934). 'Is "Goodness" a Name of a Simple Non-Natural Quality?', *Proceedings of the Aristotelian Society* 34; reprinted in Cheney (1971), pp. 106–23.

Cheney, D. (ed.) (1971). *Broad's Critical Essays in Moral Philosophy*. London: George Allen & Unwin.

Dancy, J. (1993). *Moral Reasons*. Oxford: Blackwell.

—— (2004). *Ethics Without Principles*. Oxford: Oxford University Press.

Darwall, S., A. Gibbard, and P. Railton (1992). 'Toward Fin de Siècle Ethics: Some Trends', *The Philosophical Review* 101: 115–89.

Davidson, D. (1967). 'Truth and Meaning', *Synthese* 17: 304–23.

Edwards, P. (1955). *The Logic of Moral Discourse*. New York: Free Press.

Ewing, A. C. (1959). *Second Thoughts in Moral Philosophy*. London: Routledge & Kegan Paul.

Foot, P. (1958). 'Moral Arguments', *Mind* 67: 502–13.

Frege, G. (1892). 'On Sense and Reference'. In M. Beaney (ed.), *The Frege Reader*. Oxford: Blackwell, 1997, pp. 151–71.

Geach, P. T. (1960). 'Ascriptivism', *The Philosophical Review* 69: 221–5.

Gibbard, A. (1990). *Wise Choices, Apt Feelings*. Oxford: Clarendon Press.

——(2003). *Thinking How To Live*. Cambridge, MA: Harvard University Press.

Hare, R. M. (1952). *The Language of Morals*. Oxford: Clarendon Press.

——(1963). *Freedom and Reason*. Oxford: Oxford University Press.

——(1973). 'Critical Study: Rawls' Theory of Justice', *The Philosophical Quarterly* 23: 144–55 and 241–52.

——(1981). *Moral Thinking*. Oxford: Oxford University Press.

Joseph, H. W. B. (1931). *Some Problems in Ethics*. Oxford: Clarendon Press.

Korsgaard, C. (2003). 'Realism and Constructivism in Twentieth-Century Philosophy', *The Journal of Philosophical Research*, APA Centennial Supplement, Philosophy in America at the End of the Century: 99–122. Repr. in Korsgaard, *The Constitution of Agency*. Oxford: Clarendon Press, 2008, pp. 302–26.

Kripke, S. (1980). *Naming and Necessity*. Oxford: Blackwell. Previously published in D. Davidson and G. Harman (eds.), *The Semantics of Natural Language*. Dordrecht: Reidel, 1972, pp. 253–355, 763–9.

McDowell, J. (1978). 'Are Moral Requirements Hypothetical Imperatives?', *Proceedings of the Aristotelian Society, Supp. Vol.* 52: 13–29; repr. in McDowell (1998), pp. 77–94.

——(1979). 'Virtue And Reason', *The Monist* 62: 331–50; repr. in McDowell (1998), pp. 50–73.

—— (1981). 'Non-Cognitivism and Rule-Following'. In S. Holzman and C. Leich (eds.), *Wittgenstein: To Follow a Rule*. London: Routledge & Kegan Paul, pp. 141–62; repr. in McDowell (1998), pp. 198–218.

——(1994). *Mind and World*. Cambridge, MA: Harvard University Press.

——(1996). 'Two Sorts of Naturalism'. In R. Hursthouse *et al.* (eds.), *Virtues and Reasons: Philippa Foot and Moral Theory*. Oxford: Clarendon Press; repr. in McDowell (1998), pp. 167–97.

——(1998). *Mind, Value, and Reality*. Cambridge, MA: Harvard University Press.

Moore, G. E. (1903). *Principia Ethica*. Cambridge: Cambridge University Press.

——(1912). *Ethics*. London: Home University Library.

Ogden, C. K. and I. A. Richards (1923). *The Meaning of Meaning*. London: Routledge & Kegan Paul.

O'Neill, O. (2003). 'Constructivism in Rawls and Kant'. In S. Freeman (ed.), *The Cambridge Companion to Rawls*. Cambridge: Cambridge University Press, pp. 347–67.

Platts, M. (1979). *Ways of Meaning*. London: Routledge & Kegan Paul.

Prichard, H. A. (1912). 'Does Moral Philosophy Rest on a Mistake?', *Mind* 21: 21–37; repr. in Prichard (2002), pp. 7–20.

——(2002). *Moral Writings*, ed. J. MacAdam. Oxford: Clarendon Press.

Railton, P. (1986). 'Moral Realism', *The Philosophical Review* 95: 163–207; repr. in Railton, *Facts, Values, and Norms: Essays Towards a Morality of Consequence*. Cambridge: Cambridge University Press, 2003, pp. 3–42.

Rawls, J. (1951). 'Outline of a Decision Procedure for Ethics', *The Philosophical Review* 60: 177–97.

——(1971). *A Theory of Justice.* Cambridge, MA: Harvard University Press.

Ross, W. D. (1930). *The Right and The Good.* Oxford: Clarendon Press.

——(1939). *Foundations of Ethics.* Oxford: Clarendon Press.

Scanlon, T. (1998). *What We Owe to Each Other.* Cambridge, MA: Harvard University Press.

Sidgwick, H. (1907). *Methods of Ethics,* 7th edn. London: Macmillan.

Stevenson, C. L. (1944). *Ethics and Language.* New Haven: Yale University Press.

——(1948). 'The Nature of Ethical Disagreement', *Sigma* 8–9; repr. in J. Rachels (ed.), *Ethical Theory 1: The Question of Objectivity.* Oxford: Oxford University Press, 1998, pp. 61–8.

Sturgeon, N. L. (1985). 'Moral Explanations'. In D. Copp and D. Zimmerman (eds.), *Morality, Reason and Truth.* Totowa, NJ: Rowman & Allanheld, pp. 49–78; repr. in G. Sayre-McCord (ed.), *Essays on Moral Realism.* Ithaca, NY: Cornell University Press, 1988, pp. 229–55.

Warnock, G. J. (1967). *Contemporary Moral Philosophy.* London: Macmillan.

Wiggins, D. (1976). 'Truth, Invention and the Meaning of Life', *Proceedings of the British Academy* 62: 331–78; repr. in Wiggins, *Needs, Values, Truth: Essays in the Philosophy of Value.* Oxford: Blackwell, 1987, pp. 87–137.

——(1984). 'The Sense and Reference of Predicates: A Running Repair to Frege's Doctrine and a Plea for the Copula', *The Philosophical Quarterly* 34: 311–28.

CHAPTER 25

....

NORMATIVE ETHICAL THEORY IN THE TWENTIETH CENTURY

....

JULIA DRIVER

NORMATIVE ethical theory underwent a period of refinement in some areas and proliferation in others during the twentieth century. Theories prominent in the nineteenth century, such as Utilitarianism, underwent refinement in light of criticisms; other approaches, such as normative intuitionism and virtue ethics, were developed in new directions, ones that reflected the sophistication of analytical techniques developed by philosophers in the twentieth century, particularly in ordinary language philosophy. The middle of the twentieth century was marked by an interest in conceptual analysis and what could be revealed about our concepts in the analysis of 'ordinary' language appeals to those concepts. For example, Gilbert Ryle argued that the hope of clearing up our concepts via formalizing them was futile, and instead the task of philosophy was to clear up confusions present in the ordinary use of concepts, concepts employed by ordinary people as well as specialists in a given area.

Normative ethicists in the very early part of the twentieth century had not yet adopted a 'scientizing' attitude to philosophy. They believed, for example, that one could rely on intuition in formulating ethical theories.[1] Theorists in the early part of the century were also optimistic about the prospects of systematizing normative ethics in a way that would be faithful to our common-sense normative judgements. This began, largely, with a critical look at Utilitarianism.

---

[1] See Thomas Hurka, 'Normative Ethics: Back to the Future', in Brian Leiter (ed.), *The Future for Philosophy* (Oxford: Oxford University Press, 2004), pp. 246–64, for a discussion of this trend in twentieth-century normative ethics.

25.1 UTILITARIANISM

At the opening of the twentieth century, in the Western tradition, normative ethics was dominated by Utilitarianism. Though the work of the Classical Utilitarians, Jeremy Bentham and John Stuart Mill, had been rejected by philosophers dissatisfied with its commitment to hedonism, most writers worked within the tradition articulating variations on the basic structure. In *Principia Ethica*, for example, G. E. Moore developed Ideal Utilitarianism. Though Moore was best known for his work in meta-ethics—work that appeared to influence later non-cognitivists such as Ayer and Stevenson—his work in normative ethics is also notable.[2] He shared with the classical Utilitarians the view that value is agent-neutral, though he differed on the specific nature of intrinsic value. Even Mill's modified hedonism, which incorporated various perfectionist intuitions to avoid some of Bentham's problems, was attacked as too narrow.

Moore's discussion of intrinsic value influenced later work in value theory. Notably, people were interested in how it is that we can make determinations of intrinsic value, and Moore's work led to improvements over how to identify intrinsic value. Earlier methodologies relied on a finding of explanatory primacy. Try to think of 'good' things, and then ask 'what makes x good?' Good is then reducible to the terms of explanation. The hedonists believed that this method reduced good to pleasure and avoidance of pain. But Moore challenged this with another test—the isolation test. He believed that intrinsic value, whatever it is, must be an intrinsic *property*. A pleasure state with a bad object is not intrinsically good. If it were, then we would be committed to judging it good in the absence of bad effects (i.e. in isolation from the normal consequences of, for example, sadistic pleasure, or pleasure in causing pain to others). Since this is not the case, pleasure is not the sole intrinsic good. Consciousness of pleasure is, at best, a slight intrinsic good on his view.[3]

Moore's attack on hedonism set the stage for a surge of interest in the issue of intrinsic value. Moore himself believed that 'good' was unanalysable. This was hotly contested. Writers shortly after Moore, such as W. D. Ross and A. C. Ewing, regarded the good, or intrinsic value, as analysed in terms of what is worthy of being valued—so they give an attitude-based account. But the issue of value became a major topic of discussion in the twentieth century, leading to numerous ways of avoiding the problems raised for hedonism. These analyses can be broadly classified as subjective or objective. Subjective accounts hold that what has intrinsic value must be subjective—such as pleasure, or preference or

---

[2] See William Shaw's *Moore on Right and Wrong: The Normative Ethics of G. E. Moore* (New York: Springer, 1995) for a discussion of Moore's neglected normative ethics. See Dancy's chapter in this volume for a discussion of Moore's meta-ethical work.

[3] G. E. Moore, *Principia Ethica*, 2nd edn., ed. T. Baldwin (Cambridge: Cambridge University Press, 1993), p. 212.

desire satisfaction. Some argue that, on the contrary, it must be objective—for example, the actual embodiment of a virtue state regardless of the agent's beliefs and desires. Each approach to value has its own set of problems—Derek Parfit, for example, showed the difficulty of coming up with a theory of value that could satisfactorily avoid serious problems, such as the repugnant conclusion and the non-identity problem, among others.[4]

Value is just one component of consequentialism (indeed, it is a distinct issue, though of significant importance to particular consequentialist accounts of rightness). The other component is the approach to value taken by the theory. For the classical Utilitarians, that approach was maximization, and Moore's work did not attack this aspect of the theory. However, other writers such as Ross and Prichard would attack this aspect of the theory by holding that moral norms are, in fact, pluralistic and, further, that maximizing along a single parameter is mistaken (see below).

The attacks on classical Utilitarianism led to more sophisticated developments of the theory in the latter half of the twentieth century. For example, R. M. Hare developed a sophisticated two-level approach to Utilitarianism (1981). Hare's insight involved recognizing that human beings are flawed reasoners. If we were better reasoners, if we could make reliable decisions quickly and impartially, then it might make sense to consciously employ the principle of utility on every occasion we are called on to make a moral decision. However, this is not compatible with a realistic view of human nature. Hare dubbed the perfect reasoner the 'Archangel'—what we ought to do, what the right thing to do in the circumstances, is what the Archangel would advise one to do. But people don't have access to this perspective. Hare distinguishes between two levels of moral thought—the intuitive and the critical. Given our limitations in most contexts it pays to rely on the intuitive level—these are norms we've inculcated which rest on prima facie principles, ones that are overridable, but which generally lead to the best results. Of course, in situations where we have plenty of time, and access to a lot of information, relying on these principles rather than consciously applying the principle of utility itself, may not be the best option. Sometimes we will need to adopt the critical perspective of consciously employing Utilitarianism to examine our intuitive commitments, and whether they properly apply in a given case.

Hare's account responds to a variety of earlier criticisms. Note that on this view one is not supposed to think consciously in Utilitarian terms, unless, of course, that produces the best result in the specific case at hand. Indeed, it is better for most people to rely on intuitive principles. Hare's account explains why doing the right thing may not feel right. When intuitive principles conflict—such as one ought not to lie and one ought to be loyal to one's friends—because there is a commitment to these principles a person who violates one will feel bad about it, even though the choice may have been the right one. Hare's account explains why we might actually blame someone for doing the right thing, because we may feel that the action reveals a lack of commitment to the best intuitive-level principles.

---

[4] Derek Parfit, *Reasons and Persons* (Oxford: Oxford University Press, 1984).

Another development was clearer articulation of the rule-utilitarian alternative to act-utilitarianism. Act-utilitarianism holds that the right action is the action that produces maximally good effects. Rule-utilitarianism holds that the right action is the action performed in accordance with a system of rules that maximize the good. Rule-utilitarianism is an indirect type of utilitarianism, since the rightness of an action is not determined by its own effects but, rather, by the effects of something else associated with the action (in this particular case, a system of rules). The advantage of this approach is that it is seen to avoid the problems of act-utilitarianism in that it will not recommend all actions that maximize utility. In principle, the act-utilitarian must concede that it may be obligatory to kill an innocent person to save the lives of even more innocent people. The rule-utilitarian, on the other hand, is not committed to this at all, since killing an innocent person would violate a rule in the best system of rules. Richard Brandt spelled this out in his *A Theory of the Good and the Right*. There he argues that 'right action' is best thought of in terms of the question: 'Which actions would be permitted by the moral code which a fully rational person would most strongly tend to support, for a society in which he expected to live a lifetime?'[5] There are many objections to this approach. Some argue that, when the rules are fully specified so as to be plausible, the account collapses into act-utilitarianism. To avoid the collapse, the rule-utilitarians need to insist on no violations of the rules, no matter the consequences, and this seems like a form of irrational 'rule-worship'. Rule-utilitarians argue that one can avoid this unpalatable result by keeping the rules of the system fairly simple, so that the inculcation costs are fairly low, while allowing for an 'avoid disaster' clause in the account. Thus, one can break the rule 'Don't kill an innocent person' if that is necessary to avoid a 'disaster'.[6]

Hare and Brandt weren't alone in developing more sophisticated versions of Utilitarianism, though writers were moving away from explicitly Utilitarian views and embracing a more general form of consequentialism—not committed, for example, to subjective value theory nor even to maximization of the good.[7]

Reasons for challenging Utilitarianism came from without the theory as well as from within. In her essay 'Modern Moral Philosophy' Anscombe criticized the theory for its seeming recommendation of vicious actions in virtue of their promotion of good effects. This is the criticism that Utilitarianism, or consequentialist approaches in general, are basically incompatible with justice since the consequentialist justifies actions on the basis of reasons that are forward looking. This means that, in principle, consequentialists would be open to 'punishment' of the innocent if the effects of the 'punishment' were good enough. This, on Anscombe's view, is completely outrageous and places the theory beyond the pale. Her work in *Intention* had lent much weight to these sorts of

---

5 (Amherst, NY: Prometheus Books, 1998), p. 224.

6 See, for example, Brad Hooker's discussion of how to avoid this problem for rule consequentialism in his *Ideal Code, Real World* (New York: Oxford University Press, 2000).

7 For example, Michael Slote would develop a 'satisficing' view of consequentialism which denied both a rational and moral imperative to maximize the good. See his *Beyond Optimizing* (Cambridge, MA: Harvard University Press, 1989).

criticisms. There she greatly advanced discussion of philosophical psychology in ways directly relevant to normative ethics, and in ways used to show that consequentialism, on her view, was inadequate in its failure to account for reasons for action that are essentially backward looking. Some contemporary consequentialists have tried to develop accounts that would avoid this particular problem. Fred Feldman, for example, believes that consequentialism can be so structured that past events are taken into consideration in providing justification for action.[8]

25.2 Virtues

Though on my view Anscombe was not advocating a return to virtue ethics, there is no doubt that 'Modern Moral Philosophy' generated much renewed interest in virtues and directly led to the investigation of this theoretical alternative. One feature of the latter part of the twentieth century is that increased attention was focused on developing a virtue ethics as an alternative to consequentialism and Kantian ethics. Some dissatisfaction with these approaches, however, had more to do with a general dissatisfaction with moral theory. Bernard Williams, for example, was a harsh critic of Utilitarianism but was not arguing in favour of another *moral* theory, at least as moral theory is traditionally understood as providing an account of what makes an action right or wrong, what principles we should live by, and what gives moral praise and blame their genuine normative force.[9] Williams was suspicious of morality, not just particular representations of morality. His view was similar to Anscombe's in that he felt that normative ethicists were assuming an authority to terms like 'morally right' that they were not entitled to. There were very many points that Williams made against the standard way of conceiving morality, and I cannot discuss all of them here. However, an important point of criticism was his view that morality is viewed, mistakenly, as *inescapable*.[10] This has the unfortunate tendency to make everything into an obligation—to expand the scope of morality.

On my view, the mistake Williams makes is to conflate morality with moralism. There's no doubt that people cite moral reasons inappropriately. They do so in part to harness the 'overridingness' of moral reasons to their own advantage. But this is, itself, incompatible with morality. One would not condemn logic because some people call perfectly good arguments 'illogical' as a way of criticizing them illegitimately. Thus, we need to distinguish a pervasiveness claim from the overridingness, or inescapability claim. To say that moral reasons are overriding or inescapable is not to say they are pervasive.

---

[8] See Fred Feldman, *Utilitarianism, Hedonism, and Desert* (New York: Cambridge University Press, 1997).

[9] See his discussion, with J. J. C. Smart, in *Utilitarianism: For and Against* (Cambridge: Cambridge University Press, 1973).

[10] *Ethics and the Limits of Philosophy* (Cambridge, MA: Harvard University Press, 1985), p. 177.

Further, one can regard moral reasons as overriding *relative to other types of reasons*, and also not view morality as too demanding, depending on how one understands the scope of moral reasons. If Alice has moral reasons to help the needy and moral reasons to promote her (morally acceptable) talents, then the issue is one of weighing reasons, not whether or not moral reasons are overriding with respect to other sorts of reasons.[11]

While not themselves virtue ethicists, Susan Wolf and Michael Stocker wrote on aspects of our moral lives, and our lives in general, that resisted analysis on consequentialist and Kantian accounts of normativity.[12] Their work, like Anscombe's, helped to fuel dissatisfaction with these approaches that, in turn, helped to make virtue ethics appear more attractive as an alternative. Thus, when virtue ethics first appeared on the scene it was in the context of providing such an alternative. Wolf argued that the perfect Utilitarian and the perfect Kantian were people whose lives were, overall, defective, in that living up to the demands of their respective theories would conflict with personal ideals, the sorts of ideals that make one's life flourish, and that enrich the lives of the people one is close to. Stocker argued that Utilitarianism and Kantian ethics, due to their commitment to impartiality, in effect alienate the moral agent from central values, such as friendship. This is because Utilitarianism, for example, requires that one either take an instrumental attitude towards friends, which is incompatible with the nature of friendship itself, or act on reasons that are not instrumental, in which case their actions are justified only by other reasons—not the ones they actually use in justifying their action to themselves. A parallel type of criticism can be made against the Kantian, who also either needs to appeal to impartial justification of partial norms, or discount partial norms altogether.

In some cases, such as Alastair MacIntyre's, there was a concern that ethical theory had presented a false unification of moral phenomena. Earlier works by Iris Murdoch and Thomas Nagel had cast some doubt on there really being a unified conception of value.[13] The doubt was carried over to ethical theory more generally by MacIntyre, who also noted that there was a great deal of cultural relativity in specifications of virtue.[14]

Those who favoured virtue ethics tended to favour a return to an Aristotelian view of the 'good life', informed by a conception of the good, or *eudaimonia*. On this conception of the good life, a central role is played by practical reason. A person with good, but natural, unregulated, inclinations can actually lead to behaviours that are destructive

---

[11] I discuss this further in 'Moralism', in C. A. J. Coady (ed.), *What's Wrong with Moralism?* (Cambirdge, MA: Wiley-Blackwell 2006), pp. 37–51. The volume was first published as a special issue of *The Journal of Applied Philosophy* (Vol. 22(2)).

[12] See, particularly, Susan Wolf's 'Moral Saints', *Journal of Philosophy* 79 (1982): 419–39; Michael Stocker's 'The Schizophrenia of Modern Ethical Theory', *Journal of Philosophy* 73 (1976): 453–66.

[13] See Iris Murdoch, 'The Sovereignty of the Good Over Other Concepts', reprinted in Michael Slote and Roger Crisp (eds.), *Virtue Ethics* (New York: Oxford University Press, 1997), pp. 99–117; Thomas Nagel, 'The Fragmentation of Value', reprinted in *Mortal Questions* (New York: Cambridge University Press, 1979), pp. 128–41.

[14] *After Virtue* (London: Duckworth, 1981). Philippa Foot also engaged in work that led to greater interest in virtue evaluation. See her 'Virtues and Vices', in *Virtues and Vices* (Berkeley: University of California Press, 1978), pp. 1–18.

and harmful to others. What distinguishes human activity from that of other creatures is reason, and the fact that our behaviours can be regulated by reason.

John McDowell identified virtue with perceptual knowledge.[15] McDowell was motivated by meta-ethical concerns, but the account he articulated has normative implications. On his view, virtue is perceptual knowledge of what is morally relevant. The virtuous person does not follow, or apply, rules in exercising virtue. The virtuous person sees what is morally relevant and acts appropriately. This leads to a kind of *motivational* internalism, holding that the knowledge of what is morally relevant *motivates*. The normative implications are several. First, McDowell was inspired by general Wittgensteinian scepticism on rule-following and this, in turn, led to scepticism about it in ethics. This would cut against rule-based accounts, such as consequentialism was perceived to be at the time, as well as Kantian ethics, which centred on application of the Categorical Imperative (see below). The perceptual sensitivity model was picked up on by virtue ethicists and feminist ethicists. The ethics of care, for example, in the Gilligan mould, was often viewed as involving a kind of sensitivity to what the moral agent perceived as morally significant, rather than mere application of a rule, such as the principle of utility. Further, the McDowell account viewed virtue as a kind of knowledge. This helped to cement the Aristotelian approach to virtue ethics, which viewed practical wisdom as essential to virtue, and knowledge as crucial to distinguishing true virtue from mere good inclinations. Martha Nussbaum's work on virtue also accepted this view that there is, at the basis of virtue, a kind of perceptual knowledge.[16] This knowledge condition was attacked, however, as failing to adequately model the virtues. Some virtues seem to need a negative characterization—they rely on the agent not knowing, or being aware of, features of the context that are morally relevant.[17] An awareness of one's full merits, for example, can generate social ill-will if it is detected by others in one's social group. This is one reason sincere forms of modesty are often viewed favourably. The general approach to viewing virtue as perceptual sensitivity has also come under attack by social psychologists who point out that empirical research indicates that people pick up on reasons that justify their behaviour, at best, after the fact. And, often, they can't accurately articulate the reasons that actually caused, or explain, their actions. Thus, there seems to be a disconnect between the reasons that justify the person's action and the reasons that actually cause or explain the person's actions. The famous example of this has to do with findings that show that nice smells, such as the smells of cookies baking, make it more likely that the person smelling them will act benevolently.[18] Of course, the person may see that

---

[15] 'Virtue and Reason', *The Monist* 62 (1979): 331–50.

[16] See her discussion in *Love's Knowledge* (New York: Oxford University Press, 1990). She characterizes the sort of perception crucial to practical deliberation as '... the ability to discern, acutely and responsively, the salient features of one's particular situation', p. 37.

[17] See my *Uneasy Virtue* for a discussion of such virtues as modesty and blind charity (New York: Cambridge University Press, 2001).

[18] John Doris discusses this literature in *Lack of Character* (New York: Cambridge University Press, 2002), pp. 30 ff. Specifically, he discusses the work of R. A. Baron and J. Thomley, 'A Whiff of Reality: Positive Affect as a Potential Mediator of the Effects of Pleasant Fragrances on Task Performance and Helping', *Environment and Behavior* 26 (1994): 766–84.

morality demands the benevolent act in that given situation, but these findings suggest a disconnect between that perception all by itself and motivation. Still other examples, such as the 'reasons' given by the villagers in Le Chambon for saving children from the Nazis, make it seem that even though people fortunately do respond to the right sorts of reasons they often don't perceive their own actions this way. Thus, they don't have knowledge, again, of the full facts of their motivation.

The work of writers like Anscombe and McDowell helped spur virtue ethics. The Aristotelian model would be refined by writers such as Rosalind Hursthouse (1999) who developed a neo-Aristotelian account of virtue-based ethics—which, interestingly, did not denounce rule following or suggest 'moral right' eliminativism, but, rather, tried to fold those aspects of the standard approach into virtue ethics.[19] However, later writers working in virtue theory rather than virtue ethics challenged the classical, Aristotelian, approach as placing too many psychological requirements on virtue.[20] This type of criticism would also be pursued by writers who looked at the empirical literature in psychology on the nature of our virtue ascriptions (see below).

25.3 THE KANTIAN STRAND

Moore also discussed the work of Immanuel Kant, arguing against Kant's view of biblical love, for example, as being solely motivated by duty.[21] This observation was also made, later, by those who argued that virtue ethics was superior to 'impartial' ethics such as Kantian ethics, which seemed to make no room for the role of emotion in morality.[22] This charge would be rebutted by those who noted that Kant does have a place for emotion in morality, though its value seems to be instrumental—for example, cheerfulness in doing one's duty makes one more likely to actually do it. But the failure of Kant's view to *rest* morality on emotion is considered a strength of his view as well, since it renders morality immune to the apparent fickleness of emotion.

It is uncontroversial that the work of John Rawls did much to expand the influence of Kant's ethical thought on the development of ethical theory in the last century. Rawls was interested in drawing out a view of Kantian contractarianism, or 'contractualism', that offered an innovative contrast to standard Hobbesian contractarianism.[23]

Rawls' approach, however, was restricted to political issues of justice in society. The Kantian approach in normative ethics was developed more by writers such as Barbara Herman, Tom Hill, Jr., Marcia Baron, Christine Korsgaard, Onora O'Neill, and Allen Wood. Still, Rawls' work on Kantian contractualism highlighted features of Kant's

---

[19] *On Virtue Ethics* (Oxford: Oxford University Press, 1999).

[20] Julia Driver, *Uneasy Virtue* (New York: Cambridge University Press, 2001) and Nomy Arpaly *Unprincipled Virtue* (New York: Oxford University Press, 2003).

[21] *Principia Ethica*, Chapter V: 'Ethics in relation to conduct'.

[22] Justin Oakley, *Morality and the Emotions* (New York: Routledge, 1992).

[23] *A Theory of Justice* (Cambridge, MA: Harvard University Press, 1971).

ethics that sharply distinguished Kant's approach from other approaches. One sharp distinction is that of procedure and outcome. The consequentialist approaches are often (though not always) outcome oriented. The right is understood in terms of achievement of the good. On Kant's view, however, one fulfils one's obligations procedurally, by conforming one's will to the Categorical Imperative (CI). As long as one engages in this exercise, one has acted rightly, even if the actual outcome of the action is disastrously bad. In reading Kant himself we can see that one reason why this seems so compelling is that it insulates agents from moral luck. Since consequences are ultimately beyond our control we can't be held responsible for *them*, nor can they affect the moral quality of our actions. It is only the content of our wills that matters *morally*. However, this strength is also a weakness in that it seems to run counter to strongly held intuitions to the effect that the person who kills has done something much worse, morally, than the person who tries to kill but fails.[24]

The Categorical Imperative itself has several formulations. The two that are most frequently discussed are the universalizability formulation and the principle of humanity. The universalizability formulation is the following: 'Act only according to that maxim whereby you can at the same time will that it should become a universal law.'[25] The principle of humanity formulation is: 'Act in such a way that you treat humanity, whether in your own person or in the person of another, always at the same time as an end and never simply as a means.'[26] Kant apparently held that the various formulations all came down to the same thing—a core respect for rational nature. However, various commentators pointed out conflicts between formulations. For example, Christine Korsgaard noted that one could universalize a maxim of something like 'lie to save an innocent life' but such a maxim would fail the principle of humanity (see below). Some work in the latter part of the twentieth century on Kantian ethics has sought principled ways to reconcile the formulations.

Also in the latter part of the twentieth century work on Kantian ethics has been motivated by a desire to work out Kantian accounts of moral practice that contrast favourably with alternatives such as Utilitarianism. Tom Hill, for example, has written widely on integrity and respect. Respect is a key idea in Kantian philosophy since the fundamental moral duty is taken to be one of respect for the autonomous nature of other rational beings. He noted that one attractive feature of Kant's view on respect is that self-respect is treated as a moral issue. And, intuitively, this seems right. Hill considers the case of the subservient, over-deferential housewife who sacrifices for the sake of others out of low self-esteem. This is a moral failing, not just a failure of prudence.[27]

---

[24] For a detailed discussion of moral luck and Kantian intuition see Thomas Nagel's 'Moral Luck', in *Mortal Questions*, pp. 24–38.

[25] *Grounding of the Metaphysics of Morals*, trans. James Ellington (Indianapolis, IN: Hackett, 1981), p. 30.

[26] *Grounding of the Metaphysics of Morals*, p. 36.

[27] Thomas E. Hill, Jr., 'Servility and Self-Respect', reprinted in *Autonomy and Self-Respect* (New York: Cambridge University Press, 1991), pp. 4–18.

Contemporary Kantians have also been concerned to defend the Kantian approach from criticisms. Some of those criticisms are levelled against the absolutism of the moral theory. Kant famously held that one ought never to tell a lie, no matter what good effects could be realized as a result of the lie. While there is a positive aspect to absolutism with respect to some of our intuitions—for example, it seems wrong to kill an innocent person *simply* to maximize happiness—and the absolutist can easily account for this, absolutism seems wildly implausible in other cases. The classic case used against Kant is the lie that is used to save the life of an innocent person. This is because, even if one is lying to a bad person, one is certainly still manipulating him, which violates the principle of humanity formulation of the Categorical Imperative. Christine Korsgaard has tried to defend Kantian ethics against these sorts of criticisms, arguing that, though the principle of humanity does condemn lying under any circumstances, it is intended to apply in ideal circumstances in which human beings live in cooperation and harmony, and are not trying to hurt and manipulate each other.[28]

Many of the same criticisms used against Utilitarianism were levelled against the Kantian. The theory had no role for emotion. The theory was committed to impartiality. The theory was rule-based. Many of the same strategies used by the Utilitarian could be used by the Kantian, particularly those that attacked impartiality and rule-based ethics. But Kantians kept to the spirit of Kant on emotion. It is important to note that Kant is not committed to a view that emotion is bad, or that we shouldn't have it in our lives. Rather, the view is that actions with moral worth are performed because they conform to the CI, and that is it. Emotion doesn't enter into the picture in any fundamental justificatory way. And, the argument is, that is good. It is good because, on the Kantian view, emotions are fickle and unstable, but the ground of morality is not. It is good because our emotional responses—even the ones normal for human beings in general—are highly contingent on how we developed, on our nature. Yet, moral truth is not. But Kant recognized that emotions, as part of human nature, could be cultivated in such a way as to support morality.

25.4 EMOTION AND IMPARTIALITY

The interest in moral psychology sparked by Anscombe's work inspired not just virtue ethicists, but other writers who sought alternatives to the prevailing theories. Some would look to psychology itself for inspiration, and find it in the work of Carol Gilligan, whose work on gender differences in moral thinking led to interest in feminist moral philosophy. Gilligan was not engaged in analysis, or philosophical psychology. She was engaged in an empirical study of the behaviour and attitudes of girls and boys regarding moral issues. She noted the differing responses of girls and boys to moral dilemma

---

[28] See her *Creating the Kingdom of Ends* (New York: Cambridge University Press, 1996).

cases and hypothesized that these differences reflected different moral points of view. Her methodology was attacked as flawed, since her samples were small and not randomly chosen. But the claim itself that she was making seemed to appeal to those who thought that women had, unfairly, been regarded as less morally developed than men, since men seemed to exhibit a greater adherence to norms of justice as opposed to norms of caring. This in turn raised the issue of developing an entire ethics based on caring, or sympathetic engagement with others, that was thought to be in tension with a system that advocated cold and impartial adherence to rules.[29] Indeed, feminist philosophers as well as virtue ethicists criticized the impartialist approaches exemplified by Kantian ethics and consequentialism. How, for example, can one be a good friend, or a good parent, if one is impartial in one's dealings with others? Impartiality seems utterly incompatible with the nature of these relationships, and it also seems completely obvious that these relationships have a moral dimension. However, while it is true that there is a partiality in these relationships, it is also true that they are not without impartial norms. Jean Hampton noted that one needs justice in personal relationships as well. Any parent of more than one child knows that issues of justice crop up within these relationships—benefits and burdens must still be distributed *equitably*. Likewise, consequentialists and Kantians can argue that the partiality itself is limited by higher order impartiality.[30] Miranda may have reason to prefer her children, and if reasonable she recognizes that others have reason to prefer their own children, rather than hers.

The huge literature on special obligations and the role of emotions in ethics generated pressure on impartialist approaches to at least signal how their theories accommodate these features of our moral lives. There was widespread scepticism that consequentialism was up to the task. Some writers felt that the theory led to a kind of schizophrenia in practical deliberation in that if the agent is not motivated by consequentialist reasons, but instead is motivated by reasons of, let's say, friendship plain and simple, then the agent is alienated in some way from his own view of justification. There is the added assumption that this sort of alienation is disturbing and bad.[31] Of course, even if it is disturbing, that doesn't make the theory itself false. At worst it may mean that we have one reason to not accept the theory even if it is true.

But these worries, among others, led some consequentialists to develop views that more plausibly reflected actual modes of practical deliberation on moral matters.

Peter Railton made a case for what he termed 'objective consequentialism'—arguing that the best outcome, or the right action, might be more likely obtained if agents don't employ explicitly consequentialist reasoning. In this he and Hare agreed. However, there were features of Railton's approach that were more radical than Hare's. Railton

---

[29] See Nel Noddings, *Caring: A Feminine Approach to Ethics and Moral Education* (Berkeley and Los Angeles: University of California Press, 1984); Michael Slote, *The Ethics of Care and Empathy* (New York: Routledge, 2007).

[30] Marcia Baron, 'Impartiality and Friendship', *Ethics* 101 (1991): 836–57; Julia Driver, 'Consequentialism and Feminist Ethics', *Hypatia* 20 (2005): 183–99.

[31] This line was developed in Michael Stocker, 'The Schizophrenia of Modern Ethical Theory'.

draws the distinction between subjective and objective consequentialism in the following way:

> *Subjective consequentialism* is the view that whenever one faces a choice of actions, one should attempt to determine which act of those available would most promote the good, and should then try to act accordingly.... *Objective consequentialism* is the view that the criterion of the rightness of an act or course of action is whether it in fact would most promote the good of those acts available to the agent.[32]

Other writers later pointed out that this wasn't the clearest way to make the distinction. David Sosa notes that what Railton means to say when characterizing subjective consequentialism is simply that this view holds that all right actions involve explicit consequentialist deliberation, and this has really got to be false. Sosa argues that it really should be termed something like 'deliberationism'. Most subjective consequentialists simply hold that for an action to be right the agent needs to be exhibiting the right kind of subjective state—so, for example, one might hold that the right action is the action that the agent *expects* will bring about the best consequences amongst the range of alternatives open to her. When the distinction is drawn this way the contrast between subjective and objective is understood in terms of the contrast between what the agent has in mind about the good produced by the action, and the good that is actually produced by the action. But one could also hold that the right action is the action that produces the best *foreseeable* consequences. Here one doesn't appeal to what the agent is actually thinking, but rather what is *foreseeable* by the agent—whether or not she actually does foresee the good effects. Understood this way, the contrast is between what a reasonable agent would have in mind about the good produced, and what good is actually produced regardless of what a reasonable person would foresee.

Frank Jackson makes an appeal to the phenomenology of practical deliberation when he argues against what he calls the objective view.

> When we act we must perforce use what is available to us at the time, not what may be available to us in the future or what is available to someone else, and least of all not what is available to a God-like being who knows everything about what would, will, and did happen.[33]

I share Jackson's concerns. But sticking to what is available needn't commit one to the rejection of the objective standard any more than the fact that one doesn't have a ruler commits one to rejecting the standard that the ruler sets for 'one foot'. Commitment to the standard commits one to doing the best one can (given a host of efficiency considerations that exist in real life situations). Further, as noted earlier, the objective consequentialist simply maintains that what determines the rightness or the wrongness of the agent's action is not the set of psychological states of the agent *at the time* of performing

---

[32] Peter Railton, 'Alienation, Consequentialism, and the Demands of Morality', *Philosophy & Public Affairs* 13 (1984): 134–71 (p. 152).

[33] Frank Jackson, 'Decision-theoretic Consequentialism and the Nearest and Dearest Objection', *Ethics* 101 (1991): 461–82 (p. 472).

the action, though that will determine whether or not the agent is blameworthy for performing the action. However, the standard of 'right' may involve reference to what the agent could reasonably be expected to know, or the attitude the agent could reasonably be expected to have under the circumstances. It may not refer to the agent's actual psychology but, rather, some idealized form of that psychology, even in some very indirect way.

25.5 INTUITIONISM

Probably one of the major challenges to consequentialism occurred via intuitionistic approaches to moral philosophy that were inspired by the work of H. A. Prichard and W. D. Ross, and grew out of 'natural law' approaches which held that the methodology used in answering moral questions had to do with a careful teasing out of normative principles from intuitions about given cases, particularly those presenting structural dilemmas. This branch grew from the work in the middle of the century by Philippa Foot, which was taken up by writers such as Warren Quinn and Judith Thompson, and later by Frances Kamm.

H. A. Prichard made the earliest twentieth-century case for this approach in his 1912 article 'Does Moral Philosophy Rest on a Mistake?' On his view we do not apprehend our moral obligations, or moral rightness, through arguments, but through a kind of immediate apprehension of them:

> The sense of obligation to do, or of the rightness of, an action of a particular kind is absolutely underivative or immediate. The rightness of an action consists in its being the origination of something of a certain kind in a situation of a certain kind, a situation in a certain relation B of the agent to others or to his own nature.... This apprehension is immediate, in precisely the sense in which a mathematical apprehension is immediate, e.g., the apprehension that this three-sided figure, in virtue of its being three-sided, must have three angles. Both apprehensions are immediate in the sense that in both insight into the nature of the subject directly leads us to recognize its possession of the predicate; and it is only stating this fact from the other side to say that in both cases the fact apprehended is self-evident.[34]

An implication of the general view is that right is not a matter of what is good; it isn't reducible to the good. We know what's right when we see it, and it is epistemic seeing—we see that something is right and that just is one side of seeing it as obligatory.

> The negative side of all this is, of course, that we do not come to appreciate an obligation by an *argument*, *i.e.* by a process of non-moral thinking, and that, in particular, we do not do so by an argument of which the premise is the ethical but not moral activity of appreciating the goodness either of the act or of a consequence of the act.[35]

---

[34] H. A. Prichard, 'Does Moral Philosophy Rest on a Mistake', *Mind* 81 (1912): 21–37 (pp. 27–8).
[35] Prichard, 'Does Moral Philosophy Rest on a Mistake?', p. 29.

Prichard's work had interesting implications for meta-ethics.[36] However, in this chapter we focus on the normative ethics. Prichard's work helped to launch normative intuitionism, particularly as a competitor to Utilitarianism or consequentialism. But some care is needed in unpacking Prichard's claims. His view is that rightness is directly apprehended, one isn't argued into it. However, Prichard clearly thought that, in actual moral practice in presenting a case for x rather than y, one gave reasons and there were reasons to morally prefer x to y. A right action can be justified. So, it makes perfect sense to say 'You shouldn't do that because it would hurt Mark's feelings', the 'because' providing the relevant reason, and we directly apprehend the normative force of this (the wrongness) within the specified context. What one cannot do is argue that the hurt feelings have force via reduction to something like pain, which is bad. To do so would involve, in Prichard's view, an unwarranted assumption. It is the assumption that what is good '… ought to be …' and, conversely, what is bad ought not to be. It is the 'obligatoriness' of the act once it has been fully specified that we directly apprehend in light of apprehending the features of the act. Information about consequences of the action, the agent's relation to others, and relational features of the action itself (it is in response to a gift, for example) are all relevant bits of information in understanding the nature of the action in question.

This general approach was also developed by W. D. Ross in that he, too, believed that there was no underlying theoretical basis to our normative commitments. Ross held that consequentialism was false, though there was a kernel of truth to the approach in that a consideration of the effects of one's actions is one relevant factor in determining the action's moral quality.[37] Ross also disagreed with the Kantian, who held that we had duties to avoid certain things, like lying, no matter the consequences. Unlike Anscombe, he was not an absolutist. Indeed, Ross seems to have been trying to carve out a compromise between the consequentialist and the Kantian by acknowledging the validity of portions of each. His theory relied on intuitionism in that he held that we do know, intuitively, that certain actions are right or wrong irrespective of their consequences— this is like the Kantian insight, except that it relies on intuitions themselves as a basis as opposed to the sorts of arguments we see Kant making. However, though consequences are not the only things that matter morally, they do still matter. But consequences vie with many other factors that are given in our *pro tanto* duties.[38] One may have a duty to tell the truth, but one also has a duty to save an innocent person from being killed. The weightier one is the one where a life is at stake, so it will be permissible for someone to tell a lie to save an innocent person from death, though lying is still something which one has a reason to avoid doing. Ross criticizes Moore, who was a consequentialist, for

---

[36] For further discussion, see Dancy's chapter in the present volume.

[37] *The Right and the Good*, ed. Philip Stratton-Lake (London: Oxford University Press, 1930).

[38] Ross calls them '*prima facie*' but he actually means '*pro tanto*'. As Shelly Kagan notes, *prima facie* duties are only duties 'at first blush' that, on closer inspection, one can see are not actually duties in that context. *Pro tanto* duties, on the other hand, have genuine weight though they can be overridden by weightier duties. Shelly Kagan, *The Limits of Morality* (Oxford: Oxford University Press, 1989), p. 17.

mischaracterizing our morally significant relations to others. According to Ross, Moore claims:

> in effect, that the only morally significant relation in which my neighbors stand to me is that of being possible beneficiaries by my action. They do stand in this relation to me, and this relation is morally significant. But they may also stand to me in the relation of promisee to promisor, of creditor to debtor, of wife to husband, of child to parent, of friend to friend, of fellow countrymen to fellow countrymen, and the like; and each of these relations is the foundation of a prima facie duty.[39]

Ross provides a non-exhaustive list of such duties via what he terms *prima facie principles* (which are actually *pro tanto*): fidelity, gratitude, justice, beneficence, self-improvement, non-maleficence. We can understand moral dilemmas in terms of conflicts between principles and duties. After careful scrutiny, dilemmas can be solved by considering which duty is the weightier one in the particular situation.

But precisely these sorts of cases pose the question of *how* to weigh moral concerns. One way to go is to argue that what underlies the force of Ross' normative system is just consequentialism—once it is clearly articulated. We really do weigh up the duties against each other on the basis of the effects generated by living up to one rather than the other, in dilemma situations. This strategy, which is rejected by Ross, certainly views the system as a veneer over a consequentialist basis or platform.

Ross' theory is considered a kind of middle ground between consequentialism, which seems too permissive, and absolutism, which seems much too rigid. Consider the standard case of lying. On the consequentialist view there will of course be a presumption against the morality of telling a lie since usually those are bad in that they lead to bad effects. But, of course, this is only a presumption and will be overridden when it is clear that the effects of the lie will, overall, be good effects. The absolutist holds that there is more than a presumption against lying, morally. There is a genuine prohibition such that weighing the effects is morally irrelevant to the moral quality of the lie. We don't need to weigh the effects at all—if the agent's utterance is a lie, it is wrong, period. Ross' compromise, if you will, is to hold that there is a very strong presumption against lying, but that we also have a *pro tanto* duty against, for example, allowing harm. In cases where these conflict, as in the standard lying-to-save-an-innocent-life case, we consider the case and it becomes clear that the weightier is the duty to help another, the duty to save a life. Very many find this compromise intuitively satisfying.

And Ross doesn't just rely on raw intuition in making his case. He provides some interesting arguments against consequentialism. One argument asks us to consider the consequentialist view on lying versus telling the truth, when the effects of each are exactly the same (his case is actually that of promise breaking, which he views as the same as lying). Clearly the lie would be wrong, he argues, though the consequentialist is compelled to hold that both are equal in terms of moral quality. If faced with each

---

[39] Ross, *The Right and the Good*, p. 19.

and an alternative, one could go either way. This, he believes, shows that the consequentialist cannot adequately account for the true presumption against lying.

Thomas Carson has provided a limited defence of the consequentialist against Ross' criticisms.[40] He argues that cases that satisfy this description are hard to imagine. However, he notes that one can imagine lying-to-stranger cases where the effects will be much more limited than in the typical cases:

> Suppose that I lie about my age to a stranger on a train or airplane—I tell her that I am 52 years old, when, in fact, I am 54 years old. It's hard to see how being misinformed about my age could possibly harm her or anyone else ... utilitarians can claim that, since lying almost *always* harms one's character, there is almost always a moral presumption against lying.[41]

But, he then goes on to note that Ross can avoid this by considering cases where the lie actually produces a tiny amount of good comparable to the erosion of one's character in telling the lie.

But another way to go, which is in keeping with Ross' views, and which also sets the stage for the Trolley Problem literature, is to hold that there are *principles* which are intuitively plausible and which can guide us in making these determinations. These principles have no underlying justification in effects on the world. The rightness or wrongness of some actions will be independent of effects. Again, this is not to deny the relevance of effects, it is simply to deny their exhaustive relevance. This brings us into the mid-to-late twentieth century, and into the development of normative intuitionism generated by the Trolley Problem. The trolley case was first introduced by Philippa Foot in 'The Problem of Abortion and the Doctrine of Double Effect', when she argued that it would be permissible for a tram operator to turn a trolley onto another track to save five people, even if that meant killing one.

The case was picked up and extensively discussed by later writers, including Judith Jarvis Thomson, who used it in the most well-known example of the Trolley Problem. In 'Killing, Letting Die, and the Trolley Problem', she asks us to consider the following cases, juxtaposed, the trolley case and the transplant case, respectively:

> Edward is the driver of a trolley, whose brakes have just failed. On the track ahead of him are five people; the banks are so steep that they will not be able to get off the track in time. The track has a spur leading off to the right, and Edward can turn the trolley onto it. Unfortunately there is one person on the right-hand track. Edward can turn the trolley, killing the one; or he can refrain from turning the trolley, killing the five.[42]

---

[40] Thomas L. Carson, 'Ross and Utilitarianism on Promise Keeping and Lying: Self-evidence and the Data of Ethics', *Philosophical Issues* 15 (2005): 140–57.

[41] Carson, 'Ross and Utilitarianism on Promise Keeping and Lying: Self-evidence and the Data of Ethics', p. 146.

[42] Judith Jarvis Thomson, 'Killing, Letting Die, and the Trolley Problem', in *Rights, Restitution, and Risk* [RRR], ed. William Parent (Cambridge, MA: Harvard University Press, 1986), pp. 80–1.

David is a great transplant surgeon. Five of his patients need new parts—one needs a new heart, the others need, respectively, liver, stomach, spleen, and spinal cord—but all are of the same, relatively rare, blood type. David can take the healthy specimen's parts, killing him, and install them in his patients, saving them. Or he can refrain from taking the healthy specimen's parts, letting his patients die.[43]

These cases are structurally similar, and yet our verdicts are quite different. Intuitively, like Foot, most people believe that it is permissible to steer the trolley onto the track with one person, thereby saving the other five. Thus, they believe in this case that it is better for one to die than five. However, most have the completely opposite opinion in the transplant case. In this case, if David killed one to save five he would be acting monstrously. The problem for the intuitionist approach is to devise *principles* that will adjudicate such cases in a consistent way. A plethora of writers have suggested various principles. Thomson's own suggestion was the distributive exemption principle (DEP), which holds that it is '... not morally required of us that we let a burden descend out of the blue onto five when we can make it instead descend onto the one only if we can make it instead descend onto the one by means which do not themselves constitute infringements of rights of the one'.[44] This led to a cottage industry in which various principles and distinctions were suggested as a way of reconciling these, and other, cases in which, again, the structures of the cases were similar, and yet intuitive verdicts varied.[45]

This problem highlights not simply an approach to a particular problem regarding how to rightly distribute burdens, it also illustrates the moral methodology employed by intuitionists—a method of comparing cases to determine what features might make a genuine moral difference when our intuitions seem to clash about structurally similar cases. The close of the twentieth century would see this method in normative ethics— that is, the relying on simple givens of our intuitions as the raw data for principles—cast somewhat into doubt by empirical research in moral psychology. In a way, this represents the scientizing trend, so alien at the opening of the century, in its extreme. We will return to this at the close of the essay.

Intuitionists were united in their opposition to consequentialism. Whatever one thinks about the ultimate failure of the positive project, the approach led to some compelling problems for consequentialism, and put serious pressure on the view. In the classic Trolley Problem, it would seem that the straightforward consequentialist is committed to *requiring* David to transplant, to kill one to save five. Thus, the consequentialist would seem to be in a position of requiring the agent to perform the action that

---

[43] Thomson, 'Killing, Letting Die, and the Trolley Problem', 80.

[44] Judith Jarvis Thomson, 'The Trolley Problem', in RRR, 180.

[45] Prominent examples include Warren Quinn, 'Actions, Intentions, and Consequences: The Doctrine of Doing and Allowing', *The Philosophical Review* 48 (July 1989): 287–312 and Frances Kamm, *Intricate Ethics* (New York: Oxford University Press, 2007). For some interesting literature debunking the deontic take on the Trolley Problem see Alastair Norcross, 'Off Her Trolley? Frances Kamm and the Metaphysics of Morality', *Utilitas* 20 (2008): 65–80 and Joshua Greene, 'The Secret Joke of Kant's Soul', in Walter Sinnott-Armstrong (ed.), *Moral Psychology, Volume 3* (Cambridge, MA: MIT Press, 2007), pp. 35–80.

almost all would agree is morally outrageous. This can be added to the requirement of judicial murder, and twisting a child's arm, in the list of cases against the consequentialist.[46] There are many different ways to formulate the point of these lines of criticism, but probably the most common is to hold that they demonstrate that consequentialism has no place for rights as an essential core element of the theory. At best, rights can be grounded in the instrumental good they promote, but, the thought goes, they are therefore overridable at the drop of a hat. Thus, they are very insecure.

25.6 THE EMPIRICAL TURN

At the very end of the twentieth century, as consequentialists and Kantians were defending their views against virtue ethical attacks, normative ethics began to be influenced by empirical moral psychology. In actuality, of course, philosophers had long taken an empirical approach—Aristotle is perhaps the classic example of a philosopher who viewed the good of an organism to be a matter of proper functioning, which can be determined empirically. Hume, also quite famously, held that morality was subject to the same type of inquiry and scrutiny as prevails in the empirical sciences. But at the end of the twentieth century a trend to bring in work from psychological research and show its direct relevance to normative ethics was started. This trend paralleled the use of psychology and cognitive science in the philosophy of mind. As mentioned earlier, Carol Gilligan's work was taken to have great significance for the development of feminist ethics and the ethics of care.[47] Owen Flanagan, in *Varieties of Moral Personality*, argued that normative ethics must be psychologically realistic, and, as such, needs to consider the actual research done in the psychology of morality.[48] Gilbert Harman argued that the field of 'situationism' in psychology fatally undermined virtue ethics.[49]

As an example of this trend I'll consider Harman's attack on virtue ethics.[50] Harman drew on research in psychology that seemed to support the view that *there are no character traits*. This is extremely surprising, and of course would be very bad news for virtue ethicists, since they seem committed to the existence of virtues.[51] The research Harman pointed to was that of the situationists, so-called because the hypothesis which best

---

[46] I refer here to Anscombe's criticism of Utilitarianism in 'Modern Moral Philosophy', *Philosophy* 33 (1958): 1–19 and Thomas Nagel's criticism of Utilitarianism in *The View From Nowhere* (New York: Oxford University Press, 1986).

[47] Carol Gilligan, *In a Different Voice* (Cambridge, MA: Harvard University Press, 1982). Gilligan's work greatly influenced Nel Noddings in her development of an ethics of care.

[48] Owen Flanagan, *Varieties of Moral Personality: Ethics and Psychological Realism* (Cambridge, MA: Harvard University Press, 1993).

[49] Gilbert Harman, 'Moral Philosophy Meets Social Psychology: Virtue Ethics and the Fundamental Attribution Error', *Proceedings of the Aristotelian Society*, New Series, 99 (1999): 315–31.

[50] This attack was followed up by John Doris in *Lack of Character*.

[51] This isn't quite true. The virtue ethicist could claim that even if virtues don't exist they can constitute an ideal.

explains an agent's behaviour, they argue, is that the agent's situation determines what behaviour is most likely for the agent. Consider an experiment cited by Nesbitt and Ross in their work on situationism—the experiment at Princeton Theological Seminary in 1963. This experiment seemed to show that factors such as time available, whether the talk was a job talk, and so forth, could be used to predict and explain behaviour. Since the behaviour varied according to these factors, the hypothesis was that it was these external, situational, factors that lead to the behaviour, and that character traits play no role. If they play no role in prediction or explanation they are superfluous, we don't need them. This gives us good reason to doubt their existence. It seems as though we can use character traits to explain and predict, but it is really a stable situation of the agent that is doing the work. Vary the situation and one can get dramatic variances in behaviour.

Numerous writers criticized this approach, noting, for one thing, that it doesn't show at all that character traits don't exist. Even if one accepted the empirical data as reported, it wouldn't establish that radical a conclusion. Perhaps human beings are fairly homogeneous in terms of their character, for example. Others used the situationist material to hold that a corresponding epistemological thesis could be supported: maybe virtues exist, maybe they don't. But we aren't justified in believing in them if situationism is true.[52] However, both of these approaches—the one sceptical of the existence of virtues and the other sceptical of our being justified in believing they exist—suffer from the fact that situationism is, itself, a view which is not empirically supported in the sense that there are very many ways to interpret the available evidence that are completely compatible with, and even supportive of, the existence of character traits. In the virtue ethics literature the situationist critique of the theory is often presented as the only approach compatible with research on character traits in psychology, and this is simply not true.[53] This radical interpretation of the significance of the situationist data regarding character traits is incompatible with other empirical research in psychology.

The work of Gilbert Harman and John Doris in this area has heralded a broader challenge to features of 'folk' morality.[54] Again, one can see a parallel with challenges to 'folk' psychology in the philosophy of mind. This challenge has had greater effect, though, on

---

[52] Peter Vranas takes this approach in his 'Against Moral Character Evaluations: The Undetectability of Virtue and Vice', *Journal of Ethics* 13 (2009): 213–33.

[53] For example, in 'Moral Philosophy Meets Social Psychology: Virtue Ethics and the Fundamental Attribution Error', *Proceedings of the Aristotelian Society* 99 (1999): 315–31 (p. 316), Gilbert Harman writes:

> Empirical studies designed to test whether people behave differently in ways that might reflect their having different character traits have failed to find relevant differences.... the existing studies have had negative results. Since it is possible to explain our ordinary belief in character traits as deriving from certain illusions, we must conclude that there is no empirical basis for the existence of character traits.

But this is much too strong a conclusion to draw from the situationist evidence. What one might be able to say instead is simply that the evidence underdetermines the correct theory.

[54] See Doris, *Lack of Character*.

intuitionist approaches in challenging the methodology intuitionists employ in arguing for principles of moral evaluation and guidance.

25.7 CONCLUSION

At the end of the twentieth century we also saw new developments in the major normative theories, Utilitarianism, Kantian ethics, and normative intuitionism, as well as the redeployment of virtue ethics. The century began with many ethicists convinced that naturalism with respect to normative enterprises would fail, and, while many philosophers still believe this to be the case, the scientizing approach has gained ground. By the end of the twentieth century, even in normative ethics, there was a push to incorporate empirical findings into the methodology of examining normative ethical theories.

CHAPTER 26

....

ANALYTIC AESTHETICS

....

PETER LAMARQUE

ANALYTIC philosophy gave serious attention to aesthetics relatively late and initial encounters were far from auspicious. In 1951 John Passmore published his paper 'The Dreariness of Aesthetics' in *Mind* and the often quoted title, more than the content itself, seemed to capture a widely shared attitude, at least among analytic philosophers. In 1952, Stuart Hampshire's 'Logic and Appreciation' questioned whether there really was a genuine subject of aesthetics, comparing it unfavourably with ethics. Hampshire wrote of the 'poverty and weakness' of earlier contributions to aesthetics, a view that chimed with Passmore's judgement that 'if books on aesthetics do not quite take the prize for dreariness, at least they stand very high on the list' (Elton 1954, pp. 36–7). These two essays were collected in an influential anthology, *Aesthetics and Language*, edited by William Elton (1954). Other contributors were W. B. Gallie, Gilbert Ryle, Beryl Lake, Arnold Isenberg, O. K. Bouwsma, Margaret MacDonald, Helen Knight, and Paul Ziff. In his introduction Elton endorses Passmore's and Hampshire's low opinion of aesthetics—echoed by Isenberg, who derides the 'present stone age of aesthetic inquiry'—and succinctly states the purpose of the anthology: 'to diagnose and clarify some aesthetic confusions, which it holds to be mainly linguistic in origin' and 'to provide philosophers and their students with a number of pieces that may serve as models of analytical procedure in aesthetics' (Elton 1954, p. 1).

Elton's *Aesthetics and Language* marks a convenient entry point for analytic aesthetics, as the first systematic and self-conscious effort to bring linguistic methods of analysis to bear on aesthetics. However, the position in reality is not quite as simple as that. Throughout the 1920s, 1930s, and 1940s there was a steady trickle of articles on aesthetics in prominent journals such as *Mind*, *Philosophical Review*, and *Proceedings of the Aristotelian Society*, among others. The majority of these articles, true to the editorial modes of the journals concerned, were written with all the rigour, clarity, and attention to argument demanded by the analytical school, as well as an awareness of 'analytical procedure'. Philosophers such as C. I. Lewis (e.g. in *Mind and the World Order* 1929), Charles Morris, David W. Prall, Louis Arnaud Reid, John Hospers, and T. E. Jessop were contributing to debate in aesthetics in these decades and Prall's books *Aesthetic*

Judgment (1929) and *Aesthetic Analysis* (1936), as well as Hospers' *Meaning and Truth in the Arts* (1946), were well attuned to the new analytical methods. The North American *Journal of Aesthetics and Art Criticism* was established in 1942. And to suppose that the two classic English-language works on aesthetics from this period, John Dewey's *Art as Experience* (1934) and R. G. Collingwood's *Principles of Art* (1938) were merely 'woolly' and 'dreary' is preposterous.

The truth is that Elton's anthology had the character of a manifesto. It sought a new beginning. It was deliberately provocative and polemical. Its targets were probably not the earlier English-language contributions so much as those from continental Europe, notably France, Germany, and Italy, where, as Passmore notes, aesthetics was 'intensively cultivated'. Passmore exemplifies what he takes to be the worst kinds of 'woolliness' by quoting passages not from English language works but from Jacques Maritain's *Art and Poetry* [*Frontières de la poésie*] (1935): 'Why should a musical work ever finish? ... Let us say that as the time of the world shall one day emerge into an instant of eternity, so music should cease only by emerging into a silence of another order, filled with a substantial voice, where the soul for a moment tastes that time no longer is' (Elton 1954, p. 43). This seemed to epitomize all that analytical philosophers were trying to overcome. In turn Elton approves William James' put-down 'Why does the *Æsthetik* of every German philosopher seem to the artist like the abomination of desolation?' and shares his contributors' distaste for the 'Crocean and Idealist *mythos*' (referring to the Italian philosopher and idealist aesthetician Benedetto Croce). Continental aesthetics, then, was taking the brunt of the attack, partly for its supposed tendency to vacuity of expression, partly for its metaphysical bent, and partly for its failure to employ the favoured linguistic method of analysis. The manifesto objected to other factors as well. Too often, one of the contributors remarks, claims about art are 'irrefutable and non-empirical' as with Croce's 'Art is expression' or Clive Bell's 'Art is significant form'. Aestheticians, it was thought, are particularly prone to what Ludwig Wittgenstein called a 'craving for generality', rather than noting important distinctions (for example, between different art forms). They wrongly seek out an 'essence' of art, they draw on 'misleading analogies' (e.g. as Hampshire emphasizes, between the aesthetic and the moral), they do not attend carefully to the language of criticism and evaluation, and they tend towards reductive theories of art especially in terms of psychology. To meet these undesirable tendencies Elton and his contributors propose a fresh start, drawing on the new analytical paradigm:

> While it is difficult to affix on to these essayists a general label, and certainly incorrect to associate them with positivism or other dogmatic, procrustean attitudes toward meaningfulness, one may say that they share the climate of analysis to which such men as Gottlob Frege, Bertrand Russell, G. E. Moore, and, especially, Ludwig Wittgenstein contributed. (Elton 1954, p. 11)

If aesthetics was to become respectable it needed to align itself to the doctrines and methods of such philosophers. Broadly speaking, analytic aesthetics has held true to that aspiration, for better or worse, ever since.

26.1 THE ANALYTIC FRAMEWORK

Although, strikingly, few of the contributions in *Aesthetics and Language* proved lastingly influential, the decade after the anthology's publication saw immense strides in the direction recommended. In 1956 Morris Weitz's Wittgensteinian-inspired paper 'The Role of Theory in Aesthetics' came out in the *Journal of Aesthetics and Art Criticism*; in 1958 Monroe C. Beardsley published his monumental *Aesthetics: Problems in the Philosophy of Criticism*; in 1959 Frank N. Sibley's article 'Aesthetic Concepts' appeared in the *Philosophical Review*; and in 1960 the *British Journal of Aesthetics* was founded, by Harold Osborne. By the time Arthur Danto's paper 'The Artworld' was published in 1964 in the *Journal of Philosophy* all talk of 'dreariness' had disappeared, as had the apologetic tone about aesthetics.

The best way to give focus to the distinctively 'analytical' mode of analytic aesthetics is not merely to list the major landmarks but to break down the subject into those areas in which analytic philosophy itself has made its most significant contributions: the analysis of concepts, philosophy of language and mind, metaphysics, epistemology, and ethics. It is not surprising that analytical philosophers drawn to aesthetics should seek to apply the methods, ideas, and principal advances from these other, more heavily worked, areas. It is under those headings that we can best see the strengths—also arguably, in some cases, the weaknesses—of the analytical approach.

Two provisos are needed at the outset to clarify the broader picture of developments within aesthetics over the past sixty years. The first is that there has been an increasing tendency (say, for the past 25 years or so) to mark a distinction between aesthetics, properly so-called, and the philosophy of art. In the early years of analytic aesthetics this distinction was not noted and 'aesthetics' was used largely to mean what is now called 'philosophy of art'. In other words the attention of aestheticians was directed almost exclusively at the arts. This focus on art is sometimes attributed to Hegel in contrast to the focus on natural beauty found in Kant. Kant sought to characterize the peculiar features of aesthetic judgements (judgements of beauty) wherever applied, whereas Hegel saw the history of art as a striking manifestation of the more general history of Spirit. Analytic aestheticians came to see that questions about beauty (or other aesthetic concepts) and the experiences or values associated with beauty are by no means exhausted by an examination of art; indeed art, it was argued, might have no essential connection with beauty or with the aesthetic realm. Thus a range of questions about art came to be studied—these will be exemplified later—which, while belonging to the philosophy of art, seemed to have little to do with aesthetics narrowly conceived. Likewise questions about aesthetic value or aesthetic properties were raised and debated (e.g. in relation to nature or the environment) which had nothing to do with art.

The second proviso comes out of this. While the philosophy of art was gaining a kind of autonomy from aesthetics, increasingly attention came to be directed at specific art forms. Thus philosophy of art subdivided into philosophy of music, film, literature, dance, visual art, photography, architecture, sculpture, and so forth. Interestingly, Passmore had recommended just such a move in his 1951 paper, in an attempt to overcome the vacuity of overgeneralization. So it is that a map of current analytic aesthetics would look rather different from a map of the subject sixty years ago. There are sharper divisions. A narrower band of issues are clearly demarcated as 'aesthetic'; these relate to aesthetic experience, aesthetic properties, or aesthetic values, wherever applied. There is a growing branch of aesthetics concerned specifically with the appreciation of nature or the environment. The label 'philosophy of art' is retained for questions arising about all the arts, for example, about the nature of art itself. But philosophies of the individual arts have thrown up art-specific questions—for example, about depiction in painting, expression in music, truth in literature, or transparency in photography.

26.2 ANALYSIS OF CONCEPTS

Analysing concepts has been a central preoccupation of analytical philosophy since its earliest years but the forms that this exercise has taken have differed radically: think of Frege's analysis of *number*, Russell's of *name*, Moore's of *good*, Wittgenstein's of *seeing-as*, Ryle's of *mind*, J. L. Austin's of *truth*, H. P. Grice's of *meaning*, Saul Kripke's of *necessity*, Edmund Gettier's of *knowledge*, and so on. In what follows two exemplary cases in aesthetics will be examined, exhibiting their own differences: analyses of the concept of art, and analyses of the class of aesthetic concepts.

26.2.1 The Concept of Art

Let us start with the concept of art. In the (pre-analytic) history of aesthetics it was common to seek an 'essence' of art in some single feature, such as mimesis or expression or play or 'significant form'. Most such efforts, however, seemed to fit some forms of art better than others: painting, perhaps, or poetry or music, or representational but not abstract art. Early analytic philosophers, as noted above, criticized sweeping and grandiose claims about art as either vacuous or untestable. Any substantial common essence across the arts proved elusive. Morris Weitz in his 1956 paper took the failure to find an essence of art as further evidence that the whole enterprise of trying to define 'art' or capture its essence was misplaced. 'Art', he argued, is an 'open concept', not subject to necessary and sufficient conditions, allowing for radically new kinds of instantiation. Weitz proposed that all that binds together the disparate products called 'art' are loosely connected 'family resemblances', a notion drawn from Wittgenstein's *Philosophical Investigations* (1953). Weitz was one of the first philosophers to recognize the difficulty posed for philosophy of art by the rapid proliferation of art movements in the twentieth century, from modernism to Dadaism. If the 'readymades' (a urinal, a snow shovel, a bottle rack, etc.) of the avant garde artist Marcel Duchamp (1887–1968) could count as art then traditional conceptions seemed inadequate and the search for historically invariant commonalities all the more doomed.

Nevertheless, Weitz's sceptical anti-essentialism was soon to be challenged and new ways sought to accommodate artistic innovation. Perhaps the essence of art was being looked for in the wrong place, focusing too much on inherent or perceptual properties of art objects. Danto in his 1964 paper was one of the first to develop this line of thought, suggesting that what makes something art is not what it *looks* like but what role it plays in an 'artworld'. This is a striking repudiation of a long-standing assumption that art-works are distinctive in virtue of their perceptible qualities. The properties that matter, Danto proposed, are *relational* not intrinsic. Objects become works of art not in virtue of how they look but by occupying a role in a social institution. Danto famously used Andy Warhol's facsimile Brillo Boxes to illustrate the point. There is nothing about the look of Warhol's Brillo Boxes that distinguishes them from their commercial counter-parts or determines their status as art but only their embeddedness in a 'theory' or 'art-world', which makes possible their having a special kind of artistic significance. Danto also developed his own ingenious thought-experiments seeking to show that two objects might be perceptually indiscernible but nevertheless distinct works of art (Danto 1981).

While Danto did not see himself as offering a strict definition of art, it was not long before similar ideas evolved into 'institutional' definitions (for a useful overview of dif-ferent kinds of definitions in this context, see Davies 1991). Thus George Dickie (1969, 1974, 1984) revived the idea that the concept of art could be defined. 'A work of art', he pronounced (the full theory is developed in Dickie 1974), 'in the classificatory sense is (1) an artefact (2) a set of the aspects of which has had conferred upon it the status of candidate for appreciation by some person or persons acting on behalf of a certain social institution (the artworld)' (Dickie 2003 [1983], pp. 49–50). Although Dickie saw the artworld or 'art circle' as merely a loosely knit community of artists, critics, and art appreciators, without any formal processes of 'conferral', he modified this initial defini-tion, which seemed to have that implication, into a simpler version (developed in Dickie 1984): 'A work of art is an artefact of a kind created to be presented to an artworld public' (Dickie 2003 [1983], p. 53). The appeal of this spare definition is that it puts no restric-tions on what kinds of things might count as art, thereby meeting the 'openness' require-ment from Weitz. Yet for many the definition was just too spare: too empty, too void of value components, too lacking in explanatory power, also too suspiciously circular, to afford any deep insight into the nature of art.

If Dickie's institutionalism was often criticized, the key idea of appealing to relational properties gained wide support. Analytic philosophers have by no means abandoned the quest for a definition of art. An important variant are historical definitions, which ground the concept of art not in an 'artworld' but in the preceding history of art. The subtle idea is to explain the *meaning* of 'art' with reference to the *extension* of 'art' (i.e. the set of objects to which the word 'art' has applied in the past, as determined, in effect, by art historians). Jerrold Levinson, the main proponent of the historical approach, defines art as follows: 'X is an artwork = X is an object that a person or persons having the appropriate proprietary right over X, nonpassingly intends for regard-as-a-work-of-art, i.e. regard in any way (or ways) in which prior artworks are or were correctly (or standardly) regarded' (Levinson 1979, p. 236). A distinct, but similarly motivated, suggestion by Noël Carroll (2001) is that art can be identified by means of *narrative*. An object qualifies as art only to the extent that a plausible and coherent narrative can be found that connects the object to previous artworks.

Institutional or historical definitions differ importantly from *functional* definitions (Davies 1991), as best exemplified by Monroe C. Beardsley's analysis which makes an essential link between art and the aesthetic: 'An artwork is something produced with the intention of giving it the capacity to satisfy the aesthetic interest' (Beardsley 2003 [1983], p. 98). Depending on how broadly or narrowly 'aesthetic' is taken, this approach is in danger of pitting the philosopher against the artist. Conceptual artists, of whom Duchamp was perhaps a forerunner, overtly reject the aesthetic in their work.

26.2.2 Aesthetic Concepts

If the analysis of the concept of art primarily took the form of a search for definitions, the analysis of aesthetic concepts sought more to characterize distinctive features of a class of concepts, thereby locating them on a map of other similar looking concepts. The idea of conceptual analysis as a kind of 'logical geography' was associated with Oxford in the 1940s and 1950s (it appears, for example, in Gilbert Ryle's *Concept of Mind*) and it is no coincidence that the principal contributor to the analysis of aesthetic concepts, Frank Sibley, should have been trained in Oxford during this period. Sibley, in his important 1959 paper 'Aesthetic Concepts', sought to establish a clear distinction between aesthetic and non-aesthetic concepts. Examples of the former include (Sibley's list) *beautiful, unified, balanced, integrated, lifeless, serene, sombre, dynamic, powerful, vivid, delicate, moving, trite, sentimental, tragic*. These contrast with non-aesthetic descriptions, for example, concerning the colours or shapes in a painting, the number of characters in a novel and the fact that it is set in an industrial town, the fact that 'a theme in a fugue is inverted at such a point', and so forth. While the latter are accessible to anyone with normal perception and intelligence, the correct application of the former, Sibley argues, calls for a special kind of perceptiveness or discrimination, which he labels 'taste'. Aesthetic concepts are not 'condition-governed', in the sense that there are no general principles, either deductive or inductive, that license inferences from the non-aesthetic to the aesthetic: 'no non-aesthetic features ... serve in *any* circumstances as logically *sufficient conditions* for applying aesthetic terms' (Sibley 2003 [1959], p. 128). Sibley allows, however, that there can be *negative* conditions: for example, pale pastel shades in a painting could never be characterized as 'garish'.

Sibley's analysis of aesthetic concepts proved of immense significance in analytic aesthetics. His 1959 paper totally lacked the negative and rebarbative tone of some of the articles in Elton's anthology and was to prove more of a model for later aestheticians. It opened up new fields of inquiry, not least by broadening the scope of aesthetics beyond the single aesthetic term 'beauty'. Few philosophers took up the suggestion of reviving the notion of 'taste' to characterize aesthetic perception and there were challenges both to the sharpness of the aesthetic/non-aesthetic divide (Cohen 1973) and to the non-condition-governed status of aesthetic concepts (Kivy 1973). But the inquiry soon took off from the narrowly linguistic level of usage to the ontological level of aesthetic *properties*, whether or not these are 'real' and objective, then to epistemological issues about perception and reasons and truth appraisal. Questions about evaluation were not far behind. Sibley developed and refined his views in a sequence of papers (Sibley 2001) where he offered a tentative taxonomy of aesthetic concepts, identified levels of evaluative salience in aesthetic characterizations, explored the relation between the particular and the general in aesthetics, and examined the possibility of general criteria for aesthetic description. His work always epitomized analytical methods: careful, thorough, narrowly focused, aiming to establish firm footholds on what he knew to be permanently slippery ground.

26.3 Representation, Meaning, and Reference

Another key figure in the early development of analytic aesthetics, along with Beardsley, Sibley, and Danto, is Nelson Goodman. Goodman's *Languages of Art* (1968) made a considerable impact not just through its content but from the fact that it was written by a distinguished logician known for his austere nominalist ontology and his work with W. V. O. Quine. This seemed further confirmation that aesthetics had reached the mainstream of analytic philosophy. Goodman saw works of art as belonging to complex symbol systems not different in kind from those found elsewhere, including the sciences. Both art and science can contribute to our understanding of the world; both, as he would put it later, are forms of 'worldmaking' (Goodman 1978). Goodman's work in aesthetics is hugely rich but some ideas achieved special prominence and continue to be debated (we shall return to some in the discussion of ontology).

One controversial idea is that pictorial representation is a kind of denotation, similar to naming. A picture depicts not in virtue of its resemblance to its subject matter, but because it denotes its subject in an entirely conventional manner. Realist portrayal only looks natural because of the 'familiarity' of certain symbol systems. What about pictures of fictional entities, such as unicorns or Mr Pickwick? Goodman rejects the postulation of Meinongian-style 'nonexistent objects' or non-actual possibles as 'objects' of depiction, insisting that all such pictures have the same denotation, that is, a null denotation. Of course a picture of a unicorn differs from a picture of Mr Pickwick and Goodman nicely captures the difference in terms of the kinds of pictures they are. Thus, to use his idiom, a unicorn-picture is different from a Pickwick-picture. This device of classifying pictures does not apply only to a fictitious subject matter. A picture might denote the Duke of Wellington and be a man-picture.

The theory of pictorial representation as a kind of denotation has not been widely adopted and various versions of 'resemblance' theories or at least theories based on the perceptual experiences of pictures have been proposed in opposition to Goodman. One such is Richard Wollheim's account of representation in terms of a distinctive kind of visual experience he calls 'seeing-in' (Wollheim 1980). This experience involves a double aspect or 'twofoldness' constituted by an awareness of the picture's surface, the 'configurational' aspect, and awareness of the picture's subject, the 'recognitional' aspect (Wollheim 1998). The analogy is with seeing a face in the clouds although of course a crucial difference is that in the art case an artist's intention must play a role. Other philosophers, like Flint Schier (1986), Malcolm Budd (1993), and Robert Hopkins (1999), have revived resemblance accounts based on the idea of experienced resemblance (as opposed to the multiple unspecified resemblances that, as Goodman pointed out, any two things are likely to share). Pictorial depiction has become a central topic for analytical study with recent notable works including Lopes (1996), Dilworth (2004), Lopes (2005), and Hyman (2006).

Goodman tackled the difficult problem of fictions in his theory of representation and this has been an issue widely debated among analytic aestheticians, more in relation to narrative (e.g. literature) than pictures. The starting point is a problem in logic and semantics about apparent referring expressions that have no reference ('Pickwick', 'the highest prime', 'the present king of France'). Russell (1905) had addressed the matter, with his Theory of Descriptions, independent of any interest in aesthetics. He sought to show how such expressions could be paraphrased away leaving only variables and predicates. Sentences 'about fictional characters' turned out to be false, on Russell's account, because they implied existence claims that were themselves false. A passing reference to literature from Gottlob Frege suggested a different approach and became influential for subsequent treatments of literary fictions. In his seminal paper 'On Sense and Reference' (1892) Frege wrote:

> In hearing an epic poem … apart from the euphony of the language we are only interested in the sense of the sentences and the images and feelings thereby aroused. The question of truth would cause us to abandon aesthetic delight for the attitude of scientific investigation. Hence it is a matter of no concern to us whether the name 'Odysseus', for instance, has reference, so long as we accept the poem as a work of art. (Frege 1960, p. 63)

The thought that literary fictions should be treated not as false assertions, indeed not as assertions at all, but as different kinds of 'speech acts', became something of an orthodoxy in aesthetics. John Searle, for example, explained fictional discourse, the telling of stories, in terms of pretending to make assertions (or other illocutionary acts) following conventions of story telling (Searle 1979). The idea recalls Sir Philip Sidney's often quoted line (from his *Defence of Poesie* 1595): 'Now for the poet, he nothing affirmeth, and therefore never lieth'.

However, there remains a question of how to analyse discourse about fiction (as opposed to story telling) that does seem to aspire to truth, as when critics make claims about story content ('Odysseus returned to Ithaca') or when a distinction is needed between obvious truths ('Holmes smoked a pipe') and obvious falsehoods ('Holmes was unintelligent') in relation to fiction. Do not such claims seem to make a commitment to the 'reality' of fictional characters? How could there be truths about what does not exist? A considerable amount of analytical ingenuity has been expended on this problem, with eliminativists on the one hand trying to avoid unwelcome ontological commitments and realists on the other prepared to countenance some suitable mode of existence for fictitious entities.

Kendall Walton's eliminativist strategy (Walton 1990) draws on his wider theory of representation in the arts, based on the idea of 'games of make-believe'. To be fictional, he holds, is to be a prop in a game of make-believe. When critics or others appear to be making assertions about fictional characters in fact they are just engaging in pretence: it is only fictional or make-believe that what they say is true. Not only does Walton deny any kind of existence to fictional 'entities' but he also denies there are even any propositions about them. There is no proposition that Holmes smoked a pipe.

In sharp contrast, other theorists of fiction propose that fictional characters do have some kind of being, for example, as abstract entities. They insist that it seems quite unobjectionable to allow a literal construal of some sentences 'about characters', such as: 'Some characters in nineteenth-century fiction are more realistic than any characters in medieval fiction'. Different versions of the abstract entities view have been offered. Peter van Inwagen (1977), for example, takes characters to be 'theoretical entities of literary criticism' comparable to plots and rhyme schemes. Nicholas Wolterstorff (1980) sees them as kinds, specifically 'person-kinds' (as distinct from kinds of persons). These kinds are not created so much as discovered. Amie Thomasson (1999) argues that characters are indeed created and can go out of existence (when their grounding narratives disappear) and they are contingent (they might not have existed); she calls them 'abstract artefacts'. The trouble now is that simple claims like 'Sherlock Holmes does not exist', which seem to be true, turn out to be literally false (Holmes does exist, as an abstract entity). Once again some paraphrase is needed to preserve the truth: something like 'There is no such person as Holmes'.

These theories of reference and ontology reflect core issues in analytic philosophy. But arguably they are fairly remote from concerns in aesthetics traditionally conceived. Even as topics in philosophy of art they can seem marginal, not least because they do not shed much light on the artistic qualities of the works—e.g. works of literature—they discuss. It is not fortuitous that the examples are often drawn from popular fictions like the Sherlock Holmes stories. Literary critics seem to have little interest in the ontology of fictional characters or the referential status of fictional names. It would be wrong, however, to dismiss these questions as irrelevant to the philosophy of art (or the philosophy of literature) and as merely manifestations of problems from adjacent areas, such as philosophy of language. After all, a great many works of representational art (not just literary works) are fictional in content and analytic philosophy is well equipped to cast light on the idea of fiction. What is needed, though, and is not always in evidence, is an attempt to draw out the consequences of theories of reference or ontology for works of art considered as art: addressing issues perhaps about creativity, or narrative perspective, or character identity across works, or about the idea of a 'world' in fiction, and so on (see Lamarque 2009).

Questions about meaning have also had extensive treatment in aesthetics or philosophy of art. Again, as might be expected on this topic, borrowings are common from other areas of philosophy, most obviously philosophy of language. What kinds of meaning can works of art convey? What is it to find meaning in art? What are the constraints on interpretation in art criticism? The term 'meaning' has different applications in this context, not least as applied to different art forms. Thus meaning in music, for example, is often associated with music's expressiveness. Music has a unique power to express emotions and therein lies much of its value and endurance. Yet it is far from clear how this power can be explained. Psychologists of course offer their own accounts but there seem to be 'logical' issues as well. Philosophers have asked how emotional terms—'sad', 'cheerful', 'melancholic'—can be applied to works of music, which are after all merely structures of sound. It is by no means always the case that these attributions can be re-assigned directly either to the composer or the audience; sad music need not imply sadness in its creator or in those who appreciate its musical qualities. Analytic philosophers of music, like Malcolm Budd (1985), Peter Kivy (1993), Stephen Davies (1994), Roger Scruton (1997), and Derek Matravers (1998), among others, have brought sophisticated analyses to bear on the problem.

'Meaning' in other art forms can refer to significance, purpose, or subject matter. Inevitably, though, it is linguistic meaning that has had the primary focus in analytic aesthetics. Thus it is to the literary arts, embodied in language, that discussion has most often gravitated. How do works of literature have meaning? Appeals to theories within philosophy of language are common in approaching literature. For example, speech act theory has been used in attempts to define literature: 'A literary work is a discourse whose sentences lack the illocutionary forces that would normally attach to them. Its illocutionary force is *mimetic* ...' (Ohmann 1971, p. 14). A similar view, that literature is an 'imitation' of illocutionary acts, is advanced by Monroe Beardsley (1970), and recalls Searle's theory of fiction as pretended illocutionary acts. Beardsley also proposed a 'semantic' definition, the idea that literary works are distinctive in possessing a high degree of 'semantic density' or 'implicit meaning'. These ideas chimed well with the New Criticism of the 1940s and 1950s, which emphasized such linguistic qualities as ambiguity, paradox, tension, and irony in literary works viewed as autonomous 'verbal icons'. However, several problems have been raised about purely linguistic or formalistic definitions of this kind (Olsen 1987). They often run together literature and fiction, they fail to account for the evaluative conception of literature (there is no intrinsic value in imitating illocutionary acts or possessing semantic density), they seem to apply better to some kinds of works (poetry) than others (realist novels), and they appeal to phenomena also found outside the literary realm.

It is the New Critics' attack on the relevance of intention in literary interpretation that has most preoccupied analytic philosophers addressing problems about meaning in the arts. To what extent, if any, should an author's or artist's meaning intentions be a constraint on interpretation? Monroe Beardsley's article 'The Intentional Fallacy' (1946), co-authored with the literary critic William Wimsatt (Wimsatt and Beardsley 1976), set the scene for a debate that continues unresolved to this day. Beardsley and Wimsatt put the anti-intentionalist case arguing that a literary work is autonomous, 'detached from the author at birth', and bears only those meanings grounded in a public language and culture. Critics should support their interpretations by appeal to evidence 'internal' to the work (principally the language the work uses), not to externally discovered sources about what the author 'really' had in mind. This was part of the wider negative programme of the New Critics: to reject biographical criticism, to reject undue emphasis on the personality of the author, and more generally to reject romantic conceptions of literature as personal expression. Beardsley later (1970) elaborated his account by drawing on a distinction in philosophy of language between 'speaker's meaning' and 'sentence meaning', insisting that critics should attend only to the latter, in the form of 'textual meaning'.

Although the anti-intentionalism of New Criticism became the orthodoxy in critical practice for fifty years after 'The Intentional Fallacy', encouraged no doubt by other strands of critical theory, like structuralism, poststructuralism, and Marxism, that in different ways also played down the role of the author's biography and psychology, there has nevertheless been a persistent pro-intention movement that has never quite been submerged. It is a fair generalization to say that, broadly speaking, it has been analytic philosophers who have most vigorously (perhaps most convincingly) promoted intentionalism in its various forms (Iseminger 1992). For example, analytic philosophers have drawn on Wittgenstein and Gilbert Ryle to support a view of intention that makes it look a lot less 'mentalistic' or inaccessible than might be implied by Cartesian or dualistic theories of the mind. Intentions, these philosophers point out, need not be thought to reside in a hidden private world of an author's mind but are discernible in different forms of publicly observable behaviour, including linguistic behaviour. A literary work, on this view, should be thought of as an 'intentional act' bearing its meaning (its intended meaning) in its outward linguistic structure. This focus on intention itself was certainly an important development in the debate, although questions about the source of evidence for critical reading still remained.

Analytic philosophers have also appealed to H. P. Grice's work on meaning to advance the intentionalist case. Grice in a series of papers (Grice 1989) gave an account of 'non-natural meaning' that grounds linguistic meaning ultimately in intention. Admittedly he allowed room for conventional meanings in a language and for the possibility that a speaker might mean something different on an occasion from what the sentence itself means in the language. But he thought that even conventional meanings must in the end be explained in term of what speakers intend. If right, this suggestion that meaning is inseparable from intention again might seem to strengthen the pro-intention line. In fact philosophers who have used Grice in this context have disagreed about whether literary meaning is an instance of 'utterer's meaning' or 'utterance meaning', the former resting entirely on intentions, the latter combining intention, linguistic convention, and context of utterance, in a way that allows for a constructed utterance meaning to diverge from a directly intended meaning (for example, in cases where an intended meaning fails, for whatever reason). Out of this distinction has arisen another distinction, between related but different species of intentionalism, named 'actual intentionalism' and 'hypothetical intentionalism'. The hypothetical intentionalist, whose chief proponent is Jerrold Levinson, holds that 'the core of literary meaning ... is not the meaning (the many meanings) of the words taken in abstraction from the author, or precisely of necessity the meaning that the author actually intended to put across, but our best hypothetical attribution of such, formed from the position of the intended audience' (Levinson 1992, p. 224). Levinson allows that, in rare cases, this hypothesized intention might diverge from the author's actual intentions when the outcome seems more satisfactory or more in line with background knowledge that an audience has about the author's oeuvre in general and the literary context in which it is embedded.

It is plain that the enduring debate about the relevance of intentions in criticism reflects disagreements on fundamental questions about the nature of literature and the aims of criticism. Defenders of 'actual intentionalism' (Stecker 1997; Carroll 2001) often stress the 'conversational' aspects of literary works and the continuity between literary and other kinds of communication. New Critics, in contrast, emphasized the 'autonomy' of the literary work, in effect the radical separateness of literary discourse from other modes of discourse. The stance of the New Critics should be distinguished from that of theorists like Roland Barthes (1977) who proclaim the 'death of the author'. Barthes' theory rests less on 'autonomy', more on a conception of 'writing' (écriture), which allows for a 'text' to mean virtually anything that the language permits, regardless of context or intention. A different line altogether has come from those who question the very terms of the debate itself. These philosophers, who prefer to highlight aesthetic aspects of literature, or literature as art, reject the priority given to 'meaning' in criticism, saying that it distorts the special kind of 'appreciation' that literature calls for (Olsen 1987; Lamarque 2009). After all, it seems stretched to describe, say, a long Victorian novel as an 'utterance' as if it had anything like the same kind of 'meaning' that a remark in a conversation might have. Arguably this Gricean paradigm brought to the aesthetics of literature from philosophy of language obscures rather than clarifies the special character of literature.

Finally, on the topic of meaning, Richard Wollheim has proposed a conception of criticism as 'retrieval' which goes beyond a narrow view of intention and applies across all the arts. For Wollheim 'the task of criticism is the reconstruction of the creative process', where that 'includes the many background beliefs, conventions, and modes of artistic production against which the artist forms his intentions' (Wollheim 1980, p. 185). A critic, he allows, 'is justified in using both theory and hindsight unavailable to the artist if thereby he can arrive at an account of what the artist was doing that is maximally explanatory'. This permits interpretations, for example, using psychoanalytic or Marxist theory even when the terminology might seem anachronistic or inaccessible to the artists themselves. In general, though, analytic philosophers have been wary of endorsing interpretative schemes—such as psychoanalysis, Marxism, or deconstruction—which can seem to be more imposed on a work than discovered in it. Without independent verification of the schemes themselves it is thought unwise to appropriate them into critical practice. However, it should be noted, from the other side, that defenders of these styles of criticism are sometimes equally sceptical of the importation of terminology from analytic philosophy of language.

26.4 METAPHYSICS AND ONTOLOGY

If philosophy of language has dominated discussion of meaning in the literary arts so analytical metaphysics has played a major role not just in clarifying but largely in creating that branch of aesthetics concerned with the ontology of art. On the face of it works of art are a motley: paintings, sculptures, prints, photographs, films, music, literature, drama, architecture, dance, multi-media works, performance art, conceptual art, etc. What kind of entities are these? What ontological categories do they fall under? Is there any underlying unity in this apparent multiplicity?

Some of the complexities of the ontological debate can be seen in the variety of ways we talk about different art forms. For some kinds of works—e.g. music, drama, dance—we distinguish the work itself from *performances* of the work. Indeed there could be properties of a performance, even aesthetic properties, that are not properties of the work itself; a musical performance could be 'sluggish', 'listless', or 'boisterous' where the work itself is not properly so described. Performances can be better or worse, more or less true to the original. We speak of *copies* of literary works, *reproductions* (as well as *copies*) of paintings, *impressions* of prints, *screenings* of movies, *productions* of plays, *castings* of sculptures, and so forth. Furthermore, there can be *translations* of literary works, as well as *adaptations*, and there can be *versions* and *transcriptions* of musical works. Care needs to be taken in characterizing exactly what these relations are. For example, to read a *copy* of a literary work is sufficient to have read the work itself; there is no need to read the original manuscript and indeed the manuscript might be lost without affecting the continued existence of the work. Yet to see a *copy* or *reproduction* of a painting is not strictly to have seen the painting itself. In this case seeing the 'original' seems to matter. On the other hand, to see an *impression* of a print does count as seeing the print itself, as long as the impression is taken from the original printer's block (a *reproduction* of a print might not be a true impression). The same is true of a *casting* of a cast-sculpture. In contrast, carved sculptures are more like paintings where again copies should be distinguished from the original. As for *translations*, it seems natural to suppose that to have read a translation of *War and Peace* is to have read *War and Peace*, even if none of the words read appear in the original text.

Nelson Goodman (1976 [1968]) was one of the first analytic philosophers to attempt to bring some order to this complexity. He introduced two distinctions that have been widely adopted: between *singular* vs. *multiple* art forms and between *autographic* vs. *allographic* art forms. An art form is singular if there is some unique object, such as a painting or a carved sculpture, which counts as the work or serves to identify the work; an art form is multiple if, as with music, dance, prints, and novels, the work can be multiply instantiated (e.g. in performances, impressions, copies, etc). The autographic/allographic distinction is not the same and is drawn in terms of what can and cannot be forged (forged, that is, by producing an identical replica). Thus 'a work of art is autographic if and only if the distinction between original and forgery of it is significant; or better, if and only if even the most exact duplication of it does not thereby count as genuine' (Goodman 1976, p. 113). A painting or a carved sculpture is autographic; the identity of a painting, say, the *Mona Lisa*, depends entirely on the relation of the object to its creator (Leonardo). However accurate a replica, if it does not have the right history of production, it cannot count as the *Mona Lisa*. Music and poetry, in contrast, are 'allographic' (that is, not autographic) because the composer or the poet need not have created the physical score in front of a performer or the copy of a poem before a reader. For Goodman you cannot forge a poem by producing a copy of it. Note, however, that musical performances, original scores, and original manuscripts are themselves autographic and could be forged. They are not identical with the works. The reason the two distinctions are not the same is that prints, for example, are multiple art forms yet autographic. An impression of a print that does not have the right history of production cannot count as an 'original' and could be a forgery. Allographic works that can be multiply instantiated gain their identity through a notation. Thus a musical work is the class of performances compliant with a score. Any instantiation that complies with the notation in a score is an instantiation of the work and likewise any performance that deviates from the notation in even the smallest way (e.g. one misplayed note) cannot count as a performance of the work. Goodman dismissed criticism that this latter claim poses far too strict a criterion on performance identity, arguing that he wasn't trying to reflect (or prescribe) ordinary language: 'I am no more recommending that in ordinary discourse we refuse to say that a pianist who misses a note has performed a Chopin Polonaise than that we refuse to call a whale a fish, the earth spherical, or a grayish-pink human white' (Goodman 1976, p. 187).

Although Goodman's influence is still strongly felt, his work in the ontology of art has not gone unchallenged. The distinction between autographic and allographic has come under scrutiny, not least by those who find a more important role than does Goodman for history of production among allographic arts (Levinson 1990; Currie 1989). Perhaps most attention has been given to the ontological status of music. The relation of a musical work to its performances has been characterized in different ways. For Wollheim (1980) the work is a *type* of which the performances are *tokens* and he shows how some but not all properties of the type can be manifested in a token. Wolterstorff (1980) prefers the terminology of *kinds*, specifically what he calls *norm kinds*. A work specifies rules for a *correct* performance but, unlike Goodman, Wolterstorff leaves room for the possibility of an incorrect performance. Both Wollheim and Wolterstorff reject Goodman's view that a musical work is a class of performances. The idea in any case is counterintuitive as it disallows unperformed works (or strictly it makes all unperformed works identical, as the null-class).

Before pursuing Goodman's distinction between singular and multiple works, on which again there has been much discussion, it is useful to reflect a bit further on analytic work on the ontology of music because in many ways this is paradigmatic of the new kind of interests that analytic philosophers have brought to aesthetics. There is general agreement that musical works (the same holds for literary works) are *abstract* entities of some kind. Even the nominalist Goodman seems to accept this in identifying such works with classes (although no doubt in the final reckoning he would seek a nominalist re-characterization of this). Attempts to identify works with non-abstract entities, like physical scores, sound waves, performance events, or psychological states seem doomed to failure. So the central question has become: what *kind* of abstract entities are they? Here a major divide has emerged between those 'Platonists' on the one hand who regard musical works as timeless universals, selected or discovered by composers but not strictly created by them, and on the other those who regard music as necessarily created (by humans) and so seek some non-Platonistic conception of abstract entities. Examples of the former include Wolterstorff (1980), Peter Kivy (1993), and Julian Dodd (2007); examples of the latter are Jerrold Levinson (1990) and Robert Howell (2002). Platonists do not deny that composers are 'creative', denying only that they strictly 'create' in the sense of bringing something that previously didn't exist into existence; the parallel is drawn with mathematicians who *discover* theorems yet are hailed as creative geniuses.

Levinson offers a subtle alternative. He insists that composers do bring musical works into existence, while retaining the idea that the works are abstract types. He proposes that not all types are timeless, some are 'initiated types', including, in his examples, the Ford Thunderbird, the Lincoln penny, and indeed musical works. These are 'initiated' by an intentional human act. In the case of music a 'sound structure type' is 'indicated' by a composer at a particular time and what results is a new entity: a 'sound-structure-type-as-indicated-by-X-at t', where 'X' is the composer and 't' the time of composition. One consequence of this account is that a musical work (as an 'indicated structure') is essentially linked to its composer and to a time. The 'Moonlight' Sonata could not (metaphysically could not) have been created by anyone other than Beethoven or at a different time. If some other composer had, by massive coincidence, 'indicated' the identical structure (i.e. produced a notationally identical score—other than by wilful copying) then that would be a different work and would have different aesthetic properties (because such properties are partially dependent on the musico-historical context in which the work is heard and appreciated). Levinson's account has been much discussed and has found considerable support, even though questions remain about the status of 'indicated structures' and the perhaps overly strict identity conditions for works (in fact Levinson has suggested ways of making these somewhat less strict).

While it seems hard to resist the conclusion that music is, in Goodman's terminology, a 'multiple' art form, whereby multiple performances can in some way or other 'instantiate' a work, there is no consensus on the ontological status of the so-called 'singular' arts, notably paintings and carved sculptures. In a rare contribution to aesthetics, the distinguished analytic philosopher P. F. Strawson argued, controversially, that 'all works of art ... are equally types and not particulars' (Strawson 1966, p. 10). His reason is that it is a merely contingent fact that 'we are, for all practical purposes, quite unable to make reproductions of pictures and statues which are completely indistinguishable, by direct sensory inspection, from the originals' (Strawson 1966, p. 9). If we were able to make such exact reproductions then, he argues, our interest in the originals would be no different from our interest in the original manuscripts or scores of poets or composers. Others have taken up the idea that all works of art are types rather than particulars, in effect that there are only multiple art forms. For example, Gregory Currie (1989) has argued that works of art are all 'action types', the action being that of discovering a certain structure—of colours, sounds, words, etc.—via a certain 'heuristic path', i.e. a particular artistic process. Behind Currie's proposal lies the thought, similar to Levinson's view of music, that a work's identity does not reside only in some observable structure but also in the precise means by which the structure was arrived at. Facts about a work's provenance or history of production are essential to determining the work it is, although Currie, unlike Levinson, allows in principle that different people could compose the same work.

David Davies (2004) has developed a refinement of this 'process' view of art, yet reverts to particulars rather than types. For Davies a work is identical with a particular 'performance', not with an end-product such as the painting seen or the music heard, etc., which he describes as the 'focus of appreciation'. A curious consequence is that strictly speaking, on Davies' account, works of art are virtually never seen or heard by audiences. However, even those who think of paintings as particular objects (not performances) do not always think of them as identical to the physical objects that are hung on gallery walls. Joseph Margolis (1980), for example, takes them to be 'culturally emergent entities' that are 'embodied' in physical objects but not identical to those objects. The *Mona Lisa* as a work of art has intentional properties (being a representation, being beautiful, etc.), so Margolis argues, that the mere canvas and pigment do not possess. What analytical approaches to the ontology of art show quite strikingly is how vulnerable are common intuitions about art under hard philosophical questioning. This of course in turn raises difficult issues about constraints on theorizing in ontology (Thomasson 2005).

26.5 TRUTH AND KNOWLEDGE

It is not surprising that analytic philosophers, given their strong focus on language, should give attention to truth in relation to the arts. Indeed some of the earliest contributions to analytic aesthetics (Hospers 1946; Beardsley 1958) tackled this subject and it has been a major point of interest ever since. The issue of whether the arts can convey knowledge of some distinct kind and should be valued accordingly goes back to the ancient Greek philosophers and to a large extent the framework of the modern debate reflects that of Plato and Aristotle. Plato's distinction between the rational, truth-seeking discourse of philosophy and the irrational, emotion-inducing discourse of poetry anticipates the positivistic divide (e.g. in Ogden and Richards 1923) between 'referential' and 'emotive' functions of language that relegated poetry to the realm of 'pseudo-statements' (Richards 1926). Aristotle's well-known response that 'poetry is something more philosophic and of graver import than history, since its statements are of the nature rather of universals, whereas those of history are singulars' and that 'by a universal statement I mean one as to what such or such a kind of man will probably or necessarily say or do' (Aristotle, *The Poetics*, 1451^b, 2–10, tr. W. D. Ross) in turn anticipates analytic philosophers' efforts to characterize a 'cognitive' function for literature beyond a merely 'emotive' one.

Analytic approaches to the subject of truth in the arts differ markedly from contemporaneous approaches from continental philosophers, although there is no more unity among the latter than among the former. While in both kinds of approaches it is possible to discern a broad division between defenders of truth and its detractors in this context, the considerations offered for and against are significantly different. For example, appeal to ideological conceptions of truth in art found in versions of Marxist philosophy is almost entirely absent from analytic accounts, as are more metaphysical conceptions, like that of Martin Heidegger, of truth as 'unconcealment', revealing the 'hiddenness' of being. Likewise attacks on 'artistic truth' tend to be differently grounded. Scepticism about truth itself, as sometimes manifested in, say, Friedrich Nietzsche or later poststructuralist or postmodernist writers, rarely underlies analytical discussion and there is little inclination among analytical aestheticians to challenge a broadly 'humanistic' conception of literature in particular (or art in general) or the distinction between literature and other kinds of discourse or indeed notions of the self, or meaning, or value that provide a foundation for the humanistic view.

Analytic aestheticians have been more inclined to approach the subject by way of 'clearing the ground'—asking what might be *meant* by saying that art conveys truth or what kinds of examples best illustrate this or whether the delivery of truth is a fundamental value in all the arts or just a contingent by-product of some. Much of the focus has been on literature, although claims for other art forms have been made (see Hospers 1946; Beardsley 1958; Graham 1997). Beardsley (1958) offers an important ground-clearing exercise in distinguishing 'reports' and 'reflections', 'themes' and 'theses' in literary works. His concern was, partly, to identify possible truth bearers within literary fiction, *candidates* for truth assessment, to counter the general positivistic thought that novels, being works of fiction, are *ipso facto* outside the purview of truth altogether. Beardsley's starting point, typically for an analytic philosopher, was a propositional conception of truth. Reports and reflections, on his account, can be explicit, i.e. actually contained in the work, or implicit, i.e. derivable from the work by inference. Reports are simply sentences in indicative form, which might, but need not, have fictional content or make fictional reference. The treatment of 'fictional sentences' (containing fictional reference) need not be the same as the treatment of non-fictional report sentences, those, for example, which describe a real world setting (London, perhaps, or an actual battle or a historical figure). There is no doubt that the latter can be literally true or false but the issue, as Beardsley rightly notes, is rather whether the truth or falsehood *matters* in valuing the work. How should we view factual falsity in a work's setting (Lamarque 2009)?

Reflections are also candidates for truth-valuation, as with the famous opening sentence of *Anna Karenina* 'All happy families are alike but an unhappy family is unhappy after its own fashion.' Sometimes reflections are not explicit but elicited through interpretation, as when we say that it is implicit in Kafka's *The Trial* that human beings are victims of impersonal and indifferent forces outside their control. Reflections of this kind can also count as 'theses' propounded by a work. A work's 'thesis', Beardsley argues, is not the same as its 'themes' because themes do not need to be expressed in propositional form: the conflict of love and duty might be a theme or simply jealousy or despair. Such themes are not amenable to truth assessment. Reflections can be judged for their truth and again the question arises whether the literal truth of its reflections matters to a work's value. Clearly if a reflection or thesis is patently absurd or improbable then a special reason for this would be needed to prevent a negative judgement of the work. But reflections of the *Anna Karenina* or *The Trial* kind are too general to admit of straightforward verification and even those who reject the pessimistic vision of Kafka's novel might still value the work highly for its imaginative exploration of the idea.

The identification of propositional truths in works of literature and questions about their status have been at the core of analytic approaches to the subject. But analytic philosophers have also sought non-propositional conceptions of truth in aesthetics, on the grounds that art, in particular literature, is not primarily in the business of advancing propositions, and thus not in direct competition with science or philosophy. I. A. Richards (1926), for example, denies that the 'scientific sense' of 'truth' is relevant to the arts and suggests that within criticism 'truth' most often means 'acceptability' and 'sincerity'. A related conception is that of 'authenticity' (Walsh 1969), where truth is connected not to correspondence to the facts but to truthfulness, honesty, or lack of sentimentality. John Hospers (1958) develops the idea of literature as 'true to life', a notion similar to that of 'verisimilitude', a conception of truth implying 'realistic' description, 'ringing true', or resemblance to perceived reality. Others have sought literature's cognitive powers in special kinds of knowledge, such as 'knowing how' (Novitz 1987) or 'knowing what it is like' (Walsh 1969). Iris Murdoch describes truth in art as 'a kind of transcendence', 'something we recognize in good art when we are led to a juster, clearer, more detailed, more refined understanding' (Murdoch 1992, p. 321). Such notions are often carefully worked out but nevertheless are open to the charge that in weakening the idea of truth, from its propositional paradigm, they obscure rather than illuminate art's truth-telling potential.

A different kind of approach to the cognitive value of art is to stress wider epistemological factors rather than give narrow focus to 'truth', however defined. The question now becomes what learning possibilities art can afford. One suggestion is that art encourages us to see the world (and other people) more clearly and honestly. Iris Murdoch (1970) writes that 'the greatest art … shows us the world … with a clarity which startles and delights us simply because we are not used to looking at the real world at all' (p. 65). This conception is connected to Wittgensteinian approaches to ethics and aesthetics, as represented by D. Z. Phillips (1982) and R. M. Beardsmore (1971), that stress the *particularity of moral situations* and the idea of acquiring from art a new vision or perspective on life. The thought is not that we learn determinate moral principles from art but that the very specificity of artistic (usually narrative) representation forces us to attend to the particular and the complex, thereby, perhaps, coming to reshape our moral outlook. A similar thought is that art can educate the emotions, offering in effect training in emotional response. Martha Nussbaum (1990) has developed this suggestion as has Jenefer Robinson (2005) and Susan Feagin (1996). Robinson (2005) writes that 'it is only through an emotional experience of a novel that one can genuinely learn from it' (p. 156), calling this a 'sentimental education'. Noël Carroll (2001) has introduced the idea of 'clarificationism' to capture another kind of learning function of art, a notion, he says, which 'does not claim that, in the standard case, we acquire interesting new propositional knowledge from artworks, but rather that the artworks in question can deepen our moral understanding by, among other things, encouraging us to apply our moral knowledge and emotions to specific cases' (Carroll 2001, p. 283).

All such accounts aspire to give substance to the intuition that art has cognitive benefits, that it enriches our understanding of the world even if it does not do so through advancing propositions. But the question remains how far these benefits should be viewed as somehow integral to the achievements of works of art *as art*, or how far they are merely instrumental values found only in certain kinds of works (notably those based in narrative). Some analytic philosophers have resisted giving too much emphasis to the learning or educative function of art, being sceptical of attempts to appropriate values from the sciences in characterizing the unique contribution of the arts and literature (Lamarque and Olsen 1994; Stolnitz 1992). The grounding thought here, that radically different 'practices' underpin the activities of artists and scientists, originates from Wittgenstein (1953).

26.6 ETHICS AND VALUE

The final topic that demands at least brief consideration in a survey of analytic aesthetics is the relation of art and ethics, and more generally the values of art. Some of these issues have been touched on already. Analytic philosophers, unlike some of their structuralist or poststructuralist contemporaries, have not shown reluctance to engage questions of value or to appeal to the ethical in evaluations of art. Analytic philosophy has powerful resources to help clarify the terms of debates about value even if it fails to reach consensus on key controversies. Distinctions like that between objective and subjective, relative and absolute, evaluative and non-evaluative concepts, fact and value, the valued and the valuable, provide a framework for discussion and often help to tie down sources of disagreement, perhaps in presuppositions or the classification of terms. There is a considerable analytic literature on ideas like critical reasoning, critical principles, criteria of judgements, aesthetic vs. artistic value, and indeed the grounds of all kinds of human values. Beardsley (1958) was not unusual in seeking objective criteria of artistic value—he cited unity, intensity, and complexity as fundamental values—but there has been no general agreement on what such criteria might be or where the basis of objectivity lies. Several full-length studies by analytic philosophers on artistic and aesthetic value are notable, including Anthony Savile's *The Test of Time* (1982), Mary Mothersill's *Beauty Restored* (1984), George Dickie's *Evaluating Art* (1988), and Malcolm Budd's *Values of Art: Pictures, Poetry and Music* (1995).

The relation between art and ethics has long been contested. The ancient Greeks saw a strong connection, not least in the great tragedies, between ethical concerns and mimesis. For Kant beauty serves as the 'symbol' of morality but since Kant there has been a tendency to keep the aesthetic at a distance from the ethical. The dominance of formalism in twentieth-century criticism—including New Criticism, structuralism, and deconstruction—rejected any role for ethical criticism, while Marxism and feminism reinstated a version of it in their rather special contexts. Stuart Hampshire in his polemical essay 'Logic and Appreciation' (in Elton 1954) insisted on a clear distinction between aesthetic and moral judgements, rejecting any analogy between 'principles of criticism' and 'principles of conduct'. However, there have been marked efforts more recently within analytic aesthetics to incorporate an ethical dimension into art criticism.

Martha Nussbaum, for example, has argued that certain novels can themselves count as contributions to moral philosophy and should be evaluated as such (Nussbaum 1990)—she has in mind, in particular, some of Henry James' novels. She has also claimed that 'the activities of imagination and emotion that the involved reader performs during the time of reading are not just instrumental to moral conduct, they are also examples of moral conduct' (Nussbaum 1998, p. 355). This putative relation between novels and moral philosophy has been challenged (e.g. Lamarque and Olsen 1994).

Another debate about the relation of art and ethics is that between 'autonomists' and 'moralists' (or 'ethicists'). Broadly speaking autonomism holds that art is valuable for its own sake and judgements of artistic value are largely independent of others kinds of values, in particular instrumental values such as moral improvement. A work's value as art is logically distinct from, say, its moral stance. Moralists, in contrast, think that aesthetic and moral values are closely intertwined. A strong moralist might hold that a work's aesthetic value is always dependent on its moral vision. A 'moderate' moralist, as exemplified by Noël Carroll (1998a), holds that 'in some instances a moral defect in an artwork can be an aesthetic defect, and ... sometimes a moral virtue can count as an aesthetic virtue' (Carroll 1998a, p. 419). Carroll's principal argument is that sometimes a work's immorality 'subverts the possibility of uptake' and therefore subverts the work as a work of art making it aesthetically defective. A similar position has been named 'ethicism' by Berys Gaut (1998), who first formulated it. Gaut claims that if a work prescribes a moral attitude that is reprehensible, the work is for that reason weakened aesthetically; his argument is that if a work prescribes a response that is unmerited (for example, because of its morally reprehensible nature), then the work has to that extent failed as a work of art, in the way that a tragedy fails it if does not merit a response of pity and fear. The arguments for moderate moralism and ethicism are subtle and have been developed and modified at length (e.g. Gaut 2007). They have, though, met with resistance (Anderson and Dean 1998). A third position, distinct from moralism and autonomism, is 'immoralism', the view that sometimes the *immorality* of a work might be reason for valuing it highly (Jakobson 2006).

A final word should be given to a relatively recent development in analytic aesthetics, that of the aesthetics of nature and the environment. As noted earlier, when analytic aesthetics first took shape no clear distinction was drawn between 'aesthetics' and 'philosophy of art' and nearly all the debates concerned issues about art. A seminal paper by Ronald Hepburn (1966) sought to reignite an interest in the aesthetics of nature that had after all been prominent in the eighteenth century. Hepburn laid out some important differences between the appreciation of art and the appreciation of nature, not least that art is 'framed' in a way that nature is not and nature offers more all-embracing experiences than those afforded by any single art form. The special characteristics of an aesthetic appreciation of nature have been the centre of a great deal of study. One important approach has been pioneered by Allen Carlson (2000), who proposes an 'environmental aesthetics' based on a cognitive element in our appreciation of the natural world. An adequate aesthetic response, he suggests, should be an 'emotionally and cognitively rich engagement with an environment, created by natural and cultural forces, informed by both scientific knowledge and cultural traditions' (Carlson 2002, pp. 432–3). In other words, appreciation is richer if it rests on knowledge about how a particular environment came to be as it is. The idea contrasts with the Kantian conception of aesthetic pleasure as a pure disinterested contemplation of objects about which nothing need be known.

The broadening of analytic aesthetics beyond philosophy of art into the aesthetics of the environment is a mark of how far the subject has come in its relatively short lifespan. But there is plenty of other evidence for the huge strides taken. There are now fully fledged areas of inquiry covering virtually every art form, from readymades to rock music (Gracyk 1996), from theatre (Hamilton 2007) to film (Currie 1995), from dance (McFee 2011) to mass art (Carroll 1998b), from conceptual art (Goldie and Schellekens 2007) to computer art (Lopes 2009). There is also interest in narrative identity (Hutto 2007), in feminist aesthetics (Korsmeyer 2004), in gardens (Cooper 2006), in jokes (Cohen 1999), in forgery (Dutton 1983), in sentimentality (Solomon 2004), even in pornography (Kieran 2001). There is little sign of dreariness now.

REFERENCES

Anderson, James and Jeffrey Dean (1998). 'Moderate Autonomism', *British Journal of Aesthetics* 38: 150–66.

Barthes, Roland (1977). 'The Death of the Author'. In Barthes, *Image-Music-Text*, tr. Stephen Heath. London: Fontana/Collins, pp. 142–8.

Beardsley, Monroe C. (1970). *The Possibility of Criticism*. Detroit, MI: Wayne State University Press.

—— (1981) [1958]. *Aesthetics: Problems in the Philosophy of Criticism,* 2nd edn. Indianapolis: Hackett.

—— (2003) [1983]. 'An Aesthetic Definition of Art'. In Lamarque and Olsen (2003), pp. 55–62. Originally published in Hugh Curtler (ed.), *What Is Art?* New York: Haven Publications, 1983.

Beardsmore, R. W. (1971). *Art and Morality.* London: Macmillan.

Budd, Malcolm (1985). *Music and the Emotions: The Philosophical Theories.* London: Routledge.

——(1993). 'How Pictures Look'. In D. Knowles and J. Skorupski (eds.), *Virtue and Taste.* Oxford: Blackwell, pp. 154–75.

——(1995). *Values of Art: Pictures, Poetry and Music.* Harmondsworth: Penguin.

Carlson, Allen (2000). *Aesthetics and the Environment: The Appreciation of Nature, Art, and Architecture.* London: Routledge.

—— (2002). 'Environmental Aesthetics'. In B. Gaut and D.M Lopes (eds.), *The Routledge Companion to Aesthetics.* Abingdon: Routledge, pp. 423–36.

Carroll, Noël (1998a). 'Moderate Moralism versus Moderate Autonomism', *British Journal of Aesthetics* 38: 419–24.

——(1998b). *A Philosophy of Mass Art.* Oxford: Oxford University Press.

——(2001). *Beyond Aesthetics: Philosophical Essays.* Cambridge: Cambridge University Press,.

Cohen, Ted (1973). 'Aesthetic/Non-Aesthetic and the Concept of Taste', *Theoria* 39: 113–52.

——(1999). *Jokes.* Chicago: University of Chicago Press.

Collingwood, R. G. (1938). *The Principles of Art.* Oxford: Clarendon Press.

Cooper, David E. (2006). *A Philosophy of Gardens.* Oxford: Clarendon Press.

Currie, Gregory (1989). *An Ontology of Art.* Basingstoke: Macmillan.

—— (1995). *Image and Mind: Film, Philosophy and Cognitive Science.* Cambridge: Cambridge University Press.

Danto, Arthur C. (1964). 'The Artworld', *Journal of Philosophy* 61: 571–84.

—— (1981). *The Transfiguration of the Commonplace.* Cambridge, MA: Harvard University Press.

Davies, David (2004). *Art as Performance.* Oxford: Blackwell.

Davies, Stephen (1991). *Definitions of Art.* Ithaca, NY: Cornell University Press.

——(1994). *Musical Meaning and Expression.* Ithaca, NY: Cornell University Press.

Dewey, John (1934). *Art as Experience.* New York: Minton, Balch & Co.

Dickie, George (1969). 'Defining Art', *American Philosophical Quarterly* 6: 253–6.

—— (1974). *Art and the Aesthetic: An Institutional Analysis.* Ithaca, NY: Cornell University Press.

——(1984). *The Art Circle.* New York: Haven Publications.

——(1988). *Evaluating Art.* Philadelphia, PA: Temple University Press.

—— (2003) [1983]. 'The New Institutional Theory of Art'. In Lamarque and Olsen (2003), pp. 47–54. Originally published in *Proceedings of the 8th International Wittgenstein Symposium* 10 (1983): 57–64.

Dilworth, John (2004). *The Double Content of Art.* New York: Prometheus Books.

Dodd, Julian (2007). *Works of Music: An Essay in Ontology.* Oxford: Oxford University Press.

Dutton, Denis (ed.) (1983). *The Forger's Art: Forgery and the Philosophy of Art.* Berkeley, CA: University of California Press.

Elton, William (ed.) (1954). *Aesthetics and Language.* Oxford: Blackwell.

Feagin, Susan (1996). *Reading With Feeling: The Aesthetics of Appreciation*. Ithaca, NY: Cornell University Press.

Frege, Gottlob (1960) [1892]. 'On Sense and Reference'. In *Philosophical Writings of Gottlob Frege*, tr. and ed. Peter Geach and Max Black, 2nd edn. Oxford: Blackwell, pp. 56–78.

Gaut, Berys (1998). 'The Ethical Criticism of Art'. In Jerrold Levinson (ed.), *Aesthetics and Ethics*. Cambridge: Cambridge University Press, pp. 182–203.

——(2007). *Art, Emotion, and Ethics*. Oxford: Clarendon Press.

Goldie, Peter and Elisabeth Schellekens (eds.) (2007). *Philosophy and Conceptual Art*. Oxford: Oxford University Press.

Goodman, Nelson (1976) [1968]. *Languages of Art: An Approach to a General Theory of Symbols*, 2nd expanded edn. Indianapolis: Bobbs-Merrill.

——(1978). *Ways of Worldmaking*. Indianapolis: Hackett.

Gracyk, Ted (1996). *Rhythm and Noise: An Aesthetics of Rock*. Durham, NC: Duke University Press.

Graham, Gordon (1997). *Philosophy of the Arts: An Introduction to Aesthetics*. London and New York: Routledge.

Grice, H. P. (1989). *Studies in the Way of Words*. Cambridge, MA: Harvard University Press.

Hamilton, James R. (2007). *The Art of Theater*. Oxford: Blackwell.

Hampshire, Stuart (1954) [1952]. 'Logic and Appreciation'. In Elton (1954), pp. 161–9. Originally published in *World Review* (October 1952).

Hepburn, Ronald (1966). 'Contemporary Aesthetics and the Neglect of Natural Beauty'. In Bernard Williams and Alan Montifiore (eds.), *British Analytical Philosophy*. London: Routledge & Kegan Paul, pp. 285–310.

Hopkins, Robert (1999). *Picture, Image and Experience: A Philosophical Inquiry*. Cambridge: Cambridge University Press.

Hospers, John (1946). *Meaning and Truth in the Arts*. Chapel Hill, NC: University of North Carolina Press.

——(1958). 'Literature and Human Nature', *Journal of Aesthetics and Art Criticism* 17: 45–57.

Howell, Robert (2002). 'Types, Indicated and Initiated', *British Journal of Aesthetics* 42: 105–27.

Hutto, Dan (ed.) (2007). *Narrative and Understanding Persons*. Cambridge: Cambridge University Press.

Hyman, John (2006). *The Objective Eye: Color, Form, and Reality in the Theory of Art*. Chicago: University of Chicago Press.

Iseminger, Gary (ed.) (1992). *Intention and Interpretation*. Philadelphia, PA: Temple University Press.

Jakobson, Daniel (2006). 'Ethical Criticism and the Vice of Moderation'. In Matthew Kieran (ed.), *Contemporary Debates in Aesthetics and the Philosophy of Art*. Oxford: Blackwell, pp. 342–55.

Kieran, Matthew (2001). 'Pornographic Art', *Philosophy and Literature* 25: 31–45.

Kivy, Peter (1973). *Speaking of Art*. The Hague: Martinus Nijhoff.

——(1993). *The Fine Art of Repetition: Essays in the Philosophy of Music*. Cambridge: Cambridge University Press.

Korsmeyer, Carolyn (2004). *Gender and Aesthetics: An Introduction*. New York: Routledge.

Lamarque, Peter (2009). *The Philosophy of Literature*. Oxford: Blackwell.

Lamarque, Peter and Stein Haugom Olsen (1994). *Truth, Fiction, and Literature: A Philosophical Perspective*. Oxford: Clarendon Press.

—— —— (eds.) (2003). *Aesthetics and the Philosophy of Art: The Analytic Tradition—An Anthology*. Oxford: Blackwell.

Levinson, Jerrold. (1979). 'Defining Art Historically', *British Journal of Aesthetics* 19: 232–50.

——(1990). *Music, Art, & Metaphysics*. Ithaca, NY: Cornell University Press.

——(1992). 'Intention and Interpretation: A Last Look'. In Iseminger (1992), pp. 221–56.

Lewis, C. I. (1929). *Mind and the World Order: An Outline of a Theory of Knowledge*. New York: Charles Scribner's Sons.

Lopes, Dominic McIver (1996). *Understanding Pictures*. Oxford: Oxford University Press.

——(2005). *Sight and Sensibility: Evaluating Pictures*. Oxford: Oxford University Press.

——(2009). *A Philosophy of Computer Art*. London: Routledge.

McFee, Graham (2011). *The Philosophical Aesthetics of Dance: Identity, Performance and Understanding*. Alton: Dance Books Ltd.

Margolis, Joseph (1980). *Art and Philosophy: Conceptual Issues in Philosophy*. Atlantic Highlands, NJ: Humanities Press.

Matravers, Derek (1998). *Art and Emotion*. Oxford: Oxford University Press.

Mothersill, Mary (1984). *Beauty Restored*. Oxford: Clarendon Press.

Murdoch, Iris (1970). *The Sovereignty of Good*. London: Routledge.

——(1992). *Metaphysics as a Guide to Morals*. Harmondsworth: Penguin.

Novitz, David (1987). *Knowledge, Fiction and Imagination*. Philadelphia, PA: Temple University Press.

Nussbaum, Martha (1990). *Love's Knowledge: Essays on Philosophy and Literature*. Oxford: Oxford University Press.

——(1998). 'Exactly and Responsibly: A Defense of Ethical Criticism', *Philosophy and Literature* 22: 343–65.

Ogden, C. K. and I. A. Richards (1923). *The Meaning of Meaning: A Study of the Influence of Language Upon Thought and of the Science of Symbolism*. London: Routledge & Kegan Paul.

Ohmann, Richard (1971). 'Speech Acts and the Definition of Literature', *Philosophy and Rhetoric* 4: 1–19.

Olsen, Stein Haugom (1987). *The End of Literary Theory*. Cambridge: Cambridge University Press.

Passmore, John (1954) [1951]. 'The Dreariness of Aesthetics'. In Elton (1954), pp. 36–55. Originally published in *Mind* 60: 318–35.

Phillips, D. Z. (1982). *Through a Darkening Glass: Philosophy, Literature, and Cultural Change*. Oxford: Blackwell

Prall, David W. (1929). *Aesthetic Judgment*. New York: Thomas Y. Crowell.

——(1936). *Aesthetic Analysis*. New York: Thomas Y. Crowell.

Richards, I. A. (1926). *Principles of Literary Criticism*, 2nd edn. London: Routledge & Kegan Paul.

Robinson, Jenefer (2005). *Deeper than Reason*. Oxford: Oxford University Press.

Russell, Bertrand (1905). 'On Denoting', *Mind* 14: 479–93.

Savile, Anthony (1982). *The Test of Time*. Oxford: Clarendon Press.

Schier, Flint (1986). *Deeper into Pictures: An Essay on Pictorial Representation*. Cambridge: Cambridge University Press.

Scruton, Roger (1997). *The Aesthetics of Music*. Oxford: Oxford University Press.

Searle, John R. (1979). 'The Logical Status of Fictional Discourse'. In Searle, *Expression and Meaning: Studies in the Theory of Speech Acts*. Cambridge: Cambridge University Press, pp. 58–75.

Sibley, Frank (2001). *Approaches to Aesthetics: Collected Papers on Philosophical Aesthetics*, ed. J. Benson, B. Redfern, and J. Roxbee Cox. Oxford: Oxford University Press.

—— (2003) [1959]. 'Aesthetic Concepts'. In Lamarque and Olsen (2003), pp. 127–41. Originally published, with some slight differences, in *Philosophical Review* 68 (1959): 421–50.

Solomon, Robert (2004). *In Defence of Sentimentality*. New York: Oxford University Press.

Stecker, Robert (1997). *Artworks: Definition, Meaning, Value*. University Park, PA: Penn State University Press.

Stolnitz, Jerome (1992). 'On the Cognitive Triviality of Art', *British Journal of Aesthetics* 32: 191–200.

Strawson, P. F. (1966). 'Aesthetic Appraisal and Works of Art', *Oxford Review* 3: 5–13.

Thomasson, Amie L. (1999). *Fiction and Metaphysics*. Cambridge: Cambridge University Press.

—— (2005). 'The Ontology of Art and Knowledge in Aesthetics', *Journal of Aesthetics and Art Criticism* 63: 221–9.

van Inwagen, Peter (1977). 'Creatures of Fiction', *American Philosophical Quarterly* 14: 299–308.

Walsh, Dorothy (1969). *Literature and Knowledge*. Middletown, CT: Wesleyan University Press.

Walton, Kendall L. (1990). *Mimesis as Make-Believe: On the Foundations of the Representational Arts*. Cambridge, MA: Harvard University Press.

Weitz, Morris (1956). 'The Role of Theory in Aesthetics', *Journal of Aesthetics and Art Criticism* 15: 27–35.

Wimsatt, William K. and Monroe C. Beardsley (1976) [1946]. 'The Intentional Fallacy'. In D. Newton-de Molina (ed.), *On Literary Intention*. Edinburgh: Edinburgh University Press, pp. 1–13.

Wollheim, Richard (1980). *Art and Its Objects*, 2nd edn. Cambridge: Cambridge University Press.

—— (1998). 'On Pictorial Representation', *Journal of Aesthetics and Art Criticism* 56: 217–26.

Wolterstorff, Nicholas (1980). *Works and Worlds of Art*. Oxford: Clarendon Press.

Wittgenstein, Ludwig (1953). *Philosophical Investigations*, tr. G. E. M. Anscombe. Oxford: Blackwell.

CHAPTER 27

....

ANALYTIC POLITICAL
PHILOSOPHY

....

JONATHAN WOLFF

27.1 POLITICAL PHILOSOPHY AND THE
FOUNDERS OF ANALYTIC PHILOSOPHY

Political philosophy is not, initially, easy to place in terms of the foundation and early development of analytic philosophy. If, following the traditional understanding, one takes analytic philosophy to have been founded by Frege, Russell, Moore, and Wittgenstein, it is not obvious what influence these figures have had on the subsequent development of the discipline. To take them in turn, Frege did not write professionally on any political or social topics (although famously Dummett (1981, p. xii) reports his shock and dismay at finding anti-Semitic comments in Frege's diaries; these diaries are now published (Frege 1994), as are some suggestions Frege (2000) made about an electoral system). Russell is more complex. As a public intellectual he was known primarily as a political campaigner, especially for his pacifism and opposition to nuclear arms, and indeed, was imprisoned for his views during the First World War. He wrote widely on political topics, and gave the first Reith Lectures for the BBC, later published as *Authority and the Individual* (Russell 1949). Yet *The Problems of Philosophy* (Russell 1912) does not have any discussion of political philosophy, and it is not mentioned in his *My Philosophical Development* (Russell 1959). Russell's political writings have had very little, if any, influence on subsequent debates. Despite the attention given to political philosophy in Russell's *History of Western Philosophy* (1945), and the fact that his first published book was *German Social Democracy* (1896), Russell appeared to consider political writing as something rather separate from philosophy.

Moore's reputation as a moral philosopher in a way holds out more hope that he would have made a contribution to political philosophy, but even in his case he did not explicitly write on these topics, and one struggles to find more than a few scattered remarks. Wittgenstein, of course, had little to say about political and legal matters in his early writings. His later writings, such as *Culture and Value* (1980), do bear on politics, and other writers in political philosophy, such as Hanna Pitkin in *Wittgenstein and Justice* (1972), David Rubinstein in *Marx and Wittgenstein* (1981), and, from a very different perspective, even Jean-Paul Lyotard, who makes extensive use of the term 'language game' in *Just Gaming* (Lyotard and Thébaud 1985), have found inspiration in *Philosophical Investigations*. However, it would be hard to argue that Wittgenstein's later writings remain firmly within the analytic tradition.

Casting the net more widely, Carnap and Neurath bear some interesting similarities to Russell in holding radical political beliefs and contributing to intense contemporary political debates, while never becoming part of a tradition of academic political philosophy. One way in which they differed from Russell was in claiming that their anti-metaphysical contributions to philosophy were somehow continuous with emancipatory political struggle, although how exactly this connection is to be made, and especially whether they developed a 'left philosophy of science', remains a topic of contemporary debate (Uebel 2005; Richardson 2009; Uebel 2010). Another point of difference was that Neurath engaged in and contributed to academic debates in political theory, as well as taking part in political activism and holding political office. Yet there is little trace of attention to Neurath at least in English-language political philosophy, except as a figure worthy of scholarly interest and, perhaps, rediscovery (Cartwright *et al.* 1996; O'Neill 2003).

A. J. Ayer, who also was a political activist, albeit in a more conventional party-political vein, and lectured on political theory in the late 1930s, explains his own lack of writing in political philosophy with the comment that he found that concepts such as 'the social contract' and 'the general will' 'did not repay minute analysis', but he had nothing of his own to replace them with (Ayer 1977, p. 184). He did, however, later publish an essay entitled 'The Concept of Freedom' in which he offers an analysis of the measurement of freedom (Ayer 1944).

Ayer claims that his friend Isaiah Berlin turned to political philosophy because, according to Ayer, Berlin's lack of knowledge of mathematical logic made him come to the view that to work in central areas of philosophy was 'beyond his grasp' (Ayer 1977, p. 98). This explanation, however, does not quite tally with Berlin's own, in which it was the non-substantive ambitions of contemporary philosophy that led to his disillusionment and turn to the history of ideas. (Ignatieff 1998, p. 131). We will, though, return to Berlin's writings later. Despite Ayer's evident interest in political matters, his own brand of positivism bears on political philosophy in possibly devastating fashion, apparently by reducing arguments in political philosophy to either disagreement about facts, to be resolved by the social sciences, or subjective expression of emotions, about which there can be no rational debate (Ayer 1936). All that is left, it appears, is logical analysis of concepts. Again we shall return to this below.

The impression, therefore, is that most of the central figures in the foundation and further development of analytic philosophy—even those with strongly held and argued political views—did not see political philosophy as part of their activity as philosophers. Indeed, at least in the case of Ayer, their philosophical position appears to rule out the possibility of political philosophy at least as a normative discipline. The only major exception to this is Karl Popper who is known for his contributions to both philosophy of science and political philosophy. Popper's *The Poverty of Historicism*, first published as a series of articles in 1944–5, dates back, he says in the 'Historical Note' accompanying the first publication in book form, to 1919–20 (Popper 1957). His major two-volume *The Open Society and Its Enemies* (Popper 1945a, 1945b), which, with *The Poverty of Historicism*, he described as his 'war effort' (Popper 1974/1992, p. 115), famously argues in favour of the 'open society' and against the possibility of 'historical prophecy' and in favour of 'piecemeal social engineering'. *The Open Society*, Popper says, was 'well received in England, far beyond my expectations' (Popper 1974/1992, p. 122). Yet although scholars were prepared to engage, highly critically, with Popper's readings of Plato (Levinson 1953) and Marx (Cornforth 1968) few political philosophers seem to have responded to the substantive content of Popper's own position.

In some ways it seems strange that Popper remained on the sidelines to the development of academic political philosophy, despite the wider recognition of the power of his work. Indeed in social science and broader political theory Popper is regarded as a major contributor, especially for his theory of the demarcation between science and pseudoscience (Popper 1935/1959, 1963) in addition to the themes mentioned above. Yet he was largely ignored by political philosophers. In the Preface to the first volume of the series Philosophy, Politics and Society, the founding editor Peter Laslettt, in 1956, refers to Popper as 'perhaps the most influential of contemporary philosophers who have addressed themselves to politics' (Laslett 1956a, p. xii). In this series, however, which we will discuss in detail shortly, not only does Popper not appear in any of the volumes, but his work is not engaged with in any of the 70 or so papers in the seven volumes that have appeared to date. Neither did Popper publish in the yearbook of the American Society of Political and Legal Society, *Nomos*, the first number of which appeared in 1958 and has been published annually since (Friedrich 1958).

27.2 POLITICAL PHILOSOPHY AND THE FOCAL POINTS OF EARLY ANALYTIC PHILOSOPHY

Even if few of the major figures in the early rise of analytic philosophy attended to political philosophy, this does not exclude the possibility that others would do such work inspired by developments elsewhere. Here we confront the question of what constitutes the emergence of analytic philosophy. This complex story is told elsewhere within this volume, but to simplify, it may be possible to identify three initial strands, which I will term the rejection of idealism, the introduction of the new logic, and, distinctly, the insistence on conceptual analysis.

The first strand, then, is a negative one: the rejection of forms of idealism descending from Hegel. In the context of political philosophy the leading text is Hegel's *Philosophy of Right*, first published in 1821, although not translated into English until 1896 (Hegel 1821/1896). Such delay may indicate a neglect of Hegel in the mid-nineteenth century, but may also be a consequence of the facility of British scholars in the nineteenth century to read German, and their habit of interacting with German scholars.

The most influential works of the major idealist political philosophers include T. H. Green's 'Lecture on Liberal Legislation and Freedom of Contract', and *Lectures on the Principles of Political Obligation* which were included in the volumes of his works published between 1883 and 1885, shortly after his death in 1882 (Green 1883–5). Also important is Bernard Bosanquet's *Philosophical Theory of the State*, first published 1899, with the fourth and final edition published in 1923 (Bosanquet 1899/1923), as well as F. H. Bradley, including his essay 'My Station and Its Duties' in *Ethical Studies*, first published in 1876 (Bradley 1876). Hastings Rashdall's *Theory of Good and Evil* (1907) also bears on many political issues.

Idealism, as understood in Hegelian terms, has for a long time remained largely of historical interest in contemporary thought. Although there has been a revival of interest in idealist political thought, it still remains only on the fringes of Anglo-American political philosophy, except as an object of intellectual history. It seems that we are yet to see any serious attempt to revive any strong form of neo-Hegelianism in political philosophy, although some of Hegel's ideas about moral community have influenced current criticisms of liberal thought. Hegelian idealism is notable for its social holism: the idea that the state or society exists as a moral and metaphysical entity in its own right. As developed in the UK, idealism took many forms, and it would be wrong to think that it is defined by any one doctrine or position. However, Russell's account of his own reasons for departing from idealism is instructive. Key to idealism, argues Russell, is the doctrine of 'internal relations': that 'every relation between two terms expresses, primarily, intrinsic properties of the two terms and, in ultimate analysis, a property of the whole of which the two compose' (Russell 1959, p. 42). Russell accepts that this is plausible for some relations, such as love, but argues against generalizing it to all. In particular it cannot apply to asymmetrical relations as are common in mathematics. Accordingly, Russell replaces it with the doctrine of 'external relations' allowing for contingent relations between objects (Griffin, this volume; Candlish 2007, ch. 6).

It is clear that the doctrine of internal relations leads to a form of holism, in which all must be seen as components of a whole, and thus, in political philosophy, it is natural that the legacy of the rejection of idealism appears (at least) two-fold, in the implicit adoption of two forms of individualism. First, there is an assumption that some sort of high regard must be given to the moral importance of the individual, running from utilitarianism in which total value is a simple sum of individual values, to rights theories in which autonomy must not be violated. Second, a form of methodological individualism appears also to be widely assumed, in which it is presumed that explanations of social facts should be conducted in terms of facts about individuals. Of course a wide range of positions can be held, but the general tenor of contemporary political philosophy is to give moral and explanatory priority to individuals over social collectives. This dramatically contrasts with Bradley's famous doctrine that the individual is a bare abstraction

(Bradley 1876). While it is also often noted that Rawls, in *A Theory of Justice*, quotes Bradley approvingly (Rawls 1971, p. 110), it has to be recognized that Rawls reads this phrase largely in institutional terms—i.e. what duties you have depends on institutional facts—rather than in the metaphysical and moral terms implied by holistic forms of idealism.

A second part of the initial foundation of analytic philosophy is the invention of modern logic, especially quantification and the predicate calculus, with Frege and Russell (Frege 1879; Russell 1903, 1905; Whitehead and Russell 1910–13) and the application of logical techniques to other areas of philosophy. Here it is hard to see how such concerns immediately exerted any influence on political philosophy, in that it is hard to find examples before the 1950s of any attempt to use any form of formal theory in moral and political philosophy. Matters changed to some degree with the publication of Arrow's *Social Choice and Individual Values* (1951) and, to a lesser extent, Luce and Raiffa's *Theory of Games and Decisions* (1957), in that political philosophers felt that they had at least to acknowledge the existence of such work. Yet few seriously attempted to use formal methods until Braithwaite's *Theory of Games as a Tool for the Moral Philosopher* (1955), and James Buchanan and Gordon Tulloch's *The Calculus of Consent* (1962). Braithwaite's, though, was a somewhat anomalous work in that Braithwaite, a philosopher of science, had been appointed to the Knightbridge Chair at Cambridge, at that time considered to be a chair in moral philosophy, and for his inaugural lecture apparently felt that he should make a contribution to the subject. And indeed this lecture seems to have been Braithwaite's only attempt to connect with moral philosophy. Others, such as Brian Barry, David Gauthier, Amartya Sen, and John Rawls would see possible applications of game and decision theory (Barry 1965; Gauthier 1969; Sen 1970; Rawls 1971). This strand of political philosophy remains alive and active, although its connection with logical developments in philosophy is much less marked than its debt to game theory, rational decision theory, and social choice theory.

However, a third strand is often claimed also to be central to analytic philosophy, the use of conceptual analysis, as exemplified by Moore (1903), as distinct from the logical analysis of Frege and Russell. Whether this amounts to an innovation, however, is not obvious. At its most prescriptive, it would be the project of analysing concepts by providing a set of necessary and sufficient conditions for their application, or, at least, to make as much progress in this direction as the subject matter allows. However, it is not clear how this differs from the project of seeing the philosopher's task as including the provision of definitions, which has been part of philosophy since the ancient Greeks. If, on the other hand, conceptual analysis is thought to be a term to describe a broader approach to philosophy which emphasizes rigour, argument, and attempts to achieve conceptual clarity, then it is equally hard to see it as anything new. After all, Jeremy Bentham (e.g. Bentham 1781/1970) and Henry Sidgwick, whose *Methods of Ethics*, first published in 1874, and going through seven editions, the last of which was published in 1907 (Sidgwick, 1874/1907), exemplified these virtues arguably to a higher degree than Moore. Indeed, outside political philosophy, Bentham's 'theory of fictions' was later recognized as anticipating Russell's theory of descriptions (Wisdom 1931; Quine 1981; Beaney 2003/2009).

However, to return to the first strand, it appears that the rejection of idealism left a void in political philosophy, rather than an alternative programme. When one looks for major works of political philosophy published between the wars, it is hard to find anything of comparable importance to those published at the turn of the century. Harold Laski produced a stream of books during this period (e.g. Laski 1925), yet he is rarely referred to within contemporary legal and political philosophy. Similar remarks can be made with respect to John Dewey's prolific output. Tawney's *Equality* (1931) remains a point of reference, yet it would be a great exaggeration to claim that it has been central to the development of political philosophy. Also notable is Plamenatz's *Consent, Freedom and Political Obligation* (1938), although this is an interesting transitional work, engaging with Green and Bosanquet, yet producing a contribution to the liberal individualist approach to political obligation that still receives notice today. Perhaps Marxism made more enduring contributions, with Lukács' *History and Class Consciousness* (1923/1967) and the first writings emanating from the Frankfurt School. In passing it is worth also noting that T. S. Eliot, who wrote his Ph.D. thesis on Bradley, delivered the lectures that became *The Idea of A Christian Society*, in 1939 (Eliot 1939). This work, idealist in general conception, also gives a powerful sense of a struggle between three competing ideologies and political systems—liberal democracy of the USA, UK, and France, fascism of Germany and Italy, and communism of the Soviet bloc—dominating world politics. Eliot seemed far from certain, as he wrote, which would prevail. It is extraordinary to contrast the uncertainty and tensions of the world Eliot was writing in with the relative stability of our own. Perhaps, between the wars, political theory took a back seat to real world political conflict.

But in considering the development of political philosophy in the twentieth century it is important also to consider the place of utilitarianism. At the start of the twentieth century, idealism vied with utilitarianism, especially in the version defended by Sidgwick, as leading approaches to ethics (Driver, this volume). At least in some quarters, however, utilitarianism was seen as outdated; Russell ruefully remembered that as a young man he and his friends referred to Sidgwick as 'old Sidg' (Russell 1959, p. 30). On the other hand it is sometimes thought that the lack of substantive progress in political philosophy before Rawls is somehow related to the dominance utilitarian thinking had on political philosophy, which, it is said, obtained a kind of 'dominance-by-default in the English-speaking liberal democracies in the twentieth century' (Miller and Dagger 2003, p. 449). Yet whether utilitarianism remained dominant as a theory in political philosophy (as distinct from economics and public life) in the decades before Rawls is not obvious. Utilitarianism was most obviously represented by Sidgwick's *Elements of Politics*, which was published in 1891 and reprinted several times, including in 1919 (Sidgwick 1891). In terms of the development of utilitarianism the most significant innovation may be the paper of the economist Roy Harrod setting out a version of rule-utilitarianism (Harrod 1936), and utilitarianism was taken very seriously within economics. Yet if one looks at the political philosophy textbooks of the 1930s and 1940s there is no sign of a discipline in the grip of utilitarianism. E. F. Carritt's *Morals and Politics* (1935) provides a history of the subject from Hobbes to Bosanquet without even a mention of Bentham, Mill, or Sidgwick, while in his later *Ethical and Political Thinking* utilitarianism appears in a chapter entitled 'Crude Moral Theories' and Carritt presents several objections to utilitarianism, including a version of the now notorious 'scapegoat' objection in which under certain circumstances utilitarianism would justify punishing an innocent person (Carritt 1947, p. 65). Indeed Rawls critically responds to this argument in his most utilitarian early paper, 'Two Concepts of Rules' (Rawls 1955, pp. 10–11). In Mabbott's *The State and the Citizen* (1948/1967) Bentham and Mill are mentioned primarily for their errors and Sidgwick is ignored entirely. T. D. Weldon's *States and Morals* contains no significant discussion of utilitarianism and only passing mention of Mill and Sidgwick (Weldon 1946). If utilitarianism was dominant, it is hard to find evidence.

Despite this, the idea that contemporary analytic political philosophy owes a great deal to utilitarianism is very plausible, if the claim is interpreted as a comment about form rather than content. We have noted several times that the distinctive virtues of analytic political philosophy were already present in the writings of Bentham, Mill, and Sidgwick. Agree with it or not, utilitarianism offered a model of what a clear and rigorous political philosophy could be, and how it would be established.[1]

27.3 Post-War Analytic Political and Legal Philosophy: *Philosophy, Politics and Society*

Although Hayek's *Road to Serfdom* was published in 1944, the immediate post-war period saw little revival of political philosophy, to the point where in 1956, in the preface to *Philosophy, Politics and Society* (First Series) the historian Peter Laslett famously wrote that the long tradition of political philosophy, 'from Hobbes to Bosanquet', appeared to have stopped, notoriously observing 'For the moment, anyway, political philosophy is dead' (Laslett 1956a, p. vii). Laslett's volume was conceived as a parallel to Flew's Logic and Language series, which, encouragingly, contained papers in political and legal philosophy by Margaret Macdonald and H. L. A. Hart (Flew 1951). Yet for the editor of a collection of papers in political philosophy to announce the subject 'dead' is quite extraordinary, especially when important work was still been done not only by Hayek, but also, for example, Adorno and Horkheimer in their *Dialectic of Enlightenment* (1944/1997), although to be fair to Laslett he restricts the scope of his claim to writing in English. Laslett considers three possible diagnoses of the situation. First, the horrors

---

[1] I owe this point to Alan Hamlin.

of the Second World War. 'Faced with Hiroshima and with Belsen, a man is unlikely to address himself to a neat and original theory of political obligation' (Laslett 1956a p. vii). Second, the rise of sociological thought, including Marxism, has tended to explain away political philosophy as sociologically determined by its context, and hence as a symptom of deeper causes to be understood through social analysis (Laslett 1956a, p. viii). But finally, and most importantly, 'The Logical Positivists [killed political philosophy]. It was Russell and Wittgenstein, Ayer and Ryle who convinced the philosophers that they must withdraw unto themselves for a time and re-examine their logical and linguistic apparatus.... [This re-examination] called into question the logical status of all ethical statements ... and [raised the question] of whether political philosophy is possible at all' (Laslett 1956a, p. ix).

The first of these explanations, though often repeated, may seem, however, uncompelling. Popper, as we noted earlier, referred to his writings in political philosophy as his 'war effort' (Popper 1974/1992, p. 115), and, as Laslett himself notes, it seems just as likely that a war of such magnitude should inspire reflection on political matters rather than suppress it. The second—where ideology is a reduced to a subject of sociological study—may well be more significant in undermining political theory as an autonomous discipline. The third—the rise of positivism (though here rolled together with logical atomism and ordinary language philosophy)—again looks a promising explanation but we will see that it is also more problematic than it looks. But still the appearance is a powerful one especially when combined with the introspections of ordinary language philosophy, with its concentration on clarification of questions rather than proposing solutions. Each could have a dampening effect on the prospects for political philosophy; together they threaten to be stultifying.

The particular implications of positivism for political philosophy are said, by Laslett, to have been drawn out by T. D. Weldon, whose *Vocabulary of Politics* (1953) is summarized by Weldon in a paper entitled 'Political Principles'. This is included as the second essay in Laslett's collection (Weldon 1956), after an elegant, and now well-known essay by Michael Oakeshott, on 'Political Education'. Clearly untouched by logical positivism, Oakeshott makes the case for the priority of tradition over ideology, and conversation over argument (Oakeshott 1956). By contrast, in 'Political Principles' Weldon, in a somewhat irritated tone, applies a fairly direct form of logical positivism to deflate the ambitions of traditional political philosophy, arguing that political principles have no firmer epistemological foundation than individual judgement or collective agreement.

Laslett subtly describes 'Political Principles' as a 'terser' form of the argument of Weldon's 1953 book *The Vocabulary of Politics*. The term 'terse' is accurate both in the sense of the paper being more concise but also rather brusque in tone. *The Vocabulary of Politics* was published in a series edited by Ayer, and in his editorial foreword Ayer suggests that Weldon aims to 'exhibit the logic of the statements which characteristically figure in discourse about politics'. Certainly Weldon makes what appear to be straightforward assertions of a logical positivist creed. In certain places Weldon argues that the role of the philosopher in respect to politics is not to answer what have been taken to be the traditional questions, but to clarify the meaning of the vocabulary in which they are couched. He even goes as far as to say that '[W]hen verbal confusions are tidied up most of the questions of traditional political philosophy are not unanswerable. All of them are confused formulations of purely empirical difficulties' (Weldon 1953, p. 192). Yet, as is the case so often, Weldon's own analysis rather betrays his theoretical claims. Much of Weldon's argument is that traditional political philosophy has implicitly accepted a type of Platonism, in which terms like 'freedom' and 'the state' stand for concepts with real essences, and that the task of the political philosopher is to discover such essences, which then will provide 'philosophical foundations' for particular political ideologies. Weldon claims that this approach is mistaken: there are no essences or foundations.

Weldon plausibly links the search for 'foundations' with the fear of subjectivism. In 1953 this manifests itself as the concern that unless it is possible to find philosophical foundations for Western liberal democracy, one would have nothing to say in opposition to Soviet communism, or, indeed, the Nazi regime which of course was a very recent memory. Weldon attempts to disarm this line of objection by the plausible contention that it is possible to support and oppose political positions with reasons even if there is no definitive set of foundations or philosophical test against which any political position can be judged.

At the same time, Weldon suggests, it does not follow that politics collapses into individual subjectivism; foundations are not necessary for rational politics. Rather he sketches an account in which politics is a practice with its own internal standards of excellence (although Weldon does not use this language himself) rather like art criticism or wine tasting, in which there can be genuine judgements. Weldon also takes time to sketch out the virtues of a statesman, and how such a person compares with experts in other fields. In this respect Weldon appears far closer to Oakeshott than to Ayer or Ryle. More generally, Weldon curiously combines a great respect for the genius of many of the great political philosophers, with a readiness to accuse them of rather simple logical errors and mistakes of philosophical grammar.

Still, it is evident that Weldon's relation to logical positivism and linguistic analysis is a complex one. The analytic project of conceptual analysis is sometimes implicitly guilty of the Platonism which Weldon rejects, and he is very keen to avoid the accusation that rejecting Platonism leaves one only with a 'boo-hurrah' approach to political philosophy. Indeed, the special difficulties of applying positivism to political philosophy were pointed out even before Hiroshima and Belsen, in a paper called 'The Language of Political Theory' by Margaret Macdonald (Macdonald 1940–1). Macdonald points out that political disagreement does not always seem to be based on empirical questions or linguistic confusion, and remaining disagreements can have enormous impact on human lives. Implicitly, she seems to admit that crude application of logical positivism is insufficient to diagnose all disagreement in political philosophy. By way of case study, she turns her attention to the problem of political obligation, arguing that none of the leading accounts—social contract, tradition, utilitarian—provide a general answer, and that instead each holds part of the truth and there is an indefinite set of vaguely shifting criteria, differing for different times and circumstances:

> The value of the political theorists, however, is not in the general information they give about the basis of political obligation but in their skill in emphasizing at a critical moment a criterion which is tending to be overlooked or denied. (Macdonald 1940–1, p. 112)

Macdonald's better known paper, 'Natural Rights', first published in 1947, is reprinted by Laslett, and given the historical importance of the Laslett volume it is worth looking at all the papers in the volume, if briefly. In her contribution Macdonald argues against both the idea that natural rights can be founded on the natural law, revealed by reason, and a crude 'boo-hurrah' positivism (Macdonald 1947). Like Weldon at his best, Macdonald struggles to find a middle ground. The view she presents is that statements of natural rights are akin to decisions, declaring 'here I stand', and, like Weldon, uses an analogy with another area of critical judgement—in her case literary appreciation—to point out the possibility of rational argument through the presentation of reasons. With both Weldon and Macdonald, while it is clear that a positivist orientation and concentration on questions of language strongly inform their thinking, neither is prepared simply to apply a positivist formula, and both make contributions to political philosophy of a pragmatist, contextualist, form which are independent of considerations of linguistic analysis.

More generally, many of the essays in this volume have a tendency to try to explain away disagreement in political philosophy on the grounds not of substantial doctrinal difference, but in terms of confusion about the logic or grammar of concepts. One example is Rees' essay, first published in 1950, which is an application of a type of linguistic philosophy to diagnose apparent philosophical disagreements about the nature, importance, and use of the concept of sovereignty as resulting from a failure to distinguish different concepts of state and sovereign. Although by no means a simple application of positivism, Rees' argument shows a positivist spirit by its general architecture: essentially that once linguistic confusions are cleared up then remaining disagreements can generally be settled in empirical terms (Rees 1950). Quinton, in his paper that was first published in the journal *Analysis* in 1954, presents a somewhat similar methodological approach, albeit with, potentially, a more interesting pay-off. He attempts to reconcile retributive and utilitarian doctrines of punishment by claiming that the former is a logical doctrine concerning the use of a word, and the latter a moral doctrine about the justification of punishment (Quinton 1954).

Bambrough makes a methodologically self-conscious attempt to apply new modes of linguistic analysis to Plato's use of analogies, with the 'dual purpose of making Plato's doctrines clear and making a contribution to the understanding of the logic of political theories' (Bambrough 1956, p. 99). Indeed Bambrough's discussion of Plato is exceptionally illuminating, but it is very unclear that it depends in any way on a new philosophical method. The essay concludes with a much more methodological discussion, focusing on the issue of what follows from the recognition that questions in politics and ethics are not factual questions with empirically verifiable answers. Here Bambrough has even less to offer than Weldon and Macdonald on the topic, merely suggesting that such deliberative questions require decisions, but can be reasonable if made with thought and knowledge.

Gallie, in a paper published first in *Philosophy* in 1949, as a methodological preliminary, considers the debate between those who hold the 'monarchic' view of ethics—that there is one true theory for all times and places—and the 'polyarchic' view, which claims that different moralities are valid in different times and places, and he argues that considerations of 'the logic of ethics' cannot settle this dispute as any questions about logic are internal to a language and cannot rule on whether there is more than one possible language. The rest of the paper is devoted to trying to defend the claim that there are distinct liberal and socialist moralities, which not only conflict with each other but can also both be found within the moral thought of each individual in contemporary society (Gallie 1949). It is worth noting that the argument has some affinities with Gallie's much better known paper, 'Essentially Contested Concepts', published the same year as the Laslett collection (Gallie 1955–6).

Other papers, though, seem somewhat less bound by their historical context. Bernard Mayo's very short paper (first published 1950), on the general will, assumes an anti-metaphysical account of an individual, and of the notion of individual will, which is then applied to society as an entity. Mayo suggests—in a move that anticipates later philosophy of mind—that the interpretative attitude we take to individuals can also be applied to societies. Just as we posit an individual will to make sense of individual behaviour, we are equally justified in positing a 'general will' to make sense of social action (Mayo 1950). Laslett's own contribution to the volume is a lengthy exposition of the important point that modern society is not the sort of 'face to face' society theorized by Plato or even Rousseau. However, this is offered as a type of rebuke to sociologically and historically ill-informed political theorists rather than an insight of which creative use can then be made (Laslett 1956b).

The overriding character of the essays in the book (with some exceptions) is a conviction that previous theorists, for all their genius, went badly wrong often because they were confused about the meaning, logic, or grammar of particular words or concepts. But very little, if any, real use of logic is made: one might think that 'logic' is used in the sense in which it appears in the title of Ayer's *Language, Truth and Logic*, rather than that of Frege or Russell. Certainly there is no sense of modern logic having a transforming effect on the presentation of political philosophy. Indeed the mood is much more one of linguistic, rather than analytic, philosophy, in any obvious sense. But it is also unclear that there is much, in terms of methods of argument, that marks a break with, say, Hobbes and Bentham, who each sought out clarity and rigour in argument, and were equally prepared to accuse their predecessors of confusion.

27.4 THE REVIVAL OF ADVOCACY

There is a character to the writings of the First Series of *Philosophy, Politics and Society* that is brought out very well in the Introduction to the Second Series, published in 1962, this time edited by the sociologist Runciman, alongside the historian Laslett. The editors contend that the papers of the first volume, and other writings of the time, are much more concerned with diagnosis than with advocacy (Laslett and Runciman 1962, pp. viii–ix). And indeed, looking back to the First Series there is virtually no assertion or defence of a substantive position in political philosophy.

The mood, however, had changed to some degree by 1962, and between 1956 and 1962 there had been significant developments in the area. For one, Isaiah Berlin's classic paper 'Two Concepts of Liberty' was presented as an Inaugural Lecture and published in 1958 (Berlin 1958/1969). The tone and general character of Berlin's writing make him an unlikely champion of analytic philosophy, especially in the light of Berlin's warning against attempting to impose methods of logical and linguistic analysis in political philosophy:

> To neglect the field of political thought, because its unstable subject-matter, with its blurred edges, is not to be caught by the fixed concepts, abstract models and fine instruments suitable to logic or to linguistic analysis—to demand a unity of method in philosophy, and reject whatever the method cannot successfully manage—is merely to allow oneself to remain at the mercy of primitive and uncriticised political beliefs. (Berlin 1958/1969, p. 119)

Yet the central contrast of his paper is very interesting for our purposes. In distinguishing positive from negative liberty, Berlin is distinguishing a collectivist view of liberty, in which, for example, the state knows best what makes you free, from an individualist notion in which liberty involves the pursuit of a plan of one's own. The collectivist view is associated by Berlin with Hegel, Fichte, Bradley, Bosanquet, and Green, the individualist notion with Hobbes, Locke, Smith, Bentham, and Mill. In other words, Berlin's essay is one of the main sites in which analytic political philosophy emphasized its decisive break with the idealist tradition, and by reviving an older tradition, Berlin is helping support a new one.

A second development was the publication of the major text *Social Principles and the Democratic State* by Stanley Benn and Richard Peters in 1959, which, on the first page of Chapter 1, asserts its analytic credentials with a phrase later to be made famous by Margaret Thatcher: 'The first and obvious observation to make is that there is no such thing as society' (Benn and Peters 1959, p. 13). However, rather than an assertion of a form of individualism it is part of a programme of conceptual analysis in which a series of political concepts, such as equality, democracy, authority, and freedom are probed in depth, as an attempt to introduce a form of analytic reasoning into issues of politics.

Another highly significant event during this period was the publication of H. L. A. Hart's *The Concept of Law* (1961/1994). This work, the founding text of analytic jurisprudence, also has to be regarded as a classic of analytic philosophy. Hart explicitly describes his book as an exercise in 'analytic jurisprudence', as well as, more surprisingly, 'descriptive sociology', and develops a version of legal positivism, rejecting both natural law theory and the crude 'command' theory of law identified with earlier positivist views. Legal positivism is a form of positivism in that it makes central use of a fact/value distinction, asserting that the existence of law does not depend on its moral content (the 'Separation Thesis'). Hart introduces the idea that any legal system needs a 'rule of recognition' by which new laws are made and legitimized, and that the existence of law depends on the social facts by which it is recognized (the 'Social Thesis'). Despite the power of argument and general clarity of expression, however, Hart's own view has been surprisingly resistant to precise capture, especially in light of the inclusion of an unfinished postscript to the second edition of the work (published in 1994), primarily responding to Dworkin's criticisms.

It is also worth noting that Hart's important paper 'Are There Any Natural Rights?' was published as early as 1955, a year before the First Series of *Philosophy, Politics and Society*, and much more constructive than most of the papers in that volume (Hart 1955). In addition to the substantive contributions Hart makes to the theory of rights, and, by means of his 'principle of fair play' to the theory of political obligation, this paper is notable for perhaps one of the clearest statements of the methodological assumptions of post-positivist conceptual analysis, included in the following statement, 'Perhaps few would now deny, as some have, that there are moral rights; for the point of that denial was usually to object to some philosophical claim as to the "ontological status" of rights, and this objection is now expressed not as a denial that there are any moral rights but as a denial of some assumed logical similarity between sentences used to assert the existence of rights and other kinds of sentences' (Hart 1955, p. 176).

Both Berlin and Hart are included in the Second Series of *Politics, Philosophy and Society*. The preface of the Second Series includes a reflection on the remark in the preface to the first concerning the alleged death of political philosophy (indeed all other volumes in the series either discuss or allude to this remark). The 'heyday of Weldonism' was said to have ended (Laslett and Runciman 1962, p. vii) and Weldon in fact had died in 1958, according to some accounts taking his own life (King 1994). The Second Series contains much of interest. Berlin's contribution is his famous paper 'Does Political Philosophy Still Exist?' (Berlin 1962). Here he continues his sideswipe against prescriptive methodology, mentioned above, suggesting that political philosophy arises out of disagreements about the conception of man, and while it can be suppressed, it cannot be legislated out of existence. Berlin is able to convey a sense of history in which positivist strictures are a passing fad which cannot suppress human curiosity and inventiveness. Berlin invites us to observe that in a historical perspective such concerns will eventually appear parochial, local, and a product of their time. Yet Berlin is still somewhat guarded about the current state of political philosophy, observing that no 'commanding work' had been published in the twentieth century (Berlin 1962, p. 1).

The Second Series of *Politics, Philosophy and Society* includes a number of papers that have exerted an influence on subsequent debates, and in several cases continue to do so. Richard Wollheim's 'A Paradox in the Theory of Democracy' (1962) set off a small industry, and Bernard Williams' 'The Idea of Equality' is widely reprinted and still discussed (Williams 1962). Hart's 'Prolegomenon to the Principles of Punishment' (reprinted from 1959/60) is thorough, illuminating, and informed by detailed understanding of both political theory and practices of criminal law (Hart 1959/60). In passing, it is interesting to note that the editors remark that they asked Bertrand Russell to contribute a piece on nuclear disarmament, but he declined to do so, although, perhaps, the fact that he would then have been around 90 years old may have had some bearing on his decision (Laslett and Runciman 1962, p. ix).

Part of the explicit agenda of the volume is to bring the social sciences into contact with political philosophy. Here, I think, we have to say that the volume is not entirely success-ful. MacIntyre's 'A Mistake About Causality in Social Science' is much more a contribu-tion to the philosophy of social science, rather than a contribution to social science or an attempt to show how social science can be of use to philosophers (MacIntyre 1962). But the volume does contain several papers by social scientists, including Runciman (the co-editor), Dahrendorf, and Reinhard Bendix, all of whom draw on empirical research or sociological theory to attempt to illuminate questions of issues of democracy and of inequality.

However, there is little doubt that the highlight of the collection is the reprint of Rawls' 'Justice as Fairness', first published in the *Philosophical Review* (Rawls 1958). The editors seem clear that Rawls is doing something new, and highly stimulating, and even at that time there seems to be a sense that the future health of the discipline is in his hands. The character of Rawls' paper is quite different to anything else in the first two volumes. First, it is the only paper in the volume to set out and defend a particular substantive conclu-sion. Second, it has a distinct approach to methodology. Many other authors of the era chide previous philosophers through the application of methodological dogma, and then find themselves hamstrung by their own methodological strictures. By contrast, Rawls lays out elements of a methodology, and then uses it to constructive effect. Third, Rawls' relation to the previous history of the subject is to find inspiration in it, rather than either to ignore it, or to treat it as a series of informative mistakes. So, for example, Rawls rather over-generously suggests that 'a similar analysis' to his principles of justice can be found in the now largely forgotten work *The Principles of Moral Judgement*, by W. D. Lamont (Lamont 1946) (Rawls 1962, p. 134n). Indeed the original *Philosophical Review* version of Rawls' paper contains many more referenced footnotes, and clearly demonstrates Rawls' exhaustive engagement with the recent literature. Fourth, Rawls does not restrict himself to philosophical texts, but is quite happy to make use of work in related fields, such as welfare economics. With Rawls, under the influence of Hart, Berlin, and Stuart Hampshire, whom Rawls encountered in Oxford in the academic year 1952–3 (Pogge 2007: 16), one sees political philosophy rediscovering its confidence.

One has to ask, though, whether political philosophy in the United States ever suf-fered the same degree of loss as confidence as it did in the UK. The first volume of *Nomos*, the yearbook of the American Society of Political and Legal Philosophy, was published in 1958, with a collection of essays on Authority by a range of authors including Frank Knight, Hannah Arendt, Bertrand de Jouvenal, and Talcott Parsons (Friedrich 1958). The general character of the volume is one of historical reflection and conceptual anal-ysis, with little, if anything, of the spectre of 'Weldonism' that haunted British politi-cal philosophers at the time. Volumes continued to be produced on an annual basis, and Volume VI, Justice, produced in 1963, is a particular highlight with Joel Feinberg's 'Justice and Personal Desert' perhaps the most enduring of the papers included, alongside other important contributions such as John Rawls' 'Constitutional Liberty and the Concept of Justice', Robert Tucker's 'Marx and Distributive Justice', and Hugo Bedau's 'Justice and Classical Utilitarianism' (Friedrich and Chapman 1963).

27.5 Oxford Readings and Laslett Third to Fifth Series

The Third Series of *Philosophy, Politics and Society*, again edited by Laslett and Runciman, appeared in 1967, the same year that Quinton produced the edited collection *Political Philosophy* for the Oxford Readings in Philosophy series. Quinton included Hart's 'Natural Rights' paper as well as Berlin's 'Two Concepts of Liberty'. Other highlights include a symposium between R. S. Peters and Peter Winch on 'Authority', and two papers by Brian Barry, 'The Public Interest' and 'Justice and the Common Good'. Barry's *Political Argument*, a major work of analytic political philosophy, had recently also been published (Barry 1965). Indeed in the first paragraph of *Political Argument* Barry explicitly describes his approach as 'analytical', which, interestingly, he contrasts with 'causal', by which he appears to mean the collection of data or historical information for purposes of scientific explanation (Barry 1965, p. xvii). Clearly Barry's intention is to use a method of analysis, involving arguments, objections to the arguments of others, and distinctions, rather than supporting or undermining theories through the accumulation of evidence.

Two more methodological papers are included by Quinton: John Plamenatz's 'The Use of Political Theory' and P. H. Partridge's 'Politics, Philosophy, Ideology'. These both respond to the allegation that political philosophy is dead. Plamenatz appears to agree with his contemporaries that most of the great philosophers of the past were hopelessly confused; nevertheless, he claims, political philosophy is a branch of practical philosophy, needed to guide conduct, despite the claims of the positivists (Plamenatz 1960). Partridge suggests that one reason for the apparent decline of morally informed political philosophy is the triumph of democracy, and the development of a broad political consensus. Nevertheless, he argues, political theory of other sorts flourishes (Partridge 1961).

For present purposes, however, Quinton's introduction to the volume is of greatest interest. He begins by inquiring after the nature of the subject of political philosophy, suggesting that the 'most uncontroversial way of defining political philosophy is as the common topic of a series of famous books' (Quinton 1967, p. 1). But Quinton then suggests that 'a comparatively definite place has now been marked out for philosophy within the total range of man's intellectual activities'. This place is 'the task of classifying and analysing the terms, statements and arguments of the substantive, first-order disciplines' (Quinton 1967, p. 1). From this, Quinton concludes, remarkably, that 'the works that make up the great tradition of political philosophy are ... only to a small, though commonly crucial, extent works of philosophy in the strict sense' (Quinton 1967, p. 1). For, as Quinton remarks, they also contain factual or descriptive elements falling under the heading of 'political science' and recommendations of ideal ends, which he calls 'ideology'.

Returning to *Philosophy, Politics and Society* Third Series, the editors report a subject in a productive phase, with a good number of books and important articles appearing in recent years. As with previous volumes, the contributions range over a variety of subjects, but there is a greater awareness that positivism is a theory that needs to be engaged with critically, rather than a formula or straitjacket. Interestingly, the collection begins with a paper by Ayer, 'Man as a Subject for Science', which asks why the social sciences have failed to achieve the apparent success of the natural sciences. Ayer's conclusion is relatively modest: the fact that human action has a social meaning does not rule out the type of determinism that would allow scientific explanation of human behaviour (Ayer 1967). However, a more critical engagement with positivism appears in the following essay, Charles Taylor's 'Neutrality in Political Science', which attempts to undermine the fact/value distinction by arguing that certain combinations of descriptions and value judgements cannot coherently be combined, and thus it is mistaken to suppose that questions of facts and values are entirely separable (Taylor 1967). This is complemented by the interesting inclusion of Hannah Arendt's 'Truth and Politics'. Without making the point exactly in these terms, Arendt provides an important counterweight to the naïvety of a positivistic approach to politics that supposes that scientific inquiry will be sufficient to settle empirical conflict. In contrast, Arendt shows with some plausibility how impotent a dispassionate search for empirical truth can be in the face of political power that has an interest in an opposing view (Arendt 1967).

The collection also includes contributions from Arrow, summarizing his impossibility theorem, C. B. MacPherson, R. M. Hare, Stephen Lukes, John Plamenatz, and Bernard Crick. But once more the highlight of the volume is Rawls' paper, this time 'Distributive Justice', in which he argues that a competitive market, if appropriately regulated, can be made to satisfy his two principles of justice (Rawls 1967). Much of this paper, if not the main thrust of the argument, reappears later in *A Theory of Justice*.

For the Fourth Series, published in 1972, Laslett and Runciman are joined as editor by Quentin Skinner (Laslett, Runciman, and Skinner, 1972). It is, presumably, no coincidence that the Cambridge School of the history of political thought is well represented here with papers by Skinner, John Dunn, and Richard Tuck (then aged 23). The preface comments that the recovery of political philosophy was partly a matter of rebutting the 'end-of-ideology' theorists who proclaimed ideology to be over, on the basis of 'a high degree of governmental stability [in Western democracies together] with a high degree of popular apathy' (Laslett, Runciman, and Skinner 1972, p. 1). It is curious, however, that the end-of-ideology theorists, by which the editors presumably mean Daniel Bell and followers, were neither represented nor discussed in any detail in the earlier volumes, although they were discussed by Partridge in the Quinton collection. Another previous bogey—crude positivism, as so often problematically attributed to Weldon among others—is said to have been overcome by the realization by Taylor, Foot, Hampshire, and others that identification of 'the facts' often involves a description which is 'normatively weighted' (Laslett, Runciman, and Skinner 1972, p. 3). The overwhelming impression given in the Introduction is relief at the defeat of the smothering forces of the 'end-of-ideology' and positivism, and the resurrection of political philosophy, which now takes on a variety of forms. Yet it is worth noting that the preface makes no mention of Rawls. Presumably the volume went to press before the publication of *A Theory of Justice* (Rawls 1971), published in 1972 in the UK, and so at this point nothing usefully could be said. Once more the collection reprints some highly notable papers, such as Hanna Pitkin's 'Obligation and Consent' (first published 1965 and 1966), Robert Nozick's 'Coercion' (first published 1969), and Gerald MacCallum's 'Negative and Positive Freedom' (first published 1967), with other contributions from Alasdair MacIntyre, James Cornford, Alan Ryan, and James Coleman.

Before moving on it is worth adding a very brief word about Skinner's paper ' "Social Meaning" and the Explanation of Social Action', for this is part of a programme of work by Skinner that may well be among the most ambitious attempts to connect political philosophy with other work in contemporary philosophy. Drawing on the work of Austin, Strawson, Grice, and Davidson, alongside Winch and Hollis, Skinner attempts to apply Austin's notion of 'illocutionary force' in analysing the social meaning of action (Skinner 1972).

For the Fifth Series, published in 1979, co-edited this time by James Fishkin alongside Laslett, political philosophy has clearly entered its Rawlsian phase (Laslett and Fishkin 1979). The preface begins by suggesting that the existence of *A Theory of Justice* at last falsifies Berlin's earlier contention that no commanding work of political philosophy of the twentieth century exists (Laslett and Fishkin 1979, p. 1). The editors also note the importance of the publication of Nozick's *Anarchy, State, and Utopia* (Nozick 1974), and the foundation in 1971 of the journal, *Philosophy and Public Affairs*. The editors comment that they have a 'twinge of regret' that so little of the work that has led to the revival of the subject was conducted in the UK. Indeed, of the work they present only two papers were produced by authors based in the UK: Laslett himself and the relatively unknown Geoffrey Harrison of the University of Reading, whose paper 'Relativism and Toleration', first published in *Ethics* in 1976, is really a work of moral philosophy. Brian Barry, who has a paper in the volume, was then based in Chicago. On the other hand, they say, they are delighted that the field is now flourishing. As noted earlier, however, it is unclear that political philosophy in the United States ever went through the paralysing methodological anxieties suffered in the UK. It may well be that the dominance of linguistic philosophy in Oxford exerted an effect on political philosophy in a way that was not experienced elsewhere. To take one example, the Oxford obsession with the question of whether a claim in philosophy is analytic or synthetic may have forced discussion into unpromising culs-de-sac, whereas elsewhere in the world, especially at Harvard under the influence of Quine, the straitjacket was applied with a lower degree of pressure, and political philosophers felt freer to advance their case by whatever means were at hand (for related reflections see Cohen 2000, pp. 17–19).

The Fifth Series was published at what may well be close to the high point of political philosophy in the twentieth century. The previous few years had seen, as we have noted, the publication of Rawls' and Nozick's major works, and within two years (1981) Dworkin's two papers 'What is Equality? Part 1 and Part 2' would also appear (Dworkin 1981a, 1981b). The years 1971–81 are rarely celebrated, but they are the years in which the contemporary canon in political philosophy was created.

Laslett and Fishkin speculate that three causes, in addition to Rawls' towering work, brought political philosophy to its new vibrant state. The first is the growth of human populations and its effect on the environment. The second they cryptically call 'arithmetic humanity in relation to politics' by which they mean what would now be called global ethics and problems concerning our duties to future generations. Finally, they list concerns over the obligations owed by the 'subjects of contemporary authoritarian states', especially in relation to the Soviet Union (Laslett and Fishkin 1979, p. 2). The second of the themes is well represented by the reprint of Peter Singer's famous 1971 paper 'Famine, Affluence and Morality' and also Laslett's 'The Conversation Between the Generations', although the first theme (environmental concerns) is not to be found in the volume, and the third (authoritarianism) only partially. It is true that several papers discuss democracy and the limits of authority, yet only Fishkin's own contribution 'Tyranny and Democratic Theory' expressly takes non-liberal societies as its object. Perhaps for this reason it is worth comparing Laslett and Runciman's account of the revival of political philosophy with one which is now more familiar. This is the claim that the US civil rights movement and American involvement in the Vietnam War created a series of urgent problems concerning the goals and limits of state power, sparking a variety of critical responses including defences of anarchism (Wolff 1970/72), detailed reflection on the nature of a just war (Walzer 1977), and extensive discussions of civil disobedience and freedom of expression. On this view, these urgent problems not only drew the finest philosophical minds in to the debate but also rendered any last vestiges of positivistic subjectivism an irrelevance.

Returning to Laslett and Fishkin's introduction, they also raise the question of whether the series has now served its purpose and ask whether there will be any point in the future in producing such a general work collecting together papers in political philosophy. In fact the series still continues, but changed in form so as to be focused on a single topic in each volume. The next volume, also edited by Laslett and Fishkin, appeared in 1992 and, for the first time, had a substantive title: *Justice Between Age Groups and Generations* (Laslett and Fishkin 1992). This was followed by *Debating Deliberative Democracy*, in 2003 (Laslett and Fishkin 2003). Laslett, sadly, died in 2001, but the series continues, with *Population and Political Theory*, edited by Fishkin and Robert Goodin published in 2010 (Fishkin and Goodin 2010).

Comparing the later volumes with the earlier parts of the series, the most obvious point is that the subject had developed to a point where a short volume devoted to political philosophy generally had little purpose. To some degree the same development occurred with the Oxford Readings series, where *Political Philosophy*, edited by Quinton, published in 1967, can be compared to Jeremy Waldron's much more focused edited collection *Theories of Rights* (Waldron 1985). The second change is the shift from what the editors of the second series aptly called diagnosis to advocacy: arguments for substantive views, which re-emerged with Rawls and gave others the courage to continue. This, I think, is a matter more of overcoming some of the dogmas of positivism and linguistic philosophy rather than applying other aspects of analytic philosophy. The third development concerns the engagement of the papers with the social sciences. The editors throughout the series made various valiant attempts to connect political philosophy with allied subjects such as history and sociology. Over the decades it may be possible to detect the rising importance to political philosophy of economics, rational choice theory, and formal models, and possibly the diminishing importance of qualitative social science, especially sociology. To some degree this may be part of the remaining legacy of positivism for political philosophy: the refusal to countenance empirical theory unless it yields determinate predictions that can be tested by observational or statistical methods. However, a powerful counter-current also exists in the work of writers such as Michael Walzer, Bernard Williams, and Charles Taylor who act on a much more inclusive view of what counts as successful and useful social science (see, for example, Walzer 1983; Williams 2005; Taylor 1990).

27.6 ANALYTIC POLITICAL PHILOSOPHY SINCE 1970

We noted in the opening section of this chapter that, at its foundation, it is possible to define analytic philosophy in terms of the rejection of idealism, and the use of the new logic and of conceptual analysis. In recent decades, however, analytic philosophy has tended to be defined much more in terms of its Other: continental philosophy. Yet how exactly to characterize this distinction in relation to political philosophy is contested (Glock 2008, pp. 179–203). So, for example, it is often thought that analytic political philosophy aims at conceptual clarification, while continental political philosophy is more politically engaged. While this is plausible as a tendency it will hardly do as a criterion. Equally, it may often appear that analytic philosophy looks towards mathematics and the empirical sciences for models of methodology, whereas continental philosophy looks more towards literary and interpretative studies. Again this seems fair as a broad characterization, although there are many counterexamples. Perhaps the best we can do is to say that a broad distinction can be seen in that there is a line of intellectual tradition that runs from John Stuart Mill and another from Hegel.

Any list of 'leading contemporary analytic political philosophers' is bound to be contested. Yet it is possible to identify a broad grouping of political philosophers who have in common respect for a particular type of discipline of thought, in which argument,

distinctions, thesis, and counterexample characterize their work, and there is a self-conscious attempt to achieve rigour and clarity. They also take each other's work extremely
seriously, and will naturally attempt to position their own contributions in the light of
the positions they attribute to others in this group. Yet there is a great deal of difference
in their styles of writing too. One thing that is especially striking is their use of examples. Rawls, in *A Theory of Justice*, is relatively sparing (Rawls 1971). *Anarchy, State, and
Utopia*, by contrast, bristles with examples, almost all of which are stark, small-scale,
abstract, and entirely fictional, and many carry a great deal of argumentative weight,
especially by way of counterexample (Nozick 1974). This approach is also to found in
Dworkin, Cohen, and some work of Sen (although in other work Sen also uses many
real-world cases too, as for example in Sen 1999). Nozick notes that his approach to
political philosophy may strike some as troubling:

> I write in the mode of much contemporary philosophical work in epistemology or
> metaphysics: there are elaborate arguments, claims rebutted by unlikely counterex-
> amples, surprising theses, puzzles, abstract structural conditions, challenges to find
> another theory which fits a specified range of cases, startling conclusions, and so on.
> Though this makes for intellectual interest and excitement (I hope) some may feel
> that the truth about ethics and political philosophy is too serious and important to
> be obtained by such 'flashy' tools. Nevertheless, it may be that correctness in ethics
> is not found in what we usually think. (Nozick 1974 p. x)

Many political philosophers now argue in the style brought out most clearly and
explicitly by Nozick, although it had already been pioneered by Judith Jarvis Thomson,
most notably in her 'A Defence of Abortion', published in the first issue of *Philosophy
and Public Affairs* in 1971 (Thomson 1971), and, to some degree, in work published by
H. L. A. Hart and Philippa Foot in the *Oxford Review* (Hart 1967; Foot 1967). Such use
of abstract, generally fictional, examples is one half of what often is most distinctive in
contemporary analytic political theory. In this respect, although Rawls' theory has been
far more influential than Nozick's in the substantive development of subsequent political philosophy, much of contemporary political philosophy is written in a style far closer
to Nozick than to Rawls.

If the elaborate use of abstract, fictional examples is one half of what is most distinctive about contemporary analytic political philosophy, the other half is abstraction of
another sort: the largely unstated ambition to develop theories with the precision and
economy one finds among scientists or economists, with fewest possible concepts, all as
clear as they can be made, and with widest possible application. As with the use of conceptual analysis, the search for a concise but powerful theory is not new but nevertheless
it is a type of paradigm of rigour which characterizes many of the writings most recognizable as contributions to the tradition of contemporary analytic political philosophy.
It is often accompanied by a lack of comprehension of, or respect for, writing that does
not conform to this model, supposing that it is somehow deliberately obscurantist, eva-
sive, or otherwise of poor quality.

Such a negative attitude to other approaches is exemplified in one of the very few movements within political philosophy which has self-consciously termed itself 'analytic': 'analytic Marxism'. The theorists comprising this group included G. A. Cohen, Jon Elster, John Roemer, Erik Wright, Hillel Steiner, Philippe van Parijs, and Robert van der Veen, among others (see in particular Cohen 1978/2000; Roemer 1982; Elster 1985). These theorists were attracted, albeit to considerably different degrees, to elements of Marx's thought but were also united in their dissatisfaction with the standards of rigour with which Marxist topics were treated in the literature, especially by those influenced by the French Marxist Louis Althusser (Althusser 1965/1969; Althusser and Balibar 1968/1979). So, for example, in a footnote Cohen quotes the following from Etienne Balibar: 'This is precisely the first meaning to which we can give the idea of dialectic: a logic or form of explanation specifically adapted to the determinant intervention of class struggle in the very fabric of history.' Cohen comments, 'If you read a sentence like that quickly it can sound pretty good. The remedy is to read it more slowly' (Cohen 1978/2000, p. xxiii).

Elster, in his review of Cohen's *Karl Marx's Theory of History: A Defence*, wrote that it 'sets a new standard for Marxist philosophy' (Elster 1980, p. 121). In a similar vein, Allen Wood commented, in reference to his own excellent book on Marx published in 1981 'while it is easy to write an above average book on Marx, it is very difficult to write a good one' (Wood 1981, p. x). Cohen writes in the preface to the first edition of *Karl Marx's Theory of History* that in his attempt to state Marx's theory he will be guided both by what Marx actually wrote and by standards of clarity and rigour of analytic philosophy. He remarks: 'it is a perhaps a matter of regret that logical positivism, with its insistence on precision of intellectual commitment, never caught on in Paris' (Cohen 1978/2000, p. x).

Cohen's introduction to the 2000 revised edition contains a substantial discussion of the nature and history of Analytic Marxism. Here he introduces the term 'analytic' by means of two contrasts. In what Cohen calls a 'broad sense', analytic is opposed to 'dialectic' thinking, and in a narrow sense opposed to 'holistic' thinking. Cohen suggests that Marxism has been hampered by the assumption that it had its own 'dialectic' methodology, and thereby eschewed other, powerful, methodologies that had developed in the analytic tradition of philosophy and social science: logical and linguistic analysis, neo-classical economics, and rational choice theory. Analytic philosophy in the supposed narrower sense of the rejection of holism is to adopt a form of methodological individualism in explanation; in essence an important part of the rejection of idealism identified above (Cohen 2000, pp. xx–xxv). The work of Elster (1985) and Roemer (1982) equally deploy such methodology, and indeed Elster has criticized Cohen (in his adoption of functional explanation) for being insufficiently rigorous (Elster 1980).

Part of Analytic Marxism's motivation for making its methodology so explicit is its competition with, and antagonism to, a 'dialectical' school, influenced by Hegel and by French Marxism, each side contesting the other's right to stake their claim on the same subject matter of inquiry. Subsequently, this group has produced a significant body of important writings that are not about Marx but continue to be characterized

by a number of the features of the analytic style we have identified: rejection of idealism, preference for quantitative over qualitative social science, use of abstract examples
and simplified models, methodological and moral individualism, self-conscious search
for clarity and precision of thesis and argument, intolerance of the claimed obscurity
of others, and the ambition of presenting simple theories or principles of great power
and application. Philippe van Parijs' *Real Freedom for All* (1995) and Cohen's later work
Rescuing Justice and Equality (2008) are excellent examples, containing many of these
features. But Hillel Steiner's *An Essay on Rights* may well be the purest example of such a
methodology, in which the most of the main features we have identified are deployed at
length. For example, explaining his focus on rights as a means to illuminating issues of
justice, Steiner suggests, 'A sensible strategy, it seems to me, is to begin at the elementary
particles, since all big things are made from small ones. The elementary particles of justice are rights' (Steiner 1994, p. 2). In an echo of Nozick's comment cited above, Steiner
remarks that those concerned with oppression, exploitation, discrimination, and poverty may find his treatment of these topics abstract and detached from the real issues,
even to the point of frivolity. But, he replies, conceptual analysis must be done, by the
most effective means, if the issues are to be dealt with in a suitably rigorous fashion.

27.7 Conclusion

It could be argued that the emergence of analytic philosophy was not, initially, a helpful
development for political philosophy. The most prominent early contribution was the
rejection of idealism, especially the work of writers such as Bosanquet and Green. Yet,
as we have seen, such rejection was not accompanied by the acceptance of an alternative approach, or at least not on any significant scale. The new logic had no influence on
political philosophy, and the confines of linguistic philosophy and logical positivism left
political philosophers with a very narrow understanding of their discipline: so much
so that, as we noted above, in 1967 Quinton went as far as to suggest that many of the
historically great works of political philosophy were only in small part strictly speaking
political philosophy at all (Quinton 1967, p. 1). Political philosophy became introspective and unambitious, although not averse to criticizing the apparently crude errors of
the great theorists of the past. With a few exceptions, such as the work of Hayek and
Popper, it was not until the publication of Rawls' *A Theory of Justice* in 1971 that political
philosophers began to return to write on a broad canvas and pursue advocacy of substantive positions. Since then, the subject has flourished and a distinctive methodology
of analytic philosophy has developed, although much more in the idiom of Nozick than
Rawls, and most self-consciously by Analytic Marxism.

Alongside, of course, has also developed a counter-tendency, objecting to the abstraction, individualism, ahistoricism, reductionism, over-simplifying tendencies, and,
sometimes, the apparent frivolity, of analytic political philosophy, or, at least, of some
examples of it. Yet often even the counter-works, such as Elizabeth Anderson's important

paper 'What is the Point of Equality?' (Anderson 1999) display many of the methodological characteristics of analytic political philosophy and by means of entering into critical debate can be thought to be part of the same methodological tradition. In a sense it may appear that analytic political philosophy is almost inescapable, unless one self-consciously adopts a 'continental' style. Yet it is also possible to see what it would be to write in a manner which is less obviously analytic. So, for example, the writings of Michael Walzer, Amartya Sen, and Martha Nussbaum (Walzer 1983; Sen 1999; Nussbaum 2000), taking sociology and history seriously, and attempting to be politically engaged, provide different approaches which, at the least, are on the outer fringes of analytic political philosophy, without being identifiable as continental philosophy. The abstract, politically unengaged, and ahistoric character of much analytic political philosophy affords it certain advantages in terms of sorting valid from invalid arguments and coherent from incoherent propositions. Nevertheless it would be a great pity if other styles of thinking about political questions, informed by history and sociology, and not only neo-classical economics and rational choice theory, disappeared from the menu available to political philosophers.[2]

References

Adorno, Theodor and Max Horkheimer (1944/1997). *The Dialectic of Enlightenment*. London: Verso.

Althusser, Louis (1965/1969). *For Marx*. London: Allen Lane.

Althusser, Louis and Etienne Balibar (1968/1970). *Reading Capital*. London: New Left Books.

Anderson, Elizabeth (1999). 'What is the Point of Equality?' *Ethics* 109: 287–337.

Arendt, Hannah (1967). 'Truth and Politics'. In Peter Laslett and W. G. Runciman (eds.), *Philosophy, Politics and Society (Third Series)*. Oxford: Blackwell, pp. 104–33.

Arrow, Kenneth J. (1951). *Social Choice and Individual Values*. New York: Wiley.

Ayer, A. J. (1936). *Language, Truth and Logic*. London: Victor Gollancz.

——(1944). 'The Concept of Freedom', *Horizon* 52: 228–37.

——(1967). 'Man as a Subject for Science'. In Peter Laslett and W. G. Runciman (eds.), *Philosophy, Politics and Society (Third Series)*. Oxford: Blackwell, pp. 6–24.

——(1977). *Part of My Life*. London: Collins.

Bambrough, Renford (1956). 'Plato's Political Analogies'. In Peter Laslett (ed.), *Philosophy, Politics and Society*. Oxford: Blackwell, pp. 98–115.

Barry, Brian (1965). *Political Argument*. London: Routledge.

Beaney, Michael (2003/2009). 'Analysis'. *The Stanford Encyclopedia of Philosophy (Summer 2009 Edition)*, ed. Edward N. Zalta. Available at: <http://plato.stanford.edu/archives/sum2009/

[2] I am extremely grateful to Michael Rosen, Michael Beaney, Zofia Stempslowska, Hillel Steiner, Shepley Orr, Michael Otsuka, Alex Voorhoeve, Andrea Sangiovanni, Leif Wenar, Paul Kelly, Alan Haworth, David Lloyd Thomas, Alan Hamlin, Geraint Perry, Ian Carter, Paul Snowdon, Matthew Kramer, David Miller, and members of audiences in London and Manchester for exceptionally helpful comments on earlier versions of this chapter. My great regret is that it is now too late to discuss the issues with Brian Barry and Jerry Cohen.

entries/analysis/> (accessed 29 December 2012).

Benn, S. I. and R. S. Peters (1959). *Social Principles and the Democratic State*. London: George Allen & Unwin.

Bentham, Jeremy (1781/1970). *Introduction to the Principles of Morals and Legislation*. London: Athlone Press.

Berlin, Isaiah (1958/1969). 'Two Concepts of Liberty'. In Berlin, *Four Essays on Liberty*. Oxford: Oxford University Press, pp. 118–79. Revised from Inaugural Lecture, Oxford University. Oxford: Clarendon Press, 1958.

—— (1962). 'Does Political Theory Still Exist?' In Peter Laslett and W. G. Runciman (eds.), *Philosophy, Politics and Society (Second Series)*. Oxford: Blackwell, pp. 1–33. Revised from French edition, first published in *Revue Française de Science Politique* 11, 1961.

Bosanquet, Bernard (1899/1923). *Philosophical Theory of the State*, 4th edn. London: Macmillan.

Bradley, F. H. (1876). *Ethical Studies*. London: Oxford University Press.

Braithwaite, R. B. (1955). *Theory of Games as a Tool for the Moral Philosopher*. Cambridge: Cambridge University Press.

Buchanan, James and Gordon Tulloch (1962). *The Calculus of Consent*. Ann Arbor: University of Michigan Press.

Candlish, Stewart (2007). *The Russell/Bradley Dispute and its Significance for Twentieth-Century Philosophy*. Basingstoke: Palgrave Macmillan.

Carritt, E. F. (1935). *Morals and Politics*. Oxford: Oxford University Press.

—— (1947). *Ethical and Political Thinking*. Oxford: Oxford University Press.

Cartwright, Nancy, Jordi Cat, Lola Fleck, and Thomas Uebel (1996). *Otto Neurath: Philosophy Between Science and Politics*. Cambridge: Cambridge University Press.

Cohen, G. A. (1978/2000). *Karl Marx's Theory of History: A Defence*, rev. edn. Oxford: Oxford University Press.

—— (2000). *If You're an Egalitarian How Come You're So Rich?* Cambridge, MA: Harvard University Press.

—— (2008). *Rescuing Justice and Equality*. Cambridge, MA: Harvard University Press.

Cornforth, Maurice (1968). *The Open Philosophy and the Open Society: A Reply to Dr Popper's Critique of Marxism*. London: Lawrence & Wishart.

Dummett, Michael (1981). *Frege: Philosophy of Language*, 2nd edn. London: Duckworth.

Dworkin, Ronald (1981a). 'What is Equality? Part 1: Equality of Welfare', *Philosophy & Public Affairs* 10: 228–40.

—— (1981b). 'What is Equality? Part 2: Equality of Resources', *Philosophy & Public Affairs* 10: 283–345.

Eliot, T. S. (1939). *The Idea of a Christian Society*. London: Faber and Faber.

Elster, Jon (1980). Review of G. A. Cohen *Karl Marx's Theory of History: A Defence, Political Studies* 28: 121–8.

—— (1985). *Making Sense of Marx*. Cambridge: Cambridge University Press.

Fishkin, James and Robert Goodin (eds.) (2010). *Population and Political Theory: Philosophy, Politics and Society 8*. Oxford: Wiley-Blackwell.

Flew, A. G. N. (ed.) (1951). *Essays in Logic and Language*. Oxford: Blackwell.

Foot, Philippa (1967). 'The Problem of Abortion and the Doctrine of the Double Effect', *Oxford Review* 5: pp. 5–15. Repr. in Philippa Foot, *Virtues and Vices*. Oxford: Blackwell, 1978, pp. 19–33.

Frege, Gottlob (1879). *Begriffsschrift, eine der arithmetischen nachgebildete Formelsprache des reinen Denkens*. Halle a. S.: Louis Nebert. Tr. S. Bauer-Mengelberg as *Concept Script, a Formal*

Language of Pure Thought Modelled upon that of Arithmetic, in J. van Heijenoort (ed.), *From Frege to Gödel: A Source Book in Mathematical Logic, 1879–1931*. Cambridge, MA: Harvard University Press, 1967, pp. 5–82.

—— (1994). 'Gottlob Freges politisches Tagebuch', ed. and introd. G. Gabriel and W. Kienzler, *Deutsche Zeitschrift für Philosophie* 42: 1057–98.

—— (2000). 'Vorschläge für ein Wahlgesetz', ed. U. Dathe and W. Kienzler, in G. Gabriel and U. Dathe, *Gottlob Frege—Werk und Wirkung*. Paderborn: Mentis, pp. 297–313.

Friedrich, Carl J. (1958). *Nomos 1: Authority*. Cambridge, MA: Harvard University Press.

Friedrich, Carl J. and John W. Chapman (1963). *Nomos VI: Justice*. New York: Prentice Hall.

Gallie, W. B. (1949). 'Liberal Morality and Socialist Morality', *Philosophy* 24: 318–34. Repr. in Peter Laslett (ed.), *Philosophy, Politics and Society*. Oxford: Blackwell, 1956.

—— (1955–6). 'Essentially Contested Concepts', *Proceedings of the Aristotelian Society* 56: 167–98.

Gauthier, David (1969). *The Logic of Leviathan*. Oxford: Oxford University Press.

Glock, Hans-Johann (2008). *What is Analytic Philosophy?* Cambridge: Cambridge University Press.

Green, T. H. (1883–5). *Works*, 3 vols., ed. R. L. Nettleship. London: Longmans.

Harrod, Roy (1936). 'Utilitarianism Revised', *Mind* 45: 137–56.

Hart, H. L. A (1955). 'Are There Any Natural Rights?', *The Philosophical Review* 64: 175–91.

—— (1959–60). 'Prolegomena to the Theory of Punishment', *Proceedings of the Aristotelian Society* 60: 1–26. Repr. in Peter Laslett and W. G. Runciman (eds.), *Philosophy, Politics and Society (Second Series)*. Oxford: Blackwell, 1962, pp. 158–82.

—— (1961/1994). *The Concept of Law*, 2nd edn. 1994. Oxford: Oxford University Press.

—— (1967). 'Intention and Punishment', *Oxford Review* 4: 5–22. Repr. in H. L. A. Hart, *Punishment and Responsibility*. Oxford: Oxford University Press, 1968.

Hayek, Friedrich (1944). *The Road to Serfdom*. London: Routledge.

Hegel, Georg Wilhelm Friedrich (1821/1896). *The Philosophy of Right*. London: George Bell.

Ignatieff, Michael (1998). *Isaiah Berlin: A Life*. London: Chatto & Windus.

King, Anthony (1994). 'How Many Lives Was It Worth?' *Times Higher Education Supplement*, 25 November. Available at <http://www.timeshighereducation.co.uk/story.asp?storyCode=154211&sectioncode=26> (accessed 15 December 2009).

Lamont, W. D. (1946). *The Principles of Moral Judgement*. Oxford: Clarendon Press.

Laski, Harold (1925). *A Grammar of Politics*. London: George Allen & Unwin.

Laslett, Peter (ed.) (1956a). *Philosophy, Politics and Society*. Oxford: Blackwell.

—— (1956b). 'The Face to Face Society'. In Peter Laslett (ed.), *Philosophy, Politics and Society*. Oxford: Blackwell, pp. 157–84.

Laslett, Peter, and James Fishkin (eds.) (1979). *Philosophy, Politics and Society (Fifth Series)*. Oxford: Blackwell.

—— —— (eds.) (1992). *Philosophy, Politics and Society (Sixth Series): Justice Between Age Groups and Generations*. New Haven: Yale University Press.

—— —— (eds.) (2003). *Philosophy, Politics and Society 7: Debating Deliberative Democracy*. Oxford: Blackwell.

Laslett, Peter and W. G. Runciman (eds.) (1962). *Philosophy, Politics and Society (Second Series)*. Oxford: Blackwell.

—— —— (eds.) (1967). *Philosophy, Politics and Society (Third Series)*. Oxford: Blackwell.

Laslett, Peter, W. G. Runciman, and Quentin Skinner (eds.) (1972). *Philosophy, Politics and Society (Fourth Series)*. Oxford: Blackwell.

Levinson, R. B. (1953). *In Defence of Plato*. Oxford: Oxford University Press.

Luce, R. D. and H. Raiffa (1957). *Theory of Games and Decisions*. New York: Wiley.

Lukács, Georg (1923/1967). *History and Class Consciousness*. London: Merlin Press.

Lyotard Jean-François and Jean-Loup Thébaud (1985). *Just Gaming*. Minneapolis: University of Minnesota Press.

Mabbott, J. D. (1948/1967). *The State and the Citizen*. London: Hutchinson.

MacCallum, G. (1967). 'Negative and Positive Freedom', *The Philosophical Review* 76: 312–34. Repr. in Peter Laslett, W. G. Runciman, and Quentin Skinner (eds.), *Philosophy, Politics and Society (Fourth Series)*. Oxford: Blackwell, 1972, pp. 174–93.

Macdonald, Margaret (1940–1). 'The Language of Political Theory', *Proceedings of the Aristotelian Society* 41: 91–112.

—— (1947–8). 'Natural Rights', *Proceedings of the Aristotelian Society* 47: 225–50. Repr. in Peter Laslett (ed.), *Philosophy, Politics and Society*. Oxford: Blackwell, 1956, pp. 35–55.

MacIntyre, Alasdair (1962). 'A Mistake About Causality in Social Science'. In Peter Laslett and W. G. Runciman (eds.), *Philosophy Politics and Society (Second Series)*. Oxford: Blackwell, pp. 48–70.

Matravers, Matthew (2008). 'Twentieth-Century Political Philosophy'. In Dermot Moran (ed.), *The Routledge Companion to Twentieth-Century Philosophy*. London: Routledge, pp. 883–912.

Mayo, Bernard (1950). 'Is There A Case for the General Will?' *Philosophy* 25: 247–52. Repr. in Peter Laslett (ed.), *Philosophy, Politics and Society*. Oxford: Blackwell, 1956, pp. 92–7.

Miller, David and Richard Dagger (2003). 'Utilitarianism and Beyond: Contemporary Analytic Political Theory'. In T. Ball and R. Bellamy (eds.), *The Cambridge History of Twentieth Century Political Thought*. Cambridge: Cambridge University Press, pp. 446–69.

Moore, G. E. (1903). *Principia Ethica*. Cambridge: Cambridge University Press.

Nozick, Robert (1969). 'Coercion'. In S. Morgenbesser, P. Suppes, and M. White (eds.), Philosophy, Science and Method. New York: St Martin's Press, pp. 440–72. Repr. in Peter Laslett, W. G. Runciman, and Quentin Skinner (eds.), *Philosophy, Politics and Society (Fourth Series)*. Oxford: Blackwell, 1972, pp. 101–35.

—— (1974). *Anarchy, State and Utopia*. New York: Basic Books.

Nussbaum, Martha (2000). *Women and Human Development*. Cambridge: Cambridge University Press.

Oakeshott, Michael (1956). 'Political Education'. In Peter Laslett (ed.), *Philosophy, Politics and Society*. Oxford: Blackwell, pp. 1–21.

O'Neill, John (2003). 'Unified Science as Political Philosophy: Positivism, Pluralism and Liberalism', *Studies in History and Philosophy of Science* 34: 575–96.

Partridge, P. H. (1961). 'Politics, Philosophy, Ideology', *Political Studies* 9: 217–35. Repr. in Anthony Quinton (ed.), *Political Philosophy*. Oxford: Oxford University Press, 1967, pp. 32–52.

Pitkin, Hannah (1965). 'Obligation and Consent I', *The American Political Science Review* 59: 990–9. Repr. in Peter Laslett, W. G. Runciman, and Quentin Skinner (eds.), *Philosophy, Politics and Society (Fourth Series)*. Oxford: Blackwell, 1972, pp. 45–85.

—— (1966). 'Obligation and Consent II', *The American Political Science Review* 60: 39–52. Repr. in Peter Laslett, W. G. Runciman, and Quentin Skinner (eds.), *Philosophy, Politics and Society (Fourth Series)*. Oxford: Blackwell, 1972, pp, 45–85.

—— (1972). *Wittgenstein and Justice*. Berkeley and Los Angeles: University of California Press.

Plamenatz, John (1938). *Consent, Freedom and Political Obligation*. Oxford: Oxford University Press.

—— (1960). 'The Use of Political Theory', *Political Studies* 8: 37–47. Repr. in Anthony Quinton (ed.), *Political Philosophy*. Oxford: Oxford University Press, 1967, pp. 19–31.

Pogge, Thomas (2007). *John Rawls: His Life and Theory of Justice*. Oxford: Oxford University Press.

Popper, Karl (1935/1959). *The Logic of Scientific Discovery*. London: Hutchinson.

—— (1945a). *The Open Society and Its Enemies, Volume 1: Plato*. London: Routledge & Kegan Paul.

—— (1945b). *The Open Society and Its Enemies, Volume 2: Hegel and Marx*. London: Routledge & Kegan Paul.

—— (1957). *The Poverty of Historicism*. London: Routledge & Kegan Paul.

—— (1963). *Conjectures and Refutations*. London: Routledge & Kegan Paul.

—— (1974/1992). *Unended Quest*. London: Routledge.

Quine, W. V. O. (1981). 'Five Milestones of Empiricism'. In Quine, *Theories and Things*. Cambridge, MA: Harvard University Press, pp. 67–72.

Quinton, Anthony (1954). 'On Punishment', *Analysis* 14: 133–42. Repr. in Peter Laslett (ed.), *Philosophy, Politics and Society*. Oxford: Blackwell, 1956, pp. 83–91.

—— (ed.) (1967). *Political Philosophy*. Oxford: Oxford University Press.

Rashdall, Hastings (1907). *The Theory of Good and Evil*. London: Oxford University Press.

Rawls, John (1955). 'Two Concepts of Rules', *The Philosophical Review* 64: 3–32.

—— (1958). 'Justice as Fairness', *The Philosophical Review* 67: 174–94. Repr. in P. Laslett and W. G. Runciman (eds.), *Philosophy, Politics and Society (Second Series)*. Oxford: Blackwell, 1962, pp. 132–57.

—— (1967). 'Distributive Justice'. In Peter Laslett and W. G. Runciman (eds.), *Philosophy, Politics and Society (Third Series)*. Oxford: Blackwell, pp. 58–82.

—— (1971). *A Theory of Justice*. Cambridge MA: Harvard University Press.

Rees, W. J. (1950). 'The Theory of Sovereignty Restated', *Mind* 59: 495–521. Repr. in Peter Laslett (ed.), *Philosophy, Politics and Society*. Oxford: Blackwell, 1956, pp. 58–82.

Richardson, S. (2009). 'The Left Vienna Circle, Part 1: Carnap, Neurath, and the Left Vienna Circle Thesis', *Studies in History and Philosophy of Science* 40: 14–24.

Roemer, John (1982). *A General Theory of Exploitation and Class*. Cambridge, MA: Harvard University Press.

Rubinstein, David (1981). *Marx and Wittgenstein*. London: Routledge & Kegan Paul.

Russell, Bertrand (1896). *German Social Democracy*. London: Longmans, Green.

—— (1903). *The Principles of Mathematics*. Cambridge: Cambridge University Press.

—— (1905). 'On Denoting', *Mind* 14: 479–3.

—— (1912) *The Problems of Philosophy*. London: Williams and Norgate.

—— (1945). *History of Western Philosophy*. New York: Simon & Schuster.

—— (1949). *Authority and the Individual*. London: George Allen & Unwin.

—— (1959). *My Philosophical Development*. London: George Allen & Unwin.

Sen, A. K. (1970). *Collective Choice and Social Welfare*. San Francisco: Holden Day.

—— (1999). *Development as Freedom*. Oxford: Oxford University Press.

Sidgwick, Henry (1874/1907). *The Methods of Ethics*. London: Macmillan.

—— (1891) *The Elements of Politics*. London: Macmillan.

Skinner, Quentin (1972). '"Social Meaning" and the Explanation of Social Action'. In Peter Laslett, W. G. Runciman, and Quentin Skinner (eds.), *Philosophy, Politics and Society (Fourth Series)*. Oxford: Blackwell, pp. 136–57.

Steiner, Hillel (1994). *An Essay on Rights*. Oxford: Blackwell.

Tawney, R. H. (1931). *Equality*. London: George Allen & Unwin.

Taylor, Charles (1967). 'Neutrality in Political Science'. In Peter Laslett and W. G. Runciman (eds.), *Philosophy, Politics and Society (Third Series)*. Oxford: Blackwell, pp. 25–57.

—— (1990). *Sources of the Self*. Cambridge, MA: Harvard University Press.

Thomson, Judith Jarvis (1971). 'A Defence of Abortion', *Philosophy and Public Affairs* 1: 47–66.

Uebel, T. (2005). 'Political Philosophy of Science in Logical Empiricism: The Left Vienna Circle', *Studies in History and Philosophy of Science* 36: 754–73.

—— (2010). 'What's Right About the Left Vienna Circle Thesis? A Refutation', *Studies in History and Philosophy of Science* 41: 214–21.

Van Parijs, Philippe (1995). *Real Freedom for All: What (if Anything) Can Justify Capitalism?* Oxford: Oxford University Press.

Waldron, Jeremy (ed.) (1985). *Theories of Rights*. Oxford: Oxford University Press.

Walzer, Michael (1977). *Just and Unjust Wars*. New York: Basic Books.

—— (1983). *Spheres of Justice*. New York: Basic Books.

Weldon, T. D. (1946). *States and Morals*. London: John Murray.

—— (1953). *The Vocabulary of Politics*. London: Penguin.

—— (1956). 'Political Principles'. In Peter Laslett (ed.), *Philosophy, Politics and Society*. Oxford: Blackwell, pp. 22–34.

Whitehead, Alfred North and Bertrand Russell (1910–13). *Principia Mathematica,* 3 vols. Cambridge: Cambridge University Press.

Williams, Bernard (1962). 'The Idea of Equality'. In Peter Laslett and W. G. Runciman (eds.), *Philosophy, Politics and Society (Second Series)*. Oxford: Blackwell, pp. 110–31.

—— (2005). *In the Beginning Was the Deed: Realism and Moralism in Political Argument*, ed. Geoffrey Hawthorn. Princeton, NJ: Princeton University Press.

Wisdom, John (1931). *Interpretation and Analysis in Relation to Bentham's Theory of Definition*. London: Kegan Paul.

Wittgenstein, Ludwig (1980). *Culture and Value*. Oxford: Blackwell.

Wolff, Robert Paul (1970/1972). *In Defence of Anarchism*. New York: Harper & Row.

Wollheim, Richard (1962). 'A Paradox in the Theory of Democracy'. In Peter Laslett and W. G. Runciman (eds.), *Philosophy, Politics and Society (Second Series)*. Oxford: Blackwell, pp. 71–87.

Wood, Allen (1981). *Karl Marx*. London: Routledge & Kegan Paul.

PART 3

THEMES IN THE HISTORY OF ANALYTIC PHILOSOPHY

CHAPTER 28

THE FUNCTION IS UNSATURATED

RICHARD G. HECK, JR. AND ROBERT MAY

28.1 OPENING

That there is a fundamental difference between objects and functions (among which are concepts) is among the most famous of Frege's mature views; it is the view encapsulated in the slogan that entitles this chapter. It is also among the most puzzling of Frege's views. Commentators, we think it is fair to say, have by and large had very little idea what to make of it, perhaps with good reason. But we are going to suggest here that this doctrine is not only easy enough to understand, it is also in some sense so deeply embedded in contemporary logic and semantics that it is hard to imagine life without it. That is the reason for our perplexity: We do not understand the view Frege was opposing. To understand the doctrine of *unsaturatedness*, we must thus uncover its origin.

As we shall see, the notion of function with which Frege operates in 1879, in *Begriffsschrift*, is rather different from what we find in *Grundgestze* in 1893. The evolution of Frege's mature conception begins soon after the publication of the former volume, and is largely in place by 1882. What drives this development is Frege's confrontation with the work of George Boole. Ernst Schröder had argued in a scathing review of *Begriffsschrift* that Frege had simply replicated the work of the Boolean school—of which Schröder just happened to be the most prominent German member—in a new and excessively cumbersome notation:

> With the exception of what is said … about 'function' and 'generality' and up to [Part III], the book is devoted to the establishment of a formula language that essentially coincides with Boole's mode of presenting judgements and Boole's calculus of judgements, and which certainly in no way achieves more. (Schröder 1972, p. 221, emphasis removed)

John Venn—he of the Venn diagram—does not even mention Frege's notation for generality and simply dismisses Frege's system as clearly inferior to Boole's (Venn 1972, p. 234). Both Schröder (1972, p. 220) and Venn (1972, p. 234) speculate that Frege was simply unfamiliar with Boole's writings, and they were probably right. As Terrell Bynum points out in the introduction to his translation of *Begriffsschrift*, Frege took no courses in logic as a student, and some of his claims about the originality of his own system reveal ignorance of Boole's work (Bynum 1972, pp. 77–8).

But Frege's ignorance did not last for long: He wrote several papers over the next few years in which he compared his logic to those of Boole and his followers (Frege 1972b, 1979a, 1979b). As one would expect, Frege argues that Schröder has failed to appreciate the significance of his views about functions and generality and that his notation for generality is far more powerful than anything available to his opponents. But Frege's criticisms of the Booleans were not limited to this familiar point. It is from these other criticisms that the notion of unsaturatedness emerges.

28.2 FUNCTION AND ARGUMENT IN *BEGRIFFSSCHRIFT*

In his mature period, Frege speaks of the distinction between function and object in broadly metaphysical terms. But Frege also regards the distinction between function and object as one that is central to logic, so much so that the very first section of *Grundgesetze*[1] is devoted to elucidating what it means for a function to be unsaturated. The distinction between function and object makes itself most clearly felt, however, in that functions, but not objects, are stratified into levels, a topic to which Frege devotes several sections of *Grundgesetze* (Frege 1962, §§ 19, 21–4). In this discussion, Frege holds that functions are so different from objects that a function could not take both functions and objects as arguments.[2] A function's level is thus determined by the sort of argument it takes: A function is *first-level* if it takes objects as arguments; a function is *second-level* if it takes first-level functions as arguments; and so forth.

An apparently similar distinction—between function and *argument*—is equally central to the logical theory of *Begriffsschrift*. It is in terms of it that Frege introduces the notion of quantification:

---

[1] There is an introductory section preceding this one. It is given the number zero in Furth's translation (Frege 1964), but it has no number in the German original.

[2] We are speaking here only of monadic functions. Similar remarks of course apply to polyadic functions.

In the expression of a judgement we can always regard the combination of signs to the right of ⊢ as a function of one of the signs occurring in it. If we replace this argument by a German letter and if in the content stroke we introduce a concavity with this German letter in it, as in

$$\vdash\!\!\!-\!\!\!\overset{\mathfrak{a}}{\cup}\!- \Phi(\mathfrak{a})$$

this stands for the judgement that, whatever we may take for its argument, the function is a fact. (Frege 1967, § 11, emphasis removed)

The two sections of *Begriffsschrift* that immediately precede these remarks are devoted to the explanation of the very general notion of function that Frege is using here.

Although the distinction between function and argument is put to similar use in *Begriffsschrift* and *Grundgesetze*, Frege understood that distinction very differently in 1893 from how he had understood it in 1879. Frege mentions this fact himself in the introduction to *Grundgesetze*:

[T]he nature of the function, as distinguished from the object, is characterized more sharply here than in *Begriffsschrift*. From this results further the distinction between first- and second-level functions. (Frege 1962, p. x)

Frege implies here that there was no distinction between levels in *Begriffsschrift*, and we shall see shortly that, indeed, there was not. Perhaps more interesting is Frege's remark concerning why there is no distinction between levels in *Begriffsschrift*: The distinction between function and object was not characterized sufficiently 'sharply' there. But why would that have obscured the distinction of levels? Since the difference between first- and second-level functions is parasitic on the difference between their arguments, we will distinguish first- from second-level functions only if we have sharply distinguished functions from objects—only, that is, if functions differ so fundamentally from objects that it is impossible for a single (monadic) function to take both functions and objects as arguments. Frege's point is thus not that the distinction between function and object is drawn with more precision in *Grundgesetze* than in *Begriffsschrift*, though it certainly is. His point is that the distinction between function and object is *enforced* in his later work in a way that it was not in his early work. Or more strongly: Frege is telling us that there isn't really a distinction between function and object in *Begriffsschrift*, and accordingly that there is no distinction between levels, although there is a distinction between function and *argument*.

Familiarly, both what we would now call 'first-order' and what we would now call 'second-order' quantification appear to be available in Frege's formal language, both in *Grundgesetze* and in *Begriffsschrift*. In *Grundgesetze*, these two sorts of quantification are clearly distinguished, both by notation (miniscule versus majuscule gothic letters) and by the axioms that govern them: The axiom of universal instantiation comes in both a first-order form (Basic Law IIa) and a second-order form (Basic Law IIb).[3] The two sorts of quantification are separately introduced, as well: First-order quantification is introduced in § 8; second-order quantification is not introduced until § 20, and Frege's official statement of the meaning of his second-order quantifier does not appear until § 24. It reads as follows:

> If after a concavity with a Gothic function-letter, there follows a combination of signs composed of the name of a second-level function of one argument and this [Gothic] function-letter, which fills the argument-places, then the whole denotes the True if the value of that second-level function is the True for every fitting argument [that is, for every function of appropriate type]; in all other cases, it denotes the False. (Frege 1962, § 24)

It is thus clear that Frege's explanation of second-order quantification depends upon the distinction between levels, and that is why the explanation has to wait until § 24. The preceding sections contain a detailed explanation of the distinction between first- and second-level functions (Frege 1962, §§ 21–3). At the very least, then, Frege cannot have understood the distinction between first- and second-order quantification in *Begriffsschrift*, where there is no distinction of levels, the same way he understood it in *Grundgesetze*, where there is.

In fact, there is no distinction at all between first- and second-order quantification in *Begriffsschrift*. Frege's initial explanation of the quantifier in *Begriffsschrift*, partially quoted above, continues as follows:

> Since a letter used as a sign for a function, such as Φ in $\Phi(A)$, can itself be regarded as the argument of a function, its place can be taken, in the manner just specified, by a German letter. (Frege, 1967, § 11)

That is to say, we can also write:

$$\vdash \overset{\mathfrak{I}}{\frown} \mathfrak{F}(a)$$

In this passage, Frege is not suggesting that 'function quantification' is significantly different from 'argument quantification'. To the contrary, there is but one axiom of universal instantiation in the formal theory of *Begriffsschrift*, proposition 58:

$$\vdash \overset{}{\underset{a}{\smile}}\begin{array}{l} f(c) \\ f(\mathfrak{a}) \end{array}$$

---

[3] The rule of universal generalization, rule (5) in the list given in §48, does not need separate formulations, since Frege can speak quite generally of 'Gothic letters' and 'Roman letters', without specifying which sort of letter is at issue.

To a modern reader, this formula may appear to involve a first-order quantifier, but it does not. Frege is as happy to cite proposition 58 to justify inferences involving what we would regard as second-order quantifiers as he is to cite it to justify inferences involving what we would regard as first-order quantifiers.[4] Thus from proposition 58, we may infer:

$$\vdash\!\!\!\begin{array}{l}\rule{1.5em}{0.4pt}\, f(a) \\[-0.2em] \mathfrak{F}\!\!\rule{1em}{0.4pt}\, \mathfrak{F}(a)\end{array}$$

Frege regards the changes that have been made here as *substitutions*, and he would have indicated them as follows: We have replaced '*a*' with '$\mathfrak{F}$'; we have replaced '$f(\Gamma)$' with '$\Gamma(a)$'; and we have replaced '*c*' with '*f*'. Apparently, argument-symbols are being freely substituted for function-symbols and vice versa.

How can Frege enjoy such freedom in *Begriffsschrift*? Of his mature distinction between function and *object*, Frege wrote that it 'is not made arbitrarily, but founded deep in the nature of things' (Frege 1984c, op. 31). But concerning the distinction between function and *argument*, Frege insists that it 'has nothing to do with the conceptual content [but] comes about only because we view the expression [of that conceptual content] in a particular way' (Frege 1967, § 9). That is, what, on one way of viewing such an expression, we regard as a function, on another way of viewing it, we may regard as an argument (Frege 1967, § 10). Consider, for example, the expression 'John swims'. If we imagine 'John' replaced by other expressions, then we are regarding 'John' as the argument. But we may also imagine 'swims' replaced by other expressions. Then we would be regarding it as the argument.[5]

Something similar is also true on Frege's mature view. The sentence 'John swims,' he would later hold, is most fundamentally composed of a name, 'John', and a concept-expression, 'ξ swims', where 'ξ' indicates the 'incompleteness' that Frege then understood such expressions to have. But one can also regard the sentence as saying something like: Swimming is something John does. So to regard the sentence is—allowing ourselves an un-Fregean idiom for a moment—to take the original sentence's subject to be 'ξ swims' and its predicate to be a 'second-level' concept-expression we might write 'John$_x(\Phi x)$'.[6] Here, the capital phi and bound variable '*x*' together indicate what sort of incompleteness this expression has: Its argument-place must be filled by a first-level concept-expression. But this way of understanding what it means to treat 'swims' as the argument cannot be how Frege understood it in *Begriffsschrift*: Doing so requires us to

---

[4] The actual examples in *Begriffsschrift* are needlessly complex for our purposes; see for instance Frege's instantiation of (60) just after (92).

[5] Those who are bothered by the sloppiness about use and mention are congratulated and asked to be patient.

[6] Our notation here borrows from Frege's, which he introduces in *Grundgeseze* §25; here Frege is clearly anticipating λ-abstraction. The analysis gestures to that of Montague (1974).

distinguish levels of functions in a way he simply doesn't then distinguish them. How, then, did Frege understand what it means to treat 'swims' as the argument in 1879?

The most general statement of the distinction between function and argument in *Begriffsschrift* reads as follows:

> If in an expression ... a simple or a compound sign has one or more occurrences and if we regard that sign as replaceable in all or some of these occurrences by something else ... then we call that part that remains invariant in the expression a function, and the replaceable part the argument of the function. (Frege 1967, § 9)

This explanation says quite plainly that functions are *expressions*, and similar passages can be found throughout *Begriffsschrift*. Nonetheless, we think it would be uncharitable to insist that Frege positively regarded functions as being expressions. What we can say is that Frege simply does not distinguish use from mention in *Begriffsschrift* at all clearly, and so tends to conflate functions with the expressions that name them. Perhaps the most charitable reading would note that, since the conceptual notation is intended transparently to represent functions and arguments, Frege's usage may be regarded as a transposition to the formal mode (Baker 2001; May 2011). On the other hand, however, in his exposition of Frege's work, Philip Jourdain mentions, in his list of 'advances made by Frege from 1879 to 1893', that 'the traces of formalism in the *Begriffsschrift* vanished: a function ceased to be called a name or expression' (Jourdain 1980, p. 204). Frege himself commented extensively on Jourdain's piece, and many of his comments were included by Jourdain as (sometimes very long) footnotes. Given Frege's aversion to formalism, it seems unlikely that he would not have corrected Jourdain if he had regarded this remark as incorrect. Accordingly, in *Begriffsschrift*, Frege treats the distinction between function and argument as purely linguistic. In contrast, in his mature work, he regards the distinction between function and object as metaphysical.

Frege does not say explicitly what he regards as 'that part that remains invariant' when 'John' is imagined to vary in 'John swims'. In discussing examples, he tends to use gerunds and infinitives. Thus, he might have said that what remains fixed when 'John' varies is 'to swim' or 'swimming'. Frege does not use any notation in *Begriffsschrift* that would indicate any incompleteness in such an expression. On the contrary, gerunds and infinitives are *prima facie* complete in a way the finite form 'swims' is not: Gerunds and infinitives occur as subjects in such sentences as 'Swimming is exhausting' and 'To swim is more difficult than to float'; the finite form cannot.[7]

What 'remains invariant' when we vary 'swims', then? The obvious thing to say is that, when 'swims' is varied, what remains invariant is just 'John'. Nothing Frege says in *Begriffsschrift* contradicts this interpretation. The only relevant passage appears to be this one:

---

[7] Whether gerunds and infinitives are really incomplete is of course an empirical question. In linguistic theory, they are generally supposed to have lexically null pronominal subjects, as opposed to finite clauses.

Since the sign Φ occurs in the expression $\Phi(A)$ and since we can imagine that it is replaced by other signs, Ψ or X, which would then express other functions of the argument A, we can also regard $\Phi(A)$ as a function of the argument Φ. (Frege 1967, § 10)

Frege simply does not say here what familiarity with his mature views would lead one to expect him to say: that, when we so regard $\Phi(A)$, the function is something *other* than A itself. But if he had held this view, surely he would have said so: It would have needed a great deal of explanation, the sort of explanation it gets in *Grundgesetze*. Frege's view in *Begriffsschrift* thus seems to have been that a sentence like 'John swims' is composed of two parts, 'John' and 'to swim', each of which can be regarded either as argument or as function, with 'to swim' being the function if 'John' is the argument and vice versa. And so, indeed, we can see why Frege insisted that the distinction between function and argument 'has nothing to do with the conceptual content [but] comes about only because we view the expression in a particular way' (Frege 1967, § 9).

The distinction between function and argument, as that distinction is used in mathematics, is every bit as fluid as the distinction we are attributing to the early Frege. Given any group G, for example, we may consider the set I_G of group isomorphisms on G: These are 1–1 functions on the underlying set that preserve the group operation; that is, if + is the operation, we must have $\phi(a + b) = \phi(a) + \phi(b)$. Now taking composition as our operation, we may regard I_G as constituting a new group, a so-called permutation group. Permutation groups are of mathematical interest because the properties of a group's permutation group reflect properties of the original group in ways that can be systematically studied. On Frege's mature view, however, the permutation group is *not* a group in the same sense that the original group was a group: If the elements of the original group were objects, then the members of the permutation group are first-level functions, and so the group operations are first-level functions and second-level functions, respectively. That is not a natural view. The natural view is the one that reflects how mathematicians usually speak.[8]

There are, to be sure, differences between argument- and function-symbols in *Begriffsschrift*. When Frege is substituting something for a function-symbol—be it a name or a term—he always indicates the argument, thus: $f(\Gamma)$. One might compare this to his later convention of always writing '$f(\xi)$' rather than just 'f', so that the incompleteness of the function-symbol is indicated. The purpose of the capital gamma is, however, completely different. If we are going to replace a free variable 'f' with a more complex expression, we need to indicate what the argument-places of that expression are to be: We cannot just say that 'f' is to be replaced by '$g \rightarrow ha$', for it would not be clear, for

---

[8] Frege would of course have said that, if we think of the isomorphism group as a group in the original sense, then we are taking its elements to be the value-ranges of the isomorphisms. And so this would be another example, he would have claimed, of mathematicians' tacit reliance upon his Basic Law V.

example, whether '*h*' was a one- or two-place predicate. Hence Frege would have us say that we are replacing '*f*(Γ)' with '*g*(Γ) → *ha*Γ', and now it is clear what is intended. Some such notational convention is obviously required if Frege is to indicate explicitly what substitutions he is making. What we are suggesting, however, is that Frege regarded it *merely* as a notational convention and so of no greater significance. One indication of this fact is that Frege only seems to think it necessary to indicate the argument-places of function-symbols when he is substituting something *for* a function-symbol: He does not indicate the argument-places of the function-symbol when he is substituting a function-symbol for a term. (That is why we said earlier, on page 829, that we were substituting '*f*' for '*c*', not '*f*(Γ)' for 'Γ(*c*)'.)

The differences in how Frege understands quantification, early and late, run even deeper than has been indicated so far. In *Grundgesetze*, the quantifiers are themselves regarded as higher-level functions: The second-order quantifier is a third-level function; the first-order quantifier is a second-level function (Frege 1962, § 31). From the point of view of *Grundgesetze*, then, the first-order universal quantifier is but one among many second-level functions. The value-range operator is another, and so is the existential quantifier. Though Frege has no primitive symbol for it, it would be easy enough for him to define one, perhaps:

$$\text{Ⴢ}\, Fa \overset{df}{\equiv} \neg \overset{a}{\smile} \neg Fa$$

Frege's mature view thus has much in common with how we understand quantifiers today, especially in light of the work on generalized quantifiers begun by Andrzej Mostowski (1957).

But this sort of view is wholly absent from *Begriffsschrift*, in which the purpose of the 'concavity' is conceived very differently.[9] Frege writes at the beginning of *Begriffsschrift*:

> The signs customarily employed in the general theory of magnitudes are of two kinds. The first consists of letters, of which each represents either a number left indeterminate or a function left indeterminate. This indeterminacy makes it possible to use letters to express the universal validity of propositions, as in
>
> $$(a+b)c = ab+ac$$
>
> The other kind consists of signs such as +, −, √, 0, 1, and 2, of which each has its particular meaning.
> *I adopt this basic idea of distinguishing two kinds of signs … in order to apply it in the more comprehensive domain of pure thought in general.* I therefore divide all signs that I use into *those by which we may understand different objects and those that have*

---

[9] We have a dim memory of having encountered this point elsewhere, perhaps in the work of Peter Geach.

a completely determinate meaning. The former are *letters* and they will serve chiefly to express *generality*. (1967, § 1, emphasis in original)

It is important to read this afresh. What Frege is telling us is that '$(a + b)c = ac + bc$' is adequate, *on its own*, to express one form of the distributive law. What express generality here are the *letters* that occur in the formula. Generality is *not* expressed by the concavity. The concavity is necessary only because of cases like

$$\begin{array}{l} \rule{0pt}{0pt}\\[-6pt] \text{---} \; m = 16 \\ \text{---} \; x^4 = m \\ \text{---} \; x^2 = 4 \end{array}$$

of which Frege writes: '... the generality to be expressed by means of the x must not govern the whole ... but must be restricted to' the antecedent of the outer conditional (Frege 1979a, pp. 19–20). The sole purpose of the concavity is thus to 'delimit[ ] the scope that the generality *indicated by the letter* covers' (Frege 1967, § 11, our emphasis). In that sense, then, the concavity itself has no independent meaning, and it is not a quantifier, but rather a syntactic scope indicator. Indeed, there are no quantifiers in *Begriffsschrift*. For the same reason, it would simply have been impossible, at that time, for Frege to introduce the upside-down concavity as a symbol for the existential quantifier. He could of course have introduced it as a kind of abbreviation, but there is a sense in which he could not have *defined* it. Generality is expressed by variables, and that generality is always universal.

28.3 FROM FUNCTION AND ARGUMENT TO CONCEPT AND OBJECT

The familiar Fregean doctrine that functions differ fundamentally from objects is thus absent from *Begriffsschrift*. All we find there is the more basic logico-linguistic distinction between function and argument. The former distinction, however, is undoubtedly present in *Die Grundlagen*. One of the 'three fundamental principles' Frege lists as shaping *Die Grundlagen* is 'never to lose sight of the distinction between concept and object' (Frege 1980a, p. x). Moreover, Frege explicitly distinguishes first- from second-order concepts in *Die Grundlagen*, including existence and 'oneness' among the second-order concepts (Frege 1980a, § 53).[10] And, as noted above, the distinction between first- and second-level functions is necessary only once we have sharply distinguished functions from objects, as Frege himself notes (Frege 1962, p. x).

---

[10] Frege's terminology changes over time: He uses '*Ordnung*' early and '*Stufe*' later.

Frege does not use the language of 'unsaturatedness' or 'incompleteness' in *Die Grundlagen*, although it does figure prominently in his letter to Marty, written in August 1882: 'A concept is unsaturated in that it requires something to fall under it; hence it cannot exist on its own' (Frege 1980b, p. 101). Frege remarks later in the letter that '... Kant's refutation of the ontological argument becomes very obvious when presented in my way ...' (Frege 1980b, p. 102), foreshadowing his claim, in *Die Grundlagen*, that '[b]ecause existence is a property of concepts the ontological argument for the existence of God breaks down' (Frege 1980a, § 53). It would thus appear that both the doctrine that concepts are unsaturated and the distinction of levels were in place by 1882, just three years after the publication of *Begriffsschrift*. What happened?

The remark from the letter to Marty just cited, which contains Frege's earliest use of the term 'unsaturated' (in the extant writings), occurs in the context of a lengthy explanation of his 'distinction between individual and concept':

> [T]his distinction has not always been observed (for Boole only concepts exist). The relation of subordination of a concept under a concept is quite different from that of an individual's falling under a concept. It seems to me that logicians have clung too much to the linguistic schema of subject and predicate, which surely contains what are logically quite different relations. I regard it as essential for a concept that the question whether something falls under it have a sense. Thus I would call 'Christianity' a concept only in the sense in which it is used in the proposition 'this (this way of acting) is Christianity', but not in the proposition 'Christianity continues to spread'. A concept is unsaturated in that it requires something to fall under it; hence it cannot exist on its own. That an individual falls under the concept is a judgeable content, and here the concept appears as predicative and is always predicative. In this case, where the subject is an individual, the relation of subject to predicate is not a third thing added to the two, but it belongs to the content of the predicate, which is what makes the predicate unsatisfied.... In general, I represent the falling of an individual under a concept by $F(x)$, where x is the subject (argument) and $F(\ )$ is the predicate (function), and where the empty place in the parentheses after F indicates non-saturation. The subordination of a concept $\Psi(\ )$ under a concept $\Phi(\ )$ is expressed by

$$\vdash^{a} \begin{array}{l} \Phi(a) \\ \Psi(a) \end{array}$$

> which makes obvious the difference between subordination and an individual's falling under a concept. Without the strict distinction between individual and concept, it is impossible to express particular and existential judgements accurately and in such a way as to make their close relationship obvious. For every particular judgement is an existential judgement.

$$\vdash \negthinspace{}^{a} \negthinspace{}_{\top} a^2 = 4$$

means: 'There is at least one square root of 4'.

$$\vdash \!\!-\!\!\stackrel{\mathfrak{a}}{\frown}\!\!\top\!\! \begin{array}{l} \mathfrak{a}^2 = 4 \\ \mathfrak{a}^3 = 8 \end{array}$$

means: 'Some (at least one) cube roots of 8 are square roots of 4'.... Existential judgements thus take their place among other judgements. (Frege 1980b, pp. 100–2)

We have quoted this passage at length to make it clear how wholly intertwined this early discussion of the distinction between concept and object—or, as Frege says here, concept and 'individual'—is with fundamental questions in *logic*. Our task now is to understand what those questions are.

Given the manner in which Frege begins his remarks, it is tempting to read this passage in light of his earlier discussion in § 3 of *Begriffsschrift*, where he famously insists that the distinction between subject and predicate is of no logical significance. But that discussion is limited to the contrast between active and passive voice: Frege tells us that logic need not represent the difference between 'The Greeks defeated the Persians' and 'The Persians were defeated by the Greeks', the indifference he later labels 'equipollence'. Frege does not suggest in *Begriffsschrift* that the subject–predicate form is actually ambiguous, that is, that 'the linguistic schema of subject and predicate ... contains what are logically quite different relations' (Frege 1980b, p. 101). The topic here, then, is different, and that is because Frege has a new opponent: George Boole.

Boole[11] divides all judgements into two types. On the one hand, there are primary propositions, which express the sorts of relations between concepts studied in Aristotelian logic; on the other, there are secondary propositions, which concern the sorts of relations between judgements studied in sentential logic. The theory of the former is the 'calculus of concepts'; the theory of the latter is the 'calculus of judgements'. Given the dominance of this perspective in 1879, it is no surprise that Schröder, in his review of *Begriffsschrift*, should attempt to impose it on Frege's system. Doing so, he concluded that '... Frege's "conceptual notation" actually has almost nothing in common with ... the Boolean calculus of concepts; but it certainly does have something in common with ... the Boolean calculus of judgements' (Schröder 1972, p. 224).

In 'Boole's Logical Calculus and the Concept-Script', which Frege thrice submitted for publication, he argues in response that his notation for generality allows him to express everything that can be expressed in Boole's calculus of concepts. But there is a more serious charge he wishes to bring against the Booleans:

> The real difference [between my system and Boole's] is that I avoid such a division into two parts ... and give a homogeneous presentation of the lot. In Boole, the two

---

[11] Our rendition of Boole's view is intended to represent Frege's understanding of Boole, given that our present topic is the development of Frege's views. How accurately Frege might have understood Boole is an interesting question, but not one for the present chapter.

parts run alongside one another, so that one is like the mirror image of the other, but for that reason stands in no organic relation to it. (Frege 1979a, p. 15)

The point here is partly aesthetic, but there is a logical point to be made, too.

Boole (and others) had tried to unify the treatment of primary and secondary propositions. Both the calculus of concepts and the calculus of judgements result from the imposition of an interpretation onto what is originally an uninterpreted formalism, a purely abstract algebra. For that reason, the two calculi are syntactically identical: Both contain expressions of the forms '$A \times B$', '$A + B$', and '$\bar{A}$', for example.[12] In the calculus of concepts, the letters are taken to denote classes, or extensions of concepts, and the operations are then interpreted set-theoretically, in the now familiar way: Multiplication is intersection; addition is union;[13] the bar represents the relative complement. The formula '$A \times B = A$' then means: All A are B.

Precisely how the operations were to be interpreted in the calculus of judgements appears to have been a matter of some controversy, and Boole himself takes different views in *The Mathematical Analysis of Logic* (Boole 1847) and *The Laws of Thought* (Boole 1854). But, in both works, Boole takes the letters in this case, too, to denote classes. Schröder explains the view Boole held in the later work this way:

> [L]et 1 stand for the time segment during which the presuppositions of an investigation to be conducted are satisfied. Then let $a, b, c, \ldots$ be considered *judgements* ... and at the same time, as soon as one constructs formulae or calculates (a small change of meaning taking place), the time segments during which these propositions are true. (Schröder 1972, p. 224)

The virtue of this idea is that it allows for a reduction of the calculus of judgements to the calculus of classes, that is, of secondary propositions to primary propositions. To quote Boole:

> Let us take, as an instance for examination, the conditional proposition 'If the proposition X is true, the proposition Y is true'. An undoubted meaning of this proposition is, that the *time* in which the proposition X is true, is *time* in which the proposition Y is true. (Boole 1854, ch. XI, § 5)

That is to say: All times at which X is true are times at which Y is true. The conditional proposition has thus become a universal affirmative proposition, and so '$A \times B = A$' now means: If A, then B.

---

[12] The actual notation varies from logician to logician. We have here used something we hope will be familiar to modern readers.

[13] In some authors, it is something like a disjoint union, corresponding to exclusive disjunction.

It is clear enough both why and to what extent this idea works. The sentential operators are being treated as expressing set-theoretic operations on sets of times. The algebra
so determined is of course a Boolean algebra, and so it satisfies the laws of classical logic.
Now, it is surely safe to say that, just as Schröder had underestimated the importance
of Frege's notion of generality, so Frege just as badly underestimated the importance of
this parallel, that is, of the notion of a Boolean algebra: Frege has nothing positive to
say about it. But we must surely also agree with Frege that the attempted reduction of
sentential logic to quantification theory is a failure, and not only for the case of 'eternal
truths such as those of mathematics' (Frege 1979a, p. 15).

Having rejected Boole's reduction, Frege then proceeds to turn the matter on its
head, and 'reduce [Boole's] *primary propositions* to the *secondary* ones' (Frege 1979a, p.
17). The paradigmatic primary proposition is one expressing the subordination of one
concept to another: Frege expresses such a judgement as a generalized conditional and
thereby 'set[s] up a simple and appropriate organic relation between Boole's two parts'
(Frege 1979a, p. 18).[14] Why the emphasis on the need to establish such an 'organic relation'? Frege does not make his concern explicit, but it seems fairly obvious what is both-
ering him. Boole, he is implicitly claiming, cannot properly account for relationships
between primary and secondary propositions: Boole's treatment does not, for example,
reveal the relationship, clearly represented in Frege's system, between universal affirmative propositions and hypothetical judgements. As a consequence, Boole cannot account
for the validity of inferences in which both primary and secondary propositions essentially occur. The simplest example of such an inference would, again, be that from a universal affirmative proposition to a hypothetical judgement. In Frege's logic, the premise
and conclusion of such an inference would be represented as

$$\vdash\!\!\stackrel{\mathfrak{a}}{\smile}\!\!\!-\!\!\begin{array}{l} \Phi(\mathfrak{a}) \\ \Psi(\mathfrak{a}) \end{array}$$

and

$$\vdash\!\!-\!\!\begin{array}{l} \Phi(a) \\ \Psi(a) \end{array}$$

respectively. In Boolean logic, one can represent them both as '$A \times B = A$'. But the letters
that occur in the two cases have nothing to do with one another: In one case, A is a concept; in the other, a set of times.

---

[14] Frege remarks, in a similar spirit, that '[t]he precisely defined hypothetical relation between possible
contents of judgement'—that is, the conditional—'has a similar significance for the foundation of my
conceptual notation that identity of extensions has for Boolean logic' (Frege 1979a, p. 16). (The reference to
'identity of extensions' reflects a feature of Boole's logic that is peculiar to his treatment: Frege might just as
well have mentioned subordination.) One of the points Frege is making here is thus that sentential logic is
more fundamental than predicate logic, a point to which we'll return.

Having explained his reduction of primary propositions to secondary ones, Frege continues as follows:

> [O]n this view, we do justice to the distinction between concept and individual, which is completely obliterated in Boole. Taken strictly, his letters never mean individuals but always extensions of concepts. That is, we must distinguish between concept and thing, even when only one thing falls under a concept. In the case of a concept, it is always possible to ask whether something, and if so what, falls under it, questions which are senseless in the case of an individual. (Frege 1979a, p. 18)

Frege does not make the connection between these remarks and the preceding ones terribly clear. In what way does Boole fail to respect the distinction between concept and object? How does Frege's view allow us to respect it? The connection is revealed by what Frege says next:[15]

> We must likewise distinguish the case of one concept's being subordinate to another from that of a thing falling under a concept, although the same form of words is used for both. The examples ...

$$\vdash \begin{cases} x^4 = 16 \\ x^2 = 4 \end{cases}$$

> and

$$\vdash 2^4 = 16$$

> show the distinction in the conceptual notation. (Frege 1979a, p. 18)

Frege is alluding here to an aspect of Boole's logic that he does not explicitly mention but which would have been well known to his contemporaries. Boole, as was then common, regards such propositions as 'The sun shines' as expressing relations between concepts:

> To say, 'The sun shines', is to say, 'The sun is that which shines', and it expresses *a relation between two classes of things*, viz., 'the sun' and 'things which shine'. (Boole 1854, ch. IV, § 1, our emphasis)

---

[15] Between the previous quotation and this one, Frege gives a brief argument that we must distinguish concept from thing. The argument is of significant independent interest, but to consider it here would distract us from the point at issue. We have discussed it elsewhere (Heck and May 2010, pp. 136–7).

We can see, in retrospect, that Boole is attempting to reduce what we would now call 'atomic' propositions to universal affirmative propositions, that is, to one sort of primary proposition.[16] In a sense, he has no choice: Such propositions clearly are not secondary propositions—they express no relation between propositions—so there is nothing for them to be but primary ones.

From Frege's perspective, this treatment of atomic propositions is completely misconceived. His diagnosis of the problem is made most explicit in a passage from the letter to Marty, quoted earlier:

> The relation of subordination of a concept under a concept is quite different from that of an individual's falling under a concept. It seems that logicians have clung too long to the linguistic schema of subject and predicate, which surely contains what are logically quite different relations. I regard it as essential for a concept that the question whether something falls under it have a sense. (Frege 1980b, pp. 100–1)

It should now be obvious what point Frege is making here, but it is worth spelling out explicitly. Frege is claiming that, whatever similarity of form there may be between 'Dolphins are mammals' and 'Flipper is a dolphin', it is a mistake to regard this similarity as logically significant: The relation between the subject and predicate in the first is very different from the relation between subject and predicate in the second. A proper treatment of the logic of these sentences will therefore require us to represent them differently, as Frege does in his conceptual notation.

The difference between subject and predicate is a topic Frege discusses in 'Boole's Logical Calculus' on the pages just preceding the ones we have just been discussing ourselves. Boole, Frege says, takes concepts to be the basic building-blocks of logic and regards judgements as constructed from them. Frege, on the other hand, 'start[s] out from judgements and their contents, not from concepts', and he explains how concepts are formed from judgements in a way reminiscent of his explanation of the distinction between function and argument in *Begriffsschrift*:

> If ... you imagine the 2 in the content of possible judgement

$$2^4 = 16$$

> to be replaceable by something else, by -2 or by 3 say, which may be indicated by putting an x in place of the 2:

$$x^4 = 16,$$

---

[16] Part of what lies behind Boole's failure, we suspect, at least in Frege's eyes, is a failure to distinguish classes from aggregates: Frege accuses Schröder of this conflation (Frege 1984b).

the content of possible judgement is thus split into a constant and a variable part. The former, regarded in its own right but holding a place open for the latter, gives the concept '4th root of 16'. (Frege 1979a, p. 16)

Frege goes on to explain that we may regard 4 as replaceable, rather than 2, or even in addition to 2, thus arriving at a different concept or at a relation. He then continues:

And so instead of putting a judgement together out of an individual as subject and an already formed concept as predicate, we do the opposite and arrive at a concept by splitting up the content of possible judgement. Of course, if the expression of the content of possible judgement is to be analysable in this way, it must already be itself articulated. We may infer from this that at least the properties and relations which are not further analysable must have their own simple designations. But it doesn't follow from this that the ideas of these properties and relations are formed apart from objects: on the contrary they arise with the first judgement in which they are ascribed to things. Hence, in the conceptual notation, their designations never occur on their own, but always in combinations which express contents of possible judgement. I could compare this with the behavior of the atom: we suppose an atom never to be found on its own, but only combined with others, moving out of one combination only in order to enter immediately into another. A sign for a property never appears without a thing to which it might belong being at least indicated, a designation of a relation never without indication of the things which might stand in it. (Frege 1979a, p. 17)

Frege's mature account of the distinction between concept and object is not quite present here. He does not use the term 'unsaturated', for example, nor any equivalent, as he does in the letter to Marty. But the germ of that idea is present in the suggestion that a concept is what results when we vary an argument and regard what remains constant 'in its own right but holding a place open for' the argument.

There are several other points to note about these remarks. One is that Frege is clearly moving away from his earlier view that the distinction between function and argument 'has nothing to do with the conceptual content ...' (Frege 1967, § 9). If it is to make any sense at all to speak of replacing the object '2 in the content of possible judgement $2^4 = 16$' with other objects, then the object 2 must itself occur in that content—it must somehow be a part of it—as must what remains constant when it is varied.[17] Another point is that Frege is no longer conflating functions with the expressions that denote them. On the contrary, he is carefully distinguishing the two and arguing that (what he would later call) the unsaturatedness of properties and relations has implications for the behaviour of the expressions that denote them: It is *because* 'the ideas of these properties and relations are [not] formed apart from objects' that 'in the conceptual notation, their designations never occur on their own'.

---

[17] It is a corollary of this point that Frege's insistence that we must begin with judgements rather than concepts does not express any view to the effect that judgements are intrinsically unstructured, as it is often taken to do.

But the really crucial point is that this entire discussion, which constitutes the earliest appearance of something like the notion of unsaturatedness, occurs in a discussion of the differences between Frege's logic and the dominant logic of his day, which of course was Boole's. That is to say, the distinction between concept and object arises out of Frege's attempts to motivate and explain the crucial differences between these systems, as he understood them. If we want to understand the notion of unsaturatedness, then, what we need to understand is the *logical* point Frege is using it to make.

28.4 UNSATURATEDNESS

What is that logical point? It has several aspects: Boole's secondary propositions are more fundamental than his primary ones; subsumption (an object's falling under a concept) is more fundamental than subordination (one concept's falling within another); judgements are more fundamental than concepts. These are the points to which Frege returns time and again in his discussions of Boole and out of which the distinction between concept and object arises. What underlies and unifies these various doctrines? The answer, we want to suggest, is something we now take largely for granted: From the standpoint of logical theory, the most basic sort of proposition is neither the primary proposition nor the secondary proposition but the *atomic* proposition; all other propositions are constructed from atomic propositions by means of certain syntactic operations.

Some of the operations by means of which propositions are constructed are common to Frege's and Boole's logics. Given some propositions, they may be related to one another in various ways: We may negate a proposition, form a conditional or disjunction from two propositions, or what have you. It is with respect to what Boole regarded as the primary propositions that disagreement arises. For Boole, such a proposition arises when we put concepts into relation with one another. In a sense, Frege does not disagree. But for Boole, concepts were logically primitive. Frege insists, by contrast, that to take concepts as primitive is to ignore one of the main questions an adequate logic must address, namely, how 'true concept formation' is possible (Frege 1979a, p. 35). Frege would have insisted, for example, that there is a straightforward sense in which the concept of a prime number is *not* primitive but derivative, or defined, and he would have expected Boole to agree. But the way this concept is constructed from other concepts is something Boole cannot explain. The concept of prime number is, in Sir Michael Dummett's apt phrase, *extracted from* such a judgement as

$$\forall x \left[\exists y (x \times y = 873) \rightarrow x = 1 \vee x = 873 \right]$$

when we allow the argument 873 to 'become indeterminate'. To form the concept of a prime number thus involves perceiving a pattern in this judgement that it has in common with certain other judgements, such as:

$$\forall x \big[\exists y (x \times y = 26) \rightarrow x = 1 \vee x = 26 \big].$$

And, according to Frege, this process of extraction is the key to an explanation of how scientifically fruitful concepts are formed (Frege 1979a, p. 34).

But this non-Boolean mode of concept formation has a yet more basic role to play in Frege's logic: It is involved in almost every statement in which generality is expressed. For Frege, a universal affirmative proposition will take this sort of form:

$$\vdash^{\!\!\mathfrak{a}}\!\!-\!\!\begin{array}{l} \mathfrak{a}^3 = 8 \\ \mathfrak{a}^2 = 4 \end{array}$$

Such a formula, Frege tells us in *Begriffsschrift*, expresses 'the judgement that, whatever we may take for its argument, *the function* is a fact' (Frege 1967, § 11, our emphasis). But what does Frege mean here by *the* function the formula contains? Isn't Frege's view in *Begriffsschrift* that the distinction between function and argument 'has nothing to do with the conceptual content [but] comes about only because we view the expression in a particular way' (Frege 1967, § 9)? Well, yes, that is his view about some cases, but not about all:

> [T]he different ways in which the same conceptual content can be considered as a function of this or that argument have no importance so long as function and argument are completely determinate. But if the argument becomes *indeterminate*, ... then the distinction between function and argument acquires a *substantive* significance.... [T]hrough the opposition of the *determinate* and the *indeterminate*, the whole splits up into function and argument according to its own content, and not just according to our way of looking at it. (Frege 1967, § 9, emphasis in original)

Every general statement thus involves a particular function essentially. For example, the statement displayed above essentially involves the concept: *number whose cube is eight if its square is four*. Such functions cannot in general be primitive but must be formed by extraction. The just-mentioned concept, for example, may be extracted from the sentence

$$\vdash\!\!-\!\!\begin{array}{l} 5^2 = 16 \\ 5^3 = 4 \end{array}$$

by allowing the argument 5 to vary.

These remarks from *Begriffsschrift* once again conflate functions and the expressions that denote them. As we have seen, Frege quickly remedies that flaw. But, as we have also seen, Frege insists, from the moment he clearly distinguishes them, that *both* functions *and* the expressions that denote them[18] are in some sense incomplete. The obvious question is how these two sorts of incompleteness are supposed to be related.

Frege seems to answer this question three different ways. At the beginning, in 1881, his answer has a strikingly epistemological cast. The linguistic thesis that '[a] sign for a property never appears without a thing to which it might belong being at least indicated' is derived from the epistemological premise that ideas of properties 'arise simultaneously with the first judgement in which they are ascribed to things' (Frege 1979a, p. 17); if a metaphysical conception of unsaturatedness is present at all, it surfaces only in Frege's remarks about 'the behavior of the atom', which are clearly intended as analogical. But things have changed already by 1882. In the letter to Marty, Frege's focus is on the metaphysical thesis that '[a] concept is unsaturated' and so 'cannot exist on its own' (Frege 1980b, p. 101). The epistemological doctrine that '... concept formation can[not] precede judgement ...' (Frege 1980b, p. 101) is present here, too, but it is not presented as fundamental. Rather, it is derived from the metaphysical thesis: 'I do not believe that concept formation can precede judgement *because this would presuppose the independent existence of concepts*' (Frege 1980b, p. 101, our emphasis).[19] By Frege's mature period, the epistemological thesis seems to have disappeared completely. We suggest, in fact, that Frege would then have regarded his earlier attempt to ground the distinction between concept and object in the priority of judgements over concept-formation as unacceptably psychologistic.[20]

Frege's mature view differs in another way, too. The direct way Frege tried to explain the incompleteness of concepts in 1881, by asking us to imagine replacing the number 2 in the content of the sentence '$2^4 = 16$', is no longer available to him once he has distinguished sense from reference: The content of the sentence is the thought it expresses, and objects simply do not occur in thoughts.[21] When Frege explains his view that functions are unsaturated in his mature period, then, what he explains first is always his view that

---

[18] In his mature period, he will further insist that the senses of such expressions are also incomplete. What this might mean is a topic we have explored elsewhere (Heck and May, 2010).

[19] Even the linguistic thesis evolves between 1881 and 1882. Frege now indicates the fact that a predicate can occur only with an indication of its argument by using the notation: '$F(\ )$', 'where the empty place in the parentheses after F indicates nonsaturation' (Frege 1980b, p. 101). No such notation occurs in the (extant) papers on Boole.

[20] That Frege gives his distinction between concept and object an epistemological cast in 1881 may again be due to his reading of Boole, whose discussion of logic has, overall, a strongly psychologistic cast. Indeed, *The Laws of Thought* begins with the remark: 'The design of the following treatise is to investigate the fundamental laws of those operations of the mind by which reasoning is performed ...' (Boole 1854, ch. I, §1). It is a nice question to what extent Boole is among Frege's targets in his anti-psychologistic rants.

[21] See the famous exchange about Mont Blanc and its snowfields in Frege's letter to Russell of 13 November 1904 (Frege 1980b, p. 163) and Russell's reply of 12 December 1904 (Frege 1980b, p. 169).

functional *expressions* are unsaturated; he then explains the unsaturatedness of functions in terms of the unsaturatedness of the expressions that denote them.[22, 23]

> [O]ne can always speak of the name of a function as having empty places, since what fills them does not, strictly speaking, belong to it. *Accordingly* I call the function itself unsaturated, or in need of supplementation, *because* its name has first to be completed with the sign of an argument if we are to obtain a meaning that is complete in itself. (Frege 1979c, p. 119, our emphasis)

So, in the end, it is the unsaturatedness of the *expression* that is basic. The unsaturatedness of functions and concepts is to be explained in terms of the unsaturatedness of the expressions that denote them.

So we have two distinctions: There is the distinction between function and object, which is broadly metaphysical; and there is the distinction between a name and a predicate, which is essentially syntactic; the former is to be explained in terms of the latter. That can easily make it seem as if Frege is just conflating the incompleteness of predicates with the incompleteness of their denotations, but surely he is not: He draws this very distinction himself. Is the incompleteness of predicates simply being 'projected' onto their denotations, then? That would be unfortunate.

The answer, we want to suggest, is very simple. If the fact that predicates are unsaturated is to have any consequence whatsoever for the nature of what they denote—and, as we have said, in Frege's mature work, the unsaturatedness of concepts is explained in terms of the unsaturatedness of predicates—then surely such consequences must issue from the nature of the *connection* between predicates and what they denote, that is, from something about the *semantics* of predicates. The incompleteness of predicates manifests itself in the conceptual notation in the fact that predicates never appear without an argument's at least being indicated. If so, however, then any adequate account of the meaning of predicates must take note of this crucial fact about them: that they cannot occur without an appropriate argument.

One might therefore say that on Frege's view we do not need to answer the question what a predicate denotes, since a predicate can never occur on its own, anyway: We need only answer the question what the denotation is of a complete expression that is formed by inserting appropriate expressions into its argument-places. The semantic clause for 'swims', then, should not take the form:

'swims' denotes …,

but rather:

---

[22] One finds similar remarks in *Function and Concept* (Frege 1984c, opp. 5ff.), 'On Concept and Object' (Frege 1984d, opp. 194–5), and 'What is a Function?' (Frege, 1984e, op. 665).

[23] The translation of the passage that follows has the last word of the first sentence being 'them', as if it were anaphoric on 'empty places'. It is clear, however, that what Frege means is, as he puts it in *Function and Concept*, that 'the argument does not belong with a function' (Frege 1984c, op. 6).

⌜Δ swims⌝ denotes ...

where Δ is a syntactic variable ranging over expressions that might occur as arguments.[24] This, indeed, is how Frege himself proceeds in *Grundgesetze*.[25] A Frege-inspired clause for 'swims' might therefore look like:

(1) ⌜Δ swims⌝ denotes the True iff, for some x, denotes (Δ, x) and x swims.

But while clauses like (1) directly reflect the unsaturatedness of predicates, it is not clear what they imply about predicates' denotations, since they do not explicitly assign denotations to predicates at all. The most obvious way of doing so would be:

(2) The predicate 'swims' denotes the concept *swimming*.

But that leads directly to the infamous problem of the concept *horse*.

One might want to deny that (1) assigns 'swims' a denotation at all. But Frege would not agree: His semantics for quantification—especially for higher-order quantification—requires it to do so. And it is clear that Frege thought that a relation between a predicate and a concept was at least implied by (1). In § 5 of *Grundgesetze*, for example, Frege explains the horizontal as follows:

—Δ is the True if Δ is the True; on the other hand, it is the False if Δ is not the True,

and he takes this stipulation to be sufficient to assign the horizontal a function as its denotation, continuing: 'Accordingly, —ξ is a function whose value is always a truth-value ...'.

The impression that (1) does not assign a denotation to 'swims' is presumably a consequence of the fact that it does not take the form 'This predicate denotes this concept'. But, if one thinks it must take that form, then one is not thinking clearly about the logical structure of the relation of denotation itself. The relation that holds between a one-place predicate and its denotation is a relation of 'mixed level', taking as arguments

---

[24] More formally, Δ ranges over what may be called 'auxiliary names': We suppose that the language can always be expanded by the addition of a new name, whose reference may then be any object one wishes. Formally, a truth-definition using such a device requires us to quantify over languages that expand the original one (Heck 1999). Frege uses some such device, and we have borrowed this use of Greek capitals from him. It is not clear, however, how Frege regarded these expressions, whose use he never explains. Sometimes, they seem to act like meta-linguistic variables ranging over objects; but then they also occur in quotation-marks, as in the semantic clause for identity in §7 of *Grundgesetze*, which suggests that they are substitutional variables. Auxiliary names let us have the best of both worlds.

[25] We will quote one of Frege's semantic clauses below, that for the horizontal. It is in no way exceptional. Regarding the other primitives, the clause for negation is in §6; identity, §7; the first-order universal quantifier, §8; the smooth breathing, §9; the definite article, §11; the conditional, §12; and the second-order universal quantifier, §24.

an object—the predicate itself—and a concept: its denotation. So an expression denoting this relation must take as arguments a proper name denoting the predicate and a predicate denoting the concept. This predicate, being unsaturated, must occur with an argument, or at least the 'indication' of one, which is what we have in this case: the argument will be indicated by a bound variable. Thus, a 'denotation clause' for a predicate that is compatible with Frege's commitments must have the following form:

(3) denotes$_x$('ξ swims', x swims)

Now, suppose we formulate our semantic theory using clauses of this form rather than clauses like (1). To characterize the truth of an atomic sentence, we will then also need a compositional principle such as:

(4) $\ulcorner \Phi(\Delta) \urcorner$ denotes the True if, and only if, for some ϕ and x, denotes$_x$ ($\Phi(\xi), \phi x$) and denotes(Δ, x) and ϕx.

We can now prove:[26]

(5) denotes$_x$($\Phi(\xi), \phi x$)iff, for every Δ, $\ulcorner \Phi(\Delta) \urcorner$ denotes the True iff, for some x, denotes (Δ, x) and ϕx.

It follows that (1) is indeed sufficient to determine the denotation of 'swims', since (1) just is the right-hand side of the relevant instance of (5). It might therefore be thought that the question whether the semantics of predicates should be given by clauses like (1) or instead by clauses like (3) is of no real significance. We can take the latter as basic, in which case (3) and (4) obviously imply (1); or we can take (1) as basic, define denotation using (5), and then prove both (3) and (4). In that case, we could still regard (1) as assigning a denotation to 'swims' as directly as it is possible to assign one, since, as already noted, (1) is the right-hand side of an instance of (5).

From Frege's perspective, however, the question whether (1) or (3) is more fundamental is critical. Recall the following remarks from the letter to Marty:

> A concept is unsaturated in that it requires something to fall under it; hence it cannot exist on its own. That an individual falls under it is a judgeable content, and here the concept appears as predicative and is always predicative. In this case, where the subject is an individual, the relation of subject to predicate is not a third thing added to the two, but it belongs to the content of the predicate, which is what makes the predicate unsatisfied. (Frege 1980b, p. 101)

---

[26] For the proof, we also need a principle stating that every predicate denotes at most one concept: denotes$_x$ ($\Phi\xi, \phi x$) $\wedge$ denotes$_x$ ($\Phi x, \psi x$) $\rightarrow \forall x(\phi x \equiv \psi x)$. But we need such a principle anyway, since we'd otherwise not be able to prove, say, that 'o = 1' is false: For that argument, we need to know that '=' denotes *only* the relation of identity. With this principle in place, we could then introduce an expression true-of(t, y), read 't is true of y', as equivalent to: $\exists F$ (denotes$_x$ (t, Fx) $\wedge$ Fy).

Frege speaks here of 'this case, where the subject is an individual'. What is the other case, in which it is not? The contrast, as we have seen, is between Frege's position and Boole's. The other case is thus the one traditional logic takes as fundamental, the case in which the subject is itself a concept. So this is a form of Frege's claim that 'the linguistic schema of subject and predicate … contains what are logically quite different relations' (Frege 1980b, p. 101). The relation that is present when the subject is an individual is the one he calls 'falling under'; the relation that is present when the subject is a concept is the one he calls 'subordination'. And in a proposition expressing subordination, Frege is insisting, the relation between subject and predicate *is* a 'third thing added to the two', so it is something an adequate logical theory must make explicit. In the conceptual notation, the relation of subordination is of course represented as:

$$\underset{a}{\smallsmile}\!\!\top\!\!\begin{array}{l}\Phi a\\ \Psi a\end{array}$$

Part of what Frege is claiming here is thus, again, that 'atomic' sentences are what are fundamental for logic. As he writes about a decade later: 'The fundamental logical relation is that of an object's falling under a concept: all relations between concepts can be reduced to this' (Frege 1979c, p. 118).

If atomic sentences are *truly* fundamental, however, then they cannot assert the existence of a *relation* between the subject and the predicate. The correct analysis of 'Bob swims' is not: falls-under(S, b). That is, in effect, simply a version of the traditional view. The correct analysis is just: $S(b)$. That is the sense in which a concept must contain the relation of predication within itself. But if we take the semantics of predicates to be given by clauses like (3), then we are *not* treating 'the relation of subject to predicate' as something that 'belongs to the content of the predicate'. On the contrary, it is a 'third thing' that must be 'added to the two', and what must be added is made explicit by (4), which treats predication as a relation between the denotation of the predicate and the denotation of the subject. Frege's preference is thus for (1), which makes predication 'internal' to the concept.

In what sense is the denotation Frege assigns to 'swims' incomplete, then? As we have seen, Frege uses the notion of incompleteness in an effort to explain certain crucial respects in which his logic differs from Boole's. One can try to press the notion into service here, too: What is assigned as the predicate's denotation is that part of the content expressed by (1) that is specific to the case of 'swims' and that remains constant as the argument is varied, that is, that part expressed by 'ξ swims'; it is unsaturated because its argument is missing. But if the metaphor now seems to be doing no useful work, perhaps that is because its work is done, because it is no longer needed.

Frege says explicitly that these 'figures of speech' are intended to play only a heuristic role (Frege 1984d, op. 205): He uses them when he is struggling to explain what he means by a 'concept' and, in particular, when he is trying to explain what was then a new understanding of concepts, different from the traditional one. But we hardly need such an explanation now. If there is something *we* need help understanding, it is not

Frege's notion of a concept but Boole's. More seriously: We no longer need the metaphor of incompleteness because the claim that concepts are 'incomplete' is far more adequately expressed by the semantic thesis that the meaning of a predicate should be given by stating the meaning of an arbitrary atomic sentence in which it occurs, that is, that the proper form for a semantic clause governing a predicate is (1). The same goes for Frege's thesis that predicates are incomplete. We no longer need that metaphor because that thesis is more adequately expressed by the syntactic doctrine that a predicate must always occur with its argument.

28.5 Conclusion

In the Introduction to *Grundgesetze*, Frege describes the 'progress' that he has made on the project he 'had in view as early as my *Begriffsschrift* of 1879 and announced in my *Grundlagen der Arithmetik* of 1884' (Frege 1962, p. viii): the reduction of arithmetic to logic. On his list of areas of significant progress is the understanding of 'the nature of functions', which are now 'characterized more precisely' by sharply distinguishing functions from objects. The result of this precision, Frege observes, is that functions can be stratified into levels, and that this result can be generalized to the case of primary logical interest by identifying concepts with functions whose values are truth-values. The notions of unsaturated and saturated, and of falling-under and falling-within, arise as aspects of Frege's nomenclature for elucidating these characteristics of functions.

As we have seen, Frege came by this elaboration through his engagement with Boolean logic. As Frege viewed the dispute, it was over a central point about logic: the primacy of atomic propositions. What blinded Booleans to this, on Frege's view, was their lack of appreciation of the predicative nature of such propositions. To Frege, it was essential that we understand the logical form of atomic propostions to be $P(a)$. This logical form, composed of unsaturated and saturated parts, in itself represents predication. It would be a mistake, according to Frege, to think that some additional factor is needed to relate these parts predicationally. In this regard the Boolean analysis of atomic propositions is in error; so too would be analysis in Fregean terms as their having the logical form: falls-under(P, a). In neither way is predication inherently expressed, precisely because what is effaced is the distinction between concept and object: 'P' as it occurs here is just as much a saturated term as 'a'. We could, of course, give an analysis of the relation of falling under as predicational, but this is not Frege's concern. Rather, his concerns lie with the *semantics* of predication; this is what needs to be clearly articulated in order to understand the logical primacy of atomic propositions. What Frege is describing in *Grundgesetze* are the central advances in his thinking about functions that contribute to this goal.

For Frege, then, the function is unsaturated, but this notion only has significance in the context of predication; '$P(\xi)$' refers to a concept only when it occurs in the context '$P(a)$', with an argument at least indicated. Outside this context, by itself, it does not denote a function; it is an empty term, one that has no place in the conceptual notation. As early as his first explicit discussion of the matter in his letter to Marty, Frege insists that a term for a function has no denotation unless accompanied by a term for its argument. The generalization of this insistence is the Context Principle of *Die Grundlagen*, 'never to ask for the meaning (*Beduetung*) of a word in isolation, but only in the context of a proposition', and Frege does not waver from this position, reiterating (and elaborating) it in *Grundgesetze*: 'We can inquire about reference only if the signs are constituent parts of sentences expressing thoughts' (Frege 1962, v. II, § 97). Unsaturatedness is the notion through which Frege characterizes this composition: '$P(a)$' is composed of an unsaturated part '$P(\xi)$', whose reference in the context of '$P(a)$' is a concept, and a saturated part 'a', whose reference in that context is an object. And it is this notion of composition—predication—that sits at the core of Frege's conception of logic. It is only when we have recognized this structure, as it is represented in the conceptual notation, that we can appreciate the proper analysis of generality and so secure a notion of proof adequate to the needs of mathematics.

REFERENCES

Baker, G. (2001). ' "Function" in Frege's *Begriffsschrift*: Dissolving the Problem', *British Journal for the History of Philosophy* 9: 525–44.

Boole, G. (1847). *The Mathematical Analysis of Logic*. Cambridge: Macmillan, Barclay, & Macmillan.

——(1854). *The Laws of Thought*. London: Walton and Maberly.

Bynum, T. (1972). 'Editor's Introduction'. In Frege (1972a), pp. 55–80.

Frege, G. (1962). *Grundgesetze der Arithmetik*. Hildesheim: Georg Olms Verlagsbuchhandlung. Translations of Part I are in Frege (1964), and of portions of Part III in Frege (1970). Extracts appear in Frege (1997), pp. 194–223.

——(1964). *The Basic Laws of Arithmetic: Exposition of the System*. Berkeley, CA: University of California Press.

——(1967). 'Begriffsschrift: A Formula Language Modeled upon that of Arithmetic, for Pure Thought'. In J. van Heijenoort (ed.), *From Frege to Gödel: A Sourcebook in Mathematical Logic*. Cambridge, MA: Harvard University Press, pp. 5–82.

——(1970). *Translations from the Philosophical Writings of Gottlob Frege*. Oxford: Blackwell.

——(1972a). *Conceptual Notation and Related Articles*. New York: Oxford University Press.

——(1972b). 'On the Aim of the Conceptual Notation'. In Frege (1972a), pp. 90–100.

——(1979a). 'Boole's Logical Calculus and the Concept-Script'. In Frege (1979d), pp. 9–52.

——(1979b). 'Boole's Logical Formula-Language and My Concept-Script'. In Frege (1979d), pp. 47–52.

——(1979c). 'Comments on Sense and Meaning'. In Frege (1979d), pp. 118–25. Also in Frege (1997), pp. 172–80.

——(1979d). *Posthumous Writings*. Chicago: University of Chicago Press.

——(1980a). *The Foundations of Arithmetic*, 2nd rev. edn. Evanston, IL: Northwestern University Press.

——(1980b). *Philosophical and Mathematical Correspondence*. Chicago: University of Chicago Press.

——(1984a). *Collected Papers on Mathematics, Logic, and Philosophy.* Oxford: Basil Blackwell.

——(1984b). 'A Critical Elucidation of Some Points in E. Schröder, *Vorlesungen Über die Algebra der Logik'.* In Frege (1984a), pp. 210–28.

—— (1984c). 'Function and Concept'. In Frege (1984a), pp. 137–56. Also in Frege (1997), pp. 130–48.

—— (1984d). 'On Concept and Object'. In Frege (1984a), pp. 182–94. Also in Frege (1997), pp. 181–93.

——(1984e). 'What is a Function?' In Frege (1984a), pp. 285–92.

——(1997). *The Frege Reader,* ed. and introd. M. Beaney. Oxford: Blackwell.

Heck, R. G. (1999). '*Grundgesetze der Arithmetik* I § 10', *Philosophia Mathematica* 7: 258–92.

Heck, R. G. and R. May (2010). 'The Composition of Thoughts', *Noûs* 45: 126–66.

Jourdain, P. E. B. (1980). 'Gottlob Frege'. In Frege (1980b), pp. 179–206.

May, R. (2011). 'Leibniz's problem, Frege's puzzle'. Draft, University of California, Davis.

Montague, R. (1974). 'The Proper Treatment of Quantification in Ordinary English'. In R. Thomason (ed.), *Formal Philosophy: Selected Papers of Richard Montague.* New Haven: Yale University Press, pp. 247–70.

Mostowski, A. (1957). 'On a Generalization of Quantifiers', *Fundamenta Mathematicae* 44: 12–36.

Schröder, E. (1972). Review of Frege's *Conceptual Notation.* In Frege (1972a), pp. 218–32.

Venn, J. (1972). Review of Frege's *Conceptual Notation.* In Frege (1972a), pp. 234–5.

CHAPTER 29

WHEN LOGICAL ATOMISM MET THE *THEAETETUS*: RYLE ON NAMING AND SAYING

RICHARD GASKIN

> Plato in his late dialogues was concerned with some of the same cardinal problems as those which exercised Frege and the young Russell, problems, namely, about the relations between naming and saying; between the meanings of words and the sense of sentences; about the composition of truths and falsehoods; about the role of 'not'; about the difference between contradictories and opposites; and in the end, I think, about what is expressed by 'if' and 'therefore'.
>
> (Ryle 1971, I, p. 71)

29.1 OVERVIEW

Thus Gilbert Ryle in his 1960 paper 'Letters and Syllables in Plato', stating what he had been urging for at least two decades, namely that Plato's interests in his later dialogues, and in particular in the *Parmenides*, the *Theaetetus*, and the *Sophist*, coincided significantly with those of the founding fathers of modern analytic philosophy. My initial focus in this chapter will be on a particular aspect of that coincidence—one which greatly exercised Ryle—namely the supposed commonalities of purpose and outlook between Socrates' dream in the *Theaetetus*, on the one hand, and the logical atomism of the early Wittgenstein and early Russell, on the other (§ 29.2). An examination of that topic leads on naturally to a consideration of the extent to which the 'object and designation' model of meaning is applicable to sentences and their semantically significant parts, and correspondingly whether Ryle is right to maintain that naming and saying are entirely distinct (§§ 29.3–29.4). I conclude with some reflections on the place of these issues in Ryle's philosophy more generally, and on the bearing of Ryle's treatment of the alleged naming–saying dichotomy on the problem of propositional unity (§ 29.5).

29.2 LOGICAL ATOMISM AND THE THEORY OF SOCRATES' DREAM

According to the dream theory of the *Theaetetus*, the primary elements, 'of which we and everything else are composed', have no 'account' (*logos*), but can only be named. An account of a primary element would inevitably use words that apply to other things, and so would not be proprietary to that element: hence we must affirm of such an element that 'a name is the only thing it has'. But several names 'woven together' (*sumplakenta*) can form an account of the complexes composed of the named elements. For 'a weaving together (*sumplokē*) of names is the being of an account'. The elements, we are told, are unknowable, though perceivable; complexes formed from these elements are 'knowable and expressible in an account and judgeable in a true judgement'. According to the theory, knowledge consists in true judgement with an account (*Theaetetus* 201d8–202c6).[1]

In my opening quotation Ryle alludes to Frege and the early Russell, and certainly no one familiar with, say, Russell's 1918 lectures on logical atomism could fail to be impressed by the similarities between some of the doctrines propounded therein and the position set out in the dream.[2] But one figure conspicuous by his absence from the quotation is Wittgenstein: Ryle's failure to mention him is curious in the light of the statement at the end of his seminal 1939 paper 'Plato's *Parmenides*' that there are affinities not only between late Plato, on the one hand, and Hume's and Kant's accounts of existence and judgement, on the other, but also between the relevant dialogues and 'Russell's doctrine of propositional functions and theory of types, and, perhaps, more than any other, nearly the whole of Wittgenstein's *Tractatus Logico-Philosophicus*' (1971, I, p. 44). Indeed Wittgenstein himself was to remark on the similarity that is here in question in the first part of the *Philosophical Investigations*, at § 46, where, having reproduced the essential part of Socrates' dream, he adds laconically: 'Both Russell's "individuals" and my "objects" (*Log. Phil. Abh.*) were such *Urelemente*.' And certainly the commonalities that the dream theory shares with the *Tractatus* are at least as striking as those it shares with Russell's lectures on logical atomism, which is hardly surprising, given Russell's profound and amply acknowledged debt to Wittgenstein in those lectures.

That Ryle construed the *Theaetetus* through the medium of logical atomism emerges clearly not only from the papers I have already alluded to, but also and especially from his posthumously published paper 'Logical Atomism in Plato's *Theaetetus*' (Ryle 1990). This paper gives the text of a talk delivered to the Oxford Philological Society in 1952; its contents were widely known, and the paper itself even discussed in print, long before it was finally published in 1990 (see Burnyeat's foreword to the paper, pp. 21–2). One particular strand of its influence concerns me here: in the preface to his commentary on

---

[1] I have used McDowell's translation (1973).

[2] For some of the correspondences, see Chappell 2005, p. 208.

the *Theaetetus*, published in 1973, John McDowell thanks Ryle, 'who let me see a copy of his famous, but, alas, unpublished paper on Socrates' dream, and some of his lecture notes'. And it is in the part of McDowell's commentary dealing with the dream that Ryle's presence in the background is most sensibly felt. For McDowell follows Ryle in offering a *propositional* interpretation of the dream, one that aims to bring it into line with some of the main tenets of Russellian and Wittgensteinian logical atomism. According to this interpretation, 'the being of an account', which elementary names combine to form, is the propositional structure of a statement or declarative sentence. What in effect the dream theorist is trying to achieve, on this view, is the drawing of a distinction between *saying*, which requires propositional complexity, and mere *mentioning*, which does not: names merely mention their referents, whereas statements—*logoi*, the word standardly translated as 'accounts'—say something. (See, e.g., Russell 1956, pp. 187–8; Wittgenstein 1922, §§ 3.14–3.142, 3.144, 3.221.)

Ryle and McDowell have plainly been influenced by a verbal similarity between the dream theory's treatment of the *logos* as an interweaving of names and the way the same metaphor is deployed in a passage occurring towards the end of the *Sophist* (262d3–6), where the Eleatic Stranger describes the composition of a basic *logos*, which in this context clearly has to mean something like 'sentence'. As Ryle translates the crucial text,

> A sentence (*logos*) does not merely name but gets you somewhere (*perainei ti*) by weaving together verbs with names [or nouns?]. Hence we say that it says (*legei*) [or tells or states] something and does not merely name something, and in fact it is to this woven fabric (*plegmati*) that we give the name 'sentence' (*logos*). (Ryle 1990, pp. 42–3. Cf. Burnyeat 1990, p. 197)

And the metaphor, following its enthusiastic adoption by Aristotle in the *Categories*, entered the tradition. When Wittgenstein sought an image in the *Tractatus* to convey the way names are combined in an elementary sentence he admittedly chose a different metaphor:

> Im Sachverhalt hängen die Gegenstände ineinander, wie die Glieder einer Kette.... Der Elementarsatz besteht aus Namen. Er ist ein Zusammenhang, eine Verkettung, von Namen.

> In the state of affairs the objects hang in one another, like the links of a chain.... The elementary sentence consists of names. It is a nexus, a concatenation, of names. (1922, §§ 2.03, 4.22)

But one feels that he might just as well have written Verflechtung ('interweaving') instead of Verkettung ('linkage'). (Where Wittgenstein, exploiting the natural genius of the German language, can have the root word 'Kette' reappear in 'Verkettung', English, following its natural genius, can deploy a neat *figura etymologica* in the correlates 'chain' and 'con*cate*nation'.)

Despite the superficial similarity between the language of the dream and the theory of discourse put forward at the end of the *Sophist*, it is clear on closer examination that the metaphor of interweaving is in fact deployed quite differently by the two dialogues, and that Ryle's and McDowell's propositional reading of the dream is, purely as a matter of exegesis, misguided. The dream theorist aims to tell us what knowledge, not meaningful discourse in general, is, and he does so in terms of the formula 'knowledge is true judgement together with a *logos*'. But if *logos* here meant 'sentence', that would imply that a true judgement as such was not yet in propositional form, which is absurd, and is in any case explicitly rejected by Socrates in his subsequent discussion of the dream (206d–e). Hence the 'account' that the dream theorist adds to true judgement to obtain knowledge cannot be mere propositional form; it must be something like an analysis or definition of the object of knowledge.[3] But my present interest in the propositional interpretation of the dream concerns not the question of its exegetical adequacy but its significance as an intertextual move in the modern reception of the *Theaetetus* and of the logical atomists. For if the Platonic justification of the interpretation derives from the supposed echoes of the dream theory in the *Sophist*, there can be no doubt that, both for Ryle and for McDowell, at a subliminal level the propositional reading is really being driven by the interesting, if not quite exact, parallels that we can draw between the dream's atomistic posture and what we find in the *Tractatus* and Russell's 1918 lectures.

Interesting parallels, but not quite exact. McDowell urges caution on us before we leap too readily to the conclusion that the dream theory anticipates the Tractarian doctrine that the elementary sentence is a concatenation of names. He mentions two apparent difficulties in the way of that conclusion (McDowell 1973, pp. 232–4). First, the dream seems to confuse 'know' in the sense of *savoir* with 'know' in the sense of *connaître*; we ought to be concerned with the former sense, but the only elucidation the dream offers of what complexes are ('we and everything else') seems to take us to the latter sense. In fact the dream theorist appears to be concerned with the analysis not of sentences or propositions, but of physical objects. (This of course raises an apparent difficulty for the propositional interpretation of the dream (Bostock 1988, p. 206), but McDowell does not appear to register that point.) Secondly, a proper anticipation of the *Tractatus* on the part of the dream theorist would require

> a clear understanding of the sort of complexity which a form of words must have in order to express a proposition. Now the dream theory, on the [propositional reading] shows awareness of the point that mentioning an individual thing does not constitute saying anything: cf. Wittgenstein, *Philosophical Investigations*, § 49. But its author seems to regard the difference between an account and a name as lying fundamentally in the fact that an account consists of several names. Hence we can

---

[3] See here Bostock 1988, pp. 207–8. Oddly, though Bostock rejects the propositional interpretation of the dream, his overall reading of the *Theaetetus* imposes on it the task of addressing the problem of the unity of the proposition (his own solution to which involves following Frege and Russell in according a special status to predicates/verbs: pp. 274–9). So in Bostock's story Ryle is trounced at the tactical level only to return strategically triumphant.

object as follows. If mentioning an individual thing does not constitute saying any-thing, mentioning several things, successively, does not constitute saying anything either. That performance might, perhaps, amount to mentioning a single complex thing; but saying something is not the same as mentioning a single complex thing. (McDowell 1973, pp. 232–3)

The *Tractatus*, by contrast, does not, according to McDowell, obscure the distinction between naming and saying. That is because, whereas 'the significance of an account in the dream theory' is 'exhausted by the significance of its names', a Tractarian elementary sentence is a *concatenation*, not a mere list, of names, and the fact that the names are concatenated in the way they are *says that* the corresponding objects are configured in a particular way.[4] McDowell considers the possibility that the weaving image of the dream might serve the same function in its theory as the doctrine of concatenation does in the *Tractatus*, namely to secure propositional structure for what would otherwise be a mere congeries of words. But he rejects the suggestion, and concludes that 'the resemblances between the dream theory and the *Tractatus*, though superficially quite striking, are not, ultimately, very important' (McDowell 1973, p. 234).

In making these points McDowell is to a large extent following Ryle, who repeatedly insists both on the non-reducibility of knowing in the sense of *savoir* to knowing in the sense of *connaître* (see, e.g., Ryle 1990, pp. 26–7), and on a distinction between merely mentioning several things and saying something (see, e.g., Ryle 1990, pp. 30–42). One difference between them is this. McDowell thinks that Plato corrects the second mistake in the *Sophist*, at 261c–262e, where the Eleatic Stranger distinguishes a part of the basic *logos* (the name) whose function is to mention its topic from a part of the *logos* (the verb) whose function is to say something about that topic, by contrast with the dream the-ory, whose basic *logos* comprises an undifferentiated class of names; Ryle, on the other hand, appears to think that the dream theory already implicitly has the *Sophist*'s dis-tinction.[5] But that difference is perhaps less significant than might at first sight appear, since McDowell allows that, though indeed 'for the purpose of clarifying a distinction between saying and mentioning which is to be applicable to the language which we actually speak, the line to follow is that of the *Sophist* rather than that of the *Tractatus*' (McDowell 1973, p. 234), reflection on the picture theory of the *Tractatus* shows that 'in order to distinguish saying from mentioning, it is not essential that one should, as in the *Sophist*, distinguish different kinds of constituent in the verbal expression of a proposi-tion' (McDowell 1973, p. 233).

Neither of these attempts to drive a wedge between the dream theory, on the propo-sitional interpretation of it, and the *Tractatus*, seems to me cogent. As to the first, it is possible to read Plato, at least in the *Theaetetus*, as subscribing to the view that 'we and

---

[4] McDowell 1973, pp. 233–4. Cf. Griffin 1964, pp. 124–6.

[5] See Ryle 1990, pp. 25, 28, where Ryle seems to think that the *Theaetetus* already contains the message that 'a mistake cannot be the misidentification of a subject-piece A with a predicate-piece B; nor, by implication, can a truth be the identification of a subject-piece A with a predicate-piece B'. Cf. Burnyeat 1990, p. 155.

everything else' are propositionally structured, or at any rate structured in such a way that an analysis of language down to elementary sentences, along Tractarian lines, would disclose that structure (see here Burnyeat 1990, pp. 159–64). Secondly, Wittgenstein says no more about the relation of concatenation than the dream theorist says about his weaving image. It is true that, according to the picture theory of the *Tractatus*, the fact that a sentence is a *concatenation* of names—it is itself a fact, not a mere jumble of words (*Wörtergemisch*)—is supposed to account for the unity of the sentence (Wittgenstein 1922, §§ 3.14–3.142), in concert, perhaps, with the point that a sentence is a *function* of its component expressions (Wittgenstein 1922, §§ 3.318, 4.24). But Wittgenstein tells us next to nothing about how the unified sentence is established—how we should answer his own question, *wie kommt der Satzverband zustande?* (Wittgenstein 1922, § 4.221)—and the fact that mere lists *also* concatenate their component words, and are *also* (presumably) to be conceived as functions of them, should warn us not to credit Wittgenstein with a high degree of clarity on this issue: in effect he really gets no further with his doctrine of concatenation than the dream theorist does with his weaving image. Both accounts remain at an essentially metaphorical level.

29.3 SENTENCES AND COMPLEX NAMES

In the long passage quoted above, McDowell concludes that 'saying something is not the same as mentioning a single complex thing'. There is clearly a fallacy at work in the progress to this conclusion. In its general form it is the fallacy of composition: it simply does not follow, from the premiss that mentioning one primary element does not amount to saying anything, that mentioning several such elements does not do so either; still less does it follow that mentioning a single *complex* thing does not amount to saying anything. Parts and wholes do not have to have—indeed necessarily do not have—the same properties. Surprisingly, we encounter versions of this fallacy quite commonly in McDowell's writings.[6] And Ryle commits it as well. He considers the suggestion that sentences are themselves names, and comments that

> since names are not statements, they cannot do what statements can, namely express knowledge (savoir) or belief; and they cannot be true or false. But now we are told that statements are themselves higher-order names, names of unitary objects of a queer sort. But if so construed, then they in their turn cannot express knowledge (savoir) or belief. Uttering them would just be *nominating* or *mentioning* these queer complex objects and so could not be true or false telling—and therefore not telling at all.... What is said or told in a sentence is not just *another* subject of predication. Saying or telling is one thing, naming is another. (1990, p. 34)[7]

---

[6] For another example in the *Theaetetus* commentary, see pp. 256–7; for occurrences of the fallacy elsewhere in McDowell's œuvre, see Gaskin 2006, pp. 121–7.

[7] Cf. Ryle 1971, II, p. 358: 'Saying is not naming and naming is not saying.'

Again, we see a movement from the idea that since elementary names are not statements, complex names cannot be statements either: but this just does not follow.

In order to pin the fallacy on Ryle, I have glossed his use of 'names' in the first clause of the quotation as 'elementary names'. That seems to me not only exegetically correct but also dialectically fair, for the following reason. Ryle clearly agrees with the dilemmatic argument which Socrates offers against the dream theorist at *Theaetetus* 203a–205e. The dream theorist claimed that elements are unknowable, complexes knowable. Against this, Socrates contends that if, on the one hand, a complex has parts, then it is identical with those parts and so is knowable or unknowable to just the same extent as they are, but that if, on the other hand, a complex does not have parts then it is not a whole made up of parts, and so is simple, in which case, again, it will not differ from other simples in point of knowability or unknowability. But a complex either has parts or it does not; whichever of these options we choose, it seems that the complex cannot be differentiated from elements along the lines proposed by the dream. This argument evidently commits (in establishing the first horn of the dilemma) a version of the fallacy that is here in question (see Burnyeat 1990, pp. 191–205). But Ryle fails to notice the fallacy, and endorses the argument on more than one occasion (1971, I, pp. 37–41; 1990, pp. 30–4). So it seems reasonable to suppose that in offering the argument I quoted above, Ryle is again being taken in by Socrates' fallacious refutation of the dream. McDowell, by contrast, recognizes the faultiness of Socrates' reasoning (1973, p. 243), so that the occurrence of the fallacy of composition in his comparison between Plato's dream theory and Wittgenstein's picture theory must be independently motivated (and can be so motivated, I have suggested, by noting the fact that he succumbs to it on several independent occasions).

In opposition to the fallacious deduction urged by Ryle and McDowell, that mentioning several things, or a single complex thing, cannot amount to saying anything given that mentioning a single individual thing does not do so, we have Moore's view that

> a proposition is nothing other than a complex concept. The difference between a concept and a proposition, in virtue of which alone the latter can be called true or false, would seem to lie merely in the simplicity of the former. A proposition is a synthesis of concepts. (Moore 1993, p. 5; Ryle 1990, p. 36)

Note that we are not talking about sentences here, but about propositions in the modern sense, that is, the meanings of declarative sentences. With that proviso, Moore's 'synthesis of concepts' is surely just a notational variant of the dream theorist's interweaving of names, and of Wittgenstein's concatenation of names. I see no reason to deny that if, as McDowell thinks, in Wittgenstein's case the sheer relation of concatenation is enough to unify the elementary sentence, then, contra McDowell, the dream theorist's interweaving of names is enough to unify his *logos*, and likewise (shifting levels of discourse) Moore's synthesis of concepts is enough to unify the proposition.

But these things are not enough. A concatenation, or interweaving, or synthesis of names or of their referents is insufficient to constitute the unity of the sentence or of its corresponding proposition because these linguistic or ontological features can be duplicated by a mere list of names at the level of symbolic language and by a mere aggregate of objects at the level of expressed meaning. And, as I have urged elsewhere (Gaskin 2008, esp. § 5), the fact that, as Plato notices in the *Sophist*, words in natural language do not all have a uniform grammatical function but serve a multiplicity of different syntactic and semantic tasks, does not, contrary to an implication of McDowell's (quoted above: 1973, p. 234), help. For a mere list can duplicate not merely a concatenation of grammatically congruent names—such as, we may presume, compose the elementary sentences of the *Tractatus* and perhaps also the *logoi* of Socrates' dream—but a concatenation of words discharging any grammatical functions, such as 'Theaetetus' and 'sits', arranged in that order. In other words, the grammatical congruence of concatenated words does not suffice for their combined unity in the relevant sense: there is nothing in the sheer concatenated group of words 'Theaetetus sits' that makes it a sentence rather than a list. Our account of sentential and propositional unity must draw its sustenance from elsewhere.[8]

Of course, the fact that the sheer concatenation of grammatically congruent words does not, in itself, suffice to constitute a sentence as opposed to a mere list does not mean that sentences cannot *be* such concatenations of words, just that their status as sentences has its source in more than their identity *as* such concatenations. Obviously sentences are *at least* such concatenations, and the point applies to elementary Tractarian sentences and to the *logoi* of Socrates' dream as much as it does to sentences of natural language like 'Theaetetus sits'. So sentences can indeed *be* composed of sheer names: it is not that, as perhaps Ryle thought, the dream theory can only be rescued from incoherence if the syntactic sophistication of the *Sophist*—the claim that, in the basic case, the *logos* comprises a name and a verb—is read back into it. McDowell is right that the picture theory of the *Tractatus* provides a means to construe strings of grammatically undifferentiated names as saying something; he was only wrong to deny the same resource to the dream theorist.

But why, in that case, does Ryle think, with McDowell's concurrence, that sentences cannot be, as he puts it, 'higher-order names' referring to complex objects (1990, p. 38), and that uttering such names 'would just be *nominating* or *mentioning* these queer complex objects and so could not be true or false telling—and therefore not telling at all' (1990, p. 34)? For it is clear that, even waiving the fallacious argument that led him there, Ryle thinks that the relevant complex objects are 'queer' (1990, pp. 33, 34), and that the true ones have 'the queer *extra* property of being Factual' (1990, p. 35). But the thesis that sentences are not higher-order names is not at all obvious. On the contrary, while certainly there is a distinction between a sentence and a list, and something must constitute that difference, it by no means follows from that acknowledgement that a sentence is not a name—a special sort of name, one that refers to a special sort of object. A sentence is not an *elementary* name: that much is agreed on all sides. But it could still be a *complex* name, as well as being simple in a higher-order respect: that is, though in one

---

[8] In fact, as I argue at length in my *The Unity of the Proposition*, that unity resides in the way that the proposition (by contrast with a mere aggregate) generates Bradley's regress, which thereby emerges as an innocent, constitutive regress; predictably, Ryle regards it as vicious (1990, p. 38).

sense the sentence would be composite, the upshot of its being unified in the relevant way would be to overlay a higher-order simplicity on its lower-level complexity, and correspondingly in respect of its complex referent. *Any* unity is, in that sense, both complex and simple.

Sentences cannot be elementary names, because we need to discern semantic structure in them if we are to accommodate their role in inference (see Gaskin 2008, § 6). The logical atomists denied that sentences are names of any sort, even complex names, because, in part, they were working with a semantical model that ruled out the possibility that a piece of symbolic language might *both* be a name *and* say something. And they recognized, correctly, that complex linguistic expressions *do* say that the referents of their components are configured in some particular way. But if we drop the unwarranted segregation of (complex) naming from saying, we can allow that such expressions both name their (complex) referents and say that the components of those referents are configured in some particular way. It must be agreed, I think, that the higher-order complexes in question are true or false in a primitive sense, as Moore states in the passage we have quoted; but does that make them 'queer'? Does Ryle's insistence that sentences are *not* names supply him with an explanatory account of what their truth or falsity consists in? The doctrine that truth and falsity attach primitively to worldly complexes (and, correspondingly, to sentences taken as names of these complexes) might be undermined if it could be shown that there was better to be had, but that prospect is something about which we are entitled to be rather sceptical,[9] and certainly Ryle makes no move that I can see, in his various discussions of the dream, to indicate how he thinks such an explanatory account would go. Notice that Ryle cheats when he speaks of higher-order complexes in question as having 'the queer *extra* property of being Factual': in spelling 'factual' with an upper-case 'F', he first foists a queerness on the extra property only to 'discover' it in the sequel. But there is no call for the mystification: the complexes in question are factual, when they are, in a quite ordinary, lower-case sense.

Why was it not evident to Ryle that his claim 'What is said or told in a sentence is not just *another* subject of predication' is false?[10] After all, if I say '*That Socrates is wise* is true' or '... is familiar to all readers of Plato', it is surely obvious that I am predicating truth, or its familiarity to Plato's readers, of *that Socrates is wise*. There are, I think, two principal reasons why it might be held—and why Ryle and McDowell do hold—that a sentence cannot be a complex name, and that mentioning a complex object is not the same thing as saying something: the first has to do with the *savoir–connaître* distinction, the second with the problem of falsity. There is, in addition, a widespread confusion which may lend a specious plausibility to the error, as I take it to be. In the remainder of this section I shall look at these points in turn.

First, it might be thought that someone who took sentences to be names of complex entities—let us call them propositions—would be obliged to conflate knowing a truth,

---

[9] See here again Gaskin 2006, ch. VI, § 4, and 2008, §§ 23–4.

[10] Cf. 1971, I, p. 187: 'The senses of complete or incomplete sense-conveying expressions cannot have said about them any of the things that can be said about Socrates.'

which is really an exercise of *savoir*, with being acquainted with (*connaître*) a true proposition (Ryle 1990, pp. 33–5). And of course it is easy to show that these two achievements are *toto caelo* distinct: I am acquainted with the (true) proposition that Socrates is wise just by virtue of understanding the sentence 'Socrates is wise'; but that knowledge is not enough to assure me of that sentence's truth. And obviously it will not help to insert an explicit mention of truth into the relevant sentence: being acquainted with the proposition *that it is true that Socrates is wise* does not suffice for knowing (*savoir*) the truth of either that proposition or the simple proposition *that Socrates is wise*. As Ryle puts it: 'knowing or believing is not just being aware of or grasping an atomic or a molecular object' (1990, pp. 35–6). This point is correct, but I do not see that it tells against applying an 'object and designation' model to sentential meaning (cf. Wittgenstein 1958, I, § 293). *Savoir* is one status, *connaître* another, and no one need be saddled with the mistaken view that either is reducible to the other—or at any rate that the former is reducible to the latter.

The second reason why Ryle and McDowell think that the 'object and designation' model of sentential reference is problematic is that the approach allegedly makes difficulties for falsity. How can there be false propositions, or false objectives (to use Meinong's terminology) *in re*? Ryle again:

> With this sort of view of the import of propositions there really does arise Socrates' early question: How can I believe the thing that is not? For, on this view, a false statement means something and so denotes a perfectly genuine molecular object and one which I grasp or have in mind when I make or understand the statement. It really is there for me to grasp. But if so, then what I grasp is a real object (though a molecular one). How then am I wrong or mistaken if I do not merely grasp it but accept or believe it? Conversely, if I *am* wrong or mistaken in believing it, it seems to follow that there must not exist the objective to be grasped. But how could I believe what isn't there even for me to have in mind? (1990, p. 36. Cf. McDowell 1982, pp. 129–32; Burnyeat 1990, p. 78)

There are two points to be made in reply to these questions. First, the implied argument would prove too much: for even if sentences do not name anything, nominalizations of sentences presumably do, and what they name can be objects of belief or knowledge (cf. Bostock 1988, p. 195 n36). Nothing that Ryle says in the above quotation would not apply to the complex object *Theaetetus' flight*, conceived as the referent of the nominalization of the sentence 'Theaetetus flies'. Presumably there is a good answer to the question: how can I grasp the complex object denoted by the nominalization 'Theaetetus' flight', namely *Theaetetus' flight*, when there is no such thing as *Theaetetus' flight*? And presumably, if there is a good answer to that question, it will also serve to deal with Ryle's difficulties. Nothing is gained by denying that sentences are referring expressions on the basis of an alleged problem about falsity if exactly the same problem—assuming that it is a problem—confronts us anyway in connection with linguistic items that everyone must admit to be referring expressions. That takes us to our second point in response to Ryle, which is that the answer to our question about complex objects like *Theaetetus' flight*, and the answer to the parallel question about propositions *in re*, is that being the meaning of a linguistic expression and being true or obtaining are two quite different things. The proposition *that Theaetetus flies* exists as the meaning or referent of the sentence 'Theaetetus flies', and in that sense is a perfectly good worldly object, but it does not follow that it is true. Similarly, the complex object *Theaetetus' flight* exists as the meaning or referent of the nominal phrase 'Theaetetus' flight', and in that sense is a perfectly good worldly object, but it does not follow that it obtains. Being in the world is one thing; being factual is quite another.

Similar issues arise in connection with negation, and here too we find Ryle arguing that the phenomenon of negation presents an obstacle to construing sentences as referring expressions (1990, p. 30). And he is by no means alone. David Wiggins asks how we should represent the meaning of 'It is not the case that Theaetetus is flying', given that 'Theaetetus is flying' displays or refers to the proposition or situation of Theaetetus' flying, which he represents as <flying Theaetetus> (Wiggins 1971, p. 282). He points out correctly that, if the one proposition or situation is genuinely to *negate* the other, 'we must somehow make <flying Theaetetus> into a *constituent* of <Theaetetus does not fly>'. He continues:

> We then reach something like <not <Theaetetus flies>>—which is presumably the situation of there 'being no such situation as <Theaetetus flies>'. But how exactly does the designation '<Theaetetus flies>' figure in the designation '<There is no such situation as the situation <Theaetetus flies>>', which is surely the only reading we can give '<not <Theaetetus flies>>'? By itself, '<Theaetetus flies>' is by the nature of the theory an ostension or display of a situation.... But this cannot be its role in '<not <Theaetetus flies>>'. For here the use of this complex designation would commit the user both to display flying Theaetetus, and simultaneously to display the non-displayability of flying Theaetetus. But this is an utterly self-undermining project.... What we have to conclude from this is that in our < ... > notation '<not <Theaetetus flies>>' does not display <Theaetetus flies> at all, ... [W]hatever alternative role we assign to '<Theaetetus flies>' within the more complex designation, it cannot be the same role as it has when it figures by itself. But that was what we needed in order to explain negation. It follows that there is something wrong with what we intended in the first place by the < ... > notation. (1971, pp. 282–3)

Something must have gone awry here: we can assure ourselves of that by showing that, once again, the argument proves too much. There is nothing in Wiggins's argument that would not apply to nominalizations of sentences and their complex objectual referents: starting from 'Theaetetus' flight' and 'Theaetetus' non-flight', we can repeat the argument, *mutatis mutandis*, to show that it is illicit to construe such nominalizations as names of situations or states of affairs. But that is an unacceptable conclusion, by anybody's lights; so the argument must contain a mistake. What has gone wrong, in detail, is that Wiggins is mistaken in his identification of

<not <Theaetetus flies>>

with

<There is no such situation as the situation <Theaetetus flies>>.

The former situation is the meaning of 'Theaetetus is not flying', the latter the meaning of 'There is no such situation as the situation <Theaetetus flies>', and these two meanings are not at all the same. The former meaning does indeed presuppose the existence— the *existence*, not the *truth* or *obtaining*—of the situation <Theaetetus flies>; so indeed does the latter meaning, but since this latter meaning purports to be the situation of the former meaning's *not existing*, it is absurd. So Wiggins is right to brand the latter meaning (<There is no such situation as the situation <Theaetetus flies>>) as absurd, but since it is the former meaning (<not <Theaetetus flies>>) that is the negation *in re* of the situation <Theaetetus flies>, and since the former does not amount to the latter, no absurdity from the direction of negation threatens the doctrine that declarative sentences refer to what Wiggins calls situations, and what I have called propositions.

There is another reason—a diagnostic reason this time, rather than one they would proffer themselves—why commentators have been misled into denying that mentioning a complex object can amount to saying something. They are prone to confuse semantics with pragmatics: in particular, they conflate *saying* and *asserting*. Of course it is correct that mentioning an object does not amount to *asserting* anything. But it is irrelevant to bring pragmatic considerations to bear in this context, where we are exclusively concerned with semantics, and in particular with the question what is distinctive of the declarative sentence. What is distinctive of it, as Aristotle taught us (*De Interpretatione* 17a2–3), is that it can be true or false. But that property of the declarative sentence has nothing to do with whether it is asserted on any occasion. When, for instance, I utter a conditional sentence, the antecedent of my conditional (which is a declarative sentence) is not something I assert, but it is something I say. Depending on context, the conditional as a whole may also be something I say but do not assert. In some of its uses, 'say' functions as a synonym of 'assert', but not in all, as the above examples illustrate. Had commentators reflected on this kind of example, they might have been less ready to hold that saying is semantically distinct from referring to a complex object.[11] If, with Ryle and McDowell, we read Socrates' dream through Tractarian spectacles, then however anachronistic and exegetically mistaken this exercise may be, it at least shows us that we may think of sentences as complex names, without detriment to their capacity to say something true or false.

29.4 LETTERS, SYLLABLES, AND THE CONTEXT PRINCIPLE

Ryle likes to connect what he takes to be a fundamental distinction between names and sentences with Plato's model of letters and syllables, which makes a number of

---

[11] For an especially clear case of the muddle, see Wiggins 1971, pp. 280–1. Note that Ryle is not always guilty of the confusion: see Ryle 1963, p. 245.

appearances in the late dialogues.[12] And he argues that that model has a further purpose in Plato's thought, namely to represent something like the point of Frege's context principle. Thus we are told in his paper on letters and syllables that

> Word meanings or concepts are not proposition components but propositional differences. They are distinguishables, not detachables; abstractables, not extractables—as are the audible contributions made to the voiced monosyllable 'box' by the consonants 'b' and 'x'. (1971, I, p. 58. Cf. I, pp. 183–4; II, pp. 358–9)

The idea, familiar from the exegesis of Frege, is that words and their meanings are not isolable components of the sentence and proposition; they are not independent building blocks out of which sentence and proposition can be conceived to be constructed, as though words and their meanings came first and then, as Bentham, in splendid satiric vein, continues the absurd saga, 'finding these terms endowed, each of them, somehow or other, with a signification of its own, at a subsequent period some ingenious persons took them in hand, and formed them into propositions' (Bentham 1843, vi, § 1, p. 322). Rather, the sentence is theoretically prior to the word, and the proposition theoretically prior to the word meaning. Sentences and propositions come first, and words and their meanings are abstracted therefrom. One of Ryle's expositions of the point is every bit as eloquent as Bentham's: 'Thought does not begin with a vocabulary and then trick this vocabulary out with a syntax; its vocabulary is syntactical from the start' (1971, I, p. 221). The point is well taken, though I am not sure how far Plato can be credited with having discovered it.

Actually, Ryle's position is slightly subtler than this account indicates. He distinguishes between spoken and written syllables, arguing that the former provide a model of the context principle in its application to sentences and words, but that the latter do not. Individual spoken sounds are abstractions from spoken syllables; written syllables, by contrast, are constructed out of antecedently identifiable written letters. Spoken sounds are features, not isolable parts, of the spoken syllables from which they are abstracted; written letters are straightforwardly parts of the written syllables they go to compose (Ryle 1990, pp. 33, 43–4). Now although Ryle is right to interpret the context principle in the way he does, and the analogy with spoken syllables may be helpful in elucidating the point at issue, he is wrong, as we have seen, to argue for the theoretical priority of the sentence on the basis of Socrates' fallacious refutation of the dream. He is wrong to suppose that, if the sentence *were* composed of antecedently constituted, independently available words, then it would be a mere complex name and so unfit to say anything. And it is a good thing that Ryle is wrong about this, because we *do* want there to be a sense in which words are constituted in advance of their entering into sentences. This sense is an epistemological one and is what Dummett calls the priority of words over sentences in the 'order of recognition': that is, if we are to understand a sentence, we already need to

---

[12] See, e.g., 1971, I, p. 56; 1990, p. 31. Cf. McDowell 1973, p. 248.

know what its component words are and how they are put together. This priority does not conflict, but is perfectly consistent, with the opposite priority which the context principle insists on. This opposite priority is a metaphysical one, and is what Dummett calls the priority of sentences over words in the 'order of explanation': that is, words get their theoretical point by virtue of their capacity to figure in sentences (Dummett 1981, p. 4). So we might improve on Ryle's position by offering the relation between written syllables and their component letters as an analogy for the epistemological priority of the word, and spoken syllables and their component sounds as an analogy for the metaphysical priority of the sentence.

But what is odd about the way Ryle expounds the analogy, in the paper on letters and syllables, between sentences and spoken syllables is that, though he starts by applying the lesson of the context principle uniformly to *all* words—they are all said to be 'distinguishables, not detachables; abstractables, not extractables'—he soon shifts to applying it differentially to grammatically nominal and non-nominal parts of the sentence. Thus we are told that 'live verbs'—that is, inflected verbs—

> are snatches from speech, that is, from the *using* of words. Live verbs could not feature in lists. They occur only in contexts; … What we automatically see to hold of the meanings of live verbs, we can then without difficulty see to hold also of 'and', 'if', 'therefore', 'not', 'some', 'any', 'a', and 'the'. It would be as vain an enterprise to try to examine the meanings of these words out of any sentence context as to try to examine the noise for which the character 'b' stands, out of the phonetic context of any syllable. Russell was forced by this sort of consideration … to realize, with Frege, that the notion of the sense of an integral sentence … is prior to the notion of the senses of at least some words in it. To ask after the meaning of a live verb or of a conjunction or of 'not' is to ask what *would* be being said with it if someone did put it to work. (1971, I, p. 68)

But the doctrine no longer applies, apparently, to words like 'Socrates' or 'wisdom'. Or does it? Consulting parallel passages in Ryle's writings brings no illumination on this question, but only a recurrence of the exegetical problem. In the posthumously published paper on logical atomism, having assured us that both nouns and verbs can be, as he often puts it, 'algebraized away' (see, e.g., 1971, I, p. 70)—that is, replaced by a variable—he goes on to affirm that verbs, adjectives, conjunctions, particles, adverbs, prepositions, and the word 'not', are special in that they 'quite patently flourish sentential-strings' (1990, pp. 24, 45–6). These claims are in tension, because if verbs as well as nouns can be 'algebraized away', that surely implies that nouns as well as verbs can 'flourish sentential-strings', in which case there would be nothing special about the fact that verbs, adjectives, and so on do so. Again, in some of Ryle's discussions of phenomenology we find the same uneasy opposition between hints that the context principle applies to all words, on the one hand, and restrictions of it to 'live' verbs, adjectives, and the rest of the inventory of non-nominal expressions, on the other: general terms like 'pleasure', 'conscience', and 'hope' are admitted to the charmed circle of words that, as Russell put it, 'bring in the form of the proposition' (1956, p. 205), but only because these are—so

Ryle thinks—obviously nominalizations of live verbs, and so only in virtue of an alleged underlying predicative form (see 1971, I, pp. 183–8, 220–1; II, p. 14).

But the restricted position is hopeless: if the context principle applies to any words, then it applies to all of them without distinction. In any sense in which we cannot give the meaning of 'sits' in isolation from its role in a complete sentence, in just the same sense we cannot give the meaning of 'Theaetetus' either (see further Gaskin 2008, esp. chs. 3 and 4). Conversely, in any sense in which a name like 'Theaetetus' can be 'algebraized away', in just the same sense verbs, conjunctions, and the rest can also be 'algebraized away', as developments in formal logic in the twentieth century have shown. These developments simply gave concrete expression to what was already fully clear to Bentham and even, in some moods, to Frege, despite his unfortunate doctrine of the peculiarly saturated status of names: that is to say, it was clear to Frege at least sometimes that names enjoy no exemption from the full force of the context principle. Ryle too, it seems, on occasion sees the point that verbs as well as nouns can be 'algebraized away', though he forgets that impartiality at moments of heightened Fregean fervour.

That impartiality is forgotten, or perhaps ignored, because Ryle thinks the non-nominal status of certain words is crucial to the solution of the unity problem (1971, I, p. 220), and because only if we recognize that status can we pursue conceptual investigations properly:

> For the philosopher has apparently to try not just to deploy but to describe the concepts with which he is concerned. He has to try to say what Pleasure and Existence are. He has to try, necessarily in vain, to attach object-characterizing predicates to non-object-mentioning expressions. But by no prestidigitation can the live verb 'enjoys' or the live verb 'exists' (except in inverted commas), be made grammatical subjects to live verbs. The philosopher's description of a concept is bound to terminate in a stammer. (1971, I, p. 187)

But both of these motivations are insufficient. The first fails because, as we recall from the dream theory and the *Tractatus*, sentences *can* be exclusively composed of names, which shows that 'bringing in the form of the proposition' cannot really be proprietary to verbs or other non-nominal expressions. The second reason fails because the claim that all words are names need not be a grammatical claim but a logical one, and so need not be upset by the observation that non-nominal words are not congruent with nouns. The suggestion is that we have no good reason to reserve the philosophically pregnant name–object duo to our treatment of the semantics of some words and not of others; on the contrary, the context principle gives us good reason precisely not to do this. And, if we are in the business of pursuing conceptual investigations, it hardly seems to make any difference whether we think about the meaning of the allegedly non-nominal 'exists' as opposed to examining the abstract object existence, or to be intellectually sounder to reflect on the allegedly syncategorematic functions of 'not' and 'if' rather than on the properties of negation and conditionality.

29.5 Names and the Unity of the Proposition

So far as my polemical purposes in this chapter are concerned, I have been defending the theses (i) that the context principle gives us good reason to say that all words are names, and (ii) that we may also characterize sentences as (complex) names, without detriment to the unity of the proposition or to the possibility of falsity. We have seen that the considerations raised by Ryle, and following him by McDowell, against these two theses are not compelling. In his paper 'The Theory of Meaning', Ryle called the view that all words are names a 'monstrous howler' (1971, II, p. 353), and one of his most familiar contributions to the analytic tradition has been his drawing of our attention to the so-called 'Fido'/Fido fallacy, which is precisely the error, as Ryle takes it to be, of assimilating all words to names. Ryle's presumptive exposure of this fallacy is linked in his wider thinking to a characteristic—indeed fateful—move in the analytic tradition: the idea that surface syntax is or can be a misleading index of underlying logical form, the thesis that there are such things as—to borrow the title of one of Ryle's best-known papers—'systematically misleading expressions', expressions whose semantic properties are in some way concealed or misrepresented by their syntax. The conviction that there are such expressions is, one might say, a central tenet of early analytic philosophy, and in Ryle's hands it manifests itself in two principal ways: he suggests, famously, that sensation words are not, despite appearances, names of sensations; and he argues, as we have seen, that the nominal appearance of general terms gives way, on analysis, to an underlying predicative form.

In the case of the language of sensations, Ryle's rejection of the objectual status of sensations and correspondingly of the nominal status of words such as 'pain' and 'twinge' is driven by his hostility to what he calls 'Descartes' myth'—the myth of the ghost in the machine (see Ryle 1963, *passim*, esp. pp. 199 and 204). But to suppose that one needs to deny that sensations are objects and that sensation words are their names in order to dismantle the Cartesian myth is to overshoot the target. I can refer to my headache as a bona-fide object without any implication that it is a private object in the philosophically repugnant sense explored by the later Wittgenstein. Interestingly, we find a very similar excess of zeal in Wittgenstein's own discussion of privacy, where in the notorious 'beetle in the box' passage we are told, quite generally, that 'if we construe the grammar of the expression of sensation on the model of "object and designation", the object drops out of consideration as irrelevant' (Wittgenstein 1958, I, § 293). What Wittgenstein should have said—but it is clear from other remarks in the vicinity of this passage that his failure to do so was not a mere slip on his part—was that if we construe the grammar of the purported expression of *private* sensation on the model of 'object and designation', then the *putative private* object drops out of consideration as irrelevant.[13]

---

[13] See on this point McDowell 1998, p. 283; and Gaskin 2006, p. 146.

As for Ryle's animus against general terms, his eliminative programme, like so much early analytic philosophy, is inspired by Russell's Theory of Descriptions, for he agrees with the early Wittgenstein that 'It is Russell's merit to have shown that the apparent logical form of a sentence need not be its real form' (Wittgenstein 1922, § 4.0031). As well as universals, Ryle thinks that the analytical method will demonstrate the spurious nature of the claims to objecthood of places, ideas, thoughts, meanings, concepts, and propositions.[14] The notion that sentences mislead us as to their underlying logical form—the notion that there *is* such a thing as underlying logical form, potentially diverging from surface syntax—is, when one stops to think about it, an extremely odd one, though it is so familiar that it has the status of the merest platitude, not only in modern philosophy of language, but also in syntax theory in the Chomskian tradition, where it takes the shape of the 'displacement' principle, the thesis that expressions may need to undergo syntactic movement before they can be interpreted.[15] I cannot here address the issue of logical form in full generality. As far as Ryle is concerned, we have seen that one of his motivations for rejecting the theses (i) and (ii) that I mentioned at the beginning of this section was that he believed that if we do not repudiate them we forfeit our entitlement to the unity of the proposition, and it is on this point that I wish to focus in closing.

Ryle castigates Russell for his failure to sense the impending forfeiture—in effect for his failure to descry the full import of his own revolutionary treatment of definite descriptions: 'Russell early realized the point which Mill did not very explicitly make, though Plato had made it, that a sentence is not a list. It says one thing; it is not just an inventory of a lot of things. But only much later, if at all, did Russell see the full implication of this' (1971, II, p. 359). Russell's doctrine that definite descriptions are 'incomplete symbols' took him in the right direction, Ryle opines, but not far enough:

> The very treatment which had since the Middle Ages been given to such little words as 'and', 'not', 'the', 'some' and 'is' was now given to some other kinds of expressions as well. In effect, though not explicitly, Russell was saying that, e.g., descriptive phrases were as syncategorematic as 'not', 'and' and 'is' had always been allowed to be. Here Russell was on the brink of allowing that the meanings or significations of many kinds of expressions are matters not of *naming* things but of *saying* things. But he was, I think, still held up by the idea that saying is itself just another variety of naming, i.e. naming a complex or an 'objective' or a proposition or a fact—some sort of postulated *Fido rationis*. (1971, II, p. 362)

I have argued here that saying *is* a variety of naming—or at least that the considerations adduced by Ryle and McDowell do not show that it is not. Elsewhere I have suggested

---

[14] 1971, II, pp. 16, 47–9, 54–6. As Michael Beaney points out to me, Ryle later repudiated the particular analytical method he had employed in his paper 'Systematically Misleading Expressions': see Rorty 1967, 305. But it is not clear that he meant thereby to reinstate meanings, propositions, and the rest as genuine objects.

[15] See, e.g., Hornstein, Nunes, and Grohmann 2005, p. 7, who list displacement as being an 'uncontentious' datum of syntactic theory, alongside such theses as the primacy of the sentence, the principle of compositionality, and the recursive nature of language.

that, if the concept of the syncategorematic is to be deployed at all, the context principle forces us to say that all words, not just a select bunch, are syncategorematic (see Gaskin 2008, ch. 3). And this we can affirm without risk of undermining the thesis that all words are names.

Interestingly, in the same paper from which the above quotations were drawn Ryle unwittingly comes close to conceding my main contention. Having told us that the assumption that all words are names is 'easy to demolish', he writes that

> if every single word were a name, then a sentence composed of five words, say 'three is a prime number', would be a list of the five objects named by those five words. But a list, like 'Plato, Aristotle, Aquinas, Locke, Berkeley' is not a sentence. It says nothing, true or false. A sentence, on the contrary, may say something—some one thing—which is true or false. So the words combined into a sentence at least do something jointly which is different from their severally naming the several things that they name if they do name any things. What a sentence means is not decomposable into the set of things which the words in it stand for, if they do stand for things. (1971, II, p. 354)

The passage begins badly with an outrageously poor piece of argumentation. To be sure, a list of names *like the one Ryle mentions* ('Plato, Aristotle, Aquinas, Locke, Berkeley') is not a sentence; but to suppose that from 'Not all *F*s are *G*s' ('Not all lists are sentences') we can deduce 'Not all *G*s are *F*s' ('Not all sentences are lists') is one of the oldest fallacies in the book. So it does not follow, as Ryle implies, that something that *is* a sentence, such as 'Three is a prime number', is not exclusively made up of names. As if in tacit acknowledgement of this point, Ryle proceeds in the second half of the passage as though sentences indeed *could* be exclusively composed of names. For he argues that words combined into a sentence do something jointly which is different from their severally naming the things that they name, if they do name any things, and that what a sentence means— say, a proposition—is not decomposable into the set of things which the words in it stand for. But these points are obviously compatible not only with a sentence's being composed of names, but also with a proposition's being a complex object made up of the things named by the corresponding sentence's component words. For, as we have explored in detail above, it would be fallacious to suppose that, because a bunch of words *severally* name things, they cannot achieve more than that *jointly* when they are put together. And, as I have suggested, when words, which severally are indeed names, come together in a sentence, the first thing they can do is name a complex object; and the second thing they can do is say something. But the complex object named by a sentence—the proposition expressed—is plainly more than just a set or congeries of objects. The point that Ryle is really aiming for here, namely that a sentence is not a *mere* list of names, is compatible, as he almost sees, with its being *at least* a list of names. Despite its unpromising beginning, the above passage seems to come within an ace of conceding that we may assert all words to be names without jeopardizing the unity of the proposition.[16]

---

[16]   I am grateful to the editor for his helpful comments on earlier versions of this chapter.

References

Bentham, J. (1843). *Essay on Language*. In *The Works of Jeremy Bentham*, vol. 8, ed. J. Bowring. Edinburgh: Tait, pp. 94–338.

Bostock, D. (1988). *Plato's Theaetetus*. Oxford: Clarendon Press.

Burnyeat, M. (1990). *The Theaetetus of Plato*. Indianapolis: Hackett.

Chappell, T. (2005). *Reading Plato's Theaetetus*. Indianapolis: Hackett.

Dummett, M. (1981). *Frege: Philosophy of Language*, 2nd edn. London: Duckworth.

Gaskin, R. (2006). *Experience and the World's Own Language: A Critique of John McDowell's Empiricism*. Oxford: Clarendon Press.

—— (2008). *The Unity of the Proposition*. Oxford: Oxford University Press.

Griffin, J. (1964). *Wittgenstein's Logical Atomism*. Oxford: Clarendon Press.

Hornstein, N., J. Nunes, and K. Grohmann (2005). *Understanding Minimalism*. Cambridge: Cambridge University Press.

McDowell, J. (tr.) (1973). *Plato: Theaetetus*. Oxford: Clarendon Press.

—— (1982). 'Falsehood and Not-Being in Plato's *Sophist*'. In M. Schofield and M. Nussbaum (eds.), *Language and Logos: Studies in Ancient Greek Philosophy*. Cambridge: Cambridge University Press, pp. 115–34.

—— (1998). *Mind, Value, and Reality*. Cambridge, MA: Harvard University Press.

Moore, G. E. (1993). 'The Nature of Judgment'. In *G. E. Moore: Selected Writings*, ed. T. Baldwin. London: Routledge, pp. 1–19.

Rorty, R. (ed.) (1967). *The Linguistic Turn: Recent Essays in Philosophical Method*. Chicago: University of Chicago Press.

Russell, B. (1956). 'The Philosophy of Logical Atomism'. In Russell, *Logic and Knowledge: Essays 1901–1950*, ed. R. C. Marsh. London: George Allen & Unwin, pp. 177–281.

Ryle, G. (1963). *The Concept of Mind*. London: Penguin.

—— (1971). *Collected Papers*, 2 vols. London: Hutchinson.

—— (1990). 'Logical Atomism in Plato's *Theaetetus*', *Phronesis* 35: 21–46.

Wiggins, D. (1971). 'Sentence Meaning, Negation, and Plato's Problem of Non-Being'. In G. Vlastos (ed.), *Plato I: Metaphysics and Epistemology*. Garden City, NY: Doubleday, pp. 268–303.

Wittgenstein, L. (1922). *Tractatus Logico-Philosophicus*, tr. C. K. Ogden. London: Routledge & Kegan Paul.

—— (1958). *Philosophische Untersuchungen*, tr. G. E. M. Anscombe as *Philosophical Investigations*, 2nd edn. Oxford: Blackwell.

....

CHAPTER 30

READING THE *TRACTATUS* WITH G. E. M. ANSCOMBE

....

CORA DIAMOND

WITTGENSTEIN wrote in the Preface to the *Tractatus* (*TLP*) that he believed the book to show that the reason philosophical problems are posed is that 'the logic of our language is misunderstood'. At the end of the Preface, he said that he took himself to have in essence arrived at a definitive solution of such problems. The book was meant to revolutionize philosophical thinking. In *An Introduction to Wittgenstein's 'Tractatus'* (1963), Elizabeth Anscombe wrote that almost everything that had been published about the *Tractatus* 'has been wildly irrelevant'.[1] She meant to inaugurate a rethinking of what sort of book the *Tractatus* was and how it should be understood. In this chapter, I want to look at these two intentions together: Wittgenstein's intention of bringing about a revolution in philosophical thinking and Anscombe's of inaugurating a radical change in how the *Tractatus* was read. Looking at Anscombe's intention and at what she does in carrying it out will help us to see what Wittgenstein was hoping to achieve.

In the introduction to her book, Anscombe explains why virtually all that has been said about the *Tractatus* has been fraught with misunderstanding. But the story she tells has problems, and they are the subject of section 30.1 of this chapter. If, however, we look at Anscombe's account of the picture theory, we can take it to demonstrate how she thought the *Tractatus* should be read; and there are lessons to be drawn about what was wrong with the kinds of reading she rejected. The transformation which Anscombe hoped to bring about in how the book was read helped to transform also the study of both Frege and Russell. This latter transformation can help us to see what underlies her claim in the introduction that it was neglect of Frege and over-dependence on Russell that led to the irrelevance of so much of what had been written about the *Tractatus*. An approach to the *Tractatus* can be Russellian in two different senses. It can depend upon reading Russell himself as a Humean thinker, as 'imbued' with empiricism; or it can take

---

[1] I use '*IWT*' as an abbreviation of the title.

from Russell, or at any rate share with Russell, a form of thinking which goes deeper and is not dependent on his empiricism, however nicely it fits with empiricism. I mean the kind of thinking which is described (by Warren Goldfarb and Peter Hylton) as Russell's 'object-based' approach to metaphysics and meaning, and which can be contrasted with Frege's 'judgment-based' approach.[2] Anscombe's reading of the *Tractatus* is un-Russell-ian, in both senses. Section 30.2 is meant to lay out the issues here, first by summarizing Anscombe's account of the picture theory, and then by showing the importance of the contrast between 'object-based' and 'judgment-based' accounts of meaning—its importance for understanding what Anscombe was trying to achieve, and how she differs not just from the readers of Wittgenstein whom she plainly did have in her sights, but also from such later readers as David Pears and Norman Malcolm. Her account of the contrast between Russell and Frege, in her argument for the importance of not neglecting Frege, does not reach to the largely implicit understanding of the contrast that is evident in her treatment of the picture theory. I shall not argue for this, but it seems to me that the character of the contrast begins to come out explicitly in Hidé Ishiguro's 'Use and Reference of Names' (1969). Much of the criticism of that essay (for example in Malcolm 1986, ch. 2) can be seen to be directed at a view which is already present in Anscombe's book. Section 30.3 of my chapter is about how to understand Anscombe's achievement, not just as a reader of Wittgenstein but as someone engaged in the practice of philosophy as Wittgenstein conceived it. The larger aim of this part of the chapter is to show how Anscombe's philosophical practice can lead us into further questions about Wittgenstein's understanding of philosophical activity. Sections 30.4 and 30.5 are about how we can be helped thereby to see the aims and achievements of the *Tractatus*. One of my aims in this chapter is to suggest a revision in the history laid out by Warren Goldfarb in 'Das Überwinden: Anti-metaphysical Readings of the *Tractatus*' (2011). I shall have some brief words about that in the concluding section, 30.6.

30.1 ANSCOMBE, RUSSELL, FREGE

An Introduction to Wittgenstein's 'Tractatus' was published in 1959, and drew on material that Anscombe had developed in lectures over successive years up to 1957–8. In his 1956 study of the history of philosophical analysis, J. O. Urmson presents an interpretation of the *Tractatus* of exactly the sort Anscombe criticizes.[3] He mentions that some philosophers (unnamed, but presumably including Anscombe) have called into question the kind of interpretation of the *Tractatus* which he presents. He goes on that, whatever the accuracy of that interpretation, it is the 'received' view, the view generally accepted in the period going up to the Second World War (pp. ix–x). A central feature of the interpretation he presents is that the *Tractatus* is read with Russell's *Lectures*

---

[2] Goldfarb 2002, especially pp. 190–1; Hylton 2005, especially pp. 177–8.
[3] On the 'old' interpretation of the *Tractatus*, cf. Griffin 1964, pp. 4–5, 15.

on Logical Atomism; both works are seen as fundamentally Humean in character. Both Russell and Wittgenstein are seen as empiricists, updating empiricism with the aid of recent developments in logic.

That reading of the *Tractatus* is the main target of Anscombe's remark about the irrelevance of most of what had been written about the book. If this irrelevance has any one cause, she says, the cause is neglect of Frege 'and of the new direction he gave to philosophy' (*IWT*, p. 12). She adds that 'empiricist and idealist preconceptions, such as have been most common in philosophy for a long time, are a thorough impediment to the understanding of either Frege or the *Tractatus*' (pp. 12–13). She makes a contrast between Frege and Russell, the point of which is that readers of Wittgenstein have tended to see him as resembling Russell in respects in which he is much closer to Frege. Frege, she notes, is engaged in inquiries that are 'in no way psychological'; he had no interest in 'private mental contents', while Russell, unlike Frege, is concerned with immediate experience and with private mental contents, and introduces those notions into his account of language and his theory of judgment. He is 'thoroughly imbued with the traditions of British empiricism'; many readers of Wittgenstein share that background with Russell, and it leads them to misunderstandings of Wittgenstein's concerns in the *Tractatus* (p. 14). In the following chapter, Anscombe develops further her account of the usual, and (as she sees it) deeply mistaken, reading of the *Tractatus*. She quotes Karl Popper's summary of the *Tractatus*, which ascribes to Wittgenstein a version of the verifiability criterion of meaning. Popper treats Wittgenstein's *Elementarsätze* as statements describing directly observable states of affairs; and adds that, for Wittgenstein, 'every genuine proposition must be a truth-function of and therefore deducible from, observation statements' (quoted on p. 25). Anscombe mentions that Popper's account fits with a further feature of the usual reading of the *Tractatus*, which sees it as combining two independent theories: a 'picture-theory' of elementary propositions and a truth-functional account of non-elementary propositions. Before she turns to her own positive discussion of Wittgenstein on elementary propositions, Anscombe argues briefly against Popper's view of them as observation statements like, for example, 'Red patch here', and mentions another respect in which the empiricist tradition may lead to misreadings of the *Tractatus*. Unlike Russell, and unlike the logical positivists and contemporary British readers of Wittgenstein, Wittgenstein was not concerned with epistemological issues, which he took to be irrelevant to 'the foundations of logic and the theory of meaning' (pp. 25–8).[4] Anscombe's account of Wittgenstein's view of epistemology is meant to connect with her earlier remark about the cause of the misreading of the *Tractatus* being neglect of Frege and 'the new direction he gave to philosophy'. That is, for the 'old direction' in philosophy, epistemology is central; but the questions with which Frege is concerned, and which we should see as significant for Wittgenstein, are not epistemological.

In explaining the sorts of question with which Wittgenstein was concerned, Anscombe gives as an example the question of the relation to reality of what I say, as for example if

---

[4] For discussion of Anscombe's argument, see Ishiguro 1969.

I say that Russell is a clever philosopher. The relation cannot be explained in terms of the truth of what I say, since even if my statement had been false, it would still have said something. As Anscombe notes, Wittgenstein was concerned with this problem throughout his life. She mentions that Russell discusses many of the problems that Frege discusses, and indeed this last question, which is meant to exemplify Wittgenstein's sort of concern, is a central question for Russell. What then of her contrast between a reading of the *Tractatus* which sees it as Russellian in its approach to philosophical questions and one which sees it as Fregean? The contrast (if it cannot rest on a difference between Russell's sort of question and Frege's) has to rest on the difference between Russell's psychologism and Frege's anti-psychologism, and between the direction of philosophy as understood in the light of Russell's empiricism and the new direction given to philosophy by Frege. But it is far from clear that the contrast can be made out in that way. Peter Hylton (1990) has argued in detail that the conception of Russell generally accepted by British philosophers involved a misleading assimilation of his views in the period before the First World War to those of traditional empiricism, and Anscombe herself takes the view of Russell criticized by Hylton. She passes by Russell's anti-psychologism and the complicated character of his move away from it. Here I want to quote part of a paragraph of Hylton's about Platonic Atomism, the view developed by Moore and Russell when they gave up the Idealist views which they had earlier accepted. The period about which Hylton is writing includes the period during which Russell wrote *Principles of Mathematics*:

> The anti-psychologism of Platonic Atomism … is complete and thoroughgoing. Platonic Atomism does … imply or suggest a picture of the mind and its capacities, but this picture is very much a by-product of the view. There is no overt concern at all with the nature of thought or the mind or experience, in any sense. It is not that Moore and Russell are concerned to advance a view of these notions which is different from that of the Idealists, it is rather that these notions almost cease to be the subject of explicit philosophical concern. This seems to be because the notions are looked on as psychological, and for this reason of no interest to philosophy. (1990, p. 108)

Hylton's remarks suggest that, if we look for a source of Wittgenstein's anti-psychologism in the *Tractatus*, Frege's views are no more obviously the source than are Russell's, though Russell begins what Hylton calls a 'turn towards the psychological' in the years after the publication of *Principles*. If Russell is the source, it would be Russell in his Platonic Atomist or idealist periods. Kant's anti-psychologism is itself in the background of Frege's and in that of idealists like Bradley.[5] It is not obvious that Wittgenstein's anti-psychologism in the *Tractatus* should be thought of as belonging to a new direction given to philosophy by Frege. Among idealist 'preconceptions', one might be said to be that a main thing wrong with empiricism was its psychologizing tendencies.

---

[5] See also Griffin 1964, pp. 120–3 on the 'descent' of anti-psychologistic critique of philosophy from Bradley through Moore to Wittgenstein.

Anscombe's brief account of the importance of Frege for an understanding of the *Tractatus* involves also a problematic contrast between 'empiricist and idealist preconceptions' and the 'new direction' given to philosophy by Frege. We can see one of the problems if we consider Anscombe's discussion of the question whether, when I say that Russell is a clever philosopher, I mention both Russell and what I say about him, that he is clever. If I do mention it, what is the connection between the two mentioned things? And, if I do not mention it, what account should be given of the words expressing what I say about Russell? This is one of Anscombe's examples of the sorts of question which contrast with those which are central for us if we start off with empiricist or idealist preconceptions. But here we can note that the questions mentioned by Anscombe are important for Bradley, and indeed his discussion of them is famous; further, his account of judgment stresses questions about how judgment is related to reality, questions again of exactly the sort which Anscombe is suggesting we need to be struck by if we want to understand the *Tractatus*. Idealist preconceptions would not stop us seeing the force of such questions. The other part of the contrast between 'empiricist and idealist preconceptions' and the 'new direction' given to philosophy by Frege does not work much better. Epistemological concerns are supposed to belong to the 'empiricist and idealist preconceptions', but epistemological questions are not ignored by Frege. This point is perhaps clearer in the light of material in Frege's *Nachlass* that was not available to Anscombe when she wrote the *Introduction*, but *Foundations of Arithmetic* would in any case suggest that Frege was deeply interested in the question of the source of our knowledge of arithmetic. The contrast with Russell on the matter of interest in epistemology is indeed complicated.[6]

Nothing that I have said would cast doubt on Anscombe's argument that Popper and the logical positivists had misread the *Tractatus*, and that they were in part responsible for the prevalent misreadings of the book. But I have tried to show problems for her argument that it is neglect of Frege, more than anything, that underlies the irrelevance of most of what had been written about the *Tractatus*. The features of Frege's views which she emphasizes can't bear the weight of the argument. The sorts of question which she suggests we need to think about when we read the *Tractatus*, questions like that of how a proposition hangs together, and that of how thought and reality are related, are of concern to Bradley and (as Anscombe herself notes) also to Russell; they are not more especially problems that should be associated with Frege; they are in no way out of place in the thinking of those with 'empiricist or idealist preconceptions', if that is meant to cover Bradley and Russell. While anti-psychologism is profoundly characteristic of Frege, it can be found within the idealist tradition and in Russell's idealist and post-idealist views; and the turn away from epistemology is by no means as marked in Frege as

---

[6] For the significance of epistemology for Frege, see, e.g., Weiner 1999, ch. 2. On the development of Russell's interest in epistemology, see Hylton 2005; for Russell's pre-1905 view, see Hylton 1990, p. 197, note 33. Hylton argues that Kant and the logical positivists 'share an interest in knowledge, and a conception of what it is to account for it, which is not to be found in Russell's work' in the period during which he wrote *Principles*. See also pp. 361–2, where Hylton, writing about Russell's interest in knowledge after 1910, says of Russell's earlier works that they 'show no sign at all of any such interest'; also p. 235, where Hylton explains the changing role given to acquaintance as Russell's views change after 1905.

Anscombe's discussion of the period suggests. Russell wasn't the empiricist Anscombe paints him as being, though his views were becoming more like those of the empiricists during the period in which he was working with Wittgenstein. There are all sorts of problems with the picture Anscombe gives us, of idealists and empiricists on one side, with their preconceptions and their familiar sorts of question, and Frege on the other side, giving a new direction to philosophy, and asking questions much more like those of ancient philosophy than like those that had concerned earlier thinkers. What I want to argue is that, despite the fact that practically everything Anscombe says in sketching why neglect of Frege will lead us astray needs qualification, her intention of following out what she takes to be Fregean in Wittgenstein's thought leads her right to the heart of the book. But how does she turn out to be right, if her account of the history is, as it stands, unconvincing?

30.2 Anscombe's Reading of the *Tractatus*

The heart of Anscombe's reading of the *Tractatus* is her account of the 'picture theory'[7] of the proposition in the first six chapters of her book. The view that she rejects is that the 'whole theory of propositions' in the *Tractatus* is 'a merely external combination of two theories: a "picture theory" of elementary propositions ... and the theory of truth-functions as an account of non-elementary propositions' (pp. 25–6). She had argued in her introductory chapter that, in order to understand Frege or Wittgenstein, it is best not to start with philosophical preconceptions, but rather to be capable of 'being naively struck' by questions like the one, mentioned above, of what the relation to reality is of the statement that Russell is a clever philosopher. The two central chapters of Anscombe's presentation of the picture theory begin with questions of just the sort she had claimed we need to be naively struck by. They are questions that arise from the usual explanations, in logic books, of truth-functional composition. 'It is usual for us to be told [... that] propositions are whatever can be true or false'; that 'propositions can be combined in certain ways to form further propositions'; and that 'in developing the truth-functional calculus, we are not interested in the internal structure' of the component propositions. One question which may then strike us is whether 'the property of being true or false, which belongs to the truth-functions, [is] the very same property as the property of being true or false that belongs to the propositions whose internal structure does not interest us'. And, further, if that is so, 'is it to be regarded as an ultimate fact that propositions combine to form further propositions, much as metals combine to form alloys which still display a good many of the properties of metals?' I shall quote her comment:

> In short, is there not an impression as it were of logical chemistry about these explanations? It is this conception that Wittgenstein opposes in the *Tractatus* at 6.111:

---

[7] The inverted commas around 'picture theory' are Anscombe's, p. 19; also pp. 25 and 41.

'Theories that make a proposition of logic appear substantial are always wrong. It might be thought, for example, that the words "true" and "false" denote two properties among other properties, and then it would look like a remarkable fact that every proposition possesses one of these properties. This now looks no more a matter of course than the proposition "all roses are either red or yellow" would sound, even if it were true'. (p. 53)

Here, interestingly, in the opposition to 'logical chemistry', we can see Anscombe picking out a feature of Wittgenstein's philosophizing that is highly distinctive, and not apparently derived from Russell or Frege or any of the other thinkers whose influence on Wittgenstein can be discerned. (She quite explicitly argues that Frege, for example, in discussing whether every well-formed sentence the names in which are not empty has a truth-value, takes for granted a kind of logical-chemistry view of the nature of concepts.) Anscombe's own reading of the *Tractatus* reflects a sense, not just of what sort of questions one needs to be struck by, but also of what constitutes a genuinely satisfying resolution of the puzzlement expressed in the questions. Hence the importance of her treatment of negation. It is not just a pivotal topic for Wittgenstein's early thought but one through which she can demonstrate what is involved in reaching the kind of clarity at which he aimed. If we think about ordinary pictures, she says, we shall be able to see how the possibility of using a picture to represent that things are so goes with the possibility of using the very same picture to represent that that is how things are not. We can, that is, see in ordinary pictures the possibility of being used in two opposite ways, to say two opposite things. What is central in her account of what a picture is is that 'the way the elements are connected in the picture is the same as the way [the picture] sets forth the things as being connected'. Hence the possibility of things being connected that way is in the picture itself. It is then, as occurring in such a picture-context, that the elements can have the use of representing this or that thing. We can move from that initial insight to an understanding of negation which does not appeal to some kind of ultimate logical fact. The basic idea is that the possibility of using a picture in two opposite ways, to say this is how things are, and alternatively to say that that is how they aren't, depends upon correlating elements of the picture with things; and such correlating is something we can do so far as we take some way in which the marks or figures are related to each other to be significant. Only so far as they stand in such significant connections are these items elements of a picture; only in such connections can the picture-elements stand for this or that person or object or whatever it may be. Here is her summary: 'Only in the connections that make up the picture can the elements of the picture stand for objects' (p. 67). The picture-character of an ordinary picture is then what makes it possible, once correlations have been made, for there to be a *this*, such that there are two opposed ways of representing how things are: '*This* is how things are'; '*this* is how things aren't', where the *this* in question is the same. And Anscombe's account of the picture theory is then that that picture-character that is in ordinary pictures is also in propositions. Only in the connection that makes up the proposition do the expressions in it stand for anything. It is through the significant connection of its parts that it can say that anything is the case; and so far as those significant connections make it possible to represent that *this* is how things stand, those same connections make it possible to represent that *this* is not how things stand. If what a picture represents as being so is its sense (*TLP* 2.221), we can say that a picture's sense is reversible: it can represent the opposite as being the case. We can see what propositional sense is, if we see propositions to have the reversibility that belongs to pictures, if (that is) we see in propositions the possibility that belongs to pictures of representing that *this* is how things are, or (the *this* being the same) that *this* is how they aren't. (See *TLP* 4.05–4.0621, where the point that reality can be compared with propositions is tied to the reversibility of sense of propositions.)

Two chapters after her account of the picture theory, Anscombe summarizes that account, and connects it with Wittgenstein's remarks about how a symbol can be presented:

> we have to remember the central point of the picture theory which we have already explained: 'Only in the context of a proposition has a name reference'; 'Only in the context of a proposition has an expression reference.' This prohibits us from thinking that we can *first* somehow characterize 'a', 'R' and 'b' as symbolic signs, and *then* lay it down how we can build propositions out of them. If 'a' is a symbolic sign only in the context of a proposition, then the symbol 'a' will be properly presented, not by putting it down and saying it is a symbol of such and such a kind, but by representing the whole class of the propositions in which it can occur. (p. 93)

There Anscombe quotes *Tractatus* 3.3 and *Tractatus* 3.314, two statements of the 'context principle', to give the heart of the picture theory as she had earlier explained it. Here we should pause and ask some questions. The context principle, as it occurs in the *Tractatus*, certainly appears to mark a connection with Frege's appeals to the context principle in *The Foundations of Arithmetic*. But what then is the connection? Warren Goldfarb has argued that it is not clear how far some apparently Fregean features of the *Tractatus* reflect the influence of Frege's thought on Wittgenstein.[8] It may be that Wittgenstein started with views which were profoundly influenced by Russell, but, in working through the difficulties of those views, came to a position which is close to Frege's in significant respects. I shall leave open the question whether these 'Fregean' features of his thought reflect the direct influence of Frege. I want instead to ask what these features are, and how they are important for Anscombe's reading of the *Tractatus*. Goldfarb is very helpful here in laying out differences between Frege's thought and Russell's. Goldfarb connects Frege's commitment to the context principle with what he calls the 'judgement-based nature' of Frege's view. Frege does not think of judgments as put together from parts which have some prior independent logical character. In a remark that has become well known (but which was not available in any of Frege's published writings when Anscombe wrote her *Introduction to Wittgenstein's 'Tractatus'*), Frege said 'I do not begin with concepts and put them together to form a thought or a judgment; I come by the parts of a thought by analyzing the thought' (1979, p. 253). While that remark concerns the parts of a thought, a parallel point holds, on Frege's view, for propositions: the parts of a proposition which

---

[8] Goldfarb 2002, *passim* but see especially pp. 187 and 197.

have reference are identifiable only through the logical relations of the proposition to other propositions. Goldfarb notes the sharp contrast with Russell's approach: For Russell, the primitive parts of propositions 'subsist in and of themselves'. They are put together into propositions, but are recognizable on their own, independently of their role in propositions. Russell's account of propositions and their constituents is described by Goldfarb as 'object-based', in contrast to Frege's 'judgment-based' view. As a feature of Russell's thought, it can be found as early as *The Principles of Mathematics*. Its presence doesn't indicate that Russell was an empiricist, though such a view of propositions and their parts is indeed found in the writings of empiricists.[9]

In section 30.1, I argued that, although Anscombe had claimed that neglect of Frege was the main explanation why what had been written about the *Tractatus* had been for the most part wildly irrelevant, her account of the differences between Frege and Russell left it unclear why neglect of Frege should have so distorted understanding of Wittgenstein. But her presentation of the picture theory and the connection that she makes there with Wittgenstein's version of the context principle show (I think) why she sees Frege as leading us in the right direction. My suggestion is that Goldfarb's contrast between Frege's judgment-based view and Russell's object-based approach, although it doesn't correspond to anything Anscombe explicitly says in laying out the contrast between Frege and Russell, lets us see why Anscombe insists on the importance of Frege for an understanding of the *Tractatus*. Consider the remarks that I quoted in section 30.1, that Russell differs from Frege 'by introducing the notion of immediate experience, and hence that of private mental contents, into his explanations of meaning and his theory of judgment'; for he is, she says, 'thoroughly imbued with the traditions of British empiricism'. We should, I think, read those remarks as containing three distinct points, about immediate experience, private contents, and empiricism. If we use 'experience' to include what Russell means by 'acquaintance', we could then say that Russell introduces into his account of meaning and judgment a notion of immediate experience, but we cannot then go on: 'hence of private mental contents'. There is no 'hence', since one can have a notion of immediate acquaintance (even: of immediate acquaintance conceived on the model of acquaintance with the taste of a pineapple) in which the objects with which one is immediately acquainted need not be private mental entities, but may be such things as the indefinables of logic and universals. Indeed, even sense-data need not be conceived as 'private mental contents' on a Russellian view of acquaintance. A notion of immediate acquaintance can play a central role in a philosophical account of meaning and judgment, which may be quite far from empiricism in various ways, or indeed opposed to it.[10] So one needs to separate from each other Anscombe's point that

---

[9] A classic statement of the view can be found in Chapter I of John Stuart Mill 1843.

[10] On these issues, see Hylton 1990, especially pp. 328–33. As Hylton notes, even as late as 1913, the point of acquaintance, for Russell, is that it is to be 'an unproblematic meeting ground between the mind and what is outside it' (p. 331). That the notion of acquaintance is not tied to empiricism is also evident in the writings of Gareth Evans and those who are influenced by him, who use the idea of the direct availability of something for thought, an idea developed from Russellian acquaintance.

Russell worked with a notion of immediate acquaintance and her characterization of his views as thoroughly empiricist. Anscombe is certainly right that the *Tractatus* was misunderstood by her contemporaries in large part because they saw it as a working out of a radically empiricist view; they saw Russell as arguing for a very similar kind of empiricism. But we need to focus here on the notion of acquaintance, and in particular on Russell's principle that one can understand a proposition only if one is acquainted with its constituents. The principle is stated in 'On Denoting' and repeated in *Problems of Philosophy* and 'Knowledge by Acquaintance and Knowledge by Description'.[11] The idea that understanding a proposition depends on acquaintance with its constituents goes with the point mentioned by Goldfarb in characterizing Russell's views: the primitive parts of propositions subsist on their own, and are recognizable independently of the propositions of which they are parts.

Although I am in the middle of a line of argument here, I shall introduce a digression to indicate where the argument is going. Some years after the publication of Anscombe's book, Hidé Ishiguro, B. F. McGuinness, and Peter Winch developed readings of the *Tractatus* which explicitly reject the idea that the connections between names and objects are supposed to be established prior to the use of the names in propositions; on the reading that they reject, Wittgenstein held that the logical form of the object with which a name was correlated determines how the name can be correctly combined with other names in propositions. Their readings depended on taking seriously Wittgenstein's expression of the context principle at *TLP* 3.3.[12] It thus became incumbent on anyone who wanted to read the *Tractatus* as committed to the idea that objects have their own independent nature, and that it is first of all through the connection between names and such objects that language has its connection with reality, to explain what sort of force the context principle has, since it at least appears to imply that there is no such thing as a name having meaning prior to its use in propositions. It will be helpful if I summarize here, very briefly, one such line of response, that of David Pears. He argues that it is possible to interpret the context principle so that it is consistent with the idea that contact between names and things is prior to the occurrence of names in propositions; the principle implies merely that the association between a name and the object it names is 'annulled' if the name occurs in a context that doesn't correspond to a genuine possibility for the object.[13] Pears's treatment of the context principle is developed in the course of his criticism of Ishiguro and McGuinness, and is meant as a basis for rejecting their

[11] Russell 1956, p. 56; 1967, p. 32; 1932, p. 219. Cf. also Hylton 1990, p. 246: the principle of acquaintance is, he writes, implicit in *Principles of Mathematics*.

[12] Ishiguro 1969, see, e.g., p. 22; McGuinness 1981 especially pp. 65–6; Winch, 1987, especially pp. 8–10.

[13] Pears 1987, vol. 1, pp. 75–6, 102–3. Cf. also Malcolm 1986, pp. 28–31; Malcolm appears to hold both that there is no such thing as a 'preliminary preparation' for language in which signs are correlated with objects outside of propositions and that, if I am to construct a proposition using a name for an object, I must know its possible combinations with other objects. The correlations settle for me the propositional contexts in which that name can occur. This latter point appears to involve granting to correlation-making a kind of logical priority close to the kind of 'preparation' for language which he had explicitly ruled out three pages earlier. The idea is certainly that the correlations between names and objects allow certain sign-combinations and disallow others.

understanding of the context principle and of the relation between names and objects. Anscombe does not share that understanding, but Pears's account, if correct, would equally constitute an objection to Anscombe's view.

Anscombe's account of the picture theory is incompatible with any idea that setting up the connections between names and things is prior to putting the names into significant combinations. As she says, only if significant relations hold among the elements of a picture can we correlate the elements with things, so that the picture-elements stand for the things, and so that their arrangement shows a way in which the things can stand. When she wrote that the Russellian connection leads to misunderstandings of the *Tractatus*, one of the main things she had in mind was this: that if you read into the *Tractatus* Russell's view that the intelligibility of propositions depends upon acquaintance with their constituents, you cannot understand the picture theory. But what would block understanding of the picture theory is not merely Russell's doctrines about acquaintance and meaning: if Anscombe is right about the picture theory, it is incompatible not just with Russell's own views and his version of logical atomism but also with any object-based account of meaning. Thus, for example, David Pears takes himself to be disagreeing with any strongly Russellian reading of the *Tractatus*, because he does not think that the objects of the *Tractatus* can be identified with sense-data and their properties, but whether an account is object-based has nothing to do with the question what sorts of thing the objects are; and Pears's account is a paradigmatically object-based account of meaning.[14] For Pears, as for Russell, the primitive parts of propositions subsist on their own; and the initial correlation between names and things is prior to the use of the name in propositions.

Consider also Anscombe's point, quoted above, that a symbolic sign 'a' is properly presented, 'not by putting it down and saying it is a symbol of such and such a kind, but by representing the whole class of propositions in which it can occur'. Here the recognition of some occurrence of the sign 'a' as an occurrence of that symbol is dependent on its occurrence in a proposition of the class in question, and there is no question of setting up which propositions it can occur in by considering its correlation with an object, taken to impose restrictions on its use, allowing some combinations of signs and disallowing others. The logical characteristics of what 'a' means are plain from its role in the propositions in which it can occur.[15] It is a consequence of this view that there is no logical error in using the sign 'a' in other sorts of proposition; for in those contexts it would not be the same symbol. There is here a substantial difference from the approach taken later by David Pears, who speaks of the occurrence of a name in a context which doesn't correspond to a genuine possibility for the object named as 'annulling' the

---

[14] See also McGinn 2006, pp. 271–2, n. 6.

[15] Anscombe's view, that logical characteristics of what a symbol means are plain from its role in propositions, is weaker than the views of Winch, Ishiguro, and McGuinness. Anscombe's view leaves room for a distinction between presenting what kind of thing a symbol means and settling which thing of that kind it means; but Winch, Ishiguro, and McGuinness give accounts of the *Tractatus* which don't leave room for that distinction, at any rate in the case of simple names.

connection between name and object (1987, vol. 1, p. 75). It is hard to see how this way of speaking can be connected either to Wittgenstein's (and Anscombe's) talk of signs or to Wittgenstein's (and Anscombe's) talk of symbols. The name-with-its-connection-annulled isn't a mere sign, in their sense: for the supposed name, if it is thought of as a name at all, is being thought of as if it had at any rate a shadow of an attachment to an object of a particular kind. Otherwise one could not speak of *its* connection with some object being annulled. But a mere sign has no logical connection to any particular kind of object. But isn't that the status of the name after the connection is 'annulled', on Pears's view? The trouble with that reply is that the connection can't be 'annulled' unless it is there to be annulled; and if the connection is there, then what has the connection is a symbol, not a sign; and if it is indeed a symbol, then it is in use in the sort of context of which such symbols are features, and there would then be no question of the connection being 'annulled' by the name's being in the wrong sort of context.

The difficulty in an attempt to explain Pears's view is that the context principle in the *Tractatus*, as Anscombe points out, appears to rule out the idea that we can identify a sign as a name of some particular object, and then go on to note that the combinatorial possibilities of that object permit such-and-such propositional occurrences of the name, and rule out others. The context principle is closely tied to the distinction between a mere sign and a symbol; but Pears's account of what is involved in putting a name into a propositional combination of the 'wrong' sort cannot coherently be explained in terms either of the name as a mere sign or of the name as a symbol. The word 'resolute' has been given a use in discussions of the *Tractatus*, in connection with the interpretation of Wittgenstein on sense and nonsense, but I want to suggest that, in the contrast between Anscombe's treatment of the context principle and that of Pears, we can see another sort of issue of resolution and irresolution. Pears's interpretation of the *Tractatus* allows the context principle to rule out the idea that 'a' can occur genuinely as a name anywhere except in senseful propositional combinations; but the idea of the name as occurring in the 'wrong' sort of context, and thereby having its connection with the object 'annulled', employs the idea of a name-object connection that is *there*, independently of the occurrence of the name in propositions. *This* connection requires that the name itself not be thought of either as a sign or as a symbol, if a symbol is a symbol only in the context of a proposition. The sign/symbol contrast helps us to be clear about what we want to say and about when we are dithering and not saying anything. There is (I am suggesting) a wiggle or dither in Pears's account, that operates in what is only apparently a space of possible philosophical conceptions.[16] The fundamental difficulty is the attempt to combine an object-based understanding of language, shared with Russell, and the context principle. But a weakened version of the context principle is quite different from the version of the context principle that is reflected in the distinction between sign and symbol. Putting this point another way: there is no room for the *Tractatus* understanding of what a symbol is if one tries to read into the book an object-based understanding of

---

[16] A corresponding problem emerges in Malcolm 1986, if one works through Malcolm's treatment of the context principle and tries to connect it with Wittgenstein's distinction between signs and symbols.

names. Pears supports his reading of the context principle (as consistent with an object-based understanding of names) by reference to passages in Wittgenstein's *Notebooks* from November 1914. These passages are hardly unambiguous, but more important, they were written well before Wittgenstein began to take the context principle seriously. If one takes Wittgenstein's views to have been evolving during the years before the final version of the *Tractatus* was written, and in particular, if one takes his treatment of the context principle (and of the relation between the meaning of a name and its occurrence in propositional contexts) to be among the things that changed, it becomes questionable how far remarks from November 1914, or from elsewhere in the *Notebooks*, can be taken to impose on the context principle in the *Tractatus* an interpretation weak enough to make it consistent with object-based readings of the *Tractatus*.[17]

A strong version of the context principle, like that which Anscombe ascribes to Wittgenstein, has been held by some philosophers of language and some commentators on Wittgenstein to be incompatible with the compositionality of language. So (on this view) if Wittgenstein did hold such a version of the context principle, his account of language is in trouble. It is far from obvious, though, that there is such an incompatibility, and there are good arguments against it (Bronzo 2011). I shall not, however, examine the issues here.

I have argued that there is indeed a fundamentally Russellian way of reading the *Tractatus*, and that it is common to the interpretations Anscombe criticized and to later readings like that of David Pears. Part of my argument has been that what being 'Russellian' in this context amounts to becomes clear only later, in a line of discussion which develops from Anscombe herself, and which includes the writings of (among others) Hidé Ishiguro, Warren Goldfarb, Thomas Ricketts, and Peter Hylton. Anscombe's interpretation of the *Tractatus* can be described as Fregean, not in that she claims that Wittgenstein's approach was in relevant respects derived from Frege (which it might or might not have been) but in that Wittgenstein, as she reads him, came to share with Frege an approach later described as 'judgement-based'. I have also argued that there is an important feature of Anscombe's understanding of the central ideas of the *Tractatus*, a feature which is neither Russellian nor Fregean. I mean her treatment of the idea of 'logical chemistry'. I quoted her discussion of *Tractatus* 6.111, where Wittgenstein says that theories that make a proposition of logic appear substantial are always wrong, and where he criticizes any account of logic that makes it look like a queer sort of fact that every proposition is either true or false. Anscombe's account of the picture theory is meant to make the truth or falsity of propositions fall out of what it is for propositions to be pictures. There is to be no 'logical chemistry'; and her argument is that, if we think through the analogy with pictures, and take as central the way ordinary pictures can be used to say that something is so, or used to say the opposite, we can see how the logical character of propositions is thereby made 'extremely intelligible'. What she speaks of as the 'grounds for being struck even to the point of conviction' by the account is that it

[17] On the development of Wittgenstein's treatment of the context principle and of his understanding of its consequences, see Kremer 1997.

opens up the logical character of propositions, without appeal to ultimate logical facts of any sort. If, at the end of her second chapter on negation, she says that there is surely something right about the picture theory even if it is not correct as it stands, her conviction that there is something right about it comes from being 'struck even to the point of conviction' by the 'extreme intelligibility' given to the logical character of propositions. The idea is not, I think, that we have antecedently available a conception of philosophical clarity, and that the *Tractatus* account of propositions provides that sort of clarity. Rather, the making intelligible of the logical character of propositions provides a way of understanding what philosophical clarity can be. My account of Anscombe's reading of the 'picture theory' is not intended to be complete. The most important thing that I have omitted is her discussion of elementary propositions—a discussion which is essential to her claim that the *Tractatus* makes 'extremely intelligible' the logical character of propositions.[18] Without going over all that matters in her account, I have tried to show the kind of change she hoped to make in how the *Tractatus* was understood. In the next three sections, I shall be following out a line of thought that starts from what Anscombe actually does in presenting the picture theory. That will put me in a position to discuss, in section 30.6, how Anscombe's approach fits into the history laid out by Warren Goldfarb of antimetaphysical readings of the *Tractatus*.

30.3 ANSCOMBE AND PHILOSOPHICAL METHOD

> Wittgenstein's view of philosophical method is touched on by Anscombe, but it is not one of her aims [in *An Introduction to Wittgenstein's 'Tractatus'*] to make clear what he thought about method, or in what way the method of the *Tractatus* is connected with Wittgenstein's more specific philosophical ideas in the book, or what the importance to the reader should be of his apparently methodological remarks. (Diamond 2003, p. 172)

That now seems to me a stupid and misleading thing to have said. I was too impressed by a very partial truth, and failed altogether to see the kind of attention to methodology in Anscombe's own approach. What, after all, does she *do* in the book—in that part of it that I have been considering? She lays out, makes open to view, a way of using words, the picture-proposition use. She is not simply expounding a theory held by Wittgenstein; she is attempting to put before the reader with the 'extreme intelligibility' with which the account can (she thinks) be presented, what it is to say that something is so, on analogy with using a picture to say that *this* is so, a picture capable of being used also to say that *this* isn't so. I mentioned her having quoted Wittgenstein's criticism of any account of logic that makes it look like a queer sort of fact that every proposition is either true or false. She herself is presenting a use of language, the picture-proposition

---

[18] See also Ricketts 1996, especially part iv, on logical interconnectedness.

use, which will *not* make it look like a queer sort of fact that every proposition is either true or false, but will instead make obvious, open to view, the connection between picturing and the possibility of truth and falsehood, and which will also make it clear, open to view, how such picture-propositions can be combined to form others, which will also be true or false.

In section 30.2, I quoted Anscombe's statement that, if 'a' is a symbolic sign only in the context of a proposition, then the symbol 'a' will be properly presented not by putting it down and saying that it is a symbol of such-and-such a kind, but by representing the whole class of the propositions in which it can occur. There are various ways in which we might represent such a class of propositions; but what such a presentation of the class will do is make evident what the entire class has in common. Wherever a class of propositions has a feature in common, it can be presented in some such way; and although the point as Anscombe makes it concerns sub-sentential expressions, it is also applicable to the entire class of picture-propositions. What they have in common can be laid out. They have in common *saying that something is so*. Anscombe's account of the picture theory, I am suggesting, can be taken to be a specification of a use of signs. Presenting the use of signs to *say that something is so* gives one case, indeed a quite special case, of presenting a class of propositions with something in common, of presenting a class so that what the members have in common is open to view. In any such case, the propositions in question are all values of some variable; and making plain what the values of the variable are is the way in which the variable itself is given.

I am suggesting that Anscombe's presentation of the picture theory can be taken to be a case of making plain what the values of a variable are, where the values of the variable are propositions. This is a case of making plain a use of signs, and is not (in that respect) different in principle from the case Anscombe mentions, of presenting the symbol 'a' by representing the whole class of propositions in which it can occur—the class of propositions which have in common the presence in them of that symbol. If (as the *Tractatus* has it) anything essential to their sense that propositions can have in common with one another is an expression or symbol, then picture-propositionhood is itself a symbol common to picture-propositions, a common formal feature (propositional form), and the class of propositions with that feature (all propositions) can be presented; and this is what Anscombe has done. In fact, Anscombe presents this class of propositions twice over in her book, as does Wittgenstein in the *Tractatus*. In the *Tractatus*, the presentation of picturing and of truth-functional construction leads up to *TLP* 4.5: Symbols constructed in the way described are sayings that *this is how things stand*. And Wittgenstein also claims that that class of symbols can be given by specifying a formal series the members of which are the symbols in question. Anscombe's account of the picture theory in the first part of her book gives the class of symbols and what they have in common informally; her chapter on formal concepts and formal series indicates how the symbols can be given as members of a formal series. There are questions about whether Wittgenstein actually succeeds in giving such a variable, and whether, if he does, what its use would be (Sullivan 2004). I have discussed these questions elsewhere (2012), and here I take for granted that the word 'proposition' can be used in a logical sense in ordinary talk without philosophical confusion, and that, in such cases, it would (on Wittgenstein's view) go over in a conceptual notation to a variable.

In the rest of section 30.3, I draw out two consequences of this way of looking at Anscombe's philosophical method in her account of the picture theory: as a matter of presenting a use of signs, the picture-proposition use. I shall also adduce another example of the method, before turning in sections 30.4 and 30.5 to some questions about it.

1. *Connection between this method and the context principle.* The idea that any symbolic feature that signs can have in common, essential to their sense, can be given by representing the entire class of propositions that have the feature is based on the context principle. (See *TLP* 3.3–3.317, and *IWT*, p. 93.) So, if we view *giving the picture-proposition use of signs*, their use to say that something is so, as a case of presenting a class of propositions with something in common, and thereby presenting the common feature, we can see the philosophical method in use in such a laying out of a class of propositions as an application of the context principle.

2. *Connection with Wittgenstein's remarks on philosophy.* Wittgenstein says, at *TLP* 4.112, that philosophy is an activity that results in the clarification of propositions. One way in which philosophy can do this is by making plain what expressions have in common, and also by making plain differences between expressions. Later in the *Tractatus*, Wittgenstein suggests that the activity of philosophy is, properly speaking, appropriate only in response to philosophical confusion, when the activity involves showing the confused person that he hasn't given meaning to some signs in his propositions. Taking this suggestion seriously would mean that one might, for example, present the symbol 'a' to a person who was using the sign 'a' without a meaning in his propositions, to show that person the emptiness of his employment of 'a'. Presenting to that person the class of propositions of which the symbol 'a' is the common feature might help him to see that he was not using that symbol at all, since his proposition was not in the class in question. This picture of philosophical activity doesn't have the implication that there would be no other sort of occasion for presenting the symbol 'a' (for example to someone learning a language), but the implication would be that such occasions were not cases of philosophical activity. If this is the way to understand what constitutes a philosophically appropriate sort of case of presenting the use of an expression, it would follow that Wittgenstein's own presentation of the picture-proposition use, and similarly Anscombe's presentation of the picture-proposition use, are appropriate if the activity helps to show that we are using some words with no meaning. The 'picture theory' then can be taken to be a case (indeed a rather special case, but a case nevertheless) of presenting to people a class of propositions with a common feature, unclarity about which is reflected in their (or, rather, our) use of words with no determinate meaning.

I am suggesting that the *Tractatus* can be read as a manual for philosophical activity, for philosophical clarification. You clarify by making plain commonalities and differences. I shall not here go into details about making differences plain, but one way of doing so is by making commonalities plain: if you make plain, for example, what is shared by all uses of 'is' as an expression for existence, and what is shared by all uses of 'is' as the copula, you may thereby make plain the difference between the uses. A shareable feature of propositions is represented by a variable, which can be presented by specifying its values in such a way as to make plain what they all have in common. I am also suggesting, then, that the relevance of Anscombe's book to the question of the *Tractatus* understanding of philosophical method is in part that the book provides an example of philosophical activity in presenting the picture-proposition use of signs.

It will be helpful here to look briefly at Peter Sullivan's account of the picture theory (2001). His approach is in some respects unlike Anscombe's, but there are interesting similarities which I want to bring out. Like Anscombe, Sullivan takes questions about the relation between thought, the meaningfulness of propositions, and truth to be important in his account of the aims of the picture theory. He uses the metaphor of logical space to explain how a proposition's meaning something is independent of its truth: its 'coordinates' determine a place in logical space. But his examination of the metaphor leads him to the question why we can count on it that what we can think to be so is genuinely a possibility for reality. Why should the possible combinations in which we use the names in our language enable us to represent genuine possibilities of existence for the objects named? It looks, Sullivan notes, as if it would be a kind of leap of faith, or superstition, to think that this was so. That is, it looks as if our capacity genuinely to represent possibilities for reality in our language depends on a kind of magical getting right of the logical character of the names, getting their possibilities to match those of the objects.[19] Sullivan responds by explaining the *Tractatus* conception of pictorial form, using the idea of a kind of transparency in representation. Transparency is exemplified by the use of colour in a naturalistic painting, in contrast with the use of colour to represent which nation (say) has sovereignty over some part of the world, as with maps in which the British Empire was coloured red. In the first or 'transparent' case, colour 'represents nothing other than itself'; 'a feature of reality has simply been taken up into the system of representation' (pp. 107–8). It is that notion of transparency, in its most abstract form, which is at the heart of the picture theory. In a transparent representation, the arrangement of the proxies for objects is the arrangement the objects are represented as having. A name then is a name, is a proxy for an object, in the context of a representation with such transparency. This account of the picture theory leads Sullivan to remark that Wittgenstein might well have taken the context principle to be his fundamental thought, since it underlies the idea of pictorial form as common to picture and what is pictured (p. 109). Although Anscombe and Sullivan give somewhat different accounts of

[19] Sullivan 2001, p. 100. Cf. Goldfarb, unpublished, on the question what assurance we have that the sentences we put together express genuine possibilities.

the picture theory, both of them take the context principle to be absolutely central to it.[20] What I want to emphasize is the role the context principle thus has, for both of them, in their account of how the picture theory makes propositionhood 'extremely intelligible'. The logical characteristics of propositions, their capacity for truth and falsehood, their relation to reality, can be made clear without appeal to substantial metaphysical facts, which would have to turn out right if our thought is genuinely to be in contact with reality. In somewhat different ways, Sullivan and Anscombe lay out the picture-proposition use of signs. We can take both of them to be engaged in laying out a use of signs in such a way as to achieve philosophical/logical clarity, and thereby to reshape our understanding of what we need in order to solve our philosophical problems. They each start with questions that may seem to demand answers in terms of logical and metaphysical facts; but in response they provide what we might call a perspicuous presentation of a way of using words, and for both of them, the context principle is at the heart of this perspicuous presentation. Obviously, I am pushing a certain way of reading what they are up to. And I'll push it further: they are responding to the *Tractatus* by doing what the *Tractatus* does, and doing philosophy in the sense in which the activity of philosophy is described in the *Tractatus*.

30.4 PROBLEMS ABOUT PHILOSOPHY

There is an important contrast between two ways of taking talk of presenting a use of signs. If I lay out a use of signs, I might claim that what I have laid out is the use of *propositions*. Or I can simply lay out a way of using signs, say, the picture-proposition use, and make no such claims. In the first case, it looks as if I will have achieved what I claim to have achieved if the use that I have laid out is indeed the use of *propositions*. It looks, that is, as if something out there, the way propositions are indeed used, makes my account right or wrong. But what items are we to take to be the ones the use of which makes my account right or wrong? If 'proposition' is what Wittgenstein calls a formal concept, then what falls under it are the values of a variable, a variable which can be given by specifying its values. But that is what the account itself purports to do. Underlying the idea that the laying out of the use (say, the picture-proposition use) might be compared with the way we genuinely do use *propositions* there is an unclarity about what philosophy can accomplish. The problem can be put as a dilemma. If what I have done is simply lay out a use of signs, what is its interest? Unless I make a claim about what sort of symbol it is, the use of which I am laying out, how is what I have done relevant to any philosophical

---

[20] Anscombe (1989) gives an account of the central ideas of the *Tractatus* which makes rather more explicit (than does *IWT*) some points of resemblance between her reading and that of Sullivan. Some of the features of her reading had indeed changed, but the claim that she makes, that Wittgenstein had in the picture theory solved the ancient problem of the relation between thought and reality 'by the thesis of the *identity* of the possibility of the structure of a proposition and the possibility of the structure of a fact' does not seem to me to mark a change, except in explicitness, from her earlier account.

problem? But if I do make such a claim, for example that what I have laid out is the way *propositions* are used, I use a term, in this case 'propositions', to pick out, or try to pick out, a class of symbols, but how can I take myself to have done *that*? Do I take myself to have, independently of specifying the use of a class of symbols, some way of understanding 'propositions'? But if my best specification of the use of the class is just precisely what I have given, I don't have some other specification up my sleeve by which to give content to my claim that I have given the use of *that* class of symbols. Nor can the difficulty be avoided by saying that the symbols, the use of which I have laid out, are those we would call 'propositions'. For that certainly isn't correct, since all sorts of sentences and sentence-constructions, used in a variety of ways, may be called 'propositions', and what I have attempted to lay out is a class which can be distinguished from the rest by the logical characteristics of its members, which of course are what I have attempted to lay out. The dilemma then, is this: how can a philosophical presentation of a use be illuminating, if it is not accompanied by such claims? But how can such claims be understood? In sections 30.4 and 30.5 I shall be discussing this problem; section 30.6 contains a brief discussion of a corresponding problem for Frege's treatment of *concepts*. In this second half of the chapter, I shall be making problematic my own way of talking in the first half, in which I have unselfconsciously spoken of the *Tractatus* view of *propositions*, and of Anscombe as giving an account of the logical features of *propositions*.[21]

It has been suggested that we can view (at least some) *Tractatus* propositions as having a function akin to what Wittgenstein later spoke of as grammatical propositions, and that they are nonsense only in a technical sense. On this view, one use of 'nonsense' is simply as a label for propositions that give the characteristics of senseful propositions.[22] It might seem that such an approach could resolve the difficulty I have sketched, by leaving room to say that the use that has been laid out is that of *propositions*, and that saying so is nonsense, but nonsense only in a technical sense. But such an approach cannot actually resolve the difficulty; for its source is a genuine unclarity about what one wants to say if one characterizes a use as that of *propositions*. In any case, what from the *Tractatus* point of view corresponds to what Wittgenstein later spoke of as making clear the grammar of some term is *specifying the values of a propositional variable*. That is how a way of using signs is presented. It is then about that kind of presentation that the question arises whether we can say that the use presented is that of *propositions*. The suggestion that *Tractatus* propositions themselves should be taken to have a function analogous to that of grammatical clarifications in Wittgenstein's later writings seems to depend on not noticing that there already is something else that genuinely does have a comparable function from the point of view of the *Tractatus*: the specification of the values of a propositional variable. In any case, the supposed parallel between *Tractatus* propositions and grammatical remarks would hardly resolve the difficulty, since questions parallel

---

[21] On the issues raised in this paragraph, see Floyd 2007, p. 184.

[22] Moyal-Sharrock 2007. In discussing her view I look only at reasons why it does not provide a solution to the difficulty with which I am concerned. There are other problems with Moyal-Sharrock's account connected with the topics of section 30.4, but I cannot examine these problems here.

to those which arise about presentations of use in the *Tractatus* can arise about grammatical remarks. There is indeed a further objection to the idea that *Tractatus* propositions are nonsense only in a technical sense, and are actually in the same business as are Wittgenstein's grammatical remarks in the later writings. The objection is that saying that a remark is only technically nonsensical hardly makes clear how it is to be understood, if it is not clear that there is any way to arrive at what it means through familiarity with the meaning of its parts. If we are to understand it, surely we must have some way of understanding the words in it, in their context. But do we have any such way of understanding the words in the case of the sort of *Tractatus* remarks that are in question? A good example is *TLP* 5, 'Propositions are truth-functions of elementary propositions'. If that is only 'technically' nonsense, the first word must mean something, in its occurrence *in that context*. It looks as if it is meant to be a formal concept word, but it also appears not to have the use, in that context, of a formal concept word. (See *TLP* 4.1272: formal concept words don't have the use of words for functions or classes.) If the remark is supposed to give part of the grammar of 'propositions', the problem is that it plainly isn't meant to give even part of the grammar of all that we might call 'propositions', since obviously many sentence-constructions which might get called 'propositions' don't have the use that Wittgenstein is aiming to present, and he certainly didn't think they did. If he meant to characterize any linguistic items, it was linguistic items used in a certain way. What way? Well, as truth-functions of elementary-propositions. But it is not going to be a grammatical remark to point out that truth-functions of elementary propositions are truth-functions of elementary propositions. The trouble with the idea that the *Tractatus* remarks are merely 'technical' nonsense is that, at the very least, when a sentence is called nonsensical, this should make one worry about whether one might be mistaking a conceptual blur for a meaningful remark. To characterize a sentence like 'Propositions are truth-functions of elementary propositions' as 'grammatical clarification' may make it appear that the only problem with such a remark is the label 'nonsensical', which (as being merely a label) is not a genuine problem. Hence the real problem what it means, where there is indeed such a problem, disappears from view.

Two remarks in the *Tractatus* can help us with the difficulty I have sketched: *TLP* 3.317 and 4.126. At 4.126, Wittgenstein says that the sign for the characteristics of a formal concept is a distinctive feature of all symbols whose meanings (*Bedeutungen*) fall under the concept. I take this remark to imply that the formal concept *proposition* has, falling under it, symbols with a characteristic kind of *Bedeutung*. In this context, the word '*Bedeutung*' is used so that, not just names, but also symbols other than names can be spoken of as having *Bedeutung*.[23] At 3.317, Wittgenstein says that when one gives the values of a propositional variable, and in that way gives the variable, one gives a description of the propositions whose common characteristic the variable is, and such a stipulation of the values of the variable will be concerned only with symbols, not with their meaning (*Bedeutung*). I am interested in the implication of these remarks for the case in which we are laying out what I have called the picture-proposition use of signs. I take the

---

[23] On Wittgenstein's use of '*Bedeutung*', see Kremer 2002, pp. 283–4.

remarks to imply that we should not add that signs with the picture-proposition use that has been laid out are *propositions*, for that appears to be a specification of the *Bedeutung* of the symbols.

Even if what I have said is correct as a bit of *Tractatus* exposition, it hardly resolves the dilemma about what the philosophical relevance can be of laying out the use of an expression. If Wittgenstein indeed implies that we should not characterize the use which has been laid out as that of *propositions*, some alternative story has to be told of what the value can be of such an activity. But we should note anyway that the view which I have ascribed to Wittgenstein has an important consequence. If there is no saying that such-and-such use is that of *propositions*, there is also no saying that, so far as you use words in some other way, then what you are uttering is not *genuinely a proposition*. So far as laying out a use is nothing but laying out a use, it can exclude nothing. And yet, of course, the *Tractatus* is usually thought of as excluding something, or some things. How does it exclude anything, if it is in the business of laying out a use, and if laying out a use excludes no other use?

Suppose, then, that I lay out the picture-proposition use of words. For a sentence to have this use is for it to have 'logical form', where that means that the connection of its elements sets forth that things are connected in the same way as the elements; hence the connection itself shows the possibility both of things being as they are represented as being and of their not being as they are represented as being. The two possibilities for the things represented are thus internal to this way of using signs. The laying out of such a use doesn't exclude any other use of signs, but rather helps to bring out a certain kind of confusion, in which one is at one and the same time using, or apparently attempting to use, signs in such a way, and also not using them in that way. The laying out of the picture-proposition use of signs makes clear how the two possibilities—things being as represented, or their not being as represented—are part of that use of signs, part of the proposition's being a representation in logical space. If you want to give to words the use of expressing a *substantial necessary truth* (let us say), what you need to do is make clear what it is for what you say to be how things are, how they *necessarily* are. You need to do that without letting yourself slide into relying on what it is to use words in the picture-proposition way. *That* use does provide a way of saying how things are, but you are not going to be able to appeal to it. What is excluded by laying out the picture-proposition use is a kind of unconscious slipperiness, in which you take for granted the picture-proposition use and its abrogation at the same time, in which you take yourself to be saying something that really is *so*, necessarily so, and slippery-slide into a conception of a space in which this is said to be so, a space in which there is an opposite way things might be said to be, but they *cannot* be that way. This is a space in which there lie certain cases that are *excluded*, a space in which what is impossible can be thought of as impossible. But, as Wittgenstein points out at *TLP* 5.61, there is only confusion that lies in this direction. It can unmisleadingly be said that the *Tractatus* excludes substantial necessary truth only if it doesn't mean that some way of using words is excluded. Again: no use of words is excluded by laying out a use of words; but laying out a use of words can be meant to sharpen our eyes to the fact that a supposed way of using words is not anything at all. Let me briefly specify more clearly what I mean and what I don't mean by saying that laying out a use of words does not exclude any way of using words. I don't mean that, once you have laid out the use of picture-propositions, you cannot *say* that certain other ways of using words are excluded because they are not genuine propositions, although indeed they are excluded. I mean simply that, if you lay out a use of words, you have not thereby excluded anything. If you lay out the picture-proposition use, put it clearly before us, the only thing that is thereby made clear about other uses is that they are not that use. If there is to be any 'exclusion' going on, it is at any rate not done by laying out a use. It is important, in reading the *Tractatus*, whether one takes it to exclude certain uses of words as not genuine propositions. Such readings, among which would be Anscombe's, might be labelled 'exclusionary'. I shall have more to say about such readings in sections 30.5 and 30.6, but shall first turn back to the problem of describing what the *Tractatus* does.

30.5 MORE ABOUT THE PROBLEM OF PART 4

Before trying a different approach, I shall restate the problem. One can say that Wittgenstein in the *Tractatus* was giving *the essence of propositions*, but what he was giving the essence *of* can only be made clear by giving that essence itself—that is, by giving a variable the values of which have 'propositional form' in common. To think that one might helpfully convey something by saying 'What he is giving the essence of is *propositions*' is nonsense; not nonsense because it doesn't count as a proper proposition, but nonsense because of the incoherent demands that we make on what the word 'proposition' can be thought to do. But that point leads right back to the question how it can be philosophically illuminating to lay out the picture-proposition use, if there is no claim that what is laid out is *propositionhood*. After discussing this problem again, I shall end this section by showing how philosophical activity, as I have been describing it, is connected with questions about nonsense. Although in this section I shall be wrestling with Anscombe, my aim is to think about what she herself does in presenting the picture theory. I see her philosophical *doing* as in tension with what she says about what the picture theory was supposed to accomplish, and in tension, in particular, with her exclusionary reading of the theory.

Consider again the philosophical activity of laying out the picture-proposition use. We are invited to have before our minds an ordinary picture: perhaps a realistic picture of a tree, perhaps a schematic diagram of people fencing. We are then led to *take* that picture differently. The ordinary picture that is used as an example will be one in which it is easy to see that the connection of the picture-elements that represent things is the connection that those things are represented as having. It will be easy to see that the possibility of such a connection of the things is there in the picture itself, in the connection of its picture-elements. By being led to note these features of the ordinary picture, we can be led to *take it in as a logical picture*, to take it in as having logico-pictorial form. I want to suggest that this transformation to *logical taking-in* is central in the way the ordinary picture is used in the philosophical activity. This transformation is not a matter of taking in the picture as having a property of which we had been unaware. When we come to see something as having a property of which we had been unaware, we can grasp that other things can also have the property; the grasp of such generality is part of what is involved in recognition of a property. But the generality involved in the transformation of our understanding of an ordinary picture is different. To take in an ordinary picture as a logical picture is to see something generalizable in it, but the generality of 'logical picture-hood' is not that of a property. When Wittgenstein says, in the *Tractatus*, that every picture is also a logical picture (2.182) this doesn't mean that, for all x, if x is a such-and-such, it is also a thus-and-so. In being led to take in the ordinary picture as a logical picture, we see the logical kind in the particular case; we see in it a logical shareable. To take in the picture as having logico-pictorial form is to take it in as having a logical characteristic that can be present in cases which do not share the particular pictorial form of the simple example from which we started, but which share only the most general logical feature of the example, namely that the way things are represented as being is the way the picture-elements are themselves connected, and the possibility of the things being that way is present in the connection of picture-elements. This identity may be present in only the most abstract sense, in contrast with the ordinary kinds of case used as examples, in which the identity of form is identity in the role of colour or spatial relations in the representation and in what is represented. Consider now what Wittgenstein does in introducing the idea of propositions as themselves pictures. He invites the reader to consider a case in which *taking in* a proposition as a logical picture will be easy: the case in which the propositional sign is composed of spatial objects rather than written signs (*TLP* 3.1431). Just as we can be led to *take in* an ordinary picture as a logical picture, the core of which is its logico-pictorial form, we can be led to *take in* the spatial-object proposition as a logical picture, led (that is) to *take it in* as having logico-pictorial form. In both cases we are led to recognize a kind of generality (that of a logical kind) through a transformed taking-in of a simple case. In both cases, what we are supposedly able to see clearly after the philosophical activity is not something of which we can be thought to have been totally unaware beforehand. We could hardly operate with pictures without any awareness of their logical character; we could hardly say what was the case without being able to take in, to some degree, what Wittgenstein means when he says that in a proposition a situation is in a sense constructed by way of experiment. But the point is that such takings-in of the logical features of propositions and pictures are inchoate. What is essentially in common to all such cases is not seen.[24] The philosophical activity, focusing at first on simple cases, is meant to open our eyes to what I have called a logical

---

[24] See *TLP* 4.012, where Wittgenstein says that it is obvious that we take in a proposition of the form 'aRb' as a picture. We take in the two names, and that they are combined in such-and-such relation in the proposition, and that is indeed why we take the proposition to signify the holding of a relation between a and b. But no more is implied; to see such a proposition as a picture in this minimal sense does not involve awareness of any logical characteristics shared with other symbols.

shareable. It can be represented by means of a variable, the values of which are all the symbols that share the logical characteristic in question.

In section 30.3, I suggested that Anscombe's account of the picture theory lays out a way of using language, the picture-proposition use, and that what she does can also be described as making plain the values of a variable. I've been arguing here that, when the picture-proposition use is laid out, the starting point is a transformation of our way of taking in ordinary pictures; we are led to take them in as logical pictures, led to see them as characterized by a logically shareable feature. That's the starting point, but it is also the point that lets us see the significance of laying out the picture-proposition use. When I take in the ordinary picture as a logical picture, I take it in as exemplifying a logical characteristic. I take in, in this case, *picturing*. The laying out of the picture-proposition use gives the reach (as it were), the logical generality, of the feature which I originally take in when I conceive an ordinary picture as having an identity of form with what it represents. The significance of 'laying out the picture-proposition use' should be tied particularly to *TLP* 2.1, the first *Tractatus* remark about picturing. 'We make to ourselves pictures of facts'. We are meant to take in what we thus do in simple cases; we are meant ultimately to see *that* in its full generality. Suppose I come to see it so: I take that feature, in its logical generality, to reach through my thought, through my language, through my world. What I have called 'laying out the use of picture-propositions' is meant to connect with my self-understanding; it is meant to let me see an essence in my own thought, what it has 'within' it, 'what we see when we look *into* the thing' (*Philosophical Investigations* § 92). It is this reconception of the ordinary, as having within it something hidden, special, and with a unique total generality, that is indeed the target of Wittgenstein's later thinking.[25] In one of the early drafts of the *Investigations*, Wittgenstein spoke of how we take a 'clearly intuitive' case, and treat it as an exemplar of *all* cases; we take in a single proposition as a picture, and think that we have thereby grasped an all-comprehending essence, lying *beneath* the surface.[26]

All kinds of expressions are called propositions in ordinary talk; and Wittgenstein's remarks about propositions being pictures plainly don't imply that mathematical propositions, or logical propositions (etc.) are pictures. But note now that it cannot be said that the reason his remarks don't apply to such cases is that he is making clear what is a *genuine proposition*, as opposed to those other things. What constantly guides our thought

---

[25] Marie McGinn 1999 also emphasizes the role of a reconception of the ordinary in Wittgenstein's method. Her account differs from mine in drawing a distinction between elucidations which make possible the disappearance of philosophical problems through the kind of reconception of the ordinary to which they lead us and remarks which reflect Wittgenstein's theoretical preconceptions, including centrally the idea of logical form as expressed in a variable. I think that Wittgenstein's understanding of logical generality (the generality of a variable) is not separable from the kind of reconception of the ordinary at which he aimed in the *Tractatus* and which he took to be capable of resolving philosophical problems, but I cannot here go into my reasons for disagreeing with McGinn.

[26] Wittgenstein 2000, TS 220 §93/MS 142 §§105–6; cf. also *Zettel* §444. Wittgenstein also in these remarks says that it is a characteristic of the sort of theory that he accepted that it doesn't present itself as a theory; one takes oneself merely to have seen what is there *in* the clear intuitive case.

here, and constantly leads us in a wrong direction, is the idea that we have a concept of *propositions* and Wittgenstein is clarifying it, or trying to show what is involved in it. We constantly think in terms of a *concept* here, and what genuinely falls under it; but what we have to do with is a *formal concept*, that is to say, *not* a concept. As long as we think of the *Tractatus* as doing something or other with *the concept of a proposition*, we set ourselves up to miss what he is doing. An essential contrast for the book is that between a property and a logical shareable; and what lacks a particular logical shareable is not thereby shown in any way to be 'rejected' or 'excluded'.

That last point is important when we think about Wittgenstein's later criticism of the *Tractatus*. For it is sometimes said, as Anscombe herself says, that what was wrong with the picture-theory is that 'it is correct only within a restricted area'; the idea is that there are various sorts of expressions that are genuine propositions, but that are excluded from the realm of propositions, because they are not in the 'restricted area' to which the picture theory applies. But this criticism depends upon taking the picture theory to be at one and the same time a presentation of a logical shareable (which it is) and a general account of propositionhood or sense (understood in some other way). For the idea is of a 'larger area', including both the 'restricted area' and what has been left out of it; and if the 'restricted area' is that of picture-propositions, i.e., the region characterized by the logical shareable, the larger area must be understood differently. Wittgenstein's own criticism is quite different; it is that the supposed 'logical shareable' was actually part of the form of description of a multitude of very different cases; it was read into them, not discovered in them. And he rejected also the idea that a logical kind was presented by a variable, the values of which shared a logical characteristic.

It might be objected to my claim that laying out a use doesn't exclude anything that it misses the point, since the *Tractatus* is engaged not just in laying out the picture-proposition use, but in characterizing all other kinds of cases of proposition-like constructions, apart from tautologies and contradictions, as nonsensical. What is this if not some kind of exclusion? And, indeed, doesn't the image that I used in explaining Wittgenstein's aim, that the reader should come to think of logico-pictorial form as reaching, in its generality, right through 'my thought, my language, my world' suggest that everything that lacks logico-pictorial form is pushed out into outer darkness? Consider here Anscombe's way of thinking, as it emerges in her treatment of sentences of the form "'p' says that p'. Wittgenstein had said that 'A believes that p' is of the same form as "'p' says that p'. She says that Wittgenstein thereby gives us "'p' says that p' as a possible form of proposition, and that therefore, if Wittgenstein has not been careless, 'it must fit his general account of propositions—that is, it must have true-false poles' (p. 88). That is (on her view), a proposition of this form is plainly not a tautology, and so, if it is not nonsensical, it must be a bipolar proposition, what I have here called a picture-proposition. There is, as she is presenting the case, no room for sentences to 'fit in' if they don't fit in as tautologies or contradictions or bipolar propositions. But we should, I think, follow Michael Kremer (2002) in reading the *Tractatus* to allow for various kinds of sentences which, like tautologies and contradictions, guide us in inferring non-logical propositions from non-logical propositions. These auxiliaries to inference are without sense, but not nonsensical;

far from it. They have an important kind of use, but it is not the use of saying how things are. I believe that there are quite a number of different types of auxiliaries to ordinary talk (*Behelfe der Darstellung*) recognized in the *Tractatus*, and there is no reason to think that other sorts of auxiliaries would not also be capable of 'fitting in' to the overall picture. Thus, for example, the sentence '*Aus, bei, mit, nach, seit, von*, and *zu* take the dative', if it is taken to express a rule (rather than a generalization about German-speakers) can be regarded as an auxiliary to description, in the sense that it guides the construction of propositions. Indeed, one could read *TLP* 3.343, which says that definitions are rules for translating from one language into another, as introducing a quite broad category of rules of translation, which would include the rule about German prepositions. It would, I think, be wrong to take the *Tractatus* to imply that such rules are nonsensical. Kremer discusses in detail the *Tractatus* account of identities and of mathematical equations. He argues that such expressions fit in to the overall *Tractatus* view in roughly the same kind of way as do tautologies and contradictions, and should be taken to be senseless, rather than nonsensical.[27] Other cases, discussed in the *Tractatus*, of auxiliaries to description include the presentation of an expression by means of a variable whose values are the propositions containing the expression, and again also the stipulation of the values of a variable. Besides those cases, there are the laws of mechanics, which are not logical pictures of the world, but give forms in which descriptions can be cast.[28] Wittgenstein's later discussions of 'hypotheses' suggest a similar sort of use of sentences which may look like descriptions but which function as a kind of auxiliary to description. My point here, in opposition to Anscombe, is not that propositions of the form '"p" says that p' *should* be treated as rules, but only that there is much more room in the *Tractatus* for miscellaneous uses of language than we might think. It follows that, when a kind of sentence can be seen not to have the use of a picture-proposition, nor to be tautologous or contradictory, it is not thereby cast into outer darkness. It is indeed excluded from the realm of picture-propositions, of sentences that are used as such sentences are, sentences that represent a situation in logical space. But the question what use it has, if any, is open.

Anscombe's discussions of what is allegedly excluded by the *Tractatus* account of propositions are somewhat puzzling, in any case. For consider what she says about 'Red is a colour' (p. 82). She says that, for such a case as this, the point is easily made that the sentence cannot express anything that might be false, since there are not two possibilities: that red is and that it isn't a colour, of which the first happens to be the case. Here she sees the sentence as being excluded from sensefulness because it is not bipolar; but she herself has given, as Wittgenstein's view, that we present a symbol, not by putting it down and saying that it is a symbol of such-and-such a kind, but by representing the class of

---

[27] See *TLP* 5.5303, where Wittgenstein contrasts two sorts of case of sentences that are not senseful, one sort being nonsense and the other 'saying nothing', i.e., being senseless. Here he plainly allows for sentences which do not have sense but are not nonsense, though not tautologies or contradictions. The passage seems inconsistent with readings that ascribe to Wittgenstein the view that the only sorts of sentences that lack sense but are not nonsensical are tautologies and contradictions. See Kremer 2002 for further discussion of *TLP* 5.5303.

[28] Cf. Griffin 1964, Ch. 8, § 5, esp. pp. 102–3.

propositions in which that symbol occurs. What, then, if we take the symbol 'red' that is used in colour-attributions, and think of presenting it through the class of propositions in which it occurs as that symbol? The symbol is a mark of a form and content that propositions can have in common, but 'Red is a colour' isn't one of the propositions with that shareable form and content. It has only the sign in common with those propositions, and the practice of using 'red' as a colour-word in those propositions doesn't settle what meaning, if any, it has in 'Red is a colour'.[29] There is a further question about the formal concept *colour*. Anscombe's view appears to be that the reason why formal concepts can't be presented by a function is that the attempt to do so (as in the attempt to treat being a colour as a property of *red*) leads us to construct propositions that cannot express anything that might be false. But that is not the problem. That is, the problem isn't that falling under a formal concept is a matter of having a property that *can't be said* to hold of the things in question. It is rather that it honestly and truly isn't a matter of a property *at all*, but is seen in a shared feature of a class of senseful propositions. A logical kind isn't a kind that things necessarily belong to; it's not a kind that you can't say things fall into; its difference from *kinds*, as we think of them, goes deeper than that. The word 'colour', in Anscombe's example, does not have the use of a formal concept word, and it has not been given any alternative meaning as a property word. It is not clear that the word 'colour' has any meaning in that context. Anscombe's illustration of the kind of sentence that is excluded from sensefulness on the *Tractatus* view was meant to show that the *Tractatus* view covers only some of the territory of what we take ourselves to be able to say; but the *Tractatus* does not imply that 'Red is a colour' is not capable of being false, and that it is, for that reason, excluded from sense. An argument based on the *Tractatus* would investigate what use, if any, had been given to the words in 'Red is a colour' which were taken over from a context in which they had a different sort of use.[30]

Most of Wittgenstein's propositions in the *Tractatus* use words like 'object' and 'proposition' which have an unproblematic use in everyday talk as formal concepts. In conceptual notation, he says, the use of these terms would go over to variables. But in the *Tractatus*, these words are not used as they are in ordinary talk, and the *Tractatus* remarks would not go over in a conceptual notation to formulae with variables. The contrast is clear in Wittgenstein's own pair of examples (*TLP* 4.1272): 'There are two objects which…' and 'There are objects'. The trouble with the latter proposition is not that it

---

[29] The sign 'Red' in any case has a variety of uses: it is a nickname, and people also may say that Red is what it is worse to be than to be dead, or that Red is what Virginia ceased to be in 2008. One might try to rule out such uses of 'Red' by saying 'The *colour* Red is a colour', but that spoils the example by making the sentence appear to be totally empty. The example is meant to be a sentence that appears not to be empty, but which also appears not to be capable of being false. See also Wittgenstein (1956, I, § 105) on the use of colour-words as names of colours in contexts like 'Black is darker than white'. Although Wittgenstein does not there use the contrast between sign and symbol, the point he makes is that there is a question what the use, if any, is of 'Black is darker than white', since the words 'Black', 'white', and 'darker than' are plainly not being used as they are in ordinary useful statements.

[30] Anscombe has another example, '"Someone" is not the name of someone' (p. 85), which I discuss in Diamond 2004. I consider the *Tractatus* treatment of necessary truths in Diamond 2011.

is not capable of being false; it is that 'objects', in that context, seems not to have any meaning. In 'There are objects', 'objects' hasn't got the use it has in 'There are two objects which ...', which goes over, in conceptual notation, to a formula with quantifiers and variables. The sentence 'There are objects' appears to give to 'objects' a logical role of the same sort as that of 'books' in 'There are books'. If 'objects' in 'There are objects' were given an appropriate sort of meaning, as a word for a kind of thing, the sentence would be meaningful. The fact that in other contexts the word is a formal concept word doesn't carry over to its use in 'There are objects', which has only the sign, not the symbol, in common with such other sentential contexts. The difficulty is, of course, that we don't want to give the word 'objects' some other meaning; we want it to carry with it its role as a formal concept word, and to mean, in 'There are objects', the logical kind *objects*. And similarly with *Tractatus* remarks containing the word 'propositions'. We read the word as meaning *propositions*, regardless of the fact that the word does not occur in these remarks as a formal concept word. We don't read those remarks with any doubt or suspicion about what the word means *in them*. But the *Tractatus* view is that the word 'propositions' occurs with the meaning that we unthinkingly suppose it to have in those remarks when it is used in a certain way: when it occurs in a sentence which would go over in conceptual notation to a formula containing the variable given in *TLP* 6, 'the general form of proposition'. I think it can be shown, for example, that 'Every proposition uttered by Cheney is false' is, on the *Tractatus* view, translatable into a sentence with that variable.[31] In that sentence, the word 'proposition' has the use of a word for a formal concept, just as, in 'There are two objects which ...', the word 'object' has the use of a word for a formal concept. But the *Tractatus* remarks containing the word 'proposition' do not use the word as a formal concept word. It is used, one might say, as a word pretending to be a formal concept word, and it is not given any other use. The remarks do not convey a content of a special sort which cannot be put into senseful language; they contain words with no meaning and are nonsense. They have a function within the context of the book, a book meant not only to present a use but to lead its readers to *take* their own thought and language to have in it the logical shareable that the book presents. Their function within the context of the book is described by the metaphor of the ladder that is thrown away. They are helps on the way to recognition of the contrast between logical shareables and kinds of things, a contrast the recognition of which undoes the impression they initially make of conveying a content. The recognition of that contrast is not a matter of taking *being a proposition* to be something we can't speak of; it is a matter of getting the point of philosophy as a kind of practice, in which logical shareables are displayed, as in the case of the laying out of the picture-proposition use of words.[32]

A full discussion of exclusionary readings of the *Tractatus* would have to look at Wittgenstein's treatment of the limits of language. Exclusionary readings take Wittgenstein's talk of limits to involve a conception of what lies outside, what cannot

---

[31] The sentence does not involve quantifying over propositions, although it looks as if it would do so. It involves the use of operations to construct a new proposition. See Diamond 2012.

[32] See note 37 below on my use of the contrasting pair of predicates 'logical shareable' and 'property'.

be said, and what sorts of attempted sayings fail because they are attempts to speak of what lies outside. Such readings involve what Peter Sullivan has called a *contrastive* understanding of the notion of a limit. There are then questions how far, and in what ways, such an understanding might be taken to be undercut by the *Tractatus*. Peter Sullivan (2011), A. W. Moore (2007), Juliet Floyd (2007), and I (2012) have discussed these questions, but to have gone into them here would have doubled the length of this chapter.

30.6 CONCLUSIONS

The technique, of sharpening the reader's eyes to a logical shareable through attention to linguistic patterns and their ties to inference, is Fregean, as is the connection between the recognition of a logical shareable and the use of the context principle. Frege also (in 'On Concept and Object') confronts the problem that I have been discussing. He presents a logical shareable, call it 'Fregean concepthood', and makes clear that he is not attempting to capture what is usually meant by the term 'concept', which, as he notes, is used in various ways (1984, p. 182). He is not suggesting, that is, that all and only Fregean concepts are *concepts*. At the end of his reply to Benno Kerry, he says that Kerry can use the words 'concept' and 'object' however he likes, but Frege too has a right to use 'concept' and 'object' in the way he has laid out (p. 193). But then the question arises, if what he has laid out is his way of using the terms, and if he is not giving an account of *concepthood*, what is the significance of what he has done? We have, he thinks, only a 'vague notion' of what is involved in our own thinking and inferring (1979, p. 253). We can take his logical distinctions up into our understanding, and thereby bring the logical characteristics of our thinking into focus, at the same time separating off what is inessential, and what is the result of psychologistic accretions.

Wittgenstein takes over from Frege, or simply gets on his own, the connection between the idea of a logical shareable and the context principle. He takes over from Frege, or simply gets on his own, the idea that laying out features of our use of words can make 'extremely intelligible' what we might otherwise have taken to be a kind of ultimate logical fact, as for example that every proposition has exactly one negation. There is already in Frege a conception of a technique by which thought itself can be clarified, the technique of making plain logical having-in-common, a technique we can see already in *Begriffsschrift*, in the suggestion that we think of 'subtracting' from a proposition a part or parts that can be thought to vary, leaving a part that is *logically in common* with other propositions. Wittgenstein's distinction between signs and symbols (where symbols are logical shareables) is an application of the context principle, and a corresponding distinction is clearly at work in Frege, in 'On Concept and Object' and elsewhere. But Wittgenstein gives the sign–symbol distinction a particular twist, by applying it to the question what it is for us to be using a word for a logical kind. What is shared by words used for a logical kind, when they are used for a logical kind, is clear if the propositions in which they occur are thought of as they would appear in a conceptual notation, in which sameness of sign invariably does indicate sameness of symbol, unlike the situation in ordinary language. In a conceptual notation, words that in ordinary language are genuinely in use as words for a logical kind go over to an appropriate variable. In this notational point there is reflected the profound difference between words for logical kinds and words for ordinary kinds. Now put together the Fregean point and the Wittgenstein twist.[33] We can clarify logical features of our thought by making plain logical having-in-common, as in laying out the picture-proposition use of words. If, on the other hand, we think of ourselves as trying to give a theory of *propositionhood* (say), we can come to see that, in doing so, we will use the word 'proposition', which we want to use as a word for a logical kind, in a way which defeats our purpose. When theorizing about propositionhood, we use the word 'proposition' so that it is not the equivalent of a variable, but a word with the grammar of a word for an ordinary kind. Because we want to investigate a logical kind, we are not going to give 'proposition', in these investigations, a use as a word for something else; but since it is (in the context of these investigations) not a word for a logical kind, and not a word for anything else, what we say is nonsense. It is noteworthy that in criticizing Wittgenstein's account of language, we may find ourselves doing exactly the same thing, and thereby missing a fundamental point of the book. We think of the *Tractatus* as an attempt to convey that thus-and-such is *what propositions are*, but the point is rather this: If you talk about *propositions* as you want to, you will not be saying anything at all. You misunderstand what you are after: you want to speak of a logical kind, and you also want to theorize about it in the language of ordinary kinds; and these two aims together will lead you to talk *real rubbish*.[34] The same point can be made about other topics of philosophical investigation. Philosophical investigation is self-defeating when it aims at an understanding of logical kinds, but investigates them in language which is not logical-kind language. You can show understanding of the aim of the book in turning from philosophical theorizing to a form of philosophical activity that can illuminate logical shareables by laying out the ways in which we use language. This is a very different kind of procedure, as comes out especially in the fact that laying out a use does not exclude anything, but can lead us to a different way of conceiving what had appeared problematic. Juliet Floyd (2007, Part 2) makes a related point about Wittgenstein's understanding of how philosophical problems are posed. Philosophical problems are those 'whose very formulation contains terms that require interrogation, or reconception, in order to be solved' (pp. 189–90), and she connects Wittgenstein's conception in the *Tractatus* of philosophical problems with his lifelong interest in the contrast between searching when you have a framework

---

[33] The 'Wittgensteinian twist' is still very Fregean. See Ricketts 2010, Part 5, on the 'self-stultifying' character of the attempt to use the predicates 'concept' and 'object' to make clear the distinction between concepts and objects.

[34] The expression 'real rubbish' comes from Anscombe's discussion (1989, pp. 10–11) of the contrast between ethical nonsense of the sort for which Wittgenstein had great respect and ethical nonsense which he would have liked to see disappear. But I am not using the term in exactly the way she does.

for finding an answer and searching when you do not know in advance what will count as a solution.[35]

Philosophical activity, as Wittgenstein understands it, reshapes desire. We start off wanting to know *the essence of propositions*, or how *thought* is connected with *reality*. So long as we use the language in which the problems present themselves, we will get nowhere; the questions are not the sorts of questions we take them for. The activity of presenting a logical shareable, of putting it into a sharp focus, can put the logic of our thinking before us, and we can recognize in what we thus come to see (although it wasn't the sort of answer we had been in search of) what we had wanted. If we let the philosophical activity shape our self-understanding in this way, we may give the logical shareable a label. What I have in mind is illustrated by labelling Fregean concepts 'concepts' and by labelling picture-propositions 'propositions'. The word 'proposition' can be taken over from its use in our attempts to discover *what propositions are*. It can be turned into a label for the picture-proposition use, where the choice of such a label reflects seeing our own thought through the logical-organizing lens of the logical shareable, and seeing the importance (the reach through our thought) of that logical shareable. This (I'm suggesting) is not a matter of our taking ourselves to have discovered what propositions are; and speaking of Fregean concepts as concepts isn't taking ourselves to have discovered what concepts are; we are sharpening our focus on a logical form, and seeing it in, or seeing it 'into', our thought. The label itself is no more than a reminder; it points us towards a previous clarification of a logical shareable. Wittgenstein can say 'Here is the general form of the proposition', but this is not the discovery of *what propositions are*, and a fortiori not the discovery of *what is excluded from being a proposition*. Sentences which are not picture-propositions are not picture-propositions. That's what they aren't. It won't be all that they aren't (they may also not be heroic couplets, quotations from Hume, or whatever) but there's nothing that, in not being picture-propositions, they thereby aren't. I want to pick up a Fregean way of putting these issues from Thomas Ricketts. Frege's elucidations make use of 'concept' and 'object' as a contrasting pair of predicates. Once his intended audience has mastered his conceptual notation, the confusion latent in the elucidations becomes manifest, as they try to paraphrase the remarks into the notation; but they find no thought to which 'No object is a concept' (for example) corresponds. A master of the notation is free to discard the contrasting use, in Frege's elucidations, of the predicates 'concept' and 'object', free to take the elucidations to be so much hand-waving. There isn't then something left over that is not expressed in the notation.[36] What corresponds in the case we have been considering is the contrasting pair, 'proposition' 'not a senseful proposition', as predicates in the *Tractatus*. When we have mastered what Wittgenstein is presenting through elucidatory propositions that use such predicates, we are free to

---

[35] See also Floyd 1995 and Floyd 2000.

[36] Ricketts 2010, pp. 191–3. I have stayed very close to Ricketts's wording in this summary of his account of how we are meant to take Frege's elucidations of 'concept' and 'object', but I have departed too far from his exact words to use quotation marks.

drop the predicates, and to take the elucidations to be so much hand-waving. There isn't then something left over that we haven't been able to put into words.[37]

Anscombe wanted her book to change how people read the *Tractatus*. In section 30.1 of this chapter, I brought out problems in her story about what was wrong with earlier readings. I tried to show that her account of the picture theory points us to fundamental connections between Frege's approach and Wittgenstein's. While the sorts of reading she attacked are less popular than they once were, her critique can be taken to be directed also against many later readings—readings which resemble those of her contemporaries in their dependence on an object-based understanding of language and thought, which they read into Wittgenstein. I have also argued that the *Tractatus* is meant to lead its readers to a different kind of practice of philosophy, and that, although Anscombe doesn't say much about philosophical activity, what she actually does in her account of the picture theory can be thought of as exemplifying the kind of philosophical activity to which the *Tractatus* was meant to lead. In sections 30.5 and 30.6, I tried to set against each other some of Anscombe's own remarks about the *Tractatus* and ideas to which one can be led by following out what is implicit (I claimed) in her philosophical practice. I tried to show the tension between her remarks about what Wittgenstein's conception of propositions *excludes* and her own insistence on the central importance of Frege and the context principle for a reading of the book. For it is just such an approach that helps us to see problems with the word 'proposition', as it is used in claims about what Wittgenstein's theory excludes from propositionhood, helps us to see how the word can cover over a blur in our thought. I should want to claim that, if we follow out ideas implicit in Anscombe's practice, together with points she makes about 'logical chemistry' and about how symbols can be presented, we can get a good idea how Wittgenstein hoped his book would revolutionize philosophy.

In his study of anti-metaphysical readings of the *Tractatus*, Warren Goldfarb (2011) includes Anscombe among metaphysical readers, along with Peter Geach, David Pears, Norman Malcolm, and Peter Hacker. He traces the development of anti-metaphysical readings of the book, beginning in 1969 with Hidé Ishiguro's 'Use and Reference of Names'. As he mentions, it is the realism of readings like those of Malcolm, Pears, and Hacker that was at first the focus of criticism. Anscombe's position is very interesting and in some ways anomalous. She would have found unexceptionable the statement of Hacker's that Goldfarb uses to set out the metaphysical reading. Hacker says, and Anscombe would agree, that Wittgenstein was committed in the *Tractatus* 'to a host of claims about logic, language, thought and the logical structure of the world, which cannot be stated in well-formed sentences of language' (2000, p. 383). But it is not clear how much further Anscombe's agreement goes—not clear whether she takes

---

[37] The case is similar with my use of the contrasting pair of predicates, 'logical shareable' and 'property'. Like the use of 'concept' and 'object' as a contrasting pair of predicates, such talk can serve a purpose, despite the confusion latent in it. It can help point us to philosophical activity in which differences can be perspicuously presented; and (as with 'concept' and 'object'), there isn't then an unexpressed something that is left over.

the Hacker–Pears–Malcolm view that Wittgenstein's 'objects' are independent of us and prior to language, and impose on language the structure it must have in order for what we say to express genuine possibilities.[38] But besides the question how close Anscombe really is to the metaphysical readers, there is the question how close she is to the anti-metaphysical interpreters.[39] The starting point of Ishiguro's essay is the ascription to Wittgenstein of a view that the meaning of a name cannot 'be secured independently of its use in propositions by some method which links it to an object, as many, including Russell have thought' (p. 20); but that contrast between Wittgenstein and Russell is already present in Anscombe's interpretation, and is central in her exposition of the picture theory. I should want to take Anscombe out of the group with which Goldfarb puts her, and treat her as in important ways an inaugurator of the anti-metaphysical readings. I'm suggesting that metaphysical readings like those of Hacker, Pears, and Malcolm combine the ascription to Wittgenstein of a Russellian object-based view of language and thought with the idea, sometimes labelled the 'ineffabilist view', that the *Tractatus* is committed to substantial claims about propositions, objects, facts, and so on, claims which Wittgenstein is supposed to have taken to be correct although not statable in significant language. Although Anscombe accepts such a view, it is (I think) under far greater pressure within the overall context of her interpretation than it is in the writings of Hacker, Pears, and Malcolm. We do not need to appeal to any specifically *Tractarian* views to see the kind of pressure, for we can simply look to Frege. Frege is, quite explicitly, not telling us about *concepts*; he is constructing for us an understanding of 'concept' as a logical shareable, to be thought of as 'arising from the decomposition of a judgeable content' (1980, p. 101). He isn't getting *concepts* right; and Wittgenstein isn't getting *propositions* wrong (say) by excluding too much; he isn't getting *propositions* right by getting just the right things in. In that sense he is not making substantial claims 'about propositions', but constructing for us an understanding of 'proposition' as a logical shareable. If an expression has the use of a picture-proposition, it doesn't 'show' that *it is a proposition*. What shows in its use as a picture-proposition is simply *that*.[40]

Exclusionary readings and ineffabilist readings are closely linked. The ineffabilist reading ascribes to Wittgenstein a view of *what propositions are*, a view that cannot be stated but can be communicated despite its unsayability. And the idea that the *Tractatus* excludes from propositionhood sentences that are not bipolar (or whatever the excluding criterion is supposed to be) depends upon the idea that Wittgenstein held in the *Tractatus*, but took to be unsayable, the claim that thus-and-such is what genuine propositions are, and that all other putative propositions are excluded from genuine propositionhood.[41] Against this, I have argued that Wittgenstein, like Frege, presents logical

---

[38] There is one sentence of Anscombe's which might be read as implying something like the realist reading, on *IWT* p. 110, where she refers to objects as the 'original seat' of form, but her sentence is meant simply to summarize *TLP* 2.0121. I don't think it should be taken to indicate agreement with the kind of object-based readings given by Hacker, Pears, and Malcolm.

[39] See McManus 2006, p. 68, n 5, for comments on a related issue.

[40] See Kremer 2007, especially the discussion of 'features', pp. 159–62.

[41] For a good illustration of how ineffabilist and exclusionary readings may be linked, see Hacker 2000, especially pp. 353–6.

shareables, and that to do so is to invite a kind of reconceptualization of one's own prac-tice-of-thinking-and-inferring; one sees the logical shareable reaching through that practice. As a result, features of thought that had appeared philosophically puzzling can come to be seen as unproblematic; this, at any rate, is the hope. Peter Geach had argued that there is a test whether someone has *got* the differences in logical kind that Frege was trying to convey through his elucidations. The test (which could be carried out by uni-versity examiners, say) would be whether she can work properly with a logical notation like Frege's (1976, p. 70). A test for whether someone has got the point of Wittgenstein's elucidations would be what she went on to do when she took herself to be engaging in philosophy.

In our thinking, speaking, and inferring—in such doings—logical shareables are dis-played. Learning to see these shareables clearly is a kind of philosophical achievement—on a remarkable and interesting and highly original conception of philosophy. An appreciation of the dangers of this conception of philosophy came later for Wittgenstein. When Wittgenstein said that the way we pose philosophical problems reflects misunder-standing of the logic of our language, he did not mean that we go around saying things that are excluded from the realm of sense; he meant that the misrepresentation of logical kinds is deep in our understanding of our problems.[42]

REFERENCES

Anscombe, G. E. M. (1963). *An Introduction to Wittgenstein's 'Tractatus'*, 2nd edn. London: Hutchinson University Library. 1st edn. London: Hutchinson University Library, 1959.
——(1989). 'The Simplicity of the *Tractatus*', *Critica* 21: 3–14.
Bronzo, Silver (2011). 'Context, Compositionality, and Nonsense in Wittgenstein's *Tractatus*'. In Rupert Read and Matthew A. Lavery (eds.), *Beyond the Tractatus Wars: The New Wittgenstein Debate*. London: Routledge, pp. 84–111.
Crary, Alice (ed.) (2007). *Wittgenstein and the Moral Life*. Cambridge, MA: MIT Press.
Crary, Alice and Rupert Read (eds.) (2000). *The New Wittgenstein*. London: Routledge.
Diamond, Cora (2003). 'Finding One's Way Into the *Tractatus*', *Sats* 4: 165–82.
——(2004). 'Saying and Showing: An Example from Anscombe'. In Barry Stocker (ed.), *Post-Analytic Tractatus*. Aldershot: Ashgate, pp. 151–66.
——(2011). 'The *Tractatus* and the Limits of Sense'. In Oskari Kuusela and Marie McGinn (eds.), *The Oxford Handbook of Wittgenstein*. Oxford: Oxford University Press, pp. 240–75.
——(2012). 'What Can You Do With the General Form of Proposition?' In José Zalabardo (ed.), *Wittgenstein's Early Philosophy*. Oxford: Oxford University Press, pp. 151–94.
Floyd, Juliet (1995). 'On Saying What You Really Want to Say: Wittgenstein, Gödel, and the Trisection of the Angle'. In J. Hintikka (ed.), *From Dedekind to Gödel: Essays on the Foundations of Mathematics*. Dordrecht: Kluwer, pp. 373–426.
——(2000). 'Wittgenstein, Mathematics, Philosophy'. In Crary and Read (2000), pp. 232–61.
——(2007). 'Wittgenstein and the Inexpressible'. In Crary (2007), pp. 177–234.

[42] I am grateful to James Conant, Michael Beaney, and Alice Crary for their comments and suggestions.

Frege, Gottlob (1979). 'Notes for Ludwig Darmstaedter', tr. P. Long and R. White. In Frege, *Posthumous Writings*, ed. Hans Hermes *et al.* Oxford: Blackwell, pp. 253–7. Originally written 1919.

—— (1980). Letter to Anton Marty, tr. H. Kaal. In Frege, *Philosophical and Mathematical Correspondence*, ed. Brian McGuinness. Oxford: Blackwell, pp. 99–102. Originally written 1882.

——(1984). 'On Concept and Object', tr. Peter Geach. In Frege, *Collected Papers on Mathematics, Logic, and Philosophy*, ed. Brian McGuinness. Oxford: Blackwell, pp. 182–94. Originally published in *Vierteljahrsschrift für wissenschaftliche Philosophie* 16 (1892): 192–205.

Geach, P. T. (1976). 'Saying and Showing in Frege and Wittgenstein'. In J. Hintikka (ed.), *Essays on Wittgenstein in Honour of G. H. von Wright*, *Acta Philosophica Fennica* 28: 54–70.

Goldfarb, Warren (2002). 'Wittgenstein's Understanding of Frege: The Pre-Tractarian Evidence'. In Erich H. Reck (ed.), *From Frege to Wittgenstein*. New York: Oxford University Press, pp. 185–200.

—— (2011). 'Das Überwinden: Anti-metaphysical Readings of the *Tractatus*'. In Rupert Read and Matthew A. Lavery (eds.), *Beyond the Tractatus Wars: The New Wittgenstein Debate*. London: Routledge, pp. 6–21.

——(Unpublished). 'Objects, Names, and Realism in the *Tractatus*'.

Griffin, James (1964). *Wittgenstein's Logical Atomism*. Oxford: Clarendon Press.

Hacker, P. M. S. (2000). 'Was He Trying To Whistle It?' In Crary and Read (2000), pp. 353–88.

Hylton, Peter (1990). *Russell, Idealism and the Emergence of Analytic Philosophy*. Oxford: Clarendon Press.

——(2005). 'Frege and Russell'. In Hylton, *Propositions, Functions, and Analysis: Selected Essays on Russell's Philosophy*. Oxford: Clarendon Press, pp. 153–84.

Ishiguro, Hidé (1969). 'Use and Reference of Names'. In Peter Winch (ed.), *Studies in the Philosophy of Wittgenstein*. London: Routledge & Kegan Paul, pp. 20–50.

Kremer, Michael (1997). 'Contextualism and Holism in the Early Wittgenstein: From *Prototractatus* to *Tractatus*', *Philosophical Topics* 25: 87–120.

—— (2002). 'Mathematics and Meaning in the *Tractatus*', *Philosophical Investigations* 25: 272–303.

——(2007). 'The Cardinal Problem of Philosophy'. In Crary (2007), pp. 143–76.

McGinn, Marie (1999). 'Between Metaphysics and Nonsense: Elucidation in Wittgenstein's *Tractatus*', *Philosophical Quarterly* 49: 491–513.

——(2006). *Elucidating the Tractatus*. Oxford: Clarendon Press.

McGuinness, B. F. (1981). 'The So-Called Realism of Wittgenstein's *Tractatus*'. In Irving Block (ed.), *Perspectives on the Philosophy of Wittgenstein*. Oxford: Blackwell, pp. 60–73.

McManus, Denis (2006). *The Enchantment of Words*. Oxford: Clarendon Press.

Malcolm, Norman (1986). *Nothing is Hidden: Wittgenstein's Criticism of his Early Thought*. Oxford: Blackwell.

Mill, John Stuart (1843). *A System of Logic*. London: John W. Parker.

Moore, A. W. (2007). 'Wittgenstein and Transcendental Idealism'. In Guy Kahane *et al.* (eds.), *Wittgenstein and His Interpreters*. Oxford: Blackwell, pp. 174–99.

Moyal-Sharrock, Daniele (2007). 'The Good Sense of Nonsense', *Philosophy* 82: 147–77.

Pears, David (1987). *False Prison: A Study of the Development of Wittgenstein's Philosophy*, 2 vols. Oxford: Clarendon Press.

Ricketts, Thomas (1996). 'Pictures, Logic, and the Limits of Sense'. In Hans Sluga and David Stern (eds.), *The Cambridge Companion to Wittgenstein*. Cambridge: Cambridge University Press, pp. 59–99.

—— (2010). 'Concepts, Objects and the Context Principle'. In Michael Potter and Thomas Ricketts (eds.), *The Cambridge Companion to Frege*. Cambridge: Cambridge University Press, pp. 149–219.

Russell, Bertrand (1932). 'Knowledge by Acquaintance and Knowledge by Description'. In Russell, *Mysticism and Logic*. London: Allen & Unwin, pp. 209–32. Originally published in *Proceedings of the Aristotelian Society* 11 (1910–11): 108–28.

—— (1956). 'On Denoting'. In Russell, *Logic and Knowledge*, ed. R. Marsh. London: Allen & Unwin, pp. 41–56. Originally published in *Mind* 14 (1905):. 479–93.

—— (1967). *Problems of Philosophy*. Oxford: Oxford University Press. Originally published in Home University Library. London: Williams & Norgate, 1912.

Sullivan, Peter (2001). 'A Version of the Picture Theory'. In Wilhelm Vossenkuhl (ed.), *Ludwig Wittgenstein: Tractatus Logico-Philosophicus*. Berlin: Akademie Verlag, pp. 89–110.

—— (2004). '"The general propositional form is a variable" (*Tractatus* 4.53)', *Mind* 113: 43–56.

—— (2011). 'Synthesizing Without Concepts'. In Rupert Read and Matthew A. Lavery (eds.), *Beyond the Tractatus Wars: The New Wittgenstein Debate*. London: Routledge, pp. 171–89.

Urmson, J. O. (1956). *Philosophical Analysis: Its Development between the Two World Wars*. Oxford: Clarendon Press.

Weiner, Joan (1999). *Frege*. New York: Oxford University Press.

Winch, Peter (1987). 'Language, Thought and World in Wittgenstein's *Tractatus*'. In Winch, *Trying to Make Sense*. Oxford: Blackwell, pp. 3–17.

Wittgenstein, Ludwig (1953). *Philosophical Investigations*, ed. G. E. M. Anscombe and R. Rhees, tr. G. E. M. Anscombe. Oxford: Blackwell.

—— (1956). *Remarks on the Foundations of Mathematics*, ed. G. H. von Wright *et al.*, tr. G. E. M. Anscombe. Oxford: Blackwell.

—— (1963). *Tractatus Logico-Philosophicus*, tr. D. F. Pears and B. F. McGuinness. London: Routledge & Kegan Paul.

—— (1967). *Zettel*, ed. G. E. M. Anscombe and G. H. von Wright, tr. G. E. M. Anscombe. Oxford: Blackwell.

—— (2000). *Wittgenstein's Nachlass: The Bergen Electronic Edition*. Oxford: Oxford University Press.

CHAPTER 31

IDEAS OF A LOGICALLY PERFECT LANGUAGE IN ANALYTIC PHILOSOPHY

PETER HYLTON

31.1 METAPHYSICS AND ANTI-METAPHYSICS

There is a recurrent opposition within analytic philosophy between those who put forward metaphysical views and those who oppose all metaphysics, in some cases dismissing it as nonsensical. Among those who employ the tools of modern (post-Fregean) logic, and related conceptions of philosophical analysis, some have sought to use them to discover the true nature of reality; others to use them to banish the idea that there is such a thing to be discovered. In the case of two central figures in early analytic philosophy—Frege and Wittgenstein—recent commentators differ as to whether we should read them as metaphysical or anti-metaphysical. (It should perhaps strike us as remarkable that first-rate commentators differ on what might seem like an absolutely fundamental interpretive question.)

My primary focus, in the bulk of this essay, is on metaphysical uses of the idea of a logically perfect language, and analogous ideas. Before getting to that discussion, however, I will very briefly discuss anti-metaphysical uses of the idea and, first of all, the disputed cases.

In the case of Frege, to begin with, both the metaphysical reading and the anti-metaphysical face significant difficulties. He uses the expression 'a logically perfect language' (*eine logische vollkommenere Sprache*) in a number of places.[1] It is perhaps natural to suppose

---

[1] See 'Über Sinn und Bedeutung', p. 41; the notes that Frege wrote for Ludwig Darmstaedter (*Nachgelassene Schriften*, p. 277); 'Meine grundlegenden logischen Einsichten' (*Nachgelassene Schriften*, p. 272); 'Über die Grundlagen der Geometrie, II', p. 427. I am grateful to Joan Weiner for calling my attention to these passages.

that he thinks of his *Begriffsschrift* as such a language but in fact the evidence for this is not wholly clear. One of the passages just cited certainly suggests that view but in the Preface to Frege's book called *Begriffsschrift* he says explicitly that the language developed there 'does not reproduce ideas in pure form'.[2] If Frege's *Begriffsschrift* (the formal language, not the book) is taken as a logically perfect language then we might think that it has metaphysical significance, that Frege is setting forth or presupposing fundamental distinctions within reality which correspond to the distinctions made in that language—between concepts and objects, for example. On such a reading, Frege should be counted among those who have used the idea of a logically perfect language for metaphysical ends. But there are reasons to doubt this view. One has already been noted, and further doubts arise from the fact that a sentence such as 'Concepts are not objects' cannot itself be stated in *Begriffsschrift*. If *Begriffsschrift* is indeed a logically perfect language, one might think, then only what can be stated within it is even a candidate for being the sort of full-blooded truth about reality that the metaphysician claims to offer us. This line of thought leads to the idea that Frege's version of a logically perfect language is *anti*-metaphysical: it functions to rule out what might otherwise be candidates for metaphysical truths.[3] Interpreting *Begriffsschrift* as anti-metaphysical in this way, rather than perhaps as neutral on the question of metaphysics, also has difficulties, however. It might seem to involve the claim that what cannot be stated in *Begriffsschrift* cannot be a full-blooded truth. To maintain the anti-metaphysical view of Frege, one would then have to defend that claim without making metaphysical commitments.

Similar doubts and disputes arise over the work of Wittgenstein which culminates in his *Tractatus Logico-Philosophicus*. Here the issues are perhaps better known, and I shall be yet briefer. There are those who see him as putting forward something like a logically perfect language which is based on certain ultimate facts about the world—facts which cannot themselves be stated in the language, or in any language, but which will nonetheless be evident to the careful reader. ('There is indeed the inexpressible. It makes itself manifest [*zeigt sich*] ...'.)[4] There are those who think, to the contrary, that the point of the book is to show that the very idea of unstatable facts undermines itself, and the apparent claims of the book—including apparent intimations of a logically perfect language—are straightforwardly nonsensical. Such commentators emphasize Wittgenstein's statement that anyone who understands him will eventually recognize his statements as nonsense ('*am Ende als unsinnig erkennt*').[5] Then there are those who seek a middle way, holding that the book is an exploration of necessary features of any system of representation but

---

[2] *Begriffsschrift*, Preface, pp. vi–vii.

[3] Notable among those who seem to advocate a 'metaphysical' reading of Frege is Tyler Burge. See his 'Frege on Knowing the Third Realm' and other essays reprinted in his *Truth, Thought, Reason: Essays on Frege*. For an 'anti-metaphysical' response see, for example, Joan Weiner, 'Burge's Literal Interpretation of Frege' and 'Realism bei Frege: Reply to Burge'.

[4] 6.552, my own translation. For a defence of this kind of reading, see for example Peter Hacker, *Insight and Illusion*, especially chs. 1 and 3, and 'Was He Trying To Whistle It?'

[5] 6.54. For this 'anti-metaphysical' reading, see Cora Diamond, 'Throwing Away the Ladder: How to Read the *Tractatus*' and much subsequent literature, including James Conant 'The Method of the *Tractatus*'.

draws no conclusions about the nature of the world (and, indeed, dismisses any attempt to formulate such conclusions as nonsensical).[6]

In the case of some other philosophers, there is no doubt but they have tried to use something like the idea of a logically perfect language in opposition to metaphysics. Richard Rorty discusses some such attempts in the influential introduction to his 1967 book, *The Linguistic Turn*.[7] He sees the emphasis on language from which the book takes its name as anti-metaphysical, as 'a reaction against the notion of philosophy as a discipline which attempts the solution of certain traditional problems' (p. 23). Within this general strategy of using reflections on language to argue against the possibility of metaphysics, he distinguishes two quite different methods. One is what he calls 'Ideal Language philosophy'; the other is 'Ordinary Language philosophy'. It is, of course, the first of these which draws on something analogous to the idea of a logically perfect language. The claim is that if we spoke only the 'Ideal Language' then we should find philosophical problems harder, or even impossible, to formulate; and that this fact undermines the view that such problems are genuine. Thus Rorty says: '... to find the "logical syntax" or the "logical form" of an expression is simply to find another expression which, if adopted in place of the original, makes it harder to raise traditional philosophical problems' (pp. 21–2). The implication here is that our ordinary expressions have an underlying logical form or logical syntax which would presumably be made fully explicit in the Ideal Language, with anti-metaphysical consequences.

There is an evident difficulty with an anti-metaphysical use of the idea of a logically perfect language. If one rejects metaphysics, how can one defend the idea that a given language is indeed the logically perfect language? (This is the general version of the question raised at the end of the brief discussion of Frege, three paragraphs back.) The point might be pressed further: what sense can be made of the very idea that one language is logically perfect (or ideal) without resorting to what might be labelled as metaphysics?

One might attempt to avoid this sort of difficulty by making a weaker claim: that there is a reformulated language in which the business of science, or of everyday life, could be carried out and that this language does not permit the formulation of metaphysical problems. (This sort of view might be attributed to Carnap; see § 31.3, below.) That might show that our ordinary business does not—or at least need not—involve us in metaphysical problems. Here there is no claim that the given language is logically perfect, or ideal, and so no need to defend such a claim. This would not show that metaphysics is impossible for it does not yield a knock-down argument against metaphysics, or a demonstration that its claims make no sense, or anything of that sort. But it would perhaps show that metaphysics is *optional*: that its questions do not force themselves upon us in the course of our non-philosophical activities. (Some proponents of this line may have assumed that once this was shown sensible people would choose to refrain from discussion of the useless and unresolvable questions of metaphysics; history suggests, however, that this assumption is too optimistic.)

---

[6]   See Marie McGinn, *Elucidating the Tractatus*.
[7]   I am indebted to Juliet Floyd for urging me to discuss this work in this context.

In the rest of the essay, I shall, as indicated, focus on uses of the idea of a logically perfect language which are bound up with metaphysics. To begin with, I shall discuss that idea as it occurs in Russell's work. This will give us a paradigm with which the work of other philosophers may be usefully compared. I will then briefly consider Carnap, who, in his mature work, is *not* usefully thought of as accepting anything analogous to the idea of a logically perfect language. Seeing why not will help to clarify the idea. It will also prepare the way for a discussion of Quine. In his work, I shall argue, some version of the idea does play an important role, but it is a version of the idea that differs from Russell's in crucial respects. Finally, I will very briefly consider the revival of metaphysics in the wake of Quine's rejection of Logical Positivism. Here too, I shall claim, some analogous idea is often presupposed.

31.2 RUSSELL

I begin, then, with Russell. (My concern is with the work of his most influential period, roughly 1903–19, and especially with the last few years of that period.) We can get a good sense of the idea of a logically perfect language, as I am interested in it in this essay, by looking at a passage from the second of his lectures on 'The Philosophy of Logical Atomism':

> In a logically perfect language the words in a proposition would correspond one by one with the components of the corresponding fact, with the exception of such words as 'or', 'not', 'if', 'then', which have a different function. In a logically perfect language, there will be one word and no more for every simple object, and everything that is not simple will be expressed by a combination of words...derived, of course, from the words for the simple things that enter in, one word for each simple component. A language of that sort...will show at a glance the logical structure of the facts asserted or denied. The language that is set forth in *Principia Mathematica*...aims at being that sort of language that, if you add a vocabulary, would be a logically perfect language. Actual languages are not logically perfect in this sense, and they cannot possibly be, if they are to serve the purposes of daily life. A logically perfect language, if it could be constructed, would not only be intolerably prolix, but, as regards its vocabulary, would be very largely private to one speaker. (p. 176)

It is clear from this passage that Russell's logically perfect language would show us something about the ontology of the world. It has, as I shall say, *metaphysical significance*. The justification for thinking that there is a language of this kind is not clear from this passage, and I shall revert to it shortly. But it is clear that every term in that language (except 'or' and so on) would correspond to an entity in the world. Every sentence of that language, if true, would correspond to a fact, and the structure of the sentence would show the structure of the corresponding (putative) fact—including the entities that make it up.

Something of the importance of this can be seen from the example of the reduction of arithmetic to the theory of classes—and thence to the theory of propositional functions. (This reduction functions as a paradigm in Russell's thought.) If we accept the truths of arithmetic, what entities are we thereby committed to accepting as really existing? The answer to this question is to be found not by taking the sentences of arithmetic as they stand, in ordinary language, but by analysing them. *Principia Mathematica* sets out the results of the analysis, according to which even simple arithmetical statements express very complex propositions, quite unlike the ordinary sentences which express them. According to Russell, the point is quite general. Almost every sentence, taken as it stands, as it is used in ordinary language, is misleading; taking it at face value gives the wrong account of what we would be committed to if we asserted it. Only after we have transformed it into a sentence in the logically perfect language can we read off from it what fact, what entities standing in what relations, would make it true.

The passage quoted indicates two other noteworthy features Russell's of logically perfect language. One is that the logically perfect language will be quite different from the ordinary language which serves 'the purposes of daily life'. It is extremely plausible to think that any logically perfect language which has metaphysical significance must differ from ordinary language, even if not as drastically as Russell's does. Ordinary language, taken as it is actually spoken, is a very poor candidate for a language which has metaphysical implications. Most obviously, it contains many nouns which do not seem to correspond to objects which can plausibly be thought to exist. Quine's famous example is that for each person, *A*, we can form the noun phrase: '*A*'s sake', yet we may well be reluctant to accept that there really are all those sakes in the world; further examples can be manufactured without great difficulty.

The second feature is the emphasis on *logic*. Clearly Russell is envisaging the logic of *Principia Mathematica* as forming the framework, the syntax, of the logically perfect language: (ramified) type theory plus a suitable non-logical vocabulary gives you the logically perfect language. It is perhaps only with modern logic that we can formulate a language which is both simple enough and powerful enough to make it plausible that the nature of the world can be determined from truths expressed in that language. The emphasis on logic also plays a crucial role in making the idea of a logically perfect language appealing. Paraphrasing sentences into the syntax of logic reveals and makes perspicuous many inferential connections which we accept independent of the paraphrase; it makes those connections a matter of an antecedently well-understood logic. This fact, I think, plays a significant role in making it seem as the paraphrased version does indeed capture what the ordinary sentence *really says*.

Is the clarification of inferential relations enough to justify the idea of a logically perfect language, and to justify the claim of a particular candidate for that role? If one thinks, with Russell, that the language has metaphysical significance then it may seem as if it is not. Certainly Russell himself would not think it was a sufficient answer. Given his strong realism, the fact that a given language best represents our inferential practices does not guarantee that it accurately reflects the world. The answer that Russell in fact gives is bound up with a view of how we can know anything at all about the world; discussing it will require an excursus into his epistemology.

Our only contact with the world, in Russell's view, is through a direct and immediate cognitive relation, which he calls 'acquaintance'. This is an idea which assumes very great importance in his thought. In *Problems of Philosophy*, for example, he says: 'The faculty of being acquainted with things other than itself is the main characteristic of a mind.' He goes on: 'Acquaintance with objects essentially consists in a relation between the mind and something other than the mind; it is this that constitutes the mind's power of knowing things.'[8] All knowledge rests on acquaintance, which he takes to be a direct and immediate cognitive relation between the mind and certain entities outside the mind (as well as some entities inside the mind). He takes this relation as unproblematic and as fundamental; there is no room for the question *how* the mind is acquainted with certain things—it just is. (We might say, indeed, that the point of the idea of acquaintance is precisely to turn aside such questions.)

Acquaintance, on Russell's account, is thus the only point of contact between the mind and things outside it. It is thus not only his answer to the question how we can have *true* beliefs about the world; it is also his answer to the prior question: how we can have any beliefs which are *about the world* at all. In other words, it is the basis for his views about meaning and understanding as well as about knowledge. How can my words or my thoughts reach out beyond my own mind to the world, and make claims which are true or false according as the world is this way or that way? Russell's answer is that this is possible only because I am acquainted with certain entities outside my mind. This enables me to use certain psychic elements to stand for those entities, and I can then assemble the psychic elements into thoughts.[9] A sentence in the logically perfect language mirrors the structure of the thought which it expresses and also of the fact which makes it true (if it is true). Our ability to form the thought, and thus to give meaning to the words, depends on our being acquainted with the entities which make up the corresponding fact (or which would make it up, if the thought were true).

This is the point of what I shall call 'the Principle of Acquaintance', which Russell sets out in several places. In *Problems of Philosophy* he puts it like this: '*Every proposition which we can understand must be composed wholly of constituents with which we are acquainted.*' It is, he says, 'the fundamental principle in the analysis of propositions'.[10] What Russell means by this it is not that we must be acquainted with the *words* in every sentence that we understand but rather that we must be acquainted with the entities for

---

[8] p. 42. It is particularly striking that Russell, the logician, took acquaintance rather than thought or reasoning to be 'the main characteristic of a mind'. This indicates the fundamental role that acquaintance plays in his philosophy during the period which is my concern here.

[9] Before 1906 he holds a rather different view, which involves our being acquainted with propositions, conceived of as objective and mind-independent entities. This shift in his view does not affect the issues we are concerned with here.

[10] p. 58; italics in original; see also 'On Denoting' (especially the penultimate paragraph) and 'Knowledge by Acquaintance and Knowledge by Description'.

which those words stand. (In 1918, under the influence of Wittgenstein, Russell made an exception for 'such words as "or", "not", "if", "then"', as we saw.)

To this point, I have mostly phrased the discussion of acquaintance in the first-person plural, as Russell consistently does, but in fact the first-person singular would be more apt. Since different people are acquainted with different entities, there is not a single logically perfect language but rather a different one for each person. (This is why he says that a logically perfect language would be 'as regards its vocabulary...very largely private to one speaker'.) Strictly, we should speak rather of this or that person's logically perfect language, not of *the* logically perfect language. He does, however, assume that we are acquainted with many of the same abstract entities; since he thinks logic depends on such entities, he holds that there is a single logical framework to which different people will add different non-logical vocabularies. Russell also assumes that although different people will be acquainted with different things, the *sorts* of things with which one person is acquainted will be the same as the sorts of things with which any other person is acquainted. The capacity for acquaintance, so to speak, is common to us all.

The Principle of Acquaintance is thus really the requirement that any sentence that a given person can understand must express—and in principle be analysable into—a sentence of that person's logically perfect language, i.e. a sentence in which non-logical terms name objects with which the person is acquainted. This is a principle about *meaningfulness*. It says that a sentence, as uttered by me, say, is only meaningful if it expresses a sentence of my logically perfect language.

How stringent is the requirement embodied in the Principle of Acquaintance? It depends, of course, on what entities you think we can be acquainted with. In the very first phase of his realism, say 1899–1903, Russell was usually willing to assume that just about every name—even the names of fictional characters or Homer's gods—names an object with which we can be acquainted. (See *Principles of Mathematics*, p. 449, § 427.) Rather quickly, however, he comes to find this view implausible; he comes to think of fewer types of things as possible objects of acquaintance. This development in his thought begins earlier than the Theory of Descriptions but the narrowing of the sphere of acquaintance is perhaps encouraged by that theory. In 'On Denoting' he rejects the idea that we can be acquainted either with physical objects or with the minds of other people—in short with most of the things that we think we usually talk about. He continues to think, however, that we can be acquainted with many abstract objects, such as those involved in logic.

Given this view, the Principle of Acquaintance imposes very severe constraints indeed. Almost no sentences in our ordinary language, other than those about logic, will obey these constraints. I understand the sentence 'Socrates was snub-nosed' but I am not acquainted with Socrates. What this shows is that the sentence is not fully analysed, is not a sentence in the logically perfect language. It is for this reason that the Principle of Acquaintance is fundamental to analysis: it shows you when further analysis is needed, and when you have completed the process of analysis and attained a fully analysed sentence—a sentence in the logically perfect language. When I utter the sentence 'Socrates is snub-nosed' I express a thought which would be accurately expressed by the fully analysed sentence, if I could but produce it. The fully analysed sentence, or the thought which it would accurately express, is what stands behind our ordinary language, so to speak, and underpins the meaningfulness of its sentences.

Russell's idea of a logically perfect language is thus bound up with an account of what makes language possible at all. It is for that reason that his logically perfect language goes along with an idea of meaningfulness: only what is expressible in the (given person's) logically perfect language is meaningful (for that person); anything else is nonsense. Equally, we might say that for a given person (at a given time) there is only one language. The person may in the ordinary sense be multi-lingual. Any two sentences which she understands, however, even if they are in different languages, are expressions of sentences in one and the same logically perfect language which is thus, in a sense, that person's only language. It is apparent from this that Russell's idea of a logically perfect language goes along with a clear idea of synonymy, as well as of meaningfulness: two ordinary sentences are synonymous just in case they express the same sentence of the logically perfect language.

31.3 CARNAP AND QUINE

Carnap is known as a leading exponent of the idea that the use of artificial languages will bring philosophical clarity and insight to whatever subject is under discussion. So one might think that he is an advocate of something like a logically perfect language. There may be some justification for this in some of his relatively early work. In the late 1920s he seems to hold a view according to which there is a single unique system of legitimate concepts. Thus in a lecture which he gave in June 1929 he speaks of 'the concept-system, an all-comprehending conceptual space' and says 'here there has to be a connecting path to each concept from the contents of my experience.... Everything of which one can speak has to be traceable back to things experienced by me' ('Von Gott und Seele: Scheinfragen in Metaphysik und Theologie', p. 12).

In the early 1930s, however, Carnap develops a different view, quite antithetical to the idea of a logically perfect language. Central to this view, and to his thought thereafter, is what he sometimes calls 'the Principle of Tolerance'.[11] One of the best-known statements of the principle reads as follows:

> *In logic there are no morals.* Everyone is at liberty to build up his own logic, i.e. his own form of language, as he wishes. All that is required of him is that, if he wishes to discuss it, he must state his methods clearly, and give syntactical rules instead of philosophical arguments. (*Logical Syntax of Language*, p. 52)

---

[11] The first clear sign of this view in Carnap's published writings is in 'Über Protokollsätze'. The view is stated in a form which is quite explicit and general in *Logischer Syntax der Sprache*.

The point of this is that the choice of a language, of the framework within which our thought and our knowledge takes place, is not to be judged as correct or incorrect, as right or wrong. We may, of course, find that a given language is more or less suitable for a given purpose than some other language. Making the language explicit—giving its 'syntactical rules'—is essential if we are to make sure that we are indeed speaking the same language, rather than talking at cross-purposes. But that concerns the idea that one language may be better than another *for a certain purpose*. There is no room for the idea of a uniquely correct (or perfect) language, hence no room for 'philosophical arguments' to establish that one language is the correct one. (Note that Carnap does *not* say that we are to give syntactical rules *as well as* philosophical arguments; he holds that philosophical arguments are altogether out of place in this context.)

The conflict between the Principle of Tolerance and the idea of a logically perfect language is clearest if one focuses on the idea that the latter is a language with metaphysical significance. This idea presupposes that there is such a thing as the nature of reality, and that the logically perfect language in some way reflects it or corresponds to it. The point of the Principle of Tolerance is precisely to avoid any such metaphysical commitments. Since we cannot make any claims without presupposing some language, and since the notion of correctness does not apply to choice of language, all our claims are language-relative. So any attempt to talk in an absolute way about the structure of reality simply misfires. In Carnap's view, the concepts in terms of which one might make metaphysical claims are relative to the choice of a logic and a language, and that choice is itself not a matter about which we can be right or wrong. On his conception there are various languages; one may be better or worse than another for this or that task but there is no one logically perfect language—indeed the very idea of such a language makes no sense.

Carnap certainly holds that for many purposes it is useful to paraphrase stretches of our discourse in one or another artificial language. Doing so may, for example, clarify the relation between those sentences closest to observation and those of a more theoretical character; or it may show that we could carry out science using a language in which metaphysical questions cannot be formulated, thereby suggesting that such questions are avoidable. (Here, perhaps, we get some idea of why 'Ideal Language philosophy' might be thought of as anti-metaphysical.) But no artificial language, on Carnap's account, can be logically perfect in the sense of reflecting the structure of reality: that is just the kind of metaphysics which he wishes to avoid.

Unlike Carnap, Quine is usefully seen as employing something analogous to the idea of a logically perfect language. The crucial difference between the two philosophers, for present purposes, is that Quine rejects anything like Carnap's Principle of Tolerance. That principle is based on the idea that there is a clear distinction between acceptance of a theory within a language, and acceptance of a language (or language-and-logic). The former is subject to rules of justification and is theoretical, a matter of right or wrong. The latter is not rule-governed but practical, purpose-relative, and not a matter of right or wrong; it is, Carnap says, a 'practical problem', albeit one 'disguised in the form of a theoretical question' ('Empiricism, Semantics, and Ontology', p. 209). Quine rejects that distinction. For him, all such acceptances are in principle of the same very general sort:

each is justified if it contributes to an overall theory which, taken as a whole, enables us to deal better with experience than any other that we have. There is thus, from Quine's point of view, no more reason to be tolerant about different languages than about different scientific theories within a given language—no reason, that is to say, to accept anything like Carnap's Principle of Tolerance.

Quine's rejection of the principle is evident in the 1950 essay, 'Identity, Ostension, and Hypostasis'. He says:

> the purpose of concepts and of language is efficacy in communication and in prediction. Such is the ultimate duty of language, science, and philosophy, and it is in relation to that duty that a conceptual scheme has finally to be appraised. (p. 79)

Choice of a 'conceptual scheme' here is clearly not a matter for tolerance—or at least it is no more a matter for tolerance than is the choice of a theory. Each 'choice' is of the same kind, and aims at performing the same 'ultimate duty'. Similarly, but now in explicit opposition to Carnap, Quine in 'Two Dogmas of Empiricism' famously advocates 'a more thorough pragmatism'. His point is that the pragmatic factors which Carnap takes to operate in choice of a language also operate in choice of a theory; there is no principled distinction here.[12]

Carnap and Quine agree that our account of what there is, is in part fixed by choice of language. This point alone, however, does not give us reason to accept Carnap's view that there is no such subject as ontology. His argument also requires the Principle of Tolerance, i.e. the idea choice of language is a matter of convention, not a matter on which one can be right or wrong. On this point, as we have just seen, he and Quine differ. On Quine's view, we should adopt the best language available to us. The adoption, moreover, will have ontological implications. As he says in 'On What There Is': 'Our ontology is determined once we have fixed upon the over-all conceptual scheme which is to accommodate science in the broadest sense....' (p. 17). For Quine, part of the task of the philosopher and the scientist is to choose the best language. Given that choice, the question of ontology can be answered; since the choice was not a matter of convention, the ontology is not language-relative.

What Quine in *Word and Object* calls 'canonical notation' thus functions in some ways like Russell's logically perfect language. Like the latter, it is significantly different from ordinary language. It lacks tenses, for example, and indexicals, and does not postulate such entities as beliefs or meanings. Also, logic is central to that notation: first-order logic is the syntax of Quine's regimented theory. Regimentation involves transforming sentences so that they use only the vocabulary of logic together with extra-logical predicates; the process will facilitate inference, which contributes to the advantages of regimented theory.

---

[12] Quine's use of the word 'pragmatism' should not be taken to indicate any very specific doctrine; in a later essay he denies knowing anything about Pragmatism and says 'I was simply taking Carnap's word and handing it back to him.' See 'Two Dogmas in Retrospect', p. 272.

Quine's canonical notation, moreover, has metaphysical significance, at least on a broad view of what counts as metaphysics.[13] Most obviously, it has ontological significance. Quine's work is full of what certainly appear to be ontological claims. He accepts that there are sets, for example, but denies that there are properties. What is the status and the basis of such claims in his work? The answer appeals to the idea of what our best and most objective knowledge would look like if clarified and systematized to the greatest possible extent. The process of clarifying and systematizing will involve both what one might think of as the theory and what one might think of as the language in which the theory is expressed; both, on Quine's account, are involved in the single scientific and philosophical task. What exists is what that language-cum-theory would quantify over. In the case of properties, Quine argues that the cost of including talk of such alleged entities within regimented theory exceeds the benefits; it would make our theory as a whole significantly more complex and less clear. On that basis he excludes such talk from that theory; this, for him, means that there are no such entities. It is not merely that he claims, in Carnapian fashion, to have shown that for some purposes we have reason to prefer a language which does not talk of properties; he goes further and denies that there are any properties.

What is at stake here, for Quine as for Russell, is nothing less than the nature of reality. Quine rejects Carnap's attempt to undercut that issue. He maintains that regimented theory in his sense—a comprehensive physicalist theory, set in the framework of first-order logic with identity—is the best available guide to the way the world is. His canonical notation, Quine says, is the language to use when the 'ultimate structure of reality' (*Word and Object*, p. 221) is our concern.

For Quine, as for Russell, there are questions of justification: Why we should accept that there is a logically perfect language, i.e. a language which has metaphysical significance in this way? And why we should accept his criteria for choosing that language? Quine holds that his regimented theory is the best way—the clearest, simplest, and most economical way—to organize and systematize our knowledge. One might, of course, argue that he is wrong on this or that specific point: that the best way of organizing our knowledge should in fact include this or that entity which Quine excludes—that it should, perhaps, be friendlier to mental entities of various sorts. This relatively detailed kind of argument, however, is not my concern here. My concern is rather with the question: Why should we accept that the best way of organizing our knowledge, whether it turn out to be Quine's or some other, has metaphysical significance? Let us suppose, for the sake of argument, that Quine is correct in thinking that the clearest and simplest

---

[13] For a narrower view, compare Robert Stalnaker, in the Introduction to *Ways a World Might Be*. Discussing the possibility of metaphysics, he says: 'Is there really anything substantive to be said at a completely general level, a level that transcends even the most general empirical science, about what the world is like? And if there is, what gives philosophers the expertise to address such questions? How can a priori reflection and argument yield substantive truths about the world?' (p. 1). As will be evident from what follows, Quine certainly does not attempt to transcend 'even the most general empirical science'; crucially, however, he also does not see philosophy as distinct from that enterprise.

conceptual scheme has no room for properties. Why, having accepted that, must we also accept that there are no properties? Why is reality constrained by our best conceptual scheme?

As we saw, Russell's answer to the analogous question relies on acquaintance. In his logically perfect language every term names an object with which I am acquainted; it is metaphysically significant because an object cannot be given to me in acquaintance unless it really does exist. I can know that there is an entity of a given kind only if I am acquainted with it or I can infer its existence from that of things with which I am acquainted. Quine, however, rejects any such idea of givenness, of direct and immediate knowledge of entities. He sometimes expresses this denial that any entities are simply given by saying that all entities are *posited* by us, in constructing our theories (see *Word and Object*, p. 22). So how does Quine justify his analogue of the idea of a logically perfect language?

The answer to this question takes us to the heart of Quine's philosophy—what he calls 'naturalism'. At one point he sums up that view as 'the recognition that it is within science itself, and not in some prior philosophy, that reality is to be identified and described' ('Things and Their Place in Theory', p. 21). 'Within science' here means within the totality of our ordinary and scientific knowledge, organized in the best fashion—that is, framed within canonical notation. Quine's point here is that this idea gives us the best purchase that we have on the idea of reality. Science, in this sense, develops; what was part of our best overall theory at one time may not be at another. What Quine denies, however, is that there is a standpoint external to that of science, in this sense, from which we can make sense of the idea of truth or reality. 'Truth is immanent, and there is no higher. We must speak from within a theory...' ('Things and Their Place in Theory', pp. 21f.). The result is a view that might be described, in Kantian terms, as 'empirical realism' rather than 'transcendental realism'. Quine himself claims he adheres to 'a robust realism' ('Things and Their Place in Theory', p. 21), for he barely makes sense of the idea of a stronger form of realism. 'What evaporates is the transcendental question of the reality of the external world—the question whether or in how far our science measures up to the *Ding an sich*' ('Things and Their Place in Theory', p. 22).[14]

This view goes along with Quine's denial that any entities are immediately given. All entities are posited as part of some theory. Since nothing has a higher ontological status than this, however, saying that an entity is posited does not accord it a second-rate status. As he memorably says: 'To call a posit a posit is not to patronize it' (*Word and Object*, p. 22). Expanding on the aphorism, he says: 'Everything to which we concede existence is a posit from the point of view of the theory-building process, and simultaneously real from the point of view of the theory being built. *Nor let us look down on the standpoint of theory as make-believe, for we can never do better than occupy the standpoint of some theory or other, the best we can muster at the time*' (*Word and Object*, p. 22; emphasis added) No entities are *given* in anything like the sense that Russell assumes.

---

[14] For further discussion of these issues, see the present author's 'Rorty and Quine on Scheme and Content' as well as *Quine*, especially pp. 18–23.

On Quine's account, therefore, we have no alternative but to accept as real the objects of some theory, stated in some language. Which theory-cum-language?

At this point, it is crucial that Quine does not take the language in which our knowledge is usually expressed at face value. Regimented theory is not ordinary language. It is supposed to be the best systematization of our knowledge as a whole and the process of systematization will involves significant—in some cases drastic—changes. The process, moreover, aims at yielding the most objective account of the world that we can attain; the account will differ not only from ordinary language but also from the language of working scientists. In 'The Scope and Language of Science' he discusses the distorting effect which language is likely to have on our view of the world and comments:

> To some degree...the scientist can enhance objectivity and diminish the interference of language, by his very choice of language. And we [meaning we philosophers, we scientists at the abstract and philosophical end of the spectrum], concerned to distill the essence of scientific discourse, can profitably purify the language of science beyond what might reasonably be urged upon the practicing scientist. (p. 235)

So we are justified in assuming that the entities mentioned in regimented theory exist—and that those excluded from it do not exist—because it is the best and most objective theory available to us, and because we must judge of existence and reality from 'the standpoint of some theory or other, the best we can muster at the time'.

At this point, another difference between Russell's logically perfect language and Quine's regimented theory is relevant. The former, as emphasized above, goes along with a clear criterion of meaningfulness, and thus of nonsense. A sentence of the (or a given person's) logically perfect language is meaningful because it is composed of elements each of which refers to an entity with which we are (or the given person is) acquainted. That is the only source of meaning; an ordinary sentence is meaningful only insofar as it expresses a sentence of the logically perfect language. Nothing of the sort is true for Quine.

Consider indirect discourse, i.e. statements of the form 'So-and-so said that ...' where what follows is not presented as a simple repetition of so-and-so's words but rather a paraphrase of those words. Quine argues that the idiom which enables us to form such statements should be excluded from regimented theory because the truth of such a statement is in many cases purpose-relative, or relative to the background knowledge of the one who asks, and to assumptions about *why* he or she is asking, etc. And in some cases, even given full knowledge of the purposes and circumstances of the one who makes the statement, it may still be impossible to classify it either as true or as false. For those reasons, Quine holds that the idiom has no place in our best and most objective theory of the world, that it is too vague or unclear to be used in a theory which aims at 'limning the true and ultimate structure of reality' (*Word and Object*, p. 221) and at setting down 'all traits of reality worthy of the name' (*Word and Object*, p. 221)—in short, he holds that it should be excluded from regimented theory. But this is not to say that Quine thinks that such statements are meaningless, or even that he thinks that we should try to exclude them from our ordinary discourse. To the contrary: he explicitly recognizes that we could not manage without them, saying that they are not 'humanly dispensable' (*Word and Object*, p. 218). In Quine's view, however, the fact that idioms of propositional attitude are humanly indispensable is clearly not enough to show that they report objective features of the world. The statements we make using such idioms have their place, certainly; but what Quine denies, however, is that their place is in regimented theory. That theory, or theory-cum-language, is the one best suited for giving an objective account of the world but it makes no exclusive claims to meaningfulness.

31.4 POST-QUINEAN METAPHYSICS

In the last section, I argued that an idea somewhat analogous to Russell's idea of a logically perfect language plays an important role in Quine's thought. In this section, I shall claim that an analogous idea is also presupposed by certain of Quine's more overtly metaphysical successors, and that the justification for their use of the idea is, at best, unclear. These are larger claims than can be made out in a few pages; still, I shall try to make them plausible. As an example, I shall consider some of the work of David Lewis. Certain remarks he make seem to me revealing, and to suggest broader trends; I shall not, however, attempt a balanced account of Lewis's work.

In my account, Quine could be thought of as a metaphysician of a certain kind, although certainly not of a traditional kind. His metaphysics, if we call it such, is constrained by the idea of a theory in which our best knowledge is set in the clearest and simplest overall framework; it is, one might say, metaphysics naturalized. This Quinean revival of (what might be called) metaphysics is facilitated by his attack on Logical Positivism and, in particular, his rejection of the Principle of Tolerance. More broadly, it is also facilitated by his rejection of any philosophically useful idea of nonsense. These aspects of his work, however, also opened the way for a revival of something more like traditional speculative metaphysics. (There is a deep irony here: although Quine's work prepared the way for this revival, nothing could have been less welcome to Quine himself.)

The idea of philosophical analysis plays a crucial role in the work of metaphysically inclined philosophers who were influenced by Quine. Consider, for example, the first two sentences of David Lewis's *Counterfactuals*:

> '*If kangaroos had no tails, they would topple over*' seems to me to mean something like this: in any possible state of affairs in which kangaroos have no tails, and which resembles our actual state of affairs as much as kangaroos having no tails permits it to, the kangaroos topple over. I shall give a general analysis of counterfactual conditionals along these lines. (p. 1; italics in the original)

Lewis sees this kind of analysis as having ontological significance, as telling us what entities are involved in the fact represented by the original sentence—just as Russell's analysis of arithmetical truths tells us what entities are really involved in the corresponding facts. In particular, as is well known, Lewis holds that his analysis gives us reason to believe in possible worlds other than our own. The movement of thought here is from some more or less ordinary sentence to an analysis of that sentence to the idea that we have reason to believe in the entities invoked by that analysis. In short, ontological conclusions are drawn from the philosophical analysis of an ordinary sentence.

To get some perspective on this, let us consider the idea of philosophical analysis—or at least some of the various ideas that go under that name. Understood in as untendentious a fashion as possible, the process of philosophical analysis involves going from one sentence, the unanalysed one, to another, the analysed version; the two sentences are said to stand in some relation to one another which makes it useful or necessary to replace the unanalysed one with the analysed one, at least in certain contexts or for certain purposes. But why does transforming the one sentence into the other constitute philosophical progress? A variety of answers are possible; in some cases it is perhaps unclear which one is being assumed.

The least ambitious answer is simply the claim that, in a given case, the analysed version of a given sentence is clearer—less ambiguous, less vague, generally more efficacious in communication, etc.—than the unanalysed version. Any such claim will be tied not only to a particular sentence but also, presumably to a particular communicative situation. It is hard to see how the idea of analysis, understood in this way, could have any positive philosophical significance. It might, however, have *negative* philosophical significance; some philosophers argue that some or all philosophical problems arise only because our language is unclear or misleading in some other way, and that philosophical analysis shows how we can achieve our (non-philosophical) purposes with a language in which philosophical questions simply do not arise.[15]

An overlapping answer is that the role of analysis is to clarify our ordinary (unanalysed) sentences in order to reveal inferential relations among those sentences. A strong version of this idea would be the claim that for our language, standard early twenty-first century English, say, there is a unique best analysis of each sentence; and that carrying out all the analyses will reveal inferential relations to the maximum possible extent. The result would be what we might call a logically perfect version of *our* language. If the restriction to a single language is genuine, however, then this idea too is fairly modest in its philosophical significance. (It is hard to imagine how the argument for uniqueness would go. The present point, however, is that, even granted uniqueness, the philosophical significance of the language would be modest.) In particular, it is hard to justify attributing ontological significance to the analysed sentence if one accepts that other equally good languages might be analysed in quite different ways; the correct ontology is presumably unique.

---

[15] Here, of course, there are connections with the work of Carnap, already briefly discussed, as well as with the later work of Wittgenstein. See, in particular, *Philosophical Investigations*, §§ 90–1, quoted in part in the next note, below.

It is, however, easy to move from the idea of clarifying and revealing inferential relations to a far more ambitious view of the idea of analysis.[16] It is easy to think the analysed sentence does more than facilitate communication on a given occasion, more than reveal inferential relations within a particular language; it is easy to think that it gets at the 'real meaning' of the sentence which is analysed and that it thereby shows the real constituents of the fact which makes the sentence true if it is true. This is exactly how Lewis seems to think of the matter in the passage quoted above. It is here that an analogue of the idea of a logically perfect language is presupposed. Analysis, on this metaphysically loaded conception, is not merely clarificatory; it reveals the way things are. The result of analysis, in any given case, is presumably a sentence which explicitly shows what there must be in the world if the sentence is to be true. (On some accounts, it also shows what entities there must be if the sentence is to be meaningful.) The totality of such fully analysed sentences thus constitutes something like a logically perfect language. Just as in the case of Russell's logically perfect language, a sentence in that language will make it evident what entities make up the corresponding fact. The language is also, for the same reason, unique up to perfect inter-translatability, since there is, presumably, a single world that all our true sentences are about.[17]

How is a particular instance of philosophical analysis to be justified? If one of the less ambitious conceptions of analysis is in play, the answer is relatively unproblematic. An analysis which is supposed to have metaphysical implications, however, cannot be justified in these ways. Analysis of this sort goes along with the idea of a logically perfect language which would be metaphysically significant in something like the way in which Russell's logically perfect language is. What could justify us in thinking that there is such a language, or in thinking that a given candidate is indeed the logically perfect language? We saw the quite different answers that Russell and Quine give to these questions. In the case of Russell, the answer rests on the idea of acquaintance, understood as direct and unmediated access to reality as it is in itself. Perhaps for some post-Quinean philosophers (though not for Lewis) the term 'intuition' is meant to play a similar role—rather than meaning, as clearly it often does, merely what we are at first inclined to think or to say. Or perhaps the charm of the word is precisely that it seems to promise to bridge the gulf between the weaker meaning and the stronger. However that may be, it seems to

---

[16] On the temptation to make this sort of transition, see again Wittgenstein's *Philosophical Investigations*, §§ 90–1:

> Misunderstandings concerning the use of words.... Some of them can be removed by substituting one form of expression for another; this may be called an 'analysis' of our forms of expression ...
>
> But now it may come to look as if there were something like a final analysis of our forms of language, and so a *single* completely resolved form of every expression. That is, as if our usual forms of expression were, essentially, unanalysed; as if there were something hidden in them that had to be brought to light.

[17] Strictly speaking, one has to add here that the languages are complete, i.e. capable of stating all facts. Otherwise inter-translatability might fail because each language could state facts which the other could not. In such a case, however, there would be an obvious remedy: to extend each language to make it capable of stating the given facts.

me that once we spell out the demands that Russell places on the idea of acquaintance it becomes hard to defend any idea which can play a similar role.

Quine's answers to these questions of justification depend on his unqualified scientific naturalism. One aspect here is that, according to Quine, the idea of a theory which sets out our knowledge in the clearest and most objective fashion provides the only grasp that we have on the idea of reality, the way the world is. As we saw, he rejects 'the transcendental question of the reality of the external world' (see p. 917f, above). Lewis, like other post-Quinean metaphysicians, seems to aspire to a stronger sense of realism.[18] That fact alone might undercut any attempt to give Quinean answers to the questions of justification. I shall not dwell on this point, however, but will emphasize a second aspect of Quine's justification.

Quine's regimented theory is constructed with the aim of embodying our most objective kinds of knowledge; accordingly, it excludes those whose objectivity is dubious. (It was on these grounds, as we saw in § 31.3, that he argues that the idiom of indirect discourse has no place in regimented theory.) This fact is crucial to the idea that Quine's regimented theory is not merely a convenient or otherwise interesting reformulation of our ordinary knowledge but has metaphysical significance: we are committed to accepting the existence of entities which that theory quantifies over and, perhaps more to the point, we are *not* committed to accepting the existence of entities which that theory does not quantify over.

In some passages, at least, Lewis does not place the same kind of emphasis on objectivity and seems simply to assume that most of what we ordinarily say will have a place in the fully analysed language. He says that we come to philosophy with 'a stock of opinions', and that 'the business of philosophy' is 'to try to discover ways of expanding them into an orderly system' (*Counterfactuals*, p. 88). In the same passage, he takes 'the metaphysician's analysis of mind' as an example, and says '[i]t succeeds to the extent that (1) it is systematic, and (2) it respects those of our pre-philosophical opinions to which we are firmly attached' (*Counterfactuals*, p. 88). In a later work, he speaks, along the same lines, of 'improv[ing] the unity and economy of the theory that is our professional concern—total theory, the whole of what we take to be true' (*On the Plurality of Worlds*, p. 4). These passages suggest a much greater deference towards our pre-philosophical beliefs, taken at face-value, than Quine shows. The aim here seems to be something like a systematization of what we already believe, whereas Quine is more ready to modify or discard pre-existing views in the interest of the kind of objectivity that science brings.

The point is illustrated by a well-known passage in which Lewis is defending the existence of possible worlds:

> It is uncontroversially true that things might have been otherwise than they are. I believe, and do to you, that things could have been different in countless ways. But

---

[18] Compare his comment on Putnam, he says: 'Internal realism, I take it, is realism feigned' ('Putnam's Paradox', p. 70). Putnam's 'internal realism' is not Quine's 'immanent realism' (as we might call it) but they share a rejection of any transcendent sense of reality.

what does this mean? Ordinary language permits the paraphrase: there are many ways things could have been besides the way that they actually are... I therefore believe in the existence of entities which might be called 'ways things could have been'. I prefer to call them 'possible worlds'. (*Counterfactuals*, p. 83)

Surely most of us would, in most contexts, agree that things might have been different from the way they are. What Lewis says here suggests that that is enough to settle the matter. For Quine, by contrast, the mere fact that an idiom is in use does not show that we need to take it seriously for metaphysical purposes. As we saw in § 30.3, indeed, even the fact that an idiom is humanly indispensable does not show that. Quine, I think, would argue that the 'might have been' idiom, like the idiom of indirect discourse, enables us to form sentences the truth-value of which is purpose-relative, context-dependent, and generally unfixed and that this gives us reason to exclude such idioms from regimented theory. Quine's insistence on this kind of objectivity goes along with the idea that regimented theory has metaphysical implications. A mere systematization of what we ordinarily say, without regard to how objective the various parts of that discourse are, might be of philosophical interest but it is hard to see how one could justify taking it as revealing anything about the world independent of us.

The upshot of this discussion is that it is by no means clear that Lewis can avail himself of the sorts of reasons that Quine can give for according metaphysical significance to regimented theory. Nor is it clear what other sorts of reasons Lewis can offer us to think that the results of his analyses—or the logically perfect language which would presumably result from all such analyses—are metaphysically significant. The same holds, I would claim, of many others who draw metaphysical conclusions from philosophical analysis. Lurking behind such attempts is Russell's idea of a logically perfect language, an idea which lingers on after the justification for it is gone.[19]

References

Burge, Tyler. 'Frege on Knowing the Third Realm', repr. in *Truth, Thought, Reason: Essays on Frege*, pp. 299–316; orig. pub. 1992.

—— *Truth, Thought, Reason: Essays on Frege*. Oxford: Oxford University Press, 2005.

Carnap, Rudolf. 'Von Gott und Seele: Scheinfragen in Metaphysik und Theologie', lecture, given in June 1929. Held in the Archives of Scientific Philosophy at the University of Pittsburgh. Quoted in Carus 2007, p. 183.

—— 'Über Protokollsätze', *Erkenntnis* 3 (1932): 215–28; tr. R. Creath and R. Nollan as 'On Protocol Sentence', *Noûs* 21 (1987): 457–70.

—— *Logischer Syntax der Sprache*. Vienna: Springer, 1934; tr. Amethe Smeaton as *The Logical Syntax of Language*. London: Routledge, 1934.

—— 'Empiricism, Semantics, and Ontology', *Revue Internationale de Philosophie* 4 (1950): 20–40; repr. in Carnap, *Meaning and Necessity*, pp. 205–2.

[19]   I would like to thank Andrew Lugg for his comments on earlier drafts of this essay.

—— *Meaning and Necessity*, 2nd edn. Chicago: University of Chicago Press, 1956.

Carus, André. *Carnap and Twentieth Century Thought*. Cambridge: Cambridge University Press, 2007.

Conant, James. 'The Method of the *Tractatus*'. In Erich H. Reck (ed.), *From Frege to Wittgenstein*. Oxford: Oxford University Press, 2002, pp. 374–462.

Diamond, Cora. 'Throwing Away the Ladder: How to Read the *Tractatus*', repr. in her *Realism and the Realistic Spirit*. Cambridge, MA: MIT Press, 1991, pp. 179–204; orig. pub. 1988.

Frege, Gottlob. *Begriffsschrift, eine der arithmetischen nachgebildete Formelsprache des reinen Denkens*. Halle: Nebert, 1879; tr. and ed. Terrell Ward Bynum in *Conceptual Notation and Related Articles*. Oxford: Oxford University Press, 1972, pp. 101–203.

—— 'Über Sinn und Bedeutung', *Zeitschrift für Philosophie und philosophische Kritk* 100 (1892): 25–50; very widely translated in, for example, Frege, *Collected Papers*, ed. Brian McGuiness. Oxford: Basil Blackwell, 1984, pp. 157–77.

—— 'Über die Grundlagen der Geometrie, II', *Jahresbericht der Deutschen Mathematiker-Vereinigung* 15 (1906): 377–403; tr. in Frege, *Collected Papers*, ed. Brian McGuiness. Oxford: Basil Blackwell, 1984, pp. 293–81.

—— 'Meine grundlichen logischen Einsichten' [written in 1915], *Nachgelassene Schriften*, pp. 271–2; tr. as 'My Basic Logical Insights' in *Posthumous Writings*, pp. 251–2.

—— 'Notes for Ludwig Darmstaedter' [written in July 1919], *Nachgelassene Schriften*, pp. 273–7; tr. in *Posthumous Writings*, pp. 253–7.

—— *Nachgelassene Schriften*, ed. Hans Hermes *et al.* Hamburg: Meiner, 1969; tr. Peter Long and Roger White as Gottlob Frege, *Posthumous Writings*. Chicago: University of Chicago Press, 1979.

Hacker, Peter. *Insight and Illusion*. Oxford: Oxford University Press, 1972; revised 2nd edn. 1986.

—— 'Was He Trying To Whistle It?' In Alice Crary and Rupert Read (eds.), *The New Wittgenstein*. London: Routledge, 2007, pp. 353–88.

Hylton, Peter. 'Rorty and Quine on Scheme and Content', *Philosophical Topics* 25 (1997): 67–86.

—— *Quine*. London: Routledge, 2007.

Lewis, David. *Counterfactuals*. Cambridge, MA: Harvard University Press, 1973.

—— *On the Plurality of Worlds*. Oxford: Basil Blackwell, 1986.

—— 'Putnam's Paradox'. In *Papers in Metaphysics and Epistemology*. Cambridge: Cambridge University Press, 1999, pp. 56–77.

McGinn, Marie. *Elucidating the Tractatus*. Oxford: Oxford University Press, 2007.

Quine, W. V. O., *From a Logical Point of View*. Cambridge, MA: Harvard University Press, 1953, rev. edn. 1980.

—— 'The Scope and Language of Science', *British Journal for Philosophy of Science* 8 (1957): 1–17; repr. in *Ways of Paradox*, pp. 228–45.

—— *Word and Object*. Cambridge, MA: MIT Press, 1960.

—— *Ways of Paradox*. New York: Random House, 1966; 2nd enlarged edn. Cambridge, MA: Harvard University Press, 1976.

—— *Theories and Things*. Cambridge, MA: Harvard University Press, 1981.

—— 'Two Dogmas in Retrospect', *Canadian Journal of Philosophy* 21 (1991): 265–74.

—— 'On What There Is', Chapter I of *From a Logical Point of View*.

—— 'Identity, Ostension, and Hypostasis', Chapter IV of *From a Logical Point of View*.

—— 'Things and Their Place in Theory', Chapter 1 of *Theories and Things*.

Rorty, Richard (ed.). *The Linguistic Turn: Recent Essays in Philosophical Method*. Chicago: University of Chicago Press, 1967.

Russell, Bertrand. *Principles of Mathematics*. Cambridge: Cambridge University Press, 1903.

—— 'On Denoting', *Mind* 14 (1905): 479–93; repr. in *Collected Papers, Volume 4*, pp. 415–27.

—— 'Knowledge by Acquaintance and Knowledge by Description', *Proceedings of the Aristotelian Society* 11 (1911): 108–28; repr. in *Collected Papers, Volume 6*, pp. 148–61.

—— *Problems of Philosophy*. London: Williams and Norgate, 1912; repr. Home University Library. Oxford: Oxford University Press, 1946.

—— 'The Philosophy of Logical Atomism', *The Monist* 28 (1918): 495–527 and 29: 32–63, 190–222, 345–80; repr. in *Collected Papers, Volume. 8*, pp. 160–244.

—— *Collected Papers v. 8, The Philosophy of Logical Atomism and Other Essays: 1914–19*, ed. John G. Slater (London: George Allen and Unwin, 1986).

—— *Collected Papers, Volume 6: Logical and Philosophical Papers, 1909–13*, ed. John G. Slater. London: George Allen & Unwin, 1992.

—— *Collected Papers, Volume 4: Foundations of a New Logic, 1903–05*, ed. Alistair Urquhart. London: Routledge, 1994.

Stalnaker, Robert. *Ways a World Might Be*. Oxford: Oxford University Press, 2003.

Weiner, Joan. 'Burge's Literal Interpretation of Frege', *Mind* 104 (1995): 585–97.

—— 'Realism bei Frege: Reply to Burge', *Synthese* 102 (1995): 363–82.

Whitehead, Alfred North and Bertrand Russell. *Principia Mathematica*, 3 vols. Cambridge: Cambridge University Press, 1910–1913, 2nd edn., 1925–7.

Wittgenstein, Ludwig. *Tractatus Logico-Philosophicus, Annalen der Naturphilosophie* (1921), tr. C. K. Ogden. London: Routledge & Kegan Paul, 1922; corrected edition 1933, and also by D. F. Pears and B. McGuiness. London: Routledge & Kegan Paul, 1961.

—— *Philosophical Investigations*, tr. G. E. M. Anscombe. Oxford: Basil Blackwell, 1953; 2nd edn. 1958.

CHAPTER 32

THE LINGUISTIC TURN IN ANALYTIC PHILOSOPHY

P. M. S. HACKER

32.1 TERMINOLOGICAL CLARIFICATION

The expression 'the linguistic turn' was introduced by Gustav Bergmann in his review of Strawson's *Individuals* in 1960. Bergmann (1906–87) was a member of the Vienna Circle and regular attendant at its meetings in the late 1920s and the 1930s. In 1937 he fled from Austria to the USA, where he taught at the University of Iowa from 1940 until his retirement. He was best known for his idiosyncratic writings on ontology and for the school of Iowa ontologists he inspired. His review article, published in the *Journal of Philosophy*, was entitled 'Strawson's Ontology', and was largely concerned with outlining Bergmann's own methodology and conception of philosophy. Bergmann used the expression again in subsequent articles such as 'The Glory and Misery of Ludwig Wittgenstein' (*Rivista di Filosofia* 52 (1961)) and 'Stenius on the *Tractatus*' (*Theoria* 29 (1963)).[1]

The linguistic turn, according to Bergmann, is a 'fundamental gambit as to method' agreed upon by two different groups of linguistic philosophers: 'ordinary language philosophers' (exemplified, in Bergmann's view, by Strawson) and 'ideal language philosophers' (such as Bergmann himself). The methodological gambit is to talk about the world by talking about a suitable language. The disagreement between the two groups of philosophers turns, according to Bergmann, on what is to count as *a language* and what makes it *suitable* as an object of investigation that will shed light for philosophical purposes on the nature of the world, in particular on ontology. Why should the linguistic turn be taken? In Bergmann's view, for three reasons. First, words are used either ordinarily, i.e. 'commonsensically', or philosophically. Philosophical uses of words are *prima facie* unintelligible, and require commonsensical explication. That

---

[1] All these papers are to be found in G. Bergmann, *Logic and Reality* (Madison, WI: University of Wisconsin Press, 1964).

is a requirement of the method. Second, much of the obscurity of pre-linguistic philosophy stems from failure to distinguish linguistic statements from meta-linguistic statements. The method is the safest way to avoid the ensuing confusions. Third, there are some things which any language can only show. For example, the relation of exemplification shows itself by subject predicate juxtaposition (e.g. '*a* is *F*' shows that the property *F* is exemplified by the object *a*). Such things, however (*pace* Wittgenstein), are not ineffable. Rather they can be spoken about, as we have just done, in a meta-linguistic discussion of the syntax and interpretation of a language. Hence, again, the linguistic turn.

Ordinary language philosophers, according to Bergmann, talk about the language we speak. They study communication, explore how we learn language, and how we communicate by using it. This, he declared, is a psychological study. In the hands of 'extremists', like J. L. Austin, that is all it is. Since we use ordinary language to communicate about the world, there is some sense in which it 'must therefore be a picture of the world', and must, in a minimal sense, be a 'suitable' language by the study of which one can engage in ontological investigation. If that purpose is disregarded, and the three reasons for the linguistic turn neglected, then ordinary language philosophy degenerates into trivial linguistics—this being Bergmann's judgement on Austin. But because the primary use of ordinary language is communication, it is actually most *unsuitable* as a philosophical tool. What is needed is an 'ideal language', or, more accurately, a schema of a language, which adequately pictures the world. And that is the instrumental goal of ideal language philosophers. If it is not, then ideal language philosophy degenerates into trivial design of calculi—this being (presumably) Bergmann's judgement on Carnap's philosophy.

The misconstruals of both the Carnapian wing of the Vienna Circle (who can be deemed 'ideal language philosophers') and of Strawson and others of the Oxford group of post-war philosophers (whose classification as 'ordinary language philosophers' requires clarification, and was rejected by Strawson himself) are startling. Carnap did not construct artificial calculi for ontological purposes. Indeed, in 'Empiricism, Semantics, and Ontology', he argued that ontological questions are no more than questions about the framework of the language one chose to use—questions about a language and its utility, not questions about reality.[2] Far from inventing artificial calculi for ontological purposes, he invented them in order to shed light on the language of science and to resolve philosophical problems and dissolve pseudo-problems. So called ordinary language philosophers, who would better be denominated 'natural language philosophers' (in contrast to ideal language philosophers) were not engaging in psychology or in linguistics. The reasons Bergmann gave for the so-called linguistic turn are equally spurious. There is indeed something that might be called the linguistic turn in philosophy, but, as we shall see, the reasons for it are very far removed from Bergmann's peculiar list.

---

[2] R. Carnap, 'Empiricism, Semantics, and Ontology', repr. in his *Meaning and Necessity*, enlarged edition (Chicago: University of Chicago Press, 1956).

Had the matter rested with Bergmann, the expression 'the linguistic turn' would very likely never have been heard again. But the name appealed to Richard Rorty—and he put it to good use in an eponymous anthology of writings he edited in 1967. *The Linguistic Turn: Recent Essays in Philosophical Method* contained 37 essays (some of which are replies to others) by many of the leading analytic philosophers of the day (and of the previous thirty years). The book was divided into four parts. The first consisted of essays by Schlick, Carnap, Bergmann, Ryle, Wisdom, and Malcolm. These all argued, in very different ways and for very different reasons, that philosophical questions are, in a sense which they duly tried to elucidate, 'questions of language'. Part II was entitled 'Metaphilosophical Problems of Ideal Language Philosophy' and consisted of essays by Copi, Bergmann, Black, Ambrose, Chisholm, Cornman, and Quine. Part III was called 'Metaphilosophical Problems of Ordinary Language Philosophy' in which a symposium on Austin (who had recently died) was given pride of place, and various criticisms of so-called ordinary language philosophy were examined. And the final part of the anthology was 'Recapitulations, Reconsiderations, and Future Prospects' in which Shapere, Hampshire, Urmson, Strawson, Black, Katz, and Bar-Hillel severally attempted an overview of the state of play in analytic philosophy.

It is clear from this description of the contents of his anthology that Rorty took from Bergmann the division of the linguistic turn into a dual carriageway, one lane of which was 'ordinary language philosophy' and the other 'ideal language philosophy'. Wisely, he did not repeat Bergmann's confused characterization of these two tendencies. Rorty, perfectly correctly, appreciated that a sea-change had occurred in analytic philosophy in the 1930s, and had continued after the Second World War. He characterized philosophers who participated in this change as 'linguistic philosophers' and restricted his selection largely to philosophers active in Britain and America. This included of course some of the émigré Austrian and German logical empiricists who had fled the Nazis and had brought about a powerful synthesis of the spirit of logical empiricism with American pragmatism. Rorty announced that the purpose of his anthology was to provide materials for reflection on linguistic philosophy, which he described as 'the most recent philosophical revolution'. The revolutionaries were held to include many who would have been loath to accept the banner 'linguistic philosophy', such as Carnap, Quine, and Bar-Hillel. For the name 'linguistic philosophy' was already associated with the group of Oxford philosophers in the post-war years whom Bergmann had (misleadingly) characterized as 'ordinary language philosophers'. But Rorty was well guarded against any accusation of misdescription. He characterized linguistic philosophy as 'the view that philosophical problems are problems that may be solved (or dissolved) either by reforming language or by understanding more about the language we presently use'—and the first disjunct could safely be held to include the so-called ideal-language philosophers such as Carnap and regimented-language philosophers such as Quine (who did indeed have ontological preoccupations that approximate Bergmann's specifications).

So, according to Rorty, the linguistic turn in philosophy is exhibited by the distinctive methodologies of two different strands within 'linguistic' philosophy. However, there were further claims afoot in both Bergmann's paper and Rorty's essay and anthology.

For it is clearly not *only* a pair of methods that is associated with the philosophical movement that they called linguistic philosophy. The methods go hand in hand with the claim that the source (or, at least, one major source) of the problems of philosophy lies in the misleading forms of natural languages. And linked with that is the suggestion that philosophical questions are questions *of* language (*vide* the title of Part I of Rorty's anthology 'Classic Statements of the Thesis that Philosophical Questions are Questions of Language'). The latter supposition stands in need of much clarification. Does it mean that philosophical questions are questions *about* language? If so, does it follow that philosophy is just a branch of linguistics? Does it mean that philosophical theories and theses are theories and theses about language? Or does it just recapitulate the methodological claim that philosophical problems—whatever they are—are solved or resolved by one or the other of the two methods suggested?

As we progress, we shall attend to a number of distinct questions:

What, according to linguistic philosophers thus understood, is the subject matter of philosophy?

What is a philosophical problem and how is it to be distinguished from other kinds of problems, e.g. in science or mathematics?

What is the source (or sources) of the problems of philosophy?

What is the appropriate method (or methods) for the solution of philosophical problems?

What is the result of successful philosophical investigations? Is it philosophical truths (akin to the truths produced by successful scientific investigations)? If so, how are they to be characterized? And if it is not, what is it?

What was distinctive about what Bergmann and Rorty called the linguistic turn in philosophy is evident in the kinds of answers given by analytic philosophers to these questions. The linguistic turn was in fact a phase (or more accurately a number of phases) in the development of analytic philosophy in the twentieth century. There was nothing novel about the claim that misleading features of natural languages are responsible for philosophical confusions (Plato and Aristotle pointed *that* out). Nor was there anything new about the suggestion that careful scrutiny of the use of the terms that lead to confusion will help dispel it (Aristotle excelled at *that*). These, out of context, are platitudes that should be known to every philosopher and philosophy student. To see what *was* new about this distinctive movement in philosophy, it has to be located in its historical context.

32.2 HISTORICAL STAGE-SETTING

It is evident that the expression 'the linguistic turn in philosophy' is used as a characterization of a change of direction in the development of analytic philosophy. It is worthwhile briefly locating analytic philosophy in relation to the development of European philosophy in the nineteenth century.

The linguistic turn that occurred in the 1920s was preceded by a logistic turn that occurred in the mid-nineteenth century, prior to the rise of analytic philosophy. The study of logic had been almost totally neglected from Descartes onward (with the exception of Leibniz)—indeed so much so that Kant, at the end of the eighteenth century, could declare that logic, since Aristotle, 'has not been able to advance a step and is thus to all appearance complete and perfect' (*Critique of Pure Reason* B viii). This illusion (which, incidentally, displayed complete ignorance of Stoic and medieval logic) was to be dispelled by a group of mathematicians and mathematically minded philosophers in the mid-nineteenth century, namely de Morgan, Boole, Venn, Jevons, and Schröder in Britain and Germany, and Huntington and Peirce in the USA. Mathematical logic, as de Morgan called it in 1858, was designed to represent the forms of thought by the mathematicization of logic. Boole invented logical algebra, which presented logic as a branch of abstract algebra, and his idea was taken up by Venn, Jevons, Schröder, and others. A quarter of a century later, logical algebra was superseded by Frege's invention of function-theoretic logic, which generalized the mathematical theory of functions in order to show not that logic was reducible to arithmetic, but rather that arithmetic was reducible to logic. Frege's great advances in mathematical logic, e.g. the introduction of the quantifier/bound variable technique for presenting general and existential statements and statements involving multiple generality, the complete formalization of the propositional calculus, and the axiomatization of the first-order predicate calculus with identity, were followed by those of Russell and Whitehead in *Principia Mathematica*. The invention of modern mathematical logic inaugurated a century of intense logical research and the creation of further forms of logic such as modal, tense, and deontic logics.

Frege's primary concern was to demonstrate that arithmetic is derivable from logic. It was to that end that he invented his function-theoretic logic. He conceived of his logical system as an ideal language for logical and proof-theoretic purposes. It was, he suggested, related to natural languages as the microscope to the eye. His philosophical attitude to natural language as a tool for the purpose of the philosophy of logic and mathematics was one of contempt. Natural languages did not evolve for the purposes of logical proofs; for that purpose one needs to invent a logically perfect language— which is what he presented his 'conceptual notation' as. This, broadly speaking, was also Russell's view. He conceived of the Peano-derived symbolism and of the formation rules of *Principia* as the syntax of a logically ideal language.

Does this make Frege into the originator of the linguistic turn in philosophy—belonging to the ideal language wing of the movement? That would be mistaken. First, if the mere invention of formal calculi and ideal languages for logical and proof-theoretic purposes is to introduce the linguistic turn, then many earlier philosophers made the linguistic turn, and it ceases to be a crucial aspect of, and phase in, the development of twentieth-century analytic philosophy. Those whom Rorty called 'ideal language philosophers' (e.g. Carnap and Quine) had a much larger and philosophically more ambitions agenda than that. Secondly, Frege had no *general* view of the sources of, nature of, or methods of solving, philosophical problems. He did not hold that all or even most philosophical questions are questions of language (which, according to Rorty, is one aspect of the linguistic turn). Nor did he claim that all or even most philosophical questions are to be answered or resolved by either examining the use of natural language or by inventing an ideal language (which, Rorty held, characterizes the linguistic turn). His concerns were exclusively with the philosophy of mathematics, logic, and philosophical logic. And he invented his conceptual notation for purposes of his logicist project—not to solve or resolve the problems of epistemology, metaphysics, philosophy of mind, etc.

What is true is that the function-theoretic logic that Frege and Russell devised was the source of the preoccupation of twentieth-century analytic philosophy with logic and the philosophy of logic. Moreover, the powerful logic they invented made it possible for their successors, once the linguistic turn had been taken, to devise a variety of putatively ideal languages for the purposes of philosophical analysis. There is no doubt that Frege and Russell were the main influences on the young Wittgenstein, who was stimulated by their work into demolishing much of its alleged philosophical import in the *Tractatus* and replacing it with a quite different vision, as well as on Carnap, who constructed his programme of logical syntax and later logical semantics on foundations they and Wittgenstein had laid. Insofar as one lane of the linguistic turn is conceived to be that of ideal or regimented language-construction, then that lane emerged from the confluence of two roads—the logistic turn, on the one hand, and analytic philosophy on the other.

Analytic philosophy, understood as the name of a distinctive philosophical movement of the twentieth century, had its roots in Cambridge at the very end of the nineteenth century. For its origins lay in the revolt of the young Moore and Russell against the Hegelianism of Absolute Idealism that then dominated British philosophy. It was initially luxuriantly pluralistic by contrast with the monism of the Absolute Idealists. Moore engaged in what he called 'conceptual analysis' (which had nothing to do with the analysis of linguistic usage). Russell, inspired by the conceptual elucidations of mathematicians such as Weierstrass, Dedekind, and Cantor, practised logical analysis (which he did not conceive of as merely tabulating and analysing the uses of expressions in natural language). Both Moore and Russell thought of themselves as *analysing the elements of reality*—the constituents and forms of facts, and as aiming to describe and catalogue the logical forms of the world. Analysis, as they understood it, involved the decomposition of facts into their ultimate simple constituents and the revelation of their logical forms. How intelligible this idea was is debatable, but it was given support by Russell's theory of descriptions (1905) in which he purported to show by analysis how sentences containing singular definite descriptions which appear to refer to an object do not really do so. *Decompositional analysis* characterized the first stages of analytic philosophy, including Moore, Russell, and the young Wittgenstein as well as some members of the later Cambridge school of analysis in the 1920s.

After the completion of *Principia* (1910), Russell turned his attention to epistemology (*Problems of Philosophy* (1912) and *Theory of Knowledge* (written in 1913)), logical construction, and to advocating what he thought of as 'scientific method' in philosophy (*Our Knowledge of the External World* (1914)). It was during this phase in Russell's development that he contended that 'Every philosophical problem, when it is subjected to the necessary analysis and purification, is found not to be philosophical at all, or else to be, in the sense in which we are using the word, logical.'[3] Philosophical method is to determine by logical analysis what kinds of facts there are and how they are related to each other. Philosophy, like science, aims to achieve a theoretical understanding of the world. It was partly under the impact of discussions with young Wittgenstein that Russell moved on to the next phase in his analytical philosophy, namely logical atomism.

Wittgenstein came to Cambridge to study with Russell in 1911/12. While in Cambridge he began work on what was to become his first masterpiece: the *Tractatus Logico-Philosophicus* (1921). It is above all this book and its impact upon the Vienna Circle and the Cambridge school of analysis in the 1920s that is the source of the linguistic turn in analytic philosophy.

32.3 THE *TRACTATUS* STARTS THE TURN

Wittgenstein conceived of the *Tractatus* as solving the most fundamental problems of philosophy (TLP, Preface).[4] The intention of the book was to bring the logistic turn into the heart of philosophy. His work, he observed, 'extended from the foundations of logic to the nature of the world'.[5] Where Frege and Russell had thought of natural languages as logically defective and of their artificial languages as logically perfect, Wittgenstein conceived of logic as a transcendental condition of representation, and hence as constituting the depth-grammar of *any* possible language. Hence natural language 'is all right as it is'—a language *cannot* be logically defective, for if it were its sentences would not express a sense, and so it would be no language at all. But the surface grammar of natural language is deeply misleading, and it is the task of analysis to reveal its depth structure, for which the essence of the proposition and hence logic itself (which follows from it) provide the adamantine foundations. 'All philosophy', Wittgenstein wrote, 'is a "critique" of language' (TLP 4.0031). This remark heralds the linguistic turn in twentieth-century philosophy. Wittgenstein later laid out the general programme for philosophy that was consequent upon the achievement of the *Tractatus*:

> The idea is to express in an appropriate symbolism what in ordinary language leads to endless misunderstandings. That is to say, where ordinary language disguises logical structure, where it allows the formation of pseudo-propositions, where it uses one term in an infinity of different meanings, we must replace it by a symbolism

---

[3] B. Russell, *Our Knowledge of the External World as a Field for Scientific Method in Philosophy* (Chicago and London: Open Court, 1914), p. 33.

[4] References to the *Tractatus* will be given in the text with the abbreviation 'TLP'.

[5] L. Wittgenstein, *Notebooks 1914–1916* (Oxford: Blackwell, 1969), p. 79.

which gives a clear picture of the logical structure, excludes pseudo-propositions, and uses its terms unambiguously.[6]

This imaginary symbolism was not an ideal language, but an ideally perspicuous notation that would display the depth grammar of language. This, however, was a task for the future (and was never fulfilled). What the *Tractatus* itself aimed to do was above all to disclose the nature of logical necessity, the essence of representation, and the limits of thought.

In six different respects, the *Tractatus* introduced the linguistic turn in analytic philosophy, marking a sharp break with the conception of analysis advocated by Moore and Russell.[7]

(i) Most of the propositions and questions in past philosophy are not false but nonsensical—transgressing the bounds of sense. Most of the propositions and questions of philosophers arise from failure to grasp the logic of our language (TLP 4.003). So the roots of most philosophical problems lie in misleading features of the surface grammar of natural language, and they can be resolved only by logico-linguistic analysis.

(ii) Although the book aimed to set the limits of thought (TLP, Preface), this, Wittgenstein argued, can be done only by setting the limits of *language*, i.e. by determining the boundary between sense and nonsense. This put language and its forms, the conditions of sense, and the relationship between language and reality at the centre of philosophical investigation.

(iii) The key to achieving this goal was the clarification of the essential nature of the *propositional-sign* (TLP 3.1431). That was done by determining the general propositional form—i.e. by giving 'a description of the propositions of *any sign-language whatsoever* in such a way that every possible sense can be expressed by a symbol satisfying the description, and every symbol satisfying the description can express a sense, provided that the meanings of names are suitably chosen' (TLP 4.5).

(iv) The most influential achievement of the book was its clarification of the nature of logical truth. This was done by an investigation of *symbolism*. It was argued that the 'peculiar mark of logical propositions [is] that one can recognize that they are true from the symbol alone, and this fact contains in itself the whole philosophy of logic' (TLP 6.113). Contrary to what both Frege and Russell thought, the propositions of logic are not essentially general (but essentially true), they say nothing at all, but are rather senseless, i.e. limiting cases of propositions with a sense. In particular, they are not descriptions of relations between thoughts as

---

[6] L. Wittgenstein, 'Some Remarks on Logical Form', *Proceedings of the Aristotelian Society* 9 (1929), p. 163.

[7] For a more detailed discussion, see P. M. S. Hacker, *Wittgenstein's Place in Twentieth Century Analytic Philosophy* (Oxford: Blackwell, 1996), ch. 2, from which the following observations are taken.

Frege supposed, nor are they descriptions of the most general facts in the universe as Russell had suggested.

(v) The positive programme for future philosophy was committed to logico-linguistic analysis of propositions, i.e. *sentences with a sense*. The task of philosophy is the logical clarification of thoughts, which is to be done by the clarification of *sentences* (TLP 4.112).

(vi) The negative programme for future philosophy was to demonstrate the illegitimacy of metaphysical assertions. This is to be done by demonstrating how the attempt to say something metaphysical, i.e. necessary truths about essential features of the world and about essential features of representation by means of language, inevitably transgress the bounds of what can be said in any language. Such truths, by the very nature of *language* cannot be said (although they are shown by well-formed propositions of language).

A corollary of these points is a dramatic curtailing of the aspirations of philosophy. Since philosophy cannot deliver any metaphysical truths or say anything at all about the essence of the world, since the only expressible necessity is the vacuous necessity of the tautologies of logic, *there are no philosophical propositions*. Any attempt to propound philosophical propositions, as manifest in traditional philosophy and in the *Tractatus* itself, results in nonsense, since it unavoidably employs formal or categorial concepts as if they were material concepts. But formal concepts are akin to unbound variables, and nonsense—an ill-formed word-sequence—ensues. Philosophy is not a cognitive discipline, but a critical and elucidatory one. The analysis of propositions delivers no new truths about the world, but only clarifications of existing propositions and exposure of metaphysical nonsense. This unprecedented idea was pivotal to the ensuing linguistic turn.

These methodological claims, the achievement of the book in clarifying the nature of logic, and the programme for future philosophy had an immense influence upon the next two phases of analytic philosophy—the logical empiricism of the Vienna Circle and its affiliates, and the short-lived school of Cambridge analysis (e.g. Ramsey, Wisdom, Braithwaite, as well as Moore from the older generation), which cannot be discussed here.

It would be disingenuous to hold that the *Tractatus* itself completed the linguistic turn. It was too deeply rooted in the idea that there are things that can be shown but not said—in particular things about the essence of the world and the essential nature of representation. The whole of the *Tractatus* was concerned with elaborating such deep truths—therein lay its grandeur. The conception of representation that informs the book is rooted in a metaphysical vision of the world, as well as a metaphysics of symbolism (e.g. that only simple names can represent simple things, that only relations can represent relations, and that only facts can represent facts). Of course, the book grants at the end that its very attempt to describe the conditions of representation and the limits of thought and its expression are themselves things that cannot be said but are shown by well-formed propositions with a sense. It is only when this ineffable metaphysical baggage is jettisoned, as it was by the Vienna Circle, the Cambridge analysts, and Wittgenstein himself in the 1930s that the linguistic turn was completed.

32.4 LOGICAL EMPIRICISM AND THE LINGUISTIC TURN

The Vienna Circle was a group of philosopher-scientists and philosophically minded mathematicians gathered around Moritz Schlick in Vienna from 1924 until their dispersal by the rising tides of Nazism. They were the fountainhead of logical empiricism, which was a further phase in the development of analytic philosophy. There were affiliated groups in Germany (especially the Berlin Society of Scientific Philosophy), Poland, Czechoslovakia, and Scandinavia, and a few followers in the USA. The Circle's philosophical outlook was marked by the scientific or mathematical training that most of its members had enjoyed. Their philosophical roots were in the nineteenth-century empiricism of Avenarius and Mach, and also in the neo-Kantianism of the day. They shared a distaste for metaphysics and its attempts to derive substantive (synthetic a priori) truths about the world independently of experience, and shared an interest in logic, philosophy of logic, and philosophy of science. The Circle represents the convergence of the logistic turn with budding analytic philosophy, marrying classical empiricism to the techniques of logico-linguistic analysis. This produced logical positivism (or, more accurately, logical empiricism), which was fated to be the most influential philosophical movement within twentieth-century analytic philosophy—largely due to the flight of most members of the Circle to the USA and the great impact they had there on American philosophy.

The explicit goal of the Circle was to articulate a form of consistent empiricism and to advance the reductive programme of 'unified science' as a part of the scientific worldview which they advocated. The main barrier to this was the lack of an adequate account of linguistic meaning robust enough to exclude propositions of metaphysics as meaningless, the need for an explanation of the nature of necessary truths of logic, arithmetic, and geometry which did not appeal to synthetic a priori truths accessible to pure reason or intuition independently of experience, and a convincing account of the nature and limits of philosophy. The main influence upon members of the Circle was Wittgenstein, first via the *Tractatus*, which they read and discussed line by line at their weekly meetings in the academic year of 1924/5 and again in 1926/7, and later via Schlick and Waismann, who met Wittgenstein regularly on his visits to Vienna between 1929 and 1935.[8] What impressed them above all was that the *Tractatus* seemed to have solved the question as to the status and nature of logical truths. Hahn wrote 'To me, the *Tractatus* has explained

---

[8] Schlick wrote of the *Tractatus* 'This book in my unshakeable conviction is the most significant work of our time ... The new insights are absolutely crucial to the destiny of philosophy' (in his 1929 introduction to the projected book by Waismann and Wittgenstein, *Logik, Sprache, Philosophie*). J. Jörgensen, in a history of the Circle wrote that the *Tractatus* 'contributed essentially to the formation of logical positivism', and V. Kraft, in a survey of the work of the Circle wrote 'A common starting point was provided also by the philosophy of language which Ludwig Wittgenstein had developed.' For elaboration, see Hacker, *Wittgenstein's Place in Twentieth-Century Analytic Philosophy*, ch. 3.

the role of logic'[9] and Carnap remarked similarly that Wittgenstein had shown that logical truths 'are tautological, that is, that they hold necessarily in every possible case, therefore they do not exclude any case and do not say anything about the facts of the world'.[10] The consequence of this, Carnap averred, was 'that it became possible for the first time to combine the basic tenets of empiricism with a satisfactory explanation of the nature of logic and mathematics'. The members of the Circle thought that logicism (albeit with further refinements), together with the *Tractatus* insights into logic, explained the nature of arithmetic.[11] They thought that Hilbert had successfully elucidated the conventional nature of pure geometry; and that Wittgenstein had explained the tautological nature of logic. As for metaphysics, they excluded metaphysical utterances as devoid of (cognitive) meaning either on the basis of the principle of verification, which they derived from discussions with Wittgenstein in 1929/30, or on the basis of *Tractatus* considerations pertaining to the logical syntax of language. Carnap later wrote 'the most decisive development in my view of metaphysics occurred later, in the Vienna period, chiefly under the influence of Wittgenstein'.[12]

The upshot was that the members of the Circle adopted a set of methodological and substantive doctrines that might well be thought to characterize 'the linguistic turn in analytic philosophy'.

It was generally accepted that philosophy is not a cognitive discipline that may add to the body of human knowledge. There are no special philosophical propositions in the sense in which there are propositions of the natural sciences. Moreover, there is no such thing as first philosophy which provides the foundations for empirical science.

The traditional problems of philosophy (especially of metaphysics) are pseudo-problems that arise through (i) misleading features of natural language, and (ii) the misguided idea that thought can yield substantive knowledge independently of experience.

Philosophy is an activity of clarification of problems that arise out of misleading features of natural language. Its method is the clarification of sentences of natural language that give rise to philosophical problems (Schlick and Waismann, under the influence of Wittgenstein in the early 1930s), or the logical analysis of language and the investigation of the logical syntax of the language of science (Carnap and Neurath). 'The logic of science', Carnap wrote, 'takes the place of the inextricable tangle of problems which is known as philosophy',[13] and the logic of science just is the logical syntax of the language of science. This polarity within the Circle was associated with a parallel divergence of views in respect of the project of unified science which was Neurath's dream.

---

[9] A re3mark reported by Karl Menger in his introduction to Hahn's *Philosophical Papers* (Dordrecht: Reidel, 1980), p. xii.

[10] R. Carnap, 'Intellectual Autobiography', in P. A. Schilpp (ed.), *The Philosophy of Rudolph Carnap* (La Salle, IL: Open Court, 1963), p. 46.

[11] Carnap and Hahn both thought that the difference between tautologies and arithmetical propositions are insignificant. This was never Wittgenstein's view.

[12] Carnap, 'Intellectual Autobiography', p. 45.

[13] R. Carnap, *The Logical Syntax of Language* (London: Routledge & Kegan Paul, 1937), p. 279.

The result of philosophy, Schlick claimed (very much under Wittgenstein's influence), is that some of its problems 'will disappear by being shown to be mistakes and misunderstandings of our language and others will be found to be ordinary scientific questions in disguise. These remarks, I think, determine the whole future of philosophy.'[14] Carnap had a less negative conception. 'In our discussions in the Vienna Circle', he wrote later, 'it had turned out that any attempt at formulating more precisely the philosophical problems in which we were interested ended up with problems in the logical analysis of language. Since in our view the issue in philosophical problems concerned the language not the world, these problems should be formulated, not in the object language, but in the meta-language.'[15] This conviction led to the writing of *The Logical Syntax of Language* (1934), and subsequently, under the influence of Tarski, to the development of Carnap's formal semantical methods that culminate with *Meaning and Necessity* (1947).

It is this divergence between Schlick and Waismann (most influenced by the middle Wittgenstein), on the one hand, and Carnap and Neurath, on the other, that warranted Bergmann and Rorty in distinguishing two streams within what they termed 'linguistic philosophy'—the so-called ordinary language philosophers and the ideal language philosophers. But, of course, by the time they were writing (in the 1960s) the Vienna Circle had disappeared, and so-called ordinary language philosophy was represented by Oxford philosophers and their followers in the years after 1945. Ideal language philosophers, on the other hand, were represented by Carnap and Bergmann and their followers in the USA, as well as by Quine. Quine was a self-confessed apostate from the logical empiricism of the Circle, denying the distinction between analytic propositions and empirical ones, hence denying any sharp differentiation of scientific from a priori propositions, and denying that the task of philosophy is purely elucidatory. It is part and parcel of the general human endeavour to achieve knowledge of the world. Nevertheless, he advocated the regimentation of natural language. His idea was that translating our 'theories' into the first-order predicate calculus will reveal our ontological commitments. Redundant commitments can be eliminated by a canonical notation. His goal was as austere an ontology as possible consistent with having a regimented language adequate for all scientific purposes.

I have suggested that it was through Wittgenstein that the logistic turn of the nineteenth century and the linguistic turn initiated by the *Tractatus* merged for a time. The synthesis was transmitted to later phases of analytic philosophy. The route ran via the Vienna Circle and the emigration of many of their members to the USA. Logical pragmatism was a consequence of the marriage of logical positivism with the homegrown American pragmatist tradition. In time this resulted in the Quinean naturalism characteristic of much of late twentieth-century American philosophy, in the quest for a theory of meaning for a natural language that was the main enterprise of the most influential of Quine's followers, Donald Davidson, and in possible world semantics.

---

[14] M. Schlick, 'The Turning Point in Philosophy', repr. in A. J. Ayer (ed.), *Logical Positivism* (Glencoe, IL: Free Press, 1959), p. 131.

[15] Carnap, 'Intellectual Autobiography', p. 54.

32.5 LATER WITTGENSTEIN AND THE LINGUISTIC TURN

After his return to philosophy in 1929 Wittgenstein rapidly became disillusioned with his first philosophy, dismantled it, and started the long process of developing his second philosophy that came to fruition in his posthumous *Philosophical Investigations* (1953). Although he published nothing after 1929, his influence on British philosophy was immense. He conveyed his new and revolutionary ideas in his classes at Cambridge, and his pupils in due course transmitted them in their own teachings and writings. In addition, the dictations he gave, the *Blue and the Brown Books*, were circulated in Cambridge, Oxford, and elsewhere. His criticisms of the *Tractatus* are not pertinent to the tale of the development of linguistic philosophy.[16] All that is necessary in this context is to delineate in what sense the middle and later Wittgenstein contributed to the linguistic turn—taking it in directions not dreamt of by members of the Vienna Circle other than Schlick and Waismann, who followed Wittgenstein's ideas closely until 1936.

According to Wittgenstein's later view, the major source of philosophical problems lies in the forms of natural languages and the immense difficulty of attaining a surveyable representation of the meaning-determining rules of grammar, familiar though they are.

The term 'natural language' is more appropriate here than 'ordinary language' (even though Wittgenstein did not use it). Ordinary language stands in contrast to the technical language of the sciences,[17] whereas natural language stands in contrast to artificial language (such as the concept-scripts of Frege and Russell, or the artificial languages devised by Carnap). Of course, the technical terminology of the sciences gives rise to philosophical, conceptual, problems no less than does non-technical language. Terms such as 'the unconscious mind' in psychoanalysis, 'force' in Newtonian physics, 'transfinite cardinal' in transfinite arithmetic, 'law of excluded middle' in formal logic, 'neural map' in cognitive neuroscience, 'depth-grammar' in Chomskian linguistics are technical terms, all of which notoriously generate conceptual bafflement and confusion. So too do terms of ordinary language, such as 'mind', 'force' (as that over the use of which the state has a legal monopoly), 'number', 'infinite', which are all pregnant with philosophical, conceptual, problems. Finally, terms of artificial languages, as opposed to natural languages, generate philosophical problems too. It is not for nothing that philosophers of language and logic have spent so much effort on comparing the logical connectives of the calculus with corresponding terms of natural language, or have laboured so hard to

---

[16] For examination of Wittgenstein's criticisms of the *Tractatus*, see Hacker, *Wittgenstein's Place in Twentieth-Century Analytic Philosophy*, pp. 76–86.

[17] See G. Ryle, 'Ordinary Language', repr. in his *Collected Papers* (London: Hutchinson, 1971), vol. 2, pp. 301–18, for a detailed discussion of the differences between ordinary and technical language, and the quite different contrast between ordinary uses of language and the varieties of non-ordinary (metaphorical, figurative, etc.) uses of language.

compare the use of the existential quantifier with that of natural language expressions such as 'exists' and 'is', or have striven so futilely to find ways of representing plural reference in the calculus.[18]

Nevertheless, it would be an exaggeration to suggest that *all* the problems of philosophy arise out of misleading features of language. For, as Wittgenstein pointed out, philosophical problems may arise through:

A. New scientific discoveries and theories (such as the theory of relativity).
B. Advances in the a priori disciplines (such as transfinite set theory, the predicate calculus, or Gödel's incompleteness theorem).
C. Technological inventions, such as automata in the sixteenth and seventeenth centuries or computers in the twentieth.
D. Natural dispositions of the human mind, such as:
   (i) The craving for generality (which is fundamental to our scientific endeavours);
   (ii) The demand for explanation on the model of scientific explanation, where what is really needed is description and comparison;
   (iii) The disposition to cleave to an explanatory paradigm or model (e.g. to conceive of the mental on the pattern of the physical, and so to think that mental objects, states, and processes are just like physical ones only mental, or to conceive of transfinite cardinals on the model of cardinal numbers, only vastly greater) and hence to extend its usefulness beyond its natural limits;
   (iv) The will to illusion.

What then is the subject matter of 'theoretical' (as opposed to 'practical')[19] philosophy? In the sense in which the natural sciences have a subject matter the successful investigation of which yields empirical truths and a body of established knowledge, philosophy has none. In another sense, one may say that the subject matter of philosophy consists of the peculiar problems of philosophy. What then is a philosophical problem? Wittgenstein wisely eschewed a definition, instead giving an array of uncontroversially philosophical problems as examples. These, to be sure, do share some features. Philosophical problems are a priori, not empirical. So philosophy is sharply distinct from the natural sciences. Philosophical problems can no more be solved by experiment and observation than can problems of mathematics. They are conceptual

---

[18] For a brilliant investigation of the problems of representing plural reference in the predicate calculus, see H. Ben-Yami, *Logic and Natural Language: On Plural Reference and its Semantic and Logical Significance* (Aldershot: Ashgate, 2004).

[19] The debates about the nature of philosophy in the twentieth century were focused largely upon what Kant called 'theoretical' philosophy, i.e. philosophy of logic and language, metaphysics and epistemology, philosophy of mind as well as the philosophies of special sciences (e.g. of biology, physics, mathematics, social sciences). How those debates bear upon practical philosophy (i.e. ethics, political and legal philosophy), its aims, methods, and limits, is worth discussing, but not in this context.

problems—difficulties that result from some unclarity or entanglement in our concepts that may, as we have just seen, have multiple and diverse roots, mostly in misleading features of language. These lead us, both in the formulation of philosophical problems and in our often bungled attempts to resolve them, to transgress the bounds of sense in subtle and commonly unnoticed ways.

The methods of philosophy are manifold. They are descriptive and comparative-descriptive, not hypothetical or hypothetico-deductive like the natural sciences. Central among them is the assembling of familiar rules for the use of words, which Wittgenstein idiosyncratically called grammatical propositions. These are familiar meaning-rules for the use of words, given typically in the material mode, e.g. 'Pain is a sensation', 'Different people may have the same pain', 'To mean something by a word is not an act'. The careful selection of such propositions and their ordering in a surveyable representation is tailored to the specific philosophical problem at hand. But the recollection and marshalling of ordinary (or even technical) usage is not the sole method available to the philosopher. Wittgenstein introduced and made use of the method of invented language-games—imaginary linguistic activities that are invoked to shed light on our own linguistic practices by way of both similarities and differences. He often invited his readers to reflect on how an expression might be taught to a learner in order to shed light on the primitive core of its use. He insisted on paying less attention to grammatical form and more attention to the role and purpose of expressions. His aim of uncovering the sources of philosophical confusion in a misleading analogy or mesmerizing paradigm that is inapplicable, or in a transposition of a grammatical articulation that obtains in one domain of grammar (or language-game) to another involves a further battery of methods. All these are subservient to the goals of philosophy.

Philosophy has two very general goals, the one subordinate to the other. Its primary task is the resolution and dissolution of philosophical problems. Since these problems are symptomatic of conceptual confusions and bafflement, which may be compared to a kind of intellectual disease, their resolution may be conceived metaphorically as a kind of intellectual therapy. Philosophy, one may then say, is a cure for diseases of the understanding. Its result is not new knowledge of the world, but the disentangling of the knots we tie in our understanding. Its second goal is to attain an overview of a concept and to produce a surveyable representation of the relevant field of concepts that will facilitate the resolution of the philosophical problems at hand. This he compared to drawing a map—a map that will help us find our way around in the field of our concepts and conceptual structures.

Wittgenstein's work was a major influence upon the further development of linguistic philosophy after the Second World War. His pupils and followers, such as von Wright, Wisdom, and Anscombe, who succeeded him in his chair in Cambridge, and Ambrose, Black, Malcolm, and Bouwsma in the USA ensured the further spread of his ideas and methods. But the centre from which most further advances in linguistic philosophy ('ordinary language philosophy', to use Bergmann's and Rorty's misleading phrase) came was Oxford.

32.6 Oxford Philosophy and the Linguistic Turn

For a quarter of a century after the war, Oxford was the centre of analytic philosophy in the world. 'Oxford philosophy' was not a school. Unlike the Vienna Circle, it issued no manifesto. It had no ideology akin to the 'Unified Science' of the Circle. Some of the philosophers at Oxford were influenced by Wittgenstein to a greater or lesser extent (e.g. Ryle and Strawson), some were his pupils (Waismann, Paul, and Anscombe), and others developed their views quite independently (e.g. Austin, Grice). But Oxford was more of a flourishing field fertilized by Wittgenstein's ideas than bare soil in which Wittgenstein's seeds grew. Unlike both the Circle and Wittgenstein, Oxford philosophers were fairly relaxed about the use of the term 'theory' in connection with philosophy, as long as a 'philosophical theory' was not assumed to be analogous to a scientific theory. They were equally relaxed about the idea of philosophical propositions and their truth or falsity, as long as it was realized that they are not empirical propositions. The leading figures at Oxford exhibited a variety of viewpoints united primarily by agreed meta-philosophical and methodological ideas, as well as a commitment to clarity of expression, perspicuity of argument, and detestation of obfuscation. The following methodological points would have been accepted by almost all:

(i) Philosophy is distinct from the empirical sciences, and its problems cannot be solved by observation, experiment, and hypothetico-deductive theory. Its problems are a priori, conceptual ones.

(ii) Formal calculi, such as the predicate calculus, are neither the depth grammar of any possible language nor ideal languages that illuminate or mirror the logical structure of the world (among other things, the world has no logical structure). Their usefulness in philosophy is very limited indeed. (What venerable philosophical problems have been solved by recourse to an artificial language?)

(iii) Metaphysics, understood as an investigation into the essential nature of reality is an incoherent enterprise. Admittedly, in *Individuals* (1959), Strawson introduced the term 'descriptive metaphysics', which made the word 'metaphysics' philosophically 'correct' again after some decades on the Index. But it was misleading of him to do so, since descriptive metaphysics is just more analytic description of the structure of our conceptual scheme, not synthetic description of the structure of the world.

(iv) A major source of philosophical problems lies in the misleading forms of natural languages. But there are other sources too—including the misleading forms of artificial calculi.

(v) The task of philosophy is the clarification of our concepts and conceptual structures, partly for its intrinsic interest, partly to solve or dissolve philosophical problems.

(vi) First and foremost among the methods of philosophy is the descriptive analysis of the uses of words. There are, to be sure, other methods too, but this is a *sine qua non* for successful conceptual investigation.

The latter methodological commitment received divergent descriptions from four of the leading members of the Oxford faculty.[20]

Ryle, following Wittgenstein, characterized his methods as charting the 'logical geography' of concepts, describing their logical powers and mapping their connections, compatibilities, and incompatibilities. Initially he connected this with the idea of rectifying category mistakes and type-confusions, but later saw that this was no more than an analogy with formal systems. 'Like a geographical survey', he wrote, 'a philosophical survey is necessarily synoptic. Philosophical problems cannot be posed or solved piecemeal.'[21] Austin (influenced by Moore and altogether unimpressed by Wittgenstein) would perhaps not have gone so far, although it is noteworthy that the only two books he wrote—*Sense and Sensibilia* (1962) and *How to Do Things with Words* (1962)—provided exemplary synoptic surveys. Be that as it may, in his occasional papers he exhibited great skill in detecting distinctions and differences of usage both in the large and in the small. Where our language is rich, subtle, and diverse, e.g. in the field of excuses, then it makes sense, in his view, to proceed from ordinary language 'by examining what we should say when, what words we should use in what situations'.[22] He was, as von Wright later wrote of him, the *doctor subtilis* of his day, and by his skill, and perhaps by his acerbic wit, aroused immense animosity towards what became the favoured term of abuse by its enemies, 'Oxford linguistic philosophy' or 'Ordinary language philosophy'. This was unwarranted. Proceeding from ordinary language, Austin stressed, is *one* method in philosophy, apt for the investigation of excuses or perception, but out of place for the investigation, for example, of time. He characterized it, tongue in cheek, as *linguistic phenomenology*. But he was careful not to exaggerate its powers. Certainly, he wrote, 'ordinary language is *not* the last word: in principle it can be everywhere superseded. Only remember it is the *first* word.' Grice (not in the least influenced by Wittgenstein—and far more prone to construct philosophical 'theories' than his peers) said that a proposition that would have commanded universal assent in Oxford at the time was that 'a careful examination of the detailed features of ordinary discourse is required as a foundation for philosophical thinking', and wrote of Austin's methods that

---

[20] I am, of course, disregarding many important Oxford philosophers whose contribution to philosophy in mid-century was second to none, but in less central domains, and also others who, though no less important, were not at Oxford, but belonged to the same broad movement in the heyday of analytic philosophy in Britain. For more detailed discussion, see *Wittgenstein's Place in Twentieth-Century Analytic Philosophy*, ch. 6.

[21] G. Ryle, 'Philosophical Arguments', repr. in his *Collected Papers*, vol. 2, p. 202.

[22] J. L. Austin, 'A Plea for Excuses', repr. in his *Philosophical Papers* (Oxford: Clarendon Press, 1961), p. 130.

When put to work, this conception of ordinary language seemed to offer fresh and manageable approaches to philosophical ideas and problems ... When properly regulated and directed, 'linguistic botanizing' seems to me to provide a valuable initiation to the philosophical treatment of a concept, particularly if what is under examination (and it is arguable that this should always be the case) is a family of different but related concepts. Indeed, I shall go further, and proclaim it as my belief that linguistic botanizing is indispensable, at a certain stage, in a philosophical inquiry, and that it is lamentable that this lesson has been forgotten, or has never been learned.[23]

Strawson was less inclined to the careful examination of usage than Austin, but, unlike his old tutor Grice, he was markedly influenced by Wittgenstein. He described what he conceived as the most appropriate method of philosophy as *connective analysis*. Connective analysis was presented as the appropriate replacement for the discredited forms of decompositional and reductive analysis characteristic of the early phases of analytic philosophy, and for their equally discredited successor—logical construction (e.g. Carnap's *Logische Aufbau der Welt* and Goodman's *The Structure of Appearances*). Instead of 'decomposing' or 'constructing' anything, connective analysis aimed to describe appropriate fragments of the network of our conceptual scheme, tracing the connections between a given problematic concept and adjacent concepts with which it is linked. This was to be done by describing the salient features of the uses of expressions and their logical dependencies, compatibilities, incompatibilities, and implications, their presuppositions and forms of contextual dependencies—all in order to resolve philosophical problems, to explode philosophical illusions, and illuminate aspects of our conceptual scheme.[24] This method has remarkable affinities with much of Wittgenstein's practice—although in Strawson's hands connective analysis was put to fewer diagnostic and 'therapeutic' purposes. Logical geography, linguistic phenomenology, linguistic botanizing, and connective analysis flourished side by side—the differences of detail being minimal and tolerated. No one thought that philosophy was exclusively *about* language (save for 'philosophy of language'—a term then virtually unknown),[25] nobody thought that philosophy was *a branch of linguistics*, and no one thought that scrutiny of linguistic usage was the *sole* method of philosophy.

Philosophers at Oxford from 1945 until the mid-1970s, and their pupils and followers throughout the English-speaking world brought the 'natural language' branch of the linguistic turn in philosophy to an apogee. Though none of them used the phrase 'the linguistic turn', and few if any of them called themselves 'ordinary language philosophers', there was remarkable unanimity with regard to their conception of the nature of philosophy and the methodology of philosophical investigation.

[23] H. P. Grice, 'Reply to Richards', in R. E. Grandy and R. Warner (eds.), *Philosophical Grounds of Rationality* (Oxford: Clarendon Press, 1986), p. 57.

[24] P. F. Strawson, *Analysis and Metaphysics* (Oxford: Oxford University Press, 1992), ch. 2.

[25] What we now call philosophy of language was then known as philosophical logic.

32.7 The Aftermath, an Overview, and Two Mistaken Criticisms

After the mid-1970s linguistic philosophy declined. The centre of gravity of Anglophone philosophy shifted to the USA. Quinean and Davidsonian logical pragmatism flourished.[26] For a couple of decades theories of meaning for a natural language occupied centre-stage, enjoying, together with Chomsky's linguistic theory, the thrills of seeking the depth grammar of language and the inner workings of the human mind. The excitement faded as promise exceeded performance. Philosophy of language was gradually displaced from centre-stage by various forms of physicalist philosophy of mind that in turn transmuted into 'cognitive science'. This was thought to be a synthesis of the best in philosophy of psychology, neuroscience, theoretical linguistics, and artificial intelligence. (Critics responded, like Bentham to Blackstone on the mixed British constitution, by wondering whether it might not be a synthesis of the worst in each.) In the USA Quinean naturalism came to dominate the scene. Quine's superficial criticisms of the analytic/synthetic distinction led to an unreflective acceptance of the old Russellian idea that philosophy is continuous with and in the same cognitive business as science. (It was a sore misconception of Quine's to suppose that the sharp distinction between philosophical and scientific investigation turned on the viability of Carnap's distinction between analytic and synthetic statements.) But perhaps this *scientistic* drift was unsurprising in an intellectual culture prone to adulate empirical science as the repository of all that we know and understand about ourselves and the world. The upshot was the dispersal of the broad stream of analytic philosophy that had flowed so powerfully for almost a century into a multitude of rivulets meandering through a delta with little sense of direction or purpose. At its worst, analytic philosophy moved into a characteristically scholastic phase in which pedantry displaced vision, and all that was left of an era of philosophical achievement were empty forms—the employment of the technical tools of analytic philosophy. Misunderstandings of what the linguistic turn had consisted in, and even deeper misconceptions of what Oxford linguistic (or 'ordinary language') philosophy had been, became widespread. So, before concluding, an overview may be helpful.

As we have seen, the expression 'the linguistic turn' is useful to signal an important shift in meta-philosophical reflection and in philosophical methodology that occurred in the 1920s. This merged for a while with the logistic turn that had arisen in the mid-nineteenth century, producing the ideal- and regimenting-language philosophy characteristic of logical positivism and logical pragmatism. This gave rise to the pursuit of theories of meaning for a natural language. The other, and perhaps more fruitful, branch

---

[26] See H.-J. Glock, *Quine and Davidson on Language, Thought and Reality* (Cambridge: Cambridge University Press, 2003).

of the linguistic turn was natural language philosophy, which eschewed the construction of formal languages and pursued connective analysis for purposes of philosophical elucidation and insight.

The meta-philosophical commitment was above all that philosophy is neither a science nor an extension of science. It is *sui generis*. Philosophy is a conceptual investigation that results in the description and clarification of conceptual structures and in the elimination of conceptual confusions. It is not a contribution to human knowledge, as the natural and social sciences are, but a contribution to a distinctive form of human understanding. Some (such as the logical positivists and Wittgenstein) held that there are no philosophical propositions in the sense in which there are propositions of natural science; others (such as Ryle and Strawson) were less fastidious, but held the propositions they advanced to be a priori conceptual truths. This difference is not deep.

The primary methodological commitment was to meticulous examination of linguistic usage (ordinary or technical as the case may be)[27] as a *sine qua non* for successful philosophical investigation. What was then to be done with the conceptual data thus obtained differed importantly both between the two branches of the linguistic turn (e.g. contrast Carnapian explication with Strawsonian connective analysis)[28] and within each branch (contrast Austin with Grice). And, to be sure, this also depended greatly on the skills of the philosophers in marshalling the linguistic/conceptual data.

There was also a diagnostic consensus that surface features of the sentences of natural language are one major source of philosophical confusion. This, of course, was no novelty. What was novel was the manner in which these confusing features were winkled out, arrayed, and used to shed light upon the conceptual problems of philosophy and to explain what leads us to build houses of cards.

The linguistic turn, linguistic philosophy, and so-called ordinary language philosophers were and still are subject to much criticism from many who have not properly followed the linguistic turn. Viewed cursorily and unsympathetically from afar, one cannot see the twists and turns of the linguistic turn, let alone the panoramas to which it gave access and the views across philosophical landscapes that it made possible. I shall conclude by briefly warning against two common, but misconceived, criticisms.

One is the supposition that in order to describe linguistic usage one needs to consult one's linguistic intuitions. And, it is then queried, why should one's own intuitions—especially those of Oxford dons—be preferable to anyone else's? The second, and consequent idea is that if one wants to determine usage, one should do proper empirical surveys in which one would ask people to fill out questionnaires like any other decent social scientist. Then 'ordinary language philosophy' would be revealed as what it is, namely no more than a debased form of sociology of language.

---

[27] One could hardly investigate the concept of transfinite cardinal by examining *ordinary* usage.

[28] For a fascinating confrontation, see Strawson's 'Carnap's Views on Constructed Systems versus Natural Languages in Analytic Philosophy', in Schilpp (ed.), *The Philosophy of Rudolf Carnap*, pp. 503–18 and Carnap's response, pp. 933–9.

The idea that in order to say what the correct use of a word or phrase is one has to consult one's intuitions is akin to supposing that in order to play chess a chess-master has to consult his intuitions on the rules of chess, or that a skilled mathematician has to consult his intuitions on what 12×12 is. An intuition is just a *hunch* or *guess*—and it is no more a hunch of a competent speaker that one says 'he was in the field' not 'he were in the field', than it is a hunch of a chess-master that the chess-king moves one square at a time or of a mathematician that 12×12 is 144.

It is precisely because of this that the idea that to specify the correct use of a familiar word one needs to do social surveys is misguided. A competent speaker of a natural language by definition knows how to use the common (and, if he is a specialist, the technical) words he uses, just as a competent chess-player or mathematician knows the rules constitutive of their expertise. That does not mean that he may not slip occasionally, overlook some familiar feature or other, or hesitate over borderline cases. What it does mean is that in marshalling grammatical rules in order to pinpoint the differences between, say, accident and mistake, or perception and sensation, or mental images and photographic images, one does not need to consult anyone—only to reflect, and occasionally to use a good dictionary to jolt one's memory. (If one encounters disagreement over usage, that itself is an important datum—and one may proceed from there.) Philosophical skill does not consist merely in remembering features of usage with which any competent speaker or technical practitioner is familiar, but in selecting and marshalling those features of usage that will illuminate the problem at hand and show what linguistic analogies led one up the garden path. This may be no more than the first steps in one's philosophical endeavours. But unless one learns *how* to take them, and then *takes* them, one will continue barking up the wrong tree.[29]

[29] I am grateful to the editor, to Professor Hans Oberdiek, and to Professor Herman Philipse for their helpful comments.

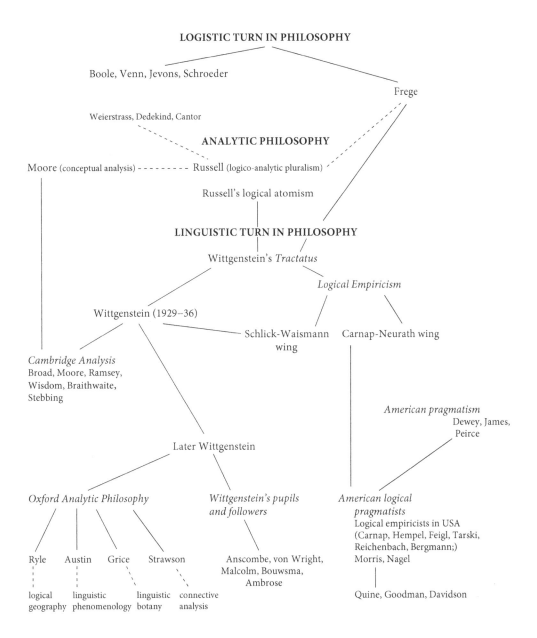

LOGISTIC TURN IN PHILOSOPHY

Boole, Venn, Jevons, Schroeder

Frege

Weierstrass, Dedekind, Cantor

ANALYTIC PHILOSOPHY

Moore (conceptual analysis) - - - - - - - - Russell (logico-analytic pluralism)

Russell's logical atomism

LINGUISTIC TURN IN PHILOSOPHY

Wittgenstein's *Tractatus*

Logical Empiricism

Wittgenstein (1929–36)

Schlick-Waismann   Carnap-Neurath wing
wing

Cambridge Analysis
Broad, Moore, Ramsey,
Wisdom, Braithwaite,
Stebbing

American pragmatism
Dewey, James,
Peirce

Later Wittgenstein

Oxford Analytic Philosophy

*Wittgenstein's pupils
and followers*

*American logical
pragmatists*
Logical empiricists in USA
(Carnap, Hempel, Feigl, Tarski,
Reichenbach, Bergmann;)
Morris, Nagel

Ryle   Austin   Grice   Strawson

Anscombe, von Wright,
Malcolm, Bouwsma,
Ambrose

logical   linguistic   linguistic   connective
geography   phenomenology botany   analysis

Quine, Goodman, Davidson

A diagram of the history of the linguistic turn

CHAPTER 33

....

PERCEPTION AND
SENSE-DATA

....

GARY HATFIELD

ANALYTIC philosophy arose in the early decades of the twentieth century, with Bertrand Russell and G. E. Moore leading the way. Although some accounts emphasize the role of logic and language in the origin of analytic philosophy, of equal importance is the theme of perception, sense-data, and knowledge, which dominated systematic philosophical discussion in the first two decades of the twentieth century in both Britain and America. Perception and knowledge persisted as central topics in the analytic tradition into the early 1970s. After a decade or two in which philosophy of language took a leading role, perception is again an area of expansion in what is still deemed 'analytic philosophy'.

Although interest in perception intensified early in the twentieth century, perception and the external world had been under discussion continuously since Descartes. When Moore and Russell turned to the problem, they sometimes invoked previous positions as reference points, especially those of Locke, Berkeley, Hume, and Reid. Many topics that Moore and Russell addressed were already prevalent by 1890, including the relation between the perceptual act of the subject and a distinct object of perception, the distinction between primary and secondary qualities, the dependence of perceived spatial structures on the distance and orientation of objects (James 1890, 2: 238–40), the dependence of colour on distance and lighting (James 1890, 1: 231), and the spectre of scepticism in relation to the external world.

Given that perception was already under active discussion, we may ask what Moore, Russell, and their contemporaries added so as to initiate an 'analytic' tradition of work on perception. Is it merely that 'analytic philosophers' took up perception because it was already a, or the, central problem in metaphysics and epistemology? There is something to that, but it is not the whole story. Moore and Russell promoted distinctive positions on perception and knowledge—distinctive positions of realism about sense-data, versus the idealism of Bradley and McTaggart among others. For a time, this realism dominated the new circle of discussion, although some analytic philosophers later adopted phenomenalism, including A. J. Ayer (1940). A second contribution of Moore and Russell was the adoption of methods that were explicitly or retrospectively deemed 'analytic'. Each had his own method of analysis, one grounded in 'common sense' and conceptual analysis, the other using the natural sciences as a source of inspiration and of philosophical substance in seeking what is analytically primitive or basic.

This chapter surveys work on perception and sense-data in the analytic tradition in the first half of the twentieth century. After sketching the situation before and just after 1900, it turns to Moore, Russell, and their interlocutors in the teens and twenties, addresses the American scene, looks to subsequent developments in the 1930s and beyond, and finally considers the fates of sense-data and the 'given' and of the topic of perception more generally.

33.1 Perception and the External World at the End of the Nineteenth Century

The immediate context for the birth of analytic philosophy is the late nineteenth-century Cambridge of Russell and Moore. Russell was the elder student. He was studying mathematics and philosophy ('moral sciences') and advised Moore, who came to study classics, also to stand for Part II of the moral sciences tripos, as had he. They shared tutors, including McTaggart, James Ward, and G. F. Stout (the latter two were psychologists as well as philosophers). Russell visited William James at Harvard in 1896 and Moore (1942a, p. 29) later read James's *Principles* 'with a good deal of attention'.

Much is rightly made of Moore's and Russell's early adherence to British Idealism, as conveyed to them by McTaggart and as represented by F. H. Bradley and T. H. Green at Oxford (e.g., Hylton 1990). Their rejections of idealism in the late 1890s—and so of meaning holism and the idealistic denial of the independence of perceptual object from perceiving subject—are well documented. In this regard, one can see their subsequent positions as developed in opposition to the idealism of their youth.

Nonetheless, idealism was not the only philosophical presence at Cambridge and Oxford or in Anglophone philosophical letters. The philosophical scene in Britain was varied. In England, for much of the nineteenth century creative philosophical work was produced outside the universities (Pattison 1876), by the likes of James Mill (a Scottish expatriate), John Stuart Mill, Herbert Spencer, George Henry Lewes, and Shadworth Hodgson, whose works were discussed at Cambridge. Hodgson was a founder of the Aristotelian Society in 1880 and its first president (1880–94). The Society, meeting in London, facilitated discussion of various philosophical positions (idealistic and non) by philosophers inside and outside university walls, and including topics such as the problem of the external world, the relation between subject and object, and the distinction between primary and secondary qualities. Such topics entered the pages of *Mind* (founded in 1876), which was no idealistic rag.

In comparison, the universities of Scotland produced original philosophy from the early eighteenth century on, when the professorial system replaced the regency or tutorial system. Concerning perception, Thomas Reid was a leading figure, followed by William Hamilton in the nineteenth century (Veitch 1877). They were known for their 'natural realism', developed by Hamilton (1861) as the view that, in the 'data' of consciousness, both the ego and a material non-ego are immediately given as independent and distinct. This Scottish realism was widely discussed in the latter half of the century. Mill's *Examination of Sir William Hamilton's Philosophy* (1872) prompted further debate; at Cambridge, it was recommended for the moral sciences tripos into the 1890s (Cambridge University 1893, p. xvii). The Oxford philosophers Thomas Case (1888) and L. T. Hobhouse (1896) developed their own perceptual realisms as revisions of Hamilton's. Case taught Hobhouse and the influential John Cook Wilson. Russell read Hobhouse's *Theory of Knowledge* in 1896,[1] the year it appeared, and the work garnered sufficient notice to be listed for Part I of the moral sciences tripos (Cambridge University 1908, p. xxxvii).

New thought about the relations between act and object—or consciousness and object, or subject and presentation—was represented at Cambridge by Ward and Stout, who introduced to a British audience the Austrian brand of phenomenology stemming especially from the work of Franz Brentano.[2] In addition to explicating the distinction between act and object, Ward (1886) and Stout (1890, 1900–1) played an active role in discussions of the problem of the external world. Further, Stout, with his *Analytic Psychology* (1896), represented the theoretical attitude, widely found in both the new British and the new German psychology, of analysing complex mental processes and achievements into simples and then seeking to explain the complexes through laws or processes for combining the simples—an outlook that was certainly a relative of the subsequent analytic bent in Moore and Russell.

Philosophical education at Oxford and Cambridge included many 'greats'.[3] It is no accident that Moore and Russell could situate their positions in relation to Locke, Berkeley, Hume, and Reid. Study of the greats engaged ongoing controversies over the structure of perceptual consciousness, the status of the object of perception, the problem of the external world, and the distinction between primary and secondary qualities.

In his article on metaphysics for the eleventh edition of the *Britannica*, Case surveyed the positions of the past two centuries, emphasizing the nineteenth. He divided previous philosophy into three types: materialism, idealism, and realism. He dispatched the

---

[1] A list of books read by Russell and sometimes his first wife, Alys Pearsall Smith, is found in Russell 1983, pp. 345–70 (for Hobhouse, p. 358).

[2] Ward (1919, p. viii) mentions Brentano with respect and credits him with helping to form his outlook, but, by contrast with Stout, rarely cites him explicitly (Ward 1876, p. 459; 1892, p. 537). On some Austrian influences in the early formation of Moore and Russell as analytic philosophers, see Bell 1999.

[3] On philosophical education at Oxford, Pattison 1876; on Cambridge, Sidgwick 1876 and the book list for the moral sciences tripos, Cambridge University 1870, including works by Plato, Aristotle, Cicero, Descartes, Locke, Kant, Hamilton, and Mill (p. 38).

recent scientific materialism quickly and left his favoured position, realism, to the end. That left the various idealisms: metaphysical, noumenal, phenomenal, and English. Case saw all idealism, from Berkeley to Mill and Bradley, as stemming from an assumption shared by Descartes and Locke (who, in his view, inconsistently adopted representative realism over idealism): the position of 'psychological idealism', which 'assumes without proof that we perceive nothing but mental objects' (1911, p. 228). Case echoed the diagnosis of Reid and Hamilton on modern philosophy's wrong turn. In his estimation, once the immediate object of perception is taken to be mental, idealism cannot be avoided, since Berkeley was right that material objects cannot properly be inferred or proven from behind the veil of sensory ideas. It remained only to decide what form of idealism to adopt: awareness of a finite self with an inference to God with Berkeley; experience of an infinite absolute with Bradley (1897); or a retreat to phenomenalism with Hume and Mill (1872). Both Bradley and Mill, as also Ward and Stout, accepted a phenomenal distinction between self and object, or ego and non-ego; they denied that this non-ego is immediately known and ultimately that it is independent of the mental.[4]

Against idealism, Case (1888) asserted a direct awareness of an external, non-mental object—joining Hamilton and later being joined by Hobhouse, Moore, and Russell. These realisms differed among themselves. In Hamilton's 'intuitive' or 'natural' realism, we are immediately aware of an external object. In visual perception, this object is not the external object at a distance, as later naïve realists such as Cook Wilson and Samuel Alexander would have it, but the light falling on the retina. There is no awareness at a distance, but there is awareness of something external to the body, if only just so.

Case did not start from the immediate data of consciousness, as had Hamilton, but from reflection on what science tells us about the external world and how we know it. We know that the world is constituted by particulate matter and that our sensory awareness of this world is mediated by the nervous system. Hence, we should conclude that the immediate object of external sense perception is the nervous system itself. It is external to the mind but not to the body. From our apprehension of the nervous system and its qualities (it turns red or white when we see red or white), we infer a world of external objects. Case called his position 'physical realism' to distinguish it from Hamilton's. It was 'physical' in starting from physical science, rather than from intuitive inspection of the data of consciousness. It was 'realistic' in affirming a world of matter beyond the mind. Hobhouse (1896) followed Case in rendering his realism as non-intuitive, but he did not restrict the objects of sense to nerve states or retinal images; he gives 'a hard, coloured surface' (p. 520) as an immediate datum. Moore and Russell's positions, which posited non-mental sense-data as immediate objects of perception, are discussed below.

Moore sometimes is credited with coining the term 'sense-data'. But it was already in use. An earlier form, 'data of sense', occurs from 1876 (Stewart 1876, p. 447; Veitch 1877, p. 221) and in Case's 1888 book. The related 'data of consciousness' recurs throughout Hamilton's *Metaphysics* and in discussions of his work (Veitch 1877, p. 224). The term

---

[4] On the distinction between act and object in Mill, Ward, Stout, and others, see Hatfield (2013).

'sense-data' itself occurs in *Mind* in the early 1880s (Royce 1882; Sidgwick 1883), was used by James (1887) and Russell (1897, p. 327) in that journal, and by Hobhouse (1896). Moreover, Moore was already discussing perception of the external world and of sensory intermediaries before using the term 'sense-data' (1909–10). Hence, use of that term *per se* does not mark the rise of 'analytic' discussions of perception. As to 'analytic philosophy', that term was also in use. Case subtitled his 1888 *Physical Realism* 'an analytical philosophy from the physical objects of science to the physical data of sense'. That the topic of sense-data in early analytic philosophy is so closely allied to Moore and Russell results in part from their prominence, visibility, and influence. But each also exemplified, and sometimes reflected on, a distinctive method of philosophizing that was in some way identified as 'analytic', and each made sense-data a central topic of concern.

33.2 MOORE, SENSE-DATA, AND THE EXTERNAL WORLD

Moore broke with idealism in 1898 and his 'Refutation of Idealism' appeared in 1903. He had not yet adopted the concept of sense-data, but he had introduced the distinction that made him a realist, which he maintained throughout his life. He distinguished the object of sensation (as non-mental) from the act of sensation. He repeatedly argued for, or asserted, this distinction in subsequent papers, including those distinguishing sense-data from the act of sensation.

His argument in the 'Refutation' was similar to that of Hamilton and the Scottish realists. He contended that, in every case of sensation, we are aware of two distinct elements, one common to all sensations and the other differing among them. The common element he called 'consciousness'. It is common between the sensation of blue and the sensation of green. The other element is the 'object' of sensation. It is blue in one case, green in the other. He argued that the common element, consciousness, must in fact be distinct and separate from the object (contrary to the idealist view that the two, though phenomenally distinct, are in some way 'inseparable'). He did not claim to prove that the object is what it seems to be: a material object at a distance. But he endeavoured to show that the existence of spirit is no better supported than that of matter: we are (or seem to be) directly aware of both, that is, of our consciousness and its object. He in effect endorsed a naïve realism, according to which we are directly aware of 'the existence of a table in space' in the same way in which we are directly aware of the conscious element that accompanies every mental fact (1903, p. 453).

Moore later disparaged this paper, which is less developed than two subsequent papers, the first introducing the concept of sense-data without the term and the second invoking the term. He introduced the concept in 'The Nature and Reality of Objects of Perception', presented to the Aristotelian Society in 1905. It assesses what evidence there may be for the existence of other perceivers having perceptions similar to our own. He

contends (1) that we have such evidence only if our perceptions reveal to us really existent things that are distinct from our thoughts and perceptions; and (2) that, generalizing
from relations between our own thoughts and experiences and bodily movements—as
when we grab our foot in pain or use words to convey thoughts—we can infer that similar movements in other bodies have the same type of preceding mental conditions. In
support of (1), he isolated a minimum characterization of what is 'actually observed' or
'directly perceived' in our visual experiences (p. 101).

Moore argued that in perception we are directly aware of two sorts of content: our
own thoughts and feelings, and, for vision, the items that are 'actually seen'. These last he
restricted to colour patches and their spatial relations:

> Most of us are familiar with the experience which we should describe by saying that
> we had seen a red book and a blue book side by side upon a shelf. What exactly can
> we be said to observe or directly perceive when we have such an experience? We
> certainly observe one colour, which we call blue, and a different colour, which we
> call red; each of these we observe as having a particular size and shape; and we ob-
> serve also these two coloured patches as having to one another the spatial relation
> which we express by saying that they are side by side. All this we certainly see or
> directly perceive *now*, whatever may have been the process by which we have come
> to perceive so much. (1905–6, p. 101)

His notion of 'directness' is epistemic. We know immediately the sizes, shapes, and
colours found in experience, independent of whatever physiological or psychological
processes underlie this experience. He called these items 'sense-contents' (p. 111) and
contrasted them with perceptions, thoughts, and feelings (which he later called 'mental acts'). He argued that in order to infer that other persons exist having thoughts and
perceptions similar to our own, it will not do simply to believe that our own perceptions exist and that colours and so forth are part of them. Colour patches must 'actually
exist' apart from being perceived. He did not claim to prove that they exist *unperceived*
(although he believed it, p. 122); even if they exist only while perceived, they must be
accepted as existing (at that very moment) apart from the perceiving of them. By this he
means that they exist in space, where they seem to be (pp. 120–6). This minimum degree
of mind-independent realism is required to establish that other minds exist.

Moore (1905–6, p. 120) acknowledged that his position was compatible with a
stronger form of realism, which he attributed to Reid, that identifies colours in objects
with collections of particles that affect light in a certain way. He allowed that the same
argument he used to infer other minds might also be used to support a belief in material
objects (as causes of the colours we immediately perceive). Both beliefs rely on a prior
premise, which is his main objective: the conclusion that colour patches exist in space,
distinct from thoughts and perceptions. He did not try to determine what such patches
are. He subsequently renamed these 'sense-contents' as 'sense-data', perhaps in order to
distinguish his position from uses of 'content' for something mental.

In December, 1909, Moore gave a paper at the Aristotelian Society on distinguishing the mental from the non-mental. He again divided 'mental acts' from their objects,

including so-called 'sense-data', using a now familiar argument: when we perceive one colour and then another, the act of consciousness is the same (of the same type), whereas the objects (the two colours) differ. Hence, the act of consciousness is distinct from its object. Such acts can differ in quality (one mental act may be a perceiving, another a willing, etc.), and sometimes many mental acts are conjoined to form a complex mental entity. But he maintained that mental acts are distinct from their objects, even if it happens that those objects exist only when we perceive them, as some people (Moore reports) believe about colours. He then explains his notion of 'sense-data':

> By sense-data I understand a class of entities of which we are very often direct-ly conscious, and with many of which we are extremely familiar. They include the colours, of all sorts of different shades, which I actually see when I look about me; the sounds which I actually hear; the peculiar sort of entity of which I am directly conscious when I feel the pain of a toothache, and which I call 'the pain'; and many others which I need not enumerate. But I wish also to include among them those en-tities called 'images', of which I am directly conscious when I dream and often also when awake; which resemble the former in respect of the fact that they *are* colours, sounds, etc.; but which seem, as a rule, like rather faint copies of the colours, sounds, etc., actually seen or heard, and which, whether fainter or not, differ from them in respect of the fact that we should not say we actually saw or heard them, and the fact that they are not, in the strictest sense of the words, 'given by the senses.' All these entities I propose to call sense-data. And in their case there is, of course, no question whether there *are* such entities. The entities meant certainly *are*, whether or not they be rightly described as 'sensations', 'sense-presentations', 'sense-data', etc. Here the only question can be, whether they are 'mental.' (1909–10, 57)

Moore's remarks are not in the spirit of *proving* that sense-data exist but of *drawing our attention* to their obvious existence; his argument concerns whether they are mental. Moore observes (p. 58) that philosophers such as Stout regard sense-data as mental because they fail to distinguish act from object, consciousness of blue from the blue of which we are conscious.

Moore introduced the term 'sense-data' to describe what minimally must exist when we are conscious of perceiving, imagining, or remembering. He intended the term to provide a neutral description for whatever is the immediate object of our awareness, without entailing a specific position concerning the character of the external world itself. Over the next five decades, he considered various theories about how sense-data might relate to physical objects. In these discussions, he sometimes used 'sensibles' as a more general term, to include unsensed sense-data—not because he thought it improper to speak of unsensed sense-data, but because others might get confused (1913–14, pp. 357–8). His preferred theory shifted from time to time, but I do not chart those swings in detail. Rather, I consider the various positions he discussed and indicate those he generally preferred.

Moore considered five relations that sense-data might have to physical objects (Moore 1913–14, 1918–19, 1925, 1957). Physical objects might (1) simply be collections of sensed and unsensed (or possibly sensed) sense-data, and nothing more. This position he contrasted with views according to which sense-data are the product of a distinct causal source. These sources might be (2) a spiritual entity (as in Berkeleian idealism); (3) an unknown thing in itself; or (4) physical objects, as in Locke's view of representative realism. In (4), sense-data stand in a relation to physical objects, called 'relation R' (Moore 1925, 1957). Finally, Moore considered that a sense-datum might (5) be a part of the surface of a physical object.

In discussing these positions, Moore introduced certain facts about how physical objects look to observers, including differences that illustrate the 'relativity' of perception. In an example using coins (I'll use US coins), a penny is smaller than a quarter and both are round. Some observers (including Moore) report that when they look at the coins from any angle other than perpendicular to the line of the sight, they appear more or less elliptical (becoming thin rectangles when seen edge-on). They also report that the quarter, when seen at sufficiently greater distance than the penny, appears smaller than it. Moore wanted to account for (what he took to be) these facts, while also preserving some widely held beliefs that are thought to constitute knowledge: that we really do, on some occasions, see coins; that the coins really are round; that they have an inside and a lower side, even though these aren't presently seen; that the quarter is really larger than the penny; and that the coins exist when we aren't looking at them.

Moore found that some of the positions (1) to (5) better preserve these beliefs than others. Position (1) he described as a 'Mill–Russell' sort of view, which denies that material objects, as ordinarily conceived, exist, and invokes sensed and possibly sensed sense-data (Mill) or treats material objects as constructions out of sensed and unsensed sense-data (sensibilia, sensibles) as in Russell (1914a, 1914b). Moore realized that this position was committed to a vast number of sense-data existing, and to various sense-data (of one degree of ellipticality or another) existing in the same place. He didn't mind that so much, but he disliked this position because it captured the widely held beliefs in a merely 'Pickwickian' sense (1913–14, p. 376). Nonetheless, he granted that it might be the true theory and favoured it over (2) and (3), which, in making the real thing something spiritual or something wholly unknown, are even further removed from the belief in a real, round penny. His ultimate preferences vacillated between (4) and (5).

Position (4), a form of representative realism,[5] accounts for the perceptual relativity that makes us want to distinguish the immediate object of perception from the properties we ascribe to physical objects. The immediate object is elliptical, the penny round. With Moore's famous envelope (1910–11/1953, ch. 2), the immediate object exhibits differing shades of colour to different observers, but the envelope itself is uniformly white. Although accommodating relativity, this position makes it difficult to explain how we know the properties of the physical object, which remains at one remove from perception.

---

[5] It differs from standard representative realism in not regarding the representing sense-datum as mental.

Position (5) equates the sense-datum with a portion of the surface of the object. In order to account for perceptual relativity, Moore now violates his basic tenet about sense-data: that we know them immediately as they are. If the penny is round and we are aware of its surface immediately (even when viewed at an angle), we are aware of a round thing. But, Moore holds, it looks elliptical. Hence, in holding (5), one must distinguish the actual properties of the directly seen surface from the properties it seems to have. There is no actually elliptical datum; rather, the circular datum simply seems to be elliptical (1918–19, p. 24). Moore did his best to uphold a direct realism in (5) and at times favoured it. But in his final writings (1957), he endorsed (4) instead.

Moore used the term 'analysis' thrice in an early paper on freedom (1898, pp. 186, 201), in disputing Kant's 'analysis of human volition'. He used it several times in a paper on judgement (1899), anent analysing judgements, concepts, and things into their constituents. Subsequently, Moore frequently described himself as undertaking analysis in order to find what may plausibly be asserted on a topic. An analysis of sensory perception yields mental acts and objects; an analysis of common sense yields some basic commitments; an analysis of propositions may reveal more basic propositions.

What can be said of Moore's method? He reflected on method in lectures from 1910–11 (Moore 1953, ch. 1) and the Schilpp volume (1942b), and he displayed his method in various papers. Analysis, in his sense, was not of verbal expressions, but of concepts, propositions, and things (1942b, pp. 660–7). Although he respected common sense and wanted to preserve its commitments where possible, he did not restrict philosophical analysis to common sense. Nor did he prioritize science. Rather, he got many of his problems and some of his terms and concepts from previous philosophy (1942a, p. 14). Other terms and concepts, if he did not invent them, he shaped to his own purposes. 'Sense-data' is one of those. Moore used that term with a definite sense, to mean an object of perception of which we as subjects are directly aware. His colleague Russell at first followed this position but then, using his own method, which drew on logic and natural science, developed a different account of sense-data and the related notion of a momentary particular.

33.3 RUSSELL, SENSE-DATA, AND ANALYSIS

Apart from an early discussion of whether quantity is a 'sense-datum' (1897), Russell's initial engagement with that term and concept arose in his analysis of propositions and reference. He described sense-data as particulars with which we are directly acquainted, or of which we have 'knowledge by acquaintance' (see Linsky, this volume). He shared with Moore a pluralistic realism: the real is not one but many and sense-data are the best known particular existents (Russell 1910–11). I am not concerned with these early discussions, but with Russell's invocation of sense-data and related notions in the period from 1912 to 1927, when his principal philosophical concerns focused on metaphysics and epistemology and especially the nature of matter, the analysis of mind, and our knowledge of the external world.

Russell's initial discussions in this period made epistemology primary. Consider the opening sentence of his 1912 popular book, *The Problems of Philosophy*: 'Is there any knowledge in the world which is so certain that no reasonable man could doubt it?' (1912, p. 7). The first instance he offers is knowledge of sense-data. The operative knowledge is not bare knowledge by acquaintance, for, although bare acquaintance is not subject to error, it also does not assert any truth or constitute 'knowledge that' something is the case (1912, p. 46). But we know basic facts about sense-data. In obtaining sense-data of a brown table, we know: that we have an appearance of brown ('a brown colour is being seen', p. 19) or perhaps of a whitish sheen, or an appearance of one or another trapezoidal surface. Knowledge by acquaintance does not itself involve judgement (pp. 44–5), but we make judgements about the items of our acquaintance (such as that they are brown or trapezoidal, or next to one another). Russell subsequently affirms that among the 'hard data' discovered by epistemological analysis are 'facts of sense', including spatial and temporal relations (within the specious present) and comparisons between sensory qualities (1914a, pp. 71–2).

Going forward, Russell retained the view that sense-data (or their counterparts) provide epistemological bedrock. His positions changed on the metaphysics of sense-data in relation to the knowing subject and material objects. In *Problems*, he treated material objects as items that could be known by inference from sense-data to their causes. Soon, he treated such objects as logical constructions out of sense-data, and he subsequently changed positions on the status of the perceiving subject, as well.

I am concerned not so much with Russell's efforts to construct physical objects and theoretical entities from sense-data, but with the data themselves from which the construction begins. Russell's realism about sense-data entailed their mind-independence; they exist independently of our perception, even while we perceive them. In *Our Knowledge of the External World* (the Lowell Lectures), Russell described sense-data as physiologically conditioned but mind-independent:

> I think it must be admitted as probable that the immediate objects of sense depend for their existence upon physiological conditions in ourselves, and that, for example, the coloured surfaces which we see cease to exist when we shut our eyes. But it would be a mistake to infer that they are dependent on the mind, not real while we see them, or not the sole basis for our knowledge of the external world. (1914a, p. 64)

In 'The Relation of Sense-Data to Physics' (1914b), he asserted that sense-data are 'physical' not mental, by which he meant that they are mind-independent, not that they consist of elementary particles.

Why posit sense-data as distinct from ordinary external objects or microscopic physical processes? Russell accepted the arguments from perceptual relativity as sufficient grounds for distinguishing sense-data from ordinary objects.[6] The table offers various appearances of colour and shape from different points of view, but we believe the material table has a single colour and shape. The coin appears now elliptical, now circular, now larger, now smaller, depending on viewing angle and distance. Convinced that the data of sense are non-mental but also are not parts of objects themselves, in *Problems* Russell posited them as third things, in addition to the mental acts that apprehend them and to the table itself, as material object (1912, ch. 2).

Russell soon upheld a more economical position that reduced the number of things to two: subjects (or mental acts) and data. The ordinary objects and microphysical processes previously known by inference would now be regarded as logical constructions. We have already met with a prime motivation for Russell's retaining sense-data and jettisoning physical matter: sense-data are very well known. They are the 'hard data' on which we base the logical constructions of common sense and science. These hard data are psychologically primitive appearances; psychology aids epistemology in disentangling such appearances from accretions, such as beliefs in ordinary physical objects (1914a, lec. 3). Such hard data may themselves be physiologically and psychologically conditioned; but, within adult experience, they should be rendered epistemically basic.

In calling the common-sense 'thing' a 'mere logical construction' (1914a, p. 89) or 'fiction' (1914b, 1915), Russell meant that it doesn't exist (or that we needn't believe that it does). The only particulars that exist are sense-data, subjective acts of apprehension, and, most likely, sensibilia—entities very like sense-data occurring at places where there is no one to see them (1914b). Sensibilia are not physiologically conditioned, which is why they are only similar to sense-data. The fact of physiological conditioning is an empirical regularity within our sense-data: staring at a bright light yields an afterimage that affects our visual experience for several minutes in ways explicable through the fictional language of physics and physiology.

If sense-data provide the hard data Russell took them to, if they are well-known items supporting all other knowledge of the external world, then Russell should be clear about their properties. For vision, these properties are colours, shapes, distances, and sizes. Russell worked on the structure of sense-data and their spatial interrelations in 1912–14. In January, 1914, he had a 'breakthrough', provoking alterations in the manuscript of the Lowell Lectures (Blackwell 1973). This breakthrough yielded a six-dimensional spatial construction relating the private spaces of sense-data to public space (Russell 1914a, 1914b, 1915). I want to explore the spatial structure especially of the private spaces, as they are the (allegedly) very well-known data at the foundation of Russell's system.

The six-dimensional spatial structure includes a 'private' space or 'perspective' of three-dimensions, had by each percipient, and a public space constructed in relation to the private spaces. Each private space corresponds to a point of view and is structured into a place 'from which' and a place 'at which'. The from-which is the vantage point of

---

[6] On perceptual relativity, see Dicker 1980, ch. 2.

the observer, located 'in the head' (1914b, p. 120),[7] perhaps just behind the eyes and centred between them. The at-which is the location of the sense-datum that presents an aspect of the object: the circular or elliptical penny at a distance from the observer. The perspectives have three dimensions to accommodate the distance from the vantage point to the surface aspect.

The various loci of from-which vantage points can be compared among observers in relation to series of at-which sense-data structures that exhibit similarities among themselves. Thus, in having experiences as of the same table, observers may report various trapezoids of different sizes that vary with the from-which. This allows the perspectives to be ordered and compared, thereby permitting the construction of a three-dimensional public or physical space consisting of points 'from which' placed into a continuous spatial structure (interpolating possible vantage points between actual ones).[8]

The Lowell Lectures credit psychologists with having shown that 'we instinctively infer the "real" size and shape of a visible object from its apparent size and shape, according to its distance and point of view' (1914a, p. 68). Russell here recounts the standard nineteenth-century textbook account of size and distance perception, according to which a penny may project a small ellipse at the back of the eye which the visual system then locates at a distance in the experience of a slanted round penny (Hatfield 1990, p. 154; Stout 1899, pp. 364–5, 378–9). In the standard theory, the projective size and the resulting operations on it are habitual and unconscious, which is what Russell seems to mean in saying that we 'instinctively infer' (a psychological process) size and shape according to distance (1914a, p. 68). We perceive the phenomenal result of this process as a coloured surface 'there' as opposed to 'here' in three-dimensional private space (p. 73). Russell held it 'probable that distances, provided they are not too great, are actually given more or less roughly in sight' (p. 73). On the usual form of the standard theory, size–distance and shape–slant invariance relations hold: if we perceive the distance correctly, we experience the real size and shape of the object; if we under-perceive the

---

[7] The distinction between from-which and at-which can guide interpretation of Russell's (1927a) statement that 'the whole of my perceptual world is, from the standpoint of physics, in my head' (p. 145; also, p. 336). The causal basis of the percept is in the head, which also is the place from which the experience occurs. But the percept presents a space that is 'external' (p. 198) and gives us 'the view of the world from a given place' (p. 258); this spatially external world is the at-which.

[8] Russell developed his six-dimensional analysis in response to a controversy between Stout and Nunn (among others) over whether contrary sensory qualities can exist 'in the same place' at the same time (Nasim 2008). Stout (1908–9) argued that, because they can't, sensory contents such as colour must be mental, whereas Nunn (1909–10) argued that sense-data with different qualities can co-exist in a place. Russell's many private spaces provided loci for various sense-data as of the same thing to exist separately while also being co-located in relation to public space (Nasim 2008, ch. 5). The from-whiches that constitute this public space are so many points 'from which' the world is viewed. Presumably, only one datum exists per moment at a given from-which point, although at successive times the same from-which location may be host to sense-data that look toward (or are oriented toward) the variety of directions in which the world may be viewed from that point. This entails that many unsensed perspectives (oriented toward different directions) coincide at a specific from-which point-location at a given time. Russell does not say how these coinciding perspectives are to be integrated in constructing the one public space. (Thanks to Alistair Isaac for pressing this point.)

distance, the object appears smaller and closer; if we don't correctly perceive the slant, the penny appears elliptical rather than as a circle-at-a-slant.

Some difficulties remain concerning the precise geometrical structures that Russell ascribed to the private spaces. In his descriptions (1914a, 1914b), the at-whiches are normally co-located in relation to the public space at the juncture of the lines along which series of shape-similar from-whiches are ordered (varying in size). Accordingly, Russell says that the penny looks smaller from a distance and looks elliptical (produces elliptical sense-data). However, if he has accepted the size-distance and shape-slant invariance relations, then the penny can look smaller only if appearing at less than its veridical distance, and it can appear elliptical only if not seen at its true slant. There is nothing in the optics of the situation that requires objects to appear smaller with increasing distance, or for circles to appear elliptical when slanted (Hatfield 2009b). If the distance and slant are correctly perceived and combined with projective values, then what psychologists subsequently called 'full size and shape constancy' would ensue and the object would be perceived with its true size and shape (not smaller or elliptical).

In speaking of a penny that looks smaller at a distance and appears elliptical, Russell may simply have reported his own visual experience. Things do look smaller at a distance and, in some circumstances, circular objects appear elliptical when viewed at a slant. In order to square these appearances with what the psychologists had shown, Russell would need to complicate his six-dimensional structure. He could retain the system of from-whiches, but the at-whiches would require adjustment. That is, Russell would need to suppose that the perceiver, in viewing the penny at increasing distances, under-perceives the distance and so experiences the penny as ever smaller and less distant than it is (in public space). That accommodates the penny's looking smaller. But this alteration complicates the construction of the public space, which depends on intersubjective comparisons of at-whiches. Still, by emphasizing close-up perceptions, a system of from-whiches might be established so as to yield a public space. There is no evidence that Russell ever became sensitive to this concern. Although becoming tentative about the depth of visual space, he continued to allow that near distances are experienced 'by sight alone' (1927b, p. 138), which means he continued to face this challenge, whether he recognized it or not.

By 1920, Russell found that he could achieve even greater ontological economy, beyond jettisoning material objects or reducing them to sensibilia. He gave up mental acts (or the experiencing subject) as distinct from sense-data. This meant that the 'data' were no longer given to a distinct subject and so were improperly named; henceforth, he spoke of 'momentary particulars' or 'events'. In accordance with James's (1904) position, both the self and the ordinary furniture of the world (as well as the microstructures of physics) were to be constructed from one neutral stuff—momentary particulars, characterized by perceptual qualities such as colour and shape (for visual particulars). In passing from the neutral monism of the *Analysis of Mind* (1921) to a fuller accounting of physical theory in the *Analysis of Matter* (1927a), he did not alter his basic position (1927a, pp. 10, 382). However, in the second work he offered a finer-grained analysis of the unsensed momentary particulars that occupy places without perceivers, that is, places that don't form a from-which in the construction of any actual perceiver's successive vantage points. These momentary particulars, whose intrinsic properties are reached through analogy with perceived momentary particulars, are assigned structures as described in physical theory—the hypothetical entities of physics, such as electrons, being constructions from these particulars together with the sensed ones, along with the relations among such particulars (1927a, pp. 227, 271, ch. 38).

Russell's method differed from Moore's. Although he gave some weight to intuitive beliefs shared by much of humankind, who affirm the reality of what they see, such beliefs did not strongly constrain his philosophical analyses and theories. For Russell, philosophy is an analytical exercise. It concerns itself with general statements in logic and with

> the analysis and enumeration of logical *forms*, i.e. with the kinds of propositions that may occur, with the various types of facts, and with the classification of the constituents of facts. In this way logic provides an inventory of possibilities, a repertory of abstractly tenable hypotheses. (1914c, p. 18)

The notion of logical form is liberal. It includes formal logic, but also classifications of facts and of constituents. As with Moore, 'analysis' is broad: it can be directed at 'ideas', beliefs or assertions, and things. The analysis involved in the epistemology and metaphysics of matter seeks the fundamental constituents that are best known (sense-data or momentary particulars). Contrary to Moore, Russell called on the sciences for help. In the Lowell Lectures, he presents epistemology as seeking 'hard data' of perception that are both logically and psychologically primitive. At the beginning of analysis, the logically primitive (non-inferred) beliefs concern the objects of common sense. Psychology helps reveal what is perceptually basic: an appearance or sense-datum. The epistemologist then adopts these entities as the basis for a new set of logically primitive (non-inferred) judgements, which may depart from common sense and facilitate the replacement of ordinary beliefs by clearer and better supported ones.

As he later showed, Russell had little patience for 'ordinary' or 'common sense' beliefs as ultimate arbiters for philosophical theory (1953). Rather, he brought the resources of logic and science to bear on common-sense beliefs and on previous philosophy, hoping to replace the obscure and ill-supported with explicit and clear theories that started from simple and well-known constituents.

33.4 THE REST OF THE STORY

Russell and Moore are classified as 'new realists' (Metz 1938), even though Russell after 1912 viewed material objects as logical constructions and Moore considered viable (but not preferred) a 'Russell-type' theory of material objects. The sense of 'realism' in play was in contrast to the idealism (or mental monistic realism) of British Idealism. This new realism held that the immediate object of perception is an existing mind-independent object having the characteristics it is perceived to have (e.g., brown with an elliptical shape). The American 'new realists' expressed a similar notion of realism in publishing a 'cooperative philosophy' (Holt *et al.* 1912). Although the American new realists were not in full agreement among themselves, Perry and Holt joined in developing James's neutral monism, according to which only 'neutral stuff' (Russell's momentary particulars) exists and minds as well as ordinary objects are ways of patterning such stuff.

Other types of realism offered other answers to the arguments from perceptual relativity employed by Russell and Moore. Naïve realists responded by suggesting that what is immediately seen is the penny or the surface of the table, which presents an ellipse or a trapezoid from a point of view even though the surface that is seen is circular or rectangular (respectively). They dispatched with sense-data as 'third things' and retained only two, but not the same two as the middle Russell: they were left with minds (or mental acts) and physical objects as seen from a point of view. Such theorists were called 'modified' naïve realists.[9] I discuss two examples.

Samuel Alexander, who protested that he was not a 'naïve' realist because he gave arguments for his position (1909–10, p. 2), held that in vision we perceive objects (including their colours) directly. Taking the example of perceiving a tree, he analysed perception into two things: 'the act of perceiving, which is consciousness, and the external or physical thing, tree' (1909–10, p. 2). The aspects of a thing, such as the tree appearing smaller from a distance, are explained by the fact that the relation between mind and object varies. Alexander spoke of the mind 'selecting' from among the objective appearances that a thing sustains. All of the appearances that can be had of a thing are ever present for selection.

Perhaps the most influential of the modified naïve realists was John Cook Wilson, who published little but was an effective teacher at Oxford as Professor of Logic (1889–1915). His *Nachlass* appeared in 1926 and included a letter responding to an article by Stout on primary and secondary qualities. Stout (1903–4) regarded the immediate objects of awareness as mental contents, including colours and visible extensions, which he distinguished from the property that colour sensations represent in objects and from the real physical extension of the object. Cook Wilson (1926) disagreed on both counts, in ways that further 'modify' naïve realism. For secondary qualities such as colour, he distinguished (a) the physical property (as described by science) that causes (b) colour sensations from (c) the property that we take to be in objects, which has the character of phenomenal colour. In this case, we fall prey to an illusion of locating the secondary-quality sensation in the object (1926, pp. 777, 781). Unlike some naïve realists, he does not treat colour as a quality actually inhering in objects.

For space, Cook Wilson affirmed that we do directly see the real spatial extension of objects. To Stout, he asked what science could tell us about spatial properties that would correspond to its telling us that motion constitutes heat in objects or that electromagnetic waves cause colour sensations. Extension is not a hidden cause but a manifest property that we see directly:

---

[9] Price (1932) described such theories as 'modifications' of naïve realism.

we always assume that the extension in the thing is exactly the same kind as the visual extension, and the science of geometry entirely depends on this.… There could be no science of the 'extension in itself' any more than of the thing in itself. Moreover, science assumes *not* that the extension of the blot that I see is *like* the extension in the thing, or *represents* the extension, but that it *is* the actual extension in the body. It is visual extension simply as real extension *seen*. (1926, p. 780)

Cook Wilson especially takes on Stout's claim that perceptual relativity requires that spatial appearances are distinct from actual spatial extension, as when things appear smaller at a distance.

In order to show that the phenomenal facts of visual space perception accord with naïve direct realism, Cook Wilson (1926, p. 790) produced Figure 33.1. It represents a plane rectangle formed by the tops of four posts (A, B, C, D), viewed from point E in the horizontal plane of the post tops. He accounted for the (in his view) misleading statement that AB 'looks smaller' than CD by appeal to the facts of 'perspective'. In particular, point A is seen along the line EA, which cuts CD at *a*, and B is seen along EB, which cuts CD at *b*. The segment *ab* is thus seen between C and D and is manifestly shorter than CD, leading us to say that AB 'looks smaller'. In reality, he thinks, although there are facts of the matter about the sizes, shapes, and distances of the things that we see and these facts describe what we see (the sizes, shapes, and distances are present visually), we actually perceive the size only by placing a ruler along the edge of an object in our visual field; otherwise, our metric descriptions are 'guesses' (1926, pp. 791–4).

Cook Wilson's diagram shows that things are seen from a point of view. His account of things 'looking smaller' at a distance draws attention to the facts that we see things in a direction and that in normal circumstances (no mirrors or refraction) we perceive physical directions veridically. Point A really is to the left of point C as both are seen from E, and point B is seen to the right of D. But it is not clear that his analysis establishes his point against Stout.

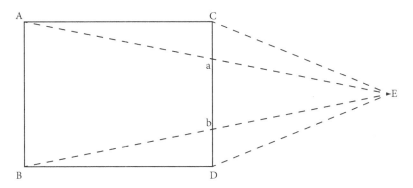

FIGURE 33.1 A plane rectangle formed by points standing in for the tops of four posts (A, B, C, D), viewed from point E in the same horizontal plane. (From Cook Wilson 1926, p. 790; public domain.)

Cook Wilson's attention to visual direction and relations of visual angles (such as AEC and BED) is penetrating as far as it goes. But the analysis is incomplete as a discussion of the geometry of visibles and their sizes. In his scheme, Figure 33.1 represents both the physical facts of the relations among A, B, C, D, and E and the visual facts that A and B are seen along EA and EB, which cut CD at *a* and *b*. Further, all the visual facts about sizes and distances of the post tops are supposed to coincide with the physical facts, making it unnecessary to introduce a subjective or phenomenal space that diverges from the physical structure. Presumably, Cook Wilson's diagram is supposed to reveal how a rectangular table top can mistakenly be taken to appear trapezoidal (because we mistakenly conclude that the back edge looks smaller than the front one).

But, in fact, as psychologists had observed, the question of whether the visual extension of AB equals that of CD is separate from the angular relations. Given the angular relations from E, AB could be seen at its true distance, in which case it would be phenomenally as wide as CD (leaving our 'guesses' aside). Perhaps Cook Wilson assumed that this is what happens, and that we then compare *ab* to CD and mistakenly say that AB looks smaller. Be that as it may, as psychologists were finding at this time, in perception we often undervalue distance.[10] In the diagram, this would lead to the phenomenal convergence of CA and DB, as when railway tracks appear to converge. Such apparent convergence can occur even if visual directions and angles are perceived veridically. Hence, although Cook Wilson's observations are insightful, they do not settle the question between him and Stout on whether there is need for a visual space that differs geometrically from the physical space of the four post tops. Settling that question is partly an empirical matter.

Cook Wilson's influence on Oxford philosophers is well documented (Metz 1938; Passmore 1957; Marion 2000). Among those he taught, H. A. Prichard is most noteworthy. In *Kant's Theory of Knowledge* (1909) and subsequent articles (1915, 1950), he advanced a modified naïve realism of the sort espoused by Cook Wilson. He accepted that we see the spatial extension of bodies directly and that secondary quality sensations are mere appearances (1909, pp. 85–9) that we mistakenly ascribe to the surfaces of things (1950). He accounted for perceptual relativity through Cook Wilson's notion that we see bodies 'subject to conditions of perspective' (1909, p. 84). He meant two things by this phrase, which he did not clearly distinguish. First, he meant that, from a given standpoint, we cannot see all of a body at once; we are limited to a 'point of view'. But, second, he invoked 'conditions of perspective' to explain why, except when we are looking straight down at a short section of a railway, the rails 'look convergent' (1909, p. 81).

[10] Hillebrand (1902) conducted an alley experiment that found the inverse of phenomenal convergence (the observer, instructed to make black cords on a white table appear parallel when viewed from table's end, made the cords diverge). Cook Wilson could not be expected to know this literature (which blossomed in Germany; Boring 1942, pp. 294–6). But he could well have known the size–distance relation as discussed by Stout and others (see above), and so be positioned to ask whether the distances in his diagram are veridically present, as demanded if visual space is to coincide with physical space as he implied.

As we have seen, the laws of optics, although specifying that receding rails are seen under smaller visual angles, do not specify that the appearance must therefore be of converging lines, since they don't specify whether we respond accurately to the physical distance. With accurate distance perception and full phenomenal size constancy, a viewer would experience the lines as remaining an equal distance apart at all distances and hence as phenomenally parallel. For convergence, distance must be under-perceived.

The 'critical realists' offered yet a different response to perceptual relativity. The term 'critical realism' was used by philosophers in Germany (Riehl), England (Dawes Hicks), and the US (R. W. Sellars, among others) (Passmore 1957, ch. 12). They agreed that in perceiving there are only two things, minds (or mental states) and physical objects. But they held that physical objects are perceived by means of mental states possessing various perceptual qualities as contents, including colour and spatial qualities. Some called these intermediaries 'sense-data', while denying the new realist and naïve realist premise that such data are mind-independent. They avoided saying that we 'see' such data. Rather, by means of mental content and cognitive attention to the object, we directly perceive the external object. Or so Sellars (1920) held. To emphasize this point, he characterized his position as a direct realism (1920, p. 194). Such critical realists differed from traditional sense-data theory in denying that sense-data are entities; rather, they are phenomenally characterized mental contents.

Other theorists retained the Moore–Russell view that sense-data are non-mental existents. Broad (1923) and Price (1932) were realists who acknowledged both sense-data and material objects. Or in any case Broad explored the position of 'critical scientific realism' by elaborating the notion of sense-data as taken over from Russell and others, together with Whitehead's event realism. This critical scientific realism was in some ways akin to traditional representative realism, although Broad denied that material objects are inferred from sense-data or, as he preferred, 'sensa'. Rather, sensing sensa induces us to form a belief in mind-independent physical objects. Science, as reinterpreted by philosophy, then teaches us to distinguish primary from secondary qualities and to view the former as physically basic.

Price's book on *Perception* (1932) is an especially probing account of sense-data, their ontological status and cognitive role. Against the 'causal' theory of perception (effectively, representative realism), Price argues that the concept of cause is neither necessary nor sufficient for our belief in physical objects, that only in some cases (even in spatial perception) do sense-data resemble physical objects, and that in any case material objects are not inferred from sense-data. He further maintains that although sense-data are distinct from material objects (contra naïve realism) and their existence may require the existence of minds, they are not mental (1932, pp. 117–27, 316–17). Against phenomenalism, he argues that physical objects exist with causal powers and are partial causes of sense-data. He elaborates notions of perceptual acceptance and perceptual assurance to describe the (non-inferential) cognitive acts through which we accept and believe that material objects exist. The belief in material objects consists in the construction of a 'standard solid' from sense-data (a spatial structure that fits the outer shape of a physical object), together with belief in a causally efficacious 'physical occupant' of this location. Along the way, he reconstructs the cognitive development of philosophical belief in the given, starting from naïve realism and introducing sense-data at a later stage. He also elaborates only to discard several positions in the philosophy of perception, including an adverbial approach.

A. J. Ayer (1940) offered a distinctive position. He argued, contra Price and others, that the existence of sense-data is not a factual question but a matter of linguistic convention. He alleged that all theorists of perception agree on the facts about sense-data (or other perceptual phenomena), providing no empirical basis for distinguishing among theories. Hence the theories become recommendations about perceptual language. Ayer himself chose to develop phenomenalism, in which statements about objects are understood as statements about actual and hypothetical sense-data. In his scheme, even though sense-data do not exist unsensed, they need not be classed as mental states (1940, p. 76).

Price (1932) and Ayer (1940) are responsible for the popular view that sense-data rest on an 'argument from illusion'. According to Price, if the penny looks elliptical or the table trapezoidal, these are illusions, since the penny is round and the table rectangular. By contrast, when Russell, Moore, Broad, and others spoke of perceptual relativity, they did not treat the elliptical appearance as illusory. Further, although they may have alleged the phenomenal indistinguishability of illusory appearances (such as the bent stick in water) and ordinary appearances, this was not the basic argument for sense-data. Their basic argument came from perceptual relativity.

33.5 THE GIVEN AND THE 'MYTH' OF THE GIVEN

From the beginning, many authors held that a great advantage of sense-data is that they are very well known (perhaps incorrigibly, perhaps only especially well). Moore and Russell emphasized these aspects, as did Broad and Ayer. Some theorists, such as Alexander (1909–10) and Price (1932), countered that perception is not in itself a species of knowledge. Still others contended that Russell's knowledge by acquaintance is not knowledge, since by hypothesis it involves no judgement, conceptual application, or affirmation of any proposition (Lewis 1929, ch. 5; Parker 1945).

Russell and others sometimes spoke of sense-data as being 'given'. In Russell's case, we have seen that he did not restrict the 'hard data' of epistemology to bare data of acquaintance but included various facts of sense, such as judgements of relations among sense-data. These judgements involve both the particular to which we are related by acquaintance and one or more predicate terms, which, in a case such as 'this is red', involve the universal redness. Russell (1912, ch. 10) held that such universals are known by acquaintance (some are so known a priori) and that sensory universals are acquired by abstraction. Hence, knowledge of facts rests on judgements that depend on acquired abilities. In contrast, Broad (1923, p. 268) held that belief in physical objects is logically primitive and is not reached by inference or any other cognitive process. The subject is primitively and originally able to render judgements about sense-data.

Price (1932) discussed the notion of the given at some length, as did C. I. Lewis (1929). They both acknowledged that, among adult perceivers, sense-data are probably not ever found in consciousness in the absence of a conceptual response. For Lewis, perceivers share a common sensory given to which they apply a socially transmitted conceptual scheme. The initial classification of the given is incorrigible (and makes no assertion); after that, any judgement must be subject to error and typically concerns expectations of changes in the given. For Price, the conceptual response is not, in the first instance, a reflective judgement or inference, but a cognitive state concerning the existence of material things that he calls 'perceptual acceptance'. Unlike Lewis, he allows that the given itself may already show effects of past experience through 'associations' or other psychological processes. Price (1932, p. 169) differed from Lewis in allowing that some part of the conceptual framework of 'material thinghood' is innate.

Wilfrid Sellars famously questioned the 'myth' of a pure given to which subjects can respond atomistically. It is interesting to speculate which philosophers he believed were subscribers to his myth. His examples in 'Empiricism and the Philosophy of Mind' (1956) draw mainly from early modern philosophy (Descartes and Locke). He also criticizes Ayer's linguistic analysis and alludes to Broad and Price.

According to Sellars (1956), the 'classical' sense-datum position holds that 's is red' can be known non-inferentially (primitively, atomically). Classical sense-data philosophers 'have taken givenness to be a fact which presupposes no learning, no forming of associations, no setting up of stimulus-response connections' (§ 6). Such philosophers are committed to the following 'inconsistent triad':

A. *X senses red sense content s entails x non-inferentially knows that that s is red.*
B. The ability to sense sense contents is unacquired.
C. The ability to know facts of the form *x is* ϕ is acquired.
A and B together entail not-C; B and C entail not-A; A and C entail not-B. (§ 6)

Locke may have held all three propositions; it is doubtful that Descartes, who distinguished sensing from judging, would endorse A. Among Sellars's twentieth-century predecessors, all or most would deny A, distinguishing sensing and 'acquaintance' from 'knowing that'; sensing red may usually and non-inferentially lead to knowing that s is red, but not as a matter of entailment. Russell would have denied a cognitive reading of B (a reading suggested by A); sensing may be unacquired but 'knowing that' involves judging, not mere sensing. Lewis, with his acquired conceptual scheme for classifying and judging the given, rejects a cognitive reading of B. Sellars himself rejects B, adopting (by assumption) a position of 'psychological nominalism', according to which kindterms are learned as part of a linguistic and conceptual web of meaning.

In 'Empiricism', Sellars constructs his own myth of cognitive development, which, although not explicitly starting from naïve realism, starts from the judgement 'x is red' as applied to material objects. In his myth, humankind initially are behaviourists with an expanded vocabulary to include thought-attributions or attributions of intentionality in describing one another's verbal behaviour. They then learn to treat thoughts as internal states of one another and subsequently to self-report their own thoughts. Next, they posit internal sensory impressions that are modelled on coloured extents; these are mental counterparts of sense-data as third things, but are mental 'states' of the perceiver, not particular entities (1956, § 61). Finally, they treat coloured areas as theoretically posited intentional objects (in the form of particulars, such as red-impressions). This view differs from the classical Moore–Russell position in making the ability to be aware of red sense experiences depend on the acquisition of a sophisticated web of meaning and theory; this ability is not 'given', precluding an epistemically basic 'given' that grounds knowledge (as in Russell's 'hard data', which are not given by acquaintance but which allegedly arise through easy and secure judgements). Sellars asserts that 'instead of coming to have a concept of something because we have noticed that sort of thing, to have the ability to notice a sort of thing is already to have the concept of that sort of thing, and cannot account for it' (1956, § 45). For Sellars, the advantage is that, through the social process of acquisition, sense impressions lose 'absolute privacy' and become objects of intersubjective knowledge (1956, § 62).

In 1947, J. L. Austin began offering lectures in Oxford on topics in the philosophy of perception, subsequently entitled 'Sense and Sensibilia'. Using Austin's notes and those of students, G. J. Warnock published the reconstructed lectures (Austin 1962). Austin focuses especially on Ayer (1940), with secondary attention to Price (1932) and a section on Warnock (1953). He seeks to explode the doctrine that 'we never see or otherwise perceive (or "sense"), or anyhow we never directly perceive or sense, material objects (or material things), but only sense-data' (1962, p. 2). He suggests that sense-data are mental, by assimilating them to the 'ideas' of Descartes, Locke, and Berkeley (1962, pp. 2, 60). Austin accuses Ayer, Price, and others of adopting a 'scholastic' view that focuses on a few poorly understood and ill-described words and a few 'half-studied "facts"'. In response, he promises to show 'that our ordinary words are much subtler in their uses, and mark many more distinctions, than philosophers have realized; and that the facts of perception, as discovered by, for instance, psychologists but also as noted by common mortals, are much more diverse and complicated than has been allowed for' (1962, p. 3).

Austin invokes an interesting variety of perceptual phenomena in noting that 'the ordinary man' does not limit what he sees to 'moderately sized specimens of dry goods' such as tables and chairs but considers as things perceived 'people, people's voices, rivers, mountains, flames, rainbows, shadows, pictures on the screen at the cinema, pictures in books or hung on walls, vapours, gases' (1962, p. 8). As to 'facts' from psychologists, his two examples are: that perceptual discrimination is heavily influenced by physical context (1962, p. 53), and that things can be seen in different ways, or 'seen as' one thing or another, a point that he credits to unnamed psychologists (who must include the Gestalt psychologists) and to Wittgenstein (1962, p. 100).

More generally, Austin's criticisms focus rather narrowly on the linguistic side of things, even though he disagrees with Ayer that the matter is merely a 'choice of language'. Austin focuses on the 'argument from illusion' from Ayer (also citing Price), and complains that ordinary cases of perceptual relativity (as in the elliptical penny) are not normally taken to be illusions. On this point, many earlier sense-data theorists would agree.

But Austin has little to say about the argument from perceptual relativity from the classical sense-data discussions. He affirms that we see distant objects (not sense-data) even if they appear as specks but does not explain why he countenances 'the speck is a star' but not 'the star is a speck' (1962, pp. 98–9). He attacks the penny example as atypical because pennies have stable and sharply bounded shapes whereas many objects, such as cats, do not. He also denies that in reporting on elliptical appearances one adopts a special sense of 'see' that (1) does not require that an elliptical material object must exist, but (2) does affirm that something elliptical (which turns out to be a sense-datum) must exist. Austin's criticisms focus on whether this sense of 'see' is found in ordinary language; he refuses to engage the philosophical motivations that led Price and others to distinguish different senses of perception words, ostensibly because attention to ordinary language shows that such theoretical coinages are otiose, nor does he consider the sense-data theorists who say that we see material things via sense-data (e.g., Broad 1923, p. 248).

Although Austin is sometimes credited with bringing sense-data talk to an end (e.g., Martin 2003), I doubt that his book, focused mainly on Ayer, could or should have done so. Part of the credit must surely go to: the popularity of the logical empiricist physical thing-language in place of a phenomenal observation language (e.g., Carnap 1938); the eliminativism of Quine (1973); and the effective eliminativism of Australians such as Armstrong (1961) and Smart (1962). But since, as discussed below, these did not eradicate all phenomenally oriented philosophy of perception, other factors were at work. The truly classical sense-data theories (Moore sometimes; Russell at first; Broad; Price) treated sense-data as third things (along with subjects and material objects), a posit that might have seemed ontologically bloated and epistemically limiting. For those who retained three things, their positions were forms of representative realism in which the data are non-mental; some philosophers developed a distaste for such theories as facilitating the 'sceptic's wedge'. These latter two factors might explain the ongoing presence of the critical direct realism of R. W. Sellars (1920, 1961) and his son Wilfrid (1963, p. 90), and its independent revival by Maurice Mandelbaum (1964), as an alternative to classical sense-data (see Hatfield 2010).

33.6 OTHER TRENDS

The third decade of the twentieth century saw new developments in philosophy and psychology that have only been touched upon. These include, in psychology, major statements of Gestalt theories of perception by Kurt Koffka (1922; also, 1935) and Wolfgang Köhler (1929). These authors, together with their mentor Max Wertheimer, emphasized the occurrence of structure and organization within perception and the phenomenal manifestation of meaning or functional significance in typical instances of perceiving things. Things are phenomenally given as objects with functional possibilities. The phenomenal field in vision is not a patchwork of coloured surfaces, but is organized into figure/ground relations that include coherent three-dimensional 'wholes' with surface boundaries that distinguish them from their surround.

The new ideas of the Gestalt psychologists were taken up by several philosophers. Carnap (1928/1967) used Gestalt notions of perceptual organization to characterize the sensory given in his *Aufbau*, an early work in what became a transoceanic philosophical movement, logical empiricism. Carnap soon turned away from phenomenal experience, first in favour of (micro) physicalism (1934) and then an observable physical thing-language (1938). Ayer (1940) invoked the Gestalt notion that the sensory field is holistically organized and not constituted of elemental sensations that remain the same in every context. Wittgenstein (1953/2001, 1982–92) was fascinated by Gestalt notions of organization and phenomenal meaning, as shown in Part II of the *Investigations* and throughout the manuscript writings.

The turn away from representative realism mentioned in the previous section was manifest in the work of Chisholm, who also helped bring phenomenology and the work of Brentano to an Anglophone audience (1960). Chisholm himself (1957) rejected sense-data and analysed seeing in terms of appearances: we see objects by having them appear to us in some way. Farber (1959) and Gurwitsch (1964) further elaborated Anglophone phenomenology, with Gurwitsch developing the psychological phenomenology of the Gestaltists (which avoided 'bracketing' the material world). From another direction, Dretske (1969) defended an epistemological direct realism, paying special attention to practices of scientific observation.

Nonetheless, the impact of behaviourism on philosophy remained strong in the middle decades of the twentieth century (including Ryle 1949). It was never completely dominant in psychology, as the study of perception kept mentalistic notions of experience and awareness in use. When analytic philosophy sought to revive mentalistic language in connection with cognitive science, it at first adopted a functionalism that was a kind of cognitive behaviourism. Input and output functions were described in relation to internal causal states, but initially these were functionally characterized in terms of their causal roles, leaving aside any phenomenal manifestation (Hatfield 2002).

At the turn of the twenty-first century, philosophical work on perception was on the upswing. This includes streams of work that engage scientific theories of perception, especially colour perception (Hardin 1988; Mausfeld and Heyer 2003) but ever more including also spatial perception (Eilan *et al.* 1993; Hatfield and Allred 2012). Perception is again a principal topic of theoretical or speculative philosophy, and a range of positions are under discussion, including echoes of critical direct realism (Hatfield 2009a), new defences of sense-data (Robinson 1994), a new naïve realism (Brewer 2004; Campbell 2002), and a sophisticated direct realism (Smith 2002).

REFERENCES

Alexander, Samuel (1909–10). 'On Sensations and Images', *Proceedings of the Aristotelian Society* 10: 1–35.

Armstrong, D. M. (1961). *Perception and the Physical World*. London: Routledge & Kegan Paul.

Austin, J. L. (1962). *Sense and Sensibilia*, ed. G. J. Warnock. London: Oxford University Press.

Ayer, A. J. (1940). *The Foundations of Empirical Knowledge*. New York: Macmillan.

Bell, David (1999). 'The Revolution of Moore and Russell: A Very British Coup?' In Anthony O'Hear (ed.), *German Philosophy since Kant*. Cambridge: Cambridge University Press, pp. 193–208.

Blackwell, Kenneth (1973). 'Our Knowledge of Our Knowledge', *Russell: The Journal of Bertrand Russell Studies* 93(4): 11–13.

Boring, E. G. (1942). *Sensation and Perception in the History of Experimental Psychology*. New York: Appleton-Century.

Bradley, F. H. (1897). *Appearance and Reality: A Metaphysical Essay*, 2nd edn. Oxford: Clarendon Press.

Brewer, Bill (2004). 'Realism and the Nature of Perceptual Experience', *Philosophical Issues* 14: 61–77.

Broad, C. D. (1923). *Scientific Thought*. London: Routledge & Kegan Paul.

Cambridge University (1870). *Calendar*. Cambridge: Deighton, Bell.

—— (1893). *Calendar*. Cambridge: Deighton, Bell.

—— (1908). *Calendar*. Cambridge: Deighton, Bell.

Campbell, John (2002). *Reference and Consciousness*. Oxford: Clarendon Press.

Carnap, Rudolf (1934). *The Unity of Science*, tr. Max Black. London: Kegan Paul, Trench, Trubner. Original German publication, 1932.

—— (1938). 'Logical Foundations of the Unity of Science'. In Otto Neurath, Rudolf Carnap, and Charles Morris (eds.), *International Encyclopedia of Unified Science, Volume 1, Part 1*. Chicago: University of Chicago Press, pp. 42–62.

—— (1967). *The Logical Structure of the World*, tr. R. A. George. Berkeley: University of California Press. Original German work, 1928.

Case, Thomas (1888). *Physical Realism, Being an Analytical Philosophy from the Physical Objects of Science to the Physical Data of Sense*. London: Longmans, Green.

—— (1911). 'Metaphysics'. In *Encyclopædia Britannica, Vol. 18*, 11th edn. Cambridge: Cambridge University Press, pp. 224–53.

Chisholm, Roderick M. (1957). *Perceiving: A Philosophical Study*. Ithaca: Cornell University Press.

—— (ed.) (1960). *Realism and the Background of Phenomenology*. Glencoe, IL: Free Press.

Cook Wilson, John (1926). 'Letter in Criticism of a Paper on Primary and Secondary Qualities'. In Cook Wilson, *Statement and Inference, with Other Philosophical Papers*, 2 vols. Oxford: Clarendon Press, vol. 2, pp. 764–800.

Dicker, Georges (1980). *Perceptual Knowledge: An Analytical Historical Study*. Dordrecht: Reidel.

Dretske, Fred I. (1969). *Seeing and Knowing*. Chicago: University of Chicago Press.

Eilan, Naomi, Rosaleen McCarthy, and Bill Brewer (eds.) (1993). *Spatial Representation: Problems in Philosophy of Psychology*. Oxford: Oxford University Press.

Farber, Marvin (1959). *Naturalism and Subjectivism*. Springfield, IL: C. C. Thomas.

Gurwitsch, A. (1964). *The Field of Consciousness*. Pittsburgh: Duquesne University Press.

Hamilton, William (1861). *Lectures on Metaphysics*, 2 vols. Edinburgh: Blackwood.

Hardin, C. L. (1988). *Color for Philosophers: Unweaving the Rainbow*. Indianapolis: Hackett.

Hatfield, Gary (1990). *The Natural and the Normative: Theories of Spatial Perception from Kant to Helmholtz*. Cambridge, MA: MIT Press.

—— (2002). 'Psychology, Philosophy, and Cognitive Science: Reflections on the History and Philosophy of Experimental Psychology', *Mind and Language* 17: 207–32.

—— (2009a). 'Introduction: Philosophy and Science of Visual Perception and Cognition'. In Hatfield, *Perception and Cognition: Essays in the Philosophy of Psychology*. Oxford: Clarendon Press, pp. 1–35.

—— (2009b). 'On Perceptual Constancy'. In Hatfield, *Perception and Cognition: Essays in the Philosophy of Psychology*. Oxford: Clarendon Press, pp. 178–211.

—— (2010). 'Mandelbaum's Critical Realism'. In Ian Verstegen (ed.), *Maurice Mandelbaum and American Critical Realism*. London: Routledge, pp. 46–64.

—— (2013). 'Psychology, Epistemology, and the Problem of the External World: Russell and Before'. In Erich Reck (ed.), *The Historical Turn in Analytic Philosophy*. Basingstoke: Palgrave Macmillan, pp. 171–200.

Hatfield, Gary and Sarah Allred (eds.) (2012). *Visual Experience: Sensation, Cognition, and Constancy*. Oxford: Oxford University Press.

Hillebrand, Franz (1902). 'Theorie der scheinbaren Grösse beim binokularen Sehen', *Denkschrift der Kaiserlichen Akademie der Wissenschaften Wien, Mathematisch-Naturwissenschaftliche Classe* 72: 255–307.

Hobhouse, L. T. (1896). *The Theory of Knowledge*. London: Methuen.

Holt, Edwin B., Walter T. Marvin, William Pepperell Montague, Ralph Barton Perry, Walter B. Pitkin, and Edward Gleason Spaulding (1912). *The New Realism: Cooperative Studies in Philosophy*. New York: Macmillan.

Hylton, Peter (1990). *Russell, Idealism, and the Emergence of Analytic Philosophy*. Oxford: Clarendon Press.

James, William (1887). 'The Perception of Space (I)', *Mind* 12: 1–30.

—— (1890). *The Principles of Psychology*, 2 vols. New York: Henry Holt.

—— (1904). 'Does "Consciousness" Exist?' *Journal of Philosophy, Psychology and Scientific Methods* 1: 477–91.

Koffka, Kurt (1922). 'Perception: An Introduction to the Gestalt-Theorie', *Psychological Bulletin* 19: 531–85.

—— (1935). *Principles of Gestalt Psychology*. New York: Harcourt, Brace.

Köhler, Wolfgang (1929). *Gestalt Psychology*. New York: Liveright.

Lewis, C. I. (1929). *Mind and the World-Order: Outline of a Theory of Knowledge*. New York: Scribner's.

Mandelbaum, Maurice (1964). *Philosophy, Science, and Sense Perception: Historical and Critical Studies*. Baltimore: Johns Hopkins Press.

Marion, Mathieu (2000). 'Oxford Realism: Knowledge and Perception', *British Journal for the History of Philosophy* 8: 299–338, 485–519.

Martin, Michael (2003). 'Sensible Appearances'. In Thomas Baldwin (ed.), *Cambridge History of Philosophy, 1870–1945*. Cambridge: Cambridge University Press, pp. 521–32.

Mausfeld, Rainer, and Dieter Heyer (eds.) (2003). *Colour Perception: Mind and the Physical World*. Oxford: Oxford University Press.

Metz, Rudolf (1938). *A Hundred Years of British Philosophy*, ed. J. H. Muirhead. London: George Allen & Unwin.

Mill, John Stuart (1872). *An Examination of Sir William Hamilton's Philosophy*, 4th edn. London: Longmans, Green.

Moore, G. E. (1898). 'Freedom', *Mind* NS 7: 179–204.

—— (1899). 'The Nature of Judgment', *Mind* NS 8: 176–93.

—— (1903). 'The Refutation of Idealism', *Mind* NS 12: 433–53.

—— (1905–6). 'The Nature and Reality of Objects of Perception', *Proceedings of the Aristotelian Society* 6: 68–127.

—— (1909–10). 'The Subject-Matter of Psychology', *Proceedings of the Aristotelian Society* 10: 36–62.

—— (1913–14). 'The Status of Sense-Data', *Proceedings of the Aristotelian Society* 14: 355–80.

—— (1918–19). 'Some Judgments of Perception', *Proceedings of the Aristotelian Society* 19: 1–29.

—— (1925). 'A Defence of Common Sense'. In J. H. Muirhead (ed.), *Contemporary British Philosophy*, second series. London: Allen & Unwin, pp. 193–223.

—— (1942a). 'Autobiography'. In Paul Arthur Schilpp (ed.), *Philosophy of G. E. Moore*. Evanston: Northwestern University Press, pp. 3–39.

—— (1942b). 'Reply to My Critics'. In Paul Arthur Schilpp (ed.), *Philosophy of G. E. Moore*. Evanston: Northwestern University Press, pp. 535–677.

—— (1953). *Some Main Problems of Philosophy*. London: Allen & Unwin. Lectures first given in 1910–11.

—— (1957). 'Visual Sense Data'. In C. A. Mace (ed.), *British Philosophy in the Mid-Century*. London: George Allen & Unwin, pp. 203–12.

Nasim, Omar W. (2008). *Bertrand Russell and the Edwardian Philosophers*. Basingstoke: Palgrave Macmillan.

Nunn, T. P. (1909–10). 'Are Secondary Qualities Independent of Perception?' *Proceedings of the Aristotelian Society* 10: 191–218.

Parker, DeWitt H. (1945). 'Knowledge by Acquaintance', *Philosophical Review* 54: 1–18.

Passmore, John (1957). *A Hundred Years of Philosophy*. London: Duckworth.

Pattison, Mark (1876). 'Philosophy at Oxford', *Mind* 1: 82–97.

Price, H. H. (1932). *Perception*. London: Methuen.

Prichard, H. A. (1909). *Kant's Theory of Knowledge*. Oxford: Clarendon Press.

—— (1915). 'Mr. Bertrand Russell on our Knowledge of the External World', *Mind* 24: 145–85.

—— (1950). 'Perception'. In Prichard, *Knowledge and Perception: Essays and Lectures*. Oxford: Clarendon Press, pp. 52–68.

Quine, W. V. O. (1973). *The Roots of Reference*. LaSalle, IL: Open Court.

Robinson, Howard (1994). *Perception*. London: Routledge.

Royce, Josiah (1882). 'Mind and Reality', *Mind* 7: 30–54.

Russell, Bertrand (1897). 'On the Relations of Number and Quantity', *Mind* NS 6: 326–41.

—— (1910–11). 'Knowledge by Acquaintance and Knowledge by Description', *Proceedings of the Aristotelian Society* 11: 108–28.

—— (1912). *The Problems of Philosophy*. London: Williams and Norgate.

—— (1914a). *Our Knowledge of the External World as a Field for Scientific Method in Philosophy*. Chicago: Open Court.

—— (1914b). 'The Relation of Sense-Data to Physics', *Scientia* 16: 1–27.

—— (1914c). *Scientific Method in Philosophy*. Oxford: Clarendon Press.

—— (1915). 'The Ultimate Constituents of Matter', *Monist* 25: 399–417.

—— (1921). *The Analysis of Mind*. London: George Allen & Unwin.

—— (1927a). *The Analysis of Matter*. London: Kegan Paul, Trench, Trubner.

—— (1927b). *Philosophy*. New York: Norton.

—— (1953). 'The Cult of "Common Usage"', *British Journal for the Philosophy of Science* 3: 303–7.

—— (1983). *Cambridge Essays, 1888–99*. London: George Allen & Unwin.

Ryle, Gilbert (1949). *The Concept of Mind*. London: Hutchinson.

Sellars, Roy Wood (1920). 'Knowledge and Its Categories'. In Durant Drake (ed.), *Essays in Critical Realism*. London: Macmillan, pp. 187–219.

——(1961). 'Referential Transcendence', *Philosophy and Phenomenological Research* 22: 1–15.

Sellars, Wilfrid (1956). 'Empiricism and the Philosophy of Mind'. In Herbert Feigl and Michael Scriven (eds.), *Foundations of Science and the Concepts of Psychology and Psychoanalysis*. Minneapolis: University of Minnesota Press, pp. 253–329.

——(1963). 'Phenomenalism'. In Sellars, *Science, Perception and Reality*. London: Routledge & Kegan Paul, pp. 60–105.

Sidgwick, Henry (1876). 'Philosophy at Cambridge', *Mind* 1: 235–46.

——(1883). 'A Criticism of the Critical Philosophy', *Mind* 8: 313–37.

Smart, J. J. C. (1962). 'Sensations and Brain Processes'. In V. C. Chappell (ed.), *Philosophy of Mind*. Englewood Cliffs, NJ: Prentice-Hall, pp. 160–72.

Smith, A. D. (2002). *The Problem of Perception*. Cambridge, MA: Harvard University Press.

Stewart, J. A. (1876). 'Psychology—A Science or a Method?' *Mind* 1: 445–51.

Stout, G. F. (1890). 'The Genesis of the Cognition of Physical Reality', *Mind* 15: 22–45.

——(1896). *Analytic Psychology*, 2 vols. London: Swan Sonnenschein.

——(1899). *A Manual of Psychology*. London: Clive.

——(1900–1). 'Presidential Address: The Common-Sense Conception of a Material Thing', *Proceedings of the Aristotelian Society* NS 1: 1–17.

——(1903–4). 'Primary and Secondary Qualities', *Proceedings of the Aristotelian Society* 4: 141–60.

——(1908–9). 'Are Presentations Mental or Physical? A Reply to Prof. Alexander', *Proceedings of the Aristotelian Society* 9: 226–47.

Veitch, John (1877). 'Philosophy in the Scottish Universities (II)', *Mind* 2: 207–34.

Ward, James (1876). 'An Attempt to Interpret Fechner's Law', *Mind* 1: 452–66.

——(1886). 'Psychology'. In *Encyclopaedia Britannica, Vol. 20*, 9th edn. Philadelphia: Stoddart.

——(1892). '*Text-Book of Psychology*, by William James', *Mind* NS 1: 531–9.

——(1919). *Psychological Principles*. Cambridge: Cambridge University Press.

Warnock, G. J. (1953). *Berkeley*. Melbourne: Penguin Books.

Wittgenstein, Ludwig (1982–92). *Last Writings on the Philosophy of Psychology*, ed. G. H. von Wright and Heikki Nyman, 2 vols. Chicago: University of Chicago Press.

——(2001). *Philosophical Investigations*, tr. G. E. M. Anscombe, 3rd edn. Malden, MA: Blackwell. Originally published 1953.

....

CHAPTER 34

SCEPTICISM AND KNOWLEDGE: MOORE'S PROOF OF AN EXTERNAL WORLD

....

ANNALISA COLIVA

A profitable way of approaching the issue of analytic philosophy's reflections on scepticism and knowledge is by looking at the history of Moore's 'Proof of an External World'. The paper first appeared in 1939, has been the object of different and contrasting interpretations since then, and is nowadays at the core of a large debate in epistemology. In § 34.1 I will present the paper to place it in its proper context, in § 34.2 I will consider some classical interpretations of it, and in § 34.3 the ones which have fostered the ongoing debate. In so doing I will assess all of them from a historical point of view, pointing out how they are all somewhat wanting as renditions of Moore's strategy. In § 34.4 I will put forward my own interpretation of the historical Moore, as it were. Finally in § 34.5, I will return to the present-day debate and sketch a further interpretation—Wittgensteinian in spirit—which may be of interest to contemporary discussions on the topic.

34.1 MOORE'S PROOF OF AN EXTERNAL WORLD

....

Moore's proof of an external world is often presented without mentioning its original context and, moreover, as if it was directed against scepticism about the external world. Things aren't that simple, though. For 'Proof of an External World' (PEW) is a long essay divided into two parts. In the first and much longer one, Moore takes his lead from Kant's famous observation, in the *Critique of Pure Reason*:

> It still remains a scandal to philosophy … that the existence of things outside of us … must be accepted merely on *faith*, and that, if anyone thinks good to doubt their existence, we are unable to counter his doubts by any satisfactory proof. (B xxxix)

Moore claims that Kant wasn't able to give a successful proof of the existence of things outside of us and that his own proof will remedy the situation. However, before presenting it, he introduces a series of terminological distinctions, meant to clarify the meaning of the expression 'things outside of us'. According to Moore, the philosophical tradition in general, and Kant in particular, erroneously believe that the following expressions are equivalent:

(A) 'things outside of us';
(B) 'external things';
(C) 'things which are external to our minds';
(D) 'things which can be met in space';
(E) 'things presented in space'.

According to Kant, all these locutions are synonymous because they make reference to phenomena as opposed to noumena. The former are necessarily presented in space—the pure form of sensibility which allows us to perceive outer things. In contrast, according to Moore, these expressions can't be equivalent because he doesn't subscribe to Kant's transcendentalism, either about empirical objects or about space.

Hence, according to Moore, (E) doesn't entail (D), although (D) entails (E). For there may be things which are presented in space and yet can't be met within it. For instance, pains or itches are presented in a part of one's body, yet can't be met in space. Moreover, according to Moore, (C) doesn't entail (D), although (D) entails (C). For example, animals' pains are external to our minds, yet can't be met in space. Finally, with respect to (A) and (B), if they are taken to be equivalent to (C), the point just made would hold in their case too. But they could also be taken as synonymous with (D). Hence both points just made would hold for them as well. Be that as it may, since for Moore 'physical object' means 'an object which exists independently of being perceived by us (human beings)', he thinks that by giving a proof of the existence of physical objects he will *ipso facto* prove that there are things which can be met in space and that are external to us, no matter how (A) and (B) are read. However, this latter claim is *prima facie* problematical. For Moore himself points out that animals' pains are external to human minds as we can't perceive them. But it doesn't follow from this that they are what we intuitively regard as physical objects. Thus, the right thing to say is that a physical object is everything *that we could perceive*, which, however, exists independently of the fact that we actually perceive it. With this clarification in hand, let us now turn to the proof itself.

By holding up his hands in front of himself and in clear view, Moore makes a gesture with the right hand and says:

(1) 'Here is a hand';

then, making the same gesture with the left hand, he says:

(2) 'Here is another';

he then concludes:

(3) 'There are at present two human hands'.

Since the conclusion concerns the existence of objects which can be met in space, Moore claims that (3) entails

(4) 'There are physical objects';

and hence, that he has proved

(5) 'There is an external world'.

It must be stressed that up to this point Moore's proof is directed against an idealist who denies that there is an external world, by denying that there are objects that exist independently of the fact that we actually perceive them. Furthermore, the proof is clearly based on the idea of presenting instances of physical objects, in order to support the claim that there is an external world. Thus, it proceeds just like a proof of, say, there being misprints in a book—that is, by presenting specific instances of the category of misprint.

Still, it is clear that an idealist could concede both premises—(1) and (2)—and the conclusion—(3)—and yet deny that that entails that there are physical objects—(4)—if by 'physical object' one meant objects existing independently of being perceived by us. Hence, an idealist wouldn't take Moore's performance to show the truth of (5).[1]

Moreover, it must be noticed that up to this point nothing has been done to show that the premises are *known* to be true and aren't merely assumed to be such; nor to show that the conclusion of the argument is known. Hence, up to now, Moore's proof has no bearing whatsoever against scepticism. In fact, some years later, Moore himself maintained, in response to his critics (see RMC 668), that his proof was directed merely at an idealist and not against a sceptic. For, in his opinion, in order to take issue with a sceptic he

---

[1] Alternatively, if by 'physical objects' one meant something compatible with idealist theses, such as objects that afford the possibility of occurrent perceptions, (4) would follow, but not (5), if by 'external world' one meant a world populated by objects that exist independently of being perceived by us. Obviously, since Moore has painstakingly defined 'physical object' and 'external world', the alternative reading just presented is *not* the intended reading of Moore's proof, as he himself made clear in 'A Reply to my Critics' (RMC 669–70).

should have *proved* that he knew its premises. In particular, he should have proved that he wasn't dreaming. But Moore himself candidly acknowledged that he couldn't have proved such a thing. For all his evidence would have been compatible with the hypothesis that he might be dreaming of it.[2]

The interesting question is therefore the following. How come that most readers of Moore's paper have taken his proof as directed at a sceptic?[3] Furthermore, given Moore's explicit pronouncements, is this reading legitimate? In order to answer both these questions, we have to take into consideration the sequel of Moore's paper where he claims that his proof is a rigorous one because:

(a) the premises are different from the conclusion;
(b) they are known to be true and aren't merely believed to be true;
(c) the conclusion really follows from the premises.

For, given (b) and the fact that the inference is valid, it follows that also the conclusion of the argument is known.[4] Hence, if it is true that Moore knew that there were two hands, it follows that he also knew that there was an external world and *this* is clearly an anti-sceptical thesis.

This, however, raises the following issue: how could Moore maintain that he knew that his premises were true, from which it follows that he also knew the conclusion of his argument, while holding that he was unable to prove that he knew them, and that that was necessary in order convincingly to oppose scepticism?

I think the most charitable interpretation of Moore's claim, which can also explain the interest Moore's work stirred in other philosophers such as Wittgenstein, is as follows. If one is a philosopher of common sense, it doesn't matter how much a sceptic can press one to give a justification for one's *claims* to knowledge. Hence, it doesn't matter if one doesn't know *how* one knows that here there are two human hands, or, more precisely (cf. § 34.4), if one can't *prove* that one knows it. For such ignorance is entirely consistent with the fact that one *does know* such a thing (as Wittgenstein himself had already argued in the *Tractatus*). In support of this interpretation consider what Moore in effect writes in PEW:

---

[2] PEW 149: 'How am I to prove now that "Here's one hand and here's another"? I do not believe I can do it. In order to do it, I should need to prove for one thing, as Descartes pointed out, that I am not now dreaming. But how can I prove that I am not? I have, no doubt, conclusive reasons for asserting that I am not now dreaming; I have conclusive evidence that I am awake: but that is a very different thing from being able to prove it. I could not tell you what all my evidence is; and I should require to do this at least, in order to give you a proof.' In fact the problem is not that one could not mention all of one's available evidence in favor of 'I am not now dreaming', contrary to what Sosa 2007 claims. Rather, it lies in the fact that, for a Cartesian sceptic, all that evidence would be compatible with the hypothesis that one were merely dreaming of it.

[3] A notable exception is Sosa 2007, 52.

[4] Unless one denied the Principle of Closure for knowledge—according to which, if you know that p and you know that p entails q, you know that q—as Dretske 1970 and Nozick 1981 did. Moore, however, never proposed such a thing.

I certainly did at the moment [in which the proof was given] *know* that which I expressed by the combination of certain gestures with saying the words 'There is one hand and here is another'. I *knew* that there was one hand in the place indicated by combining a certain gesture with my first utterance of 'here' and that there was another in the different place indicated by combining a certain gesture with my second utterance of 'here'. How absurd it would be to suggest that I did not know it, but only believed it, and that perhaps it was not the case! (146)

I can know things, which I cannot prove; and among things which I certainly did know, even if (as I think) I could not prove them, were the premises of my ... [proof]. (150)

We will come back to this issue in § 34.4. Before doing so, however, let us now turn to some influential interpretations and assessments of Moore's proof. As we shall see, they are all interesting both as attempts to make sense of it and for their conceptual relevance for subsequent and contemporary epistemology. Yet—I will argue—they all somehow fail to take proper measure of Moore's strategy.

34.2 Some Classical Interpretations of Moore's Proof

34.2.1 Norman Malcolm: Ordinary Language and Common Sense

In his 1942 paper 'Moore and Ordinary Language' Norman Malcolm aims to show, contrary appearances notwithstanding, how Moore's proof of an external world is both a confutation of scepticism and a good response as such. According to him, the real essence of Moore's strategy consists in clarifying how sceptical doubts, once made explicit, go against *ordinary language*. In his view, that suffices to confute them.

According to Malcolm, when a sceptic says 'It cannot be known with certainty that physical objects exist' or 'We can't know with certainty that statements about physical objects are true' he isn't expressing empirical judgements, but making grammatical statements. For they don't say that it is a contingent empirical fact that *sometimes*, when certain statements about material objects are made and prefixed by the verb 'to know', what is said is false. Rather, they say that such statements are *always* false. This is so, according to Malcolm, because any empirical proposition is liable to an infinite number of verifications that can't (logically) be exhausted. Hence, our knowledge of empirical claims can only be probable and not certain. According to Malcolm, who follows Ayer (1940, 44) on this, a sceptic then proposes a *revision* of our ordinary language which consists in forbidding any expression of the form 'I know with certainty that *p*', where *p* is an empirical proposition, and substituting it with an expression such as 'It is highly probable that *p*'.

Moore's response to scepticism, on Malcolm's reading of it, is thus as follows. Let us consider a *paradigmatic case* of sure-fire knowledge, such as that this, which I hold up in front of me in good lighting conditions, while I am cognitively lucid, is my hand. It would be nonsense to say 'It is highly probable that there is a hand here'. If a child who was learning language said such a thing, we would correct him by saying 'It is *certain* that there is a hand here and it is not just merely probable'. According to Malcolm, Moore's answer to the sceptic appeals to our *language sense*, reminding him of the fact that there is an ordinary use of the locution 'to know with certainty' in which it is applied to empirical statements. But, then, if 'I know with certainty that *p*', where *p* is an empirical statement, is an expression of our ordinary language—that is to say, it has a perfectly accepted usage within our linguistic community—it can't be maintained, with a sceptic, that it is self-contradictory. For, otherwise, it couldn't be used to describe any kind of situation and couldn't have the ordinary use it does in fact have—as Moore reminds us of. The only partial criticism that Malcolm raises against Moore is that it fails to convince the sceptic of his mistake because he doesn't clarify that his argument is a logico-linguistic one, rather than an epistemic-empirical one and also because it fails to make explicit the origin of the sceptical mistake.

Malcolm's understanding of the sceptical position is surely contentious, though. For a sceptic usually takes for granted our ordinary use of 'to know (with certainty)'. He does so in order to show how it seems to be a necessary condition upon the correct usage of those expressions that one be able to give reasons in favour of what one claims to know (with certainty). He then maintains that, with respect to beliefs about physical objects, it may be shown—in different ways depending on which sceptical argument is at stake— that one doesn't really have a justification to believe what one takes to know. Hence, assuming the classical tripartite definition of knowledge as justified true belief, a sceptic concludes that one doesn't know what one claims to know.

As we saw, however, Malcolm bases his interpretation of scepticism on Ayer's understanding of it. So—it may be argued—his considerations may well be effective against at least that particular kind of sceptic. We will come back to this counter in a moment. What must be stressed for now, however, is, first, that there is no textual evidence that Moore's sceptic is whom Malcolm (and Ayer) take(s) him to be. Secondly, that even if it were, Moore's response, on Malcolm's interpretation of it, would leave out a great number of sceptical positions and would engage with one of the least interesting ones. For Malcolm's sceptic's position depends on the finitude of human cognitive capacities. So it leaves it open in principle that a creature without such cognitive shortcomings, yet exercising *the same kind of cognitive faculty*, could have sure-fire knowledge of propositions about material objects. However, the best sceptical arguments—such as the Cartesian and the Humean ones—purport to establish a stronger result. Namely, that by exercising the very same cognitive capacities we usually employ—however freed from all defects and limitations ours might have—*nobody* could get to know with certainty a proposition about physical objects.[5]

---

[5] For the distinction between Cartesian and Humean scepticism cf. § 34.3.1.

Moreover, Moore's proof, on Malcolm's understanding of it, could hardly be effective against its opponent, even as Malcolm represents him, because it would be based on a *petitio principii*. For Moore would be trying to counter a sceptic by saying that he does have certain knowledge of an empirical proposition and that it would be nonsense to claim that it is only probable. This, however, would mean assuming in the premise what one should prove.

Let me point out, however, that Moore's position is subtler than that. For, on the one hand, he sharply distinguishes between knowledge and the conditions of its obtainment and, on the other, the possibility of *proving* that they are indeed satisfied. He also recognizes that the latter is what needs to be done in order to confront scepticism. However, Moore also thinks that acknowledging the impossibility of meeting this challenge doesn't impugn the fact the he knows the premises of his proof and hence its conclusion. So, first of all, Moore proposes a gambit, which, if successful, would diminish the impact of sceptical arguments. For, if one can somehow stop the inference from the impossibility of proving that one knows that *p* to the fact that one doesn't know that *p*, one would have greatly lessened the force of sceptical arguments which make play with such an inference. Secondly, he also puts forward some considerations to try and meet the sceptical challenge. For he argues that the sceptical— evidently Cartesian—argument which appeals to the hypothesis of dreaming in order to cast doubt on the fact that we may be able to prove that we are not dreaming, and thus on the fact that we have knowledge of some ordinary empirical propositions, isn't *reasonable*. For either there are absolutely *no* reasons to think that we might be dreaming in the circumstance of Moore's proof;[6] or they are indeed *weaker* than the reasons we have to think that we are not dreaming.[7] Hence, admitting such a hypothesis wouldn't be *sensible*.

---

[6] FFS 222: 'I don't see any reason to abandon my view that I do know for certain ... that I am not dreaming now. And the mere proposition, which I admit, that percepts of the same kind *in certain respects* do sometimes occur in dreams, is, I am quite certain, no good reason for saying: this percept *may* be one which is occurring in a dream.' See also PEW 149: 'I have, no doubt, conclusive reasons for asserting that I am not now dreaming; I have conclusive evidence that I am awake: but that is a very different thing from being able to prove it.'

[7] FFS 220: 'It seems to me *more* certain that I *do* know that this is a pencil and that you are conscious, than that any single one of these four assumptions [from which it would follow that he didn't know that] is true, let alone all four.... Of no one of [them] do I feel *as* certain as that I do know for certain that this is a pencil. Nay more: I do not think it is *rational* to be as certain of any one of [them], as of the proposition that I do know that this is a pencil. And how on earth is it to be decided which of the two things it is *rational* to be most certain of?'

See also C 247: 'I agree, therefore, with that part of this argument which asserts that if I don't know now that I'm not dreaming, it follows that I don't *know* that I am standing up, even if I both actually am and think that I am. But this first part of the argument is a consideration which cuts both ways. For, if it is true, it follows that it is also true that if I *do* know that I am standing up, then I do know that I am not dreaming. I can therefore just as well argue: since I do know that I'm standing up, it follows that I do know that I'm not dreaming; as my opponent can argue: since you don't know that you're not dreaming, it follows that you don't know that you're standing up. The one argument is just as good as the other, unless my opponent can give *better* [my italics] reasons for asserting that I don't know that I'm not dreaming, than I can give for asserting that I do know that I am standing up.'

Now, I don't mean to suggest that Moore's gambit and counter to the sceptic are successful. Yet, he had at least the merit of devising a move, which, if successful, would greatly weaken the force of the sceptical challenge. On Malcolm's reading of him, in contrast, he would simply be begging the question and be doing so in an utterly obvious way.

In a later paper—'Defending Common Sense' (1949)—Malcolm raises totally different criticisms against Moore's proof.[8] There, he focuses on the use that Moore makes of the verb 'to know' in relation to his truisms. According to Malcolm, the correct use of the expression 'I know (with certainty) that p' requires:

(i) That there be an open question and a doubt to be removed;
(ii) That the person who makes the assertion be able to produce reasons in favour of his claim to knowledge;
(iii) That it be possible to make an inquiry that could determine whether p is the case.

According to Malcolm, none of these features is respected by Moore's use of that expression. The first one isn't because when Moore says 'I know that there is a hand here', there is no doubt that it be so. An objection that Malcolm takes into account is that Moore is here responding to *a philosophical kind of doubt*—to the question 'How do you know that there is a hand here?' Clearly, however, Moore would merely believe he was answering the sceptic, for it can only be an ironic response to the question 'How do you know it?' to answer 'Because I know it'. This, however, according to Malcolm, shows that a sceptic raises a doubt where there is no reason to do so. According to Malcolm, then, the second feature of the grammar of 'to know' is violated by the fact that Moore claims to know that he has a hand, but he is unable to give reasons in favour of that, or indeed a proof of it. Finally, according to Malcolm, Moore goes against the third feature of the correct use of 'I know' for there is no inquiry that could determine that that really is a hand. For touching and observing it would make it plain that one had misunderstood the nature of sceptical doubts, which can't be silenced by ordinary empirical investigations.

Several things are worth noticing. First, regarding Malcolm's contention that Moore's use of 'to know' hasn't respected (i)—that there be a doubt to be removed—it has to be observed that of course there was no 'real' or 'ordinary' doubt. Indeed, Moore would very much agree on that. If, then, one considers a sceptical doubt, it should be kept in mind that its removal wasn't Moore's aim in PEW. Moreover, he was perfectly aware that he couldn't have responded to such a kind a doubt—which depends on asking for a proof of the fact that he knew the premises of his proof—just by saying 'because I know it'.

---

[8] For a reconstruction of the genesis of this paper, and its relationship to Wittgenstein's conception of claims to knowledge with respect to psychological self-ascriptions and to *On Certainty*, see Coliva 2010b, ch. 2

Secondly, regarding the allegation that Moore didn't give reasons in favour of his claim to knowledge, it should be noticed that he repeatedly said that he knew there were two hands because of his perceptual evidence.[9] Hence, an inquiry could have settled the 'ordinary' issue of whether that was the case—(iii). However, that wouldn't have settled the philosophical issue of proving that he really knew that there were two hands. But, as we have seen, Moore never thought or claimed he had done so.

Finally and more generally, one could object, and Moore himself did so, that his use of 'I know' was *peculiar*, given the circumstances of its use, where there was no doubt about the existence of his hands, but not mistaken. As Moore wrote to Malcolm in 1949 (LM 214), despite this oddity he was using 'I know' *in the sense* in which it is ordinarily used. This, in turn, clarifies how Moore's and Malcolm's conceptions of meaning are utterly different. In Moore's view, an expression maintains its usual meaning even if it is used in circumstances other than the ones in which it is typically employed. In Malcolm's view, in contrast, just like for the later Wittgenstein, the meaning of words is given by the rules which govern the various circumstances of their use.

The same difference may be noted by considering Moore's and Malcolm's debate over philosophical doubts. Malcolm maintains that a philosophical doubt arises where there is no real doubt about the fact that, for instance, there is a hand here. One may then think that it would be correct to say 'There is no doubt that there is a hand here' and hold that that would be equivalent to 'I know that there is a hand here' or even to 'It is certain that there is a hand here'. From this, it would follow that Moore would be right in saying 'It is certain that there is a hand here'. But, according to Malcolm, a sceptic's mistake isn't that of doubting where one doesn't usually do so, but, rather, of doubting where a doubt *cannot be raised*, on pain of nonsense. Hence, in such a context, 'There is no doubt that there is a hand here' isn't equivalent to 'It is certain that there is a hand here'; rather, it means 'To doubt that there is a hand here would be nonsense'. Thus, it is clear how, on Malcolm's reading of him, Moore's mistake would consist in failing to see how the impossibility of meaningfully raising doubts in such a context goes together with the impossibility of making any meaningful claim to knowledge. This, from a logico-linguistic point of view, for Malcolm (and Wittgenstein), boils down to the view that if one cannot say that something isn't known, one cannot say that it is known either (OC 58).

In his letter to Malcolm (LM 215–16), Moore discusses this objection and points out how the crucial difference between him and Malcolm (and hence between Wittgenstein and him) is a different conception of meaning and of the legitimacy of philosophical doubts. As already remarked, for Moore words retain their meaning even when employed outside the usual contexts of their use. Moreover, according to Moore,

---

[9] In support of this reading of Moore, see C 243: 'A third characteristic which was common to all those seven propositions [viz. propositions about material objects in Moore's surroundings] was one which I am going to express by saying that I had for each of them, at the time when I made it, *the evidence of my senses* … In other words, in all seven cases, what I said was at least partly *based* on "the then present evidence of my senses".'

contrary to Malcolm and Wittgenstein, philosophical doubts are nonsensical because they go against the common-sense picture of the world. But they are not nonsense because they violate some linguistic norm. Therefore, Moore thinks it legitimate to oppose them by maintaining that the common-sense picture of the world is indeed certain, despite a sceptic's claims to the contrary.

34.2.2 Thompson Clarke and Barry Stroud: at the Origins of Contextualism

In the paper 'The Legacy of Skepticism' (1972) Thompson Clarke introduced a distinction between plain talk and philosophical talk. In his view, the former is what is produced within all our usual linguistic practices, with their characteristic embedment in non-linguistic activities. The latter, in contrast, is what is produced while doing philosophy. Philosophical talk extrapolates from any ordinary practice and from non-linguistic activities, to consider language in its own right. While in plain talk the conditions of meaningful discourse are subject to pragmatic constraints—such as relevance, and other forms of appropriateness (see Grice 1957)—in philosophical talk these limitations are removed and words are considered as such. Any well-formed sentence of natural language can be subject to philosophical analysis. A philosophical question, like the sceptical question about the foundations of our knowledge, is formulated within philosophical talk and, according to Clarke, it is perfectly legitimate, since it satisfies a deep intellectual need that isn't fulfilled by any of its counterparts in plain talk (1972, 292).

According to Clarke, Malcolm's interpretation of Moore (as well as Wittgenstein's) conflates the peculiarity of Moore's use of 'to know' with its alleged lack of sense. Clarke then points out that if Moore's use is taken to be part of plain talk, it reveals a *philosophical lobotomy*, since Moore means to oppose philosophical theses. If, in contrast, it is taken as part of philosophical talk, it is *dogmatic*, since it doesn't face the sceptical challenge of explaining *how* he knows that there are two hands where he seems to see them (and consequently, that there is an external world) and simply counters 'Because I do'.

Barry Stroud's interpretation of Moore's proof closely resembles Clarke's, which is explicitly mentioned as its inspirational source. However, according to Stroud, Moore's proof is given within plain talk. If so, it is a *good proof*, but, obviously, it can't have any anti-sceptical bearing, since it doesn't even face the sceptical challenge. From the inside, it is a good proof because it appeals to the greater degree of certainty possessed by the premises of Moore's argument over the degree of certainty possessed by those premises which, within plain talk, would be necessary in order to maintain that he may only be dreaming of having two hands. Still, none of this shows that a doubt about Moore's knowledge of his premises is *impossible*. Hence, the proof fails to address the philosophical issue and, for this reason, when it is considered from the outside, in the way in which confronting the sceptical challenge requires, it can't be successful.

Hence, the 'internal'/'external' dialectic is as follows: it is possible to doubt from the inside only when there are *actual reasons* to doubt that *p*, or when there are *stronger* reasons to doubt it than the ones one can produce in favour of one's claim to know that *p*. Since, however, with respect to the premises of Moore's proof there are no such reasons—or at any rate, they aren't stronger than the ones in favour of holding those premises—any form of scepticism appears, from the inside, totally misguided.

From the outside, in contrast, any doubt is legitimate, inasmuch as it is possible or conceivable. Thus, it is perfectly right to doubt the fact that the premises of Moore's argument are known, because one can raise hypotheses, such as the one from dreaming, that would call into question any supposed instance of sensory-based knowledge regarding physical objects. Therefore Moore, by failing to show why a merely possible doubt—like the Cartesian one—is illegitimate or, in effect, no doubt at all, doesn't address the sceptic, whose challenge is raised at the purely philosophical level. According to Stroud, Moore's strategy is wanting because it provides no account of why our knowledge from the inside is legitimate and because it offers no diagnosis and solution (or dissolution) of what, in his view, the sceptical mistake would amount to.

This way, Stroud introduces a sort of *evaluative lobotomy* that, however, can help clarify the relationship between *ordinary* and *philosophical discourse*. This, in turn, is, on Stroud's view, what is really at stake in the debate over scepticism and common sense. From such a perspective, Moore's proof is interesting because—its failure notwithstanding—it *contradicts* scepticism while being *compatible* with it. It contradicts it because it claims that we do have knowledge both of its premises and of its conclusion. Still, it is compatible with it because such a claim is made in a context other than the sceptical one. Similar considerations would apply in the other direction too—that is, scepticism contradicts common sense, yet it is compatible with it.[10]

Hence, on Stroud's view, Moore's mistake consists in failing to appreciate that if this is the right description of the relationship between ordinary and philosophical discourse, then his negation of the sceptical thesis can't be a confutation of scepticism. Thus, 'the price of philosophical skepticism's immunity … would be the corresponding immunity of all our ordinary assertions to philosophical attack' (1984, 127).

It is worth noticing how Clarke's and Stroud's interpretations somehow connect with contemporary contextualist as well as relativist positions about knowledge ascriptions.[11] According to contextualism, there are different contexts, determined by different standards about what must be the case in order for knowledge to obtain. So, what may be known in a context may turn out not to be so in a different one. Accordingly, this is

---

[10] Intuitively, however, Stroud's claims are dubious. For, if 'knowledge' is context-sensitive in the way proposed, there would be no real contradiction between scepticism and common sense, because, in order to have a contradiction, *p* should be both known and not known *in the same context*.

[11] Cohen 1999; DeRose 1992; MacFarlane 2005. Travis 1989 too, but under the influence of some Wittgensteinian elements as well. For a discussion of the latter, in connection with Wittgenstein, see Coliva 2010b, ch. 2.

what happens in the passage from ordinary contexts to philosophical ones. Moore's proof could thus be correct in the ordinary context, yet fail as an anti-sceptical weapon. Contemporary contextualism therefore provides only a strategy of damage limitation against scepticism, rather than a rebuttal of it. For, as we just saw, the price to pay to philosophical scepticism, in order to make our ordinary knowledge immune to it, is to let it turn out right in its own context. A corollary of this view is that, contrary appearances notwithstanding, 'knowledge' is a context-sensitive term (or concept), like ordinary indexical terms such as 'I' and 'yesterday', which pick out different people and days, respectively, according to the context of their utterance. Therefore, also the extension of 'knowledge' varies according to shifts in context of utterance (or of assessment, on the relativist variant of contextualism).[12]

Let us now consider Clarke's and Stroud's interpretations from a historical point of view, by turning to the issue of whether their readings tally with Moore's explicit pronouncements. As we saw before, in his letter to Malcolm Moore claims that he is using the verb 'to know' according to its ordinary meaning. Furthermore, he maintains that his use of 'I know' in relation to the premises of his proof is meant to engage with his philosophical opponents, contrary to what Stroud says.[13] Hence, on the one hand, according to Moore, it is with an ordinary conceptual repertoire that one enters philosophical discourse, contrary to what Clarke claims. On the other, in his view, there is no separation between philosophy and common sense, in such a way that statements respectively made in those different contexts could contradict each other yet somehow be compatible with one another, as opposed to what Stroud holds. These two claims together amount to the view that, according to Moore, the concept of knowledge isn't context-sensitive;[14] nor is there any hint that he may have favoured a relative view of truth, in such a way that opposite knowledge ascriptions could turn out both to be true, when assessed on the basis of different standards of evaluation, respectively held by common sense and scepticism.

Finally, and most importantly, on Moore's own understanding of scepticism, the latter arises when the issue of showing *how* one can know what one claims to know, and thus *prove* that one does indeed know it, is raised. To ask such a question doesn't show the context-sensitivity of knowledge, let alone the relativity of knowledge ascriptions to different standards of evaluation. On the contrary, it depends on making use of an invariant concept and yet on asking *a different question*—not whether it is known that *p*, but, rather, *how* one can *prove* that *p* is known (if indeed it is). Moore, moreover, agrees that he isn't able to answer such a question. Yet, as we have repeatedly seen, he refuses to agree with the sceptic that because one can't answer it, it follows that one doesn't know that *p*. This,

[12] This may be a problematic claim for it seems to entail that speakers are blind to the semantics of 'to know' in a way in which they aren't to the semantics of indexicals and demonstratives.

[13] For a similar objection to Stroud's interpretation of Moore, see McGinn 1989, ch. 3.

[14] Travis 1989, 165–6, who is sympathetic to Moore's claim that he knows the premises of his proof, and who supports contextualism about knowledge ascriptions, clearly recognizes this point and actually deems it the source of the failure of Moore's anti-sceptical strategy.

however, isn't simply a dogmatic and unphilosophical position, as Clarke claims.[15] Rather, it depends on a specific conception of the relationship between the conditions of knowledge and their obtainment and the possibility of proving that they are in fact the case.[16]

Thus, to conclude: Clarke's and Stroud's interpretations of Moore's proof—though interesting in their own right, as well as in light of contemporary debates on semantic contextualism and relativism—are deeply at odds with Moore's own understanding of his proof. Thus they can't be taken as faithful interpretations of what Moore was up to.

34.3 THE CONTEMPORARY DEBATE ON MOORE'S PROOF: WRIGHT AND PRYOR

Let us now turn to the interpretations of Moore's proof that are at the origin of much contemporary debate on the topic.

34.3.1 Moore and Humean Scepticism: Wright's Interpretation of the Proof

In a paper titled 'Facts and Certainty' (1985) Crispin Wright has put forward another reading of Moore's proof, which is widely debated nowadays, although mostly from a conceptual point of view, rather than as an interpretation of Moore's actual thought. According to him, it is important to make explicit the *grounds* on which Moore claims to

---

[15] McGinn 1989, 49–53 rightly notes that Moore is directly engaging with scepticism and isn't confining his claims to knowledge merely to ordinary contexts. Yet, she herself shares the view that he is being dogmatic and, hence, somewhat unphilosophical, by failing to diagnose what is wrong with scepticism. In contrast, and as will become apparent in the following, I think Moore is proposing a subtler, though not obviously successful move.

[16] According to Travis (1989, 192–6), however, Moore appreciated the context-sensitivity of *proofs*, though he confined it to the premises of his own proof of an external world. So, on Travis' reading of PEW, Moore agreed with a sceptic that he could not prove 'Here is one hand' and 'Here is another'. Yet, he claimed that he knew them nonetheless, because, according to Travis, he thought that, *in given contexts*, they simply couldn't be proved. Still, he held that in different ones they might well be. From a textual point of view, however, Travis' interpretation of Moore as a proto-contextualist about proof has nothing on its side. For he never explicitly claimed that, in different contexts, such a proof could in fact be given. As Michael Williams has repeatedly claimed, this was actually one of Wittgenstein's intuitions, not Moore's. Nor did Moore ever claim that he lacked evidence for holding the premises of his proof (fn. 9). Hence, if he thought that no proof of the premises of PEW could be given, he thought so while having in mind a rather special notion of proof, whose absence was compatible with his having evidence and grounds for those very premises. Thus, I think we can safely conclude that Moore was neither a contextualist about knowledge nor about proof.

know the premises of his proof in the circumstances in which the proof was offered. As is apparent, in those circumstances, the assertion 'Here is a hand' was based on his *sensory evidence*. Indeed, Moore himself made clear, though not in PEW, that his claim was based on those very grounds (cf. fn. 9).

That Moore was basing his claim on his available evidence may appear obvious, but it isn't within the historiography on the proof. For it has been denied that Moore made explicit the *criterion* on the basis of which he could assert his premises.[17] In response to such a claim, it must be noted that Moore certainly said he couldn't prove that he knew his premises, but, as we have repeatedly seen, he equally denied that that entailed the fact he didn't know them *in those very circumstances*—that is to say, when he was holding up his hands in front of him, in clear view, and could thus perfectly well *see* them. Hence, Moore didn't mean to deny that he was justified in holding his premises. Rather, he denied that the inability to prove, against a sceptic, that his grounds were sure-fire could impugn his knowledge—on whatever bases the latter might have been achieved.

According to Wright, then, if Moore's grounds are made explicit, it becomes immediately evident why the proof fails. He reconstructs it as follows:

   (I) A given proposition describes the salient aspects of my experience at the time in question;
   (II) I have a hand;
   (III) Therefore, there is an external world.

In fact (I) amounts to saying that there is a proposition which correctly describes the relevant aspects of Moore's experience in the circumstances in which his proof was given. For instance: 'I am perceiving (what I take to be) my hand'. According to Wright, (II) is then inferred from (I) and (III) follows from (II) since a hand is a physical object. Moreover, given that the premises are known, according to Moore, so would be the conclusion.[18]

However, on Wright's view, it is clear that (I) can ground (II) only if one can already take it for granted that one's experience is being produced by causal interaction with physical objects. Hence, any sensory experience can warrant a belief about empirical objects only if it is already assumed that there is an external world. However, in order *justifiably* to go from (I) to (II), one needs already to have a *warrant* for (III). Hence, the proof is *epistemically circular* (or *question begging*). For antecedent and independent

---

[18] Wright 2002 puts forward another possible rendition of Moore's proof where (II) isn't *inferred* from a proposition about one's experience such as (I). Rather, it is simply grounded in one's experience. On Wright's view that makes no difference with respect to the eventual diagnosis of the proof because in this case too one's perceptual warrant would depend not just on one's available experience but also on having independent warrant that there is an external world.

warrant for (III) is needed in order to have warrant for (II) in the first place,[19] given one's current sensory experience, as described in (I).

Ironically enough, then, Moore's proof—on Wright's understanding of it—rather than being a response to scepticism instantiates the template of a powerful form of scepticism, that Wright calls 'Humean', as opposed to 'Cartesian'. The difference between these two forms of scepticism resides in the fact that while the latter makes play with uncongenial scenarios, such as the hypothesis that one may be the victim of a sustained and lucid dream, whereby one would be systematically unable to tell whether one is dreaming or not, the former doesn't. From such a starting point, the Cartesian sceptic then claims that for any specific empirical proposition we take ourselves to know on the basis of our sensory experience, it is metaphysically possible that it be produced in a non-standard way. From the impossibility of excluding that this is the case, he takes it to follow that we don't know *any* such empirical proposition. Consequently, that we don't know (III)— that there is an external world.[20]

Humean scepticism, in contrast, merely draws on the kind of epistemic gap between having a certain kind of evidence, and warrantedly forming a belief about a domain which goes beyond the one immediately testified by one's experience, presented by inferences such as the (I)–(II)–(III) argument just offered, or indeed inductive inferences—whence the title of 'Humean' for this form of scepticism. To repeat, in order warrantedly to go from the first premise, which is about one's sensory experience, to the second, which is about an object whose existence is independent of one's experience, warrant for the conclusion of the argument—that there is an external world—must be independently available. Since, however, by sceptical lights, there is no way of getting such an independent warrant, the argument fails to provide warrant for its conclusion. Wright calls this phenomenon 'failure of transmission of warrant'. For the need of an antecedent warrant for the conclusion in order warrantedly to go from (I) to (II) prevents the warrant one *may* after all have for (II)—if somehow the sceptic was wrong in claiming that independent warrant for (III) could not be attained—to be *transmitted* to (III). That is to say, Moore's proof cannot either give one a *first* warrant to believe (III), or *further epistemic support* for the warrant one might already have to believe it.[21]

---

[19] Warrant for (II) is a necessary condition for having knowledge of it, on the tripartite conception of knowledge. Since nowhere to my knowledge does Moore impugn the tripartite account, lack of such a warrant would impugn one's alleged knowledge of (II), also by Moore's lights. So, the fact that Wright is talking about warrant while Moore talks of knowledge, though certainly inaccurate from a historical point of view, makes no substantial difference from a conceptual one—or so it seems to me.

[20] Cf. Wright 1985, 2004a, 2004b; Coliva 2008, 2010a.

[21] These qualifications are important in order to clarify the difference between 'transmission failure' and the failure of the Principle of Closure for epistemic operators (fn. 4). There is an ongoing discussion about whether, once granted the specific conception of the architecture of empirical warrants recommended by Wright, Moore's proof could at least enhance the previous warrant one might have for (III), once the Principle of Closure is retained. Be that as it may, there is substantial agreement that, given that conception of empirical warrants, the proof couldn't give one a first warrant to believe its conclusion.

If Wright's reading of Moore's proof were correct, it would be devastating. For, regardless of Moore's insistence that despite being unable to prove that he knew his premises he knew them nonetheless and notwithstanding the fact that—given the Principle of Closure—one would know the conclusion, he may have indeed had the former piece of knowledge, without actually being in a position to *acquire* knowledge of the conclusion, or indeed somehow *enhance* it, *by running his proof*. So, interpreted this way, Moore's proof would simply be no proof whatever of (III)—viz. that there is an external world. For, characteristically, proofs are means which allow us to *extend* our knowledge from their premises to their conclusions and thus provide us with reasons for *first* believing them, or else with reasons which should *enhance* our epistemic support for believing them. On Wright's reading of it, in contrast, Moore's 'proof' would dramatically fail to do so.

Now, two things are worth pointing out. First, things might be different if Wright's attack were meant to impugn merely Moore's ability to *redeem* his knowledge of (III)—viz. the ability of *proving* that he did really have it—as Wright's more recent discussions of Moore's proof seem sometimes to suggest (2004a, 167, 210–11; 2007), and if this de-coupling could be matched by endorsing an externalist notion of knowledge (and/or warrant). In such a case Moore's proof could establish that its conclusion is known—since its premises would be—and yet, just as Moore held, fail at *proving*, against scepticism, that either the premises or the conclusion be known. We will come back to this issue in § 34.4.

Secondly, Jim Pryor has recently challenged the correctness of Wright's views upon the structure of empirical warrants. If Pryor were right, it would certainly come as a relief for the proof's prospects of success. Hence, we must now turn to a discussion of this rejoinder.

34.3.2 Moore's Comeback: Pryor's Dogmatist Interpretation

Jim Pryor in 'What's Wrong with Moore's Argument?' (2004) claims that the proof is fine, from an epistemological point of view. In particular, it doesn't exhibit failure of warrant transmission. For, on Pryor's understanding of the structure of perceptual warrants, it suffices, in order to possess such a warrant, merely to have a certain course of experience while lacking any reason to doubt that there may be an external world, at least when what is at stake is the justification of what he takes to be *perceptually basic beliefs*.[22] Hence, there is no need, on his view, to possess an independent warrant for the conclusion of that argument, viz. that there is an external world.

---

[22] 'Here is a hand' would be such a perceptually basic belief. If one found this claim odd, Pryor would allow substituting it with 'Here is a pinkish expanse'. I am not sure whether Moore himself would be happy with that substitution. Be that as it may, the important point (for both) is that perceptually basic beliefs would be about physical objects.

Pryor, however, thinks that although Moore's proof is perfectly in order from an epis-temic point of view, it is not successful against a sceptic. In particular, it is *dialectically ineffective* for, according to him, a sceptic will think it is (likely) *false*[23] that there is an external world. For such a reason he will not consider Moore's experience as of a hand in front of him sufficient for warrant of the corresponding empirical belief. Starting off with an unwarranted premise—at least by a sceptic's lights—the proof won't be able to confer warrant upon its conclusion and hence to convince a sceptic that there is an external world.

Pryor, however, doesn't think that the sceptical doubt is legitimate. He holds it is a 'disease' we shouldn't catch, or else cure ourselves of (2004, 368). Yet, this judgement is at odds with the claim that Moore's proof would fail for dialectical reasons when propounded against a sceptic. For reflect: if Pryor is right in thinking that the proof is epistemically correct, by being presented with it one should—if rational—give up one's disbelief in the existence of an external world. Hence, on Pryor's account of the proof, it could be dialectically ineffective only against a—as it were—*stubborn* kind of sceptic (Coliva 2010a). That is to say, it would be ineffective only against a sceptic who resolutely—and by Pryor's lights, irrationally—denied that just by having a certain course of experience one would thereby get a warrant for a belief about a specific mate-rial object like 'Here is a hand', and could thus discard hypotheses that are incompatible with it—e.g. the dreaming hypothesis—while also acquiring a warrant for the conclu-sion of the argument, i.e. 'There is an external world'.

Although such an outcome would be very sympathetic to Moore's proof a few things must be noticed, if Pryor's story were meant to provide a historically faithful interpre-tation of the proof.[24] First, Moore never explicitly argued for the view about percep-tual warrants that Pryor sees as the key to the proof's epistemic success. No doubt he made explicit the grounds of his proof—that is, the fact that he believed its premises on the basis of his perceptual evidence. But he never said that that would be sufficient, by itself, to give one a warrant—or indeed knowledge—of certain propositions about physical objects such as 'Here is a hand'. On the contrary, one of the main tenets of Moore's philosophy of perception is his appeal to sense-data. Now, it merits emphasis that any such account would entail a conception of perceptual warrant (and there-fore knowledge) as dependent on some extra element beside the occurrence of the

---

[23] This is indeed a contentious rendition of the sceptical position, for a sceptic is no idealist! Rather, on the basis of philosophical arguments he holds an *agnostic position* and, in particular, that it can't be warrantedly believed either that there is an external world, or that that there isn't. But, as already noticed, Cartesian and Humean sceptics reach this position for slightly different reasons. The former think that since all our perceptual evidence is compatible with the hypothesis that we might be dreaming of it, no single belief about specific physical objects can be warranted and therefore known. From that, they conclude that our belief about the fact that the whole category of physical objects isn't empty is unwarranted and unknowable. Humean scepticism, in contrast, directly shows the latter belief to be unwarrantable and thus unknowable because any warrant one may produce for it would in turn depend on already having warrant for it. See Coliva 2008, 2010a.

[24] Which is something Pryor may well not be interested in doing.

sense-datum itself—at least unless the latter were taken to be identical with some part or other of a physical object.[25] Such an extra element would presumably be the (warranted) assumption that the experience one is having be produced by causal interaction with physical objects.

Indeed in FFS Moore explicitly said that he agreed with Russell that propositions about specific material objects in one's surroundings aren't known *immediately*, but always on the basis of some 'analogical or inductive argument' (FFS 226). Thus, it is almost certain that he didn't endorse in PEW[26] the conception of the structure of empirical warrants (or of knowledge) that Pryor has recently put forward and which has served as basis for his interpretation of Moore's proof.

Moreover, it should be kept in mind that Moore raised the issue of having to prove that he wasn't dreaming because he realized that that was what stood in the way of *his opponent's* recognition that the premises of his proof were known. If so, however, and this brings us to the second point worth noticing, Pryor's and Moore's understanding of what would be needed to confront a sceptic would dramatically diverge. For, on Pryor's account it would suffice simply to remind him that in order to possess a perceptual warrant for 'Here is a hand' it is enough to have a certain course of experience, when there is in fact no reason to doubt that there is an external world *and* that the conditions are such that no doubt of that kind is reasonable. On Moore's view, in contrast, it should be *proved* that, on those circumstances, such a doubt would be unreasonable. Indeed Moore thought he could make some gesture in that direction, and accordingly said that the *grounds* for thinking that he might have been dreaming of his hand were *weaker* than the ones available to him to claim knowledge of his premises, or even totally *non-existent*.[27]

True, this move is unsuccessful, once coupled with other things Moore says. For, if it is legitimate to distinguish between, on the one hand, knowledge and the conditions of its obtainment and, on the other, the ability to prove that they are satisfied, as Moore claims, and if, as he argues, the sceptical challenge concerns such a proof, merely to insist that one does know that there are hands and that, given one's evidence, the hypothesis that one may be dreaming is less supported, or even unsupported by it, can't exclude the metaphysical possibility that it be the case. Hence, Moore didn't succeed in proving that he wasn't dreaming. Accordingly, he also failed to prove that he knew the premises of his proof, contrary to what he thought he should have done in order to counter a sceptic. Still, it is clear that he saw and characterized the sceptical position not as a 'disease', but as a genuine challenge, that arises out of asking a kind of question that can't be answered by simply exposing the structure of empirical warrants. It is to such a question and to its legitimacy that we shall now turn.

---

[25] A view that Moore considered and rejected in DCS iv.
[26] But it should be kept in mind that Moore wrote FFS between 1940 and 1944, thus after PEW.
[27] See fn. 6–7.

34.4 Having Knowledge and Being Able to Prove that One Does

In order finally to assess Moore's proof from a historical point of view, we need to consider the issue of the relationship between, on the one hand, having knowledge and the conditions of its obtainment and, on the other, the possibility of *proving* that those conditions do in fact obtain and thus that one really has that knowledge one takes oneself to have, in such a way as to be able rationally to claim or redeem it. The 'How do you know?' kind of question that the sceptic typically asks is meant to raise that issue. Hence, that question, when voiced by a sceptic, isn't a simple request of what the *grounds* of one's knowledge are. Rather, it is meant as a request of a proof of what one claims to know. To exemplify once more with the premises of Moore's proof, Moore can say that his ground for holding that there is a hand in front of him is his current visual experience. A sceptic, however, is precisely questioning Moore's ability to prove that his experience is indeed veridical in those circumstances.

Hence, according to Moore, the sceptic holds the following view of the relationship between having knowledge and being able rationally to redeem it:

> (1) If you can't show how you know that *p*—that is, *prove* that you do know it—and can't, therefore, rationally redeem your claim to knowledge, you don't know that *p*.

Moore, however, thinks that this entailment doesn't hold. Why? I submit that it is because he was in fact endorsing a *somewhat externalist* conception of knowledge. The *caveat* is apposite because he never proposed anything which would suggest his leaning towards one of the views that, *later on*, would have been qualified as externalist—let it be reliabilism, relevant alternative theories, counterfactual analyses, etc. All he seems to have done is to introduce a certain kind of move, which would then become the typical externalist manoeuvre. Namely, the move according to which one can know that *p* even if one is unable to prove that one does. In other words, Moore denied (1).

The evidence in Moore's writings that he would deny (1) is plenty.[28] For instance, in PEW, he quite explicitly said that neither he nor anyone else *may have been able to prove* the truth of his premises:

> [If what is required is a general proof for the existence of physical objects], (t)his, of course, I haven't given; and I do not believe it can be given: if that is what is meant by proof of the existence of external things, I do not believe that any proof of the existence of external things is possible. (149)

---

[28] Sosa 2007, 50 concurs with this appraisal.

Yet, he was adamant that such an impossibility wouldn't have impaired the fact that he did know them. To repeat the relevant quotation:

> I can know things which I cannot prove; and among the things which I certainly did know, even if (as I think) I could not prove them, were the premises of my ... [proof]. (150)

In the recent literature on scepticism it is often remarked that if one makes this kind of move, one will then face some 'crisis of intellectual conscience' or 'angst'.[29] That is to say, it is conceded that one may know that p, even if one is unable to prove it. Yet, one wouldn't be able to reassure oneself that one does. Scepticism, on this reading, wouldn't directly challenge one's knowledge but, rather, one's ability rationally to *redeem* it. Hence, scepticism wouldn't be characterized by (1), but by:

> (2) If you can't show how you know that p—that is *prove* that you know it—and can't therefore, rationally redeem your claim to knowledge, you may know that p, but you can't reassure yourself of it.

Thus, scepticism brings about an 'intellectual crisis', at least *prima facie*, because, even supposing that through a gift of nature, as it were, we knew that p, we would also feel the intellectual need to be able to prove that we really do.

The problem then becomes that of explaining the sources and legitimacy of this intellectual need. The issue is subtle, yet, I believe, of the utmost epistemological and meta-epistemological significance. In particular, a supporter of this view will have to claim that we have just an externalist notion of knowledge—which makes us hold that we know that p even if we can't say how—and then a sort of self-reflective spontaneous attitude which forces us to look for an explanation of how that knowledge may have come about. Scepticism would thus be due to such a deeply rooted human attitude. Yet, it would have no bearing on whether we possess knowledge. One may then try to explain why, adaptively, it would be useful for us to have such an attitude; by saying, for instance, that it forces us to make inquiries, which sometimes show that we don't really know what we thought we knew. Hence, that attitude prevents us from indulging in mistakes. Moreover, such inquiries into the sources of our knowledge may actually increase it, by providing an explanation of how it comes about. A case in point, which exemplifies both aspects, is that of chicken sex tellers. For, by inquiring into their ability, it was discovered that it is based on the operations of the sense of smell and, thereby, the incorrect belief that it depended on sight and touch was removed. One may then say that the price to pay, its advantages notwithstanding, is that at times such a self-reflective attitude gets in the way of our recognition of our real epistemic status and makes us worry when

---

[29] The former phrase is Wright's (2004a, 167, 210–11); the latter is Pritchard's (2005); similar remarks have been made by Stroud 1994.

there is no need to. The circumstances in which Moore claimed to know that there was a hand where he seemed to see it would just be an example of this down-side of our self-reflective attitude. For clearly he knew that there was a hand in what appeared to be cognitively optimal conditions. But, of course, if our self-reflective attitude kicks in and demands that we provide a proof of the fact that those are indeed optimal conditions, how could we accomplish such a task? We could only set into operation the same cognitive faculties in the same kind of optimal conditions for which the problem of how we could prove them to be reliable and optimal respectively was raised. Hence, we would be caught up in a circle which would prevent us from being able to prove that we know what we take ourselves to know.[30]

Faced with this charge, an externalist could either insist and say that, provided one does know that here is one's hand, one would also be able to prove, via (successive steps of something like) Moore's proof, that one does know that one's sense organs are working reliably, that one isn't dreaming, and so forth. Surely we won't be able to settle the issue against an opponent that *doubts* that our sense organs are working reliably, that we aren't victims of lucid and sustained dreams, etc., because such an opponent would not concede that we know that there is a hand in the first place. But this is simply a dialectical failure which doesn't impugn our knowledge. Furthermore, an externalist should notice that the sceptic would raise a doubt that, on closer inspection, is illegitimate because it would be grounded on a mistaken conception of knowledge. Or else, an externalist should concede that we do have knowledge but can't actually prove that we know that our sense organs are working reliably and that we aren't victims of lucid and sustained dreams. He should, moreover, recommend that we had better tame our self-reflective attitude whenever its setting into motion would get in our way by raising challenges that can't, *in principle*, be met. Be that as it may, both kinds of explanation would also have a meta-epistemological consequence: that of casting doubt—albeit for different reasons—on the legitimacy of the sceptical challenge.

In my view, Moore somehow anticipated, in many respects, the kind of approach that epistemic externalists have developed after him. It remains, however, that most of his contemporaries, and in particular Wittgenstein, were firmly rooted in an internalist conception of knowledge and, accordingly, thought that Moore was altogether missing the point. Equally, it is true that Moore did not develop that 'externalist' strategy and, in particular, while discarding what nowadays is somewhat the standard externalist response to 'bootstrapping' arguments, he did not offer a diagnosis of why the sceptical challenge would be illegitimate by the lights of an externalist epistemologist. All these factors may explain both why he was criticized by his contemporaries and why, also nowadays, quite independently of one's epistemological preferences, which may even go in that very same direction, one may find Moore's strategy somewhat unconvincing. Yet, it is obvious that he had the great merit of individuating a series of propositions, in

---

[30] For a discussion and different appraisals of these forms of 'bootstrapping' arguments, see Sosa 1994; Cohen 2002, 2005; Vogel 2000, 2008; and Wedgwood forthcoming.

PEW as well as in DCS, for which it is a genuine challenge to understand whether we bear an epistemic relation to them. Moreover, he had the merit of expressing, perhaps inappropriately, the commonsensical intuition that no matter how unprovable these propositions turn out to be, we would never give them up. This was the important lesson Wittgenstein learnt from Moore and which, I think, can be of interest to contemporary epistemology as well, once further developed.

34.5 Moore's Proof: A Wittgensteinian Assessment

So much for the 'historical' Moore, as it were, which has let us see that his views would best be developed within a broadly externalist framework about knowledge (and/or warrant), which addressed also the issue of the legitimacy of the sceptical challenge of proving that one knows the premises of the proof.[31]

However, Moore's proof could be of interest also to theorists of an internalist persuasion. They would presumably be united in thinking that it ultimately teaches us that our warranted or even known empirical beliefs rest on assumptions which can't in turn be known or (at least evidentially) warranted. The problem, from their point of view, would then be whether this lesson is after all compatible with an anti-sceptical position; or whether it would play straight into a sceptic's hands.

I actually believe this is one of the main problems Wittgenstein was addressing in *On Certainty*. Before looking at his proposed solution, however, let me point out that it is often thought that his assessment of the proof was rather disparaging and probably based on several misunderstandings or, at least, on different views about meaning and knowledge, which caused him and Moore to pass each other by. I think this assessment is largely correct, if we focus on Wittgenstein's claims in OC about Moore's use of 'I know' in relation to the premises of his proof and if we insist on his failure to distinguish between the conditions that must be fulfilled in order for *knowledge* to be attained and what makes *claims* to knowledge correct.[32] I won't go over this aspect of Wittgenstein's critique here,[33] for we have already seen at least the gist of it by presenting Malcolm's assessment of the proof (§ 34.2.1). What I would like to point out, rather, is what Wittgenstein thought Moore's proof could nevertheless teach us. One negative lesson we have already seen by discussing Wright is that the proof can't give one a warrant

---

[31] Sosa 1994 and Pritchard 2005, 2007 provide, in my opinion, such a development, though in different ways.

[32] In Coliva 2010b, ch. 2 I have addressed more fully these views and criticized those readings of OC, such as Morawetz (1978), Williams (2004a, 2004b), and Pritchard (2011) that argue that in OC Wittgenstein drew such a distinction.

[33] I have done it at length in Coliva 2010b, ch. 2.

to believe its conclusion. For, in order to have a perceptual warrant for one's specific empirical beliefs, it is necessary already to *assume*—at least—that there is an external world, while having a certain course of experience. Wittgenstein, however, never thought that such an assumption could rationally be grounded, let alone known. Rather, he held the view that our relationship to 'There is an external world' wasn't epistemic in nature and that this was, positively, what paying attention to Moore's proof would teach us. Namely, that at the bottom of our epistemic practices lie assumptions which can't be warranted or known, yet can't be doubted either, contrary to what a Humean sceptic would have us believe.

But why, on a Wittgensteinian perspective, can't assumptions such as 'There is an external world' be doubted? In Wittgenstein's view, this can't be due to the fact that since this is a proposition of common sense (or is at least entailed by it), it is known no matter what, as Moore held. Nor could it be because we have some kind of non-evidential warrant—call it 'entitlement'—for it, as Wright has been arguing for lately (2004a), partly followed by Williams.[34] For it is true that Wittgenstein wrote that 'it belongs to the *logic* [my emphasis] of our scientific investigations that certain things are *in deed* not doubted' (OC 341). However, it would be a mistake to infer from this that he thought that we would be non-evidentially warranted in assuming propositions such as 'There is an external world'. In fact Wittgenstein resolutely denied that our basic assumptions are either true or false (OC 196–206), either justified or unjustified, known or unknown (OC 110, 121, 130, 166) and, lastly, either rational or not rational (OC 559). Furthermore, it should be kept in mind that by the time of OC, Wittgenstein was using the term 'logic' (mostly) as a synonym of 'grammar', which was in turn understood in a broad sense so as to include not only linguistic rules but also other kinds of *norms*, such as those of *evidential significance*.[35] That is to say, those 'hinges' (OC 342) that must stay put if our experience is to give us a warrant for ordinary empirical beliefs. So, I take the gist of OC to be that our relationship to propositions like 'There is an external world' is resolutely *non-epistemic*. For they are normative in nature—though rules of evidential significance rather than of meaning—and can't therefore be sensibly doubted.

Moreover, since assuming 'There is an external world' is, according to Wittgenstein, a condition of possibility of all empirical warrants both in favour of specific empirical propositions and of reasonable doubt about them, that proposition is susceptible neither of epistemic support, nor of doubt, since all empirical reasons—including those which would make a doubt about it *rational*—would presuppose taking it for granted. Yet, for Wittgenstein, a doubt which *can't* be supported by reasons would also violate the

---

[34] Williams 2004a, 2004b. Williams exploits the idea of non-evidential warrants and further argues that in OC Wittgenstein thought that the presuppositions of our epistemic language-games are true. He then concludes that Wittgenstein held they were known, even if they couldn't be claimed to be known. Notice, however, that for Williams this doesn't apply to 'There is an external world', as he argues that Wittgenstein thought that it was sheer nonsense. I beg to disagree, though I can't expound on this issue here. I discuss Wright's and Williams' positions at length in Coliva 2010b, ch. 3.

[35] Wright 1985 and Moyal-Sharrock 2005 have made this point.

criteria that govern the use of 'to doubt' and would thus be *meaningless*. Therefore, no rational and intelligible doubt could be raised with respect to 'There is an external world' in his view.

Of course, nowadays, not many epistemologists would agree with the claim that 'There is an external world' is a norm and with a conception of meaning whereby if doubt is unsupported by reasons it is meaningless. In these respects contemporary epistemology is much more Moorean in spirit than Wittgensteinian. So, an interesting question is how much of Wittgenstein's overall, radically non-epistemic approach to Moore's proof one could retain in the context of a present-day, broadly internalist epistemology.

My own view[36]—which I can only sketch here—is that a new Wittgensteinian should abandon the normative conception of assumptions such as 'There is an external world', while insisting that that proposition can't be warranted—either evidentially or non-evidentially. In order not to play straight into a sceptic's hands, however, he should then point out that that assumption is constitutive of what we, as well as sceptics, take *epistemic rationality* to be. For epistemic rationality constitutively depends on the practice of producing, assessing, and withdrawing from empirical beliefs. Such a practice, in its turn, depends on taking for granted that there is an external world, so that we can take our sensory evidence to speak for or against beliefs about physical objects in our surroundings. A new Wittgensteinian should then insist that the assumption that there is an external world—as unwarranted as it is—lies *within* the scope of epistemic rationality if only at its *limit*, for it is its condition of possibility. To notice this, moreover, allows a new Wittgensteinian to diagnose the (Humean) sceptical mistake as due to the failure of appreciating the width of our own notion of epistemic rationality, which extends also to those assumptions that—while unwarranted and unwarrantable—make it possible.[37] Finally, a new Wittgensteinian should maintain that to say that an unwarrantable assumption is constitutive of epistemic rationality does not provide one with a non-evidential warrant for that very assumption, contrary to what Wright and Williams have recently claimed. Rather, it simply provides one with a reason for the second-order claim, as it were, that sceptics are wrong to think that just because that assumption isn't warranted, it falls outside the scope of epistemic rationality.[38] A new Wittgensteinian should also point out that that assumption is needed in order to have perceptual warrants. Hence, a sceptic would be wrong in holding that only if it were warranted in its turn could we have warrants for ordinary beliefs about empirical objects. Thus, the sceptical challenge would in fact be *dissolved*, rather than solved.

---

[36] See Coliva 2010c, already anticipated in Coliva 2007 and further developed in Coliva 2011, 2012, and forthcoming.

[37] Wright's diagnosis, in contrast, is that it consists in failing to see the width of our notion of *warrant*, which would include both evidential and non-evidential warrants.

[38] Hence, I submit, our notion of epistemic rationality is captured by the following disjunction: holding an empirical proposition true is epistemically rational if (and only if) either we have evidential warrant for it or, while unwarrantable, it is itself a condition of possibility of acquiring evidential warrants for other empirical propositions.

It wouldn't be solved because no warrant for the assumption that there is an external world would be provided. Yet, it would be dissolved because the entailment from the lack of warrant for such an assumption to its lying outside the scope of epistemic rationality would be blocked. Similarly, the entailment from the lack of warrant for that assumption to the unwarrantedness of our ordinary beliefs in propositions about specific empirical objects, such as 'Here is a hand', would be blocked.

It is worth pointing out how such a new Wittgensteinian account would have a bearing also on the assessment of Moore's proof. For, as I have argued elsewhere (Coliva 2011), it would lead one to acknowledge that the proof exemplifies a deeper and more basic kind of failure of transmission of warrant than the one first presented by Wright. Accordingly, an argument such as Moore's would exhibit this new kind of failure of warrant transmission because merely *assuming* its conclusion—as opposed to also *having warrant* for it[39]—would be necessary in order to have warrant for its premises in the first place. Therefore, Moore's proof could not be used to produce warrant for its very conclusion. If so, however—and this is indeed an important consequence—we would also explain why, in a limited amount of cases, the Principle of Closure across known entailment for epistemic operators such as warrant would fail. For Moore's proof would be a valid argument whose premises are warranted—given the assumption that there is an external world and a certain course of experience. Yet, by allowing for such a kind of transmission failure, it would then turn out that the warrant one does have for its premises can't give one warrant for the conclusion. Thus, by going Wittgensteinian we would also—surprisingly, perhaps—vindicate Fred Dretske's and Robert Nozick's views on the Principle of Closure.

So, to sum up and conclude, the study of Moore's proof from a historical point of view points out two broad ways of understanding it, which we may call, for convenience, 'externalist' and 'internalist', respectively. The former, which, to my mind, is more philologically accurate and sympathetic to Moore's overall strategy, needs to be developed along two dimensions. For it will have to rely on an externalist notion of knowledge and develop a response against the legitimacy of the sceptical challenge. The latter, in contrast, will find epistemic fault in Moore's proof, yet will take it to show an important point; namely that we can't have (at least evidential) warrants for assumptions such as 'There is an external world'. This opens up the problem of explaining how such an outcome is compatible with an anti-sceptical position and, I have argued, one profitable way of meeting this challenge is to endorse what I have called a new Wittgensteinian position, alternative in many important respects to both Wright's and Williams' readings of *On Certainty*. Whatever the fate of such an account, it remains that it bears testimony to the interest and relevance that Moore's proof, as well as Wittgenstein's work, still have for contemporary epistemology.

---

[39] The reader will recall that this is in fact Wright's account of transmission failure we briefly presented in § 34.3.1.

References

Works by Moore and list of abbreviations

C   'Certainty', 1959, in PP, 227–51.
DCS   'A Defence of Common Sense', in J. H. Muirhead (ed.), *Contemporary British Philosophy* (2nd series). London: George Allen & Unwin, 1925, 193–223; reprinted in PP, 32–59.
FFS   'Four Forms of Scepticism', 1959, in PP, 196–226.
LM   'Letter to Malcolm', 1949, in SW, 213–16.
PEW   'Proof of an External World', *Proceedings of the British Academy* 25, 1939, 273–300; reprinted in PP, 127–50.
PP   *Philosophical Papers*. London: George Allen & Unwin, 1959.
RMC   'A Reply to my Critics', in P. A. Schillp (ed.), *The Philosophy of G. E. Moore*. Evanston and Chicago: Northwestern University Press, 1942.
SW   *Selected Writings*. London and New York: Routledge, 1993.

Works by Wittgenstein and list of abbreviations

OC   *On Certainty*. Oxford: Blackwell, 1969.

Other references

Ayer, A. J. (1940). *The Foundations of Empirical Knowledge*. London: Macmillan.
Baldwin, T. (1990). *G. E. Moore*. London: Routledge.
Clarke, T. (1972). 'The Legacy of Skepticism', *The Journal of Philosophy* 69(20): 754–69; repr. in M. Williams (ed.), *Scepticism*. Aldershot: Dartmouth, 1993, pp. 287–302.
Cohen, S. (1999). 'Contextualism, Skepticism and the Structure of Reasons', *Philosophical Perspectives* 13: 57–89.
—— (2002). 'Basic Knowledge and the Problem of Easy Knowledge', *Philosophy and Phenomenological Research* 65(2): 309–29.
—— (2005). 'Why Basic Knowledge is Easy Knowledge', *Philosophy and Phenomenological Research* 70: 417–30.
Coliva, A. (2007). 'Lo scetticismo sul mondo esterno'. In A. Coliva (ed.), *Filosofia analitica. Temi e problemi*. Rome: Carocci, pp. 255–80.
—— (2008). 'The Paradox of Moore's Proof', *The Philosophical Quarterly* 58(231): 234–43.
—— (2010a). 'Moore's Proof and Martin Davies' Epistemic Projects', *Australasian Journal of Philosophy* 88(1): 101–16.
—— (2010b). *Moore and Wittgenstein: Scepticism, Certainty and Common Sense*. Basingstoke: Palgrave Macmillan.
—— (2011). 'Varieties of Failure (of Warrant Transmission—What Else?!)', *Synthese*. 189(2), pp. 235–54.
—— (2012). 'Moore's Proof, Liberals, and Conservatives: Is There a (Wittgensteinian) Third Way?' In A. Coliva (ed.), *Mind, Meaning and Knowledge: Themes from the Philosophy of Crispin Wright*. Oxford: Oxford University Press, pp. 323–51.
—— (Forthcoming). 'Moderatism, Transmission Failures, Closure and Humean Scepticism'. In E. Zardini and D. Dodd (eds.), *Contemporary Perspectives on Scepticism and Perceptual Justification*. Oxford: Oxford University Press.

DeRose, K. (1992). 'Contextualism and Knowledge Attributions', *Philosophy and Phenomenological Research* 52(4): 913–29.

Dretske, F. (1970). 'Epistemic Operators', *Journal of Philosophy* 67: 1007–23.

Grice, P. (1957). 'Meaning', *Philosophical Review* 66: 377–88.

Kant, I. (1787). *Kritik der reinen Vernunft*, tr. Norman Kemp Smith as *Critique of Pure Reason*. London: Macmillan, 1929.

MacFarlane, J. (2005). 'The Assessment Sensitivity of Knowledge Attributions'. In T. S. Gendler and J. Hawthorne (eds.), *Oxford Studies in Epistemology 1*. Oxford: Oxford University Press, pp. 197–233.

McGinn, M. (1989). *Sense and Certainty: A Dissolution of Scepticism*. Oxford: Blackwell.

McManus, D. (ed.) (2004). *Wittgenstein and Scepticism*. London and New York: Routledge.

Malcolm, N. (1942). 'Moore and Ordinary Language'. In P. Schillp (ed.), *The Philosophy of G. E. Moore*. Evanston and Chicago: Northwestern University Press, pp. 345–68.

——(1949). 'Defending Common Sense', *Philosophical Review* 58: 201–20; repr. in E. D. Klemke (ed.), *Studies in the Philosophy of G. E. Moore*. Urbana: University of Illinois Press, 1969, pp. 200–19.

Morawetz, T. (1978). *Wittgenstein and Knowledge: The Importance of* On Certainty. Atlantic Highlands, NJ: Humanities Press.

Moyal-Sharrock, D. (2005). *Understanding Wittgenstein's* On Certainty. Basingstoke: Palgrave Macmillan.

Nozick, R. (1981). *Philosophical Explanations*. Cambridge, MA: Harvard University Press.

Nuccetelli, S. and G. Seay (eds.) (2007). *Themes from G. E. Moore: New Essays in Epistemology and Ethics*. Oxford: Oxford University Press.

Pritchard, D. (2005). 'Scepticism, Epistemic Luck and Epistemic *Angst*', *Australasian Journal of Philosophy* 83(2): 185–205.

——(2007). 'How to be a neo-Moorean'. In S. Goldberg (ed.), *Internalism and Externalism in Semantics and Epistemology*. Oxford: Oxford University Press, pp. 68–99.

——(2011). 'Wittgenstein on Scepticism'. In M. McGinn and O. Kuusela (eds.), *The Oxford Handbook of Wittgenstein*. Oxford: Oxford University Press, pp. 523–49.

Pryor, J. (2004). 'What's Wrong with Moore's Argument?', *Philosophical Issues* 14: 349–78.

Sosa, E. (1994). 'Philosophical Skepticism and Epistemic Circularity', *Proceedings of the Aristotelian Society, Supplementary Volume* 68: 263–90.

——(2007). 'Moore's Proof'. In Nuccetelli and Seay (2007), pp. 49–61.

Stroll, A. (1994). *Moore and Wittgenstein on Certainty*. New York: Oxford University Press.

Stroud, B. (1984). *The Significance of Philosophical Scepticism*. Oxford: Clarendon Press.

——(1994). 'Scepticism, "Externalism", and the Goal of Epistemology', *Proceedings of the Aristotelian Society, Supplementary Volume* 68: 291–307.

Travis, C. (1989). *The Uses of Sense*. Oxford: Oxford University Press.

Vogel, J. (2000). 'Reliabilism Leveled', *Journal of Philosophy* 97: 602–23.

——(2008). 'Epistemic Bootstrapping', *Journal of Philosophy* 105: 518–39.

Wedgwood, R. (forthcoming). 'A Priori Bootstrapping'. In A. Casullo and J. Thurow (eds.), *The Apriori in Philosophy*. Oxford: Oxford University Press.

Williams, M. (1992). *Unnatural Doubts: Epistemological Realism and the Basis of Skepticism*. Cambridge, MA: Wiley-Blackwell.

——(2004a). 'Wittgenstein's Refutation of Idealism'. In McManus (2004), pp. 76–96.

——(2004b). 'Wittgenstein, Truth and Certainty'. In M. Kölbel and B. Weiss (eds.), *Wittgenstein's Lasting Significance*. London and New York: Routledge, pp. 249–84.

Wright, C. (1985). 'Facts and Certainty', *Proceedings of the British Academy* 71: 429–72.

—— (2002). 'Anti-Sceptics Simple and Subtle: G. E. Moore and John MacDowell', *Philosophy and Phenomenological Research* 65(2): 330–48.

—— (2004a). 'Warrant for Nothing (and Foundations for Free)?', *Proceedings of the Aristotelian Society, Supplementary Volume* 78: 167–212.

—— (2004b). 'Wittgensteinian Certainties'. In McManus (2004), pp. 22–55.

—— (2007). 'The Perils of Dogmatism'. In Nuccetelli and Seay (2007), pp. 25–48.

CHAPTER 35

THE VARIETIES OF RIGOROUS EXPERIENCE

JULIET FLOYD

THIS essay explores some of the varieties of rigorous experience encountered in modern mathematical philosophy. By 'experience' I do not mean anything phenomenological or psychological, but rather an historical and philosophical investigation of a term of criticism that was central to the early analytic tradition's self-image. I shall explore the question 'How rigorous?', not along a single scale ('How *rigorous*?'), but in terms of a complex, multi-faceted quality ('*How* rigorous?').[1]

I shall not call into question something typical and perfectly acceptable to assume in certain contexts, namely, that the core locale and prerequisite for evaluating the notion of rigour as it is presently used in logic and philosophy is the use of familiar techniques of syntactic and semantic rigorization to achieve gap-free, fully explicit forms of reasoning; precisifications and titrations of consistency strength; conceptual clarification; purification of method; and more. What I seek rather is to place this assumption itself—the nearly automatic equation of 'rigour' with this family of formal techniques in general parlance—into philosophical and historical perspective, reflecting upon some of what it involves and assumes about the history of early analytic and modern mathematical philosophy.

My method is partly historiographical. I propose a widened frame for the history for early analytic philosophy, following a trend in recent work on the history and philosophy of logic and mathematics that questions the oft-repeated assumption that early analytic philosophy began in 1879, with Frege's *Begriffsschrift*, and ended more or less in 1931,

---

[1] In German 'rigorous' may be expressed by '*streng*', as in Frege 1879 (iv), Husserl 1911/1965, *Philosophie als strenge Wissenschaft*, or the famous Wittgenstein remark 'For how can logic lose its rigor (*Strenge*)? Of course not by our bargaining any of its rigor out of it' (2001: §108). But related terms are also linked: '*hart*' and '*rigoros*' (Wittgenstein 2001: §437; 1978: I, §121; VI §49, 'the hardness (*Härte*) of the logical must'). In French '*rigoureux*' may be used, as it is in English, for harshness or difficulty, as in 'the rigours of a cold winter' (see below on *de rigueur*).

with Gödel's incompleteness theorems.[2] The historiographical suggestion—effectively implemented in a number of the pieces I refer to below—is that we ought to press further back in time, exploring nineteenth-century scientific, philosophical, cultural, and mathematical roots.

There is one especially valuable idea in this literature that I shall draw upon below—with debts to others working this vein, occasional hesitations expressed about some of their conclusions along the way, and a number of avenues broached but not developed. The excellent suggestion, due to Sieg, is that we begin the relevant history in 1854, the year of Dedekind's *Habilitationsschrift*, and end it in 1954, when Turing, in the final year of his life, published a popular scientific article in *Science News*, 'Solvable and Unsolvable Problems'. Dedekind and Turing thus form a new pair of parentheses around the history of modern mathematical philosophy, framing what Sieg has called a '*centuria mirabilis*' (2013, p.8).

Here I use Sieg's idea of the *centuria mirabilis* to generate a more purely philosophical interpretation of the period. The point is to reorient our conception of early analytic (and later analytic) philosophy by focusing reflectively on the concept of rigour. In the course of my investigation I draw a tentative set of conclusions. From these, other reframings of the vast literature on rigorization might follow—as well as reframings of early twentieth-century philosophy, the history of modern philosophy generally, and perhaps also of modernism as a cultural phenomenon. Here I have sufficient space only to sketch a number of suggestions that have so far sprung to mind. I wish, however, to urge that larger prospects lie before us for revisiting and reframing the early analytic tradition, and the history of philosophy more generally, in new and instructive ways.

35.1 RIGOUR AND RESIDUE

A heightened insistence on the centrality of the notion of rigour is often and rightly said to be fundamental to, and characteristic of, the analytic tradition in philosophy (see, e.g., Soames 2003: xiii). But how are we to understand this? The usual story emphasizes principled norms of argumentation and clarity, but this hardly suffices to illuminate the notion of rigour without elaboration. Other traditions in philosophy and mathematics, and even within the arts, can claim to have achieved this much. Within philosophy proper, not only the most famed of the early analytic philosophers (Frege, Moore, Russell, and early Wittgenstein), but also the phenomenologists fastened on the notion's importance to foundations (Husserl 1911/1965), and there were mathematicians, e.g., Poincaré and Brouwer, who denied that rigour could appropriately be reduced within the terms of formal analyses of mathematics (Goldfarb 1985; Detlefsen 1993, 2010;

---

[2] In Floyd 2009, I criticized both Soames and Hacker for not going back sufficiently far enough, i.e., to Frege. Here I go further.

Mancosu 1998). In fact, contested notions of rigour informed, quite explicitly, the parting of the ways between early analytic philosophy and phenomenology that became explicit by the mid-1920s.[3]

Obviously the question 'What is the nature of rigour?' admits of no general answer. As a quality, the notion attaches to all kinds of representations, systems of belief, arguments, norms, procedures, methods, and manners of articulation. In the history of mathematics it indexes what might be called the 'culture' of proof (Chemla 2003; Gray 2008), but there is not one notion here, because the notion evolves (Kleiner 1991; Crowe 1988). Different philosophers and mathematicians use the term for different purposes, and there is much debate, even for single philosophers, about how best to understand uses of the notion. Rigour is an ideal or value attaching to different practices, problems, and purposes, taking on different colourings on different occasions.

There is then a question whether the term 'rigour' is ambiguous in an interesting or in an uninteresting way. Clearly in practice the nature and value of *philosophical* rigour lie to a significant extent in the eye of the beholder. As Aristotle insisted, however, these lie also in the nature of the subject matter at hand. Though I shall insist that the notion of rigour is purposive, historically framed, and reflective, I shall not take uses of the notion to be occasion-sensitive in quite the ways that, arguably, the semantics of colour terms, shapes, and human actions are (cf. Travis 2008). Trailing its way through the contested territory of the concept of rigour is, instead, a set of notions that evince a unity that matters for philosophy, a unity to which nearly every participant in the history of mathematics and philosophy would have agreed. At least there are sufficiently recognizable affinities among uses of the notion to let us see that norms of trust, tradition, authority, control, precision, systematicity, purity, strictness, clarity, reflectiveness, simplification, articulation, and communication are involved near its centre.

What I wish to resist here is a tendency—among analytic philosophers as well as philosophically minded historians of early analytic philosophy and mathematics—to assume that the notion of rigour is relatively clear, perhaps even admitting of a kind of 'absolute' measure (Ferreirós and Gray 2006). Philosophically, logically, and historically speaking, this idea strikes me to be in need of proper framing. This framing, as we shall see, involves us in interesting, distinctively philosophical reflection on our aims and capacities. This itself highlights an important fact: every analysis, and every rigorization, leaves an interpretive need behind, the trail where the human serpent brings philosophy and knowledge into the garden.

An important outcome of the formalization of deductive reasoning provided by Frege, Russell and Whitehead, Hilbert, and others is that philosophers and philosophically minded mathematicians have become quite self-conscious—as I shall argue here, more rigorous—about the status of appeals to (what they call by turns) commonsensical,

---

[3] Heidegger took modern uses of the notion to be dominated by scientific ideals of representational accuracy, mathematization, and precision, ideals lacking a pre-modern emphasis on facticity (1929, 1938). Carnap 1937 embraced this story, but advocated the modern, scientific perspective.

intuitive, pragmatic, elucidatory, explicative, contextual, heuristic, phenomenological, and informal aspects of argument. There has tended to be a certain heightened insistence on being scrupulous about informality at the basic level of foundational questions, i.e., places where currently recognizable methods of rigorization (definition, formalization, axiomatization) give out, or where the propaedeutics of science as such begin. Following a pattern of prior usage, I shall call this whole issue, very loosely, one of *residue*.[4]

The point of focusing on residue is certainly not to reject the idea of rigour as formalization. Yet among philosophical lessons to be drawn from my focus here is the idea that true rigour involves seeing certain concepts, mathematical developments, and idealizations with a realistic, reflective, and yet critical eye (Wittgenstein 1978: VI §23; Diamond 1991). This tends to involve one in articulating the *point* (or *purposes*) of identifying a logical shareable in a certain context or contexts. We need to be able to articulate in each case—however differently—something about why we care about rigour, and what makes it appropriate or inappropriate as a demand. Identifying or qualifying or contesting the naturalness or satisfactoriness or range of applicability of a generalization, reduction, or novel conceptual systematization is not a simple matter of an undifferentiated category of pragmatics. It contributes and requires rigour as well, sometimes of a distinctively philosophical, sometimes of a distinctively logical or mathematical kind. Sometimes these kinds overlap, and in subtle ways. For, in the end, rigour is a *purposive* notion. As such it is a *reflective* one: it illuminates, and depends upon, *us*: our ideas, demands, interests, and articulations.

One pattern I shall emphasize here is the task of articulating how to recognize the familiar in a rigorization: that aspect of the notion stressing intersubjective communicability as part and parcel of our notion of the objective. Beginning with Moore, naturalness and common sense were explicitly pursued within the analytic tradition, as is often noted. But not, as I shall be arguing, for their own sakes. Instead, their pursuit emerged within the framework of a more generally modernist objective of rigour, encompassing a drive to recognize ideals in the concrete, as self-standing and directly presented to us in an inclusive, rather than an esoteric, way.

The pursuit continued through the later development of analytic philosophy, for example in so-called 'ordinary language' philosophy. Far from overturning or trivializing the contributions of modern mathematical logic, this tradition, inspired in significant part by Ryle, Austin, and Wittgenstein, may be seen to have attempted to qualify and situate formal logic's tools with respect to our conceptions (and practices) of utterance—another form of rigorization, to be sure, but a form of rigorization nonetheless.

---

[4] Here 'residue' is not a natural kind, but a higgledy-piggledy job lot of a notion, fashioned as shorthand. It includes, e.g., metaphors or stipulations appealed to in motivating particular precisifications, as well as a sense of experience involved in the use of the term by Turing: the 'residue' of initiative, experience, and intuition that we may more broadly aim to copy or offload onto or encode in machines (Turing 1948/1992: 125; cf. Sieg 2007). It might also include philosophical uses of the notion tied directly either to Kant or to intuitionism (Heyting 1956: 106) or to attacks upon formalism as a philosophy of mathematics (cf. Wang 1961, on which see Floyd 2011), though I do not regard these as fundamental for my purposes.

Wittgenstein argued explicitly that without the friction of design constraints from some direction or other, without some room to discuss our purposes (or at least possible purposes) in analysing, as well as our errors and interests, formal or logical rigour has insufficient foothold (2001: §§107, 242). This was not, as I see it, intended to face us with a methodological choice between ordinary language and artificial or formalized languages—much less a choice between rigour and non-rigour, or between the end of philosophy or logic, as we know them, and their pursuit. Instead, it was to advise us to look to the newfound complexities of their interplay as we pursue and articulate philosophy first-order: avoiding the temptation to reduce philosophy to a taxonomy of 'isms' or philosophy of 'philosophy'. 'First-order', in this sense, is a constraint, i.e., the laying down of a demand for a certain kind of rigour.

My method, applying this advice, will be to look to the purposes shaping rigorizations within the rise of modern mathematical philosophy. I shall argue that the effort to regain the familiar—some form of appropriate friction for the notion of rigour—had a formal counterpart that emerged *within* the development of the modern mathematical tradition. I take Turing's success in analysing the very notion of a formal system by way of his human-oriented model, the 'Turing machine', to have provided a formal counterpart to the idea of looking to our purposes and the everyday in using logic, i.e., a focus on our capacity for making objects, standards, and procedures intelligible to ourselves and communicable when we 'rigorize'. Turing rigorized the very idea of formally rigorizing precisely by so looking. This, as I see it, had fundamental philosophical—and not merely mathematical or scientific or psychological—value.

35.2 MODERNISM

The very idea of an absolute or complete measure of rigour is characteristic of modernism generally, whether we are speaking of the arts or the sciences. But what senses of 'absolute' are at stake? And what are we to understand modernism to be, such that attention to rigour is characteristic of it?

As the twentieth century progressed, throughout the sciences, mathematics, and the arts and humanities generally, the rhetoric of rigour was connected with an aspiration to become specialized and fully thoroughgoing, unified, self-critical, grounded, and systematic, especially at the foundations. This aspiration expressed itself in the idea of making philosophy (and other subjects, such as history and the social sciences) 'scientific' and/or 'rigorous' (cf. Putnam 1997; Schorske 1997). There were of course competing ideas about what these aims involved and required. But even among those who questioned the idea of philosophy modelled on natural science (e.g., Dilthey, Heidegger, and their followers), an effort was made to rigorize under the banner of philosophy, to shore thought up in the face of the eclecticism, historicism, idealism, and revolutionary transformations at work in late nineteenth-century thought.

The notion of rigour is *reflective* insofar as it crucially involves us in setting forth standards of procedure for ourselves, fitting means to ends, settling on standards that are suited to a particular subject matter and to ourselves—of course given present methods, problems, and aims (cf. Aristotle 1985: Bk. I, §2). Its use carries with it a presumption that we face choices and contingencies in our design of standards, that we have ends and interests, both cognitive and practical, and that we are better off attempting to control the production of what we want rather than allowing it to emerge haphazardly or with piecemeal guesswork alone.

The shift toward 'modernism', linked with a shift toward scientism, was one in which concrete, familiar objects previously known and encountered would be asked to display the very concept of an object, concept, theory, system, or method. In this display, form—coincident now with content—would follow function or end. Extraneous ornament and any needless machinery of eclecticism would be excised. This forced a reconsideration of the very idea of what it is to represent, what it is to be a system or object of thought, and what it *is* to fit an everyday object into the articulated parameters of a system.

This general emphasis on precisification of standards was rooted, of course, in earlier developments internal to specific subjects. But mathematics led the way. As Kant had insisted, 'there is only so much science in a subject as there is mathematics'; for this reason, he argued, there could never be a science of the soul, or inner sense (1786/2004: 7). During the late nineteenth and early twentieth centuries mathematics was transformed into a 'modern', if not an intensively self-reflective, 'modernist' subject.[5] The subject had been vastly enriched for over a century: it was an exceptional period, described by Russell as one culminating in 'the discovery of pure mathematics' (1901).

The backdrop to modernist mathematics was one of quantitative and qualitative richness, variety, and eclecticism, not purity in the sense of uniformity. What appeared were novel projections and characterizations of known concepts and theories, widened generalizations and combinations of subjects, new forms of domain extension, model construction and unification, geometrical and computational sophistication, generalized algebraic thinking, increased sophistication in the applications of mathematics, and, finally, entirely new subjects (set theory, topology, mathematical logic; cf. Hallett 2003: 128ff.). Mathematics changed from a subject dealing with apparently natural, traditional objects and familiar patterns of reasoning (numbers, Euclidean geometrical constructions, space, quantity, magnitude, algebraic equations) into a subject preoccupied with confronting its own modes of reasoning and ways of demarcating and securing its objects and domains using novel reconceptualizations and novel objects (e.g., 'system', 'transformation', 'duality', 'set', 'group', 'space', 'lattice', 'structure', and 'model').[6]

---

[5] Benis-Sinaceur 2002; Kennedy and Van Atten 2004; Ferreirós and Gray 2006; Ferreirós 2007: 463–5; Gray 2008. Ferreirós and Gray (2006: 1ff.) date the modernist period 1890–1930. Broadly cultural analyses of modernism include Gray 2006; Richardson 2002; Galison 1990, 1996; Corry forthcoming; and Epple and Müller forthcoming.

[6] The newness and strangeness of sets as objects in the nineteenth century is stressed in Kanamori (1996); this has been disputed by Ferreirós (2011).

In 1902 Husserl, responding to these trends, characterized mathematics (not logic) as the science of theoretical systems in general, as opposed to the old mathematics of *Quantitätsmathematik*.[7] And Peirce took himself to be bringing what he called 'modern' mathematics to bear on logic, by which he meant, not merely post-Cartesian mathematics, but modern 'abstract' algebra and topology (2010: xvi, 68ff., 87, 177, 209).

In the end, it was the appearance of new kinds of definitions, structural approaches, styles of comparison, conceptual recarvings,[8] proof methods, and axiomatizations in analysis, number theory, algebra, and geometry that brought a focus on deductive methods onto centre stage to a degree not seen since the Greeks. The impulse to organize an understanding of proof methods and to manifestly display our concept of objecthood as such were responses, not to a loss of certainty in the face of paradox, sloppiness, or ontological profligacy, but to the rising variegation within mathematics as a whole. Demands for rigour in deductive articulation emerged from the overall need to compare and contrast theories as much as from the emergence of particular contradictions encountered in the precisification of logic.[9]

This need, and the attendant drives are, of course, quite traditional. Analysis's long and unified history in mathematics and philosophy lies in the idea of the regressive method (cf. Beaney 2007b, 2003/2009). Implemented in the context of the axiomatic method, it offers a nuanced and complex conception of the purpose(s) of rigorization, a conception capable of illustrating and instantiating larger themes. The general procedural idea is that first, one distils the basic, underlying notions and principles through analysis beginning at the 'naïve' level, working 'backwards' to the assumptions and articulation of the basic definitions, notions, and principles. And then one proceeds 'progressively' or 'synthetically', deducing new truths and, to the greatest (clearest) extent possible, recapturing and representing (re-presenting) the original 'naïve' notions. The entire process takes place in the context of some kind of question, body of theory, or structure of inquiry (such as Euclidean geometrical analysis), and is intended to unearth new questions, notions, and principles as one proceeds, not merely to isolate primitive notions or eliminate uncertainty (cf. Peckhaus 2002).

From Euclid to Kant to Frege to Sartre this general idea of regression and progression to and from principles has shaped the articulation of philosophical and mathematical method. Yet any application of the regressive method involves reinterpretation, or at least resituating, of naïvely or fundamentally given notions, as Russell in particular explicitly emphasized (1907/1973). Analysis involves a confrontation between practice—what one does—and what one says about what one does, all in the name of systematicity, intelligibility, and coherence. A crucial point is that the original, naïve level must be recognizable at the end of the inquiry, remaining captured or seen to be established in some way or other in the analysis.[10] Notions and objects and facts are

---

[7] Husserl 1900/2001: 1–2; cf. Hartimo 2006, 2010, 2011, 2012; Centrone 2010.

[8] For the impact on Frege of this see Wilson (1992/1995, 2005, 2010) and Tappenden (1995).

[9] Cf. Hallett 2003; on the influences of the paradoxes in Göttingen see Mancosu 1998; Peckhaus 2004.

[10] Psychoanalysis took up this idea: the neurotic is to be cured by bringing scattered bits of freely associated experience together, so that they can be incorporated and made familiar and ordinary, systematized fruitfully within a more coherent, truly spontaneous, and integrated self.

recognized, not merely in the sense of being re-cognized, re-individuated, re-presented, re-identified as the same (*erkennen*, in German), but also in the sense of being acknowledged, i.e., tendered or accredited or granted or seen to have been granted an established dominion of some kind (*anerkennen*, in German).[11] In fact the two aspects of the verb 'to recognize' are not wholly separable. But just here is where philosophy tends to enter in, the room for debate. We are to see ourselves leaving from Kansas, and then returning at the end, seeing the place where we began anew. But can we ever go home? Did we ever leave it? What is it to recognize a place as home?

Such questions mark the provenance of modernism as a general cultural and philosophical phenomenon. They serve to illuminate those marks and features of the ordinary concept of rigour that students of early analytic and modern mathematical philosophy should bear in mind. Eliot's famous line that 'We cannot say at what point "technique" begins, and where it ends' is highly relevant to the very idea of modernism and its discontents (1928/1997: ix). To call a poem 'rigorous' may point to features of its structure, means, method, style, and/or theme that are admirably, thoroughly, correctly or cleanly executed, and concisely, recognizably, transparently, or directly conveyed. But application of a technique is not everything, and is usually insufficient to clinch the poem's value as a poem—rigour can be overdone, indicating merely formal dexterousness, superficial finesse, or over-refinement detached from expressive connection with the purpose at hand. At the same time (so for Eliot in 1928), a return to explicit or familiar forms or structures to tighten standards in a practice can instil a heightened sense of rigour, the value of proceeding with limited patterns or means, of doing more with less, or revisiting, recontextualizing, and recovering a sense of lost or more familiar, well-established standards.[12]

Still, it is hardly optimal to be forced to demand agreement on the value of a particular canon of rigour *per se*. Rigour is a value, often an epistemic and sometimes an aesthetic or pedagogic one, but, crucially, it is not everything. It is, to repeat, a reflective and purposive notion, for it is applied when we need to make adjustments in matching means to ends in the pursuit of knowledge. Rigour must be fitted to an object or concept or procedure or branch of knowledge more or less appropriately or adequately. Unlike truth, justification, understanding, and fruitfulness, it is never

---

[11] *Reconnaître* in French, like *recognize* in English, covers both. I avoid the word 'certify', since this invites an image of proof framers as border guards of the true and the false, stamping passports. True recognition requires something more: a systematic articulation, perceivable as such (cf. the history of the notion of *recognition* in nineteenth-century Idealist philosophy).

[12] In the history of painting, loose brushwork must be said, relative to a certain quality of precise representational accuracy, to display its own rigour, especially if it somehow is felt to distil or explain or simplify, showing us a better way of realizing what was essential to the aim of an earlier standard of representational precision, or separating out what was inessential in that former approach to achieve its aims (Rembrandt, the Impressionists, the Cubists, the Abstract Expressionists …). But in other cases deviating from well-known and accepted ('academic') standards of rigour or representational precision may impugn the value of a work. Art itself may of course reflectively (or reflexively) comment on these issues (e.g., Jasper Johns' *Three Flags* 1958, Pop Art).

an end in itself, though its pursuit may crucially serve the acquisition of other ends. Rigour is a virtue to be weighed against and among others, just like simplicity and consistency (with which it is sometimes too easily equated), and its moral or religious roots should not be forgotten. Too much single-minded emphasis upon it, too simple a characterization or handling of it, can stifle its contributions, as well as those of other virtues, and actually hold progress up (*rigor mortis*, failure to evolve) or lead to fanaticism (Kant 1790/2000: 5:275). Rigour begets rigour, but rigour must critique and qualify rigour: reflection on our human powers of conceptual development and systematization keeps knowledge organized, but also organizes us, by keeping an image of human intelligibility, with all its limits and imperfections and contingencies, before us.

Assuming that rationality matters, it is not always rational to place rigour first among virtues, and it is not at all clear that mathematicians ever did so, even during the period of the arithmetization of the calculus that is usually understood as the paradigm example of 'rigorization' (Kitcher 1981). Nor is it obvious that the only possible route to rigour in mathematics is *via* pursuit of the axiomatic method, although in a broad sense this might be a defensible claim (cf. Tait 2005). As I am arguing, rigour is not to be reduced to the identification of elementary patterns of reasoning that identify what are taken to be definitory principles for rationality or knowledge—though there is a long-standing tendency in philosophy, logic, and mathematics of doing this, at least insofar as some hold that the domain of proofs, extensionally speaking, must conform to formal standards of rigour.[13] Even if one holds this, rigour is not reducible to justification, if we mean by that the flat claim that there is some justification or other for a judgement. For the claim that there exists (or does not exist) a proof of a certain kind from certain principles may be established more rigorously than not. And insight may be conveyed more rigorously in an unformalized setting than in a formalized one.

At the same time, being accused of being 'unrigorous' is especially damning. Rigour is connected with *de minimus* conditions of presentation, argumentation, simplicity, or procedure in a practice (*de rigueur*, conforming to current etiquette). Also with routinization, the elimination or reduction of guesswork, *ad hocness*, haphazardness, and potential error. One interest it serves is the transmission of standards in a practice from one generation to the next. It is then often used, not only to shape future practitioners, but also to exclude that which falls out of step. Because of its strong ties to notions of systematicity and intelligibility, rigour is also often associated with heightened normative ideals for epistemic and/or persuasive and/or communicative success: achieving adequacy, eliminating or controlling vagueness, proving where others took principles as self-evident, doing more with less, cutting away unnecessary dross through simplification.

---

[13] Even the anti-deductivist Kitcher (1981, 1984) assumed (at least in this period) that rigour is both a *sine qua non* of the rationality of mathematics and generally tied to the articulation of forms of reasoning which sharpen what is taken to be an elementary logical step.

It is easy to underestimate the fact that modernism—including modernist mathematics and modernist twentieth-century philosophy generally—maintains the presence of a drive toward reconfiguring and incorporating the familiar in the name of defeating esotericism. But as Cavell once argued with regard to modernism in music and the other arts, so in modern mathematical philosophy: the rise of modernism retranslates traditions of composition into its own terms, heightening and making problematic issues of rigour and of trust (1967/1976: 182ff.). Whether we are speaking of the arts, or of mathematics and philosophy, 'modernism only makes explicit and bare what has always been true' (Cavell 1967/1976: 189): the potential for philosophical reflection and dispute that are always embedded in rigorization. Modernist 'rigorizations' led to a certain alienation from the familiar, but also, therefore, to a quest to make the familiar appear in the garb of the fundamental—partly in anticipation of charges of disbelief, or even fraudulence (in the history of mathematics, we must remember Kronecker). The demand for recognition at the *naïve* level that had always been embedded in the use of the regressive method thus remained in modernism, but now heightened and laid bare. This in turn necessitated the quest for reflective recovery, from within broader systematizations, of what was frequently called *naturalness*, *naïveté* or *common sense*.

The modernist aims of recovering naturalness, generality, and perspicuity are not merely, on this view, a matter of focusing on 'the object as such' or 'mere form', a reflection of a wide-ranging interest in 'formalism'. Nor do they evince purely romantic demands for direct, unprecisified confrontations with life.[14] They express, more fundamentally, an enlightenment ideal of communicability, one that earmarks the very idea of the intersubjective validity of the domain of the objective, as Cavell also emphasized (1965). Rigour invokes a set of norms involving the importance of the communicability and intersubjective shareability of knowledge and experience, as well as norms of adequacy and precision. Thus it can be defeated by false or overly precisified forms of rigour, the kind of pseudo-machinery of rigorization that can occur when particular standards are applied or articulated too single-mindedly, with insufficient attention to phenomena of residue.

If one may say that the communicative, humanly intersubjective aspects of the notion of rigour are radicalized in the formal developments that were a prerequisite for the development of modern proof theory and logic (Sieg 2006a), one may also say that these formed a quite traditional ideal, just newly thematized, negotiated, transposed, and exploited (cf. Stein 1988). Here, I shall take this to imply that certain aspirations to philosophical rigour cannot be reduced without qualification to a foundational ideal of deductive explicitness, precisification of vague or intuitive ideas, minimization of principles, or formalization—much less to ideals of rationality and/or intuition—any more

---

[14] There is, however, a relation to the history of romanticism, as Cavell has also long emphasized (1988); cf. Beaney (2003/2009) on 'romantic' objections to decompositional analyses.

than mathematical rigour in general can be. Ideals of reasonableness, in the Rawlsian sense, enter into many of these notions' uses in practice, as do ideals of adequacy, accuracy, suitability, transparency, completeness, simplicity, and vividness.[15] Although rigour is in no way reducible to these notions in every case, their frequent presence as aspects of the notion should be highlighted.

35.3 MOORE

We have as good an example of modernist philosophy as any in G. E. Moore. Moore made a modernist move when he claimed that his proof of the external world, deduced from ostension of his hand, is a 'perfectly rigorous one; and that it is perhaps impossible to find a better or more rigorous proof of anything whatever' (Moore 1939/1959: 146; cf. 145–7). He meant, minimally, that his series of claims possessed as well as any other the expected virtues and form of an argument: rigour means here that the premises are all different from the conclusion, the conclusion follows by logic from the premises, the claims are not vague, but direct and to the point, and that he knew his premises to be true. Yet it is also clear that he took himself to have reached an ultimate point, logically speaking, vis-à-vis the sceptic, idealist, or insister on the mind-dependence of truth. He achieved—or appeared to achieve—something: not only a remarkable philosophical simplification, but also successful critique of the overuse of certain logical methods of argumentation in philosophy. This was achieved by disentangling the notions of rigour and conclusiveness from their false rendition in the logical machinery of Idealism.

For Moore rejected the request of some philosophers to say how it was that he knew his premises to be true. He invoked a notion of rigour in rejecting the need for any (further) proof of the existence of the external world, *punkt*. His claim to the rigour of his exhibition lay in the fact that he intended his argument to be in some way reductive, boiling the question as to the existence of the external world down to the simplest, most conclusive, most lucid, and most direct, self-reflective and transparent elements. He thereby highlighted the need for at least some judgements to be held fixed in discussion if the notions of proof, truth, and argument are to be applicable. Moore embraced the principle that philosophy is not to overturn the obvious, or make what is fundamental seem not to be so. But he was also an advocate of a certain heightened sense of rigour,

---

[15] For Rawls the reasonable has to do with terms that can be offered to an interlocutor that that interlocutor could reasonably be expected to share, accept, and adhere to. It cannot be equated with the idea of 'whatever allows us to avoid error' in designing social institutions, though it is arguably an element of rigour in democratic theory Rawls conceptualizes as central. Importantly, the notion of the reasonable is neither definable nor reducible to the rational (Rawls 1997/1999). I find it analogous in status to the idea of a *sensus communis*, or common sense, at work in Kant's third *Critique* (see Floyd 2007).

reaching for a communicable fundamental, perceivable as such, and perceivable there-fore as free-standing—i.e., not dependent upon, or anyway minimally dependent upon, a metaphysical or logical or epistemic theory (cf. Rawls 1985/1999, 1996 for the idea of a 'free-standing' conception).

The difficulty in Moore's case, of course, is that his 'proof', in all its vividness and concreteness, has seemed to many utterly unpersuasive and darkly difficult to under-stand, despite being the sort of proof that can be reproduced, producing smiles, for just about any audience. Is what Moore proves capable of proof? (Real proof, con-vincing proof, not merely formal arrangements of sentences we take or assume to be known, as Wittgenstein stressed (1974: §1).) The primary problem with Moore's argument lies not, I think, in the fact that he had insufficiently analysed the notions involved (e.g., that of physical object, or perceived thing, or knowledge, or proof), or the role played by the circumstances of his utterance—though it is true, as he admit-ted, that he had not, and this in itself provided an invitation for later philosophers to ponder how such analyses might help to clarify ('rigorize') his proof.[16] Rather, I think one must question Moore's notion of 'perfect' rigour itself. Is this an illuminating notion?

Russell, for one, suggested that it was not, being a 'scarcely attainable ideal' even in mathematics (1993: 144). But Moore felt Russell's standards were either too high or wrongheaded, reducing the idea of perfect rigour to something like absolute certainty, proved to be such—a Fata Morgana, as he saw it. One lesson to draw from Moore then (not, perhaps, his own) would be that any form of perfect rigour, even conceived as an unattainable ideal, is inevitably subject to a lasting residue of interpretation and argu-mentation. Rigour, even perfect rigour, has to be articulated and seen to have a point: it must be recognizable. Furthermore, any articulation takes place on a certain occasion, even if what is articulated (and extrapolated from that articulation) is a generalizable technique, concept, proposition, principle, or method. So there must always be some-thing further to say, on a given occasion (or in a given historical period) even about the structure of what is in fact perfectly plain.

Moore opened early analytic epistemology up to this possibility, to the philo-sophical difficulty facing any articulation or communication of the structure (or the circle, in something akin to the sense of the Cartesian one) of the plain or the obvious itself. He showed us its philosophical significance.[17] He bequeathed to ana-lytic epistemology the question of how to see what is obvious as obvious and still be able to see and successfully to say (without dogmatism or unclarity or inability to critique it) what precisely one is doing (or saying) on a given occasion in calling something obvious.

---

[16] Moore himself stressed the distinction between understanding something and knowing its correct analysis: one could have the first without the second. But Wittgenstein explicitly questioned whether the everyday sentence 'I can't be making a mistake' *can* be understood in a wholly rigorous sense (*in ganz strengem Sinne*) (1974: §669).

[17] Cf. Clarke 1972; Stroud 1972/2000, 1984; Hamawaki 2014.

There may be no hope of such an articulation without some prior understandings among us. This itself is a familiar idea, often drawn from Wittgenstein (cf., e.g., Travis 2006). My question here, however, is more self-reflexive and more deeply entwined with the very idea of logic as foundational: Is there a formal counterpart to Moore's move? That is: can a modern, mathematically articulated formal system of logic be regarded as something perfectly plain? What *is* a formal system, in general? What *is* the notion of taking a step in a formalized language? How are we to make rigorous sense of these ideas themselves? What prior understandings among us about rigour—in this case deductive rigour—need to be in place to get the logical into proper view?

Here is a cluster of modernist questions *par excellence*.

35.4 LIMITATIVE RESULTS

There is of course a mathematical way of taking the idea of residue. In the end, as is well known, the work of Frege, Russell, Hilbert, Gödel, Tarski, Carnap, Church, Turing, and others defeated the idea of a single instrument articulable in the frame of a formal system for resolving problems in the foundations of mathematics once and for all. The fact that there is no single elementary point of view was balanced, of course, by the mathematical development of proof theory, model theory, and computability theory. But this balance remains one to be negotiated in specific contexts, as we now see. This reinforces the idea that part and parcel of the notion of rigour, even if we understand by that formal deductive rigour, means being clear about the limitations of that very concept of rigour itself, qualifying its scope and application. Rigour may beget further rigour, but rigour is also sometimes required to rigorously understand the nature of standards of rigour.

In an essay published in the last year of his life (one in which he aimed to make the recent limitative results user-friendly) Turing stated that an implication of the incompleteness theorems is that an appeal to 'common sense' is inevitable for a mathematician:

> These [limitative] results, and some other results of mathematical logic may be regarded as going some way towards a demonstration, within mathematics itself, of the inadequacy of 'reason' unsupported by common sense. (1954: 595)

By 'reason' (in scare quotes) Turing meant, minimally, a formal system of the usual type (a type, as I have already emphasized, that he had already clarified long before). But the scare quotes distance him from an overly traditional conception of this: he is granting a term only for the sake of argument, and not endorsing any particular use. For him, it belongs to the notion of the human, as it may also to a machine, that infallibility is not a necessary part of intelligence, and in both cases in a down-to-earth sense. As he wrote,

'If a machine is expected to be infallible, it cannot also be intelligent' (1947: 124). So with a human being.[18]

It is important to stress, of course, that none of the above points undermine the fact that there are canonical norms of presentation for proofs in deductive science by now, and these rely upon the use of formalized languages to explicitly present the deductive architecture of theories, as well as proofs (sometimes model-theoretic) of the uniqueness, categoricity, completeness, incompleteness, and consistency of theories, aided and abetted by Tarski's truth-definition (truth rigorization), which allows the uses of formalized theories for such ends by rigorizing the notion of definability.[19]

The syntactically rigorized model of proofs, classically employed, is a mathematical and 'rigorous' one (in the sense that its properties have been well analysed by the mathematical tradition). Of course it makes things, in a sense, much harder, because it is so abstract. Unarticulated or improperly motivated, it leaves out much mathematical experience, and virtually all features of vividness and clarity that appeal to informal elements that are in practice crucial to the presentation and communication of proofs, especially in the pre-modern period. It is not in general anything like a representation or description of proof, but at best a model.

At the same time, it is a meaningful model, put to work in the application to ordinary mathematics of the famous unprovability results. For it is a means to extrude extra-logical considerations from the articulation and assessment of possible deductive argument, and so provides a rigorization of the very notion of a possible deductive argument for purposes of proving universal negative generalizations. Here there is no precise commitment, either to the view that all informal proofs can be formalized, or even that they can be taken always to 'indicate' formal proofs in any sense of rigour commensurate with the traditional formal one.

One could take as residue, as eluding formal reduction, the very idea that for every proof in the mathematician's sense one may infer the existence of a deduction or proof derivation in the logician's syntactic sense (nowadays this often means in first-order logic plus a supplementary theory, e.g., Zermelo–Fraenkel set theory). This assumption has been dubbed 'Hilbert's Thesis' by Burgess (1992), and much discussed (see, e.g., Azzouni 2004; Rav 2007). It has been called a 'thesis', not a theorem: something intuitively clear, but not proved. Differently put, it is a pure existence claim, and hardly

---

[18]   I suspect there is a connection between Turing's ideas as expressed here and Wittgenstein's otherwise impenetrable remark (written after his exchanges with Turing 1937–9): 'I have not yet made the role of miscalculating clear. The role of the proposition: "I must have miscalculated". It is really the key to an understanding of the "foundations" of mathematics' (1978: III §90). Cf. Mühlhölzer 2010 for a more detailed reading.

[19]   I do think that both Wittgenstein and Turing underestimated the importance of Tarski's work. This may be an indirect effect of their not having a direct focus on the notion of truth to begin with, rather than notions like 'effective'. However, as I emphasize below, even Dedekind (1854) stressed the centrality of the notion of truth while also emphasizing the notions of effectiveness and rigour as far more central to our concept of science, *sub specie humanitatis*. Wittgenstein's remarks on Dedekind are among his weakest (cf. Mühlhölzer 2010).

the sort of thing that is plausibly rigorously demonstrable by formal methods them-selves, however interesting the practice of actually formalizing mathematics in pro-gramming languages has become as a branch of mathematics (cf., e.g., Hales 2008; Asperti and Avigad 2011). Burgess takes its status to be analogous to 'Church's Thesis' (sometimes called the 'Church–Turing thesis'), the 'thesis' that all (humanly, or rele-vantly) computable functions are Turing computable, in the technical sense. But such 'theses' ought hardly, ideally, to be theses in a doctrinal sense.[20] Assumptions, hypoth-eses, and stipulations are neither themselves beliefs nor capable of supporting beliefs directly. In fact Turing's analysis of the general notion of taking a step in a formal sys-tem should be taken to presuppose, not any such 'thesis', but rather a set of simplify-ing assumptions that can be mathematized by being axiomatized (Gandy 1980; Sieg 2005, 2008b; Hodges 2006a). I would regard the notion of a Turing Machine, more generally, to have been offered in the spirit of a perspicuous presentation, i.e., a simpli-fied snapshot of a limited portion of human cognitive behaviour offered for a purpose, i.e., to shed light, as an object of comparison, on a particular problem, viz., Hilbert's *Entscheidungsproblem* (Davis 1982; Gandy 1988,1996). As such, it rigorizes, and pre-cisely because it is free-standing (in Rawls's sense): it is independent of choice of par-ticular formal framework, metaphysical position, or disputable logical principles, and yet widely applicable (Floyd 2012a, 2012b, 2013). It is also convincing *because* it is vivid and natural and familiar. That is part of its rigour, part of how it works to articu-late a certain region of residue that emerged within the tradition. 'Hilbert's Thesis' is employed as a rigorizing model of *unprovability*. It gives us a rigorous way to respond to certain general representations about what, e.g., the continuum or the truths of arithmetic are or must be.

For the sake of rigour one should go beyond the notions of 'thesis', 'stipulation', 'hypothesis', or 'convention', each of which involve comparisons that can be misleading. In what follows I shall forswear any special discussion of the 'Church–Turing' thesis, focusing instead on a series of what I take to be more elusive and sometimes underem-phasized philosophical points. By 1937, when Turing published his (negative) resolution of Hilbert's *Entscheidungsproblem*, a certain closing punctuation mark was placed on the classical period of the mathematical tradition in early analytic philosophy. Wholly new areas of research were made available, of course, by this work, and the traditional schools of logicism, proof theory, and intuitionism continued to be developed. But for philosophy the most important outcome of the development of modern mathemati-cal philosophy was or should have been self-reflective, a certain philosophical refine-ment about the very nature of the rigour to be gained by analysis using techniques of formalization inherited from Frege, Russell, and Hilbert. Howard Stein has called the philosophical outcome conducive to a certain increased 'modesty' about the nature of the human capacities revealed in the practice of mathematics: we have learned, at least,

---

[20] Though they are widely discussed as such. See Olszewski *et al.* 2006 for a recent collection of illuminating articles.

something about what that capacity is not (Stein 1988: 238–9). I concur. I would also call this outcome itself an increase of 'rigour', though one of a distinctive and philosophically significant kind.[21]

35.5 FREGE

It might be claimed that Frege, in formally articulating the language of modern quantificational logic, established standards for rigour that were unprecedented in philosophy, and nearly unprecedented in mathematics (Weiner 1990; Burge 2005: 12). The idea that these standards were distinctively philosophical, rather than recognizably mathematical, might, in turn, be questioned (Benacerraf 1981; Tappenden 1997; cf. Jeshion 2001, 2004; Weiner 2004; Ricketts 1996), as well as the idea that the mathematical formalization and application of the logical principles was all that crucial, or all that novel, philosophically and mathematically speaking (Ferreirós 2007).

Of course it would be foolish to pretend that nothing of philosophical worth had been in play with regard to foundational questions in mathematics before Frege showed us how to crisply formulate philosophical questions in his *Begriffsschrift* (my answer to Ferreirós and Gray 2006: 8 n10). Yet the distinctiveness of Frege's philosophy is only to be underscored, I think, if we ask with sufficient sensitivity and clarity about the continuous history of philosophical ideals at work in mathematicians who preceded and followed him. For those mathematicians, in turn, held certain common (and yet certainly not neutral) philosophical ideals, as some of the best recent literature on the development of conceptualist approaches in nineteenth-century mathematics makes clear.[22] Frege's philosophy spelled out, whatever else it did, a commonly held set of ideas about rigour, though it implemented and articulated them with newly rigorous terms of a distinctive philosophy.

---

[21] On 'informal' rigour: first-order quantification theory, with its neat properties of completeness and compactness, emerged about 1918 as a kind of softly canonical, simple, and rigorous core or touchstone for proceeding. It forms no more, and of course no less, than a widely transportable, schematic module for explicating and titrating theories. It shows us how things would be *if* they were simple. Of course, it is a familiar mark of the need for 'informal rigour' that the notion of validity for first-order logic mandates the use of non-standard, non-isomorphic models of theories (Kreisel 1967), and this may be taken to show that the familiar first-order quantifier has no univocal interpretation (Putnam 2001: 153). Other logical systems, with other meta-theoretic properties, may and have been developed for other purposes, and of course first-order logic itself was extracted a posteriori, historically speaking, from the higher order context on which Frege relied. That higher-order logic, despite its inconsistent initial presentation, is still preferred by many for its ontological fertility and applications in discourse about concepts and plurals. Fragments are studied, and with differing motivations. So there is no claim to fundamentality for all purposes (even in his syntax period Carnap admitted that informal, pragmatic assumptions played a role in logic (Lavers 2008)). My focus here is not, however, on the issue of logical pluralism, but instead on the notion of rigour. Here it is worth stressing that the articulations of two quite different logics (or ontologies) may be equally rigorous. Or not. It will be, in part, the role of residue that decides this.

[22] I have learned especially from Webb 1980; Kanamori 1996; Ferreirós 2007; Sieg and Schlimm 2005.

We have already seen from a glance at Moore and the limitative results of the 1930s that proof, if it is to convince us, cannot be a merely inert, purely formal thing. Formalization, to be rigorous, must be understood in purposive terms, though not merely conventional or stipulative ones. It is important that Frege would not have disagreed, and that his philosophical articulation of logicism furthers these ideas.

Frege was careful to emphasize rigour as one value among many, and an ideal to be pursued, not a mere fact or property. He compared his *Begriffsschrift* to a microscope, a device 'invented for certain scientific purposes', namely, to offer sharpened resolution, formulation, and recognition of logical distinctions and relations and principles, for the sake of explicit flagging of assumptions, clarity of epistemological basis, and gap-free presentation of deductive relations among thoughts (1879: 6). His formalized language was not to be condemned, he argued, on the ground that it is only suited to certain ends. After all, he pointed out, given certain purposes the human eye is superior to the microscope: it is superior in the range of its uses and its versatility. But this in no way condemns the microscope, used in its proper place.

So Frege appealed to vivid metaphors in explicating what might be conceived of as residue. His ideal of purposiveness had a philosophical, as well as a mathematical and logical significance. The specific *locus* of that ideal was for him the articulation of logic as a science of truth, and not the concept of rigour; the latter was only an instrument, and never a value as such. My intention here, however, is not to pursue an interpretation of *these* distinctive parts of Frege's philosophy. It is rather to emphasize as philosophically relevant the very fact that Frege takes purposiveness to belong to the notion of rigour as it is used in mathematics and logic.

Like Dedekind, Frege held that it was a requirement of rigour to prove truths where possible. But there is a conceptual problem, with respect to the notion of rigour, about which notions of completeness and extent are involved in this ideal. The remark raises the fundamental issue of what cannot, or not really, *be* proved, and thus, what we are to take ourselves to mean by 'proof', and by 'capable'. It raises the issue, not merely of how far rigour includes the *extent* and *scope* of our reasoning, its numerical fruitfulness with respect to truths, so to speak, but also the nature of the application of the above modal, which was duly stressed by Hilbert (cf. Hallett 2010).[23] Rigour at the foundations requires an articulation of such issues. And for that there must be understandings of what the syntactic-cum-semantic articulation achieves or is designed to achieve, a probing of its possible uses.

Frege considered it to be of central philosophical importance to motivate and draw into familiar parlance notions he took to receive their best systematization in his *Begriffsschrift* formulation of logic. Here he admitted that he had to ask the reader to meet him 'halfway' as he presented in German his elucidations of the undefined notions, including those of truth, function, and concept—notions that were, after all,

---

[23] Compare the idea, broached and reflected on in Cavell 1967: 187, that modernist music is not to be defended because it incorporates *more* sounds, rhythms, and so on. Also in Stein 1988, that the 'second birth' of modern mathematics was not due to its sheer fertility.

relatively everyday notions in the philosophy, mathematics, and logic of his day. To draw these everyday notions into a systematic articulation of the laws of deductive science, to exhibit their logical place, was a crucial part of his aim, even if he was also clear that the *Begriffsschrift* was needed in cases where ordinary language tended to find itself unable to articulate logical relations clearly. Frege was of the opinion that at the fundamental level, in the primitive notions of mathematics and logic, the only reasonable modes of communication are hints, winks, analogies, colourful metaphors, and 'elucidations'— though not intuitions.[24] This is a mark of rigour in his philosophy, for it qualifies the nature of his own remarks. Part of the purpose of these elucidations was, however, communicative, a function of rigour in the broad sense I am construing it: to make the *Begriffsschrift* familiar enough, as a symbolism, that our understanding of the notions it analyses and its purposes may be furthered, sharpened, and also recognized for what they are, epistemologically speaking.

Russell also brought out the importance of the 'indefinables' of logic in its presentation and articulation. Impressed by the potentially infinite regress of explicit principles for the drawing of logical inference in Carroll (1895), he insisted that logic couldn't be completely formalized, drawing on analogies with everyday notions (e.g., 'the taste of pineapple', 'acquaintance') to convey the basic notions (1903/1938: §§ 19, 38: Whitehead and Russell 1910: chapter 1, 8–9).

So not only a survey of principles, but also their motivation and articulation in terms that could be seen to be familiar, were essential to the project of logicism. So was a mathematically and logically relevant fundamental point, which few if any would have contested. One requirement of reason, as Frege argued, is that we be able to grasp all first principles in a finite survey (1884: §5). This is not a psychological point, but a logical one about the point of rigorization, and one essential, in turn, for extruding empirical psychology from the foundations of mathematics and logic. Even Kant would have taken it to be wholly unrigorous simply to take all the infinitely many truths of arithmetic, individually speaking, as axioms: this would have meant for him not really using 'axioms' at all. But why not? Because such an 'articulation' would shed no light for *us* on the deductive articulation of number theory or the conceptual organization of the subject of logic itself. Hilbert too, incorporating Kronecker's concerns with the new conceptualism in mathematics, expressed the opinion that the 'whole meaning' of rigour in mathematical proof lies in the finitistic (constructively acceptable) aspect of the deductive architecture, even calling it 'a universal philosophical necessity of our understanding' (1900/1996: 1099).

What Frege did not do was to raise the formal-as-plain question as a problem that logic *itself* must address. It was difficult enough, after all, for him to devise the first fully formalized logical language. He gave no account of what it *is* to work with such a thing in general, focusing instead on an articulation of how his *Begriffsschrift* in particular, and logic in general, should be viewed in relation to truth. What was wanted, however, was

---

[24] Frege 1892/1984,1914/1979, 1980: 37; cf. Ricketts 1997; Weiner 2001, 2005; Beaney 2006: 56.

an analysis of what a 'formal system' *is*, and what the idea *is* of a human cognizer taking a 'step' in such a system. This required reflection on what it was that one wanted to use these notions *for*, and as I have said Turing resolved this in a generally satisfactory way.

Long before Turing, however, the road was paved with a fairly robust and widely shared sense of the philosophical constraints and standards that were to be met in resolving such questions. To see this, we need to go back to Kant.

35.6 Kant

That rigour is reflective, purposive, and oriented toward a perspective *sub specie human-itatis* emerged explicitly for the tradition in Kant's remarkable treatment of the power of 'reflective judgment' in his *Critique of Judgment* (1790/2000). Here Kant ascribed to human beings a primitive intellectual capacity for developing analogies and conceptual articulations into intelligible and communicable rigorizations, a purposiveness without any particular causal or intentional or God-given purpose (*Zweckmässigkeit ohne Zweck*).

In arguing that the power of reflective judgement is a fundamental cognitive capacity, Kant argued, following Hume, that the actual course of human experience is, at least potentially, infinitely manifold and haphazard (1790/2000: 5:183, 20:203). We have no a priori way to know that we will be able to devise a unitary classificatory system adequate to the objects of knowledge. To develop science rigorously, we must create suitably fitting generalizations, demanding that the objects of knowledge are organized so as to satisfy our own conceptual, classificatory methods by something better than accident. Thus we must proceed *as if* the phenomena were designed with our own procedures in mind, providing genuine criteria of correctness. Our cognitive capacity is not to be seen as slight, and our use of analogy not always as frail, as Hume held.[25] Both pure deduction and induction presuppose our capacity to creatively devise concepts and principles so as to develop science as a system.

Kant construed reflective judgement as the capacity for 'ordinary critique' in everyday life: the ability to refine, sagaciously devise, and correctly apply well-chosen, suitably systematizable concepts to objects in particular situations (1790/2000: 20, 169). This notion is normative, and not merely heuristic or psychological. It belongs *constitutively*

---

[25] Hume states that reasoning by analogy in the law is a 'frail' capacity in his *Enquiry Concerning the Principles of Morals*, §III, part II, ¶10 (1777/1975). Quoting the passage, Burgess (2014) views this kind of reasoning as a classic example of the use of 'heuristic' intuition in the ordinary mathematician's sense. While Burgess admits that this forms an important element of the mathematician's everyday understanding of 'intuition', he is concerned, following Hume, to question how rigorous this notion really is. In the third *Critique* Kant is especially concerned to emphasize that our capacity to judge has more to it than the merely sceptical and/or psychologically instrumental import Hume emphasizes, though like Hume and Burgess he stresses that there is absolutely no a priori guarantee that our heuristics will yield true generalizations (Floyd 1998).

as a rule to 'the logical use' of judgement (1790/2000: 20:214). Kant explicitly insisted that it would be 'contrary to the sense' of reflective judgement if we were to reduce it to mere psychology (as Hume did) or to a merely deductive power (as Leibniz had done) (1790/2000: 20:182). Hume, despairing of the latter to take account of knowledge, had insisted on the former, seeing our modes of generalization as habitual, mechanical, automatic mechanisms of the mind. Kant insisted, against Hume, that reflective judgement is purposive, proceeding according to a demand for intelligibly, 'not schematically, but **technically**, not as it were merely mechanically, like an instrument, but **artistically**, in accordance with the general but at the same time indeterminate principle of a purposive arrangement of nature in a system' (1790/2000: 20:214). [26]

Part of what is needed beyond pure rationality in the garnering of knowledge are *criticism* and *refinement*. This is inevitable when we face the fact that human knowledge requires sagaciousness and skill in choosing conceptual *motifs*. In order to realize the systematicity and communicability of knowledge, we face the work of science, and this faces us with choices. These choices, Kant argues, require *Urteilskraft*, the capacity to judge, well or poorly. This is a capacity that cannot be reduced to a set of rules or axioms, because it is itself the very capacity we have for formulating rules, applying them to cases, and developing new concepts to further the human knowledge in the face of a possibly infinite array of (at least) empirical possibilities. The capacity is creative, reflective, in a way circular, sometimes analogical, teleological, and partly (not wholly) aesthetic in nature, yet it belongs to the foundations of logic, science, ethics, philosophy, and mathematics nevertheless.[27] Kant lays explicit and repeated emphasis upon the human demand for developing what he calls *sound and common human understanding*. The principle of reflective judgement is nothing more, though nothing less, than a self-picturing of the human activity of sagaciously rendering experience and knowledge systematic and intelligible to ourselves through a demand of intersubjective communicability.

Kant's model is a legal one, though he mentions many empirical sciences—e.g., mineralogy, chemistry, and physics—as he emphasizes the importance of reflective judgement to the development of science. Faced with a particular case, a judge must render a verdict, but not by merely quoting the law in a 'mechanical' manner. Instead, wherever

[26] Husserl too emphasized the 'teleological' character of the development of science with respect to evidence at the foundations (1969: 160; cf. Hartimo 2011: 11).

[27] Cf. Floyd 1998. An appreciation of Kant's 'Critique of Aesthetic Judgment', the first half of *The Critique of Judgment*, was central to the modernist conception of Clement Greenberg. On Greenberg's modernism, see Jones 2005 and Corry forthcoming. As for mathematics: although Kant denied that causal teleological reasoning is used in mathematics, and insisted that there could be no such thing as a beautiful proof, he certainly admitted that in mathematics there was purposiveness, i.e., well-designedness, though he held it to be formal in nature, rather than metaphysical, sensory, inductive, or moral (cf. 1790/2000: 5:364). He denied also, of course, that logic relied upon axioms, which he regarded as synthetic a priori judgements held to be immediately true or self-evident: if axioms were formulated for logic, they would cover merely formal logic, and be empty of content, or even tautologous (Dreben and Floyd 1991).

alternative rulings seem plausible, a judge exercises judgement, adjudicating by articulating an argument as to why the case does or does not fall under a rule (1790/2000: 5:211). New concepts and criteria may need to be formulated, an analysis of the case given to eliminate arbitrariness, the appearance of thoughtlessness, or haphazard bias. Similarly in science: the concept of *granite*, for example, may or may not be suitable or rigorous in the development of a particular science: it is useful in mineralogy, but not in chemistry (1790/2000: 20:216).

35.7 DEDEKIND I

Dedekind and Turing both appreciated and emphasized the artfulness involved in transforming analogies into correspondences in the course of mathematics and science (Dedekind 1872/1996, 770; Hodges 1983). After Kant, it would be important to rigorize the very distinction he relied upon, symbolically and metaphorically, in setting out his conception of reflective judgement, namely, that between the *infinite* and the *finite*. This required getting clear about the relation between two apparently quite different notions, that of the *infinite* and the *formal*.

Arguably Frege and the early analytic philosophers were not pioneers in rigorizing the distinction between the finite and the infinite (Tait 2005: chapter 10). It was Dedekind who most strikingly drew the notion of the infinite into mathematics, by treating *actually* infinite objects as unpathological and subjecting them to systematic conceptualization (cf. Sieg and Schlimm 2005; Ferreirós 2007; Kanamori 2012). Dedekind articulated the theory of the infinite mathematically, in a non-empirical, positive, and definite, yet non-constructive and non-temporal way, showing how to transform Aristotle's 'potential', 'empirically limited', more psychologistic conception of the infinite (arguably also Kant's) into a definite, positive property.[28] Moreover, he provided materials to rid mathematical philosophy of its reliance on an ancient analogical image of the infinite—the repeated iteration of human mental operations *ad nauseum*, without limit[29]—if only by exposing for subsequent philosophers and mathematicians the very place where the relevant existence assertions would have to come in. For Dedekind was the first to analyse the notion of a recursive process and subject it, *via* his notion of a *chain*, to deductive and mathematical analysis. When it came to rigorous reflection on the structure of what continuity in general *is*, or what a real or a natural number *is*, one had to subject the notions of the infinite, the finite, and number to rigorization, i.e., definition and analysis.

---

[28] To say that a system (or set) P is Dedekind-infinite (what he calls 'simply infinite') is to say that there *exists* a 1–1 mapping from P onto a proper subset of itself.

[29] This is a frequent move in the history of empiricism, e.g., in Locke (Webb 1980). A more recent appeal to what he would admit is a kind of 'Just So' story was made in Kitcher's 1984. Steiner (1984) pointed out that this story falls foul of rule-following concerns.

(One also ultimately had to face, as Dedekind, Frege, and Russell did, what sense of 'is' one wishes to treat as fundamental.)[30]

What of logicism? It may be conceived to be a broad nineteenth-century tradition, both mathematical and philosophical, implicitly and explicitly differing with Kant. As we have seen, Kant maintained that there is only so much natural science in a subject as there is mathematics. Hilbert would follow him here, in a general and updated sense.[31] Kant's mathematics was that of Euclidean geometry and arithmetic, which he regarded as sciences of constructions exploring the a priori and general forms of space and time. So for Kant, mathematics and natural science were tied at the foundations to the domain of physics, or at least our possible experience of nature as some system of empirical laws or other—and not to logic. Gauss, who initiated the primacy of number theory as a modern mathematical pursuit, divided the theory of number from that of space and time, regarding the theory of number as a product of pure intellect, and quite different in status from geometry, which he regarded as dependent upon external reality for its structure.[32] Thus was set in motion a project, logicist in nature, to see how number and arithmetic could be analysed and developed purely, without the spectacles of Kant's philosophy (i.e., independently of theories of space and time) and portrayed as internal to our very conception of thought. Dedekind would later express the idea as 'a demand that arithmetic develop out of itself'.[33]

The problem was in a broad sense one of rigorization. First, how to capture the nature of number and space, apart from a prior philosophical theory's assumptions. Second, how to show that the theory of number (naturals, integers, rationals, real and complex) may be developed independently of assumptions imported from geometry or kinematics. Third, to see how geometry could be developed in an abstract manner, receiving rigorous articulation in light of its more complex relation to empirical reality and apart from the Euclidean framework. Fourth, to learn how to portray a branch of knowledge

---

[30] Frege and Russell view the theory of cardinal number as more general and fundamental, because they aim to tell us what the numbers are, as objects, and how they figure in applications of number words. We have a standoff here analogous to one between those who argue (like Frege and Russell) that the notion of 'recognize' has its fundamental meaning in connection with re-identification of particulars (either by identity or classificatory conception), and those who would emphasize (with Dedekind) the legitimizing notion of 'recognition', which derives from legal acknowledgement of dominion or ownership over an area. See Dedekind (1888a/1996: 791) on this notion of recognition.

[31] Hilbert 1930/1996: 1163: '... our entire modern culture, insofar as it rests on the penetration and utilization of nature, has its foundation in mathematics'.

[32] Gauss 1830: 302; cf. Hallett 2003: 130. Gauss reported that he had developed non-Euclidean geometry, which would of course only have reinforced this idea.

[33] Dedekind (1872/1996: 771). Cf. Demopoulos 1994/5: Hallett 2003. Webb (1980: 40 n) traces the idea that numbers are more 'inner' to our thought than geometry back to Proclus, Leibniz, Berkeley, and Kant, as well as to Gauss (whom he reads as using 'philosophically neutral language' in the above quote). As is nicely stressed by Reck (2008/2011), within this aspect of his work the distinctive contribution of Dedekind was to bring the irrational numbers within the systematic development of this genetic approach, thereby bridging the ancient gap between numbers as quantities (units of pluralities) and numbers as magnitudes (ratios). Tappenden 1995, 2006 explore the geometrical and Riemannian background to Frege, another factor.

(in this case, arithmetic) as *inner* to the nature of human thought itself, rather than drawn from the contingent and possibly haphazard course of human experience, or from godly implantation of an idea—but without making mathematics rely on a (controversial) theory of the mind or empirical psychology.

Hence the motto of Dedekind's 1872, 'humanity always arithmetizes' (1872: 796), one self-consciously opposed to Plato's 'God always arithmetizes' (for a discussion cf. Ferreirós 2007: 245). Dedekind repeated the motto more than once (1888a/1996: 792; Ewald 1996: II, 837). He kept before him an image of the human practitioner of science *as* human, and as more than a creature of particular, haphazard historical or empirical forces. This drawing forward of an image of the human as such remained with the tradition, down through Hilbert and Turing.

Dedekind was clear from the outset of his career that an unrigorous metaphorical gesture toward potentially unlimited iterated powers of idealized human agents or constructing minds would not do, and that science itself demands more than lucky guesses and loose analogies for its systematization. Like Kant (and later Turing and Wittgenstein) he jettisons the very idea of infallibility or self-evidence in generalizing or inferring. Even if we cannot be sure that he read Kant (Reck 2008/2011), it must be said that the opening of Dedekind's *Habilitationsschrift* (read before Gauss and Weber) strikingly echoes Kant's account of reflective judgement in his introduction to *The Critique of Judgment*.[34] Like Kant, Dedekind stresses that while science itself is 'infinitely manifold' as an historical phenomenon, it is constantly subjected to the limitations of human intellectual powers, which, since they are not capable of 'unbounded understanding' or instantaneous grasp of deductive inference, are imperfect (1854/1996: 753–4 §3). This is why, he says, the careful 'turning over' of definitions, the introduction of new '*motifs*' and concepts for arranging the system of science, is an art of proposing 'hypotheses concerning the inner nature of a science', that is, hypotheses which must be tested for fruitfulness and systematizing power in the further development of the science. The development of science itself answers as to the value of a rigorization, whose worth is measured in terms

---

[34] Of course, this purely philosophical background is neither exhaustive nor perhaps decisive, and I claim no more than an allusion, which may not have been conscious on Dedekind's part. Nevertheless, the background in Kant's discussion of systematicity in the third *Critique*, influential as it was on both the science and the Idealistic philosophy of Dedekind's day, strikes me as perhaps more important to consider when reflecting on Dedekind's idea of 'free creation' than anything in Kant's *Critique of Pure Reason*, which has so far been the main focus of scholars. There is a large literature relating Dedekind to Kant. Some have tried to argue that Dedekind's notion of 'free creation' bears the stamp of notions such as intuition or purely logical abstraction. Ferreirós 2007: 17 is right to emphasize that scientists learned from philosophers not necessarily directly, as scholars, but as scientists; nevertheless, in stressing the importance of Riemann to Dedekind, he suggests that Hamilton's Kantian-sounding view was a possible stimulus to Dedekind (Ferreirós 2007: 220–1; cf. Sieg and Schlimm 2005: 160 n16). Webb 1980 and McCarty 1995 read Dedekind's axiom of cuts (discussed below) in terms of Kant's epistemology of the *Ding an Sich* and formalism, while Potter 2000 brings a Kantian mentalistic reading to bear on Dedekind's famous Theorem 66 and on Dedekind's mention of 'divinity' in his 1888b. For non-Kantian discussions, see Sieg and Schlimm 2005, especially at 125; Tappenden 2008.

of 'the greater or lesser *effectiveness*' of the concept(s), i.e., the successfully systematizing *motifs*, we create (1854/1996: 756 §3).

Reflective conceptual creativity is useful in any science, he says; like Kant, he mentions law, mineralogy, chemistry, and the difficulty of distinguishing superficial from systematic *Merkmale* so as to extend the scope of systematized science. 'The greatest art of the systematizer', he writes, 'lies in this turning and manipulation of definitions for the sake of the discovered laws or truths in which they play a role' (1854/1996: 756 §4).[35] But, he argues, mathematics is special. Its new definitions and laws must 'follow with compelling necessity' from earlier definitions, 'no longer allowing scope for arbitrariness', and provably holding of 'freely created' objects with general validity (1854/1996: 757). This is a demand, not simply for deductively articulated explicitness or ontological accuracy, but also for *intelligibility*, a demand that extensions of science 'make sense' (1854/1996: 758). Wherever possible, assumptions should be flagged and proofs found, exhibiting them as part of the 'organism' of the science (1854/1996: 756 §5). Again like Kant, Dedekind views science as, ideally, organically organized in terms of its systematic development and communicability.

That is why Dedekind insists that this demand for intelligibility requires sensitivity, as a constraint, to what he would later call the 'naïve point of view'. This, applied to the most basic level in mathematics, would turn out to be the 'natural' numbers themselves (1888a/1996).[36] A novel fundamental system of conceptualization should, ideally, require no technical knowledge beyond 'common sense' when it comes to the basis, i.e., it should as much as possible recover and not displace our best naïve ideas about numbers, but exhibit these as part of the purely intellectual structure of human thought as such. Modernist mathematician that he was, Dedekind would seek to systematize the theory of natural numbers at the basis, but still demand that within his analysis that both the continuum and even the natural numbers would reappear, to be recognized once again as 'faithful and familiar friends', through the use of 'common place thinking' or 'good common sense', i.e., thought not depending upon any 'technical, or mathematical, or philosophical knowledge in the least degree' (1972/1996: 771; 1888a/1996: 791).

On Dedekind's general view of science, then—one I am arguing he shared with Kant, and, later on, many others, including Turing—analysis consists of conceptual innovation, the art of the 'turning over definitions' to present truths of the known domain in a newly systematic way through deriving consequences or extensions of domains to which known operations would apply in a controlled, uniform, and intelligible (rigorous) way (cf. Sieg and Schlimm 2005: 125). Dedekind's conception involved intelligibility and systematicity, as well as fruitfulness. Already in his *Habilitationsschrift* he was announcing

---

[35] Much later he would write in *Was Sind?* (1888a/1996: 792, Preface to the 1st edition) that 'the greatest and most fruitful advances in mathematics and other sciences have invariably been made by the creation and introduction of new concepts, rendered necessary by the frequent recurrence of complex phenomena which could be mastered by the old notions only with difficulty'.

[36] In 1872/1878/1976 Dedekind wrote drafts of *Was Sind?* entitled 'Attempt to analyze the number concept from the naïve point of view'; see Ferreirós 2007: 107; Sieg and Schlimm 2005: 130ff. for discussions of the methodology and manuscripts.

a research programme designed to give a uniform account of the introduction of new numbers and functions into mathematics, so that they would not appear to be arbitrary, *ad hoc,* or based upon forms of knowledge dependent upon something other than the structure of our intellect alone. The strategy is 'genetic', involving a controlled introduction of domains coupled with composition from vivid and familiar parts: to show how from the addition of positive numbers we get subtraction, from subtraction integers, from multiplication division, from division rational numbers, and so on. But its ultimate outcome, by 1888, would be axiomatic, yielding a principled basis for the natural numbers.[37]

A certain method of 'naïve' analysis emerged within analytic philosophy by the later 1930s in work of Austin, Wittgenstein, and others, but it is worth stressing that this kind of methodological need for 'naïve' descriptions as part of a step in analysis had already arisen long before, and quite explicitly within the emerging tradition of modern mathematical philosophy. Dedekind, as I have said, was explicit on the point, emphasizing the 'protracted labor' that this step initiates when we ask what the 'natural' numbers are and should (be conceived to) be (1890/1967).[38] His famous monograph of 1888 answers the question what the numbers are *for* in this sense (Stein 1988; Ferreirós 2007: 217). The point of the 'naïve' description is to return initially to mathematical experience as it presents itself. Not, of course, to question our knowledge, or to tie it to an empiricist's or phenomenologist's theory, but to analyse it with an eye on its further rigorous development as an autonomous ('freely created')[39] system, intelligible in terms reflecting a 'common understanding' of how notions are used.

Dedekind had to struggle to achieve such a rigorous description in this sense: he is quite clear that the 'naïve analysis' is needed even if the notion of ordinal number is assumed as 'immediately evident to "inner intuition"' (Dedekind 1872/1878/1976: 293; cf. Sieg and Schlimm 2005: 131). His analysis of the 'natural' numbers came last in his

---

[37] Hilbert did not recognize this as an instance of the axiomatic method, but the influence on Hilbert was profound, and in retrospect, one can see that the spirit and means are broadly axiomatic. Thus the apparently different methods of approach to rigorization are not incompatible. On this topic see the very interesting exchange between Sieg and Schlimm 2005 and Ferreirós 2007 (Appendix to 2nd edition).

[38] Later, in correspondence with Weber (1888b/1996, 835) Dedekind explicitly states that his ordinal numbers are not always used in ordinary grammar in the way adjectival, cardinal constructions are, though he regards them nevertheless as fundamental. So the 'naïve' point of view is not about ordinary grammar alone. But what we ordinarily say is not irrelevant. He reminds Weber about his own argument from lack of coincidence in ways of speaking: it leads him to state that his analysis of the continuum does not tell us what the *real* nature of space is, but instead reflects our own concepts in rigorizing and representing it.

[39] When Dedekind speaks of the 'free creation' of number realms in the *Habilitationsschrift,* he is appealing to freedom in the Kantian (*Critique of Judgment*) sense, not of *autonomy,* but of *heautonomy*: the giving of non-arbitrary, constitutive laws of the intellect by the intellect to itself through reflection on contingently given particular objects and generalizations over them. (See his letter to Keferstein (1890/1967); cf. Floyd 1998.) As Sieg and Schlimm 2005 emphasize, however, the emphasis on 'freedom' evolved. After Kronecker and the controversies surrounding Dedekind's abstract approach, it takes on more the sense of unfettered postulation by powerful methods, with (as Minkowski famously put it) 'a maximum of insight and a minimum of blind calculation'.

long career, not first. It was needed in order fully to implement his motto, enunciated in his (1872/1996): 'where possible, find proofs'. His strategy, as he later reconstructed it for (his critic) Keferstein (1890/1967), was a classical pursuit of the regressive method of analysis, applied at the basis. The goal was to analyse the fundamental concepts and principles of number in such a way that the whole theory of number could be presented in terms of proofs of its truths from fundamental 'laws of thought' in a step-by-step way that is *pure*, i.e., recognizably purely intellectual and free of geometrical reasoning and any 'foreign' elements (1872/1996: 768,771).

35.8 DEDEKIND II

In his *Habilitationsschrift* Dedekind had isolated, naïvely so to speak, the notion of 'immediate successor in the number series'. As he writes, 'the successive progress from one member of the sequence of positive integers to the next is the first and simplest operation of arithmetic; all other operations rest on it'. 'If one collects into a single act the multiply-repeated performance of this elementary operation, one arrives at the concept of addition', he points out, and then similarly multiplication and exponentiation (1854: 756ff.).

But a problem arises how to intelligibly construct the other operations. For subtraction and division, the inverse operations, it is required that we 'create the entire existing domain of numbers anew', that is to say, that we ensure that 'the inverse operations of subtraction, division and the like be unconditionally applicable'. Whence the negative integers? And then what to say about their addition and multiplication and exponentiation? A subtle circularity is faced: the extension of the operations assumes that the new domain will be subject to them, and presumes as well the very notions of extension and operation (cf. Sieg and Schlimm 2005: 127; cf. Kanamori 2012: 6). What Dedekind did initially was to carefully obtain new domains through unrestricted inversions of operations, but then prove that theorems of addition and multiplication still hold in the extended domain, ensuring lawful and non-arbitrary extension. He would articulate the modern algebraic notion of a field.

The step to showing an intelligible development of irrational numbers from rationals was taken in Dedekind's famous treatise 'Continuity and Irrational Numbers' (1872/1996). Dedekind begins by reporting on his experience teaching calculus to prospective teachers at the Polytechnic School in Zürich. In the course of lecturing, he had 'recourse to geometric evidence', something he regarded as 'indispensable' from a didactic standpoint of efficiency. But it seemed obvious to him that this way of introducing the calculus 'can make no claim to being scientific'. Here rigour is a reflection of the need to articulate a science whose principles can be displayed as rigorous, and clearly communicated. (Gauss never taught a large audience; Cauchy and Dedekind did. When one does, one faces questions.) So Dedekind sought to articulate 'a perfectly rigorous foundation for the principles of infinitesimal analysis' (1872/1996: 766ff.).

So emerged his well-known 'Dedekind cuts'. These he used to define the notion of continuity and to completely characterize the system of real numbers. He proved that all relevant numerical features of the geometric line could be represented in a fully arithmetical way, the laws of real numbers treated wholly in terms of operations on systems of rational numbers. (For example, it was now possible to state, and to prove, that every bounded set of numbers has a least upper bound.) Dedekind showed that for every real number on the geometrical line there *corresponds* a representation which is a cut—some of these would be irrational numbers, and some rational, but the totality would fit into the 'inner necessity' of the science of the real numbers.

An analogy has been converted into a correspondence. Yet Dedekind held that he was 'utterly unable to adduce any proof' of the correctness of this definition of continuity relative to the actual geometrical line (1872/1996: 771). He held, in fact, that this is unprovable. If space has a real existence, he wrote, it is not necessary for it to be continuous, so what one really has is an 'axiom by which we attribute to the line its continuity, by which we find continuity in the line', and this axiom, he stated, expresses only 'a commonplace' thought (1872/1996: 771). What is striking is that at nearly the same time there were a number of different though comparable rigorizations given of the real numbers and the notion of continuity. In 1872 Cantor gave the most subsequently influential characterization of continuity, framed in terms of Cauchy sequences. Interestingly, Cantor too formulated what he called an 'axiom' about these sets of sequences, in the same way insisting that his representation of the geometrical line was not to be identified with it. Dedekind acknowledges Cantor's articulation of the axiom, and it is known as the axiom of Cantor–Dedekind (Cantor 1872: 128; Dedekind 1872/1996: 771).

The axiom has been called a kind of 'Church's Thesis' for the continuum (Kanamori 1996: 3). This invites the question, once again: Is an axiom really best understood as a 'thesis'? Certainly it is a form of residue, in my sense of the term, and like most residue, it has occasioned much discussion. Were Dedekind and Cantor following a tradition initiated by Riemann, according to which the geometrical, spatial line must in no way be reduced to the theory of real numbers (Ferreirós 2007)? Was Dedekind merely demanding that our naïve ideas about real numbers remain largely intact because he was objecting to the identification, on grounds that certain properties we would say hold of the cuts (e.g., containing infinite elements) do not hold of the real numbers? Did Dedekind think that the actual structure of space was a 'thing in itself', and so unknowable (Webb 1980; McCarty 1995)? Was he advocating a kind of structuralism, according to which numbers are nothing but positions in a structure, or according to which the kind of objects have no inner essence or nature, but are figments of a system (Shapiro 1997; Potter 2000; Parsons 2008)? Was he a kind of sophisticated formalist (Webb 1980)? Was he groping his way toward the very idea of a model for a set of axioms (Sieg and Schlimm 2005)? Or was he merely expressing a kind of logicizing indifference to identifying the objects in a way quite characteristic of modern mathematics (Burgess 2014; cf. Kanamori 2012)?

Russell alleged that Dedekind's analysis amounted to 'theft over honest toil' (1993: 71). A logicist demands an analysis that will structure the application of cardinal number words in propositions (e.g., about space and time) and will display numbers themselves as logical objects, and Dedekind takes ordinality to be fundamental, treating cardinality as deriving from that. Nevertheless, despite Russell's idea that his logicism was a more general approach, there were methodological, analytic, and conceptual toils Dedekind had to undertake that were serious and rigorous. Whether he did or should have developed a theory of what the real numbers *are* as opposed to all other objects is an opinion that divides neo-logicists from structuralists and others to this day, a dispute that could be viewed as an issue of rigour, of systematicity.

But what then of the ultimate bedrock of Dedekind's analysis, the infinity of the structure of the natural numbers? Peano thought that the axioms he extracted from a reading of Dedekind (1888a/1996)[40] formed a *definition* of the natural numbers, but Dedekind had already seen that this was not so, having grasped that in general the transformation of a recursive specification into an explicit definition required a *theorem*, that is, Dedekind's 'recursion theorem' (1888a/1996: 817ff., theorem 126), later derived by Frege in his *Grundgesetze* after he had read Dedekind's *Was Sind?* (cf. Heck 1995, 1998; Beaney 2006: 56). Implementing his conception of rigour Dedekind would articulate and successfully further certain crucial elements of the modern axiomatic method, including the strategy of exhibiting a model to show consistency, an insistence on distinguishing between representation and thing modelled, a formulation of categoricity and a use of what we can see in retrospect to be sets ('systems') to characterize, systematize, justify, and analyse notions such as mapping, function, infinity, finitude, ordinal and cardinal number, and to justify such principles as proof by mathematical induction and definition by recursion.

The difficulty had been in even conceiving of arithmetic as a branch of mathematics to be interestingly subject to axiomatization: Kant had explicitly denied that this was possible. Those who made the first attempts made piecemeal steps lacking a systematic articulation.[41] Dedekind took crucial steps beyond them, most vividly in separating the 'successor operation' from addition in the second version of his 1872/1878. Consider a series of 'naïve' ways of representing the 'system' of natural numbers to be analysed:[42]

(a) 1st, 2nd, 3rd, …

(b) $1, 1 + 1, 1 + 1 + 1, \ldots$

(c) $a + (b + 1) = (a + b) + 1$[43]

(d) $1, \phi(1) = 2, \phi(2) = 3 \ldots$

(e) $a + 1 = \phi(a)$
     $a + \phi(b) = \phi(a + b)$

---

[40] Though Dedekind's method of rigorization was not explicitly presented in terms of an axiomatic system, such is easily extracted from his proofs, and this is apparently what Peano did, rendering in formal symbols what are known as the 'Dedekind–Peano' axioms of arithmetic (Peano's was rigorization as symbolic transcription—another variety pursued nowadays in the formalization of known proofs).

[41] Grassman, perhaps the earliest mathematician to attempt to axiomatize arithmetic in a 'logicist' fashion (1860), attempted to formulate recursive specifications of the basic arithmetic operations, but he only got so far. See Wang 1957; Webb 1980, 44ff.; Sieg and Schlimm 2005; Ferreirós 2007.

[42] Cf. the presentation in Sieg and Schlimm 2005: 132ff.

[43] Grassman's idea, criticized by Frege (1884/1974: 5).

At each point in the development of these formulations, Dedekind struggled to achieve the appropriate level of systematization to formulate principles from which theorems could be proved. The addition symbol enters in at steps (b) and (c), even as generality of the definition increases. A breakthrough occurs at step (d), for here that function has dropped out, analysed away, and the concept of the structure of natural numbers as an actually infinite system, one capable (according to Dedekind's definition) of being mapped into itself, is laid bare. This presentation in turn enables the canonical form of a recursive definition to be framed, at (e).

Once this rigorization is achieved, two questions could emerge that would prove crucial to the development of computability theory and the analysis of the general notion of a formal system in the relevant sense of rigorization. This happened *via* the wedding of Frege's formalization of logic to Hilbert's meta-mathematical idea of an *effective* or *finitary* procedure—an idea linked directly to the notion of 'definite method' in a sense Hilbert would later make central to his *Entscheidungsproblem*: the question (linked explicitly by Hilbert to a necessary feature of our common human understanding) whether every well-posed mathematical question could be decided *by us*, by we human cognizers, *according to a definite or systematic method*. Historically this whole tradition was rooted, as we see, in Dedekind's earlier *Habilitationsschrift* idea of the *effectiveness* of a concept for science, and in a certain picture the notion of rigour demanded of the human activity of rendering science systematic.

The questions that would eventually emerge were, then, first,

'Does a well-defined function correspond to *any* set of recursive equations in the form of (e.)?'

and second—perhaps 'the most difficult question of all' (Webb 1980: 46),

'Do equations exist (that can be written down in an acceptably effective way by *us*) for every intuitively effective or computable or step-by-step recursive function in the relevant sense?'

The first question Dedekind answered with his proof of the recursion theorem. (Having allowed that his analysis in terms of infinite systems gives us a rigorization of what the natural numbers really *are*, he then presented his notorious 'Theorem' 66, the proof that there *exists* at least one actually infinite system, to ensure application).[44]

---

[44] Dedekind's 'proof' adduces the series of a thought of his self, a thought of that thought, a thought of the thought of that thought, *and so on*: a system then could be seen to exist that was mapped into a proper subsystem of itself, in a pure way, based solely upon considerations drawn from the structure of thought alone. There has been much discussion of this proof. Does it defeat logicism? (cf. Boolos 1998); is it too psychologistic? (cf. Webb 1980 vs. Sieg and Schlimm 2005). Of course, Dedekind failed to take account of a mathematical or logical problem later excavated by Russell: that the totality would itself be a system creates something contradictory. As has been noted, we may take Theorem 66 to be acquiescing in the demand, familiar in mathematics, to produce a consistency proof through exhibition of a model (Ferreirós 2007: 246; Sieg and Schlimm 2005). Later on, it would of course be acknowledged that an axiom of infinity is needed in order to avoid appeal to this kind of model, or to self-evidence of its existence. This is a matter, of course, of rigour.

The second question was solved only by Gödel, Herbrand, Church Kleene, and, in the end—*via* the transformation of a strikingly ordinary analogy or comparison into mathematics—by Turing.

35.9 TURING

Turing resisted, quite explicitly, what he thought of as the refusal of some logicians (e.g., Quine) to encourage liaisons between mathematical logic and everyday ways of using mathematics (Turing 1944–5, cf. Floyd 2013). He was quite explicit that he took the aspiration to what he called 'common sense' and communicability to be important to the nature of logic (Floyd 2012a). When he attended Wittgenstein's 1939 Cambridge lectures on the foundations of mathematics, he suggested that Wittgenstein too appeared to be relying on this idea (1989: 219ff.). Although Wittgenstein at first vehemently denied this, he revisited the issue sympathetically in the subsequent lecture, admitting that he did want to say something 'similar' (1989: 223ff.). Of course, reacting to Moore, Russell, and others, Wittgenstein was inclined to subject the notion of 'common sense' to critical scrutiny, as any good philosopher would. But he shared with Turing an ideal of rigour that included concrete attention to what makes sense by the lights of our current purposes, needs, and 'common sense' ways of thinking—including those couched in the language of ordinary mathematics. Rather than being against one another on matters of principle or method, Wittgenstein and Turing were in agreement, but having a civil quarrel about how best to formulate a conception in light of developments within formal logic in the 1930s.[45]

Instead of speaking, as Turing did, of a 'common sense basis' for developing mathematical logic, one might emphasize the value for mathematics and science of making 'very clear statements of the fundamental nature of the symbols', as Turing explicitly also urged (1944/5). The strong value he placed on the vernacular here, on lucidity and communicability, on perspicuity, and the 'naïve' level, is one that Turing and Wittgenstein shared, as I have argued, with the tradition.

This shows that we do not have quite the stark methodological disagreement that some will say forced (and still forces) a revolutionary choice between rigorous methods of analysis using ideal languages, on the one hand, and unrigorous methods of analysis using spoken and used ones—or for that matter, between specifically mathematical methods and philosophical or logical (foundational) ones. Both are rigorous, each in their own way, and both belong to an integrated set of aspects of the notion of rigour.

The most popular example to invoke nowadays as a paradigm of residue, because the room for play about what has been analysed is relatively clear, is the so-called

---

[45] Cf. Floyd 2012b. Here I am differing with the portrait painted by Monk of the Wittgenstein–Turing 1939 exchanges in his otherwise marvellous biography (1990).

'Church–Turing thesis', the thesis that all computable functions are Turing computable. But this is the converse of Turing's problem in 1936, which was to prove that his model completely systematized and captured all the classes of functions that had so far been offered. He worked regressively, looking backwards, so to speak, from the 'naïve' level, in order to proceed forward and show that he could resolve Hilbert's problem by appeal to something familiar.

Turing was a master simplifier, a master modernist, and a master rigorizor of the very idea of rigour. He pursued 'naïve' analysis in Dedekind's sense, and without postulating any completed infinite or importing any psychological theory into the foundations of mathematics. His analysis of computability by means of the notion of a Turing Machine is 'profoundly ordinary' (Hodges 1983: 96). It is more vivid, more pertinent and (as Gödel himself maintained) more epistemologically satisfying than Church's or Gödel's extensionally equivalent demarcations of the class of recursive functions (1986: 195). This is because, as a way of thinking, it is not entangled with the limitations of any particular formal system. Instead, it *makes the whole idea of a formal system plain*. It is everyday, perspicuous, simple, direct, or 'commonsensical', and the focus is on the user, the human end. To rigorize the traditional notion of a 'definite method' in the sense of Hilbert's *Entscheidungsproblem*, we had to bring ourselves back into the picture, and tie that picture in, thus *remodelling* the relevant definitions in just the creative way that Kant and Dedekind stated science demands generally in rigorizations (cf. Dedekind 1888a/1996: 795 for 'remodelling' language).

Although it is true that a Turing Machine may and must be provably shown to be readable as just another formal system, its capacity *as a remodelling* to systematize involves a quite distinctive sense of 'rigour' that cannot be reduced to the terms of just *one* formal system. Differently put: in order to rigorize the general notion of a formal system, one could not simply write down another formal system. One had instead to articulate a point of view from which we could see the general idea of what a formal system *is*. Turing's analysis is certainly conceptual in approach, and satisfies the Moorean ideal with which we began—though it is a piece of mathematics all the same. A Turing Machine lends itself, intentionally and conceptually, to a double point of view: it is both a formal system and a remodelling. Crucially, his model is dependent neither upon a choice of logic nor upon a choice of linguistic framework, nor upon the development or presentation of any particular formalized language or technique of formalization, and perhaps for this reason Carnap never once mentioned it, even though it is often adduced as a nearly perfect example of Carnapian 'explication' (Floyd 2012a). The idea of a Turing Machine abstracts away from the idiosyncratic features of any particular formalized language, from any particular philosophical position on a choice of logic or the use of logical principles or axioms (such as the law of the excluded middle), and from any particular philosophical account of logic or the mind, and from ascent to any particular meta-language. This is first-order philosophy. It is able to set into view the very idea of a definite method by exhibiting to us (and by means of us) just what it is that mathematicians and logicians designed such languages *for*.

For Gödel it offered a 'precise and unquestionably adequate definition of the general concept of formal system' which allowed his incompleteness theorem to be 'proved rigorously for every consistent formal system containing a certain amount of finitary number theory'.[46] But no analysis is unquestionable. Instead, Turing rigorized Gödel's incompleteness theorem by showing us its *point*. He settled its range of applicability within the Hilbertian tradition of proof theory, as it conceived of the human enterprise of generating definite methods for the solutions of certain problems (Sieg 2007). He also settled the range of applicability of that tradition to a certain class of ideal machines. The initial point was a suggestion about how to conceive of computable numbers, and Hilbert's decision problem was only an 'application' of the Turing Machine model. But since the formalization of incompleteness can occur within any formal system in which every Turing machine can be expressed by an equation, one might also say that what Turing shows is that the class of (relevant) machines cannot be described in a certain way by means of a single formal system (Webb 1980).

Gödel also wrote that with Turing's notion of a machine one had 'for the first time succeeded in giving an absolute definition of an interesting epistemological notion, i.e., one not depending on the formalism chosen'.[47] By 'absolute' is meant here the idea that the class of computable functions (or computable numbers, as in Turing (1937)) is robust in the sense that it does not change when it is represented in this or that formal system of the relevant Hilbertian kind: because of partially defined computable functions, one cannot diagonalize out of the class, and Turing managed to devise a universally applicable parameter for measuring the (relevant) idea of a *step* in a formal system. Yet in a more purely philosophical sense, absoluteness also turns on the fact that Turing's analysis artfully dodges controversies between constructivists, intuitionists, and classical logicians. This is connected with the anthropocentric comparison embedded in Turing's model of computation. For it is not part of the notion of a 'definite method', not part of our concept of the ordinary activity of a human computer, or the general concept of a person working within a formal system of the relevant kind, that the person takes a stance on the law of the excluded middle or holds a philosophical theory.

Turing provided what I would regard as a 'perspicuous presentation' of the idea of a definite method, a plain perspective on the notion of a formal system, by providing an 'object of comparison'. Crucially, he proceeds without an underlying theory of mind or logic or mathematics or thought as such. He returns, as Wittgenstein observed in 1947, to the human (Wittgenstein 1980: §§1096–7; cf. Sieg 1994; Floyd 2012b). The Turing Machine is a model that offers a simplified snapshot of a limited portion of human cognitive behaviour. In its language-game character, it is a model, available to common

---

[46] Gödel 1986: 195; Gödel here means a formal system of the *relevant* (recursively axiomatizable, finitary language) kind.

[47] See Gödel's (1946) 'Remarks before the Princeton bicentennial conference on problems in mathematics', in Gödel 1990: 150–3; compare the Postscriptum to his (1936a) essay 'On the Length of Proofs', 1990: 399. See also Sieg 2006a (472ff.) and 2006b.

understanding and yet 'pure', in spite of its spectacular suggestiveness and connections to certain subsequent technological and scientific developments.

Turing's work helps to show that not every formalization affords an increase in philosophical rigour in the same way. Sometimes what is involved is a new arrangement of concepts and principles. Sometimes what is sought is simply the plain. More generally, not every example of successful rigorization in philosophy involves an increase in order among our concepts, principles, or definitions in just one dimension. It is sometimes enough, especially in modernist situations, to be reminded of the integrity of the familiar.[48]

REFERENCES

Aristotle (1985). *Nicomachean Ethics*. In *The Complete Works of Aristotle*, ed. J. Barnes. Princeton, NJ: Princeton University Press, vol. 2, pp. 1729–867.

Asperti, A. and J. Avigad (2011). 'Zen and the Art of Formalization', *Mathematical Structures in Computer Science* 21(4): 671–7.

Aspray, W. and P. Kitcher (eds.) (1988). *History and Philosophy of Modern Mathematics*. Minnesota Studies in the Philosophy of Science. Minneapolis, MN: University of Minnesota Press.

Azzouni, J. (2004). 'The Derivation-Indicator View of Mathematical Practice', *Philosophia Mathematica* 12(3): 81–105.

Beaney, M. (2003/2009). 'Analysis'. In *The Stanford Encyclopedia of Philosophy*. Available at: <http://plato.stanford.edu/entries/analysis> (accessed 14 March 2012).

—— (2006). 'Frege and the Role of Historical Elucidation: Methodology and the Foundations of Mathematics'. In Ferreirós and Gray (2006), pp. 47–66.

—— (ed.) (2007a). *The Analytic Turn: Analysis in Early Analytic Philosophy and Phenomenology*. London: Routledge.

—— (2007b). 'Conceptions of Analysis in the Early Analytic and Phenomenological Traditions: Some Comparisons and Relationships'. In Beaney (2007a), pp. 196–216.

Benacerraf, P. (1981). 'Frege: The Last Logicist'. In P. A. French, T. E. Uehling, and H. K. Wettstein (eds.), *The Foundations of Analytic Philosophy*. Minneapolis, MN: University of Minnesota Press, pp. 17–36.

Benis-Sinaceur, H. (2002). 'Modernité mathématique: Quelques invariants épistémologiques' [Modernity in Mathematics: Some Epistemological Invariants], *Revue d'histoire des sciences* 55(1): 83–100.

Boolos, G. (1998). 'The Standard of Equality of Numbers'. In Boolos, *Logic, Logic and Logic*, ed. R. Jeffrey. Cambridge, MA: Harvard University Press, pp. 202–20.

[48] I am indebted for research support provided in 2009–10 by the Deutsche Forschungsgemeinschaft in the framework of the Lichtenberg-Kolleg of the Georg-August-Universität Göttingen, especially to my colleagues there, Felix Mühlhölzer, Norma Goethe, and Akihiro Kanamori. Michael Beaney suggested the essay's topic and gave me substantial help and much patience, for which I am truly grateful. Thanks are also due to Robert Bowditch, Stanley Cavell, Jean Philippe Narboux, Katerina Paplomata, Sanford Shieh, Judson Webb, and Harvey Friedman for many helpful conversations about rigour.

Burge, T. (2005). *Truth, Thought, Reason: Essays on Frege*. New York: Oxford University Press.

Burgess, J. P. (1992). 'Proofs about Proofs: A Defense of Classical Logic. Part I: The Aims of Classical Logic'. In M. Detlefsen (ed.), *Proof, Logic and Formalization*. New York: Routledge, pp. 8–23.

—— (2014). 'Intuitions of Three Kinds in Gödel's Views on the Continuum'. In J. Kennedy (ed.), *Interpreting Gödel*. New York and Cambridge: Cambridge University Press, pp. 11–31.

—— (2015). *Rigor and Structure*. Oxford: Oxford University Press.

Cantor, G. (1872). 'Über die Ausdehnung eines Satzes aus der Theorie der trigonometrischen Reihen', *Mathematische Annalen* 5: 123–32.

Carnap, R. (1937). *The Logical Syntax of Language*. London: Routledge & Kegan Paul.

Carroll, L. (1895). 'What the Tortoise Said to Achilles', *Mind* 4: 278–80.

Cavell, S. (1965/1976). 'Aesthetic Problems of Modern Philosophy'. In Cavell, *Must We Mean What We Say? A Book of Essays*. Cambridge: Cambridge University Press, pp. 73–96.

—— (1967/1976). 'Music Discomposed'. In Cavell, *Must We Mean What We Say? A Book of Essays*. Cambridge: Cambridge University Press, pp. 180–212.

—— (1988). *In Quest of the Ordinary: Lines of Skepticism and Romanticism*. Chicago: University of Chicago Press.

Centrone, S. (2010). *Logic and Philosophy of Mathematics in the Early Husserl*. Dordrecht: Springer.

Chemla, K. (2003). 'Generality above Abstraction: The General Expressed in Terms of the Paradigmatic in Mathematics in Ancient China', *Science in Context* 16(3): 413–58.

Clarke, T. (1972). 'The Legacy of Skepticism', *The Journal of Philosophy* 69(20): 754–69.

Corry, L. (Forthcoming). 'How Useful is the Term "Modernism" for Understanding the History of Early Twentieth-Century Mathematics?' In Epple and Müller (forthcoming).

Crowe, M. J. (1988). 'Ten Misconceptions about Mathematics and Its History'. In Aspray and Kitcher (1988), pp. 260–77.

Davis, M. (1982). 'Why Gödel Didn't Have Church's Thesis', *Information and Control* 54: 3–24.

Dedekind, R. (1854/1996). 'On the Introduction of New Functions in Mathematics'. In Ewald (1996), vol. 2, pp. 753–61.

—— (1872/1878/1976). *Was sind und was Sollen die Zahlen? [Erster Entwurf]*: Attempt to analyze the number concept from the naive point of view (Versuch einer Analyse des Azhlbegriffs vom naiven Standpuncte aus). In P. Dugac (ed.), *Richard Dedekind et les fondements des mathématiques*. Paris: Vrin, pp. 293–309.

—— (1872/1996). *Continuity and Irrational Numbers*. Oxford and New York: Oxford University Press.

—— (1888a/1996). *Was sind und was sollen die Zahlen?* In Ewald (1996), vol. 2, pp. 790–833.

—— (1888b/1996). Letter to Heinrich Weber, 24 January 1888. In Ewald (1996), vol. 2, pp. 834–5.

—— (1890/1967). Letter to Keferstein. In J. van Heijenoort (ed.), *From Frege to Gödel: A Sourcebook in Mathematical Logic, 1879-1931*. Cambridge, MA: Harvard University Press, pp. 98–103.

Detlefsen, M. (1993). 'Poincare vs Russell on the Role of Logic in Mathematics', *Philosophia Mathematica* 1(1): 24–49.

—— (2010). 'Rigor, Re-proof and Bolzano's Critical Program'. In P. E. A. Bour (ed.), *Construction, Festschrift for Gerhard Heinzmann*. London: King's College Publications, pp. 171–84.

Demopoulos, W. (1994/5). 'Frege and the Rigorization of Analysis'. In Demopoulos (1995), pp. 68–88.

—— (ed.) (1995). *Frege's Philosophy of Mathematics*. Cambridge, MA and London: Harvard University Press.

Diamond, C. (1991). *The Realistic Spirit: Wittgenstein, Philosophy and the Mind*. Cambridge, MA: MIT Press.

Dreben, B. and J. Floyd (1991). 'Tautology: How Not to Use A Word', *Synthese* 87(1): 23–50.

Eliot, T. S. (1928/1997). *The Sacred Wood: Essays on Poetry and Criticism*. London: Faber & Faber; orig. pub. London: Methuen, 1928.

Epple, M. and F. Müller (forthcoming). *Modernism in the Sciences, ca. 1900–1940*. Berlin: Walter de Gruyter.

Ewald, W. (ed.) (1996). *From Kant to Hilbert: A Source Book in the Foundations of Mathematics*, 2 vols. New York: Oxford University Press.

Ferreirós, J. (2007). *Labyrinth of Thought: A History of Set Theory and Its Role in Modern Mathematics*. Basel: Birkhaüser.

—— (2011). 'On Arbitrary Sets and ZFC', *The Bulletin of Symbolic Logic* 17(3): 361–93.

Ferreirós, J. and J. J. Gray (eds.) (2006). *The Architecture of Modern Mathematics*. New York and Oxford: Oxford University Press.

Floyd, J. (1998). 'Heautonomy and the Critique of Sound Judgment: Kant on Reflective Judgment and Systematicity'. In H. Parrett (ed.), *Kant's Aesthetics*. Berlin and New York: Walter de Gruyter, pp. 192–218.

—— (2007). 'Rawls's Restatement of Justice as Fairness: An Introductory Overview'. In K. Dethloff, N. Charlotte, R. Staubmann, and A. Weiberg (eds.), *Humane Existenz. Reflexionen zur Ethik in einer pluralistischen Gesellschaft*. Berlin: Parerga Verlag, pp. 17–35.

—— (2009). 'Recent Themes in the History of Early Analytic Philosophy', *Journal of the History of Philosophy* 47(2): 157–200.

—— (2011). 'Wang and Wittgenstein'. In C. Parsons and M. Link (eds.), *Hao Wang: Logician and Philosopher*. London: College Publications, pp. 145–94.

—— (2012a). 'Wittgenstein, Carnap, and Turing: Contrasting Notions of Analysis'. In P. Wagner (ed.), *Carnap's Ideal of Explication and Naturalism*. Basingstoke: Palgrave Macmillan, pp. 34–46.

—— (2012b). 'Wittgenstein's Diagonal Argument: A Variation on Cantor and Turing'. In P. Dybjer, S. Lindström, E. Palmgren, and G. Sundholm (eds.), *Epistemology versus Ontology: Essays on the Philosophy and Foundations of Mathematics in Honour of Pe Martin-Löf*. Dordrecht: Springer, pp. 25–44.

—— (2013). 'Turing, Wittgenstein, and Types: Philosophical Aspects of Turing's "The Reform of Mathematical Notation and Phraseology" (1944-5)'. In S. B. Cooper and J. V. Leuven (eds.), *Alan Turing: His Work and Impact*. Amsterdam: Elsevier, pp. 250–253.

Frege, G. (1879/1967). 'Begriffsschrift: A Formula Language of Pure Thought Modelled on That of Arithmetic'. In J. van Heijenoort (ed.), *From Frege to Gödel: A Sourcebook in Mathematical Logic 1879–1931*. Cambridge, MA: Harvard University Press, pp. 1–82.

—— (1884/1974). *The Foundations of Arithmetic*. Evanston, IL: Northwestern University Press.

—— (1892/1984). 'On Concept and Object'. In Frege, *Collected Papers on Mathematics, Logic, and Philosophy*, tr. M. Black *et al.*, ed. B. McGuinness. Oxford: Blackwell, pp. 182–94.

—— (1906/1984). 'The Foundations of Geometry', Second Series. In Frege, *Collected Papers on Mathematics, Logic, and Philosophy*, tr. M. Black *et al.*, ed. B. McGuinness. Oxford: Blackwell, pp. 293–340.

—— (1914/1979). 'Logic in Mathematics'. In *Gottlob Frege: Posthumous Writings*, ed. H. E. A. Hermes. Chicago: University of Chicago Press; Oxford: Blackwell, pp. 201–52.

—— (1980). *Gottlob Frege: Philosophical and Mathematical Correspondence*, tr. H. Kaal, ed. B. McGuinness. Chicago: University of Chicago Press.

Galison, P. (1990). 'Aufbau/Bauhaus: Logical Positivism and Architectural Modernism', *Critical Inquiry* 16: 709–52.

—— (1996). 'Constructing Modernism: The Cultural Location of *Aufbau*'. In R. N. Giere and A. Richardson (eds.), *Origins of Logical Empiricism*. Minneapolis, MN: University of Minnesota Press, pp. 17–44.

Gandy, R. O. (1980). 'Church's Thesis and Principles for Mechanisms'. In J. Barwise, D. Kaplan, H. J. Keisler, P. Suppes, and A. S. Troelstra (eds.), *The Kleene Symposium*. Amsterdam: North-Holland, pp. 123–48.

—— (1988). 'The Confluence of Ideas in 1936'. In R. Herken (ed.), *The Universal Turing Machine: A Half-Century Survey*. New York: Oxford University Press, pp. 55–112.

—— (1996). 'Human versus Mechanical Intelligence'. In P. Millican and A. Clark (eds.), *Machines and Thought: The Legacy of Alan Turing, volume 1*. Oxford and New York: Oxford University Press, pp. 125–36.

Gauss, C. F. (1830). Letter to Bessell, 9 April 1830. In Ewald (1996), vol. 1, p. 302.

Gödel, K. (1986). *Kurt Gödel Collected Works, Volume I: Publications 1929–1936*. New York: Oxford University Press.

—— (1990). *Kurt Gödel Collected Works, Volume II: Publications 1938–1974*. New York: Oxford University Press.

Goldfarb, W. (1985). 'Poincaré against the Logicists'. In Aspray and Kitcher (1988), pp. 61–81.

Grassmann, H. (1860). *Lehrbuch der Mathematik für höhere Lehranstalten, Part I. Arithmetik*. Stettin.

Gray, J. J. (2006). 'Modern Mathematics as a Cultural Phenomenon'. In Ferreirós and Gray (2006), pp. 371–96.

—— (2008). *Plato's Ghost: The Modernist Transformation of Mathematics*. Princeton, NJ: Princeton University Press.

Hales, T. C. (2008). 'Formal Proof', *Notices of the American Mathematical Society* 55(11): 1370–80.

Hallett, M. (2003). 'Foundations of Mathematics'. In T. Baldwin (ed.), *The Cambridge History of Philosophy 1870–1945*. Cambridge: Cambridge University Press, pp. 128–56; 833–7.

—— (2010). 'Frege and Hilbert'. In Potter and Ricketts (2010), pp. 413–64.

Hamawaki, A. (2014). 'In Search of the Plain and the Philosophical: Skepticism, Self-Knowledge and Transcendental Illusion', *International Journal for Skepticism*, 4(3): 35–62.

Hartimo, M. (2006). 'Mathematical Roots of Phenomenology: Husserl and the Concept of Number', *History and Philosophy of Logic* 27(4): 319–37.

—— (ed.) (2010). *Phenomenology and Mathematics*. New York: Springer.

—— (2011). 'Husserl's Pluralistic Phenomenology of Mathematics', *Philosophia Mathematica* 20(1): 86–110.

—— (2012). 'Husserl and the Algebra of Logic: Husserl's 1896 Lectures', *Axiomathes* 22(1): 121–33.

Heck, R. G. (1995). 'Definition by Induction in Frege's Grundgesetze der Arithmetik'. In Demopoulos (1995), pp. 295–33.

—— (1998). 'The finite and the infinite in Frege's Grundgetze der Arithmetik'. In M. Schirn (ed.), *The Philosophy of Mathematics Today*. New York: Oxford University Press, pp. 429–66.

Heidegger, M. (1929/1993). 'What is Metaphysics?' In Heidegger, *Basic Writings*, ed. David F. Krell. London: Routledge, pp. 89–110.

—— (1938). 'Age of the World Picture'. In Heidegger, *The Question Concerning Technology and Other Essays*. New York: Harper Torchbooks, pp. 115–54.

Heyting, A. (1956). *Intuitionism: An Introduction*. Amsterdam, North-Holland.

Hilbert, D. (1900/1996). 'Mathematical Problems'. In Ewald (1996), vol. 2, pp. 1096–105.

—— (1930/1996). 'Logic and the Knowledge of Nature'. In Ewald (1996), vol. 2, pp. 1157–65.

Hodges, A. (1983). *Alan Turing the Enigma of Intelligence*. New York: Touchstone.

—— (2006a). 'Did Church and Turing Have a Thesis About Machines?' In Olszewski *et al.* (2006), pp. 242–52.

—— (2006b). 'Book Review, *The Essential Turing*, ed. J. Copeland', *Notices of the American Mathematical Society* 53(10): 1190–9.

Hume, D. (1777/1975). *Enquiry Concerning Human Understanding and Concerning the Principles of Morals*. Oxford and New York: Oxford University Press.

Husserl, E. (1900/2001). *Logical Investigations, Volume 1*. London: Routledge.

—— (1911/1965). *Phenomenology and the Crisis of Philosophy: Philosophy as a Rigorous Science, and Philosophy and the Crisis of European Man*. New York: Harper & Row.

—— (1969). *Formal and Transcendental Logic*. The Hague: Martinus Nijhoff.

Jeshion, R. (2001). 'Frege's Notions of Self-Evidence', *Mind* 110(440): 937–76.

—— (2004). 'Frege: Evidence for Self-Evidence', *Mind* 113(449): 131–8.

Jones, C. A. (2005). *Eyesight Alone: Clement Greenberg's Modernism and the Bureaucratization of the Senses*. Chicago: University of Chicago Press.

Kanamori, A. (1996). 'The Mathematical Development of Set Theory from Cantor to Cohen', *Bulletin of Symbolic Logic* 2(1): 1–71.

—— (2012). 'In Praise of Replacement', *Bulletin of Symbolic Logic* 18: 46–90.

Kant, I. (1786/2004). *Metaphysical Foundations of Natural Science*. Cambridge and New York: Cambridge University Press.

—— (1790/2000). *Critique of the Power of Judgment,* tr. and ed. P. Guyer. Cambridge and New York: Cambridge University Press.

Kennedy, J. and M. Van Atten (2004). 'Gödel's Modernism: On Set-Theoretic Incompleteness', *Graduate Faculty Philosophy Journal* 25(2): 289–349.

Kitcher, P. (1981). 'Mathematical Rigor—Who Needs It?' *Noûs* 15(4): 469–93.

—— (1984). *The Nature of Mathematical Knowledge*. New York: Oxford University Press.

Kleiner, I. (1991). 'Rigor and Proof in Mathematics: A Historical Perspective', *Mathematics Magazine* 64(5): 291–314.

Kreisel, G. (1967). 'Informal Rigour and Completeness Proofs'. In I. Lakatos (ed.), *Problems in the Philosophy of Mathematics*. Amsterdam: North-Holland Publishing Company, pp. 138–57.

Lavers, G. (2008). 'Carnap, Formalism, and Informal Rigour', *Philosophia Mathematica* 3(16): 4–24.

McCarty, D. (1995). 'The Mysteries of Richard Dedekind'. In J. Hintikka (ed.), *From Dedekind to Gödel: Essays on the Development of the Foundations of Mathematics*. New York: Springer, pp. 53–96.

Mancosu, P. (1998). *From Brouwer to Hilbert: The Debate on the Foundations of Mathematics in the 1920s*. New York: Oxford University Press.

Monk, R. (1990). *Ludwig Wittgenstein: The Duty of Genius*. New York: Free Press; London: Jonathan Cape.

Moore, G. E. (1939/1959). 'Proof of an External World'. In Moore, *Philosophical Papers*. London: George Allen & Unwin, pp. 127–50.

Mühlhölzer, F. (2010). *Braucht die Mathematik eine Grundlegung? Ein Kommentar des Teils III von Wittgensteins Bemerkungen über die Grundlagen der Mathematik*. Frankfurt am Main: Vittorio Klostermann.

Olszewski, A., J. Wolenski, and R. Janusz (eds.) (2006). *Church's Thesis After 70 Years*. Heusenstamm: Ontos Verlag.

Parsons, C. (2008). *Mathematical Thought and Its Objects*. Cambridge and New York: Cambridge University Press.

Peckhaus, V. (2002). 'Regressive Analysis', *Logical Analysis and the History of Philosophy* 4: 97–110. Available at <http://kw.uni-paderborn.de/fileadmin/kw/institute/Philosophie/Personal/Peckhaus/Texte_zum_Download/regressive_analysis.pdf> (accessed 14 March 2012).

——(2004). 'Paradoxes in Göttingen'. In G. Link (ed.), *One Hundred Years of Russell's Paradox: Mathematics, Logic, Philosophy*. Berlin and New York: Walter de Gruyter, pp. 501–15.

Peirce, C. S. (2010). *Philosophy of Mathematics: Selected Writings*. Bloomington, IN: Indiana University Press.

Potter, M. (2000). *Reason's Nearest Kin: Philosophies of Arithmetic from Kant to Carnap*. New York: Oxford University Press.

Potter, M. and T. Ricketts (eds.) (2010). *The Cambridge Companion to Frege*. Cambridge: Cambridge University Press.

Putnam, H. (1997). 'A Half Century of Philosophy, Viewed from Within', *Daedalus* 126: 175–208.

——(2001). 'Was Wittgenstein *Really* an Anti-Realist about Mathematics?' In T. G. McCarthy and S. C. Stidd (eds.), *Wittgenstein in America*. New York and Oxford: Oxford University Press, pp. 140–94.

Rav, Y. (2007). 'A Critique of a Formalist-Mechanist Version of the Justification of Arguments in Mathematicians' Proof Practices', *Philosophia Mathematica* 15(3): 291–320.

Rawls, J. (1985/1999). 'Justice as Fairness: Political not Metaphysical'. In *John Rawls: Collected Works*, ed. S. Freeman. Cambridge, MA and London: Harvard University Press, pp. 388–414.

——(1996). *Political Liberalism*. New York: Columbia University Press.

——(1997/1999). 'The Idea of Public Reason Revisited'. In *John Rawls: Collected Papers*, ed. S. Freeman. Cambridge, MA and London: Harvard University Press, pp. 573–615.

Reck, E. (2008/2011). 'Dedekind's Contributions to the Foundations of Mathematics'. In *The Stanford Encyclopedia of Philosophy*. Available at: <http://plato.stanford.edu/entries/dedekind-foundations/> (accessed 14 March 2012).

Richardson, A. (2002). 'Philosophy as Science: The Modernist Agenda of Philosophy of Science, 1900–1950'. In P. Gardenfors, J. Wolenski, and K. Kijania Placek (eds.), *The Scope of Logic, Methodology, and Philosophy of Science, Volume. 2*. Dordrecht and New York: Kluwer, pp. 621–39.

Ricketts, T. (1996). 'Logic and Truth in Frege', *The Aristotelian Society, Supplementary Volume* 70: 121–40.

——(1997). 'Frege's 1906 Foray into Metalogic', *Philosophical Topics* 25(2): 169–87.

Russell, B. (1901). 'Recent Work on the Principles of Mathematics', *International Monthly* 4: 83–101.

——(1903/1938). *The Principles of Mathematics*. Cambridge: Cambridge University Press.

——(1907/1973). 'The Regressive Method of Discovering the Premises of Mathematics'. In Russell, *Essays in Analysis*, ed. D. Lackey. London: George Allan & Unwin, pp. 272–83.

—— (1993). *Introduction to Mathematical Philosophy*. London and New York: Routledge.

Schorske, C. E. (1997). 'The New Rigorism in the Human Sciences, 1940–1960', *Daedalus: Journal of the American Academy of Arts and Sciences* 126(1): 289–309.

Shapiro, S. (1997). *Mathematics: Structure and Ontology*. New York and Oxford: Oxford University Press.

Sieg, W. (1994). 'Mechanical Procedures and Mathematical Experience'. In A. George (ed.), *Mathematics and Mind*. New York and Oxford: Oxford University Press, pp. 91–117.

—— (2006a). 'Gödel on Computability', *Philosophia Mathematica* 14(2): 189–207.

—— (2006b). 'Step by Recursive Step: Church's Analysis of Effective Calculability'. In Olszewski *et al.* (2006), pp. 456–85.

—— (2007). 'On Mind and Turing's Machines', *Natural Computing* 6: 187–205.

—— (2008a). 'On Computability'. In A. Irvine (ed.), *Handbook of the Philosophy of Science: Philosophy of Mathematics*. Amsterdam: Elsevier BV, pp. 535–630.

—— (2008b). 'Church Without Dogma: Axioms for Computability'. In B. S. Cooper, B. Löwe, and A. Sorbi (eds.), *New Computational Paradigms: Changing Conceptions of What is Computable*. New York: Springer, pp. 139–52.

—— (2013). *Hilbert's Programs and Beyond*. Oxford and New York: Oxford University Press.

Sieg, W. and D. Schlimm (2005). 'Dedekind's Analysis of Number: Systems and Axioms', *Synthese* 147: 121–70.

Soames, S. (2003). *Philosophical Analysis in the Twentieth Century: The Dawn of Analysis*. Princeton, NJ: Princeton University Press.

Stein, H. (1988). '*Logos*, Logic, and *Logistiké*: Some Philosophical Remarks on Nineteenth-Century Transformation of Mathematics'. In Aspray and Kitcher (1988), pp. 238–59.

Steiner, M. (1984). 'Review of Philip Kitcher, *The Nature of Mathematical Knowledge*', *Journal of Philosophy* 81: 449–56.

Stroud, B. (1972/2000). 'Doubts About the Legacy of Scepticism'. In Stroud, *Understanding Human Knowledge*. New York and Oxford: Oxford University Press, pp. 26–37.

—— (1984). *The Significance of Philosophical Scepticism for Everyday Life*. Oxford: Clarendon Press.

Tait, W. W. (2005). *The Provenance of Pure Reason: Essays in the Philosophy of Mathematics and its History*. Oxford and New York: Oxford University Press.

Tappenden, J. (1995). 'Geometry and Generality in Frege's Philosophy of Arithmetic', *Synthese* 102: 319–61.

—— (1997). 'Metatheory and Mathematical Practice in Frege', *Philosophical Topics* 25: 213–64.

—— (2006). 'The Riemannian Background to Frege's Philosophy'. In Ferreirós and Gray (2006), pp. 97–132.

—— (2008). 'Mathematical Concepts and Definitions: Fruitfulness and Naturalness'. In P. Mancosu (ed.), *The Philosophy of Mathematical Practice*. Oxford and New York: Oxford University Press, pp. 276–301.

Travis, C. (2000). 'Philosophy's Twentieth Century: A Revolutionary Path', *Disputatio* 8 (June): 3–16.

—— (2006). *Thought's Footing*. New York: Oxford University Press.

—— (2008). *Occasion-Sensitivity: Selected Essays*. Oxford and New York: Oxford University Press.

—— (2011). *Objectivity and the Parochial*. New York and Oxford: Oxford University Press.

Turing, A. M. (1937). 'On Computable Numbers, with an Application to the Entscheidungs problem', *Proceedings of the London Mathematical Society* 2(42): 230–65.

—— (1944–5). 'The Reform of Mathematical Notation and Phraseology'. Repr. in *The Collected Works of A. M. Turing: Mathematical Logic*, ed. R. O. Gandy and C. E. M. Yates. Amsterdam: North-Holland/Elsevier Science, 2001, pp. 211–22.

—— (1947). 'Lecture to the London Mathematical Society, 20 February 1947'. Repr. in *The Collected Works of A. M. Turing: Mechanical Intelligence*, ed. D. C. Ince. Amsterdam: North-Holland, 1992, pp. 87–106.

—— (1948/1992). 'Intelligent Machinery'. Repr. in *The Collected Works of A.M. Turing: Mechanical Intelligence*, ed. D. C. Ince. Amsterdam: North-Holland, 1992, pp. 107–28.

—— (1954). 'Solvable and Unsolvable Problems', *Science News* 31: 7–23.

Wang, H. (1957). 'The Axiomatization of Arithmetic', *The Journal of Symbolic Logic* 22(2): 145–58.

—— (1961). 'Process and Existence in Mathematics'. In Y. Bar-Hillel, E. I. J. Poznanski, M. O. Rabin, and A. Robinson (eds.), *Essays on the Foundations of Mathematics, dedicated to Prof. A. A. Fraenkel on his 70th anniversary*. Jerusalem: Magnes Press, pp. 328–51.

Webb, J. C. (1980). *Mechanism, Mentalism, and Metamathematics: An Essay on Finitism*. Dordrecht and Boston: D. Reidel.

Weiner, J. (1990). *Frege in Perspective*. Ithaca, NY: Cornell University Press.

—— (2001). 'Theory and Elucidation: The End of the Age of Innocence'. In J. Floyd and S. Shieh (eds.), *Future Pasts: The Analytic Tradition in Twentieth Century Philosophy*. New York: Oxford University Press, pp. 43–66.

—— (2004). 'What was Frege Trying to Prove? A Response to Jeshion', *Mind* 113(449): 115–29.

—— (2005). 'On Fregean Elucidation'. In M. Beaney and E. H. Reck (eds.), *Gottlob Frege: Critical Assessments*. New York: Routledge, pp. 197–214.

Whitehead, A. N. and B. Russell (1910). *Principia Mathematica*. Cambridge: Cambridge University Press.

Wilson, M. (1992/1995). 'Frege: The Royal Road from Geometry'. In Demopoulos (1995), pp. 108–62.

—— (2005). 'Ghost World: A Context for Frege's Context Principle'. In M. Beaney and E. H. Reck (eds.), *Gottlob Frege: Critical Assessments*. New York: Routledge, pp. 157–76.

—— (2010). 'Frege's Mathematical Setting'. In Potter and Ricketts (2010), pp. 379–412.

Wittgenstein, L. (1974). *On Certainty/Über Gewissheit*. Oxford and Malden, MA: Blackwell.

—— (1978). *Remarks on the Foundations of Mathematics*. Cambridge, MA: MIT Press.

—— (2001). *Philosophical Investigations*, tr. G. E. M. Anscombe, 3rd edn. Oxford: Wiley-Blackwell.

Wittgenstein, L. and C. Diamond (1989). *Wittgenstein's Lectures on the Foundations of Mathematics: Cambridge, 1939*. Chicago and London: University of Chicago Press.

Wittgenstein, L., G. H. Von Wright *et al.* (1980). *Remarks on the Philosophy of Psychology, Volume 1 [RPP I]*. Chicago: University of Chicago Press; Oxford: Blackwell.

CHAPTER 36

....

MODALITY

....

SANFORD SHIEH

MODAL concepts, especially the Leibnizian notion of possible worlds, are central in contemporary analytic philosophy. Quite the opposite was the case earlier. Until the 1970s, the default attitude towards modality among analytic philosophers was some degree of suspicion. My aim in this chapter is to provide an overview of the main forms of this distrust, and the ways in which it faded from the mainstream.

The period of analytic philosophy closest to us contains the heyday of logical positivism and its decline. Since many contemporary analytic philosophical preoccupations arose in reaction to positivism, we have an understandable, and not altogether unjustifiable, tendency to think of positivism as an amalgam of easily identifiable philosophical mistakes, and to project these mistakes onto all of our predecessors.[1] Thus, we take suspicion of modality to have been based on the now discredited anti-metaphysical empiricist criterion of significance: there are no sensory or observational grounds for modal sentences, so the only respectable species of necessity consists of a priori analytic truths that are a product of the meanings conventionally attached to linguistic expressions. With the demise of the criterion of significance, opposition to modality collapsed.[2]

The analytic tradition is a complex interweaving of many strands of thought, so this picture is not entirely false, even of positivism. But it undoubtedly fails to fit the founders of analytic philosophy, Gottlob Frege, G. E. Moore, and Bertrand Russell, all of whom opposed empiricism and held no brief against metaphysics. For them lack of empirical grounds is no basis for denial of mind-independent objectivity. So while they took necessity and possibility to be reducible to more fundamental logical notions, logic for these thinkers consists of truths about a mind- and language-independent reality extending beyond the empirical world. In addition, their conceptions of the relations among the notions of necessity, analyticity, and apriority differ significantly from the positivists' views.

---

[1] A paradigm of this tendency is Soames (2003), chapters 12 and 13.
[2] See Rosen (2001) for a clear account of this view.

Thus there were, in the history of the analytic tradition, at least two main forms of reductionism or eliminativism about modality. Correspondingly, there were two major phases in the passing of anti-modal stances. In the first phase it was argued that modal notions are not reducible to logical ones because logic itself requires modal notions. In the second phase it was argued that modal properties are mind- and language-independent features of the world.

I begin with a brief account of Frege, Moore, and Russell. I turn then to two critiques of Russell's conception of logic that constitute the first phase: C. I. Lewis's rejection of Russell's material implication, and more briefly Ludwig Wittgenstein's rejection, in *Tractatus Logico-Philosophicus* (1922 [1921]), of Russell's view of the nature of logic. Next I outline Rudolf Carnap's pragmatically motivated account of modal terms as expressing pseudo-object properties, properties which appear to be of objects, but can be construed as holding of their designations. Quine's sharpening and critique of Lewis's and Carnap's accounts of necessity as analyticity is a pivotal moment in the history recounted here, since the second phase arose in response to Quine's critique. Two central planks of Quine's critique—the difficulties of quantifying into modal contexts, and the need to resort to essentialism to overcome these difficulties—originate in Carnap's notion of pseudo-object property.

Opposition to Quine's modal scepticism appeared as soon as Quine published his arguments in 1943, but it wasn't until the 1960s that there was a sustained movement away from Quine's views. Among the main works opposing Quine in this period are Ruth Barcan Marcus (1961), Dagfinn Føllesdal (1961, 1965), Jaakko Hintikka (1963, 1969), A. N. Prior (1963), N. L. Wilson (1965), Bede Rundle (1965), Richard Cartwright (1968), Leonard Linsky (1969), Alvin Plantinga (1969, 1970), and Saul Kripke (1971, 1972). Since this work is relatively well-known, and since it's obviously not possible to provide adequate analyses of all these texts here, I give merely a brief outline of two of the most significant factors in dispelling the Quinean attitude to modality. These are Marcus's rejection of necessity as analyticity through a directly referential conception of naming and Kripke's use of our intuitive understanding of modal statements to support the cogency of essentialism.[3]

In general I have chosen, at the expense of completeness of coverage, to isolate a few central lines of development, focusing on philosophically significant views and arguments. Limitations of space force me to forgo consideration of a number of salient philosophical developments. Apart from the works already mentioned, I particularly regret not discussing the role of modality in motivating Jan Łukasiewicz's work in many-valued logic,[4] work on modal expressions in the ordinary language philosophy tradition,[5] and Wilfrid Sellars's (1948) view of laws. Finally, I don't treat connected developments in modal logic.

---

[3] Some further discussion of the works I do not treat can be found in Neale (1999). I am very much indebted to the historical section of this paper; in many cases it oriented my thinking, even where I disagree with Neale's emphases and conclusions.

[4] The classic statement is Łukasiewicz (1930).

[5] For instance, Austin (1979 [1956]).

36.1 REDUCTIONISM ABOUT MODALITY: FREGE, MOORE, AND RUSSELL

As noted above, modal notions are neither central nor foundational in the philosophical projects that inaugurated analytic philosophy: Frege's use of higher-order quantificational logic in logicism, and Moore's and Russell's collaborative rejection of British Idealism. These philosophers treated modal notions reductively or eliminatively, explaining them away in terms of logical notions.

One of Frege's concerns in the early sections of *Begriffsschrift* (1970 [1879]) is to set out *his* notions of judgment, proposition, and conceptual content in contrast to the corresponding notions in traditional logic. In § 4 Frege asserts that his notion of conceptual content does not distinguish between the traditional notions of apodictic and assertoric judgments. From Frege's perspective, a judgment in apodictic form merely 'suggests the existence of universal judgments from which [it] can be inferred', so in characterizing a proposition as necessary one merely gives 'a hint about the grounds for' one's judgment (13). Similarly, in characterizing a proposition as possible 'either the speaker is suspending judgment by suggesting that he knows no laws from which the negation of the proposition would follow or he says that the generalization of this negation is false' (13). Thus for Frege modal predicates do not contribute to the conceptual contents of judgments in whose expressions they occur, but merely 'hint at', or 'suggest' the existence of deductive relations between those contents and laws or generalizations, and so perhaps contribute to 'coloring and shading' (1984 [1892], 161). To the extent that such hints are objective features of assertions, they might be eliminated by explicitly stating these deductive relations.[6]

In *The Foundations of Arithmetic* (1980 [1884], § 3), Frege provides accounts of the analytic/synthetic and a priori/a posteriori distinctions in terms of kinds of deductive justification. A truth is analytic if its proof rests ultimately 'only on general logical laws and on definitions', synthetic if its proof also depends on 'truths which are not of a general logical nature, but belong to the sphere of some special science' (3). The notion of analyticity here is recognizable as an ancestor of semantic accounts of analyticity; but it differs from such accounts since for Frege definitions are supposed to reflect analyses of concepts, and so are not arbitrarily adopted but have to be justified.[7] A truth is a posteriori if its proof requires appeal to 'truths which cannot be proved and are not general, since they contain assertions about particular objects', a priori 'if ... its proof can be derived exclusively from general laws' (3). These accounts obviously do not rule out

---

[6] If Frege's notions of universal judgment and of law have irreducibly modal components, then, of course, these accounts would not succeed in eliminating modal notions. But the consensus is that for Frege universal judgments and laws are simply universal quantificational generalizations understood purely extensionally. Danielle Macbeth argues against this consensus in *Frege's Logic* (2005); for critical discussion of her arguments see Shieh (2005).

[7] Frege apparently changed his mind on the arbitrariness of definitions. See Shieh (2008).

truths whose justification depends on general but non-logical laws, and Frege explicitly agrees with Kant in holding that 'the truths of geometry [are] synthetic and *a priori*' (§ 88, 101). Moreover, the distinction between a priori and a posteriori turns simply on the generality or particularity of grounds, and so does not imply anything about whether sensory experience or observation is required. Finally, Frege's views don't rule out necessary propositions that are a posteriori. The 'suggestion' that a judgment can be inferred from general laws entails neither that its ultimate grounds *in fact* contain general laws, nor, even if they do, that they do not *also* contain particular truths.

Central to Moore and Russell's rejection of idealism is a theory of propositions first articulated in Moore's 'The Nature of Judgment' (1899).[8] Propositions are composed of the very entities, called 'concepts', that they are about.[9] Truth is an unanalysable property of propositions not constituted by correspondence to facts in the world. Instead, existence, reality, and fact are explained in terms of true propositions.[10] On the basis of this view Moore claims that Kant's a posteriori/a priori distinction is really a distinction between propositions containing empirical concepts, 'which can exist in parts of time' (1899, 187), and those which don't. He goes on to reject Kant's identification of necessity with apriority: *all* true empirical propositions, even those about occurrences of sensations, are necessary. The implicit argument rests on the nature of truth. The *existence* of an alternative to a proposition P's being true consists of such *facts* as P's being true at another moment of time t, or at another possible world w. But each of these facts is nothing more than a related but distinct proposition P', about t or w being true *simpliciter*. Hence, fundamentally, there is no conception of any alternatives to a true proposition's being true.[11]

From *The Philosophy of Leibniz* (1900) to *The Principles of Mathematics* (1903) Russell adopts Moore's position: 'there seems to be no true proposition of which there is any sense in saying that it might have been false', whence necessity marks no distinction among truths, every proposition is 'a mere fact' (1903, 454), and 'the notion of necessity is shorn of most of its importance' (1900, 24).

Moore was not satisfied with this view for long. In 'Necessity' (1900) he advances a new account on which 'no proposition is necessary in itself', but only in virtue of being 'connected in a certain way with other propositions' (302). The connection is called 'presupposition', 'implication', or 'logical priority' and, in typical Moorean fashion, elucidated by examples: 'when we say: Here are two chairs, and there are two chairs, and therefore, in all, there are four chairs ... we presuppose in our conclusion that $2 + 2 = 4$' (301). The arithmetical truth is logically prior to the particular inference.

---

[8] For extensive discussion of this theory see Griffin (1980), Hylton (1990), and Cartwright (2003), on which the present account is based.

[9] A significant qualification for Russell on this point is his theory of denoting concepts, constituents of propositions which are not about those concepts but what they denote.

[10] On existence see Moore (1899, 180); on reality see Moore (1901, 717); on fact see Russell (1904, 523; 1994a [1905], 495).

[11] I give a full reconstruction of this argument in Shieh (forthcoming).

Strictly for Moore no proposition is necessary *simpliciter*, but one proposition is more necessary than another if it is logically prior to the other but not vice versa.

In an unpublished paper, 'Necessity and Possibility' (1994b [1905]), Russell rejects both of Moore's reductionist accounts of necessity and presents a nuanced and thoroughgoing critique of modality from which Russell never departed.[12] The main argument treats four modal intuitions or 'feeling[s] of necessity' (520). In each case Russell proposes precise accounts of the intuition, in logical terms, and shows that they fail in one of three ways: they mark no logically significant distinction among propositions, they don't distinguish necessary from contingent truth, or, they don't accord with all our modal intuitions. Russell concludes that 'there is no one fundamental logical notion of necessity, [hence] the subject of modality ought to be banished from logic, since propositions are simply true or false, and there is no such comparative and superlative of truth as is implied by the notions of contingency and necessity' (520).

One of Russell's accounts is important for our subsequent discussion. It is an explication of the intuition that a proposition is necessary if its truth 'can be deduced from the laws of logic' (520). Russell's proposal for making the notion of 'deducibility' precise is: 'q is deducible from p if it can be shown by means of the [axioms of logic] that p implies q' (515).[13] He then defines *analytic* propositions as just those deducible from the axioms of logic; here analyticity has nothing to do with meaning or synonymy. A 'necessary proposition is an analytic proposition, and a possible proposition is one of which the contradictory is not analytic' (517). Russell rejects this account because propositions such as 'If a thing is good, it is not bad', are 'felt to be necessary', but 'are not analytic' since 'mere logic will never prove that *good* and *bad*' are incompatible (517).

36.2 C. I. LEWIS AGAINST RUSSELL

Modern modal logic began with C. I. Lewis's criticisms of the propositional logic of Whitehead's and Russell's *Principia Mathematica* (1910).[14] Lewis's critique is the first significant reversal of the attitude, just canvassed, that modal notions are to be explained away rather than used in philosophical explanations. I begin my account of Lewis with

---

[12] Many aspects of Russell's position in (1994b [1905]) are sketched in (1904).

[13] Russell's use of letters 'p', 'q', etc. in formulas and of quotation marks is an especially controversial matter in view of Quine's accusation that he and Whitehead confused use and mention. I won't attempt a defensible Russellian usage, but my general policy is to use single quotes to reproduce Russell's text, and no quotes when using Russell's formulas in discussing his views, taking these formulas to be intended as expressing generalizations about non-linguistic (propositional) entities.

[14] Lewis is not alone in adopting modal notions in logic as a reaction to *Principia*; Jan Łukasiewicz (1930) is another. In a series of papers leading up to (1906), Hugh MacColl also formulated logical systems with modal implication connectives. See Russell's (1906) review of MacColl (1906), MacColl's (1908) criticism of Russell (1903), and Russell's reply (1908).

a sketch of the key background of his critique, some aspects of Russell's conception of propositional logic in the period from *Principles* to *Principia*.[15]

Russell held that logic is 'essentially concerned with inference in general, and is distinguished from various special branches of mathematics mainly by its generality.… What symbolic logic does investigate is the general rules by which inferences are made …' (1903, 11). The generality of logic consists in the applicability of its principles of inference to *all* subject matters—they are universally applicable norms of inference.[16] Let's call this feature of logic 'maximal generality of application'.

The part of logic that is the propositional calculus 'studies the relation of *implication* between propositions' (14).[17] The context for this claim is the Moore–Russell theory of propositions mentioned in the last section. Propositions are themselves entities, and one of the relations in which *these* entities can stand is the relation of implication.[18] The relation of implication is just as indefinable as the properties of truth and falsity (§ 16), and is the basis of valid inference (33). A rule of inference is a general proposition about propositions standing in the relation of implication. Being a proposition, it is, of course, objectively true or false. When it is in fact true, inferences we draw in accordance with it are correct. Since logic is maximally general in application, it comprises those rules of inference that describe how propositions are related by implication, in virtue of being propositions, *simpliciter*, not in virtue of being about this or that subject matter.[19]

Note that implication is not the only relation among propositions figuring in logic. Propositions related by implication themselves have certain structures given by occurrences of logical constants. For example, axiom (5) of *Principles* § 18, '$p.q \supset p$', states that

---

[15] Russell of course is famous for his many changes of mind, and so strictly speaking he did not hold a single view of logic even in this fairly limited period of philosophical development. I simplify in order to focus on what Lewis might have taken to be Russell's conception of logic. Moreover, my story does incorporate a significant change in Russell's views.

[16] Russell's conception of the generality of logic is similar to the normative sense in which Frege takes logic to be maximally general; see MacFarlane (2002, 35–7). Consider, e.g., Frege's claim that logical laws are 'the most general laws' because they 'prescribe universally the way in which one ought to think if one is to think at all' (1964 [1893], xv). If we gloss the phrase, 'if one is to think at all', as 'no matter what one is thinking about', then we have in essence Russell's view.

[17] The following account of Russell's view of logic owes much to Hylton (1990), especially Part II, Chapter 4, and Griffin (1980).

[18] Indeed, Russell in *Principles* holds that only propositions can stand in this relation; see Russell (1903), § 16, 15, § 18, axioms (2) and (3).

[19] I would like to situate my account with respect to a recent controversy over whether Frege or Russell held 'universalist' conceptions of logic which preclude semantic theorizing about logic: van Heijenoort (1967), Ricketts (1986), Stanley (1996), Tappenden (1997), and Proops (2007). It should be obvious that I'm *not* claiming that in order to be a principle of logic for Russell, a proposition must quantify over all items whatsoever in his ontology. It is clear that Russell takes some pains in *Principles* to formulate some principles of deduction as generalizations in which 'the variables have an absolutely unrestricted field: any conceivable entity may be substituted for any one of our variables' (§ 7). However, it is *not this* feature of those generalizations, but rather the fact that they range over *all propositions*, that is necessary for them to be principles of logic. The only sense in which Russell's logic is maximally general on my account is maximal generality of application as norms of inference.

every proposition is borne the relation of implication by all those propositions in which it stands in the relation of conjunction to some proposition (§ 18, 6).

A consequence of this view of logic is that, since the principles of logic are themselves propositions, they can also stand in the relation of implication. Because logic is maximally general in application, i.e., because the principles of logic describe how propositions, purely in virtue of being propositions, are related by implication, they must describe the facts about how the propositions that are logical rules of inference are related by implication to other propositions. That is to say, the rules of inference that comprise logic have to be applicable to those very rules, have to govern reasoning about those very rules.

Between *Principles* and *Principia*, Russell's conception of logic changed in a number of significant ways, only one of which is directly relevant to our concerns.[20] Russell no longer took the relation of implication to be indefinable, but '"p implies q" is ... defined to mean: "Either p is false or q is true"' (Whitehead and Russell 1910, 94). In spite of these changes, Russell continues to maintain the generality of logic; he describes Part I, the very beginning of *Principia*, as 'dealing with such topics as belong traditionally to symbolic logic ... in virtue of their generality' (87). Moreover, Russell continues to take valid inference to track implication. 'The Theory of Deduction', which opens Part I, is 'the theory of how one proposition can be inferred from another', and Russell tells us that 'in order that one proposition may be inferred from another, it is necessary that the two should have that relation which makes the one a consequence of the other. When a proposition q is a consequence of a proposition p, we say that p implies q. Thus *deduction depends upon the relation of implication*' (90).[21]

Russell sets out the following reasons for defining implication. He acknowledges that 'there are other legitimate meanings' of implication, but claims that his definition yields a more 'convenient' meaning (90). Russell's definition captures '[t]he essential property that we require of implication', namely, true propositions do not imply false ones (90). This property is essential to implication because it is 'in virtue of this property that implication yields proofs' (90). What Russell has in mind here depends on his conception of proof, which consists of establishing truths by inferring them from true premises[22] by *modus ponens*: if p implies q and p is true, then, provided that true propositions do not imply false ones, q must be true. It follows that *any* non-empty relation R between propositions such that for any propositions p and q if

$$p \text{ is true and } q \text{ is false} \tag{1}$$

---

[20] Two other major changes are the 'ramified' theory of types and the multiple-relation theory of judgment, on which propositions, like classes, are analysed away.

[21] It is not clear that the multiple-relations theory of judgment mentioned in *Principia* is compatible with this talk of implication as a relation among propositions. But of course it is a vexed question whether the multiple-relations theory is consistent with the quantification over propositions and propositional functions apparently required by the logic of *Principia*. For contrasting views see, e.g., Ricketts (2001, 101–21) versus Landini (1998) and Klement (2004).

[22] Thus, arguments by *reductio* are strictly speaking not proofs; but Russell thinks that all such arguments can be converted into genuine proofs.

then p does *not* stand in R to q, 'yields proofs.' It should be clear that there are many (extensionally) distinct relations that satisfy these requirements, differing on which of the propositions p and q that fail condition (1) count as standing in that relation. Russell's definition of implication in essence picks out from among these relations the one which holds of the most propositions: *whenever* any propositions p and q fail to satisfy (1), p materially implies q. This is why Russell takes his definition to give 'the most general meaning compatible with the preservation of' the essential characteristic of implication. The definition is 'convenient' because it does not require distinguishing among ordered pairs of propositions that fail (1).[23]

But Russell's justification of his definition of implication raises a question. How are the logical axioms of *Principia* selected? These axioms are supposed to describe which implications hold and so license deductions. Since in *Principia* Russell adopts material implication, one might expect that Russell's reason for thinking that, e.g. $q \supset q \vee p$, is an axiom is that, of any two propositions, q and $q \vee p$, either the first is false or the second is true. But if so, why does Russell not set forth these reasons when he presents the logical axioms? Why does Russell, in contrast to Frege, never give elucidatory arguments for accepting his axioms?[24] We will come back to this question below.

I turn now to Lewis. In his early writings on logic, Lewis was in many ways a faithful Russellian. Three points stand out. First, like Russell, Lewis takes the propositions of logic to be descriptive generalizations which 'state' 'implication relations' (1913, 428). Second, for Lewis as for Russell implication is 'that relation which is present when we "validly" pass from one assertion, or set of assertions, to another assertion' (428). Finally, Lewis holds that 'while other branches [of knowledge] find their organon of proof in … logic, this discipline supplies its own' (429). That is, logic is *the* instrument of proof in all disciplines, including itself, which is to say that it is maximally general in application.

In 'Implication and the Algebra of Logic' (1912), Lewis presents his most well-known disagreement with Russell over 'the paradoxes of material implication,' '$\sim p \supset (p \supset q)$' and '$q \supset (p \supset q)$'—which Russell himself in *Principles* read as 'false propositions imply all propositions, and true propositions are implied by all propositions' (1903, 15). Lewis's point is that, since we don't ordinarily accept that every statement is a logical consequence of any false statement, or that any true statement is deducible from every statement, these theorems of *Principia* show that *Principia* does not correctly describe the relation of implication.

It's unclear how much force this criticism has against Russell. Russell's logicist project is to *prove* the truths of mathematics from the truths of logic, and for Russell, as we saw above, all genuine proof rests on truths. So, Russell is constrained *not* to use, in *Principia*,

---

[23] Is there an explanation of how Russell came to accept these reasons for the definability of implication? I argue in Shieh (forthcoming) that in fact there is less change in Russell's views than meets the eye.

[24] What I mean by 'elucidatory argument' is a line of reasoning by going through which one comes simultaneously to grasp a thought and to see that it is true. I follow Burge (2005) in holding that the arguments Frege sets out in discussing his basic laws are precisely such arguments.

any of the implications from falsehoods that he accepts as perfectly valid. For the purposes of Russellian logicism, an implication relation need only be truth-preserving, and not reflect other aspects of our deductive practice.

But the 'paradoxes' are not the only basis for Lewis's criticism. A less well-known argument against material implication is that it is *not useful* in inference. A material conditional can be established on the basis that its antecedent is false, but then one would not be able to use it in inferring the consequent by *modus ponens*. Alternatively, it can be established on the basis that its consequent is true, but then there would be no point in inferring the consequent by *modus ponens*.[25]

Russell himself explicitly addresses this argument:

> In fact, inference only arises when 'not-*p* or *q*' can be known without our knowing already which of the two alternatives it is that makes the disjunction true. Now, the circumstances under which this occurs are those in which certain *relations of form* exist between *p* and *q* ... which enables us to *know* that the first implies the second, without having first to know that the first is false or to know that the second is true. (1919, 153; emphases mine)

The 'relations of form' hold between *p* and *q* just in case *q* is deducible from *p* by the axioms of *Principia*,[26] in the sense of deducibility outlined in the previous section.

Lewis's counter-argument to this Russellian reply takes us to the heart of his objection to material implication.[27] Lewis asks, how do we know that the axioms of *Principia* can be known without first knowing the truth-values of their antecedents or consequents? Consider one way in which we can explain the truth of Russell's fifth axiom, $(q \supset r) \supset ((p \lor q) \supset (p \lor r))$, by giving the following argument. $q \supset r$ is either true or false. If $q \supset r$ is false, then by definition the implication $(q \supset r) \supset ((p \lor q) \supset (p \lor r))$ is true. So suppose that it is true. Then either *q* is false or *r* is true. We have now to show that the consequent $(p \lor q) \supset (p \lor r)$ is true. If *r* is true, then $p \lor r$ has to be true, so $(p \lor q) \supset (p \lor r)$ is true. So now let's suppose that *q* is false. It follows that $p \lor q$ is true if *p* is true, false if *p* is false. If $p \lor q$ is false, then $(p \lor q) \supset (p \lor r)$ is true. So suppose that *p* is true. Then $p \lor r$ is true, so again $(p \lor q) \supset (p \lor r)$ is true.

In this argument there are three steps in which we move from a supposition that some proposition is false to another claim. If these three steps are all inferences, and if our inferences are to be governed by facts about material implication, then, since a false proposition materially implies any proposition, each of the conclusions in these transitions can legitimately be the negation of the one actually stated. For example, an

---

[25] This argument is discussed in one of the best accounts of Lewis's strict implication, Curley (1975), at 521–2.

[26] In this text Russell calls these axioms 'formal principles of deduction' (1919, 149).

[27] The following argument is based on a reading of Lewis's (1917) response to Norbert Wiener's (1916) criticism of Lewis's rejection of the logic of *Principia*. I give a full account of this argument and its textual bases in Shieh (forthcoming)

equally legitimate alternative inference to the first step of the argument would be: if $q \supset r$ is false, then $(q \supset r) \supset ((p \lor q) \supset (p \lor r))$ is also false. But then, the truth of the fifth axiom is not established on this supposition. Nor can we argue that since it follows by material implication from the falsity of $q \supset r$ that $(q \supset r) \supset ((p \lor q) \supset (p \lor r))$ is both true and false, we can, by *reductio*, conclude that $q \supset r$ is true. For, if we allow this form of argument, then we can establish the truth of every implication from the assumption of its falsity. So, if we reason in accordance with material implication, then it's *not* clear that we can see that, or explain how, the (propositional) axioms of *Principia* are true. That is to say, the inferential resources required to demonstrate that the propositional axioms of *Principia* are true on the basis of Russell's definition of implication are in conflict with the principles of deduction that can be derived from these axioms. This incoherence internal to the logic of the *Principia* is the deepest source of Lewis's criticism of material implication. This is why Lewis says that one cannot demonstrate the logical connections articulated in the postulates of *Principia* 'without calling on principles outside the system' (1917, 356). But this then puts in question whether Russell's axioms and theorems can count as logic. Since logic is maximally general in application, it must be its own instrument of proof, and so it must supply any principles needed to establish or explain the correctness of its axioms. Thus Russell's system of material implication fails to be logic, and moreover, fails according to an aspect of his own conception of logic.

It is in response to this incoherence in Russell's logic that Lewis introduces modal notions, especially the notion of strict implication, into logic. Let's go back to our explanatory argument for the truth of Russell's fifth propositional axiom. The problem this argument poses for material implication is that one notorious purported rule of inference based on that implication allows too much to be inferred from assumptions of the falsity of some proposition. So, what we need, in order to describe the inferential standards that are implicit in this argument, are principles of implication that limit what may be inferred from such assumptions of falsity. Lewis tried out several formulations, settling eventually on ones based on the notion of impossibility.[28] That is, he construes, e.g., the first step in the argument as based on this fact: given the definition of material implication, it is impossible for $q \supset r$ to be false and $(q \supset r) \supset ((p \lor q) \supset (p \lor r))$ not to be true. That is to say, the falsity of $q \supset r$ *strictly implies* the truth of $(q \supset r) \supset ((p \lor q) \supset (p \lor r))$. This impossibility precludes the correctness of inferring, from the falsity of $q \supset r$, anything incompatible with the truth of $(q \supset r) \supset ((p \lor q) \supset (p \lor r))$.

In developing the systems of strict implication, Lewis did not provide much explanation of these modal notions. After *A Survey of Symbolic Logic* (1918), Lewis embraced a version of pragmatism, and developed a view of the a priori as based on meaning (see in particular Lewis 1923, 1929). He then took necessity to be based ultimately on the meanings that we associate with our inferential vocabulary. I here pass over the details

---

[28] Lewis starts with 'intensional disjunction' in (1912), goes to 'strict implication' in (1913), and reaches 'impossibility' in (1914); he stays with 'impossibility' in (1918), and makes the slight change to 'possibility' in Lewis and Langford (1932).

of Lewis's views, noting only that it was assimilated, mainly by Quine, to the positivists' account of necessity in terms of analyticity, which will be treated below.

36.3 Wittgenstein's *Tractatus*

Wittgenstein's *Tractatus Logico-Philosophicus* (1922 [1921])[29] is one of the most enigmatic philosophical texts of the twentieth century, and there is controversy over just about every aspect of it. Here considerations of space preclude more than a sketch of an account of logical necessity shared by many opposed readings of the *Tractatus*,[30] which displays its connections with Lewis's critique of Russell and its influence on the conceptions of modality of the Vienna Circle and Carnap.

To begin with, just as Lewis was led to strict implication by criticism of Russell's logic, so the tautologousness of the propositions of logic in the *Tractatus* is motivated by dissatisfaction with Russell's view of logic.[31] In particular, Wittgenstein rejected Russell's view of logic as descriptive generalizations for failing to square with the *inconceivability*, and so *impossibility*, of the falsity of any proposition of logic. The conception of tautology in the *Tractatus* accounts for this modal status of logic.

The conception rests on the picture theory of propositions.[32] Propositions are pictures of facts, and what it is to *be* a picture is to agree or disagree with the facts, so it is essential to a proposition to be either true or false of the facts. There are two levels of picturing in language. At the most fundamental level are elementary propositions representing possible atomic facts. A non-elementary proposition is analysed into elementary ones, and represents by agreeing or disagreeing with each of the combinations of possibilities for truth or falsity of the elementary propositions in question. So a non-elementary proposition corresponds to a class of truth-possibilities of elementary propositions.

There are two important features of non-elementary propositions. First, one and the same class of truth-possibilities of elementary propositions can be expressed in different ways, in which different 'logical constant' signs occur. So the logical signs make no difference to the picturing of the world by propositions, and are not representatives of anything in the world (4.0312). Second, for any set of elementary propositions there is a class that contains every truth-possibility. So for any set of elementary propositions there is a proposition that agrees with every truth-possibility. These propositions are tautologies (4.46).

---

[29] References to the *Tractatus* will be by remark number.

[30] For example, this view is discernible in both Diamond (1988) and Hacker (1986), which otherwise disagree completely about the *Tractatus*.

[31] This claim is relatively uncontroversial; see Griffin (1980), Ricketts (1996, 2002), and Proops (2002).

[32] The following sketch owes much to Warren Goldfarb's (amazingly still) unpublished paper, 'Objects, Names, and Realism in the *Tractatus*'. Note that on Goldfarb's view, the *Tractatus* seems to present what appears to be a conception of logic, but only in order to display its ultimate incoherence.

A tautology is true no matter which elementary propositions are true; that is, it is true no matter what atomic facts obtain, no matter how the world is. So it is not true in virtue of correctly picturing the world, but in virtue of the mechanism of propositional representation. Hence tautologies 'lack sense' (4.461), and 'do not represent any possible situations' (4.462). It is inconceivable for a tautology to be false, for two reasons: to be a proposition is to agree or disagree with truth-possibilities of elementary propositions, and it makes no sense to think that it might not be possible to agree with all truth possibilities. The essence of propositional representation is prior to and determines the necessity of the propositions of logic.

I pause to note briefly the relation of Tractarian necessity to apriority and analyticity. First, tautologies are not in any obvious way true in virtue of the meanings of the logical constants, since for Wittgenstein the constants are not representatives of entities and have no sense.[33] Thus it is a fallacy to argue that since what makes Wittgenstein's tautologies true is not the world, it must be their meanings. Second, since tautologies are not analytic, *if* they are a priori their apriority does not rest on analyticity. In fact Tractarian tautologies *are* a priori, but what this comes to is that since they do not depict facts of any sort, knowledge of them doesn't depend on any kind of access to facts, be it sensory experience or rational intuition. In sum, the Tractarian conception of necessity has little if anything in common with the conception popularly attributed to logical positivism.

This sketch of the conception of necessity in the *Tractatus* is subject to a major caveat posed by Wittgenstein's say/show distinction. Terms such as 'fact' 'signify formal concepts' (4.1272), which are 'pseudo-concepts'; the use of such terms as 'proper concept word[s]' lead to 'nonsensical pseudo-propositions' (4.1272). The nonsensicality of pseudo-propositions differs from the senselessness of tautologies. Alongside formal concepts are formal properties, which also lead to pseudo-propositions if one attempts to ascribe them. The only legitimate expression of a formal property 'is a feature of certain symbols' (4.126) which shows itself in any adequate notation. The most important instances of formal properties for us are 'internal properties': '[a] property is internal if it is unthinkable that its object does not possess it' (4.123). We have taken one basis of the necessity of logic to be the inconceivability of an elementary proposition's failing to be either true or false. So we have attempted to ascribe an internal property of elementary propositions, and our words would then, by Wittgenstein's lights, be nonsense.[34]

---

[33] An objection might be based on Hylton's (1997) argument that Tractarian logical symbols express operations mapping patterns of agreements with truth-possibilities to other such patterns. I cannot go into this issue here any further here than to say that operations are *our* means of recognizing that a proposition is a tautology, not that in virtue of which that proposition is a tautology.

In addition, although Wittgensteinian tautologies are not analytic in the sense popularly attributed to logical positivism, they can be understood as analytic according to the Leibnizian–Kantian conception of analyticity as conceptual containment. See Dreben and Floyd (1991).

[34] In Shieh (forthcoming) I argue against the more or less standard picture of Tractarian logical necessity sketched in this section. I hold that, in fact, in the *Tractatus* the necessity of logic is not a mode of truth at all. It is, rather, the non-arbitrary ('nicht willkürlich', 3.342, see also 6.124) identities and differences in any system of representations of the world. These non-arbitrary *features* constitute what Wittgenstein calls 'logischen Syntax' (3.325, 3.327, 3.33, 3.334, 3.344, and 6.124) and show forth in our use of symbols.

36.4 THE VIENNA CIRCLE AND CARNAP'S *LOGICAL SYNTAX OF LANGUAGE*

There are, we now know, significant synchronic and diachronic differences among the doctrines held by members of the Vienna Circle.[35] Here my focus will be on the *Tractatus*'s influence on the Vienna Circle's, and in particular on Carnap's, views of modality.[36]

Through the influence of A. J. Ayer's *Language, Truth, and Logic* (1936), logical positivism is nowadays frequently taken to be an updating of Humean empiricism with the techniques of modern mathematical logic. The Vienna Circle held that sense experience is the only source of genuine knowledge about the world, and rejected metaphysics as, not false, but meaningless nonsense, on the basis of verificationism: a sentence can be meaningful only if it is associated with a method of verification ultimately based on sensory experience. The main problem that the Circle saw for empiricism is how to account for knowledge of logic and mathematics, both indispensable to modern science. Experience might always be different from the way it is, so any truth based on experience is contingent. In contrast, we have no clear conception of how logical and mathematical truths might be false. Thus, logico-mathematical knowledge seems a priori, and so to require some faculty of rational intuition, paving the way to metaphysics. Indeed, logic and mathematics seem no better able to pass the verifiability test than metaphysics.

The Circle saw, in the Tractarian view of logic as tautology, the key to a consistent empiricism. Since tautologies owe their truth, not to correct depiction of the world, but to the nature of linguistic representation, our knowledge of logic does not rest on the sensory sources of genuine knowledge of worldly facts. Rather, it rests on knowledge of how we represent the world in language. The apparent apriority and necessity of logic can now be taken to have a linguistic, rather than factual, origin. Of course the sentences of metaphysics also have no empirical content. The rejection of metaphysics is based on the Tractarian distinction between the senseless and the nonsensical. The nonsense of metaphysics results from violations of the rules of language, while the senselessness of tautologies is a by-product of rules of the language (see in particular Carnap 1931).

The view just outlined—call it classical positivism—was indeed briefly espoused by the Circle. But the positivists themselves were aware of an array of difficulties with these classical doctrines, and soon moved away in a number of diverging directions. For our purposes, the most salient problem of classical positivism is to show that

---

[35] For discussion of some of them, see Uebel, in the present volume. See also, *inter alia*, Coffa (1991), Friedman (1999), Creath (1999), Richardson (2004), Goldfarb and Ricketts (1992), Awodey and Carus (2007), and Carus (2007).

[36] For a balanced and informative account of how the Vienna Circle received Wittgenstein's *Tractatus*, see Uebel (2011).

mathematics, like logic, is tautologous,[37] that is, to carry out a type of logicist reduction of mathematics, to tautologies rather than Frege's or Russell's formulations of logic. Carnap attempted such a reduction, using David Hilbert's idea of meta-mathematics. Technical difficulties eventually led Carnap to abandon many details of the Tractarian framework.[38] Language becomes conceived as 'a system of rules' (Carnap 1937, 4) not explained in more fundamental terms of picturing extra-linguistic facts. The study of language thus conceived is 'logical syntax'. The notion of tautology, sentences true in virtue of the mechanism of representation, is replaced by a *syntactic* notion of *analyticity*, sentences formally derivable from the rules of language alone. Logico-mathematical sentences are analytic, mere auxiliaries for the confirmation of theoretical empirical sentences.

At first these changes still subserve the project of a consistent empiricism. By *Syntax*, Carnap has (mostly) abandoned classical positivism.[39] For our story, I focus on a form of criticism directed, not only at metaphysics, but at controversies over the foundations of mathematics among philosophers of an anti-metaphysical orientation, including members of the Vienna Circle. Carnap found these debates just as intractable and confused as traditional metaphysical disputes (1963, 45ff.; 1937, xiv–xv), and he seems to take their sterility to stem from a kind of illusion over the subject matter of philosophical sentences. These sentences 'seem to concern ... objects, such as the structure of space and time, the relation between cause and effect ... the necessity, contingency, possibility or impossibility of conditions, and the like', but they 'really concern linguistic forms' (Carnap 1935, 59–60).[40]

One source of this diagnosis is the Tractarian notion of formal properties, ascription of which results in nonsense (4.124): '[t]he expression of a formal property is a feature of certain symbols' (4.126). Carnap rejects Wittgenstein's say/show distinction and takes what is shown in language to be features of expressions that can be described in a meta-language. So formal properties become syntactical properties of expressions that appear to be properties of objects. Carnap calls them 'pseudo-object' or 'quasi-syntactical' properties. Ascriptions of pseudo-object properties comprise 'the material mode of speech'. They are 'like object-sentences as to their form, but like syntactical sentences as to their contents' (Carnap 1935, 59–60).

In the case of foundational debates, 'in the material mode we speak about numbers instead of numerical expressions', and this tempts us 'to raise questions as to the real essence of numbers' (78–9). Once such questions arise, so does the possibility of such irresoluble disputes as that between logicists and formalists. The way out of such impasses is to translate pseudo-object-sentences into their syntactic correlates, sentences in 'the formal mode of speech'. The dispute just mentioned is then dissolved by

---

[37] This goes against the *Tractatus*. See Floyd (2005) for arguments against taking the *Tractatus* to espouse any form of logicism.

[38] For details see especially Awodey and Carus (2007) and Carus (2007).

[39] See Carus (2007) for a detailed examination of tensions in *Syntax*.

[40] Compare the title of chapter VII of Hacker (1972): 'Metaphysics as the Shadow of Grammar'.

transformation into two mutually compatible claims about numerical expressions in distinct formal languages.

Modal sentences are also 'veiled syntactical sentences' (73). We 'usually apply modalities … to conditions, states, events, and such like' (73), using sentences like

That A is older than B, and B is older than A, is an impossible state.

The formal mode translation of this sentence is:

The sentence 'A is older than B, and B is older than A' is contradictory.

More generally, '[i]mpossibility is a quality to which there is a parallel syntactical quality, namely contradictoriness, because always and only when a state is impossible, is the sentence which describes this state contradictory'; hence it is a pseudo-object property. The translations of other modal expressions into syntactical terms are straightforward: 'As possibility is the opposite of impossibility, obviously the parallel syntactical term to "logically possible" is "non-contradictory" … Analogously, we translate "logically necessary" into "analytic"' (77).

So far Carnap's diagnosis of philosophical illusion seems to presuppose that the material mode 'suggests something *false* … and … the formal mode … tells the unvarnished *truth*' (Coffa 1991, 325; emphases mine). In particular, the claim that modal predicates are quasi-syntactical seems to be that necessity, for instance, *really is* analyticity, and that's precisely what, according to popular wisdom, positivism holds. But this view of Carnap's criticisms is problematic. Carnap uses phrases such as 'really about' and 'object' to formulate his criticism, but these are the very words that generate paradigmatic pseudo-object sentences.[41] So these criticisms are, by Carnap's own standards, themselves in the material mode of speech, i.e., they contain pseudo-object sentences. Carnap takes no pains to hide this; he explicitly notes in Part V of *Syntax* that '[e]ven in this book, and especially in this Part, the material mode of speech has often been employed' (1937, § 81, 312). Carnap specifically characterizes his remarks about what pseudo-object properties really apply to and about philosophical illusion as 'informal', in contrast to the formal syntactic definition of quasi-syntacticality (1937, § 63). Thus when Carnap says that philosophical sentences are really about language, he recognizes that this is no less potentially misleading than those very philosophical sentences.

What then is Carnap's ground for preferring the formal mode? Note to begin with that according to Carnap the '*material mode of speech is not in itself erroneous*; it only readily lends itself to wrong use' (1937, 312). Indeed, 'if suitable definitions and *rules* for the material mode of speech are laid down and systematically applied, no obscurities or contradictions arise' (312; my emphasis). The reason why questions generated by material-mode talk lead to apparently irresoluble disputes is that they are posed in natural languages, which are 'too irregular and too complicated to be actually comprehended in a system of rules' (312).

---

[41] On 'about' see Carnap (1937, 290), example 12a; 'object' is a 'universal word' which, used in the material mode of speech, produces pseudo-object sentences, see Carnap (1937, 293–5).

This points to Carnap's view of 'controversies in traditional metaphysics': 'there seemed hardly any chance of mutual understanding, let alone of agreement, because there was not even a common criterion for deciding the controversy' (1963, 44–5). If indeed there are no common criteria for deciding metaphysical controversies, then it would be pointless, irrational, to continue these disputes in the form of trying to find out who is right. A 'question of right or wrong must always refer to a system of rules' (1939: § 4, 7), and logical syntax is the construction of languages as systems of rules. Thus the aim of syntax is to set out criteria that would rationalize pointless philosophical debates. Specifically, Carnap offers the parties to philosophical disputes the possibilities of adopting a common set of rules for adjudicating their disagreement, or of reconceiving their opposition, not as a disagreement over the truth of a doctrine, but as different recommendations about what language, what system of rules, to adopt. Either way, the dispute would acquire a clear point. This is the reason for preferring the formal mode.

Now it is natural, at this point, to ask: what is the basis of Carnap's view of the rationality of disputes? It's a short step from such a question to intractable philosophical debates over the true nature of rationality. Thus, Carnap's conception of rationality is also not a theoretical claim but a practical proposal. We can take Carnap to ask his audience to compare the state of their philosophical debates with that of his precise syntactical investigations, and to offer philosophers a way out of the fruitless debates in which they are stuck. He in effect says to philosophers: you don't *have to* take yourself to be advancing a substantive thesis about reality against other such substantive theses, because I can offer you a way of looking at what you want, in which it will no longer be unclear what exactly getting it involves, because you'll be doing something other than what you took yourself to be doing. In the words of another philosopher, Carnap aims to 'shew the fly the way out of the fly-bottle' (Wittgenstein 2001 [1953], § 309). Thus, Carnap is not engaged in the same enterprise as traditional philosophy at all; rather, he proposes an activity, syntactical investigation, to *replace* traditional philosophizing; he urges philosophers to 'change the subject'.[42]

The upshot of this radical pragmatism for Carnap's theory of modality is that any claim to the effect that, e.g., for Carnap the property of necessity is *really* analyticity is in the material mode and misleading. The significance of Carnap's theory consists in the philosophical perplexities displaced by the syntactic explication of necessity as analyticity. Let's look at two philosophical tangles that Carnap proposes to treat with his theory of modality in *Syntax*.

First, Carnap sees the dispute between Russell and Lewis on the nature of implication as similar to debates over the foundations of mathematics. He characterizes Russell's 'opinion' that implication 'is a relation between propositions' as a material mode claim that is correct if 'proposition' is understood as 'that which is designated by a sentence' (1937, 253). Once we think of implication in such a way, we are tempted to ask, what exactly is this relation? Since, ' "to imply" in the English language means the

---

[42] Rorty (1982, xiv). Carnap's attitude towards traditional philosophy is of a piece with his Principle of Tolerance (1937, § 17, 52).

same as "to contain" or "to involve", we are tempted to take it to be 'the consequence-relation' (255). Succumbing to this temptation, 'Lewis and Russell—they are agreed on this point—look upon the consequence-relation ... as ... on the same footing as sentential connectives' (254). This leads to wrangles about which propositions containing the implication symbol correctly describe the logical consequence relation, i.e., which logical system is correct.

The dissolution of this dispute rests on Carnap's explications of ordinary imprecise conceptions of logical consequence in precise syntactical meta-linguistic terms. From the perspective of such explications, Carnap takes Lewis to be right in the following sense. If the consequence relation is to be expressed by a 'sentential connective', say '<', so that ' "A < B" is demonstrable if "B" is a consequence of "A" ', then neither 'Russell's implication' nor any 'of the so-called truth-functions ... can express the consequence-relation at all' (254) Thus, Lewis 'believed himself compelled to introduce intensional sentential connectives, namely, those of strict implication and of the modality-terms' (254) But, given Carnap's explications of consequence, one sees that Lewis's move is not compulsory. One can, instead, distinguish 'the consequence-relation [as] a relation between sentences' from '*implication [which] is not a relation between sentences*'; in the formal mode, ' "consequence" [is] a predicate of the syntax-language', while ' "⊃" is a symbol of the object-language' (253–4; emphases in the text). Thus, *pace* Lewis, we are not forced to 'think that the symbol of implication ought really to express the consequence-relation, and count it as a failure on the part of this symbol that it does not do so' (255). The language of *Principia* is perfectly 'adequate for the construction both of logic and of mathematics', and 'in it necessarily valid sentences can be proved and a sentence which follows from another can be derived from the former' (253). While there is nothing objectionable in the 'requirement that a language be capable of expressing necessity, possibility, the consequence-relation, etc.', we do not, in the case of *Principia*, have to insist that to satisfy this requirement we need 'anything supplementary to [it]', because we can simply 'formulat[e its] syntax' (253–4).[43]

Given this context for Carnap's theory of modality in *Syntax*, we can see that Carnap is *not claiming* that necessity is a syntactic property, but rather *proposing* the use of the meta-linguistic predicate 'analytic' in the place of the object language predicate 'necessary', in order to explicate our imprecise ideas of logical consequence. Carnap's aim is to show Russellian extensional logicians and Lewisian modal logicians that there is no need to argue over whose logic is the right one.[44]

---

[43] Carnap's view here bears comparison with Robert Brandom's (1994, 2000) view that logical vocabulary play primarily an expressive role in making inferential proprieties explicit. The syntactic correlate of Lewis's strict implication connective is the consequence predicate of the syntax language, and we have already seen what syntax language predicates are the correlates of Lewis's other modal connectives: the impossibility connective is correlated with 'contradictory', the possibility connective with 'non-contradictory', and the necessity connective with 'analytic' (Carnap (1935, 73–4, 77; 1937, § 69, 250–1)).

[44] I am very much indebted to discussion with Gary Ebbs for the formulation of this point.

Second, Carnap addresses a problem deriving from what he takes to be Wittgenstein's notions of essential or internal properties. Expressed in the material mode, a 'property of an object c is called an *essential* property of c, if it is inconceivable that c should not possess it' (1937, 304). This problem is particularly significant in the subsequent history of modality:

> Let us take as the object c ... the father of Charles. [B]eing related to Charles is an essential property of c, since it is inconceivable that the father of Charles should not be related to Charles. But being a landowner is not an essential property of the father of Charles. For, even if he is a landowner, it is conceivable that he might not be one. On the other hand ... it is inconceivable that the owner of this piece of land should not be a landowner. Now, however, it happens to be the father of Charles who is the owner of this piece of land. [Thus] it is both an essential and not an essential property of this man to be a landowner. (304)

Carnap proposes to dissolve this apparent contradiction by translation of the second-order pseudo-object property of being an essential property to the syntactical property of *relative analyticity*: a predicate is analytic relative to a sequence of 'object designations' just in case the sentence resulting from filling the place-holders of the predicate with these terms is analytic. Applying this translation scheme to the problematic essential properties of the example, the contradiction disappears because ' "landowner" is an analytic predicate in relation to the object-designation "the owner of this piece of land", but it is not an analytic predicate in relation to the object-designation "the father of Charles" ' (304). We now see that the 'fault of' the material mode definition of essential property 'lies in the fact that it is referred to the one *object* instead of to the *object-designations*, which may be *different* even when the object is the same' (304).

36.5 Quine, I: The Carnapian Background

The roots of Quine's critiques of modality go back to the phase of his philosophical development when he was 'very much [Carnap's] disciple' (1976, 41). Specifically, in lectures in 1934 expounding Carnap's *Syntax* views,[45] Quine characterizes modal expressions as a 'quasi-syntactic' 'material idiom' whose use leads us to lose

> sight of what we are talking about; ... we appear to be talking about certain non-linguistic objects, when all we *need* be talking about is the ... signs ... used for

---

[45] The significance of these lectures was brought to my attention by Hylton (2001).

denoting those objects. [T]he expressions of modality ... are for all the world properties not of names, or sentences, but of things or situations. These modality-properties or pseudo-properties then involve us in difficulties from which we turn to metaphysics for extrication. (1990, 98)

In particular, use of modal expressions lead us to 'talk of a realm of possibility as distinct from the realm of actuality', and this raises 'problems as to how fragments of the possible are actualized, and what it means for a possibility to be actualized, and why certain possibilities are actualized rather than others' (94–5). The remedy, naturally, is syntax; when 'the syntactic formulation is used, so that whatever *in effect* concerns language is made explicitly to concern language, these difficulties vanish' (98; emphases mine). As we will see, Quine's rejection of modality is decisively shaped by this Carnapian view that modal properties are pseudo-object properties, and by Carnap's replacement of necessity by (syntactic) analyticity.

The idea of 'losing sight of what we are talking about' suggests that the problem is forming a *false* view of what we're talking about. This suggestion seems confirmed by Quine's going on to say, 'in the quasi-syntactic idiom we *appear* to be talking about certain nonlinguistic objects'. At this point one expects Quine to go on to tell us what we are *really* talking about. But that's *not* what Quine tells us. Instead, he says that we *don't have to be* talking about what we might think we're talking about. That is to say, there is an alternative to our conception of the subject matter of our modal discourse. Moreover, Quine urges that this alternative conception is better, because it does not lead to metaphysical difficulties. In other words, this alternative is better, *not* because it is correct, identifies the true subject of our talk, *but* because it keeps us out of trouble. This is confirmed by what Quine says at the end of the passage, that in syntactic formulation 'whatever *in effect* concerns language is made explicitly to concern language'. Quine does *not* say that the quasi-syntactical idiom 'in fact' concerns language, but only 'in effect'. That is, Quine suggests that we don't actually know what quasi-syntactical sentences are about, but also that, given a syntactic translation, we can take them 'in effect' to be about language. Thus, Quine's standard for favouring the syntactic over the quasi-syntactic alternative is a pragmatic one, just as Carnap's is.

But Quine's pragmatism is not quite the same as Carnap's. Carnapian pragmatism, as we saw, operates at the level of a choice between pursuing traditional philosophical problems and constructing linguistic frameworks. The choice is: do we change the subject or not? The successor subject could be based on explications, in Carnap's sense,[46] of notions figuring in the predecessor subject, but it needn't be. Quinean pragmatism, in contrast, applies to the choice between competing scientific hypotheses. One hypothesis is that our talk of possibility and impossibility commits us to positing a realm of possibilia and impossibilia alongside actual things. The other hypothesis is that this talk only commits us to actual concrete and abstract entities, including the objects of syntactic

---

[46] The classic statement of explication is in Carnap (1950).

claims. The first hypothesis not only multiplies entities, and so runs afoul of Occam's Razor, but involves us in intractable issues about, *inter alia*, the properties and individuation of these entities. The second has neither the additional ontological commitments nor the burden of answering these additional questions. Thus, our best scientific methodology dictates that we adopt the second hypothesis over the first.[47]

One of the metaphysical problems of modality Quine mentions is: what does it *mean* for a possibility to be actualized? Much of Quine's critique of modality stems from this problem. Quine's objection, at bottom, is that he doesn't see any clear meaning in claims about what is possible or necessary. Quine divides such claims into two types, and his criticisms fall correspondingly into two groups. The first type consists of claims ascribing necessity or possibility to statements, in traditional terminology, ascriptions of necessity *de dicto*. The second type consists of claims ascribing modal properties to individuals, traditionally termed claims of necessity *de re*, and generalizations involving modal properties.

As I mentioned, the target of Quine's critique rests on an account of necessity in terms of analyticity that he takes from Lewis and Carnap (1960, 195). The principal thesis of the account is that 'the result of applying "necessarily" to a statement is true if, and only if, the original statement is analytic' (Quine 1943, 121). Analyticity here is not Carnap's syntactic conception but Quine's well-known account: 'a statement is *analytic* if by putting synonyms for synonyms ... it can be turned into a logical truth', where a 'logical truth is ... deducible by the logic of truth functions and quantification from true statements containing only logical signs'.[48] In addition, note that although Quine rarely explicitly mentions it, there is a link between analyticity and apriority.[49] This goes through a view of the relation between synonymy and understanding: '[t]o determine the synonymity of two names or other expressions it should be sufficient to understand the expressions; but to determine that two names designate the same object, it is commonly necessary to investigate the world' (Quine 1943, 119). Let's call this view the synonymy thesis. Given this thesis and the account of analyticity, it follows that an analytic statement can be determined as true without investigating the world.

Quine argues, against *de dicto* modal claims, that there is no clear distinction between necessary truth and plain truth, because there is no clear distinction between analytic truth and plain truth. I will not discuss these Quinean criticisms, since they rest on

---

[47] In one sense, this is also a charge of illusion. But the illusion is of the same kind as the illusion we were under when we thought that aether explains certain electromagnetic phenomena. From Quine's perspective the danger of the material mode is that it may lead us to commitments that are to be rejected as *false* on our best theory of the world. Quine's rejection of modality is a rejection of the apparent commitments of modal talk in the material mode, and so with it that material mode talk altogether.

[48] Quine (1947, 44, 3). Note that for Quine here deducibility 'can be expanded into purely syntactical terms by an enumeration of the familiar rules, which are known to be complete; and the reference to "logical signs" can likewise be expanded by enumeration of the familiar primitives' (Quine (1947, 43)). Note in addition that Quine later gave what he takes to be a more general characterization of logical truth in terms of substitution and grammar (1986, chapter 4).

[49] So far as I can tell, the term 'a priori' appears only once in Quine's writings on modality, in (1953b, 159).

Quine's rejection of a clear analytic/synthetic distinction, a topic with no specific connection with modality. The problem with *de re* modal claims is that if one tried to make sense of them in terms of the analyticity conception of necessity, then they either do not describe concrete material objects, or do not have determinate truth conditions. Moreover, to make sense of such claims one must abandon the analyticity conception of necessity, and adopt questionable non-trivial forms of essentialism, what Quine calls 'Aristotelian' essentialism.

36.6 QUINE II: THE SUBSTITUTION AND QUANTIFICATION ARGUMENTS

As first presented in 'Notes on Existence and Necessity' (1943),[50] Quine's critique seems to be a two-part argument. The first part is based on two things. One is the logical law of the '*indiscernibility of identicals*' (1943, 113; Quine's emphases). The other is the notion of *purely designative* occurrences of a singular term, a 'name' in Quine's terminology. He writes, 'The relation of name to the object whose name it is, is called *designation*.... An occurrence of the name in which the name refers simply to the object designated, I shall call *purely designative*' (114). If a name occurs purely designatively in a statement, then that statement says something, truly or falsely, of the object designated by that name. Moreover, if an object is designated by two names, then 'whatever can be said about' it by a statement in which one of its names occur purely designatively is exactly the same as what is said about it by any statement that results from replacing that name by the other name. So if one of these statements says something true of the object, what the other statement says 'should be equally true of' the object.[51] Quine assumes that if a statement of identity is true, then the names occurring in it designate the same object. The conclusion of this line of reasoning is the principle of substitutivity: '*given a true statement of identity, one of its two terms may be substituted for the other in any true statement* [in which they occur purely designatively] *and the result will be true*' (113; emphases in text).

On the basis of the substitutivity principle, Quine argues that whenever mutual substitution, in a statement, of names occurring on two sides of a true identity fails to preserve truth-value—whenever, as I shall put it, there is a substitution failure—'the occurrence

---

[50] This is Quine's first presentation of his critique in English; it was first put forward in Portuguese, but published later than the English translation, in (1944). In addition, a very compressed version of part of the argument appears in footnote 22 of Quine (1941, 16).

[51] Quine (1943, 114). On this construal the indiscernibility of identicals is used twice: first to show that the same thing is said by the two statements, and again to show that the single item that is said is true. Note also that here it is the (onto)logical law governing properties of identity that underlies the principle governing substitution inferences.

to be supplanted is not purely designative, and ... the statement depends not only upon the object but on the form of the name. For it is clear that whatever can be affirmed about the *object* remains true when we refer to the object by any other name' (114).

Quine applies this general thesis to modality by arguing for a by-now famous case of modal substitution failure.

The identity:

$$\text{The number of planets} = 9 \tag{2}$$

is a truth ... of astronomy. The names 'the number of planets' and '9' are not synonymous.... This fact is emphasized by the possibility, ever present, that (2) be refuted by the discovery of another planet.[52] (119)
... The statement:

$$\text{9 is necessarily greater than 7} \tag{3}$$

is equivalent to

'$9 > 7$' is analytic

and is therefore true (if we recognize the reducibility of arithmetic to logic).
On the other hand the statement...:

$$\text{The number of planets is necessarily greater than 7,} \tag{4}$$

[is] false, since ...

The number of planets is greater than 7

[is] true only because of circumstances outside logic. (121)

Hence 'the occurrence of the name "9" in (3) is not purely designative' (123). Let's call this first part of Quine's critique 'the substitution argument'.

The second part of Quine's argument also begins at a general level. He starts by arguing that existential generalization is justified only from purely designative occurrences of names: '[t]he idea behind such inference is that whatever is true of the object designated by a given substantive is true of something; and clearly the inference loses its justification when the substantive in question does not happen to designate' (116). It follows that whenever there is substitution failure, existential generalization is not warranted. At this point it seems that Quine can simply apply this general claim to the modal substitution failures that he had already established, to conclude that that existential generalization

---

[52] Or by the adoption of a resolution: the identity sentence (2) came to express a falsehood on 24 August 2006, when the XXVIth General Assembly of the International Astronomical Union passed the final resolution on the definition of a planet.

from singular terms in modal contexts is unwarranted. But this is not how Quine proceeds. Instead, he propounds a problem with specifying the object that makes true an existential generalization into a modal context:

> [T]he expression:
>
> $$\sim (x) \sim x \text{ is necessarily greater than 7,}$$
>
> that is, 'There is something which is necessarily greater than 7', is meaningless. For, would 9, that is, the number of planets, be one of the numbers necessarily greater than 7? But such an affirmation would be at once true in the form (3) and false in the form (4). (123)

It's not immediately clear what role this problem plays in Quine's criticism, and so not clear how exactly the second part of the criticism works. Let's call the second part, however it works, 'the quantification argument'. Quine does eventually make more explicit that these apparently extra considerations are not superfluous, and that his objection to quantifying into modal contexts is *not* a straightforward application of the conclusion of the substitution argument. But before getting to that, let's survey the first responses to Quine's critique, which can be broadly divided into Fregean and Russellian objections.

36.7 INITIAL REPLIES TO QUINE

Fregean objections, first proposed by Alonzo Church in a review of 'Notes' (1943) claim that singular terms do not have the same references in modal contexts as they do in non-modal ones. Church specifically suggests that in modal contexts singular terms designate, not their ordinary denotations, but their ordinary senses. Since the designations of singular terms in true identities differ from their designations in modal contexts, the indiscernibility of identicals no longer justifies the principle of substitutivity. Moreover, quantification into modal contexts is legitimate because the variable of quantification in such contexts ranges over intensional entities such as senses and attributes.[53]

Russellian objections, also first advanced by Church (1942), are based on applying Russell's theory of descriptions to definite descriptions in identity and modal statements. Church points out that if one applies Russell's theory to eliminate the descriptions occurring in Quine's purported substitution failure, the result no longer has the logical form of a substitution inference. Moreover, as Smullyan (1948) observes, there are two possible scopes for the description 'the number of planets' with respect to the modal phrase 'necessarily' in the conclusion of Quine's example. Smullyan shows that when this description has wide scope, the result of eliminating it using Russell's theory

---

[53] Carnap advances what seems to be a similar reply in (1947) in terms of the 'method of extension and intension'.

is derivable, in the logic of *Principia*, from the premises of the example. Thus Quine's example is not unambiguously an invalid inference.[54]

Neither objection is decisive. Quine argues, against the Fregean introduction of intensional entities, that it 'purifie[s the] universe' of material objects and leaves only intensional objects.[55] The argument is based on a theorem of quantified modal logic, as first formulated by Marcus,[56] a theorem that has come to be known as the necessity of identity:[57]

$$(\forall x)(\forall y)(x = y \supset \Box(x = y)) \tag{5}$$

Quine argues that in order for (5) to be true, any distinct designations, a and b, of an element of the domain of quantification must be synonymous. For such terms, $\ulcorner a = b \urcorner$ is true, so $\ulcorner \Box(a = b) \urcorner$ must be true for (5) to be true. So $\ulcorner a = b \urcorner$ has to be analytic, which requires that a and b be synonymous. This condition is not, however, satisfied by 'concrete material objects'. Such objects, in general, may have distinct designations such that it takes empirical investigation for us to know that they refer to a single object. Hence, by the synonymy thesis, these terms are not synonymous.

Against Smullyan's Russellian objection, Quine points out that the Russellian analysis of the wide-scope reading of the conclusion is an existential quantification into a modal context (Quine 1969, 338).[58] So, Smullyan must presuppose that such quantifications are meaningful. But this assumption begs the question against Quine's overall conclusion that such quantifications are meaningless. Of course, if Quine's overall conclusion is based on the thesis that singular terms occurring in modal contexts are not purely designative, and so ultimately on the existence of substitution failures in modal contexts, then, from Smullyan's perspective, it is Quine who has begged the question. For Smullyan can take his argument to show that if modal quantifications are meaningful,

---

[54] Smullyan (1947, 140) advances another objection to Quine's arguments, based on what nowadays is called a Millian view of names: 'if "Evening Star" and "Morning Star" proper-name the same individual they are synonymous'. Unfortunately, with the notable exception of Marcus's review of Smullyan's paper, this early and prescient objection to Quine had little immediate influence.

[55] The argument appears in 'Reference and Modality', an essay that has three distinct versions, Quine (1953, 1961b, 1980); the quoted phrase appears at 150 in all versions. I present a reconstruction of Quine's argument.

[56] In Barcan (1946a, 1946b, 1947). Marcus provides extensions of two of the Lewis systems—S2 and S4—with axioms for quantification and identity, and an axiom governing quantifiers and modal operators now known as the Barcan formula. Three months after the first two of Marcus's papers appeared in print, Carnap (1946) sets out a quite different account of quantification and modality, based on a semantic construction whose relation to the Lewis axioms systems is not obvious.

[57] In Barcan (1947), Theorem 2.33 and an immediate corollary of it assert that material identity is strictly equivalent to both strict identity and the necessity of strict identity.

[58] Quine's initial replies to Smullyan are undermined by mistakes about the theory of descriptions in *Principia*. Quine claimed that Smullyan's solution requires an 'alteration' in the treatment of descriptions in *Principia*, because in *Principia* all wide and narrow scope eliminations of descriptions are provably equivalent (1953, 155; 1961b, 154). But in fact in *Principia* the equivalence is established only for extensional contexts; Quine's claim is removed from the third (1980) version of the paper. For more details see Marcus (1990) and Neale (1999).

then Quine's examples are not genuine cases of substitution failure. So, in order to take his examples as genuine substitution failures, Quine must already reject the meaningfulness of modal quantifications. Neither side, it seems, has provided an argument that is compelling for the other.

36.8 Quine III: The Quantification Argument Revisited

The standoff at the end of the last section assumes that Quine's only ground against quantifying in is substitution failure. In this section we'll see that this assumption is false.

Let's come back to the question we left hanging at the end of section 36.6: how exactly *does* substitution failure bear on the meaninglessness of quantification? A moment of reflection suggests a problem.[59] Suppose we accept that *if* both '9' and 'the number of planets' occur designatively in

$$9 \text{ is necessarily greater than } 7 \tag{3}$$

and

$$\text{The number of planets is necessarily greater than } 7 \tag{4}$$

then these sentences do not differ in truth-value. Now, given that they do differ in truth-value, we can conclude that *not both* '9' and 'the number of planets' occur designatively, i.e., that *at least one* does not. However, it is compatible with this conclusion that one of these two terms *does* occur designatively. If that's the case, then the truth-value of *one of the two* affirmations of the predicate 'necessarily greater than 7', i.e., one of (3) and (4), *is* determined only by the object designated. Thus it doesn't follow that whether this predicate is truly affirmed of an entity is *invariably* determined by the terms used to single out those entities, and so it doesn't follow that there is no account of the truth conditions of existential generalizations from (3) or (4).

Recall that in 'Notes' Quine does not explicitly base the quantification argument on the substitution argument, but rather raises a problem of specifying the objects that satisfy the matrices of the quantifications. In a 1946 letter to Carnap Quine elaborates this problem:

> I'm going to try to make the essential theoretical point of my article ['Notes'] without use either of the term 'designation' ... or of the formal theory of identity.
>   Let us agree ... to regard the following statement as true:

---

[59] David Kaplan discusses a considerably more intricate version of this problem in (1986), section III.

It is impossible that the capital city of Venezuela be outside Venezuela   (6)

From this it would seem natural, by existential generalization, to infer ...:

∃x it is impossible that x be outside Venezuela   (7)

Now just what is the object x that is considered, in inferring (7) from (6), to be incapable of being outside Venezuela? .... It is a certain mass of adobe et al., viz, the capital city itself. And it is this mass of adobe that is (*apparently*) affirmed, in (6), to be incapable of being outside Venezuela. Hence the *apparent* justice, intuitively, of the inference of (7) from (6). However, that same mass of adobe et al. is affirmed in the following true statement (*apparently*) to be capable of being outside Venezuela:

It is possible that the native city of Bolivar be outside Venezuela   (8)

Justification of (7) by (6) is thwarted by (8), for (8) has just as much right to consideration as (6) so far as the mass of adobe in question is concerned. (Carnap and Quine 1990, 326; emphases mine)

Let's start with Quine's claim that in (6), it is a city, a mass of adobe, etc., that is *apparently affirmed* to have a certain modal property. That is, (6) *seems to be* an ascription of a property to a city. Moreover, if (6) is indeed such an ascription, then it *does warrant* the conclusion that something has that property, since that property *appears to be* a property which cities have. But, Quine asks, is (6) *in fact* the ascription of a property of cities to a city? If it is, then the correctness of this ascription should not be sensitive to 'the form of the name' of that object. However, if (6) ascribes a property to a city, is there any reason to think that (8) does not? If not, then (8) has 'as much' a claim as (6) to being an ascription of the very same property that is ascribed in (6) to the very same city mentioned by (8). But (8) has a different truth-value from (6). Since a single city is designated in these two sentences, this difference in truth-values cannot be accounted for if the truth conditions of the sentences consist in a single predicate's being true of that city. Some other features of the two singular terms must play a role; equivalently, the applicability of the predicate must be sensitive to those other features. The obvious feature in which these terms differ is their syntactic form. Hence I take Quine to reason that, in the absence of a different account, we have to think that whether the predicate is true of an object is fixed by the syntactic form of designations of those objects. So the property ascribed in (6) is not a genuine property of cities after all.[60]

Now, all this talk of what property *seems to be* ascribed, and what property *is in fact* ascribed should remind us of the notion of pseudo-object property, which *seems to be* a property of objects, but is in fact a property of linguistic expressions. Let's recall,

---

[60] Plantinga (1974, Appendix) presents a closely related account of why, according to Quine, modalized predicates do not express genuine properties.

furthermore, that according to Carnap what makes a property φ pseudo-object is that whether φ holds of an object is determined by whether a syntactical property correlated with φ holds of that object's designations, that is, it is determined by the syntactical *forms* of those designations. Thus, the difference in truth-value between (6) and (8), in spite of the identity of the object mentioned in these sentences, shows that they are ascriptions of a pseudo-object property. That is, the modal property of being possibly outside Venezuela is a pseudo-object property.

So what then is the problem with quantifying into modal contexts? The problem is an instance of a general problem of generalizing over pseudo-object properties. Affirmations of pseudo-object properties of specific objects are unproblematic; they can be eliminated in favour of translations into formal mode sentences.[61] But with (objectual) quantification the situation is different. The truth-value of a quantification ⌜something is φ⌝ is determined by whether the predicate φ is truly affirmed of each member of the universe of discourse, independently of what terms, if any, designate that member. But, whether an object has a pseudo-object property can vary depending on how that object is designated *and* there is no account of how to determine whether a designation-less object has that property. So quantificational generalizations about pseudo-object properties have no determinate truth conditions.

The present quantification argument clearly is not independent of substitution failures. But it is not based on the conclusion of the substitution argument, namely, that the singular terms involved in a substitution failure are not purely referential. One might put the point in this way. According to the present argument, substitution failure shows, not that there is something non-standard about the functioning of the singular terms in question, but that there is something non-standard about the functioning of the predicate in question.[62]

However, since the argument is still based on substitution failures, it is open to Church's and Smullyan's Russellian objections. In particular, since in Quine's sentences (6) and (8) the singular terms are descriptions, one might hold that neither of these sentences is an ascription of a property to a city. Hence the difference in their truth-values has no implications for the nature of the property expressed by the predicate occurring in these sentences.

In answer, Quine writes,

> Whatever is greater than 7 is a number, and any given number x greater than 7 can be uniquely determined by any of various conditions, some of which have '$x > 7$' as

---

[61] Around the time that Quine formulated these arguments Carnap came to adopt semantics, and so to give up the notions of pseudo-object and quasi-syntactical property. Nevertheless Carnap continued to work with a successor notion, that of a quasi-logical property. A reformulation of Quine's arguments in terms of quasi-logical properties introduces a number of complications that I can't go into here.

[62] In Shieh (forthcoming) I show on the basis of this point that Quine's argument is not affected by the view that variables are directly referential, or the view that the coherence of an account of the satisfaction of open sentences is independent of designative properties of singular terms.

a *necessary* consequence and some of which do not. One and the same number x is uniquely determined by the condition:

$$x = \sqrt{x} + \sqrt{x} + \sqrt{x} \neq \sqrt{x} \qquad (9)$$

and by the condition:

$$\text{There are exactly } x \text{ planets} \qquad (10)$$

but (9) has '$x > 7$' as a necessary consequence while (10) does not. *Necessary* greaterness than 7 makes no sense as applied to a *number x*; necessity attaches only to the connection between '$x > 7$' and the particular method (9), as opposed to (10), of specifying x. (1953a, 149)

This is yet another version of the quantification argument. The conclusion, again, is that since whether an object has the property of being necessarily greater than 7 depends on which open sentence it satisfies, this property is pseudo-object.

Let's look at the quantification arguments in a slightly different way. As we saw, Quine began by accepting Carnap's explication of necessity, considered as a pseudo-object property of states of affairs, in terms of meta-linguistic predicates of sentences describing these states of affairs. *Modulo* doubts about analyticity, Quine never rejects this explication. His critique of modality relates to Carnap's explication of necessary properties of objects in terms of relative analyticity. As we saw above, Carnap explicates the claim that something has a necessary property by the (meta-linguistic) claim that a sentence formed by putting a designation of the object in the placeholder of a predicate expressing the corresponding non-modal property is analytic. Since different designations or specifications lead to different verdicts about the analyticity of the resulting sentences, and so different verdicts about whether the necessary property holds of the object, it follows from this Carnapian account that modal properties are pseudo-object properties as well. This is hardly a surprising conclusion to reach from the view that necessity is a pseudo-object property of states of affairs. Quine, however, goes on from this conclusion to argue that (objectual) quantificational generalizations over pseudo-object properties have no determinate truth conditions. But then there is no meaningful explication of modal properties of objects.[63]

36.9 QUINE IV: ANTI-ESSENTIALISM

In face of the revised quantification arguments, how could one confer determinate truth conditions on a generalization involving a modal predicate, when different verdicts on whether this predicate is true or false of an object result from different specifications of

---

[63] Burgess (1997) and Neale (1999) also argue that Quine's argument against quantifying in is independent of substitution failures. They do not discuss its connection to Carnap's notion of relative analyticity in *Syntax*.

that object? One way to accomplish this is, for each object, to retain all the positive verdicts and throw out all the negative ones, or vice versa. This is what Quine means by 'adopting an invidious attitude toward certain ways of uniquely specifying [the object], and favoring other ways' (1961b, 155). But, Quine asks, what basis is available for rejecting some specifications and retaining others? All these conditions are, after all, *ex hypothesi* satisfied by the object. It is at this point that Quine brings in 'Aristotelian essentialism': the favoured specifications are those 'somehow better revealing the "essence" of the object' (155).

What Quine has in mind is a feature of a traditional conception of essential properties: if an object loses an essential property then it ceases to exist.[64] Let's illustrate Quine's line of thinking with an example. Suppose the specification of 8 as the successor of 7 expresses an essential property of 8, and suppose that being even follows analytically from being the successor of 7. Consider now the claim that 8 is not even. Since being even follows analytically from being the successor of 7, it follows from this claim that 8 is not the successor of 7. But since being the successor of 7 is essential to 8, anything distinct from the successor of 7 is not 8. So we reach the logical contradiction that 8 is not 8. Thus the claim that 8 is not even is contradictory; hence being even is a necessary property of 8. Consider now, in contrast, the non-essential property of 8 of numbering the planets. Being a non-essential property of 8, failure to number the planets is not sufficient for diversity from 8, and so the claim that 8 does not number the planets fails to lead to any contradiction. Strictly this line of reasoning does not show that the notion of essential property is required to confer determinate truth conditions on quantificational generalizations over modal properties; essence merely suffices for determinate truth conditions. Quine's conclusion should then be a challenge to explain objectual quantification over modal properties without invoking the notion of essential property.

Of course the force of this challenge depends on whether there is anything wrong with essentialism. Quine's most well known objection to essentialism is based on a version of the example motivating Carnap's explication of essential property:

> Mathematicians may conceivably be said to be necessarily rational and not necessarily two-legged; and cyclists necessarily two-legged and not necessarily rational. But what of an individual who counts among his eccentricities both mathematics and cycling? Is this concrete individual necessarily rational and contingently two-legged or vice versa? (1960, 199)

The Carnapian background is key to understanding Quine's challenge. Recall that Carnap took the case of the landowning father, c, to lead to an apparent contradiction

---

[64] Many are sceptical of the Aristotelian pedigree of Quine's essentialism. But Aristotle would surely accept that a thing couldn't exist without having any of its essential properties. Now, on Aristotle's conception, this modal feature is not sufficient for the property to be essential, because essential properties have explanatory priority with respect to other properties with this modal feature. (See Shields (2007, 99–105) for a fuller account of Aristotle on essence.) So all Aristotelian essential properties are Quinean, but not vice versa.

via Wittgenstein's account of essential property: c is both essentially a landowner and not essentially a landowner. Carnap resolves this contradiction by appeal to relative analyticity, so that c is essentially a landowner relative to one description but not relative to another. But essentialism abjures appeal to descriptions or conditions satisfied by objects for determining whether they possess essential properties. So the Carnapian method of resolving such apparent contradictions is no longer available. In terms of Quine's example, if, in accordance with essentialism, we are barred from appealing to the conditions of being a mathematician and being a cyclist, nothing stands in the way of inferring that mathematical cyclists are both necessarily rational and not necessarily rational.

This argument is hardly conclusive. An obvious essentialist response is that the supposed contradiction arises only because Quine's basis for claiming that a mathematical cyclist is necessarily rational is a condition—being a mathematician—which she satisfies only contingently.[65] So essentialists can resist the supposed contradiction, by claiming that mathematical cyclists are not necessarily rational, because not essentially mathematicians. But from Quine's perspective this response takes us to another question: what justifies, without any appeal to conditions that someone satisfies, the claim that she is not essentially a mathematician? This question has particular weight for Carnap. Obviously Carnap has no objection to the notion of essence so long as it is explicated in precise terms. But Carnap's explication of essence is precisely that which essentialism rejects. So, for Carnap, unless there is some way other than essentialism for providing modal quantifications with determinate truth conditions, it's unclear why the use of modal expressions should not simply be rejected altogether.

Quine's argument plausibly has force not only against Carnap. If one rejects Carnap's relative analyticity as the basis for predicating essential and contingent properties, what should be put in its place? Thus, at bottom, Quine is not claiming that essentialism is objectionable because it leads to contradictions. Quine is, rather, posing a challenge to essentialism: what coherent and non-arbitrary standards are there for determining the correctness of ascriptions of essential properties, and for doing so with no appeal to conditions satisfied by the object of the ascriptions?

36.10 MARCUS AND THE REJECTION OF THE ANALYTICITY CONCEPTION OF NECESSITY

Marcus's 'Modalities and Intensional Languages' (1961) marks the beginnings of a sea-change in our philosophical conception of modality. In particular, we can see, in her defence of the necessity of identity against Quine's criticism, a rejection of the conception of necessity as analyticity. As before, limitations of space enjoin a mere sketch of my reading with little explanation or argument.

---

[65] See in particular Marcus (1961, 317–19).

Marcus begins by supposing that $\ulcorner a = b \urcorner$, with a and b distinct expressions, is a 'genuine' true statement of identity. It follows that a and b denote a single thing. But then $\ulcorner a = b \urcorner$ says the same thing as $\ulcorner a = a \urcorner$. But $\ulcorner a = a \urcorner$ is a tautology. Hence $\ulcorner a = b \urcorner$ is also a tautology, and thus is necessarily true.[66] For Marcus an identity is genuine just in case the expressions flanking '=' function like certain artificial singular terms she calls 'tags'.[67] Tags provide an idealized model of the referential aspect of ordinary singular terms: they are merely correlated with objects, and have 'no meaning' (1961, 309).

In order to understand this argument, we have to grasp the notions of saying the same thing and of tautology. For Marcus what a statement says is the state of affairs that it represents. The two true identities $\ulcorner a = b \urcorner$ and $\ulcorner a = a \urcorner$ say the same thing because they both depict one and the same entity as self-identical. Since these identities are supposed to be tautologies, they obviously are *not* Tractarian tautologies, which do not represent anything.[68] Nor is the tautology $\ulcorner a = b \urcorner$ true in virtue of its meaning, because tags have no meanings,[69] and so it can't be turned into a truth of logic by substituting synonymous tags for one another. In other words, for Marcus tautologousness is not Quinean analyticity.[70] Rather, a statement is a tautology just in case the state of affairs it depicts holds as a matter of logic. In particular, the state of affairs depicted by a true identity statement is the self-identity of some object; since it is a logical law that every object is self-identical, this state of affairs holds as a matter of logic. Tautologies are necessary, then, not because they are true in virtue of meaning, but because they depict states of affairs that hold as a matter of logic. It follows, in particular, that statements concerning ordinary material objects can be tautologous, and so necessary, in virtue of describing facts involving such objects that hold as a matter of logic.

Since for Marcus the necessity of genuine identities does not rest on analyticity, she does not face the question why knowledge of certain identities requires empirical investigation, rather than mere knowledge of meaning or linguistic reflection. But if for her true identities between tags are necessary because logically true, she faces a variant of this objection. As Quine puts it, 'We may tag the planet Venus, some fine evening, with the proper name "Hesperus". We may tag the same planet again, some day before

[66] Marcus's argument is closely connected to one advanced by Russell (1918, 212).

[67] Tagging is the result of putting some (finite) set of randomly generated natural numbers in a one-to one correspondence with 'all the entities countenanced as things by some particular culture through its own language', Marcus (1961, 310). If we take Marcus at her word here, we have to take tagging to be what Carnap calls a syntactic correlation, between the singular or descriptive referring expressions of the language of a culture with a set of numbers.

[68] Although I cannot discuss this here, it is a mistake to take Marcus's inference from the tautologousness of $\ulcorner a = a \urcorner$ to the tautologousness of $\ulcorner a = b \urcorner$ to be based on the view that since tautologies represent nothing, they all, vacuously, represent the same thing.

[69] Again, although I cannot go into it here, it is a mistake to think that Marcus's argument for the necessity of true identities between tags must after all depend on synonymy because if tags have no meaning they are all vacuously synonymous.

[70] Thus, one should not infer, from Marcus's claim that 'to say of an identity ... that it is true, it must be tautologically true or analytically true' (1961, 309–10), that she subscribes to the analyticity conception of necessity that Quine is attacking.

sunrise, with the proper name "Phosphorus". When at last we discover that we have tagged the same planet twice, our discovery is empirical' (1961a, 327). If this identity between two tags can be established only by empirical investigation, how could it be logically true? If it is logically true, wouldn't we be able to establish its truth by deductive reasoning alone, without appeal to empirical evidence?

Implicit in the text of (1961) is a reply to this objection.[71] Marcus accepts that in Quine's scenario, 'we may both be surprised that as an empirical fact, the same thing is' tagged twice (1961, 310). But she insists that 'it is not an empirical fact that' Phosphorus = Phosphorus or that Phosphorus = Hesperus. That is, Marcus holds that what requires empirical investigation to establish is not the single, non-empirical fact—the self-identity of an object—described by two true identities, $\ulcorner a = b \urcorner$ and $\ulcorner a = a \urcorner$. *Rather*, what requires empirical investigation to establish is the fact that this self-identity is depicted by the statement $\ulcorner a = b \urcorner$, by establishing that a and b tag a single object.

36.11 KRIPKE AND THE PASSING OF QUINEAN ANTI-ESSENTIALISM

Marcus's arguments in (1961) provide a conception of necessity not tied to analyticity, and a view of how objects as such, independent of conditions they satisfy, can possess necessary properties such as self-identity. But, as Quine makes clear in a letter to Carnap in 1943, these are not the properties existential statements about which are problematic: 'I had argued that ... the "N" of necessity ... could not govern matrices whose variables were quantified in a wider context. Naturally I did not hold that trouble would always arise, regardless of what matrix followed "N"; for, trivial and harmless cases could readily be got by letting the matrix contain its variable merely in such a manner as "x = x"' (Carnap and Quine 1990, 371). The modal properties to which Quine objects are those whose ascriptions are fixed, not by logic, but by Carnapian relative analyticity. For these, as we saw in section 36.9 above, Quine propounds a dilemma: either existential statements purportedly about them have no determinate truth conditions, or there is no principled essentialist account of their ascription to objects. So Quine overstates his case by suggesting that his argument rules out *all* quantification into modal contexts.

Moreover, until Quine's contribution to the discussion on Marcus's 'Modalities', he did not make clear what he meant by claiming quantified modal logic is committed to essentialism. In that discussion Quine explicitly disavowed claiming that essentialist statements are theorems of quantified modal logic, either syntactically or semantically

---

[71] It is arguable that, at the time Marcus presented this paper at the Boston Colloquium in the Philosophy of Science, she did not have a fully worked out reply based on the material in 'Modalities'.

characterized (Marcus *et al.* 1962, 140). What Quine means, as we saw above, is that some quantifications into modal contexts can be furnished with determinate truth conditions by assuming essential properties.[72]

Finally, as we saw in section 36.9 above, Quine's objection to essentialism is not that essential properties lead to contradictions and so are incoherent, but that without something like relative analyticity it's an open question what principled grounds underlie attributions of essential properties.

Quine's overstatements and unclarities led to the impression that he holds that all quantification into modal contexts require essentialism, that essentialist claims are theorems of quantified modal logics, and that essential properties, to use Kantian language, generate antinomies. This impression led to illuminating work by Marcus and Terence Parsons making precise and distinguishing clearly notions of essential property, and showing that essentialist claims are not theorems of systems of quantified modal logic as characterized by Kripke semantics.[73] This work, together with the contributions in the 1960s mentioned in my introductory remarks, made it increasingly plausible that essentialism is no minefield of antinomies. Of course the intelligibility of essentialism in *this* sense doesn't answer Quine's underlying demand for principled grounds for the ascription of essential properties that do not rely on conditions satisfied by the objects of these ascriptions. But it contributed to a growing sense that it's unclear *why* such Quinean questions *have to be* answered. As Marcus puts it, a 'sorting of attributes (or properties) as essential or inessential to an object or objects is not wholly a fabrication of metaphysicians', since the 'distinction is frequently used by philosophers and nonphilosophers alike without untoward perplexity' (1971, 187).

The most influential expression of the growing consensus against Quinean doubts about essentialism is in Kripke's 'Naming and Necessity' (1972):

> [I]t is very far from being true that [the idea that a property can meaningfully be held to be essential or accidental to an object independently of its description] is a notion which has no intuitive content, which means nothing to the ordinary man. Suppose that someone said, pointing to Nixon, 'That's the guy who might have lost'. Someone else says 'Oh no, if you describe him as "Nixon", then he might have lost; but, of course, describing him as the winner, then it is not true that he might have lost'. Now which one is being the philosopher, here, the unintuitive man? It seems to me obviously to be the second. (265)

Kripke here points to a pervasive pre-philosophical and intuitive agreement on ascriptions of essential and accidental properties to objects, independent of how they're described. Thus Kripke's answer to Quine's challenge is like Grice's and Strawson's (1956) reply to Quine's attack on the analytic/synthetic distinction. In the presence of

---

[72] On this point compare Ballarin (2004).

[73] Marcus (1961, 1967, 1971); Parsons (1967, 1969).

systematic non-collusive agreement on essentialist claims, there is no need to specify the principles underlying these claims in order to justify their use.

Once essentialism is in place, Kripke advances familiar, much-discussed, arguments for a sharp distinction between, on the one hand, necessity as underwritten by essential properties, and, on the other, apriority and analyticity, neither of which characterizes our epistemic access to these essential properties.[74] The relationship between these arguments and Marcus's rejection of the analyticity conception of necessity is not straightforward, but it is matter for another occasion. With the absorption of Kripke's attitude towards Quine's challenge to modality and the acceptance of its consequences, the rehabilitation of modal concepts in analytic philosophy is complete. Whether the attitude itself is indeed sufficient as a reply to Quine is also matter for another occasion.

REFERENCES

Austin, J. L. (1979 [1956]). 'Ifs and Cans'. In Austin, *Philosophical Papers*, 3rd edn., ed. J. O. Urmson and G. J. Warnock. Oxford: Oxford University Press, pp. 205–32.

Awodey, Steve and André Carus (2007). 'The Turning Point and the Revolution'. In A. Richardson and T. Uebel (eds.), *The Cambridge Companion to Logical Empiricism*. Cambridge: Cambridge University Press, pp. 165–92.

Ayer, A. J. (1936). *Language, Truth and Logic*. London: Victor Gollancz.

Ballarin, Roberta (2004). 'The Interpretation of Necessity and the Necessity of Interpretation', *Journal of Philosophy* 101(12): 609–38.

Barcan, Ruth C. (1946a). 'A Functional Calculus of First Order Based on Strict Implication', *Journal of Symbolic Logic* 11: 1–16.

—— (1946b). 'The Deduction Theorem in a Functional Calculus of First Order Based on Strict Implication', *Journal of Symbolic Logic* 11: 115–18.

—— (1947). 'The Identity of Individuals in a Strict Functional Calculus of Second Order', *Journal of Symbolic Logic* 12: 12–15.

Brandom, Robert (1994). *Making it Explicit: Reasoning, Representing, and Discursive Commitment*. Cambridge, MA: Harvard University Press.

—— (2000). *Articulating Reasons: An Introduction to Inferentialism*. Cambridge, MA: Harvard University Press.

Burge, Tyler (2005). 'Frege on Knowing the Foundation'. In Burge, *Truth, Thought, Reason: Essays on Frege*. Oxford: Oxford University Press, pp. 317–55.

Burgess, John (1997). 'Quinus ab Omni Naevo Vindicatus', *Canadian Journal of Philosophy, Supplement* 23: 25–65.

Carnap, Rudolf (1931). 'Überwindung der Metaphysik durch logische Analyse der Sprache', *Erkenntnis* 2: 219–41.

—— (1935). *Philosophy and Logical Syntax*. London: K. Paul, Trench, Trubner & Co.

—— (1937). *The Logical Syntax of Language*, tr. Amethe Smeaton (Countess von Zeppelin). London: K. Paul, Trench, Trubner & Co.

---

[74] That essentialism is the key premise in Kripke's defence of the existence of necessary truths not knowable a priori is very clear in (1971).

—— (1939). *Foundations of Logic and Mathematics*. Chicago, IL: University of Chicago Press.

—— (1946). 'Modalities and Quantification', *Journal of Symbolic Logic* 11: 33–64.

—— (1947). *Meaning and Necessity: A Study in Semantics and Modal Logic*. Chicago, IL: University of Chicago Press.

—— (1950). *Logical Foundations of Probability*. Chicago, IL: University of Chicago Press.

—— (1963). 'Intellectual Autobiography'. In Paul Arthur Schilpp (ed.), *The Philosophy of Rudolf Carnap*. La Salle, IL: Open Court, pp. 1–84.

Carnap, Rudolf and W. V. Quine (1990). *Dear Carnap, Dear Van: The Quine–Carnap Correspondence and Related Works*, ed. Richard Creath. Berkeley, CA: University of California Press.

Cartwright, Richard (1968). 'Some Remarks on Essentialism', *Journal of Philosophy* 65: 615–26.

—— (2003). 'Russell and Moore, 1898–1905'. In Nicholas Griffin (ed.), *The Cambridge Companion to Bertrand Russell*. Cambridge: Cambridge University Press, pp. 108–27.

Carus, André (2007). *Carnap and Twentieth-Century Thought*. Cambridge: Cambridge University Press.

Church, Alonzo (1942). Review of W. V. Quine, 'Whitehead and the Rise of Modern Logic', *Journal of Symbolic Logic* 7(2): 100–1.

—— (1943). Review of W. V. Quine, 'Notes on Existence and Necessity', *Journal of Symbolic Logic* 8(1): 45–7.

Coffa, Alberto (1991). *The Semantic Tradition from Kant to Carnap: To the Vienna Station*. Cambridge: Cambridge University Press.

Creath, Richard (1999). 'Carnap's Move to Semantics: Gains and Losses'. In J. Woleński and E. Köhler (eds.), *Alfred Tarski and the Vienna Circle: Austro-Polish Connections in Logical Empiricism*. Dordrecht: Kluwer, pp. 65–76.

Curley, E. M. (1975). 'The Development of Lewis's Theory of Strict Implication', *Notre Dame Journal of Formal Logic* 16: 517–27.

Diamond, Cora (1988). 'Throwing Away the Ladder'. In Diamond, *The Realistic Spirit: Wittgenstein, Philosophy, and the Mind*. Cambridge, MA: MIT Press, pp. 179–204.

Dreben, Burton and Juliet Floyd (1991). 'Tautology: How Not to Use a Word', *Synthese* 87: 23–49.

Floyd, Juliet (2005). 'Wittgenstein on Philosophy of Logic and Mathematics'. In Stewart Shapiro (ed.), *The Oxford Handbook of Philosophy of Mathematics and Logic*. Oxford: Oxford University Press, pp. 75–128.

Føllesdal, Dagfinn (1961). 'Referential Opacity and Modal Logic'. Ph.D. Thesis, Harvard University.

—— (1965). 'Quantification into Causal Contexts'. In R. S. Cohen and M. W. Wartofsky (eds.), *Boston Studies in the Philosophy of Science*. New York: Humanities Press, pp. 263–74.

Frege, Gottlob (1964 [1893]). *The Basic Laws of Arithmetic: Exposition of the System*, tr. Montgomery Furth. Berkeley, CA: University of California Press.

—— (1970 [1879]). '*Begriffsschrift*, a Formula Language, Modeled Upon That of Arithmetic, for Pure Thought'. In Jean Van Heijenoort (ed.), *Frege and Gödel: Two Fundamental Texts in Mathematical Logic*. Cambridge, MA: Harvard University Press, pp. 1–82.

—— (1980 [1884]). *The Foundations of Arithmetic: A Logico-Mathematical Enquiry into the Concept of Number*, 2nd rev. edn., tr. J. L. Austin. Evanston, IL: Northwestern University Press.

—— (1984 [1892]). 'On Sense and Meaning'. In Frege, *Collected Papers on Mathematics, Logic, and Philosophy*, ed. Brian McGuinness. Oxford: Blackwell, pp. 157–77.

Friedman, Michael (1999). *Reconsidering Logical Positivism*. Cambridge: Cambridge University Press.

Goldfarb, Warren and Thomas Ricketts (1992). 'Carnap and the Philosophy of Mathematics'. In D. Bell and W. Vossenkuhl (eds.), *Science and Subjectivity*. Berlin: Akademieverlag, pp. 61–78.

Grice, H. Paul and P. F. Strawson (1956). 'In Defense of a Dogma', *The Philosophical Review* 65(2): 141–58.

Griffin, Nicholas (1980). 'Russell on the Nature of Logic (1903–1913)', *Synthese* 45: 117–88.

Hacker, P. M. S. (1986). *Insight and Illusion: Themes in the Philosophy of Wittgenstein*, 2nd rev. edn. Oxford: Oxford University Press.

Hintikka, Jaakko (1963). 'Modes of Modality', *Acta Philosophica Fennica* 16: 65–82.

—— (1969). 'Semantics for Propositional Attitudes'. In J. W. Davis, D. J. Hockney, and W. K. Wilson (eds.), *Philosophical Logic*. Dordrecht: Reidel, pp. 21–45.

Hylton, Peter (1990). *Russell, Idealism, and the Emergence of Analytic Philosophy*. Oxford: Oxford University Press.

—— (1997). 'Functions, Operations, and Sense in Wittgenstein's *Tractatus*'. In William W. Tait (ed.), *Early Analytic Philosophy: Frege, Russell and Wittgenstein. Essays in Honor of Leonard Linsky*. La Salle, IL: Open Court, pp. 91–106.

—— (2001). ' "The Defensible Province of Philosophy": Quine's 1934 Lectures on Carnap'. In J. Floyd and S. Shieh (eds.), *Future Pasts: The Analytic Tradition in Twentieth-Century Philosophy*. New York: Oxford University Press, pp. 257–76.

Kaplan, David (1986). 'Opacity'. In L. E. Hahn and P. A. Schilpp (eds.), *The Philosophy of W. V. Quine*. La Salle, IL: Open Court, pp. 229–89.

Klement, Kevin (2004). 'Putting Form Before Function: Logical Grammar in Frege, Russell and Wittgenstein', *Philosopher's Imprint* 4(2): 1–47.

Kripke, Saul A. (1971). 'Identity and Necessity'. In Milton Munitz (ed.), *Identity and Individuation*. New York: New York University Press, pp. 66–101.

—— (1972). 'Naming and Necessity'. In Donald Davidson and Gilbert Harman (eds.), *Semantics of Natural Language*. Dordrecht: Reidel, pp. 253–355.

Landini, Gregory (1998). *Russell's Hidden Substitutional Theory*. Oxford: Oxford University Press.

Lewis, C. I. (1912). 'Implication and the Algebra of Logic', *Mind* 21(84): 522–31.

—— (1913). 'A New Algebra of Implications and Some Consequences', *Journal of Philosophy* 10(16): 428–38.

—— (1914). 'The Matrix Algebra for Implications', *Journal of Philosophy* 11(22): 589–600.

—— (1917). 'The Issues Concerning Material Implication', *Journal of Philosophy* 14(13): 350–6.

—— (1918). *A Survey of Symbolic Logic*. Berkeley, CA: University of California Press.

—— (1923). 'A Pragmatic Conception of the *A Priori*', *The Journal of Philosophy* 20(7): 169–77.

—— (1929). *Mind and the World-Order: Outline of a Theory of Knowledge*. New York: C. Scribner's Sons.

Lewis, C. I. and C. H. Langford (1932). *Symbolic Logic*. New York and London: The Century Co.

Linsky, Leonard (1969). 'Reference, Essentialism, and Modality', *Journal of Philosophy* 66: 687–700.

Łukasiewicz, Jan (1930). 'Philosophische Bemerkungen zu mehrwertigen Systemen des Aussagenkalküls', *Comptes Rendus de la Société des Sciences et des Lettres de Varsovie* 3(23): 51–77.

Macbeth, Danielle (2005). *Frege's Logic*. Cambridge, MA: Harvard University Press.

MacColl, Hugh (1906). *Symbolic Logic and its Applications*. London, Longmans, Green and Co.

—— (1908). '"If" and "Imply"', *Mind* 17(65): 151–2.

MacFarlane, John (2002). 'Frege, Kant, and the Logic in Logicism', *The Philosophical Review* 111: 25–65.

Marcus, Ruth Barcan (1961). 'Modalities and Intensional Languages', *Synthese* 13: 303–22.

—— (1967). 'Essentialism in Modal Logic', *Noûs* 1: 90–6.

—— (1971). 'Essential Attribution', *The Journal of Philosophy* 68(8): 187–202.

—— (1990). 'A Backward Look at Quine's Animadversions on Modalities'. In Robert B. Barrett and Roger F. Gibson (eds.), *Perspectives on Quine*. Oxford: Blackwell, pp. 230–43.

Marcus, Ruth Barcan, *et al.* (1962). 'Discussion on the Paper of Ruth B. Marcus', *Synthese* 14: 132–43.

Moore, G. E. (1899). 'The Nature of Judgment', *Mind* 8(30): 176–93.

—— (1900). 'Necessity', *Mind* 9(35): 289–304.

—— (1901). 'Truth and Falsity'. In John Mark Baldwin (ed.), *Dictionary of Philosophy and Psychology*. New York: Macmillan, pp. 716–18.

Neale, Stephen (1999). 'On a Milestone of Empiricism'. In A. Orenstein and P. Kotatko (eds), *Knowledge, Language and Logic*. Dordrecht: Kluwer, pp. 237–346.

Parsons, Terence (1967). 'Grades of Essentialism in Quantified Modal Logic', *Noûs* 1: 181–200.

—— (1969). 'Essentialism and Quantified Modal Logic', *The Philosophical Review* 78: 35–52.

Plantinga, Alvin (1969). 'De Re et De Dicto', *Noûs* 3: 235–58.

—— (1970). 'World and Essence', *The Philosophical Review* 79: 461–92.

—— (1974). *The Nature of Necessity*. Oxford: Oxford University Press.

Prior, A. N. (1963). 'Is the Concept of Referential Opacity Really Necessary?', *Acta Philosophica Fennica* 16: 189–200.

Proops, Ian (2002). 'The *Tractatus* on Inference and Entailment'. In Erich H. Reck (ed.), *From Frege to Wittgenstein: Perspectives on Early Analytic Philosophy*. Oxford: Oxford University Press, pp. 283–307.

—— (2007). 'Russell and the Universalist Conception of Logic', *Noûs* 41(1): 1–32.

Quine, W. V. (1941). 'Whitehead and the Rise of Modern Logic'. In Quine, *Selected Logic Papers*, enlarged edn. Cambridge, MA: Harvard University Press, pp. 3–36.

—— (1943). 'Notes on Existence and Necessity', *Journal of Philosophy* 40: 113–26.

—— (1944). *O sentido da nova lógica*. São Paulo: Livraria Martins Editora.

—— (1947). 'The Problem of Interpreting Modal Logic', *Journal of Symbolic Logic* 12: 43–8.

—— (1953a). 'Reference and Modality'. In Quine, *From a Logical Point of View: Nine Logico-Philosophical Essays*. Cambridge, MA: Harvard University Press, pp. 139–59.

—— (1953b). 'Three Grades of Modal Involvement'. In *Proceedings of the XIth International Congress of Philosophy*, vol. 14. Amsterdam: North-Holland, pp. 65–81.

—— (1960). *Word and Object*. Cambridge, MA: MIT Press.

—— (1961a). 'Reply to Professor Marcus's "Modalities and Intensional Languages"', *Synthese* 13: 323–30.

—— (1961b). 'Reference and Modality'. In Quine, *From a Logical Point of View: Nine Logico-Philosophical Essays*, 2nd edn. Cambridge, MA: Harvard University Press, pp. 139–59.

—— (1969). 'Replies'. In Donald Davidson and Jaakko Hintikka (eds.), *Words and Objections*. Dordrecht: Reidel, pp. 292–352.

—— (1976). 'Homage to Rudolf Carnap'. In Quine, *The Ways of Paradox and Other Essays*, rev. and enlarged edn. Cambridge, MA: Harvard University Press, pp. 40–3.

—— (1980). 'Reference and Modality'. In Quine, *From a Logical Point of View: Nine Logico-Philosophical Essays*, 2nd rev. edn. Cambridge, MA: Harvard University Press, pp. 139–59.

—— (1986). *Philosophy of Logic*, 2nd edn. Cambridge, MA: Harvard University Press.

—— (1990). 'Lectures on Carnap'. In Rudolf Carnap and W. V. Quine, *Dear Carnap, Dear Van: The Quine-Carnap Correspondence and Related Works*, ed. Richard Creath. Berkeley, CA: University of California Press, pp. 47–103.

Richardson, Alan (2004). 'Tolerating Semantics: Carnap's Philosophical Point of View'. In S. Awodey and C. Klein (eds.), *Carnap Brought Home: The View from Jena*. Chicago: Open Court, pp. 63–78.

Ricketts, Thomas (1986). 'Objectivity and Objecthood: Frege's Metaphysics of Judgement'. In Leila Haaparanta and Jaakko Hintikka (eds.), *Frege Synthesized*. Dordrecht: Reidel, pp. 65–95.

—— (1996). 'Pictures, Logic, and the Limits of Sense in Wittgenstein's *Tractatus*'. In Hans Sluga (ed.), *The Cambridge Companion to Wittgenstein*. Cambridge: Cambridge University Press, pp. 59–99.

—— (2001). 'Truth and Propositional Unity in Early Russell'. In Juliet Floyd and Sanford Shieh (eds.), *Future Pasts: The Analytic Tradition in Twentieth-Century Philosophy*. Oxford: Oxford University Press, pp. 101–21.

—— (2002). 'Wittgenstein against Frege and Russell'. In Erich H. Reck (ed.), *From Frege to Wittgenstein: Perspectives on Early Analytic Philosophy*. Oxford: Oxford University Press, pp. 227–51.

Rorty, Richard (1982). *Consequences of Pragmatism: Essays, 1972–1980*. Minneapolis: University of Minnesota Press.

Rosen, Gideon (2001). 'Brandom on Modality, Normativity and Intentionality', *Philosophy and Phenomenological Research* 63(3): 611–23.

Rundle, Bede (1965). 'Modality and Quantification'. In R. J. Butler (ed.), *Analytical Philosophy, Second Series*. Oxford: Blackwell, pp. 27–39.

Russell, Bertrand (1900). *A Critical Exposition of the Philosophy of Leibniz, with an Appendix of Leading Passages*. London: George Allen & Unwin.

—— (1903). *The Principles of Mathematics*. Cambridge: Cambridge University Press.

—— (1904). 'Meinong's Theory of Complexes and Assumptions (III)', *Mind* 13(51): 509–24.

—— (1906). Review of Hugh MacColl, *Symbolic Logic and Its Applications*, *Mind* 15(58): 255–60.

—— (1908). '"If" and "Imply", a Reply to Mr. MacColl', *Mind* 17(66): 300–1.

—— (1918). 'The Philosophy of Logical Atomism', *The Monist* 28, 29: 495–7, 32–63, 190–222, 345–80.

—— (1919). *Introduction to Mathematical Philosophy*. London: George Allen & Unwin.

—— (1994a [1905]). 'The Nature of Truth'. In *The Collected Papers of Bertrand Russell, Volume 4: Logical and Philosophical Papers, 1903–05*, ed. Alasdair Urquhart and Albert Lewis. London and New York: Routledge, pp. 490–506.

—— (1994b [1905]). 'Necessity and Possibility'. In *The Collected Papers of Bertrand Russell, Volume 4: Logical and Philosophical Papers, 1903–05*, ed. Alasdair Urquhart and Albert Lewis. London and New York: Routledge, pp. 507–20.

Sellars, Wilfrid (1948). 'Concepts as Involving Laws, and Inconceivable without Them', *Philosophy of Science* 15(4): 287–315.

Shieh, Sanford (2005). Review of Danielle Macbeth, *Frege's Logic*, Notre Dame Philosophical Reviews. Available at: <http://ndpr.nd.edu/review.cfm?id=4641> (accessed 14 March 2012).

—— (2008). 'Frege on Definitions', *Philosophy Compass* 3(5): 992–1012.

—— (forthcoming). *Modality and Logic in Early Analytic Philosophy*. Oxford: Oxford University Press.

Shields, Christopher (2007). *Aristotle*. London and New York: Routledge.

Smullyan, Arthur Francis (1947). Review of W. V. Quine, 'The Problem of Interpreting Modal Logic', *Journal of Symbolic Logic* 12(4): 139–41.

—— (1948). 'Modality and Description', *Journal of Symbolic Logic* 13(1): 31–7.

Soames, Scott (2003). *Philosophical Analysis in the Twentieth Century*, 2 vols. Princeton, NJ: Princeton University Press.

Stanley, Jason (1996). 'Truth and Metatheory in Frege', *Pacific Philosophical Quarterly* 77(1): 45–70.

Tappenden, Jamie (1997). 'Metatheory and Mathematical Practice in Frege', *Philosophical Topics* 25(2): 213–63.

Uebel, Thomas (2011). 'Vienna Circle', *Stanford Encyclopedia of Philosophy*. Available at: <http://plato.stanford.edu/entries/vienna-circle/> (accessed 14 March 2012).

van Heijenoort, Jean (1967). 'Logic as Calculus and Logic as Language', *Synthese* 17: 324–30.

Whitehead, Alfred North and Bertrand Russell (1910). *Principia Mathematica*. Cambridge: Cambridge University Press.

Wiener, Norbert (1916). 'Mr. Lewis and Implication', *Journal of Philosophy* 13: 656–62.

Wilson, N. L. (1965). 'Modality and Identity: A Defense', *Journal of Philosophy* 62(18): 471–7.

Wittgenstein, Ludwig (1922 [1921]). *Tractatus Logico-Philosophicus*, tr.. C. K. Ogden. London: K. Paul, Trench, Trubner & Co.

—— (2001 [1953]). *Philosophical Investigations*, 3rd edn., tr. G. E. M. Anscombe. Oxford: Blackwell.

CHAPTER 37

INFERENTIALISM AND NORMATIVITY

JAROSLAV PEREGRIN

37.1 INFERENTIALISM VS. REPRESENTATIONALISM

The term 'inferentialism' was coined by Robert Brandom, as a name for his own sweeping and ambitious philosophical doctrine, which drew strongly on the ideas of Brandom's mentor Wilfrid Sellars. It may be characterized as the conviction that to be meaningful, in the distinctively human way, or to possess 'conceptual content', is to be governed by a certain kind of inferential rules. However, Brandomian inferentialism can be seen as a culmination of certain trends already latent within both logic and philosophy of language since the outset of modern logic and analytic philosophy.

The rationale for articulating inferentialism as a fully-fledged philosophical position is to emphasize its distinctness from the more traditional *representationalism*. The tradition of basing the explanation of human mind and the semantics of human languages on the idea of representation is long and rich. The basic representationalist picture tells us that we are confronted with things of the world, acquire mental contents representing these things, and by making our words express these contents we make the words stand for the things (individual philosophers have different views, of course, about what is to be understood by *stand for*). Many twentieth-century philosophers took some form of representationalism for granted, seeing no viable alternative basis for semantics; others had more specific reasons for entertaining one or another form of it.

Inferentialism is closely connected with the conviction that any kind of human meaning is essentially, in Sellars's often quoted words, 'fraught with ought'. It follows that when describing phenomena that have to do with meaning (language, mind, etc.) we cannot make do with the language of natural science. This is not because some additional concepts are lacking, but because claims concerning meaning are often not indicative claims—as Brandom would put it, they do not ascribe properties, but rather establish proprieties. We may tend to compress this view into the slogan *meaning is normative*, but this slogan can mislead, as the point at issue is not that meaning is a specific, normative kind of thing, but rather that meaning is not really a thing at all, for the talk about it is not really a description.

37.2 INFERENTIALIST TRENDS IN CLASSICAL ANALYTIC PHILOSOPHY

As dawn glimmered for analytic philosophy, Frege (1879, pp. 2–3 in original) gave the following account of conceptual content:

> The contents of two judgments may differ in two ways: either the consequences derivable from the first, when it is combined with certain other judgments, always follow also from the second, when it is combined with these same judgments, [and conversely,] or this is not the case. The two propositions 'The Greeks defeated the Persians at Plataea' and 'The Persians were defeated by the Greeks at Plataea' differ in the first way. Even if one can detect a slight difference in meaning, the agreement outweighs it. Now I call that part of the content that is the same in both the conceptual content.

This means that two judgments A and B share their conceptual content iff for every sequence of judgments $A_1, \ldots, A_{i-1}, A_{i+1}, \ldots A_n, A_{n+1}$ it is the case that $A_1, \ldots, A_{i-1}, A, A_{i+1}, \ldots A_n \vdash A_{n+1}$ if and only if $A_1, \ldots, A_{i-1}, B, A_{i+1}, \ldots A_n \vdash A_{n+1}$. Hence A and B share their conceptual content iff they share their *inferential role*;[1] and it would seem that hence we can identify the content with the inferential role. Thus, this account ties in with the inferentialist *credo* formulated much later by Brandom (1994, p. 144):

> It is only insofar as it is appealed to in explaining the circumstances under which judgments and inferences are properly made and the proper consequences of doing so that something associated by the theorist with interpreted states or expressions qualifies as a *semantic* interpretant, or deserves to be called a theoretical concept of a *content*.

---

[1] The condition Frege gives states, in effect, that whatever is inferable from A (given some collateral premises) is also inferable from B (given the same collateral premises) and vice versa; and we might think that to reach a true inferential role we need to supplement it by the condition that B is inferable from whatever A is inferable from and vice versa, i.e. that for every sequence of judgments $A_1, \ldots, A_n$ it is the case that $A_1, \ldots, A_n \vdash A$ if and only if $A_1, \ldots, A_n \vdash B$. However, this supplementary condition already follows from Frege's, given the relatively modest assumptions that every judgment is inferable from itself and that the relation of inferability is transitive: then $B \vdash B$, hence according to Frege's condition $A \vdash B$, and hence if $A_1, \ldots, A_n \vdash A$, then $A_1, \ldots, A_n \vdash B$ due to the transitivity of $\vdash$.

However, Frege's characterization of content quoted above is often dismissed as a fruit of his immaturity (even Brandom 2000, Ch. 1, sees the mature Frege as switching from his early inferentialist view of content to a truth-theoretical version): at the time he was writing his *Begriffsschrift*, he did not pay any systematic attention to semantic issues and hence his proclamation cannot be taken too seriously. When Frege (1892a, p. 31 in original) did turn his explicit attention to semantics, he talks differently:

> A proper name (word, sign, combination of signs, expression) *expresses* its sense, *stands for* [*bedeutet*] or designates [*bezeichnet*] its *Bedeutung*, By employing a sign we express its sense and designate its *Bedeutung*.

This seems to be an outline of the representational paradigm of semantics, according to which to *mean something* is *to stand for this something*,[2] which was accepted as almost self-evident and further elaborated by many of his followers. Thus, Russell (1912, p. 91) stresses:

> We must attach some meaning to the words we use, if we are to speak significantly and not utter mere noise; and the meaning we attach to our words must be something with which we are acquainted.

Here the representational picture is straightforward: to make a word meaningful, we have to let it stand for (represent) an entity we are confronted with. The same train of thought prompted Carnap (1942) to isolate semantics as that part of the theory of language which has to do with expressions' denoting objects:

> When we observe an application of language, we observe an organism, usually a human being, producing a sound, mark, gesture, or the like as an expression in order to refer by it to something, e.g. an object. Thus we may distinguish three factors involved: the speaker, the expression and what is referred to, which we shall call the *designatum* of the expression.... If we abstract from the user of the language and analyze only the expressions and their designata, we are in the field of *semantics*.... *Semantics* contains the theory of what is usually called the meaning of expressions ... (pp. 8–10)

However, not *everybody* who was attracted by the representational (or *semiotic*, as I called it elsewhere; 2001a) picture of language took the representationalism entirely for granted. Thus Wittgenstein, whose *Tractatus* (1922) exposed the language–world relationship as congenial to Russell's view, clearly saw that his Tractarian depiction of *names* as standing for *objects* cannot be taken at face value; as he famously claimed, it is rather merely a ladder that must be thrown away, after one has climbed up on it. The

---

[2] There are, however, objections to taking Frege, even in this later period, as a straightforward representationalist, let alone ascribing to him the Platonist view that our expressions generally *stand for* the senses they express in the way that proper names stand for people who have been allocated their names by baptism. Cf. Mendonça and Stekeler-Weithofer (1987).

trouble Wittgenstein perceived, unlike most of his fellow founding-fathers of analytic philosophy, was that a thing cannot come to stand for something else by being *proclaimed* to stand for it; for this would lead to an infinite regress.[3] Trying explicitly to make something into a representation, according to Wittgenstein, is trying to *say* something that can only be *shown*.[4]

Kenny (1972, p. 36) describes the troubles Wittgenstein had with semantics, using as an example the semantically ill-formed sentence *The class of men is a man*:

> Shall we say that the symbols 'the class of men' and '… is a man' cannot be combined to make a sensible sentence? This seems to offer us a way out, but does not. For if the expressions in quotes refer to the sounds then again we are just expressing a trivial empirical truth. On the other hand, if it refers to the sounds with their meaning, to the symbols with their logical properties, what can we mean by 'combination' when we say that they cannot be combined in a certain way? The most plausible account is: 'the class of men', meaning what it does in English, cannot be the subject of a sentence whose predicate is '… is a man', meaning what that does in English. We may doubt whether this in turn is meaningful, but even if it is, it may well only postpone the evil day. For can we account for the meaning of the fragmentary expressions without giving an account of the sentences in which they can occur? If not, all our earlier problems will meet us again.

Kenny's verdict is that 'Wittgenstein's way out of this difficulty is to lay down that the rules of logic must be entirely syntactical rules, i.e. rules about the manipulation of symbols.' Such a view is quite close to the inferentialist *credo* (though we should be alert to the elusiveness of the term *syntactical* here);[5] and independently of whether Kenny characterizes the position of *Wittgenstein* accurately, there is little doubt that what he puts forward is an accurate characterization of the moral *Carnap* drew from the *Tractatus* and developed in the 1930s.[6]

---

[3] This created much misunderstanding among those logicians who took logic, in terms of van Heijenoort's (1967) famous distinction, 'as a calculus'. Wittgenstein, who took it 'as a language', did not accept that the assumption that for any language of logic we can have a meta-language, can be taken for granted.

[4] To avoid misunderstanding: of course it *is* possible to make something into a representation by means of an explicit convention. But this presupposes some means of establishing the convention, a language or at least something language-like, hence something that is already meaningful. Therefore, Wittgenstein dismisses this case as uninteresting; his interest is exclusively for the case where this regress comes to an end, i.e. where we establish meaningfulness without presupposing anything already meaningful.

[5] The trouble is that the term is dangerously ambiguous—using the terminology of Carnap (1934), explained below, we can say that in the narrow sense it refers merely to the formation rules of language, whereas in the wide sense it encompasses also the transformation rules.

[6] Thus, Carnap and Wittgenstein, in a sense, moved in opposite directions. Whereas Wittgenstein started to move away from his (tentative) representationalism in the 1930s, later reaching his use-theory of meaning, Carnap, in the 1930s, rejected representationalism with a vengeance, only to embrace it later, under the influence of Tarski. For a discussion of the influence of the *Tractatus* on Carnap's *Logical Syntax* see Awodey and Carus (2009).

In his *Logical Syntax of Language* (1934) Carnap presented a thoroughly inferentialist picture of language. Language is constituted by two kinds of rules, *formation* rules (which constitute syntax in a narrow sense, determining well-formedness), and *transformation* rules (constituting 'logical syntax', being, in effect, rules of inference). Any tractable aspect of language must be a matter of these two kinds of rules. Thus even the concept of consequence (later taken, by Tarski, for a paradigmatically non-syntactic notion), if it is to make any sense at all, must be definable in terms of inference.

In the case of his Language I, one of the two prototype languages Carnap discusses in the book, the difference between consequence and inference was accounted for in terms of the *omega rule* (the rule allowing us to derive the conclusion that all natural numbers have a property P from the infinite number of premises containing the claim $P(n)$ for every natural number n): consequence amounts to derivability by means of the rules of inference plus this infinitist rule. In the case of Language II, the relation becomes more complex and Carnap's resulting definition of consequence comes near to the semantic definition of Tarski (1936) (though Carnap is still convinced that he managed not to leave the level of syntax).[7]

Thus, Carnap's project in this book has a lot to do with inferentialism—he tries to account for all those aspects of a language that may be relevant for *logic* exclusively in terms of his logical syntax, viz. inference. However, it is nothing like the Brandomian general inferentialism, where any kind of *meaning* is a matter of inference. In contrast to Brandom, Carnap claims that even if we settle all logical properties of a language, the language will still be unusable for communication, because it lacks *interpretation* (*Deutung*). (For Carnap, there are just two ways to interpret it: either by translation into another, already interpreted language, or a purely practical way.) However, his book explored many of the paths rediscovered by later inferentialists.

37.3 PROOF THEORY AND LOGICAL INFERENTIALISM

Since the founding fathers of modern logic, the paradigmatic examples of logical constants, such as classical conjunction, were characterized in two ways: in terms of axioms (presented by Frege, Russell, …) and in terms of truth tables (Post, Wittgenstein, …). This foreshadowed the later distinction between what is now called *proof theory* and *model theory*. In the 1930s, Tarski argued that only semantic methods could offer an ultimate grip on the concepts of truth and consequence that

---

[7] See Coffa (1991, Ch. 16) for a thorough discussion.

underlie the whole of logic; he developed formal semantics which later mutated into model theory.[8] Tarski (1986) thereafter offered a general semantic theory of logical constants.

Under Tarski's influence, studies of proving, and of axiomatic systems, were relegated increasingly to the sphere of the instrumental—to what logicians must use, given our human predicament, to get an incomplete, though useful grip on concepts that are ultimately accountable for only by means of explicitly semantic methods. Proof theory was first established as an ambitious research program by Hilbert (see Kreisel 1964); but its campaign was soon compromised when faced with the well-known result of Gödel (1931). However, another version of proof theory, based not on the Hilbertian notion of axiomatic system, but on the notion of a system of natural deduction, was developed by Gentzen (1934, 1936).

Gentzen presented, for each usual logical constant of elementary logic, an inferential pattern that he claimed to be constitutive of it. Each such pattern consisted of an *introduction* rule or rules, showing which statements a complex statement built by means of the constant may be inferred from, and *elimination* rules, giving what can be inferred from such a statement. Thus, for example *implication* was characterized by the introduction rule stating that if B is derivable from A, then we can derive $A{\rightarrow}B$; and the elimination rule amounting to *modus ponens*:

$$\frac{\begin{array}{c}[A]\\B\end{array}}{A \rightarrow B} \qquad\qquad \frac{A \qquad A{\rightarrow} B}{B}$$

Moreover, Gentzen claimed that there is a sense in which only the introduction rules are really substantial, that there is a sense in which the elimination rules are already 'contained' in them.[9]

This laid the foundations for an inferentialist account of logical constants. (It is important to realize that this logical kind of inferentialism must be classified as a special case of general inferentialism not just because it is restricted to logical constants, but also because strict constraints are posed on the inferential patterns that can constitute the (meanings of the) logical constants. By contrast, general inferentialism only claims that the meaning of a word is its role vis-à-vis an inferential pattern; there is no claim that each word must have its own constitutive inferential pattern, let alone a claim that this pattern must be of a shape prescribed by Gentzen.)

The idea that the meaning of a logical constant may be a matter of the inferential rules governing it was vigorously attacked by a succinct paper of Prior (1960/1).

---

[8] Formal semantics was first addressed by Tarski (1939); the establishment of model theory is described by Vaught (1974) and Chang (1974).

[9] See the discussion given by Koslow (1992, Part I).

Prior showed that we may have an inferential pattern, and especially an inferential pattern within the bounds of inferential constraints, that introduces a constant whose very presence in a language makes this language automatically inconsistent. And though it is not clear why the existence of such 'malign' inferential patterns should be seen as deadly to the very idea of inferentialism (which Prior himself takes it to be—see also Prior 1964), it is undoubtedly something an inferentialist should be able to account for.

In particular, the inferentialist should be concerned with distinguishing such malign patterns from the benign ones, which he sees as truly meaning-conferring expedients. One way of doing this can be found in the reply that Belnap (1962) gave to Prior: he argued that the benign patterns are marked by their *conservativity*, i.e. by the property that the new inferential links they institute are restricted to just the sentences containing the new constants. Thus, if $\vdash$ is the relation of inference of a language and $\vdash^*$ the relation of inference of the language extended by some new logical constants, then $A_1, ..., A_n \vdash^* A$ if and only if either some of the $A_1, ..., A_n, A$ contain the new constants or $A_1, ..., A_n \vdash A$ (hence no new links emerge among old sentences). Later logicians characterized the benign patterns in terms of the so-called *harmony* between their introduction and their elimination rules (Dummett 1991), or in terms of the so-called *normalizability* of proofs to which such inferential rules can add up (Prawitz 1965).

A characterization of logical constants couched exclusively in proof-theoretic terms was offered by Hacking (1979) and though this exposition may not be entirely flawless (cf. Sundholm 1981), it clearly showed that there is a viable purely proof-theoretical account of the nature of logic. Dummett (1978) generalized the basic proof-theoretical insights (as they manifest themselves especially within intuitionist logic) beyond the boundaries of logic to general semantics and philosophy of language; and recent reconsiderations of the theories of Gentzen and Prawitz have yielded the widely discussed idea of *proof-theoretic semantics* (see Prawitz 2006; Schroeder-Heister 2006).

It turns out that the logical constants that are most straightforwardly accounted for in proof-theoretical terms are those of intuitionist logic.[10] Constants of classical logic are slightly more problematic: although they can be delimited inferentially in the sense that we have sound and complete axiomatization of classical logic (which, since axioms can be seen as inferences with empty antecedents, can be seen as a collection of inferential rules), already Carnap pointed out that this does *not* mean that the axioms would pin down the semantics of the constants to their classical meanings.[11]

---

[10] See Peregrin (2008a).

[11] The axioms of classical logic do not exclude cases of disjunction of two false disjuncts being true; just as they do not exclude the negation of a false statement being false. See Carnap (1943).

37.4 Inferentialism as a General Philosophical Project: Sellars and Brandom

To craft inferentialism into a general philosophical project, Brandom (1994), following Sellars (1949, 1953, 1969), did three crucial things:

1. He applied the inferential paradigm to the whole of our vocabulary indiscriminately. This made him face problems absent from purely logical inferentialism, especially the problem of what kind of inferences can confer meaning on *empirical* words and how we account for the obvious *representational* powers of our language.

2. He provided for a 'sociological' reduction of the concept of *inference* to the concepts of *commitment* and *entitlement*. The idea is that our speech acts may, on the one hand, presuppose various kinds of commitments or entitlements, whereas, on the other hand, they may institute new commitments and entitlements. An order, for example, presupposes an entitlement on the part of the orderer and institutes a commitment on the part the orderee; an assertion creates commitment on the part of the assertor (the commitment to justify the assertion if challenged) and offers an entitlement to anybody to reassert it deferring its justification to its original assertor. Viewed from this perspective, linguistic interchange is seen as effectively a traffic of normative statuses and corresponding normative links.[12]

   In this way, he aligns our linguistic practices with other varieties of social practices, accounting for language as just one specific kind of human rule-governed enterprise. Brandom follows Sellars in regarding this specific kind as essentially characteristic of the distinctively human way of coping with the world—in believing that, in Sellars's (1949, p. 311) words, that 'to say that man is a rational animal is to say that man is a creature not of *habits*, but of *rules*'.

3. Thus he embedded the question about the nature of meaning into the broader context of the nature of distinctively human practices and the nature of human reason.

How does language, according to Brandom, work? Just as in the case of logical constants, any word is meaningful in virtue of being governed by a collection of rules. (However, in the case of empirical words, it is not merely inferential rules in the usual

---

[12] This may even lead to a normative version of the speech act theory, such as outlined by Kukla and Lance (2009).

narrow sense; we must also engage rules somehow 'involving' the extralinguistic world.)[13] Anyway, there is no (human kind of) meaningfulness aside of inferential articulation. The most basic kinds of inferences are *material* ones, inferences that are not logical but rather crucially involving extralogical vocabulary; inferences such as

(1) *This is a dog*
     This is an animal

or (an example frequently employed by Sellars)

(2) *Lightning now*
     Thunder shortly.

These inferences are, in essence, a matter of preserving normative statuses—especially commitments and entitlements. Hence to say that *This is an animal* is correctly inferable from *This is a dog* may be to say that the commitment instituted by asserting the latter sentence involves the commitment instituted by asserting the former one.[14]

Logic comes into play only later. Thus logical inferences are not something underlying material ones—in the sense that inference (1) would then be only an oblique form of the inference

(1*) *This is a dog*
      Every dog is an animal
      This is an animal.

Instead, they stand wholly on their own feet. Logical inference is what makes the material ones explicit: the claim *Every dog is an animal* enables us to *say* explicitly what we were previously only able implicitly to *do* by endorsing the inference from *This is a dog* to *This is an animal*. Hence the role of the logical vocabulary is merely *expressive*. (But saying *merely* here might be misleading, for making the inferences explicit is no insignificant achievement. It fosters what Brandom 2000 calls our 'semantic self-consciousness'.)

This view (the roots of which again go back to Sellars 1953) wholly inverts the usual view of the relationship between logical and material inferences. It is often assumed that the only truly valid inferences are logical ones, and that what we call material inferences are only oblique (or, using Aristotle's term, *enthymematic*) forms of logical inferences

---

[13] Given this, the term *inferentialism* may seem a misnomer. Calling the rule that it is correct to claim *This is a dog* when pointing at a dog an *inference* (perhaps from world to language) appears to be stretching the term beyond reasonable limits. (Admittedly, Sellars would not want to talk about an *inference* here. Sellars, 1954, compares the kind of correctness that is in play here to the correctness of the way pieces are arranged in the starting position of the game.) Maybe, from this viewpoint, *normativism* would be less misleading.

[14] Brandom (2000) claims that considering the fine structure of the interplay between commitments and entitlements yields us three layers in inference: commitment-preservation, entitlement-preservation, and inference induced by incompatibility. However, his grounds for this assertion are somewhat unclear (cf. Peregrin, 2001b).

(hence that (1) can be seen as a valid inference only if we see it as implicitly containing the 'hidden' premise *Every dog is an animal*). But why should this be so?

It is clear that the inference (1*), which is logically valid due to being an instance of the general schema

> *X is an A*
> *Every A is a B*
> *X is a B,*

is valid only assuming that the words *every*, *is*, etc. mean what they do in English. Conversely, these words' meaning what they do suffices to make the inference valid. And similarly it is sufficient that these words, together with the words *dog* and *animal*, mean what they do in English for (1) to be valid. There is no need to add the premise *Every dog is an animal*, for it is involved by the assumption that the words mean what they do.

Not all material inferences are of this kind, though. Take the other one mentioned above, namely (2). From the viewpoint of logic, such an inference can be considered to hold at most *ceteris paribus*. It is certainly not the case that *whenever* I see lightning, I will hear thunder shortly. So inferentialism does not merely turn logic 'upside down', in the sense that it sees logical inferences as being underlaid by material ones rather than vice versa. In addition to this, it challenges also the claim that the most basic kinds of inferences are the deductively valid ones. In our ordinary linguistic practices, we rely on an abundance of inferences that are merely inductive, *ceteris paribus*, or contextually bound.

Hence the inferential structure of language, essentially, rests on *material* inferences; however, the fact that pieces of language, viz. sentences, are caught into the web of these inferential relationships makes these pieces into vertices of a logical space and makes their content acquire the shape we call *propositional*. It is for this reason that it is not generally *normative*, but rather especially *inferential* relationships that are crucial for the semantics of our language.

It is essential to realize that by becoming this general, inferentialism becomes a doctrine no longer restricted to the semantics of logical constants, nor even to semantics—its ambition is to provide for a general theory of the conceptual and hence of the distinctively human reason. This is why Brandom thinks that inferentialism is not merely a matter of language, it is a general theory of what makes us humans special, namely of the trinity reason/language/concepts.

37.5 Meaning and Normativity

The most distinctive characteristic feature of the inferentialist construal of meaning is that it is essentially *normative*—that it is 'fraught with ought'. Thus, meaning is not a thing stood for by an expression (as the representationalists would have it), and nor is it, in fact, a thing at all—it is rather a *role* the expression assumes vis-à-vis the rules that govern it.[15]

This may be a deeper deviation from usual paradigms than it *prima facie* seems. It is not a mere variation on the older theme of the 'use theory of meaning'.[16] It involves the view that saying an expression means thus and so may sometimes be not claiming that something is the case, but rather urging that something *ought to be* the case.

As Sellars put it in his letter to R. Chisholm:

> My solution is that
> '...' means —
> is the core of a unique mode of discourse which is as distinct from the *description* and *explanation* of empirical fact, as is the language of *prescription* and *justification*. (Chisholm and Sellars, 1958, p. 527)

The situation becomes more perspicuous when we confront language with chess. If, during a chess game, I say 'This is a king!', then what I am likely to be expressing is not (merely) a fact, but (also) an urge—'you cannot move the piece like this, for this would violate the rules this piece is governed by!' Hence the slogan *meaning is normative* (widely discussed these days, appreciated by some philosophers and rejected by others),[17] may be less misleadingly interpreted not as saying that meanings are some peculiar, 'normative' kind of objects, but rather as saying that the talk about meanings is not a talk about any kind of object at all, for it involves subscribing to rules.

This does not mean that we cannot *treat* meanings as objects. Aside of *urging* rules we can also *report* on the fact that a community endorses some rules—i.e. state this *as a fact*. Being governed by a set of rules makes an object, especially a linguistic expression, assume a role vis-à-vis the rules, and we can explicate this role in terms of an object—perhaps a mathematical function.[18] But when we do this, we do not necessarily mean that this object is what the expression *stands for*—it is rather an encapsulation of its role, especially its inferential role.

In this sense, the reality of meanings is 'virtual'—they become real objects only if we disregard semantic discourse being 'fraught with ought' and take it as purely indicative and hence 'fact-reporting'.[19] Indeed, by the same change of visual angle there emerges

---

[15] See Peregrin (2008b, 2012).

[16] Here we must avoid conflating this normative inferentialism with what is sometimes called 'inferential role semantics' (Boghossian 1993) and which construes meaning as constituted not by *rules* of inference, but rather by inferences as instances of mental processes actually carried out by speakers or thinkers; thus being, unlike normative inferentialism, a subspecies of functionalism well-known from the philosophy of mind.

[17] See Boghossian (2005), Whitting (2008), or Glüer and Wikforss (2009).

[18] It was in this way that Frege (1892b) introduced his 'mathematical' explication of the meanings of predicates. For more about this, see Peregrin (2001a, Ch. 8).

[19] In a sense, their reality can be seen as a kind of Kantian 'transcendental illusion'—we take the project of the human world, that is an essentially *open* and *never finished* project, and in this sense an essential *potentiality*, as a completed *actuality*.

the whole of what Sellars (1962) calls the 'manifest image' of the world—an image which is different from the 'scientific image' because it contains many entities not existing within the causal order (such as meanings, and also persons as something over and above mere organisms, actions and deeds as something over and above mere functioning and behaviour, etc.). These entities are not supernatural or ghostly, but arise from our normative engagement with the world.

Hence the normativity of meaning is carried by the *normative* attitudes of the community of speakers. Some actions of a speaker elicit praise, encouragement, or reward; others meet with disagreement, contempt, or even sanctions and are liable to corrections or rectifications. As Wittgenstein (1953, § 54) points out, our experience of such attitudes is so basic that we might even recognize them when observing speakers of a language we do not understand:

> But how does the observer distinguish in this case between players' mistakes and correct play?—There are characteristic signs of it in the players' behaviour. Think of the behaviour characteristic of correcting a slip of the tongue. It would be possible to recognize that someone was doing so even without knowing his language.

Can we identify these attitudes with mere patterns of behaviour, and hence does this approach lead to a naturalization of meaning? Not really. We cannot say that an utterance is (in)correct if and only if it faces, as a matter of fact, certain normative attitudes—it is (in)correct if these specific normative attitudes towards it are *correct*. But now this might appear to open a *reductio ad absurdum* of the whole normativist approach to meaning, for it seems to lead to a vicious circle, or at least to render correctness as something completely esoteric, wholly unleashed from what speakers of the language in question do.

The point, however, is that what we humans use language for is much more than 'reporting facts'; and that some of the utterances we make, despite having the form of indicative sentences, are not really reports. And what is behind the untranslatability of the normative idiom into the indicative one (and hence the reduction of 'norms' to 'facts') is precisely this. Utterances that I will call *genuine normatives* are, despite appearances, not fact-reporting statements, but (slightly, but importantly) different kinds of speech acts—they are essentially 'fraught with ought'.

Let us return to the case of chess; and let us consider the statement *One should not move a rook diagonally*. This is the kind of statement I will call a *normative*. There are basically two ways of employing a statement of this kind. As we already pointed out, one can state the fact that this kind of rule is in force in some community. This is, as it were, an 'outsider' statement; a statement made by a disengaged observer describing the practices of the community in question. Besides this, one can state this as an 'insider': which does not amount to (or does not amount *only* to) stating a fact, but also to *upholding* the rule, urging its propriety or at least confirming its legitimacy. And *genuine* normatives are normatives posed precisely from this perspective.[20]

---

[20] The exposition of normativity presented here is close to that of Lance and O'Leary-Hawthorne (1997).

It follows that the talk about the *existence* of rules is better seen as a metaphor: of course they do not exist in the way rocks, trees, or dolphins do. To say that a rule exists is to take genuine normatives for ordinary indicative statements. And though it seems to be our human way to do this, we should not forget that this sense of *existence* differs from the one in which we use the word when we talk about the existence of spatio-temporal particulars and their constellations. Hence we people tend to live, besides the causal world explored by natural science, also in a different kind of world, in the world that Kant termed 'the realm of the concept of freedom' and which Sellars dubbed 'the manifest image'.

But how can correctness as such transcend our overt normative attitudes (expressed explicitly as genuine normatives, or otherwise), so that it is, on the one hand, carried by them, while being, on the other hand, not reducible to them? We must see that any verdict we reach regarding correctness is at best tentative; it belongs to the nature of the concept that the verdict is considered as always amendable by our successors (cf. Gauker 2007). They can discover later that what we held for *correct* is in fact *incorrect*, but unlike in the case of terms such as 'blue', 'fish', or 'iron', whose past apparent misapplication may have been caused either by an error of application, or by a subsequent shift of the term's meaning, in the case of the term 'correct' there is a third possibility: we can subsequently revise our standards of correctness and project them back to the past.

Thus, if future researchers find out that something we hitherto held to be a fish is really a mammal, they will conclude that we applied the concept of fish wrongly, because we were ignorant of some facts that were hitherto extant, but had remained undiscovered. This is what it takes to deal with *objective nature*, independent of us. In contrast to this, if our descendants come to the conclusion that something we currently hold as correct is in fact incorrect (think of the past cases of slavery or of denying women's suffrage), they may take it likewise as a discovery of a kind of objective fact, but not a fact objective in the same sense as a *natural* fact. The difference is that in our current time there is *nothing* in the external world that could make us recognize that we are making an error—indeed from our current perspective we are *not* making an error. The point is that the structure of the concept of correctness is such that if we see *the normative* as a *reality*, then we must conclude that we *make* this kind of reality, we establish standards with which to assess even past generations.

37.6 THE NORMATIVE INNERVATION OF THE HUMAN WORLD

Inferentialism holds that any content cannot but be born from a network of *rules*; and that the propositional content that dominates our language and our reason is born from certain kinds of networks of *inferential* rules. Moreover, it sees networks of rules as the animating nervous system breathing life into the causal world, thus making it into the 'meaningful' kind of world we humans inhabit. It is because of the work of rules that we not only live among *organisms* that *behave* in certain ways, but also among *persons* that *act responsibly,* that *reason,* and that *talk meaningfully.* The nature of our *manifest image* of the world, in contrast to the *scientific image,* is, as Sellars claimed, essentially normative.

It follows that any kind of meaningfulness we want to understand must be traced back to the rules that gave it birth. The meaningfulness of expressions of our languages must be traced back to the inferential rules that govern the words of our language and the ways they are composed together. And the rules must be scrutinized for their role within the kinematics of deontic statuses they constitute, and within the practices they regulate. And as rules are essentially social institutions—indeed they underlie our very sociality—this excavation of the normative innervation of the human world has much to tell us about who we humans really are. At least, this is what the inferentialists believe.[21]

References

Awodey, S. and A. W. Carus (2009). 'From Wittgenstein's Prison to the Boundless Ocean: Carnap's Dream of Logical Syntax'. In P. Wagner (ed.), *Carnap's Logical Syntax of Language.* Basingstoke: Palgrave Macmillan, pp. 79–106.

Belnap, N. (1962). 'Tonk, Plonk and Plink', *Analysis* 22: 130–4.

Boghossian, P. A. (1993). 'Does an Inferential Role Semantics Rest Upon a Mistake?'. In A. Villanueva (ed.), *Philosophical Issues* 3. Atascadero, CA: Ridgeview, pp. 73–88.

——(2005). 'Is Meaning Normative?'. In C. Nimtz and A. Beckermann (eds.), *Philosophie und/ als Wissenschaft.* Mentis, Paderborn, 205–18.

Brandom, R. (1994). *Making It Explicit.* Cambridge, MA: Harvard University Press.

——(2000). *Articulating Reasons.* Cambridge, MA: Harvard University Press.

Carnap, R. (1934). *Logische Syntax der Sprache.* Vienna: Springer. English translation *Logical Syntax of Language,* London: Kegan Paul, 1937.

——(1942). *Introduction to Semantics.* Cambridge, MA: Harvard University Press.

——(1943). *Formalization of Logic.* Cambridge, MA: Harvard University Press.

Chang, C. C. (1974). 'Model Theory 1945–1971'. In L. Henkin *et al.* (eds.), *Proceedings of the Tarski symposium (Proceedings of Symposia in Pure Mathematics XXV).* American Mathematical Society, pp. 173–86.

Chisholm, R. M. and W. Sellars (1958). 'Intentionality and the Mental: Chisholm–Sellars Correspondence on Intentionality'. In H. Feigl, M. Scriven, and G. Maxwell (eds.), *Minnesota Studies in the Philosophy of Science,* vol. II. Minneapolis: University of Minnesota Press, pp. 521–39.

Coffa, A. (1991). *The Semantic Tradition from Kant to Carnap.* Cambridge: Cambridge University Press.

Dummett, M. (1978). *Truth and Other Enigmas.* London: Duckworth.

——(1991). *The Logical Basis of Metaphysics.* Cambridge, MA: Harvard University Press.

[21] Work on this chapter was supported by research grant No. P401/10/0146 of the Czech Science Foundation. I am grateful to Vladimír Svoboda for helpful critical comments.

Frege, G. (1879). *Begriffsschrift*. Halle: Nebert. English translation *Concept Script* in J. van Heijenoort (ed.), *From Frege to Gödel: A Source Book from Mathematical Logic*. Cambridge, MA: Harvard University Press, 1971, pp. 1–82.

—— (1892a). 'Über Sinn und Bedeutung', *Zeitschrift für Philosophie und philosophische Kritik* 100: 25–50. English translation 'On Sense and Reference' in P. Geach and M. Black (eds.), *Translations from the Philosophical Writings of Gottlob Frege*, 2nd edn. Oxford: Blackwell, 1960, pp. 56–78.

——(1892b). 'Über Begriff und Gegenstand', *Vierteljahrschrift für wissentschaftliche Philosophie* 16: 192–205. English translation 'On Concept and Object' in P. Geach and M. Black (eds.), *Translations from the Philosophical Writings of Gottlob Frege*, 3rd edn. Oxford: Blackwell, 1980, pp. 42–55.

Gauker, C. (2007). 'The Circle of Deference Proves the Normativity Semantics', *Rivista di Estetica* 47: 181–98.

Gentzen, G. (1934). 'Untersuchungen über das logische Schliessen I', *Mathematische Zeitschrift* 39: 176–210.

—— (1936). 'Untersuchungen über das logische Schliessen II', *Mathematische Zeitschrift* 41: 405–31.

Glüer, K. and A. Wikforss (2009). 'Against Content Normativity', *Mind* 118: 31–70.

Gödel, K. (1931). 'Über formal unentscheidbare Sätze der Principia Mathematica und verwandter Systeme I', *Monatshefte für Mathematik und Physik* 38: 173–98.

Hacking, I. (1979). 'What is Logic?', *Journal of Philosophy* 76: 285–319.

Kenny, A. (1972). *Wittgenstein*. London: Penguin.

Koslow, A. (1992). *A Structuralist Theory of Logic*. Cambridge: Cambridge University Press.

Kreisel, G. (1964). 'Hilbert's Programme'. In P. Benacerraf and H. Putnam (eds.), *Philosophy of Mathematics*. Englewood Cliffs, NJ: Prentice-Hall, pp. 157–80.

Kukla, R. and M. Lance (2009). *'Yo!' and 'Lo!': The Pragmatic Topography of the Space of Reasons*. Cambridge, MA: Harvard University Press.

Lance, M. N. and J. O'Leary-Hawthorne (1997). *The Grammar of Meaning*. Cambridge: Cambridge University Press.

Mendonça, W. P. and P. Stekeler-Weithofer (1987). 'Frege—ein Platonist?', *Ratio* 29: 157–69.

Peregrin, J. (2001a). *Meaning and Structure*. Aldershot: Ashgate.

——(2001b). 'Review of Brandom: *Articulating Reasons*', *Erkenntnis* 55: 121–7.

——(2008a). 'What is the Logic of Inference?', *Studia Logica* 88: 263–94.

——(2008b). 'Inferentialist Approach to Semantics', *Philosophy Compass* 3: 1208–23.

—— (2012). 'The Normative Dimension of Discourse'. In K. Allan and K. Jasczolt (eds.), *Cambridge Handbook of Pragmatics*. Cambridge: Cambridge University Press, pp. 209–25.

Prawitz, D. (1965). *Natural Deduction*. Stockholm: Almqvist & Wiksell.

——(2006). 'Meaning Approached via Proofs', *Synthèse* 148: 507–24.

Prior, A. N. (1960/1). 'Runabout Inference Ticket', *Analysis* 21: 38–9.

——(1964). 'Conjunction and Contonktion Revisited', *Analysis* 24: 191–5.

Russell, B. (1912). *The Problems of Philosophy*. London: Williams and Norgate.

Schroeder-Heister, P. (2006). 'Validity Concepts in Proof-Theoretic Semantics', *Synthèse* 148: 525–71.

Sellars, W. (1949). 'Language, Rules and Behavior'. In S. Hook (ed.), *John Dewey: Philosopher of Science and Freedom*. New York: Dial Press, pp. 289–315.

——(1953). 'Inference and Meaning', *Mind* 62: 313–38.

——(1954). 'Some Reflections on Language Games', *Philosophy of Science* 21: 204–28.

—— (1962). 'Philosophy and the Scientific Image of Man'. In R. Colodny (ed.), *Frontiers of Science and Philosophy*. Pittsburgh: University of Pittsburgh Press, pp. 35–78.

—— (1969). 'Language as Thought and as Communication', *Philosophy and Phenomenological Research* 29: 506–27.

Sundholm, G. (1981). 'Hacking's Logic', *The Journal of Philosophy* 78: 160–8.

Tarski, A. (1936). 'Über den Begriff der logischen Folgerung', *Actes du Congrès International de Philosophique Scientifique* 7: 1–11. English translation 'On the Concept of Logical Consequence' in Tarski (1956), pp. 409–20.

—— (1939). 'O ugruntowaniu naukowej semantyki', *Przeglad Filosoficzny* 39: 50–7. English translation 'The Establishment of Scientific Semantics' in Tarski (1956), pp. 401–8.

—— (1956). *Logic, Semantics, Metamathematics*. Oxford: Clarendon Press.

—— (1986). 'What are Logical Notions?', *History and Philosophy of Logic* 7: 143–54.

van Heijenoort, J. (1967). 'Logic as Calculus and Logic as Language', *Synthèse* 17: 324–30.

Vaught, R. V. (1974). 'Model Theory before 1945'. In L. Henkin *et al.* (eds.), *Proceedings of the Tarski symposium (Proceedings of Symposia in Pure Mathematics XXV)*. American Mathematical Society, pp. 153–72.

Whitting, D. (2008). 'On Epistemic Conceptions of Meaning: Use, Meaning and Normativity', *European Journal of Philosophy* 17: 416–34.

Wittgenstein, L. (1922). *Tractatus Logico-Philosophicus*. London: Routledge. English translation included in the same edition.

—— (1953). *Philosophische Untersuchungen*. Oxford: Blackwell. English translation *Philosophical Investigations*. Oxford: Blackwell, 1953.

CHAPTER 38

··

PRAGMATISM AND ANALYTIC PHILOSOPHY[1]

··

CHERYL MISAK

38.1 THE RECEIVED VIEW

Richard Rorty articulates and upholds the received view of the relationship between pragmatism and analytic philosophy:

> Along about 1945, American philosophers were, for better or worse, *bored* with Dewey, and thus with pragmatism. They were sick of being told that pragmatism was the philosophy of American democracy, that Dewey was the great American intellectual figure of their century, and the like. They wanted something new, something they could get their philosophical teeth into. What showed up, thanks to Hitler and various other historical contingencies, was logical empiricism, an early version of what we now call 'analytic philosophy'. (Rorty 1995: 70)

The received view has it that when the logical empiricists hit America's shores, there was a straightforward replacement of pragmatism with a radically different view. Logical empiricism became the dominant force in American philosophy departments, bullying and chasing out the home-grown pragmatism.

Louis Menand reaffirms this view in his best-selling and Pulitzer Prize winning history of American pragmatism, *The Metaphysical Club*—which was the reading group in the 1860s in which Chauncey Wright, Charles Peirce, Williams James, Oliver Wendell Homes, and others first hammered out pragmatist ideas. Menand holds that pragmatism is anti-analytic and 'belongs to a disestablishmentarian impulse in American culture'. On this picture, pragmatism is Rorty's position that there is no certainty, no truth, and no objectivity to be had, only agreement within a community (2001: 89).

---

[1] This chapter is a whirlwind tour of an argument I make in *The American Pragmatists* (Oxford University Press, 2013).

Menand's argument is that the American Civil War was, amongst other things, a failure of ideas. It 'swept away almost the whole intellectual culture of the North' and 'it took nearly half a century for the United States to find a culture to replace it, to find a set of ideas, and a way of thinking, that would help people cope with the conditions of modern life' (2001: x). That set of ideas was pragmatism. After the trauma of the Civil War, in which the lesson was 'certitude leads to violence', people were not in the mood for absolutist philosophies (2001: 61). Pragmatism thus arose and flourished until its fallibilism and tolerance were thrown into suspicion by the intellectual climate of the Cold War of the 1950s (2001: 439). James and Dewey came to be seen then as 'naïve, and even a little dangerous' (2001: 439). With the end of the Cold War, uncertainty was allowable again—hence Rorty's revival of pragmatism during the 1980s and '90s. 'For in the post-Cold War world, where there are many competing belief systems, not just two, skepticism about the finality of any particular set of beliefs has begun to seem to some people an important value again' (2001: 441).

But the story is not, as Menand and Rorty would have it, a straightforward replacement of pragmatism with what was perceived as a safer view (Menand) or as a more exciting view (Rorty). Scott Soames (2008) is right to say that the pragmatist reverence for logic, respect for science, suspicion of metaphysics, and emphasis on practical consequences made for fertile soil in which logical empiricism could grow. Indeed, the burden of this chapter will be to show that many of the central tenets of logical empiricism, and analytic philosophy more generally, were already present in early American pragmatism and continued to flourish in the pragmatist views of C. I. Lewis and Quine. It is only when Rorty resolutely follows one of the less analytic of the early pragmatists (William James) that things go awry.

On the James–Rorty understanding of pragmatism, on which truth and objectivity are to be replaced by something like agreement, pragmatism is indeed in tension with the kind of analytic philosophy exemplified by certain of the logical empiricists—those who tried to show how objectivity was possible by bringing together all genuine inquiry under the umbrella of science and the new mathematical logic. Inquiry was to be unified and progress made possible with all branches of inquiry conducted in the same straightforward, logical, observational language. The verifiability principle did most of the heavy lifting here: it required all meaningful beliefs and theories to be reducible, via formal deductive logic, to statements that are empirically verifiable. Since metaphysics does not meet this test, aspersion was cast upon it.

I will show, however, that many of these themes were already present in early American philosophy. If we are to see how the received view of the relationship between pragmatism and analytic philosophy is wrong-headed, we need to carefully examine this history. I will then offer an account of the fate of pragmatism that differs substantially from the received view but which is, I submit, not only more accurate, but much more interesting.

I should note what will already be obvious. I am not taking 'analytic philosophy' to be philosophical analysis, where the philosopher's job of unpacking of the meaning of words is engaged prior to first-order inquiry. On this version of analytic philosophy, philosophy is discontinuous with science and is a non-empirical venture. This is the analytic philosophy, on which one term is to be reduced to another set of terms and rendered clear without residue, that is often caricatured as Oxford ordinary language philosophy. Rather, I am taking analytic philosophy to be that which was born with Frege and Russell's delivery of a new and powerful logic, spent its youth in the optimistic excitement of logical empiricism in the 1930s and 1940s, went through a period of disillusionment when the strong programme of logical empiricism started to unravel, came into maturity with the likes of Quine, and is now perhaps showing itself to be immortal as the dominant methodology of philosophy. That is, the term 'analytic philosophy' marks a way of doing philosophy that has argumentative rigour, logic, and a focus on science and its methodology at its centre. I will show that some of the classical pragmatists are not only completely at home here, but helped to build the house in which modern analytic philosophy now lives.

38.2 Chauncey Wright: Science, Mathematics, and the Suspicion of Metaphysics

Chauncey Wright is an under-rated figure, known only to aficionados of American philosophy. While a student at Harvard he made a great impression on many of his contemporaries and on the Professor of Mathematics—Benjamin Peirce, who was Charles Peirce's father. After graduation, he became a computer for the American Nautical Almanac, cramming a year's work into three or four months and then devoting himself to philosophy. He died in 1875, when he was 45, after suffering from general poor health, abuse of stimulants, and terrible sleep habits.

Wright's thought was influenced by the work of the psychologist Alexander Bain, and by Hume, Mill, and Darwin. One thing these thinkers have in common is that they direct their attention to first-order inquiry and take observation seriously. They treat their subject matter, whether it be chemistry, philosophy, or religion, as 'a science of causes and effects' (Wright 1873: 417). Wright rails against the 'a priori school' of philosophy, aligning himself firmly with the 'positive mode of thought', which investigates the world by observation, experiment, and verification (1865a: 44). He is set against metaphysics, unknown inscrutable powers, intuitions, innate ideas, laws of the faculty of mind, and primitive convictions—those supposed truths that have the mark of self-evidence, necessity, and universality (1865b: 330). These kinds of phenomena are not verifiable and hence they cannot be the objects of scientific study. He thinks that 'a priori too often means no more than *ab ignorantia et indolentia*' (1875: 393)—an expression translatable even for those without any Latin at all.

Wright sees the difficulties and subtleties involved in the verificationist idea straight off the bat. As Edward Madden (1963: 108ff.) notes, he anticipates a major innovation in verificationism made 60 years after his death. Instead of requiring every hypothesis to be directly testable by experience, Wright has it that hypotheses must 'show credentials from the senses, either by affording from themselves consequences capable of sensuous verification or by yielding such consequences in conjunction with ideas which by themselves are verifiable' (1865a: 46). Decades later, the logical empiricists, under relentless pressure to make their verifiability criterion stand up to excellent objections, conceded that a theoretical concept can receive some or all of its meaning from the theory in which it occurs. Carnap, for instance, says that there is in the strict sense no refutation or confirmation of an hypothesis—tests apply '*at bottom, not to a single hypothesis but to the whole system of physics as a system of hypotheses*' (1937: 318). The logical empiricists moved, that is, towards what Quine called holism. We need to look to a whole system of interconnected concepts and hypotheses and then require that theory to be verifiable.

Wright is of the same view. In the paper in which he expresses it, he presages another devastating objection to logical empiricism:

> It is indisputable that verification is essential to the completeness of scientific method; but there is still room for debate as to what constitutes verification in the various departments of philosophical inquiry. So long as the philosophy of method fails to give a complete inventory of our primary sources of knowledge, and cannot decide authoritatively what are the origins of first truths, or the truths of observation, so long will it remain uncertain what is a legitimate appeal to observation, or what is a real verification. (1865a: 45)

To assume that direct reports from our senses are the sum total of what counts as legitimate verification is to blithely assume the answer to some very hard questions.

Unlike Comte, the verificationist most discussed in Wright's time, Wright does not think that we can assume that philosophy and theology are superseded by science. They can in principle coexist with science. But in Wright's view, science was just coming to maturity and it promised 'to throw a flood of light' on subjects such as history, society, laws, and morality (1865a: 54). He is the first to set out a defining feature of pragmatism. This is the idea that experience goes beyond what our five senses deliver; that experience must be conceived of broadly; that all inquiry must and can be thought of as being a part of a seamless whole.

He is also the first to articulate the pragmatic account of truth, which he thought arose naturally once the new science was taken seriously. He thinks that 'our knowledges and rational beliefs result, *truly and literally*, from the survival of the fittest among our original and spontaneous beliefs' (1870: 116).

38.3 Charles Sanders Peirce: Truth and Inquiry

Peirce was by all accounts a very difficult and brilliant man, who found it impossible to get a permanent position in the academy. He did manage to get a part-time post at Johns Hopkins, where he taught logic and had a great impact on a select and excellent group of students. But in 1884, after four years there, he was fired, never able to return to a paid position in a university despite his desperation to do so and his manifest talent. A scandal around his infidelity and the collapse of his marriage seems to have sealed his fate. What money he had, from then on, was acquired from his day job as a scientist for the US Coast and Geodetic Survey and from charity organized by William James. During his 31 years at the Survey, he made significant advances in pendulum studies to determine the shape of the earth, in photometric research on stars, and in chromatics.

Peirce conceived of himself first and foremost as a logician. He says that Jevons, along with Boole, Whewell, Berkeley, Glanville, Ockham, and Duns Scotus would capture 'the purpose of my memoirs'. That purpose is 'to lay a solid foundation upon which may be erected a new logic fit for the life of twentieth century science' (CP 7.161, 1902).[2] Logic, for Peirce, is a normative science. He was forever outlining proposals for a grand book on logic that had at its centre the study of inquiry aimed at the truth. This is not what we today take logic to be, but Peirce was also a brilliant logician in the modern sense. He developed a quantified first-order logic independently of and at the same time as Frege; discovered the Sheffer stroke decades before Sheffer; and made lasting advances in the logic of statistical reasoning.

Peirce shares Wright's commitment to science and to a kind of verificationist principle. Add to that his ability in formal logic and the resemblance to the logical empiricist expression of analytic philosophy is striking. But, as with Wright, there is some distance between the verificationism of Peirce and that of the logical empiricists. In 'How to Make Our Ideas Clear', one of the few papers Peirce managed to publish, he identifies pragmatism as a way of clarifying our ideas so that they are not subject to metaphysical 'deceptions'. Here is that famous, or perhaps infamous, statement: 'Consider what effects, which might conceivably have practical bearings, we conceive the object of our conception to have. Then, our conception of these is the whole of our conception of the object' (W3: 266).

In this essay, the effects Peirce is concerned with are 'effects, direct or indirect, upon our senses' (W3: 266). He asks about the meaning of 'this diamond is hard' and finds that it amounts to 'it will not be scratched by many other substances' (W3: 266). He says, setting up pragmatism for trouble for a century to come: 'There is absolutely no difference between a hard thing and a soft thing so long as they are not brought to the test. Suppose, then, that a diamond could be crystallized in the midst of a cushion of soft cotton, and should remain there until it was finally burned up' (W3: 266). His suggestion is that it is meaningless to speak of such a diamond as being hard.

He tinkered with and improved this published account of the pragmatic maxim over the course of many years. He sees, for instance, that the use of the indicative conditional—it *will* not be scratched—is highly problematic and is insistent on replacing

---

[2] References to Peirce's *Collected Papers* are in standard form: volume number, followed by paragraph number. Reference to Peirce's *Writings* are in the form: volume number, followed by page number.

the 'will-be' with a 'would-be'.[3] But even in 'How to Make our Ideas Clear', it wasn't obvious that the principle Peirce was articulating was designed to be a semantic principle about the very meaning of our concepts. As the very title of the paper suggests, the maxim is about achieving clarity. Pierce took his contribution to be one in a well-worn debate. 'The books', he says, 'are right in making familiarity with a notion the first step toward clearness of apprehension, and the defining of it the second' (W3: 260). He wants to add an important third 'grade of clearness' or grade of 'apprehensions of the meanings of words': knowing what to expect if hypotheses containing the concept are true.

The pragmatic maxim, that is, is designed to just capture one—albeit very important—aspect of what it is to understand something. In addition to connotation and denotation, Peirce thinks that there is a third thing that someone needs to understand when they understand a concept. They have to know what to expect if beliefs containing the concept are true or false. If a belief has no consequences—if there is nothing we would expect would be different if it were true or false—then it lacks a dimension we would have had to get right were we to fully understand it.

Rather than take that snappy summary provided in 'How to Make Our Ideas Clear' as capturing Peirce's intentions, we should focus rather on the following kinds of expressions. We 'must look to the upshot of our concepts in order to rightly apprehend them' (CP 5.4, 1901). In order to get a complete grasp of a concept, we must connect it to that with which we have 'dealings' (CP 5.416, 1905). Or: 'we must not begin by talking of pure ideas,—vagabond thoughts that tramp the public roads without any human habitation,—but must begin with men and their conversation' (CP 8.112, 1900). Peirce's idea is nicely articulated by David Wiggins (2002: 316). When a concept is 'already fundamental to human thought and long since possessed of an autonomous interest', it is pointless to try to define it. Rather, we ought to attempt to get leverage on the concept, or a fix on it, by exploring its connections with practice. This is the insight at the very heart of Peircean pragmatism.

When Peirce shines the light of the pragmatic maxim on the concept of truth, the upshot is an aversion to 'transcendental' accounts of truth, such as the correspondence theory, on which a true belief is one that corresponds to, or gets right, or mirrors the believer-independent world (CP 5.572, 1901). Such accounts of truth are examples of those 'vagabond thoughts'. They make truth the subject of empty metaphysics. For the very idea of the believer-independent world, and the items within it to which beliefs or sentences might correspond, seem graspable only if we could somehow step outside of our corpus of belief, our practices, or that with which we have dealings. We would do better to illuminate truth by considering its linkages with inquiry, assertion, and belief, for those are the human dealings relevant to truth. Peirce's view of truth is a naturalist view—we should not add anything metaphysical to science, or to any other first-order inquiry. We have to extract the concept of truth from our practices of inquiry, reason-giving, and deliberation.

---

[3] See CP 5.453, 5.457, 8.208.

That concept of truth is as follows. A belief is true if it would be 'indefeasible'; or would not be improved upon; or would never lead to disappointment; or would forever meet the challenges of reasons, argument, and evidence. A true belief is the belief we would come to, were we to inquire as far as we could on a matter. Peirce initially put this idea in the following unhelpful way: a true belief is one which would be agreed upon at the hypothetical or 'fated' end of inquiry (see W3: 273, 1878). But his considered and much better formulation is this: a true belief is one which would withstand doubt, were we to inquire as far as we fruitfully could into the matter. A true belief is such that, no matter how much further we were to investigate and debate, it would not be overturned by recalcitrant experience and argument (CP 5.569, 1901, 6.485, 1908). On the whole, he tries to stay away from unhelpful ideas such as the final end of inquiry, perfect evidence, and the like.

As Peirce's thoughts about the pragmatic maxim matured, he also made amendments regarding the nature of the practical consequences required by the pragmatic maxim. He tries to divert our focus from sensory experience and direct it to a broader notion of experience. Experience, he argues, is that which is compelling, surprising, unchosen, involuntary, or forceful. This extremely generous conception of experience is clearly going to allow for a criterion of legitimacy that encompasses more than beliefs directly verifiable by the senses. For one thing, Peirce thought that mathematical and logical beliefs were connected to experience in the requisite way. They have consequences in diagrammatic contexts—when we manipulate diagrams, we can find ourselves compelled and surprised.

This thought certainly pulls against the logical empiricist's distinction between observational and logical statements and against their requirement that sensory experience is the only testing ground for belief. A. J. Ayer is right to think that Peirce's pragmatic maxim was a clear predecessor of the verifiability criterion: it 'allows no truck with metaphysics. Its standpoint is closely akin to that which was later to be adopted by the logical positivists' (Ayer 1968: 45). But he is wrong to think that the maxim is 'identical … with the physicalist interpretation of the verification principle' (1968: 45). For Peirce offered a much broader account of experience than the verificationists ever envisioned and he was very clear that he was talking about an aspect of meaningfulness, not the whole of it.

Ayer discovered Peirce long after the height of logical empiricism's popularity. But even at the apex of logical empiricism, Peirce was seen by those who knew of him as a kindred spirit. Ernest Nagel, at the fifth International Conference for the Unity of Science held at Harvard in 1940, gave a talk titled 'Charles S. Peirce: Pioneer of Modern Empiricism'. There he asserted:

> One is not minimizing the contributions of the Vienna Circle in pointing out that many of its recent views have been taken for granted for some time by American colleagues, largely because the latter have come to intellectual maturity under the influence of Peirce. (Nagel 1940: 70)

Nagel points to the antipathy to metaphysical speculation, the emphasis on cooperative scientific research, and the fact that the pragmatic maxim 'was offered to philosophers in order to bring to an end disputes which no observation of facts could settle because they involved terms with no definite meaning' (1940: 73).

But, as we shall see below, another stream of pragmatism took a turn away from analytic philosophy. It took this turn during Peirce's lifetime, causing him to bemoan that the term 'pragmatism'

> gets abused in the merciless way that words have to expect when they fall into literary clutches.... So then, the writer, finding his bantling 'pragmatism' so promoted, feels that it is time to kiss his child good-by and relinquish it to its higher destiny; while to serve the precise purpose of expressing the original definition, he begs to announce the birth of the word 'pragmaticism', which is ugly enough to be safe from kidnappers. (CP 5.414, 1905)

'Pragmaticism', he says, should be used in a narrow sense—for his own doctrine only—and '"pragmatism" should ... be used somewhat loosely to signify affiliation with Schiller, James, Dewey, Royce' and others who have drifted away from what Peirce saw as the spirit of pragmatism as he and Chauncey Wright envisioned it (CP 8.205, 1903).

38.4 WILLIAM JAMES: TRUTH AND USEFULNESS

William James's version of the pragmatic maxim makes short work of many long-standing and seemingly intractable philosophical problems. 'If no practical difference whatsoever can be traced, then the alternatives mean practically the same thing, and all dispute is idle' (James 1907 [1949]: 45). Once you trace the consequences of two views, you might very well find them empirically equivalent. Hence all sorts of philosophical problems will be seen to be pseudo-problems, to use the language of the logical empiricists.

But while Peirce is the archetype of what James called a 'technical' philosopher, James makes it clear at the beginning of *Pragmatism* that he is not interested in being one: 'the philosophy which is so important to each of us is not a technical matter; it is our more or less dumb sense of what life honestly and deeply means' (1907 [1949]: 5). He goes on: 'I have heard friends and colleagues try to popularize philosophy in this very hall, but they soon grew dry, and then technical, and the results were only partially encouraging.' James was not good at the new formal methods, but he was very successful in getting philosophy to the educated masses. This popularizing ambition tended not to impress professional philosophers. In his rather bad-tempered (indeed, generally bad) *Anti-Pragmatism*, Albert Schinz rants: 'Popular science, popular art, popular theology— only one thing was lacking—popular philosophy. And now they give that to us. What a triumph for a weak cause!' (Schinz 1909: xvi).

Two very different versions of the pragmatic account of truth and objectivity arise from applying the pragmatic maxim to the concept of truth. One is the naturalism which originates in Wright and Peirce. It focuses on the practices of inquiry and tries to capture our cognitive aspirations to objectivity. It is this view that manifests itself in Quine and then almost drops out of sight as a recognizably pragmatist view. That is, it ceases to be thought of as pragmatism.

The other orginates with James. It is the view which took root in Rorty, and which became identified with pragmatism between the 1970s and 1990s. James argues that truth is what works for us: 'Any idea upon which we can ride ... any idea that will carry us prosperously from any one part of our experience to any other part, linking things satisfactorily, working securely, simplifying, saving labor, is ... true *instrumentally*' (1907 [1949]: 58). 'Satisfactorily', for James, 'means more satisfactorily to ourselves, and individuals will emphasize their points of satisfaction differently. To a certain degree, therefore, everything here is plastic' (1907 [1949]: 61). Sometimes he puts his position as follows: 'True ideas are those that we can assimilate, validate, corroborate and verify'; 'truth *happens* to an idea' (1907 [1949]: 200). He rather infamously suggested that if the belief in God made a positive impact on someone's life, then it could reasonably be taken as true by that person.

Two giants of analytic philosophy—Bertrand Russell and G. E. Moore—took a kind of glee in dismantling James's view. Russell notes in 1910 that he is sympathetic with pragmatism's turning its back on a priori reasoning and towards concrete facts and consequences (1966 [1992]: 196). Nonetheless, he thinks that James's account of truth is seriously defective. Russell turns the pragmatist account of truth on itself, as it were, and notes that if it is to be useful, there must be a way of telling when the consequences of a belief are useful or good (1966 [1992]: 201):

> We must suppose that this means that the consequences of entertaining the belief are better than those of rejecting it. In order to know this, we must know what are the consequences of entertaining it, and what are the consequences of rejecting it; we must know also what consequences are good, what bad, what consequences are better, and what worse. (Russell 1966 [1992]: 201)

This, of course, is a very tall order, illustrated by Russell with two examples. First, the consequences of believing the doctrine of the Catholic faith might make one happy 'at the expense of a certain amount of stupidity and priestly domination' (1966 [1992]: 201). It is unclear how we are to weigh these benefits and burdens against each other. Second, the effects of Rousseau's doctrines were far-reaching—Europe is a different place from what it would have been without them. But how do we disentangle what the effects have been? And even if we could do that, whether we take them to be good or bad depends on our political views.

In a related objection, Russell points that one can take 'works' or 'pays' in two very different ways. In science, a hypothesis works if we can deduce a number of verifiable hypotheses from it. But for James, a hypothesis works if

> the effects of believing it are good, including among the effects ... the emotions entailed by it or its perceived consequences, and the actions to which we are prompted by it or its perceived consequences. This is a totally different conception

of 'working', and one for which the authority of scientific procedure cannot be invoked. (Russell 1966 [1992]: 210)[4]

Moore reviewed James's *Pragmatism* in the 1907 *Proceedings of the Aristotelian Society*. The review is harsh, with Moore finding James's assertions to be 'silly' (1907: 49). Here is a catalogue of his objections to James's view. First, he points to a problem that dogs all pragmatist views of truth. If truth is tightly connected to what we can verify, what do we think about statements for which the evidence has been destroyed, or statements that are so trivial that no one has bothered to collect any evidence for them, or statements the evidence for which lies buried deep in the past? (1907: 36–9).[5] Second, with Russell, Moore interrogates the linkage between the true and the useful. If usefulness is a property that may come and go, then (in James's own words) 'a belief, which occurs at several different times, may be true at some of the times at which it occurs, and yet untrue at others' (1907: 61). The truth of a belief, that is, seems to vary from time to time and from culture to culture. Truth is not a stable property of beliefs and that, Moore thinks, is an anathema. Third, Moore takes on James's claim that we make the truth: 'I think he certainly means to suggest that we not only make our true beliefs, but also that we *make them true*' (1907: 72). Moore thinks that it is crazy to suggest that my belief that *p* makes it true that *p*. My (correct) belief that it rained today did not make it rain today.

One can see that under a barrage of well-formed criticism such as this, pragmatism's reputation across the Atlantic was bound to suffer. It came under similar stress at home.

James Pratt is the American critic who takes the most care with James's view. He sees two ambitious claims at the heart of it. The first is about truth: 'in morality and metaphysics and religion, as well as in science, we are justified in testing the truth of a belief by its usefulness' (1909: 13). A true claim is a 'verified human claim' (1909: 83). The second is about meaning: 'the meaning of any philosophical proposition can always be brought down to some particular consequence in our future practical experience' (1909: 25).

Pratt, like Russell, asks whether the pragmatist account of truth is itself true. It is certainly useful to pragmatists, he says, but not to others (1909: 127). The fact that pragmatists will want to respond by saying that the truth of pragmatism consists in something more robust shows that they too think that there is some more transcendental account of truth in play—the pragmatist is 'making use of the very conception of truth which he is trying to refute' (1909: 129).

Pratt also tackles James's view that religious hypotheses are true if they are good for us to believe. Here he echoes Moore's distinction between the two senses of what works or what is good. Pragmatism, Pratt says,

---

[4] Frank Ramsey, another icon of analytic philosophy, made the same objection to James's view, and then went on to put forward a pragmatist account of truth that was very much like Peirce's (and indeed, was heavily influenced by Peirce). See Misak (forthcoming).

[5] Peirce worried about this set of issues. See Misak (1991) for his careful attempt at resolving them.

seeks to prove the truth of religion by its good and satisfactory consequences. Here, however, a distinction must be made; namely between the 'good', harmonious, and logically confirmatory consequences of religious concepts as such, and the good and pleasant consequences which come from believing these concepts. It is one thing to say a belief is true because the logical consequences that flow from it fit in harmoniously with our otherwise grounded knowledge; and quite another to call it true because it is pleasant to believe. (Pratt 1909: 186–7)

The difference between the views of Peirce and James can be nicely summarized by Pratt's distinction. Peirce holds that 'a belief is true because the logical consequences that flow from it fit in harmoniously with our otherwise grounded knowledge' and James seems to hold that a belief is true 'because it is pleasant to believe'.[6] Indeed, Peirce anticipated and tried to avoid or work through the catalogue of objections set out above (see Misak 1991). James, on the other hand, tended to merely rail against them, claiming that they had a 'fantastic' and 'slanderous' character and were based on wilful misinterpretation (1909 [1914]: xv, 180). Paul Carus captures the general attitude towards James's protestations: 'He seems to be in the habit of sometimes saying what he does not mean and then blames the world for misunderstanding him' (1911: 23). Pragmatism struggled, from this point onward, to shake its unhappy reputation amongst analytic philosophers.

38.5 John Dewey and Logical Empiricism

John Dewey's long life and working span connected him to both classical pragmatism and to modern analytic philosophy. He studied with Peirce during Peirce's brief stint at Johns Hopkins and although the logical empiricists arrived in America after Dewey's retirement from Columbia in 1929, he actively engaged with them. Although Dewey, on the received view, is seen as standing against the rising and dangerous tide of analytic philosophy, it is important to understand that he shared the central concern of the logical empiricists: to unify all inquiry through the experimental method.

This affinity was fully noticed during the rise of logical empiricism. In 1933, before the mass immigration of the Vienna Circle, Otto Neurath started *The International Encyclopedia of Unified Science* and this, teamed with a set of influential conferences on the unity of science, was for a long time the official forum for logical empiricism—its 'organized contemporary expression', as Neurath put it (Neurath *et al.* 1938: 2). Once

---

⁶ There are two caveats. The first is that Peirce insisted on a subjunctive formulation: a belief is true if the logical consequences *would* fit harmoniously with our otherwise grounded knowledge, were we to pursue our investigations as far as they could fruitfully go. The second caveat is that James sometimes put forward a more careful and subtle account of truth, one that was much closer to Peirce's. He was concerned to characterize truth as something that was of human value, without making a true belief what this or that human finds valuable at this or that time. The true, he says, is 'the expedient', but the expedient 'in the long run and on the whole, of course' (James 1909 [1914]: vii).

the logical empiricists hit the shores of America, Dewey was immediately seen as a kindred spirit. He was on the *Encyclopedia*'s Advisory Committee, he was one of the introducers of the very first volume of the new series (alongside Otto Neurath, Niels Bohr, Bertrand Russell, Rudoph Carnap, and Charles Morris), and in 1939 he was the sole author of a volume—*Theory of Valuation*—which tried to bring values under the umbrella of science.

One subtle difference between Dewey and the logical empiricists is found in their attitude towards value. Dewey wanted to find a place for value in the scientific world-view. The project of the logical empiricists, on the other hand, was to work out the implications of the scientific world-view, without a prior requirement that a place be held for value. Many of the logical empiricists thought that the unifying project left little room for value, while Dewey thought that it left plenty of room. One exception here is Neurath, who, as Alan Richardson (2008) notes, is remarkably similar to Dewey in thinking that an increasingly scientized world is one which will be socially progressive.

In *Theory of Valuation* Dewey argued that value judgements must be understood operationally or in terms of behaviour. Dewey set this scientific account of value against that favoured by many of the logical empiricists: the boo-hurrah (or as Dewey puts it, 'ejaculatory') theory of value, on which to say that something is good is to applaud it and to say that something is bad is to say 'boo-hiss' to it. On this view, statements about value are statements about how one feels; they are not candidates for truth, falsity, warranted assertion, or rational belief in the way that statements about the world are candidates for such normative concepts.

This debate, it is important to notice, was a debate within the circle of those who insisted that value judgements, if they are to be legitimate, must be empirical. While there was some disagreement between Dewey, Ayer, Neurath, and Carnap on how to conceive of ethics, the disagreement can be described as interfamilial.[7] But as interfamilial relations often are, this one was tense. Dewey was upset at the logical empiricists sparking what he saw as the loss of relevance of philosophy. In the 1948 introduction to the new edition of *Reconstruction in Philosophy* he bemoaned what he saw as contemporary philosophy's concern 'for the improvement of techniques' and a 'withdrawal from the present scene' (1920 [1948]: vi–vii).

As Morton White, an analytic pragmatist who lived through these times, puts it, the 1940s were marked by polemics in which 'liberalism, Communism, pragmatism, and positivism often did battle with each other on political and personal levels' (1999: 87). The fact that Dewey was not a technically proficient logician, and yet spoke against the use of logical techniques, did not help. In Dewey's hands, pragmatism seemed to be out of step with the new methods, despite its being in step with the general aims of logical empiricism.

But as logical empiricism modified itself in response to relentless criticism from within the analytic tradition, it moved closer and closer to adopting the pragmatist epistemology and account of truth. Neurath's famous image of inquirers having to

---

⁷ Although Reisch does not use this term, see his (2005: 92).

rebuild our boat of knowledge plank by plank while at sea carries precisely the same message as Peirce's central metaphor: that of inquirers walking on a bog, saying only 'this ground seems to hold for the present. Here I will stay until it begins to give way' (CP 5.589, 1898).

Indeed, what gets called the left wing of logical empiricism in the end expressly embraced the pragmatist account of truth. Hans Hahn says: 'As against the metaphysical view that truth consists in an agreement with reality—though this agreement cannot be established—we advocate the pragmatic view that the truth of a statement consists in its confirmation' (1933 [1987]: 43).[8] And here is Philipp Frank:

> The physicist in his own scientific activity has never employed any other concept of truth than that of pragmatism. The 'agreement of thoughts with their object', which the school philosophy requires, cannot be established by any concrete experiment.... In reality, physicists compare only experiences with other experiences. They test the truth of a theory by what it has become customary to call 'agreements'. (Frank 1930b [1949]: 101–2)

38.6 QUINE: EMPIRICISM, NATURALISM, AND HOLISM

Not only did logical empiricism come very close to pragmatism, but the next major move in analytic philosophy came even more so. Willard Van Orman Quine arrived at Harvard in 1930 as a graduate student in philosophy, with a BA in mathematics. Two of his courses during his intense graduate introduction to philosophy were taught by C. I. Lewis, the inheritor of Peirce's analytic pragmatism. It was here that Quine acquired his introduction to pragmatism (Quine 1990: 292). Indeed, he pretty much adopted his teacher's views.[9] Quine was never a scholar of texts—he was not, that is, terribly interested in the history of pragmatist ideas. He told Morton White that reading Josiah Royce was like going through muck. White tried to persuade him otherwise, with no success (White 1999: 121–4). But the naturalized, holist epistemology that Quine was to make famous was taken, almost word for word and unacknowledged, from Lewis.[10] For his part, Lewis got his view straight from Peirce, duly acknowledged. When he arrived at Harvard as a faculty member in 1920, he 'practically lived with' the 'manuscript remains' of Peirce for two years. This massive bulk of papers had been left to Harvard in a state of disarray by Peirce's widow and there was some hope that Lewis would start to put them into order (Lewis 1968: 16). He was already on a Peircean path, guided there by Royce. Lewis came to the view that

---

[8] The translation is Uebel's (2004).
[9] See Misak (2013) for this argument.
[10] See Misak (2013) for the details.

the 'originality and wealth' of this 'legendary figure' was not fully evident in Peirce's meagre published writings and not well represented by those who were influenced by him—James and Royce (1970 [1930c]: 78). It is very clear that he studied and absorbed these papers closely.

Quine ushered in the next stage in analytic pragmatism. When he first put his position forward, he was happy placing it firmly in the pragmatist camp. In the abstract of his famous 'Two Dogmas of Empiricism', he asserts that one upshot of the paper is 'a shift towards pragmatism' (1980: 20). He argues that our entire belief system must be seen as an interconnected web. Mathematics and logic are at the centre, gradually shading into the theoretical sentences of science, and then to specific observation sentences at the periphery. When faced with recalcitrant experience, we must choose where to make adjustments in our web of belief. No sentence is immune from revision. Indeed, it was Quine who made famous Neurath's metaphor: we are like sailors adrift at sea, never able to return to dry dock to reconstruct our boat out of the finest materials. We work with what we have, replacing our boat of knowledge plank by plank, as required by the surprise of experience. Quine unpacks that metaphor as follows:

> The naturalistic philosopher begins his reasoning within the inherited world theory as a going concern. He tentatively believes all of it, but believes also that some unidentified portions are wrong. He tries to improve, clarify, and understand the system from within. (Quine 1981: 28)

Here are two later Quinean pragmatist thoughts:

> As an empiricist I continue to think of the conceptual scheme of science as a tool, ultimately for predicting future experience in the light of past experience. Physical objects are conceptually imported into the situation as convenient intermediaries—not by definition in terms of experience, but simply as irreducible posits comparable, epistemologically, to the gods of Homer. For my part I do, qua lay physicist, believe in physical objects and not in Homer's gods ... But in point of epistemological footing the physical objects and the gods enter our conceptions only as cultural posits. The myth of physical objects is superior to most in that it has proved more efficacious than other myths as a device for working a manageable structure into the flux of experience. (Quine 1980: 44)
>
> Philosophically I am bound to Dewey by the naturalism that dominated his last three decades. With Dewey I hold that knowledge, mind, and meaning are part of the same world that they have to do with, and that they are to be studied in the same empirical spirit that animates natural science. There is no place for a priori philosophy. (Quine 1969: 26)

But Quine's relationship to pragmatism is complex. He often distances himself from the position, taking it to be the Jamsesian view that truth is what works for individuals.[11]

---

[11] See, for instance, Quine (1981).

And as White notes, Quine recoiled from extending his holism, to include ethics (2002: 53). Quine asserted that 'apart from a salient marker or two' one found only 'uncharted moral wastes' there (Quine 1987: 5). Much more often than not, Quine declined to call his position 'pragmatist'.

38.7 RICHARD RORTY AND THE FORTUNES OF PRAGMATISM

When Quine abandoned the pragmatist camp, he left the ground wide open to be taken over by a new Jamesian in the person of Richard Rorty. In the late 1970s and early 1980s Richard Rorty turned pragmatism away from the analytic Peircean variety that took science and logic to be important and towards the less analytic Jamesian variety (Rorty 1995: 71). Indeed, Rorty goes farther than James. He argues that if we look at the practices of first-order inquiry, we see that notions of truth and objectivity are irrelevant to inquirers. What we aim at is not truth, but solidarity or agreement with our peers. Truth and objectivity are plastic—they are what our peers will let us get away with saying (1979: 176). What he would like to see is a 'post-philosophical culture' in which there are no appeals to authority of any kind, including appeals to truth and rationality (1982: xlii). We are to 'substitute the idea of "unforced agreement" for that of "objectivity"' in every domain of inquiry—science as well as morals and politics (1991: 36, 38).

While the young Rorty worked, in sometimes an uneasy way, within analytic philosophy, by the early 1970s he had become an explicit opponent of it. Analytic philosophy, he argued, had installed itself as the dominant view and it was exiling other genres of philosophy, such as pragmatism and the history of philosophy.[12] Rorty was not alone in his dislike for analytic philosophy. The 1960s and 1970s saw a movement of 'pluralist' philosophers, who wanted to see more diversity in the kinds of papers presented at the American Philosophical Association meetings and in the kind of hires made in top departments. In 1979 Rorty was president of the Eastern Division of the APA and faced an unheard-of nomination from the floor for his successor. The pluralists had packed the business meeting to back John E. Smith, a Yale scholar of American pragmatism. There were questions about the legitimacy of the manoeuvre and about procedural irregularities but in the end Rorty declared the election valid. He thus became even more publicly identified with the challenge to the dominance of analytic methods. The episode made the *New York Times*.[13]

Rorty also delivered that year's Presidential Address—'Pragmatism, Relativism and Irrationalism'—calling on philosophers to revisit the American pragmatists. He noted

---

[12] See Gross (2008: 192–8).
[13] 30 December 1979. See Gross (2008: 219–27) for a blow-by-blow account.

that the pragmatists were acknowledged by analytic philosophers for having made 'various holistic corrections of the atomistic doctrines of the early logical empiricists' (Rorty 1982: 160). But he argued that what is really going on in Dewey and James is a wholesale rejection of the aims of analytic philosophy, not an attempt at making it better. Pragmatists, he argued, urge the abandonment of the ideas of truth and objectivity.

Of course analytic philosophy cannot be identified with the reductionist, foundationalist philosophy of the early logical empiricists. Rorty does not always make this mistake:

> Even at Yale the suspicion was growing that Carnap and Quine might be riding the wave of the future. So I began looking around for analytic philosophers who were less reductionistic and less positivisitic than they, less convinced that philosophy had only recently come of age. This led me to the work of Sellars, whose work I have spent the rest of my life trying to clear and broaden. Sellars combined a Carnapian style (lots of numbered premises, bedecked with lots of quantifiers) both with a thorough acquaintance with the history of philosophy and with an exuberant metaphysical imagination. That mixture of logic-worship, erudition and romance was reminiscent of Peirce … (Gross 2008: 312–13)

This is a telling passage. Wilfrid Sellars was very much an analytic pragmatist in the spirit of Peirce and Lewis.[14] Had Rorty stuck more closely to this kind of pragmatism, pragmatism and analytic philosophy would never have seemed to have parted ways. Rorty's mark on the history of pragmatism is deeply interesting in that he is almost single-handedly responsible for the currently perceived cleavage between analytic philosophy and pragmatism and for the reintroduction and promotion of the looser, more relativist, pragmatist view. In the 1970s pragmatism became identified with the Rortian–Jamesian position and it stepped out of the mainstream.

The analytic pragmatism I have traced in this chapter is, however, still alive and well. These pragmatists continue to emphasize fallible first-order inquiry while arguing that the fact that standards of objectivity are historically situated (they come into being and evolve over time) does not detract from their objectivity.[15] They include Arthur Fine, Isaac Levi, Susan Haack, Huw Price, Jeffrey Stout, and, I would argue, Ian Hacking. These philosophers agree with James that the trail of the human serpent is over everything—standards of truth and objectivity are our standards. But as James himself did not always see, this does not toss us into the sea of arbitrariness, where truth varies from person to person and culture to culture. Nor does it require us to abandon our concepts of truth and objectivity.

All pragmatists argue that we are always immersed in a context of inquiry, where the decision to be made is a decision about what to believe from here, not what to believe were we able to start from scratch—from certain infallible foundations. But as Fine

---

[14] See Misak (2013) for this argument.
[15] See the essays collected in Misak (2007).

(2007) puts it, we do not go forward arbitrarily. The central and deep pragmatist question is how we should go from present practice to a future practice, where our very standards themselves may be thrown into question. How can we come to genuinely normative concepts in science, in mathematics, and in morals, when we have nothing to go on but our actual practices? That is a question that will never disappear from philosophy and it is the question that the analytic pragmatists—Wright, Peirce, Lewis, Quine, Sellars, and their successors—engage with rigour and precision.

REFERENCES

Ayer, A. J. (1968). *The Origins of Pragmatism*. London: Macmillan.

Carnap, Rudolf (1937). *The Logical Syntax of Language*. London: Routledge & Kegan Paul.

Carus, Paul (1911). *Truth on Trial: An Exposition of the Nature of Truth*. Chicago: Open Court. Repr. in volume 3 of Shook (2001), pp. 1–143.

Dewey, John (1920 [1948]). *Reconstruction in Philosophy*. Boston: Beacon Press.

—— (1939). *Theory of Valuation. International Encyclopedia of Unified Science*, vol. II, no. 4. Chicago: University of Chicago Press.

Fine, Arthur (2007). 'Relativism, Pragmatism, and the Practice of Science'. In Misak (2007), pp. 50–67.

Frank, Philipp (1930a [1949]). *Modern Science and Its Philosophy*. Cambridge, MA: Harvard University Press.

—— (1930b [1949]). 'Physical Theories of the 20th Century and School Philosophy'. In Frank (1930a [1949]), pp. 90–121.

Gross, Neil (2008). *Richard Rorty: The Making of an American Philosopher*. Chicago: University of Chicago Press.

Hahn, Hans (1933 [1987]). *Logik, Mathematik, Naturerkennen*. Vienna: Wolf.

James, William (1891 [1979]). 'The Moral Philosopher and the Moral Life'. In *The Will to Believe and Other Essays in Popular Philosophy, The Works of William James*, volume 6, ed. Frederick H. Burkhardt, Fredson Bowers, and Ignas K. Skrupskelis. Cambridge, MA: Harvard University Press, pp. 141–62.

—— (1907 [1949]). *Pragmatism: A New Name for Some Old Ways of Thinking*. New York: Longmans, Green and Co.

—— (1909 [1914]). *The Meaning of Truth: A Sequel to Pragmatism*. New York: Longmans, Green and Co.

Lewis, Clarence Irving (1968). 'Autobiography'. In Paul Schlipp (ed.), *The Philosophy of C. I. Lewis*. La Salle: Open Court, pp. 1–21.

Madden, Edward (1963). *Chauncey Wright and the Foundations of Pragmatism*. Seattle: University of Washington Press.

Menand, Louis (2001). *The Metaphysical Club: A Story of Ideas in America*. New York: Farrar, Straus and Giroux.

Misak, Cheryl (1991). *Truth and the End of Inquiry: A Peircean Account of Truth*. Oxford: Clarendon Press.

—— (ed.) (2007). *New Pragmatists*. Oxford: Oxford University Press.

—— (ed.) (2008). *The Oxford Handbook of American Philosophy*. Oxford: Oxford University Press.

—— (2013). *The American Pragmatists*. Oxford: Oxford University Press.

—— (forthcoming). *Cambridge Pragmatism*. Oxford: Oxford University Press.

Moore, G. E. (1907). 'Professor James's "Pragmatism"', *Proceedings of the Aristotelian Society* 8: 33–77.

Nagel, Ernest (1940). 'Charles S. Peirce: Pioneer of Modern Empiricism', *Philosophy of Science* 7(1): 69–80.

Neurath, Otto, Niels Bohr, John Dewey, Bertrand Russell, Rudolf Carnap, and Charles Morris (1938). *Encyclopedia and Unified Science*. International Encyclopedia of Unified Science, vol. I, no. 1. Chicago: University of Chicago Press.

Olin, Doris (ed.) (1992). *William James's Pragmatism in Focus*. London: Routledge.

Peirce, Charles Sanders (1931–58). *Collected Papers of Charles Sanders Peirce*, vols. I–IV, ed. C. Hartshorne and P. Weiss, 1931–35; vols. VII–VIII, ed. A. Burks. Cambridge, MA: Belknap Press of Harvard University Press.

—— (1982). *The Writings of Charles S. Peirce: A Chronological Edition*, gen. ed. N. Houser. Bloomington: Indiana University Press.

—— Microfilm: *Charles S. Peirce Papers,* Houghton Library, Harvard University.

Pratt, James B. (1909). *What is Pragmatism?* Repr. in volume 1 of Shook (2001), pp. 1–269.

Quine, Willard Van Orman (1969). *Ontological Relativity and Other Essays*. New York: Columbia University Press,

—— (1980). 'Two Dogmas of Empiricism'. In Quine, *From a Logical Point of View*, 2nd edn. Cambridge MA: Harvard University Press, pp. 20–46.

—— (1981). 'The Pragmatist's Place in Empiricism'. In Robert J. Mulvaney and Philip M. Zeltner (eds.), *Pragmatism: Its Sources and Prospects*. Columbia, SC: University of South Carolina Press, pp. 21–39.

—— (1987). *Quiddities*. Cambridge, MA: Harvard University Press.

—— (1990). 'Comments on Parsons'. In Roger Gibson and Robert Barrett (eds.), *Perspectives on Quine*. Oxford: Blackwell, pp. 291–3.

Reisch, George (2005). *How the Cold War Transformed Philosophy of Science: To the Icy Slopes of Logic*. Cambridge: Cambridge University Press.

Richardson, Alan (2008). 'Philosophy of Science in America'. In C. Misak (ed.), *The Oxford Handbook of American Philosophy*. Oxford: Oxford University Press, pp. 339–74.

Rorty, Richard (1979). *Philosophy and the Mirror of Nature*. Princeton, NJ: Princeton University Press.

—— (1982). *Consequences of Pragmatism*. Minneapolis: University of Minnesota Press.

—— (1991). *Objectivity, Relativism, and Truth: Philosophical Papers, volume 1*. Cambridge: Cambridge University Press.

—— (1995). 'Response to Richard Bernstein'. In H. J. Saakamp (ed.), *Rorty and Pragmatism: The Philosopher Responds to his Critics*. Nashville: Vanderbilt University Press, pp. 68–71.

Russell, Bertrand (1966 [1992]). 'William James's Conception of Truth'. In Russell, *Philosophical Essays*. London: George Allen & Unwin. Repr. in Olin (1992), pp. 196–211.

Schinz, Albert (1909). *Anti-Pragmatism: An Examination into the Respective Rights of Intellectual Aristocracy and Social Democracy*. Boston: Small, Maynard and Company. Repr. as volume 2 of Shook (2001).

Shook, John R., (ed.) (2001). *Early Critics of Pragmatism, 3 vols*. Bristol: Thoemmes Continuum.

Soames, Scott (2008). 'Analytic Philosophy in America'. In C. Misak (ed.), *The Oxford Handbook of American Philosophy*. Oxford: Oxford University Press, pp. 449–81.

Thayer, James Bradley (1878 [1971]). *Letters of Chauncey Wright: With Some Account of his Life*. New York: Lennox Hill.

Uebel, Thomas (2004). 'Carnap, the Left Vienna Circle and Neopositivist Antimetaphysics'. In S. Awodey and C. Klein (eds.), *Carnap Brought Home: The View from Jena*. Chicago: Open Court, pp. 247–77.

White, Morton (1999). *A Philosopher's Story*. University Park, PA: University of Pennsylvania Press.

——(2002). *A Philosophy of Culture: The Scope of Holistic Pragmatism*. Princeton, NJ: Princeton University Press.

Wiggins, David (2002). 'An Indefinibilist cum Normative View of Truth and the Marks of Truth'. In R. Schantz (ed.), *What is Truth?* Berlin: Walter de Gruyter, pp. 316–33.

Wright, Chauncey (1865a). 'The Philosophy of Herbert Spencer'. In Wright (1877 [1971]), pp. 43–96.

——(1865b). 'McCosh on Intuitions'. In Wright (1877 [1971]), pp. 329–41.

——(1870). 'Limits of Natural Selection'. In Wright (1877 [1971]), pp. 97–127.

——(1873). 'John Stuart Mill: A Commemorative Notice'. In Wright (1877 [1971]), pp. 414–28.

——(1875). 'Speculative Dynamics'. In Wright (1877 [1971]), pp. 385–93.

—— (1877 [1971]). *Philosophical Discussions*, ed. Charles Eliot Norton. New York: Burt Franklin.

CHAPTER 39

THE ROLE OF PHENOMENOLOGY IN ANALYTIC PHILOSOPHY

DAVID WOODRUFF SMITH

39.1 PROLEGOMENA: IT'S ABOUT MEANING; IT'S ABOUT CONTENT

The tradition of analytic philosophy has many concerns, but one theme is clearly deep and central. Philosophy in this tradition is about meaning, the analysis of meaning. Meaning is expressed in language, and modern logic articulates structures of language that carry meaning (however conceived—intensionally, extensionally, pragmatically). At the same time, meaning is (by any other name) the content of thought and experience, not least conceptual content (but also perceptual content *inter alia*). Indeed, when not looking specifically at forms of language, we often speak of conceptual analysis, analysis of conceptual structures at work in philosophical thought about nature, mind, value, number.

Where we see the role of meaning analysis in the history of analytic philosophy, we should see the role of phenomenology in that history. Indeed, before there was a cultural divide between phenomenology and analytic philosophy, the founding figures of the two traditions were in communication about common concerns of how to develop a rigorous analysis of meaning or content, where meaning is not merely subjective, but something objective, public, highly structured, and amenable to careful, scientific, philosophical analysis.

Here we explore the historical and conceptual trail of phenomenology in what came to be called analytic philosophy. While logical theory dominated much of analytic philosophy in the first half of the twentieth century, philosophy of mind has dominated much of analytic philosophy in the latter part of the twentieth century. Accordingly, phenomenology is returning to the fore in contemporary analytic philosophy of mind. Ironically, phenomenology was already interwoven with early logical theory in the analytic tradition. The irony will settle in as we track the role of phenomenology proper in the evolving tradition of analytic philosophy, leading into current issues in philosophy of mind.

39.2 THE ORIGINS OF PHENOMENOLOGY AND ANALYTIC PHILOSOPHY

At the historical origins of analytic philosophy lie the historical origins of phenomenology, as late nineteenth-century philosophy led into early twentieth-century philosophy. Gottlob Frege's work in logic played a seminal role, arguably the principal role, in launching the tradition now called analytic philosophy. In the same era, Edmund Husserl's work explicitly founded the discipline of phenomenology—integrating *inter alia* logical theory, epistemology, and descriptive psychology. Central to both Frege and Husserl were kindred notions of meaning or sense (*Sinn*), sharply distinguished from mental or psychological processes. In the background were key logical notions in the air among prior nineteenth-century logicians, especially Bernard Bolzano's notion of objective ideas (*Vorstellungen*) or propositions (*Sätze*) (developed in Bolzano 1837): a notion that cut against the 'psychologizing' of logic and stood as a predecessor to the conceptions of *Sinn* in Frege and in Husserl. Husserl especially praised Bolzano, after Frege had pressed Husserl to move away from psychologism. (On relations between Frege and Husserl, and their historical context, see: Føllesdal 1958, 1969, 1982; Mohanty 1982a, 1982b; Simons 1992.)

Equally in the background were continuing concerns of epistemology, from Descartes to Locke to Hume to Kant, leading into late nineteenth-century positivist, scientific epistemologies, notably in Ernst Mach and Hermann von Helmholtz. (See B. Smith 1994; Friedman 1999; Hyder 2002.) The emerging field of empirical psychology took shape in this context, not least in the work of Franz Brentano. Brentano promoted 'exact' philosophy, and in conceiving psychology as a new and exact science Brentano integrated an empiricist epistemology with an Aristotelian ontology. (See B. Smith 1994 on Brentano's legacy, and his relation to logical theory.) At stake in this epistemological–psychological milieu were concerns of how the mind represents and cognizes objects: how 'phenomena'—from Kant to Brentano—or, better, objective meanings—from Bolzano to Frege and Husserl—structure thought and experience of objects. These epistemological and logical concerns were common ground for both Frege and Husserl, and for the continuing legacy of how meaning is treated in philosophy where logical, epistemological, and phenomenological theory converge. (Compare Friedman 2000 on how the same concerns of objectivity of meaning and cognition continued in subsequent debates within neo-Kantian schools in Germany. See B. Smith

1994 on contrasting trends in Austrian vis-à-vis German philosophy in the late nineteenth century.)

Thus, where analytic philosophy took root, with the new logic at the turn of the twentieth century, phenomenology took root in the same soil. As logical theory developed, on the more philosophical as opposed to mathematical side, the conception of meaning (and subsequent reactions against the 'intensional') played a consistent role in the grounding of both analytic and phenomenological philosophy. By the century's end, the conception of 'content' in thought and perception continued the resonance of 'meaning'. In Husserl's work circa 1900, integrating logical theory with his emergent conception of phenomenology, we find intentional content and linguistic meaning already in harmony—an instructive model for interpreting the role of phenomenological ideas (by any other name) in analytic philosophy. Moreover, in point of history, Husserl interacted significantly with key analytic philosophers from Frege onward (as we observe along our way below).

In the last decades of the twentieth century phenomenology has played an increasingly important role in philosophy of mind within the analytic tradition. That story is unfolding even today, revolving around both consciousness and intentional content, which is to say meaning in experience. The present study will lead up to that story, which must be told elsewhere. (See Smith and Thomasson 2005, for starters.)

It is worth noting that the term 'analytic phenomenology' has gradually taken root, signifying the practice of phenomenology where informed by, and interacting with, both philosophical logic *cum* philosophy of language and philosophy of mind *cum* consciousness studies and cognitive science. There is now an online journal called *Analytic Phenomenology* (edited by Gianfranco Soldati and Fabian Dorsch, reviving the spirit of Husserl's early journal). There is also a journal called *Phenomenology and the Cognitive Sciences* (edited by Shaun Gallagher and Dan Zahavi). Broadly analytic and phenomenological themes interweave thusly in contemporary philosophy. (And see Huemer 2005, whose subtitle is 'A Study in Analytic Phenomenology'.)

When we look for the evolving theory of meaning or content, we see how phenomenology weaves in and out of the course of analytic philosophy over the twentieth century.… We might ask why? What is it about the phenomenon of meaning that drives the ebb and flow of analytic philosophy—and of phenomenology?

39.3 RETHINKING THE HISTORY OF TWENTIETH-CENTURY PHILOSOPHY

Since the middle of the twentieth century a picture of analytic versus phenomenological philosophy has dominated the *Zeitgeist* in European and American (and also Latin American) philosophy. The picture goes roughly like this. The tradition of analytic philosophy began with Frege, Russell, *et al.*, centred in the new logic, leading into logical or conceptual analysis of knowledge, belief, reference, truth, value, etc. Meanwhile, the very different tradition of phenomenology began with Husserl, Heidegger, *et al.*, centred on analysis of consciousness, and the meaning things have for us in our experience, leading into appraisal of phenomena of intentionality, perception, self and other, freedom, society, etc. Both traditions were emerging by 1900 and have followed different trajectories for a full century, defined by different philosophers and disjoint literatures. So goes the familiar historiography.

However, as we dig into the history of early twentieth-century philosophy, in Europe and America, a very different picture emerges. In the early decades of the century there was no split between 'analytic' philosophy and what came to be called 'continental' philosophy, the former grounded initially in logic and the latter in phenomenology. Instead, there were interlocking themes and motivations, and concrete historical links between key thinkers in what later became two traditions. (On the common origins of the two traditions, see the essays in Horgan *et al.* 2002.)

We need to distinguish, clearly, between the tradition of phenomenology and the discipline of phenomenology. The phenomenological movement or tradition is defined by such figures as Brentano, Husserl, Heidegger, Sartre, Merleau-Ponty, and many others, extending into recent thinkers such as Føllesdal, Dreyfus, and others. The *discipline* of phenomenology is defined, rather, by themes and methods: most basically, phenomenology is the study of consciousness from the first-person perspective (on a broadly Husserlian characterization). What has this to do, we may ask, with logic and linguistic analysis in the historic literature of analytic philosophy? At issue, we shall see, are basic conceptions of meaning.

In the interaction of phenomenology with twentieth-century analytic philosophy, there are many more figures and lines of influence than we shall be able to address here. Interestingly, the history of ethical theory in analytic philosophy includes in its own way the search for meaning: in seeking the foundation of values in emotion (on emotivist and sentimentalist views), in practical reason or judgment (on Kantian constructivist and rationality-based views), or in self-determination (on neo-existentialist and related views). (Compare Smith 2007, Chapter 8.) However, we shall have our hands full in treating the role of meaning in thought and language. Accordingly, our study will be guided by themes of meaning, representation, and consciousness in language and thought.

39.4 FROM LOGIC TO PHENOMENOLOGY: HUSSERL'S PROGRAMME VIS-À-VIS FREGE'S

Dagfinn Føllesdal's study of Husserl and Frege, circa 1960, opened the door to understanding anew the conceptual and historical relations between phenomenology and analytic philosophy. The focus of Føllesdal's approach was the relation between logical theory and phenomenological theory. (See Føllesdal 1958, 1969, 1982.) In the formative years of phenomenology and early analytic philosophy, ca. 1880–1930, this linkage would not have surprised Frege, Husserl, and their theoretical compatriots. Indeed, Husserl interacted with many of the era's philosophical mathematical-scientific thinkers: not only Frege, but also Georg Cantor, David Hilbert, Herman Weyl, and others, whose work shaped set theory, number theory, mathematical logic, even Einstein's general relativity theory. And the great mathematical logicians Kurt Gödel and Alfred Tarski had read Husserl, Gödel finding in Husserl's phenomenology a compelling framework for his own broadly Platonistic philosophy of logic and mathematics. (See Simons 1992, Hill and Rosado Haddock 2000, and Tieszen 2005 on Husserl's ties to logicians; see Richardson 1998 and Friedman 1999 on Husserl's ties to Carnap; and see Ryckman 2005 on ties between Husserlian transcendental phenomenology, Weyl, and Einstein's relativity theory.)

By 1960, however, analytic philosophy had 'forgotten' its roots, which needed to be rediscovered and reconceived.... But we are getting ahead of our story.

Broadly, Husserl entered philosophy from a historical context of mathematics and logic. His initial philosophy of mathematics drew him into the study of associated mental activities. It was within that theoretical matrix that Husserl developed the discipline of phenomenology.

Specifically, Husserl's conception of phenomenology evolved in the wake of Brentano's conception of the new science of psychology. In his *Psychology from an Empirical Standpoint* (1874/1995), Brentano divided psychology into genetic and descriptive psychology. Genetic psychology studies the causal genesis or aetiology of mental states, whereas descriptive psychology studies the basic types and characters of mental states. In a way, then, descriptive psychology is more fundamental than genetic. Brentano later called descriptive psychology 'phenomenology', and Husserl went on to develop the foundations of phenomenology in his own framework, sharply separating phenomenology from empirical psychology. (See B. Smith 1994 on the scope of Brentano's philosophy and influence.)

Husserl's earliest work, his *Philosophy of Arithmetic* (1891/2003, developed from his 1886 Habilitation), concerned philosophy of mathematics. There he tied numbers to mental activities such as counting. His view was received as an exercise in 'psychologism', reducing numbers themselves to psychological activities (in a form of nineteenth-century idealism). Frege in particular wrote a strongly critical review charging Husserl with psychologism. (See Føllesdal 1958 on the Frege–Husserl connections, and further Mohanty 1982b and Føllesdal 1982 on the Frege–Husserl interchange.) Partly in response to that charge of psychologism (compare writings gathered in Husserl 1994), Husserl set out on the decade-long project of writing his *Logical Investigations* (1900–01/2001). In that 1,000-page study Husserl argued strongly against psychologism in the foundations of logic. He then developed a theory of language founded on consciousness, and laid out the fundamentals of his new theory of intentionality, the directedness of consciousness towards objects in the world. Central to Husserl's theory of intentionality is his own model of 'ideal' meaning or *Sinn*, explicitly inspired by Bolzano's notion of 'objective' ideas (*Vorstellungen*)—and prompted, famously, by Frege's critique. We note that Frege's explicit doctrine of *Sinn* was detailed in his 'On *Sinn* and *Bedeutung*' (1892/1997). So it is in the same years that Frege and Husserl unfurled their respective conceptions of *Sinn*, and in fact they exchanged letters on these views. An important difference, we shall see, was how tightly *Sinn* was to be tied to language on their respective views.

There is a concrete historical linkage, then, between logic and phenomenology, in this famous interaction between Husserl and Frege. Moreover, as we find below, there are specific conceptual links between the evolved views of Husserl and Frege, in particular, concerning the nature of *Sinn* and its relations to mind and to language. Kindred issues arose already in Husserl's early foray into philosophy of arithmetic. As Dallas Willard has observed, in the Introduction to his translation of Husserl's *Philosophy of Arithmetic* (1891/2003), Husserl was in fact struggling to bring together the nature of number (or any mathematical object) and the intentionality of thinking of a number. Brentano's model of intentionality famously held that the object of an act of consciousness is 'intentionally in-existent', that is, it exists intentionally 'in' the mind—in some way. Husserl's aim was not, as commonly inferred, to reduce numbers to mental phenomena, but rather to set numbers in relation to intentionality. However, Husserl had not yet developed his theory of the structure of intentionality. That theory was developed at length in the course of the *Logical Investigations* (1900–01/2001), and later enhanced in *Ideas* I (1913/1969/1983).

As the phenomenological tradition evolved, the focus of phenomenological analysis expanded far beyond the focal issues of logic—prominently, in the rich analyses of time-consciousness, embodied experience, and experience of self and others, analyses central in the works of Husserl, then Martin Heidegger, Maurice Merleau-Ponty, and Jean-Paul Sartre. Yet the fundamental concept of meaning remained evident on every page of such works: '*Sinn*' in German, '*sens*' in French. Nearly forgotten is the way that Heidegger—widely perceived as the antithesis of a logic-minded philosopher—began his philosophical development with the project of avoiding psychologism in logic, endorsing Husserl's objective conception of *Sinn*, and subsequently tilling the 'grounds' of meaning (and thus of 'being') throughout his career (from his conception of phenomenology as 'fundamental ontology' into his late work on language as 'the house of being'). (See Friedman 2000, pp. 41 ff., on Heidegger's early wrestling with neo-Kantian philosophy from his 1913 dissertation onward.) Even as Husserl developed his later 'transcendental' phenomenology, his concern with logic remained in play, re-cast in his *Formal and Transcendental Logic* (1929/1969), where logic (qua transcendental) is ultimately grounded in intentionality and thus in ideal meaning.

So we should thus see an important interplay—both historical and conceptual—between logic and phenomenology in the work of Husserl and Frege starting in the 1890s. Where Frege articulated the mind-independence of *Sinn*, crucial for logic, Husserl went on to place mind-independent *Sinn* in the very structure of intentionality, the heart of phenomenology. From the side of logic we define the objective character of meaning; from the side of phenomenology we define the role of objective meaning in the intentionality of consciousness. And with phenomenology in hand we can return to phenomenological themes in philosophical logic, looking for relations between language and mind, where meaning plays its role in language and in thought.

39.5 INTENTIONALITY VIS-À-VIS REFERENCE: HUSSERL VIS-À-VIS FREGE

Working in both phenomenology and logic, Føllesdal approached Husserl's theory of intentionality—the foundation of Husserlian phenomenology—from a logical point of view. Føllesdal's strategy was to draw a parallel with Frege's theory of reference, a theory that was familiar to analytic philosophers. Noting historical links between Husserl and Frege, Føllesdal drew a structural parallel between linguistic reference and intentionality. (Føllesdal 1958, 1969/1982, 1972. See also the other essays by Føllesdal in Dreyfus and Hall 1982. Smith and McIntyre 1982 extends the approach begun by Føllesdal and Dreyfus.) Interestingly, Føllesdal has contributed to modal logic and to the philosophical interpretation of reference in various logics (already in his doctoral dissertation, Føllesdal 1961/2004). In effect, then, Føllesdal has championed 'intensional' notions of meaning and modality in both logical theory and phenomenological theory. There are other readings of Husserl, often emphasizing epistemological themes. However, Føllesdal's reading explicitly brought phenomenology and logical theory into alignment. And that perspective is crucial for understanding Husserl's forgotten role in early analytic philosophy. (Some recent studies have focused specifically on Husserl and Frege and on reference, meaning, and intentionality: Fisette 1994; Soldati 1994; Beyer 2000.)

For Husserl, consciousness is characteristically a consciousness 'of' something. In that sense, an act of consciousness is *intentional*, or directed towards an object. If you will, consciousness represents an object—Husserl prefers to say consciousness 'intends' or 'means' (*meinen, vermeinen*) an object, and so is 'intentionally' related to an object if such object exists. Similarly, linguistic reference consists in a relation whereby an expression refers to, or represents, an object. On Frege's model of reference, his famous theory of *Sinn* and *Bedeutung*: an expression *expresses* a sense or *Sinn*, the sense determines an object, if such object exists, and the expression stands for or *refers* to that object, called the referent or *Bedeutung* of the expression. For example, the term 'the morning star' expresses a sense that specifies Venus and so the term *refers* to Venus.

For Frege, on Føllesdal's understanding: reference consists in a three-place relation of an expression to a sense and thereby to a referent, if such referent exists. Frege's theory of *Sinn* and *Bedeutung* is not always read in this way, where reference is a three-term relation formed by composition from the relation of expression to sense and the relation of sense to referent. (An alternative reading simply assigns two entities to an expression, its sense and its referent.) So Føllesdal's conception of the formal structure of reference *à la* Frege is already a significant step in logical theory. In a diagram:

Expression 'the morning star' — sense → object Venus.

Similarly, for Husserl, Føllesdal proposes: intentionality, or 'intention', consists in a relation of an act of consciousness to a sense and thereby to an object of consciousness. For example, an act of thinking of 'the morning star' has a sense—the ideal content or meaning of the act of thinking—that specifies or 'means' Venus, which is thus the object of the act. In a diagram:

Act of thinking of 'the morning star' — sense → object Venus.

The ideal, shareable content of an act of consciousness Husserl called the noema, or noematic sense (*Sinn*), of the act of consciousness. The structure Føllesdal formalized is this three-place form of representation: for reference on the one hand, for intentionality on the other. As an expression reaches through its *Sinn* towards its referent, so consciousness reaches through its noematic *Sinn* towards its object. In a comparative diagram:

expression — sense → object,
act — sense → object.

There is much more to Husserl's theory of intentionality and his conception of phenomenology, and Føllesdal has long lectured on the full range of Husserl's philosophy. In any event, this structural parallel between reference via sense and intentionality via sense (or noema) is a cornerstone of Føllesdal's 'analytic' reading of Husserl and phenomenology.

Føllesdal's aim was not to reduce consciousness to language, or intentionality to linguistic reference, or Husserlian phenomenology to Fregean logic. For the focus of Husserl's phenomenology was the characterization of lived experience, not linguistic constructions. Rather, Føllesdal proposed the Husserl–Frege parallel as a way of clarifying the formal structure of intentionality on Husserl's model, by comparison with the Fregean model of reference familiar in logical theory. (The title of the essay, Føllesdal 1972, is 'An Introduction to Phenomenology for Analytic Philosophers'.)

Beyond the systematic parallel, however, Føllesdal noted concrete historical ties between Husserl and Frege, in letters written to each other. J. N. Mohanty also pursued the historical relations between the two thinkers (Mohanty 1982a, 1982b), noting that Husserl had his own conception of meaning and reference, so Husserl was not merely responding to Frege's critique of the early Husserl's tendency to psychologism. Husserl himself, as we noted, broadened his scope as he crafted the *Logical Investigations*, emphasizing the ideality of meaning as intentional content, whether expressed in language or not.

As more detail is added to the portrait of the times at which Frege and Husserl wrote, we see ever more clearly that both Husserl's phenomenology and Frege's logic were born of related concerns in a common era. Moreover, conceptually, the concerns of Husserl's phenomenology—ideal meaning, its relation to consciousness, and its relation to language—were at the heart of Frege's concerns.

As the so-called 'Fregean' or 'analytic' conception of Husserlian phenomenology unfolded, a good number of Husserl interpreters resisted the logical view of ideal meaning as playing the role of intentional content of consciousness. In *Ideas* I (1913), with no logical fanfare, Husserl introduced the Greek term 'noema' for the ideal intentional content of an act of consciousness (§§ 88ff.). Husserl characterized the noema of an act in two different ways: (a) as 'noematic *Sinn*', and (b) as 'the object as intended' ('as perceived', 'as remembered', etc., echoing similar terms in the *Logical Investigations*, 1900–01). These two characterizations seem to lead in very different directions. In one direction lies lived experience and the way an object of consciousness is 'given' in subjective experience—the domain of phenomenology proper. In another direction lies the quasi-mathematical objective structure that determines reference and truth—the domain of logic proper.

Yet, in Frege's own understanding of *Sinn*, we find the core of a phenomenological conception of *Sinn*, phrased in terms similar to Husserl's. Mostly, Frege expounds on what a *Sinn* does in relation to a referent: a *Sinn* 'determines' a referent or *Bedeutung*, and determines it in a certain way, with a certain 'mode of determination' (*Bestimmungsweise*). Yet, when he seeks to explicate what a *Sinn* is, Frege says a *Sinn* includes a 'mode of presentation' or 'manner of givenness' of the specified referent: in the German, an *Art des Gegebenseins* (Frege 1892/1997, p. 152). 'Given' can only mean given in consciousness. Frege distinguishes, for an expression, its sense or *Sinn*, its referent or *Bedeutung*, and an associated 'idea' or *Vorstellung*—the established German term for ideas in the mind, in consciousness, translated variously as 'idea', 'presentation', or 'representation' (Frege 1892/1997, pp. 154ff.). Indeed, Frege speaks explicitly of 'consciousness' (*Bewusstsein*) when discussing *Sinn*. (Compare Frege 1918/1997, where Frege argues for the objective character of 'thoughts', or *Gedanken*.) There can be no question, then, that Frege and Husserl were within conversing distance of one another on the notion of *Sinn*, whether digging into the foundations of logic (Frege, also Husserl) or the foundations of phenomenology (Husserl). Yet there are important differences, not least concerning the relation between mind and language. (And, on a different theme, Beyer 2000 argues that Husserl's account of demonstratives introduces an externalist element not evident in Frege.)

39.6 Language vis-à-vis Mind: Frege vis-à-vis Husserl

Michael Dummett—an influential figure in analytic philosophy—has crafted an important interpretation of the development of analytic philosophy in the early decades of the tradition. In his *Origins of Analytical Philosophy* (1993, 1998) Dummett explores the conceptual and historical ties between Frege and Husserl at the origin of analytic philosophy as Dummett conceives it, noting Brentano's legacy. Dummett rightly views Husserl as the prime mover of early phenomenology and Frege as the prime mover of early analytic philosophy. (Let's drop the 'al' from 'analytical'; both terms are used, perhaps with some variation in connotation.) These Frege–Husserl connections Dummett approaches from a perspective on philosophical logic, having written extensively on Frege and logi-cal notions including truth. The same Frege–Husserl ties Dagfinn Føllesdal approaches from a perspective on phenomenology informed by logical theory. This convergence of perspectives, drawn respectively from analytic philosophy and from phenomenology, underscores the way that logical theory circa 1880–1900 lay at the origin and founda-tion of both phenomenology and analytic philosophy.

On Dummett's interpretation, what made analytic philosophy as such possible was the 'linguistic turn'. There was no one time or text wherein philosophers explicitly began taking this turn to language. However, as Dummett observes (1998, Chapter 2), Frege the mathematician clearly assumes, in *The Foundations of Arithmetic* (1884/1978, see section 62), that logic is to be done within a particular language, an idealized symbolic or formal language. Of course, the technical constructions that define modern symbolic logic are central and essential to its practice. Thus, in the new logic, we reason explicitly in a formalized language. Ancient Aristotelian logic, the theory of syllogism, can of course be rendered in formal terms. But the new logic abstracts still further from the familiar forms of ordinary language. And in this mathematizing of the language in which rea-soning is expressed we find a crucial achievement: mathematical logic launched in the works of Frege, and fellow logicians Peirce, Peano, Russell and Whitehead, leading into Gödel, Tarski, *et al*. Noteworthy in the new symbolism, quite at home in idioms of math-ematics, were the quantifiers (read as 'for all x' and 'for some x') and the relational predi-cate form that mirrors a mathematical functional notation ('R(x,y,z)' for a three-place relational predicate). Beyond issues of syntax were issues of semantics, notably in Frege's model of *Sinn* and *Bedeutung*—though the idiom of 'syntax' and 'semantics' had not set in when Frege and Husserl wrote.

By around 1950 analytic philosophers refocused on ordinary language, having found more to meaning than is fully captured in the idiom of symbolic logic. In his posthu-mous *Philosophical Investigations* (1953/2001), Ludwig Wittgenstein's methodology—where to know the use of an expression is to know its meaning—brought home the force of ordinary language. In *The Concept of Mind* (1949), Gilbert Ryle followed this practice of meaning analysis, or conceptual analysis, in appraising our concepts of mental activ-ity as expressed in our language about belief, sensation, etc. (See Thomasson 2002 and Brandl 2002 on relations between Ryle and Husserl on phenomenology.) In *Empiricism and the Philosophy of Mind* (1956/2000), Wilfrid Sellars pursued the traditional issues of empiricism, in relation to philosophy of language and now the emerging field of phi-losophy of mind, considering methodological behaviourism along the way. Sellars very deliberately followed the practice of analysing forms of language about sensation, mind, and knowledge, famously treating thought as 'inner speech'. It is significant that both Ryle and Sellars had studied Husserl, in effect practising a linguistic variant on phenom-enology. Moreover, Wittgenstein had already declared, 'Phenomenology is Grammar', insofar as examining the rules of our language is tantamount to 'the construction of a phenomenological language'. (See Hintikka and Hintikka 1986, pp. 142, 159–160, on Wittgenstein's middle-period text called 'The Big Typescript'.) It is not known whether Wittgenstein had read Husserl or vice versa, but 'phenomenology' was clearly in the air when Wittgenstein wrote. In *Individuals: An Essay in Descriptive Metaphysics* (1959), P. F. Strawson took analytic philosophy into the forbidden land of metaphysics, forbidden since the late 1920s by the logical positivism of the Vienna Circle, imported to Oxford by A. J. Ayer (Ayer 1936), and further discouraged by the resolute focus on language in Wittgenstein's wake. Strawson pursued the metaphysics of individuals or particulars, persons, bodies, and minds through a 'descriptive'—logical or 'grammatical' or conceptual—analysis appraising our language about such things. Strawson's big picture was Kantian, set against a background of early modern figures, but with no reference to Brentano, Husserl, *et al.* In effect, Strawson's analysis was a linguistic mode of Kantian transcendental philosophy—thus tantamount to a logico-linguistic phenomenology of 'individuals', 'persons', etc. Subsequently, in *Word and Object* (1960), W. V. Quine famously championed the syntax of first-order logic as a 'regimentation' of parts of everyday language, addressing meaning and evidence only as expressed in language, while sceptical of Brentano's 'autonomous science of intention' (p. 221), the progenitor of Husserlian phenomenology. A leaning towards then-fashionable behaviourism was commonly ascribed to Wittgenstein, Ryle, Sellars, and Quine, though their views on the relation between language and experience were in fact much more subtle than any behaviourism. (See Candlish and Damnjanovic, this volume.) What is salient in these philosophers, at any rate, is the emphasis on language as the window on mind, meaning, inference, knowledge.

Thus, in retrospect, Dummett sees in Frege's early logic the pivotal move that, for Dummett, defines analytic philosophy: Philosophy is to proceed through *analysis of language*, whether formal or ordinary language. That is what makes this type of philosophy 'analytic'. (Compare Beaney 2002 and Thomasson 2002 on types of 'analysis'.)

Accordingly, philosophy of language came to play a central role in analytic philosophy over the years, as in the writings of Bertrand Russell, G. E. Moore, Wittgenstein, Ryle, J. L. Austin, P. F. Strawson, John Searle, and many others. In recent decades, though, philosophy of mind has been a dominant force in analytic philosophy—not only or primarily through analysis of our idioms about various types of mental state, but through analysis of the ontological relation between a mental state and its neural substrate as well as its causal interaction with the environment. The locus of 'analysis' has thus shifted in these studies.... In any event, theory of mind and theory of language were joined at the hip in Husserl's *Logical Investigations* circa 1900. And this connection leads into deeper ties between early analytic philosophy and early phenomenology.

39.7 Meaning, Mind, and Language: Frege, Husserl, and Successors

As Dummett emphasizes (Dummett 1998, Chapter 4), Frege argued for what Dummett calls the 'extrusion' of meaning (*Sinn*) and in particular thoughts (*Gedanken*, propositional meanings) from the mind. For Frege, thoughts themselves form a 'third realm' distinct from both physical objects and mental processes (*Vorstellungen*). (See Frege 1892/1997, 'On *Sinn* and *Bedeutung*', and Frege 1918/1997, 'Thought'.) Moreover, for Frege, logic is properly about thoughts and their conditions of truth—though, to be sure, we express thoughts in a well-formed language and practice logic by studying appropriate forms of expression. Husserl concurred that logic is about ideal meaning, pressing the case in the Prolegomena to the *Logical Investigations* (1900–1/2001). There Husserl explicitly cites Bolzano—while responding, in effect, to Frege's charge that Husserl's *Philosophy of Arithmetic* (1891/2003) had lapsed into 'psychologism' (purportedly reducing the logical structure of number to the psychological structure of thinking about number). Yet, where they agreed on the objectivity of meaning, Husserl and Frege differed on the relation between language and mind. Part of the difference is due to the fact that Frege did not have a theory of intentionality, whereas Husserl developed in tandem his theory of linguistic representation and mental representation, or intentionality.

For Husserl, language parallels and is founded on thought. In the *Logical Investigations* (First Investigation), Husserl holds that when you assert 'p', your speech act (yes, Husserl's term) is founded on an act of judging or thinking that p, and that underlying act of thinking 'lends' its sense to the expression uttered: the expression's meaning is precisely that sense (though sometimes modified for language, Husserl allows). So, for Husserl, meaning resides most fundamentally in acts of consciousness, and language brings meaning to the public sphere for communication. As the *Investigations* unfold (in the Fifth Investigation), Husserl develops his full theory of intentionality, on which his theory of linguistic expression and assertion rests. (On Husserl's theory of the relation between language and intentional thought, see: McIntyre and Smith 1975/1982; Smith and McIntyre 1982, Chapter IV; and Simons 1995.)

By contrast, when Frege talks about mental activities, or *Vorstellungen*, he seems to think only of sensations (Frege 1892/1997, 1918/1997). He does not seem to think that mental processes themselves have the power to represent objects: that power belongs to *Sinn*. It is as if he thinks that when one says 'the morning star is a planet', one may have associated sensory images surrounding the term 'the morning star', but one's sensory mental processes themselves do not have meaning that stands for something. The expression has a sense that determines an object (Venus), but one's associated *Vorstellungen* do not represent or mean (*bedeutet*) anything—in Husserlian terms they are not intentional. Frege held that we 'grasp' a thought or sense, but that is a different matter. Perhaps the logician grasps a thought while evaluating its truth-value. But this grasping has no place, Frege seems to think, in the *Vorstellungen* that may or may not pass through one's consciousness when one utters the sentence 'the morning star is a planet'. These issues of how language is related to mind or consciousness receive only cursory hints in Frege's writing.

However, as noted, Husserl goes to great length to characterize the activities of consciousness wherein one thinks that the morning star is a planet and asserts, 'The morning star is a planet'. Thus, when so thinking about the morning star, my act of thinking carries a proposition (*Satz*), or propositional *Sinn*, which includes a component *Sinn* that represents Venus. My act of thinking is itself directed towards Venus, and the state of affairs that it is a planet. And so my uttering the expression 'the morning star is a planet' is directed towards the state of affairs that it is a planet… All the classical phenomenologists—Husserl, Heidegger, Sartre, Merleau-Ponty—approached language as a form of experience and action, thus part of the subject matter of phenomenology as a discipline. Not infrequently, this phenomenological approach to language is compared to the later Wittgenstein's study of 'language games' as 'forms of life', in the *Philosophical Investigations* (1953/2001). At any rate, the early Husserl took a more formal approach to language, in light of the new logic and its mathematical side (from set theory onward).

In the end Dummett sides with Frege over Husserl in granting language a certain autonomy over mind. To a certain extent Dummett wants to decouple language from mind, rather in the spirit of the later Wittgenstein. Given Dummett's own emphasis on language, he worries that Husserl tied language too closely to mind, treading close to the Humpty Dumpty view (Dummett 1993). In Lewis Carroll's *Through the Looking Glass*, Dummett reminds us (1998, pp. 44–6), Humpty Dumpty sniffs, 'When *I* use a word, it means just what I choose it to mean—neither more nor less.' But surely that is not what Husserl intended. When I say, 'The sun has set', thinking that the sun has set as I look over the ocean, the Husserlian view is not that I wilfully choose to mean that. The Husserlian claim is rather that my conscious act of assertion is founded or dependent on my conscious act of thinking as I utter the words, 'The sun has set'. Husserl's point is a point about consciousness in speech, and it is only natural to assume that when one thinks in a language and expresses what one thinks, then normally one is following the traditional use of the words. And surely that is what makes Humpty Dumpty's pronouncement so amusing.

The complexities of exactly how natural language is founded on thought remain to be worked out in contemporary theory. Still, what Husserl brings to the table is a proper theory of intentionality, at work in language and thought. And so we find the structure of intentionality, the heart of Husserl's phenomenology, at work in the logical structure of language, the centrepiece of Frege's logic in early analytic philosophy.

Whether language has priority over mind, or vice versa, remained an active concern in analytic philosophy. In 'Intentionality and the Mental' (1957), Roderick Chisholm and Wilfrid Sellars debated the issue in a famous dialogue. Chisholm, drawing on Brentano, argued that intentional thought is more basic than language; Sellars, drawing on Wittgenstein and Ryle, argued that language is more basic than thought. Both views, in any event, rest on the crucial notion of intentionality, which was developed in phenomenology and focuses directly on mind rather than language about mind. In his *Philosophical Investigations* (1953) Wittgenstein wrestled with the problem whether 'private', or subjective, experience can be brought to public language, seeming to argue that it cannot, hence the meaning of an expression is tantamount to its overt use in speech. In the *Logical Investigations* (1900–01), we observed, Husserl developed a detailed theory of how meaning in language is aligned with intentional content of consciousness. Yet Husserl further held that language modifies intentional content (*Ideas* I, 1913, § 124). (Livingston 2004 traces the recurring problem of subjectivity through key junctures in the history of philosophy of mind in the twentieth century, with some echoes of Wittgenstein's privacy problem.)

In the evolving tradition of analytic philosophy, interestingly, John Searle turned from a focus on language in his *Speech Acts* (1969) to the theory of intentionality proper in *Intentionality: An Essay in the Philosophy of Mind* (1983) and to consciousness itself in *The Rediscovery of the Mind* (1992). In Searle's mature view, consciousness and its intentionality are more basic than language, which itself is a product of collective intentionality, on Searle's analysis in *The Construction of Social Reality* (1995). In this way the evolution of Searle's perspective follows and contributes to the evolution of the tradition of analytic philosophy. But then analytic philosophy cannot be defined as exclusively concerned with analysis of language.

Indeed, in recent decades philosophy of mind has arguably displaced philosophy of language as the centre of gravity of contemporary analytic philosophy. Dummett rejects this perspective that would favour mind over language as the central focus of analytic philosophy. In fact, within the Oxford tradition language was, shall we say, re-infused with mind or experience, notably, in P. F. Strawson's 'descriptive metaphysics' in *Individuals* (1959), where Kantian themes took on a linguistic face. Then Gareth Evans, in *The Varieties of Reference* (1982), turned the focus of language somewise to perception, thus to mind. For Strawson and Evans, demonstrative reference was tied to concrete perceptual experience—as it was for Husserl (1900–01/2001, I, § 26, VI, § 5). Noting this tilt towards mind over language, Dummett declares that Evans, in his account of reference, is no longer practising analytic philosophy, which is to be focused on language. What are we to say, then, about the robust literature in philosophy of mind after Ryle? The writings of David Armstrong, Jerry Fodor, the later John Searle, and many others address the ontology of mental states vis-à-vis brain states, quite apart from analyses of language. In common parlance these works belong to 'analytic' philosophy. Dummett's interpretation of what defines analytic philosophy captures the early impetus of the tradition. But later developments, especially in philosophy of mind, extend the tradition beyond concerns with language. With that wider purview in mind, we turn to a prior perspective on the relation between phenomenology and analytic philosophy, between experience and logic. Interestingly, the ascendancy of philosophy of mind, and ultimately of consciousness studies, rejoins the early, but later repressed, role of phenomenology at the origins of analytic philosophy: in the work of Rudolf Carnap.

39.8 Phenomenology in Logical Empiricism: Carnap vis-à-vis Husserl

Phenomenology and logical empiricism (or logical positivism)—how could any two movements be more antithetical? In the 1920s, spilling over into the 1930s, the Vienna Circle spread the gospel of positivism infused with the new logic: all knowledge is ultimately empirical, to be developed in the 'positive' sciences, notably physics, and to be expressed most precisely in the idiom of the new mathematical logic. How does the practice of phenomenology square with that programme? Were not the practitioners of phenomenology and logical positivism squarely in opposition, the two traditions pulling sharply apart by the 1920s?

Well, the history is rather different. The great statement of logical empiricism was Rudolf Carnap's *The Logical Construction of the World* (1928/2003), i.e., *Der logische Aufbau der Welt*, known as the *Aufbau*. Carnap was not only working, so obviously, with the logic and mathematics of the day, considering the physics of the day (general relativity). He was also, less obviously, developing an 'explication' or 'rational reconstruction' in that logically rigorous mould of philosophical ideas much discussed in Husserlian phenomenology as well as competitor models in the contemporary neo-Kantian schools of Germany. The Kantian historical and philosophical environs of Carnap's *Aufbau* have been charted recently. But not all roads lead from Kant. The legacy of Bolzano (who argued against Kant) inspired Husserl's focus on 'pure logic' in framing his conception of phenomenology, which in turn influenced Carnap's *Aufbau*. (See Coffa 1991 on the rise of the theory of meaning and its influence on Carnap. See Friedman, 1999, 2000, on the background of Carnap's *Aufbau*; compare Richardson 1998. See Friedman 2000, Beaney 2002, and Friedman and Ryckman forthcoming on Carnap's relation to Husserl, also on Lotze's influence on late nineteenth-century logical theory.)

In 1924–25 Carnap attended lectures by Husserl in Freiburg, even as Carnap was working on the project that became the 1928 *Aufbau*. In fact, Carnap's *Aufbau* develops a formal explication of a 'constitution theory' of knowledge that closely and explicitly parallels Husserl's phenomenological theory of knowledge in *Ideas* I (1913), wherein Husserl follows groundwork laid in the longer course of the *Logical Investigations* but now presented in a 'transcendental' idiom (see Smith 2007). Once we observe this background, Carnap's project takes on a new look. (Again, see Friedman *et al.* above.)

Carnap's logical empiricism grounds knowledge in sensation (thus empiricism) where knowledge is expressed in terms of the new logic (following on Frege's logicism, where the mathematics of physics is articulated in Fregean logic). The *Aufbau* project has been widely seen as developing a logical 'construction' of the world out of simpler entities, beginning (as one option) with sensory data, thus producing a form of phenomenalism. (Another option, Carnap allowed, was a 'physicalist' reduction.) Indeed, Wittgenstein felt Carnap simply lifted the picture from Wittgenstein's *Tractatus*, which was well known in the Vienna Circle. (See Hintikka and Hintikka 1986 on Wittgenstein's *Tractatus*, its ostensible assumption of sense-data as the elementary objects, and his response to Carnap.) However, Carnap's inspiration lay elsewhere.

Broadly, Carnap sought to synthesize empiricism with rationalism, the goal of Kant's transcendental idealism. In a Kantian spirit, Carnap explicitly remained neutral on the 'metaphysics' of the objects represented in the logical formalism of the *Aufbau*—objects as represented in the formalism are, as it were, the 'phenomena' of the system (and 'noumena' need not apply). Carnap's opposition to 'metaphysics' is of course legendary. However, his metaphysical neutrality in the *Aufbau* explicitly adopts a Husserlian phenomenological perspective writ in symbolic language. Carnap's own conception of the *Aufbau* programme was Husserlian. (See Roy 2004.)

Carnap's 'methodological solipsism' (his metaphysical neutrality) echoed Husserl's trumpeted phenomenological method of 'bracketing' or *epoché*, whereby we are to bracket the thesis of the existence of the natural world and describe the way objects in nature are presented in our subjective experience (*Ideas* I, §§ 27ff.). Indeed, the phenomenal 'world' spelled out in the *Aufbau* was structured along lines that exactly parallel the lines of Husserl's system in *Ideas* I, where the phenomenology is framed by a novel formal ontology (see the opening chapter). The formal structure of the *Aufbau* system defines 'objects'—i.e. concepts of objects expressed in the logical idiom—through a system of 'step forms' within the logic of relations. That formal structure governs the material structure of three domains, just as Husserl's 'formal ontology' governs his 'material ontology' of three 'regions'. Carnap's formal definition of 'objects' thus governs the 'constitution' of objects in three domains: subjective 'autopsychological objects' (Husserl's region of 'pure consciousness'); 'physical objects' (Husserl's region of 'nature'); and intersubjective 'heteropsychological and cultural objects' (Husserl's region of *Geist* or culture). As these distinctions are developed in the course of the *Aufbau*, Carnap's footnotes reference Husserl's *Ideas* I, indicating (succinctly) that Carnap was a careful reader of *Ideas* I. (See Smith 1995 and 2007 on how Husserl's phenomenology is framed by his formal and material ontology in *Ideas* I.)

Carnap's own German spoke not of the 'construction' of such objects in the world, but of the 'constitution' (*Konstitution*) of such objects—the term 'constitution' being central in Husserlian transcendental phenomenology and *au currant* in 1920s German neo-Kantian schools of transcendental idealism. Carnap's title for the project that became the *Aufbau* was 'Outline of a Constitution Theory of the Objects of Cognition', i.e. *Entwurf einer Konstitutionstheorie der Erkenntnisgegenstände*. So we need to re-read the English translation of the *Aufbau* while replacing the term 'construction' with the term 'constitution'. But what does the phenomenological term 'constitution' mean if not the constructing of higher-level objects out of lower-level objects in an onto-phenomeno-logical composition? (The title term '*Aufbau*', literally building-up, does not occur in the text of the *Aufbau*, but was apparently urged on Carnap by Moritz Schlick, the ring-leader of the Vienna Circle. See Friedman 2000, pp. 70 ff., on Carnap's neutral conception of 'constitution'. See Smith 1995 and 2007 on Husserl's conception of formal versus material ontology. With these perspectives revisit Carnap's *Aufbau*.)

On Husserl's model in *Ideas* I (1913), with roots in the *Logical Investigations*, we find that an object such as a tree is 'constituted' in consciousness insofar as an 'horizon' of further possible experiences presents the same object in different ways, for example, as one walks around the same tree and sees it from different perspectives. Husserl's model does not reduce the tree to a series of visual appearances from different perspectives, much less a series of mere sensory data. Rather, the object is presented through a 'manifold' of noematic meanings that present the same object in different ways. (See Smith 2007 on the details of this meaning-based model of constitution, employing Husserl's adaptation of the mathematical notion of 'manifold', or *Mannigfaltigkeit*. That account extends the account of horizon developed in Smith and McIntyre 1982.)

Carnap's 'constitution system', then, is a system of linguistic expressions (especially sentences) that stand proxy for a structure of types of experience, hence intentional contents or noematic meanings, that present objects in appropriate ways. Carnap's technical formulations are extensional (*Aufbau*, section 44); in effect, the expressions do the work of *Sinn*—leaving *Sinn* in the background until we use a sentence denoting a *Sinn* (section 44).… But there is more, for Carnap's concern is the 'constitution' of 'objects of cognition' (as represented symbolically), not simply 'objects' (as represented).

For Husserl, an 'intuition' (*Anschauung*), or self-evident experience, carries both *Sinn* and 'evidence' (*Evidenz*). (For Kant, *Anschauung* is formed from concepts plus a manifold of sensations.) Hence, from a Husserlian perspective, Carnap's 'constitution system' tracks a structured 'manifold' of object-representations carrying a trail of evidential support. Evidential support is tracked step-wise up from the most elementary types of experience through higher-level types of experience presenting different levels of objects—that is, as expressed in Carnap's formalism. This pattern is in effect a symbolic record of structures of cognitive experience, not a 'logical' composition of objects in the world. The *Aufbau* is thus a formalized system of phenomenology.

39.9 Phenomenology in the Semantic Tradition: Truth and Meaning, Modality and Intentionality

Frege's 'On *Sinn* and *Bedeutung*' appeared in 1892. Husserl's theory of reference and intentionality via sense was developed in his *Logical Investigations* of 1900–01. Yet it was not until decades later that *semantics* took its now-recognized place in the philosophy of logic and language. And only after the ascendancy of semantics per se could the 'semantic' character of intentionality in phenomenology come to the fore (starting with the work of Føllesdal in the 1960s, as discussed above).

Alberto Coffa has aptly circumscribed an evolving approach to meaning, in *The Semantic Tradition from Kant to Carnap: To the Vienna Station* (1991). Logic and epistemology—and proto-phenomenology (I would note)—interweave in Coffa's fascinating historiography. A vital philosophical thread he traces is the notion of ideal meaning or sense. Indeed, it is Coffa's retrospective insight to factor out of nineteenth-century philosophy what he dubs the *semantic* tradition: 'Semanticists are easily detected: they devote an uncommon amount of attention to concepts, propositions, senses—to the content and structure of what we say [or, let us add, think], as opposed to the psychic acts in which we say [or think] it' (p. 1). Coffa wends his way through the problems of Kant, Bolzano, Frege, Husserl, Russell, Wittgenstein, Carnap, and others. But 'semantics' was not so clearly recognized in their day. Indeed, the term was not used by Frege, Husserl, *et al.* And it was only in the 1940s that logical theory was factored into syntax (defining forms of expression), semantics (assigning meanings, referents, and truth to appropriate expressions), and pragmatics (studying use of expressions). It is interesting where the impetus to semantics came from, on the heels of Carnap's non-metaphysical practice of 'logistic', as he termed modern symbolic logic.

Carnap's *Aufbau* system of 1928 mapped out forms of expression, but steered clear of the 'metaphysics' of sense and reference and truth—and so stopped short of what we today call semantics, i.e. the correlation of expressions with meanings and objects, which was already an explicit part of Husserl's 'pure logic'. It was not long before meaning re-entered logical theory, followed in three decades by intentionality.

Contemporary logical semantics emerged from Alfred Tarski's 'semantic' theory of truth. During the 1930s Tarski had developed a mathematical model of truth for certain formalized languages, presented in a study known as the *Wahrheitsbegriff* (Tarski 1933/1935/1983). In 1935, while visiting Vienna, Tarski convinced Carnap that semantics could be done in a rigorous way that met the mathematical and empirical ideals Carnap had stressed. (See Feferman and Feferman 2004: pp. 95ff., on the relations between Tarski and Carnap and Tarski's development of his theory of truth, of meta-mathematics, and of model theory; pp. 109–23 on his theory of truth. See Reck, this volume.) In 'The Semantic Conception of Truth and the Foundations of Semantics' (1944/2001), Tarski then presented a broadly philosophical account of his theory of truth. A sentence in a well-formulated language is true, on Tarski's account, if and only if certain conditions in the world obtain. For example, the sentence 'snow is white' is true in English if and only if snow is white. These well-specified truth-conditions spell out the semantics of the language: the correlations of forms of expressions with appropriate objects (referents or extensions) in relevant conditions in the world.

But Tarski was a self-declared nominalist (see Feferman and Feferman, p. 52). Where then, in Tarskian semantics, do we find anything like ideal meaning *à la* Frege and Husserl? The effect of *Sinn* is approximated in set-theoretic machinery: the *Sinn* of an expression is, if you like, reduced to a function that assigns to the expression an appropriate object (object, set, or truth-value). Indeed, Tarski's theory of truth led into the development of mathematical model theory. In that scheme, a sentence is said to be true in a 'model', that is, a set-theoretic structure mirroring what Husserl and Wittgenstein called a state of affairs (*Sachverhalt*)—an ontological structure formed from objects standing in a relation. (See Smith 2002 and 2005 on Husserl vis-à-vis Wittgenstein and Tarski.)

Now, Tarski's theory of truth was not without influence from Husserlian ideas on intentionality and meaning. Tarski studied in Warsaw partly under a student of Kasimir Twardowski, who taught in Lvov after studying Brentano's philosophy in Vienna. (See B. Smith 1994, Chapter 6, on Twardowski's work in Vienna and his influence on Polish philosophy, including Tarski. Also see Feferman and Feferman 2004 on Tarski's early studies.) In 1894 Twardowski published an important treatise called *On the Content and Object of Presentations* [*Vorstellungen*]: *A Psychological Investigation* (1894/1977). Twardowski's distinction among a presentation, its content, and its object is a forerunner of Husserl's distinction among an act of consciousness, its content, and its object. But Husserl criticized Twardowski for leaving content a 'psychological' entity. (See B. Smith 1994, p. 175.) Husserl charged that Twardowski had not yet drawn the distinction between psychological content and ideal meaning—which Husserl would soon emphasize in the *Logical Investigations* (1900–01). In his scheme of 'pure logic', Husserl proposed a systematic correlation among categories of expression, categories of meaning, and categories of object (Husserl 1900–1, Prolegomena, Chapter 11). Well, as a matter of fact, Tarski (1933/1935/1983) cited Husserl's notion of categories in the *Logical Investigations*, presumably drawing inspiration from Husserl's notion of correlation among categories. Tarski's truth-theoretic semantics thus mirrored the structure of intentionality, albeit shifting the focus from experiences ('presentations') to expressions.

By the 1960s, with a more ontological flair, truth-theoretic semantics defined truth in a 'possible world', a possible state of affairs or state of the world. Moreover, Jaakko Hintikka, one of the founders of possible-worlds semantics, focused specifically on the intentional attitudes. Hintikka developed systems of possible-worlds semantics to explicate attributions of belief, knowledge, and perception (Hintikka 1962, 1969, 1975). On Hintikka's model, say, for the logic of perception: the sentence 'Smith sees that the moon is full' is true in a world W if and only if the sentence 'the moon is full' is true in every world compatible with what Smith sees (in the appropriate context in W). This style of possible-worlds semantics offered an explication of the intentionality of perception or other intentional acts of consciousness. In effect, an act of consciousness is directed towards appropriate objects in appropriate 'possible worlds', worlds defined by intentional content or meaning. Thus, the Fregean notion of meaning was thereby recast as a function from possible worlds to extensions in worlds: the *Sinn* of 'the morning star' specifies Venus in the actual world, or another celestial body in an alternative world. (See Hintikka 1975 on meanings, meaning functions, Husserlian noemata, and intentionality. See Smith and McIntyre 1982 on relations between Husserl's theory of intentionality and Hintikka's possible-worlds semantics for sentences ascribing intentional acts of perception, etc. For the record, both Smith and McIntyre wrote 1970 doctoral dissertations at Stanford on intentionality in relation to semantic theories, under the supervision of Føllesdal and Hintikka.)

Phenomenology reappears in logical theory, then, with the logic of intentionality. And Hintikka explicitly interacted with Husserlian ideas in pressing the philosophical significance of his models for intentional modalities.

39.10 PHENOMENOLOGY IN PHILOSOPHY OF MIND: INTENTIONALITY, SUBJECTIVITY, SELF-CONSCIOUSNESS

We have focused on the theory of meaning in phenomenology and analytic philosophy. Meaning serves as content in *subjective* activities of conscious thought, perception, and action. Yet meaning itself is an *objective* structure at work in mind and in language. And language is a social practice where meaning is communicated and even produced in *intersubjective* understanding. All these phenomena of meaning—involving subjectivity, objectivity, intersubjectivity—were richly analysed in classical phenomenology, in the writings of Husserl, Heidegger, Merleau-Ponty, Sartre, *et al.* The same issues worked their way through seminal writings in the history of early analytic philosophy, in Frege, Carnap, Wittgenstein, Ryle. Meanwhile, phenomenology has assumed a new role in recent philosophy of mind, with the growth of consciousness studies.

In the analytic tradition, philosophy of mind developed prominently following Ryle's *The Concept of Mind* (1949). Already, as we noted, Carnap's 'constitution' theory in the *Aufbau* (1928) had addressed forms of experience, with an eye to Husserlian phenomenology (*Ideas* I 1913). Also, empiricist epistemology had long focused on sense-data in sensory experience. And Frege's early notion of *Sinn* (1892) involved the proto-phenomenological notion of a 'mode of presentation' (i.e. in consciousness) of what the *Sinn* refers to. By the 1960s materialist or physicalist theories of mind were resurgent (see Armstrong 1968, 1999). In the 1970s functionalism flourished, identifying mental states with what a brain or computer does regardless of its physical implementation. Mental representation was the focus in this era of philosophy of mind and early cognitive science. Accordingly, parallels with Husserl's theory of intentionality were explored in reflection on that milieu (see Dreyfus and Hall 1982), though of course Husserl would oppose both materialism and functionalism.

By the late 1980s analytic philosophers of mind were turning to the subjectivity of consciousness, starting with sensory 'qualia' and then awareness in 'higher-order monitoring'. In that literature there was seldom any reference to phenomenology per se, either the discipline or the tradition (see Block et al. 1997). But gradually analytic philosophers of consciousness took up bona fide phenomenological issues. Consciousness, it was argued, does not simply reduce to neural process, much less computational function, even in a fundamentally physical universe. Accordingly, phenomenological characters of consciousness were rediscovered, as it were, in the analytic tradition: notably, in works by Thomas Nagel (1974), John Searle (1983, 1992), Galen Strawson (1994 and 2009), and David Chalmers (1996). Amid the renewed interest in consciousness, ideas from Brentano, Husserl, Heidegger, Merleau-Ponty, and Sartre gradually mixed with ideas born of analytic philosophy. (See the essays in Smith and Thomasson 2005 and in Kriegel and Williford 2006.)

In particular, the problem of self-consciousness has loomed large in recent philosophy of mind, drawing in phenomenology proper—both the discipline and the tradition. What makes a mental activity *conscious*, on a classical view, is the subject's awareness of the activity: consciousness is in its essence *self-consciousness*—as Locke held. In a sharp development of this view, Brentano held that consciousness involves a primary consciousness of its object and a secondary 'inner consciousness' of that primary consciousness. Husserl followed with a detailed analysis of 'inner time-consciousness', where consciousness tracks the flow of experience through 'retentions' (and 'protentions') of 'impressions' of sounds, etc. Sartre followed with his view of the 'pre-reflective cogito', where consciousness essentially includes a pre-reflective consciousness of itself. These classical phenomenological views have been coming together with views of 'higher-order monitoring' in analytic philosophy of mind. (For variations on higher-order monitoring within the broadly physicalist mould, see the essays by Armstrong, Rosenthal, and Lycan in Block *et al.* 1997.)

Some three or four models of self-consciousness have been detailed in this emerging area. On one model (with several variations), awareness of mental activity consists in a *higher-order* monitoring of the activity. A second model keeps the awareness on the same level, a *same-order monitoring* that is a proper part of the act of consciousness, following Brentano's account. A variation on this model articulates self-consciousness as the fine structure of time-consciousness, following Husserl's account. A third model sees self-consciousness as an auxiliary *self-representation* built into a conscious mental state. A fourth model articulates self-consciousness as a *reflexive modal* structure, wherein the subject is aware 'in this very experience' of thinking or seeing such-and-such. (All these models are discussed in essays in Kriegel and Williford 2006. The self-representational approach is elaborated in Kriegel 2009; an interesting revision is in Kidd 2011. The modal model is detailed in Smith 2004, Chapter 3, initially introduced in Smith 1986, amplified in Smith 1989.)

Now, what does the phenomenological problem of self-consciousness have to do with the theory of *meaning* we have tracked in analytic philosophy? The ideal phenomenological structure of consciousness is precisely what we are calling meaning, what Husserl called noema or noematic sense, a generalization of *Sinn*. The 'modal' model of self-consciousness (sketched by the present author) explicitly begins with Husserl's articulation of different parts of an act's noema, informed by an intuitive notion of intentional modalities (indicated above in Hintikka's logic of perception, belief, etc.) And the self-representation sought in response to higher-order and same-order models of self-consciousness is explicitly a 'logical' part of the act (per Kriegel's essay in Kriegel and Williford 2006; cf. Kidd 2011). So the theory of self-consciousness takes the form of a theory of the ideal 'logical' or better 'phenomeno-logical' structure wherein one is aware of one's ongoing conscious activity of thinking, perceiving, or acting (bodily).

And so we close our study of the role of phenomenology in analytic philosophy—with a moment of historical self-consciousness in the evolving tradition(s).

39.11 CONCLUSION: WHY MEANING?

The phenomenon of meaning flows historically through the heart of twentieth-century philosophy, in phenomenology and in analytic philosophy. What is it about meaning that gives it this vital role in twentieth-century philosophy?

Meaning, we might propose, is the condition of the possibility of knowledge formation—in logic, in science, in phenomenology, in philosophy itself. This ('transcendental'?) meta-theory can be seen emerging through the interaction of phenomenology with analytic philosophy of mind and language and science. (See Smith 2007 on the role of meaning in Husserl's meta-theory, and compare Friedman and Ryckman forthcoming on transcendental themes in early phenomenology and analytic philosophy.)

The 'analytic' conception of philosophy was made possible by the methods of modern logic, with its perspective on the foundations of mathematics, of the natural sciences, and of broadly scientific theorizing. The phenomenological conception of philosophy, on the other hand, was made possible by the methods of phenomenological reflection on our experience, including our intentional activities in the practice of science and in the formation of knowledge generally. The theory of meaning emerged accordingly in both logical theory and phenomenology, but with a certain division of labour.

Hindsight is beautiful. In the mid-1930s Tarski was formulating a mathematical theory of truth in the *Wahrheitsbegriff* (1933/1936/1983), conceived as a 'semantic' theory of truth (1944/2001)—truth being the logician's equivalent of successful intentionality. Meanwhile, in the same years, Husserl was worrying about the way that physics 'mathematizes' nature in the theory of space-time. In his late work, gathered in the posthumous volume called *The Crisis of the European Sciences and Transcendental Phenomenology* (1935–38/1970), Husserl argues that the mathematization of nature abstracts away from the way we normally experience spatio-temporal things in nature, thus from the meaning that spatio-temporal things have in our everyday intentional experience in the 'life-world' (*Lebenswelt*). This critique can be pressed further. The mathematization of logic itself loses touch with the foundation of logic in intentionality theory, where meaning is drawn from ideal intentional content. Indeed, in his 1929 treatise *Formal and Transcendental Logic* (1929/1969), Husserl calls for 'transcendental' logic to ground 'formal' logic: in effect, mathematical logic is to be philosophically founded in a phenomenological theory of intentionality, whereby symbolic linguistic structures are to be seen as abstracted from ideal structures of meaning in intentional experience. And today we can press the critique still further. The mathematization of mind in computational models in neuroscience, we would find, abstracts away from the subjective character of mental activity in consciousness and from its 'lived' ideal contents, i.e., meanings. The point is not to discount the mathematical models of truth, intentionality, and even subjectivity, but rather to ground these formal models in the structure of lived experience. And, in the semantic tradition, that means: in ideal meaning structures. (The essays in Hyder and Rheinberger 2009 explore the significance of Husserl's *Crisis* for various themes in analytic philosophy.)

If this line of historical critique is correct, then we can see why the phenomenon of meaning is so evidently the driving force in the history of phenomenology and analytic philosophy—even in our self-conscious interpretation of that history. If you will, meaning is both the medium and the message in this flow of philosophy.[1]

[1] I should like to thank Mike Beaney and Johannes Brandl for helpful comments on the penultimate draft. I thank Clinton Tolley for discussion of the line of interpretation here explored. For innumerable discussions over many years, concerning historical and conceptual ideas here pursued, I am indebted to Dagfinn Føllesdal, Jaakko Hintikka, Ronald McIntyre, Amie Thomasson, Jeffrey Yoshimi, and Paul Livingston. For their studies of the Austrian tradition from Bolzano to Brentano to Husserl, and many discussions thereof, I am grateful to Edgar Morscher, Peter Simons, Barry Smith, Kevin Mulligan, and Johannes Brandl. On alternative models of self-consciousness, I appreciate discussions with Jason Ford, Chad Kidd, Uriah Kriegel, Christopher Lay, and Michelle Montague. Less obviously, I am indebted to my encounter with Tarski's theory of truth, already in my pre-philosophy undergraduate days (while studying mathematics and engineering at Northwestern).

REFERENCES

Armstrong, D. M. (1968). *A Materialist Theory of the Mind*. London: Routledge & Kegan Paul.

—— (1999). *The Mind-Body Problem: An Opinionated Introduction*. Boulder, CO: Westview.

Ayer, Alfred Jules (1936). *Language, Truth and Logic*. London: Gollancz.

Beaney, Michael (2002). 'Decompositions and Transformations: Conceptions of Analysis in the Early Analytic and Phenomenological Traditions'. In Horgan *et al.* (2002), pp. 53–99.

Beyer, Christian (2000). *Intentionalität und Referenz: Eine sprachanalytische Studie du Husserls transzendentaler Phänomenologie*. Paderborn: Mentis.

Block, Ned, Owen Flanagan, and Güven Güzeldere (eds.) (1997). *The Nature of Consciousness*. Cambridge, MA: MIT Press.

Bolzano, Bernard (1837/1972). *Theory of Science: Attempt at a Detailed and in the main Novel Exposition of Logic with Constant Attention to Earlier Authors*, ed. and tr. Rolf George. Berkeley and Los Angeles: University of California Press, 1972. A partial translation of Bolzano's *Wissenschaftslehre*, original German 1837.

Brandl, Johannes L. (2002). 'Gilbert Ryle: A Mediator between Analytic Philosophy and Phenomenology'. In Horgan *et al.* (2002), pp. 143–51.

Brentano, Franz (1874/1995). *Psychology from an Empirical Standpoint*, tr. A. C. Rancurello, D. B. Terrell, and L. L. McAlister. London and New York: Routledge.

Carnap, Rudolf (1928/2003). *The Logical Structure of the World and Pseudoproblems in Philosophy*, tr. Rolf George. Chicago and La Salle, IL: Open Court. From the German original, *Der logische Aufbau der Welt*, 1928. Nicknamed the *Aufbau*.

Chalmers, David (1996). *The Conscious Mind*. Oxford and New York: Oxford University Press.

Coffa, J. Alberto (1991). *The Semantic Tradition from Kant to Carnap: To the Vienna Station*, ed. Linda Wessels. Cambridge and New York: Cambridge University Press.

Dreyfus, Hubert L. and Harrison Hall (eds.) (1982). *Husserl, Intentionality and Cognitive Science*. Cambridge, MA: MIT Press.

Dummett, Michael (1993/1998). *Origins of Analytical Philosophy*. Cambridge, Massachusetts: Harvard University Press.

Evans, Gareth (1982). *The Varieties of Reference*. Oxford: Oxford University Press.

Feferman, Anita Burdman and Solomon Feferman (2004). *Alfred Tarski: Life and Logic*. Cambridge and New York: Cambridge University Press.

Fisette, Denis (1994). *Lecture frégéenne de la phénoménologie*. Paris: Editions de l'eclat.

Føllesdal, Dagfinn (1958). *Husserl und Frege*. Oslo: Aschehoug.

—— (1961/2004). *Referential Opacity and Modal Logic*. New York and London: Routledge. Publication, with a new Introduction, of the author's 1961 Ph.D. thesis at Harvard under the supervision of W. V. Quine.

—— (1969/1982). 'Husserl's Notion of Noema'. Repr. in Dreyfus and Hall (1982), pp. 73–80. First published in *The Journal of Philosophy* 66 (1969): 680–7.

—— (1972). 'An Introduction to Phenomenology for Analytic Philosophers'. In Raymond E. Olson and Anthony M. Paul (eds.), *Contemporary Philosophy in Scandinavia*. Baltimore: Johns Hopkins Press, pp. 417–29.

—— (1982). 'Response' to J. N. Mohanty on 'Husserl and Frege'. See Mohanty and Føllesdal. In Dreyfus and Harrison (1982), pp. 52–6.

Frege, Gottlob (1884/1978). *The Foundations of Arithmetic*, tr. J. L. Austin. German and English, 2nd revised edn. Oxford: Oxford University Press. German original, *Die Grundlagen der Arithmetik*. Breslau: W. Koebner, 1884.

—— (1892/1997). 'On *Sinn* and *Bedeutung*'. In *The Frege Reader*, ed. Michael Beaney. Oxford and Malden, MA: Blackwell, 1997, pp. 151–71. German original, 1892. Key terms sometimes translated as: sense (*Sinn*) and reference (*Bedeutung*).

—— (1918/1997). 'Thought', tr. Peter Geach and R H. Stoothoff. In *The Frege Reader*, ed. Micheal Beaney. Oxford and Malden, MA: Blackwell, 1997, pp. 325–45. German original, 'Der Gedanke', published in 1918–19.

Friedman, Michael (1999). *Reconsidering Logical Positivism*. Cambridge and New York: Cambridge University Press.

—— (2000). *A Parting of Ways: Carnap, Cassirer, and Heidegger*. Chicago and LaSalle, IL: Open Court.

Friedman, Michael and Thomas Ryckman (forthcoming). 'Analytic and Continental Traditions: Frege, Husserl, Carnap, and Heidegger'.

Hill, Claire Ortiz and Guillermo E. Rosado Haddock (2000). *Husserl or Frege? Meaning, Objectivity, and Mathematics*. Chicago and LaSalle, IL: Open Court.

Hintikka, Jaakko (1962). *Knowledge and Belief*. Ithaca, NY: Cornell University Press.

—— (1969). *Models for Modalities*. Dordrecht and Boston: D. Reidel.

—— (1975). *The Intentions of Intentionality and other New Models for Modalities*. Dordrecht and Boston: D. Reidel.

Hintikka, Merrill B. and Jaakko Hintikka (1986). *Investigating Wittgenstein*. Oxford and New York: Blackwell.

Horgan, Terry, John Tienson, and Matjaz Potre (eds.) (2002). *Origins: The Common Sources of the Analytic and Phenomenological Traditions. The Southern Journal of Philosophy*, Supplement 2002. Proceedings of the Spindel Conference 2001. Memphis: Department of Philosophy, University of Memphis.

Huemer, Wolfgang (2005). *The Constitution of Consciousness: A Study in Analytic Phenomenology*. London and New York: Routledge.

Husserl, Edmund (1891/2003). *Philosophy of Arithmetic: Psychological and Logical Investigations with Supplementary Texts from 1887–1901*, tr. Dallas Willard. Dordrecht and Boston: Kluwer Academic Publishers (now: New York: Springer), 2003. German original, 1891.

—— (1900–01/2001). *Logical Investigations*, vols. 1 and 2, tr. J. N. Findlay, ed. and rev. Dermot Moran. London and New York: Routledge, 2001. German original, first edition, 1900–01; second edition, 1913, 1920. English translation, first edition, 1970.

—— (1913/1969/1983). *Ideas* I. With two English translations: (a) *Ideas pertaining to a Pure Phenomenology and a Phenomenological Philosophy, First Book: General Introduction to Pure Phenomenology*, tr. Fred Kersten. Dordrecht and Boston: Kluwer Academic Publishers (now: New York: Springer), 1991. German original called *Ideas* I, 1913/1983. (b) *Ideas* [*toward a Pure Phenomenology and Phenomenological Philosophy, First Book*]: *General Introduction to Pure Phenomenology*, tr. W. R. Boyce Gibson. London: George Allen & Unwin, and New York: Humanities Press, 1969. First English edition, 1931. A prior translation of *Ideas* I. 1913/1969.

—— (1929/1969). *Formal and Transcendental Logic*, tr. Dorion Cairns. The Hague: Martinus Nijhoff (now: New York: Springer), 1969. German original 1929.

—— (1935–38/1970). *The Crisis of European Sciences and Transcendental Phenomenology: An Introduction to Phenomenological Philosophy*, tr. David Carr. Evanston: Northwestern University Press, 1970. Original German manuscripts written 1935–8. German edition first published 1954.

—— (1994). *Early Writings in the Philosophy of Logic and Mathematics*, tr. Dallas Willard. Dordrecht and Boston: Kluwer Academic Publishers (now: New York: Springer).

Hyder, David (2002). *The Mechanics of Meaning*. Berlin and New York: Walter de Gruyter.

Hyder, David and Hans-Jörg Rheinberger (eds.) (2009). *Science and the Life-World: Essays on Husserl's Crisis of the European Sciences*. Stanford: Stanford University Press.

Kidd, Chad (2011). 'Phenomenal Consciousness with Infallible Self-Representation', *Philosophical Studies* 152: 361–83.

Kriegel, Uriah (2009). *Subjective Consciousness: A Self-Representational Approach*. Oxford and New York: Oxford University Press.

Kriegel, Uriah and Kenneth Williford (eds.) (2006). *Self-Representational Approaches to Consciousness*. Cambridge, MA: MIT Press.

Livingston, Paul M. (2004). *Philosophical History and the Problem of Consciousness*. Cambridge and New York: Cambridge University Press.

McIntyre, Ronald and David Woodruff Smith (1975/1982). 'Husserl's Identification of Meaning and Noema', *The Monist* 59(1) (January 1975): 115–32. Repr. in Dreyfus and Harrison (1982), pp. 81–92.

Mohanty, J. N. (1982a). *Husserl and Frege*. Bloomington: Indiana University Press.

——(1982b). 'Husserl and Frege: A New Look at Their Relationship', with response by Dagfinn Føllesdal. In Dreyfus and Harrison (1982), pp. 43–56.

Nagel, Thomas (1974/1997). 'What is it Like to be a Bat?' *Philosophical Review* 83: 435–50. Repr. in Block *et al.* (1997), pp. 519–28.

Quine, Willard Van Orman (1960). *Word and Object*. Cambridge, MA: MIT Press.

Richardson, Alan W. (1998). *Carnap's Construction of the World: The Aufbau and the Emergence of Logical Empiricism*. Cambridge and New York: Cambridge University Press.

Roy, Jean-Michel (2004). 'Carnap's Husserlian Reading of the *Aufbau*'. In Steven Awodey and Carsten Klein (eds.), *Carnap Brought Home: The View from Jena*. Chicago and LaSalle, IL: Open Court, pp. 41–62.

Ryckman, Thomas (2005). *The Reign of Relativity: Philosophy in Physics 1915–1925*. Oxford and New York: Oxford University Press.

Ryle, Gilbert (1949/1965). *The Concept of Mind*. New York: Barnes and Noble. First published in 1949.

Searle, John R. (1969). *Speech Acts*. Cambridge: Cambridge University Press.

—— (1983). *Intentionality: An Essay in the Philosophy of Mind*. Cambridge and New York: Cambridge University Press.

——(1992). *The Rediscovery of the Mind*. Cambridge, MA: MIT Press.

——(1995). *The Construction of Social Reality*. New York: The Free Press.

Sellars, Wilfrid (1956/2000). *Empiricism and the Philosophy of Mind*. Introduction by Richard Rorty, Study Guide by Robert Brandom. Cambridge, MA: Harvard University Press, 1997, repr. 2000. Originally published in *Minnesota Studies in the Philosophy of Science*, Vol. 1, ed. Herbert Feigl and Michael Scriven. Minneapolis: University of Minnesota Press, 1956, pp. 253–329.

Sellars, Wilfrid and Roderick M. Chisholm (1957). 'Intentionality and the Mental: A Correspondence', *Minnesota Studies in the Philosophy of Science*, Vol. 2, ed. Herbert Feigl, Michael Scriven, and Grover Maxwell. Minneapolis: University of Minnesota Press, pp. 507–39.

Simons, Peter (1992). *Philosophy and Logic in Central Europe from Bolzano to Tarski*. Dordrecht and Boston: Kluwer Academic Publishers.

——(1995). 'Meaning and Language'. In Smith and Smith (1995), pp. 106–37.

Smith, Barry (1994). *Austrian Philosophy: The Legacy of Franz Brentano*. Chicago and LaSalle, IL: Open Court.

Smith, Barry and David Woodruff Smith (eds.) (1995). *The Cambridge Companion to Husserl*. Cambridge and New York: Cambridge University Press.

Smith, David Woodruff (1986). 'The Structure of (Self-) Consciousness', *Topoi* 5: 149–56

——(1989). *The Circle of Acquaintance: Perception, Consciousness, and Empathy*. Dordrecht and Boston: Kluwer Academic Publishers (now: New York: Springer).

——(1995). 'Mind and Body'. In Smith and Smith (1995), pp. 323–93.

——(2002). 'Intentionality and Picturing: Early Husserl *vis-à-vis* Early Wittgenstein'. In Terry Horgan, John Tienson, and Matjaz Potrc (eds.), *Origins: The Common Sources of the Analytic and Phenomenological Traditions, The Southern Journal of Philosophy* 40, *Supplement*, Proceedings of the Spindel Conference 2001, published by the Department of Philosophy, University of Memphis, pp. 153–80.

—— (2005). 'Truth and Experience: Tarski vis-à-vis Husserl'. In M. E. Reicher and J. C. Marek (eds.), *Experience and Analysis. Erfahrung und Analyse. The Proceedings of the 27th International Wittgenstein Symposium*. Vienna: ÖBV & HPT, pp. 270–84.

——(2007). *Husserl*. London and New York: Routledge.

Smith, David Woodruff and Ronald McIntyre (1982). *Husserl and Intentionality: A Study of Mind, Meaning, and Language*. Dordrecht and Boston: D. Reidel (now New York: Springer).

Smith, David Woodruff and Amie L. Thomasson (eds.) (2005). *Phenomenology and Philosophy of Mind*. Oxford and New York: Oxford University Press.

Soldati, Giancarlo (1994). *Bedeutung und psychischer Gehalt: Zur sprachanalytischen Kritik von Husserl's Früher Phänomenologie*. Paderborn: Schöningh, Mentis.

Strawson, Galen (1994). *Mental Reality*. Cambridge, MA: MIT Press.

—— (2009). *Selves: An Essay in Revisionary Metaphysics*. Oxford and New York: Oxford University Press.

Strawson, P. F. (1959). *Individuals: An Essay in Descriptive Metaphysics*. London: Methuen.

Tarski, Alfred (1933/1935/1983). 'The Concept of Truth in Formalized Languages'. In Tarski, *Logic, Semantics, Metamathematics: Papers from 1923 to 1938*, ed. and tr. J. H. Woodger. Oxford: Clarendon Press, pp. 152–278. Known as the *Wahrheitsbegriff*, from the German title. Original Polish edition, 1933.

—— (1944/2001). 'The Semantic Conception of Truth and the Foundations of Semantics'. In Michael P. Lynch (ed.), *The Nature of Truth*. Cambridge, MA: MIT Press, 2001, pp. 331–63. Repr. from *Philosophy and Phenomenological Research* 4 (1944): 341–76.

Thomasson, Amie L. (2002). 'Phenomenology and the Development of Analytic Philosophy'. In Horgan *et al.* (2002), pp. 115–42.

Tieszen, Richard (2005). *Phenomenology, Logic, and the Philosophy of Mathematics*. Cambridge and New York: Cambridge University Press.

Twardowski, Kasimir (1894/1977). *On the Content and Object of Presentations: A Psychological Investigation*, tr. R. Grossmann. The Hague: Martinus Nijhoff (now: New York: Springer). German original, *Zur Lehre vom Inhalt und Gegenstand der Vorstellungen: Eine psychologische Untersuchung*, 1894.

Wittgenstein, Ludwig (1953/2001). *Philosophical Investigations*. The German Text, with a Revised English Translation, 3rd edn., tr. G. E. M. Anscombe. Oxford and Malden, MA: Blackwell. First published in 1953, in German with English translation.

INDEX

Lightning Source UK Ltd
Milton Keynes UK
UKOW07f1223160915

258723UK00001B/1/P